Great Events from History

The Ancient World

Prehistory - 476 C.E.

Great Events from History

The Ancient World

Prehistory - 476 C.E.

Volume 2
312 B.C.E. - 476 C.E.
Indexes

Editor
Mark W. Chavalas
University of Wisconsin-La Crosse

Consulting Editors
Mark S. Aldenderfer, *University of California, Santa Barbara*
Carole A. Barrett, *University of Mary*
Jeffrey W. Dippmann, *Central Washington University*
Christopher Ehret, *University of California, Los Angeles*
Katherine Anne Harper, *Loyola Marymount University*

SALEM PRESS
Pasadena, California   Hackensack, New Jersey

Editor in Chief: Dawn P. Dawson *Acquisitions Editor:* Mark Rehn
Editorial Director: Christina J. Moose *Research Supervisor:* Jeffry Jensen
Project Editor: Rowena Wildin *Research Assistant:* Desiree Dreeuws
Copy Editor: Leslie Ellen Jones *Production Editor:* Cynthia Beres
Assistant Editor: Andrea E. Miller *Graphics and Design:* James Hutson
Editorial Assistant: Dana Garey *Layout:* William Zimmerman
Photograph Editor: Philip Bader

Cover photos: Library of Congress

Some of the essays in this work originally appeared in the following Salem Press sets: *Great Events from History* (1972-1980, edited by Frank N. Magill), *Chronology of European History: 15,000 B.C. to 1997* (1997, edited by John Powell; associate editors, E. G. Weltin, José M. Sánchez, Thomas P. Neill, and Edward P. Keleher), and *Great Events from History: North American Series, Revised Edition* (1997, edited by Frank N. Magill; associate editor, John L. Loos).

Library of Congress Cataloging-in-Publication Data

Great events from history. The ancient world, prehistory-476 C.E. / editor, Mark W. Chavalas ; consulting editors, Mark S. Aldenderfer . . . [et al.].
    p. cm.
Some essays previously published in Great events from history (1972-1980), Chronology of European history, 15,000 B.C. to 1997 (1997), and Great events from history, North American series (1997).
Includes bibliographical references and indexes.
ISBN 1-58765-155-6 (set : alk. paper) — ISBN 1-58765-156-4 (v. 1 : alk. paper) — ISBN 1-58765-157-2 (v. 2 : alk. paper)
1. History, Ancient. I. Title: Ancient world, prehistory-476 C.E. II. Chavalas, Mark W. (Mark William), 1954- III. Aldenderfer, Mark S.
D65.G74 2004
930—dc22

2004001360

First Printing

PRINTED IN THE UNITED STATES OF AMERICA

CONTENTS

400 - 301 B.C.E. *(continued)*

300 - 201 B.C.E.

200 - 101 B.C.E.

100 - 1 B.C.E.

Contents

1 - 100 C.E.

101 - 200 C.E.

201 - 300 C.E.

301 - 400 C.E.

CONTENTS

KEYWORD LIST OF CONTENTS

LIST OF MAPS AND TABLES

THE ORIGIN OF HUMANS, C. 4 MILLION–100,000 B.P.

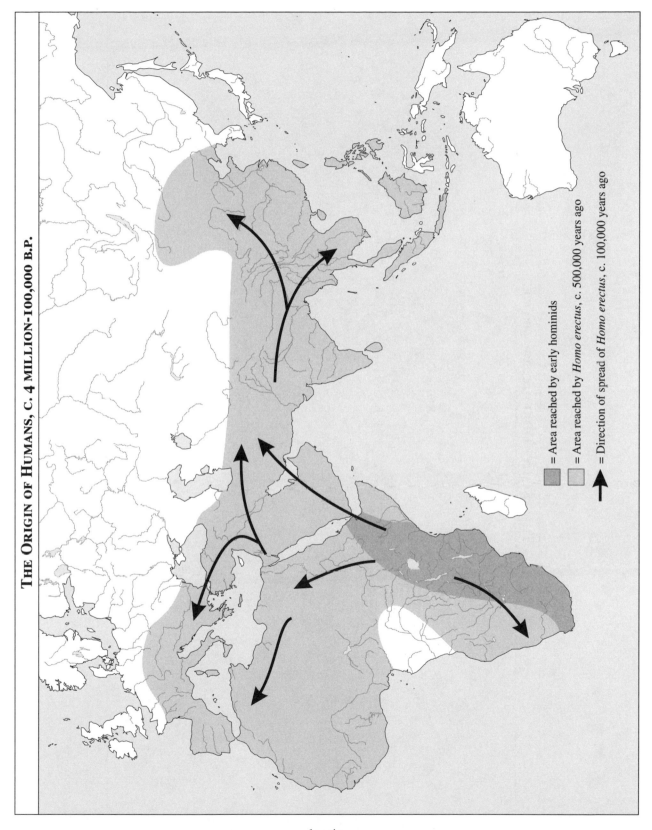

= Area reached by early hominids

= Area reached by *Homo erectus*, c. 500,000 years ago

= Direction of spread of *Homo erectus*, c. 100,000 years ago

THE ANCIENT WORLD, C. 200–500 C.E.

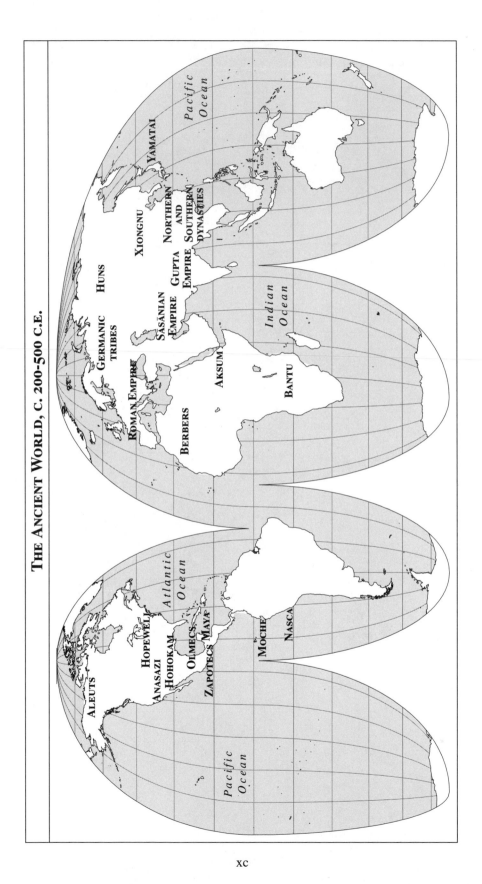

ALEUTS

ANASAZI
HOPEWELL
HOHOKAM
OLMECS
ZAPOTECS
MAYA

MOCHE

NASCA

Pacific
Ocean

Atlantic
Ocean

GERMANIC
TRIBES

HUNS

ROMAN EMPIRE

BERBERS

SASANIAN
EMPIRE

AKSUM

BANTU

Indian
Ocean

XIONGNU

GUPTA
EMPIRE

NORTHERN
AND
SOUTHERN
DYNASTIES

YAMATAI

Pacific
Ocean

ANCIENT NORTH AMERICA

Ipiutak

• Anangula

Norton Onion
Portage

ALEUTS

ARCTIC AND SUBARCTIC

PACIFIC COAST

Cape
Dorset

DORSET Port
au Choix

Head-Smashed-In

• Hoko River

CALIFORNIA

Casper

**GREAT
PLAINS**

OLD

Serpent
Mound

**RED
PAINT**

**GREAT
BASIN**

Danger Cave

COPPER

• Osceola

• Neville

EASTERN

Meadowcroft

Pacific
Ocean

ANASAZI

• Mesa Verde

MOGOLLON

Canyon de • Tularosa Cave
Chelly • Bat Cave (Cochise)

HOHOKAM

Koster

HOPEWELL

• Adena

Atlantic
Ocean

Indian Knoll

Poverty Point

WOODLAND

Blackwater Draw
(Clovis) Marksville

• Porter

Gulf
of
Mexico

ZAPOTEC

OLMEC

MAYA

• = Sites
Cultures indicated by **BOLD SMALL CAPS**

ANCIENT MESOAMERICA

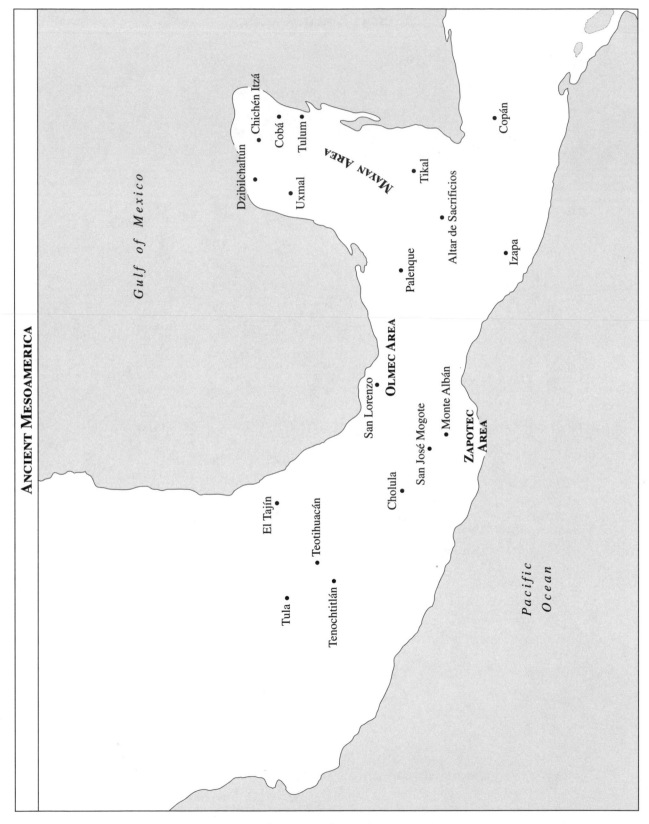

Gulf of Mexico

Pacific Ocean

Chichén Itzá
Cobá
Tulum
Dzibilchaltún
Uxmal
Copán
Tikal
Altar de Sacrificios
MAYAN AREA
Palenque
Izapa
OLMEC AREA
San Lorenzo
Monte Albán
San José Mogote
ZAPOTEC AREA
Cholula
El Tajín
Teotihuacán
Tula
Tenochtitlán

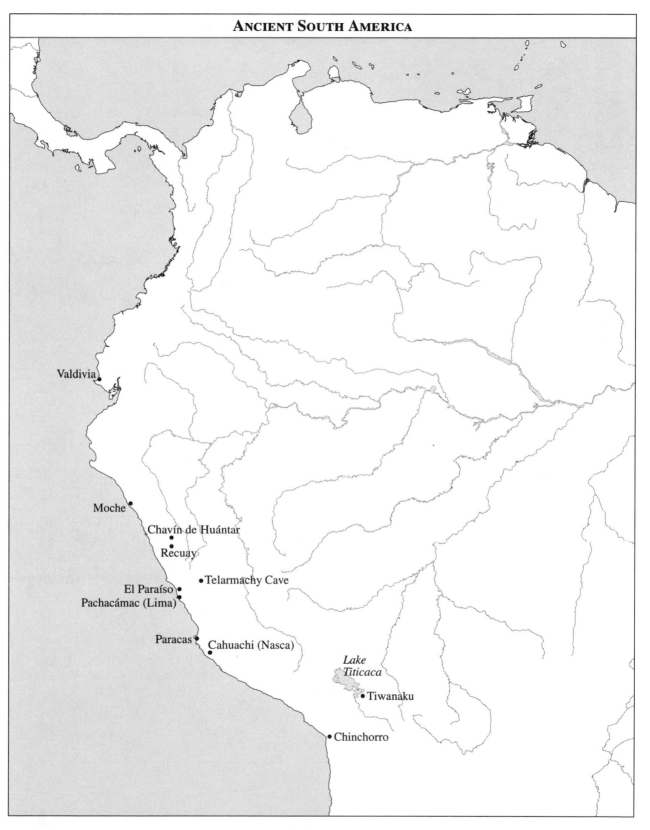

ANCIENT SOUTH AMERICA

Valdivia

Moche

Chavín de Huántar

Recuay

Telarmachy Cave

El Paraíso

Pachacámac (Lima)

Paracas

Cahuachi (Nasca)

Lake
Titicaca

Tiwanaku

Chinchorro

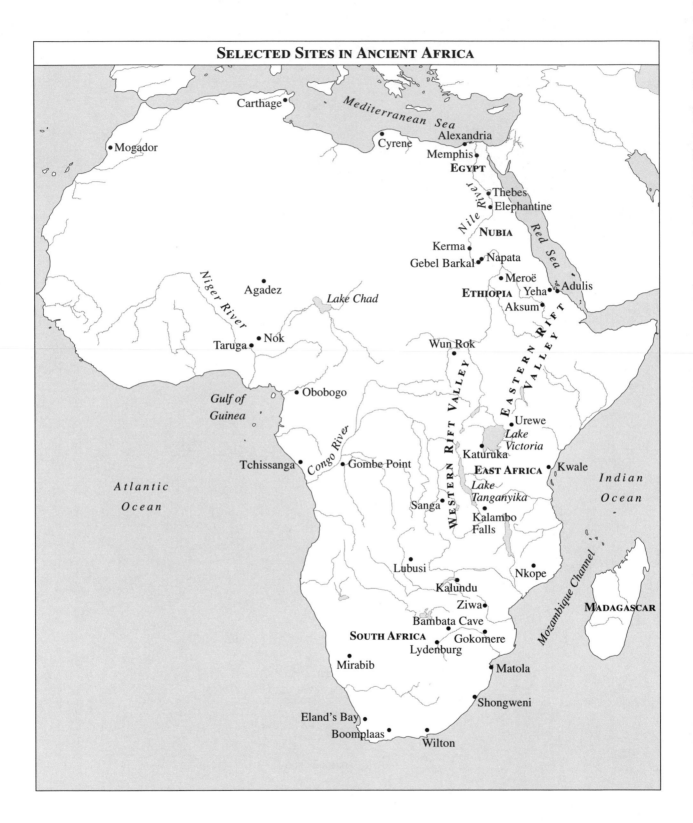

SELECTED SITES IN ANCIENT AFRICA

Mediterranean Sea

Carthage

Mogador

Cyrene

Alexandria

Memphis

EGYPT

Nile River

Thebes
Elephantine

NUBIA

Red Sea

Kerma

Gebel Barkal

Napata

Meroë

ETHIOPIA

Yeha

Adulis

Aksum

Niger River

Agadez

Lake Chad

Taruga

Nok

Wun Rok

EASTERN RIFT VALLEY

Obobogo

*Gulf of
Guinea*

Congo River

Urewe

WESTERN RIFT VALLEY

*Lake
Victoria*

Tchissanga

Gombe Point

Katuruka

EAST AFRICA

Kwale

*Indian
Ocean*

*Atlantic
Ocean*

Sanga

*Lake
Tanganyika*

Kalambo
Falls

Lubusi

Nkope

Mozambique Channel

Kalundu

MADAGASCAR

Ziwa

Bambata Cave

SOUTH AFRICA

Gokomere

Lydenburg

Mirabib

Matola

Shongweni

Eland's Bay

Boomplaas

Wilton

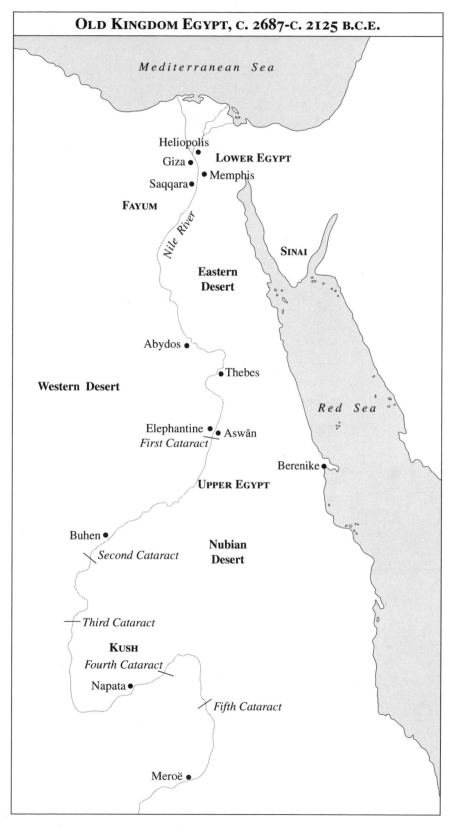

OLD KINGDOM EGYPT, C. 2687–C. 2125 B.C.E.

Mediterranean Sea

Heliopolis

LOWER EGYPT

Giza ●

● Memphis

Saqqara ●

FAYUM

Nile River

SINAI

Eastern Desert

Abydos ●

● Thebes

Red Sea

Western Desert

Elephantine ● ● Aswān
First Cataract

Berenike ●

UPPER EGYPT

Buhen ●

Nubian Desert

Second Cataract

— *Third Cataract*

KUSH

Fourth Cataract

Napata ●

Fifth Cataract

Meroë ●

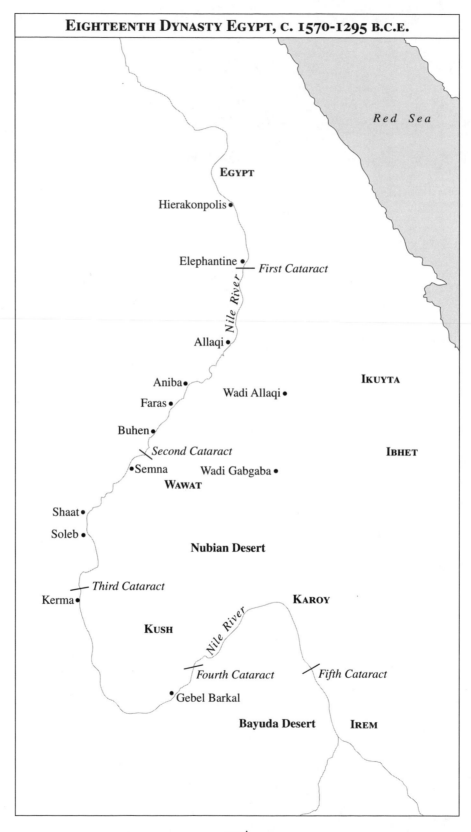

EIGHTEENTH DYNASTY EGYPT, C. 1570-1295 B.C.E.

Red Sea

EGYPT

Hierakonpolis •

Elephantine • — *First Cataract*

Nile River

Allaqi •

IKUYTA

Aniba •

Faras •   Wadi Allaqi •

Buhen •

Second Cataract

IBHET

• Semna   Wadi Gabgaba •

WAWAT

Shaat •

Soleb •

Nubian Desert

Third Cataract

Kerma •   **KAROY**

Nile River

KUSH

Fourth Cataract   *Fifth Cataract*

• Gebel Barkal

Bayuda Desert   **IREM**

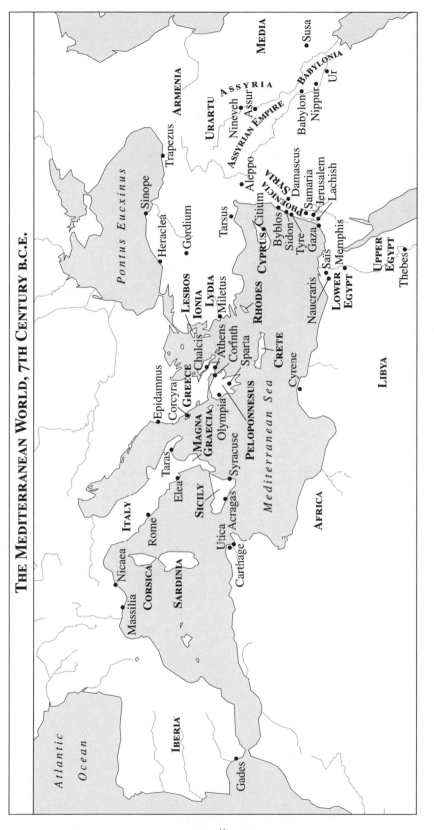

THE MEDITERRANEAN WORLD, 7TH CENTURY B.C.E.

Atlantic Ocean

Gades

IBERIA

Massilia

Nicaea

CORSICA

SARDINIA

Utica

Carthage

Acragas

SICILY

Elea

Rome

ITALY

Taras

Syracuse

Olympia

MAGNA GRAECIA

PELOPONNESUS

AFRICA

Mediterranean Sea

Epidamnus

Corcyra

GREECE

Chalcis

Athens

Corinth

Sparta

LESBOS

IONIA

LYDIA

Miletus

RHODES

CRETE

Cyrene

LIBYA

CYPRUS

Citium

Byblos

Sidon

Tyre

Gaza

Saïs

Naucraris

Memphis

LOWER EGYPT

UPPER EGYPT

Thebes

PHOENICIA

SYRIA

Damascus

Samaria

Jerusalem

Lachish

Aleppo

Tarsus

Gordium

Heraclea

Sinope

Pontus Eucxinus

Trapezus

ARMENIA

URARTU

ASSYRIA

Nineveh

Assur

ASSYRIAN EMPIRE

MEDIA

Susa

BABYLONIA

Babylon

Nippur

Ur

xcvii

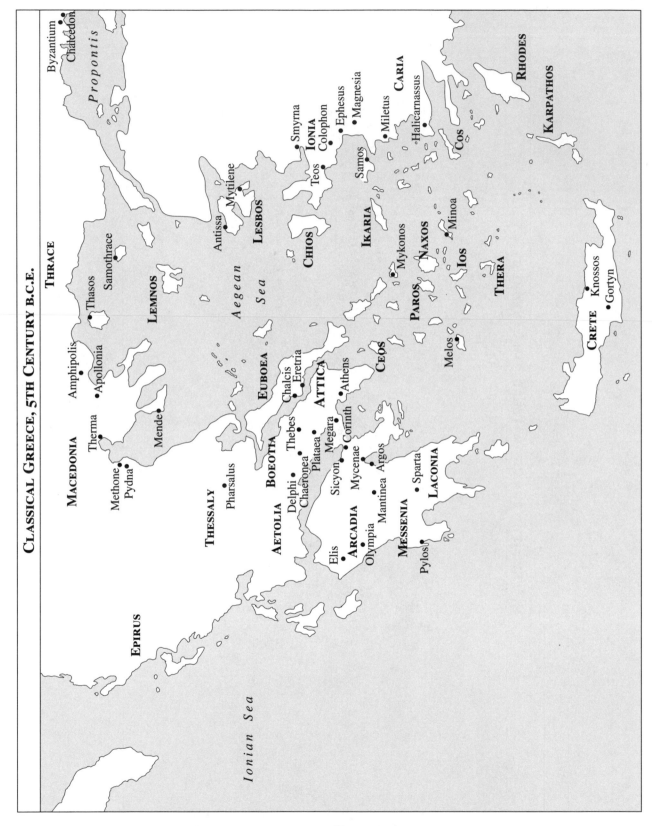

CLASSICAL GREECE, 5TH CENTURY B.C.E.

Byzantium
Chalcedon
Propontis

THRACE

EPIRUS

Ionian Sea

MACEDONIA
Amphipolis
Therma
Apollonia
Methone
Pydna
Mende

THESSALY
Pharsalus

AETOLIA

Delphi
Chaeronea
Thebes
BOEOTIA
Plataea
Chalcis
Eretria
EUBOEA

ATTICA
Athens
Megara
Corinth
Sicyon
Mycenae
Argos
Mantinea
ARCADIA
Olympia
Elis
Sparta
LACONIA
MESSENIA
Pylos

Samothrace
Thasos
LEMNOS

Antissa
Mytilene
LESBOS

CHIOS

CEOS

PAROS

Mykonos
NAXOS
Minoa
Ios
THERA

Melos

Smyrna
IONIA
Colophon
Teos
Ephesus
Magnesia
Miletus
Samos
IKARIA

CARIA
Halicarnassus
Cos

RHODES

KARPATHOS

CRETE
Knossos
Gortyn

Aegean Sea

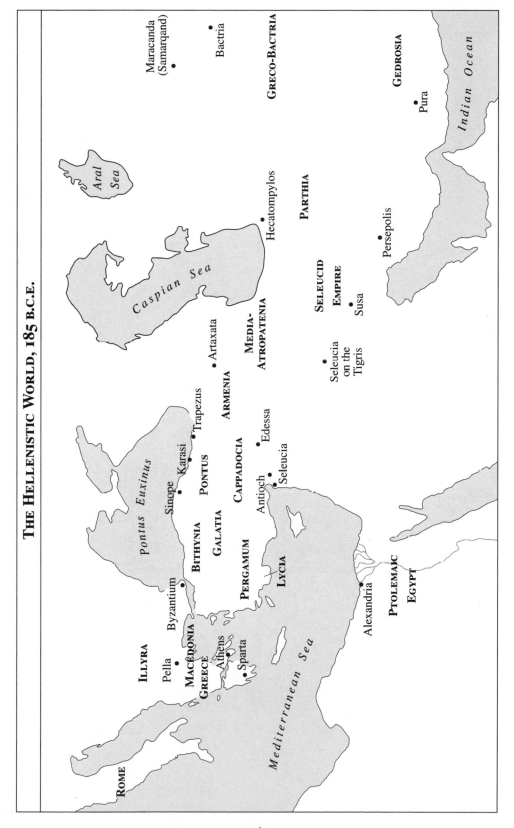

The Hellenistic World, 185 B.C.E.

ROME

ILLYRA

Pella
•

MACEDONIA

GREECE

Athens
•

Sparta
•

Byzantium
•

Pontus Euxinus

Sinope

BITHYNIA

Karasi
•

PONTUS

Trapezus
•

GALATIA

PERGAMUM

CAPPADOCIA

LYCIA

Antioch
•

Seleucia
•

Edessa
•

ARMENIA

Artaxata
•

MEDIA-ATROPATENIA

Alexandria
•

PTOLEMAIC

EGYPT

Mediterranean Sea

Aral Sea

Caspian Sea

Hecatompylos
•

PARTHIA

Seleucia on the Tigris
•

SELEUCID EMPIRE

Susa
•

Persepolis
•

MEDIA-ATROPATENIA

Maracanda (Samarqand)
•

Bactria
•

GRECO-BACTRIA

GEDROSIA

Pura
•

Indian Ocean

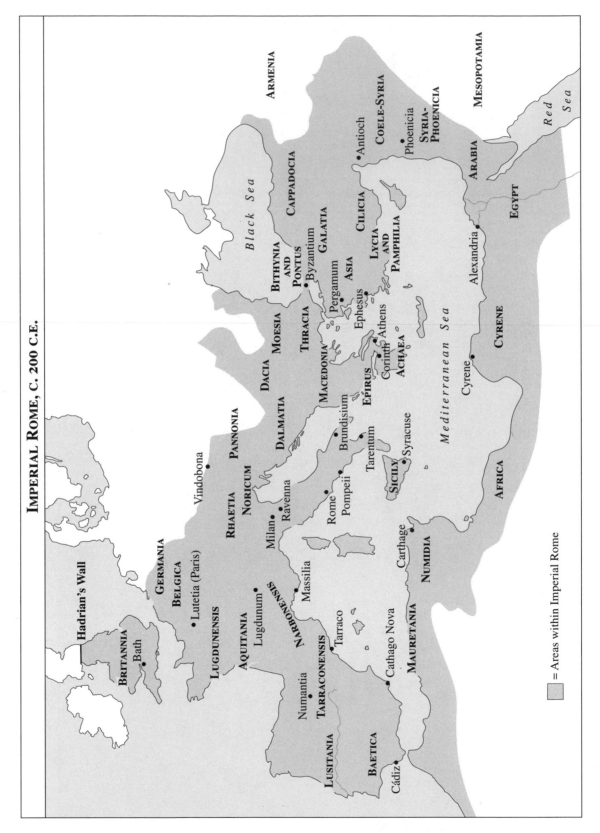

IMPERIAL ROME, C. 200 C.E.

= Areas within Imperial Rome

c

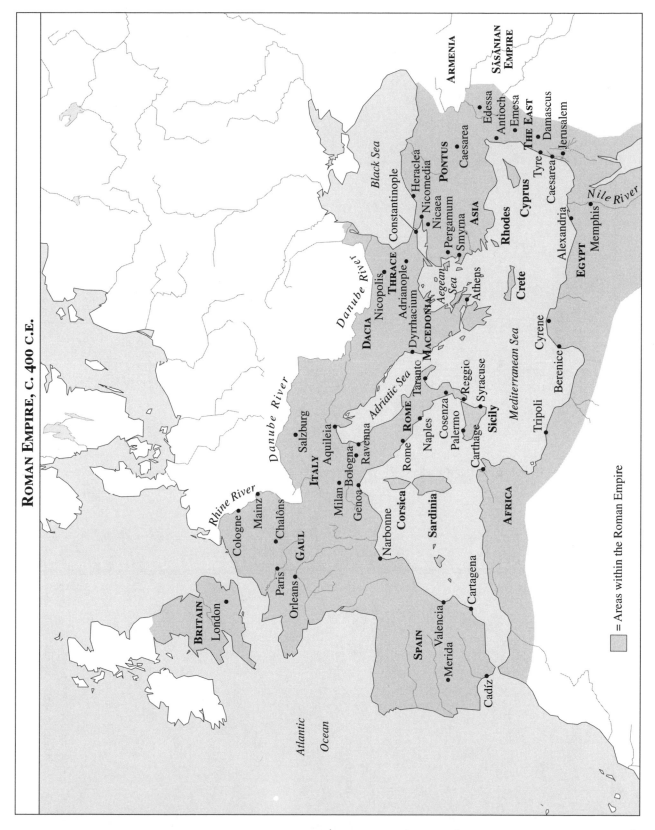

ROMAN EMPIRE, C. 400 C.E.

Atlantic
Ocean

BRITAIN
London

Rhine River

Cologne
Mainz
Chalôns
Paris
Orleans
GAUL

Narbonne

SPAIN
Valencia
Merida
Cartagena
Cadiz

Salzburg
Aquileia
ITALY
Milan
Bologna
Genoa
Ravenna

Corsica

Sardinia

AFRICA

Danube River

Danube River

DACIA

Nicopolis
THRACE
Adrianople
Dyrrhacium
MACEDONIA

Rome
ROME
Naples
Cosenza
Palermo
Carthage

Taranto
Reggio
Syracuse
Sicily

Adriatic Sea

Aegean
Sea
Athens

Black Sea

Constantinople
Heraclea
Nicomedia
Nicaea
Pergamum
Smyrna
ASIA
PONTUS
Caesarea

ARMENIA

SĀSĀNIAN
EMPIRE

Edessa
Antioch
Emesa
THE EAST
Tyre
Damascus
Caesarea
Jerusalem

Cyprus
Rhodes
Crete

Mediterranean Sea

Cyrene
Berenice

Tripoli

Nile River

Alexandria
Memphis

EGYPT

= Areas within the Roman Empire

ci

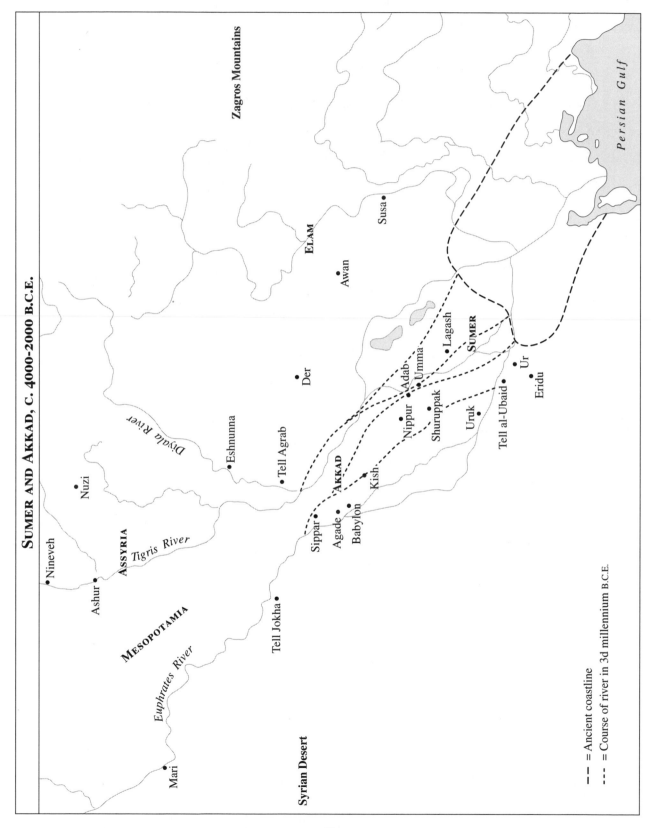

SUMER AND AKKAD, C. 4000-2000 B.C.E.

Zagros Mountains

Persian Gulf

ELAM

Susa

Awan

Der

SUMER

Lagash

Adab

Umma

Ur

Eshnunna

Nippur

Eridu

Tell Agrab

Shuruppak

Uruk

Tell al-Ubaid

Diyala River

Nuzi

Kish

AKKAD

Nineveh

ASSYRIA

Tigris River

Sippar

Ashur

Agade

Babylon

MESOPOTAMIA

Tell Jokha

Euphrates River

Syrian Desert

Mari

-- -- = Ancient coastline

- - - = Course of river in 3d millennium B.C.E.

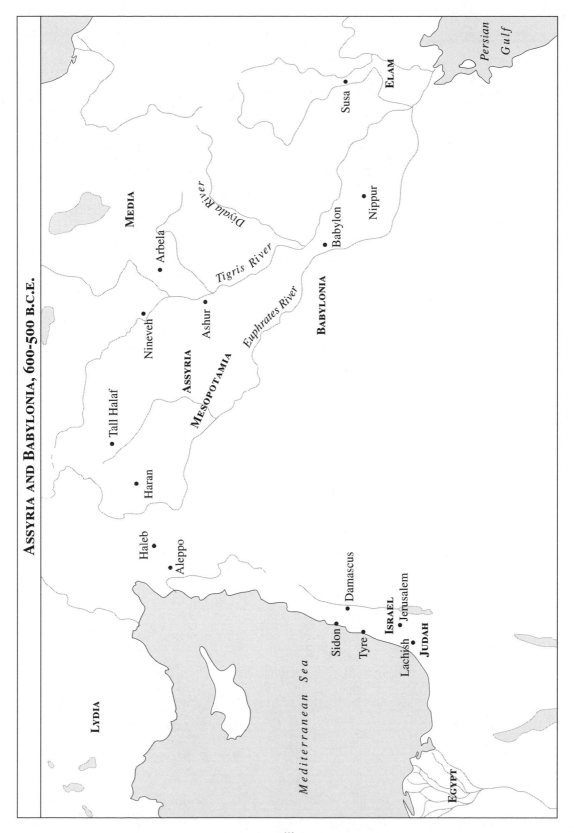

ASSYRIA AND BABYLONIA, 600–500 B.C.E.

LYDIA

Haleb

Aleppo

Tall Halaf

Haran

MESOPOTAMIA

ASSYRIA

Nineveh

Ashur

Arbela

MEDIA

Diyala River

Tigris River

Euphrates River

Babylon

Nippur

BABYLONIA

Susa

ELAM

Persian
Gulf

Mediterranean Sea

Sidon

Tyre

Damascus

ISRAEL

Lachish

Jerusalem

JUDAH

EGYPT

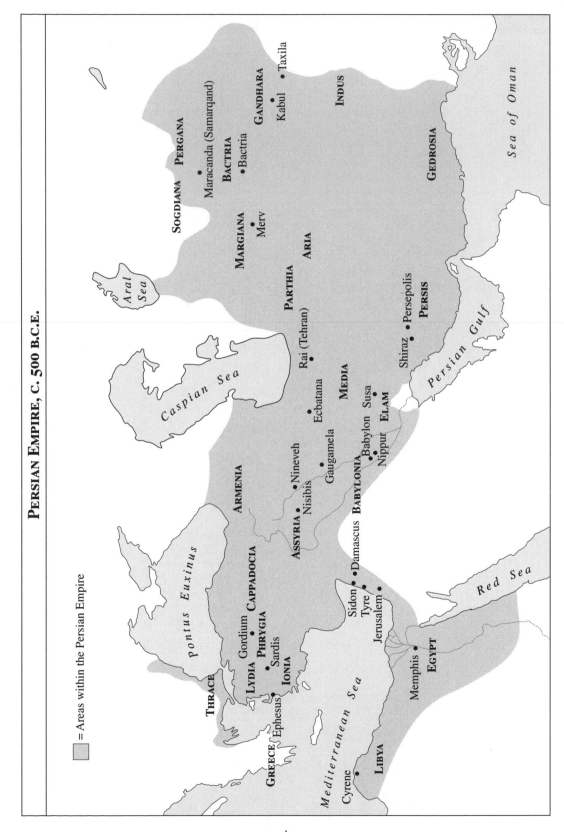

PERSIAN EMPIRE, C. 500 B.C.E.

= Areas within the Persian Empire

THRACE

Pontus Euxinus

GREECE
Ephesus
IONIA
Sardis
LYDIA Gordium
PHRYGIA CAPPADOCIA

ASSYRIA •Nineveh
Nisibis•
•Damascus

Sidon•
Tyre•
Jerusalem•

Mediterranean Sea

Cyrene•
LIBYA

Memphis•
EGYPT

Red Sea

ARMENIA

Caspian Sea

Aral
Sea

SOGDIANA
Maracanda (Samarqand)•
PERGANA

BACTRIA
•Bactria

GANDHARA
Kabul• •Taxila

INDUS

MARGIANA
Merv•

ARIA

PARTHIA

Rai (Tehran)•
Ecbatana•
MEDIA

Gaugamela•
BABYLONIA
Babylon• Susa•
Nippur• ELAM

Shiraz• •Persepolis
PERSIS

GEDROSIA

Persian Gulf

Sea of Oman

civ

PARTHIAN AND SĀSĀNIAN EMPIRES, C. 230 B.C.E.-500 C.E.

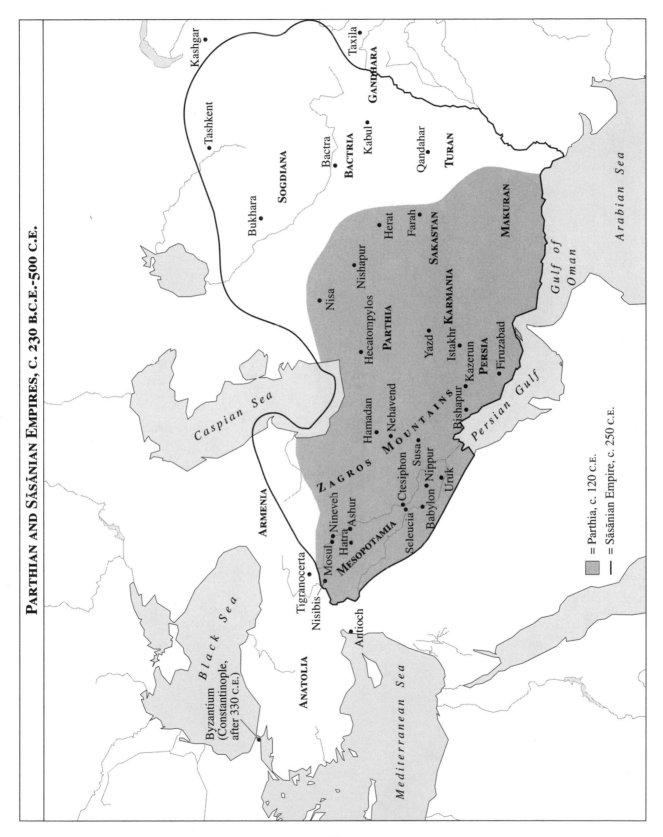

Kashgar

Taxila

Tashkent

GANDHARA

Bactra

BACTRIA

Kabul

SOGDIANA

Qandahar

TURAN

Bukhara

Herat

Farah

SAKASTAN

MAKURAN

Nishapur

Arabian Sea

Nisa

Gulf of Oman

Hecatompylos

PARTHIA

KARMANIA

Yazd

Istakhr

Caspian Sea

Kazerun

Firuzabad

PERSIA

Bishapur

Hamadan

Nehavend

Persian Gulf

MOUNTAINS

ZAGROS

Ctesiphon

Susa

Babylon Nippur

Uruk

ARMENIA

Mosul Nineveh

Hatra Ashur

MESOPOTAMIA

Seleucia

Tigranocerta

Nisibis

ANATOLIA

Black Sea

Byzantium
(Constantinople,
after 330 C.E.)

Antioch

Mediterranean Sea

= Parthia, c. 120 C.E.

= Sāsānian Empire, c. 250 C.E.

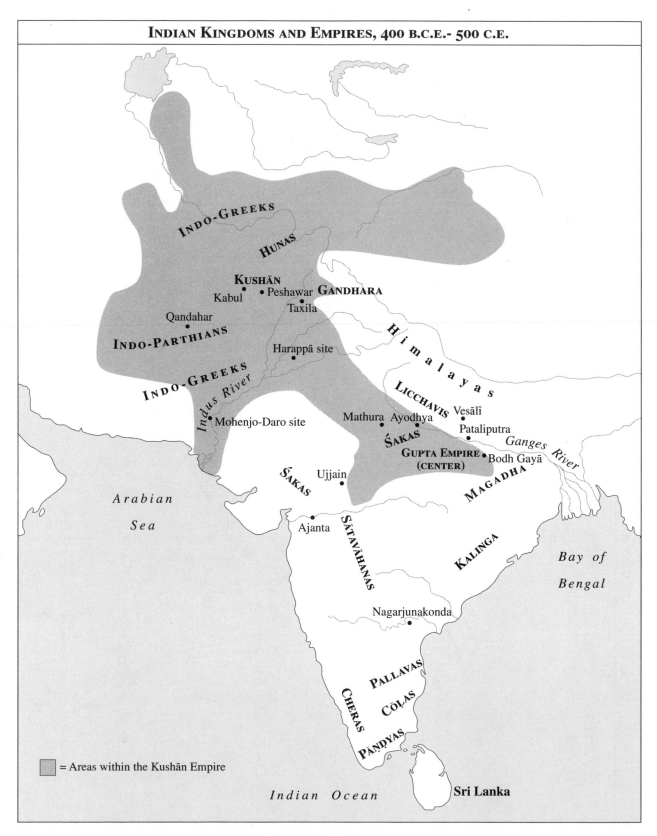

INDIAN KINGDOMS AND EMPIRES, 400 B.C.E.- 500 C.E.

INDO-GREEKS

HUNAS

KUSHĀN
Kabul • • Peshawar GANDHARA
Taxila
Qandahar

INDO-PARTHIANS
Harappā site

INDO-GREEKS

Indus River

H i m a l a y a s

LICCHAVIS
Vesālī •
Mathura • Ayodhya
Pataliputra
Mohenjo-Daro site
ŚAKAS
GUPTA EMPIRE • Bodh Gayā
(CENTER)
Ganges River

ŚAKAS
Ujjain MAGADHA

Arabian
Sea
Ajanta SATAVAHANAS
KALINGA
Bay of
Bengal

Nagarjunakonda

PALLAVAS
CHERAS CŌLAS
PANDYAS

= Areas within the Kushān Empire

Indian Ocean Sri Lanka

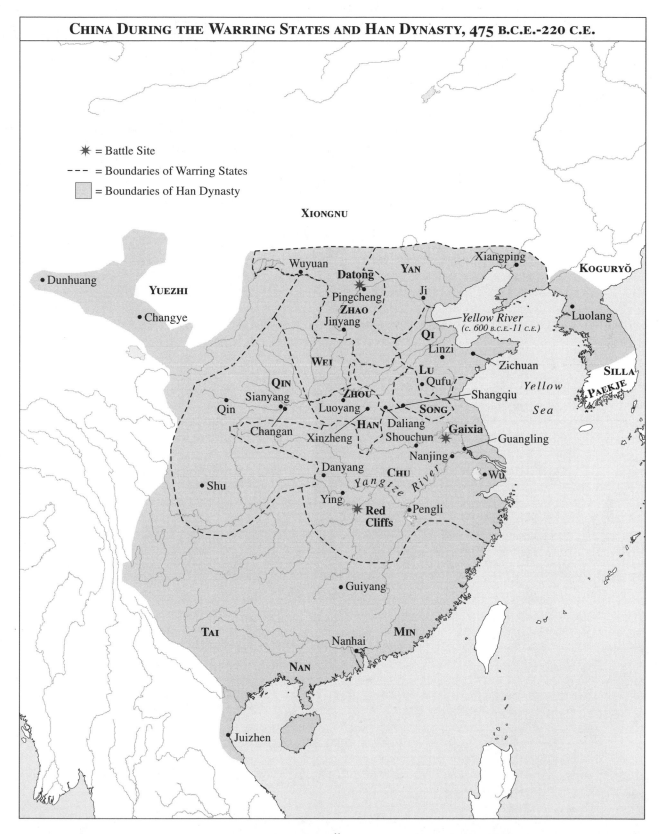

CHINA DURING THE WARRING STATES AND HAN DYNASTY, 475 B.C.E.–220 C.E.

✳ = Battle Site

- - - = Boundaries of Warring States

▢ = Boundaries of Han Dynasty

XIONGNU

Dunhuang

YUEZHI

Changye

Wuyuan

Datong

YAN

Xiangping

KOGURYŎ

Pingcheng

Ji

ZHAO

Jinyang

Yellow River
(c. 600 B.C.E.–11 C.E.)

Luolang

QI

Linzi

WEI

Zichuan

SILLA

PAEKJE

LU

Qufu

QIN

Sianyang

ZHOU

Luoyang

Shangqiu

Yellow
Sea

Qin

SONG

Changan

HAN

Daliang

Gaixia ✳

Xinzheng

Shouchun

Guangling

Nanjing

Danyang

CHU

Yangtze River

Wu

Shu

Ying

Red
Cliffs ✳

Pengli

Guiyang

TAI

MIN

Nanhai

NAN

Juizhen

The Ancient World

Prehistory - 476 C.E.

312-264 B.C.E.
BUILDING OF THE APPIAN WAY

The Appian Way, a major highway, improved transportation of people and goods within the Roman Empire.

LOCALE: Latium and Campania, south of Rome
CATEGORY: Science and technology

KEY FIGURES

Appius Claudius Caecus (fl. early fourth-late third century B.C.E.), Roman consul, censor in 312 B.C.E., and builder of the highway

Trajan (Marcus Ulpius Traianus; c. 53-117 C.E.), Roman emperor, r. c. 98-117 C.E., had highway paved to the port at Brundisium, which was 366 miles (590 kilometers) from Rome

SUMMARY OF EVENT

During the first centuries of the Roman conquest of Italy, there were no major roads to connect the growing city on the Tiber River with other areas on the peninsula.

Whereas the Persians had created a partially paved road system through their wide domain, Italian travel was limited before 300 B.C.E. In the early fourth century, short gravel or dirt trackways reached out from Rome to Alba Longa 12 miles (19 kilometers) to the south, and east to the salt beds in the mountains. Among his many duties, the Roman magistrate known as the *censor* was charged with maintaining such roads.

The earliest paved highway of any length in Italy was begun in the year 312 B.C.E., when the censor Appius Claudius Caecus took the initiative in projecting a military highway south from Rome. Appius was a vigorous patrician and two-time consul who was also credited with constructing Rome's first aqueduct and with enrolling plebeians in the senate. His chief monument, however, was the road he began, which was named the Via Appia in his honor.

Surveyors laid out the first 50 miles (80 kilometers) of the road on a straight southwest line paralleling the sea-

The Appian Way. (F. R. Niglutsch)

coast, about 12 miles (19 kilometers) inland. Rapid military access to the coast may have been one purpose for the highway. Its chief original objective, however, was the key city of Capua, in the heart of the fertile Campanian Plain. Capua had recently been captured by Roman armies, and Roman military colonies had been founded in strategic sites near Capua.

Less than 12 miles (19 kilometers) of the new road was paved immediately. On this section, laborers dug a trench 15 feet (4.6 meters) wide and 3 feet (0.9 meter) deep. Lining this with layers of loose gravel and small rock, they carefully fitted large slabs of polygonal stone into place as a surface. This segment of the road climbed to a ridge, from which it provided panoramic views of flat lands toward the sea as well as the Alban Hills to the east. An old village, Bovillae, was the first post-station at the end of the original paved area in 292 B.C.E.

Climbing and descending more steeply, travelers reached the village of Ariccia, where many travelers, including the poet Horace (65-8 B.C.E.), spent the first night out of Rome. At such points, the road was intersected by a crossroad, used by farmers to bring produce to a village market. Beyond Ariccia were the broad Pomptine Marshes, where it was necessary to drive in wooden pilings to raise a causeway 6 feet (1.8 meters) above the swamp land. At a trade center called Forum Appii, the road ended temporarily. Travelers could take boats 20 miles (32 kilometers) to Terracina or choose a long detour inland.

South of Terracina were mountains, forcing a zigzag route until a sea-level road was cut into the cliffs during imperial times. A four-arch brick bridge crossed the Liri River, and at Sinuessa the road turned sharply eastward along the Volturno River until it crossed on another massive bridge into Capua, 132 miles (213 kilometers) from the Roman Forum.

Too blind to see the finished project, Appius was said to have walked barefoot on the road to feel that the stones were well placed. Later, the highway was stretched out to Venusia, a colony settled by twenty thousand inhabitants. By 264 B.C.E., the road reached the sea at the ports of Tarentum and Brundisium, a total of 366 miles (590 kilometers) from Rome.

Other highways later shared the traffic, but the Via Appia remained the chief route south of Rome well into imperial times. About 250 B.C.E., milestones were placed at intervals measuring 5,000 Roman feet (approximately 4,860 feet or 1,480 meters). Trees planted by the roadside shaded travelers. In ancient times and later during the medieval period, rich Italians built tombs alongside the road, which eventually became lined with markets, towns, temples, monasteries, and other landmarks. One famous location was the Quo Vadis Church, where, according to legend, Saint Peter was said to have met his Lord and turned back during his flight from Rome.

SIGNIFICANCE

Finally paved to Brundisium by the emperor Trajan in 114 C.E., the Appian Way was called the Queen of Roads by the poet Statius (c. 46-96 C.E.). By that time, a complex web of roadways, built to the same pattern, crisscrossed the Roman Empire. Built to last and constructed on deep-set roadbeds resistant to flood or frost, these roads bound together Rome's conquests. Although originally used as military passageways, these roads served many other purposes. Roman civilians, such as Cicero (106-43 B.C.E.), and provincials, such as the apostle Paul (c. 10-c. 64 C.E.), traveled on these roads. It could be argued that these roads, which ensured direct, relatively easy travel between cities and among provinces, were a key element in administering and maintaining the imperial bureaucracy over such a huge territory as Rome commanded at its height.

In paving their 53,000 miles (85,500 kilometers) of roads, the Romans used many local stones. The most common type of stone found in Italy was the hard green-black volcanic basalt used along much of the Appian Way. Although floods or cultivation have obliterated the old road in many places, long stretches are still usable, paralleling more modern highways. The fact that modern highways do parallel the Roman roads is a testament to the Romans' efficiency in plotting out the most efficient route between two points.

—*Roger B. McShane, updated by Jeffrey L. Buller*

FURTHER READING

Hamblin, Dora Jane. *The Appian Way, a Journey.* New York: Random House, 1974. Part travelogue, part history, this work provides a highly readable introduction to the Appian Way. Short but useful bibliography.

MacKendrick, Paul. *The Mute Stones Speak.* 2d ed. New York: W. W. Norton, 1983. Expertly combining archaeological information with historical and social insight, this work contains a valuable short survey of Roman road construction, including the Via Appia.

Paget, Robert F. *Central Italy: An Archaeological Guide.* Park Ridge, N.J.: Noyes Press, 1973. In addition to providing a wealth of archaeological information about Italian prehistory and Villanovan, Etruscan,

Samnite, Italic, and early Roman remains, this work also discusses the ancient Roman road system.

Scullard, Howard Hayes. *A History of the Roman World: 753-146 B.C.* 5th ed. New York: Routledge, 2002. Lavishly detailed and comprehensive in scope, this book places the construction of the Via Appia in its context of Roman economic, military, and social history.

Staccioli, Romolo Augusto. *The Roads of the Romans.* New York: Oxford University Press, 2003. An amaz-

ingly detailed study of the road system of the Roman Empire, starting with the streets of Rome itself and moving outward to discuss the construction, maintenance, and importance of roads throughout the empire.

SEE ALSO: 447-438 B.C.E., Building of the Parthenon; 312 B.C.E., First Roman Aqueduct Is Built.

RELATED ARTICLE in *Great Lives from History: The Ancient World*: Trajan.

3d century B.C.E.
COMMERCIAL CITY OF JENNE IS FOUNDED ON NIGER RIVER

Excavations of a commercial city-state at Jenne on the Niger River revealed a high level of development and urbanization in Africa, long before the arrival of Islamic Arabs.

LOCALE: Jenne, Mali

CATEGORIES: Prehistory and ancient cultures; trade and commerce

SUMMARY OF EVENT

Jenne (now Djenné, Mali) was one of the first urban centers of Africa, emerging by the last millennium B.C.E. The city had a thriving economy based on economic specialization and interregional trade by the third century B.C.E. It continued to be important as a commercial and religious center for western African and trans-Saharan trade networks for twenty-three centuries after its initial emergence.

Jenne lies in the Niger floodplain just south of Timbuktu and north of the western African forests at the interface of desert, savanna, woodland, and river economies, a position that makes it ideal for trade. Transportation from Jenne was unusual because it required shifting between overland and river transport at various points. Exported and imported goods were moved overland with pack animals such as the camel or donkey and in the middle Niger Delta by boats, which moved goods to transshipment points such as Jenne for further distribution in the Saharan, Sahelian, and forest zones.

One of the most prominent historical trends south of the Sahara between 1000 and 100 B.C.E. was the emergence of long-distance trading between forest and desert communities. The major reasons for this shift from domestic agriculture to long-distance trade and commerce most likely were economic specialization and increasing dependence across the wider Sudanic belt on iron and

copper implements as common currencies of exchange. Although copper was available at sites such as Aïr in the Saharan mountains of western Africa, no major sources of copper existed in many regions of western Africa, and iron ore was scarce in the Niger Delta (metal ores were available about 60 miles, or 100 kilometers, east of Jenne). Without urban centers, people of Sudanic western Africa had to travel great distances to obtain desired metals such as copper or iron. Another product in high demand throughout western Africa was cotton cloth. Archaeology indicates that the weaving of cotton was already occurring along the Niger by 1000 B.C.E., and cotton cloth was another important commodity in Jenne's social and economic life in the third century.

With the rise of commerce in the western Sudanic belt came communities or villages, formed by social stratification or caste divisions that evolved as people adopted or were forced into roles such as artisan, ruling elite, slave, or peasant. Artisans and merchants made up the core populations of the urban centers, and villages often formed around a central city and acted as suppliers and outposts of the market centers. One of the most widely known and best examples of this kind of commercial community is the cluster of cities around Jenne.

Archaeologists have determined that a permanent settlement first became possible in the Middle Niger around 1000 B.C.E. This initial settlement was the result of southward migration from the upper inland Niger Delta, which occurred because of a markedly dry period that reached its climax between 200 and 100 B.C.E. Before this time of low rainfall, the floodwaters of the Niger and its tributaries were higher and lasted longer in the Middle Niger, discouraging any long-term village settlement in the delta. During the arid last millennium B.C.E., farmers and herders of the Upper Niger Delta moved farther southward in their quest for dependable water sources. Moving southward, migrants discovered the interior floodplain of the Middle Niger, full of rich soil and a flood region suitable for rice cultivation.

Archaeological evidence strongly suggests that as soon as the initial urban settlements of the Middle Niger were formed, they began trading with outside regions. Archaeological excavations have uncovered smithed iron in the form of jewelry and tools dating from the third through first centuries B.C.E., indicating artisans were a strong presence in Jenne. Researchers have also discovered Roman beads and stone grinders dating back to this period, which indicate long-distance trade in ancient times.

SIGNIFICANCE

The city of Jenne is one of the best sites for understanding the early history of urban development in western Africa because the site contains rich archaeological evidence of an ancient western Sudanic commercial city-state. Material culture from Jenne reveals how commerce progressed in western Africa. The city became a center for commerce in West Africa for many reasons, including its geographical location. Located on the eastern edge of the inland delta and surrounded by various channels of the Niger River, it became a major transshipment center. The Niger was a direct source of transportation of goods by boat from the east and west of the river. Jenne's position on the eastern border of the delta meant that it had the advantage of close proximity to various important long-distance overland routes and iron deposits in the east. The use of boats along the river rather than circling the river overland by foot or donkey markedly cut a trader's travel time.

As a transshipment point, Jenne was influential in the development of metalworking in other parts of western Africa. By the third century B.C.E., copper and iron, once rarities in many regions, were reaching the western Sudan from the east and traveling via boat along the Niger River. Once the copper reached the commercial center of Jenne, it would be taken south and west of the Niger by donkey along the main overland routes.

Jenne was not only a city of trade but also an agriculturally thriving locality. The city was surrounded by a moist, rich, alluvial soil along with a great floodplain, which was ideal for fishing and rice growing, even in a climatically arid phase. Jenne was an important town that exported agricultural products to the more arid regions outside the Niger Delta.

The archaeological significance of Jenne has been momentous in that it is a pre-Islamic urban and commercial center in Africa. After increased excavations of Jenne took place during the 1970's and 1980's, many earlier assumptions about the lack of a social, economic, or urban history in Africa before the common era were proven incorrect. Many archaeologists and historians once believed that the development of an urbanized commercial city-state based on long-distance trade in Africa had not taken place until after the arrival of the Islamized Arabs in North Africa during the seventh and eighth centuries. The excavations of Jenne have revealed that the rise of a commercial city-state at this site had begun at least as early as 200 B.C.E.

Jenne has important significance in the context of Africa's urban history in the latter part of the last millennium B.C.E., and from the eighth century onward, it increasingly gained currency as a center of university learning, Islamic life and culture, and artistic developments.

—Kristofor Rico

FURTHER READING

Bedaux, Rogier Michiel Alphons, and J. D. van der Waals. *Djenné: Une Ville millénaire au Mali*. Leiden: Rijksmuseum voor Volkenkunde, 1994. Examines the architecture of Djenné (Jenne) in historical perspective. In French.

McIntosh, Roderick J. "Clustered Cities of the Middle Niger: Alternative Routes to Authority in Prehistory." In *Africa's Urban Past*, edited by David Anderson. Portsmouth, N.H.: Heinemann, 2000. Examines the ancient history of Djenné as an urban settlement.

McIntosh, Susan Keech, and Roderick J. McIntosh. "Jenne-Jeno: An Ancient African City." *Archaeology* 33, no. 1 (January/February, 1980): 8-14. A discussion of the archaeology of the ancient city of Djenné in the Inland Niger Delta.

_____. "Cities Without Citadels: Understanding Urban Origins Along the Middle Niger." In *Archaeology of Africa: Food, Metals, and Towns*, edited by Thurstan Shaw et al. New York: Routledge, 1993. This source traces the history and origins of early urbanism in the western Sudan that preceded Arab and Islamic influences in the region.

SEE ALSO: c. 1000 B.C.E.-c. 300 C.E., Urban Commerce Develops in the Sudan Belt; c. 500 B.C.E.-c. 200 C.E., Libyan Garamantes Flourish as Farmers and Traders; 450-100 B.C.E., City-State of Yeha Flourishes in the Northern Ethiopian Highlands; c. 300-c. 100 B.C.E., Berber Kingdoms of Numidia and Mauretania Flourish; c. 100 B.C.E.-c. 300 C.E., East African Trading Port of Rhapta Flourishes.

3d century B.C.E. (traditionally 660 B.C.E.)
JIMMU TENNŌ BECOMES THE FIRST EMPEROR OF JAPAN

Traditionally, Japanese people consider the legendary Jimmu to be the first emperor of their nation and celebrate the day of his mythical assumption of imperial dignity, February 11, as a national holiday.

LOCALE: Kyūshū and Kinki region (especially Nara), Japan

CATEGORIES: Government and politics; expansion and land acquisition

KEY FIGURES

Jimmu Tennō (possibly fl. third century C.E.; traditionally 711-585 B.C.E.), legendary first emperor of Japan

Nagasune Hiko (traditionally d. c. 663 B.C.E.), Jimmu's most formidable adversary

Michi no Omi (traditionally fl. seventh century B.C.E.), Jimmu's most able officer

Hime Tatatara Isuzu Hime no Mikoto (traditionally fl. seventh century B.C.E.), daughter of a lightning god and a mortal, first empress of Japan, and Jimmu's wife

SUMMARY OF EVENT

According to Japanese tradition, Jimmu founded the Japanese empire on the first day of the first month of the Japanese calendar in the year 660 B.C.E., when he enthroned himself in the Kashihara Palace, believed to have stood near the contemporary city of Nara on Japan's central island of Honshū. Until the end of World War II, most Japanese took this event and the legendary struggles leading up to it as true history, discounting strong scholarly evidence that Jimmu was most likely a mythical figure, comparable to King Arthur in the Western world. Although February 11, the day of Jimmu's coronation in the Western calendar, was made a holiday again in 1967 after being abolished in 1945, the popular consensus in Japan treats Jimmu's accession to the throne as a legend based on some historical fact.

Traditionally, Kamu Yamato Iware Hiko no Mikoto was born in 711 B.C.E. on the southwestern Japanese island of Kyūshū. His father was a great-grandson of the sun goddess, Amaterasu Ōmikami, and his mother was a daughter of the sea god. The name of Jimmu, meaning "divine valor," was given to him much later, long after his death, in the eighth century C.E., but it is the name that he has been known by ever since. In 694 B.C.E., Jimmu inherited the throne of his local kingdom. He married Ahiratsu Hime, a beautiful young local noblewoman, as a consort, and they had two children.

Historically, there is evidence of the pottery-producing Yayoi culture inhabiting Kyūshū in the third century B.C.E., and Chinese sources of the period mention a feudal society existing on the island. Hence scholars believe this much later period to be closer in time to when the man who might have been Japan's first emperor actually lived.

According to tradition, in 667 B.C.E., Jimmu gathered his household and revealed his plan to conquer the Yamato region, around the present city of Nara. He justified his invasion with a divine mandate that called for him to subjugate the plain of Nara, believed to be the center of the universe. Historically, there is evidence for the invasion of Yamato (now the Kinki region in Japan) by peoples from the southwest and the subsequent establishment of a strong central authority.

As Jimmu's expedition made its way eastward from Kyūshū across the Inland Sea to its subsequent landfall near modern-day Ōsaka, the future emperor picked up more followers, who would become the ancestors of Japan's noble families ruling in the seventh and eighth centuries, when the story of Jimmu's accession was first written down. For three years, until 663 B.C.E., Jimmu rested in fortified camps and built a huge fleet. Then he took on his powerful adversary Nagasune Hiko, who ruled the fertile Nara plains.

In the first battle, Jimmu's forces were defeated at Ōsaka, and his brother Itsuse was mortally wounded by an arrow from a lowly enemy foot soldier. Retreating south by sea toward the tip of the Wakayama peninsula, Jimmu lost his remaining two brothers to the ferocious sea that swallowed them. Trying to advance toward Nara from the south, Jimmu's army was enshrouded by a poisonous vapor. The mist was lifted by the intervention of the sun goddess Amaterasu, who also sent Jimmu a three-legged sun crow, Yatagarasu, to lead his army out of the mountainous wilderness near the shore and bring it into contact with the enemy.

By force and trickery, Jimmu and his most able officer, Michi no Omi, succeeded in subduing their various enemies. Late in 663 B.C.E., Jimmu met up again with Nagasune Hiko. Their battles were inconclusive until a golden kite descended from heaven and blinded Hiko's soldiers, who abandoned the battlefield. As Nagasune Hiko asked for mercy, he was killed by his brother-in-

THE FIRST TEN LEGENDARY EMPERORS OF JAPAN, 660-30 B.C.E.

Emperor	Traditional Reign Date
Jimmu	660-585
Suizei	581-549
Annei	549-511
Itoku	510-477
Kōshō	475-393
Kōan	392-291
Kōrei	290-215
Kōgen	214-158
Kaika	158-98
Sujin	97-30

law, who then submitted their army to the victorious Jimmu.

In 662 B.C.E., Jimmu cleaned the Nara area of bandits, among them some hideous earth spider people, who were summarily executed. In spring, he decided to found a genuine empire and civilize the land and his people. In 661 B.C.E., Jimmu married Hime Tatatara Isuzu Hime no Mikoto, a noblewoman with a divine father from Nara plains.

In 660 B.C.E., in the new palace at Kashihara near modern-day Nara, Jimmu enthroned himself and his wife as Japan's first emperor and empress. At this point, the country was considered unified, and the Japanese nation was born.

Subsequently, Jimmu rewarded his followers and had two more children, one of whom would succeed him on the throne. According to tradition, he reigned for seventy-four more years, as the country prospered and grew. Jimmu reportedly died in 585 B.C.E., at the age of 126.

SIGNIFICANCE

Since the legend of Jimmu was written down in the seventh and eighth centuries B.C.E., it has been a source of pride for many Japanese, who have held that the imperial line descended from ancient times unbroken into the present. Historically, the legend of Jimmu became important as Japanese civilization came into its own, imperial rule solidified, and the young nation sought to establish a worthy native counterpart to the much older Chinese culture.

After writing was introduced to Japan via China and Korea around 404 C.E., its rulers felt a need for a written history. In the seventh century, imperial authorities wanted a history that depicted a stable rule, not civil wars and disruptions. A second major role of the written history was to establish a genealogy for the noble families that would legitimize their social rank and position, for some enterprising families had forged ancient origins. The Jimmu legend neatly fulfilled these functions. In 621 C.E., the first history of Japan was written, yet it did not survive the burning of the imperial library two decades later. It was not until 712 and 720 C.E. that the first surviving Japanese histories were written, fixing the legendary events of Jimmu's reign. These histories were the *Kojiki* (712 C.E.; *Records of Ancient Matters*, 1883) and the *Nihon shoki* (compiled 720 C.E.; *Nihongi: Chronicles of Japan from the Earliest Times to A.D. 697*, 1896).

The traditional date of Jimmu's accession as emperor is based on Chinese numerology rather than history. Calculating backward from the eighth century, 660 B.C.E. was considered a grand *kanoto tori*, a year in which universe-shaping events would take place. Consequently, the foundation of the Japanese nation was put into this special year.

Contemporary historians have come to associate Jimmu with the legendary empire-building tenth emperor, Sujin, who traditionally ruled from 97 to 30 B.C.E., still probably much earlier than reality. Some believe that Sujin, although he must have ruled much later, may have been a real ruler on whom Jimmu was later modeled. Another theory holds that Jimmu is a mythical projection of the genuine twenty-sixth historical emperor Keitai, who also had to fight his way into Yamato before he was enthroned in the sixth century.

Regardless of the rather shaky historical basis for the legend of Jimmu, the story of Japan's first emperor has enjoyed great popularity in Japan for many centuries. It helped to install pride and confidence in the young island nation and later served as a substantial pillar of national identity. Misused by the militarists before and during World War II, the Jimmu legend was criticized in the postwar period. In its revived and revised form, it serves to remind the Japanese people of the long duration of their culture and preserves a nostalgic notion of an ancient, mythical past.

—*R. C. Lutz*

FURTHER READING

Aston, W. G., trans. *Nihongi: Chronicles of Japan, from the Earliest Times to A.D. 697.* 1896. Reprint. London: George Allen and Unwin, 1956. Still the only translation of the *Nihon shoki*, originally compiled in 720, which contains one of the two original accounts of Jimmu's accession to the imperial throne of Japan.

Brown, Delmer M., ed. *Ancient Japan*. Vol. 1 in *The Cambridge History of Japan*. New York: Cambridge University Press, 1993. A collection of contemporary essays covering the latest scholarship on the rise of early imperial Japan, with an interesting reflection on ancient Japanese historical consciousness.

Lu, David J. *Japan: A Documentary History*. Armonk, N.Y.: M. E. Sharpe, 1997. Contains an abridged account of Jimmu's accession to Japan's throne and related historical documents of the period.

Philippi, Donald L., trans. *Kojiki*. Princeton, N.J.: Princeton University Press, 1968. An English translation of the first Japanese account of Jimmu's rise to power, published in 712. Philippi uses an unusual romanization system for Japanese words, which alters the spelling of many familiar names, but no other complete English translation is available.

Reischauer, Robert Karl. *Early Japanese History: Part A*. Princeton, N.J.: Princeton University Press, 1937. Reprint. Gloucester, Mass.: Peter Smith, 1967. A pre-World War II compilation of Japanese sources describing mostly legendary events.

Sansom, George B. *A History of Japan to 1334*. Stanford, Calif.: Stanford University Press, 1958. Still valuable study of the earliest, legendary period of Japanese history.

SEE ALSO: c. 10,000-c. 300 B.C.E., Jōmon Culture Thrives in Japan; c. 7500 B.C.E., Birth of Shintō; c. 300 B.C.E., Yayoi Period Begins; c. mid-3d century C.E., Himiko Rules the Yamatai; c. 300-710 C.E., Kofun Period Unifies Japan; 390-430 C.E. or later, traditionally r. 270-310, Ōjin Tennō, First Historical Emperor of Japan, Reigns.

RELATED ARTICLES in *Great Lives from History: The Ancient World*: Jimmu Tennō; Jingū; Ojin Tennō.

3d century B.C.E. (traditionally 6th century B.C.E.)
LAOZI COMPOSES THE *DAO DE JING*

The compilation of the central Daoist classic, the Dao De Jing, *provided Chinese culture with one of its most distinctive and enduringly influential statements.*

LOCALE: China
CATEGORIES: Cultural and intellectual history; philosophy; religion

KEY FIGURES

Laozi (Lao-tzu; 604-sixth century B.C.E.), Chinese philosopher and Daoist religious figure who wrote the *Dao De Jing*

Wang Bi (Wang Pi; 226-249 C.E.), influential scholar who edited and wrote a commentary on the earliest complete manuscript of the *Dao De Jing*

SUMMARY OF EVENT

The *Dao De Jing* (*Tao Te Ching*; possibly sixth century B.C.E., probably compiled late third century B.C.E.; *The Speculations on Metaphysics, Polity, and Morality of "the Old Philosopher, Lau-Tsze,"* 1868; better known as the *Dao De Jing*), traditionally considered the foundational work of Daoism (Taoism), was often simply called the *Laozi* (*Lao Tzu*), after its supposed author. It was also known as the Five Thousand Character Classic, referring to its approximate length in the received text, which was edited as part of an early commentary by Wang Bi.

The work traditionally consists of eighty-one chapters, divided into two parts: the *Dao Jing*, or "Classic of the Way" (chapters 1-37), and the *De Jing*, or "Classic of Virtue/Power" (chapters 38-81). No chapter is longer than one page, and many are only a few lines. The order of the parts, interestingly, is reversed in some of the manuscripts, which some have seen as shifting the emphasis from the traditional cosmological emphasis to a social/political interpretation.

Daoism holds that a universal principle—the *dao*, or "way"—underlies everything as a supreme pattern and a principle of growth. This *dao* may be attained by observing nature, returning to a state of infancy, practicing nonaction, and controlling the breath, which is the life force. One who possesses *dao* must appear soft and weak and conceal his or her power; the exhibition of power only reveals that one does not possess it. Possessing the *dao* makes one a sage fit to rule.

Like many ancient works, the *Dao De Jing* has been viewed as more unified than may in fact be the case. Many contemporary scholars believe the work to be a kind of anthology of sayings, perhaps from various schools of thought. The connections among the chapters, and sometimes between individual lines, are certainly not always evident. Some general themes, however, can be discerned in the work as a whole, including the importance of *wu wei*, "not acting" or acting in accordance with the *dao* rather than forcing one's will, and in general the complementarity of opposites. Whether these themes are thought to be the foundation of Daoist sensibility, or merely an influential later expression of it, depends in large part on what dates are assigned to the work.

According to tradition, Laozi (the Old Master) was an older contemporary of Confucius (Kongfuzi, K'ung-Fu-Tzu; 551-479 B.C.E.). This would place the *Dao De Jing* in the late sixth or early fifth century B.C.E. Confucius is said to have met Laozi, and this notion might seem to be confirmed by the important Daoist text *Zhuangzi* (c. 300 B.C.E.; *The Divine Classic of Nan-hua*, 1881; also known as *The Complete Works of Chuang Tzu*, 1968; commonly known as *Zhuangzi*, 1991), and also attested to by the biographical entry in the *Shiji* (first century B.C.E.; *Records of the Grand Historian*, 1960) of Sima Qian. The latter identifies Laozi as the author of "a work in two books, setting out the meaning of the way and virtue in some five thousand characters," which he is said to have written as he was leaving for the west, at the request of a gatekeeper.

Modern critics have cast doubt on all the details of this simple picture. The biography in question is late and plainly not authoritative, mixing together ill-assorted claims. The material in the *Zhuangzi* is equivocal, admitting of adulteration. If Laozi lived so early and wrote the *Dao De Jing*, as the traditional story claims, historians ask why his views are not mentioned by a philosopher such as Mencius (Mengzi, Meng Tzu, 372-289 B.C.E.), who was so concerned to reply to the critics of Confucianism.

Some scholars have doubted whether Laozi ever existed at all. Even if he did, others have questioned whether his name should really be associated with the compilation of the *Dao De Jing*, which many scholars now date to the beginning of perhaps the mid-fourth or

The Chinese philosopher Laozi, riding an ox. (Hulton|Archive)

third century B.C.E. A popular date among revisionist scholars has been 250 B.C.E., though more recent arguments (for example, on the basis of comparative poetics) have suggested that 350 B.C.E. might be a likelier date—the partial text found at Guodian in 1993 has been thought to date from about 300 B.C.E. A few scholars, however, have continued to defend dates closer to the earlier, traditional dating of the text.

SIGNIFICANCE

In his much-admired 1963 translation and commentary, *The Way of Lao Tzu*, Wing-tsit Chan suggested that "no one can understand China or be an intelligent citizen of the world without some knowledge of the *Lao Tzu*." Since its creation, the *Dao De Jing* has exerted a pervasive influence on two dozen centuries of Chinese culture, as well as on the many other cultures within the Chinese sphere of influence in Southeast Asia. During the Tang Dynasty (T'ang; 618-907 C.E.), Daoism was particularly influential, with emperors patronizing the philosophy and the deified Laozi taken as the dynasty's original ancestor.

Daoism has also proven to have broad appeal throughout the Western world during the past two centuries. It has thus served as a primary stimulus to increased interest in, and knowledge of, the central concepts of Daoist thought, as those have come to play—perhaps in part because of that stimulus—a greater role in the philosophical and religious conversations of an increasingly cosmopolitan planet. The philosophy's exoticism and attraction often lie in its direct opposition to the mainstream Western philosophy of molding nature to human will, taking direct action to change the world, and viewing the world through the lens of rigorously defined and mutually exclusive categories.

—Edward Johnson

FURTHER READING

Chan, Alan K. L. *Two Visions of the Way: A Study of the Wang Pi and the Ho-shang Kung Commentaries on the Lao-Tzu.* Albany: State University of New York Press, 1991. A comparative study of the two chief traditional commentaries on the *Dao De Jing.* Notes, glossary, bibliography, index.

Clarke, J. J. *The Tao of the West: Western Transformations of Taoist Thought.* New York: Routledge, 2000. A study of the influence of the *Dao De Jing* and Daoism on Western cultures. Chronological and linguistic appendices, bibliography, index.

Kohn, Livia, and Michael LaFargue, eds. *Lao-tzu and the "Tao-te-ching."* Albany: State University of New York Press, 1998. Important collection includes a dozen essays by leading scholars. Glossary, bibliographies, index.

Laozi. *Dao De Jing, "Making This Life Significant": A Philosophical Translation.* Translated by Roger T. Ames and David L. Hall. New York: Ballantine, 2003. Well-known experts on Chinese philosophy offer a translation based on the Mawangdui texts, but keeping the traditional order, and an interpretation in terms of a philosophy of process. Lengthy introductions, glossary, distributed commentary, appendix, bibliography, thematic index.

_____. *Dao De Jing: The Book of the Way.* Translated by Moss Roberts. Berkeley: University of California Press, 2001. This version attempts to combine impressive scholarship with a poetic approach to the text. Introduction, detailed distributed commentary, notes, bibliography of Chinese and English sources.

_____. *The "Daodejing" of Laozi.* Translated by Philip J. Ivanhoe. New York: Seven Bridges Press, 2002. A new scholarly translation of the traditional Wang Bi text. Introduction, notes, bibliography, index, and an appendix that examines different ways of translating the first chapter.

_____. *Lao Tzu's "Tao Te Ching": A Translation of the Startling New Documents Found at Guodian.* Translated by Robert G. Henricks. New York: Columbia University Press, 2000. Translation of the incomplete version, with about two thousand characters, discovered in 1993 at Guodian, written on bamboo strips and dating from about 300 B.C.E. Chinese text, introduction and notes, bibliography, index.

_____. *Tao Te Ching.* Translated by D. C. Lau, edited by Sarah Allan. New York: Alfred A. Knopf/Everyman's Library, 1994. Lau's respected translation, valuable glossary, and appendices on the problem of authorship and the nature of the work are supplemented by Allan's chronology, bibliography, and useful introduction.

_____. *Tao Te Ching: The Definitive Edition.* Translated by Jonathan Star. New York: Jeremy P. Tarcher/Putnam, 2001. Besides his translation, the author provides a word-for-word rendering, with detailed defining glosses, which makes it possible for readers to explore the text in unusual detail. Notes, concordance, list of radicals, bibliography, and a detailed commentary on translating the first chapter.

SEE ALSO: 5th-1st century B.C.E., Composition of *The Great Learning*; 500-400 B.C.E., Creation of the *Wujing*; 479 B.C.E., Confucius's Death Leads to the Creation of *The Analects*; 139-122 B.C.E., Composition of the *Huainanzi*; 142 C.E., Zhang Daoling Founds the Celestial Masters Movement; c. 3d century C.E., Wang Bi and Guo Xiang Revive Daoism; 397-402 C.E., Ge Chaofu Founds the Lingbao Tradition of Daoism.

RELATED ARTICLES in *Great Lives from History: The Ancient World:* Confucius; Laozi; Mencius; Wang Bi; Zhuangzi.

c. 300 B.C.E.
EUCLID COMPILES A TREATISE ON GEOMETRY

Euclid's Elements, *one of the most influential mathematics texts of all time, set the standard for logical mathematical thought throughout Europe and the Middle East.*

LOCALE: Alexandria (now in Egypt)
CATEGORIES: Mathematics; cultural and intellectual history; science and technology

KEY FIGURE
Euclid (c. 330-c. 270 B.C.E.), Greek mathematician

SUMMARY OF EVENT
The city of Alexandria was founded by Alexander the Great in 332 B.C.E. After Alexander's death in 323 B.C.E., his empire was divided between his generals. Alexandria came under the power of Ptolemy Soter, who founded a great library and school there. The first of what was to become a long line of mathematicians at that school was Euclid.

The only sources of information on Euclid's life are commentaries in mathematics texts, which discuss his mathematics more than his personal life. The main sources are the commentaries of Pappus, which were written in the third century C.E., and the commentaries of Proclus, which were written in the fifth century C.E., significantly later than Euclid's lifetime. What can be said about Euclid's life is that he flourished about 300 B.C.E. and probably studied mathematics in Athens at the school founded by Plato. What is certain is that he wrote the *Stoicheia* (compiled c. 300 B.C.E.; *Elements*, 1570), an elementary introduction in thirteen books to all of Greek geometry as it was known at the time.

Euclid's great task was not in the creation of that geometry, although some of the proofs of the theorems in the *Elements* are thought to be Euclid's. Rather, his accomplishment is in the collection, categorization, and simplification of the contemporary knowledge of geometry. Euclid's achievement is twofold.

First, he collected the entire corpus of ancient Greek geometry and arranged it in a logical fashion. Each theorem in the *Elements*, including those of other authors, is proved using theorems that precede it in the text. Thus the theory is built up, theorem by theorem, on a solid logical foundation.

The second, and perhaps more important, of Euclid's accomplishments is the statement of the five axioms forming the logical basis of the entire work. An axiom is

an unprovable statement, one that is simply accepted as true and is then used as the basis of a mathematical theory. Euclid's genius lay in recognizing that all of Greek geometry flowed from five simple axioms: (1) a straight line can be drawn between any two points; (2) a straight line can be extended indefinitely; (3) given any center and any radius, a circle can be drawn; (4) all right angles are equal to each other; and (5) if a line intersects two other lines, and if the sum of the interior angles made on one side of the first line is less than two right angles, then the other two lines, when extended, meet on that side of the first line. All the theorems in the *Elements* are logically based on just these five axioms.

Special note must be made of the fifth axiom. It is often called the Parallel Postulate, because in fact, it is a statement about parallel lines: If a line happens to intersect two others, and the sum of the interior angles on neither side of the first line is less than two right angles, then the other two lines do not meet; in other words, they are parallel. This axiom stands out from the others. The first four are all simply stated and quickly understood and believed; the fifth takes some time to state and to understand, and it caused much anxiety among mathematicians, ancient and modern. Many tried to prove the fifth postulate from the other four, to no avail. Finally, in the nineteenth century, it was shown that the fifth could not be proved from the other four. In fact, one can replace the fifth axiom with certain other axioms and obtain "non-Euclidean" geometries.

The geometry of Euclid covers more than the modern definition of geometry. In fact, it covers a great variety of mathematical subjects from a modern perspective. For instance, Euclid's geometry does deal with plane and solid figures, but it also deals with the application of these figures to many other problems. Plane figures such as rectangles, triangles, and circles are treated in books 1, 3, and 4 of the *Elements*. These books cover modern geometry. In books 2 and 6, geometric methods are used to solve what today are considered algebraic problems, such as solving linear and quadratic equations. The geometry of ratios of magnitudes, covered in book 5, is in today's terminology the study of rational numbers; book 10 covers the geometry of magnitudes that are not in a simple ratio, or are incommensurable, which is the study of irrational numbers. The geometry in books 7, 8, and 9 is used to do what is now called number theory, including divisibility of one whole number by another, factoring whole numbers, and treatment of prime numbers. Solid figures also appear prominently in Euclid's geometry, in books 11, 12, and 13. These books hold theorems from the most basic facts about solid figures up to the fact that there are only five regular solid figures all of whose sides are a given regular planar figure. These five figures are known as the Platonic solids.

Euclid is thought to have written nine works besides the *Elements*. These other works deal with some more specialized areas of geometry. *Data* (compiled c. 300 B.C.E.; English translation, 1751) is a text that deals further with plane geometry, expanding on books 1 through 6 of the *Elements*. *Peri Diairéson biblion* (compiled c. 300 B.C.E.; *On Divisions of Figures*, 1915) treats the taking of a single plane figure and dividing it according to a rule; for example, dividing a triangle into a quadrilateral and a triangle of certain areas, or dividing a figure bounded by two straight lines and the arc of a circle into equal parts. Parts of these two works are extant. The rest of Euclid's works are known only because they are mentioned by other mathematicians or historians. Euclid produced a work called the *Pseudaria*, or the "book of fallacies." In it he gives examples of common errors and misgivings in geometry, with the idea that later geometers could avoid these mistakes. The *Porisms* are de-

Euclid. (Library of Congress)

scribed by Pappus as "neither theorems nor problems, but . . . a species occupying a sort of intermediate position." An example of this is the task of finding the center of a circle: it can be stated as a problem, or as a theorem proving that the point found is actually the center. Euclid also wrote a work entitled *Conics*, which deals with conic sections, or the shapes obtained when one slices a cone. *Surface-Loci* deals with figures drawn on surfaces other than a plane, for example, triangles drawn on a sphere. Euclid also produced works in applied mathematics: *Phaenomena*, dealing with astronomy; *Optics*, *Caltropics*, or the theory of mirrors; and the *Elements of Music*.

SIGNIFICANCE

The influence of Euclid's *Elements* has been felt across the ages. From the rise of the Roman Empire through the early medieval period, the value of the kind of abstract intellectual thought embodied in the *Elements* was largely ignored in Europe. The Arabian world, however, had inherited Greek intellectualism and continued to study geometry, copying and translating the *Elements* and adding to geometry and mathematics in general. In the eleventh and twelfth centuries C.E., this intellectual thought was reintroduced to Europe as a result of the Crusades and the Moorish invasion of Spain. Euclid was translated into Latin, first from Arabian copies, then from older Greek copies. The rise of the universities in Europe introduced many to Euclid's *Elements*, and European intellectuals began to add to mathematical knowledge. The geometry of Euclid is studied to this very day. Although much has been added to mathematical thought in the twenty-three centuries years since the writing of the *Elements*, that text remains one of the most published and most revered of mathematical treatises.

—*Andrius Tamulis*

FURTHER READING

Artmann, Benno. *Euclid: The Creation of Mathematics*. New York: Springer Verlag, 1999. This book is, in essence, a close reading of the *Elements*, walking readers through each book and providing sample proofs, interspersed with chapters of more general commentary.

Euclid. *Elements*. 300 B.C.E. Translated with commentary by Thomas L. Heath. 1908. Reprint. New York: Dover Publications, 1956. English translations of the oldest extant Greek sources, with copious commentary.

Fauvel, John, and Jeremy Grey, eds. *The History of Mathematics: A Reader*. 1987. Reprint. Washington, D.C.: The Mathematical Association of America, 1997. Excerpts on commentaries on the *Elements*, from Pappus to modern commentators. Bibliography and index.

Grattan-Guinness, Ivor. *The Norton History of the Mathematical Sciences*. New York: W. W. Norton, 1999. A history of mathematics from the earliest beginnings to the early twentieth century. Bibliography and index.

Heath, Sir Thomas L. *A History of Greek Mathematics: From Thales to Euclid*. 1921. Reprint. New York: Dover Publications, 1981. A history specifically looking at Greek mathematics, by one of the best authors in the field. Index.

Mlodinow, Leonard. *Euclid's Window: A History of Geometry from Parallel Lines to Hyperspace*. New York: Touchstone, 2002. This history of geometry, written for a general audience, is divided into five sections, the first of which is devoted to Euclid.

SEE ALSO: 600-500 B.C.E., Greek Philosophers Formulate Theories of the Cosmos; c. 530 B.C.E., Founding of the Pythagorean Brotherhood; c. 500-400 B.C.E., Greek Physicians Begin Scientific Practice of Medicine; c. 450-c. 425 B.C.E., History Develops as a Scholarly Discipline; c. 380 B.C.E., Plato Develops His Theory of Ideas; 325-323 B.C.E., Aristotle Isolates Science as a Discipline; c. 320 B.C.E., Theophrastus Initiates the Study of Botany; c. 250 B.C.E., Discoveries of Archimedes; 415 C.E., Mathematician and Philosopher Hypatia Is Killed in Alexandria.

RELATED ARTICLES in *Great Lives from History: The Ancient World*: Apollonius of Perga; Archimedes; Diophantus; Euclid; Eudoxus of Cnidus; Hero of Alexandria; Hypatia; Pappus; Pythagoras; Thales of Miletus.

c. 300 B.C.E.
IZAPAN CIVILIZATION DOMINATES MESOAMERICA

Izapan civilization became the heart of a phenomenal cultural development, including early writing and calendrical customs; its Late Preclassic period stylistic impact was felt across the length and breadth of Mesoamerica.

LOCALE: Izapa, Chiapas, Mexico, and Pacific coastal Guatemala

CATEGORY: Prehistory and ancient cultures

SUMMARY OF EVENT

The ancient settlement of Izapa, Chiapas, Mexico, established and maintained one of the earliest and longest-lived periods of civic-ceremonial and urban development known anywhere in Mesoamerica. Established in the Early Preclassic (c. 2000-900 B.C.E.), or the period identified with the Formative era of Mesoamerican urban cultures, the site reached its zenith of construction, monumental elaboration, and pan-Mesoamerican influence by the Late Preclassic (c. 300 B.C.E. to 250 C.E.). The Izapan artistic tradition—marked by very elaborately carved bas-relief panels and a stela-altar complex (an altar placed before a stela carved with scenes from mythological narratives)—in turn peaked at 150 B.C.E. Despite this extraordinary period of urban development, culminating with the construction of some eighty platform mounds, the site remained viable and active in agricultural and commercial pursuits well into that period associated with the rise of the Mexica Aztec state c. 1400 C.E. Through-

out the course of its history, Izapa and the civilization of which it was a part remained vigorous as the direct result of its near-total monopoly of the Soconusco and Pacific coastal Guatemalan cacao trade. Positioned as it was near the Pacific coastal piedmont, Izapa apparently drew its wealth, and thereby its cultural and commercial longevity, from its role as both intermediary and source for the exchange of the highly valued cacao plant and its by-product, chocolate.

In addition to its strategic location for the exploitation of the cacao plant, Izapa was situated at a key commercial crossroads for overland transport and seaborne commercial interactions between Mesoamerica more generally, and the Guatemalan highlands and Pacific coastal piedmont more specifically. The cultural, commercial, and ritual importance of the cacao bean was clearly enhanced by virtue of its role as the basis of the primordial drink of the elite class and its widespread use as a form of currency throughout Mesoamerica. So important was the cacao plant that the early Preclassic Olmec civilization (c. 400 B.C.E.) left its stamp on the region and the much later Postclassic Mexica Aztec (c. 1375-1521 C.E.) launched imperial incursions and conquests in the region of Soconusco and Pacific coastal Guatemala for the purposes of usurping commercial and political control of this prime cacao-growing region. Combined with the fact that chocolate consumption is now dated to as early as 600 B.C.E., it now appears that the development of Izapan civilization parallels the origins and development of the cacao industry in Mesoamerica more generally.

Perhaps the most distinctive and culturally significant legacy of Izapan civilization was the development of a system of iconographic, glyphic, and calendrical forms of notation and computation in the early first century C.E. Although the original systems of notation and calendrical computation used by Izapan peoples are attributed to the Preclassic era Olmec peoples of the Gulf Coast regions of Veracruz and Tabasco, Mexico, their early use by Izapan peoples poses many questions regarding the relationships of these two groups. Clearly, the very early use of glyph-based forms of record keeping and the recording of secular narratives and dynastic histories at the core sites of Izapa, Mexico, and Abaj Takalik and El Baúl, Guatemala, have focused scholarly attention on the origins of what became a widespread pattern of monument making and civic-ceremonial embellishment through the use of glyphic texts.

Although clearly influenced by the culture and art forms of the Olmec civilization, Izapan civilization nevertheless produced some of the earliest indigenous iconographic conventions later found in Maya cities of the Guatemalan highlands, Peten lowlands, and beyond. Among the civic ceremonial elements that first make their appearance in Izapan urban centers—such as Izapa, Abaj Takalik, and Kaminaljuyú—are the early appearance of the stela-altar complex, sculpted images of the World Tree like that of Palenque, monolithic toad and frog altars or platforms like those of the later Maya site of Quirigua, sky and earth band iconographic elements, and a number of deities held prominent by the later Maya, including the gods labeled by archaeologists G1, G2, and K—the latter being the ubiquitous manikin scepter of Maya lords. In the case of the World Tree and the sky and earth bands, these are among the earliest such representations to be found anywhere in the Maya region.

Ultimately, the Izapan tradition made its mark across the length and breadth of Mesoamerica and the Maya regions of Central America. Any search of the literature on Mesoamerica will make clear that Izapan's iconographic forms and cult themes were adopted throughout the Maya region, Oaxaca, and as far afield as the Mexican Gulf Coast culture areas of El Tajin, Veracruz, and highland central Mexico. Specific cult motifs attributed to Izapan civilization include trophy heads, scroll-eyed dragon masks, U-shaped symbols, descending sky deities, the so-called long-lipped god, and a veritable array of weaponry. The general narrative style and preponderance of relief carvings comprising both violent and elab-

orate compositions serves as a hallmark of the Izapan tradition. Despite the very early narrative style, the compositions of the type-site of Izapa in particular appear to focus on supernatural and secular themes such as those reflected in bas-relief images depicting acts of violence and warfare. The monuments of Abaj Takalik, on the other hand, depict rulers and other elite personages carved in bas-relief panels or on stelae replete with historical narratives. This latter combination of portrait narratives and dynastic texts was adopted directly by the Early Classic Maya. Moreover, this same narrative tradition, with probable Mixe-Zoquean and Isthmian-Izapan affinities, makes a reappearance in the elaborately carved monument known as Stela I from La Mojarra, Veracruz. Bearing dates of 143 and 156 C.E., the monument incorporates the Mixe-Zoquean glyphic script that is now generally accepted to have been the narrative tradition of the Isthmian or Izapan peoples of Pacific coastal Guatemala. As such, scholars now argue that, while Izapan civilization evolved from the earlier Miraflores and Olmec prototypes, Izapan iconographic conventions set the standard for later Maya dynastic reckoning and monument building.

Some of the earliest dated—albeit undeciphered—monuments and glyphs thus far recorded in Mesoamerica have been recovered from Izapan sites of the Pacific coastal lowlands and Guatemalan highlands dating between 35 B.C.E. and 36 C.E. However, this early use of both glyphic and calendrical notation on Izapan monuments nevertheless emerged subsequent to the appearance of Olmec and Olmecoid traits and cultural patterns of the Isthmus of Tehuantepec and Pacific coastal Guatemala. Moreover, archaeological findings by Mary Pohl, Kevin Pope, and Christopher von Nagy provide indications for a growing body of evidence pertaining to the Olmec origin of Mesoamerican writing and calendar systems. Recent findings from the Preclassic Olmec site of La Venta, Veracruz, clearly antedate the Izapan developments; a cylinder seal and carved greenstone plaque bearing glyphs date as far back as 650 B.C.E. If the evidence for an Olmec origin of the Mixe-Zoquean glyphic and calendrical system is ultimately substantiated in other Olmec contexts as well, then age-old questions regarding the very early dates found at some Izapan settlements would prove moot.

SIGNIFICANCE

The ultimate significance of Izapan civilization lies in its pioneering development of Late Preclassic narrative traditions and monumental works of art and sculpture devoted to the reckoning of dynastic succession in glyphic and calendrical contexts. This early formula ultimately served as the prototype for the emergence of the later Maya narrative tradition and stela and altar groupings of the Early Classic era (c. 300-600 C.E.). According to art historian Mary Ellen Miller, whereas iconographic and thematic conventions established at the site of Izapa contributed directly to the evolution of the mythic imagery of the Early Classic Maya, the works of the contemporary Izapan site of Abaj Takalik fostered the prototypes and iconographic conventions and forms that served later innovations in Maya historical portraiture. So pronounced was the influence of Izapan civilization on the earliest Maya civic-ceremonial pattern that archaeologist Michael Coe has characterized the primary distinction between the Early and Late Classic Maya as the displacement of the "strong Izapan element" evident in the Early Classic by the Teotihuacán pattern so evident in the Late Classic.

—*Ruben G. Mendoza*

FURTHER READING

Coe, Michael D. *Breaking the Maya Code.* New York: Thames and Hudson, 1992. An intricately detailed and groundbreaking study of the history of decipherment of the Maya glyphic writing system.

_____. *The Maya.* 6th ed. New York: Thames & Hudson, 1999. A classic and well- illustrated overview of the rise and fall of Maya civilization.

Hassig, Ross. *War and Society in Ancient Mesoamerica.* Berkeley: University of California Press, 1992. A general overview of warfare in ancient Mesoamerica, with a discussion regarding the social dynamics of war and conflict during the Preclassic era.

Hunter, C. Bruce. *A Guide to Ancient Maya Ruins.* 2d ed. Norman: University of Oklahoma, 1986. A popular guide to the archaeological zones of the Maya region, including both Mexico and Central America.

Lowe, Gareth W., Thomas A. Lee, Jr., and Eduardo Martínez Espinoza. *Izapa: An Introduction to the Ruins and Monuments.* Provo, Utah: New World Archaeological Foundation, 1982. The most complete published study on the archaeological and art historical evidence from the cultural type-site of Izapa.

Marcus, Joyce. *Mesoamerican Writing Systems: Propaganda, Myth, and History in Four Ancient Civilizations.* Princeton, N.J.: Princeton University Press, 1992. A comprehensive and detailed overview of Mesoamerican writing systems as seen from the vantage point of four early civilizations, including those of the Maya, Zapotec, Mixtec, and Aztec.

Miller, Mary Ellen. *The Art of Mesoamerica: From Olmec to Aztec.* 3d ed. New York: Thames and Hudson, 2001. A general overview of the art and art history of ancient Mesoamerica spanning the Preclassic through Postclassic periods of Mesoamerican cultural history.

Pohl, Mary E. D., Kevin O. Pope, and Christopher von Nagy. "Olmec Origins of Mesoamerican Writing." *Science* 298 (December 6, 2002). This article reports the recovery of a radiocarbon-dated cache that included a very early glyph-inscribed cylinder seal and carved greenstone plaque from the Olmec site of La Venta, Veracruz.

SEE ALSO: c. 1530 B.C.E., Mixtec Civilization Develops in Western Oaxaca; c. 1500-c. 300 B.C.E., Olmec Civilization Rises in Southern Mexico; c. 100 B.C.E.-c. 200 C.E., Zapotec State Dominates Oaxaca; 200-900 C.E., Maya Civilization Flourishes.

c. 300 b.c.e.
HOHOKAM CULTURE ARISES IN AMERICAN SOUTHWEST

Adapting to the desert environment, the Hohokam, ancestors of the modern Pima and Tohono O'Oodham, established agricultural settlements and irrigation systems.

LOCALE: Southern Arizona
CATEGORY: Prehistory and ancient cultures

SUMMARY OF EVENT

One of four prehistoric cultures in the American Southwest, the Hohokam people, ancestors of the modern Pima and Tohono O'Oodham, lived in the fertile valleys of the Salt and Gila Rivers in what is now southern Arizona. Artifacts show that this seemingly bleak region, the Arizona-Sonora Desert, was home to the Hohokam for more than seventeen hundred years, but archaeologists are not certain where they originated. It is unknown whether they were descendants of the earlier Cochise people, who hunted and gathered in the same desert area, or if they migrated from Mexico. Much of their cultural history suggests a Mesoamerican influence; however, this could have been acquired through the extensive trade routes established by the Hohokam.

Development of Hohokam culture occurred in four phases: Pioneer, 300 B.C.E.-500 C.E.; Colonial, 500-900 C.E.; Sedentary, 900-1100 C.E.; and Classic, 1100-1400 C.E. The Hohokam culture was similar to the desert cultures of the Anasazi, Hakataya, and Mogollon, but a major difference was their complex irrigation system. Evidence from the Pioneer phase shows that the Hohokam lived in pit houses and began the cultivation of corn in their small villages. Floodplains along the rivers were rich with silt deposited from spring rains and snowmelt from nearby mountains. The earliest irrigation was probably achieved by directing the floodwaters.

About 300 B.C.E., during the Pioneer phase, the village of Skoaquick, or Snaketown, was founded on the north bank of the Gila River. The first canal was built there to divert river water to irrigate fields as far as 3 miles (5 kilometers) away. Early canals were shallow but very wide. Later, using technology from Mexico, the Hohokam built narrow, deep canals with many branches and lined them with clay to channel water more than 30 miles (48 kilometers). Gates made of woven grass mats controlled the flow from large dams throughout the canal system. Archaeological evidence suggests that construction of the canals was done by men using digging sticks and stone hoes. Earth was carried away in baskets by women and was probably used in building their pyramid ceremonial platforms.

Continual maintenance was needed to keep the canals open after floods or thunderstorms, but this full-time technology provided a reliable subsistence for the Hohokam and supported a denser population. Instead of harvesting crops from the natural habitat, the Hohokam successfully brought agriculture into their villages to develop a stable farming society in which the men tended the fields instead of hunting.

As domesticated corn moved northward from Mexico, it evolved into a new type with a floury kernel more easily crushed when dry. The Hohokam harvested their domestic corn and prepared it by traditional desert-culture methods of sun-drying, parching in baskets with coals, and grinding dried kernels. Storage in large pits kept their surplus food secure for several years. The plentiful food supply allowed time for the creation of art, including shell carving, loom weaving, and pottery making. Images of Kokopelli, the humpbacked flute player, a fertility god believed to assure a good harvest, frequently decorated the pottery. Epic poems carried Hohokam cultural history through many generations.

The archaeological record shows that the Hohokam had no weapons; their bows, arrows, and spears were used for hunting deer, rabbits, and other small game to supplement their crops. Deerskins and rabbit fur were used for ponchos, robes, and blankets. Cotton shirts and breechcloths were typical outfits for men, and apron-skirts of shredded fiber were worn by women. Both wore sandals of woven fiber and wickerwork. Other Hohokam artifacts include stone and clay pipes, cane cigarettes, noseplugs, wooden spoons, flutes, and prayer sticks. Stick and ring games, guessing games, gambling bones, and dice were also part of Hohokam culture.

SIGNIFICANCE

Later remains tell the story of how the Hohokam evolved after the ancient Pioneer phase. In addition to pottery and domestic crops, which by 600 C.E. included cotton, the Colonial phase shows the use of astronomy to calculate planting dates. Narrower, deeper canals were dug to control evaporation, ball courts were built for ceremonial use, and images of the feathered serpent were used in ceremonial art.

In the Sedentary phase, a smaller area of the desert was occupied by the Hohokam. Greater development occurred in the material culture, which showed more influence from Mexico: red-on-buff pottery, copper bells, turquoise mosaics, iron-pyrite mirrors, textiles, and bright-feathered macaws as pets in homes. During this period, Hohokam artists began the process of etching. The earliest people in the Western world to master the craft, they devised a method of covering the shells with pitch, carving the design, then dipping shells in the acidic juice of the saguaro cactus fruit. Along with salt, these shells were highly prized for exchange on the extensive trade route.

During the Classic phase, the Salados (a branch of the Anasazi people) moved into Hohokam territory, bringing a new architecture of multistory adobe houses. They introduced other varieties of corn, as well as beans and squash, and brought basketry, the newest art form. Always peaceful people, the Hohokam coexisted with the Salados, who assisted with the building of canals. By 1350 C.E., the complex network extended more than 150 miles (240 kilometers). Of great importance to the Hohokam were the new songs and ceremonies brought by the Salado, for these kept the world in balance and assured a life of abundance and harmony.

Snaketown, after its start as the year-round site of a village of about fifty families who relied on the production of domestic crops, remained the center of Hohokam culture for fifteen hundred years. During the expansive period, more than one hundred pit houses covered the 300-acre (120-hectare) site. A highly developed social organization was needed to oversee the large population, produce abundant food, and maintain the network of canals. As their culture evolved through the Classic phase, Hohokam social organization shifted from small bands to tribes to chiefdoms to states.

In the early fifteenth century, the Hohokam abandoned Snaketown and other settlements, possibly because of a long period of drought. In the nineteenth century, Mormon farmers used part of the network of canals skillfully engineered almost two thousand years earlier. Continuing the legacy, a canal at Snaketown near present-day Phoenix was reconstructed in the twentieth century to divert water from the Salt River.

The ancient Hohokam spoke Uto-Aztecan, one of the seven Southwest language families, which also included Hopi, Pima, Yaqui-Mayo, and Huichol. In the Piman language, the term "Hohokam" translates as "the vanished ones." Myths and songs about the mysterious desert whirlwinds are found in Piman culture, inherited from their Hohokam ancestors. Although the Hohokam are gone, much of their culture and some of their developments remain as their legacy.

—*Gale M. Thompson*

FURTHER READING

Abbott, David R. *Ceramics and Community Organization Among the Hohokam.* Tucson: University of Arizona Press, 2000. Covers the Hohokam culture, with emphasis on its social organization, pottery, and canals.

Clark, Jeffery J. *Tracking Prehistoric Migrations: Pueblo Settlers Among the Tonto Basin Hohokam.* Tucson: University of Arizona Press, 2001. An analysis of the migrations of the early Indian groups. Covers the Hohokam and Salado cultures. Bibliography and index.

Johnson, Jolene R. *Hohokam Ecology: The Ancient Desert People and Their Environment.* Washington, D.C.: National Park Service, 1997. An examination of the Hohokam culture and the land in which the culture lived. Bibliography.

Taylor, Colin, and William C. Sturtevant, eds. *The Native Americans: The Indigenous People of North America.* New York: Smithmark, 1991. Native American culture and lifestyle in nine culture areas, from the Arctic to the Southwest. Includes twenty-eight photographic spreads showing more than a thousand artifacts, dating from 1860 to 1920; 250 archival photographs, maps, and color plates, dating from 1850 to 1940; bibliography; catalog of artifacts; and index.

Thomas, David Hurst. *Exploring Ancient Native America: An Archaeological Guide.* New York: Macmillan, 1994. Overview of Native American cultures and the evolution of numerous Native American civilizations. References more than four hundred accessible sites in North America. Discusses new scientific data from burial mounds, petroglyphs, artifacts, and celestial observations. Photographs, drawings, maps, and index.

Underhill, Ruth M. *Red Man's America: A History of Indians in the United States.* Rev. ed. Chicago: University of Chicago Press, 1971. Concise volume surveying origins, history, and definitive accounts of social customs, material culture, religion, and mythology. Written from the perspective of the first peoples of North America. Illustrations, maps, notes, extensive bibliography, and index.

SEE ALSO: c. 9500-c. 9000 B.C.E., Clovis Culture Rises in New Mexico; c. 9000-c. 8000 B.C.E., Cochise Culture Thrives in American Southwest; c. 2100-c. 600 B.C.E., Mogollon Culture Rises in American Southwest; 200-1250 C.E.; Anasazi Civilization Flourishes in American Southwest.

c. 300 B.C.E.
STOICS CONCEPTUALIZE NATURAL LAW

By positing a universal moral law independent of cultures and religions, the Stoics established the foundations of modern conceptions of human rights and law based on human reason.

LOCALE: Athens
CATEGORIES: Cultural and intellectual history; government and politics; philosophy

KEY FIGURES
Zeno of Citium (c. 335-c. 263 B.C.E.), founder of the Stoic school of philosophy
Cleanthes (c. 331-c. 232 B.C.E.), successor of Zeno as scholar of the Stoa
Chrysippus (c. 280-c. 206 B.C.E.), third scholar of the Stoa who was chiefly responsible for the systematic formulation of the doctrines of the Old Stoa

SUMMARY OF EVENT
The formulation of the Stoic concept of natural law was the logical culmination of trends in cosmological thought and political development in the Greek world after the time of Hesiod (fl. c. 700 B.C.E.). Implicit in Hesiod's *Theogony* (c. 700 B.C.E.; English translation, 1728) is an understanding of the world order as political in nature and of physical nature as obedient to the orderly processes of thought in the human mind. Early Ionian philosophy, especially that of Anaximander (610-546/545 B.C.E.), had given explicit formulation to these implications of Hesiod's poem in the concepts of a cosmic justice governing all natural phenomena; the logos of Heraclitus of Ephesus (c. 540-c. 480 B.C.E.) expressed an active rational principle permeating all nature and directing its phenomena.

Although these cosmological ideas were themselves derived from the political framework of the polis (city-state), there seems to have been no reapplication of them to the political and moral relationships of persons within different political and ethnic communities of the world until the mid-fifth century B.C.E. At that time, the Sophists called attention to the relativity of current moral and political standards, or *nomos*, in different communities and then pointed to a common human nature, or *physis*, with laws of its own that might well conflict with laws of human communities.

As the institutions of the Greek polis were losing their power to command the loyalties of individuals, the Athenian Socrates (c. 470-399 B.C.E.) postulated an objective and rational standard of moral human behavior based on the nature of the individual man as a rational and social being. Plato (c. 427-347 B.C.E.) further developed this conception of a rational human nature and a rational moral law in the *Politeia* (388-369 B.C.E.; *Republic*, 1701) and the *Nomoi* (360-347 B.C.E.; *Laws*, 1804). Philosophy of the fourth century B.C.E. failed to realize the universalist implications of these ideas, probably because the polis remained the only obviously self-validating type of human community; but the conquests of Alexander demolished such claims for the polis and created in fact a universal human cultural community throughout the civilized areas of the eastern Mediterranean world. *Koine* Greek became a common language of international commerce and culture, and through this medium the cultural heritages of Greeks and "barbarians" cross-fertilized each other.

The earliest explicit recognition of the community of humankind seems to have been more a negative statement of the individual's rejection of ties to the local community than a positive affirmation of human brotherhood. The Cynic Diogenes (c. 412/403-c. 324/321 B.C.E.) is said to have been the first to call himself a "citizen of the world" by way of denying any personal obligation to the polis. Far from being a political idealist, Diogenes held that all humans and beasts are related inasmuch as humans are beasts. All culture is artificial; a person keenly aware of what nature requires will find contentment without heeding the conventions of the community in which the person happens to reside.

The Stoic school of philosophy was established by Zeno of Citium about 300 B.C.E. and received its name from Zeno's practice of teaching from the porch (*stoa*) at the Athenian market. It was more fully developed and disseminated by Zeno's successors, Cleanthes and Chrysippus. Stoicism was the dominant philosophy of educated persons in the Hellenic world for five hundred years until it was replaced by Christian thought, which incorporated many of its tenets, especially that of natural law. Stoicism has three main periods referred to as Old Stoicism, Middle Stoicism, and Roman Stoicism. It is the first and last periods which are important to the conception of natural law.

The basis for natural law theory developed in Old Stoicism and was given its practical application in the form of Roman law and governance during the period of Roman Stoicism. Stoicism developed out of Cynicism and

559

Seneca the Younger. (Library of Congress)

evolved more systematically the Cynic school's conception of "the life according to nature." While the Cynics, however, had set a low estimate on a person's rational capacity, the Stoic conception of persons and their place in nature laid a supreme value on this rational capacity. Taking the cosmology of Heraclitus as a physical foundation for his system, Zeno postulated a cosmic monism of a pantheistic nature in which *logos*, or "active reason," pervades all nature and determines all events and also provides a moral law. God is present in all nature, yet God, or *logos*, has consciousness only in the souls of persons and in the totality of the universe. Since God and persons as conscious participants in the events of nature and of history are thus distinguished from plants, animals, and inorganic nature, God and all persons are bound together in a natural community of all rational beings.

The Stoic ethic comprises two complementary levels of the rational life according to nature. One is the inner level of assent by the *logos* within to the pattern of events determined by the universal *logos*, a recognition of the

necessity and rationality of all that does in fact occur, contentment with fate, or in Stoic diction *apatheia*, imperturbability. Yet on the external level of practical moral response to critical choices confronting the individual, reason guides choice to fulfillment of duty. Duty is that portion of the responsibility for fulfilling the rational operation of nature and history that confronts the individual moral agent. Duty is not limited by geographic, ethnic, political, or even social boundaries. It is laid on the individual not by the state or ancestral mores but by the rational principle that governs the universe, and therefore it extends to all human beings who, since they are endowed with reason, are members of the world community, the *cosmopolis*.

Although the early Stoic concepts of *cosmopolis* and natural law defining the duties of all rational beings are stated in positive form, in the period of the Old Stoa these ideals are essentially nonpolitical; they do not lead to any positive vision of the political unity of humankind. Citizenship is not a person's highest obligation, and while it is asserted that the laws of a state ought to reflect the natural laws and ought to be disobeyed if they contradict them, Stoic idealism in the early period could not envision a universal state over which a single code of law reigned supreme. With the emergence of the Roman Empire, however, Roman rulers were confronted with the very practical problem of finding a universal law and morality that was to govern persons of diverse cultural and religious backgrounds. It was during this period that Roman philosophers, especially Cicero, Seneca the Younger, Epictetus, and Marcus Aurelius, more fully developed the practical aspects of natural law theory to provide a foundation for political, civil law based on universal moral principles. These universal principles were understood to be accessible to all persons by virtue of their participation in universal reason (the *logos*).

SIGNIFICANCE

Stoicism was so influential that Seneca served as the tutor of the emperor Nero, and Marcus Aurelius was himself emperor of Rome. The concepts of *cosmopolis* and natural law were thus ultimately influential in the formulation of the Roman imperial *ius gentium* (universal applied law). Stoic moral thought, especially the concept of natural law, was also very influential in the systematic formulation of the moral philosophy of the Christian Church, and it received formal development in the work of the medieval theologian Saint Thomas Aquinas (1224 or 1225-1274 C.E.). The entire conception of natural law became a basis for modern theories of the equality of all persons since all participate in universal reason. It also provides the primary source for modern conceptions of human rights and international law.

—*Carl W. Conrad, updated by Charles L. Kammer III*

FURTHER READING

Inwood, Brad, ed. *The Cambridge Companion to the Stoics*. New York: Cambridge University Press, 2003. A collection of fifteen essays on all aspects of Stoic philosophy. A valuable introduction.

Long, A. A. *Hellenistic Philosophy: Stoics, Epicureans, Sceptics*. 2d ed. Berkeley: University of California Press, 1986. Locates Stoicism in the context of Hellenistic philosophy and the cross influences of the various traditions.

Schofield, Malcolm. *The Stoic Idea of the City*. Reprint. Chicago: University of Chicago Press, 1999. A discussion of the Stoic ideas of political order.

Verbeke, Gerard. *The Presence of Stoicism in Medieval Thought*. Washington, D.C.: Catholic University of America Press, 1983. A discussion of Stoicism's influence on Christian thought and its role in shaping Western conceptions of ethics and natural law.

Weinreb, Lloyd. *Natural Law and Justice*. Cambridge, Mass.: Harvard University Press, 1987. A general discussion of natural law.

SEE ALSO: 445 B.C.E., Establishment of the Canuleian Law; c. 380 B.C.E., Plato Develops His Theory of Ideas; c. 335-323 B.C.E., Aristotle Writes the *Politics*; 54 B.C.E., Roman Poet Catullus Dies.

RELATED ARTICLES in *Great Lives from History: The Ancient World*: Cicero; Diogenes; Heraclitus of Ephasus; Marcus Aurelius; Plato; Seneca the Younger; Socrates; Zeno of Citium.

---

c. 300 B.C.E.

YAYOI PERIOD BEGINS

The Yayoi period marks the transition from hunting-and-gathering societies in Japan to those with a settled agricultural lifestyle, coinciding with the introduction of bronze and iron.

LOCALE: Kyūshū, Japan
CATEGORY: Prehistory and ancient cultures

SUMMARY OF EVENT

The Yayoi period is the second major prehistoric age in Japan. The name derives from Yayoi-chō, a section of the University of Tokyo campus where the first pottery unique to the period was discovered in 1884. The Yayoi is traditionally dated from 300 B.C.E. to 300 C.E., and was preceded by the Jōmon period (c. 10,000-c. 300 B.C.E.), which was marked by a hunting-and-gathering style of life. During the Yayoi, bronze and iron usage appeared for the first time, wet-rice cultivation was introduced, the population increased dramatically, and social and political organization began to emerge.

The period is broken up into three divisions. The Early Yayoi (c. 300-100 B.C.E.), centered in northern Kyūshū, represented a transitional phase during which the population adopted a mixed economy of rice cultivation and hunting and gathering. Evidence indicates that shellfish, a staple of the Jōmon diet, was still an important source of protein. Simple political divisions began

to emerge at this time, with the settlements, most located in low, marshy areas, being ruled by a variety of chieftains.

The Middle Yayoi (c. 100 B.C.E.-100 C.E.) witnessed the development of water control systems for irrigation, the movement of settlements onto higher ground purposefully cleared, and the use of a variety of new tools, including many tipped with or made entirely of iron. Evidence indicates that the culture had spread as far north as present-day Nara.

During the Late Yayoi (c. 100-300 C.E.), irrigated wet-rice cultivation was perfected, complex political units began to emerge, and the culture extended to the northernmost reaches of Honshū. As Hokkaidō is too cold for growing rice, Yayoi culture never affected the far north of the Japanese archipelago.

The two most important advances of the Yayoi period are the introduction of wet-rice cultivation and the simultaneous entrance into the Bronze and Iron Ages. It is most likely that wet-rice technology was introduced into northern Kyūshū from the late Bronze Age culture in Korea. Trade was widespread, and evidence of significant contact between the Koreans and Jōmon Japanese is abundant. As noted above, the initial stages of settlement centered on low, marshy regions, where the inhabitants could take advantage of the natural irrigation, flooding, and accessible water tables. Diked fields and drainage systems allowed for ideal conditions to grow rice. Cultivation at this stage was simplistic, with hoes, spades, and reaping knives made of wood and stone. In the transitional stage, the basic diet was supplemented by hunting, gathering, and fishing. Even at an early period, however, communities were beginning to form around the new agricultural centers, with one of the oldest sites, in Itazuke, Fukuoka, boasting at least thirty homes.

As technology advanced in the Middle Yayoi, elaborate irrigation systems were developed and iron-tipped tools introduced. Paddy cultivation became a large-scale enterprise in some communities. Excavations at Toro, in present-day Shizuoka, reveal the technology and lifestyle of a Middle Yayoi community, which had a highly developed rice cultivation system, with more than fifty paddies covering seventeen acres. Supplied by sluice-gated irrigation ditches, the paddies sloped south, with residences and a storehouse located to the north. The paddies were separated by carefully cut wooden slats, presumably cut with iron tools. As production rose, storehouses were constructed with uniform planks for the flooring and walls, and the whole structure was raised 3 to 6 feet (1 to 2 meters) above ground, with wooden collars on each of the six posts to keep rodents out.

The homes, referred to as pit houses, were typically built with semi-subterranean floors, generally 1.7 feet (0.6 meter) below the surface. The pits were oval, with a cone-shaped superstructure built of poles and topped with a thatched roof of reeds or bark. The single-room dwellings typically had a central fireplace, with the interior banked with earth, creating a bench that supported wooden planks. The average home measured 19 by 26 feet (3 by 8 meters). Inhabitants wove cloth from flax and paper-mulberry fibers, and evidence suggests that men wrapped lengths of cloth around their bodies, while women slit a single piece and slipped it over their heads. Jewelry was manufactured, with jasper and jade beads strung together into necklaces and bracelets and occasionally made into rings.

The early Yayoi depended on a variety of wooden and stone tools. Typical implements included wooden rakes and shovels, fire drills, looms, and lathed bowls and cups. Some furniture was produced, and rice paddy clogs, known as *geta*, were used when transplanting rice. Stone tools became increasingly sophisticated, the axes and adzes growing larger and more highly polished, and were increasingly used for reaping rice, chopping, and tilling.

By the middle and late periods, iron and bronze had entered Japan. As was so often the case, bronze was primarily used by the upper class, both as a status symbol and for weapons, while the lower classes used iron to fashion tools and weapons. Bronze arrowheads may have been introduced as early as the second century B.C.E., with other weapons such as halberds, daggers, and short swords appearing in Kyūshū by the first century B.C.E. Local production in sandstone molds began in northern Kyūshū and around the Inland Sea, although quality was uneven for at least a century. As a symbol of wealth and power, the majority of bronze manufactures were mirrors, bracelets, coins, vessels, shield ornaments, and bells. A large number of bells have been uncovered, and it appears as though the Kinki region may have dominated this particular market. Bells throughout Japan were manufactured from the same mold and identified with the Kinki region. The majority appear to be ritualistic in nature; a number of sites have been uncovered in which several bells are buried in hillside terraces overlooking fertile fields. The reasons behind the burials are still shrouded in mystery, but many scholars speculate that they served in some type of ritual to ensure a good harvest.

At the same time, small-scale iron smelting produced a variety of implements and weapons. By the late Yayoi, iron was being used to fashion farming implements such as plows, sickles, and hoes; iron axes, chisels, and planes allowed for more sophisticated woodworking; and arrowheads, swords, and halberds, along with spearheads and fishhooks, were also forged. As noted, these tools allowed the inhabitants to move out of the marshy lowlands to comparatively dry land, where the soil was better suited to rice cultivation. The ability to clear forests and construct elaborate paddy field systems paved the way for very labor-intensive rice cultivation, which in turn produced larger and larger harvests. Because rice has more calories per unit than other farm products produced at the time, it was able to support a much greater population. Although exact numbers are unknown, some speculate that the population grew from an estimated 250,000 in Jōmon to 600,000 in the Middle Yayoi, and perhaps as many as 2.5 million by 300 C.E.

The growing population and emergence of agricultural villages naturally led to the development of social and political organizations. According to the *Wei Zhi* (written between 280 and 297 C.E.; "The History of the Wei Kingdom," 1951), a Chinese history that provides the best glimpse of Yayoi society, Japan had become a highly stratified society by the third century C.E., with wealthy landowners ruling commoners. It also refers to

Yamatai, a kingdom ruled by the shamaness Queen Himiko, that controlled more than thirty countries (*kuni*), each with their own chieftain. Within this kingdom, taxes were collected, marketplaces served as the center of trade, and class distinctions were rigidly enforced. When passing a member of the upper class on the road, commoners were required to retire to the roadside and kneel to show their respect. Although commoners had only one wife, the nobility were allowed four or five.

SIGNIFICANCE

The Yayoi period marks a watershed in Japanese history. The Japanese transitioned from hunting and gathering to settled agricultural communities with highly structured and complex social organization and began to establish the foundations for the political, economic, and military specialization that would follow in the Kofun period (c. 300-710 C.E.).

The origins of Yayoi culture remain under study. Older theories proposing massive immigration from mainland China that overwhelmed and replaced the Jōmon have largely been abandoned. Consensus now holds that some immigration certainly took place during this period. Refugees and traders from Manchuria and Korea, along with immigrants from the Yangtze River region, undoubtedly brought the already developed technology of iron smelting and wet-rice cultivation. However, there is no evidence to suggest a wholesale replacement of the indigenous population with mainland immigrants.

The most likely scenario involves a degree of intermarriage between the Jōmon and immigrants, especially in western Japan, where the Yayoi are on average taller. In eastern Japan, the Jōmon simply adopted the new cultural elements. For example, the use of storage pits was developed in north China as early as 4000 B.C.E., and it is clear that the Yayoi imitated the production of such items as bronze mirrors and weapons, iron tools and weapons, and the building of wooden houses on posts, prominent

in south China. Once adopted, however, these techniques and technology helped turn the Japanese archipelago into a flourishing and complex society.

—*Jeffrey W. Dippmann*

FURTHER READING

Barnes, Gina L. *Protohistoric Yamato: Archaeology of the First Japanese State*. Ann Arbor: University of Michigan, Center for Japanese Studies and the Museum of Anthropology, 1988. A seminal work dealing with the process and results of archaeological work for the Yayoi period. An extensive bibliography provides an abundance of additional resources.

Hall, John Whitney, Marius B. Jansen, et al., eds. *Ancient Japan*. Vol. 1 in *The Cambridge History of Japan*. Cambridge, England: Cambridge University Press, 1993. A standard history of the period, placed into the context of Japan's earliest societies.

Imamura, Keiji. "Jomon and Yayoi: The Transition to Agriculture in Japanese Prehistory." In *The Origins and Spread of Agriculture and Pastoralism in Eurasia*, edited by David R. Harris. Washington, D.C.: Smithsonian Institution Press, 1996. An excellent analysis of the climatic and sociological factors that combined to produce an agricultural society in Kyūshū.

Kanaseki, H., and M. Sahara. "The Yayoi Period." *Asian Perspectives* 19 (1979): 15-26. Very good overview of the cultural and material aspects of the Yayoi period.

SEE ALSO: c. 10,000-c. 300 B.C.E., Jōmon Culture Thrives in Japan; c. 7500 B.C.E., Birth of Shintō; 3d century B.C.E. (traditionally 660 B.C.E.), Jimmu Tennō Becomes the First Emperor of Japan; c. mid-3d century C.E., Himiko Rules the Yamatai; c. 300-710 C.E., Kofun Period Unifies Japan.

RELATED ARTICLES in *Great Lives from History: The Ancient World*: Jingū; Jimmu Tennō.

c. 300-c. 100 B.C.E.
BERBER KINGDOMS OF NUMIDIA AND MAURETANIA FLOURISH

Numidia and Mauretania, in the Mediterranean region of northern Africa, played important roles during the spread of Roman power in this part of the African continent.

LOCALE: Northern Africa (present-day Algeria and northern Morocco)

CATEGORIES: Expansion and land acquisition; government and politics; trade and commerce; wars, uprisings, and civil unrest

KEY FIGURES
Masinissa (c. 238-148 B.C.E.), king of Numidia, r. c. 201-148 B.C.E.

Jugurtha (c. 160-104 B.C.E.), king of Numidia, r. 118-105 B.C.E.

Juba I of Numidia (c. 85-46 B.C.E.), king of Numidia, r. c. 62/50-48 B.C.E.

Bocchus (fl. late second-early first centuries B.C.E.), king of Mauretania, r. c. 110-91 B.C.E.

SUMMARY OF EVENT
Africa northwest of the Sahara gave rise to several groups of Berber people who were organized into tribes and clans and followed a seminomadic life. Of these Berbers, the Numidians were the most powerful. Their kingdom was part of the Carthaginian empire until Masinissa, the ruler of eastern Numidia, allied himself with Rome in 208 B.C.E. during the Second Punic War (218-201 B.C.E.). Rome's victory over Carthage, brought about by Publius Cornelius Scipio (d. 211 B.C.E.), enabled Masinissa to extend his rule over all of Numidia, initiating a cultural and political efflorescence. Mauretania, a land west of Numidia, came under Numidian control in the second century B.C.E. under the leadership of Bocchus. Rome involved itself in the internal affairs of Mauretania by placing Juba II on the throne. When the Mauretanians revolted against Rome, they were vanquished and later absorbed into the empire as two provinces—Mauretania Caesariensis and Mauretania Tingitana. Rome's influence was slight, however, and limited to coastal areas, with local Berber chiefs retaining control over most of the interior.

Northern Africa during the time of the Roman Republic and Empire was peopled by seminomadic Berbers, a group related by linguistic similarities. In Numidia, roughly comprising the area of present-day Algeria, people lived a seminomadic life herding small flocks of animals from one grazing area to another and cultivating grain and olives in coastal areas and in desert oases. The Numidians lived in the shade of a more powerful north African people, the Carthaginians. By the third century B.C.E., Carthage had become an economic power and a threat to Rome's dominance in the Mediterranean. In the Punic Wars fought between Carthage and Rome (264-146 B.C.E.), Numidia allied itself with Rome.

Numidia's first king was Masinissa, chief of the Massyli tribe. The Massyli inhabited the area around Cirta, a city near the Mediterranean coast. During the Second Punic War, Masinissa allied himself with Carthage but turned sides and went over to the Roman general Scipio Africanus in 206 B.C.E. In 203, Masinissa helped Scipio defeat the Carthaginian army. One year later, Scipio destroyed the Carthaginians at the Battle of Zama. Under the terms imposed on Carthage by Rome, the Carthaginians gave the kingdom of Syphax, ruler of western Numidia, to Masinissa.

Masinissa (top left). (F. R. Niglutsch)

Numidia under Masinissa was supported by Rome for approximately fifty years. In addition, Masinissa retained a close personal alliance with the Scipio family. During his reign, Numidians served in the Roman infantry and cavalry, where their skill with the javelin was noted. At home, Masinissa attempted to encourage settled farming. He also took control over Carthaginian lands with the goal of ruling all of northern Africa. Numidia experienced an influx of Carthaginian refugees when Carthage was destroyed by Rome in 146. In the aftermath of the destruction, the Romans organized the area around Carthage as the province of Africa and left the remainder to the three sons of Masinissa.

Two of Masinissa's sons died shortly after their father, leaving Micipsa as the sole ruler of Numidia. As king, Micipsa adopted Jugurtha, his illegitimate nephew and a grandson of Masinissa. The line of succession to the throne of Numidia was complicated, however, when Micipsa had two sons of his own, Adherbal and Hiempsal. In 134 B.C.E., Micipsa sent Jugurtha to command Numidian troops serving in the Roman army in the hope that he would be killed. Jugurtha survived and returned to Numidia with praise from his Roman commanders and the loyalty of Numidia's soldiers.

On the death of Micipsa in 118 B.C.E., Numidia was destined to be divided into three, with each part going to one of Micipsa's sons. The division never took place. Instead, Jugurtha had Hiempsal killed. Adherbal responded by launching a revolt against Jugurtha. The conflict between the two princes split Numidia as each side sought to convince the Roman senate as the justness of its cause.

Jugurtha then seized control of Numidia and reunited it by force of arms. In 112 B.C.E., Jugurtha sacked the city of Cirta and killed its inhabitants, many of whom were Romans. His action enraged Rome and led to an attack by his former ally. The Jugurthine War (111-105 B.C.E.) lasted six years and ended when Jugurtha was betrayed to the Romans by his father-in-law, King Bocchus of Mauretania. Jugurtha was put to death and his kingdom was reduced in size; the main portion went to Jugurtha's half brother Gauda and the western part to King Bocchus. Rome then made Numidia a client-state when it replaced Jugurtha with a king of its own choosing.

Numidia's fate became intertwined with the civil war fought between Julius Caesar (100-44 B.C.E.) and Gnaeus Pompeius (Pompey the Great; 106-48 B.C.E.). In 49 B.C.E., Juba I attempted to restore an independent kingdom of Numidia when he launched a revolt against Roman rule. Juba's attempt ended in his defeat at the hands of Julius Caesar at the Battle of Thapsus one year later. Juba committed suicide, and Numidia was broken into two: One part was added on to the Roman province of Africa, the other part was added to the kingdom of eastern Mauretania. A separate province of Numidia was created by the Roman emperor Septimius Severus (145-211 C.E.) in the second century C.E.

Like its north African neighbor to the east, the kingdom of Mauretania was first inhabited by nomadic Berbers. They were called Mauri by the Romans (a name that, misleadingly, gave rise to the English word "Moor"). As the Mauri adopted a more settled way of life, they cultivated grain and olives and established trading posts along the Mediterranean and Atlantic sea coasts. Mauri rulers established a royal court at Siga. During the Second Punic War, the king of the Mauri, Syphax, fought against the Carthaginians. In 212, Syphax underwent a change of mind (possibly because of the influence of his Carthaginian wife, Saphanbaal) and joined forces with Carthage. Syphax was killed when Scipio and Masinissa of Numidia defeated the Carthaginians in 203.

During the reign of King Bocchus I, Mauretania sided with the Romans against the Numidians and their ruler Jugurtha. During the civil war between Julius Caesar and Pompey, Mauretania's corulers, Bocchus II in the east and Bogud in the west, supported Caesar. After the deaths of Bocchus and Bogud, Octavian (the future emperor Augustus; 63 B.C.E.-14 C.E.) seized control of all of Mauretania and set up several military colonies there. Under the emperor Claudius I (10 B.C.E.-54 C.E.), Mauretania was made into two provinces of Rome: Tingitana in the west and Caesariensis in the east. Rome was now in complete control of the Roman province of Africa.

SIGNIFICANCE

The Berber kingdoms of Numidia and Mauretania were involved in Rome's struggle to extend its control over northern Africa and, specifically, to destroy Carthage. They sided with one or the other as it suited their political ends. Under Masinissa, Numidia became a client state of Rome and provided skilled soldiers to the Roman army. This special relationship was undone during the reign of Jugurtha, a former friend of Rome. Jugurtha fought a six-year war with Rome that ended with his betrayal by his Mauretanian father-in-law and the breakup of Numidia. During the civil war between Caesar and Pompey, Mauretania supported Caesar. Under the first emperors, Mauretania and Numida became absorbed into the empire as provinces.

—Adriane Ruggiero

FURTHER READING

Cherry, David. *Frontier and Society in Roman North Africa*. New York; Clarendon Press, 1998. Discusses Rome's presence in Numidia and Mauretania from c. 50 B.C.E. to 250 C.E.

Herodotus. *Histories*. Translated by Aubrey de Selincourt. New York: Penguin, 2003. The classic work by the ancient Greek historian.

Lazenby, J. F. *Hannibal's War: A Military History of the Second Punic War*. Norman: University of Oklahoma Press, 1998. A history of the wars between Carthage and Rome, focusing on the career of the Carthaginian general, Hannibal. Written by a British scholar of ancient warfare.

Moulton, Carroll, ed. *Ancient Greece and Rome: An Encyclopedia for Students*. 4 vols. New York: Charles Scribner's Sons, 1998. A multivolume reference work for students.

Raven, Susan. *Rome in Africa*. 3d ed. New York: Routledge, 1993. An expansive overview of Rome's relations with all its African colonies, subject states, and enemies. Uses both archaeological and literary sources.

Roller, Duane W. *The World of Juba II and Kleopatra Selene: Royal Scholarship on Rome's Africa Frontier*. New York: Routledge, 2003. A detailed and comprehensive study of the Mauretanian king and his queen, daughter of Cleopatra VII and Marc Antony. Portrays the complex interactions of Roman and North African cultures in the early first century C.E.

SEE ALSO: c. 2300-c. 2000 B.C.E., First Great Expansion of Berber Peoples Across North Africa; c. 1200-c. 1000 B.C.E., Berbers Expand Across North Africa; 264-225 B.C.E., First Punic War; 218-201 B.C.E., Second Punic War; 202 B.C.E., Battle of Zama; 149-146 B.C.E., Third Punic War.

RELATED ARTICLES in *Great Lives from History: The Ancient World:* Augustus; Julius Caesar; Claudius I; Hannibal; Scipio Africanus; Sophonisba of Numidia.

---

c. 300 B.C.E.-c. 100 C.E.
KHOIKHOI AND KWADI ADOPT PASTORAL LIFESTYLE

Deviating from the San hunter-gatherers of southern Africa, the Khoikhoi and Kwadi peoples realized the economic potential of pastoralism and began herding sheep and cattle.

LOCALE: Southern Africa (present-day South Africa and Namibia)

CATEGORIES: Prehistory and ancient cultures; agriculture

SUMMARY OF EVENT

Khoisan (Khwe) herders entered southern Africa in approximately 300 B.C.E., replacing the hunter-gatherer San peoples who had inhabited the area since the early first millennium B.C.E. Given the nature of the communities known as Khoisan (the name that denotes this group as one of both herders and hunter-gatherers), it is difficult to pinpoint either their exact date of arrival in the region or their specific place of origin. This is important to note because experts have repeatedly issued the caveat that too closely defining the boundaries of hunter-gathering and herding societies would be counterproductive in the effort to uncover their pasts. As there were no livestock known to have originated in southern Africa, a fundamental question is how the Khwe people and their herds came to the region. Historians traditionally believed that modern Khoisan pastoralists, namely the Khoikhoi of South Africa and the Kwadi people of Namibia, originated in northeastern Africa and traveled southward until reaching the Cape. In recent times, however, expert opinion has swung to the hypothesis that the herding people of southern Africa came from the eastern Sahelian region, in present-day Botswana and Zambia.

During the third and fourth centuries B.C.E., when the Khoisan herders came to inhabit regions previously occupied by hunter-gatherer groups, these newcomers brought with them much more than livestock. The introduction of domestic animals to southern Africa had a significant impact on life in the region. For example, while the hunter-gatherers were able to sustain themselves on very little land, the pastoralists required vast amounts of terrain to graze their livestock; weather and the seasons dictated the migration of the Khoisan herders. The pastoralists spent the summer months near the coast and then traveled inland to allow their livestock to graze on the fertile grasslands along the mountain rivers. These societies even transplanted their more permanent homes from season to season by placing them on the backs of their oxen and traveling between the inland settlements and the coast. This practice was very different from that of the hunter-gatherer societies that lived in small clans and could stay in one place for a relatively long period of time.

Despite the need for seasonal migration, herding livestock was very successful economically. True entrepreneurs, the Khoikhoi and the Kwadi realized the advantages of combining herding with hunting and gathering, and as a result their populations grew nearly four times as large as the earlier inhabitants. Because of their versatility and success in the region, the Khoisan were able to spread into Namibia and into South Africa as far as the Cape. Instead of small, family-sized clans, the Khoisan settled in larger patriclans; these larger communal societies were able to split and spread, leaving many groups of related community members around the region. Also, unlike purely hunter-gatherer societies that often experienced the hardships of drought and lack of game, the Khoisan peoples were able to supplement their diets with milk and the meat from their livestock when necessary. As scholar Christopher Ehret explains in *The Civilizations of Africa* (2002):

This 1955 photograph shows a Khoikhoi tribesman drinking water from an ostrich eggshell used as a drinking vessel. (Hulton| Archive)

> Each cultural spread was as much of an economic frontier as of people. As often as not, the new economy would have advanced because the people ahead of the economic frontier saw the advantages of the new mixed hunting and herding adaptation, accepted it, and made it their own.

As Ehret suggests, when this frontier expanded, the Khoisan inevitably encountered the hunter-gatherer societies and in many cases welcomed newcomers into their clans; their interactions with the hunters were influential and resulted in intermixing rather than confrontation or hostility. Yet with this new economy came a new way of life for much of the region. Cattle became the livelihood of these societies and the introduction of ownership and wealth changed the character of society. There was now a hierarchy that often placed hunters at the bottom of the social order and patriarchs with an abundance of cattle at the top. Also, the split-and-spread method of the herder clans led to a less cohesive community and to lineages that became more difficult to trace over time.

SIGNIFICANCE

Pastoralism, perhaps one of the most significant methods of livelihood in southern Africa, has been a topic of contention and historical inquiry for centuries. Socially and economically, the herders of southern Africa played a pivotal role in the growth and change of the region. History has recognized the Khoisan peoples' adoption of sheep and cattle herding not only as socially important but also as economically progressive. The level of sophistication and social effects that herding brought to southern Africa through the Khoikhoi and Kwadi peoples is an important subject of study because it changed the way many inhabitants of the region came to structure their society. Social order, wealth, and acquisition became the economic drive of society.

In addition, pastoralism has survived nearly thirty centuries. To this day, cattle herding is a mainstay in many regions of southern Africa, including the better part of South Africa as well as northern Namibia. The fact that pastoralism has been so successful and fundamental to the changing societies of southern Africa has prompted years of historical research on the region. Unfortunately, a lack of archaeological evidence, combined with large migration and cultural mixing, have made study of the Kwadi (more so than study of the Khoikhoi of the southern Cape) arduous. Because the introduction and spread of pastoral peoples occurred in the prehistoric era of the region, historians have had to call on various means of research and have come to a number of contentious conclusions about the origins of these cultures.

—Mellissa Betts

FURTHER READING

Ehret, Christopher. *An African Classical Age: Eastern and Southern Africa in World History, 1000 B.C. to A.D. 400*. Charlottesville: University Press of Virginia, 1998. A comprehensive study of social, agricultural, and cultural history of South and East Africa that traces the development of many cultures historically and linguistically.

_____. *The Civilizations of Africa: A History to 1800*. Charlottesville: University of Virginia Press, 2002. A general history of the continent from prehistory to 1800.

Elphick, Richard. *Krall and Castle: Khoikhoi and the Founding of White South Africa*. New Haven, Conn.: Yale University Press, 1977. An extensive study of the Khoikhoi peoples from the time of their arrival in southern Africa through much of the colonial era.

Mokhtar, G., ed. *Ancient Civilizations of Africa*. Vol. 2 in *General History of Africa*. Berkeley: University of California Press, 1981. A comprehensive study of societies from all regions of the continent during prehistory.

Reader, John. *Africa: A Biography of the Continent*. New York: Alfred A. Knopf, 1998. A textbook on Africa from before the common era to colonial times. References the colonial era as a tool for examining diverse perspectives on early inhabitants.

Vogel, Joseph O., ed. *Encyclopedia of Precolonial Africa: Archaeology, History, Languages, Cultures, and Environments*. Walnut Creek, Calif.: AltaMira Press, 1997. A key resource on the archaeology and anthropology of Africa, with more than one hundred signed essays accompanied by bibliographies, maps, illustrations, and charts.

SEE ALSO: c. 7000-c. 6000 B.C.E., Khoisan Peoples Disperse Throughout Southern Africa; c. 6500-c. 5000 B.C.E., Nilo-Saharan Farmers Spread Cultivation and Herding.

---

300 B.C.E.-600 C.E.
CONSTRUCTION OF THE MĀHABODHI TEMPLE

The Māhabodhi Temple was built to commemorate the place where the Buddha attained enlightenment. It is the most important pilgrimage site for Buddhists the world over.

LOCALE: Bodh Gayā, India
CATEGORIES: Architecture; religion

KEY FIGURES
Buddha (Siddhārtha Gautama; c. 566-c. 486 B.C.E.), founder of Buddhism
Aśoka (c. 302-c. 238 B.C.E.), Indian emperor and legendary builder of the temple, r. c. 273/265-c. 238 B.C.E.
Faxian (Fa-hsien; c. 337-422 C.E.), Buddhist monk, pilgrim, and translator of Buddhist scripture who reported finding a shrine to Buddha

SUMMARY OF EVENT

The Māhabodhi Temple in Bodh Gayā commemorates the place where the Buddha attained enlightenment. The origins of the temple are shrouded in the legends surrounding King Aśoka, who is said to have built a structure around the Bodhi tree under which the Buddha reached enlightenment. According to the *Aśokāvadāna* (third century B.C.E.; the legend of Aśoka), translated from Sanskrit to Chinese by the pilgrim Faxian, Aśoka's wife was upset that her husband spent so much time at the Bodhi tree, so she had it cut down. Aśoka then heaped up the earth on the four sides of the stump and bathed it in milk. The tree is said to have been restored to its former state. Xuanzang, another Chinese pilgrim in the seventh century, reported that Aśoka built a stone wall around the tree. In this version of the story, Aśoka burned the tree before his conversion to Buddhism, then repented and revived it with a milk bath. His queen had the tree destroyed, only to have Aśoka restore it a second time.

The earliest pictorial evidence for the temple is a relief sculpture from Bhārhut (first century B.C.E.) showing a two-story structure built around the Bodhi tree and the Vajrāsana (the Diamond seat), on which the enlightenment of the Buddha occurred. Alexander Cunningham, in his archaeological report, reported that an altar, three column bases, and a step had been found under the floor of the present temple. He assigned these remains to a rectangular temple similar to that found in the Bhārhut relief and believed that they belonged to the Aśokan temple. Later scholars have usually placed these remains somewhat later (second-first century B.C.E.) and have pointed out that the relief shows a circular, wooden structure. The construction of this structure coincided with a rise in devotion toward the Buddha and places associated with him—something that the Buddha had discouraged. Although the bodily relics of the Buddha had drawn much attention immediately after his death, it was not until after Aśoka that this devotional tendency increased. Scholars have attributed this increase to attempts of certain Buddhist sects to appeal to the laity.

When Faxian visited Bodh Gayā in the fifth century C.E., he reported that a stupa had been built at the place of enlightenment. This structure, now in stone, has been attributed to the newly arrived Kushāns (100-400 C.E.). It is probably represented on a plaque from Patna showing a statue of the Buddha within the temple. Although Faxian did not speak of a statue, it nevertheless seems probable that there would have been a statue given the emergence of images of the Buddha in the first century C.E. It is also likely that the Bodhi tree was moved outside at this time.

In the seventh century C.E., Xuanzang reported that the temple consisted of a 160-foot (49-meter) tower on a rectangular base. He also related the legendary origin of the statue of the Buddha in the temple. From his description, it is clear that the statue showed the Buddha in the *bhūmisparśa mudrā* (the earth-touching gesture). This type of statue commemorates the moment at which the Buddha overcame Māra, calling on the earth to bear witness to his enlightenment (the statue in the present temple dates from the tenth century C.E.). The temple of this time probably formed the basis for the present temple.

Sometime after the twelfth century, the temple fell into neglect. It was not until the Burmese mission to the temple in 1802 that interest in the Māhabodhi Temple revived. The Burmese mission drew the attention of the British. Francis Buchanan-Hamilton visited the site in 1811, publishing a report much later in 1836. In 1861, Alexander Cunningham suggested excavation of the site, which was carried out by Major Mead. After the Burmese mission of 1875 and in conjunction with the mission of 1880, J. D. Beglar directed a restoration of the temple based on an eleventh century miniature model of the temple. The model showed a tower and four smaller corner towers on a two-story base.

SIGNIFICANCE

The Māhabodhi temple, along with the Bodhi tree and the Vajrāsana, are the major pilgrimage sites for Buddhists. The architecture of the temple and its artwork have influenced Buddhist temples and art throughout India and other Buddhist countries. The temple itself has also been reproduced in other Buddhist countries. Two reproductions are found in Burma, the Māhabodhi Temple at Pagan (thirteenth century) and the Schwegugyi in Pegu, and two in Thailand, the Wat Chet Yot at Chiengmai and the Chiengrai Temple. The last three reproductions date from the fifteenth century. In Nepal, the Mahābauddha Temple dates from the sixteenth century.

—*Albert T. Watanabe*

FURTHER READING

Barua, Dipak K. *Bodh Gayā Temple: Its History.* Bodh Gayā, India: Buddha Gayā Temple Management Committee, 1981. Barua gives a detailed history of the development of the temple, taking all the factors of architecture, art, and literature into consideration.

Coomaraswamy, A. K. "Early Indian Architecture II. Bodhi-garas." *Eastern Art* 2 (1939): 225-235. This article discusses the early form of the Māhabodhi Temple as a tree shrine.

Cunningham, Alexander, *Māhabodhi: Or, The Great Buddhist Temple Under the Bodhi Tree at Buddha-Gayā.* London: W. H. Allen, 1892. Although the temple was not systematically excavated, archaeologist Cunningham reported on what he found before the restoration of the temple.

Leoshko, Janice, ed. *Bodh Gayā: The Site of Enlightenment.* Bombay: Marg Publications, 1988. A collection of essays on various aspects of the temple. In addition to the history of the temple, essays discuss the sculptures and votive objects at the temple. Other essays examine the relation of the temple to Sri Lanka, Southeast Asia, Nepal, and Tibet.

SEE ALSO: 6th or 5th century B.C.E., Birth of Buddhism; c. 5th-4th century B.C.E., Creation of the *Jātakas*; c. 273/265-c. 238 B.C.E., Aśoka Reigns over India; c. 250 B.C.E., Third Buddhist Council Convenes; c. 250 B.C.E., *Tipiṭaka* Is Compiled; c. 247-207 B.C.E., Buddhism Established in Sri Lanka; c. 1st century B.C.E., Indian Buddhist Nuns Compile the *Therigatha*; 1st century B.C.E.-1st century C.E., Compilation of the *Lotus Sutra*; 1st-2d century C.E., Fourth Buddhist Council Convenes; c. 60-68 C.E., Buddhism Enters China.
RELATED ARTICLES in *Great Lives from History: The Ancient World*: Aśoka; Buddha; Faxian.

287 B.C.E.
LEX HORTENSIA REFORMS THE ROMAN CONSTITUTION

The Lex Hortensia *brought about constitutional reform by making plebiscites equal to laws and enforceable on the entire community.*

LOCALE: Rome (now in Italy)
CATEGORIES: Government and politics; laws, acts, and legal history

KEY FIGURE
Quintus Hortensius (d. 287 B.C.E.), plebeian dictator in 287 B.C.E.

SUMMARY OF EVENT

Throughout the fifth and fourth centuries B.C.E., persistent class conflict raged in Rome between the privileged patrician class and the plebeians over the distribution of political rights and powers. Eventually, the plebeians managed to win increasing degrees of equality with the patricians. By means of various laws, they had gained recognition of intermarriage with patricians and the right of election to all major political offices. The patricians had also recognized the plebeians as a distinct political body within the state by granting to them the power of electing their own officials, the tribunes of the people. Most of these gains (essentially tactical concessions to the new economic and military power of the plebeians) were won only grudgingly from the patricians, who retained ultimate control over the state by dominating the legislative process.

In the early Roman constitution, a measure became law after it had been proposed to and ratified by a validly convened assembly, or *comitia*, of the community. Such assemblies had to be convoked by a consul or a praetor, could meet only on specified days after the performance of stipulated religious rituals, and could only vote "yes" or "no" to properly submitted proposals. Even after a proposal had been affirmed, it still required ratification by the patrician senators before it became valid. To ensure further patrician control over the legislative process, the main assembly in the early period was the *comitia centuriata*, in which the voting groups were unequal and a minority of wealthy patrician citizens could influence the final ballot. Once a proposal had navigated this complex process, it became law and was binding on all members of the community regardless of class affiliation, but the restrictions on the autonomy of the legislative body allowed the predominantly patrician senate (which did

not itself have the power to enact laws) to subordinate legislation to senatorial interests and programs.

From the earliest days of the Roman Republic, the plebeians had formed their own assembly (the *Concilium Plebis*), which contained only plebeian members and attended to their interests alone. Although convened by its own legitimate authority—one of the tribunes—it was not considered to be a *comitia* because it was limited to the enactment of proposals that were binding only on the plebeians themselves. Such enactments were termed plebiscites and were rigidly distinguished from laws, which obligated everyone.

The first attempt to change this situation was contained in one of the provisions of the Valerio-Horatian laws of 449 B.C.E., which stipulated that validly enacted plebiscites were to enjoy the same standing as laws and bind the entire citizen populace. The ineffectiveness of this law required a similar enactment by Quintus Publilius Philo in 339 B.C.E., which again attempted to convert plebiscites into laws. Some historians have seen both these laws as fictitious anticipations of the later *Lex Hortensia*, while others have argued that both laws were real enough but contained some qualifying condition, such as the necessity of senatorial ratification, before plebiscites became legally binding on everyone. It is likely, however, that both laws were passed without any qualification but were simply disregarded by the patricians as invalid since they had been passed without their approval.

This situation developed into a crisis in 287 B.C.E., when the plebeians, who had contributed greatly to the recent victory over the Samnites, imposed a general strike by withdrawing as a group from the city to force the patricians to meet their demands. In this emergency, the extreme measure was taken of appointing as dictator the plebeian and otherwise undistinguished Quintus Hortensius. Hortensius put through a law, called the *Lex Hortensia*, again making plebiscites equal to laws and enforceable on the entire community. The plebeians returned to the city after the acceptance of this constitutional reform by the patricians, and thereafter there was no further opposition to this particular issue by the patricians.

SIGNIFICANCE

Roman legal theorists treat subsequent plebiscites and laws as equivalent legislative enactments differing only in their point of origin. Armed with the power of making laws, the plebeians became an influential part of Roman political life; the tribunate, as the initiator of plebiscites, grew into a more powerful office; and the democratic aspects of the Roman constitution became more evident and effective.

—*George M. Pepe, updated by Jeffrey L. Buller*

FURTHER READING

Buckland, William Warwick. *A Manual of Roman Private Law*. 2d ed. New York: Cambridge University Press, 1953. Still the best source available for an analysis of the laws affecting Roman citizenship and private life.

Bush, Archie C. *Studies in Roman Social Structure*. Washington, D.C.: University Press of America, 1982. A general treatment of issues affecting Roman class and society, including marriage, the family, and kinship. The discussion of the conflicts inherent in Rome's social structure will help clarify the issues leading to the passage of the *Lex Hortensia*.

Crook, John Anthony. *Law and Life of Rome*. Ithaca, N.Y.: Cornell University Press, 1967. Discusses the evolution of Roman law within the context of social conditions.

Mitchell, Richard E. *Patricians and Plebeians: The Origin of the Roman State*. Ithaca, N.Y.: Cornell University Press, 1990. An excellent discussion of class as an issue in Roman society and its impact upon the development of Roman legal and constitutional history.

Watson, Alan. *The Evolution of Law*. Baltimore: The Johns Hopkins University Press, 1985. A good general introduction on the history and development of Roman law.

Yavetz, Zvi. *Plebs and Princeps*. Oxford: Clarendon Press, 1969. The classic study of the Roman class system. Though focusing primarily upon the imperial period, this work provides important background on social conflicts that extended early into republican society.

SEE ALSO: c. 2112 B.C.E., Ur-Nammu Establishes a Code of Law; c. 1770 B.C.E., Promulgation of Hammurabi's Code; 621 or 620 B.C.E., Draco's Code Is Instituted; 508-507 B.C.E., Reforms of Cleisthenes; 483 B.C.E., Naval Law of Themistocles Is Instituted; 445 B.C.E., Establishment of the Canuleian Law; 180 B.C.E., Establishment of the *Cursus honorum*; 90 B.C.E., Julian Law Expands Roman Citizenship; c. 50 C.E., Creation of the Roman Imperial Bureaucracy; c. 165 C.E., Gaius Creates Edition of the *Institutes* of Roman Law.

---

c. 285-c. 255 B.C.E

XUNZI DEVELOPS TEACHINGS THAT LEAD TO LEGALISM

Xunzi, a major scholar, rejected many tenets of Confucianism, creating a philosophy that, in the hands of his students, became Legalism.

LOCALE: China
CATEGORIES: Philosophy; government and politics

KEY FIGURES

Xunzi (Hsün-tzu; c. 307-c. 235 B.C.E.), philosopher, legal scholar, and educator

Hanfeizi (Han Fei-tzu; 280-233 B.C.E.), philosopher and popularizer of authoritarian Legalism, a student of Xunzi

Li Si (Li Ssu; 280?-208 B.C.E.), minister of state, 221-208 B.C.E., a student of Xunzi

SUMMARY OF EVENT

Xunzi was born in the state of Zhao (Chao) during the Warring States Period (475-221 B.C.E.). He was extremely gifted intellectually and studied at the Jixia Academy in Qi (Ch'i), the intellectual center at the time.

He traveled to different states, eventually became a great scholar, and rose to official posts, including that of magistrate.

Xunzi developed his philosophical theories in a logical manner in the *Xunzi* (compiled c. 285-c. 255 B.C.E.; *The Works of Hsuntze*, 1928; commonly known as *Xunzi*), a book of some thirty-two chapters. These might be regarded as the first collection of philosophical essays in China, as distinct from fragments (analects) or records of conversations.

According to the *Xunzi*, human nature is bad. Human nature is such that people are born with a love of profit. If they follow this inclination, they will struggle and take things from each other, and they will drive out less dominant inclinations, such as to defer or yield. People are born with fears and hatreds. If they follow them, they will become violent, and any tendencies they have toward good faith will disappear. Similarly, people are born with sensory desires that draw them to pleasant sounds and sights. If they indulge in these desires, the result will be

571

the disorder of sexual license, and ritual and moral principles will be lost. In other words, if people act in accord with human nature and follow their desires, they inevitably end up struggling, taking things, violating norms, and acting with violent abandon. Consequently, only after people are transformed by teachers and by ritual and moral principles do they defer, conform to culture, and abide in good order.

In spite of his gloomy view of humanity's original nature, Xunzi believed that people could be improved through education and through application of the proper rules of conduct. He also believed that heaven is not a realm of mystical forces embodying ethical principles (the Confucian philosopher Mencius's view) but is part of the realm of nature, indifferent to humans.

Xunzi was a major scholar who bridged Confucianism and Legalism. He lived at a pivotal time in Chinese history that produced some truly profound thinkers. What is more, he had the advantage of being taught by a number of these people at a prestigious learning academy that had access to the doctrines of numerous schools of thought. Xunzi was in a position to build on and integrate the ideas of numerous thinkers, adopting their strengths and correcting or discarding their weaknesses. He is believed to have died c. 235 B.C.E., but some scholars such as John Knoblock think that the philosopher died around 220 B.C.E.

By his teaching and writing, Xunzi established a strong reputation that ultimately brought him such talented students as Hanfeizi and Li Si. His students developed Legalism, which is very different from the earlier philosophy of Confucianism, named after its founder Confucius (Kongfuzi, K'ung-Fu-Tzu; c. 551-479 B.C.E.). Although the name given to the last classical school of philosophy developed before the Qin Dynasty is translated as Legalism, the philosophy has little to do with jurisprudence per se. The central idea of this school of political philosophy is the supremacy of authority and centralization of power in the person of the ruler.

Most of the major tenets of the Legalists were fully developed and formulated between 380 and 230 B.C.E., during the late Warring States Period. Legalists were noted for their unabashed insistence on the total subordination of the people to the ruler. Whereas Confucianism made verbal concessions to the interest of the people and justified the authority of the sovereign as ensuring the welfare of the people, the Legalists explicitly treat the people as a means for the glorification of the ruler. They were called the Legalist school because of their insistence on the importance of law as a major tool of the ruler

to maintain his authority and power. In contrast to the Confucians, who emphasized rituals, ethics, and education, the Legalists stressed the role of force and punishment.

Ironically, a number of Legalists died as the result of severe punishment. The early Legalist Shang Yang (d. c. 337 B.C.E.) implemented a series of reforms that brought about fundamental changes in social and political institutions designed to strengthen the state and to enhance the authority of the sovereign. The reforms stripped the nobles of many privileges and incurred the hatred of the aristocracy and the prince regent. After the old Qin lord died, Shang was executed by the new ruler. Two of Xunzi's students, Hanfeizi and Li Si, also met similar fates.

Hanfeizi, probably the greatest Legalist, developed the philosophy of Legalism further by elevating law to a position of supreme importance in governing human affairs. According to Hanfeizi, a victory in the competition among states depends on having the greatest force. The ruler who has great force will be paid tribute by others, and the ruler who has less force will pay tribute to others; therefore, the wise ruler cultivates force. The fifty-five-chapter work *Hanfeizi* (traditionally later half of third century B.C.E., probably compiled c. 235-c. 160 B.C.E.; *The Complete Works of Han Fei Tzu: A Classic of Chinese Legalism*, 1939-1959, 2 vols.; commonly known as *Hanfeizi*) is the work of Hanfeizi and later Han Dynasty Legalists.

Xunzi's other prominent student, Li Si, was more a practitioner than a scholar of Legalism. Li Si once offered his teacher Xunzi a position serving in the Qin court, but Xunzi declined the offer. Li Si was engaged in a rivalry with fellow student Hanfeizi, and when Li Si felt that his former schoolmate might be elevated above him by the Qin king, Li Si convinced the king that Hanfeizi posed a danger to the Qin state and had him arrested. Then Li Si had poison sent to Hanfeizi and persuaded him to commit suicide in prison.

Li Si played a very important role in helping the state of Qin defeat six other states to create the first united Chinese dynasty in 221 B.C.E. As prime minister under Shi Huangdi, the first Qin emperor, Li Si was responsible for initiating some important Legalistic reforms that had a decisive effect on the building of institutions and the bureaucracy in the Chinese empire. He was a pivotal force in Shi Huangdi's decision to abolish feudal fiefs and replace the aristocracy by an appointed, nonhereditary bureaucracy.

Li Si enabled a junior son of the Qin emperor to acquire the throne by illegitimate means. In the second year of the second Qin emperor, Li Si himself became a victim of court intrigue and was falsely accused of plotting treason. He was executed by the consorted five corporal punishments, the cruelest form of execution devised by the Legalists.

SIGNIFICANCE

Xunzi's theory of the inherent evil of human nature must have made a great impression on his Legalist disciples. Xunzi's insistence on decorum was a bridge from Confucian decorum to Legalist law, because law can be regarded as an extension of decorum in that it adds norms and a coercive element to decorum. It could be argued that the Legalists share some important ideas with the Confucians: the ideal of one unified world under the supreme authority of one ruler, the centralization of political power, a hierarchical social order, and the treatment of law as a natural extension of decorum.

Xunzi emphasized the multiple functions of decorum to such an extent that his concept of decorum appears to be almost identical to what the Legalists conceived of as law: Decorum is what the ruler uses as legal form to set measures for the conduct of the various ministers. Those who emphasize decorum and respect the virtuous will become kings, and those who stress law and love the people will become hegemonic rulers. It is significant that Xunzi, who emphasized decorum more than any other classical Chinese thinker, was the master of the two eminent Legalists Hanfeizi and Li Si. Like Confucianism, its rival school of thinking, Legalism continues to affect Chinese legal and political thinking today.

—*Guoli Liu*

FURTHER READING

Ebrey, Patricia. *Chinese Civilization: A Sourcebook*. 2d ed. New York: Free Press, 1993. Good introduction to Chinese culture; includes a concise discussion of Xunzi.

Goldin, P. R. *Rituals of the Way: The Philosophy of Xunzi*. Chicago: Open Court, 1999. A summary and analysis of Xunzi's philosophy with a focus on rituals.

Knoblock, John. *Xunzi: A Translation and Study of the Complete Works*. 3 vols. Stanford, Calif.: Stanford University Press, 1988-1994. The most comprehensive and authoritative translation and analysis of Xunzi's work.

Machle, E. J. *Nature and Heaven in the Xunzi: A Study of the Tian Lun*. Albany: State University Press of New York, 1993. An analysis of the core concept of Tian (heaven) in Xunzi's thinking.

Watson, Burton, trans. *Xunzi: Basic Writings*. New York: Columbia University Press, 2003. A good translation of selected writings by Xunzi.

Zhengyuan Fu. *China's Legalists: The Earlier Totalitarians and Their Art of Ruling*. Armonk, N.Y.: M. E. Sharpe, 1996. Examines the key viewpoints of major eminent Legalists including Li Si and Hanfeizi.

SEE ALSO: 479 B.C.E., Confucius's Death Leads to the Creation of *The Analects*; 475-221 B.C.E., China Enters Chaotic Warring States Period; 221 B.C.E., Qin Dynasty Founded in China; 221-206 B.C.E., Legalist Movement in China; 206 B.C.E., Liu Bang Captures Qin Capital, Founds Han Dynasty.

RELATED ARTICLES in *Great Lives from History: The Ancient World*: Confucius; Hanfeizi; Shi Huangdi; Xunzi.

285-160 B.C.E. (traditionally, c. 300 B.C.E.)
COMPOSITION OF THE *ZHUANGZI*

The Zhuangzi, *an early and important work, laid the foundation for the development of Daoism in later generations and shaped Chinese thinking and life for more than two thousand years.*

LOCALE: China
CATEGORIES: Cultural and intellectual history; philosophy

KEY FIGURES
Zhuangzi (Chuang-tzu; c. 365-290 B.C.E.), philosopher
Guo Xiang (Kuo Hsiang; d. 312 C.E.), writer of a commentary and compilation of the *Zhuangzi* and a Chinese government official

SUMMARY OF EVENT

The *Zhuangzi* (*The Divine Classic of Nan-hua*, 1881; also known as *The Complete Works of Chuang Tzu*, 1968; commonly known as *Zhuangzi*, 1991) is an early work on Daoism, one of the most influential philosophical schools in China. Although the thirty-three-chapter work is named after Zhuangzi (Master Zhuang) and traditionally given the compilation date of c. 300 B.C.E., it was not written by him alone and not all at once. The first seven inner chapters are traditionally thought to be the work of Zhuangzi himself, and the remaining outer and miscellaneous chapters are thought to be the contributions of Zhuangzi's followers. Although the work is a composite, its chapters are consistent in both writing style and basic philosophical orientation. The *Zhuangzi* was probably first compiled c. 285-160 B.C.E. by Zhuangzi's followers, but the work is best known as compiled by Guo Xiang, who wrote the commentary *Zhuangzizhu* (fourth century C.E.).

The composition of the *Zhuangzi* was based on the first Daoist classic, *Dao De Jing* (possibly sixth century B.C.E., probably compiled late third century B.C.E.; *The Speculations on Metaphysics, Polity, and Morality of "the Old Philosopher, Lau-Tsze,"* 1868; better known as the *Dao De Jing*), traditionally attributed to Laozi, who was supposedly a contemporary of Confucius (Kongfuzi, K'ung-Fu-Tzu; 551-479 B.C.E.). The two classics share some fundamental Daoistic beliefs—they both embrace the concepts of *dao* (the Way) and *de* (virtue), insist on the spontaneity of all things and harmony (or integration) of humankind with nature, advocate following the way of nature or nonaction (*wu wei*) in personal life and in government, disparage wisdom and knowledge and

institutions, and reject Confucianism. On the other hand, however, the *Zhuangzi* differs from the *Dao De Jing* in terms of style of expression and emphasis. The *Dao De Jing* is composed of terse and abstract statements, many of which are esoteric and subject to different interpretations. By contrast, the *Zhuangzi* illuminates sophisticated philosophic ideas by using literary devices—amusing stories, parables, and metaphors, which are often about humorous and enjoyable personalities. Furthermore, the *Dao De Jing* is primarily a political treatise addressed to the ruler who would be a sage-king and is mainly concerned with achieving a good society through harmony with nature, whereas the *Zhuangzi*, contemptuous of rulership and indifferent to social life, focuses overwhelmingly on personal happiness or personal self-realization. It only derivatively concerns social and political order.

The overriding concern of the *Zhuangzi* is a quest for personal happiness, a state in which a person enjoys absolute spiritual freedom and that is within the reach of every human being. The achievement of personal happiness is an individual matter that depends solely on an individual's understanding and following the course of nature and has nothing to do with external things such as material wealth, institutions, or supernatural forces. Any person can be happy if he or she genuinely follows the way of nature. The person who has achieved happiness is portrayed in the *Zhuangzi* as an Authentic (or True) Person (*zhenren*). This individual is happy because the person identifies with nature and models his or her conduct on the rhythm and cadence of natural change. Following the way of nature, the Authentic Person makes no distinctions between polarities such as this/that, good/bad, right/wrong, beauty/ugliness, past/present, and life/death. Instead the Authentic Person blends everything into a harmonious whole and sees all things as equal or as one. For example, life and death are one, and right and wrong are the same. Most important, the Authentic Person transcends the distinction between the self and the world, the "me" and the "non-me." Therefore, the individual has no consciousness of self (or forgets the existence of himself or herself)—the self is totally integrated with the rest of the universe.

Because the Authentic Person has transcended all distinctions, he or she is not affected by the changes of the world; not fettered by desire, hate (aversion), anxiety, and attachment; and not disturbed by things such as worldly gain and loss or good and bad luck. The Authentic Person takes no assertive or deliberate actions, so he or she has neither regret in failure nor self-complacency in success. He or she is noncontentious, not contending or competing for anything; contented, accepting whatever comes to him or her or is inevitable; and not meddling but accommodating; he or she also lives in harmony with both nature and other humans. The Authentic Person even has no anxiety about death, viewing it as just another form of existence and seeing the transformation of life and death as natural as seasonal alternations and the succession of day and night. Living, he or she feels no elation; dying, he or she offers no resistance. In this way, the Authentic Person keeps his or her mind tranquil and imperturbable and free from all concerns and, therefore, enjoys absolute spiritual freedom and personal happiness.

Although the *Zhuangzi* takes death lightly and sometimes even suggests that death is preferable to life, its emphasis is still on preservation or longevity of life. The best way for people to achieve longevity is to live in accordance with nature and do nothing artificially to increase what is already in their lives. Because death is inevitable and natural, it is futile and unnecessary to worry about it. Worrying about death, an inevitability, only hurts a person's life, while indifference to it will help preserve or prolong life.

Given its overriding concern with how to live a happy personal life, the *Zhuangzi* can be viewed as a book on the philosophy or art of living. This philosophy is naturalistic because it does not attribute personal happiness to a creator or god and does not promise immortality; rather, it stresses following nature as the only way to personal happiness and sees death as a natural change. This philosophy is also imbued with individualism in the sense that it places the individual's happiness above anything else (for example, the interests of the society or the state) and holds that such happiness can be attained by the individual.

The insistence of the authors of the *Zhuangzi* on following the course of nature led them to oppose anything that they believed to be unnatural, such as institutions (laws, governments, morals, or ethics). The *Zhuangzi* holds that institutions are nothing more than artificial structures imposed on individuals and that they constitute a primary cause of social troubles and human miseries. Institutions function to distort human nature—humankind's innate disposition to be free or to be left alone. Applying institutions to humankind is like putting a halter around a horse's neck or a string through an ox's nose; it is also like lengthening the legs of the duck or shortening those of the crane—what is natural and spontaneous is changed into something artificial. Therefore, institutions are not only unnecessary but also detrimental to the well-being of humankind.

The *Zhuangzi* is critical of other schools of thought, especially Confucianism, because these schools insist on using institutions to regulate people's behavior. For instance, it denounced the Confucian advocacy of "benevolence and righteousness" and "rituals and music" and identified this advocacy as a source of confusion and disorder. Throughout the text, Confucius is depicted as a humble and modest figure, ready to learn the *dao* (the Way) from Daoist masters, which implies that Confucianism is inferior to Daoism.

The *Zhuangzi* states that the ideal way to govern is through nonaction (*wu wei*): Rulers should refrain from interfering with people's lives and leave them alone to exercise their own natural ability fully and freely. If rulers follow this course of nonaction, the world will remain in order and people will be happy. However, if rulers act assertively and contrive to control people's lives through such means as laws and morals, punishments and rewards, and schemes and wisdoms, people will become cunning and treacherous, and the world will fall into disorder.

The *Zhuangzi* thus projects a political philosophy, which is characterized by its opposition to institutions and the stress on governing through nonaction. This political philosophy is derived from and consistent with the philosophy of living that is elaborated in the *Zhuangzi*. The two philosophies share a common theme—following what is natural is the source of all happiness and good, while following what is artificial is the source of unhappiness and bad.

SIGNIFICANCE

The composition of the *Zhuangzi* constitutes a major contribution to the development of Daoism. Through stories, parables, metaphors, and other literary devices, this work sheds light on basic Daoistic beliefs, some of which were first put forward but not well explained in the *Dao De Jing*, and it helped establish Daoism as a major school of thought.

The individualistic spirit and nonconformist attitude expressed in the *Zhuangzi* has the effect of liberating humankind's mind and thus poses a potential challenge to any established or official ideology that stresses conformity and obedience. Throughout history, the *Zhuangzi* has been popular among Chinese of different social strata. Politicians drew from it inspirations on governing, and scholars of the Profound or Mysterious Learning (*xuanxue*) from the third to sixth centuries C.E. based their theories on it. People, especially intellectuals, found comfort in it during troubled times or when they were frustrated in their careers. Daoist priests as well as others used it as a guide for self-cultivation, and writers learned its literary style of expression. Many stories from the *Zhuangzi* were included in school textbooks and thus had a direct impact on young students.

—*Yunqiu Zhang*

FURTHER READING

Ames, Roger T. *Wandering at Ease in the Zhuangzi*. Albany: State University of New York Press, 1998. A collection of essays on different themes expressed in the *Zhuangzi*.

Fung, Yu-lan, trans. *Chuang-Tzu: A New Selected Translation with an Exposition of the Philosophy of Kuo Hsiang*. Beijing: Foreign Languages Press, 1989. An English translation of the first seven chapters of the

Zhuangzi with commentaries by the translator and Guo Xiang.

Palmer, Martin, et al., trans. *The Book of Zhuangzi*. New York: Penguin Putnam, 1996. An English version of the *Zhuangzi*.

Watson, Burton, trans. *Zhuangzi: Basic Writings*. New York: Columbia University Press, 2003. A standard translation of the *Zhuangzi*.

Wu, Kuang-ming. *Chuangzi: World Philosopher at Play*. New York: Scholar Press, 1982. An analysis of various philosophical views presented in the *Zhuangzi*.

SEE ALSO: 3d century B.C.E. (traditionally 6th century B.C.E.), Laozi Composes the *Dao De Jing*; 139-122 B.C.E., Composition of the *Huainanzi*; 142 C.E., Zhang Daoling Founds the Celestial Masters Movement; c. 3d century C.E., Wang Bi and Guo Xiang Revive Daoism; 397-402 C.E., Ge Chaofu Founds the Lingbao Tradition of Daoism.

RELATED ARTICLES in *Great Lives from History: The Ancient World*: Confucius; Laozi; Wang Bi; Zhuangzi.

c. 275 B.C.E.
GREEKS ADVANCE HELLENISTIC ASTRONOMY

Advances in Hellenistic astronomy were made when the ancient Greeks considered theories of an Earth-centered and a Sun-centered universe; the geocentric epicycle-on-deferent system proved to explain the most observations.

LOCALE: Alexandria (now in Egypt)

CATEGORIES: Science and technology; cultural and intellectual history

KEY FIGURES

Heraclides of Pontus (c. 388-310 B.C.E.), Greek astronomer and head of Plato's Academy

Aristarchus of Samos (c. 310-c. 230 B.C.E.), Alexandrian astronomer and mathematician

Apollonius of Perga (c. 262-c. 190 B.C.E.), Alexandrian astronomer and mathematician

Eratosthenes of Cyrene (c. 285-c. 205 B.C.E.), Alexandrian astronomer, geographer, and mathematician

Hipparchus (190-after 127 B.C.E.), Greek astronomer and mathematician

Ptolemy (c. 100-c. 178 C.E.), Alexandrian mathematical astronomer

SUMMARY OF EVENT

That Earth was spherical was known to learned Greeks of the fourth century B.C.E. by the shape of its shadow on the moon during a lunar eclipse. The accepted view of the universe, however, was that Earth remained unmoving at its center, while around it in concentric spheres moved the seven planets of the ancient world: the Moon, Mercury, Venus, the Sun, Mars, Jupiter, and Saturn. About 340 B.C.E. at Athens, Heraclides of Pontus postulated that the earth rotated daily on its axis and that the Sun and the other planets revolved around the Earth. His work "On Things in the Heavens" is lost, so modern scholars do not know how he arrived at these conclusions.

This theory was the most advanced position taken by Greek astronomers by the time of Alexander the Great's conquest of Persia, which opened up a new world to scientists. At Babylon, Uruk, and Sippar, in Mesopotamia, fairly accurate observations of the movements of the heavenly bodies had been recorded and kept for centuries. Part of this mass of new knowledge became known to Greek scientists in the third century B.C.E. The Greeks also had their own means of acquiring data, for among the wonders of the new museum established in Alexandria as a sort of university was an observatory, a simple tower whose only instrument was a device without lenses for measuring the azimuth and angle of height of a star or planet.

From these small beginnings, Greek astronomers reached astonishing conclusions. Aristarchus of Samos, invited to Alexandria, showed by the use of observations and of plane geometry that the Sun was some three hundred times larger than Earth. This estimate was a considerable improvement over the fifth century B.C.E. estimate that the Sun was about the size of the Peloponnesus. Aristarchus demonstrated his findings through geometrical proofs in his extant treatise *Peri megethon kai apostematon heliou kai selenes* (c. early third century B.C.E.; *On the Size and Distance of the Sun and the Moon*, 1913). Having established this fact to his own satisfaction, Aristarchus went on to deduce that the Sun, apparently because it was so much larger than Earth, must itself be the unmoving center of the cosmos, with Earth and the other planets revolving about it in circles, the Moon about Earth, and Earth rotating on its axis. The unmoving fixed stars were at an infinite distance. The book in which he explained his reasons for holding these bold hypotheses is lost and, because his system violated ancient authority and common sense and predicted a shift in the position of the stars that was actually too small to be observed at that time, his ideas were not widely accepted.

Apollonius of Perga, on the other hand, made adjustments to the Earth-centered system that Greeks found to be more reasonable. He proposed the theory that the planets moved in epicycles around imaginary points on spheres called deferents. The points were also supposed to move in spherical orbits around Earth, but their centers were not Earth itself. The complex scheme accounted for variations observed in the speeds of the planets and their distances from Earth. It also explained why a planet sometimes seemed to be moving backward and why that "retrograde" motion coincided with the planet's brightest appearance.

Meanwhile, at Alexandria and Syene, Eratosthenes of Cyrene conducted an imaginative experiment during which he measured the circumference of Earth to within perhaps less than 2 percent. He noticed that at Syene on the Nile River (modern Aswān) at noon on the summer solstice, the Sun was exactly overhead. His proof began with the observation that then a vertical pole cast no shadow and the bottom of a deep well with vertical sides was completely illuminated. He arranged for an assistant at Alexandria to measure the angle cast by a vertical pole

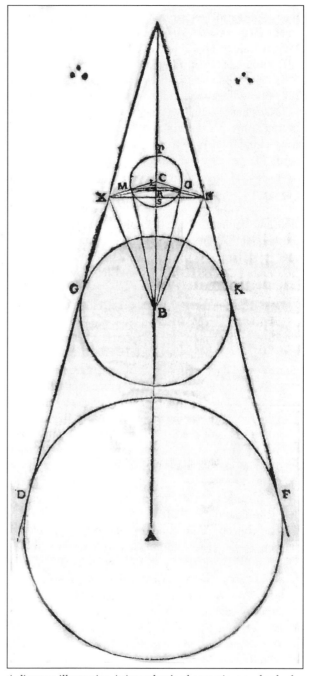

A diagram illustrating Aristarchus's observations and calculations regarding the Sun, Moon, and Earth. (Library of Congress)

there at the same time on the same day. This angle measured one-fiftieth of a complete turn (7 degrees, 12 minutes), so he concluded that the distance between Syene and Alexandria was about one-fiftieth of the circumference of the earth. Determining this land distance, Eratosthenes then calculated the circumference of the earth as 250,000 stadia. This is an error of only about 250 miles (403 kilometers) according to some scholars' estimates of the length of a stade. He later changed his estimate to 252,000 stadia, although it is not known on what basis.

Eratosthenes actually made two mistakes: He wrongly assumed that Alexandria and Syene were on the same great circle, and his measurement of the distance between the two cities was inaccurate. Fortunately the two errors tended to cancel each other out, and his method was otherwise sound. Because he also knew that the distance from Gibraltar to India was only some sixty-nine thousand stadia, he made the remarkable prediction that another continental system would be found at the Antipodes by sailing west into the Atlantic Ocean or east into the Indian Ocean, an opinion held later by Christopher Columbus (1451-1506).

Like most of these astronomers, Hipparchus of Nicaea said that he acted "to save the phenomena." Theoretically, he accepted the geocentric system, but he is most noted for numerous observational contributions. He measured the length of the solar year to within 6 minutes, 14.3 seconds, discovered the precession of the equinoxes, and cataloged more than 850 fixed stars together with their magnitudes into an accurate star map. He estimated the mass of the Sun as 1,800 times that of Earth and its distance as 1,245 Earth diameters, improvements on those of Aristarchus, whose system had otherwise faded away.

The theories of the Hellenistic astronomers reached their culmination in Ptolemy. He added circular orbits and the concept of an equant point to the epicycle-on-deferent model of Apollonius, in part to resolve difficulties raised by the observations of Hipparchus. The equant point was as far from the true center of the universe as was the earth. A planet in orbit swept out equal areas of its circle around the earth in equal times with respect to the equant point. This system, which admittedly involved some complicated mathematics, remained influential into the Renaissance.

SIGNIFICANCE

The researches of the Hellenistic astronomers laid the groundwork for modern astronomy, and also severed the association between astronomy and religion for the first time. Their investigations were intended to discover how the natural world worked for its own sake rather than to predict and interpret astronomic events as signs of a deity's intentions or wrath. While the hypothesis of a heliocentric universe was dismissed, the fact that such a hypothesis could be proposed, and that it was one of several competing hypotheses, indicates the radical change in worldview that had taken place within Greek science.

—Samuel K. Eddy,
updated by Amy Ackerberg-Hastings

FURTHER READING

Aaboe, Asger. *Episodes from the Early History of Astronomy.* New York: Springer Verlag, 2001. Chapter 2 of this short and accessible book is concerned with the Greek geometrical theories of planetary movement.

Evans, James. *The History and Practice of Ancient Astronomy.* New York: Oxford University Press, 1998. This unusual book teaches astronomy by explaining ancient theories and then setting readers experiments to carry out themselves, in order to understand exactly what the ancients were doing and thinking in elaborating their theories.

Gingerich, Owen. *The Eye of Heaven: Ptolemy, Copernicus, Kepler.* New York: Springer Verlag, 1993. Gingerich places the Hellenistic astronomers in relation to these three; he also introduces the reader to notable themes and scholars in the history of science.

Jacobsen, Theodor S. *Planetary Systems from the Ancient Greeks to Kepler.* Seattle: University of Washington Press, 1999. Reviews the astronomical theories and knowledge of all major Greek astronomers, mathematicians, and philosophers.

Toulmin, Stephen, and June Goodfield. *The Fabric of the Heavens: The Development of Astronomy and Dynamics.* Chicago: University of Chicago Press, 1999. Close to half of this history of astronomy is devoted to ancient Greek theories of the universe. Illustrations and index.

SEE ALSO: 600-500 B.C.E., Greek Philosophers Formulate Theories of the Cosmos; c. 250 B.C.E., Discoveries of Archimedes; 46 B.C.E., Establishment of the Julian Calendar.

RELATED ARTICLES in *Great Lives from History: The Ancient World*: Anaximander; Apollonius of Perga; Aristotle; Empedocles; Eratosthenes of Cyrene; Eudoxus of Cnidus; Hipparchus; Nabu-Rimmani; Ptolemy (astronomer); Pythagoras; Sosigenes; Thales of Miletus.

c. 273/265-c. 238 B.C.E.
AŚOKA REIGNS OVER INDIA

India emperor Aśoka, after a successful series of military conquests, converted to Buddhism and sought to spread the religion's nonviolent beliefs

LOCALE: India
CATEGORIES: Religion; government and politics

KEY FIGURE
Aśoka (c. 302-c. 238 B.C.E.), Indian emperor who converted to Buddhism, r. c. 273/265-c. 238 B.C.E.

SUMMARY OF EVENT

Aśoka (also spelled Ashoka) was an emperor of the Mauryan Dynasty, which united a large part of the land now known as India under a single ruler. Aśoka is chiefly remembered for his conversion to Buddhism and for his contributions to the spread of the Buddhist religion. Stories about his conversion are found in several texts, most notably in the *Aśokāvadāna* (third century B.C.E.; the legend of Aśoka), which was translated from Sanskrit to Chinese by Faxian (Fa-hsien; c. 337-422 C.E.) circa the fourth or fifth century C.E. There are also numerous references to Aśoka in the chronicles of the kingdom of Sri Lanka. In 1837, the Western scholar James Prinsep managed to translate an inscription on a stone pillar. The inscription was a series of edicts by a ruler identified as "King Piyadasi." Over the course of the nineteenth century, researchers found other stone inscriptions that pronounced legal reforms and moral principles. In 1915, an inscription that identified this king by name as the legendary Aśoka established that the ruler responsible for these edicts was the hero of the ancient Buddhist stories.

The founder of the Mauryan Dynasty was Aśoka's grandfather, Chandragupta Maurya. Chandragupta was a relatively low-caste member of the Moriya tribe who managed to seize the throne of the northern Indian kingdom of Magadha about 321 B.C.E. After bringing the rest of the valley of the Ganges River under his control, Chandragupta moved into the northwestern area of South Asia, where the recent departure of the Greek invader Alexander the Great had left a power vacuum. Chandragupta's son, Bindusāra, inherited the throne in c. 298 B.C.E. Under Bindusāra, the Mauryan territory grew to include most of the Indian subcontinent. However, the land of Kalinga, along the eastern coast of India by the Bay of Bengal, remained independent. Because Kalinga controlled the routes to southern India, it was a barrier to the consolidation of the Mauryan Empire.

Bindusāra died in 272 B.C.E. His son Aśoka, also known as Aśoka the Fierce because of his aggressive character, rushed to the imperial capital of Pataliputra and killed all of his rivals to the throne except for his brother. Popular anger against Aśoka's actions delayed his coronation until 270. He took the title of Dēvānaṃpiya Piyadasi, which means "Beloved of the Gods, the One Who Looks on With Affection." After becoming ruler, he assumed the task of defeating the Kalingans. He was ruthless, brutal, and successful. In 260 B.C.E., he attacked the territory, destroying its military forces and killing or exiling all who resisted. According to Buddhist tradition, Aśoka was so disturbed by the suffering he had caused that he converted to Buddhism and devoted the rest of his reign to supporting and spreading this religion of nonviolence.

Aśoka's conversion may not have been as dramatic and sudden as the legends suggest. He was probably a Buddhist in name for at least two years before the Kalinga campaign. He also did not desert his warlike ways immediately after that campaign. However, the edicts in stone do show him to be concerned with the moral reform of his kingdom during the latter part of his reign. In these edicts, Aśoka proclaimed his good intentions toward his subjects, whom he addressed as a father addressing his children. He apologized for the excesses of the Kalinga war and stated that he did not intend to extend his empire further. He announced the need for private morality in the lives of his subjects and for public morality in the administration of his state. Aśoka apparently reformed the empire's judicial system, with the aim of making it more humane and just. He also undertook an extensive program of public works, including the digging of wells along roads, the planting of fruit and shade trees, and the building of hostels.

During Aśoka's rule, the Buddhist Saṅgha, or community of the faithful, undertook a major effort at reorganization. Since the death of the Buddha in about the fifth century B.C.E., Buddhism had split into a number of different factions and schools. According to many historical accounts, a Third Buddhist Council was held at Pataliputra in 250 B.C.E. to establish Buddhist orthodoxy. At this council, the adherents of the Theravāda (literally, the way of the elders) school of Buddhism attempted to maintain what they believed was true Buddhism. The council is generally described as leading to the division of Buddhism into the Theravāda (also called Hīnayāna) and Mahāyāna approaches to Buddhism. Some Buddhist histories maintain that Aśoka directed or even called the Third Council, but there is no indication of the ruler's active involvement in his own stone inscriptions. Still, even if Aśoka was not behind the assembling of the council, it could not have taken place without his knowledge and approval.

The Third Buddhist Council is reported to have established the basic sacred writings of Theravāda Buddhism, known as the *Tipiṭaka* (compiled c. 250 B.C.E.; English translation in *Buddhist Scriptures*, 1913), and to have made the decision to send Buddhist envoys to other lands. Regardless of whether Aśoka participated in such a council, he certainly became active in the promulgation of Buddhism. Within his empire, Aśoka attempted to teach Buddhism to his own subjects. Many of the inscriptions on rocks or on erected pillars were located in places where crowds would gather. These inscriptions proclaimed to the people the Buddhist idea of *dhamma*, or *dharma*, which refers to universal law and the idea of justice or order. Aśoka's edicts have been found in Nepal, Pakistan, and Afghanistan, as well as in India.

Aśoka. (Hulton|Archive)

Aśoka sent his son Mahinda as a missionary to Sri Lanka. The king of Sri Lanka, Dēvānaṃpiya Tissa, took up the religion and modeled himself on the Indian emperor. Aśoka sent Tissa a branch of the tree under which the Buddha achieved enlightenment, and it is believed that a descendant of this tree still survives in modern Sri Lanka. The emperor sent other Buddhist missionaries to locations throughout India and to foreign lands. His religious missions may have reached the Ionian Greeks, Burma, Malaya, Sumatra, and the regions of the Himalayas to the north. According to his rock edicts, he maintained diplomatic contacts with such faraway rulers as Antiochus II of Syria, Ptolemy Philadelphus of Egypt, Alexander of Epirus, and Antigonus II Gonatas of Macedonia. There is some evidence, then, that the Indian emperor managed to introduce Buddhist ideas to the Mediterranean world.

Aśoka died in c. 238 B.C.E., after a reign of about thirty years. Soon afterward, the Mauryan Empire began to decline, and it broke up c. 185 B.C.E. Some historians have attributed the collapse of the empire to Aśoka's own policies, maintaining that the emperor's support of Buddhism led to a reaction by the pre-Buddhist brahman priesthood and that his nonviolence undermined the force needed to maintain an empire. However, other historians have argued that the empire was strained economically by the need to maintain its large army and that any state based primarily on personal loyalty to a ruler would tend to break up.

SIGNIFICANCE

The rule of Aśoka was significant in three ways. First, he largely completed the process, begun by his grandfather and father, of bringing the Indian subcontinent under a single rule. This contributed to the concept of India as a single place, rather than as a collection of states like Europe. Second, although Buddhism was already spreading when Aśoka came to power, his sponsorship helped the religion flourish and move on to other locations. Theravāda Buddhism, which moved into Southeast Asia under Aśoka's patronage, eventually became the dominant faith in the areas that became Burma, Laos, Thailand, and Cambodia. Sri Lanka still celebrates the mission of Aśoka's son as the origin of Buddhism in that nation. Third, Aśoka became the model of the ideal Buddhist ruler in many kingdoms and therefore played an important part in the development of ancient Asian political theory and practice. The concept of the king who represents and maintains the cosmic order of justice was central to the idea of the monarch in ancient Cambodia. It was taken up by the kings of Siam (now known as Thailand) and by rulers in other Theravāda realms.

—*Carl L. Bankston III*

FURTHER READING

Lopez, Donald S. *The Story of Buddhism: A Concise Guide to Its History and Teachings*. San Francisco: Harper, 2001. A short history of the origins and transformations of Buddhism. Pronunciation guide, bibliography, glossary, and index.

Seneviratna, Anuradha, ed. *King Aśoka and Buddhism*. Seattle: Pariyatti Press, 1995. A collection of essays on Aśoka's life and on the debates about his role in history.

Tamiah, Stanley J. *World Conqueror and World Renouncer: A Study of Buddhism and Polity in Thailand Against a Historical Background*. New York: Cambridge University Press, 1976. The classical work on the theory of the Buddhist king in Thailand. The author traces this theory from its origins in ancient India. Chapter 5 deals specifically with Aśoka as the model of the Buddhist king. Bibliography, index.

Thapar, Romila. *Aśoka and the Decline of the Mauryas*. Delhi: Oxford University Press, 1997. An updated edition of one of the most widely read histories of the Mauryan period by a prominent scholar of ancient India. Bibliography and index.

SEE ALSO: 6th or 5th century B.C.E., Birth of Buddhism; 327-325 B.C.E., Alexander the Great Invades the Indian Subcontinent; c. 323-275 B.C.E., Diadochi Divide Alexander the Great's Empire; c. 321 B.C.E., Mauryan Empire Rises in India; 300 B.C.E.-600 C.E., Construction of the Māhabodhi Temple; c. 250 B.C.E., Third Buddhist Council Convenes; c. 250 B.C.E., *Tipiṭaka* Is Compiled; c. 247-207 B.C.E., Buddhism Established in Sri Lanka.

RELATED ARTICLES in *Great Lives from History: The Ancient World*: Alexander the Great; Aśoka; Buddha; Chandragupta Maurya; Faxian; Dēvānaṃpiya Tissa.

264-225 B.C.E.
FIRST PUNIC WAR

The First Punic War pitted Roman military forces against Carthage in an effort to expand Roman authority in the Mediterranean.

LOCALE: Italy, Sicily, and Africa
CATEGORIES: Wars, uprisings, and civil unrest; expansion and land acquisition;

KEY FIGURES

Hieron II of Syracuse (c. 305-c. 215 B.C.E.), king of Syracuse, r. 270-c. 215 B.C.E.

Gaius Duilius (fl. third century B.C.E.), Roman consul who won a great naval victory in 260 B.C.E.

Regulus (c. 300-c. 249 B.C.E.), Roman consul in 267 B.C.E. and 256 B.C.E. who commanded an invasion of Africa

Appius Claudius Caudex (fl. third century B.C.E.), Roman consul in 264 B.C.E. who led the initial campaign

SUMMARY OF EVENT

The First Punic War was a milestone in Roman history. Modern scholarship rejects the old interpretation that entry into this conflict committed Rome to a policy of expansion on an altogether new scale. The Roman victory in 241 B.C.E. marked the emergence of Rome as the dominant power in the western Mediterranean. The policies Rome adopted in Sicily and elsewhere at the conclusion of the war had permanent repercussions both at home and in foreign affairs.

The Mediterranean world in the early third century B.C.E. consisted in the east of large territorial empires in areas conquered by Alexander the Great. In the west were three major states and numerous tribal peoples. Carthage, a merchant oligarchy, dominated the coast of Africa from modern Tunisia westward to Morocco, Spain, the western corner of Sicily, Sardinia, and Corsica. Rome, the second state, controlled the southern two-thirds of Italy. The portion inhabited by Roman citizens was the *ager Romanus*; the rest belonged to nominally independent allies (*socii*), of whom the Latins were relatively privileged while the majority were subordinate to Rome. As of yet, Rome had no possessions and scant interest beyond the peninsula.

The small kingdom of Syracuse in the southeast corner of Sicily, the leading Greek power in the west, was the third state. Sicily was an anachronism, certain to attract

A Roman attack during the First Punic War. (F. R. Niglutsch)

efforts on the part of the Hellenistic monarchies to attach it to one or another of the eastern empires. Carthage and Rome were equally certain to resist the establishment of Hellenistic powers in the western Mediterranean. When Pyrrhus (319-272 B.C.E.), king of Epirus, led his armies into Italy and Sicily, he first met the resistance of Rome, then of Carthage. The failure of his Italian and Sicilian campaign between 280 and 275 B.C.E. left a power vacuum little different from that which existed before, and it was only a matter of time before Rome and Carthage could be expected to come into conflict there.

The occasion of Roman involvement in Sicily, and the beginning of the First Punic War, may have seemed of relatively slight importance. The Mamertines, once mercenary soldiers of Syracuse who had seized the city of Messana and used it as a base of operations in northeast Sicily, found themselves threatened by the growing power of Hieron II, king of Syracuse. They called on the Carthaginians for aid, but then fearing domination by these traditional rivals, requested aid from Rome in order to expel the Carthaginian garrison. Rome was a land power with no navy.

The Roman senate, fearing overseas campaigns against a naval power, refused to accept the overture from the Mamertines. Rome had been almost continually at war for several generations (three Samnite Wars in 343-290 B.C.E., then the struggle against Pyrrhus). Further, Rome had no desire to get involved in Sicily, from which the Roman government occasionally purchased grain, and had long had good relations with Carthage, highlighted by treaties of friendship and trade in 507, 348, and 306 B.C.E. and a defensive pact against Pyrrhus in 279 B.C.E. Yet Rome did not want Carthage to control Sicily. The Roman assemblies, perhaps beguiled by thoughts of the prosperity to be gained from involvement in the rich territories of Sicily, perhaps merely failing to foresee the extent of the military operations they were initiating, voted to aid the Mamertines. Appius Claudius Caudex, a leader in the prowar faction, was elected consul for the year 264 B.C.E. and led an expedition to Sicily.

In the first phase of the war, the Roman forces aided Messana, while Carthage supported Syracuse. Yet this phase, and with it the original pretext for the war, was soon over. Hieron II of Syracuse had no interest in matching his power against Rome's, nor in being dominated by his erstwhile allies. In 263 B.C.E., Hieron made peace with Rome on terms that left him extensive territories as well as his independence. Syracuse and Messana gained treaties (*foedera*) by which they became allied to Rome. Yet Carthage and Rome were now in a struggle that neither cared to give up.

Between 262 and 256 B.C.E., Rome pressed hard, driving the Carthaginians into a limited number of military strongholds, and mounting the first Roman fleet, which under Gaius Duilius met with surprising success against the experienced Carthaginian navy. In 256, under Regulus, Rome transported an army into North Africa; it had initial successes, but the Carthaginians, directed by the Greek mercenary Xanthippus, succeeded the next year in destroying the forces of Rome. Regulus and his Carthaginian captors passed into legend as models of Roman adherence to their sworn word (*fides*) and Punic perfidy. Back in Sicily, the fortunes of war took many turns. Rome won most of the island but Carthage kept its naval bases in the west. At sea, the Roman navy was often victorious even though the loss of one fleet in battle and of others in storms weakened its position. By 247 B.C.E., both powers were fatigued. Peace negotiations stalled, but military efforts were at a minimum for some years.

In 244 B.C.E., the Roman government, too exhausted to build a new fleet, allowed a number of private individuals to mount one with the understanding that they should be repaid if the war were brought to a successful conclusion. In 242, this fleet arrived in Sicily. When a convoy of transports bringing supplies to Carthage's troops was captured, Carthage came to terms. The Carthaginians agreed to evacuate Sicily and pay an enormous indemnity over a long period of time.

Rome now confronted the consequences of victory. Skeptical of the volatile Sicilians' military capacities, Rome deemed it unwise either to include them among the Italian allies or to leave them free to stir up troubles among the Greeks of southern Italy, who resented their recent subordination to Rome. Nor would Rome permit Syracusan expansion throughout all Sicily. The easiest course of action was to rule Sicily directly, which Rome did by decreeing that taxes previously paid to Carthage or the Greek cities would henceforth go to Rome. Three years later, Rome evicted Carthage from Sardinia and Corsica and adopted the same policy. In 227 B.C.E., Rome increased the number of praetors from two to four, making the new ones governors of Rome's first possessions beyond Italy, Sicily and Sardinia-Corsica. A governor's

"assignment" was his *provincia*; gradually this term became a geographical concept, corresponding to the modern word "province."

Early in the Second Punic War, Hieron's grandson and successor Hieronymus switched sides and supported Carthage. Turmoil followed. Rome captured the city of Syracuse (the mathematician Archimedes was killed in the fighting) and incorporated it into the province in 211 B.C.E. All Sicily was a Roman province except for treaty-bound Messana and several other cities made "free and immune" (autonomous and exempt from the Roman taxes) as rewards for joining Rome.

SIGNIFICANCE

Rome's annexation of these islands as subject, tribute-paying territory, marked the start of the Roman Empire. By annexing a Hellenistic territory, Rome became, in a sense, a Hellenistic state, a fact that had a profound effect on Roman cultural life as well as on foreign relations. Rome's development of naval capacity made possible commercial and military involvement with all the Mediterranean world. Its need to govern conquered territory caused it to modify city-state institutions and begin constitutional developments that in the end undermined the republican form of government in Rome.

—*Zola M. Packman, updated by Thomas H. Watkins*

FURTHER READING

Bagnall, Nigel. *The Punic Wars, 264-146 B.C.* New York: Routledge, 2003. A concise history of the Punic Wars, primarily focusing on the military strategies. Includes very useful maps.

Cornell, T. J. *The Beginnings of Rome: Italy and Rome from the Bronze Age to the Punic Wars (c. 1000-264 B.C.E.).* New York: Routledge, 1995. This detailed history of early Rome analyzes expansion in Italy and relations with Carthage before the war.

Goldsworthy, Adrian. *The Punic Wars.* Cassell, 2002. A thorough history combining military analysis and biography of the main participants. Explains the military aspects clearly for nonspecialists.

Harris, W. V. *War and Imperialism in Republican Rome, 327-70 B.C.* 2d ed. Oxford: Clarendon Press, 1985. The thrust of Harris' work is Rome's almost constant aggression and readiness to annex.

Hoyos, B. D. *Unplanned Wars: The Origins of the First and Second Punic Wars.* New York: De Gruyter, 1998. Analyzes the events leading up to the first two Punic Wars. In addition to discussing the historical context of the wars, Hoyos also analyzes the inherent biases in the major sources. Includes maps, bibliography, and indexes.

Lazenby, J. F. *The First Punic War.* Stanford, Calif.: Stanford University Press, 1996. The sources for the First Punic War are scarce and frustratingly opaque; Lazenby does his best to reconstruct the reality of the war in clear terms for the nonspecialist reader.

SEE ALSO: June, 415-September, 413 B.C.E., Athenian Invasion of Sicily; 218-201 B.C.E., Second Punic War; 149-146 B.C.E., Third Punic War; 439 C.E., Vandals Seize Carthage.

RELATED ARTICLES in *Great Lives from History: The Ancient World*: Archimedes; Hamilcar Barca; Polybius.

c. 250 B.C.E.
DISCOVERIES OF ARCHIMEDES

Archimedes' theoretical and practical discoveries led to innovations in mathematical theory as well as technological inventions.

LOCALE: Syracuse, Sicily (now in Italy), and Alexandria

CATEGORIES: Cultural and intellectual history; mathematics; science and technology

KEY FIGURES

Archimedes (c. 287-212 B.C.E.), mathematician and inventor

Euclid (c. 330-c. 270 B.C.E.), Greek mathematician and pioneer geometrician

Hieron II of Syracuse (c. 305-c. 215 B.C.E.), king of Syracuse, r. 270-c. 215 B.C.E.

Marcus Claudius Marcellus (c. 268-208 B.C.E.), Roman general who led the successful siege of Syracuse from 213 to 211 B.C.E.

SUMMARY OF EVENT

By far the best-known scientist of the third century B.C.E. was Archimedes of Syracuse, a man revered in his own age for his skill as an inventor and since recognized as one of the greatest Greek mathematicians, ranking with Pythagoras (c. 580-c. 500 B.C.E.) and Euclid.

Although tradition holds that Archimedes was born in Syracuse, virtually nothing is known of the scientist's early life. No one thought of writing a biography of Archimedes during his era, and posterity has had to depend on legend, Roman historical accounts, and the inventor's own works to piece together his life story. He may well have been of aristocratic descent, for the young Archimedes spent several years in study at Alexandria in Egypt, where he was introduced to the best mathematical and mechanical researchers. While there, he seems to have become such a close associate and admirer of the astronomers Conon of Samos (fl. c. 245 B.C.E.) and Eratos-

thenes of Cyrene (c. 285-c. 205 B.C.E.) that in later years he deferred to their judgment on the publication of his own mathematical treatises. Following his stay in Egypt, Archimedes spent most of his remaining life in Syracuse, where he enjoyed the patronage of King Hieron II. It is around this monarch that many of the legendary episodes of Archimedes' life cluster, especially his development of a system of pulleys for drawing newly constructed ships into the water, his construction of military machinery, and his discovery of the fraudulent alloy in Hieron's crown.

Contemporaries and later generations of ancient writers praised Archimedes more for his colorful technical ingenuity than for his significant mathematical formulations. His discovery of the "law" of hydrostatics, or water displacement, and his application of this theory to determine the actual gold content of Hieron's crown may be true, but the exact methodology, if indeed he pursued any, is not at all clear in the ancient accounts. Similar vagueness surrounds the development of the *cochlias*, or Archimedian screw, a device by which water could be raised from a lower level to a higher level by means of a screw rotating inside a tube. Supposedly, Archimedes developed this invention in Egypt, but he may well have taken an existing mechanism and improved it. Other pieces of apparatus he either invented or constructed include a water organ and a model planetarium, the latter being the sole item of booty that the conqueror of Syracuse, Marcus Claudius Marcellus, took back to Rome.

The great historians of the Roman Republican period, such as Polybius (c. 200-c. 118 B.C.E.), Livy (59 B.C.E.-17 C.E.), and Plutarch (c. 46-after 120 C.E.), give accounts of Archimedes' genius in inventing military weapons. In his life of Marcellus in *Bioi paralleloi* (c. 105-115 B.C.E.; *Parallel Lives*, 1579), Plutarch emphasized Archimedes' dramatic role in the defense of Syracuse. In constructing military weapons, Archimedes seems to have put to use all the laws of physics at his disposal. His knowledge of levers and pulleys was applied to the construction of ballistic weapons, cranes, grappling hooks, and other devices, so that the Roman siege of Syracuse was stalemated for two years, from 213 to 211 B.C.E. Even the improbable use of large mirrors for directing sharply focused rays of sunlight in order to ignite the Roman fleet is credited to Archimedes. Doubtless, he was the mind behind the defense of Syracuse, and the Romans respected his ability. Although Marcellus wished to capture Archimedes alive, the scientist was killed by a Roman legionnaire when the city of Syracuse fell.

SIGNIFICANCE

Archimedes preferred to be remembered for his theoretical achievements rather than his discoveries in mechanics. In the third century B.C.E., Greek mathematical thought had advanced as far as it could in terms of geometric models of reasoning without algebraic notation, and the mathematical work of Archimedes appears as the culmination of Hellenistic mathematics. His work on plane curves represented an extension of Euclid's geometry, and it predicted integral calculus. Archimedes' studies included conic sections, the ratio of the volume of a cylinder to its inscribed square, and some understanding of pure numbers as opposed to the then prevalent notion of infinity. Through his sand-reckoner, Archimedes supposedly could express any integer up to 8×10^{16}.

In his own lifetime, Archimedes' works were forwarded to Alexandria, where they were studied and dispersed. Two major Greek collections of Archimedes' works made by the mathematical schools of Constantinople were later passed on to Sicily and Italy, and then to northern Europe, where they were translated into Latin and widely published after the sixth century C.E. Because none of the Greek collections is complete, Arabic collections and associated commentaries have been used to tabulate the works attributed to Archimedes. Through these legacies, modern scholars have been able to study Archimedes' work, and some modern scholars consider him to be the greatest mathematician of antiquity.

—Richard J. Wurtz, updated by Jeffrey L. Buller

Archimedes, moments before his death. (F. R. Niglutsch)

FURTHER READING

Archimedes. *The Works of Archimedes*. Translated by Sir Thomas Heath. 1897. Reprint. New York: Dover, 2002. Contains nineteenth century translations of Archimedes' work along with more contemporary commentary.

Clagett, Marshall, ed. *Archimedes in the Middle Ages*. 4 vols. Madison: University of Wisconsin Press, 1964. A series of texts in Latin, with English translation, that illustrate the continuing influence (and reinterpretation) of Archimedes in the Christian and Islamic worlds during the medieval period.

Dijksterhuis, Eduard Jan. *Archimedes*. Translated by C. Dikshoorn, with a new bibliographic essay by Wilbur R. Knorr. Princeton, N.J.: Princeton University Press, 1987. The most thorough treatment of Archimedes available. Also provides an extensive look at the development of Greek mathematics.

Netz, Reviel. *The Shaping of Deduction in Greek Mathematics: A Study in Cognitive History*. New York: Cambridge University Press, 2003. An advanced discussion of the subject that provides the intellectual context for understanding Archimedes and his work.

Stein, Sherman. *Archimedes: What Did He Do Beside Cry Eureka?* Washington, D.C.: The Mathematical Association of America, 1999. Uses high-school-level math to explain Archimedes' accomplishments.

Tuplin, C. J., and T. E. Rihll, eds. *Science and Mathematics in Ancient Greek Culture*. New York: Oxford University Press, 2002. A collection of essays that cover many specific topics touching on Archimedes' mathematics and inventions.

SEE ALSO: c. 530 B.C.E., Founding of the Pythagorean Brotherhood; 332 B.C.E., Founding of Alexandria; 325-323 B.C.E., Aristotle Isolates Science as a Discipline; c. 300 B.C.E., Euclid Compiles a Treatise on Geometry; c. 275 B.C.E., Greeks Advance Hellenistic Astronomy; 264-225 B.C.E., First Punic War; 415 C.E., Mathematician and Philosopher Hypatia Is Killed in Alexandria.

RELATED ARTICLES in *Great Lives from History: The Ancient World*: Apollonius of Perga; Archimedes; Diophantes; Euclid; Eratosthenes of Cyrene; Eudoxus of Cnidus; Hero of Alexandria; Hypatia; Pappus; Pythagoras.

---

c. 250 B.C.E.
THIRD BUDDHIST COUNCIL CONVENES

A group of Buddhist elders reportedly met under the direction of King Aśoka for the purpose of establishing the beliefs and practices appropriate to Buddhism. The meeting also was said to have resulted in Buddhist missions to lands outside of India.

LOCALE: Pataliputra (now Patna, Bihar), India
CATEGORIES: Religion; government and politics

KEY FIGURES

Aśoka (c. 302-c. 238 B.C.E.), Indian emperor, who convened Third Buddhist Council, r. c. 273/265-c. 238 B.C.E.

Moggaliputta Tissa (fl. third century B.C.E.), an elder called on by Aśoka to preside over the Third Buddhist Council

Mahinda (c. 270-c. 204 B.C.E.), son of Aśoka, who served as Buddhist missionary to Sri Lanka

SUMMARY OF EVENT

During the lifetime of the Buddha (Siddhārtha Gautama; c. 566-c. 486 B.C.E.), Buddhism consisted of his teachings. After his death, however, Buddhists began to interpret these teachings in various ways. Therefore, the Buddhists called a council about a year after the death of the Buddha to organize and interpret his teachings and to compile a code of monastic discipline. Council members also accused and criticized those who advocated views or practices they believed were inconsistent with Buddhism. For example, the Buddha's favorite disciple, Ānanda, was charged with having unorthodox ideas, including the view that Buddhists should allow the establishment of a separate order for nuns.

Roughly a century later, the Second Buddhist Council, held at Vesālī and also known as the Council of Vesālī, continued the work of trying to define and maintain Buddhist orthodoxy. However, different approaches to Buddhism continued, and these began to develop into the split that would gradually lead to the development of the two major sects or schools of Buddhism, Theravāda (also called Hīnayāna) and Mahāyāna. As Buddhism grew in popularity, it absorbed influences from other religions in India, complicating the problem of defining orthodox Buddhism.

During the third century B.C.E., Aśoka, the ruler of much of the Indian subcontinent, converted to Buddhism. Aśoka was a ruthless and cruel monarch early in his career, but he was so disturbed by the suffering caused by a military campaign that he turned to the Buddhist doctrine of nonviolence and became one of the most important early supporters of the religion. Even though Aśoka apparently treated all religions with tolerance, the fact that this was the king's religion led many people to identify themselves as Buddhists. Ancient texts in the Pāli language report that members of unorthodox sects began to enter Buddhist monasteries, and religious practices in many of these monasteries grew lax. Disputes over religion even led to rioting. In one tradition, the king's brother, who was a faithful Buddhist, died in a religious riot. According to these Pāli texts, King Aśoka sponsored the Third Council in his capital city of Pataliputra in order to establish the correct beliefs and practices of Buddhism.

A Pāli language chronicle of the history of what became Sri Lanka, known as the *Dīpavamsa* (compiled fourth century C.E.; *The Dīpavamsa: An Ancient Buddhist Historical Record*, 1879), recounts that Aśoka called on the elder Moggaliputta Tissa to convene the council. Tissa, who had been living as a hermit to escape the religious turbulence, presided over a gathering of one thousand of the wisest Buddhist elders 236 years after the Buddha's death, or about 250 B.C.E. by current historical dating. The council lasted nine months. By its end, the participants had agreed on one version of Buddhism, identified in the texts with what later became known as Theravāda (literally, the way of the elders). The monks who refused to conform to this version of the faith were expelled from the Saṅgha, the community of believers. They were forced to give up their yellow robes, the symbol of a true Buddhist monk, and put on white robes instead. The white-robed dissidents would not be allowed to live in monasteries or on temple grounds.

The Third Council is supposed to have completed the assembly of the writings that made up the basic canon of Theravāda Buddhist writings, known as the *Tipiṭaka* (compiled c. 250 B.C.E.; English translation in *Buddhist Scriptures*, 1913), or "Three Baskets" after its three divisions. To spread the newly reestablished orthodoxy, the members of the council decided to send missionaries to other lands. These lands included Gandhara (now in Pakistan), the Greek settlements of northwestern India, the Bombay coast, the Himalayas, and other territories. Most notably, King Aśoka's own son, Mahinda (sometimes

spelled Mahendra) went as a missionary to Sri Lanka, where Theravāda Buddhism put down deep roots and continues to be the majority religion. There have been claims that Buddhist missions reached even farther than the territories surrounding India and may have been in Greece and North Africa. There is little evidence for these claims, although some small molded Indian figures and stones with Buddhist symbols from approximately the era of Aśoka have been found in Egypt.

Some historians have raised doubts about whether Aśoka was behind the Third Council, and some have questioned whether it actually took place. They point out that no mention is made of this council in the inscriptions made by Aśoka on rocks and pillars around his empire. Further, doubting historians argue that although Aśoka was a Buddhist, he ruled an empire that included different religions and would have been reluctant to alienate non-Buddhists or unorthodox Buddhists. Aśoka's policy of religious tolerance would have been contrary to the goals of the council, in the view of these historians. The only descriptions of the Third Council that exist are from the Pāli language sources of the Theravāda Buddhist tradition, with the chronicles of Sri Lanka being especially important. Skeptics have suggested that the writers of those Pāli texts may have tried to create historical support for their own school of Buddhism by claiming that it had the approval and sponsorship of the great king.

The questions about the historical accuracy of traditional accounts of the council have led some historians to suggest that there may have been a local gathering in Pataliputra, without the active involvement of Aśoka, that was later exaggerated into a major event. Some evidence, though, does support the traditional view of the Third Council. Although Aśoka's inscriptions do not explicitly mention the gathering, there is a royal inscription from the period known as the Schism Edict, which threatens to expel dissenting monks from the Saṅgha and orders those who disrupt the faith to leave the monasteries and replace their yellow robes with white ones. This is consistent with the idea that the king was supporting efforts to maintain orthodoxy and that he was pursuing the kinds of policies reported to have been put in place by the council. The descriptions of the missions give the names and destinations of the missionaries, and these religious journeys are consistent with the embassies Aśoka maintained with foreign lands. Therefore, even if one accepts the possibility of some distortion and exaggeration in the Pāli records, it seems reasonable to conclude that they are based on actual events.

SIGNIFICANCE

It is unlikely that scholars will be able to resolve the arguments about the historical accuracy of the Pāli language reports of the Third Council, unless some new and unexpected archaeological evidence emerges. Still, the council represents at least three important developments in the early history of Buddhism. First, Buddhism had become a dominant religion in India by this period, with official recognition and support. Second, by the mid-third century B.C.E., variations in Buddhist belief and practice had taken the forms that would be acknowledged as the two major schools, Theravāda (Hīnayāna) and Mahāyāna. The former, the type of Buddhism reported to have been recognized by the council as orthodox, became the version of the religion that would predominate in the areas of Sri Lanka and most of Indochina, and Mahāyāna Buddhism became the version most widely practiced throughout China, Korea, and Japan. Whether the council actually was a major gathering sponsored by the king or a smaller, local affair, it marks a definite stage in the division of the religion. Finally, the third century B.C.E. was a time in which Buddhism made substantial progress in moving from India and becoming a major world religion.

—*Carl L. Bankston III*

FURTHER READING

Armstrong, Karen. *Buddha*. New York: Viking, 2001. A short, well-written biography of the Buddha and introduction to his teachings. Glossary.

Lopez, Donald S. *The Story of Buddhism: A Concise Guide to Its History and Teachings*. San Francisco: Harper, 2001. A short history of the origins and transformations of Buddhism. Pronunciation guide, bibliography, glossary, index.

Seneviratna, Anuradha, ed. *King Aśoka and Buddhism*. Seattle: Pariyatti Press, 1995. A collection of essays on Aśoka's life and on the debates about his role in history, including debates about his role in the Third Council.

Thapar, Romila. *Aśoka and the Decline of the Mauryas*. Delhi: Oxford University Press, 1997. An updated edition of one of the most widely read histories of the Mauryan period by a prominent scholar of ancient India. The second chapter contains a critical discussion of the historical arguments about the Third Council and about Aśoka's involvement in it. Bibliography, index.

c. 250 B.C.E.
TIPIṬAKA IS COMPILED

The Tipiṭaka, *a three-part work, contains the basic teachings of the Buddha in accordance with the Theravāda school of Buddhism.*

LOCALE: India and Sri Lanka
CATEGORY: Religion

SUMMARY OF EVENT

The *Tipiṭaka* (literally "three baskets"; English translation in *Buddhist Scriptures*, 1913) is the Pāli name for the threefold division of the Pāli Canon. The "baskets" (*piṭakas*) consist of the *Vinaya* (monastic rules), the *Suttas* (discourses), and the *Abhidhamma* (the higher teachings). These texts were written in Pāli, an "ecclesiastical language" based on middle Indo-Aryan dialects. The Pāli Canon is the religious text for the Theravāda (Hīnayāna) sect of Buddhism.

According to Buddhist tradition, the formation of the *Tipiṭika* originated in the First Buddhist Council held at Rājagṛha after the *parinibbāna* (final nirvana) of Śākyamuni Buddha (544 B.C.E. is the traditional date; historians have dated this event to as late as 480 B.C.E.). At this time, there was a recitation of the monastic rules (*Vinaya*) and the discourses (*Suttas*) of the Buddha. Ānanda is said to have recited the *suttas*, and Upāli recited the monastic rules. The other monks at the council approved these texts and recited them in turn. At the end of the council, the *Vinaya* was entrusted to Upāli, and the first four divisions (*nikāyas*) of the *Sutta-piṭaka* were assigned to Ānanda, Sāriputta, Mahākassapa, and Anuruddha respectively. This is probably the origin of the reciters (*bhāṇakas*), who shared the recitation of these texts.

It is unclear whether the texts recited at this time correspond exactly to the texts in their present form. According to the final sections of the *Vinaya*, which describe the first two councils, Upāli was asked to recite the twofold *Vinaya*. This is generally agreed to refer to the *Pātimokkha* rules for monks and nuns. Buddhaghosa, a prominent Buddhist thinker and commentator of the fifth century C.E., named sections of the present *Vinaya* as being recited at the First Buddhist Council but also claimed that the text at the First Buddhist Council was not the same as in his time. Clearly the accounts of the first two councils could not have formed part of the *Vinaya* of the First Buddhist Council. It is also uncertain whether the *Abhidhamma* formed any part of the canon at this council.

The Second Buddhist Council was held at Vesālī a hundred years after the *parinibbāna* of Śākyamuni Buddha. The council arose because monks in Vesālī had relaxed monastic regulations. In addition to dealing with these violations, the council read through the *Vinaya* and *Suttas*. At the end of this council, it is said that a group split off and held its own great council (*mahāsaṅgīti*). They later were called the Mahāsāṅghikas. Thus began a process that would eventually result in the division into the eighteen schools of the Hīnayāna. From this time onward, the various schools or sects kept their own versions of the *Vinaya* and *Suttas*.

The Third Buddhist Council was held, reportedly under the patronage of King Aśoka, in Pataliputra c. 250 B.C.E. The Sarvāstivādin and Vibhajjavādin sects broke off at this point. Some experts argue that the *Abhidhamma-piṭaka* was recited at this council. It is believed that the basis of the modern *Tipiṭaka* was essentially in place at this council.

The *Vinaya-piṭaka* consists of the regulations for monks and nuns of the Buddhist order. This *piṭaka* is divided into three sections: the *Suttavibhaṅga*, the *Khandaka*, and the *Parivāra*. The *Suttavibhaṅga* is divided into the *Mahāvibhaṅga*, 227 rules for monks, and the *Bhikkunīvibhaṅga*, 311 rules for nuns. These rules are embedded in stories that relate the circumstances in the life of the Buddha that led to their promulgation or that deal with related themes, along with a commentary. In the other Hīnayāna schools, these rules (without the stories of their origin) exist as a separate text, known as the *Pātimokkha* (Sanskrit: *Prātimokṣa*). *Prātimokṣa* rules have come down to modern times from the Mūlasarvāstivādins, Mahāsāṅghikas, Sarvāstivādins, and the Dharmaguptakas.

The *Khandaka* is divided into the *Mahāvagga* and the *Cullavaga*. These rules are also conveyed through a story that details their origin. Descriptions of the first two councils have been added to the text. Sections of the *Skandaka* (Sanskrit for *Khandaka*) from the Mūlasarvāstivādins, Sarvāstivādins, and Mahāsāṅghikas have been found.

The *Parivāra* is an appendix. Many believe that the work or parts of it originated later than the texts above, perhaps in the first century B.C.E. It consists of nineteen chapters. Some of the chapters take the form of catechisms on the rules of the *Vinaya*, and other chapters comment on these rules.

The *Sutta-piṭaka* consists of the discourses of the Buddha. The Pāli canon divides this *piṭaka* into five divisions (*nikāyas*). The first division is the *Dīgha-nikāya*, the Long Discourses of the Buddha. There are 34 *suttas* found in this division. Next there is the *Majjhima-nikāya*, the Middle Length Discourses. There are 152 *suttas* in this *nikāya*. The third division is the *Saṃyutta-nikāya*, the Connected Discourses. It receives its name from the fact that the *suttas* are joined by subject. There are 56 groups (*saṃyuttas*) and 2,889 *suttas*. The fourth division is the *Aṅguttara-nikāya*, "the by-one-limb-more collection." This collection is divided into 11 sections, *nipātas*; the *suttas* in each *nipāta* refer to subjects connected with the number of the section; for example, the third *nipāta* discusses subjects that are grouped in three. This *nikāya* contains well in excess of 2,000 *suttas*. The fifth division, the *Khuddaka-nikāya*, is a large miscellaneous collection of texts associated with the Buddha. By far the most well-known text from this *nikāya* is the *Dhammapada*, a collection of the sayings of the Buddha. This is perhaps the most translated text in Buddhism. The *nikāya* also has a large collection of *Jātakas*, more than 500 birth stories of the past lives of the Buddha.

Parts of Sanskrit versions of the first four *nikāyas* are preserved. Complete or almost complete Chinese translations of these Sanskrit texts exist. These collections do not always group the *suttas* in the same *nikāya* as the *Tipiṭaka* does. Furthermore, the Sanskrit versions do not divide the *suttas* into *nikāyas*, but *āgamas*. Also some of the texts of the *Khuddaka-nikāya*, such as the *Dharmapada* and *Jātakas*, have been translated into Sanskrit. For the most part, the surviving Sanskrit texts belong to the Sarvāstivādin school.

The *Abhidhamma-piṭaka* seems to have been compiled later than the other two *piṭakas*. The term *abhidhamma*, when used in the other two *piṭakas*, seems to have meant "regarding the *dhamma*" (teaching). After the *piṭaka* was compiled, the prefix *abhi* took on the meaning "higher or special," that is, "the higher *dhamma*." Buddhaghosa argued along these lines.

> [The *Abhidhamma*] excels and is distinguished by several qualities from the other *Dhamma*. . . . In the *Suttantas* (*Sutta-piṭaka*) knowledge is partially classified, not fully. . . . But in the *Abhidhamma* there is a detailed classification of knowledge after the table of contents has been thus laid down.

The *Abhidhamma-piṭaka* consists of the following seven works: *Dhammasaṅgani*, *Vibhaṅga*, *Dhātukathā*, *Puggala-paññatti*, *Kathāvatthu*, *Yamaka*, and *Paṭṭhāna*. As Buddhaghosa noted, these works offer a fuller classification of what is found in the other *piṭakas*. For example, the *Dhammasaṅgani* gives a classification of mental states. These texts are also regarded as more philosophical; for example, the *Yamaka* is a work on logic. A Sanskrit *Abhidharma* for the Sarvāstivādin school has been found, but it does not contain the same works as the Pāli version, except for the *Dhātukāya*.

SIGNIFICANCE

The *Tipiṭaka* is the Theravādin record of the discourses and the monastic rules laid down by the Buddha. The Thervādins are the only Hīnayāna school of the original eighteen that has survived until the present day. From India and Sri Lanka, the Theravāda school spread into Myanmar and Thailand in the first century C.E. and from there into Cambodia and Laos. Eventually Burmese and Thai versions of the *Tipiṭaka* were established.

—*Albert T. Watanabe*

FURTHER READING

Akira, H. *A History of Indian Buddhism from Śākyamuni to Early Mahāyāna*. Honolulu: University of Hawaii Press, 1990. A detailed analysis of the early history of Buddhism. Bibliographical essay. Bibliography and index.

Frauwallner, E. *The Earliest Vinaya and the Beginnings of Buddhist Literature*. Rome: Instituto Italiano per il Medio ed Estremo Oriente, 1956. An examination of the origins of the *Vinaya*. Frauwallner also gives accounts of the *vinaya* of the other Buddhist sects.

Norman, K. R. *Pāli Literature*. Wiesbaden, Germany: Otto Harrassowitz, 1983. This is an extremely knowledgeable survey of Pāli literature. Norman gives a brief summary of each text in the Pāli Canon, with references to editions and literature. Bibliography and indexes.

Skilton, A. *A Concise History of Buddhism*. New York: Barnes and Noble Books, 2000. A good introduction to the development of early Buddhism, including the *Tipiṭaka* and the councils. Although the chapters are concise, the bibliography gives detailed and up-to-date references on each subject. Bibliography and index.

SEE ALSO: 6th or 5th century B.C.E., Birth of Buddhism; c. 5th-4th century B.C.E., Creation of the *Jātakas*; 300 B.C.E.-600 C.E., Construction of the Māhabodhi Temple; c. 250 B.C.E., Third Buddhist Council Convenes; c. 1st century B.C.E., Indian Buddhist Nuns Compile the *Therigatha*; 1st-2d century C.E., Fourth Buddhist Council Convenes.

RELATED ARTICLES in *Great Lives from History: The Ancient World*: Ānanda; Buddha; Vattagamani.

250-130 B.C.E.
COMMISSIONING OF THE SEPTUAGINT

The translation of the Jewish Scriptures from Hebrew into vernacular Greek was intended to serve Jews outside of Palestine, but also ended up becoming the link between Judaic and Christian holy writ during late antiquity.

LOCALE: Alexandria (now in Egypt)
CATEGORY: Religion

KEY FIGURES

Ptolemy Philadelphus (308-246 B.C.E.), king of Egypt, r. 288-246 B.C.E.

Aquila (fl. second century C.E.), translator of the Old Testament

Theodotion (fl. second century C.E.), translator of the Old Testament

Origen (c. 185-c. 254 C.E.), early Christian Bible scholar

SUMMARY OF EVENT

Although there has always been resistance among Jews to reading the Holy Scriptures in any language other than Hebrew, considered by some Jewish scholars to be the holy tongue if not the original one, conditions made translations essential. The first translation of the Bible into vernacular, or *koine*, Greek was to serve nearly one million Jews living in Egypt, primarily in Alexandria, who could no longer read Hebrew. In the two thousand years since this Greek edition, the holy book has been translated into literally hundreds of languages and dialects.

The Septuagint became so venerated that its origin was glamorized with romance. The pseudepigraphic Letter of Aristeas (c. 150 B.C.E.) relates that Ptolemy Philadelphus arranged to have seventy-two Jews translate the Pentateuch into Greek for his royal library, hence the term *Septuagint*, Greek for "seventy" and the cryptic designation "LXX." The scholars, supposedly housed on the island of Pharos, completed their work according to legend in seventy-two days. A later story pictured them working in pairs in separate cells to produce thirty-six copies of the whole Old Testament, all finishing at the same moment without a single variant in their Greek texts.

Actually, the translations were made piecemeal between 250 and 130 B.C.E. by many scholars in various synagogues whenever and wherever portions of the Old Testament were needed in the vernacular. The work was complete before the Hebrew canon as a whole had been finally set.

The Septuagint was received differently in different quarters. Greek-speaking Jews such as Philo of Alexandria (c. 20 B.C.E.-c. 45 C.E.) found it indispensable. To Hebrew-speaking Jews, the work had little relevance except as an occasional textual corrective for Samuel, and to some extent for Exodus, Deuteronomy, and Jeremiah. Generally renounced by Judaism because of its Christian adoption, the Septuagint was replaced by three new Greek translations in the second century C.E. Aquila of Pontus, a Christian who later became a Jew, made a conservative and literal translation using the name Yahweh in the text but in Greek transliteration to replace the Septuagint's earlier substitution of *Kurios*, or Lord. Theodotion, probably a Jew, also revised the Septuagint in the second century, and Symmachus in the late second or early third century rendered a free translation that put more of a premium on style than on verbal accuracy.

The Septuagint differs considerably from the Hebrew text both in the order of the books and also in textual differences within them, especially in Job, 1 Samuel, and Jeremiah. Moreover, the Septuagint includes the so-called Apocrypha: Wisdom, Ecclesiasticus, Judith, Tobit, and Baruch. In general, the Greek translation tends to tone down the anthropomorphisms of the Hebrew: the "hand of God" becomes "the power of God," and "his robe" becomes "his glory."

SIGNIFICANCE

One of the purposes for translating the Old Testament into Greek seems to have been an apologetic, propagandistic one, to convince the world that Jews possessed a literature rivaling the wisdom of the Greeks. The popularity of the Septuagint, however, was chiefly among Christians. A careful examination of New Testament citations of Old Testament verses shows that statistically, the Septuagint was used more by early Christians than any other Hebrew version. Direct quotations, word usage, phraseology, and even similarity of literary form make it evident that the New Testament is the child of the Septuagint.

Christian reliance on the Septuagint persisted until the fourth century. New Testament writers quote from it, and it served as the foundation for the Old Latin version of the Scriptures used in the early Church. Origen (c. 185-c. 254 C.E.), in his work the *Hexapla* (c. 235 C.E.), was the first Christian to take an interest in checking the Septuagint text by comparing it with the Hebrew and the other three Greek versions of the second century. When Saint

Jerome (331/347-c. 420 C.E.), at the urging of Pope Damasus (c. 304-384 C.E.), restudied the Hebrew to reestablish the text of the later official Vulgate, Saint Augustine (354-450 C.E.) was disturbed. He, like most Christians, assumed that the Septuagint was divinely inspired and its variants with the Hebrew were, in his mind, divinely contrived as part of a new revelation. Finally, the Septuagint was largely responsible for the acceptance of the Apocrypha as canonical by the Western Church.

As mistrust of the Septuagint arose among the Jews, Christian writers and teachers adhered to it all the more ardently. The many commentaries written on it by the early Church Fathers attest to its continued Christian popularity up to the time of Jerome, and to its reputation as a book of equal or even greater inspiration than the original Hebrew. The Septuagint served the early Church well during the great crises in her early history, particularly in the struggles with Judaism, Marcionism, and the various schools of Gnosticism and Arianism. Even after Jerome's Vulgate appeared, the Septuagint remained important for textual criticism as the oldest translation of the Old Testament. Even the Vulgate, which was purposely based on the Hebrew text, perpetuates many of the characteristics of the Septuagint.

The fact that the Septuagint was used by Jews, not only in Palestine and Egypt but throughout West Asia and Europe as well, created, as it were, an official language of religion other than Hebrew, which Christianity as a Gentile movement could readily use to lend dignity to its New Testament. Furthermore, translation of the Old Testament into Greek set a precedent for all further translations so that as Christianity spread, the Septuagint lent itself readily to translation into Latin, Coptic, Gothic, Armenian, Slavic, Georgian, Ethiopian, and Arabic. During the Renaissance and Reformation the rebirth of interest in Greek studies caused the Septuagint to become popular again. This renewed interest was motivated by the desire of critical language study to rediscover the original archetype behind the Massoretic text and other versions of the Bible.

—Joseph R. Rosenbloom

FURTHER READING

Bartlett, John, ed. *Jews in the Hellenistic and Roman Cities*. New York: Routledge, 2002. This series of essays provides cultural background on the situation of Hellenistic Jews that led to the translation of the Septuagint.

Beck, John A. *Translators as Storytellers: A Study in Septuagint Translation Technique*. New York: P. Lang, 2000. Studies the literary aspects of the translation from Hebrew to Greek.

Brenton, Lancelot, trans. *The Septuagint with Apocrypha: Greek and English*. 1851. Reprint. Peabody, Mass.: Hendrickson, 1986. Provides the Greek on one side of the page with the English translation next to it for easy comparison.

Jobes, Karen H., and Moises Silva. *Invitation to the Septuagint*. Grand Rapids, Mich.: Baker Book House, 2000. A clear, reader-friendly introduction to the Septuagint. Includes illustrations, maps, timeline, indexes, and appendixes of organizations, research projects, reference works, glossary, and a summary of the versification differences between the Septuagint and English versions.

Tcherikover, Avigdor. *Hellenistic Civilization and the Jews*. 1959. Reprint. Peabody, Mass.: Hendrickson, 1999. An excellent account of cultural background leading to the development of the Septuagint.

SEE ALSO: c. 950 B.C.E., Composition of the Book of Genesis; c. 250 B.C.E.-70 C.E., Dead Sea Scrolls Are Composed; c. 200 B.C.E.-c. 100 C.E., Composition of the Intertestamental Jewish Apocrypha; c. 30 C.E., Preaching of the Pentecostal Gospel; c. 90 C.E., Synod of Jamnia; 200 C.E., Christian Apologists Develop Concept of Theology; c. 382-c. 405 C.E., Saint Jerome Creates the Vulgate.

RELATED ARTICLES in *Great Lives from History: The Ancient World*: Saint Augustine; Saint Jerome; Origen; Philo of Alexandria; Ptolemy Philadelphus.

c. 250 B.C.E.-70 C.E.
DEAD SEA SCROLLS ARE COMPOSED

The Dead Sea Scrolls, the oldest extant copies of the Hebrew scriptures, describe the life and thought of a sect of Judaism that lived on the shores of the Dead Sea more than two thousand years ago.

LOCALE: Northwestern shore of the Dead Sea, Israel
CATEGORY: Religion

SUMMARY OF EVENT

In 1947, some Bedouin shepherds entered caves along the northwestern shores of the Dead Sea and discovered large jars containing numerous ancient texts. Their find has been described as the greatest archaeological discovery of the twentieth century. Subsequent exploration of other caves in the area yielded more texts. In all, eleven caves in the vicinity were found to hold around nine hundred different (and mostly fragmentary) scrolls.

Nearby the caves, a set of ancient building ruins was also discovered. The excavation of the ruins was undertaken in the winter of 1951. The excavations were directed by Father Roland de Vaux of the Ecole Biblique et Archéologique Française in Jerusalem and G. Lankester Harding, the chief inspector of antiquities for Jordan. The excavations uncovered a small compound that included a central hall, a dining hall, a possible scriptorium, a watch tower, an extensive aqueduct system, ritual bathing facilities, kilns for manufacturing pottery, and a cemetery. The ruins were called Qumran after the area of the Dead Sea where they were located. De Vaux concluded that Qumran was a monastic-type settlement of the Essenes, a strict Jewish sect whose scribes had written the texts that had been discovered in the caves. De Vaux's conclusion linking the Dead Sea Scrolls with Qumran is still widely supported, given the compelling evidence of the close proximity of the caves to the ruins, the discovery of inkwells among the artifacts discovered at Qumran, the close identification of pottery found at the site and the jars holding the scrolls, and the identification by ancient author Pliny the Elder (23/24-79 C.E.) in book 5 of his *Naturalis historia* (77 C.E.; *Natural History*, 1938-1963) of a splinter Jewish community—the Essenes—located near the Dead Sea.

The scrolls themselves were mostly made of parchment (processed animal hide). A small number (about one hundred texts) were composed of papyrus. One, known as the Copper Scroll, is written on sheets of bronze. The writing was done on one side of the sheet, using a reed pen dipped in ink. There are no books or codices (wherein parchment or papyrus is written on both sides and bound together—a method adopted later by the Christian community for the New Testament). The scrolls are written mostly in Hebrew, although Aramaic and a small amount of Greek are also present. A variety of methods have been employed to date the scrolls, including paleography (analyzing styles of letter formation), carbon-14, and accelerator mass spectrometry (a more refined form of carbon-14 dating). With minor exceptions, the dating techniques were consistent in establishing dates that ranged from 250 B.C.E. to 70 C.E. In sorting out the manuscripts, a standard method of designation was agreed upon whereby a scroll is given a Q-number indicating which cave it came from; for example, 4Q means it was discovered in cave four. Then a number is added to the site designation: 4Q224 was the 224th text from cave 4. There are some exceptions to this method, including the scrolls found in cave 1 which were identified before the standard method was introduced. The scrolls from cave 1 are identified by a letter indicating the type of text represented: 1QpHab is the Pesher (Commentary) on Habbakuk from cave 1.

There are several genres of literature present in the large corpus of scrolls. All the books of the Hebrew scriptures (at least in fragments—the most complete is the scroll of the Book of Isaiah) with the exception of the Book of Esther are to be found. In addition, several books of the Apocrypha and Pseudepigrapha were found. *Apocrypha* is a Greek word that means "hidden books." The word is used to designate religious texts not included in the Hebrew Scriptures but found in the Septuagint (the Greek translation of the Hebrew scriptures) and included in Catholic but not the Protestant Old Testament. The Apocrypha present among the scrolls include Tobit and Sirach (Ecclesiastes). *Pseudepigrapha*, also a Greek term meaning "false writings," are religious texts, sometimes written under fake names or pseudonyms. Pseudepigrapha are also not included in the Hebrew scriptures nor in the Septuagint and thus do not appear in the Catholic or Protestant Old Testament. Pseudepigrapha found among the scrolls include Jubilees and Enoch.

In addition to the biblical, apocryphal, and pseudepigraphal texts, there are numerous texts written by and for the community itself. These sectarian texts include manuals for governing the community (such as the Community Rule, 1QS), halakhic or legal discussions (such as *Miqsat Ma'aseh HaTorah* or the Sectarian Manifesto,

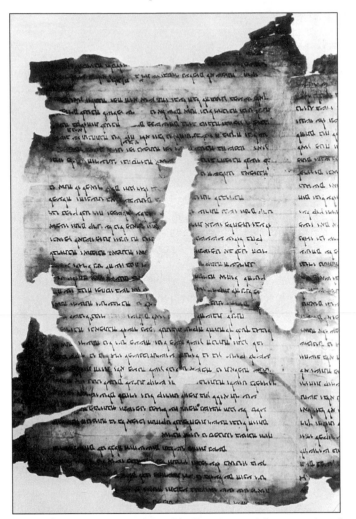

A torn portion of the Dead Sea Scrolls, recovered from a series of caves in Israel. (Hulton|Archive)

Teacher in revealing the way to victory over evil. The community (called in the scrolls the *yahad*, or unity) that stands behind the scrolls refers to itself as "the community of those who entered into the renewed covenant," and understands itself as the sole legitimate representative of biblical Israel. Imposing on itself rigorous rules of initiation, ritual purity, and sexual abstention, the community is prepared for the inevitable final war of cosmic dimensions. The community is led by the Teacher of Righteousness who, in the tradition of prophetic teaching, is led by the divine spirit and renders decisions and interpretations that are beyond debate and unconditionally binding.

The question of the identity of the community behind the scrolls has eluded a sure answer. The Jewish historian Flavius Josephus (c. 38-93 C.E.) described Judaism in Palestine in the first century B.C.E. and first century C.E. and gave the impression of a religious community broken into several competing sects. Among the several sects he identified, the one most often associated with the Dead Sea Scrolls are the Essenes. The Essene hypothesis has a number of supporters not only because of Pliny's identification of an Essene group living on the Dead Sea but also because of the striking convergence at many points of Josephus's description of the sect's beliefs and practices and the beliefs and practices evident in the scrolls. There are two significant challenges to the Essene hypothesis. One argues that the scrolls did not come from Qumran at all but are the work of priests in Jerusalem who were persecuted and forced to flee. The other argues that the residents of Qumran and the authors of the scrolls were Sadducees rather than Essenes.

4QMMT), biblical interpretations of various kinds and on various books of the Hebrew scriptures (the Pesher on Habbakuk, 1QpHab) religious poetry (Thanksgiving hymns, 1QH), calendars (the Calendar of Heavenly Signs, 4Q319), liturgical texts (the Liturgy of Blessings and Curses, 4Q286-289) and astrological texts (the Divination Text or Brontologion, 4Q318). The Copper Scroll (3Q15) tells of the hiding places for caches of precious metals and other scrolls.

The content of the sectarian scrolls is wide ranging and complex but the core message is one marked by a strong sense of determinism, the necessity of rigorous practice to ensure the purity of the elect community, the expectation of a cataclysmic struggle between forces of good and evil in the near future, and the importance of the

SIGNIFICANCE

The recovery of the Dead Sea Scrolls has proven significant for several reasons. The scrolls are the oldest Jewish texts in Hebrew or Aramaic that have been found. They have provided biblical scholars with texts that were far more ancient than had previously been the case. For example, the oldest Hebrew text of Isaiah had been the Ben Asher codex, dated to 895 C.E. The Isaiah scroll found among the Dead Sea Scrolls is around one millennium older. The scrolls have brought about a whole new period in the textual history of the Hebrew Scriptures. The scrolls have also provided apocryphal and pseudepigraphal texts that were either not known or known in different versions.

Having come to modern scholars directly from their hiding place in the desert, the scrolls have proven invaluable in reconstructing the Jewish world in the first centuries B.C.E. and C.E. The scrolls have provided direct evidence of the diversity of Judaism in this period. Moreover, as the scrolls are contemporary with the genesis of Christianity, they have provided a critical resource for understanding the origins of Christianity within Judaism in this era.

—*C. Thomas McCollough*

FURTHER READING

Golb, Norman. *Who Wrote the Dead Sea Scrolls?* New York: Scribner, 1995. The book that presents Golb's argument for a Jerusalem provenance for the scrolls.

Magness, Jodi. *The Archaeology of Qumran and the Dead Sea Scrolls.* Grand Rapids, Mich.: W. B. Eerdmans, 2002. An assessment of the architecture and the material culture of Qumran and its bearing on understanding the scrolls. Illustrations, photographs, and an annotated bibliography.

Schiffman, Lawrence. *Reclaiming the Dead Sea Scrolls.* Philadelphia: Jewish Publication Society, 1994. Schiffman offers the argument for a Sadduceean identification of the community responsible for the scrolls.

Schiffman, Lawrence, and James Vandercam, eds. *Encyclopedia of the Dead Sea Scrolls.* New York: Oxford University Press, 2000. A comprehensive guide to the scrolls and Qumran.

Vanderkam, James C. *The Dead Sea Scrolls Today.* Grand Rapids, Mich.: W. B. Eerdmans, 1994. A clear discussion of Qumran and a helpful introduction to the scrolls.

Vermes, Geza. *The Complete Dead Sea Scrolls in English.* New York: Penguin, 1997. A discussion of the Qumran community along with the English translations of the scrolls.

SEE ALSO: c. 1280 B.C.E., Israelite Exodus from Egypt; c. 1000 B.C.E., Establishment of the United Kingdom of Israel; c. 922 B.C.E., Establishment of the Kingdom of Israel; 587-423 B.C.E., Birth of Judaism; c. 538-c. 450 B.C.E., Jews Return from the Babylonian Captivity; c. 200 B.C.E.-c. 100 C.E., Composition of the Intertestamental Jewish Apocrypha; c. 6 B.C.E., Birth of Jesus Christ; c. 30 C.E., Condemnation and Crucifixion of Jesus Christ; c. 30 C.E., Preaching of the Pentecostal Gospel; September 8, 70 C.E., Roman Destruction of the Temple of Jerusalem; c. 90 C.E., Synod of Jamnia

RELATED ARTICLES in *Great Lives from History: The Ancient World*: Jesus; Flavius Josephus; Saint John the Baptist; Pontius Pilate.

---

c. 247-207 B.C.E.
BUDDHISM ESTABLISHED IN SRI LANKA

The legendary king Dēvānaṃpiya Tissa received a Buddhist mission from the Indian king Aśoka and afterward established the Buddhist religion as a central part of Sri Lankan society.

LOCALE: Sri Lanka (formerly Ceylon)
CATEGORIES: Religion; government and politics

KEY FIGURES

Dēvānaṃpiya Tissa (fl. third century B.C.E.), first Buddhist king of Sri Lanka, r. c. 247-207 B.C.E.

Aśoka (c. 302-c. 238 B.C.E.), Indian king, r. c. 273/265-c. 238 B.C.E.

Mahinda (c. 270-c. 204 B.C.E.), Buddhist missionary to Sri Lanka, Aśoka's son

Sanghamitta (b. c. 282 B.C.E.), Mahinda's sister, who, with a branch of the Bodhi tree, symbolically planted Buddhism in Sri Lanka

SUMMARY OF EVENT

The life and rule of King Dēvānaṃpiya Tissa are recorded in the chronicles of Sri Lanka. The most important of these chronicles is the *Māhavamsa* (fifth century C.E.; *The Mahāvamsa*, 1837, 1909). Dēvānaṃpiya Tissa is reported to have been the second son of King Mutasiva, who had nine other sons and two daughters. Despite having an older brother, Dēvānaṃpiya Tissa inherited the throne on his father's death because of his reputation for virtue and intelligence.

So great was Dēvānaṃpiya Tissa's merit that his consecration as ruler was accompanied by miracles, according to the *Māhavamsa*. Precious jewels that had been buried in the earth or lost in the sea rose to the surface. Strange bamboo stems in many colors and in the shapes of living creatures grew up at the foot of the mountains. Pearls washed up from the sea. The new king was delighted to see these treasures. Because generosity counted among his many virtues, he decided to send them to a king to the north in India, called "Dhammaśoka" in the chronicles. King Tissa appointed his nephew, Arittha, to lead envoys north to bring the treasures to the Indian king. Aśoka, as the Indian ruler is more commonly known, was a convert to Buddhism and was in the process of holding the Third Buddhist Council, which is credited with producing the *Tipiṭaka* (compiled c. 250 B.C.E.; English translation in *Buddhist Scriptures*, 1913), a work containing three of the most sacred Buddhist texts, and with preparing missionaries to spread Buddhism to other lands.

Aśoka sent back to Sri Lanka his son Mahinda (Mahendra, in Sanskrit). After arriving in the southern island kingdom, Mahinda and six companions met Dēvānampiya Tissa at Mihintale Hill, near the Sri Lankan capital of Anuradhapura. The son of Aśoka preached a sermon that immediately converted Dēvānampiya Tissa, and settlements for the missionaries were established at a

This Buddhist statue in Polonnaruwa, Sri Lanka, demonstrates the religion's lasting influence in the region. (PhotoDisc)

royal pavilion in Mahamegha Park. From their encampment, Mahinda and his fellow missionaries preached continually, and Buddhism spread rapidly, so that many Sri Lankans became Buddhist monks.

King Dēvānampiya Tissa proceeded to build the monastery of Mahāvihāra (literally, great temple) at Mahamegha. The prestige of this Buddhist center was enhanced even further when Mahinda's sister, Sanghamitta, arrived with a branch of the Bodhi tree under which the Buddha had attained his enlightenment. Sanghamitta planted the shoot, symbolically planting Buddhism in the Sri Lankan soil, and founded an order of nuns. With the backing of the king, missionaries spread out through the villages of Sri Lanka.

The chronicles clearly mix historical event and legend. No one knows whether Dēvānampiya Tissa was the model of virtue presented in the Sri Lankan records. Although the stone inscriptions left by Aśoka make it evident that the Indian king did convert to Buddhism and that he did support his new religion, some historians have questioned how much of a part the Indian king actually played in the Third Buddhist Council. However, a number of important points can be accepted. Aśoka and Dēvānampiya Tissa did reign in their respective kingdoms at the same time, and they would have been in contact with each other. Buddhist missionary activities to lands outside of India did take place immediately after the years of the Third Buddhist Council. Dēvānampiya Tissa became the most important patron of Buddhism in Sri Lanka, and the religion was established as a central feature of Sri Lankan society during and immediately after his reign.

The form of Buddhism planted in Sri Lanka during King Dēvānampiya Tissa's time is known as Theravāda Buddhism. The word "Theravāda" literally means "the way of the elders" in the Pāli language of ancient India, and it is generally regarded as a more conservative form of Buddhism than the Mahāyāna Buddhism that came to predominate in China, Japan, Korea, and Vietnam. Within Sri Lanka, Theravāda Buddhism gradually split into three schools, but the school of the Mahāvihāra monastery established by Dēvānampiya Tissa was the most powerful and influential for centuries.

SIGNIFICANCE

The adoption of Buddhism became the basis of political and social identity for Sri Lanka, and the idea of the Buddhist monarchy helped give legitimacy to the Sri Lankan kings. Dēvānampiya Tissa, as the legendary founder of Buddhism in the land, became the model for rulers who were seen as protectors and patrons of the faith. In modern times, the religion established during Dēvānaṃpiya Tissa's reign has become a point of conflict. Religious differences have intensified conflicts between the Buddhist Sinhalese, the majority ethnic group, and the Hindu Tamils, who settled in northern Sri Lanka from southern India centuries ago.

The Indian missionary movement that brought Buddhism to Sri Lanka also took the religion to Southeast Asia, which later received Buddhist influences from both India and Sri Lanka along trade routes. Theravāda Buddhism became the dominant form in Myanmar, Laos, Thailand, and Cambodia. These Southeast Asian nations were therefore linked to Sri Lanka by religion, and Sri Lankan Buddhism was influential throughout the region.

—*Carl L. Bankston III*

FURTHER READING

Fa-hsien. *A Record of Buddhistic Kingdoms: Being an Account by the Chinese Monk Fa-hsien of His Travels in India and Ceylon (A.D. 399-414) in Search of the Buddhist Books of Discipline*. Translated by James Legge. New York: Dover Publications, 1991. A new edition of a translation originally published in 1886. Although Faxian made his travels several centuries after Dēvānaṃpiya Tissa, the book is a firsthand account of the rituals, practices, and folklore of ancient Sri Lankan Buddhism.

Mahanama. *The Mahāvamsa: The Great Chronicle of Sri Lanka*. Translated by Douglas Bullis. Fremont, Calif.: Asian Humanities Press, 1999. A new translation of the chronicle of Sri Lanka. Readers concerned chiefly with the establishment of Buddhism by Dēvānaṃpiya Tissa will find this subject in chapter eleven. The translator has included his own historical commentary.

Mitchell, Donald W. *Buddhism: Introducing the Buddhist Experience*. New York: Oxford University Press, 2002. A good general introduction to Buddhism that has chapters on its origins in India and on Mahāyāna and Theravāda Buddhism. Particularly recommended for those seeking to understand the distinctions between those two major approaches to Buddhism.

Rahula, Wapola. *History of Buddhism in Ceylon: The Anuradhapura Period, Third Century B.C. to Tenth Century A.D.* London: Taylor & Francis, 1966. An older history, but one of the most detailed on this topic and a volume that can be found in many large libraries.

SEE ALSO: 6th or 5th century B.C.E., Birth of Buddhism; c. 5th-4th century B.C.E., Creation of the *Jātakas*; 300 B.C.E.-600 C.E., Construction of the Māhabodhi Temple; c. 273/265-c. 238 B.C.E., Aśoka Reigns over India; c. 250 B.C.E., Third Buddhist Council Convenes; c. 250 B.C.E., *Tipiṭaka* Is Compiled; 1st-2d century C.E., Fourth Buddhist Council Convenes.

RELATED ARTICLES in *Great Lives from History: The Ancient World*: Ānanda; Aśoka; Buddha; Dēvānaṃpiya Tissa.

---

c. 245 B.C.E.
DIODOTUS I FOUNDS THE GRECO-BACTRIAN KINGDOM

Diodotus I rebelled against his Seleucid overlords and created an independent kingdom between the Hindu Kush and the Oxus River, which became an important conduit of Hellenic culture into Central Asia.

LOCALE: Kingdom of Bactria (modern Afghanistan, Uzbekistan, and Tajikistan)
CATEGORIES: Government and politics; wars, uprisings, and civil unrest

KEY FIGURES
Diodotus I (d. c. 239 B.C.E.), Greek governor of Bactria who revolted against the Seleucid Dynasty and founded the Greco-Bactrian kingdom
Antiochus II (d. 246 B.C.E.), Seleucid ruler at time of Diodotus's revolt, r. 261-246 B.C.E.

SUMMARY OF EVENT
Although Diodotus I probably was instrumental in wresting Bactria from the Seleucid Dynasty and establishing it as a Greek kingdom, the evidence for the exact sequence of events is slight. Diodotus I was the satrap (governor) of the province of Bactria-Sogdiana in the Seleucid Empire. According to one school of thought, he revolted against the Seleucid ruler Antiochus II in 250 B.C.E.; according to another, his gradual progress to independence can be traced in Seleucid coinage. However, this latter, numismatic argument has itself been undermined by changing theories about the coinage of the time.

About 246 B.C.E., the year of Antiochus's death and his succession by Seleucus II, Diodotus I is said to have been bribed with marriage to a daughter of Antiochus, sister of Seleucus. This would imply that Diodotus I was still a Seleucid satrap at this time. His son, Diodotus II (d. c. 210 B.C.E.), is attested as king of Bactria by 227 or 228 B.C.E., which suggests that Diodotus I could not have died much later than 230, more likely around 239 B.C.E. The family romance gets tangled after Diodotus I's death, for Diodotus II turned against the Seleucids and joined forces with Tiridates of Parthia (r. c. 248-211 B.C.E.), the Seleucids' enemy. However, Diodotus I's widow appears to have retained allegiance to her Seleucid family and married her own daughter to Euthydemus (fl. third century B.C.E.), himself a satrap of the new Bactrian kingdom who then murdered Diodotus II.

According to the Greek historian Polybius (c. 200-c. 118 B.C.E.), Euthydemus told Antiochus the Great (242-187 B.C.E.) that he was no rebel but that he had killed the son of one. If this is a true reporting of Euthydemus's words, it would imply that Diodotus I was the rebel against the Seleucids. Other historians, however, are uncertain whether it was Diodotus I or Diodotus II who established the Bactrian kingdom. What does seem clear is that by the 230's B.C.E., Bactria was a separate kingdom; the date at which it achieved this independence may have been anywhere between 250 and 238 B.C.E.

Diodotus and his descendants have been termed "an elusive dynasty" by modern historians because of the immense prestige they enjoyed during their day, and for several centuries after, contrasted with the complete lack of documentary information surviving from the Diodotids themselves. A pottery fragment bears an incomplete Greek word that may be the beginning of the name Diodotus, but it may also be the beginning of any of several other words. Other slight bits of documentary evidence are even less convincing.

Lacking documentary sources, modern knowledge of ancient Bactria derives from archaeology, literary references in the works of outside observers, and numismatics. The archaeological evidence, for instance, reveals that Bactria was an integral part of the overall Hellenistic culture. The city of Ai Khanoum, developed between c. 280 and c. 250 B.C.E. in the confluence of the Oxus and Kochba Rivers, included a theater, a pool, a treasury, a palace, an arsenal, and a gymnasium, along with numerous mansions owned by wealthy Greeks. A monumental gate greeted visitors to a public area dominated by a sprawling palace. A limestone wine press attests to a certain level of culinary sophistication, and the public library housed Greek philosophical texts that would have been read by citizens with such Greek names as Strato,

Cosmas, Philoxenos, and Philiskos. A Greek visitor named Klearchos traveled 3,000 miles (4839 kilometers) from Greece to Ai Khanoum early in the third century B.C.E. to publicize the maxims from the Temple of Apollo at Delphi. The propagation of these maxims in Ai Khanoum was not unique, for copies were posted in the gymnasia of other cities in central Asia. Archaeological discoveries indicate that throughout the Diodotid period Ai Khanoum enjoyed peace and prosperity.

Literary sources offer another kind of insight into the Diodotid period in Bactria. The *Geōgraphica* (c. 7 B.C.E.; *Geography*, 1917-1933) of Strabo and a history of the world by Strabo's contemporary Pompeius Trogus were both probably derived from a lost work of the first century B.C.E., the *Parthika* (Parthian history) of Apollodorus of Artemita. Strabo's brief references to Diodotus I are inconsequential, but the ancient historian Justin condensed Trogus as the *Epitoma historiarum Philippicarum* (n.d.; *Epitome of the Philippic History of Pompeius Trogus*, 1853). Justin himself is a mystery; it is uncertain whether his name was M. Iunianus Iustinus or M. Iunianius Iustinus, although the latter is more likely, and he lived as early as 144 C.E. or as late as 395 C.E. Justin reports that the quarrel over the Seleucid kingdom by the royal brothers Seleucus and Antiochus made possible a rebellion, and Diodotus I (or Theodotus, as Justin calls him) took advantage of this moment to rebel himself, setting himself up as king. The population of Macedonia defected as well.

A third source of information about the Diodotids appears in their coinage, the history of which constitutes a fascinating story of intimidating complexity. The first coin minted by Diodotus turned up in France in 1835 but was not at first recognized as such because it bore the name, in Greek, of King Antiochus, and it depicted Zeus naked and hurling a thunderbolt. The first coin bearing the name King Diodotus in Greek was described in 1841 and now rests in the Bibliothèque Nationale in Paris. Gradually, a few hundred coins from Diodotid Bactria have come to light, providing perhaps the most useful evidence about the reign of the Diodotids and their place in history.

SIGNIFICANCE

By breaking free of the Near Eastern Seleucid Empire, Bactria became a conduit of Hellenistic culture—art, architecture, coinage, and writing—from Greece and the rest of the Mediterranean world into Central Asia and northwestern India. When Bactria was, in turn, conquered by the Yuezhi, a Central Asian tribal group that probably are the people called Tokharians by the Greeks,

Bactrian and Hellenistic culture were carried almost to the Great Wall of China. As Bactrian influence spread across the Hindu Kush into India, it also became a conduit for Buddhism into Central Asia. A distinctive artistic style developed from this multicultural kingdom that combined the classicism and naturalism of Greek art with the stylization of Indian religious sculpture.

—Frank Day

FURTHER READING

Holt, Frank L. *Thundering Zeus: The Making of Hellenistic Bactria*. Berkeley: University of California Press, 1999. Studies the period of Diodotus I and Diodotus II with great attention to their coinage.

Justin (Marcus Junianus Justinus). *Epitome of the Philippic History of Pompeius Trogus*. Translated by J. C. Yardley, with an introduction by R. Develin. Atlanta: Scholars Press, 1994. The classical source for the story of Diodotus I, here known as Theodotus.

Legg, Stuart. *The Heartland*. New York: Capricorn Books, 1971. Very readable account of the nomadic tribes in central Asia.

McGovern, William Montgomery. *The Early Empires of Central Asia: A Study of the Scythians and the Huns and the Part They Played in World History*. Chapel Hill: University of North Carolina Press, 1939. Summarizes the events of Diodotus I's reign.

Sherwin-White, Susan, and Amélie Kuhrt. *From Samarkand to Sardis: A New Approach to the Seleucid Empire*. Berkeley: University of California Press, 1993. An excellent and generally revisionary account of the Seleucids.

Tarn, W. W. *The Greeks in Bactria and India*. 2d ed. New York: Cambridge University Press, 1951. Tarn's account of the Seleucids and Diodotus I, long the standard, has been superseded by the research of Sherwin-White and Kuhrt and of Holt.

SEE ALSO: c. 420 B.C.E.-c. 100 C.E., Yuezhi Culture Links Persia and China; 245-140 B.C.E., Rise of Parthia; c. 155 B.C.E., Greco-Bactrian Kingdom Reaches Zenith Under Menander; c. 100-c. 127 C.E., Kushān Dynasty Expands into India.

RELATED ARTICLES in *Great Lives from History: The Ancient World*: Antiochus the Great; Menander (Greco-Bactrian ruler).

245-140 B.C.E.
RISE OF PARTHIA

The Parthians rose from obscure origins to become a dominating force in the Near East in the third and second centuries B.C.E. until colliding with the expanding Roman Empire. They became symbolic of the resistence of eastern, Greek-based culture against the encroachments of Rome.

LOCALE: Parthia (now in northwestern Iran)
CATEGORIES: Expansion and land acquisition; government and politics; wars, uprisings, and civil unrest

KEY FIGURES

Arsaces (fl. third century B.C.E.), traditional founder of the Parthian Dynasty, c. 250-c. 248 B.C.E.
Tiridates (d. 211 B.C.E.), possible founder of the Parthian Dynasty, king of Parthia, r. c. 248-211 B.C.E.
Andragoras (d. c. 238 B.C.E.), Seleucid satrap of Parthia, c. 245 B.C.E.
Antiochus the Great (c. 242-187 B.C.E.), Seleucid king, r. 223-187 B.C.E.
Mithradates I (c. 200-138 B.C.E.), king of Parthia, r. 171-138 B.C.E.

SUMMARY OF EVENT

Out of the historical mists surrounding the regions northeast of the Caspian Sea rode the vanguards of barbarian invaders of what is now Iran in the first half of the third century B.C.E. They were the Parni. Toward the middle of the century, Diodotus I, king of the Greco-Bactrian state, attacked and drove them westward into the Seleucid provinces of Hyrcania and Parthia. At that time, these districts were sparsely populated by nomadic Iranian shepherds, a few agriculturalists, and occasional brigands. Here, about 245 B.C.E., the Parni met the Seleucid satrap Andragoras and defeated him. The fact that such a small army could overcome the mighty Seleucid forces and kill their leader was no doubt largely because of contemporary Seleucid involvement in the Third Syrian War (246-241 B.C.E.) against Ptolemaic Egypt.

Their victory gave the Parni a permanent home in Parthia, and the province gave them the name by which they are known in history. Their first known king was

Arsaces, who ruled about the middle of the third century B.C.E. and apparently died while fighting. He was succeeded by Tiridates, who most likely was the real founder of the kingdom. Few details of early Parthian history are known. After the death of Tiridates, Seleucid control of Parthia was reasserted by the indefatigable campaigner Antiochus the Great, who was intent on restoring to his kingdom the territory it had possessed in the days of its founder, Seleucus I (c. 358 or 354-281 B.C.E.). Antiochus's defeat by Rome in 189 B.C.E. was followed by his own death at the hands of rebels in Elymais in 187 B.C.E., and the Arsacids seized the opportunity to throw off Seleucid suzerainty. Thereafter, Parthia grew stronger, and by 140 B.C.E., Mithradates I had overrun Media and Persis and had taken most of Babylonia from the Seleucids. These rich conquests transformed Parthia, until then a third-rate power, into an important state.

Parthia was a loosely organized monarchy with its capital sometimes at Ecbatana in Iran and sometimes at Ctesiphon in Babylonia. Its kings ruled over a feudal aristocracy of Parthians dwelling mostly in modern-day Iran. The noble families were half-independent princely clans who lived in fortified castles and held sway over Iranian serfs who toiled in the valleys below. In this eastern, Iranian, half of the state, the old institutions, customs, and culture of the Orient continued, and the Arsacids pretended to be descendants of Artaxerxes I (the Achaemenid king of Persia from 465-c. 423 B.C.E.) and worshipers of the traditional gods of Iran. In the western, Babylonian, half of the state, a different set of values obtained. There the Parthians carefully fostered good relations with the Greek cities founded by Alexander the Great, Seleucus I, and Antiochus the Great. The cities continued, as they had under Seleucid rule, to be autonomous states governing their own territory, speaking Greek and maintaining Greek institutions. To these cities, the Arsacids, Mithradates I especially, advertised themselves as Philhellenes.

Many Greeks readily accepted this new order because the military strength of the Parthians protected them from participating in the miserable wars that had begun between rival branches of the Seleucid Dynasty. Some Greeks did not take kindly to the Parthians and made gibes about their kings, said to love their horses so much that they would not dismount from them even to hold a trial. The Arsacids did develop a sincere admiration for Hellenistic culture; King Orodes II (r. c. 57-37/36 B.C.E.) was interrupted once while enjoying a performance of Euripides' *Bakchai* (c. 405 B.C.E.; *Bacchae*, 1781).

After the death of Mithradates I, Parthian power continued slowly to expand until it reached the Euphrates in northwestern Mesopotamia, where, in the middle of the first century B.C.E., it met the rapidly growing empire of the Romans. There then ensued between these two powers a series of wars that caused the periodic expenditure of the resources of both to the advantage of neither. In 53 B.C.E. the great noble Surenas defeated the Roman plunderer Marcus Licinius Crassus (c. 115-53 B.C.E.) in the bloody Battle of Carrhae by wearing down the sturdy Roman infantry under a hail of arrows shot by horse-archers. His men replenished their supply of missiles from a mobile ammunition column of camels.

Marc Antony (c. 82-30 B.C.E.) sought to avenge this disaster by invading the Parthian Empire in 36 B.C.E., but his campaign ended in a second Roman defeat. The Parthians thus appeared as the

A Parthian horse archer, c. third century B.C.E. (Kimberly L. Dawson Kurnizki)

MAJOR KINGS OF PARTHIA, C. 250 B.C.E.-224 C.E.

Ruler	Reign
Arsaces I	c. 250-c. 248 B.C.E.
Tiridates	c. 248-211
Arsaces II	211-191
Priapatios	191-176
Phraates I	176-171
Mithradates I	171-138
Phraates II	138-127
Artabanus II	127-124
Mithradates II	123-88
Gotarzes I	95-87
Orodes I	90-77
Sinatruces	77-70
Phraates III	70-57
Mithradates III	57-54
Orodes II	57-38
Phraates IV	38-2
Tiridates	29-27
Phraatakes	2 B.C.E.-4 C.E.
Orodes III	6
Vonones I	8-12
Artabanus III	12-38
Vardanes I	40-45
Gotarzes II	40-51
Vonones II	51
Vologases I	51-80
Vardanes II	55-58
Vologases II	77-80
Pakoros II	78-105
Artabanus IV	80-90
Vologases III	105-147
Osroes I	109-129
Parthamaspates	116
Mithradates IV	140
Vologases IV	147-191
Osroes II	190
Vologases V	191-208
Vologases VI	208-228
Artabanaus V	213-224

gotiated a settlement with the Arsacids. Thereafter, the Parthians were not a serious menace to Rome. Nero's great general Gnaeus Domitius Corbulo (d. 67 C.E.) inflicted severe defeats on them; the emperor Trajan (c. 53-117 C.E.) actually overran all Babylonia; and Marcus Aurelius (121-180 C.E.) and Septimius Severus (145-211 C.E.) repeated Trajan's feat. The last invasion seriously weakened Parthia, and about 224 C.E., the last Parthian king was killed by Ardashīr I of Persis (r. 224-241 C.E.), who founded the powerful Sāsānian Dynasty as the standard-bearer of revived Zoroastrianism and Iranian nationalism.

SIGNIFICANCE

The Parthians were a small feudal, military aristocracy settled in parts of modern-day Iran, lording it over the peasants, intermingling Greek and Asian civilization, extracting a derivative art from them, creating nothing original, and interested in commerce only because it could be taxed. It is a commentary on the Parthian contribution to the stock of human culture that their history is known almost entirely from Greek and Latin sources and not from Parthian literature at all, except for a small number of official administrative documents. In general, the kings of Parthia were tax gatherers, raiders, and collectors of booty, remembered only for their military accomplishments.

Parthian history is a catalogue of wars. There were Corbulo's extended campaigns from 58 to 63 C.E., which arose out of a quarrel as to whether Parthia or Rome would make Armenia its sphere of influence. Trajan made war on Parthia, using Armenia as a pretext, from 114 to 117 C.E., invading Babylonia and sacking Ctesiphon. Marcus Aurelius also invaded Babylonia from 162 to 166 C.E., again ravaging the country and taking the capital. Although this was a Roman military success, it became a human disaster, for the army became infected with plague and brought it home with catastrophic results. From 195 to 199 C.E., Septimius Severus conducted the last great offensive against the Arsacids, overrunning Babylonia for the third time in less than a century, and sacking Ctesiphon. All these Roman victories were hard on Mesopotamia, and the level of human existence there, as shown by excavations at Dura-Europus and Seleucia-on-Tigris, was reduced by these heavy-handed campaigns.

Although many scholars dismiss Parthia as a minor force in the history of Mesopotamia, others hold that the Parthians were not entirely without virtue. From a point of view that does not view the classical world as the sole

champions of eastern Greeks and of Asians alike against the rapacity of Rome. Some Hellenic historians highly approved of them in this role, and a Jewish prophet forecast that the Messiah would be nigh when a Parthian tied his horse to a tree outside Jerusalem. That dream ended when Augustus (63 B.C.E.-14 C.E.) consolidated the Roman Empire on a new and more formidable basis, and ne-

arbiter of taste, Parthian art and architecture, far from being merely degenerate Greek forms, were interesting blends of Greek and Iranian ideas. The Arsacids defended Iranian culture against the Greeks. In the third century B.C.E., Hellenism penetrated readily into Iran under the protection of the Seleucids. At that time, the population was under the spell of the victories of Alexander the Great (356-323 B.C.E.), which had so easily toppled the seemingly invincible power of the Achaemenids. The Parthians, however, by first checking and then repelling the Seleucids, served to diminish Greek influence in Iran and to afford a breathing space for the Orient.

As the power of the Seleucid Empire slowly ebbed, not least because of the military blows dealt it by Mithradates I, there was something of a revival of native Iranian culture and tradition. To this the Parthians adapted themselves and may even have supported it, although the lack of sufficient evidence does not allow a definitive judgment on this point. The Parthians, moreover, were tolerant of all religions, leading them to protect Zoroastrianism, which now slowly developed a more definite theology and detailed forms of organization than it had had in the Achaemenid period. For all this, they deserve better remembrance.

Their worst detractors were actually their native Persian successors. The Sāsānians regarded the Parthian era as an age of darkness that fell between the glory of the Achaemenids of Persis and the period of grandeur inaugurated by themselves. There is evidence of Sāsānian tampering with the tradition of Parthian history; they certainly shortened the length of time allotted Arsacid rule in Iran, possibly to make the expected reappearance of Zoroaster at the end of earthly time a more remote event.

—*Samuel K. Eddy*

FURTHER READING

Colledge, Malcolm. *The Parthians*. New York: Thames and Hudson, 1967. Part of the Ancient Peoples and Places series, this is one of the few works devoted completely to Parthian history and culture. Includes genealogies, chronology, illustrations, and maps.

Curtis, John, ed. *Mesopotamia and Iran in the Parthian and Sasanian Period: Rejection and Revival c. 238 B.C.-A.D. 642*. London: British Museum Press, 2000. A collection of essays covering many aspects of Parthian history, culture, and costume.

Curtis, Vesta Sarkhosh, Robert Hillebrand, and J. M. Rogers, eds. *The Art and Archaeology of Ancient Persia: New Light on the Parthian and Sasanian Empires*. New York: I. B. Tauris, 1998. This volume of twenty-three conference papers touches on many aspects of Parthian and Sāsānian Persia, largely through the analysis of material culture.

Wiesehöfer, Josef. *Ancient Persia*. Translated by Azizeh Azodi. New York: I. B. Tauris, 2001. This history of Persia from 550 B.C.E. to 650 C.E. devotes three chapters to the Parthians. Well written for a general audience. Includes illustrations, a bibliographical essay, a chronological table, and a list of dynasties and kings.

Yarshater, E., ed. *The Seleucid, Parthian, and Sasanid Periods*. Parts 1 and 2 of Vol. 3 in *The Cambridge History of Iran*. Reissue ed. New York: Cambridge University Press, 1993. The most compendious history of the Parthian period available.

SEE ALSO: 224 C.E., Ardashīr I Establishes the Sāsānian Empire.

RELATED ARTICLES in *Great Lives from History: The Ancient World*: Alexander the Great; Antiochus the Great; Marcus Aurelius; Seleucis I Nicator; Trajan.

From 240 B.C.E.
EXPLOITATION OF THE ARCH

The exploitation of the arch as both a structural and decorative device revolutionized architecture, making possible the building of much larger structures than those allowed by post-and-lintel construction.

LOCALE: Western Europe
CATEGORIES: Science and technology; architecture; cultural and intellectual history

KEY FIGURE
Augustus (63 B.C.E.-14 C.E.), Roman emperor, r. 27 B.C.E.-14 C.E.

SUMMARY OF EVENT

Although the structural benefits of the arch were known as early as 3500 B.C.E., both the Egyptians and later the Greeks chose a simpler form of construction. As they adapted the Greek orders, so too the Romans took the structural form of the arch and exploited it throughout the Roman Empire. Through numerous barbaric invasions the arch remained a symbol of civilization long after the power of Rome disappeared.

The earliest architects used post-and-lintel construction to create the first shelters. In this type of structure, weight is not distributed on the posts but is placed directly on the lintel, thus limiting a structure's height, weight of materials, and number of stories. Large structures required massive pieces of stone and an equally massive labor force. In 3500 B.C.E., Egyptian architects began experimenting with vaults at both Dendera and Abydos. Constructed of wedge-shaped voussoirs with the joints between radiating from the center, the arch permits weight to be dispersed directly on to the posts. Though this support system proved successful, a rigid artistic tradition relegated the arch to underground storage areas.

As in Egypt, the Greeks chose to perfect post-and-lintel construction. Using weight, iron rods, and exact measurement, architects created what appeared to be seamless monumental structures. The Greek "order" featured a simple post-and-lintel construction of column and entablature, which produced a structure of horizontal and upright stone beams, featuring the colonnade designed to suppress the wall. The Greeks disliked the arch because it gave distinctive form to a hole. It was characteristic of Greek thought to conceive of form or shape as that which determines the reality of what truly exists and to think of space or emptiness as the prime symbol of nonbeing.

The first architects to accord the arched aperture an important role in their construction were the Etruscans. These residents of Latium first used the arch in vaulted drains dating from the fourth century B.C.E. By 240 B.C.E., architects employed this technology for bridges on the Via Amerina and city gates such as the Porta Augusta in Perugia. As the Romans began to gain an upper hand in the struggle for the control of the Italian peninsula, they freely adopted cultural traits from the peoples they conquered.

Unlike either the Egyptians or Greeks, the Romans made the brick their major medium of construction. While such a small building block hampers post-and-lintel construction, it is ideal for the arch. The genius of Roman architecture lay in combining the arch and the Greek orders by building a wall pierced with arches and then placing the Greek colonnade against it, so as to show an arch between two columns that appeared to carry the entablature above. To fully ally the two elements, the impost molding was put around the pier to receive the arch, while the base moldings and the band about the arch echoed the architrave. Finally, a keystone was used as an inventive aesthetic detail to bind the arch and the Greek order at its most critical point. This architectural innovation first appeared at the beginning of the first century B.C.E. in structures such as the Tabularium and the Temple of Hercules Victor at Tivoli.

As their engineering skills increased, the Romans employed the arch in a variety of ways, ranging from the strictly utilitarian Cloaca Maxima and the Pont du Gard to the purely commemorative or monumental arches of triumph. As Rome expanded outside of the Italian peninsula, communication became vital. It was as *pontifex maximus* or "bridge builder" that the ruler could best visibly assert his authority by binding the empire together with roads and bridges. The scale of public works such as the aqueduct at Segovia, Spain, from the first century C.E., dwarfed earlier Etruscan examples.

The Etruscans first employed the arch in a city gate, but it was the Romans who isolated the gateway as a symbol of power. Augustus ordered the construction of the first triumphal arch at Rimini in 27 B.C.E. to celebrate the restoration of the highway system in northern Italy. The arch thus became a metaphor of the state's control over the passageway and its ability to regulate and control the citizen's movements. This idea is enforced by the use of the triumphal arch on imperial coinage beginning during the reigns of the Julio-Claudian Dynasty of Roman emperors (14-37 C.E.).

The pinnacle of Rome's exploitation of the arch was not visible to the average person, but it did make the grandeur of the imperial city possible. In works such as the Pantheon, begun in 27 B.C.E. by Marcus Vipsanius Agrippa and rebuilt by Hadrian (76-138 C.E.) in c. 118-128 C.E., a series of arches are used as internal buttress that support the domed rotunda. Hidden by the interior design of the building, these arches are then supported by a series of vaulted galleries. The development of the vault forced the column eventually to stand alone below this device because with this form of arch there is no place for an entablature. The first time arches were set directly on capitals of columns with no architrave was in the palace of Diocletian at Spalatum in 300 C.E.

SIGNIFICANCE

Following the shift of imperial power from the West to the East after the founding of Constantinople in 326-330 C.E., the arch played an important role in attempting to reverse the technical decline of European architecture. In 547 C.E., under Justinian's plan to reunify the Roman Empire, the Church of Saint Vitale was constructed in Ravenna. Centrally planned, its eight piers rely on two sets of arches to support the gallery and the roof.

Although Justinian's successors found it unprofitable to maintain the reconquered provinces in the West, Saint Vitale and its combination of the column and arch became an architectural model in Europe for another five hundred years. When Charlemagne began a cultural revival in 800 C.E., he used the architecture of his palace at Aachen, Germany, to express his ties to Rome. His Palatine Chapel, consecrated in 805 C.E., follows the plan of Saint Vitale with a simplified elevation, since a thorough knowledge of Rome's engineering practices had been lost among western builders. Charlemagne was not alone in his desire to employ Roman forms, because they are clearly apparent in such structures as the abbey gatehouse of Lorsch (near Frankfurt, Germany), which is meant to be a triumphal arch.

By 1140, the Roman arch and many of the vaulting forms developed during the imperial period once more appeared in many of the religious structures of Western Europe. Abbot Suger (1081-1151) made revolutionary use of the flying buttress and pointed arches at Saint-Denis, marking the first intellectual break with Christianity's architectural past. For the next four hundred years, the arch's structural and aesthetic uses were combined to create edifices of greater height with multiple window openings which were dedicated to the glory of God.

In 1421, Filippo Brunelleschi's design for the Foundling Hospital in Florence not only ushered in the Renaissance but also restored the rounded Roman arch to its place as a symbol of civilization. Expanding from Italy, both Imperial and Republican architecture were used by successive generations to express their place on the international political stage.

Although the arch has played a role as a decorative motif in the twentieth century, its last development as a structural form took place in the nineteenth. With the harnessing of steam and industrialization, architects and engineers faced new design problems. For many, Joseph Paxton's prominent use of the arch in the iron supports of the Crystal Palace demonstrated how a "noble" Roman form could be adapted for modern needs. With the advent of reinforced concrete and steel, however, the arch no longer fulfilled a structural need.

—*Norris K. Smith,*
updated by Edmund Dickenson Potter

FURTHER READING

Jones, Mark Wilson. *Principles of Roman Architecture.* New Haven, Conn.: Yale University Press, 2003. Explores the design principles used by Roman architects and the ways in which they channeled their creativity. The book is divided into a theoretical section and a set of three case studies of specific monuments.

MacDonald, William L. *The Pantheon: Design, Meaning, and Progeny.* 1992. Reprint. Cambridge, Mass.: Harvard University Press, 2002. A close study of the Pantheon and its architectural features, both technological and theoretical, including the use of arches.

Sear, Frank. *Roman Architecture.* London: Batsford, 1989. A fundamental, illustrated account integrating the arch into the development of Roman architecture.

Thorpe, Martin. *Roman Architecture.* London: Bristol Classical Press, 1995. Thorpe illustrates the vast subject of Roman architecture by focusing on several important examples.

SEE ALSO: 625-509 B.C.E., Rise of Etruscan Civilization in Rome; 312 B.C.E., First Roman Aqueduct Is Built; 312-264 B.C.E., Building of the Appian Way.

221 B.C.E.
QIN DYNASTY FOUNDED IN CHINA

The Qin Dynasty, although brutal and short, unified and centralized China politically and culturally and separated the ancient feudal history from the imperial history of China.

LOCALE: China

CATEGORY: Government and politics; expansion and land acquisition; wars, uprisings, and civil unrest

KEY FIGURES

Shi Huangdi (Shih Huang-ti; 259-210 B.C.E.), first emperor of China, r. 221-210 B.C.E.

Xunzi (Hsün-tzu; c. 307-c. 235 B.C.E.), traditional founder of Legalism

Li Si (Li Ssu; 280?-208 B.C.E.), minister of state, 221-208 B.C.E., student of Xunzi

SUMMARY OF EVENT

The Qin (Ch'in), who ruled a poor frontier province during the Eastern Zhou Dynasty (Eastern Chou; 770-256 B.C.E.), saw themselves as a hardy warrior people. In the decade before the establishment of the empire in 221 B.C.E., the Qins conquered province after province and defeated all other claimants to succeed the discredited Zhou as rulers of China. Having conquered all the warring states and united southern and northern China for the first time, King Zheng (Cheng) of the Qin proclaimed himself to be Qin Shi Huangdi (first emperor of Qin) and established the Qin Dynasty (221-206 B.C.E.).

The Qin were strongly influenced by the philosophy of Legalism. Like Confucianism, Legalism offered practical solutions to the problems of government. Unlike Confucianism, the solutions offered were rooted in ruthless practicality and pragmatism rather than the virtues of gentlemanly behavior. Legalism arose as a reaction to the disorder of the Eastern Zhou Dynasty, when weak kings allowed invasion, insurrection, and civil war to split China into several warring states. Legalists blamed the weakness of the Zhou kings for the disorder and proposed that the proper remedy to China's ills was for rulers to hold and practice absolute power. The early advocates of Legalism held that they were followers of Xunzi, who was himself a disciple of Confucius. However, Legalism was actually a number of distinct but related schools of practical thought that coalesced among philosophers and government officials. According to the Legalists, because human nature is evil, the ruler must keep the people disciplined and even suppressed if they are rebellious.

The ideal state was an authoritarian state in which the people were well treated but uneducated and barred from dissent. The ruler should appropriate their labor to feed his army and their wealth to fill his coffers. The state should possess as much power as possible and should extend it ruthlessly. All aspects of life were to be regulated in detail by laws designated to promote the economic and military power of the state. Rulers were not to be guided by traditional or Confucian virtues of humanity and righteousness but by their need for power and wealth. They were to root out all intellectual dissent or resistance and all competing political ideas. Legalism was too narrow to compete with Confucianism, but under the Qin Dynasty, all competing philosophies were repressed.

The Qin centralized the Chinese state to a degree without rival in the ancient world. They viewed the nobility as a useless holdover from the past and an undependable challenge to the authority of the emperor. Shi Huangdi forced the nobility to live in the capital and attend court, effectively removing them from local government. Their estates were reorganized into large provinces that the emperor controlled through centrally appointed governors.

During the Qin Dynasty, the textile industry grew, and increased trade led to the growth of cities. However, the traditional distrust of merchants remained and the Qin government focused mostly on the peasants. Large irrigation projects increased agricultural production. The Qin standardized weights, measures, and coinage. Regulations dictating axle widths on carts allowed for improved transportation. The Qin introduced a simplified, standardized set of written characters, which remains in use, with modifications, to the present. A population census, showing the empire contained almost sixty million people, enabled the emperor to anticipate tax revenues and to calculate the force available for military service and state building projects. Peasant land rights were expanded, in part to check the power of the large landowners and also to tie the peasants closer to the land.

Although the first Qin emperor strived to bring unity and prosperity to China, he faced constant peril from the north. The Mongolian plateau to the north of China was harsh terrain but not impassable to the Mongol-Turkic nomadic tribes. For years, the Chinese had pushed northward, driving out the nomads and settling their grasslands. Chinese encroachment on their land endangered the very survival of these nomads, who in retaliation

MAJOR EMPERORS OF THE QIN DYNASTY, 221-206 B.C.E.	
Ruler	*Reign*
Shi Huangdi	221-210
Er Shi Huangdi	209-208
San Shi Huangdi	207-206

struck back at the Chinese. Mounted horsemen plundered towns and farms, disappearing back into the vast steppes to the north before the Chinese armies could catch them. The northern provinces had been building defensive walls as early as the fourth century B.C.E. The first Qin emperor was more systematic and ordered the various stretches of wall to be linked together in one great fortification, extending from the sea three thousand miles (five thousand kilometers) inland. Hundreds of thousands are thought to have labored to build it, a demonstration of the power and organization of the Qin empire. However, an estimated one million men died from accidents, exposure, disease, and starvation while building the wall. The Great Wall brought some measure of peace to China's northern frontier, although raids continued on a limited scale. Although the Qin are generally credited with building the Great Wall, scholar Arthur Waldron points out that the Great Wall that exists today was built in the sixteenth century, under the Ming Dynasty, and that the earlier wall was probably earthen rather than stone. Therefore, the exact location of the wall built by the Qin emperor is unknown, and the amount of labor involved may have been exaggerated in order to demonstrate the cruelty and ruthlessness of the first Qin emperor.

The Qin behaved in an imperial fashion, extending Chinese rule over most of what is modern-day China, to the coast of the South China Sea and into northern Vietnam. The Qins created a highly centralized, powerful state, with a vast and highly trained imperial bureaucracy. The high level of centralization in the state established by the Qin became a characteristic of Chinese government that was retained to the present day. Shi Huangdi tolerated no dissent. According to later accounts, he buried alive several hundred scholars who had questioned his policies. He ordered that all books except official manuals and chronicles be burned. The destruction of most history and philosophy books ran counter to deep currents in Chinese culture but ensured that official policies would have no intellectual competition.

Because of high taxes, incessant demands for forced labor, and the countless deaths and misery caused by the massive building projects, the Qin were unpopular rulers. Their attacks on Confucianism and scholars brought great resentment from much of the educated classes. When Shi Huangdi died in 210 B.C.E., Li Si tried to keep news of his death a secret. Bypassing the more aggressive first son and heir, he installed the more pliable second son as a puppet emperor. However, massive revolts occurred after knowledge of the death of the first emperor became widely known. Li Si was killed in 208 B.C.E. by police, supposedly because he lacked the travel permits his own laws required. The Qin Dynasty survived only four years after the death of its founder.

Following a short period of struggle, the Han Dynasty (206 B.C.E.-220 C.E.), was established. The Han maintained the centralized state structure of the Qin Dynasty but eased the more oppressive facets of the Qin system of governing. The political and social stability that followed, along with the wealth brought by trade, gave China an unparalleled period of peace and prosperity during the height of the Han Dynasty.

SIGNIFICANCE

The Qin Dynasty was short-lived but momentous in the development of the Chinese state. The name *China* itself comes from a corruption of the name *Qin*. The first Qin ruler took the title of emperor, and thus the ascent of the Qin Dynasty marks the beginning of the Chinese empire. The Qin Dynasty ruled China roughly halfway between the origins of Chinese civilization under the perhaps mythical Xia Dynasty (Hsia; c. 2100-1600 B.C.E.) to the present. Under the Qin, Chinese rule extended over most of what is modern-day China, and China began the long practice of establishing tributary relations with neighboring states. The removal of the hereditary nobility from local government ended feudalism in China and allowed the development of a meritocracy under succeeding dynasties.

—*Barry M. Stentiford*

FURTHER READING

Bodde, Derk. *China's First Unifier: A Study of the Ch'in Dynasty as Seen in the Life of Li Ssu*. Hong Kong: Hong Kong University Press, 1967. Bodde focuses on Li as the true architect of the Chinese empire.

Sima, Qian. *Records of the Grand Historian*. Translated by Burton Watson. New York: Columbia University Press, 1995. A traditional Chinese history of pre-Qin, Qin, and early Han China, written by a court historian of the Han Dynasty.

Xuequin, Li, Hsueh-Chain Li, and K. C. Chang, trans. *Eastern Zhou and Qin Civilizations*. Early Chinese Civilizations Series. New Haven, Conn.: Yale University Press, 1986. A good introduction to the chaos of the late Zhou Dynasty and the reaction against that chaos that allowed the oppression during the Qin Dynasty.

Yang, Yuan, and Xiao Ding. *Tales of Emperor Qin Shihuang*. Chicago: Foreign Language Press, 1999. A compilation of surviving official contemporary histories of the first emperor as well as legends and stories of the first emperor from later periods.

Zhongyi, Yuan, et al. *Terra-Cotta Warriors and Horses at the Tomb of Qin Shi Huang*. Beijing: Cultural Relics Publishing House, 1983. Official Chinese government guide to relics excavated from the tomb of the first emperor. This book, with text in both English

and Chinese, is a visually oriented work, filled with color and black-and-white photos of the terra-cotta warriors.

SEE ALSO: 479 B.C.E., Confucius's Death Leads to the Creation of *The Analects*; 475-221 B.C.E., China Enters Chaotic Warring States Period; c. 285-c. 255 B.C.E, Xunzi Develops Teachings That Lead to Legalism; c. 221-211 B.C.E., Building the Great Wall of China; 221-206 B.C.E., Legalist Movement in China; 221 B.C.E.-220 C.E., Advances Are Made in Chinese Agricultural Technology; 140-87 B.C.E., Wudi Rules Han Dynasty China.

RELATED ARTICLES in *Great Lives from History: The Ancient World*: Confucius; Hanfeizi; Shi Huangdi; Xunzi.

c. 221-211 B.C.E.
BUILDING THE GREAT WALL OF CHINA

The Great Wall, a huge fortification constructed along the southern edge of the Mongolian plain, was designed to protect China from the northern barbarians.

LOCALE: Northern China
CATEGORY: Architecture

KEY FIGURE
Shi Huangdi (Shih Huang-ti; 259-210 B.C.E.), first emperor of China, r. 221-210 B.C.E.

SUMMARY OF EVENT
Although reliable records of early Chinese history are scarce, China had developed an agricultural society by 4000 B.C.E. Its northern neighbors, the Mongols, were nomads renowned for their fierceness. As small agricultural enclaves developed in China, it became necessary to defend them from their marauding neighbors to the north. The people living in these enclaves built substantial walls, within which were living accommodations for their residents and fields for cultivation.

The walls built to protect the agricultural villages ranged in height from 15 to 50 feet (5 to 15 meters) and had bases that ranged from 15 to 30 feet (5 to 9 meters). The top, which was a roadway, was wide enough to hold ten or twelve people abreast, usually about 12 feet (4 meters) in width.

The walls had narrow openings through which arrows could be shot. Most of them had elevated watchtowers at frequent intervals and had narrow entrances, seldom more than two in number, protected by heavy gates that were closed at night. Most of the walls were made of earth pounded into solid masses. These earthen outcroppings were framed in wooden planks or bamboo and faced with granite, bricks, or timber, depending on what was readily available.

During the period from about 4000 until about 235 B.C.E., China was not unified politically. In 246 B.C.E., thirteen-year-old Zheng (Cheng) became ruler of the Qin (Ch'in) state, from which China derives its name. This state was strong militarily and had succeeded in repelling the northern barbarians. The state expanded and eventually achieved supremacy.

Zheng, using his strong military forces, was not adverse to employing wholesale slaughter to achieve his ends. Through his authoritarian rule, he succeeded in uniting China before he turned forty and, on becoming emperor, changed his name to Shi Huangdi (first emperor). He imposed a standardized writing system, a uniform system of weights and measures, and standards regarding the width of thoroughfares. He abolished feudal privileges and, in 213 B.C.E., ordered that most books and other remnants of past history be destroyed. In one of the most ruthless crackdowns in ancient history, he reportedly had scholars buried alive so that they could not preserve any of the traditions of the past. Zheng wanted Chinese history to begin with him.

In 221 B.C.E., the emperor began his most ambitious project, that of building the Great Wall of China. Most existing walls were preserved and were attached to other existing walls so that a great structure would stretch for at least 1,500 miles (2,400 kilometers) across northern China. Zheng expected this structure to be impregnable.

Scholar Arthur Waldron points out that the Great Wall that exists today was built in the sixteenth century, during the Ming Dynasty, and is not what the Qin emperor had constructed. The Qin were working with earth rather than stone, and it is believed that much of the first Great Wall may not have survived into the present day. Records

regarding this first wall are minimal, and its actual path and length are difficult to determine. Waldron suggests that estimates of the numbers of workers and amount of labor required to build the wall might be exaggerations meant to demonstrate the ruthlessness of the first Qin emperor.

The Great Wall was called the Wall of Ten Thousand Li, the *li* being a measurement of about one-third of an English mile. This would make the Great Wall more than three thousand miles (about five thousand kilometers) long. Although this calculation was probably an exaggeration at the time of its building, later dynasties added to the structure, increasing its length significantly.

For the Great Wall to provide the protection its builders needed, watchtowers several stories high were placed

The Great Wall of China, as it stands today. (Digital Stock)

strategically along the wall. These watchtowers, each within sight of at least two other watchtowers, were used as beacons to signal each other of imminent threats. It is estimated that more than ten thousand such beacons were linked to each other along the Great Wall. This signaling system was highly developed and efficient.

To bring his vision to fruition, the Qin emperor is believed to have mustered a workforce of about 800,000. A military force exceeding 300,000 was formed to oversee this ambitious and harrowing project. Workers were conscripted from among the nation's criminals, troublemakers, cheats, and those in disfavor with the government. Soon, however, it was obvious that a larger workforce was required, and it became necessary to conscript teachers, scholars, musicians, artists, and others. Many of these workers were forcibly dragged from their homes and set to the strenuous and dangerous task of helping erect a huge wall over incredibly rugged terrain. Much of the wall was built along the edges of China's steepest mountains.

Shi Huangdi was a ruthless and cruel dictator who let nothing stand in the way of his obsession with completing the wall, a project that was finally finished in 211 B.C.E. The human cost of building this huge structure was incalculable. Tens of thousands of laborers were killed in accidents or died from sheer exhaustion. Dead bodies were daily dumped unceremoniously into soil that was then compressed to form the sides of the Great Wall.

Shi Huangdi's rule over a unified China lasted for just eleven years. One year after the Great Wall was completed, he died. His harsh, authoritarian government combined with the heavy taxation required to implement his civic projects, most notably the construction of the Great Wall and the construction of his massive tomb, caused considerable unrest among the citizenry, leading eventually to rebellion. In 206 B.C.E., the Qin Dynasty was overthrown and replaced by the Han Dynasty, which ruled China from 206 B.C.E. until 220 C.E.

DIMENSIONS OF THE FIRST GREAT WALL

Length:	About 1,500 miles (2,400 kilometers)
Average height:	25 feet (about 7.5 meters)
Height range:	15 to 50 feet (4.6 to 15 meters)
Average width at base:	15 to 30 feet (4.6 to 9 meters)
Average width at top:	12 feet (4 meters)
Number of watchtowers:	More than 10,000

SIGNIFICANCE

The construction of the Great Wall of China was, beyond all else, an act of unification. Protective walls existed in China for nearly four millennia before Shi Huangdi grasped power and decreed that all the existing walls be joined into one great wall. The wall would extend from the Liaodong Peninsula in the east to Lintao, some 1,500 miles (2,400 hundred kilometers) to the west. By this act, Shi Huangdi created a protective barrier for the provinces that he had unified as the Qin Dynasty. As a protective barrier, the Great Wall was in its time among the most efficient structures ever conceived of and constructed. The unification taking place at this time extended to demands that the language and writing systems be standardized and that a uniform system of weights and measures be adopted. In many respects, the Qin Dynasty marked the beginning of modern-day China.

—*R. Baird Shuman*

FURTHER READING

Jan, Michel. *The Great Wall of China*. New York: Abbeville Press, 2001. Ably translated from French by Josephine Bacon. Rich with photographs by Roland and Sabrina Michaud. Informative and lucid text.

McNeese, Tim. *The Great Wall of China*. San Diego, Calif.: Lucent Books, 1997. Aimed at a young adult audience. Clear and direct. Illustrations, particularly its maps, are useful.

Poirier, Rene. *Engineering Wonders of the World: The Stories Behind the Greatest Engineering Feats in History*. New York: Random House, 1993. Offers an interesting and useful historical perspective. Shows the Great Wall as the most monumental engineering undertaking ever recorded.

Schwartz, Daniel. *The Great Wall of China*. London: Thames and Hudson, 2001. Attractively presented. Contains 149 duotone photographs, texts by Jorge Luis Borges and Franz Kafka, and Luo Zhewen's informative essay, "The Great Wall in History."

Waldron, Arthur. *The Great Wall: From History to Myth*. New York: Cambridge University Press, 1990. Waldron approaches the traditional stories about the Great Wall with skepticism, pointing out that the current Great Wall was built at a later time and that many of the stories may be later inventions.

SEE ALSO: 221 B.C.E., Qin Dynasty Founded in China; 221 B.C.E.-220 C.E., Advances Are Made in Chinese Agricultural Technology; c. 212-202? B.C.E., Construction of the Qin Tomb; 206 B.C.E., Liu Bang Captures Qin Capital, Founds Han Dynasty.

RELATED ARTICLE in *Great Lives from History: The Ancient World*: Shi Huangdi.

221-206 B.C.E.
LEGALIST MOVEMENT IN CHINA

During the Qin Dynasty, the Legalist movement sought to move Chinese society away from its Confucian tradition toward a philosophy that favored a strict code of justice.

LOCALE: Qin, in eastern China, from modern-day Manchuria to the northern border of modern-day Vietnam

CATEGORIES: Government and politics; philosophy

KEY FIGURES

Shang Yang (d. c. 337 B.C.E.), high adviser to Qin ruler, 359-339 B.C.E.

Shi Huangdi (Shih Huang-ti; 259-210 B.C.E.), first emperor of Qin Dynasty, r. 247-201 B.C.E.

Li Si (Li Ssu; 280?-208 B.C.E.), minister to Shi Huangdi and leader of the Legalists

SUMMARY OF EVENT

Much of ancient Chinese imperial history can be understood through the lens of Confucian political thought and philosophy. The dominance of Confucian beliefs was apparent in the Zhou Dynasty (Chou; 1066-256 B.C.E.). To the west of the Zhou territory, in the state of Qin (Ch'in), arose a new movement that eventually led to the overthrow of the Zhou and the founding of the Qin Dynasty (221-206 B.C.E.). This new political ideology was known as Legalism.

The Legalist movement in China was a reaction to the legal chaos that gripped the country during the Zhou Dynasty. The Legalists attributed this chaos to the Confucian belief in the natural harmony of the society and the practice of dividing power among many local governments. Therefore, the Legalists presented a competing view to that of the Confucians.

Legalists opposed the basis of Confucian law, which assumed that society was naturally harmonious and that it could be governed by a moral authority, or *li*, that would guide everyday actions and prevent people from disrupting this natural harmony. Therefore, Confucians preferred not to threaten or take punitive measures against lawbreakers but rather to rehabilitate criminals and bring them back into the natural harmony of society. Government officials were not to act as punishers but rather as moral guides who would be models on which ordinary citizens could structure their lives. Because of their high positions, government officials were expected to lead more moral lives and serve as examples.

The Confucian idea of *li*, which had a natural law element, differed from the Legalists' view of the origin of laws. Because *li* represented the natural harmony of the universe, there was no need for government officials to enact artificial law codes. Instead, individuals would follow the law that was natural to their existence. Lawbreakers would be educated as to their faults and would reenter society and not disturb the natural harmony. Confucian law also had a distinct hierarchical flavor. Citizens were expected to remain within their political and social classes. Only by staying within those classes would the natural order continue and society flourish.

In contrast, the Legalists viewed law as a creation of humankind. Law was a necessary component of government, which used it to ensure that officials could maintain control of their subjects. Law was also a unifying tool. Confucian law tended to diffuse or spread political power among local feudal governments that would enforce the natural order with little direction from the central government.

Legalist theory and practice was developed by Shang Yang, a high adviser to the Qin leader for two decades. Shang Yang's view of the law favored punitive punishments and equality in the eyes of the law. The Legalists' views were that the law, *fa*, was central to maintaining order in a society. The Legalists believed that group punishment would serve as the best deterrent of criminal acts. People would be placed within groups of ten families who would live within a small area and report on everyone's activities to the authorities. Failure to reveal wrongdoing would bring severe punishment, sometimes death. Shang Yang also applied the law equally to all people without regard to their rank in society.

The end of the Zhou Dynasty and its replacement by the Qin Dynasty caused a sudden shift in the government's approach to law and the means of maintaining control of the population. The Zhou Dynasty had fallen because of the chaos and political divisions that seemed part of the Confucian system. The Legalists wanted to centralize power and, by doing so, to take control of the legal system from local officials and place it in the hands of the emperor. One of the initial actions of the first Qin emperor, Shi Huangdi, was to appoint governors to rule the many provinces. The emperor took power from local Zhou officials and appointed his own governors to various regions. These governors were given the task of imposing Qin legal ideas on the peasants and elite. Accompanying these governors were inspector generals, who reported directly to the emperor and supervised the governors.

Shi Huangdi was aggressive in eliminating the power of the nobility and exerting control over the population. The emperor, along with Li Si, the leader of the Legalists during the early Qin Dynasty, sought a broad-based change in Chinese society. They built roads and defensive walls, regulated the weights and measures of China, and standardized the currency and the writing system. This desire to completely change many basic parts of Chinese society made the old Confucian ideas, which tended to maintain the status quo, dangerous.

To combat the population's adherence to Confucian ideas and establish control over all learning and philosophy, Shi Huangdi developed a totalitarian state that attempted to destroy all the old knowledge and those who taught it. His adviser Li Si ordered the destruction of texts that opposed the Legalist interpretation of the law. Local governors were ordered to conduct mass book burnings and to imprison anyone who refused to destroy the texts or tried to prevent the burnings. The reeducation of Chinese society took a grisly turn when Shi Huangdi ordered that more than four hundred Confucian scholars be buried alive to prevent them from teaching their philosophy to future students. This savagery, although possibly fabricated or exaggerated by later writers, decreased the emperor's popularity and heightened the possibility of revolt if government control ever slackened.

Part of the Legalist plan was the compilation of a law code to be used throughout the empire to establish Qin control over Chinese society. Both Shi Huangdi and Li Si sought strict limitations on individual behavior that would replace the vague commands of Confucian philosophy. Many Chinese disliked the Legalist code, viewing the restrictions to be too great and the punishments too severe.

The Legalists were effective at controlling Chinese society during the reign of Shi Huangdi. However, the emperor's erratic behavior and the brutal means of control used by the Legalists produced greater and greater disenchantment among the people. The crashing of a meteor—a natural disaster usually interpreted as a prediction of a change in government leadership—was met by Shi Huangdi's orders to execute those who opposed him. Shi Huangdi died shortly after this, and the Qin Dynasty was shaken by a series of revolts and the execution of Li Si by the new emperor. The Legalists' program ended with the death of the chief minister in 208

B.C.E., and the Qin were replaced by the Han Dynasty (206 B.C.E.-220 c.e.).

SIGNIFICANCE

The Legalist movement was tied closely to the Qin Dynasty. This dynasty, which marked the beginning of the imperial period in Chinese history, ended the chaos that had broken out during the Zhou Dynasty. The Legalist movement sought to expand the central power of the Chinese government and to change the Confucian tradition in law and politics. Led by imperial adviser Li Si, the Legalists in the Qin Dynasty attempted to rewrite history and enforce a strict code of conduct backed up with harsh punishments.

Although the Qin Dynasty was short-lived and the Legalists' control of government fell with the dynasty, the movement and its philosophy continued through subsequent dynasties, challenging the Confucian ideal. The Legalists had a modernizing influence on ancient China and continued this role, working in opposition to the feudal system of government throughout the many dynasties that followed.

—*Douglas Clouatre*

FURTHER READING

Chin, Rinn-Sup, and Robert Worden. *China: A Country Study*. Washington, D.C.: U.S. Government Printing Office, 1988. An overall view of China that presents the historical background.

De Bary, William Theodore. *Sources of Chinese Tradition*. New York: Columbia University Press, 2001. A compilation of original sources that contains information on the Qin Dynasty and Legalism.

Fu, Zhongyuan. *China's Legalists: The Earliest Totalitarians and Their Art of Ruling*. New York: M. E. Sharpe, 1996. An analysis of Legalism and how it worked as a system of government.

Graham, A. C. Graham. *Disputers of the Tao: Philosophical Arguments in Ancient China*. New York: Open Court Publishing, 1999. An examination of ancient Chinese philosophy, including Confucianism and Legalism.

Han Feizi. *Han Feizi: Basic Writings*. Translated by Burton Watson. New York: Columbia University Press, 2003.

Loewe, Michael. *Cambridge Encyclopedia of China*. New York: Cambridge University Press, 2001. A general reference on China with information on Legalism, Confucianism, and the Qin Dynasty.

Maisels, Charles Keith. *Early Civilizations of the Old*

World: The Formative Histories of Egypt, the Levant, Mesopotamia, India, and China. London: Routledge Press, 2001. A history of the ancient world that includes China.

221 B.C.E.-220 C.E.
ADVANCES ARE MADE IN CHINESE AGRICULTURAL TECHNOLOGY

The short-lived Qin Dynasty and the following four-hundred-year Han Dynasty brought significant technological advancements and government policies relating to agriculture that affected China for two thousand years.

LOCALE: China
CATEGORY: Agriculture

KEY FIGURES
Shi Huangdi (Shih Huang-ti; 259-210 B.C.E.), emperor of the Qin Dynasty, r. 221-210 B.C.E.
Liu Bang (Liu Pang; 256-195 B.C.E.), founder and first emperor of the Han Dynasty, r. 206-195 B.C.E.
Wang Mang (45 B.C.E.-23 C.E.), emperor of the Xin Dynasty, r. 9-23 C.E.

SUMMARY OF EVENT
The period preceding the Qin Dynasty (Ch'in; 221-206 B.C.E.) in China was called the Chan-kuo (Ch'an K'uo), or Warring States Period (475-221 B.C.E.). All Chan-kuo states used iron for implements and weapons and irrigated and fertilized crops. These iron implements were crude but vastly superior for clearing and tilling land than their stone and wooden predecessors. The largest irrigation systems were found in the state of Qin, but extensive irrigation projects were not widespread until the Qin Dynasty and Han Dynasty (206 B.C.E.-220 C.E.). During the Chan-kuo period, suitable crops were matched to the soil and seasons, and rice was grown only in the southern region, which had naturally flooded fields.

Social and political reforms instituted by the ruler of the state of Qin, under the guidance of his adviser, Shang Yang (d. c. 337 B.C.E.), proved to be powerful catalysts for its eventual supremacy, which ended the Warring States Period. Allowing the private ownership of land made small family farmers economically important and transformed a feudalistic society into a strong, centralized monarchy. Qin military power was enhanced by giving public lands to immigrants so that they could create small farms, which allowed citizen and immigrant farmers the time to enhance their social status through military service. In 221 B.C.E., Qin prevailed over the other Chan Kuo states and established the Qin Dynasty, China's first unified empire. Shi Huangdi, the first emperor of the Qin Dynasty, extended the reforms of the state of Qin to the entire country. The effective strategy of using the productivity of free land-owning small farmers, who could advance economically and socially, to support the centralized imperial administration was adopted by the ensuing Han Dynasty and used for generations.

Liu Bang, a peasant warrior, defeated the Qin Dynasty in 206 B.C.E. and established the Han Dynasty, renaming himself Gaozu. This empire endured for more than four hundred years, interrupted briefly by the Xin (Hsin) Dynasty from 9 through 23 C.E. After seven disruptive years of civil war, the masses of dislocated citizens were encouraged to return to their areas of origin. The emperor proclaimed that their land and homes would be returned to them and that other citizens of merit would be given land and homes. Then the slow process of increasing agricultural productivity to prewar levels began.

The Han Dynasty was divided into the Western Han Dynasty (206 B.C.E.-23 C.E.) and the Eastern Han Dynasty (25-220 C.E.). The population at least doubled, and possibly quadrupled, during the Western Han period. Early in this period, population growth-related pressures prompted influential citizens to petition the government to enact policy initiatives designed to increase agricultural productivity. These entreaties were mostly ignored by Han emperors for more than a hundred years. Farmers were moving to cities in large numbers to pursue more lucrative occupations, which had the effect of slowing the pace of agricultural improvements. When the government did force the relocation of masses of urban dwellers back to farms starting in 178 B.C.E., when land was still available in all parts of the empire, the people were moved to the northern and northwestern frontiers for defense purposes rather than to the south, where their farms would have been more productive. By 140 B.C.E., available arable land was scarce, and the government opened up public land to farmers, which bore positive results for some time, but by the end of the Western Han Dynasty, this land was exhausted.

Farming in the Han Dynasty was initially based on the Qin Dynasty model, which emphasized mostly small farms that used some irrigation and fertilization but more often matched crops to natural soil conditions and employed crudely made iron implements and relatively primitive methods of tilling and sowing fields with a limited number of crops. Throughout the two Han Dynasties, new crops were added, providing Han farmers with several cereals, including beans, rice, barley, oats, wheat, and millet; a number of vegetables; and cash crops such as hemp, indigo, sesame, mulberries, and gourds. These farms became increasingly well organized and productive as crop rotation and intensive agricultural techniques and implements were developed.

As the first century B.C.E. progressed, population growth in the capital district and the increasing demand for crops such as rice and wheat that required a great deal of water led to official policies that called for and publicly supported the creation of irrigation systems. Fifty-six water control projects for irrigation and land reclamation have been documented during the Han Dynasty. The largest were created by imperial proclamation and involved tens of thousands of laborers working for years. Smaller systems were built by local administrations and private investors. These systems spread throughout the country. Han irrigation projects utilized advanced engineering technology for dam building, complex networks of troughs and trenches in fields, and siphons, water wheels, and other mechanical devices for raising water from lower to higher levels. Archaeological evidence indicates that eventually every Han household had a well with a sophisticated system for drawing water and a water tank with an opening into an irrigation ditch.

Two new dry-farming and one new wet-rice-farming technique contributed to much higher productivity for Han farmers. The *dai tian* (*tai-t'ien*) method of "ridge farming" involved plowing to produce trenches, or furrows, with the removed dirt piled beside them, creating ridges. Seeds were then planted in the furrows, and the dirt was gradually pushed back in as the plants grew. This technique was far more successful than sowing large amounts of seed on a flat field, because less seed was required, moisture was held in the furrows, and plants got more sun and were protected from the wind. The *ou zhong* (*ou chung*) method of "pit farming" involved digging small square pits on plots of land and growing well-irrigated and well-fertilized crops in them. This method made it possible to farm land that was marginal or too small for conventional plowing and reportedly resulted in dramatically increased yields. In the northern regions, improved crop yields were realized by growing rice seedlings in a nursery while other crops were grown and harvested, then planting the seedlings in the fields, which were flooded through irrigation, and harvesting the rice after a short growing season.

Available evidence indicates that most of the agricultural implements of the Western Han Dynasty were made of cast iron and were relatively small and fragile. By the Eastern Han Dynasty, apparently there had been a major breakthrough in iron technology, including the invention of the water-driven bellows, resulting in greatly improved high-grade wrought-iron implements during this period. Han plows came to be produced in many sizes and were made of materials and with new designs that made deeper plowing and the use of new farming methods such as *dai tian* practical. The government-owned iron foundries produced and distributed other high-quality implements, such as various configurations of sickles, spades, and hoes, that were necessary for maximizing agricultural output.

Citizens of the Eastern Han Dynasty apparently enjoyed a higher standard of living than their Western Han predecessors because of these advances in agricultural technology. Gaozu, Han's first emperor, encouraged land investment and created the trend of landlords controlling larger and larger areas of land, which caused privately owned farms to become rarer. Land reform initiatives in the late Western period and by Emperor Wang Mang during the Xin Dynasty were too late; thwarted by the politically powerful landlords, who also had their land removed from the tax rolls. The private ownership of family farms had once been a source of political stability, but the increasingly overtaxed peasants rebelled in 184 C.E., creating a period of civil wars that culminated in the fall of the last Han Dynasty in 220 C.E.

SIGNIFICANCE

Qin and Han Dynasty agricultural technological advancements avoided what would surely have been disastrous imbalances between food supplies and the growing population. Moreover, it was impossible for citizens during this period to have imagined what an enormous impact these developments would have on every period to follow, up to modern times. Many of these innovations—in irrigation, tilling, sowing, specialized implements, and rice growing—are still used today in China's struggle to feed a population in excess of one billion people.

—*Jack Carter*

FURTHER READING

Hsu, Cho-yun. "The Changing Relationship Between Local Society and the Central Political Power in Former Han 206 B.C.-8 A.D." *Comparative Studies in Society and History* 7, no. 4 (1965). Examines the effect of government policies on the general populace, including laws against entrepreneurs and the rise of landlordism.

_____. *Han Agriculture: The Formation of Early Chinese Agrarian Economy (206 B.C.-A.D. 220)*. Seattle: University of Washington Press, 1980. A detailed and well-documented history of the government's attempts to increase agricultural productivity during the Han Dynasty and the resulting technological developments and sociopolitical changes. Includes maps, illustrations, documents, and Chinese and Western-language bibliographies.

Wang, Zhongshu. *Han Civilization*. New Haven, Conn.: Yale University Press, 1982. A comprehensive treatment of the archaeological findings from the Han Dynasty. Includes a chapter on Han agriculture with numerous figures, an index, and a bibliography.

Yu, Ying-shih. *Trade and Expansion in Han China: A Study in the Structure of Sino-Barbarian Economic Relations*. Berkeley: University of California Press, 1967. In focusing on Han Dynasty foreign and economic policy, this work discusses agricultural and industrial advancements. Includes maps, a glossary, an index, and a bibliography.

SEE ALSO: 221 B.C.E., Qin Dynasty Founded in China; c. 221-211 B.C.E., Building the Great Wall of China; c. 212-202? B.C.E., Construction of the Qin Tomb; 206 B.C.E., Liu Bang Captures Qin Capital, Founds Han Dynasty; 140-87 B.C.E., Wudi Rules Han Dynasty China.

RELATED ARTICLE in *Great Lives from History: The Ancient World*: Shi Huangdi.

218-201 B.C.E.
SECOND PUNIC WAR

The Second Punic War allowed Rome to incorporate the Iberian Peninsula into the Roman Empire and paved the way for Roman domination of the western Mediterranean.

LOCALE: Iberian Peninsula

CATEGORIES: Wars, uprisings, and civil unrest; expansion and land acquisition

KEY FIGURES

Hamilcar Barca (c. 275-winter 229/228 B.C.E.), Carthaginian general, father of Hannibal and Hasdrubal Barca

Hasdrubal (d. 221 B.C.E.), Carthaginian general, son-in-law of Hamilcar Barca

Hannibal (247-182 B.C.E.), Carthaginian general

Hasdrubal Barca (d. 207 B.C.E.), Carthaginian general

Gnaeus Cornelius Scipio (d. 211 B.C.E.), Roman consul and general, brother of Publius Cornelius Scipio

Publius Cornelius Scipio (d. 211 B.C.E.), Roman consul and general

Scipio Africanus (236-184/183 B.C.E.), Roman proconsul and general, son of Publius Cornelius Scipio

SUMMARY OF EVENT

By 275 B.C.E., Rome controlled the Italian peninsula. The Romans then began to acquire an empire around the Mediterranean. Their expansion south brought them within 3 miles (5 kilometers) of Sicily, where Carthage, a major power situated on the Bay of Tunis on the north coast of Africa, was contending with Greek colonists for control. Its strategic location at the narrowest part of the Mediterranean helped Carthage develop into a great commercial state.

To protect and expand its commercial interest, Carthage built one of the largest navies of the time and expanded to include North Africa from Bengazi to Gibraltar, Spain, Portugal, Corsica, the Balearic Islands, and parts of Sicily. With the capture of Malta, the people of Carthage were able to exclude the Greeks, their great-

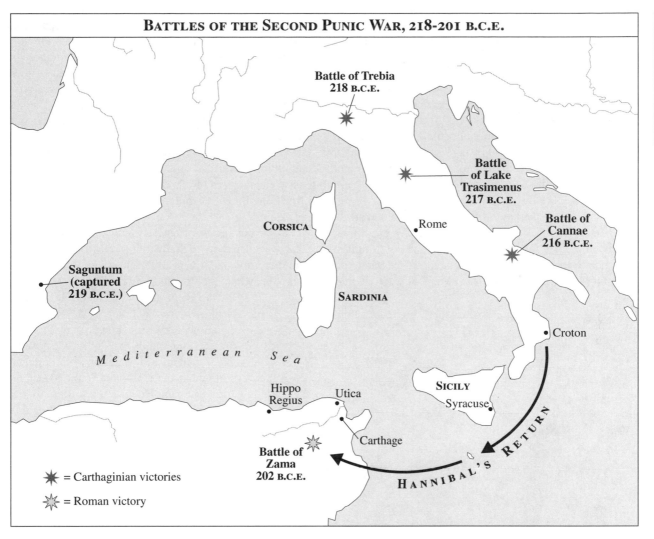

BATTLES OF THE SECOND PUNIC WAR, 218-201 B.C.E.

Battle of Trebia
218 B.C.E.

Battle of Lake Trasimenus
217 B.C.E.

Battle of Cannae
216 B.C.E.

CORSICA

Rome

Saguntum
(captured
219 B.C.E.)

SARDINIA

Croton

Mediterranean Sea

Hippo Regius

Utica

SICILY

Syracuse

Carthage

Battle of Zama
202 B.C.E.

HANNIBAL'S RETURN

= Carthaginian victories

= Roman victory

---

est commercial and colonial rivals, from the western Mediterranean.

Carthage forced the captured peoples to become tribute-paying subjects and failed to win friends and allies as Rome had done in Italy. This unwise policy caused Carthage enormous difficulties and helps explain its defeat. During the wars with Rome, revolts broke out among Carthage's subject peoples in North Africa and Spain. Even the wealth and commercial domination of Carthage were not enough to fight both internal uprisings and Rome.

Other problems contributing to the Carthaginian defeat resulted from its political and military institutions. Carthage was an oligarchic republic dominated by a small group of wealthy men who were greedy and corrupt. The Carthaginian army was composed of conscripted soldiers from the empire. Their loyalty was questionable. Additionally, Carthaginian generals who won too many battles were considered dangerous and punished, but generals who lost battles were sometimes nailed to the cross. Only the navy, manned by Carthaginians and commanded by experts, was excellent.

During the First Punic War (264-225 B.C.E.), Rome had defeated Carthage, forcing it to surrender Sicily and to pay an indemnity. Carthage's sea power and its control of the western Mediterranean were lost. Rome became a major sea power and also became politically involved in the western Mediterranean.

Following the war, Rome distrusted Carthage and continued its own imperial expansion. Carthage resented its defeat at the hands of Rome and wanted to regain its former position. To achieve this goal, Carthage turned to

Spain as a source of money, men, and supplies. Under the leadership of Hamilcar Barca, general of the Carthaginian army during the First Punic War, and his son-in-law Hasdrubal, Carthage extended its control over most of the Iberian Peninsula south of the Ebro River. Hannibal, eldest son of Hamilcar Barca, took command in Spain after Hasdrubal was assassinated in 221 B.C.E. He continued the Iberian campaign until only the city of Saguntum (Sargunto), a trading partner of Rome's ally Massilia (Marseille), remained. In 219 B.C.E., Hannibal captured Saguntum, and the Second Punic War (218-201 B.C.E.) began.

Hannibal had one large, loyal, and well-trained army but had no navy. Roman naval superiority prevented Carthage from transporting large amounts of supplies and men to the Iberian Peninsula and enabled Rome to establish beachheads when and where it wanted. Be-

cause Hannibal had only one army and only Spain as a supply base, he chose to create a single front, preferably in Italy. As long as the city of Rome was in danger, the Romans would be forced to concentrate most of their power in Italy. Hannibal also believed that an invasion of Italy would break up the Roman Confederation, and the Roman allies in central and southern Italy would join him against their Roman overlords. Sometime around May 1, 218 B.C.E., Hannibal left New Carthage (Cartagena) with about forty thousand infantry, six thousand cavalry, and sixty elephants to invade Italy. He had crossed the Ebro River, the Pyrenees, and the Rhone River by the middle of August.

Rome planned an offensive war using its naval power. Rome sent an army to Sicily to invade Africa and landed another army under Consul Publius Cornelius Scipio at Massilia, where the Roman army could either invade the Iberian Peninsula or intercept Hannibal in Gaul (modern-day France). The Roman occupation of Massilia, however, was too late to stop Hannibal. When Publius discovered that he had missed Hannibal, he ordered his brother Gnaeus Cornelius Scipio to lead the army to Spain. He returned to Italy to lead the two legions in Cisalpine Gaul against Hannibal as he crossed the Alps.

It is not known what pass Hannibal used to cross the Alps. None of the passes would have been easy, and he lost approximately one-third of his forces to dangerous terrain, deep snow, and the attacks of mountain tribes. When he reached the plain of northern Italy, Hannibal had about twenty-six thousand infantry, four thousand cavalry, and twenty elephants. Nevertheless, the Carthaginians fought well. Between 216 and 212 B.C.E., the Romans suffered a series of defeats that forced them to give up temporarily the idea of invading Africa. In 217 B.C.E., Rome gained control of the coastal waters off Spain and prevented the Carthaginians from using Spain as a supply base or from sending reinforcements to Hannibal in Italy. Hannibal could not win new allies in Italy nor protect those cities that had gone over to him, but he continued to fight in Italy until he was recalled to Carthage to stop the invasion Rome began in 204 B.C.E.

Spain was one of the major areas of the war both on land and sea. In 215 B.C.E., the

A battle in the Second Punic War. (Library of Congress)

Scipio brothers defeated Hasdrubal Barca near Iberia. Two years later, the recall of Hasdrubal to Africa to put down a Numidian revolt gave Rome an even greater opportunity to strengthen its position. Many Spaniards went over to Rome. When Hasdrubal returned shortly after Rome captured Saguntum in 211 B.C.E., the Spaniards deserted Rome, and the Carthaginians defeated the Roman army. Publius and Gnaeus were killed in separate battles.

In 210 B.C.E., Scipio Africanus was appointed proconsul and given command of the Roman forces in Spain. He reformed battle tactics and adopted the better weapons of Spain—the short sword and probably the javelin. After extensive training, his army became a more efficient battle force. In 209 B.C.E., New Carthage was captured, giving Rome a strategically located stronghold, money, ships, supplies, weapons, and the ten thousand Spanish hostages held by the Carthaginians. Scipio Africanus earned substantial good will by allowing these hostages to return home with part of the loot. Hasdrubal was defeated in 208 B.C.E., but managed to escape with his army. He joined his brother Hannibal in Italy. Scipio defeated the remaining Carthaginian generals, who were quarreling with each other. By 207 B.C.E., Carthaginian power in Spain was gone, and Rome decided to retain the peninsula to prevent any nation from using the area as a base to invade Italy. Rome also wanted Iberian wealth to help pay for the war.

Rome had difficulty subduing Spain. There were no large kingdoms or states that could be held responsible for collecting taxes or maintaining order. The interior had not been effectively controlled by Carthage or even explored. The tribes in the interior had long raided the richer and more civilized areas controlled by Carthage and now by Rome. Rome had to conquer the peninsula to actually control it or to benefit from its wealth.

Spain was divided by mountains into many small communities and separated clans. Communications and access were difficult. Rome could not conquer the tribes in a few battles. Even though the Second Punic War ended in 201 B.C.E., the Spaniards continued to fight the Romans until 133 B.C.E., and even then Spain was not fully subdued.

SIGNIFICANCE

Although Rome won the Second Punic War, the conditions of its treaty with Carthage were punitive and soon led to Carthaginian discontent. Fifty years after the end of the Second Punic War, the Third Punic War broke out when Carthage rearmed itself, against the terms of its treaty with Rome, and attempted to win back what it had

lost. However, by this time Carthage was a spent force and was defeated so roundly that the Romans leveled the city and, according to tradition, sowed the site of Carthage with salt to prevent anything from ever growing there again.

The Punic Wars were seminal in setting Rome on the road to an empire. By defeating one of the largest trading empires in the world, Rome acquired its commercial interests and had to develop a bureaucracy to administer its new possessions or else lose them to the next aggressor.

—*Robert D. Talbott*

FURTHER READING

Crawford, Michael. *The Roman Republic*. 2d ed. Cambridge, Mass.: Harvard University Press, 1993. Places the conquest of Spain in the context of the Roman expansion into the eastern and western Mediterranean. Includes a list of important dates.

Daly, Gregory. *Cannae: The Experience of Battle in the Second Punic War*. New York: Routledge, 2001. The Battle of Cannae, in which Hannibal defeated the much larger Roman army, has become known as one of the most strategically important and destructive battles of the ancient world. This account both covers the technical aspects of the battle and provides a vivid picture of the experience of war from the soldier's point of view.

Hoyos, B. D. *Unplanned Wars: The Origins of the First and Second Punic Wars*. New York: Walter de Gruyter, 1998. Provides the political background to the Punic Wars in extensive detail. Maps, bibliography, and indexes.

Lazenby, J. F. *Hannibal's War: A Military History of the Second Punic War*. Reprint. Norman: University of Oklahoma Press, 2001. A detailed history of the campaigns of the war, focusing on the battle of military wits between Hannibal and Scipio.

Prevas, John. *Hannibal Crosses the Alps: The Invasion of Italy and the Second Punic War*. New York: DaCapo Press, 2001. Focuses on the logistics of Hannibal's transalpine invasion. Includes a list of key figures, a chronology, a select bibliography, and index.

SEE ALSO: 264-225 B.C.E., First Punic War; c. 250 B.C.E., Discoveries of Archimedes; 202 B.C.E., Battle of Zama; 149-146 B.C.E., Third Punic War; 439 C.E., Vandals Seize Carthage.

RELATED ARTICLES in *Great Lives from History: The Ancient World*: Hamilcar Barca; Hannibal; Scipio Africanus.

c. 212-202? B.C.E.
CONSTRUCTION OF THE QIN TOMB

The Qin tomb and its army of terra-cotta warriors were created to represent the power of the first emperor of unified China.

LOCALE: Near Xi'an, Shaanxi Province, China
CATEGORY: Architecture

KEY FIGURES
Shi Huangdi (Shih Huang-ti; 259-210 B.C.E.), first
    emperor of China, r. 221-210 B.C.E., oversaw
    construction of the Qin tomb
Hu Hai (fl. third century B.C.E.), Shi Huangdi's son,
    who became emperor after his father's death, r. 210-
    206? B.C.E.

SUMMARY OF EVENT
Zheng (who became Shi Huangdi after becoming emperor) was born the son of the king of Qin state. After his father's death, at the age of thirteen, Zheng became king and began a crusade to reform China. By 221 B.C.E., Qin's armies had conquered the six other primary Chinese states, unifying China for the first time in its history. Zheng, now Shi Huangdi, emperor of the Qin Dynasty (Ch'in; 221-206 B.C.E.), further unified the country by deposing the remaining feudal warlords, establishing a system of prefectures administered by government officials appointed from the Qin capital, codified Chinese law, introduced standard weights and measures, issued a single national currency, and formulated a single written Chinese alphabet and language. To protect his newly unified nation, Shi Huangdi began the construction of a defensive barrier along the northern frontier, known as the Great Wall (some scholars believe that this wall is not the same as the Great Wall that stands today, which was constructed in the sixteenth century, during the Ming Dynasty).

Aside from his achievements, Shi Huangdi exhibited a streak of paranoia, megalomania, and tyranny. Proud of his national achievements, Zheng had proclaimed himself a deity, calling himself Shi Huangdi (first emperor), signifying that he had surpassed the achievements and status of the three previous emperors (San Huang) and the five great emperors of Chinese mythology (Wudi). To fulfill this grand new title, Shi Huangdi pursued a quest for immortality to ensure his status as a living god, employing medicine men, prophets, and necromancers to achieve eternal life. Qin also became obsessed with death and the representation of his achievements after his pass-

ing. As a monument to his accomplishments, Qin began construction of his tomb the same year that he unified China, presumably knowing that the grand structure would take years to complete. He chose a site in his native province for his tomb, in what is now the modern province of Shaanxi. The tomb occupies a small valley with Lishan Mountain to the south and the Weihe River to the north. Ancient historical records indicate that royal officials assembled as many as 700,000 workers to work on the tomb complex. Although construction began early in Qin's reign, the tomb was incomplete when Qin died at the age of fifty, in 210 B.C.E. Qin's son, Hu Hai, continued construction on the tomb for an additional two years, but the unpopularity of his father soon led to Hu Hai's assassination and the end of the Qin Dynasty.

The Qin tomb is the central structure in a massive funerary complex, surrounded by other facilities paying homage to the great emperor. Descriptions of the complex appear in *Shiji* (first century B.C.E.; *Records of the Grand Historian of China*, 1960, rev. ed. 1993), a history of China compiled by the historian Sima Qian a century after Shi Huangdi's death. Sima Qian recorded that the tomb was the center of what represented an idealized Chinese city. The historian described the mausoleum as constructed of waterproof vermilion stone and flanked by large treasure rooms. The ceiling depicted celestial vistas, and the walls portrayed rural scenes on one side and views of the capital city of Qin on the other. The central chamber contained a large stone sarcophagus holding Shi Huangdi's remains, surrounded by a stream of mercury representing a silvery river. In addition to Shi Huangdi's remains, there may be bodies of others in this main chamber. According to legend, Hu Hai entombed many of the tomb's workers alive within the chamber to protect its secrets. Another story states that Hu Hai had all of Qin's concubines who had yet to bear a child entombed with the emperor. Protecting the mausoleum was a dirt mound, constructed with loess soil dredged from the Weihe River, 390 feet (120 meters) high (although erosion has reduced the mound to about 213 feet, or 65 meters), covered with trees and plants to resemble a small mountain. Historians are unclear about the purpose of the dirt mound. One theory is that the mound hid the tomb from prospective robbers; and another that the mound is consistent with the ancient concept of *qi* (*ch'i*), maintaining harmony by avoiding stark contrasts or disruptions with the natural world.

Surrounding the tomb are two rings of walls. The inner wall measures 1,482 yards (1,355 meters) along the east-west axis by 635 yards (580 meters) along the north-south axis. The outer wall extends 2,370 yards (2,165 meters) by 1,030 yards (940 meters). Within the walls were structures to support and emphasize the tomb structure, placed to indicate their importance and hierarchy. An imperial palace structure existed north of the tomb, intended to house royal visitors to the great mausoleum. Little of the structure remains, but fragments of hipped roofs, royal red tile, and a foundation atop an elaborate internal plumbing system indicate its purpose. The imperial gardens stretched to the west of the tomb. Covering dozens of acres, the gardens extended past the inner defensive wall and to the edge of the outer wall. Small temples to lesser deities dotted the imperial garden, but the largest structure, the Yue Fu, served as a conservatory to house the royal musicians and as an outdoor concert hall.

Surrounding the garden and tomb were a series of sacrificial trenches. To the west, the trenches generally contained the largest and most expensive offerings, such as luxury goods, weapons, armor, and chariots. Within the inner wall on the east side of the tomb were trenches for animal sacrifices. Because of their importance, horses represent the most common sacrifice, with artifact fragments indicating the animal's place of sacrifice. Attendants slaughtered the offerings in the "middle stable," "palace stable," or "left stable" depending on the status of the donor. Figurines of stable boys flanked each of the "stable" trenches, ceremoniously accepting the gift to the emperor. Outside of the inner wall, other trenches served as sacrificial sites for the lower classes. The contents of these trenches contained a variety of smaller animals, some in figurine form but others real animals encased in small earthen caskets.

Filling the remaining space within the inner wall were many auxiliary tombs for lesser members of the royal family. The largest cluster of tombs existed to the east of the main tomb and housed the remains of twenty-eight members of the royal family. According to legend, these twenty-eight represent Hu Hai's siblings, who he had killed and buried along with their father to ensure his

These terra-cotta warriors were buried in rows to guard the Qin emperor after death. (Corbis)

claim to the throne. The largest auxiliary tomb houses the remains of Gao, Hu's brother and main competitor for the throne. Outside of the inner wall, tombs of the upper class surround the inner complex, while large primitive tomb pits outside the outer wall contain the remains of slaves and the lower class.

The most famous element of the Qin tomb, however, existed beyond the eastern walls. In 1974, workers digging a well uncovered a buried army of terra-cotta warriors in combat formation silently protecting the tomb. Since then, archaeologists have found two other buried formations. Excavations have revealed more than eight thousand figures, and more may remain undiscovered. The life-size warriors represent all ranks, social classes, and branches of service, including horses for the cavalry. Artisans could mass produce the figures by using a standardized mold for the limbs and torso, attaching the parts with a ceramic glaze. The heads, however, are unique to each figure, leading to speculation that the terra-cotta army represented real soldiers from the Qin era. The Chinese practice of burying symbolic figures with an emperor had the practical application of honoring the emperor without destroying those vital to the next ruler. The *Records of the Grand Historian of China* recorded that when Duke Mu died in 621 B.C.E., his successor entombed 177 of Mu's ministers and civil servants with him, severely damaging the efficiency of the Chinese government. Hence, the symbolic burial of servants and protectors became a more practical alternative.

SIGNIFICANCE

The construction of the Qin tomb represented a physical manifestation of not only the majesty of the Qin court but also of the new China. By surpassing the construction efforts of earlier rulers, the Qin emperor's tomb created a statement in stone that a new China existed, united under his rule, which surpassed the greatness of that of any pre-vious Chinese ruler. After the construction of the complex, the symbolism of the tomb, along with its mythology, provided a central reference point for Chinese history. Although the political capitals of China may change and the dynasties come and go, the first centralized Chinese government, symbolized by the Qin tomb, marked the beginning of China as a nation, rather than China as a divided people. As a physical structure, the Qin tomb is a notable achievement. However, as a symbol, the Qin tomb marked a milestone in Chinese history.

—*Steven J. Ramold*

FURTHER READING

Capon, Edmund. *Qin Shi Huang: Terracotta Warriors and Horses*. Sydney, Australia: International Cultural Corporation, 1983. A basic study of the terra-cotta army defending the Qin tomb.

Cotterell, Arthur. *Qin: The First Emperor of China*. New York: Penguin, 1989. A history of China's first emperor concentrating on his personality and rise to power.

Guiso, R. W. L. *The First Emperor of China*. New York: Birch Lane, 1989. A history of the first Chinese emperor from a broad Chinese cultural viewpoint.

Lazo, Caroline E. *The Terra Cotta Army of Emperor Qin*. Toronto: New Discovery Books, 1993. An advanced archaeological study of the terra-cotta army written from a more scientific and technical approach.

SEE ALSO: 221 B.C.E., Qin Dynasty Founded in China; c. 221-211 B.C.E., Building the Great Wall of China; 221 B.C.E.-220 C.E., Advances Are Made in Chinese Agricultural Technology; 206 B.C.E., Liu Bang Captures Qin Capital, Founds Han Dynasty; 140-87 B.C.E., Wudi Rules Han Dynasty China.
RELATED ARTICLES in *Great Lives from History: The Ancient World*: Shi Huangdi; Sima Qian.

209-174 B.C.E.
MAODUN CREATES A LARGE CONFEDERATION IN CENTRAL ASIA

*Maodun, leader of the Xiongnu, created a powerful
nomadic empire on the Eurasian steppe that engaged
in numerous battles with the Chinese.*

LOCALE: Mongolia, Eastern Siberia, East Turkestan,
Northern China, and Central Asia.

CATEGORY: Expansion and land acquisition; wars,
uprisings, and civil unrest

KEY FIGURES

Touman (T'ou-man; fl. third century B.C.E.), shanyu of
the Xiongnu Empire, 220-209 B.C.E.

Maodun (Mao-tun; fl. late third-second centuries B.C.E.),
shanyu of the Xiongnu Empire, 209-174 B.C.E.

Chi-Chih (Lao Shang; fl. second century B.C.E.),
shanyu of the Xiongnu Empire, 174-160 B.C.E.

Shi Huangdi (Shih Huang-ti; 259-210 B.C.E.), first
Chinese emperor and founder of Qin Dynasty,
r. 221-210 B.C.E.

Liu Bang (Liu Pang; 256-195 B.C.E.), Chinese emperor
and founder of the first Han Dynasty, r. 206-195 B.C.E.

SUMMARY OF EVENT

Maodun was the leader of an empire of pastoral nomads
called the Xiongnu (Hsiung-nu), who originated in the
Ordos region of the Eurasian steppes. One of many Mongolian tribes, they lived in tents and wagons and were
very militant. Called Asiatic Huns by the Turks, the
Xiongnu were a mixture of many tribes, both Turkic and
Mongol. Although their origins are shrouded in mystery,
the Chinese first encountered them in 318 B.C.E., when
they defeated an army of the Zhou emperor at the Battle
of Northern Xiansi (Hsien-ssi). They frequently raided
China in the fourth and third centuries B.C.E., during the
Warring States Period (475-221 B.C.E.), until Qin em-
peror Shi Huangdi completed the construction of the first
Great Wall to protect his people from those raiders. The
Xiongnu also threatened other regions of Asia, including
Dzungaria and the Altai Siberians.

Touman, Maodun's father, was probably responsible
for completing the task of organizing the Xiongnu into a
coherent state about 210 B.C.E. Assuming the title of
shanyu, meaning high chieftain, he took lands away from
the Chinese, enabling his tribespeople to use the grassy
plains for their herds. The territorial base was Mongolia
and the Xiongnu state lasted until the middle of the first
century C.E. Touman's primary attention was westward,

but standing in his way was another powerful nomadic
people called the Yuezhi (Yüeh-chih). To appease those
people, he sent them his own son, Maodun, as a hostage.
Touman marched on the Yuezhi, but it is possible that this
action was only a feint because his new wife had given
birth to another son and was hostile to Maodun.

At any rate, Maodun was able to escape, and on his return, he was given an army of ten thousand horsemen.
Then, during a training hunt, Maodun "accidentally"
killed his father with an arrow in 209 B.C.E. The traditional story is that while training his soldiers, he compelled them to shoot at whatever object he pointed toward, whether it be one of his own consorts or the favored
horse of the shanyu. Therefore, when he pointed at his
father, his soldiers instinctively obeyed his command.
Whether the result of an accident or vengeance, Maodun
attained the title of shanyu of the Xiongnu, later earning
the sobriquet Tanhu (T'an-hu), meaning "the magnificent."

Soon after his elevation as leader, Maodun launched a
successful war on neighboring nomads called the
Tonghu (T'ung-hu) in 208 B.C.E. Fearing that his forces
would be outnumbered by the Tonghu, he allowed his foe
to impose tribute on his people in an effort to relax their
defenses. His feigned weakness was successful, because
the Tonghu succumbed to a surprise attack. After his
Tonghu campaign, he defeated other tribes living in
northern Mongolia, called the Ting-Lings. Having unified the lands of the Ordos, he turned to the southwest to
defeat his former jailors, the Yuezhi, in 203 B.C.E. This
latter triumph enabled Maodun to gain control of the
wealth from the Silk Road. From these farming communities in the oases of the Tarim basin, he received grain,
fruit, and animal feed, and from the defeated nomads, he
gained herds of cattle, sheep, and horses. Within a few
years, he was able to accomplish all this and even recaptured territories seized by the Chinese.

Where his father established a state, Maodun created a
steppe empire. The Xiongnu posed a difficulty for the
Chinese armies because they had no walled cities and
were constantly moving in search of water and pastures,
engaging only slightly in farming. At Pancheng (P'an-
ch'eng) in 201 B.C.E., Maodun employed the tactic of
feigned retreat, divided his foe, and surrounded the army
of Gaodi (Liu Bang), the Chinese emperor, who was
compelled to negotiate a treaty. This culminated a three-
year war with the Han Dynasty of China, as Gaodi was

forced to pay yearly tributes to the Xiongnu, including a large amount of silk and foodstuffs, and had to cede to his foe a large territory in northern China. The Xiongnu leader never tried to invade all of China because he believed that a foreign dynasty could not rule such a vast country for a long time. Besides, for two centuries, the Xiongnu compelled the Chinese to pay them tribute. Such tribute was necessary because for a long time China refused to allow trade with the Xiongnu.

Mongolia was their home, but the Xiongnu also moved westward into Gansu (K'an-su), Xinjiang (Hsing-chiang, also commonly known as Sinkiang), and eastern Central Asia. Like his father, Maodun fought several wars with the Chinese but then turned westward to complete the conquest of western Gansu from the Yuezhi, driving the remnants of the Yuezhi into the Gobi Desert. About 177 B.C.E., Maodun drove the Yuezhi from that region to the Ili Valley, and twelve years later, they were forced south by the Wu-sun, ancestors of the Sarmatian Alanis and vassals of the Xiongnu. Part of the Yuezhi formed a confederacy and moved south to the Tibetan mountains. Most, however, occupied territories between the Amu Dar'ya and Syr Dar'ya rivers (Sogdia), driving Śaka tribes south into Khurasan and Bactria. The Yuezhi established their new capital at Kienshih (Maracanda, later Samarqand).

Maodun died in 174 B.C.E. and was succeeded by his son, Chi-Chih. The new leader completed the consolidation of the Xiongnu Empire and reunited all the tribes of Mongolia.

SIGNIFICANCE

The Xiongnu Empire was the first of the great nomad empires on the Eurasian steppe, and a prototype of others including the Mongols. During the reign of Maodun, many Turkic, Mongol, Tongusic, and Tatar tribes were brought under the Xiongnu rule. When Maodun died, his empire extended from Korea in the east, to the Aral Sea in the west, from Lake Baikal in the north, to Tibet and the Karakorum Mountains in the south. His organization of the armies according to the decimal principle and his administration techniques were later adopted by many Central Asian tribes and kaghanates.

After Maodun's death, Chi-Chih ruled for fourteen years, during which time, the Xiongnu maintained their authority. Chi-Chih married a Han princess, a feat that Maodun had earlier attempted without success. That marriage later opened Xiongnu territories to Han officials, who allegedly incited various tribes to revolt against their rulers, leading to the eventual breakup of the vast Xiongnu

Empire. The Xiongnu lost control of the Silk Road to the Han in c. 60 B.C.E., and in 54 B.C.E., they split into two separate empires in the east and west. The former then split into northern and southern factions, and the Chinese, in combination with the southern branch, destroyed the power of the north in 156 C.E. The remnants of the northern Xiongnu then migrated toward the Aral Sea, while the southern Xiongnu were finally subjugated by the Han in 216 C.E. The remnants of both Xiongnu empires lived on as scattered tribes throughout Western Turkestan for a long time, until they began migrating westward around 350 C.E. Under the leadership of their leader, Balamir, they entered the territories of the Ostrogoth Kingdom in Ukraine in 375 to found the European Hunnic Empire. Another branch of those Xiongnu remnants migrated to Afghanistan, where they established the White Hun (Hephtalite) Empire in the fifth century.

That the empire of Maodun lasted longer than any of the other steppe empires (300 years) is testimony not only to his military prowess but also to his organizational abilities. The Xiongnu military aristocracy consisted of twenty-four chiefs, each commanding an army of ten thousand horsemen. Ten successors were to follow Maodun as shanyu without civil strife.

—*John D. Windhausen*

FURTHER READING

Barfield, Thomas J. *The Perilous Frontier: Nomadic Empires and China*. Oxford: Blackwell, 1989. Provides a full account of Maodun's leadership and organizational skills. Bibliography and index.

Christian, David. *Inner Asia from Prehistory to the Mongol Empire*. Vol. 1 in *A History of Russia, Central Asia and Mongolia*. Oxford: Blackwell, 1998. A fine review of current writings. Bibliography and index.

Davis-Kimball, Jeannine, Vladimir A. Bashilov, and Leonid T. Yablonsky. *Nomads of The Eurasian Steppes in the Early Iron Age*. Berkeley, Calif.: Zinat Press, 1995. Offers analysis of Soviet archaeological works since 1960. Bibliography and index.

Edwards, I. E. S., et al., eds. *Cambridge Ancient History*. Vol 1. New York: Cambridge University Press, 1970. A traditional, indispensable work for information about the region. Bibliography and index.

Torday, Laszlo. *Mounted Archers: The Beginning of Central Asian History*. Durham, England: Durham Academic Press, 1997. An excellent discussion of the various peoples of the region with fine maps. Bibliography and index.

Yong, Ma, and Sun Yutan. "The Western Regions Under

the Xiongnu and the Han." In *The Development of Sedentary and Nomadic Civilizations: 700 B.C. to A.D. 250*, edited by B. Harmatta, N. Puri, and G. F. Etermandi. Vol. 2 in *History of Civilizations of Central Asia*. Paris: UNESCO, 1994. A comparative approach to the governance of east Turkestan. Bibliography and index.

SEE ALSO: c. 420 B.C.E.-c. 100 C.E., Yuezhi Culture Links Persia and China; 221 B.C.E., Qin Dynasty Founded in China; 206 B.C.E., Liu Bang Captures Qin Capital, Founds Han Dynasty; 2d century B.C.E., Silk Road Opens; 140-87 B.C.E., Wudi Rules Han Dynasty China. **RELATED ARTICLES** in *Great Lives from History: The Ancient World*: Shi Huangdi; Wudi.

206 B.C.E.
LIU BANG CAPTURES QIN CAPITAL, FOUNDS HAN DYNASTY

Liu Bang captured Xianyang, toppling the Qin Dynasty and founding the Han Dynasty, which was marked by expansion, the adoption of Confucianism as the state religion, and the institution of a bureaucracy based on merit.

LOCALE: China

CATEGORIES: Government and politics; wars, uprisings, and civil unrest

KEY FIGURES

Liu Bang (Liu Pang; 256-195 B.C.E.), founder of first Han Dynasty and emperor of China, r. 206-195 B.C.E.

Xiang Yu (Hsiang Yü; d. 202 B.C.E.), chief of confederacy that overthrew the Qin and rival of Liu Bang in the subsequent civil war

Lü (d. 180 B.C.E.), empress, first female ruler of China, wife of Liu Bang, and regent for their son and grandsons

SUMMARY OF EVENT

The first commoner to found a Chinese dynasty, Liu Bang came from Pei in northern China. He served as a village official during the oppressive Qin Dynasty (Ch'in; 221-206 B.C.E.), which had unified China. Widespread rebellions erupted when the feared first emperor of Qin, Shi Huangdi, died in 210 and was succeeded by his weak son. Some rebels were former aristocrats whom the Qin had defeated and degraded and who saw an opportunity to regain their lost power and status; others were ordinary people unable to bear Qin oppression any longer. Xiang Yu (Hsiang Yü), a nobleman whose family had long served Chu (Ch'u), a state in southern China, was an example of the former, and Liu Bang represented the common people. Liu joined Xiang in revolt, and the two men agreed that whoever first reached Guanzhong (Kuan-chung), the strategically important area in which the Qin capital was located, would be proclaimed king.

In 206 B.C.E., Liu Bang captured the Qin capital Xianyang (Hsien-yang) in the Guanzhong region and accepted the surrender of the last Qin ruler, thus ending that dynasty and beginning the Han Dynasty (206 B.C.E.-220 C.E.). He treated the Qin royal family kindly, spared the city from looting, and won great popular acclaim by declaring an end to the cruel Qin legal code with a simple order: Those who killed would suffer the death penalty, and those who robbed and injured others would be punished according to the gravity of their offenses. When Xiang Yu reached Xianyang later, he ordered the murder of the Qin royal family and permitted his men to loot and burn that city. As leader of the coalition, Xiang Yu proclaimed himself overall ruler of China and gave Liu Bang, his subordinate general, the title of king of Han, a region in northern China. Soon the two men went to war. Although a brilliant general, Xiang Yu alienated his subordinates with his arrogance and cruelty. He lost the civil war by 202 and committed suicide.

In 202 B.C.E., Liu accepted the title *huangdi* (*huang-ti*), or emperor, offered by his confederates, and named his new dynasty the Han, which would last until 220 C.E. At his accession, Liu Ji changed his personal name to Bang but was referred to by his title Gaodi, meaning "high emperor" until his death in 195 B.C.E. (after which he was known as Gaozu). His first acts as emperor won him widespread acclaim. He proclaimed an amnesty, demobilized the troops, gave relief to the poor, freed slaves, and lowered the land tax to one-fifteenth of the crop (down from more than half under the Qin). He chose a site near Xianyang, within the strategic passes of Guanzhong, for the capital city and named it Changan (Chang-an, present-day Xi'an). He retained the Qin government system at the central level, but for the government of the entire empire, he chose a compromise between the Qin system of commanderies (provinces) and counties and the pre-Qin system of feudal states. He established commanderies in central China and appointed officials to rule those regions under the direct control of the imperial government, but he created kingdoms and marquisates in the border regions in the east and north and appointed his allies and relatives to rule them under central government supervision.

In domestic affairs, Gaodi followed a laissez-faire policy of limited and frugal government and low taxes that allowed the people to recover and the economy to rebound. More important, he established the precedent that the ruler should act only on the advice of his ministers, which put a real limit on imperial power. Also, Gaodi recognized that the Qin lost the mandate of heaven (the divine approval of rulership) for not putting the people's interest first and that his success had been due to popular support. Finally, the defeat of Xiang Yu marked the breakdown of the ancient aristocracy. The aristocratic government that had prevailed up to that time would slowly be replaced by imperial institutions based on a meritocracy.

Gaodi had a major foreign relations problem with a northern nomadic people called the Xiongnu (Hsiungnu), related to the Huns who later invaded Europe. The Xiongnu had been defeated by the powerful Qin general Meng Tian (Meng T'ien), who, acting under the Qin emperor, linked existing walls along the northern border and extended them to form the Great Wall. The fall of the Qin and the ensuing civil wars resulted in the crumbling of the defenses built under the Qin and allowed the powerful Xiongnu leader Maodun to raid the Chinese-settled lands along the frontier. In 201 B.C.E., Gaodi personally led a campaign against Maodun, but his mainly infantry army was defeated by Maodun's cavalry, and he narrowly escaped capture. The two sides made a peace treaty, which established borders and regulated trade; the Han also agreed to give the Xiongnu lavish gifts of silk, grain, and gold. Gaodi also promised to give his only daughter by his wife, the empress Lü, in marriage to Maodun. However, because of the strong objection of the empress, the royal couple did not give their daughter but instead accorded a girl of the Liu clan the rank of princess and sent her as a substitute bride. This peace treaty was renewed many times over the next sixty years. Although the terms cost the Han prestige and money and did not end the Xiongnu's periodic raids, it did allow the Chinese an opportunity to recover from the previous era of exhausting wars.

The establishing of the Han Dynasty marked the end of the dominance of the Legalist philosophy of the Qin, with its absolutist style of government, cruel laws, high taxes, and attempts to control thought through the proscription of Confucian and other philosophies. It marked

EMPERORS OF THE WESTERN HAN DYNASTY, 206 B.C.E.-23 C.E.	
Ruler	*Reign*
Gaozu (Liu Bang)	206-195 B.C.E.
Huidi	195-188
Shaoi Kong	188-180
Shaodi Hong	188-180
Wendi	180-157
Jingdi	157-141
Wudi	140-87
Zhaodi	87-74
Xuandi	74-49
Yuandi	49-33
Chengdi	33-7
Aidi	7-1
Pingdi	1 B.C.E.-6 C.E.
Ruzi	6-9 C.E.

a gradual triumph for Confucian philosophy. Although not a Confucian himself, Gaodi had Confucians among his advisers and appointed Confucian scholars to teach his sons and to define court ceremonies and rituals to give dignity to the newly formed government. He also ordered his Confucian advisers to recommend young men of learning and good character to serve in his government. This custom expanded to become the examination system that would be regularized and expanded under his successors of the Han and under the leaders of later dynasties.

Gaodi died in 195 B.C.E. while on campaign against a rebel force. He had several young sons and was succeeded by his eldest son, whose mother was Empress Lü and who took the reign name Huidi (Hui-ti). Huidi reigned for eight years but did not rule. He was thoroughly dominated by his mother, who had become Dowager Empress Lü and appointed her brothers and nephews to powerful positions. On her death, members of her clan attempted to seize power, but their plots were foiled by government leaders who had remained faithful to the memory of Liu Bang, and most members of the Lü clan were put to death.

SIGNIFICANCE

The Han Dynasty that Liu Bang established would last four hundred years. He is remembered by Chinese historians as a good general and humane ruler who set the precedence that rulers should be mindful of the people's well-being and should heed the advice of ministers and give them credit for successes. Liu Bang is also admired for being the first commoner to establish a dynasty.

Under Gaodi's successors, the Han Dynasty gradually expanded territorially to include most of modern China, northern Vietnam, and Korea. Chinese power and prestige extended into much of central Asia. This era in Chinese history coincided with the height of Roman power in the Western world: These two contemporary empires thus dominated most of the Eurasian continent.

In establishing an empire that continued the best features of its predecessor's institutions minus its oppressive Legalist practices and in adopting Confucianism as the guiding philosophy of the Chinese state, with a nonhereditary bureaucracy whose members were recruited on merit through impartially administered examinations based on Confucian doctrines, the Han Dynasty inaugurated ideals and practices that would continue for two millennia and last to the twentieth century. Because of these achievements, even today about 94 percent of the Chinese call themselves people of the Han. These foundations were established by the first humble-born Chinese, Liu Bang, who became king of Han in 206 and emperor in 202 B.C.E.

—*Jiu-Hwa Lo Upshur*

FURTHER READING
Ch'u, T'ung-tsu. *Han Social Structure*. Seattle: University of Washington Press, 1967. Scholarly and readable work, with documents. Bibliography. Index.
Jagchid, Sechin, and Van Jay Symons. *Peace, War, and Trade Along the Great Wall: Nomadic-Chinese Interactions Through Two Millennia*. Bloomington: Indiana University Press, 1989. An overview of Chinese-nomadic relations, with a large section devoted to the Han Dynasty.
Pizzoli-t'Serstevens, Michele. *The Han Dynasty*. New York: Rizzoli, 1982. Lavishly illustrated, good maps, and well-presented text. Bibliography. Index.
Sage, Steven F. *Ancient Sichuan and the Unification of China*. Albany: State University of New York Press, 1992. On the role of Sichuan from antiquity through the Han Dynasty. Bibliography. Index.
Twitchett, Denis, and John K. Fairbank, eds. *The Ch'in and Han Empires, 221 B.C.-A.D. 220*. Vol. 1 in *The Cambridge History of China*. New York: Cambridge University Press, 1986. The definitive history of the Qin and Han Dynasties. Glossary. Index. Bibliography.
Wang, Zhongshu. *Han Civilization*. New Haven, Conn.: Yale University Press, 1982. Richly illustrated account with recent archaeological information. Bibliography. Index.

SEE ALSO: c. 285-c. 255 B.C.E., Xunzi Develops Teachings That Lead to Legalism; 221 B.C.E., Qin Dynasty Founded in China; c. 221-211 B.C.E., Building the Great Wall of China; 221-206 B.C.E., Legalist Movement in China; 209-174 B.C.E., Maodun Creates a Large Confederation in Central Asia; 140-87 B.C.E., Wudi Rules Han Dynasty China; 220 C.E., Three Kingdoms Period Begins in China.
RELATED ARTICLES in *Great Lives from History: The Ancient World*: Cao Cao; Confucius; Hanfeizi; Shi Huangdi; Wudi; Xunzi.

202 B.C.E.
BATTLE OF ZAMA

The Battle of Zama was a pivotal engagement between Roman and Carthaginian armies in the Second Punic War.

LOCALE: About 60 miles (97 kilometers) southwest of Carthage (modern Tunisia)
CATEGORIES: Wars, uprisings, and civil unrest; expansion and land acquisition

KEY FIGURES
Hannibal (247-182 B.C.E.), Carthaginian general
Hasdrubal Barca (d. 207 B.C.E.), younger brother of Hannibal
Gaius Laelius (d. after 160 B.C.E.), Roman consul in 190 B.C.E. and commander under Scipio Africanus
Masinissa (c. 238-148 B.C.E.), king of eastern Numidia, r. c. 201-148 B.C.E., and an ally of Rome
Scipio Africanus (236-184/183 B.C.E.), Roman consul and general

SUMMARY OF EVENT
After Hannibal had finally been trapped in southern Italy by the "Fabian tactics" of Rome, the tide of the Second Punic War turned against him. The victories of Scipio Africanus in Spain from 208 to 206 B.C.E. and the frustration of the efforts of Hasdrubal Barca, Hannibal's younger brother, to reinforce Hannibal in 207 B.C.E., prepared the way for an invasion of Africa by Scipio in 204 B.C.E. It was then Rome's turn to ravish the enemy's countryside

as Hannibal had done for fifteen years in Italy. With a large and well-disciplined army composed mostly of volunteers, Scipio outwitted two defense forces collected by Carthage, captured the rural areas around the city, and damaged its economy. The Carthaginians offered a truce to gain time in order to effect Hannibal's return from Italy; he succeeded in getting away with a force of more than ten thousand veterans.

Hannibal spent the winter of 203-202 B.C.E. collecting and training an army for the decisive meeting with Scipio. Because both Roman and Carthaginian cavalry were limited, the rival generals each sent out appeals for aid to various North African chieftains. Scipio turned to an old companion in arms, the wily desert sheik Masinissa, who had fought with the Romans in Spain. In 204-203 B.C.E., Scipio had helped Masinissa defeat a rival for control of a kingdom in Numidia, west of Carthage. In 202 B.C.E., however, Masinissa was slower to respond to Scipio than were other local princes who brought cavalry and elephants to aid Hannibal. As a result, Scipio moved his army inland and westward to avoid a major battle until he had secured more cavalry.

Hannibal marched his army in pursuit of the Romans, hoping to force a confrontation before Scipio was ready. When the Carthaginian army came near the village of Zama, about five days' march southwest of Carthage, Hannibal sent scouts to search out Scipio's position. These spies were captured, but after being shown through the Roman camp, they were released. By this device, Scipio hoped that their reports would discourage an immediate Carthaginian attack. The Greek historian Polybius (c. 200-c. 118 B.C.E.) reported that the two generals actually had a dramatic face-to-face meeting before the battle, alone on a plain between two opposing hills where their armies were encamped. Nevertheless, Hannibal's peace proposals were rejected by Scipio, who had recently been encouraged by the arrival of Masinissa with four thousand cavalrymen and other reinforcements.

On the following day, the two armies were drawn up for battle. They were probably roughly equal in size, although some scholars estimate that Hannibal's force was as large as fifty thousand men while Scipio's was as small as twenty-three thousand. Certainly the Roman cavalry was stronger. Hannibal placed his eighty elephants in front of his first-line troops, who were experienced mercenaries from Europe and Africa. Scipio's front line was divided into separate fighting units with gaps between them to allow the elephants to pass through without disturbing the line.

When the battle began, bugles caused the Carthagin-

ian line of elephants to stampede and then turn sideways onto Hannibal's own cavalry stationed on the wings. The Roman cavalry under Gaius Laelius and Masinissa took advantage of the confusion to drive the Carthaginian cavalry off the battlefield.

During the infantry battle that ensued, the disciplined front rank of Roman legionnaires, closely supported by their second-rank comrades, managed to penetrate Hannibal's line. The second-line troops of Carthage, apparently not as well coordinated, allowed both Punic lines to be driven back with heavy casualties. Hannibal had kept in reserve a strong third line of veterans, intending to attack with this fresh force when the Romans were exhausted, but he allowed a fatal pause during which Scipio regrouped his detachments. The final stage of the battle raged indecisively until the cavalry of Laelius and Masinissa returned to the field to attack the Carthaginians in the rear and destroy most of those encircled by this maneuver. Polybius reported that the Carthaginians suffered twenty thousand casualties, compared to only fifteen hundred Romans killed.

SIGNIFICANCE

Hannibal escaped, but Carthage was exhausted and surrendered without a siege, accepting peace terms that took away all Carthaginian possessions outside Africa, imposed a heavy indemnity, and guaranteed the autonomy of Masinissa's kingdom. Scipio returned in triumph to Rome, where he was awarded the title "Africanus." Remarkably undaunted by defeat, Hannibal led Carthage to economic recovery within a few years; later, he fled eastward to aid adversaries of Rome in further wars.

By their victory at Zama, the Romans gained supremacy in the western Mediterranean and launched an imperialistic program that eventually made them dominant throughout most of Europe and the Near East, repressing eastern leadership until the rise of Muslim power in the seventh century C.E.

—*Updated by Jeffrey L. Buller*

FURTHER READING

Hoyos, B. D. *Unplanned Wars: The Origins of the First and Second Punic Wars.* New York: Walter de Gruyter, 1998. Provides the political background to the Punic Wars in extensive detail. Maps, bibliography, and indexes.

Lancel, Serge. *Hannibal.* Translated by Antonia Nevill. Boston: Blackwell, 2000. A detailed biography of the Carthaginian general; a substantial chapter is devoted to the Battle of Zama. Illustrations, maps, chronology, bibliography, and index.

Lazenby, John Francis. *Hannibal's War: A Military History of the Second Punic War.* 1978. Reprint. Norman: University of Oklahoma Press, 2001. Thorough analysis of the Second Punic War by one of the twentieth century's recognized experts in Roman military history.

Russell, Francis H. "The Battlefield of Zama." *Archaeology* 23 (April, 1970): 120-129. An illustrated study of the Battle of Zama, with emphasis upon the role that topography played in that conflict.

Smith, Philip J. *Scipio Africanus and Rome's Invasion of Africa.* Amsterdam: Gieben, 1993. Part of McGill University's series of monographs in classical archaeology and history, this historical commentary on Book 29 of Livy's history contains a wealth of information on Scipio, Hannibal, and the site of Zama.

SEE ALSO: 264-225 B.C.E., First Punic War; c. 250 B.C.E., Discoveries of Archimedes; 218-201 B.C.E., Second Punic War; 149-146 B.C.E., Third Punic War; 439 C.E., Vandals Seize Carthage.

RELATED ARTICLES in *Great Lives from History: The Ancient World*: Hannibal; Scipio Africanus.

2d century B.C.E.
SILK ROAD OPENS

The trading route known as the Silk Road linked the civilizations of China in eastern Asia, Rome in Europe, and the rich kingdoms in between.

LOCALE: Central and Western Asia
CATEGORIES: Trade and commerce; cultural and intellectual history

KEY FIGURES
Wudi (Wu-ti; 156-87 B.C.E.), emperor of the Han Dynasty, r. 140-87 B.C.E.
Zhang Qian (Chang Ch'ien; d. 114 B.C.E.), Chinese explorer

SUMMARY OF EVENT
In the early years of the twentieth century, a handful of explorers made a series of remarkable discoveries in Central Asia. Sir Aurel Stein of Great Britain, Sven Hedin of Sweden, and a few other key figures from Europe, the United States, and Japan rediscovered what had been one of the most significant trade routes in the history of civilization. Along the way, they also recovered manuscripts, art objects, and religious artifacts that eventually made their way into the museums of the Western world. Today, their activities are regarded as little more than plundering by the Asians whose lands they penetrated, but Stein and his fellow explorers helped turn the attention of the world to what is known today as the Silk Road.

Although given its familiar name by German explorer Baron Ferdinand von Richthofen in 1877, the Silk Road had its origin more than two millennia earlier. In the second century B.C.E., Wudi, a Han Dynasty (206 B.C.E.-220 C.E.) emperor, wished to make contact with the Yuezhi (Yüeh-chih), a people living far to the west of China. He hoped to persuade them to make joint war on the Xiongnu (Hsiung-nu), the people who would become known centuries later in Europe as the Huns.

In 138 B.C.E., Zhang Qian, an officer in Wudi's household, set out to reach the Yuezhi, but he was captured almost immediately by the Xiongnu and imprisoned for ten years. After making his escape in about 128 B.C.E., he skirted the southern reaches of the great Taklimakan (Takla Makan) Desert (which the Chinese knew as Liu Sha, or moving sands) and the southern slopes of the Tian Shan (T'ien Shan), eventually locating the Yuezhi in Bactria (now northern Afghanistan).

Received cordially but finding himself unable to persuade the Yuezhi to take up arms, Zhang Qian managed to return to China only in 126 B.C.E., having been captured by the Xiongnu once again and imprisoned for a year. He had failed in his immediate goal, but his long and eventful journey revealed the existence of rich kingdoms to the west—Samarqand, Bukhara, and Fergana—all now in Uzbekistan. The explorer also brought back reports of fabulous lands farther to the west, including Persia (centered in what is now Iran), Arabia, and, apparently, the Roman Empire. Although he could not know it, Zhang Qian had reached the terminus of a network of trade routes that had existed for at least two thousand years, linking the lands of the Mediterranean with those of Central Asia.

The emperor's attention, however, was drawn to Zhang Qian's reports of the jade to be found in Hotan (Khotan) on the southern edge of the Taklimakan and of

An artist's depiction of silk making in ancient China. (F. R. Niglutsch)

the swift horses of Fergana. Jade is highly valued by the Chinese, and the horses Zhang Qian described might well give the Chinese, who rode inferior mounts, an advantage in their ongoing war with the Xiongnu.

Some ten years later, Zhang Qian was sent by Wudi on a second expedition, this time to forge an alliance with the Wu-sun, who lived north of the Tian Shan. He and his men carried with them horses, cattle, sheep, gold, and silk as gifts to the Wu-sun; they returned in 108 B.C.E., carrying gifts from the Wu-sun in return. Although he again failed to make the strategic alliance Wudi wished, Zhang Qian succeeded in dispatching envoys to Parthia and India, encouraging these civilizations to send diplomats and traders to China in turn. Pleased with his official's efforts, the emperor named him the "Great Traveler."

SIGNIFICANCE

Although western sections of the route had long been in existence, the expeditions of Zhang Qian and a few other explorers led to the establishment of what is known today as the Silk Road. Eventually stretching some 4,000 to 5,000 miles (6,500 to 8,000 kilometers) across Asia, the route served as a conduit not only for goods but also for skills and ideas, and for the first fifteen hundred years of the common era, it was the most important trade route in the world.

Just as Zhang Qian had followed several different routes in his travels, the Silk Road evolved into different branches. Because most routes passed through dry, inhospitable country, travelers depended on the maintenance of oases spaced within a day or two's march of each other. Most trade was carried out over relatively short distances, with goods passed from merchant to merchant and kingdom to kingdom, each transaction increasing the ultimate cost of the merchandise. Very few individuals probably made the entire journey, but one who did was Venetian traveler Marco Polo (1254-1324), who published a famous account of his travels in 1299.

The commodity for which the Silk Road was named was first produced in China about 3,000 B.C.E. By the first century B.C.E., it became known to the Romans, who encountered it in the hands of the nomadic Parthians in what is today Iraq, apparently traded by one of Zhang

Qian's successors. The diaphanous material proved enormously popular in the West and accounted for much of the early traffic on the road, but many other commodities were traded as well. These included ivory, precious stones (especially jade and lapis lazuli), ceramics, incense, paper, spices, horses and other animals, hides and furs, and tapestries and rugs. The route also served to introduce a number of plants into China, including grapes, pomegranates, walnuts, cucumbers, sesame, and alfalfa.

The Silk Road also became a route for the spread of religions, including Buddhism, which originated in what is now northeastern India, and Manichaeanism. Nestorian Christianity, declared a heresy in the West, became established in China in the early seventh century C.E. Perhaps equally important, the Silk Road became a means by which art and music spread and evolved. The most important example of this is perhaps the artistic style known as Serindian, a complex mixture of Chinese, Greek, and Indian elements.

The sophisticated civilizations that grew up along the Silk Road reached their zenith in the seventh, eighth, and ninth centuries C.E. After this period, deteriorating political conditions in China and worsening climatic conditions led to the gradual abandonment of settlements and of the Silk Road itself.

—Grove Koger

FURTHER READING

Ball, Warwick. "Following the Mythical Road." *Geographical Magazine* 70 (March, 1998): 18-23. Argues that there is no evidence that the Silk Road actually existed in any organized fashion and suggests that scholars and readers have been all too willing to believe in a romantic myth. An important counterweight to other sources.

Franck, Irene M., and David M. Brownstone. *The Silk Road: A History.* New York: Facts on File, 1986. Well-researched popular history, quoting a number of ancient sources and following Zhang Qian's journeys in substantial detail. Black-and-white illustrations, maps, and substantial bibliography.

Grousset, Rene. *The Empire of the Steppes: A History of Central Asia.* New Brunswick, N.J.: Rutgers University Press, 1970. Originally published in French in 1939 but unsurpassed for understanding the context of the Silk Road. Numerous maps, extensive notes.

Hopkirk, Peter. *Foreign Devils on the Silk Road: The Search for the Lost Cities and Treasures of Chinese Central Asia.* London: John Murray, 1980. A popular account of the rise and fall of the Silk Road and in particular of the explorers who rediscovered it. Maps, some black-and-white illustrations, and brief bibliography.

Juliano, Annette L., Judith A. Lerner, et al. *Monks and Merchants: Silk Road Treasures from Northwest China: Gansu and Ningxia, Fourth-Seventh Century.* New York: Abrams with The Asia Society, 2001. Sumptuous volume surveying the artistic impact in northwest China of the cultural exchange brought about by the Silk Road. Color illustrations, chronologies, and short glossary.

Mirsky, Jeannette, ed. *The Great Chinese Travelers.* New York: Random House, 1964. Includes a summary of Zhang Qian's travels drawn from a first century B.C.E. account by Chinese historian Sima Qian (Ssu-Ma Chien).

Whitfield, Susan. *Life Along the Silk Road.* Berkeley: University of California Press, 1999. Reconstructs the lives of ten individuals—merchants, monks, soldiers, and so on—who lived along the Silk Road during its heyday. Black-and-white and color illustrations, map, plans, table of rulers, and discussion of sources for further reading.

SEE ALSO: c. 420 B.C.E.-c. 100 C.E., Yuezhi Culture Links Persia and China; 209-174 B.C.E., Maodun Creates a Large Confederation in Central Asia; c. 155 B.C.E., Greco-Bactrian Kingdom Reaches Zenith Under Menander; 140-87 B.C.E., Wudi Rules Han Dynasty China.

RELATED ARTICLE in *Great Lives from History: The Ancient World*: Wudi.

c. 200 B.C.E.
BIRTH OF HINDUISM

Hinduism is the name given to the religion of India that developed historically from Brahmanism and Vedism as depicted in surviving Sanskrit texts.

LOCALE: India
CATEGORY: Religion

SUMMARY OF EVENT

Hinduism arose out of an earlier religious tradition generally called Vedism, whose oldest representative text is the *Rigveda* (also known as *Ṛgveda*, c. 1500-1000 B.C.E.; English translation, 1896-1897), and its later phase, Brahmanism, as exemplified in a class of texts called Brāhmanas (compiled eighth to fifth centuries B.C.E.; commentaries on Brahman, the sacred utterances of the Vedas). The people who produced the *Rigveda* had a tremendous interest in ritual; religious behavior was important. The word *veda* means "knowledge," the sacred knowledge found for the most part in hymns addressed to particular deities and collected in anthologies such as the *Rigveda* (the oldest of them) related to various schools and priestly functions.

The later period of Brahmanism saw a systemizing of ritual. The religious specialists who produced the Brāhmanas functioned in various priestly roles to conduct sometimes elaborate and lengthy ceremonies, as in the case of the horse sacrifice, which lasted a year. The deities worshiped in this period—Indra, Viṣṇu (or Vishnu), and others—seem impersonal: They gain from the sacrifices offered, and they give in return. Mythological details about their deeds are fuzzy and difficult to reconstruct.

The word "Hindu" was used by Muslim invaders in the eighth century C.E. to describe the people they met in India who worshiped various deities; it is not a term that appears in the texts. Today in India, the preferred term to describe the religion commonly called Hinduism is *dharma* or *sanātana-dharma* (eternal *dharma*). According to Mahatma Gandhi, the essence of Hinduism can be found expressed in the following verse from the *Īśa* Upaniṣad (c. 300 B.C.E.; literally "the secret teaching concerning the Lord," translated in *Sacred Books of the East*, 1879):

> All this, whatsoever moves on earth, is to be hidden in the Lord (the Self). When thou hast surrendered all this, then thou mayest enjoy. Do not covet the wealth of any man!

Hindu tradition also cites the sixty-sixth verse from the eighteenth chapter of the *Bhagavadgītā* (c. 200 B.C.E.-200 C.E.; *The Bhagavad Gita*, 1785) as an essential teaching:

> Go beyond all religious customs [*dharmas*], come to me as your sole refuge. I will liberate you from evil. Do not fear!

The Sanskrit word *dharma*, which appears in this stanza, is a key term. Its wide range of meaning is shown by the many English equivalents found in translations of the *The Bhagavad Gita*: duty, sacred duty, appearance, religious practice, law, and things of law (both lawful and lawless), to name a few.

The transition to Hinduism is found most clearly in a number of texts called Upaniṣads (c. 1000-c. 200 B.C.E.). The word *upaniṣad* has been taken by some scholars to signify originally "to sit near (reverentially)" and by others to mean "mystical connection." Later the word clearly came to mean "secret teaching" or "secret doctrine." Various Upaniṣads were produced that belonged to particular priestly schools. In them one reads of students approaching teachers who instruct their disciples in essential doctrines about religious behavior and the meaning of life and death. The Upaniṣads seem to have been composed in an atmosphere of debate, as if new speculations were circulating in esoteric circles. In the transition to Hinduism there is no sudden change, but rather an increasing tendency to speculate on the meanings of key words and on the ritual itself. In the Upaniṣads, rituals are given a new inner meaning and there is a new stress on an individual realization of that meaning. For example, at the beginning of one of the old Upaniṣads, one finds speculations on the cosmic meaning of the horse that is the ritual victim offered in the important horse sacrifice; in another, speculations on the universal symbolism of the word *om*, roughly equivalent to the western "amen."

At this period, new concepts arose, ideas that became central in later Hinduism. Among them were karma (meaningful actions that determine one's life), rebirth, *saṃsāra* (the world as a dismaying endless flow of existence), and *bhakti* (the stylized devotion to a chosen deity). Some scholars have seen the rise of these new ideas, rebirth and *saṃsāra* especially, as inherited from a prehistoric substratum, a remainder from the religion that

Indo-Aryan speakers found when they came to India in the second millennium B.C.E. Other historians of religion deny that view, preferring to see the newer Hinduism as a logical development from Brahmanism. The development of these new concepts is outlined in the following paragraphs.

In the Upaniṣads, the problem of "repeated death" is discussed: the idea that after attaining heaven, one might have to undergo death again. The idea of rebirth is seemingly born from this discussion, so that, in later Hindu texts such as *The Bhagavad Gita*, one learns that every individual has had many births and will have many more. In these works speculation then turns to a new problem: What sort of knowledge or method will allow one to escape the endless cycle of birth and death?

The Bhagavad Gita is a more recent Upaniṣad that reveals the practical method (yoga) for gaining liberation from the endless cycle of births through an internal realization of ultimate truth. This text also promotes devotion to a particular deity—in this case Kṛṣṇa (or Krishna), who is identified as an incarnation of Viṣṇu. In the eleventh chapter of the *The Bhagavad Gita*, Kṛṣṇa reveals himself in all his divine forms; the vision of God described there is vivid and powerful. Arjuna, the principal hero of the *Mahābhārata* (mentioned below) and the questioner of Kṛṣṇa in *The Bhagavad Gita*, is transformed by his vision; his is an individual realization, though held out as a possibility for others. Clearly the devotees of Kṛṣṇa were interested in an extremely personal and concrete God.

The idea of karma (action) assumes a new meaning also. The term originally meant "ritual action," but in the transition to Hinduism the term takes on a more generalized significance, as one Upaniṣad states: "As one does a karma, so he is born." One's actions determine his or her status in a future birth.

The two epics of India, the *Mahābhārata* (400 B.C.E.-400 C.E., present form by c. 400 C.E.; *The Mahabharata of Krishna-Dwaipayana Vyasa*, 1887-1896) and *Rāmāyaṇa* (c. 550 B.C.E.; English translation, 1870-1889; some material added later; English translation, 1870-1889), are important sources of information for the understanding of early Hinduism. One study, by Alf Hiltebeitel (published in 2001), now narrows the dating of both epics to 150 B.C.E. or later. The *Mahābhārata* especially contains many discussions of religious topics, both in its long twelfth book, the *Śānti-parvan* (the book of peace), and in the many digressions from the main heroic tale, the most famous of which is *The Bhagavad Gita* itself. The *Rāmāyaṇa* introduces Hanumān, the divine monkey

and son of the wind god Vayu, who exemplifies the perfect devotee in his relationship to Rāma, hero of the epic and incarnation of Viṣṇu. Both epics, which were recited at religious festivals, spoke to a more general and popular audience than the Upaniṣads, which were composed by and for those priestly initiates who dedicated much of their life to memorizing the Vedas.

The *Mahābhārata* and the *Rāmāyaṇa* also contain new myths, sacred stories about the gods that differ in many particulars from the stories scholars can reconstruct from the Vedic period. Pilgrimages and pilgrimage sites are also prominent, such as the section of the *Mahābhārata* that tells how the main characters took a tour of sacred fords. Religious festivals, day-to-day rituals, and influences from tribal religions appear in the texts as tantalizing glimpses. Much of this religious teaching was clearly oral: A sage comes to the court of a local ruler and is asked to relate tales of ancient gods and heroes, both for entertainment and for edification.

Another development in Hinduism, reflected in the epics, is the change of status of different deities. In the *Rigveda*, Indra is supreme, the king of the gods. At places the epic worship of Indra is mentioned; for example, a popular ritual or festival connected with an "Indra-pole." Early Buddhist texts also mention both Indra and Brahma as central gods. Mostly, however, Indra, Brahma, Vayu, and other gods important in the earlier religion become humbler in Hinduism—inferior, for instance, to Viṣṇu, who becomes more important in Hinduism than in Vedism. The *Rigveda* features a class of minor deities known as Rudras, with a slightly sinister appearance. In Hinduism, one of them, Rudra in the singular, stands out and is renamed Śiva (or Shiva), "the beneficent one." Two major divisions of the new Hinduism then developed, dedicated to the glorification of one or the other of two great gods, Viṣṇu and Śiva.

The two epics give evidence of one other important feature of Hinduism: the ascetic tradition. The earlier Upaniṣads depicted the ideal sage as a married man, one of whose duties was to produce sons. However, in the epics a new type of wise man appears, the ascetic or "sannyasin" who has abandoned family, married life, and any ordinary occupation to wander the world, seeking knowledge and liberation. This becomes also an ideal in early Buddhism, where monks are advised to "wander free as a rhinoceros."

SIGNIFICANCE

The religious concepts that arose during the birth of Hinduism became pan-Indian in importance. Both Hinduism and Buddhism adopted ideas such as rebirth (*saṃsāra*) and karma as unquestioned foundational elements of their doctrine. Hinduism never was a unified religion, but was a composite in which many sometimes divergent views were accommodated. Forms of Hinduism traveled outside the Indian subcontinent to southeast Asia, and in the twentieth century throughout the world.

—*Burt Thorp*

FURTHER READING

Basham, A. L. *The Origins and Development of Classical Hinduism*. Boston: Beacon Press, 1989. A prominent historian's final views on the subject.

Goodall, Dominic, ed. and trans. *Hindu Scriptures*. Berkeley: University of California Press, 1996. A useful collection of primary documents in translation.

Hiltebeitel, Alf. *Rethinking the Mahābhārata: A Reader's Guide to the Education of the Dharma King*. Chicago: University of Chicago Press, 2001. A recent reinterpretation, which proposes new ideas about the dating and context of composition of the two epics.

Miller, Barbara Stoler, trans. *The Bhagavad-Gita: Krishna's Counsel in Time of War*. New York: Bantam, 1986. A readable translation with an informative introduction.

Olivelle, Patrick, trans. *Upaniṣads*. New York: Oxford University Press, 1996. A scholarly translation of the principal older texts, with extensive introduction and notes.

SEE ALSO: 1500-1100 B.C.E., Compilation of the Vedas; c. 1000-c. 200 B.C.E., Compilation of the Upaniṣads; c. 550 B.C.E., Vālmīki Composes the *Rāmāyaṇa*; c. 5th-4th century B.C.E., Creation of the *Jātakas*; c. 467 B.C.E., Gośāla Maskarīputra, Founder of Ājīvika Sect, Dies; c. 400 B.C.E.-400 C.E., Composition of the *Mahābhārata*; c. 321 B.C.E., Mauryan Empire Rises in India; c. 200 B.C.E.-200 C.E., *Bhagavad Gita* Is Created; 5th or 6th century C.E., First Major Text on Hinduism's Great Goddess Is Compiled.

RELATED ARTICLES in *Great Lives from History: The Ancient World:* Aśoka the Great; Chandragupta Maurya; Vālmīki.

---

c. 200 B.C.E.-c. 100 C.E.
COMPOSITION OF THE INTERTESTAMENTAL JEWISH APOCRYPHA

Noncanonical Jewish religious writings composed in the three centuries before the emergence of the New Testament provided early Christians with a sense of continuity between Judaism and Christianity.

LOCALE: Palestine and Egypt
CATEGORY: Religion

SUMMARY OF EVENT

Between 200 B.C.E. and 100 C.E., many Jewish religious writings appeared in Palestine that were destined not only to remain outside the canon but also to be completely ignored by normative Judaism by the end of the first century in the common era. When the Synod of Jamnia closed the canon, Jewish religious thought preferred to find expression in the development of oral tradition and in rabbinical literature, rather than in the expansion of Scripture per se. To a Judaism already demoralized by the fall of Jerusalem, a closed canon precluded any adulteration of the word of God by contemporary books of dubious message and provenance, especially those of Christian origin clamoring for recognition. The decision that "no one should read" in more than the

twenty-four recognized books led, it appears, to the deliberate destruction of the Aramaic and Hebrew manuscripts of extracanonical writings.

These noncanonical compositions have been conventionally divided into two categories: the Apocrypha and Pseudepigrapha. The former, so-called outside books, always enjoyed a privileged position. Although they failed to achieve canonicity among Palestinian Jews, they were accepted by the Greek-speaking Jews of Alexandria. The long-term preservation of these Greek manuscripts, however, is due to Christians who found in the apocryphal literature, without need of any adulterating interpolations on their part, a ready-made bridge between the Old and New Testaments. These writings provided in Christian eyes the evidence for continuity of doctrinal development in the intertestamental period, making the transition to Christianity gradual and logical.

The Apocrypha is made up of Tobit, Judith, parts of Esther, the Wisdom of Solomon, Ecclesiasticus (Sirach), 1 Baruch, the Epistle of Jeremiah, three additions to Daniel (the prayer of Azariah and the Song of the three children; Susanna; and Bel and the Dragon), 1 and 2 Maccabees, 1 and 2 Esdras, and the Prayer of Manasses. It represents a variety of literary composition: history, poetry, apocalyptic writing, wisdom literature, and simple narrative.

There seem to be allusions to the apocryphal literature by authors of the New Testament: by Paul to the Wisdom of Solomon and possibly by James to the proverbs of Sirach and the Wisdom of Solomon. However, these books as a group came to be recognized by the Church in the West only gradually. The Muratorian Canon of Rome (c. 180 C.E.), for instance, accepts the Wisdom of Solomon as canonical. Early synods, such as those of Hippo (393 C.E.) and Carthage (397 C.E.), and Athanasius's Festal Letter (365 C.E.), held the Apocrypha as a privileged set of books, but Saint Augustine (354-430 C.E.), who considered the Greek Alexandrian canon a divine improvement over the Hebrew list of books and, therefore, quoted the Apocrypha probably more than any other Church Father, practically guaranteed its incorporation in the Vulgate. When the Council of Trent (1546), confirmed by Vatican I (1870), declared the Apocrypha canonical (with the exception of 1 and 2 Esdras and the Prayer of Manasses), it attempted to determine the canon finally in the face of Reformation criticism. Probably the most important book for the Roman Church was 2 Maccabees with its strong note of angelology, prayers for the dead, intercession of saints, resurrection of the bodies of the righteous, and justification of the miraculous in general.

The second set of extracanonical writings is the corpus of the so-called Pseudepigrapha, books whose authorship was deliberately but falsely ascribed to ancient authorities. Once the idea of the inspired law came to dominate the religious scene in post-Exilic Judaism, it was no longer necessary for a prophet or a representative of God to appear, except possibly as an occasional judge choosing between different factions. Writers who preferred to avoid repeating old shibboleths, or who hoped to challenge orthodoxy by suggesting new ideas or by advancing the mystic at the expense of the legal, or who wished to offer hope to oppressed Jews with new stirring apocalypses, chose to write anonymously after 200 B.C.E. and to ascribe their messages to great patriarchs of the past.

Among the many books of the Pseudepigrapha, a few deserve mention because of their importance for Christianity. The Book of Jubilees, while reflecting a strong note of legalism, emphasizes the immediate advent of the Messianic kingdom from Judaea heralded by a great ethical and physical transformation when people will live for a thousand years and find eventual immortality in the spiritual world. The famous Book of Enoch, a composite work in time and authorship, by airing conflicting views of the Messiah, the kingdom, sin, final judgment, resurrection, future life, and angelology, faithfully records the ferment of Jewish thought on these matters in the intertestamental period. Both Jude and 2 Peter seem to know Enoch well. The Testament of the Twelve Patriarchs exercised a great influence on the writers of the New Testament in the area of ethics. The Assumption of Moses, which Origen says the author of Jude used, was contemporaneous with Jesus; it stressed opposition to any alliance of religion and politics. The Apocalypse of Baruch (2) finds many parallels in the New Testament, concerned as it is with the relationship of the fall and free will, works and justification, the Messianic kingdom, and resurrection of the dead. There are still others (the Jewish Sybilline Oracles, the Psalms of Solomon, 4 Maccabees, and the Apocalypse of Elijah), which 1 Corinthians especially seems to use.

SIGNIFICANCE

Without knowledge of these extracanonical books, the transition from Judaism to Christianity is largely unintelligible. After Saint Augustine more or less assured the acceptance of canonical status for these books, they rested secure until the fourteenth century, when the Latin canon was again compared to the shorter old Hebrew Bible. Martin Luther (2483-1546) was led by his studies to isolate the Apocrypha at the end of the Bible; it was to be read by those interested in a "knowledge of history" and in instruction in godly manners but not for the purpose of eliciting any systematic theology. Although all the Reformers again put these books on a secondary list as generally superfluous, Luther considered a few of them to be superior to some regularly accepted sections of the Latin Bible as, for example, the Epistle of James. His grouping was accepted into the English Bible of 1535 and in succeeding revisions including the King James Version of 1611.

However, when opposition to these books even as a secondary corpus began to mount in England, thanks to the Puritans, the Archbishop of Canterbury felt obliged to impose a one-year prison sentence on any publisher who printed the Bible without the Apocrypha. Although an edition did appear without the addition in 1629, opposition increased after the turn of the century, the result in large part of the work of the famous English scholar John Lightfoot (1602-1675), who helped Brian Walton (1600-1661) produce the Polyglot Bible in 1657. The Puritans brought their objections to America, and by 1827 both

British and American Bible societies, dependent on funds supplied by churches and individuals hostile to the Apocrypha, stopped including the corpus in their editions. The reputation of the disputed books declined still further until J. Goodspeed and others finally rescued the Apocrypha in the 1930's from neglect by issuing excellent translations and interpretations.

The position of the Greek Orthodox Church was never made clear by any authoritative decision, although it tends to follow Saint Athanasius of Alexandria (c. 293-373 C.E.) and the Council of Trent (1545). Roman Catholics accept twelve of the fifteen books, while Jews and Protestants reject them all. The Apocrypha nonetheless had a long and pervasive influence on literature and art. Explorer Christopher Columbus (1451-1506) was encouraged to undertake his voyage by a passage in 2 Esdras; English writer John Bunyan (1628-1688) found new life through a passage in Ecclesiasticus; diarist Samuel Pepys (1633-1703) was inspired by Tobit; and such great writers as Geoffrey Chaucer (c. 1342-1400), William Shakespeare (1564-1616), John Milton (1608-1674), and Henry Wadsworth Longfellow (1807-1882) were significantly influenced by the apocryphal writings.

—*Joseph R. Rosenbloom*

FURTHER READING

Charlesworth, James H., ed. *The Old Testament Pseudepigrapha*. 2 vols. Garden City, N.Y.: Doubleday, 1983. A collection of sixty-five Pseudepigraphic texts, translated by an international team of scholars, along with commentary.

Desilva, David Arthur. *Introducing Apocrypha: Message, Context, and Significance*. Grand Rapids, Mich.: Baker Book House, 2002. A review of current scholarship and theory on the Apocrypha, written in accessible language for the nonspecialist.

Ehrman, Bart D. *Lost Christianities: The Battle for Scripture and Truth in the Early Church*. New York: Oxford University Press, 2003. Presents an overview of the proliferation of religious texts, Christian and Jewish, that were created in the first centuries C.E. Well researched and lucid.

_____., ed. *Lost Scriptures: Books that Did Not Become the New Testament*. New York: Oxford University Press. A companion to *Lost Christianities* provides the translated texts of the apocryphal scriptures discussed in that book.

Nickelsburg, George. *Jewish Literature Between the Bible and the Mishnah*. 1981. Reprint. Fortress Press, 2003. A thorough introduction to the Jewish intertestamental literature.

Schneemelcher, Wilhelm, and R. M. Wilson, eds. *New Testament Apocrypha*. Rev. ed. 2 vols. 1991. Reprint. Louisville, Ky.: John Knox Press, 2003. A translation, with commentary, of the Apocrypha.

SEE ALSO: c. 1280 B.C.E., Israelite Exodus from Egypt; c. 1000 B.C.E., Establishment of the United Kingdom of Israel; c. 950 B.C.E., Composition of the Book of Genesis; c. 922 B.C.E., Establishment of the Kingdom of Israel; c. 538-c. 450 B.C.E., Jews Return from the Babylonian Captivity; 250-130 B.C.E., Commissioning of the Septuagint; 167-142 B.C.E., Revolt of the Maccabees; c. 135 B.C.E., Rise of the Pharisees; c. 90 C.E., Synod of Jamnia.

RELATED ARTICLES in *Great Lives from History: The Ancient World:* Saint Athanasius of Alexandria; Saint Augustine; Jesus; Saint Paul.

c. 200 B.C.E.-200 C.E.
BHAGAVAD GITA IS CREATED

The Bhagavad Gita has become a central devotional text in Hinduism and is admired as a work of literature; it is preserved as an interlude in the great Hindu epic, the Mahābhārata.

LOCALE: India
CATEGORIES: Religion; cultural and intellectual history

SUMMARY OF EVENT

The *Bhagavadgītā* (*The Bhagavad Gita*, 1785; literally the divine song or song of the lord) is a brief interlude of eighteen chapters, or seven hundred Sanskrit verses, interpolated into the longest epic in all world literature, the *Mahābhārata* (400 B.C.E.-400 C.E., present form by c. 400 C.E.; *The Mahabharata of Krishna-Dwaipayana Vyasa*, 1887-1896). The authorship of the *Mahābhārata*, the great Indian epic, is traditionally attributed to the legendary Vyāsa (the compiler).

Scholars have dated *The Bhagavad Gita* from around the time of the Buddha, in the sixth century B.C.E., to as far forward as the fourth century C.E., although most estimates fall between c. 200 B.C.E. and 200 C.E. At least the major part of the work as it is known was probably created in the second century B.C.E.

The setting of the story is the battle between two divisions of a large founding family, the Pāndāvas, the aggrieved heroes, and the Kauravas, the aggressors, which takes place c. 1200 B.C.E., in northern India. The story may be linked to actual historical events that took place in Kurukshetra in northern India, the site of early Vedic culture. *The Bhagavad Gita* opens by referring to the field of *dharma* or righteousness, *Dharmakshetra*. However, to reduce the book to a search for events in history is to distort the intent of the book itself. Its importance is in the events of cultural interpretation, more exciting and more meaningful than any single battle.

According to a devotional view, *The Bhagavad Gita* is *apauruseya*, eternally existing. The work may be made up of strands and aphorisms reflecting the work of multiple poetic and religious perspectives; however, most interpreters of the work treat it as a unified poem of formal, philosophical, and religious integrity.

The plot is simple: On the battlefield, the warrior Arjuna, one of the Pāndāvas brothers, lays down his weapon and refuses to fight. He is caught in a conflict between his *dharma* (duty) to his society and his responsibility to inflict no harm. His chariot driver, Krṣṇa

(Krishna, an *avatar*, or incarnation, of the god Viṣṇu), exhorts him to perform his *dharma* without seeking the rewards of his actions. Krṣṇa reveals the value of the yogas, or ways to worship and act in the world, which are karma (work), *bhakti* (love), and *jñana* (knowledge).

The Bhagavad Gita is both continuous with and a departure from the scriptural traditions of the Vedas and the Upaniṣads. The people who developed *The Bhagavad Gita* and tucked it into the *Mahābhārata* were concerned with the dilemma of how to awaken to the divine as well as how to be a responsible part of the everyday world. The rise of *The Bhagavad Gita* as a core sacred text reflects a shift in the control of society from the Brahman (priests) to the Kṣatriya (the caste of lords and warriors). In the work, that shift is made philosophically, as a shift of the meaning of duty in relation to enlightenment.

The Bhagavad Gita is the scripture of action without entanglement in ego's desire, devotion to the source and sustaining force of all action, and the wisdom of the indivisibility of self and spirit. As with any sacred text, there are contending interpretive approaches; the two most prominent systems are Sāmkhya and Vedānta. Without endorsing a single interpretive model, one might begin to study *The Bhagavad Gita* by pursuing the following puzzles concerning the divine, the world, the self, and the self in relation to the world and the divine.

The divine, or theistic, puzzle asks, Who is Krṣṇa? He is Arjuna's kinsman, his chariot driver, and *avatar* of the god Viṣṇu, preserver of the universe. In chapter 11, Krṣṇa reveals to Arjuna his universal form, as the essence of all being, radiant and infinite. Does, then, *The Bhagavad Gita* represent the divine by means of theism (a concept of god) or nontheism (a concept of the divine that supercedes all attributes, is beyond all description)? Is Krṣṇa a theistic divinity, *saguna* (with attributes), or a means to transcend theism, apprehending the divine *nirguna* (without attributes)? Another way to put the question, is the divine in *The Bhagavad Gita* personal or transpersonal? Many interpreters of the work suggest that the figure of Krṣṇa paradoxically is both personal and impersonal.

The world, or the *māyā* (illusion), puzzle asks if the world is real or unreal. One of the arguments Krṣṇa offers to the reluctant warrior, Arjuna, is that he can neither kill nor be killed. If *The Bhagavad Gita* was written under the influence of Sāmkhya philosophy, then it reconciles *purusha* (spirit) and *prakriti* (nature). If *The Bhagavad Gita* is read as representative of Vedānta thinking, as a nondualist text, then it recognizes that *ātman* is *Brahman*, or that the self is inseparable from the divine (and everything else that seems real is *maya*, the net of illusion). In either case, according to *The Bhagavad Gita*, humanity cannot be released from acting in the world, but humans must release themselves from desiring the fruits of their actions.

The self, or the *ātman*, puzzle, related to the *maya* puzzle, asks what the self is. *The Bhagavad Gita* speaks to more than one notion of a self. First, there is the provisional self in an embodied personality. In Sāṃkhya doctrine, there are three *gunas* (strands, threads, or mental states), aspects of the personality: *sattva* (purity and selfless happiness), *rajas* (restlessness, fieriness, misery), and *tamas* (dull lethargy). Some combination of these *gunas* describes a person's character. Second, there is the universal self, or *ātman*, which is divine. Often the word *ātman* is translated as "soul," causing the term to be confused with a Western concept of personal soul, which attains eternity for the individual, transitory personality. Instead, *ātman* refers to the transpersonal aspect of the self that is beyond ephemeral self-identifications. Certainly the dialogue in *The Bhagavad Gita* draws on the range of meanings of self.

The yoga puzzle, involving the self in relation to the world and the divine, asks what people are to do. The first three puzzles, regarding the divine, the world, and self, conclude with the fourth puzzle, regarding how the self is in relation to the world and the divine. There are three primary yogas in the work: karma (action), *bhakti* (loving devotion), and *jñana* (knowledge). Many scholars contend that *The Bhagavad Gita* is fundamentally a case for karma yoga, yet *The Bhagavad Gita* clearly makes a case for all three. Can one of these methods be identified as the essence of Kṛṣṇa's teaching? In chapter 3, Arjuna must learn to work (karma) without seeking goals or rewards for his action. Kṛṣṇa tells Arjuna that action is better than inaction, that he must perform his duty free from attachment to the fruits of that work. Moreover, even though nothing is to be attained and has not been attained already, "Yet," Kṛṣṇa says, "I work." In chapter 9, Arjuna also learns that devotion is the purest form of worship. "If one offers me with *bhakti*, a leaf, a flower, fruit, or water, I accept it." In chapter 4, Arjuna learns that *jñana* is the ultimate *marga* (path). Arjuna "cuts with the sword of wisdom (*jñana*) this doubt born of ignorance, follow the means of wisdom." Finally, the distinction between these yogas, or disciplines, breaks

down, and knowledge, action, and devotion are intermingled and united.

SIGNIFICANCE

In 1785, Charles Wilkins first translated *Bhagavadgītā* into English, and although there may be no precise English equivalents either linguistically, theologically, or philosophically for many of the words used, the book has had an enduring influence on the West. The essential qualities of American nineteenth century thought, as evidenced in the works of Ralph Waldo Emerson, Henry David Thoreau, and Walt Whitman, were profoundly influenced by these writers' readings of *The Bhagavad Gita*. Mahatma Gandhi (1869-1948), who helped lead India to independence in 1947, first became interested in *The Bhagavad Gita* in an English translation; his interpretation of it became part of the very fabric of his life's work. Although *The Bhagavad Gita* takes place on a battlefield, Gandhi was certain that the book was not about the necessity of warfare but rather proved its futility. It has become the most beloved of all Hindu texts and, since its translation into European languages, has profoundly influenced Western culture as well.

—*Lynda Sexson*

FURTHER READING

Gandhi, Mohandas K. *The Gospel of Selfless Action: Or, The Gita According to Gandhi.* Translated with an introduction by Mahadev Desai. Roseville, Calif.: Dry Bones Press, 2000. Originally published for an unsophisticated audience in India, the text exemplifies the use of *The Bhagavad Gita* in Gandhi's philosophy of nonviolence.

Nicolas, Antonio de, trans. *The Bhagavad Gita.* York Beach, Maine: Nicolas-Hays, 1990. An elegant translation and an invaluable introductory essay on models of interpretation of Arjuna's crisis and liberation.

Prabhavananda, Swami, and Christopher Isherwood. *The Song of God: Bhagavad-Gita.* Introduction by Aldous Huxley. 1944. Reprint. New York: Penguin Books, 1954. This lyrical translation also includes Huxley's introduction and two appendices on cosmology and war.

Sargent, Winthrop. *The Bhagavad Gita.* New York: State University of New York Press, 1994. Each page provides one stanza in Sanskrit in the Devanagari script, in transliteration, in a literal translation, and in English.

Sharma, Arvind. *The Hindu Gita: Ancient and Classical Interpretations of the Bhagavadgītā.* La Salle, Ill.:

Open Court, 1986. A thorough guide to the major Hindu interpretations of the text, which is a reminder that there are several crucial interpretive issues in the tradition of Hinduism.

Sharpe, Eric J. *The Universal Gita: Western Images of the Bhagavad Gita.* La Salle, Ill.: Open Court, 1985.

Tells the story of the influence *The Bhagavad Gita* has had on Western culture.

SEE ALSO: 1500-1100 B.C.E., Compilation of the Vedas; c. 400 B.C.E.-400 C.E., Composition of the *Mahābhārata*; c. 200 B.C.E., Birth of Hinduism.

200 B.C.E.-200 C.E.
NASCA LINES DRAWN IN DESERT NEAR COAST OF PERU

Although many hypotheses have been advanced, the so-called Nasca lines and figures remain enigmatic. Careful analyses of the Nasca culture indicate that these figures probably served several different purposes.

LOCALE: Nasca Plain, Peru
CATEGORY: Prehistory and ancient cultures

SUMMARY OF EVENT

About 200 miles (320 kilometers) south of Lima, Peru, is the Nasca Plain, a featureless desert of red-brown pebbles located on a high, rainless plateau. Although the view from the ground is uninteresting, aerial views reveal an enduring and enigmatic human-constructed spectacle, the Nasca lines and images. Etched into the desert floor are a huge conglomeration of lines, geometric shapes, and images of animals. Although the size of the figures is gargantuan, spanning hundreds of feet, they are surprisingly well proportioned, while the lines connecting the figures extend for miles and are absolutely straight.

These markings were created by Nasca peoples some two thousand years ago, when a thin layer of dark rock was removed to reveal the lighter-colored soil beneath, enhanced by stacking the cleared stones along the border to a height of several inches. At ground level, many of the lines are difficult to see and the figures are unrecognizable. Why would these ancient people develop the skills and dedicate considerable time and energy to construct geoglyphs (ground drawings) and markings that are neither intelligible nor impressive when viewed from earth's surface? There are no nearby hills or mountains to give a higher perspective, and there is no evidence that any type of tower or viewing platform was ever constructed.

The enigma of the lines has aroused speculation ranging from scientific hypotheses to outlandish propositions devoid of archaeological support. One early suggestion was that the geoglyphs, obviously constructed to be viewed from the air, were observed from primitive hot-air balloons. This idea, however, does not explain the many straight lines, or narrow roads, that begin nowhere and lead to nowhere.

Writer Jim Woodman, convinced that constructing large drawings would have been pointless if not viewable from the air, in 1975 enlisted a British balloonist to build a balloon to demonstrate that the ancient Nascans could have flown over the plain. Constructing the balloons from materials readily available and filled with hot smoke from a fire pit, the adventurers managed, with some difficulty, a two-minute flight to a height of 300 feet (91 meters). Although this demonstration proved that balloon flight was at least a theoretical possibility, absolutely no archaeological evidence (such as remnants of huge fire pits) supports the hypothesis.

Another hypothesis, first advanced in the 1950's by British UFOlogists, was that the Nasca lines served as an airport for extraterrestrials. This idea became popular after Swiss author Erich van Daniken included it in his best-selling 1968 book, *Chariots of the Gods*. He asserted that the triangles and trapezoids were landing strips constructed and used by ancient astronauts; he even included a photograph of a Nasca "runway" with "parking bays" similar to those found at modern airports. Although widely promoted in the popular press, this hypothesis was never taken seriously by scientists. Throughout van Daniken's writings, archaeological knowledge is consistently distorted, if not ignored, and *ad hominum* arguments to discredit professional researchers abound. The concept of using the markings as aircraft landing strips is ludicrous; the surface is so insubstantial that any vehicle lacking four-wheel drive quickly becomes mired in soft sand, and intergalactic travelers would undoubtedly utilize a more sophisticated landing procedure. The so-called runway and parking bays shown in *Chariots of the Gods* is actually a photograph of the right knee and

The Nasca lines and figures include this great bird, visible from high above the ground. (Archivo Iconografico/Corbis)

four claws of a large bird. The shoddy research utilized by van Daniken renders his hypothesis completely devoid of merit and totally inadequate to account for any aspect of the Nasca Plain.

A hypothesis that was widely studied and at one time accepted is that the straight lines were laid out to align with critical rising and setting points of the Sun, Moon, and important stars or constellations, thus functioning as an astronomical calendar. For example, if a "road" lined up with the setting positions of the Sun at the solstices, priests would have an accurate means of tracking seasons, an absolute necessity for successful agriculture. The main proponent of this belief is Maria Reiche, a German mathematician who has devoted forty years of her life to studying, surveying, and protecting the fragile markings from the destructive intrusions of modern technology, such as dirt bikes and four-wheelers.

Although Reiche's calendar theory is based on sound science and decades of careful observation, it is almost certainly mistaken, even though intricate sky lore was known and practiced by the Incas. Because there are dozens of lines running in every conceivable direction, it is possible that the alignment of a path with an important astronomical event (such as the position of the setting Sun on the summer solstice) occurred by pure chance. Alternatively, the builders could have had some as yet unimagined astronomical purpose for constructing the straight lines; this idea spurred Reiche to survey and graph more than 250 lines. The results demonstrate that the lines are distributed fairly evenly along the horizon, with several slightly denser clusters of possible significance. For example, about a dozen lines point 68 to 70 degrees east of north, the direction where the Pleiades (a prominent star cluster) rose during the later stages of Nasca culture. Unfortunately, her approach was marred somewhat by including many different sorts of lines (straight roads and pieces of complex geometrical figures), all treated equally. If enough lines are included and sufficient astronomical events considered, correlation by pure chance becomes increasingly probable.

A further attempt to examine the astronomical alignment hypothesis was made by astronomer Gerald Hawkins in 1968. Earlier he had used a computer to demonstrate that the stones and other prominent features of Stonehenge (Salisbury Plain, England) aligned with major astronomical events and could be used to predict eclipses. Hawkins used the same computer program to check the alignment of 186 of the Nasca lines against the movements of the Sun, Moon, planets, and stars along the horizon during the period when the lines were constructed. Although 39 of the 186 directions accurately matched major Sun and Moon angles, half could be accounted for by pure chance. Furthermore, the results were inconsistent because some geometrical figures yielded an alignment while an identical figure elsewhere did not. Planetary and major star alignments were even less promising, causing Hawkins to conclude that the astronomical hypothesis could not account for the majority of the lines, although he admitted that several significant lines certainly could be astronomical.

Then what is the most likely explanation for the lines? To comprehend the markings, it is imperative to place the lines in the cultural context of the ancient Nasca peoples. Archaeological research has discovered that constructing lines was not unique to Nasca; similar, if less spectacular, examples can be found elsewhere in their empire, indicating broadly dispersed common motivations that could slowly have altered over time. The scarcity of water compelled the development of elaborate irrigation techniques with technology unsurpassed until the twentieth century. Their success in eking out an existence in an inhospitable environment evolved in tandem with a complex belief system employing powerful hallucinogens to supplicate supernatural animals for support in earthly endeavors. Ceremonies venerating mountain deities identified with weather phenomena and fertility are still performed at the terminuses of some lines, suggesting that a deep-rooted corpus of belief still influences actions of their descendants. The religion affirmed by these visible manifestations seems to embody more than irrational superstition; many of the legends and rites are symbolic synoptic representations distilled from centuries of vigilant observation of nature. By correlating rainfall cycles with celestial regularities, they would have been able to predict the expedient periods of the agricultural cycle to optimize the use of their limited resources.

Today, the ancient preoccupation with rituals is accepted by most scientists as the best explanation for many of the markings. Rituals for agricultural fertility, mountain worship, and the summoning of water (a regional commodity always in short supply) could explain the "roads" as paths leading to the mountain gods and the geoglyphs as sites for ceremonies worshiping supernatural animals.

SIGNIFICANCE

The Nasca lines and geogyphs are much more than a remnant of an obscure period of an inconsequential culture. Rather, the figures graphically elucidate perhaps the most remarkable achievement of an extraordinary culture: The Andean people were able, not merely to survive, but also to thrive in a hostile coastal desert where rainfall is virtually unknown. The Nasca figures are not merely a spectacular ancient conception but a symbol of the adaptability and ingenuity of the pre-Columbian civilization of the Andes.

—*George R. Plitnik*

FURTHER READING

Hadingham, Evan. *Lines to the Mountain Gods: Nazca and the Mysteries of Peru.* New York: Random House, 1987. A critical analysis of the many hypotheses proposed over the years to explain the Nasca lines and a comprehensive review of the Nascan culture presented to support the most likely explanation.

Kroeber, Alfred Louis, and Donald Collier. *The Archaeology and Pottery of Nazca, Peru: Alfred L. Kroeber's 1926 Expedition.* Edited by Patrick H. Carmichael. Walnut Creek, Calif.: AltaMira, 1998. Tells the fascinating story of Kroeber's discoveries in Peru and his excavation report, which did not see light until the end of the century. The earliest and still the primary analysis of Nasca pottery, architecture, cloth, hair bundles, and other material culture, including early descriptions and photographs of the famous Nasca lines. More than four hundred photographs and drawings, thirty-two in color.

Mason, J. Alden. *The Ancient Civilizations of Peru.* New York: Penguin Books, 1975. Traces the development of Incas' culture from their predecessors and discusses their history, economics, social organization, religion, intellectual life, and arts and crafts.

Moseley, Michael. *The Incas and Their Ancestors: The Archaeology of Peru.* London: Thames & Hudson, 2001. A survey of the development and golden age of Inca civilization emphasizing the art, architecture, and government.

Silverman, Helaine. *Cahuachi in the Ancient Nasca World.* Iowa City: University of Iowa Press, 1993. A

200 - 101 B.C.E.

full account, including discussion of the Nasca. Illustrations, maps.

Von Hagen, Adriana, and Craig Morris. *The Cities of the Ancient Andes.* London: Thames & Hudson, 2001. Although the pages devoted entirely to the Nasca Plain are few, this book offers an excellent survey of Inca cities, monuments, and culture.

SEE ALSO: c. 2500 B.C.E., Construction of Monumental Architecture at Caral in Peru; c. 1800-c. 1500 B.C.E., Construction of El Paraíso in Peru; c. 100 B.C.E.-c. 1000 C.E., Construction of the Pyramids of the Sun and Moon at Teotihuacán; c. 100-c. 700 C.E., Moche Build the Huaca del Sol and Huaca de la Luna.

c. 200 B.C.E.-c. 500 C.E.
HOPEWELL PEOPLE CONSTRUCT EARTHWORKS

Earthworks of the Hopewell Culture indicate that groups of prehistoric Native Americans shared elaborate rituals, established an extensive exchange system, and held a sophisticated understanding of astronomy and geometry.

LOCALE: Scioto River Valley (near modern Chillicothe, Ohio)

CATEGORY: Prehistory and ancient cultures

SUMMARY OF EVENT

Between approximately 200 B.C.E. and 500 C.E. independent groups of Native Americans living in eastern North America practiced similar customs and rituals, characterized by the construction of monumental earthworks and burial mounds. Collectively, these practices are referred to as the Hopewell culture.

Although influence of the Hopewell can be found throughout the Missouri, Mississippi, and Ohio River Valleys, the culture was most prominent in southwestern Ohio, with the largest concentration in the Scioto River Valley near present-day Chillicothe, Ohio. The term "Hopewell" comes from a nineteenth century farmer, Mordecai Hopewell, on whose property the complex later named the Hopewell Earthworks was located.

The most impressive manifestation of Hopewell culture is to be found in its earthworks and mounds, numbering in the tens of thousands. Geometrical enclosures, some more than 1,000 feet (305 meters) across and with walls 12 feet (3.7 meters) high, distinguish Hopewell from the earlier mound-building Adena culture as well as from Illinois Hopewell. Mounds in the shapes of animals and conical burial mounds reaching up to 30 feet (9 meters) are located in or near the enclosures. The Hopewell employed precise standards of measurement in their constructions, often aligning them with lunar and solar cycles and orienting them to the east.

Large enclosures typically included a rectangular wooden building or great house, constructed on evenly spaced posts. Separate areas within the great house were used for elaborate burial preparations. Although cremation was common, skeletal remains were entombed in log crypts inside the great house. Once the great house had served its purpose, it was dismantled or burned and a mound built over it. Other structures within the enclosures may have been used for holding ceremonies, storing cremated remains, and securing valued artifacts.

The largest enclosure, part of the Hopewell Earthworks at Paint Creek, west of Chillicothe, covers 111 acres (45 hectares) and contains the largest Hopewell burial mound, which is 34 feet (10.4 meters) high and 500 feet (152.4 meters) long. This site was first surveyed by Ephraim G. Squier and Edwin H. Davis in the 1840's. Although Squier and Davis conducted some excavation, it was not until 1892 that significant discoveries were found. An excavation arranged by Harvard archaeologist Frederick Ward Putnam, in preparation for the World's Columbian Exposition, yielded an extraordinary quantity of burial goods: jewelry, animal-shaped or effigy cutouts, ornaments of copper, mica, and gold, conch shells, carved teeth of grizzly bears, effigy pipes, and tens of thousands of freshwater pearls. The variety of materials from which these burial goods were composed reflects a vast and complex exchange network extending eastward to the Atlantic coast, south to the Gulf of Mexico, west to the Rocky Mountains, and north into Canada.

Differing types and amounts of burial goods found with remains and the variation in funeral practices indicate a class structure, with only an elite few receiving elaborate burials. Unlike Adena interments, which appear to have buried generationally, adding layers to mounds, the Hopewell erected a mound following the interment of an important person, arranging cremated and skeletal remains from earlier deaths around the central crypt. Evidence from skulls suggests many elite burials were members of one prominent family of the Ohio Hopewell.

The class structure suggests that the Hopewell, who were cultivators as well as hunter-gatherers, were more settled than earlier cultures; however, there is little evidence of large villages. Habitation sites, which have been identified by patterns of post holes and middens or trash pits, were small, often single-family households. These dwellings are believed to have been semipermanent, the inhabitants relocating every few years, presumably when nutrients in the soil had been exhausted. Graves located near habitation sites offer further proof of social stratification: Many Hopewell were buried without accompanying goods in unmarked locations.

Identifying habitation sites has been difficult, not only because dwellings were constructed of perishable material, but also because they were often scattered at a distance from the earthworks. Yet it is obvious that people came together at arranged times to erect ceremonial sites and participate in seasonal rituals. Clearly, the Hopewell had evolved a calendar, and there is some evidence of pilgrimages. In 1995, Bradley T. Lepper, an archaeologist from the Ohio Historical Society, working with maps drawn by researchers more than a century earlier, postulated the existence of a road 60 miles (97 kilometers) long linking major groupings of earthworks in Chillicothe with those in Newark, Ohio.

By the end of the fifth century C.E., the Hopewell culture disappeared. Although it is possible that it died out because of disease or migrated because of deteriorating resources, more likely it was dispersed or eliminated by invading tribes. The last examples of Hopewell earthworks are palisaded hilltop enclosures resembling forts, and the western orientation of post-Hopewell burials implies an incursion of Iriquois.

Although the ending of Hopewell culture is readily apparent, the beginnings are less easily discernible. Some researchers regard the Hopewell as descendants of the Adena; others believe the two coexisted for several centuries. Yet it is widely recognized that Hopewell is a markedly distinct culture. Even though daily life may have been similar for the two groups, their social structure and belief systems were dramatically different. The stratification of Hopewellian society evidenced in burial customs suggests that the elite functioned as intermediaries between the earth and the spiritual world, a radical departure from the apparent egalitarianism of the Adena. Further, the complexity and sophistication of the Hopewell earthworks indicate enormous changes in worldview and thought processes. What brought about these changes and why they were concentrated in one small area have yet to be determined.

SIGNIFICANCE

The earthworks of the Adena, Hopewell, and later Fort Ancient cultures commanded the attention of early Americans, such as Benjamin Franklin and Thomas Jefferson, who excavated a mound at Monticello, Jefferson's home in Virginia. However, it was generally believed that the earthworks were too complex to have been created by Native Americans, and in the absence of written records, vast speculation about their creators ensued. The researchers Squier and Davis determined that the mound builders were a lost race, not ancestors of the indigenous peoples. In 1882, newspaper publisher Ignatious Donnelly wrote that the mounds were constructed by survivors of the lost continent Atlantis. Other theories named Egyptians, Celts, Hindus, Vikings, and prehistoric masons. Attempting to settle the matter, the U.S. Congress, in 1894, allocated funds to the Federal Bureau of Ethnology, and studies conducted by its director, Cyrus Thomas, revealed conclusive evidence—some which was available to earlier scientists—that the mound builders were indeed prehistoric Native Americans. Writing in 2001, historian Thomas S. Garlington attributes the misreading of archaeological evidence to prejudice and believes the failure to identify correctly the mound-building cultures helped justify repressive policies through the nineteenth century.

Research since mid-twentieth century has firmly established the contributions of Hopewell to the progress of civilization in North America. They appear to be the earliest cultivators of maize, and their advancements in agriculture led to increasingly stable and complex social structure. Their intellectual achievements are remarkable: Without precise tools, they created exact standards of measurement, comprehended and applied geometric principles, devised calendric lore, and acquired a working knowledge of astronomy, all of which is reflected in the construction and design of their earthworks.

—K Edgington

FURTHER READING

Korp, Maureen. *The Sacred Geography of the American Mound Builders.* Lewiston, N.Y.: E. Mellen, 1990. A discussion grounded in history and physical evidence. Chapters on the Adena and Hopewell cultures draw perceptive distinctions between the two.

Romain, William F. *Mysteries of the Hopewell: Astronomer, Geometers, and Magicians of the Eastern Woodlands.* Akron, Ohio: University of Akron Press,

2000. Using precise measurements of archaeological sites, the author attempts to connect the earthworks with a highly complex worldview; he also presents convincing evidence that the Serpent Mound is a Hopewell structure rather than Adena or Fort Ancient.

Shetrone, Henry Clyde. *The Mound-Builders: A Reconstruction of the Life of a Prehistoric American Race, Through Exploration and Interpretation of Their Earth Mounds, Their Burials, and Their Cultural Remains.* New York: D. Appleton and Company, 1930. The first comprehensive text written for nonspecialists, this volume provides an overview of mound building cultures, but focuses on the Ohio valley earthworks, including one chapter devoted specifically to the Hopewell. Index, bibliography, and 299 illustrations.

Silverberg, Robert. *Mound Builders of Ancient America: The Archaeology of a Myth.* Greenwich, Conn.: New York Graphic Society, 1968. A rich examination of myths about the origins of the mound builders. The chapter on the Adena and Hopewell represents theories in place at mid-twentieth century.

Woodward, Susan L., and Herry N. McDonald. *Indian Mounds of the Middle Ohio Valley.* Blacksburg, Va.: McDonald and Woodward, 2002. An excellent guide providing maps, illustrations, and an historical overview of Adena, Hopewell, Cole, and Fort Ancient sites.

SEE ALSO: c. 1800-c. 700 B.C.E., Poverty Point Culture Builds Earthworks; c. 1000 B.C.E.-c. 100 C.E., Adena Mound Builders Live in North America; c. 1000 B.C.E.-c. 900 C.E., Woodland Culture Flourishes in Northern America; 200-1250 C.E., Anasazi Civilization Flourishes in American Southwest.

---

180 B.C.E.

ESTABLISHMENT OF THE *CURSUS HONORUM*

The establishment of the cursus honorum *restructured Roman government through new regulations governing officeholders.*

LOCALE: Rome (now in Italy)

CATEGORIES: Government and politics; laws, acts, and legal history

KEY FIGURES

Scipio Africanus (236-184/183 B.C.E.), consul in 205 B.C.E.

Lucius Villius (fl. late third-second century B.C.E.), plebeian tribune in 180 B.C.E.

SUMMARY OF EVENT

The growth of Rome from an insignificant river city to the administrative center of a far-flung empire brought with it numerous changes in the machinery of its government. Many of these changes were made gradually but some were concessions forced by new political situations. A significant stage in this process was marked by the law passed in 180 B.C.E., the *Lex villius annalis.* Understanding of its full significance, however, requires a historical description of the Roman magisterial offices.

Before the establishment of the Roman Republic, all final political power in Rome resided in the person of the king, while the executive officers of the state acted solely as his personal representatives. With the overthrow of the monarchy, these officials, called magistrates by the Romans, became effective representatives of the entire community; their powers, duties, and privileges were thought to be derived from the senate and people conjointly, even though in the early period the people were limited solely to ratifying the election of patrician candidates. At that time the most powerful officials were the two consuls, elected for terms of one year. Only patricians were eligible for this office until the Licinian laws of 367 B.C.E. threw it open to the plebeians. So strong was the aristocratic domination of Roman political life, however, that only in 172 B.C.E. were both consuls plebeians. The duties of the consuls were diverse; they were charged with conducting the affairs of the senate, maintaining public order throughout Italy, and leading the army in time of war.

The second most powerful office was the praetorship. It seems probable that the first praetor was elected in 360 B.C.E., although there are some indications that the office may have formed part of the original constitution of the republic. Plebeians first became eligible for it in 337 B.C.E. The praetor was above all the supreme civil judge. In 242 B.C.E., the number of annually elected praetors was increased to two, so that one could be placed in charge of lawsuits between Roman citizens and aliens. As Rome's overseas dominions increased, the number of praetors was raised to four in 227 B.C.E., allowing two praetors to serve as governors of the newly formed provinces of Sicily and Sardinia. In 197 B.C.E., the number was raised to six, the additional two officers being assigned to administer the two provinces of Spain.

An office not constitutionally essential for election to higher offices, but extremely influential in itself, was the aedileship. At the beginning of the Roman Republic, two aediles were appointed to supervise the temples and religious practices of the plebeians. Ultimately, they were given control over public buildings, street maintenance, the distribution of the corn supply, and, above all, production of the public games. This capacity enabled ambitious politicians to stage lavish and spectacular games in an attempt to gain popularity with the urban electorate.

The lowest political office was the quaestorship. The office was probably created at the beginning of the republic, with the number of annually elected quaestors raised to four in 421 B.C.E. At the same time, plebeians were also made eligible for the office. Ultimately the number of quaestors was fixed at twenty. Two of the quaestors had charge of the state treasury and official archives. The others were attached as aides either to generals on campaign or to provincial governors. Their duties were diverse: financial, judicial, and military.

These four offices formed the so-called *cursus honorum*, the order in which political offices had to be held, although the aedileship was not necessarily a prerequisite for election to any other office. The *cursus honorum* did not exist before 180 B.C.E., since until that time there were no age qualifications assigned to any of these offices, nor was the holding of any one office a necessary condition for election to another higher office. Thus Scipio Africanus, the conqueror of Hannibal, was elected consul for 205 B.C.E. at the age of thirty-one, and Titus Quinctius Flamininus (c. 229-174 B.C.E.), the victor at Cynoscephalae in 197 B.C.E., was elected consul in 198 B.C.E. at a similarly early age. This situation was drastically altered by a law carried in 180 B.C.E. by the tribune Lucius Villius that set fixed age qualifications for the various offices. The probable age limits established were forty for the praetor and forty-three for the consul. Although no minimum age was placed on the quaestors, it was generally understood that candidates who stood for this office would have already completed their ten-year military obligation and thus be approximately twenty-eight years old.

SIGNIFICANCE

The establishment of the *cursus honorum* placed a regular and restrained order over the advancement of all political careers and thus made it difficult for a politician to

rise to power purely through popularity or force. In an age when the average lifespan of a Roman male was around forty years, the age requirements imposed by the *cursus honorum* meant that only the elders—and presumably the wise men—of the community were eligible for leadership. The *cursus honorum* also restricted eligibility for public office by age after a period during which participation in political life was increasingly opening up to plebians, thus, at least theoretically, replacing a class-based political structure with one more amenable to rewarding talent and experience.

—George M. Pepe, updated by Jeffrey L. Buller

FURTHER READING

Adcock, F. E. *Roman Political Ideas and Practice*. 1959. Reprint. Ann Arbor: University of Michigan Press, 1994. A discussion of how theory and practice intersected in ancient Roman politics. An excellent place for the general reader to begin.

Gardner, Jane F. *Being a Roman Citizen*. London: Routledge, 1993. A good introduction to the duties and responsibilities of Roman citizenship, including the political offices of the *cursus honorum*. Written in a popular style but well researched.

Lintott, Andrew. *The Constitution of the Roman Republic*. New York: Oxford University Press, 1999. A detailed overview of Roman government, outlining the various offices and they way they worked. Also discusses the legacy of the Roman constitution in later European history.

Scullard, Howard Hayes. *A History of the Roman World: 753-146 B.C.* 5th ed. New York: Routledge, 2003. Lavishly detailed and comprehensive in scope, this book sets a discussion of Roman politics against the background of early economic, military, and social history.

SEE ALSO: c. 509 B.C.E., Roman Republic Replaces Monarchy; 494/493 B.C.E., Institution of the Plebeian Tribunate; 451-449 B.C.E., Twelve Tables of Roman Law Are Formulated; 445 B.C.E., Establishment of the Canuleian Law; 340-338 B.C.E., Origin of *Municipia*; 287 B.C.E., *Lex Hortensia* Reforms the Roman Constitution; 90 B.C.E., Julian Law Expands Roman Citizenship; 43-42 B.C.E., Second Triumvirate Enacts Proscriptions; 27-23 B.C.E., Completion of the Augustan Settlement; c. 50 C.E., Creation of the Roman Imperial Bureaucracy; 68-69 C.E., Year of the Four Emperors; c. 165 C.E., Gaius Creates Edition of the *Institutes* of Roman Law.

RELATED ARTICLE in *Great Lives from History: The Ancient World*: Scipio Africanus.

167-142 B.C.E.
REVOLT OF THE MACCABEES

The Maccabees revolted against the Seleucids, recaptured Jerusalem, and ruled Judaea until the end of the second century B.C.E.

LOCALE: Judaea (now in Israel)
CATEGORY: Wars, uprisings, and civil unrest

KEY FIGURES

Antiochus IV Epiphanes (c. 215-164 B.C.E.), Seleucid king, r. 175-164 B.C.E.

Joshua (fl. second century B.C.E.), Jewish notable, brother of Onias III, high priest, 174-172 B.C.E.

Onias III (fl. late third-second century B.C.E.), Jewish high priest, 185-174 B.C.E.

Onias (fl. second century B.C.E.), Jewish notable, high priest, 172-163/162 B.C.E.

Mattathias (d. c. 166 B.C.E.), Jewish notable of priestly rank

Judas Maccabaeus (d. 160 B.C.E.), son of Mattathias, soldier, and patriot

Jonathan (d.143/142 B.C.E.), younger brother of Judas Maccabaeus and high priest, 152-143/142 B.C.E.

SUMMARY OF EVENT

The Seleucid king Antiochus the Great (r. 223-187 B.C.E.) took Judaea from the Ptolemies of Egypt in the Fifth Syrian War (201-200) and made it part of his Asian empire. He lowered taxes and guaranteed freedom to Jews to practice their religion and follow their ancestral laws. Nevertheless, the Jews hated the Seleucids, regarding them as godless promoters of foreign customs, greedy taxers of widows and orphans, and, above all, protectors of the idols that the pagans worshiped. They failed to propagate the true worship of the Lord Yahweh. Some Jews even hoped for the return of the Ptolemies so that they might recover the lucrative official posts they had once held. On the whole, however, Seleucid rule provoked much less hostility than the Ptolemaic Dynasty had caused. More Jews collaborated than had done so under the Ptolemies because the Seleucids were milder and because the important cultural currents that had been flowing over Judaea since the beginning of the Greek period now began to bring forth fruit. Hellenism at its best was an attractive way of life, with its sensible humanism and its personal freedoms; it made Jewish dietary restrictions and the painful practice of circumcision appear to be barbaric superstitions. Conversions to Hellenism occurred, and about 180 B.C.E., Jesus ben Sirach, the author of Ecclesiasticus, had to admonish the younger generation to have greater respect for the traditional Jewish Law.

Judaea was caught up in great international events during the reign of the Seleucid Antiochus IV Epiphanes, a remarkable man: efficient, brilliant, and erratic. His father Antiochus the Great had been badly beaten in a war with Rome, and in the aftermath of that debacle, the Seleucids lost their easternmost provinces. To strengthen the weakened state, Antiochus decided to encourage the partially Hellenized towns of his empire to adopt the Greek civic institutions of gymnasia, Hellenized religious cults, and autonomous assemblies. In this way, he hoped to increase the stock of Hellenized manpower available for the defense of his empire against Rome and for the recovery of his lost eastern territory.

In 174 B.C.E. a Hellenically minded Jewish notable named Joshua, whose name was altered to the Greek form "Jason," proposed to make Jerusalem a Greek city if Antiochus would depose the high priest Onias III and install Jason in his place. Antiochus accepted this offer and granted a charter to the newly organized Jerusalem. A gymnasium was built, and Jewish youths exercised in the nude, to the dismay of conservatives. A citizen body was enrolled and debated affairs in a *gerousia*, or council, to the degradation of the Jewish law. In 172 B.C.E., Jason was outbid for his office by a man called Onias, who offered to increase the taxes paid by Judaea to Antiochus. The king straightway deposed Jason, who withdrew into sullen exile, and invested Onias as high priest under the Greek name Menelaus. Jews loyal to their law were rightly outraged at this cavalier treatment of their most sacred office, and Jews friendly to the Seleucids were disturbed to see Antiochus's sudden cancellation of his father's promise of lowered taxes.

Simultaneously, Ptolemy VI was preparing a war to recover Palestine. Antiochus, however, attacked him first, and, in the Sixth Syrian War (170-168 B.C.E.), he defeated the Egyptian forces, captured Ptolemy, and made himself king of Egypt. At this point Rome intervened, fearful that Antiochus was growing too strong, and ordered him out of Egypt on pain of instant war. Antiochus prepared to obey. His diplomatic defeat inspired a rumor reporting his death, and Joshua (Jason) decided to drive his rival Menelaus (Onias) out of Jerusalem (Antioch) at this favorable moment. Antiochus, returning to Syria, came on the city in revolt against his lawful high priest.

He suppressed the revolt by force, fined the Jews heavily, and, later in 167, decided to assist his loyal Hellenizers by forbidding the practice of the Jewish religion in Judaea. In the temple, the worship of the Syrian god Baal Shamim was substituted for that of Yahweh. This provoked armed resistance. In 167, Mattathias, a landed magnate of priestly rank, revolted. From 167 until 164, while Antiochus was campaigning in the east against Parthia with first-line Seleucid troops, Mattathias's son Judas, surnamed Maccabaeus (the Hammer), warred against Seleucid mercenaries and Hellenized Jewish militia alike, successfully establishing himself in the countryside. Even so, he had to accept a truce with the Seleucid government in the spring of 164. During this war, about 165 B.C.E., the Old Testament book of Daniel was made public in its present form. It was an important part of Jewish propaganda, looking forward to the death of Antiochus ("a mouth speaking great things"), the end of the Hellenistic Age, and the dawn of a divine fifth monarchy, presided over by a Messianic figure. Late in 164, Antiochus unexpectedly died, and Judas took advantage of this to break the truce. He entered Jerusalem and seized the temple, which in December was ritually cleansed and rededicated to Yahweh.

SIGNIFICANCE

With Antiochus dead, the Seleucid Dynasty soon suffered the disaster of the emergence of two rival lines of kings at war with each other. With the central government distracted, the courageous, skillful, and ruthless Maccabees made headway in Judaea until, in 152 B.C.E.,

both Seleucid factions recognized Jonathan, a younger brother of Judas (who had been killed in the fighting), as high priest. In 142, his brother Simon became king of newly independent Judaea, founding the Hasmonean kingdom, which lasted until Rome conquered Palestine in 63 B.C.E. This century of Jewish independence was a time of great national, cultural, and religious revival, and of growing strife between differing schools of religious thought and belief.

—Samuel K. Eddy

FURTHER READING

Bickerman, Elias. *The God of the Maccabees: Studies on the Origin and Meaning of the Maccabean Revolt.* Leiden, Netherlands: Brill, 1979. Bickerman focuses on the revolt and its significance.

_____. *The Maccabees: An Account of Their History from the Beginnings to the Fall of the House of the Hasmoneans.* New York: Shocken Books, 1947. A short but highly competent survey by an outstanding scholar.

Cohen, Shaye. *From the Maccabees to the Mishnah.* Philadelphia: Westminster John Knox Press, 1995. An examination of Jewish history, beginning with the Maccabees.

Schalit, Abraham, ed. *The Hellenistic Age: Political History of Jewish Palestine from 332 to 67 B.C.E.* New Brunswick, N.J.: Rutgers University Press, 1972. This history of Jewish Palestine covers the period in which the Maccabean rebellion occurred.

Sievers, Joseph. *The Hasmoneans and Their Supporters:*

200 - 101 B.C.E.

MILESTONES IN THE REVOLT OF THE MACCABEES, 167-142 B.C.E.	
Date	Event
167	Jewish priest Mattathias and his sons revolt against Syrians.
167	After his father's death, Judas Maccabaeus assumes leadership.
167-164	Judas wins battles at Ascent of Lebonah, Beth Horon, Emmaus, and Bethsura.
164	Maccabeans repair temple in Jerusalem.
162	Syrian regent Lysias defeats the Jews at Bethsura and Beth Zachariah.
162	Syrian general Bacchides defeats Judas and drives him from Jerusalem.
161	Judas defeats Syrians at Adasa; Judas is defeated and killed in battle at Elasa; his brother Jonathan takes command.
155	Jonathan occupies a fortress at Beth-Basi, resulting in a negotiated peace that gives him control over most of Judaea.
152	Jonathan is recognized as high priest.
143	Jonathan falls into a trap and is captured and executed at Ptolemais.
142	Jonathan's brother Simon becomes king of newly independent Judaea; he and his descendants found the Hasmonean kingdom.

From Mattathias to the Death of John Hycranus I. Atlanta: Scholars Press, 1990. Sievers examines the Hasmonean Dynasty that began with the Maccabean rebellion.

SEE ALSO: c. 1280 B.C.E., Israelite Exodus from Egypt; c. 966 B.C.E., Building of the Temple of Jerusalem;

c. 922 B.C.E., Establishment of the Kingdom of Israel; 587-423 B.C.E., Birth of Judaism; 323 B.C.E., Founding of the Ptolemaic Dynasty and Seleucid Kingdom; c. 135 B.C.E., Rise of the Pharisees.

RELATED ARTICLES in *Great Lives from History: The Ancient World:* Antiochus the Great; Herod the Great; Flavius Josephus

---

159 B.C.E.
ROMAN PLAYWRIGHT TERENCE DIES

The landscape of Roman drama changed forever following the death of Terence, whose plays influenced world literature throughout many centuries.

LOCALE: Rome (now in Italy)
CATEGORIES: Literature; cultural and intellectual history

KEY FIGURE
Terence (Publius Terentius Afer; c. 190-159 B.C.E.), Roman playwright

SUMMARY OF EVENT
The death of Terence had a profound effect on Roman drama, as it signified the end in Rome of a rich tradition of comedies that had its origin nearly three centuries earlier with the Greek New Comedy. Spectacles with gladiators, circuses, and mock sea battles soon replaced Terence's refined adaptations of Greek comedies, introduced to Romans after Rome's political and economic expansion to the rest of Italy and Sicily. The quality of Roman drama continued to deteriorate, as the main forms of entertainment during the years leading up to the fall of the Roman Empire were pantomimes, jugglers, and acrobats.

The principal source of information on Terence's life is the biography by the Roman Suetonius (70-after 122 C.E.). Two other useful sources are a collection of production notices called *didascaliae* and the prologues Terence wrote for his plays. The information contained in Suetonius's biography and the prologues, however, must be studied with some skepticism. Ancient biographies are generally considered to be anecdotal and based on suspect information. Terence used the prologues to serve as a defense against those who attacked his literary style. For example, in the prologue to his first play, *Andria* (166 B.C.E.; English translation, 1598), Terence writes:

When the poet first turned his attention to writing he thought his sole concern was that the plays he had constructed please the people. But he learns that matters turn out much differently, for he wastes his efforts on writing prologues, not to relate the plot, but to answer the slanders of a malevolent old poet.

The "old poet" whom Terence refers to is the dramatist Luscius Lanuvinus. Defending his adaptation of *Andria*, Terence addresses his critics:

Do they show by their knowledge that they know nothing? When they accuse him (Terence), they accuse Naevius, Plautus, and Ennius, whom our poet has as authorities and whose carelessness he would much rather follow than the crabbed carefulness of these detractors. Furthermore, I warn them to hold their peace henceforth and stop their slanders, so they do not find out their own misfeasances.

It is widely accepted that Terence was from Africa, as his cognomen, Afer, adopted by Terence to indicate his origin, was used in Latin to mean North African. According to Suetonius's biography, Terence traveled to Rome as a slave of the Roman senator Terentius Lucanus. The existence of a senator with this name and the custom of slaves adopting the family name of their masters support the hypothesis of Terence's birthplace. Shortly after arriving in Rome, however, the Roman senator recognized Terence's natural intellect and many talents and granted the young man his freedom. Terentius Lucanus also provided Terence with a classic Roman education. At an early age, Terence began to write Greek-cloak plays (*palliatae*). It did not take long before Roman noblemen with a love of Greek literature and culture appreciated the young playwright's talent. Among the high-ranking Romans who admired Terence's plays was Roman statesman and general Scipio Africanus Minor

(185-129 B.C.E.), with whom Terence shared an intimate friendship.

Terence adapted into Latin Greek plays from the period of the New Comedy, the name given to comedies written in the period after the death of Alexander the Great in 323 B.C.E. He based his adaptations on the New Comedy plays by Menander (c. 342-c. 291 B.C.E.), an Athenian who wrote nearly 108 plays. Terence's adaptations, however, differed from those of Plautus, Terence's immediate predecessor. While Plautus took many liberties with his adaptations, Terence modeled his plays more closely after the originals. Greek New Comedy plays consisted of five acts separated by song-and-dance routines performed by a chorus. Unlike comedies from the periods of Old and Middle Comedy, the role of the New Comedy chorus was minimal. The number of actors who spoke usually was three, although additional actors participated in smaller roles. A prologue delivered by a divine figure introduced the main characters and described the dramatic setting. The divine figure did not take part in the action of the play. Terence did not include a chorus in his adaptations and significantly changed the purpose of the prologue.

Roman theaters during Terence's lifetime were makeshift wooden structures, erected for the performance of a play. The first permanent stone theater in Rome dates to 55 B.C.E. The stage was wooden and its wide and shallow dimensions resembled the setting of a street. This design accommodated the stock character of the "running slave" and facilitated dramatic devices, such as eavesdropping and asides. The area behind the stage had a dual purpose. It served as the actors' dressing room and the facade of this area contained illustrations of three doors, each one representing a house of the street in which the action of the play took place. Stage entrances located to the left and to the right of the spectators provided access to the harbor and the center of town. Another common feature of theaters during Terence's lifetime was the presence somewhere on stage of an altar, which was a necessity for the performance of many plays. During Terence's time, spectators, who did not pay to see the plays, sat on benches and consisted of people from the different classes of society.

Production notices provide the most conclusive evidence about Terence's plays. According to these notices, the plays were produced in the following order: *Andria*

Terence. (Library of Congress)

(166 B.C.E.); *Hecyra* (165 B.C.E.; *The Mother-in-Law*, 1598), which was a failure; *Heautontimorumenos* (163 B.C.E.; *The Self-Tormentor*, 1598); *Eunouchus* (161 B.C.E.; *The Eunuch*, 1598); *Phormio* (161 B.C.E.; English translation, 1598), *The Mother-in-Law* (160 B.C.E.), again a failure; *Adelphoe* (160 B.C.E.; *The Brothers*, 1598); and *The Mother-in-Law* (160 B.C.E.), finally a successful production.

Terence adapted all of the plays except *The Mother-in-Law* and *Phormio* from works by the Greek playwright Menander. Apollodorus of Carystus (fl. third century B.C.E.) was the Greek author of *The Mother-in-Law* and *Phormio*. The performance of the first four plays took place at the Megalensian Games. The Roman Games were the occasion for the productions of *Phormio* and *The Mother-in-Law* (160 B.C.E.). Both *The Mother-in-Law* (160 B.C.E.) and *The Brothers* formed a part of the Funeral Games for Lucius Aemilius Paullus, who was Scipio Africanus Minor's father. The production notice of *The Self-Tormentor* provides insight into the circumstances surrounding the performance of this play:

Here begins *The Self-Tormentor* of Terence. It was performed at the Games for the Great Mother [*Ludi Megalenses*] in the curule aedileship of Lucius Cornelius Lentulus and Lucius Valerius Flaccus. Lucius Ambivius Turpio and Lucius Atilius Praenestinus played the leading roles. Flaccus, slave of Claudius, made the music. In the first performance it was played with unequal pipes, later with two right-handed pipes. The Greek play was by Menander. It was the third, written in the consulship of Manius Iuventius and Tiberius Sempronius.

The production notice informs the audience of the author of the Greek original, the composer and performer of the music (including the instrument) that accompanied the play, the date of the play (determined by the years of the consuls mentioned), the names of the main actors, and finally, the names of the aediles responsible for the games. Terence was thirty-four when he completed his first play. Although it is not known why Terence's career as a playwright did not begin earlier, his rivals' opposition to his abilities might explain this mystery.

SIGNIFICANCE

The circumstances surrounding Terence's death are as much a mystery as the details of his life. The only aspect of Terence's death that is not a source of debate is that he was traveling abroad, most likely to Greece. There is no debate, however, about the influence Terence had on world drama. The Saxon nun Hrosvitha modeled her tenth century Christian plays after Terence's comedies. Later, Terence's plays enjoyed success as effective moral statements during the Renaissance. Sixteenth century playwrights and teachers used Terence's comedies to support their dramatic theories. Molière (1622-1673) based two of his plays, *L'École des maris* (1661; *The School for Husbands*, 1732) and *Les Fourberies de Scapin* (1671; *The Cheats of Scapin*, 1701), on Terence's

plays *The Brothers* and *Phormio*, respectively. The English playwright William Congreve (1670-1729) considered himself a student of Terence's style. Finally, in the eighteenth century, the Frenchman Denis Diderot (1713-1784) preached that any aspiring comic playwright should imitate Terence.

—*Michael J. McGrath*

FURTHER READING

Forehand, Walter E. *Terence*. Boston: Twayne, 1985. Part of Twayne's World Authors Series, this book provides a comprehensive study of Terence's life and plays.

Norwood, Gilbert. *The Art of Terence*. New York: Russell and Russell, 1965. Analysis of Terence's plays and overview of the playwright's life and literary style. Index.

Terence. *The Eunuch*. Edited by A. J. Brothers. Warminster, England: Aris and Phillips, 2000. The Introduction to Brothers's edition of *The Eunuch* contains useful information about the life of Terence and a general overview of his plays. Includes a translation from the Latin and commentary. Bibliography and index.

_____. *Works*. Edited by John Barsby. Cambridge, Mass.: Harvard University Press, 2001. Study and translation of Terence's plays. Information about Terence's life. Bibliography and index.

SEE ALSO: c. 456/455 B.C.E., Greek Tragedian Aeschylus Dies; 406 B.C.E., Greek Dramatist Euripides Dies; c. 385 B.C.E., Greek Playwright Aristophanes Dies; c. 400 C.E., Kālidāsa Composes Sanskrit Poetry and Plays.

RELATED ARTICLES in *Great Lives from History: The Ancient World*: Aeschylus; Ennius, Quintus; Euripides; Menander (dramatist); Plautus; Terence.

c. 155 B.C.E.
GRECO-BACTRIAN KINGDOM REACHES ZENITH UNDER MENANDER

Menander expanded the Greco-Bactrian Empire to its greatest extent; he is immortalized in The Questions of King Milinda, *a Buddhist dialogue between Menander and the Buddhist sage Nāgasena.*

LOCALE: Bactria (now in Afghanistan)
CATEGORIES: Expansion and land acquisition; wars, uprisings and civil unrest; religion

KEY FIGURE
Menander (c. 210-c. 135 B.C.E.), Greco-Bactrian king, r. c. 155-c. 135 B.C.E.

SUMMARY OF EVENT
After the death of Alexander the Great in 323 B.C.E., the eastern kingdoms of his empire fell to the Seleucids. In c. 256 B.C.E., Diodotus I broke away from the Seleucids, establishing Bactria as a separate kingdom. Menander remains the most well-known of the Indo-Greek kings.

The chronology for the successors of Diodotus I has been difficult to ascertain, with various scholars positing different dates for the reigns of kings. This situation arises from the scarcity of written sources. At times the only evidence for certain kings is numismatic. Joint kingships and rival kings claiming legitimacy at the same time complicate the establishment of an exact chronology.

What seems clear from the evidence is that Diodotus I was succeeded by his son Diodotus II. Then Euthydemus I became the king, apparently revolting against Diodotus II. Antiochus the Great led a campaign against Euthydemus in an attempt to reassimilate Bactria into the Seleucid Empire. After a two-year siege of Bactria, Antiochus concluded a peace with Euthydemus, promising to give his daughter in marriage to Demetrius, the son of Euthydemus. The acknowledgment of Euthydemus's right to rule consolidated the existence of the kingdom of Bactria. Euthydemus was followed by his sons Euthydemus II and Demetrius I. It is unclear who ruled first or whether they were appointed at the same time. In any case, Demetrius, ruling in the early part of the second century B.C.E., has been credited by some with expanding the extent of the kingdom into India. Thus he is known as "Rex Indorum," king of the Indians. Antimachus was followed by Demetrius II. Evidence suggests that around this time, Pantaleon and Agathocles, perhaps brothers, were also ruling. The rise of Eucratides I (171-155 or 170-145 B.C.E.) occurred at about the same time. He and

his successors seem to have gained control of western Bactria, while Panteleon and Agathocles ruled over the eastern half of the kingdom. Eucratides was assassinated by his son Plato, who would be supplanted by another of Eucratides' sons, Heliocles I.

It was into this world of the rule of Pantaleon and Agathocles as well as Eucratides that Menander rose to power. The *Milindapañha* (first or second century C.E., some material added later, date uncertain; *The Questions of King Milinda*, 1890-1894) states that he was born in Kalasi near Alasanda, probably Alexandria-in-Caucaso (modern Begram, Afghanistan). Some, however, have argued for Alexandria in Egypt. *The Questions of King Milinda* says Menander was descended from a royal family, although the name of his father and mother are not given. It is not clear that he is descended from the Diodochi or from Euthydemus. He rose to the kingship c. 155 B.C.E., and his capital was in Sāgala (now Sialkhot, Pakistan).

Menander's major accomplishment was his invasion of India. According to the Roman historian Strabo, Apollodorus of Artemita reported that Menander advanced beyond the Hypanis (modern Gharra, a tributary of the Indus river) as far as the Imaus River (either the Yamuna or Sun Rivers).

Indian sources describe a Greek advance into India at this time without specifically naming Menander. In his *Mahābhāṣya* (second century B.C.E.; English translation, 1856), Patañjali (fl. c. 140 B.C.E.) cites references to the Greek conquest of Sāketa (Ayodhyā) and Madhyamikā. In the play *Mālavikāgnimitra* (traditionally c. 70 B.C.E., probably c. 370 C.E.; English translation, 1875), the Indian playwright and poet Kālidāsa refers to the defeat of Greek forces at the Indus River by Vāsumitra during the reign of his grandfather Puṣyamitra (d. 148 B.C.E.). The *Yuga Purāna* (n.d.; *The Yuga Purana*, 1986) in the *Gārgi Saṁhitā* (n.d.), a work on astrology, describes the Greek advance into India, which ended in the capture of Pataliputra (Patna). However, Menander was not able to consolidate his conquests and left India without retaining any territory.

The Questions of King Milinda reports that Menander withdrew from the world and left his kingdom to his son. However, Plutarch in *Ethika* (after c. 100 C.E.; *Moralia*, 1603), says that he died in camp and that his ashes were equally divided among the cities of his kingdom, where monuments were dedicated to him. Plutarch's

200 - 101 B.C.E.

649

account is reminiscent of descriptions of the dispersal of the Buddha's remains. At the time of Menander's death (c. 135 B.C.E.), Agathocleia, his wife (probably the daughter of king Agathocles), served as regent for Strato, their son, who was not of age to assume the kingship.

Two other Greco-Roman sources may also be cited at this point. Pompeius Trogus (1st century B.C.E.-1st century C.E.) also mentioned Menander in his *Philippic Histories* (around 20 B.C.E., now lost). Only the table of contents for book 41 of this work has survived. In it, Trogus is said to have described how Diodotus came to power and how during his reign the Scythians, Saraucae, and Asians invaded Bactria. The book also contained a description of affairs in India during the reigns of Apollodotus and Menander. On the whole, the passage reveals few specifics about Menander, and the account errs in placing the invasion of the Scythians and the others during Diodotus's reign instead of later.

The *Periplus Maris Erythraei* (also known as *Periplus*, first century C.E.; *Periplus of the Erythraean Sea*, 1912), written by a sea captain, recorded that the old drachmas with inscriptions of Apollodotus and Menander were marketed as bullion in Barygaza (modern Bharuch, north of Mumbai, in northwest India). The reference to coins was verified by the discovery in Gogha near Barygaza of a horde of coins, some of which were minted by Apollodotus.

The coins of Menander were bilingual (in Greek and Kharoshti). Pallas was most frequently on the reverse. His titles were "soter" (savior) and "dikaios" (just). Some scholars, however, have argued that the coins with the epithet "just" belong to another king named Menander. Menander's coins have been found in Kabul, Swat, Gandhara, Taxila, and east of Mathura. These finds seem to confirm what the literary sources suggest about the extent of his power. In the recent assessment of scholar Gerard Fussman, Menander's kingdom, at its greatest extent, included Gujarat, Rajasthan, a great part of Uttar Pradesh, the Panjab, perhaps the Sind, the Northwestern Frontier Provinces, and the regions around Kabul and Jalalabad.

In addition to the evidence of the coins, a Buddhist reliquary casket preserves the name of Menander and a mention of his regnal year. The Buddhist reliquary provides little evidence to evaluate whether Menander was a Buddhist. Menander's name is cited here only in relation to giving a date. Elsewhere on his coins, there is a wheel, which has been taken as the Buddhist *dharmacakra*, wheel of the law. However, this interpretation has not been accepted by all scholars. In the end, *The Questions*

of King Milinda is the only major piece of evidence linking Menander to Buddhism, and recent scholars have been skeptical about its historical value.

SIGNIFICANCE

With Menander, the influence of the Greco-Bactrian kings reached it zenith. His successors were unable to stay in power. In the century after Menander, more than twenty rulers are recorded. By the middle of the first century B.C.E., the Yuezhi-Kushān, Śaka, and Scytho-Parthian ethnic groups had taken over the region. In addition to his exploits, Menander's fame is assured in the portrayal of Milinda in *The Questions of King Milinda* He is the only Greek king to be mentioned in Indian literary sources.

—*Albert T. Watanabe*

FURTHER READING

Davis, Norman, and Colin M. Kraay. *The Hellenistic Kingdoms: Portrait Coins and History*. London: Thames and Hudson, 1973. This book gives an account of the coins minted by Menander, with some illustrations of the coins. Maps and plans.

Fussman, Gerard. "L'Indo-grec Menandre: Ou, Paul Demiéville Revisité." *Journal Asiatique* 281 (1993) 61-138. An up-to-date reevaluation of the evidence on Menander. Fussman rightly points out the importance of the Chinese translations of *Milindapañha*, which antedate the Pāli versions of the text. He reviews in detail the evidence of the coins issued under Menander and offers a new text and commentary of the Bajaur reliquary.

Narain, A. K. *The Coin Types of the Indo-Greek Kings*. Chicago: Argonaut, 1968. A list of the different types of coins produced by Menander.

_____. *The Indo-Greeks*. Oxford: Clarendon Press, 1962. A general history of the Greco-Bactrian kings. Maps, bibliography and indexes.

Tarn, W. W. *The Greeks in Bactria and India*. 3d ed. Chicago: Ares, 1985. While this text, originally published in 1938, may appear to be out of date, scholars on Menander, as Fussman points out, are still conducting a dialogue with Tarn and establish their positions in relation to him.

SEE ALSO: c. 245 B.C.E., Diodotus I Founds the Greco-Bactrian Kingdom.
RELATED ARTICLE in *Great Lives from History: The Ancient World*: Menander (Greco-Bactrian ruler).

149-146 B.C.E.
THIRD PUNIC WAR

The Third Punic War, the last of a series of wars between Rome and Carthage, ended with the utter destruction of Carthage.

LOCALE: Carthage (modern Tunisia)
CATEGORIES: Wars, uprisings, and civil unrest; expansion and land acquisition

KEY FIGURES

Cato the Censor (234-149 B.C.E.), Roman senator
Masinissa (c. 238-148 B.C.E.), king of Numidia, r. c. 201-148 B.C.E., and an ally of Rome
Scipio Aemilianus (c. 185/184-129 B.C.E.), Roman consul and general

SUMMARY OF EVENT

After victories in two long wars (264-241 B.C.E. and 218-201 B.C.E.), Rome had reduced Carthage to a cipher and had imposed on the defeated North African city-state a peace treaty of grinding severity. Seizing Carthaginian possessions in Spain and requiring an enormous indemnity of 10,000 talents paid out over fifty years, Rome reduced the formidable Carthaginian navy to just ten ships and forbade the city to ever again make war without permission. Prostrate before the overwhelming military might of Rome, hedged in by Roman Spain and Sicily to the north and Roman clients in North Africa, Carthage no longer posed the slightest threat to its menacing imperial neighbor. A third Punic War was inconceivable.

However, Carthage had not been erased from history, for the city itself was virtually untouched by decades of warfare, did not suffer Roman occupation, and maintained control of a prosperous North African hinterland. For the next half century, its half-million residents minded their own affairs to their immense profit. As the enterprising middlemen between Africa and the Mediterranean, they restored their lucrative maritime trade and tended their abundant fields of grains, fruits, olives, and livestock. Relieved of the burden of military spending, they grew rich. Carthage had lost its wars, but in the covetous and apprehensive eyes of certain Romans, it had won the peace, and no one knew if the future might bring a reversal of fortunes.

Meanwhile, along the eastern edges of Carthage, the Numidians under Masinissa, Rome's ally in the region, took advantage of their rival's military incapacity to poach territory along its borders. Bound by the treaty of 201 B.C.E., the Carthaginians' only recourse was protest to the unsympathetic Romans. After one of these periodic Carthaginian petitions, a Roman delegation arrived in North Africa in 153 to investigate. Among their number was Cato the Censor (also called Cato the Elder), a senator and former consul who came away unsettled by the wealth of Carthage and stirred to action. No matter the subject, every speech Cato gave in the Senate ended with the words "Carthage must be destroyed." His hatred for Carthage and hunger for revenge for events long past, especially the ravages of Hannibal (247-182 B.C.E.) during the Second Punic War, never abated. Moreover, the prospects of conquering an enemy of great riches whetted the appetites of Roman politicians, generals, and common soldiers alike, each of whom stood to profit from the looting that inevitably followed conquest. From several influential quarters, then, pressure mounted for a preemptive strike.

To satisfy the growing clamor for war, all that was needed was a sufficient provocation, which, in 151 B.C.E., Masinissa provided by goading the Carthaginians into violating the treaty of 201. In response to the Numidian's siege of one of its towns, Carthage raised twenty-five thousand troops to sally to its rescue. Even though the Carthaginian army was trounced, it had handed Rome its pretext. Panicked, the Carthaginian senate made a last-ditch effort to stave off ruination, sending envoys to Rome in 149 to offer unconditional surrender. They arrived too late; the senate had already declared war. What would be the price of peace? the unnerved delegates asked. They listened, horrified, as the Romans demanded three hundred young sons of the ruling class as hostages and reserved the right to impose further conditions in due time.

At heartbreaking expense, Carthage had frustrated the Roman design to force a war, but its groveling acceptance of Roman bullying only delayed the inevitable, for when the consuls swept into North African ports they came with secret orders from the senate to lay the city waste. The Roman army of more than eighty thousand supervised the surrender of all weapons, and the Carthaginians, disarmed and presumably powerless to resist, awaited the final Roman stipulation, so cagily withheld from the Carthaginian embassy. Soon the Romans produced their impossible demand: The people of Carthage must abandon the city and settle 10 miles (16 kilometers) inland. For a seafaring people dependent on the trade of the Mediterranean, acquiescence would have been tantamount to collective suicide, as the Romans had calculated it to be. The Carthaginians grimly took up newly forged arms and set their minds to a ferocious defense.

In the early stages of the fighting in 149 B.C.E., the Romans campaigned complacently and failed to drive their enemies' armies from before the city walls. Nor could they break the Carthaginian resolve to resist; women sheared their hair to make rope for catapults. Progress was also slow in 148, in spite of a temporary penetration of the city's walls. Finally, with the offensive stalled, Scipio Aemilianus, the adopted son of Scipio Africanus (the great hero of the Second Punic War), assumed command of the army in 147, drove the Carthaginians into the city, and built a barrier across the harbor to isolate Carthage from escape or resupply. In an audacious counterstroke, the Carthaginians constructed a fleet while excavating a new channel into the harbor. Even these heroic efforts were for naught, however. When the improvised navy issued forth, it squandered the advantage of surprise by a vainglorious display and then fought poorly. The last hope of Carthage drowned with her sailors.

In 146, Scipio carried the walls. To his astonishment, his storming of the ramparts did not lead to surrender but to bitter house-to-house fighting, an unusual occurrence in ancient warfare, when the capture of a city's walls normally brought prompt surrender and pitiable supplications for mercy. The adaptable legions learned to avoid the streets and instead clambered from rooftop to rooftop with gangplanks. Attacking from top floors down, they rooted out and slaughtered all before them. For six hard days, the Romans mopped up the harbor district and, on the seventh, closed on the last stronghold, a heavily defended citadel called the Byrsa. Scipio offered all who surrendered there their lives and, spent from exhaustion and hunger, fifty thousand Carthaginians staggered from the redoubt to be sold into slavery. Remaining behind were nine hundred Roman deserters who could expect no quarter and who made their last stand from the roof of the temple of Eshmoun, where, cornered and determined to avoid capture, they set it afire and perished. Resistance at an end, the Romans pulled down the 22 miles (35 kilometers) of walls and all the buildings.

After plundering to their satisfaction, they torched the rubble, which burned furiously for at least ten days, perhaps seventeen, depending on which Roman historian is to be believed.

As Carthage burned, Scipio is reported to have wept, not out of remorse for his actions or because he pitied the Carthaginians but for fear that the same fate might someday befall Rome. As for the moment, however, Carthage was subsumed into the new Roman province of Africa and much of its richest farm fields bought for a song by the rich Roman landowners who had pressed for one last war. Both Julius Ceasar (100-44 B.C.E.) and Augustus (63 B.C.E.-14 C.E.) rebuilt on the ruins and in 29 B.C.E. the Romans were calling their city Augustus Colonia Julia Carthago, the administrative headquarters of Roman Africa. In 439 C.E., the Vandals occupied it, and two hundred years later, Arab armies destroyed the city a second time.

This embossed steel shield depicts Scipio Aemilianus as he receives the keys of Carthage at the end of the Third Punic War. (Hulton|Archive)

SIGNIFICANCE

Overseas prizes in three Punic Wars set Rome on the path of empire but at the cost of its republic, whose institutions and virtues could not stand the strain of vast imperial expansion. Two thousand years after the Third Punic War, Ferdinand Gregorovius (1821-1891), a German medievalist, wrote that the Romans crowned their rampage of 146 by plowing under the smoldering ruins of Carthage with salt so nothing would ever again grow there, but no ancient historian substantiates the claim. Even though this often-repeated story of the city's final indignity is untrue, Carthage could have hardly endured a more humiliating and permanent exodus from history. Its Phoenician culture and heritage ended in the flames of its defeat, never to rise from its ashes. The stories, the myths, and the epics the Carthaginians may have written as a testimony to their existence were also consumed in fire; thus, their seven-hundred-year history—including their Armageddon—is known not in their authentic voice but almost entirely through the trumpeting of their most ominous foe and the destroyer of their civilization, the Romans.

—*David Allen Duncan*

FURTHER READING

Appian. *Roman History*. Translated by Horace White. Vol. 1. Cambridge, Mass.: Harvard University Press, 1972. A Roman account written more than a century after the event.

Bagnall, Nigel. *The Punic Wars, 264-146 B.C.* Oxford, England: Osprey, 2002. A brief introduction to the economies, governmental institutions, religions, and military establishments of Rome and Carthage. Bibliography and index.

Coulston, J., and M. Bishop. *Roman Military Equipment: From the Punic Wars to the Fall of Rome*. London: Batsford, 1993. A handsomely illustrated study of military technology.

Dorey, Thomas. *Rome Against Carthage*. Garden City, N.Y.: Doubleday, 1972. Stresses the clash of cultures and the Roman tendency of aggressive defense. Bibliography and index.

Lloyd, Alan. *Destroy Carthage! The Death Throes of an Ancient Culture*. London: Souvenir, 1977. Reconstructs Carthaginian culture so far as Roman sources and modern archaeology allow. Bibliography and index.

Nardo, Don. *The Punic Wars*. San Diego, Calif.: Lucent Books, 1996. A good introduction for young readers. Maps and illustrations.

Polybius. *The Rise of the Roman Empire*. Translated by Ian Scott-Kilvert. New York: Penguin, 1980. An eyewitness account of the sacking of Carthage by a friend and tutor of Scipio Aemilianus.

SEE ALSO: 264-225 B.C.E., First Punic War; 218-201 B.C.E., Second Punic War; 133 B.C.E., Pergamum Is Transferred to Rome; 58-51 B.C.E., Caesar Conquers Gaul; 51-30 B.C.E., Cleopatra VII, Last of Ptolemies, Reigns; 43-130 C.E., Roman Conquest of Britain; 439 C.E., Vandals Seize Carthage; September 4, 476 C.E., Fall of Rome.

RELATED ARTICLES in *Great Lives from History: The Ancient World*: Cato the Censor; Hamilcar Barca; Hannibal; Masinissa; Polybius; Scipio Aemelianus; Scipio Africanus.

200 - 101 B.C.E.

146 B.C.E.
SACK OF CORINTH

The sack of Corinth marked the end of Greek political autonomy and displayed the harsh tactics of mature Roman imperialism.

LOCALE: Greece
CATEGORY: Wars, uprisings, and civil unrest

KEY FIGURES

Titus Quinctius Flamininus (c. 229-174 B.C.E.), Roman general
Philopoemen (c. 252-182 B.C.E.), Achaean statesman
Callicrates (d. 149 B.C.E.), pro-Roman Achaean statesman
Diaeus (d. 146 B.C.E.), Achaean general
Quintus Caecilius Metellus (d. 115 B.C.E.), Roman general
Lucius Aurelius Orestes (fl. second century B.C.E.), Roman senator and diplomat
Critolaus (d. 146 B.C.E.), Achaean general
Lucius Mummius (fl. second century B.C.E.), Roman general who sacked Corinth in 146 B.C.E.

SUMMARY OF EVENT

Corinth's fall in the summer of 146 B.C.E. came as the final event of what the Romans called the *bellum Achaicum*, or Achaean War, the fifth Roman military intervention into the eastern Mediterranean region since 200 B.C.E. Unlike earlier invasions, which had targeted the powerful kings of Macedonia and Syria, this conflict was a war against a Greek state: the Achaean League, one of several confederacies of city-states that had come to prominence during the late classical and Hellenistic periods. Since joining the league in 243 B.C.E., Corinth had emerged as an influential member and frequently served as a site for Achaean League congresses and meetings with foreign ambassadors. As a result, Corinth was a logical target for punitive action following the Roman victory over the league. The fame of its wealth and artistic treasures made it an even more appealing victim, and its international prominence as overseer of the Panhellenic Isthmian Games heightened the lesson of its destruction.

The motives behind Rome's halting assertion of control over Greece are extremely complex, but two things must be understood: The Romans did not set out to conquer Greece, and initially the Greeks did not find the Roman presence unwelcome. For example, the Romans undertook the Second Macedonian War (200-196 B.C.E.)

against Philip V (238-179 B.C.E.) at the behest of several Greek states that had suffered Philip's depredations, and they fought the war with the support of most Greek states, including the Achaean League. Following Philip's defeat, the victorious commander Titus Quinctius Flamininus held a grand Panhellenic ceremony at Corinth at which he declared the Greek states to be free and then evacuated all Roman forces from the region. The Achaeans also supported Rome in its war against Seleucid king Antiochus the Great (r. 223-187 B.C.E.), but friction soon arose as the aggressively independent Achaean general Philopoemen ignored Roman appeals for restraint and forcibly incorporated the city-state of Sparta into the league. His death in 182 B.C.E. allowed a pro-Roman Achaean leader Callicrates to adopt a more cooperative relationship with Rome, but this stance invited charges of collaboration. Stung by these attacks, Callicrates urged the Roman senate to support their Greek friends and show displeasure with their enemies—something the Romans would do with a vengeance during their next military intervention.

The Third Macedonian War (171-167 B.C.E.) revealed a hardening of Roman attitudes, not only toward defeated opponents but also toward Greek states that had displayed lukewarm support for the Roman war effort. Thus, Illyrians and Macedonians saw their monarchies abolished and their countries divided. In Epirus, the Romans sacked seventy Greek towns that had sided with Macedonia and enslaved 150,000 people. In Boeotia, the fate of Haliartos exactly presaged the doom that would later befall Corinth: slaughter, enslavement, and destruction. With the aid of a Roman garrison, the pro-Roman faction of the Aetolian League executed 550 citizens suspected of antipathy to Rome. Some one thousand leading Achaean citizens named by Callicrates were deported to Italy, where they remained for seventeen years. The absence of these opposition leaders at first strengthened the hand of the pro-Roman faction in Achaea, but the continued holding of the hostages engendered growing resentment.

The release of the surviving Achaean captives in 150 B.C.E., along with the death of Callicrates in the following year, stiffened the Achaean League's sense of independence at a crucial time, for Sparta had chosen this moment to reassert its autonomy and appealed to Rome. Diaeus, a rival of Callicrates, defended the Achaean position before the Roman senate, which promised to send a ten-man commission to settle the dispute. Perhaps because of the senate's preoccupation with Rome's Third Punic War (149-146 B.C.E.) against Carthage, the commission was not sent for more than a year, during which the dispute intensified. At this moment, the appearance of a pretender to the Macedonian throne brought forth the army that would soon threaten Achaea. In 148 B.C.E., Quintus Caecilius Metellus defeated the pretender and stayed on with his army to complete the pacification of Macedonia. Again the Achaeans had supported the Roman campaign, but they did not respond positively to Metellus's initial request that they show restraint in their conflict with Sparta. A second embassy from Metellus finally convinced the league to call a truce and await the promised Roman commission.

Headed by Lucius Aurelius Orestes, the commission arrived at Corinth in the summer of 147 B.C.E. and delivered a stunning decision: It not only endorsed Sparta's secession from the league but also decreed that Corinth, Argos, Heracleia, and Orchomenos were to be detached as well. News of this ultimatum provoked a furious response throughout the city. The Roman commissioners tried in vain to save Spartans who had taken refuge with them and at one point were themselves pelted with filth. An outraged Orestes returned to Rome, where he claimed that the lives of the Roman commissioners had been in danger and demanded retaliation. Another Roman embassy accomplished little, and formal contacts between the league and the senate ceased at this point. The Achaean general Critolaus spent the winter of 147-146 B.C.E. preparing for war, and the senate authorized Lucius Mummius to raise an army and proceed against Achaea.

When Critolaus led the Achaean League army north in 146 to lay siege to the rebellious town of Heracleia, he was probably unaware of Mummius's preparations. On the one hand, perhaps recalling Philopoemen's successful acts of defiance, he may not have expected the Romans to back up their threats with force. Alternatively, he may have anticipated an eventual attack by Metellus but thought he had time to take up a position at Thermopylae, where he might reasonably attempt to confront Roman forces coming down from Macedonia. In any case, he was unprepared for Metellus's ferocious onslaught, which routed the Achaean army. Critolaus himself disappeared in the confusion, a victim of the battle or a suicide. Metellus then took control of the Isthmus of Corinth and tried to upstage Mummius by offering a negotiated settlement, but the Achaean leadership refused and resolved to resist with a hastily assembled force made up primar-

ily of freed slaves. At this juncture Mummius arrived, dismissed Metellus back to Macedonia, and with a fresh army overcame Diaeus and the Achaeans in battle at the Isthmus. Diaeus fled to his home city of Megalopolis, where he killed his wife and himself to avoid capture.

The destruction of Corinth followed shortly in two phases. Two days after the battle at the Isthmus, Mummius subjected the city to a brutal sack. Most of the men were killed, the women and children enslaved, and the city systematically looted. Scores of artistic treasures were shipped back to Italy, where they adorned temples and public buildings. Some weeks after this initial sack, a ten-man commission arrived from Rome to impose a final settlement. The commissioners dismembered the Achaean League and placed Greece under the oversight of the military governor in Macedonia, which was now organized as a Roman province. As for Corinth, part of its territory was declared Roman public land and reserved for exploitation by Romans; the rest was ceded to the neighboring city-state of Sicyon, which also received control of the Isthmian Games. Finally, citing as justification the insolent treatment of Orestes' commission, the commissioners ordered that the city be razed and burned.

SIGNIFICANCE

For a century, the site remained a wasteland inhabited by a few squatters and tomb robbers, who raided the cemeteries for valuables. Thus, Corinth ceased to exist, until Julius Caesar refounded the city in 44 B.C.E. as a colony for his veterans and others. Ironically, in this reincarnation, the city would later flourish as the capital of the entire Greek region, now called the Roman province of Achaea.

—*James T. Chambers*

FURTHER READING

Derow, P. S. "Rome, the Fall of Macedon, and the Sack of Corinth." In *Rome and the Mediterranean to 133 B.C.* Vol. 8 in *The Cambridge Ancient History*, edited by A. E. Asitn, F. W. Walbank, M. W. Frederiksen, and R. M. Ogilvie. 2d ed. New York: Cambridge University Press, 1990. This chapter provides an excellent study of the background to the sack.

Gruen, Eric S. *The Hellenistic World and the Coming of Rome*. 2 vols. Berkeley: University of California Press, 1984. A comprehensive study of Rome's entry into the east that stresses Rome's lack of design.

Harris, William V. *War and Imperialism in Republican Rome 327-70 B.C.* Oxford: Oxford University Press,

200 - 101 B.C.E.

1985. Harris provides a realistic look at Roman imperialism that attributes Roman expansion to a habit of war and a keen sense of war's economic rewards.

Kallet-Marx, Robert Morstein. *Hegemony to Empire: The Development of the Roman Imperium in the East from 148-62 B.C.* Berkeley: University of California Press, 1995. Exposes the complexity of the relationship between Greek culture and Roman imperialism in the late Republic.

SEE ALSO: May, 431-September, 404 B.C.E., Peloponnesian War; 340-338 B.C.E., Origin of *Municipia*; 149-146 B.C.E., Third Punic War; 133 B.C.E., Pergamum Is Transferred to Rome.

140-87 B.C.E.
WUDI RULES HAN DYNASTY CHINA

Under Wudi, China became a great power and spread its influence throughout East and Southeast Asia.

LOCALE: China
CATEGORY: Government and politics

KEY FIGURES
Wudi (Wu-ti; 156-87 B.C.E.), emperor of the Han Dynasty, r. 140-87 B.C.E.
Dong Zhongshu (Tung Chung-shu; c. 179-c. 104 B.C.E.), philosopher of history
Zhang Qian (Chang Ch'ien; d. 114 B.C.E.), Wudi's trusted general

SUMMARY OF EVENT
Wudi succeeded to the throne of the Han Dynasty (206 B.C.E.-220 C.E.) in 141 B.C.E. and became one of the most important emperors in Chinese history. He inherited a government that was politically unstable and torn apart by internal strife, and by instituting a series of reforms, he created a dynasty that would dominate East Asia for the next three centuries.

Much of the instability in the early Han Empire was connected to the political policies enacted by the Qin Dynasty (Ch'in; 221-206 B.C.E.) under the leadership of Shi Huangdi (Shih Huang-ti; 259-210 B.C.E.). The political and social upheavals of the Warring States Period (475-221 B.C.E.) caused the new dynasty to enact totalitarian political policies based on the philosophy of Legalism. This doctrine represented humanity as basically evil and promoted a social policy based on the strict enforcement of a harsh legal code.

When Liu Bang (Liu Pang; 256-195 B.C.E.) defeated the Qin and established the Han Dynasty, he chose to keep the Legalist system of government. This exacerbated an already oppressive situation and gave rise to a number of conspiracies that undermined his political power. When Wudi ascended the throne, he sought an alternative model on which to base his government. The new emperor wanted to know what factors gave rise to an oppressive regime such as that of the Qin and what actions had to be taken to prevent such a problem in the future. Wudi found the answer to these questions in the writings of the great Chinese philosopher of history, Dong Zhongshu.

Dong's worldview was based on Confucian principles and consisted of five basic concepts. He believed that universal natural laws governed the history of humankind and that all the actions of the human community were interrelated. He also believed that there is an overarching governing force that created all life on earth. Dong referred to this power as "heaven," and he stated that all kings and emperors received their right to rule from this divine power (the mandate of heaven). He wrote that all natural events, especially celestial phenomena, reflect the approval or disapproval of heaven.

Dong convinced Wudi that a system could be constructed that would ensure that the actions of a ruler would be in line with these universal laws and thus would win the mandate of heaven. Wudi responded by mandating that the Legalism of the Qin be discredited and that Dong's neo-Confucian model be accepted by the new government. This was an important turning point in the new emperor's quest for power because it established him and his policies as a rational and humane alternative to the oppression of the past.

Dong convinced Wudi to establish a national university centered on the teachings of Confucius (Kongfuzi, K'ung-Fu-Tzu; 551-479 B.C.E.) that would be used for the creation of a bureaucracy reflecting the necessary characteristics and skills that were needed to be in compliance with the natural law. The basic text in this university would be *Chunqiu* (fifth century B.C.E.; *The Ch'un Ts'ew with the Tso Chuen*, 1872; commonly known as *Spring and Autumn Annals*), believed at that time to be written by Confucius. Dong was convinced that this great text was a guidebook to the universal law of history. Within its pages, Dong believed he had found evidence that heaven intervened in the lives of human beings, distributing rewards and punishments in accordance with their actions. He also convinced Wudi that the fall of the Qin Dynasty and the ultimate failure of the early Han were the result of heavenly retribution. The new emperor accepted this concept of divine justice and began his reign determined to act in accordance with Dong's theory.

The implementation of these ideas began with Wudi's attack on the traditional aristocracy. He removed the nobles from their positions in government and created a bureaucracy based on merit. A government official's position within this new system was determined initially by the scores received on the civil service exam that was based on the new Confucian curriculum. Future individual progress would be determined by the extent that the bureaucrat followed basic Confucian principles in the execution of his duties. Wudi also attacked the rising new merchant class that was attempting to monopolize the empire's trade and commerce. He instituted a series of taxes that reduced their power and created government monopolies in selected industries, the most important of which were iron, salt, and liquor. Government control increased the effectiveness of these industries, especially in the area of iron smelting. New, high-quality iron tools increased industrial and agricultural output. This had a dramatic impact on China's population, which increased from 20 million to 60 million by the beginning of the first century C.E. This population explosion helped make China the most urbanized civilization in the world, with as many as 30 percent of its people living in cities.

Wudi's reign also witnessed the growth of domestic and foreign trade. He funded the construction of an extensive infrastructure of roads and canals that not only moved goods efficiently but also extended government control throughout the empire. China would also prosper from a series of long-distance trade networks. The most famous part of this system was the great Silk Road that connected China to the other Eurasian superpower, Rome. A wide variety of goods, ideas, religious systems, and diseases moved from one part of Eurasia to the next along this great, ancient highway. These overland routes were also linked to a series of sea lanes that connected the East China Sea and the Indian Ocean to the Persian Gulf and the Red Sea. One of the primary reasons for the great success of this trade complex was Wudi's ability to ensure the safe transportation of goods.

The success of Wudi's industrialization efforts also enabled him to create a military that could go into battle with the latest high-tech equipment, including steel swords, strong armor, and highly accurate crossbows. Like their Roman counterparts, China's armies were also trained in civil engineering. Chinese forces created a system of military roads that allowed troops to move quickly throughout the empire in times of trouble. Wudi took advantage of his military strength and launched a series of wars of conquest against Mongolia, Manchuria, southern China, Korea, and parts of Southeast Asia. He also developed plans to move against Japan, but the expense and logistics proved too much of an obstacle.

The primary focus of the emperor's foreign policy was aimed at pacifying the northern nomadic tribes, the most powerful of which were the Xiongnu (Hsiung-nu). Wudi initially constructed a great defensive wall in an attempt to control the movement of these powerful nomads. Eventually, he sent one of his trusted generals, Zhang Qian, to negotiate with the Xiongnu. Zhang's success was the primary reason China was able to open up and protect its western trade routes. In time, the Han were able to carry on extensive trade with the Roman outpost at Bactria.

Wudi's wars of expansion placed a great burden on the empire's finances. In an attempt to remedy this problem, the emperor raised taxes and began to confiscate the land of wealthy landlords. These actions exacerbated an already growing gap between the rich and poor, and a series of rebellions broke out. Later emperors would attempt unsuccessfully to ease these tensions through a series of land redistribution programs.

SIGNIFICANCE

Wudi's reign established China as the greatest power in East Asia. Over time, the stress of empire took its toll on Chinese society. The empire would suffer from nomadic invasions and the biological exchanges that were a result of its long-distance trade. Epidemics of smallpox, measles, and the bubonic plague would eventually decrease China's population by 25 percent.

The reign of Wudi was also the source of the Chinese concept of "dynastic cycle." This historical model was an attempt to explain the rise and fall of great empires. Future dynasties such as the Tang, Song, and Ming would reach great heights, only to succumb to internal political and social pressures. The factors that caused decline were always a combination of social and economic inequality, cultural decay, and threats to China's national security.

—*Richard D. Fitzgerald*

FURTHER READING

De Crespigny, Rafe. *Northern Frontier: The Policies and Strategy of the Later Han Empire.* Canberra: Australian University Press, 1984. Discusses the international relations of the Han Dynasty. Bibliography and index.

Fung, Yu-lan. *A History of Chinese Philosophy.* Princeton, N.J.: Princeton University Press, 1953. The most comprehensive guide to the history of Chinese philosophy. Bibliography, index.

Hsiao, Kung-chuan. *A History of Chinese Political Thought.* Princeton, N.J.: Princeton University Press, 1979. A comprehensive overview of Chinese political philosophy. Especially useful for the thought of Dong Zhongshu.

Loewe, Michael, and Edward L. Shaughnessy. *The Cambridge History of Ancient China: From the Origins of Civilization to 221 B.C.E.* New York: Cambridge University Press, 1999. A comprehensive overview of the history of ancient China. Maps, bibliography, and index.

SEE ALSO: 5th century B.C.E., Composition of the *Spring and Autumn Annals*; 479 B.C.E., Confucius's Death Leads to the Creation of *The Analects*; c. 285-c. 255 B.C.E, Xunzi Develops Teachings That Lead to Legalism; 221 B.C.E., Qin Dynasty Founded in China; c. 221-211 B.C.E., Building the Great Wall of China; 221-206 B.C.E., Legalist Movement in China; 221 B.C.E.-220 C.E., Advances Are Made in Chinese Agricultural Technology; 209-174 B.C.E., Maodun Creates a Large Confederation in Central Asia; 206 B.C.E., Liu Bang Captures Qin Capital, Founds Han Dynasty; 2d century B.C.E., Silk Road Opens; 139-122 B.C.E., Composition of the *Huainanzi*.

RELATED ARTICLES in *Great Lives from History: The Ancient World*: Confucius; Mencius; Shi Huangdi; Xunzi.

139-122 B.C.E.
COMPOSITION OF THE *HUAINANZI*

The Huainanzi, *a Chinese philosophical treatise, was compiled by a group of scholars at the court of Liu An, king of Huainan, in the second century B.C.E.*

LOCALE: China

CATEGORIES: Philosophy; cultural and intellectual history

KEY FIGURES

Liu An (c. 179-122 B.C.E.), king of Huainan, r. 164-122 B.C.E., compiler of the *Huainanzi*, poet, scholar

Wudi (Wu-ti; 156-87 B.C.E.), emperor of the Han Dynasty, r. 140-87 B.C.E.

SUMMARY OF EVENT

Liu An, a king of Huainan (Huai-nan; present-day Anhui), assembled at his court a group of scholars to hold discussions on matters of philosophy and science. Their deliberations resulted in numerous treatises, which were compiled into the *Huainanzi* (*Huai-nan Tzu* or *Huai-nan-tzu*; *The Tao of Politics: Lessons of the Masters of Huainan*, 1990, commonly known as *Huainanzi*). Because Liu An was a poet and man of literary abilities himself, he may have played a role in its composition. His role was similar to that of a modern-day general editor. At this time, being seen as the author of a treatise gave one political power and authority; and by virtue of the treatise, Liu An hoped to be seen as commanding all the knowledge needed for a sage ruler and, hence, fit to rule or advise the emperor.

At the time the *Huainanzi* was being written, the early Han emperors were becoming more autocratic. They were attempting to restrict the power of the kings by shrinking their authority, territories, and armies and concentrating power, including intellectual opinion and moral values, in the central court. The kingdom of Huainan was especially threatened by this centralization. Just as the Han emperors were trying to unite regions that had their own political and cultural traditions, the *Huainanzi* examines many pre-Han philosophic traditions (Confucianism, Legalism, and Daoism) and melds them into a grand synthesis of the main currents of early Han philosophy.

During a visit to court in 139 B.C.E., Liu An offered the treatise to his nephew, Wudi. Presenting the treatise was probably an attempt to gain favor with the emperor. Confucianism prevailed at the imperial court, and the treatise can also be seen as an attempt to convince the court of the merit of a Daoist-inspired government. The treatise was placed in the royal library. However, because the Han emperor was beginning a campaign to centralize power, he was no longer open to including earlier pre-Han traditions, and the *Huainanzi* remained forgotten in the archive.

In 124 B.C.E., Liu An was charged with disloyalty to the emperor, and the following year, he was accused by the emperor's officials of plotting a revolt and convicted at a trial. To avoid the humiliation of punishment, he committed suicide in 122, and his kingdom was dismantled. There is dispute whether Liu An was actually plotting a revolt or was framed by the emperor's officials. One scholar, Griet Vankeerberghen, argues that it was Liu An's claims to have the moral knowledge necessary for a sage ruler (and suggesting that those who ignored him or disagreed with his book did not) that were interpreted as signs of disloyalty or rebelliousness.

The exact date of the *Huainanzi* in its present form cannot be known for certain. It is probable that the original treatise of 139 B.C.E. continued to be revised during Liu An's lifetime, and after his death, it was probably subject to editing and revision by later scholars and commentators.

Its effort to present a synthesis of pre-Han traditions gives the *Huainanzi* two features: It covers an unusually wide range of topics, and it borrows heavily from earlier treatises. The *Huainanzi* originally contained twenty-one inner chapters (or treatises) and thirty-three outer chapters devoted to the philosophy of other schools (these are now lost). The first eight chapters deal with Daoist and yin-yang principles and the cosmos: (1) the nature of the *dao* (tao; the Way or Path); (2) cosmogony; (3) astronomy and astrology; (4) topography; (5) ritual or astrological calendars; (6) resonances (or correspondences) between things of the same kind; (7) physiology and psychology; and (8) history.

The central chapters apply these principles to social and political life from the point of view of the sage ruler: (9) rulership; (10) art of communication; (11) ritual systems, both Chinese and non-Chinese; (12) exegesis of passages from the *Dao De Jing* (possibly sixth century B.C.E., probably compiled late third century B.C.E.; *The Speculations on Metaphysics, Polity, and Morality of "the Old Philosopher, Lau-Tsze,"* 1868; better known as the *Dao De Jing*); (13-14) guidelines for the behavior of the sage ruler; (15) the military; (16-17) lists of topics useful in persuasion; (18) the causes of success and failure; (19) the importance of human effort; and (20) interactions between the cosmic and human worlds. Chapter 21 is a conclusion that spells out the book's purpose and presents the *Huainanzi* as a treatise that could be put to practical use.

Special emphasis in the *Huainanzi* is given to central

doctrines of Daoism, and the work quotes extensively from many earlier Daoist texts. For these reasons, the *Huainanzi* has often been considered a Daoist treatise. However, it should not be classified solely as one because it also includes ideas from the Confucian and Legalistic traditions. Hence, recent scholars are stressing that it should be seen and studied as a creative adaptation with its own originality.

Daoist concepts of *qi* (vapor or breath), the *dao* (tao, or the Way or Path), yin-yang (dark and light, rest and activity, cold and heat), and the doctrine of five phases (or elements) are used to explain the universe and classify Earth's living creatures. The *Huainanzi* sees the natural world as a single, seamless unit of which human beings must realize they are but a part. Everything is made of *qi*; nature works in alternating balances or interactions of the complementary dual forces of yin and yang; and natural processes of creation pass through major cycles of five phases (*wuxing*; *wu hsing*) of birth, decay, and rebirth. Hence, there is a tendency in Chinese thought to form categories and correspondences (*ganying*) of things in fives (planets, gods, colors, elements, and so on). The *dao* is the order of nature in which all those rhythms and processes operate; all human effort must conform to, harmonize with, and not contradict the *dao*.

What ties the *Huainanzi* together is its focus on defining a perfect social and political order and particularly its function as a political handbook for the ruler in governing according to the same patterns that govern the natural world. A sage ruler becomes a bridge between heaven and earth; hence, political and social order derive from a sage ruler. Because the ruler is the guardian of a cosmological balance, he must know how to perfect himself; he must understand the operation of nature not for its own sake but in order to govern. The ruler must align his actions with those of the universe and rule in accord with its natural rhythms and harmonies. He must know about the calendar, for example, because he must engage in the proper rituals according to the astronomical, meteorological, and religious characteristic of each month or else the balance of the cosmos would be upset.

The sage ruler must also practice self-cultivation. This means abandoning selfish desires or excessive attachment to material things and connecting with something higher and larger than the self, such as following the Way (the *dao*), what is right (*yi*), what is good (*shan*), and human nature (*xing*). A ruler who understands the intricate relationship between all things in the world should be able to achieve success and avoid failure. In some passages of the *Huainanzi*, though, certain actions are due to fate (*ming*). Thus, self-cultivation will produce inner contentment, and following the Way will make the sage ruler indifferent to failure.

Cultivated people or sages have within themselves guidance for their actions and standards of right and wrong. Laws, rituals, and virtues should be followed not blindly but to the extent they agree with what each person or sage finds within himself. The sage ruler must not practice only one virtue but, for example, must be kind, respectful, or courageous, depending on the circumstance. Likewise, the sage must know when rules should be bent.

SIGNIFICANCE

The *Huainanzi* is the most comprehensive philosophic and scientific work of the Han period. By offering it to Wudi, the king Liu An was both making a gesture of loyalty and demonstrating that he possessed all the knowledge needed for a sage ruler.

The treatise is a compendium of earlier pre-Han thought, drawing on Confucianism, Legalism, and Daoism, and is one of the primary sources of information about early Han Daoism. Its chapters contain a systematic explanation of the universe and its mode of operation, and show how all elements fit into the cosmic system.

The *Huainanzi* is best seen as an eclectic text that does have its own unity of thought and purpose. Its overriding purpose is to synthesize all the knowledge that is necessary for a sage ruler. It teaches rulers that to govern successfully, they must understand nature and keep themselves and their kingdoms aligned with nature and the *dao*.

—*Thomas McGeary*

FURTHER READING

Ames, Roger T. *The Art of Rulership: A Study of Ancient Chinese Political Thought*. Albany: State University of New York Press, 1994. Study of the *Huainanzi* and the political philosophy of China and translation of book 9.

Le Blanc, Charles. *"Huai-nan Tzu": Philosophical Synthesis in Early Han Thought: The Idea of Resonance ("Kan-Ying") with a Translation and Analysis of Chapter Six*. Hong Kong: Hong Kong University Press, 1985. Discussion of the treatise's philosophical system and translation of chapter 6.

Loewe, Michael. *Chinese Ideas of Life and Death: Faith, Myth, and Reason in the Han Period (202 B.C.-A.D. 220)*. London: George Allen & Unwin, 1982. Survey of Chinese cosmological and mystical ideas, with reference to the *Huainanzi*.

Major, John S. *Heaven and Earth in Early Han Thought: Chapters Three, Four, and Five of the "Huainanzi."* Albany: State University of New York Press, 1993. Detailed discussion of early Han cosmology and translation of chapters 3, 4, and 5.

Vankeerberghen, Griet. *The "Huainanzi" and Liu An's Claim to Moral Authority*. Albany: State University of New York Press, 2001. Thorough coverage of the political climate surrounding the *Huainanzi* and Liu An's rebellion.

_____. "The *Huainanzi (Huai-nan Tzu)* Text." In *Encyclopedia of Chinese Philosophy*, edited by Antonio S. Cua. New York: Routledge, 2003. Good overall summary of the text and the reason for its composition.

Wallacker, Benjamin E. *The Huai-nan-Tzu, Book Eleven: Behavior, Culture, and the Cosmos*. New Haven, Conn.: American Oriental Society, 1962. Brief introduction and translation of chapter 11.

SEE ALSO: 479 B.C.E., Confucius's Death Leads to the Creation of *The Analects*; 3d century B.C.E. (traditionally 6th century B.C.E.), Laozi Composes the *Dao De Jing*; c. 285-c. 255 B.C.E, Xunzi Develops Teachings That Lead to Legalism; 285-160 B.C.E. (traditionally, c. 300 B.C.E.), Composition of the *Zhuangzi*; 221-206 B.C.E., Legalist Movement in China; 140-87 B.C.E., Wudi Rules Han Dynasty China; 104 B.C.E., Dong Zhongshu Systematizes Confucianism; 142 C.E., Zhang Daoling Founds the Celestial Masters Movement; c. 3d century C.E., Wang Bi and Guo Xiang Revive Daoism.

RELATED ARTICLES in *Great Lives from History: The Ancient World*: Confucius; Hanfeizi; Laozi; Wudi; Xunzi; Zhuangzi.

c. 135 B.C.E.
RISE OF THE PHARISEES

The Pharisees advocated a flexible Judaism that incorporated aspects of Hellenistic civilization and accommodated cultural changes that resulted from Palestine's incorporation into a broader Mediterranean world.

LOCALE: Palestine
CATEGORY: Religion

KEY FIGURES

John Hyrcanus (c. 175-104 B.C.E.), king of Palestine, r. 135-104 B.C.E.
Shammai (fl. first century B.C.E.-first century C.E.), Pharisaic leader, contemporary of Hillel
Hillel (c. mid-first century B.C.E.-c. early first century C.E.), noted Pharisaic teacher
Zadok (fl. first century B.C.E.-first century C.E.), Pharisee who joined the Zealots c. 6 C.E.
Saint John the Baptist (c. 7 B.C.E.-27 C.E.), possible Pharisee
Jesus Christ (c. 6 B.C.E.-30 C.E.), independent critic of Pharisaic background and founder of Christianity

SUMMARY OF EVENT

Although many older scholars associate the beginning of the Pharisees with Ezra (c. 425 B.C.E.), current scholarship more accurately places their advent in the reign of the Hasmonaean John Hyrcanus (135-104 B.C.E.). After securing independence from Syria, Hyrcanus had himself designated high priest in addition to the title of king. A group of pietists were hostile to the innovation of uniting in the person of the monarch both sacerdotal and secular functions. His control over religion was particularly objectionable since he was neither of a priestly family nor of the House of David.

The objectors called themselves Pharisees, derived from the Hebrew equivalent of "separatists." Those in official religious positions who allied themselves with the government and the status quo were chiefly priests who served in the temple, members of the family of Zadok. They were called Sadducees. The Pharisees, on the positive side, sought a creative adjustment to the changes brought to Palestine by the impact of Hellenistic civilization following the conquest of Alexander the Great (356-323 B.C.E.). The Pharisees, in short, were rebelling against the old order that had prevailed in Palestine from the time of Nehemiah and the canonization of the Penta-

teuch, around 400 B.C.E., to the revolt of the Maccabees (167-142 B.C.E.).

The Pharisees sought to recognize second century developments both in doctrine and practice by supplementing the Scriptures or the written law with an oral law as developed by qualified teachers and rabbis. In this way, the Bible would remain a flexible book allowing its legal structure and ideological message to adapt to the changing intellectual, social, and economic needs of the times.

The Pharisees stressed newer concepts of God, the individual, and life after death. God was universalized as Lord of all peoples and all lands, an idea welcome to the many Jews outside Palestine and conducive to the conversion of Gentiles. The Pharisees placed greater emphasis on individuals and their needs by encouraging the spread of synagogue worship, where study and personal involvement supplanted the sacrifices and the impersonality of the temple. A more direct emphasis was laid on the individual through the consolatory doctrine of immortality and resurrection of the dead.

As time passed, divisions appeared within the ranks of the Pharisees. An early cleavage developed between conservatives and liberals. Although both factions agreed that piety was expressed through strict observance of both the written Law and oral tradition, Shammai stood for extreme rigor, while Hillel was more lenient and adaptable to changing conditions. Their attitudes were formalized by their students into schools which generally split on important issues.

Tightening of Roman control over Palestine about the beginning of the common era brought more diverse reactions among Pharisees. Around 6 C.E., the Pharisee Zadok joined a Galilean militant, Judah, to organize a body of intransigent patriots called Zealots, who were determined to end Roman domination by direct action.

Jewish historian Flavius Josephus (c. 38-93 C.E.) and the Dead Sea Scrolls (written fourth century B.C.E.-first century C.E.) reveal still another kind of Pharisaism, that of the Essenes, an extreme pietistic group that lived in monastic communities. After surviving a rigorous novitiate, members practiced celibacy, held property in common, and lived in seclusion from the troubled Hasmonaeans and the Roman occupation.

Reacting differently to the unsettled times were the "apocalyptists" such as John the Baptist, who believed that a new world order was imminent. The Baptist, seeing himself the forerunner of the Messiah, summoned the

Jesus Christ (left) addresses the Pharisees and Herodians in this depiction of a Biblical scene. (Hulton|Archive)

people to repentance and purification by immersion in the River Jordan. His most famous initiate was the Galilean Jesus Christ, reputedly the son of a Nazareth carpenter. His claim of Messiahship and his criticism of the Pharisees as hypocritical in observing vain legalism and ritualism brought him into a fatal clash with the faction.

The Pharisaic development of Judaism through the oral tradition established a new sensitivity to change on the part of the ancient religion. From this movement emerged the main stream of Jewish life as it developed in the Mishnah and the Talmud. The approach of the Sadducees was buried forever.

SIGNIFICANCE

The faith of the Pharisees lay in their attempt to understand God's will, their ideas on revelation, divine justice and mercy, their prayers, ethics, and devotion to the study of Scriptures. The key to understanding the Pharisees is their theory of Torah as given in the Pentateuch. They

correctly understood it not as a static, legalistic corpus tailored to a given situation, but rather as a deposit of faith which would deepen spiritual life and impart a strong sense of personal responsibility in a current process. The Pharisees may be seen as challenging the monopoly of the priests in behalf of a universal and democratic priesthood of the people; the synagogue's prayer and study were to be open to all in preference to the temple's sacrificial and priestly system, which centered about a faithful few.

The Pharisaic movement derived from a conflict between rural and urban Jews, a conflict that appears in all advanced civilizations. The differences between the Sadducees and the Pharisees regarding the oral tradition, resurrection, angelology, and providence arose not from academic and theological conflicts but from social and economic factors—conflicts between patricians and plebeians that date back to the time of Samuel. Samuel represented the plebeians, while Saul, betraying the rural classes to which he belonged, joined the patricians. The opposed aspirations of the patricians and the plebeians eventually crystallized into the parties of the Sadducees and the Pharisees. The messages of the prophets show them as representatives of peasants' rights which were being exploited by the patricians of Jerusalem. The Pharisees continued this prophetic strain especially in Jeremiah and 2 Isaiah but now directed it toward the urban plebeians. Proclaiming freedom to all in the cities, they were asserting, as certain prophets had asserted, equality for all social classes. The Pharisees were unique as a religious group because they achieved great influence without sacrificing their individuality or compromising their principles.

Although the Pharisees themselves limited their concerns to Israel alone, they ultimately became mentors to all humankind through their role as a determinative force in the formation of Christianity and Islam. The ideas that Paul and his fellow apostles carried to the world came from Pharisaism. The Pharisaic influence on Islam is seen as even more important. Despite the low ebb of Judaism in the seventh century C.E., there was sufficient energy left in ancient Pharisaism to kindle the spirit of the Prophet Muḥammad (c. 570-632 C.E.), and so transform ignorant idolators into ardent monotheists. Pharisaism was successful not because of its promise but because of its fulfillment of redemption from urban enslavement. Pharisaism was prophecy in action.

—*Joseph R. Rosenbloom*

FURTHER READING

Neusner, Jacob. *The Rabbinic Traditions About the Pharisees Before 70*. Boston: E. J. Brill, 1997. A meticulous compilation of literary references within rabbinic literature.

Saldarini, Anthony J. *Pharisees, Scribes, and Saducees in Palestinian Society: A Sociological Approach*. Grand Rapids, Mich.: William B. Eerdmans, 2001. An insightful study of the role of Pharisees and Saducees in their society and their relation to other religious movements of the time. Includes indexes and a glossary of sociological terms.

Stemberger, Günter. *Jewish Contemporaries of Jesus: Pharisees, Saducees, and Essenes*. Minneapolis, Minn. Fortress Press, 1995. Discusses the religious climate in Israel around the turn of the first millennium C.E., first discussing the literary sources and then establishing the teachings and history of the Pharisees and Saducees.

SEE ALSO: c. 1280 B.C.E., Israelite Exodus from Egypt; c. 1000 B.C.E., Establishment of the United Kingdom of Israel; c. 966 B.C.E., Building of the Temple of Jerusalem; c. 922 B.C.E., Establishment of the Kingdom of Israel; 587-423 B.C.E., Birth of Judaism; c. 538-c. 450 B.C.E., Jews Return from the Babylonian Captivity; c. 200 B.C.E.-c. 100 C.E., Composition of the Intertestamental Jewish Apocrypha; 167-142 B.C.E., Revolt of the Maccabees; c. 6 B.C.E., Birth of Jesus Christ; c. 30 C.E., Condemnation and Crucifixion of Jesus Christ; September 8, 70 C.E., Roman Destruction of the Temple of Jerusalem.

RELATED ARTICLES in *Great Lives from History: The Ancient World*: Jesus; Saint John the Baptist; Flavius Josephus.

133 B.C.E.
PERGAMUM IS TRANSFERRED TO ROME

Political control of the kingdom of Pergamum was transferred from the Seleucid Empire to Rome, allowing for the expansion of Roman imperialism.

LOCALE: Pergamum, northwestern Asia Minor (modern Bergama, Turkey)
CATEGORY: Government and politics

KEY FIGURES

Eumenes II (d. 160/159 B.C.E.), king of Pergamum, r. 197-160/159 B.C.E.

Attalus III (c. 170-133 B.C.E.), last king of Pergamum, r. 138-133 B.C.E., son of Eumenes II

Aristonicus (d. c. 133 B.C.E.), illegitimate claimant to the throne of Pergamum

Scipio Nasica (d. 132 B.C.E.), Gracchus's cousin who served as pontifex maximus from 141 B.C.E., as consul in 138 B.C.E., and as legate to Pergamum to supervise annexation in 132 B.C.E.

Tiberius Sempronius Gracchus (163-133 B.C.E.), plebeian tribune in 134/133 B.C.E.

Publius Licinius Crassus Dives Mucianus (c. 180-130 B.C.E.), consul in 131 B.C.E., Scipio's successor as pontifex maximus, and later proconsul in Asia

Marcus Perperna (d. 129 B.C.E.), consul in 130 B.C.E. who replaced Crassus and died while proconsul

Manius Aquillius (fl. second century B.C.E.), successor to Perperna as consul in 129 B.C.E., proconsul 128-126 B.C.E., and head of the senatorial commission that established the *provincia* of Asia

SUMMARY OF EVENT

The kingdom of Pergamum was originally part of the Seleucid state carved out of the empire of Alexander the Great (356-323 B.C.E.). When Philetaerus, a satrap (governor, a title taken over from the Persians) in the Seleucid Empire, detached the area, he founded what came to be known as the Attalid Dynasty; the name comes from the first king, Attalus I (r. 241-197 B.C.E.). In any study of the politics of the area, it must be remembered that Pergamum, along with all successor states in the east, was ruled by a Greek minority that dominated the native-born population.

In time, Pergamum came to adopt a pro-Roman policy because it became increasingly clear that Rome could be counted on to favor Greek culture and its supporters over that of the native Easterners. Attalid involvement with Rome became active during the reign of Attalus I, who early discovered that it was advantageous to favor Roman fortunes in the involved Macedonian-Seleucid conflicts of the period. It was mainly under Eumenes II, however, that the fortunes of Pergamum were cast. He first fomented a war between Rome and the Seleucid Antiochus the Great (c. 242-187 B.C.E.), and then supported Rome. At the Peace of Apamea, which concluded this Syrian war in 187 B.C.E., Rome gave him much of Anatolia west of Galatia and north of the Maeander River. Roman policy for fifty years sought to maintain a stable balance of power without direct involvement. Accordingly, Rome weakened and confined the major powers, Antigonid Macedonia and Seleucid Syria, and strengthened various lesser states, notably Pergamum but also Rhodes, Bithynia, and even Pontus. It seems to have crossed Eumenes' mind that Roman legions could be used again to advantage in suppressing any unrest fomented against the dominant Greek aristocracy by the native population, a threat that became increasingly more realistic after 200 B.C.E.

By this time, the city of Pergamum was a desirable prize. Adorned with majestic architecture and sculpture, it became more and more the home of artists and scholars. Its library rivaled that of Alexandria, and the famous Altar of Zeus further attests its artistic greatness. From Pessinus and with the help of Attalus, in 204 B.C.E. Rome obtained the fabled black stone of the Mother of the Gods, Cybele, thought to bring help in the final stages of the Second Punic War (218-201 B.C.E.). Rich in industry and agriculture, Pergamum became the trade outlet for much of the economic transactions in northern Asia Minor. Moreover, on it centered much of the balance of power in the East.

Eumenes II pursued a policy that apparently was an attempt to create a solidarity of the Greeks against the Orientals. He did at times panic, however, and employed a tortuous diplomacy that eventually cost him Roman favor, especially when he changed his mind and belatedly helped Perseus of Macedonia (c. 212-c. 165 B.C.E.), son of Rome's old enemy Philip V, in the Third Macedonian War (171-167 B.C.E.). The temporary defection cost Pergamum the loss of Galatia. Attalus II (r. 158-138 B.C.E.), his brother, restored friendship with Rome, and, in 146 B.C.E., the Pergamene navy supported Lucius Mummius, Rome's commander in the Fourth Macedonian War at Corinth. Scipio Aemilianus (c. 185/184-129 B.C.E.) made a state visit to Pergamum in 140 B.C.E., but as was true of the senate as a whole, he had little interest in or knowledge of affairs east of Macedonia. Rome's attempt at remote management by occasional diplomacy was ineffective, and the states did not regard themselves as Roman clients.

Little is known about the last Attalid king, Attalus III, who died at age thirty-six and bequeathed his kingdom to Rome. Why he did so is uncertain. Rome had shown no interest in annexation. Without substantiation, Strabo (64/63-after 23 B.C.E.) charges that Attalus III was insane. Although childless, he could have adopted a successor. The only living Attalid claimant to the throne was his half-brother Aristonicus, an illegitimate son of Eumenes II and a slave. Perhaps Attalus only designated Rome his heir to deter both Aristonicus (possibly already in revolt) and ambitious neighbors (the kings of Bithynia and Pontus) from attacking, but then died unexpectedly before making other arrangements. Less probably, he envisioned Greek and Roman cooperation in maintaining Greek culture in the east and was interested in providing a peaceful future for his people. Aristonicus evidently appointed himself leader of the submerged eastern elements. Recruiting his followers from natives, he called them "Citizens of the Sun-city" (Heliopolis), an appeal to Mithraic sentiments if not a utopian dream, in an effort to unite and inspire the local population, said to have detested Attalus. His war was under way before Roman authorities arrived.

Attalus's gift was unexpected at Rome, which had acquired all previous provinces through its own decisions at the conclusion of major wars. Consequences of the bequest follow two paths over several centuries: increasing Roman involvement in Asia Minor, culminating in direct rule over the region west of the upper Euphrates valley; and polarization of Roman domestic politics, accelerating the failure of the traditional state and leading to the Augustan Principate. The will arrived at Rome in mid-133 B.C.E., some six months after the king's

death. Reacting slowly, the senate dispatched Scipio Nasica and four others in 132 B.C.E. to oversee annexation. Alternatively, the envoys' task was to determine whether Rome would accept the legacy. The mission conveniently removed Scipio from Rome, where he had incurred widespread hatred for leading the violent suppression of the reforming tribune Tiberius Sempronius Gracchus. Scipio soon died and his successor Publius Licinius Crassus Dives Mucianus, commander of the first legions in Asia Minor since 187 B.C.E., was killed in battle in 130 B.C.E. Marcus Perperna captured Aristonicus at Stratonicea but then died at Pergamum. Manius Aquillius ended the war and, assisted by a senatorial commission, organized the area as the province of Asia. Rome minimized its obligations: It gave outlying portions of the former kingdom to the rulers of Pontus, Bithynia, and Cappadocia, and did not keep a garrison in the province.

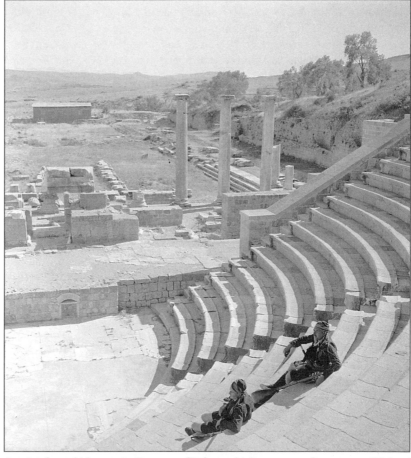

A ruined amphitheater in Bergama, Turkey, which once was Pergamum. (Hulton Archive)

KINGS OF THE ATTALID DYNASTY, c. 282-133 B.C.E.	
King	*Reign*
Philetaerus	c. 282-263
Eumenes I	263-241
Attalus I	241-197
Eumenes II	197-160/159
Attalus II	158-138
Attalus III	138-133

SIGNIFICANCE

Unfortunately, the great age of Pergamum had already passed. Its wealth became fair game for ambitious Roman speculators, as well as idealistic reformers. For example, Tiberius Sempronius Gracchus, probably with good intentions and before the senate had formally accepted the will, proposed that the Attalid treasury be used to stock new farms for the Roman poor of Italy. The bill was controversial, as it implied tribunician and legislative control over areas the senate had long regarded as its prerogative, foreign policy and finance. When Gracchus stood for reelection, his opponents labeled him a revolutionary. A mob of senators led by Scipio clubbed him and some followers to death. Gracchus's tribunate has long been seen as opening the Late Republic.

Rome would have remained disinterested in the region indefinitely had the regional kings kept the peace. Instead, the weakness of Nicomedes II of Bithynia (r. 149-91 B.C.E.) and the Ariarathrid rulers of Cappadocia tempted the territorial ambitions of Mithradates VI Eupator of Pontus (c. 134-63 B.C.E.). Gracchus's brother Gaius Sempronius Gracchus in 123-122 B.C.E. opened the door for financial exploitation. Tax farming companies sometimes combined with corrupt governors soon caused widespread hatred of the Roman regime. In 89 B.C.E., Mithradates swept through Asia as a liberator and Rome was slow to regain control. Nicomedes IV of Bithynia bequeathed his kingdom to Rome at his death in 74 B.C.E.; by 63 B.C.E., Pompey the Great (106-48 B.C.E.) eliminated Mithradates, annexed Pontus as a province and reduced the other states to client kingdoms. To the south, he annexed Syria and converted Palestine to client

status. Addition of the latter had incalculable results on Judaism and Christianity, and indeed on the entire intellectual history of the West.

—*Richard J. Wurtz, updated by Thomas H. Watkins*

FURTHER READING

Allen, R. E. *The Attalid Kingdom: A Constitutional History*. Oxford, England: Clarendon Press, 1983. A political history of the Attalids. Includes index, maps, and genealogical tables.

Boren, H. C. *The Gracchi*. New York: Twayne, 1968. Emphasizes the annexation of Pergamum in the context of the Gracchan reform program.

Dreyfus, Renée, and Ellen Schraudolf, eds. *Pergamon: The Telephos Frieze from the Great Altar*. San Francisco: Fine Arts Museums of San Francisco, 1996-1997. The essays and illustrations in this exhibit catalog give an idea of the artistic splendor of Pergamum.

Gruen, Eric S. *The Hellenistic World and the Coming of Rome*. 2 vols. Berkeley: University of California Press, 1984. Sometimes controversial analysis; excellent bibliography and notes.

Mitchell, Stephen. *The Celts in Anatolia and the Impact of Roman Rule*. Vol. 1 in *Anatolia: Land, Men, and Gods in Asia Minor*. New York: Oxford University Press, 1993. Discusses the repercussions of Rome's involvement in Asia Minor as a result of the acquisition of Pergamum.

Roller, Lynn E. *In Search of God the Mother: The Cult of Anatolian Cybele*. Berkeley: University of California Press, 1999. This study of the goddess Cybele provides insight into the Roman attitude toward the "exotic" East and their attempt to incorporate it through the adoption of Cybele as an object of worship.

Sherwin-White, A. N. *Roman Foreign Policy in the East, 168 B.C. to A.D. 1*. Norman: University of Oklahoma Press, 1984. A cautious and reliable source that stresses Roman reluctance to act.

SEE ALSO: 475-221 B.C.E., China Enters Chaotic Warring States Period; 218-201 B.C.E., Second Punic War; 146 B.C.E., Sack of Corinth; 27-23 B.C.E., Completion of the Augustan Settlement.
RELATED ARTICLES in *Great Lives from History: The Ancient World*: Antiochus the Great; Gracchi; Mithradates VI Eupator.

133 B.C.E.
TIBERIUS SEMPRONIUS GRACCHUS IS TRIBUNE

The tribunate of Tiberius Sempronius Gracchus attempted to reform Roman society, but Gracchus's murder inaugurated an era of political violence that eventually destroyed the Roman Republic.

LOCALE: Rome (now in Italy)
CATEGORY: Government and politics

KEY FIGURES

Tiberius Sempronius Gracchus (163-133 B.C.E.), Roman tribune in 134/133 B.C.E.
Marcus Octavius (fl. second century B.C.E.), Roman tribune, 133 B.C.E., opponent of Tiberius
Scipio Aemilianus (185/184-129 B.C.E.), uncle of Tiberius and the leader of senate opposition to his reforms, consul in 147 and 134 B.C.E.
Scipio Nasica (d. 132 B.C.E.), Roman senator, chief opponent and murderer of Tiberius, and consul in 138 B.C.E.

SUMMARY OF EVENT

By the 130's B.C.E., conditions in Roman Italy were deteriorating. The acquisition of empire made the posting of garrisons in distant provinces necessary and provoked a long, drawn-out war of pacification in Spain. Soldiers were conscripted for these duties from the small farmers of the Italian peninsula, and the long periods of time some of them had to spend overseas made it very difficult for them to keep their farms going at home. Many of the farms of these soldiers were ultimately sold to their wealthy creditors, who then added this land to their large rural plantations (*latifundia*), worked by non-Italian slaves taken in vast numbers during the provincial wars. For these reasons, the danger of mutiny grew in many foreign-based Roman legions. Moreover, landless citizens swelled the growing numbers of the demoralized urban proletariat, who, without property, were no longer subject to military service with the Roman field armies. This progressive pauperization of small farmers, who made up the bulk of recruits into the Roman army, threatened the long-term stability and survival of the state. A few attempts had been made to repair this situation, but they all had been blocked by the conservative Roman senate.

In December, 134 B.C.E., Tiberius Sempronius Gracchus took office as one of the ten plebeian tribunes. Shortly thereafter, he proposed passage of the Sempro-

nian Agrarian Law, a measure intended to reform the use of "public" land (land owned by the state). This land was occupied, but not owned, by farmers and ranchers, many of whom were wealthy *latifundia* proprietors. The agrarian bill stipulated that the amount of public land being used by any single individual should not exceed 300 acres (121 hectares). A man would be allowed to work an additional 150 acres (60 hectares) for each of his first two sons. The state would repossess areas above the stipulated 300 acres (121 hectares), paying compensation for improvements made by the occupier, and divide this excess into 18-acre (7-hectare) parcels that the state would then rent to landless citizens. This measure was designed to reduce the number of landless citizens in Rome and simultaneously increase the number of men eligible for military service overseas.

Tiberius presented this plan to the assembly of the people, the *Consilium Plebis*, which voted it into law. At this point, however, Marcus Octavius, one of the other tribunes, who was said to have enormous tracts of public land, exercised his legal veto and nullified the assembly's act.

Tiberius counterattacked with a legal innovation that provoked a constitutional crisis of the first order. He argued that a tribune should not hold office if he acted against the interests of the people. Whether he did act against them should be decided by the people themselves through the *Consilium Plebis*. Conservatives, led by Tiberius's own uncle Scipio Aemilianus, strongly opposed this proposal, arguing that tribunes were inviolable and therefore not subject to recall. Moreover, they argued that there was no precedent for the deposition of a tribune. Tiberius, however, ignored these constitutional objections and presented his proposal to the *Consilium Plebis*, which voted overwhelmingly to recall Octavius. The assembly then immediately voted the agrarian bill into law and appointed a commission, which included Tiberius, his brother Gaius, and another relative, to survey the public land and proceed with its redistribution.

This commission required money to function, and the conservative-dominated senate, which traditionally controlled state finances, refused to grant it sufficient funds to operate. It was at this point that the news arrived that the Hellenistic state of Pergamum had been bequeathed to Rome by its recently deceased king, Attalus III (c. 170-133 B.C.E.). Tiberius, apparently with the approval of the *Consilium Plebis*, appropriated part of the financial reserve of Pergamum and used it to finance the commission's work. This action, while necessary to implement the agrarian law, nevertheless outraged conservative Romans, who viewed it as a serious breach of constitutional practice and a threat to the traditional authority of the senate. The senate therefore made up its collective mind to resist Tiberius.

As the time for the election of magistrates for the year 132 approached, Tiberius feared that his opponents would make an effort to elect men in sympathy with their own views and attempt to then repeal the agrarian law. To head off this possibility, he presented himself for reelection as tribune, another unprecedented action because tribunes had traditionally only served a single-year term. Conservatives charged that Tiberius was implementing a nefarious strategy designed to increase his personal power every year until he was in a position to proclaim himself king.

On election day, a crowd of senators and their clients gathered in the Roman Forum. When it became clear that Tiberius was going to be returned to office, this mob, led by Scipio Nasica, stormed the crowded voting areas armed with staves and knives. They seized Tiberius, beat him to death, and then murdered more than three hundred of his supporters. Their bodies were unceremoniously flung into the Tiber River.

SIGNIFICANCE

Tiberius, in attempting to reform Roman society, had had to resort to extraconstitutional measures, which turned the senate, which included many of his relatives and former friends, sharply against him. Instead of attempting some sort of legal redress to deal with the renegade tribune, the senate resorted to the drastic expedient of murder. This act inaugurated an era of violence that gradually swelled into a full-scale civil war that would ultimately destroy the Roman Republic.

—*Samuel K. Eddy,*
updated by Christopher E. Guthrie

FURTHER READING

Brunt, P. A. "The Fall of the Roman Republic." In *The Fall of the Roman Republic and Related Essays*. Oxford: Clarendon Press, 1988. A highly original and thought-provoking essay which places Tiberius Gracchus within the larger framework of the breakdown of the republican system of government in Rome.

Hildinger, Erik. *Swords Against the Senate*. Cambridge, Mass.: DaCapo Press, 2003. Details the Republic's descent into anarchy and civil war, beginning with the time of the Gracchi. Written from the perspective of a military historian.

Scullard, Howard Hayes. *From the Gracchi to Nero: A History of Rome, 133 B.C. to A.D. 68*. 1959. Reprint. New York: Routledge, 1989. A classic study that places Tiberius Gracchus at the beginning of a process that led to the installation of the Julio-Claudian dynasty.

Shotter, David. *The Fall of the Roman Republic*. New York: Routledge, 1994. A concise and easy-to-read analysis which argues that Tiberius Gracchus was essentially an opportunist who adopted the position of social reformer to further the interests of his senatorial faction.

SEE ALSO: 494/493 B.C.E., Institution of the Plebeian Tribunate; 287 B.C.E., *Lex Hortensia* Reforms the Roman Constitution; 133 B.C.E., Pergamum Is Transferred to Rome; 90 B.C.E., Julian Law Expands Roman Citizenship.

RELATED ARTICLES in *Great Lives from History: The Ancient World*: Gracchi; Scipio Aemelianus.

107-101 B.C.E.
MARIUS CREATES A PRIVATE ARMY

The general Gaius Marius created a private army composed of volunteers rather than conscripts, thereby revolutionizing the organization of the Roman army.

LOCALE: Rome, North Africa, and north Italy
CATEGORIES: Government and politics; wars, uprisings, and civil unrest

KEY FIGURE
Gaius Marius (157-86 B.C.E.), commoner who gained high civilian status through military achievements

SUMMARY OF EVENT
Marius's reforms of the Roman army were the culmination of developments arising out of Rome's emergence as an imperial power. These reforms marked the beginning of developments that led to the civil wars of the late first century and the end of the Roman Republic.

From the earliest period, the Roman army was recruited on an ad hoc basis for specific campaigns. Levies were held in each year in which military operations were proposed; recruits were conscripted from free-born citizens whose properties enabled them to provide their own arms. Although the property qualifications for military service were often loosely observed, and although the extended campaigns required from the First Punic War onward brought about the institution of military pay for soldiers, the armies of Rome were still thought of, and in large part were still treated as, a citizen militia rather than a professional force. Possession of property, regarded as a pledge of good faith and a commitment to the nation, remained a requirement for eligibility to serve.

During the third and second centuries B.C.E., the traditional system of recruitment was subjected to increasing strain. The requirements of empire created a need for larger numbers of troops recruited for longer periods of time. Small landholders, who made up the bulk of the army, found it increasingly difficult to maintain their farms while fulfilling their military responsibilities. The importation of cheap grain from conquered territories created additional hardships for small farmers, whose small holdings fell more and more into the hand of large landowners. These prosperous landowners operated their tracts with the help of slaves and tenants who were disqualified, by lack of property, from army service. In short, the need for troops was increasing while the class of citizens who supplied that need was diminishing.

The reforms of Tiberius and Gaius Sempronius Gracchus, designed to reestablish the small farmer class, failed to achieve their purpose while creating a climate of mutual suspicion and hostility between the ruling senatorial order and the rest of the Roman population. When Gaius Marius, an experienced soldier unconnected with the senatorial order, offered to remove the conduct of the Jugurthine War (111-105 B.C.E.) from the hands of the senate-appointed generals, he was elected to office by a large popular majority. Furthermore, over the objections of the senate, Marius was entrusted with the African campaign. Seeing the difficulties of raising an army in the traditional way, and less bound by tradition than generals of higher birth, Marius refused to order a conscription. Instead, he called for volunteers, accepting all who appeared to be physically fit, with no consideration of property qualifications.

Marius's action, superb in its simplicity, solved once and for all the problems of recruiting military forces. Although the Roman countryside had been depleted of small farmers, the propertyless masses of the city had grown large. From these urban residents and from the large rural population of tenant farmers, Marius forged

Gaius Marius. (Library of Congress)

an army of volunteers who regarded military service not as a civic obligation but as a means of earning a living.

SIGNIFICANCE

The change from a citizen militia to a professional army, however, created difficulties of a new kind. Thereafter, the Roman army was not a force raised by the state, but one that had attached itself to a particular commander. Soldiers fought not to protect their possessions but to earn a living. Their advantage lay not in a quick resolution of a specific campaign but in the continuation of military action. The commander of these forces had to guarantee their pay and booty; he also had to ensure them some form of pension, usually a small landholding, at the end of their service. To offer such guarantees, he had to maintain a high degree of control over Roman policies, both foreign and domestic. So Rome came under the twin threats of civil war and military dictatorship, a situation that was not resolved until the collapse of the Roman Republic, when military and civil government were combined under the emperors.

With the creation of a truly professional army came extensive reorganizations in tactics and equipment. The Roman legion, regarded as a standing force, was given an identity symbolized by a permanent name and a legionary standard. Armor and pack were improved and standardized; training and discipline received greater attention. The maniple, a tactical unit of approximately 120 men of proven maneuverability against the larger and tighter Greek phalanx, was replaced by the cohort. This tactical unit of six hundred men proved itself more effective against the non-Greek forces that had become more common as Rome's opponents. Whatever its unfortunate effects upon the republican form of government, the professional army created by Marius served the Roman Empire well for centuries of conquest, occupation, and defense.

—*Zola M. Packman, updated by Jeffrey L. Buller*

FURTHER READING

Goldsworthy, Adrian. *The Roman Army at War: 100 B.C.-A.D. 200*. New York: Oxford University Press, 1997. An overview of the organization and operation of the Roman imperial army. Gives both practical and theoretical examples and contrasts the Roman army with its major oppositions.

Keppie, L. J. F. *The Making of the Roman Army: From Republic to Empire*. 1984. Reprint. Norman: University of Oklahoma Press, 1998. A survey of the historical development of the Roman army, tracing changes in strategy and organization as a result of political as well as military factors.

Le Bohec, Yann. *The Roman Imperial Army*. New York: Routledge, 2000. One of the best studies of the Roman army, divided into sections on its organization, its activities and functions, and its role in the maintenance of the empire.

Peddie, John. *The Roman War Machine*. Stroud, Gloucestershire, England: A. Sutton, 1994. A good general introduction to the evolution of the Roman army and navy.

Santosuosso, Antonio. *Storming the Heavens: Soldiers, Emperors, and Civilians in the Roman Empire*. Boulder, Colo.: Westview Press, 2001. Focuses on how the military was itself a source of antagonism and disorder within Roman society and contributed to the instability of imperial Roman politics.

SEE ALSO: c. 700-330 B.C.E., Phalanx Is Developed as a Military Unit; c. 550 B.C.E., Construction of Trireme Changes Naval Warfare; 264-225 B.C.E., First Punic War; 133 B.C.E., Tiberius Sempronius Gracchus Is Tribune; 58-51 B.C.E., Caesar Conquers Gaul.

RELATED ARTICLE in *Great Lives from History: The Ancient World*: Gaius Marius.

104 B.C.E.
DONG ZHONGSHU SYSTEMATIZES CONFUCIANISM

China adopted the philosophy of Confucianism developed by Dong Zhongshu and established itself as a great power in East Asia.

LOCALE: China
CATEGORIES: Government and politics; philosophy

KEY FIGURES

Dong Zhongshu (Tung Chung-shu; c. 179-c. 104 B.C.E.), Confucian scholar
Shi Huangdi (Shih Huang-ti; 259-210 B.C.E.), emperor of the Qin Dynasty, r. 221-210 B.C.E.
Wudi (Wu-ti; 156-87 B.C.E.), emperor of the Han Dynasty, r. 140-87 B.C.E.
Confucius (551-479 B.C.E.), Chinese ethicist, political philosopher, and founder of Confucianism

SUMMARY OF EVENT

At the time of his death, Dong Zhongshu was already recognized for his philosophical writings. His work reflected the attempt by intellectuals of the Han Dynasty (206 B.C.E.-220 C.E.) to create a model that would ensure that China would not suffer from the chaotic and repressive governments that were so representative of its early political history. He combined Confucian ideals with his own philosophy of history to produce an operational model that would create an environment of peace and prosperity for the Chinese people.

Dong extended his historical investigations back to the rise of the Zhou Dynasty (Chou; 1066-256 B.C.E.) in 1122 B.C.E. China's new ruler, the duke of Zhou, established the political philosophy known as the mandate of heaven, which stated that an emperor who provided an environment in which his nation and people could prosper would receive divine sanction of his rule. The emperor, who would then be known as the son of heaven, would keep this mandate as long as he maintained a virtuous government. If over time the dynasty became lax and corrupt, another noble had both the right and the duty to overthrow the existing political structure. This philosophical concept was in fact the rationale used by the duke of Zhou to depose the leaders of the Shang Dynasty (1600-1066 B.C.E.).

The rise and inevitable fall of Chinese empires resulting from their inability to maintain their mandate gave rise to the political theory known as the cycle of dynasties, which in time became an accepted historical truth among the intellectual elite of Chinese civilization and

had a major influence on the writings of Dong Zhongshu. The Zhou Dynasty's inability to prevent this historical "inevitability" led to its collapse and ushered in an era of civil war known as the Warring States Period (475-221 B.C.E.), whose events would also play a major role in the intellectual development of Dong's philosophical system.

This was a period of unprecedented disruption when leaders of seven regional Chinese kingdoms fought one another in wars of bloody conquest. The Warring States Period also witnessed an intellectual renaissance that produced an explosion of philosophical writing known as the Hundred Schools of Thought, the most prominent being Confucianism, Daoism, and Legalism. The great philosophical debates of this golden age would also have a significant impact on the thought and writings of many of China's great intellectuals, including Dong Zhongshu. Most important, Chinese philosophers saw a cause-and-effect relationship between the intellectual diversity of the period and its political and social chaos. Dong and many others would come to believe that the Hundred Schools of Thought had prevented China from developing a single unified plan to revitalize the empire.

The Warring States Period finally ended when Shi Huangdi unified China and established a repressive regime based on Legalist principles. The Legalist model focused on the belief that people were naturally selfish and rebellious and that a system of harsh laws and penalties had to be implemented to maintain order. Legalism also challenged the mandate of heaven philosophy with the belief that people were to be used for the benefit of the state.

Shi Huangdi's central bureaucracy also rejected the idea of intellectual diversity. Shortly after obtaining power, the new emperor ordered the burning of all books that did not support Legalist principles. When a number of intellectuals refused to follow the emperor's command, he had 460 of China's most respected scholars executed. The reactionary policies of the Qin Dynasty (221-206 B.C.E.) were unable to create a period of peace or prosperity, and the dynasty ended shortly after the death of its first emperor.

In time, China would be pacified under the Han Dynasty and would become one of the greatest empires in world history. It would be under the rule of Wudi that Dong Zhongshu would make his contribution to Chinese history and philosophy. His writings would propose an alternative between the inefficient, decentralized policies of the Zhou and the harsh, totalitarian model of the Qin.

Dong's new model was based on the principles of Confucianism. Confucius centered his philosophy on the idea that people could be trained to be virtuous and that these "philosophical" individuals could be the foundation of a successful government. Dong also believed that a divine power governed the actions of the universe, and that all the events of the natural world and human society were interrelated. According to Dong, extraordinary natural phenomena, especially astronomical events, were a sign of the approval or disapproval of heaven.

The importance of celestial events, especially an eclipse, had played an important role in Chinese history extending back to the beginning of the Zhou Dynasty. Dong postulated that an unexpected eclipse was a sign that the emperor had lost his mandate from heaven. This is one of the major reasons that the Chinese Astronomical Bureau played such an important role in Chinese society.

The major challenge for Dong was the creation of a model that would ensure a harmonious balance between the natural world and human society. His solution was to create a national university based on the teachings of Confucius that would develop a pool of highly intelligent, virtuous men who would provide a source of candidates for the Chinese bureaucracy. Dong believed a government run by a cadre of "philosophical" bureaucrats would make China the most successful civilization on earth.

Dong also believed his model would end the cycle of dynasties that had plagued Chinese history for so many centuries. His confidence was based on the idea that Confucian scholar bureaucrats would be guided by virtuous philosophical principles and thus would not succumb to the corruption and decadence so prevalent in past dynasties. The Han Dynasty would maintain the mandate of heaven, and peace and prosperity would become the norm.

Dong stated that virtuous habits had to be reinforced on a daily basis in order for his philosophical model to maintain its longevity. As a result, he directed that every aspect of Chinese society had to reflect the basic Confucian principles of the superior/subordinate relationships. He set in motion the development of a "great chain of filial piety" that originated in the basic structure of the family and extended up through the various levels of Chinese bureaucracy. The institutionalization of this Confucian system would be the most important accomplishment of Dong Zhongshu.

SIGNIFICANCE

The philosophical system developed by Dong Zhongshu established Confucianism as the dominant Chinese philosophical school of thought until the outbreak of the Republican Revolution in 1912. The Han Dynasty benefited greatly from Dong's system because it created a social and political structure that played a major role in unifying China after generations of conflict and oppression.

Dong's system would also prove to be a great detriment to Chinese progress. The Confucian model, with its strict set of unchanging superior/subordinate relationships, created a society that was absolutely opposed to change. By the middle of the nineteenth century, this inability to accept new ideas and modes of social behavior placed China out of the international mainstream and was one of the major reasons it fell under the control of the new European colonial powers.

—*Richard D. Fitzgerald*

FURTHER READING

Ames, Roger T. *The Art of Rulership: A Study of Chinese Political Thought.* Albany: State University of New York Press, 1994. An excellent source of early Chinese political writings. Bibliography and index.

DeBary, William Theodore, et al., eds. *Sources of Chinese Tradition.* 2d ed. New York: Columbia University Press, 1999. An excellent source for early Chinese cultural history. Index.

Fung, Yu-lan. *A History of Chinese Philosophy.* Princeton, N.J.: Princeton University Press, 1953. The most comprehensive guide to the history of Chinese philosophy. Bibliography and index.

Hsiao, Kung-chuan. *A History of Chinese Political Thought.* Princeton, N.J.: Princeton University Press, 1979. A comprehensive overview of Chinese political philosophy. Especially useful for the thought of Dong Zhongshu.

Loewe, Michael, and Edward L. Shaughnessy. *The Cambridge History of Ancient China: From the Origins of Civilization to 221 B.C.E.* New York: Cambridge University Press, 1999. A comprehensive overview of the time period. Maps, bibliography, and index.

Major, John S. *Heaven and Earth in Early Han Thought: Chapters Three, Four and Five of the "Huainanzi."* Albany: State University of New York Press, 1993. An excellent introduction to the thought of the Han period. Bibliography and index.

SEE ALSO: 479 B.C.E., Confucius's Death Leads to the Creation of *The Analects*; c. 285-c. 255 B.C.E, Xunzi

Develops Teachings That Lead to Legalism; 221 B.C.E., Qin Dynasty Founded in China; c. 221-211 B.C.E., Building the Great Wall of China; 221-206 B.C.E., Legalist Movement in China; 221 B.C.E.-220 C.E., Advances Are Made in Chinese Agricultural Technology; 209-174 B.C.E., Maodun Creates a Large Confederation in Central Asia; 206 B.C.E., Liu Bang Captures Qin Capital, Founds Han Dynasty; 2d century B.C.E., Silk Road Opens; 140-87 B.C.E., Wudi Rules Han Dynasty China; 139-122 B.C.E., Composition of the *Huainanzi*.

RELATED ARTICLES in *Great Lives from History: The Ancient World*: Confucius; Hanfeizi; Mencius; Shi Huangdi; Wudi; Xunzi.

Early 1st century B.C.E.-225 C.E.
SĀTAVĀHANA DYNASTY RISES TO POWER IN SOUTH INDIA

Sātavāhana rule marked a long and important phase in Indian history in its Brahmanical revitalization after Aśoka's great Buddhist sweep.

LOCALE: The Deccan region of India
CATEGORIES: Government and politics; cultural and intellectual history

KEY FIGURES

Simuka (fl. early first century B.C.E.-first century C.E.), traditional first Sātavāhana ruler, r. c. early first century C.E.

Kṛṣṇa (Krishna; fl. first century C.E.), brother of Simuka, traditional second ruler, r. c. early first century C.E.

Sātakarṇi (fl. second century C.E.), traditional third ruler, r. c. mid-first century C.E.

Gautamīputra Sātakarṇi (fl. second century C.E.), traditional fourth ruler, r. c. late first century C.E.

Pulumāvi (fl. late second-early third centuries C.E.), traditional fifth ruler, son of Gautamīputra Sātakarṇi, r. c. late first-early second century C.E.

SUMMARY OF EVENT

At its height in the second century C.E., the Sātavāhana Dynasty, sometimes called Sādavāhana-kula, Sātakarṇi, or Āndhra Dynasty, ruled an immense territory extending from the Vindhya Mountain range south to the border of modern-day Tamilnadu and from the Indian Ocean to the Bay of Bengal. Although the dynasty was long lived and an influential religious and political force in India, lively controversies exist concerning this dynasty's origins and the chronology of its kings because of the fragmented and sometimes contradictory evidence. The Āndhras are mentioned in records of the Mauryan Dynasty emperor Aśoka as being people over whom he governed. After the decline of Mauryan authority in the Deccan, the Āndhras rose to power in the political vacuum. The appellation Āndhra Dynasty led to the assumption that they were people who had originated in eastern Āndhradeśa (modern-day Andhra Pradesh) in the region between the Krishna and Godarvari Rivers. A more recent theory asserts that Āndhradeśa is so called because it was the last province remaining to the Sātavāhanas before their demise. The evidence indicates that their original home may have been northwestern Maharashtra, specifically the Nasik-Pune region. Their first capital was Pratiṣṭhāna (modern Paithan), a city located on the major north-south trade route crossing the subcontinent.

It is impossible, given the current state of knowledge, to supply a definitive history of the Sātavāhanas because the data are fragmentary and obscure. At best, a tentative account may be established through the use of coins, literary references in various *Purāṇas* (fourth to sixth centuries C.E.; sectarian anthologies compiled by the legendary sage Vyāsa), and some thirty-five known inscriptions in Prākrit. The chronology of kings is difficult to establish because, according to the lists of kings in various *Purāṇas*, there were either nineteen kings who ruled for approximately 350 years (short chronology) or twenty-nine kings who reigned for 456 years (the long chronology). Some specialists have suggested that the discrepancy may be attributed to the inclusion of names of some minor family members serving as governors under the Sātavāhanas, thus producing a longer chronology of rulers. There is general agreement today that the short chronology is the more viable version, although its use poses some serious questions.

Inscriptional evidence and accounts in the *Purāṇas* seem to agree that the founder of the Sātavāhana line was a Brahman named Simuka. He is mentioned in the inscription of Queen Nāganikā at Nanaghat, wife of King Sātakarṇi, as being her husband's father. Little is known of him, although he is said to have destroyed the Kāṇvas and the last of Śuṅga power, events that may have occurred early in the first century B.C.E. Launching his fam-

MAJOR RULERS OF THE SĀTAVĀHANA DYNASTY, EARLY 1ST CENTURY B.C.E.-225 C.E.

Ruler	Reign
Simuka	c. early first century B.C.E.
Kṛṣṇa	c. early first century C.E.
Sātakarṇi	c. mid-first century
Gautamīputra Sātakarṇi	c. late first century
Pulumāvi	c. late first-early second century

ily on a path of great leadership and unification of the Deccan, Simuka ruled for twenty-three years. He was succeeded by his younger brother Kṛṣṇa (Kaṇha), who ruled for eighteen years.

The third king of the line, Sātakarṇi, made the Sātavāhanas into a great power. It is recorded that he performed numerous Vedic sacrifices, including the *Rājasūya* and at least two *aśvamedhas*, ancient Vedic rituals affirming his kingship. Instituting a campaign of aggressive military expansion, he extended the eastern boundary of his kingdom to the border of modern-day Orissa and north beyond the Vindhya Range into the Malwa region. A votive inscription on the south *toraṇa*, or gateway, of the Great Stupa at Sanchi records the name of Vāsishthīputra Ānanda, foreman of the artisans of King Sātakarṇi, an indication that the western Malwa region was under the sway of the Sātavāhanas during construction of the gateway. It is also recorded that Sātakarṇi married the daughter of a Mahārāthi chieftain, a political alliance that ensured Sātavāhana power in the Deccan. Depending on which source is consulted, Sātakarṇi ruled for either ten, eighteen, or fifty-six years.

The Sātavāhana period was one of great industrial, commercial, and maritime activity and one in which the kingdom grew rich on trade with the Romans and various regions of South Asia. Hoards of Roman coins found throughout the Deccan and along coastal Andhra Pradesh indicate vigorous trade between the Sātavāhanas and Romans. Indian spices, textiles, semiprecious stones, jewelry, exotic birds and animals, and in particular ivory items were prized in the Roman world. A carved ivory mirror-handle found in the ruins of Pompeii (dating before 79 C.E.) and an ivory comb found at Tac-Gorsium, Hungary (found beneath the ruins of Roman basilica dating to the late second century C.E.) attest to the Roman fascination with exquisite Sātavāhana luxury items.

A king named Gautamīputra Sātakarṇi ruled the empire in the latter half of the first century C.E. Ptolemy, in the *Geōgraphikē hyphēgēsis* (second century C.E.; *The Geography of Ptolemy*, 1732), mentioned a king named Saraganus (probably Sātakarṇi) who administered the prosperous market town of Kalliena (modern-day Kalyana). The enemies and rivals of the Sātavāhanas were the Scythians, called Śakas, who vied for control of their lucrative trade routes and ports along India's western coast. At one point, the Śaka ruler Nahapāna, who ruled enormous tracts of land in northwest India, led successful incursions into the Sātavāhana kingdom, seizing control of the western ports. Gautamīputra's decisive response in retrieving the pillaged lands can be attested to by the vast hoard of silver coins found near Nasik, consisting of coins initially minted by Nahapāna but that had been overstruck by Gautamīputra, who was referred to in the famous Nasik inscription as the destroyer of the Śakas (Scythians), Yanas (Greeks), and Pahlavas (Parthians). His reputation reflects the protectionist policies concerning the Sātavāhanas' prosperity and control of trade. Particularly during his reign, a complex exchange network with ports along the coast supplied by inland production centers promoted the rise of a great mercantile society sustained by highly organized guilds. The inscription records that he destroyed the pride of the Kṣatriyas (warrior class), stopped contamination of the four *varṇas* (castes), and promoted the interests of Brahmans. He ruled for either twenty-one or thirty-four years.

Sātavāhana control of its northernmost holdings was brief, and Śaka rule reasserted its hegemony over lands north of the Vindhyas. Ptolemy also mentions a king Siro-Ptolemaios (Sri Pulumāvi), ruling from Pratiṣṭhāna. According to the *Purāṇas*, Pulumāvi ruled for twenty eight years. It was probably King Pulumāvi who lost the western territories to the Śakas. Deprived of the benefits of that trade, he extended control to the east and consolidated Sātavāhana rule in Āndhradeśa. He left an inscription on the Great Stupa at Amaravati, and his coins have been discovered throughout Āndhradeśa and further south. That Amaravati, ancient Dhanyakataka, became the capital from then on is confirmed by numerous inscriptions and coins.

Despite the rulers' allegiance to Hinduism, both Jainism and Buddhism flourished under Sātavāhana rule; it is recorded that the kings generously endowed land to Brahmans and Buddhists alike. The material prosperity of the Sātavāhanas was reflected in their art. In the western provinces, important monuments include the rock-cut caves at Nasik, Karle, and Kanheri. The Sātavāhanas were responsible for introducing rock-cut art to the eastern Deccan and south India. The eastern Āndhradeśa school of art was responsible for creating numerous noble monuments, including the marvelous sculptures associated with the Buddhist monuments at Amaravati, Goli, Jaggayyapeta, Gummadidurru, and Bhattiprolu. The classic southern style of sculpture with its elegant, fluid treatment of the human figure came to full expression at these early Āndhra sites. Permanently recorded in the white limestone used on the sacred Buddhist monuments, the texts of the Buddhist faith in symbolic form—the stupa, the wheel of dharma, the Bodhi tree and the footprints of the Buddha—are repeated in infinite variety.

In the heyday of Sātavāhana rule, both literary pursuits and intellectual inquiries were advanced. The great Buddhist teacher Nāgārjuna lived under the auspices of the Sātavāhanas. The primary advocate of Mādhyamika Buddhism, Nāgārjuna's main treatise was the *Madhyamikaśastra* (second century C.E.; treatise on the Middle Way). He was also interested in medical science and pharmaceutical remedies. A rationalist, he contended that if something cannot be demonstrated rationally, it cannot be completely true. A Sātavāhana king named Hāla, a contemporary of Nāgārjuna, is cited in the *Purāṇas* as being the seventeenth ruler of the Sātavāhanas. A highly literate man, he compiled the *Gāthāsaptaśati* (second century C.E., also called *Gāhākośa*; *The Prakrit Gāthā-Saptaśati*, 1971) an anthology of seven hundred verses that portrayed daily life, scenes of love, humorous situations, and descriptions of natural phenomena. Hāla was king for a mere five years, possibly between 150 and 200 C.E. The literary genius Guṇādhya, a prolific writer, lived during the first or second century C.E. He is known for writing the *Bṛihatkathā* (the great tale). The work, written in the Paiśāchi language, was an anthology of folk tales, many of which were about love. The original work has not survived, but it was so popular that sections of it were cited or copied by writers for many centuries.

By the early third century C.E., Sātavāhana rule was weakening and gradually the dynasty's territories were being overrun by vigorous new contenders for the riches of the empire. The western provinces were taken by the Ābhīras and Taikutakas. The Kalachuris usurped the northern territories. The Ikṣvāku Dynasty, in taking the fertile lands of Āndhradeśa, brought an end to Sātavāhana rule around 225 C.E.

SIGNIFICANCE

There can be no doubt that the Sātavāhanas brought unity, order, and prosperity to the Deccan. Little is known of the region before their rule, but the vast expanse seems to have been populated by widespread and diverse clans and tribes. The Sātavāhanas were responsible for consolidating Brahmanism with its social strictures as the primary religion of the empire. Nonetheless, they were enlightened and liberal rulers who encouraged religious tolerance. Perhaps their greatest contribution was the creation of a great mercantile network that ensured prosperity for their subjects.

—Katherine Anne Harper

FURTHER READING

Knox, Robert. *Amaravati: Buddhist Sculptures from the Great Stupa.* London: British Museum Trust, 1992. Provides historical background on the Sātavāhanas and excellent evaluation of Sātavāhana archaeological materials from Amaravati. Bibliography.

Sastri, Ajay Mitra, ed. *The Age of the Sātavāhanas.* 2 vols. New Delhi: Aryan Books International, 1999. Collection of essay addressing history, culture, numismatics, epigraphy, art, and archaeology of the Sātavāhanas. Plates and notes with references.

SEE ALSO: c. 321 B.C.E., Mauryan Empire Rises in India; c. 273/265-c. 238 B.C.E., Aśoka Reigns over India; c. 100-c. 127 C.E., Kushān Dynasty Expands into India.
RELATED ARTICLES in *Great Lives from History: The Ancient World*: Aśoka; Kanishka.

100 - 1 B.C.E.

c. 1st century B.C.E.
INDIAN BUDDHIST NUNS COMPILE THE *THERIGATHA*

A group of Indian Buddhist nuns compiled the
Therigatha, *a collection of poems, some of which date
back to the sixth century B.C.E.*

LOCALE: India
CATEGORIES: Religion; cultural and intellectual
   history; literature

KEY FIGURES
Buddha (Siddhārtha Gautama; c. 566-c. 486 B.C.E.),
   founder of Buddhism
Subha,
Canda,
Patacara,
Vasitthi,
Vimala,
Mutta, and
Bhadda (c. sixth-first century B.C.E.), Buddhist nuns
   whose stories comprise the *Therigatha*

SUMMARY OF EVENT
The *Therigatha* (*Psalms of the Sisters*, 1909-1913) is a
collection of seventy-three poems composed by Buddhist nuns (*bhikkhunis*) in ancient India. Tradition maintains that the poems were originally chanted. The date
and location of composition are not precisely known,
and scholars cannot ascribe authorship to any single person. Nuns mentioned as authors include Subha, Canda,
Patacara, Vasitthi, Vimala, Mutta, and Bhadda. Because
some verses relate the stories of the early female followers of the Buddha and reflect a fairly independent religious experience for women, including wandering and
alms-taking, scholars argue that some poems within the
Therigatha may have emerged as early as the sixth century B.C.E. as oral narrative.

The verses were first transcribed into the literary language of Pāli during the reign of King Vattagamani (r. c.
89-77 B.C.E.) in Sri Lanka. Around the sixth century C.E.,
the scholar Dhammapala wrote a commentary on the
Therigatha, including narrative analysis and background
information for the Buddhist women described in the
Therigatha, adding to historical lore.

The *Therigatha* describes the experiences of Buddhist nuns, particularly female elders, in contrast to the
Theragatha (c. first century B.C.E.; *Psalms of the Brethen*,
1909-1913), which relates the experiences of Buddhist
monks. Both texts are part of the Pāli canon, considered
sacred in Buddhism today. Some scholars have ques-

tioned women's ability to compose the powerful text of
the *Therigatha*, but Kathryn Blackstone's linguistic comparison of the *Therigatha* and the *Theragatha* indicates
that women authored the *Therigatha*. She argues that the
text was written by women because the *Therigatha* employs gendered images and vocabulary throughout the
text, relates personal suffering and familial relationships
on a larger scale, and generally ignores frequent references to the Buddha. At the very least, it differs markedly
from its companion text, the *Theragatha*, which centers
on men's lives.

The *Therigatha* contains powerful stories about
women in ancient India. All the verses concern women
who have reached liberation (arahanthood), the ultimate
goal of Buddhism. After renouncing families, shaving
their heads, and taking on ascetic robes, women searched
for the path that would lead them away from the world of
suffering. The poems of the *Therigatha* describe the
struggles and success stories of the Buddhist nuns and
therefore serve as a sort of manual for others seeking to
do the same. In the text, women meditate, retreat to the
forest, suffer homelessness, reject sensual pleasures, and
even sit cross-legged for seven days. Familiar themes
center around liberation from household oppression, including chores and cheating husbands, and conquering
personal suffering such as the death of a child. Many of
the poems end with tributes to relief from lifelong obses-
sions and misery and reflect a general happiness and contentment with liberation.

Although some scholars debate whether the women
depicted in the *Therigatha* were historical rather than fictional figures, most scholars argue that there is little reason to doubt the text's accuracy. Readers learn of Patacara, who taught thirty nuns; Vasitthi, who once was
mad; Vimala,who worked as a prostitute; and perhaps
most famously, Mutta, who exalted her liberation from
"pestle, mortar, and crooked husband," proclaiming "I
am free." All these women—even the courtesans, beggars, and madwomen—were capable of reaching arahanthood.

SIGNIFICANCE
The *Therigatha* is considered the first anthology of
women's literature; among world religions, it is the only
canonical text authored by women. Although the significance of women within ancient Buddhism has been
sharply debated, and the Buddha seems to have reluc-

tantly admitted women, the *Therigatha* reveals an active world of Buddhist nuns, greatly empowered by their faith. It offers telling portraits of women in ancient India, allowing readers a chance to understand this time period culturally and spiritually. Despite encountering struggles on a daily basis, these women found liberation in Buddhism and in their retreat from the world. The *Therigatha* thus retains special significance for scholars seeking to understand the past, and contemporary Buddhists, especially women, seeking liberation for themselves.

—*Shelley Wolbrink*

FURTHER READING

Barnes, Nancy. "The Nuns at the Stupa: Inscriptional Evidence for the Lives and Activities of Early Buddhist Nuns in India." In *Women's Buddhism/Buddhism's Women*, edited by Ellison Banks Findly. Boston: Wisdom Publications, 2000. Useful insights for the life of a *bhikkhuni* in early Buddhism.

Blackstone, Kathryn R. *Women in the Footsteps of the Buddha: Struggle for Liberation in the "Therigatha."* London: Curzon Press, 1998. A detailed and important linguistic analysis of the *Therigatha* and the *Theragatha* with far-reaching implications for gender studies. Index and extensive bibliography.

Lang, K. C. "Lord Death's Snare: Gender-Related Imagery in the *Theragatha* and the *Therigatha.*" *Journal of Feminist Studies in Religion* 2, no. 2 (1986): 63-79. Argues that the poems of the male and female elders vary considerably in their attitudes toward the body.

Murcott, Susan. *The First Buddhist Women: Translations and Commentary on the "Therigatha."* Berkeley: Parallax Press, 1991. Interesting thematic analysis of the *Therigatha* with some primary text. Index and bibliography.

Norman, K. R., trans. *Elders' Verses*. 2 vols. London: Luzac, 1969-1971. Volume 2 contains an English translation of the *Therigatha* in prose form. Index, bibliography, and extensive notes.

Pruitt, William, trans. *The Commentary on the Verses of the Theris*. Oxford, England: Pāli Text Society, 1999. English translation of Dhammapala's commentary on the *Therigatha*. Index.

Rhys Davids, C. A. R., trans. *Psalms of the Sisters*. 1909-1913. Reprint. London: Luzac, 1964. English translation of the *Therigatha* in verse form. Index and bibliography.

Rhys Davids, C. A. R., and K. R. Norman, trans. *Poems of the Early Buddhist Nuns*. Oxford, England: Pāli Text Society, 1997. Provides both Rhys Davids' and Norman's translations of the *Therigatha*. Index and bibliography.

Trainor, Kevin. "In the Eye of the Beholder: Nonattachment and the Body in Subha's Verse (*Therigatha* 71)." *Journal of the American Academy of Religion* 61 (1993): 57-79. Specific analysis of one poem.

SEE ALSO: 6th or 5th century B.C.E., Birth of Buddhism; c. 5th-4th century B.C.E., Creation of the *Jātakas*; c. 250 B.C.E., *Tipiṭaka* Is Compiled; 1st century B.C.E.-1st century C.E., Compilation of the *Lotus Sutra*; c. 220 C.E., Cai Yan Composes Poetry About Her Capture by Nomads.

RELATED ARTICLE in *Great Lives from History: The Ancient World*: Buddha.

100 - 1 B.C.E.

1st century B.C.E.
SIMA QIAN WRITES CHINESE HISTORY

Sima Qian's history of China, which described the events and people who had shaped the country through a Confucian viewpoint, initiated the tradition of creating histories that would guide future leaders.

LOCALE: Han Dynasty, which encompassed much of modern-day China
CATEGORY: Historiography

KEY FIGURES

Sima Qian (Ssu-ma Ch'ien; 145-86 B.C.E.), Chinese historian
Shi Huangdi (Shih Huang-ti; 259-210 B.C.E.), emperor of the Qin Dynasty, r. 221-210 B.C.E.
Dong Zhongshu (Tung Chung-shu; c. 179-c. 104 B.C.E.), Chinese philosopher and Confucian scholar
Wudi (Wu-ti; 156-87 B.C.E.), emperor of the Han Dynasty, r. 140-87 B.C.E.
Zhang Qian (Chang Ch'ien; d. 114 B.C.E.), Chinese general

SUMMARY OF EVENT

Sima Qian led one of the most productive lives in Chinese intellectual history. As the author of *Shiji* (*Records of the Grand Historian of China*, 1960, rev. ed. 1993), he laid the foundation for the Chinese historical tradition. His philosophy of history was influenced by both the political events and the major intellectual currents that dominated China during his lifetime.

Sima was born into a state that was still recovering from the great upheaval of the Warring States Period (475-221 B.C.E.). This was a time of unprecedented political and social chaos. For more than two and a half centuries, China had suffered the scourge of constant warfare. Military leaders battled each other in an attempt to become the dominant force in the region. Large standing armies of more than a quarter of a million men, armed with the latest weapons, clashed in some of the bloodiest battles in Chinese history.

The instability of this era drove China's intellectual class to search for models of good governance and individual behavior that would restore peace and prosperity to the war-torn region. Schools of philosophy bloomed like a thousand flowers, as intellectuals competed for recognition. In time, three major philosophical models—Confucianism, Legalism, and Daoism—came to dominate the intellectual landscape. The Confucian school was based on the belief that political and social stability could be found in the patriarchal social structure of the early Zhou Dynasty (Chou; 1066 B.C.E.-256 B.C.E.). Legalism vehemently rejected relying on the past and instead insisted that stability could be restored only through the harsh implementation of a strict "law and order" policy. The Daoists rejected the first two models as the vain attempt to impose human rules and regulations on the natural order of the cosmos. These intellectuals believed that stability could be achieved only by acting in harmony with the natural rhythms of the universe.

Sima followed the Confucian model, based on the teachings of China's most influential intellectual of the period, Dong Zhongshu. Dong's worldview was based on a belief in universal natural law, which governed both the cosmos and the affairs of humankind. He believed that once these laws were understood, a societal model could be developed that would create an environment in which peace and prosperity would flourish. Dong also believed in the existence of a powerful force that regulated the affairs of humankind, which he referred to as heaven. It was this divine power that bestowed the right to rule on China's leaders. If the emperor acted in accordance with natural law, China would prosper and the emperor would maintain the mandate of heaven. If, on the other hand, the emperor became corrupt and the people suffered, he would lose his divine sanction.

The concept of the mandate of heaven also elevated the importance of history because it could provide the factual explanation for the rise and fall of dynasties. Events such as famine, war, or governmental corruption could be documented by the historian and then used as evidence of the failure of a particular ruler.

Sima attempted to bring all of China's history in line with the theory of the mandate of heaven as interpreted through the Confucian worldview. His writing concentrated on both historical events and the biographies of important political and cultural figures. Unlike modern historians, Sima did not offer an interpretation of historical events. He believed it was his duty to remain neutral and to allow the reader to reach his own conclusions. Sima was convinced that through extensive training based on Dong's Confucian model, history could be an important tool in the development of a well-ordered society.

Sima's great work begins with an overview of early Chinese history, from the Five Sage Emperors (Wudi) to the fall of the Zhou Dynasty. The history of the early Zhou is of particular importance to Sima because Confucian scholars use it as a model of excellent government. He then focuses on the Qin Dynasty (Ch'in; 221-206 B.C.E.), which Sima believed was an excellent example of a government at war with the natural law. Shi Huangdi, the new emperor, rose to power at the end of the Warring States Period. In an attempt to restore stability, he installed a governmental system based on Legalist principles. Sima describes events that paint Shi Huangdi as an unfit leader. The emperor is portrayed as egotistical, greedy, and unwilling to take the advice of his ministers. Like Confucius (Kongfuzi, K'ung-Fu-Tzu; 551-479 B.C.E.), Sima believed that good government was based on virtue and that the successful ruler relied on the judgment of advisers who had proved their merit through honest and intelligent service to the state. Shi Huangdi further violated the natural law when he attacked the intellectual foundation of China by ordering the destruction of all the histories of the earlier dynasties, especially the ones pertaining to the Zhou. The emperor then compounded the outrage by ordering the execution of 460 scholars who refused to take part in the destruction of China's historical legacy. Sima interpreted these violations as the reason the emperor eventually lost heaven's mandate, which ended in the fall of his government and the rise of the Han Dynasty.

Sima focuses the majority of the remaining sections of his work on recording the major events of the Han Dynasty. In particular, he focuses on Wudi, the emperor who ruled China during the time Sima was composing *The Records of the Grand Historian*. Initially, he believed the new emperor was the answer to China's problems. Wudi embraced the philosophy of Dong Zhongshu, and he attempted to create a government based on Confucian principles. Industrial and agricultural output increased, and China's population reached an all-time high. In the area of foreign affairs, China expanded its borders and opened vast trading networks that increased the nation's prosperity. Sima viewed China's good fortune as the result of the emperor's virtuous form of government, which was in line with natural law.

One of Sima's most important biographies discussed the accomplishments of the general Zhang Qian. Sima believed Zhang was the model Confucian government official. He was a virtuous man who always placed his well-being second to the welfare of the nation. When China was embroiled in one of its many struggles against the nomadic tribes that occupied the region along its northern borders, the emperor requested a volunteer to negotiate a peace agreement on his behalf. Zhang immediately stepped forward and volunteered for the danger-

ous mission. He was subsequently captured and spent the next ten years living among these nomads. During that time, he collected valuable intelligence concerning the people and the geography of Central Asia. Zhang eventually escaped, and the information he brought back to China allowed the Han Dynasty to expand westward and establish trade networks with the Roman Empire. Zhang's exploits seemed to confirm Sima's belief in the Confucian concept that virtuous men have a positive impact on the welfare of the state.

The march of history would eventually test Sima's conviction about leading the virtuous life. One of China's great generals, who also happened to be the historian's close friend, volunteered to lead a campaign against one of China's northern rivals. Badly outnumbered and short on supplies, the general engaged the enemy; however, though he and his troops fought bravely, in the end they suffered a tragic defeat. It was traditional in classical China for a defeated general to be executed for his failure. Sima spoke out on his friend's behalf and was also sentenced to death by the angry emperor. The historian had two choices. He could accept execution and leave his great work unfinished, or he could submit to the great indignity of castration and live to finish his world history. Sima accepted humiliation in order to complete his task, which he believed could be used to train future ministers in the Confucian tradition. He spent the remainder of his life completing the work.

SIGNIFICANCE

Sima began the Chinese historical tradition that emphasized the importance of past events in the training of future virtuous leaders. He also began the tradition of Chinese intellectuals using their respected position to both criticize governmental injustice and to initiate social reform.

—*Richard D. Fitzgerald*

FURTHER READING

Durrant, Stephen. *The Cloudy Mirror: Tension and Conflict in the Writings of Sima Quin*. Albany: State University of New York Press, 1995. Discusses the major works of Sima Qian. Bibliography and index.

Hardy, Grant. *Worlds of Bronze and Bamboo: Sima Qian's Conquest of History*. New York: Columbia University Press, 1999. Discusses the major interpretations of the writings of Sima Qian. Bibliography and index.

Lowe, Michael, and Edward L. Shaughnessy. *The Cambridge History of Ancient China: From the Origins of*

Civilization to 221 B.C.E. New York: Cambridge University Press, 1999. Provides a comprehensive overview of the history of ancient China. Maps, bibliography, and index.

Watson, Burton. *Early Chinese Literature.* New York: Cambridge University Press, 1962. Discusses the importance of history in early Chinese literature. Bibliography and index.

_____. *Records of the Grand Historian:* New York: Cambridge University Press, 1993. Provides the best translation of the work of Sima Qian. Bibliography and index.

SEE ALSO: 479 B.C.E., Confucius's Death Leads to the Creation of *The Analects*; 221 B.C.E., Qin Dynasty Founded in China; 209-174 B.C.E., Maodun Creates a Large Confederation in Central Asia; 206 B.C.E., Liu Bang Captures Qin Capital, Founds Han Dynasty; 140-87 B.C.E., Wudi Rules Han Dynasty China; 104 B.C.E., Dong Zhongshu Systematizes Confucianism; c. 99-105 C.E., Ban Zhao Writes Behavior Guide for Young Women.

RELATED ARTICLES in *Great Lives from History: The Ancient World*: Confucius; Shi Huangdi; Sima Qian; Wudi.

1st century B.C.E.-1st century C.E.
COMPILATION OF THE *LOTUS SUTRA*

The Lotus Sutra, *one of the most important of Mahāyāna Buddhist texts, opened new avenues in Buddhist thought with its doctrines of expedient means and sudden enlightenment.*

LOCALE: India
CATEGORY: Religion

SUMMARY OF EVENT

The *Saddharma-puṇḍarīka Sūtra*, the *Sutra of the Lotus Flower of the Wonderful Law*, or *Lotus Sutra*, is one of the most well known of Mahāyāna texts. It forms part of the texts labeled as Prajñāpāramitā Sūtras, sutras of the perfection of wisdom of Mahāyāna Buddhism.

It has been argued that the text originated in India in the first century B.C.E. to the first century C.E. The present text is a compilation of prose and verse. Statements first made in prose are often reiterated in verse. The verse usually is more elaborate and very often offers details and points not mentioned in the prose. Scholars have argued that the original text consisted of verse in Prākrit. These verses were translated into Sanskrit, and the prose was then added. Sanskrit manuscripts of the *Lotus Sutra* have been found in Nepal, Central Asia, and Gilgit in Kashmir. Not all are complete. The earliest Sanskrit manuscripts have been dated to the fifth century C.E.

Six Chinese translations are recorded, but only three have come down to modernity. In 286 C.E., Dharmaraksha translated the work into Chinese. The most well known of the Chinese translations was that made by Kumārajīva in 401. A third translation was made by Jñānagupta and Dharmagupta in 601.

As can be seen, the earliest Chinese translations antedate the Sanskrit manuscripts. Scholars continue to examine the relation between the Sanskrit manuscripts and the Chinese translations. One significant difference between these versions is that the earliest Chinese translations have only twenty-seven chapters, omitting what is now known as chapter 12, the Devadatta chapter. Most of the Sanskrit manuscripts have this chapter. Thus it appears that Dharmaraksha and Kumārajīva drew on a Sanskrit manuscript that had only twenty-seven chapters. Somewhere toward the latter half of the sixth century, the Devadatta chapter was added to the Kumārajīva translation, and this augmented version forms the basis of modern Chinese and Japanese texts of the *Lotus Sutra*. Other smaller differences between the versions exist.

The setting for the *Lotus Sutra* is at Mount Gṛdhrakūta near Rajagriha (now Rajgir, Bihar, India). At an assembly, the Buddha sent forth a ray of light from between his eyebrows, lighting up all the worlds to the east. The bodhisattva Maitreya asked another bodhisattva, Manjushri, what was the cause of this emission of light. Manjushri explained that when these signs appeared in the distant past, the Buddha of that time preached the *Sutra of the Lotus Flower of the Wonderful Law*. Thus at the end of the first chapter, the story creates a strong expectation of hearing the *Lotus Sutra*. This expectation, however, is never fulfilled. The *Lotus Sutra* is constantly referred to but never recited.

Instead various ideas come into play. The most significant of these ideas is found in chapter 2. After the Buddha has stated that the wisdom of the Buddhas was difficult to explain, he resorted to the doctrine of "expedient or skillful means" (*upāya*). The Buddha explained: "We employ countless expedient means, discussing causes and conditions and using words of simile and parable to expound the teachings." Various means are used to suit the varying capacities of the Buddha's interlocutors. As an example of expedient means, the Buddha in chapter 3 related the parable of the rich man who saved his children from the burning house. The burning house represented the world of suffering. The rich man enticed his children out of the house with a promise to give them carts. The children rushed out of the house looking for the carts. The rich man was so relieved that he gave them one large cart. In interpreting the passage, the Buddha pointed out that the carts represent the way of the *sravakas* (voice hearers, or Hīnayāna), the way of the *pratyekabuddhas* (self-enlightened beings, who make no attempt to help others), and the way of the bodhisattva. Thus, on one level, the parable is an illustration of expedient means. However, within the parable one learns that the Hīnayāna, the way of the *pratyekabuddha*, and the bodhisattva are also expedient means, which are addressed to persons of different spiritual capacities. Ultimately the Buddha tells us there is only one way: All these expedient means lead to the same result—progress of the person toward enlightenment.

SIGNIFICANCE

The idea of expedient means first appeared in the *Lotus Sutra* and has had a decisive influence on the development of Mahāyāna Buddhism. In China, the translation of Kumārajīva assured the preeminent status of the sutra. In Japan, Saicho (767-822) and Kukai (774-835), the respective founders of the Tendai and the Shingon sects, were greatly influenced by the *Lotus Sutra*, in particular by the Devadatta chapter, in which the dragon king's daughter attained "sudden" enlightenment. The *Lotus*

Sutra forms the basis for the Nichiren sect (which emerged in the twelfth century). The Nichiren chant, *Namu myoho renge kyo* ("honor to the *Lotus Sutra*") is well known.

—Albert T. Watanabe

FURTHER READING

Kashiwahara, Y., and K. Sonoda, eds. *Shapers of Japanese Buddhism*. Tokyo: Kosei, 1994. Essays on Saicho, Kukai, and Nichiren and their relation to the *Lotus Sutra*. Bibliography and index.

Niwano, N. *A Guide to the Threefold "Lotus Sutra."* Tokyo: Kosei, 1981. A general introduction to the *Lotus Sutra* with discussion of each chapter. Glossary and index.

Pye, M. *Skillful Means: A Concept in Mahāyāna Buddhism*. London: Gerald Duckworth, 1978. The only book-length analysis of skillful or expedient means, which forms the core of the *Lotus Sutra*. Bibliography and index.

Tanabe, G., and W. Tanabe, eds. *The "Lotus Sutra" in Japanese Culture*. Honolulu: University of Hawaii Press, 1989. A useful collection of essays on the influence of the *Lotus Sutra* on Japanese Buddhism, art, and society. Bibliography and index.

SEE ALSO: 6th or 5th century B.C.E., Birth of Buddhism; c. 5th-4th century B.C.E., Creation of the *Jātakas*; 300 B.C.E.-600 C.E., Construction of the Māhabodhi Temple; c. 250 B.C.E., Third Buddhist Council Convenes; c. 250 B.C.E., *Tipiṭaka* Is Compiled; c. 1st century B.C.E., Indian Buddhist Nuns Compile the *Therigatha*; 1st-2d century C.E., Fourth Buddhist Council Convenes.

RELATED ARTICLE in *Great Lives from History: The Ancient World:* Buddha.

100 - 1 B.C.E.

c. 100 B.C.E.-c. 100 C.E.
CELTIC HILL FORTS ARE REPLACED BY *OPPIDA*

Celtic hill forts and fortified towns, used by Iron Age tribes as defense points against invading Roman armies, were superseded by unfortified religious and commercial centers known as oppida.

LOCALE: Western and central Europe
CATEGORIES: Architecture; prehistory and ancient cultures; science and technology

KEY FIGURES
Julius Caesar (100-44 B.C.E.), Roman general, statesman, and dictator, r. 49-44 B.C.E., who conquered the Celts in Gaul in 58 B.C.E.
Vercingetorix (c. 75-c. 46 B.C.E.), Celtic leader who united the Celts against Julius Caesar in Gaul in 52 B.C.E.

SUMMARY OF EVENT
By the beginning of the second century B.C.E., the Celtic expansion, which encompassed lands from Asia Minor to the British Isles, was waning. In Austria, southern Germany, and western Hungary, the fierce and warlike Celts, who spoke Indo-European languages later classified as Celtic, were beginning to feel the force of Rome. By the middle of the first century B.C.E., when the Roman legions marched into western Europe, many of the old Celtic hill forts had been replaced by newly established fortified towns. These towns, referred to by the invading Romans as *oppida*, had grown into large commercial centers as a result of lucrative trading.

The Celts—loosely related congeries of tribes whose collective label derives from their Greek name, *Keltoi*—traditionally built fortified hilltop settlements that were defended by multiple earthwork ramparts, wooden palisades, and ditches. Prehistoric people used antlers to dig the soil and willow baskets to remove it. Two hundred people could dig a ditch and erect a 13-foot-high (4-meter-high) bank topped with one thousand stakes in a matter of one hundred days. By the time of Rome's advancement, scores of Celtic hill forts were scattered throughout western Europe and were used as defenses against the Roman armies. In his *Comentarii de bello Gallico* (51-52 B.C.E.; *Commentaries*, 1609), Julius Caesar listed *oppida* belonging to twenty-nine different Gallic tribes and regarded each *oppidum* as a commercial center.

Some hill forts were permanently inhabited during the Iron Age and others were occupied only during times of crisis. The oldest date from 1500 B.C.E. Originally con-

structed as refuges, storage sites, or as domiciles for kings, many of these forts could be entered only through a series of mazes. They enclosed villages or towns of circular huts and could house permanently up to one thousand people, as well as large numbers of refugees during times of crisis. According to Caesar, the *oppidum* of Avaricum (modern-day Bourges, France) sheltered forty thousand individuals during one Roman siege. The fully enclosed weatherproofed huts measured about 36 feet (11 meters) in diameter, were roofed with thatch made of reeds, and walled with vertical wooden planks. Many large grain storage pits as deep as 10 feet (3 meters) were also dug within the forts, ensuring survival during long Roman sieges.

A 1955 excavation in Bavaria, Germany, revealed that the *oppidum* of Manching housed between one thousand and two thousand people. In southern Germany, another site known as Heuneburg Towers, which was excavated in 1876, revealed a Celtic stronghold dating back to 1500 B.C.E. By examining the layers of debris left by successive generations, scientists were able to determine that this particular hill fort had been demolished and rebuilt more than twenty times. The central building of each enclosure served as a religious shrine.

By 600 B.C.E., an era referred to by archaeologists as the Hallstatt period and named after the Austrian village where its remains were first identified, the use of iron-working technology had advanced to the point that the Celts had spread their culture and hill forts across a geographic area that covered Italy to Ireland and Spain to the Ukraine. By the fifth century B.C.E., partly as a result of trade disruptions, many of the early Hallstatt hill forts were abandoned, and the wealth of the early Celts began to fade.

By 450 B.C.E., however, the second Iron Age period of Celtic culture, known as the La Tène period, had emerged and the earlier hill fort sites were refurbished and restored.

Named after a key archaeological site on the east side of Lake Neuchâtel in Switzerland, the La Tène period was characterized by iron swords and household utensils decorated with distinctive curvilinear patterns that express the vigorous and exuberant Celtic art style. The La Tène period lasted from the mid-fifth century B.C.E. until the Roman conquest and spread across France, Germany, Austria, Switzerland, Britain, Ireland, Bohemia, parts of Iberia, and Italy.

Before 400 B.C.E., the Celtic hill forts had used natural topographic features such as cliffs for defense. After that time, the La Tène Celts constructed contour forts, in which an entire hilltop, encircled by banks and ditches, made enemy assault almost impossible. The best-known British hill forts from this period, built by a Celtic tribe known as the Western Belgae, are Hod Hill (later turned into a military establishment by the Romans), Hambledon, and the large Maiden Castle.

Maiden Castle, in Dorset, England, remains one of the best-known extant hill forts. In its many archaeological layers, it clearly demonstrates how one culture built on another on the prehistoric hill forts. Excavated by Sir Mortimer Wheeler between 1934 and 1937, the Iron Age hill fort was initially developed from a single-rampart,

15-acre (6-hectare) enclosure in about the fourth century B.C.E. By the Roman conquest in the first century C.E., however, it had grown to an immense fortress made up of four concentric ramparts that enclosed nearly 45 acres (18 hectares). Maiden Castle is believed to have surrendered to the Second Roman Legion under Vespasian shortly before 45 C.E. Yet the mighty Maiden Castle was occupied in an earlier form long before this. Neolithic constructions at the site include a prehistoric camp, enclosed by concentric ditches, and an immense earthen mound 1,805 feet (550 meters) in length. In addition, the remains of a Romano-Celtic temple attest to the mighty hill fort's later occupation by Romano-Britons in the fourth century C.E.

From the third century B.C.E., the expansive world of

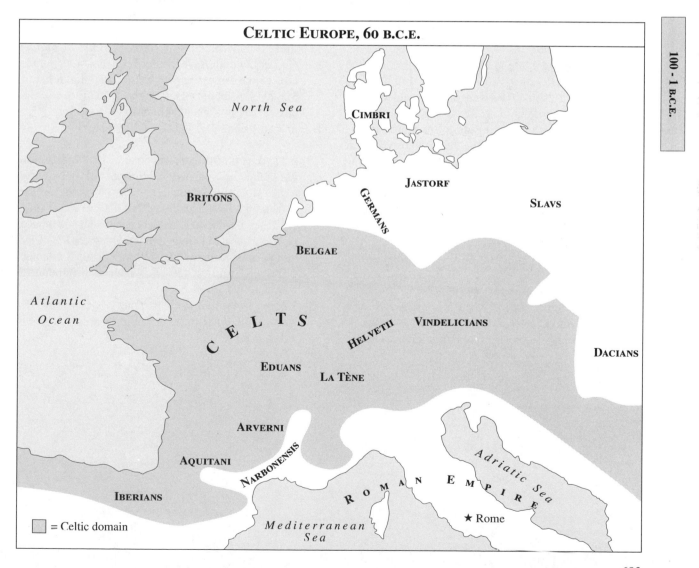

CELTIC EUROPE, 60 B.C.E.

North Sea

CIMBRI

JASTORF

SLAVS

GERMANS

BRITONS

BELGAE

Atlantic Ocean

C E L T S

HELVETII

VINDELICIANS

DACIANS

EDUANS

LA TÈNE

ARVERNI

AQUITANI

NARBONENSIS

Adriatic Sea

ROMAN EMPIRE

IBERIANS

★ Rome

Mediterranean Sea

☐ = Celtic domain

the La Tène Celts increasingly shrank until the early first century B.C.E., when Rome began to penetrate Celtic lands in Gaul (modern France). Julius Caesar first encountered the Celts in Gaul in 58 B.C.E., where he met little resistance until he finally engaged an army of united Celts under Vercingetorix at Alesia in 52 B.C.E. Victory for Caesar here meant the collapse of Celtic dominance of Gaul, which he finally subjugated in 51 B.C.E. Independent Celtic kingdoms were maintained in southern Britain until their conquest by Claudius in 43 C.E., and in Ireland and parts of Scotland up into the Middle Ages.

SIGNIFICANCE

The Roman Empire's occupation of western Europe instituted a strong central government and accelerated the development of unfortified *oppida*, resulting in the decline of independent hill forts such as the one in Dorset, England. The Celtic hill forts in unoccupied Ireland, however, remained in use for about another five hundred years. When the Romans were ousted from Britain in the fifth century C.E., some forts were again occupied by the native Britons as a defense against the invading Saxons. As Roman power declined, invading Germanic tribes— the Saxons, the Angles, and the Jutes—renewed their drive westward into the former Celtic lands. Only along the Atlantic fringe of Europe did Celtic culture survive in distinct form. The modern populations of Ireland, Scotland, Wales, Cornwall, and Brittany retain strong Celtic elements, and the sites of thousands of Celtic hill fort settlements are scattered throughout Europe.

—*M. Casey Diana*

FURTHER READING

Audouze, Françoise, and Oliver Büchenschütz. *Towns, Villages, and Countryside of Celtic Europe.* Translated by Henry Cleere. Bloomington: Indiana University Press, 1992. A scholarly but approachable work detailing many aspects of Celtic life and history.

Cunliffe, Barry. *The Ancient Celts.* New York: Oxford University Press, 1997. An excellent archaeologically based overview of Continental Celtic civilization.

_____. *English Heritage Book of Danebury.* London: B. T. Batsford, 1993. Exposition of the popular Celtic archaeological site discovered under Heathrow airport. Covers the structures erected consecutively over five hundred years.

Rankin, David. *The Celts and the Classical World.* Reprint. New York: Routledge, 1996. A very thorough assessment of the interactions between Celts and Romans from the Hallstatt era through the fall of Rome. Includes an appendix on recently discovered remains of a Roman trading outpost in southern Ireland which appears to contradict the truism that Rome never made it to Ireland.

Sharples, Niall M. *English Heritage Book of Maiden Castle.* London: B. T. Batsford, 1991. Traces the history of the largest known Celtic Iron Age hill fort: Maiden Castle, in Dorset, England. Sharples also discusses the Celts' abandonment of the fort after the Roman invasion.

SEE ALSO: 14th-9th centuries B.C.E., Urnfield Culture Flourishes in Northwestern Europe; c. 1100-c. 500 B.C.E., Hallstatt Culture Dominates Northern Europe; c. 60 B.C.E., Druidism Flourishes in Gaul and Britain; 58-51 B.C.E., Caesar Conquers Gaul; 43-130 C.E., Roman Conquest of Britain; 60 C.E., Boudicca Leads Revolt Against Roman Rule; 449 C.E., Saxon Settlement of Britain Begins; c. 450 C.E., Conversion of Ireland to Christianity.

RELATED ARTICLES in *Great Lives from History: The Ancient World*: Boudicca; Julius Caesar; Hadrian; Vercingetorix.

c. 100 B.C.E.-c. 200 C.E.
ZAPOTEC STATE DOMINATES OAXACA

The Zapotec civilization became one of the highly developed civilizations in Mesoamerica, dominating Oaxaca and the surrounding area.

LOCALE: Valley of Oaxaca, Mexico
CATEGORY: Prehistory and ancient cultures

SUMMARY OF EVENT

The Zapotec civilization developed in the Valley of Oaxaca, the only broad valley in southern Mexico. The average elevation is 5,085 feet (1,550 meters). On the east and west, it is bordered by high mountains and on the north by somewhat lower mountains. The Atoyac River and its tributaries drain the valley, which is semiarid and depends on the river for irrigation. Annual rainfall averages 22 inches (56 centimeters). Temperatures seldom fall below freezing in the southern and western arms of the wishbone-shaped valley, but because of the higher altitude of the eastern arm, frost limits the growing of corn and beans. Original vegetation included willow and alder trees near the river and evergreens farther back. The closed forest canopy limited plant growth on the floor to ferns and herbaceous plants. Vines, orchids, and ferns grew in the trees. Some distance from the river, where the water table was deeper, there was mesquite. Scrub forest and cactus grew higher on the mountainside, and farther up, where there was greater rainfall, oak and pine trees replaced the scrub forest.

There is strong evidence that the first true New World states emerged in the Mixtec and Zapotec civilizations. The state has been defined as a strong, usually highly centralized government with a professional ruling class. The bonds of kinship that characterized the leadership of simple societies are no longer present. The state can wage war, levy taxes or tribute, and draft soldiers or workers to construct public buildings, some of which are devoted to a state religion. There are priests, professional architects, and bureaucrats. States have administrative units that control regions that were formerly independent. All of these characteristics were found at Monte Albán, the Zapotec capital.

Hunter-gatherers moved into the Valley of Oaxaca around 10,000 B.C.E. By 5000-4000 B.C.E., there is evidence development had reached the ritualistic and ceremonial stage. During the Formative stage, 750-200 B.C.E., the basic skills of village life emerged. Weaving, pottery making, adobe manufacture, and stone masonry were all present. Ancestor worship, ritual bloodletting, and human sacrifice seem to have originated in this period along with the beginning of agricultural skills. Squash and later maize were domesticated. The people remained hunter-gatherers, but a stratified society and a more complex settlement pattern were developing.

The state did not come into being until the Classic period, 200 B.C.E.-100 C.E. By this time, the capital of Monte Albán had reached its peak of construction. Large palaces and public buildings were built, with audience halls and spaces for the transaction of state business. These structures required labor beyond the efforts of a single family; they were the result of extensive community cooperation and organization. An administrative hierarchy controlling outlying areas had been established, with Monte Albán as its focal point. Regional administrative centers were established in other parts of the valley. By this time the Zapotec royalty and nobles were completely separated from the commoners, with no intermarriage between the classes. Zapotec nobles married into Mixtec and Aztec noble families. Important Zapotec rulers were buried in special tombs where commemorative temples could be built over them.

By 100 B.C.E., a state religion was established. There was a professional priestly class and public structures devoted exclusively to religious purposes. Priests performed all religious functions formerly conducted by commoners. The temple was a two-room building with a slightly elevated inner room. Only priests entered the inner room, their residence. Commoners brought objects for a professional sacrifice to the outer room, where the priest accepted them and performed the ritual. The function of the ball courts was at least partly religious. These courts, shaped like a capital I, were present at Monte Albán and other secondary centers. The particulars of the ball game are not well known, but it did possess a ritual significance and probably existed and was staffed separately from the temple.

The Zapotecs at Monte Albán drafted soldiers, levied taxes, and collected tribute by the 200 B.C.E. to 100 C.E. period. Conquest was driven by the need for new sources of food to feed the increasingly large urban population. By 100 B.C.E. three quarters of the population of the Valley of Oaxaca lived in cities. Farmers in the valley could not produce enough food to feed such a large urban population. Tribute in the form of food fed the urbanites. All the conquered towns were outside the Valley of Oaxaca, and all the areas in which towns were located show

100 - 1 B.C.E.

A seated figure in Oaxaca, Mexico. (PhotoDisc)

months, but the important subdivisions were a dry and a wet season. The rainy season was May through September. The ritual calendar was divided into four parts of 65 days, a total of 260 days. Each sixty-five-day period was divided into five units of thirteen days each. Each day had its own name and number. There were thirteen number days but twenty name days, so the combination of names and numbers was nearly always unique. A special group of priests knew the properties of the days, benevolent or not, and determined the best days for marriage and other important events.

The Zapotecs used a system of writing numbers similar to the Maya. Dots and bars were written vertically beginning at the bottom. A dot represented one and a bar five. Events were recorded on stelae using pictographic symbols. As the repository for records, Monte Albán exercised a powerful influence over the area.

SIGNIFICANCE

The Zapotec state was one of the earliest examples of centralized government in Mesoamerica. It was also one of the first to experience the drawbacks of urban living, particularly the need to conquer others in order to obtain sufficient food to sustain an urban civilization. The art and architecture of Monte Albán suggests a close relationship between religion and conquest, and the religious calendar and writing system influenced later Mesoamerican civilizations such as the Mixtec.

—*Robert D. Talbott*

FURTHER READING

Blanton, Richard E., Gary H. Feinman, Stephen A. Kowslewski, and Linda M. Nicholas. *Ancient Oaxaca: The Monte Albán State.* New York: Cambridge University Press, 1999. Includes an introduction to Mesoamerican pre-Hispanic civilizations and relates the development of the Zapotec state and the importance of Monte Albán, its center.

Flannery, Kent V., and Joyce Marcus. *The Cloud People: Divergent Evolution of the Zapotec and Mixtec Civilizations.* New York: Academic Press, 1983. A collection of essays by experts on the history and development of the Zapotec and Mixtec civilizations and the rise and importance of Monte Albán.

Paddock, John, ed. *Ancient Oaxaca: Discoveries in Mexican Archeology and History.* Stanford, Calif.: Stanford University Press, 1966. Describes the early settlement of Oaxaca, the development of Oaxacan civilization, and the emergence of urban centers and the state.

Zapotec influence. As many as fifty "town conquest" slabs were carved on buildings at Monte Albán. Zapotec military superiority appears to have been memorialized at the Edificio de los Danzantes, a pyramidal platform filled with rubble. The outer walls are rectangular slabs of stone with more than three hundred carvings on them, representing single, naked men in awkward positions. The distorted poses and closed mouths and eyes indicate that the figures are corpses. Because nudity was scandalous in Zapotec society, the figures must represent slain or sacrificed captives. Some of the figures show sexual mutilation or blood flowing from severed parts. Scholars believe this scene functioned as a display of power meant to impress or intimidate the enemies of the Zapotecs.

Although the Zapotecs had already begun to develop their calendar and writing, it was during the period in which the state emerged that both reached completion. The Zapotecs had two calendars, one secular and one ritual. The secular calendar had 365 days divided into

Wiley, Gordon R. *Archeology of Southern Mesoamerica.* Vol. 4 in *Handbook of Middle American Indians.* Austin: University of Texas Press, 1965. Includes articles by experts on architecture, art, ceramics, jewelry, and metalwork of Oaxaca.

SEE ALSO: c. 1530 B.C.E., Mixtec Civilization Develops in Western Oaxaca; c. 1500-c. 300 B.C.E., Olmec Civilization Rises in Southern Mexico; c. 500 B.C.E.-c. 700 C.E., Zapotecs Build Monte Albán; c. 300 B.C.E., Izapan Civilization Dominates Mesoamerica.

c. 100 B.C.E.-c. 300 C.E.
EAST AFRICAN TRADING PORT OF RHAPTA FLOURISHES

Rhapta, an important trade town on the east African coast, flourished as an entrepôt for the commerce of the Indian Ocean through the construction of woven-plank boats for seagoing commerce.

LOCALE: East African coast of present-day Tanzania
CATEGORIES: Prehistory and ancient cultures; trade and commerce

SUMMARY OF EVENT

Rhapta is the name given to an important trade town that had become established by the closing century of the last millennium B.C.E. on the western Indian Ocean coast. The exact location of Rhapta is still unknown but it is believed to have emerged somewhere along the stretch of coast between the Tana River in Kenya and north-central Tanzania's shore, perhaps in the vicinity of modern-day Dar es Salaam. Scholars have argued for Rhapta being located in the now-swampy coastal lands off the Tana River because of information contained in travel logs and the amount of time needed to sail between known points on the Somali Peninsula, such as Ras Hafun, down the coast to the unknown point of Rhapta. Scholars have also argued for Dar es Salaam as the site because it is an ideal natural harbor, protected by bays and allowing more readily for the Malgasy-Indonesian-Rhapta trade connection.

Rhapta fell off the map some time after the fourth century C.E. as it was outranked as an entrepôt of trade by other coastal towns, or *shungwaya.* Rhapta's total decline and as-yet-undiscovered location lend credence to arguments for its existence in both the Tana swamplands and the more southern location in the Dar es Salaam vicinity. Swamplands are not well suited to the preservation of material culture. Although Dar may have served as a natural harbor, its immediate hinterland historically had few resources, according to archaeological data. In early Indian Ocean trade, a natural harbor may have been more important for landing a boat than immediately

available resources were. Over time, as competition for resources increased and as the seaborne long-distance trade became increasingly lucrative, it is presumed that traders would have sought more direct access to products by seeking out the source of supply and establishing ports more directly adjacent to those points. Thus, the Dar landscape serves as a good example of a gentle landing site without resources in its own environs but with resources in adjacent lands, which would have led to Rhapta's decline. Until further archaeological work in coastal East Africa uncovers material culture indicative of urban life of the proper era, the location of Rhapta will remain vague.

Rhapta is the only known trading port of East Africa between 100 B.C.E. and 100 C.E. Rhapta exported ivory, spices, gums, rhino horn, tortoise shell, and other locally and regionally attainable products that served as important consumer goods and raw materials for production of aphrodisiacs, medicines, luxury foods, and trinkets, as well as artistic creations throughout the Indian Ocean and Mediterranean worlds. Through this network, East Africa's coastal populations were able to import grains, wine, glass, and metal products produced in Europe, India, and the Arabian peninsula. In particular, glass beads were popular and have been uncovered in abundance in the archaeological record. Additionally, South Arabian and Mediterranean metal products such as spears, axes, knives, and other imported products have been uncovered in excavations. This importation of foreign-produced metals at the coast coincided with the spread of iron production out of the Great Lakes region into the coastal areas. Thus, there was a competition between foreign and domestic iron products in coastal and hinterland East Africa from the early first centuries of the first millennium C.E.

Periplus Maris Erythraei (also known as *Periplus,* first century C.E.; *Periplus of the Erythraean Sea,* 1912), an Egyptian sailor's log written in Greek in the first century C.E. for traders on the Indian Ocean and Mediterranean Sea, reveals that Rhapta was, at the time the *Periplus of the Erythraean Sea* was written, under the authority of the governor of Ma'afir (Mapharitis province) in the Himyar state of Yemen. It is uncertain whether this authority was actual political control, or if it signifies an economic monopoly that the governor of Ma'afir may have enjoyed the benefit of for certain products. Himyaritic script demonstrates a worship of the South Arabian moon-god in Adulis and Aksum farther north, but this same relationship is not represented in coastal East Africa's archaeological record, which may be valuable evidence in understanding the economic versus political connections between ancient Rhapta and any South Arabian kingdoms. Ironically, the history of most regions of Africa is known only through archaeological excavation, linguistic reconstruction, and comparative ethnography, yet Rhapta is known almost exclusively through written accounts, and its exact geographic location remains ambiguous in the writings.

SIGNIFICANCE

Rhapta was the first urban settlement in East Africa, emerging as a trade post on East Africa's Indian Ocean coastline, and becoming a leading site of long-distance trade on the Indian Ocean seaboard. Rhapta served as a trade emporium, exporting products to South Arabia's Aden, Alexandria, and other Indian Ocean ports. Rhapta, as the southernmost terminus of trade between 100 B.C.E. and 100 C.E., connected East Africa to a great and extensive network that linked the Mediterranean, Indian Ocean, and Red Sea trades in a system of commercial exchange.

Rhapta's importance as a city was recorded in *Periplus of the Erythraean Sea*, which details the commercial interchange that existed between Yemen, Alexandria, Rhapta, and other sites. Additionally, Ptolemy (c. 100-c. 178 B.C.E.), in his *Geōgraphikē hyphēgēsis* (second century C.E.; *The Geography of Ptolemy*, 1732), discussed Rhapta as a "metropolis," a term that gives a clear indication of its commercial importance and distinctiveness as a community stratified by wealth. The word "metropolis" may have even referred to the cosmopolitan nature of a place like Rhapta, where cultural intermixing and intermarriage were not uncommon. Linguistic exchange and intermarriage among coastal Africans and South Arabian sailors are referred to in the *Periplus of the Erythraean Sea*, which states that the foreigners were able to speak the language of Rhapta.

Rhapta was most likely settled not later than the early first century B.C.E. by the early northeast coastal Bantu and perhaps some Cushitic-speaking peoples. Africans who settled the coastal strip of eastern Africa in various stages employed sewn wooden boats for fishing, tortoise hunting, and nautilus catching. While many of the marine products harvested by coastal Bantu were probably locally consumed or dried and exported, the luxury goods that could be produced from tortoise shell and pearly nautilus were of particular interest for luxury trade in the international market that developed. The trading and fishing vessels that were produced by the coastal Bantu were distinctive enough that the foreign sailors gave the site its name, Rhapta, which is the Greek term for "sewn boats." The exact size of these early boats remains unknown, but they probably were not particularly small, as they had to be large enough to carry cargo and to sail successfully in the Indian Ocean channel rather than simply hugging the coast.

The intercontinental trade that emerged on the Indian Ocean littoral was part of one of the earliest global trade networks in human history. The commercial exchange that emerged had connections in the west to Aksum and Adulis on the Red Sea, and this trade linked the farther Mediterranean world to eastern Africa. In the east, perhaps slightly later, Rhapta was linked through commodity exchange with Omani traders, the Indian subcontinent's merchants, China's maritime expeditioners, and Indonesian traders. Rhapta certainly must have served as a transshipment point for Indonesian goods such as highly coveted spices, which most likely passed via Madagascar and the Comoros through Rhapta and then onward to other, more lucrative markets. In the 1920's, scholars calculated the value of spices in Mediterranean European markets for the early first millennium and estimated that the exchange cost of one pound of cinnamon would have been equivalent to $325 at that time, roughly $3,000 in 2002. Some legends record the maritime traders of Rhapta as being practitioners of piracy; the legends may have been a device to protect the lucrative trade by discouraging large numbers of maritime traders from getting involved. The early Indian Ocean-Mediterranean exchange network, at the end of the last millennium B.C.E., was the beginning of long-distance seaborne commerce, an entirely new economic concept and endeavor at the time; this system was part of the first global trade network.

Early settlements and commercial entrepôts such as Rhapta transformed parts of East Africa. Coastal Bantu communities that became incorporated into the trade network came to be influenced by Shirazi, South Asian, and Islamic cultural elements, which was the beginning of what has come to be referred to as the Swahili identity; Rhapta and subsequent towns that emerged for trade on the coast contributed to the spread of Swahili culture. Although Rhapta may not have been the first and certainly was not the only coastal settlement of Africans, it is a symbol of the history of the Swahili culture that emerged along the coast. Sewn boats, maritime culture, and a seafaring life prevalent in Rhapta and other coastal towns and settlements like it has been an important part of the identity of later generations of coastal Swahili.

—*Catherine Cymone Fourshey*

FURTHER READING

Allen, James de Vere. *Swahili Origins: Swahili Culture and the Shungwaya Phenomenon.* London: James Currey Press, 1993. Focuses primarily on issues of Swahili ethnicity and culture, which is, according to Allen, heavily grounded in a history of Indian Ocean trade.

Casson, Lionel. *The Periplus of the Erythraei.* Princeton, N.J.: Princeton University Press, 1989. A translation and discussion of a primary document from first century C.E. Red Sea, Indian Ocean, Mediterranean Sea trade.

Hourani, George Fadlo, and John Carswell. *Arab Seafaring in the Indian Ocean in Ancient and Early Medieval Times.* Princeton, N.J.: Princeton University Press, 1995. A history of commercial sea routes in the Indian Ocean. The primary focus is on the Arab traders who, between 500 and 1500 C.E., traded with people of the East African coast in towns like Rhapta.

Kirwan, L. P. "Rhapta, Metropolis of Azania." *Azania* 21 (1986): 99-104. Kirwan analyzes the geographical and historical evidence about Rhapta, concluding that Rhapta must have been in the vicinity of Dar es Salaam.

Reade, Julian, ed. *The Indian Ocean in Antiquity.* New York: Paul Keagan, 1996. A survey of the ancient Indian Ocean with particular attention to commercial history.

SEE ALSO: c. 1000 B.C.E.-c. 300 C.E., Urban Commerce Develops in the Sudan Belt; 1st century C.E., Kingdom of Aksum Emerges.

100 - 1 B.C.E.

95-69 B.C.E.
ARMENIAN EMPIRE REACHES ITS PEAK UNDER TIGRANES THE GREAT

Armenian king Tigranes the Great, by defeating war-weakened Parthia and the civil-strife-ridden Seleucid Empire, conquered the area from central Iran to the Mediterranean, bringing Armenia to its greatest expanse.

LOCALE: Armenia, Media (now western Iran), Assyria (now northern Iraq), Syria, Phoenicia (now Lebanon), and Cilicia (now eastern and central Turkey)

CATEGORIES: Expansion and land acquisition; wars, uprisings and civil unrest

KEY FIGURES

Tigranes the Great (c. 140-c. 55 B.C.E.), king of Armenia, r. 95-55 B.C.E.

Mithradates VI Eupator (c. 134-63 B.C.E.), king of Pontus (modern northeastern Turkey), r. 120-63 B.C.E.

Pompey the Great (106-48 B.C.E.), Roman triumvir, 60-53 B.C.E.

Lucius Licinius Lucullus (c. 117-56 B.C.E.), Roman proconsul in the province of Asia (now western Turkey), c. 75-c. 65 B.C.E.

SUMMARY OF EVENT

Ancient Armenia extended farther to the south and west of modern Armenia, including substantial portions of what is now eastern Turkey and northern Syria and Iraq. Originally under the rule of native dynasties, most of Armenia passed under the rule of Alexander the Great's general Seleucus I Nicator and his descendants in the late fourth century B.C.E. In 189 B.C.E., independence was regained under a dynasty descended from the Seleucid general Artaxias, although the neighboring kings of Pontus to the west (now in eastern Turkey) and Parthia to the east (now Iran) had substantial influence. Tigranes the Great spent the first forty years of his life as a hostage in the court of the Parthian king Mithradates II after a war between Armenia and Parthia.

Scholars have inferred from the literary sources that in 95 B.C.E., Artavasdes II, Tigranes's uncle and predecessor, died or was killed. In that year, the Armenians paid a ransom of seventy rich valleys to the Parthians for Tigranes's return. The popularity of Tigranes may in part have been due to his claim of descent from the Orontid

Dynasty of early independent Armenia as well as his proven descent from the Artaxiad kings. The sources say little of internal affairs in Armenia under Tigranes, emphasizing external relations. Parthia, threatened for the first time by Roman intervention on its western frontiers, may have hoped to set up Tigranes as a subordinate ally, but he proved to be his own man.

Shortly after taking the throne, Tigranes formed an alliance with Mithradates VI Eupator of Pontus and married the king's daughter, Cleopatra. He waged war with Parthia, regaining the lost valleys and forcing the small neighboring state to the northwest, Sophene, into tributary status. Although Parthia, temporarily weakened because of invasions on its eastern frontier (now Afghanistan and Pakistan), had attempted an alliance with Rome, after the death of the Parthian king Mithradates II in 87 B.C.E., Tigranes took advantage of Parthia's situation. He took the ancient Persian title of "king of kings," previously claimed by the Parthian monarchs, and invaded territory that is now in northern and central Iraq. In 83, Tigranes occupied Syria, Phoenicia, and Cilicia, taking advantage of civil strife in the declining Seleucid Empire. Marriage alliances were secured with local kings in the east, establishing a political pattern in the area that was to last for centuries. After 80 B.C.E., Tigranes founded a new capital, Tigranocerta, at an uncertain location in Mesopotamia (now Iraq), to secure his southern frontiers. Greek cultural influences were strong in Tigranocerta, as Greeks from some defeated cities to the west were forced to live there. Greek mercenaries as well as Armenians formed the city's garrison. The city survived a Roman attempt at its destruction in 69 B.C.E. and remained inhabited for centuries, becoming an important Christian center some five centuries later.

At about the same time as he founded his new capital, Tigranes captured the Seleucid capital, Antioch (now in southeastern Turkey but considered part of Syria until well into the twentieth century), which was then one of the largest cities in the world and a major Greek cultural center. By this time, the Armenian army numbered more than six figures. Only a narrow tongue of land (now in Syria and eastern Turkey) remained under Selucid rule until the Romans under Pompey the Great finally destroyed what remained of that empire in 60 B.C.E. At the height of his power, Tigranes ruled much of the Middle East and had no strong opponents, either internally or ex-

Tigranes the Great. (Library of Congress)

ternally. Even Ptolemaic Egypt was too weakened by internal conflict to be a threat to him.

Unfortunately for Tigranes, his unification and consolidation of the area only paved the way for Roman conquest. By 70 B.C.E., popular discontent at continual and expensive warfare as well as the humiliation of local kings, whom Tigranes had treated like domestic servants, undermined his popularity, and his subjects, especially the Greeks, began to look to Rome. In 69 B.C.E., Rome, avenging earlier defeats, sent an army under Lucius Licinius Lucullus against king Mithradates VI Eupator of Pontus, Tigranes' ally, capturing Tigranocerta and all Tigranes' conquests west of Armenia's historic borders. In 67, Tigranes again invaded Cappadocia (now in central Turkey), but the arrival of an even stronger Roman army under Pompey the Great, assisted by Tigranes' own son who had rebelled, forced the elder Tigranes to sue for peace. Under the alliance, Tigranes was forced to pay large sums to Rome, and his kingdom was reduced to its size at the time of his accession plus the seventy valleys. Greek and Roman influence became even stronger in the latter days of his reign. Tigranes died in 55 B.C.E. and was succeeded by one of his sons, Artavasdes II; Tigranes the Younger, his son by another mother, apparently had died in Roman captivity or exile.

SIGNIFICANCE

Although Tigranes the Great's external conquests proved ephemeral and despite his reputation for cruelty and terror, his lasting achievement was significant. At a time when smaller states in the Middle East were being absorbed by Pontus, Parthia, and Rome, Tigranes laid the foundations for the preservation of Armenia as an independent state ruled by the same dynasty for hundreds of years to come, even if under Roman or Parthian protection. He increased the influence of Greek civilization and arguably set the state for the spread of Christianity into Armenia in the following century. According to Armenian historians, in the fourth century C.E., a few years ahead of Rome, Armenia became the first Christian state. Factors set in motion by Tigranes would result in the preservation of ancient literature, including Christian writings, and probably the prevention of the absorption of Armenia by Islam in later centuries. Although many historians of other nations, including Rome, judged Tigranes negatively, to Armenian writers, both contemporary and later, he was a national hero.

—*Stephen A. Stertz*

FURTHER READING

Debevoise, Neilson C. *A Political History of Parthia.* 1938. Reprint. Chicago: University of Chicago Press, 1968. Discusses the general Armenian background from the viewpoint of relations to Parthia. Has not been superseded.

Sherwin-White, A. N. "Lucullus, Pompey, and the East." In *The Last Age of the Roman Republic 146-43 B.C.*, edited by John A. Crook et al. Vol. 9 in *Cambridge Ancient History*. 2d ed. New York: Cambridge University Press, 1994. Provides a brief, up-to-date, well-documented account, primarily from the Roman viewpoint.

_____. *Roman Foreign Policy in the East, 168 B.C. to A.D. 1.* Norman: University of Oklahoma Press, 1984. More detailed than the previously cited work, with some emphasis on military history.

Sullivan, Richard D. *Near Eastern Royalty and Rome 100-30 B.C.* Toronto: University of Toronto Press, 1990. Provides a highly detailed treatment and assessment of the career and importance of Tigranes the Great. Numerous references to primary and secondary sources. Also covers the general background, as implied in the title.

SEE ALSO: c. 323-275 B.C.E., Diadochi Divide Alexander the Great's Empire; 245-140 B.C.E., Rise of Parthia; 133 B.C.E., Pergamum Is Transferred to Rome.

RELATED ARTICLES in *Great Lives from History: The Ancient World*: Mithradates VI Eupator; Pompey the Great; Tigranes the Great.

---

90 B.C.E.
JULIAN LAW EXPANDS ROMAN CITIZENSHIP

The Julian Law extended Roman citizenship to the southern two-thirds of Italy, transforming the concept of citizenship and creating the first nation in history.

LOCALE: Rome and Italy
CATEGORIES: Laws, acts, and legal history; government and politics

KEY FIGURES

Marcus Livius Drusus (d. 91 B.C.E.), Roman tribune, 91 B.C.E.
Silo Pompaedius (fl. second-early first centuries B.C.E.), leader of the Italic allies, 88 B.C.E.
Lucius Julius Caesar (d. 87 B.C.E.), Roman consul, 90 B.C.E.
Gnaeus Pompeius Strabo (d. 87 B.C.E.), Roman commander who became a consul in 89 B.C.E.

Publius Sulpicius Rufus (c. 124-88 B.C.E.), Roman tribune, 88 B.C.E.
Gaius Marius (157-86 B.C.E.), Roman consul in 107, 104-100, and 86 B.C.E.

SUMMARY OF EVENT

For centuries the Romans, as did all the peoples of ancient Italy, thought of their community in ethnic rather than geographical terms: The state was a people, the *Res Publica Populi Romani*. Its members (citizens, *cives*) possessed distinct duties, privileges, and rights. The foremost duties were the payment of various taxes and compulsory service in the military; the chief privilege was eligibility for elective public office. The rights of citizenship (*civitas*) were more comprehensive and ultimately, for most people, more valuable: *conubium*, the right to contract a valid marriage; *commercium*, the right to own private property and to enter into contracts that were enforceable in court; the right of appeal in the face of cruel and arbitrary punishment by a public official; and the right to vote on proposed legislation and on candidates for elective office.

Two and a half centuries of constant warfare gave Rome domination of Italy by the end of the First Punic War in 241 B.C.E. In the course of the fighting, Rome devised a flexible three-tiered system to control its defeated rivals. Roman citizens were the first category. Nearly all Romans were citizens from birth. On rare occasions individuals received citizenship through government grant, and the children of freed slaves became citizens.

The Latins received preferential treatment; they were geographically and culturally close to Rome and prior to 338 B.C.E. were Rome's full partners. These "allies of the Latin name" (*socii nominis Latini*), the second tier, were given *commercium* and *conubium* together with limited voting rights in Rome. For a time, Latins could migrate to Rome and obtain Roman citizenship, though this right (*ius migrandi*) ceased in the 170's B.C.E. Within another fifty years, Latins who held local political office thereby won Roman citizenship. This ingenious and not altogether disinterested provision ensured each city a small ruling class, primarily loyal to Rome. All "Latins-become-Romans" had to abandon their original citizenship, for one could not be a citizen of two communities simultaneously. The Latins were numerically the smallest of the three categories. A few peoples received citizenship without the vote (*civitas sine suffragio*), a category that was close to *Latinitas*; by the end of the second century they had acquired full *civitas*.

The remaining communities of Italy were treated as allies, *socii*, bound to Rome by formal treaties that specified their obligations and rights. These peoples varied widely, from urbanized Greeks and Etruscans to the numerous tribal *populi* lacking central governments, notably the Samnites and Marsi. The common feature of this third tier was its members' cultural difference from Rome. They retained their local autonomy except in matters of foreign policy, where they had to follow the will of Rome. Although they were exempt from the payment of tribute and taxes, they had to provide troops at Rome's request even for wars that did not affect their own security directly. Furthermore, they were under the vague and general obligation to respect Rome's dignity and to preserve its power.

This threefold alliance system with its fine gradations functioned smoothly in the beginning. The efforts of the Carthaginian general Hannibal (247-182 B.C.E.) at fo-

menting insurrection among Rome's allies in the Second Punic War (218-201 B.C.E.) had insignificant results. In the course of the second century, however, the situation gradually worsened. Enormous changes swept over the peninsula. Rome established control over north Italy, called Cisalpine Gaul, whose largely Celtic population joined the number of *socii*. By this time, Rome was acquiring lands outside Italy, called provinces, and Rome compelled the Latins and Italians to provide a disproportionate share of the incessant and heavy military demands—and discriminated against them when sharing out the spoils of war.

Further, Roman citizenship had become far more valuable than earlier, and Roman officials are known to have violated the allies' treaty rights. By the 140's, the allies were demanding the protection of full citizenship, but the conservative senate and jealous Roman assemblies rejected their appeals. In 125 B.C.E., Rome destroyed the Latin colony of Fregellae when it revolted in frustration, and then the voters rejected the proposals of Marcus Fulvius Flaccus (d. 121 B.C.E.) and Gaius Sempronius Gracchus (153-121 B.C.E.) to extend the citizenship. The terms of the bills are uncertain (perhaps full *civitas* to the Latins and Latin rights to the Italians), and in any case, they failed to pass.

In 91 B.C.E., the reform program of the tribune Marcus Livius Drusus included a proposal to extend citizenship to the allies. Passions ran high on both sides. The bill failed, he was murdered, and fighting broke out. The war goes by various names: Social (from *socius*), Marsic (Marsi were among the leaders), or Italian (from the belligerents). Under the command of the Marsian Silo Pompaedius, the allies revolted and established their own confederation of Italia, with its seat at Corfinium. They began issuing their own coinage and put a huge army in the field. For a time Rome was close to disaster but slowly gained the upper hand. Several factors combined to bring about a Roman victory. With one exception, Venusia, the Latins remained loyal and Rome used their towns as strongholds. Few Etruscans, Gauls, other northern peoples, or Greeks defected. The Samnites and Marsi were the most resolute enemies, as they had been among Rome's bitterest enemies in the fourth century B.C.E. The rebels had no tradition of union and failed to coordinate effectively. Most important, Rome undercut the rebellion by judicious concessions.

In 90 B.C.E., the consul Lucius Julius Caesar, second cousin once removed of the more famous Julius Caesar, carried the *Lex Julia: De civitate Latinis et sociis danda* (Julian Law on giving citizenship to the Latins and [Italian] allies), which granted full citizenship to all communities south of Cisalpine Gaul—and the four Latin colonies in it (Piacenza, Cremona, Bologna, and Aquileia)—which had not joined in the revolt or promptly abandoned it. This was the major act of enfranchisement and it decisively changed the nature of Italy. Urbanization proceeded rapidly, and with it relative administrative uniformity, as *populi* were upgraded to *municipia* and joined the older *coloniae*. Roman citizenship was now well on the way to becoming a national institution, and Italy was distinct from the provinces.

SIGNIFICANCE

Subsequent laws supplemented the *Lex Julia*. In 89 B.C.E., Gnaeus Pompeius Strabo's *Lex Pompeia* evidently made Cisalpine Gaul a province (its southern border set at the Arno and Rubicon Rivers), granted Latin status to the mostly Celtic peoples north of the Po River, and attached them to the former Latin colonies, which were now Roman *municipia*. This extension of *Latinitas* manifests Roman flexibility: Latinity was coming to be seen as a condition halfway to full citizenship and independent of its homeland in Latium. The Gallic Latins became citizens in 49 B.C.E., and Cisalpine Gaul was incorporated into Italy in 42 B.C.E. Rome was henceforward the common *patria* of all free Italians, including women. In later centuries, both Latin status and full citizenship spread throughout the Roman Empire.

Registration of the masses of new citizens was controversial. Fearing the loss of their ability to control political life, conservatives wanted to pack them in a few of the older tribes. In 88 B.C.E., the tribune Publius Sulpicius Rufus proposed that they be distributed evenly through all thirty-five tribes. He turned to the military hero Gaius Marius for help. The sixty-eight-year-old Marius favored equitable treatment for the Italians and through marriage had become an in-law of the Caesars. Rufus transferred to him the eastern command, which the senate had as-

signed to Lucius Cornelius Sulla, one of the consuls elected in 88 B.C.E. In the ensuing civil war, Sulla marched on Rome and killed Rufus. Marius fled, returned, proscribed his enemies (including the Caesar who passed the law of 90 B.C.E.), and died in January, 86 B.C.E., two weeks into his seventh consulship. A few years later, Sulla became dictator, but accepted the distribution of the new citizens in all thirty-five tribes.

—*George M. Pepe, updated by Thomas H. Watkins*

FURTHER READING

Brunt, P. *Italian Manpower, 225 B.C.-A.D. 14*. 1971. Reprint. New York: Oxford University Press, 1993. Places the question of citizenship in the context of population trends, including emigration.

Dyson, Stephen L. *Community and Society in Roman Italy*. 1992. Reprint. Baltimore, Md.: The Johns Hopkins University Press, 2002. Examines the relationship dynamics between rural Italian communities and Rome in the period between the end of the Second Punic War and the Middle Ages. Good bibliography.

Gardner, Jane F. *Being a Roman Citizen*. New York: Routledge, 1993. A comprehensive study of Roman citizenship, discussing the differences in rights among different categories of person, especially the handicapped, women, and children.

Johnston, David. *Roman Law in Context*. New York: Cambridge University Press, 2000. This survey describes how the theoretical rights of Roman citizenship operated in practice.

SEE ALSO: 340-338 B.C.E., Origin of *Municipia*; 287 B.C.E., *Lex Hortensia* Reforms the Roman Constitution; 133 B.C.E., Tiberius Sempronius Gracchus Is Tribune; 58-51 B.C.E., Caesar Conquers Gaul.

RELATED ARTICLES in *Great Lives from History: The Ancient World*: Gracchi; Gaius Marius.

100 - 1 B.C.E.

73-71 B.C.E.
SPARTACUS LEADS SLAVE REVOLT

The legendary slave gladiator Spartacus led a slave uprising in Italy that only the Roman army could suppress, contributing to the fall of the already declining Roman Republic.

LOCALE: Italy
CATEGORIES: Wars, uprisings, and civil unrest; government and politics

KEY FIGURES

Spartacus (late second century-71 B.C.E.), Thracian slave gladiator
Marcus Licinius Crassus (c. 115-53 B.C.E.), Roman triumvir, 60-53 B.C.E.
Pompey the Great (106-48 B.C.E.), Roman triumvir, 60-53 B.C.E.

SUMMARY OF EVENT

After the Second Punic War (218-201 B.C.E.), the Roman Republic became a great empire divided by a gulf between the wealthy classes (the senatorial land owners and merchant knights) and a teeming Mediterranean population of slaves, exploited provincials, and underemployed citizens dependent on the largesse of the wealthy. Attempts by the tribal assembly to alleviate the situation of the poor citizens, the *populares*, in the late second century failed and gave rise to powerful demagogic generals. The First Civil War (88-82 B.C.E.) between the senatorial and *populare* parties was a long, bloody struggle won by the senatorial general Lucius Cornelius Sulla (138-78 B.C.E.). Sulla, in an extraordinary one-year dictatorship, introduced several laws in favor of the land-owning class. The senate, also as a result of the civil war, placed a ban on generals keeping their armies in Italy.

During the same period, two large slave revolts erupted in Sicily, the site of some of the richest senatorial estates: the First (135-132 B.C.E.) and Second (104-101 B.C.E.) Servile Wars. The Third Servile War took place in Italy beginning in 73 B.C.E. Its leader was a Thracian bandit, Spartacus, who once served in the Roman army but later, perhaps after deserting, turned to brigandage. After his capture, the Romans sold him into slavery and sent him to the gladiator school at Capua, the chief city of the wealthy region of Campagnia, to train for the arena. Along with seventy-three other gladiators, Spartacus escaped and seized weapons from travelers they encoun-

tered, including the guards sent to subdue them. The gladiators fled to Mount Vesuvius.

The senate initially sent a force of three thousand under the praetor Gaius Claudius Glaber, who set a guard at the foot of Vesuvius to wait out the slaves. However, Spartacus made ladders from the thick vines at the mountaintop and his troops stealthily descended and surprised the Romans, seizing their camp. Glaber's defeat left the rebels in control of southern Italy. Other slaves from throughout the peninsula—highly discontented Gauls, Thracians, Germans, and others—fled to join them, and Spartacus's forces grew to more than 100,000, whom he armed and supplied with booty from Glaber's camp as well as weapons they forged themselves.

Another praetor, Publius Varinius, followed Glaber. Spartacus defeated two thousand of his troops and went after Lucius Cossinius, Varinius's adjutant, seizing his camp and supplies and eventually defeating and killing him. The slaves then escaped Varinius by the ruse of propping up corpses on stakes, lighting fires, and using trumpeters to give the illusion that they were in camp while most sneaked out. When they finally met in battle, the rebels won and many of Varinius's troops fled in fear, creating great anxiety over Spartacus in Rome.

Spartacus and his second in command, Crixus, now each leading his own army, differed in their goals. Spartacus wished to return to Thrace, but Crixus wanted to remain in Italy and plunder the Roman estates. In 72 B.C.E. the senate ordered the consuls Lucius Gellius Publicola and Gnaeus Cornelius Lentulus Clodianus and the praetors Quintus Arrius and Gnaeus Manlius to attack the slave armies in force. Gellius cornered Crixus at Monte Gargano, destroying his army. However, he was unable to defeat Spartacus, who fought a more cautious and cleverer campaign. Spartacus moved his troops north toward the Alps to leave Italy, with Gellius pursuing him from the rear. Meanwhile Lentulus tried to intercept his van. In two rapid battles in Pincenum, Spartacus defeated first the latter and then the former, and then, farther north at Mutina, defeated Gaius Cassius Longinus (not to be confused with the assassin of Julius Caesar), the proconsul of Gaul. Spartacus's victory opened the way for his escape from Italy.

However, Spartacus apparently decided that bringing his people out through the Roman-controlled frontier was too difficult and returned south, where he hoped to link up with the slaves of Sicily. Spartacus tried to maintain discipline, but many of his followers, with the help of local slaves, plundered the towns through which they passed. There is speculation, which cannot be verified, that Spartacus hoped to attack Rome—a scheme that would have been doomed to failure. In fact, he retreated south to the Brutium Hills. The senate now appointed Marcus Licinius Crassus to replace the dismissed consuls and asked him to bring his troops from the provinces. Crassus added six legions to the consuls' four, which had

Spartacus. (Library of Congress)

lost as much as half of their strength in the campaigns against the slaves. Furthermore, he had one in ten of the defeated battalion executed to instill in them fear of himself rather than the rebels and then headed south to cut off Spartacus from Sicily.

Crassus conducted his pursuit with severity—punishing commanders and executing soldiers who wavered in the least. He drove Spartacus's force to Rhegium, where Gaius Verres prevented his crossing over to Sicily. However, Crassus's strategy of trying to confine the slaves behind a wall and ditch across southern Italy to starve them out failed, as Spartacus easily broke through the mountains by concentrating his assault.

Open warfare was renewed. With agitation by the populace of Rome, the senate also commissioned two generals to aid Crassus: Pompey the Great, then fighting in Spain, and Marcus Licinius Lucullus, the consul for 73 B.C.E., who had returned from a successful campaign against Mithradates VI Eupator, the king of Pontus. Crassus had originally asked the senate to send Pompey and Lucullus, but when they arrived, he was afraid of losing the honor of the victory and tried to finish the campaign quickly. After failing to escape to Sicily, Spartacus moved west to Brundisium (present-day Brindisi), but Lucullus forced him to return north and try to escape once again through the Alps. Moreover, Spartacus's comrades broke with him. In addition to Crixus, the Gauls Castus and Cannicus struck out on their own as well. Spartacus's attention was diverted to holding his troops together. After several battles, the Romans defeated the Gauls between Paestum and Venusia (near Bari). Their loss crushed Spartacus as well. He moved south, where he had a minor success, and his followers urged him to meet Crassus's legions in open battle. Unwisely, he agreed. Crassus won and Spartacus died in the action.

After the battle, Pompey arrived. Crassus reluctantly accepted his aid in rounding up the remaining slave fugitives. They captured six thousand and crucified them along the Appian Way from Capua to Rome. Some accounts say that, all told, perhaps 100,000 slaves were killed in the war. Crassus had accomplished his task in six months, although the Romans continued to chase down small bands of rebel slaves for several years afterward.

SIGNIFICANCE

The Third Servile War, like the previous two in Sicily, was not a major cause of the downfall of the Republic. It warned Rome of the danger of slave revolts, and the government took steps to avoid a repetition of gladiatorial uprisings. The damage in southern Italy was severe, but Rome recovered. The civil wars caused more damage to Rome's ancient institutions. For Crassus and Pompey, the victory over Spartacus was a stepping stone in their careers. Crassus, with justified confidence in his military ability, now felt ready to follow Gaius Marius and Sulla as a warrior leader of Rome, and although he resented Pompey imposing himself in the victory and continued to resent him for the remainder of his life, he collaborated with him on his march to power. The two shared the consulate the following year, and subsequently, in 60 B.C.E., when Pompey contested Cicero (106-43 B.C.E.) for leadership of the senatorial party, he joined again with Crassus and Julius Caesar (100-44 B.C.E.) to form the first triumvirate, which controlled Rome and eventually led to the end of the Republic.

For Spartacus, although his uprising was unsuccessful, in the long run, his name has lived on as a symbol of revolt of the downtrodden and as a hero of the political left. The left-wing splinter group of the German Social Democrats, led by Rosa Luxemburg and Karl Liebknecht, who also led an unsuccessful uprising in Berlin in 1919, called themselves the Spartacists. The Third Servile War was the subject of a novel *Spartacus* by the Marxist Howard Fast, which in turn formed the basis of a popular motion picture of the same name in 1960.

—*Frederick B. Chary*

FURTHER READING

Appian. *The Civil Wars*. Translated by John Carter. New York: Penguin, 1996. The second century Greek historian's account of the late Roman Republic.

Bradley, K. R. *Slavery and Rebellion in the Roman World, 140 B.C.-70 B.C.* Bloomington: Indiana University Press, 1998. An excellent account of all three Servile Wars by a major contemporary historian of Rome. Documentation and extensive bibliography.

Crook, J. A., Andrew Lintott, and Elizabeth Rawson, eds. *The Last Age of the Roman Republic, 146-43 B.C.* Vol. 9 in *The Cambridge Ancient History*. 2d ed. New York: Cambridge University Press, 1994. A standard work on the ancient world. Contains a detailed account of the war and the surrounding history of the major Roman politicians and generals involved. Maps, chronology, and a very extensive bibliography.

Plutarch. *Plutarch's Lives*. Translated by John Dryden, edited by Arthur Hugh Clough. Reprint. New York: Modern Library, 2001. The lives of Crassus and Pompey cover the war. The former is the best ancient source. This translation by the sixteenth century English poet is classic.

Shaw, Brent D., trans. *Spartacus and the Slave Wars: A Brief History with Documents*. New York: Palgrave Macmillan, 2001. Contains documents related to all the slave wars as well as others related to Roman history of the time. Useful appendices, illustrations and a bibliography.

SEE ALSO: 90 B.C.E., Julian Law Expands Roman Citizenship; Late 63-January 62 B.C.E., Catiline Conspiracy; 58-51 B.C.E., Caesar Conquers Gaul; 54 B.C.E., Roman Poet Catullus Dies.
RELATED ARTICLES in *Great Lives from History: The Ancient World*: Julius Caesar; Cicero; Pompey the Great; Spartacus.

Late 63-January 62 B.C.E.
CATILINE CONSPIRACY

Senator Catiline's conspiracy to overthrow the government in 63 B.C.E. was averted by the consul Cicero, who thereby preserved the Roman Republic.

LOCALE: Rome and northern Italy
CATEGORIES: Wars, uprisings, and civil unrest; government and politics

KEY FIGURES
Catiline (c. 108-62 B.C.E.), Roman senator
Cicero (106-43 B.C.E.), Roman senator, philosopher, and orator

SUMMARY OF EVENT
A key feature of Roman politics during the Republican period was the annual competition among candidates to fill prestigious government positions and to enjoy their concomitant public honors. Political campaigns became increasingly competitive during the first century B.C.E. as citizens began expending great sums of money in their attempt to be elected. Despite new legislation aimed at curtailing the expense, bribery, and violence associated with elections, the Republic was having little success in preventing scandals that threatened the integrity of the election process and the stability of the government itself.

The story of Catiline is instructive in this sense. Catiline was a member of a noble family that had once held high office but was no longer prominent. As a young man, he supported the dictator Lucius Cornelius Sulla (138-78 B.C.E.) in his war against the Roman senate and earned a reputation for brutality. Although a series of sexual scandals darkened Catiline's reputation, he appeared to be enjoying a successful political career after he entered the senate and was elected in 69 B.C.E. as praetor, one of the eight men who oversaw Rome's law courts. After serving the following two years as governor of the province of Africa, he returned to Rome to run for the office of consul, Rome's highest political office. However, charges of extortion prevented his candidacy for two years.

In 64 B.C.E. he finally stood for election as one of the two consuls, and several important senators, including Marcus Licinius Crassus and Julius Caesar (100-44 B.C.E.), openly supported Catiline. Several strong candidates vied for the consulship, including the prominent senator Cicero. Although Cicero came from humble means, he had developed a reputation as an eloquent orator and he enjoyed the backing of many influential members of the senate. The results of the election were close, but Cicero took the senior consul post and Catiline was narrowly defeated for the junior position. In September of 63 B.C.E., Catiline failed again to be elected consul, but on this occasion his defeat was decisive. Despairing of his future political chances, he made preparations to overthrow the government.

The chronology of the conspiracy itself is problematic. Ancient sources tend to believe that Catiline was contemplating an insurrection even while he was a candidate for the consulship. Modern scholars, however, tend to believe that he only turned to revolutionary means after his defeat in September of 63 B.C.E. Whatever the timing, Catiline recruited leaders of the conspiracy by assembling a group of indebted and discredited fellow senators and businessmen. He proposed to murder high government officials and seize control of the government. He tried to gather support among the masses with promises to cancel all private debts and proscribe wealthy citizens. He directed his lieutenants to recruit supporters from the lower classes of Rome, and he sent others into the countryside to raise an army among disgruntled veterans of the wars Sulla had waged in the eastern Mediterranean.

The consul Cicero was greatly concerned by rumors of the conspiracy that were circulating in the second half of 63 B.C.E. Although a few years earlier, he had contemplated a political alliance with Catiline, he now was convinced that the senator was planning for a widespread uprising. Fortunately for the consul, one of Catiline's conspirators, Quintus Curius, informed Cicero of the plot and agreed to keep the consul apprised of its progress. Cicero began to take precautions in Rome, but lacking substantial evidence, he initially could not convince the senate that Catiline was a threat to the city. However, news began filtering into Rome that Catiline's associates were recruiting soldiers and preparing insurrections throughout the provinces. Consequently, on October 21, the senate passed legislation granting Cicero emergency powers to combat the threat. Catiline was charged with preparing violent measures against the government, but he was not detained because of a lack of evidence.

Plans for the conspiracy continued despite Cicero's vigilance. On the morning of November 7, two conspirators attempted to assassinate Cicero at his house, but Quintus Curius had warned the consul in advance and he was protected from harm. On the following day, the consul convened a meeting of the senate in order to denounce Catiline. To Cicero's surprise, Catiline attended the meet-

697

ing and even took a seat among the senators; all the senators, however, moved away and left Catiline to listen to the consul's speech by himself. Cicero openly accused Catiline of treason and encouraged him to leave Rome. That evening, Catiline fled Rome to join an army of rebels in Etruria. He intended to march on Rome once conspirators in the city openly rebelled.

In Rome, Cicero redoubled his efforts to gather evidence on the conspiracy and uncover the identities of Catiline's confederates. By the middle of November, news reached Rome that Catiline had taken up arms in Etruria, and the senate declared him a public enemy. In early December, the conspiracy fell apart when envoys of a Gallic tribe informed Cicero of the identities of several conspirators. Cicero made arrangements for the envoys to gather evidence, and by December 3, he was able to arrest five conspirators. At a hastily convened meeting of the senate that morning, the arrested conspirators confessed to their actions and provided additional information about the plot. On December 5, Cicero summoned the senate to determine the punishment for the conspirators. The senator Decimus Silanus proposed that the conspirators be summarily executed, but Julius Caesar argued for clemency to be shown to them. Eventually, the senate decided on execution, and later that evening, the conspirators were taken to the prison and strangled. A grateful senate later declared Cicero *pater patriae*, "father of his country."

In the meanwhile, Catiline remained with his army outside of Rome, waiting for an uprising to occur in the city. When news arrived that Cicero had suppressed the conspiracy, he tried to withdraw his army into Gaul (modern-day France). However, a large army under Gaius Antonius trapped Catiline in northern Italy and compelled him to attempt a desperate battle. In early January near the city of Pistoria (modern Pistoia, Italy), the army of Antonius easily defeated the ill-trained and ill-equipped army of the conspirators. Catiline himself was killed in battle.

SIGNIFICANCE

Catiline's attempt to overthrow the government was symptomatic of the growing internal challenges that the Roman senate faced at the twilight of the Republican era. Men such as Catiline, Pompey, and Crassus were willing to promote their own personal interests at the expense of the senate. However, it was only with Julius Caesar that the senate's traditional authority collapsed and the stable republican government Rome had enjoyed for centuries was brought to an end.

It is possible that the insurrection championed by Catiline was not as serious a threat to the government as ancient sources indicate. Much of its fame is due to several orations of Cicero in which the consul boasted of his actions in 63 B.C.E. The historian Sallust (86-35 B.C.E.) wrote a monograph about the conspiracy, *Bellum Catilinae* (c. 42 B.C.E.; *The Conspiracy of Catiline*, 1608), presenting Catiline as a talented but evil man who nearly overthrew the Republic. Modern scholars are divided in their opinions about the conspiracy. Some judge that Catiline's threat to Rome was serious, while others believe that he was a populist primarily interested in relieving the debt of the masses. What is not controversial is that Cicero viewed Catiline as a threat to Rome and that he acted vigorously to protect the republican government.

—*David Christiansen*

FURTHER READING

Everitt, Anthony. *Cicero: The Life and Times of Rome's Greatest Politician*. New York: Random House, 2001. Everitt's biography of Cicero includes a chapter devoted exclusively to Catiline's activities in 63 B.C.E.

Gruen, Erich. *The Last Generation of the Roman Republic*. Berkeley: University of California Press, 1974. Gruen's work is indispensable for understanding the motivations of the conspirators. His conclusions about the events are erudite and informed, fitting them in the turbulent political period of the late Republic.

Hardy, Ernest. *The Catilinarian Conspiracy in Its Context*. Oxford, England: Blackwell, 1924. Despite its age, this work is important for a full understanding of the Catilinarian conspiracy. Hardy provides special attention to the controversies of the relationship that Crassus and Caesar shared with Catiline.

Hutchinson, Lester. *The Conspiracy of Catiline*. New York: Barnes and Noble, 1967. This work systematically discusses the major events and personages of the Catilinarian conspiracy. Hutchinson provides important background information about Catiline and his motivations.

Syme, Ronald. *Sallust*. Berkeley: University of California Press, 1964. Although Syme is primarily concerned with Sallust's literary account of Catiline's conspiracy, he expends considerable time distinguishing between actual events and the literary accounts of them that arose in later years.

Wiseman, T. P. "The Peasants' Revolt and the Bankrupts' Plot." In *The Last Age of the Roman Republic, 146-43 B.C.*, edited by J. A. Crook, Andrew Lintott, and Elizabeth Rawson. Vol. 9 in *The Cambridge Ancient History*. 2d ed. New York: Cambridge University Press, 1994. Wiseman's article, set within a larger chapter on the challenges the Roman Senate faced in the late Republic, establishes a clear chronology of Catiline's conspiracy and Cicero's response.

SEE ALSO: c. 509 B.C.E., Roman Republic Replaces Monarchy; 494/493 B.C.E., Institution of the Plebeian Tribunate; 451-449 B.C.E., Twelve Tables of Roman Law Are Formulated; 73-71 B.C.E., Spartacus Leads Slave Revolt; 58-51 B.C.E., Caesar Conquers Gaul; 54 B.C.E., Roman Poet Catullus Dies; 51 B.C.E., Cicero Writes *De republica*; 43-42 B.C.E., Second Triumvirate Enacts Proscriptions; 27-23 B.C.E., Completion of the Augustan Settlement.

RELATED ARTICLES in *Great Lives from History: The Ancient World*: Julius Caesar; Catiline; Cicero.

c. 60 B.C.E.

DRUIDISM FLOURISHES IN GAUL AND BRITAIN

Druids, the priestly and intellectual class of the ancient Celts, ruled on civil and criminal proceedings, performed religious ceremonies, preserved tribal history and lore, and educated the young.

LOCALE: Northwestern European continent and throughout British Isles

CATEGORIES: Prehistory and ancient cultures; religion

SUMMARY OF EVENT

Druids served as an intellectual caste of judges, prophets, and teachers at the top of the social structure of ancient Celtic culture. Because there are no written extant Druidic texts, it is difficult to be exact about either documenting the dating of their influence or even specifically defining their philosophies and ethical worldview. Indeed, it was reportedly the tradition that, although the Celts were familiar with the Greek alphabet and used it for business purposes, Druidic doctrine had to be transmitted orally, a process in which young Druid priests would commit doctrine to memory over a period of twenty years or more. As a result, contemporary information about the Druids comes from Greek and Roman commentators, while information from within the Celtic tradition comes from the post-Christian era. In both cases, therefore, information about Druidism comes from the opponents of Druidism.

The etymology of the word *druid* is contested. The second element is accepted as deriving from *wid-*, an Indo-European root connoting wisdom, knowledge, and (oracular) sight. The first element comes from an Indo-European root *deru*, which has connotations of hardness, firmness, and steadfastness, but opinions differ as to whether the *dru-* in "druid" comes from forms of the root meaning "truth" or from a form meaning "tree," especially the oak (*derw* in Welsh). Although the etymology

of Druids as purveyors of "oak wisdom" was long accepted, recent opinion has veered toward "true knowledge" as the more probable meaning.

Any contemporary understanding of the Druids and their legacies relies on archaeological evidence (including votive pits, sculpture, tools, jewelry, temples, and fortresses) as well as the writings of Greek and Roman chroniclers. Most classical writing on Druids derives from Posidonius, a Greek philosopher from Syria who lived in the first century B.C.E. and wrote of his travels among the Celts. However, his own writings are lost and all that survives is quotations in the works of later writers such as Strabo, Diodorus Siculus, and Julius Caesar, who, although he was personally acquainted with the Druid Divitiacus, as he relates in his *Comentarii de bello Gallico* (52-51 B.C.E.; *Commentaries*, 1609), apparently felt that Posidonius's work was more authoritative than his own experience.

In continental Gaul (modern-day France), Druids were exempt from taxes and were not required or expected to provide military service, although in practice there were exceptions. More often they served as sage counselors to the tribal chief and war-leader. They were the teachers of noble Celtic children as well as of Druids in training. Druids adjudicated both criminal and civil law disputes; the harshest sentence they could inflict was to ban a person from participating in sacrifices, thereby turning him into a nonperson. The Druids officiated at these sacrifices to the gods, which were said to include the sacrifice of humans. The latter practice seems to have created conflict with the Romans soon after initial contact because both Tiberius and Claudius report the Roman banishment of the Druids as a result of such profane superstitions. However, it is an open question whether human sacrifice was actually practiced, either in the past or at the time of Roman contact, or whether it was a calumny aimed at undercutting the Druids' political opposition to Rome. It is nonetheless notable that the Romans quickly outlawed Druidism, while Roman practice generally was to annex new gods and practices into its own pantheon rather than outlawing them.

Druidic teaching seems to have deemphasized the importance of the moment of death. Druids believed that the human soul is immortal and that the universe is indestructible (although they believed that it was periodically consumed in a ritual cleansing by fire and water alternately). The animal or human sacrifice was used not only to ensure the fertility or effectiveness of the ritual but also because the very manner and movement of the death of the sacrifice demanded priestly interpretation: the pattern of the blood flowing from the mortal wound or the movement made in the victim's death throes was noted and interpreted by the Druid priests.

Pliny the Elder notes in his *Naturalis historia* (77 C.E.; *Natural History*, 1938-1963) that the Druids were nature-healers who employed liberal amounts of mistletoe and other medicinal herbs in their rituals. (Pliny is the only major classical source to emphasize the ritual importance of oak trees in Druidic ritual, a connection that Robert Graves made the centerpiece of his poetically inspired but historically suspect *White Goddess*, 1948.) Pliny described elaborate formulae and taboos governing how particular ingredients should be collected—*samolus* should be plucked with the left hand only; *selago* should be picked with the right hand stretched through the left sleeve of a white robe—and even the particular phases of the moon during which such collection should occur.

Druidic belief and practice were most likely in decline in Gaul by the time of Julius Caesar's victory over the Gaulish chieftain Vercingetorix at Avaricum in 52 B.C.E. The religion persisted longer in Britain, which Caesar reported was the birthplace of Druidism and the source of its truest doctrine. Reports of Druids are common throughout the next century, until the watershed point at the end of classical Druid history, the Roman defeat of the Celts at Anglesey in 61 C.E. which destroyed the Druidic stronghold.

Over the next four centuries, the Celts of Britain and Gaul practiced a religion that mixed

elements of native belief with Roman religion. The temple at Bath in southern England is a good example of this later trend: The hot springs and their tutelary goddess Sulis had long been worshiped by the Celts, and with the advent of the Romans, Sulis became Sulis Minerva and the springs became the focal point of a magnificent Roman temple and healing spa. In Ireland, which never fell under Roman rule, Druids maintained their positions as teachers, counselors, judges, and poets until the advent of Christianity, and often appear in early saints' lives as magic-working opponents of the holy men and women.

Druidic practice was moribund throughout the Middle Ages, but the late Renaissance in France and England

An artist's conception of Druid worship in ancient Gaul. (F. R. Niglutsch)

DRUIDIC SPECIALIZED CELTIC CULTURAL ROLES

Name	Role
Bard	popular poet and singer
Brithem	judge, arbitrator, ambassador
Cainte	master of magical chants, blessings, curses, invocations, execrations, banishments
Cruitre	harpist who uses music as magic, master of the "three Noble Strains" of music, designed to invoke laughter, tears, and sleep
Deoghbaire	cup bearer with knowledge of intoxicating and hallucinogenic substances
Faith	diviner
Fili	sacred poet and diviner
Liaig	doctor who uses plants, magic, and surgery
Scelaige	keeper of myths and epics
Sencha	historian, analyst

rekindled a fascination with the mystery and antiquity of the nature-loving Druids, in large part in England because of the writings of William Stukeley (1687-1765). Stukeley's archaeological volumes *Stonehenge, a Temple Restored to the British Druids* (1740) and *Avebury* (1743) popularized the Druids in the English-speaking world as philosopher-sages responsible for these magnificent megalithic monuments, whose religion "was so extremely like Christianity, that in effect, it differed from it only in this; they believed in a Messiah who was to come into the world, as we believe in Him who has come."

SIGNIFICANCE

The Druids and their place in the Celtic pre-Christian past continue to enjoy significant attention in contemporary Western societies. In the popular imagination, reconstructed Druidic religions in various forms have been practiced since Stukeley's time. The Druids' role as public intellectuals was adopted by Celtic nationalist movements beginning in the nineteenth century, and latter-day Druids preside over the Welsh National Eisteddfod, a yearly artistic and cultural festival, and similar organizations in Cornwall and Brittany.

More important, while early Christians repressed the particulars of Druidic religious rituals and doctrines, the monks of Ireland, Scotland, Wales, Brittany, and Cornwall preserved much of the literary and historical lore that the Druids had maintained in oral tradition. Although the religious functions of the Druids were eliminated, their roles as judges, lawyers, counselors, teachers, doctors, poets, and historians remained.

—*Richard Sax*

FURTHER READING

Brunaux, Jean Louis. *The Celtic Gauls: Gods, Rites, and Sanctuaries*. Translated by Daphne Nash. London: Seaby, 1988. Presents the archaeological evidence for Druidic religion on the Continent in a clear and insightful manner.

Cunliffe, Barry. *The Ancient Celts*. New York: Oxford University Press, 1997. This comprehensive overview of Celtic culture includes significant chapters on history, community, religion, and the enduring legacy of Druidic culture in modern society. Includes many black-and-white and color plates with scholarly editing.

Freeman, Philip. *War, Women, and Druids: Eyewitness Reports and Early Accounts of the Ancient Celts*. Austin: University of Texas Press, 2002. Collects primary source material on Druids from the classical world. Given the amount of fantasizing focused on Druidism, it is useful to read the original sources of their contemporaries.

Green, Miranda J. *The World of the Druids*. New York: Thames and Hudson, 1997. Provides an introduction to the world of the Druids via Welsh and Irish myths, including excellent chapters on Celtic society, derived principally through writings of early Roman invaders and archaeological evidence.

Hutton, Ronald. *The Pagan Religions of the Ancient British Isles: Their Nature and Legacy*. Cambridge, Mass.: Blackwell, 1991. A well-researched history that aims to dispel many of the myths about Britain's pagan heritage. Chapters 5-7 deal with the development of Druidism and its confrontation and accommodation with Roman and Christian religion.

Kendrick, T. D. *Druids and Druidism*. 1960. Reprint. Mineola, N.Y.: Dover, 2003. One of the classic works on Druidism, addressing the information about and opinions of Druidism prevalent in the Greek and Roman worlds and assessing the archaeological evidence of religious practices. Although dated, Kendrick's analysis is sober and insightful.

Ó Hógáin, Dáithi. *The Sacred Isle: Belief and Religion in Pre-Christian Ireland*. Rochester, N.Y.: Boydell, 1999. Written by a well-known folklorist, this book attempts to reconstruct the religious beliefs of Irish Druidism by making connections between medieval Irish mythological narratives and modern folklore, archaeological remains, and the comparative anthropology of religion.

SEE ALSO: 14th-9th centuries B.C.E., Urnfield Culture Flourishes in Northwestern Europe; c. 1100-c. 500 B.C.E., Hallstatt Culture Dominates Northern Europe; c. 100 B.C.E.-c. 100 C.E., Celtic Hill Forts Are Replaced by *Oppida*; 58-51 B.C.E., Caesar Conquers Gaul; 60 C.E., Boudicca Leads Revolt Against Roman Rule; c. 450 C.E., Conversion of Ireland to Christianity.

RELATED ARTICLES in *Great Lives from History: The Ancient World*: Boudicca; Vercingetorix.

58-51 B.C.E.
CAESAR CONQUERS GAUL

Julius Caesar's conquest of Gaul reshaped Gallic culture, altered the nature of the Roman Empire, and propelled Caesar toward the domination of Rome.

LOCALE: Gaul (modern France, Belgium, the German Rhineland, and Switzerland)

CATEGORIES: Wars, uprisings, and civil unrest; expansion and land acquisition

KEY FIGURES

Ambiorix (fl. first century B.C.E.), Gallic chieftain whose troops slaughtered a Roman legion and who was never captured by the Romans

Julius Caesar (100-44 B.C.E.), Roman politician and general, proconsul of Gaul, 58-50 B.C.E.

Indutiomarus (d. 54 B.C.E.), chieftain of the Gallic Treveri

Publius Vatinius (d. after 42 B.C.E.), tribune in 59 B.C.E. and a political ally of Caesar

Vercingetorix (c. 75-c. 46 B.C.E.), Gallic chieftain chosen in 52 B.C.E. to lead the Gauls against Julius Caesar

SUMMARY OF EVENT

Julius Caesar's conquest of Gaul is among the most significant campaigns in Roman and Western European history. In the Roman context, Caesar's campaigns fit into the pattern of Roman imperialism. For centuries, commanders ambitious to enhance their political careers by military glory had initiated wars of aggression. For instance, Caesar's *Comenatrii de bello Gallico* (51-52 B.C.E.; *Commentaries*, 1609), released in annual books, were self-promotional press releases. The annexation of Gaul, the largest single acquisition, shifted Rome's interest from Mediterranean possessions to involvement in northwest Europe and led to campaigns across the Danube and Rhine Rivers (abandoned in 9 C.E.) and then to the conquest of Britain from 43 C.E.

For Caesar personally, his brilliance as a commander won him glory, immense (and very useful) wealth, the devotion of his soldiers, widespread popularity, and the enmity of those senators who began to fear his ultimate intentions. Having gained a strong military, financial, and political base through the wars, Caesar challenged the Roman establishment in civil war when he marched troops across the Rubicon River in January, 49 B.C.E. When the fighting ceased, Caesar had unprecedented powers as master of Rome—which led directly to his assassination. His career was fundamental in the transition from the failing Republic to the Empire.

Viewed from a different perspective, Caesar's warfare in the 50's B.C.E. also altered the culture of the Celtic tribes. Greeks had been settled in southern Gaul and spreading their culture northward since the sixth century B.C.E. Answering an appeal for help from the leading Greek city, Marseilles, Rome conquered the coastal strip in the late 120's B.C.E. and made it the province of Gallia Narbonensis, named for the colony of Narbo founded in 118 B.C.E. The recent discovery of quantities of Italian wine amphoras prove that Roman merchants were soon operating beyond the provincial boundaries. Commercial activities thus preceded Caesar's wars by fifty years and may have influenced his policies. Rome applied vari-

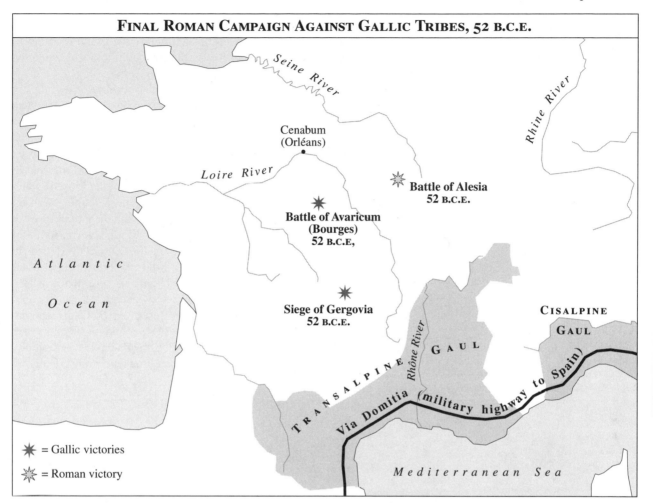

FINAL ROMAN CAMPAIGN AGAINST GALLIC TRIBES, 52 B.C.E.

Seine River

Rhine River

Cenabum
(Orléans)

Loire River

Battle of Alesia
52 B.C.E.

Battle of Avaricum
(Bourges)
52 B.C.E,

A t l a n t i c

O c e a n

Siege of Gergovia
52 B.C.E.

CISALPINE
GAUL

T R A N S A L P I N E G A U L

Rhône River

Via Domitia (military highway to Spain)

✴ = Gallic victories

✴ = Roman victory

M e d i t e r r a n e a n   S e a

ous labels to this extensive territory: Gallia Transalpina (beyond the Alps, contrasted with Cisalpina, this side of the Alps), Ultima (farthest), Comata (long-haired), and Bracata (trousered).

In 59 B.C.E., the tribune Publius Vatinius sponsored a law that gave Caesar the proconsular governorship of Cisalpine Gaul and Illyricum with three legions for five years. The opportune death of the governor of Narbonensis allowed him to tack on an amendment adding this province and another legion. North of "the Province," as Narbonensis was often known, lay most of Gaul, a diverse but fertile area between the Rhine River and the Pyrenees and inhabited mostly by Celts. Divided into more than one hundred tribes, the Gauls were unstable politically, with a feuding nobility and rival factions even within tribes.

In the spring of 58 B.C.E. the Helvetii, a group of tribes in western Switzerland, were migrating in search of

richer lands and requested the right to pass through the Roman province. Perceiving an opportunity use his newly formed legions and gain military renown, Caesar rushed from Rome to Geneva to block the Helvetii at the Rhone River. Those he did not annihilate he forced to return to their Alpine homes. Later that year, under the pretext of defending Gallic allies, Caesar boldly marched northward to drive back across the Rhine a Germanic chieftain whose aggressions were threatening central Gaul as well as Roman political and presumably economic interests.

Recruiting additional legions in the winter and gaining more Gallic allies, Caesar in 57 B.C.E. ravaged Belgic territory in northern Gaul, overwhelming one tribe after another. When one town resisted a siege, he sold more than fifty thousand of the Belgae into slavery. The following year, building a fleet, Caesar crushed the Veneti who lived along the Atlantic coast. Thus by the end of 56

B.C.E., he had ruthlessly asserted Roman dominance in most of Gaul.

Back at Rome, Caesar's political enemies charged that he had far exceeded his authority. In 56 B.C.E., however, his political allies obtained the extension of Caesar's proconsulship for another five years, which encouraged him to press on toward permanent occupation of northern Gaul.

In 55 B.C.E., two German tribes crossed the Rhine seeking land. When their leaders came to Caesar to negotiate, he detained them and by a surprise attack massacred the Germans, his cavalry hunting down even their women and children. Caesar's enemy Cato the Younger (95-46 B.C.E.) demanded in the senate at Rome that Caesar be handed over to the Germans to atone for his butchery. Bridging the Rhine, Caesar's forces briefly invaded Germany, to forestall further Germanic inroads. That same summer, he led two legions in a reconnaissance of Britain, and in the following year, 54 B.C.E., he led a large-scale invasion army across the English Channel, receiving the nominal submission of a British king north of the Thames River. Although Caesar claimed victories, Rome gained no lasting control in Britain or Germany and paid little attention to the island for almost a century. Nevertheless, these expeditions were impressive features in Caesar's reports to Rome.

Many Gallic tribes refused to accept Roman rule, and Caesar faced several dangerous rebellions in the years 54-52 B.C.E. One crafty chieftain, Ambiorix of the Belgic Eburones, wiped out a Roman legion; Roman merchants as well as Roman supply trains were butchered by the Gauls. Simultaneously, Indutiomarus of the nearby Treveri threatened Rome's control in the Moselle valley and along the left bank of the Rhine. Enlarging his army to ten legions or about fifty thousand men, Caesar vowed vengeance. Yet a new leader, Vercingetorix, unified a Gallic coalition. His scorched-earth policy forced the Romans to besiege Gallic hill forts. Frustrated, Caesar's men massacred the inhabitants of several towns. His siege of a stronghold at Gergovia, however, failed miserably, encouraging further desertions by Gauls who had once supported Rome. Only by employing German mercenary cavalry and by dogged discipline and shrewd strategy did Caesar finally outmaneuver and corner Ver-

Vercingetorix, mounted, heads toward a meeting with Caesar. (F. R. Niglutsch)

cingetorix. After a bitter and bloody siege the Gallic hero surrendered. Caesar had him executed after his triumph in 46 B.C.E.

SIGNIFICANCE

For Caesar, this eight-year campaign brought prominence and increased ambition. His reports to Rome cleverly justified his actions, and his veteran army, intensely loyal to him, enabled him to return to Italy to seize sole power after a civil war. Caesar never had time to do more than begin recovery. Gaul was devastated, perhaps more than half its men of military age slaughtered or enslaved, and its agriculture and towns badly damaged. Scholars are uncertain as to what Caesar's plans were. By playing on inter- and intratribal enmities, he had won the allegiance of some Gauls. Many Gauls were soon named Julii; they or their ancestors won Roman citizenship through Caesar's grants. (Most others obtained it from Augustus.) Using demobilized veterans as settlers, Caesar reinforced the colony at Narbo and founded new ones at Baeterrae (Beziers), Arelate (Arles), and probably Noviodunum (Nyon). Evidently following Caesar's intentions, one of his former officers founded colonies at Raurica (Augst near Basel) on the Rhine and Lugdunum (Lyon) at the confluence of the Rhone and Saône. Because of renewed civil wars, general recuperation only began after 30 B.C.E.

Caesar's great-nephew and adopted son Octavian, better known as Rome's first emperor, Augustus (63 B.C.E.-14 C.E.), established the basic administrative structure of the newly conquered lands. Three provinces lay north of Narbonensis: Aquitania, Lugdunensis, and Belgica. Each was divided into administrative units called *civitates* (cantons), created out of the old tribes. Two military zones, Upper and Lower Germany, ran along the west bank of the Rhine; they became provinces in the early 90's C.E. Augustus founded several more colonies in Narbonensis, notably Forum Julii (Fréjus) and Arausio (Orange). A network of roads, linked to Narbonensis, radiated from Lugdunum, the chief city of the north. Roman rule soon brought relative peace and order, economic prosperity, and the development of this extensive, agriculturally rich, and prosperous land.

—*Roger B. McShane, updated by Thomas H. Watkins*

FURTHER READING

Caesar, Julius. *The Gallic War.* Translated by Carolyn Hammond. New York: Oxford University Press, 1996. One of the earliest significant descriptions of Gallic society. Although Caesar's point of view is biased, much of his description is substantiated by archaeological evidence.

Cunliffe, Barry. *The Ancient Celts.* New York: Oxford University Press, 1997. Well-illustrated overview of Celtic culture and the changes caused by contact with the Greeks and Romans.

Mathison, Ralph, ed. *Roman Aristocrats in Barbarian Gaul: Strategies for Survival in an Age of Transition.* Austin: University of Texas Press, 1993. Discusses the many ways in which individuals from one of the most sophisticated cities in the ancient world adapted to life in one of the more uncivilized areas of Europe.

Woolf, Greg. *Becoming Roman.* New York: Cambridge University Press, 1998. Studies the cultural history of Gaul between 200 B.C.E. and 300 C.E., describing the process of cultural synthesis that created a unique Gallo-Roman civilization. Illustrations, bibliography, index.

SEE ALSO: 107-101 B.C.E., Marius Creates a Private Army; c. 60 B.C.E., Druidism Flourishes in Gaul and Britain; 15 B.C.E.-15 C.E., Rhine-Danube Frontier Is Established; 43-130 C.E., Roman Conquest of Britain; 60 C.E., Boudicca Leads Revolt Against Roman Rule.

RELATED ARTICLES in *Great Lives from History: The Ancient World*: Julius Caesar; Vercingetorix.

100 - 1 B.C.E.

54 B.C.E.
ROMAN POET CATULLUS DIES

Catullus epitomized an innovative cultural movement in Rome that forsook traditional literary forms for livelier, intensely personal poetry, a movement that was politically at odds with traditionalist patricians.

LOCALE: Verona, Rome
CATEGORIES: Literature; cultural and intellectual history

KEY FIGURES
Catullus (c. 84-c. 54 B.C.E.), Roman poet
Clodia (c. 95-after 45 B.C.E.), literary patron, Catullus's lover, and an indirect influence on Roman politics
Cicero (106-43 B.C.E.), Roman orator, philosopher, and senator
Julius Caesar (100-44 B.C.E.), Roman soldier, politician, and dictator, r. 49-44 B.C.E.

SUMMARY OF EVENT
Little is known with certainty about the life of Catullus. He was born c. 84 B.C.E. (possibly 87 B.C.E.) into a wealthy family of Verona having the rank of *eques* (knight). From 57 to 56 B.C.E., he served in the retinue of the governor of Bithynia (now part of northern Turkey), where he visited the grave of his brother. Although he complains in his poetry about his poverty, he apparently was well enough off to own a yacht and a lakeside villa near Sirmio (Sirmione in northern Italy). Catullus probably died in 54 B.C.E.

Well-educated in Verona, Catullus apparently moved to Rome to continue his studies before the age of twenty and thereafter regarded it as his home. He made the acquaintance of leading literary and political figures and became involved in a loosely knit group of poets who constellated around the patrician Publius Clodius Pulcher (c. 92-52 B.C.E.) and his sister Clodia. Although trained in traditional Roman literary forms, these poets borrowed from Greek lyric poets, such as Callimachus (c. 305-c. 240 B.C.E.) and Sappho (c. 630-c. 580 B.C.E.), to introduce a greater variety of rhythms into Latin verse. In their poems, often written as if they were letters to each other, they sometimes treated lofty philosophical and mythical themes but more often wrote about their own immediate affairs. They wrote love poetry, scurrilous lampoons of enemies, elegies, wedding hymns, and narratives. Word play, topical and literary allusions, and elegant turns of phrase characterized the style. Whether

their diction was colloquial, even obscene, or formal, the guiding principle was its aptness and force; the phrasing was rhetorically calculated for balance and emphasis, qualities reinforced by the assonance of the words and the rhythm.

Cicero referred to this group, somewhat dismissively, as "the new poets," and so they have become known to posterity (sometimes referred to as the neoterics). Catullus gained fame in his lifetime as one of them, and he is the only who remains widely read. In fact, he is held to be among the greatest lyric poets of antiquity.

Clodia and Catullus became lovers. She figures most often of all his contemporaries in his surviving 113 poems, in which he refers to her as Lesbia. She apparently had other lovers at the same time, and her fickleness tormented him. His poems range in tone from playful, delicate love poems to enraged denunciations of her faithlessness and despair at his helpless passion for her. However, more was involved than frustrated love. Clodia and her brother were central figures in a political faction that wanted to loosen some of the traditional patrician prerogatives of the Roman Republic. Bitterly opposed to this faction were such commanding figures as Cicero and Julius Caesar, the latter of whom was then nearing the height of his political power. During a trial instigated by Clodia against a friend of his, Cicero went out of his way to blacken her character by implying that she was guilty of abundant promiscuity, even incest.

Whatever his political convictions, Catullus wrote poems belittling the traditionalists, sometimes accusing them of outrageous sexual misbehavior and sometimes making fun of them as stupid or pompous, as is the case in a poem addressing Cicero. Romans placed great value on poetry as a cultural force. Invective and satirical verse were particularly popular (even some later emperors wrote such) and could have damaging effects on the person attacked. One of Catullus's targets was Caesar, who felt his prestige endangered by Catullus's poems. Catullus's father was friendly toward Caesar, on one occasion acting as his host, and perhaps for that reason Caesar sought to make friends with Catullus. They reconciled not long before the poet's death. However, Catullus had made other enemies with his "fierce iambs" who did not forgive him. How Catullus died is unknown, but he belonged to a time of vigorous intrigue when some of his own friends died at the hands of political enemies, and he himself could have been the victim of revenge.

SIGNIFICANCE

Catullus's poetry exerted an immediate, powerful influence on Roman literature. The generation that succeeded his included some of Rome's greatest poets, such as Vergil (70-19 B.C.E.), Propertius (54/47-16 B.C.E.), Horace (65-8 B.C.E.), and Ovid (43 B.C.E.-17 C.E.), and each of them imitated Catullus's style. In fact, judging from the number of times he quotes him, Catullus was Vergil's favorite Latin poet.

Catullus is also mentioned by Roman historians and commentators, such as Suetonius (70-after 122 C.E.), Apuleius (c. 125-after 170 C.E.), and Saint Jerome (331/347-c. 420 C.E.). However, in late Imperial Rome, he had apparently ceased to be popular among the literati. His was very seldom mentioned after the beginning of the second century. One poem appears in a ninth century anthology, but Catullus is otherwise only an obscure name in classical literature until the early Renaissance. About 1290, a manuscript, whose origin is unknown, was found in a wine cask. It was subsequently lost again, but not before two copies were made that are the source of all modern texts. The manuscript apparently combined three separate collections of Catullus's poems, which are collectively known as the *Carmina Catulli* (*The Adventures of Catullus, and the History of His Amours with Lesbia*, 1707).

The influence of the rediscovered poems was swift and lasting, even though some poems were left out of editions and translations because of their sexual content. Petrarch (1304-1374) read them and clearly borrowed from Catullus. Specifically, as Catullus spoke to his literary lover, Lesbia, in a series of poems, so did Petrarch in addressing sonnets to Laura, although she is an idealized figure. Likewise, the dark lady of the *Sonnets* (1609) of William Shakespeare (1564-1616) belongs to this same literary tradition of serial love poems. The same may be said of works by Robert Herrick (1591-1674), Thomas Campion (1567-1620), John Donne (1572-1631), Edmund Waller (1606-1687), and many other European poets, for along with Sappho, Catullus was the most imitated love poet from classical literature.

The style of Catullus's epistolary poems also found early imitators, particularly in Ben Jonson (1573-1637). A proponent of the "plain style," Jonson used ordinary

100 - 1 B.C.E.

The poet Catullus recites his works before a group of listeners. (F. R. Niglutsch)

diction, rather than elevated literary language, in addressing short, often nakedly emotional poems to family and friends. As was true of Catullus, Jonson's wording may sound conversational, even vulgar, yet it appears in verse that is carefully contrived to carry home the complex emotional overtone of the message. For both Catullus and Jonson, such techniques as word play, parallelism, metaphor, innuendo, and natural symbolism are artistic representations of personal self-searching that arises directly from experience. The plain style stands in sharp contrast to that of the heroic, philosophical, or religious poetry that treated overarching communal themes, such as war, the relation of humankind to God, or social problems.

Catullus continued to inspire writers through the twentieth century, not only as a love poet but also in his use of the epistolary poem and, especially, plainspoken diction. Poets who represented a wide variety of stylistic schools paid homage to him directly, such as the free verse poet Louis Zukofsky (1904-1978) and the dramatic poet Archibald MacLeish (1892-1982). However, those proponents of the plain style who also wrote in traditional verse forms imitated Catullus most overtly, particularly J. V. Cunningham (1911-1985).

—*Roger Smith*

FURTHER READING

Catullus. *The Complete Poetry of Catullus*. Edited and translated by David Mulroy. Madison: University of Wisconsin Press, 2002. A translation of Catullus's poems with invaluable commentary and a concise, readable introduction concerning the poet's life, textual problems, and basic Latin prosody. Short bibliography.

Ferguson, John. *Catullus*. New York: Clarendon Press, 1988. A booklet discussing the overarching themes in Catullus's poetry and twentieth century scholarly criticism. Bibliography.

Fitzgerald, William. *Catullan Provocations: Lyric Poetry and the Drama of Position*. Berkeley: University of California Press, 1995. Examines Catullus's poetry within its cultural context and assesses its prestige among modern writers. Bibliography.

Janan, Michael. *"When the Lamp Is Shattered": Desire and Narrative in Catullus*. Carbondale: Southern Illinois University Press, 1994. Argues that in his poems about Lesbia, Catullus is examining gender roles in his society. Bibliography.

Jaro, Benita Kane. *The Key*. New York: Dodd, Mead, 1988. A novel. Not to be taken as factual, although based loosely upon the facts, this fictional treatment is a vividly entertaining conjecture about Catullus and the intellectual and political milieu of ancient Rome.

Petrini, Mark. *The Child and the Hero: Coming of Age in Catullus and Vergil*. Ann Arbor: University of Michigan Press, 1997. Arguing that Catullus was Vergil's favorite writer, Petrini traces Vergil's use of Catullan themes, a study that elucidates Roman literary styles. Bibliography.

Wiseman, T. P. *Catullus and His World: A Reappraisal*. New York: Cambridge University Press, 1985. Following chapters sketching the lives of Marcus Caelus Rufus, Catullus's rival, and Clodia, Wiseman combs Catullus's verse for biographical and cultural information. Bibliography.

SEE ALSO: c. 438 B.C.E., Greek Lyric Poet Pindar Dies; 19 B.C.E., Roman Poet Vergil Dies; November 27, 8 B.C.E., Roman Lyric Poet Horace Dies; 8 C.E., Ovid's *Metamorphoses* Is Published; 100-127 C.E., Roman Juvenal Composes *Satires*; 159 B.C.E., Roman Playwright Terence Dies.

RELATED ARTICLES in *Great Lives from History: The Ancient World*: Julius Caesar; Callimachus; Catullus; Cicero; Clodia; Saint Jerome; Ovid; Propertius; Sappho; Vergil.

51 B.C.E.
CICERO WRITES *DE REPUBLICA*

In his De republica, *Cicero argued that the mixed constitution of the Roman state was the perfect government because it evolved naturally and was not the creation of a single lawgiver.*

LOCALE: Rome (now in Italy)
CATEGORIES: Cultural and intellectual history; government and politics

KEY FIGURE
Cicero (106-43 B.C.E.), Roman orator, philosopher, and statesman, consul in 63 B.C.E.

SUMMARY OF EVENT
For centuries, the only known substantial portion of *De republica* (51 B.C.E.; *On the State*, 1817, commonly known as *De republica*) was the "Dream of Scipio" (*Somnium Scipionis*). Scattered quotations, many in Saint Augustine's *De civitate Dei* (413-427 C.E.; *The City of God*, 1610), provided hints of the main text. In 1820, a manuscript of much of the rest was found in the Vatican Library. Although scholars still do not possess the full text of *De republica*, it is sufficiently intact to reveal its main argumentation and to justify an assessment of its contribution to political theory. ("On the commonwealth" is a more accurate rendering of Cicero's title; the Roman state was not a republic in the modern sense of the word.)

It is fairly certain that Cicero had completed the writing of the *De republica* before his term as the governor of the province of Cilicia in Asia Minor in 51 B.C.E. This date is decisive for proper appraisal of the work. Cicero's political career had peaked when he suppressed the Catiline conspiracy as consul in 63 B.C.E. Politics were turbulent. Cicero had a powerful enemy in Publius Clodius Pulcher (c. 92-52 B.C.E.). In 59 B.C.E., Julius Caesar (100-44 B.C.E.) was consul and formed the first triumvirate with Gnaeus Pompeius Magnus (Pompey the Great; 106-48 B.C.E.) and Marcus Licinius Crassus (c. 115-53 B.C.E.). Cicero opposed this coalition and Caesar's readiness to use violence to gain passage of measures he supported. The next year, Clodius was tribune and exiled Cicero, ostensibly because he had summarily executed some of the Catiline conspirators without a trial (although with the moral support of the senate) at the end of 63 B.C.E. Although Cicero was recalled to Rome the next year, his political initiative was henceforth curtailed severely. The triumvirs forced him into submission in 56

B.C.E. and compelled him to speak on behalf of some of their allies, although Caesar always sought to keep Cicero a friendly neutral. By 54 B.C.E., Cicero had essentially dropped out of politics. During this period, as he himself records, he turned to philosophy, especially to Plato (c. 427-347 B.C.E.), for consolation. The result was *De republica*, to which was added later a companion piece on the nature of law, the *De legibus* (which was never completed).

Cicero's efforts are not to be seen as translations of Plato. Both works have a Roman setting and famous Romans as the interlocutors of the dialogues. In *De republica*, the chief speaker is one of Cicero's heroes, Scipio Aemilianus, the most distinguished Roman of his generation (184/184-129 B.C.E.; consul in 147 and 134 B.C.E., censor in 142 B.C.E., and *princeps senatus*); he is best known as the conqueror of Carthage in 146 B.C.E. The remaining eight participants are his political allies and clients. *De republica* is set in 129 B.C.E., shortly before Scipio's death. Cicero himself leads the discussion in *De legibus*, so his role corresponds to that of Scipio; his brother Quintus and friend Titus Pomponius Atticus (109-32 B.C.E.) are the other participants in the discussion.

The two works are not merely Roman replicas of Greek originals. In both works, Cicero is more dependent on Platonic format (the dialogue form and concluding dream) than content. He draws on the teaching of many other philosophical schools, especially Stoic philosophy, and on the Greek historian Polybius (c. 200-c. 118 B.C.E.), a friend of Scipio, to form his own conception of the ideal state and of the nature of law. Above all, Cicero utilizes his own experiences as Roman patriot, statesman, and theoretician. Cicero, for all his wisdom and patriotism, is fundamentally romantic. Politics in Scipio's time were much more complex than Cicero presents them. As history the work is flawed, but as theory it was intended to be practical, not utopian.

Cicero's *De republica* is composed of six books. Unlike Plato's *Politeia* (388-368 B.C.E.; *Republic*, 1701), its theme is not the nature of justice reflected in the workings of the perfect state, but the state itself reflected in its constitution and government. In book 1, Scipio examines the three types of government: monarchy, aristocracy, and democracy. He shows that the best state is formed from a mixture of elements drawn from the three separate types. In book 2, he shows how the Roman state, itself a mixed form of government, achieved in the course of history this composite form. Book 3 discusses the nature of justice and its relation to the state. Book 4 treats education, while books 5 and 6 portray the ideal statesman (variously styled *princeps*, *moderator*, or *rector*), who guides the state by the force of personal integrity and reputation (*auctoritas*). The work ends with an almost mystic vision of the rewards to be enjoyed in the afterlife by those who have administered the state properly.

This last section had a life separate from the rest of the dialogue as the *Somnium Scipionis*. In it, Scipio has a dream in which he discourses with two distinguished Roman senators, his adoptive grandfather (Scipio Africanus Major, or the Elder, 236-184/183 B.C.E.) and his real father (Lucius Aemilius Paulus, d. 216), and learns of the eternal fame and deification of the true statesman. Cicero's propensity to simplify complexities, to idealize those he regarded as good and vilify those he thought bad, proved fatal, for in 44-43 B.C.E., seeing himself as *rector*, his vitriolic attacks on Marc Antony (c. 82-30 B.C.E.) led to the civil war many sought to prevent and to his own death.

SIGNIFICANCE

Two aspects of *De republica* have been especially influential among later thinkers: the theory of the mixed constitution, and the relation of justice to the state. Cicero was not the originator of either idea, but he is primarily responsible for transmitting them to later ages. A third aspect is controversial. Cicero's theory may have influenced Augustus (63 B.C.E.-14 C.E.) and his advisers in the early 20's B.C.E. to model Augustus's role as *princeps* on the Ciceronian *princeps* or *rector*, who guides by *auctoritas* (prestige) instead of ruling through *potestas* or *imperium* (power).

The virtue of the mixed constitution is that it is immune to the defects inherent in the three types of government. In ancient political theory there was an inevitable cycle in which monarchy degenerated into tyranny, aristocracy into oligarchy, and democracy into anarchic mob rule. Yet if the three types are combined into a single system of government, their differences interact with one another and form a series of checks and balances to prevent the dominance and subsequent degeneration of any one type. The influence of this theory is readily apparent in the structure of the U.S. Constitution.

Cicero's treatment of the role of justice within the state is equally relevant. The initial argument is that justice is inimical to the efficient operation of the state because it is opposed to self-interest. Because each state has diverse laws and customs, there is no universal con-

Cicero. (Library of Congress)

cept of justice that all states can follow. Among states as among men, the accepted principle is that the stronger dominate and exploit the weaker to ensure their own security and self-interest. If a state attempts to observe justice, it will only expose itself to mediocrity and external control. Against this view it is argued that justice forms the very fabric of the state, without which the state cannot even exist, since by definition the state is the union of persons who are joined by a common agreement about law and rights and by a desire to share mutual advantages. Yet justice is concerned precisely with the due observance of law and rights. Without justice, the members of the state can have nothing to share in and can only become a band of mutual exploiters. Cicero thus placed as the bedrock of his republic the inextricable bond of justice and law, and he transmitted to the West the concept that the very existence of the state depends on its being just; indeed, the unjust state has no right to continue.

Plato's *Republic* has appealed to political thinkers more as an allegory than as a practical treatise for real politicians. Cicero's *De republica* and his *De officiis* (44 B.C.E.; *On Duties*, 1534), however, typified a Roman practicality tempered by moderate idealism urging on men a role of action as statesmen. To the philosophers, Cicero remained the ideal of the active man, a thinker in action, in spite of the faulty policy that led to his death in the proscription on December 7, 43 B.C.E.

—*George M. Pepe, updated by Thomas H. Watkins*

FURTHER READING

Cicero, Marcus Tullius. *The Republic and the Laws*. Edited by Jonathan Powell and translated by Niall Rudd. New York: Oxford University Press, 1998. A modern translation that provides an excellent introduction, a table of dates, notes on the Roman constitution, and an index of names.

Everitt, Anthony. *Cicero: The Life and Times of Rome's Greatest Politician*. New York: Random House, 2002. A biography aimed at the general reader, which concentrates on portraying Cicero the man, in the context of his times.

Powell, Jonathan, ed. *Cicero the Philosopher: Twelve Papers*. New York: Oxford University Press, 1997. A collection of essays that focus on Cicero as a philosopher rather than a political theorist. Several essays consider aspects of *De republica*.

Mitchell, Thomas N. *Cicero: The Ascending Years*. New Haven, Conn.: Yale University Press, 1989.

_____. *Cicero: The Senior Statesman*. New Haven, Conn.: Yale University Press, 1991. This two-volume biography lucidly explains Cicero's political life and thought. The work is notable for its thoroughness and its careful use of sources.

Rawson, E. D. *Cicero: A Portrait*. Ithaca, N.Y.: Cornell University Press, 1975. Reliable overview of the life and work of Cicero.

SEE ALSO: c. 380 B.C.E., Plato Develops His Theory of Ideas; c. 300 B.C.E., Stoics Conceptualize Natural Law; 264-225 B.C.E., First Punic War; 218-201 B.C.E., Second Punic War; 149-146 B.C.E., Third Punic War; Late 63-January 62 B.C.E., Catiline Conspiracy; 43-42 B.C.E., Second Triumvirate Enacts Proscriptions; 27-23 B.C.E., Completion of the Augustan Settlement.

RELATED ARTICLES in *Great Lives from History: The Ancient World*: Marc Antony; Julius Caesar; Catiline; Cicero; Plato; Polybius; Pompey the Great; Scipio Aemelianus; Scipio Africanus.

100 - 1 B.C.E.

51-30 B.C.E.
CLEOPATRA VII, LAST OF PTOLEMIES, REIGNS

Cleopatra VII became joint ruler of Egypt with her brother, Ptolemy XIII; her reign signified the nexus of Roman and Hellenistic cultures and the end of the Greek domination of Egypt.

LOCALE: Egypt
CATEGORIES: Government and politics; wars, uprisings, and civil unrest

KEY FIGURES

Cleopatra VII (69-30 B.C.E.), queen, diplomat, and the last Ptolemaic ruler, r. 51-30 B.C.E.
Julius Caesar (100-44 B.C.E.), Roman general, statesman, and dictator, r. 49-44 B.C.E., lover of Cleopatra
Marc Antony (c. 82-30 B.C.E.), Roman general, member of the Second Triumvirate, lover of Cleopatra
Octavian (63 B.C.E.-14 C.E.), greatnephew and heir of Julius Caesar, who became Augustus, first Roman emperor, r. 27 B.C.E.-14 C.E.

SUMMARY OF EVENT

Numerous accounts have been propagated about Cleopatra VII since her life, many of them based on myth or fiction rather than fact. The Egyptian queen has fascinated European artists and writers for many epochs.

Cleopatra hailed from the Lagides family, which entrenched itself as a ruling class monarchy in ancient Egypt starting in 323 B.C.E., with Ptolemy (later Ptolemy Soter), son of Lagos and a close associate of Alexander the Great. Ptolemy established a kingdom that extended over the eastern Mediterranean, with Alexandria as its capital. Though the Hellenistic culture was all encompassing in most Greek colonies, the Egyptians refused to surrender their indigenous culture and tenaciously held on to their autochthonous practices and mores.

The Ptolemaic era was characterized by formidable queens, starting with Ptolemy II Philadelphus's sister and consort Arsinoe II Philadelphus around 274 B.C.E. Cleopatra VII entered the queenship as part of this continuity of strong queens. She was probably born around

The court of Cleopatra VII. (F. R. Niglutsch)

69 B.C.E., the daughter and third child of Ptolemy XII Neos Dionysos (Auletes). She was distinctive among her preceding monarchical peers in that she possessed a superlative intellect and received a rigorous education. Benefitting from the Egyptian pharaonic tradition in which girls received an education identical to that of boys, she read the epic poetry of Homer, the tragedies of Euripides, the comedies of Menander, and the histories of Herodotus and Thucydides. She studied arithmetic, geometry, astronomy, and medicine. She mastered several languages, including the indigenous Egyptian language, Mdw Ntr, Hebrew, Aramaic, Arabic, Ethiopian, Median, Partian, and Latin, enabling her to be a skilled diplomat with political savvy. In contrast, not one of her predecessors spoke the Egyptian language.

Cleopatra VII co-ruled with her father, Ptolemy XII. Following his death, he was succeeded by Ptolemy XIII. Adhering to the tradition of her predecessors, Cleopatra VII co-ruled by edicts and decrees, aided by courtiers and close associates. Their rule was initially characterized by perennial obstacles: The indigenous Egyptians were asserting rebellious nationalist sentiment against the Greek monarchy; poverty was rife, with the peasantry decimated by famine; the Egyptian currency had been significantly devalued; and most troubling of all, Rome had become the principal sustainer of Egypt. The Ptolemaic Empire, which had once encompassed places as far as Asia Minor in the north and Syria in the east, had become confined to Egypt alone. Compounding these difficulties were rivalries from Cleopatra VII's sister, Arsinoe, who desired the throne, and her brother-husband, who had grown hostile to her. Skillfully exercising her political mettle, she devalued the currency by a third to make exports more attractive, initiated social and land reforms, and launched a strategy to assuage Rome so that war would be prevented. She was challenged by the boy-king Ptolemy XIII, who was placed under the tutelage of the Roman leader, Pompey the Great, following the military assistance extended by Ptolemy XIII to Pompey against Julius Caesar. Following disputes between Cleopatra VII and Ptolemy XIII, she was removed from the throne and forced to flee to Syria in 48 B.C.E.

In early June, 48 B.C.E., Caesar and his troops routed Pompey at Pharsalus in Thessaly. Pompey fled to Egypt, hoping to exact revenge on Caesar with help from Ptolemy XIII. However, he was quickly assassinated. Soon thereafter, Caesar sailed into Alexandria. Caesar treacherously sought to obtain financial returns from occupying Alexandria, realizing that Egypt's riches were vast. He forced Ptolemy XIII to withdraw his army from the frontier, leaving the ruler little choice as he had become a prisoner of Caesar's Roman troops.

When Cleopatra heard that Caesar was in Alexandria, she was determined to see him but realized that Achillas, commander of the Egyptian forces, would not permit her return. She thus surreptitiously bundled herself into a rolled-up carpet, and with the aid of a faithful servant, Apollodorus, was carried, undetected, into Caesar's quarters. The Roman general was initially shocked but captivated by both Cleopatra VII's wit and beauty. However, he insisted that he arbitrate between Cleopatra VII and Ptolemy XIII. Caesar publicly read the testament from Ptolemy XIII in view of the two rulers and the assembly of people, emphasizing the role that Rome was accorded in the administration of Egypt. He assured the gathering that Cleopatra VII and Ptolemy XIII were the joint rulers of Egypt, and declared that he was restoring the island of Cyprus to Egypt, to be jointly ruled by the younger brother, Ptolemy XIV, and his sister, Berenice. Caesar thus returned control of a land that Rome had controlled for a decade, underscoring the personal relationship that quickly developed between Cleopatra VII and him. Cleopatra VII had successfully manipulated the leader of the strongest empire in the world at that time, to her defense.

Caesar returned to Rome to continue with his colonial conquests. Cleopatra VII gave birth to a son named Ptolemy Caesar, even though there is no clear evidence that the child was fathered by Caesar. Caesar was killed in 44 B.C.E.

Cleopatra VII returned to Alexandria to the duty of ruling. She devoted the following three years to administering rule over Egypt, even in the face of the dwindling waters of the Nile. She was asked to provide and did deliver assistance to both Cassius and Marcus Junius Brutus, Caesar's assassins, and to Marc Antony, Caesar's consul, who teamed up with Octavius, Caesar's nineteen-year-old son and adopted nephew.

Thus began a long relationship of political interdependence and sexual passion between Cleopatra VII and Marc Antony, who left his wife, Fulvia, to spend time with Cleopatra in Alexandria. Antony married Octavius's sister, Octavia, following Fulvia's death and had an ongoing relationship with Cleopatra VII, who had

three children by him. Cleopatra, fully conscious of the fragile political path she was treading with Antony, was nevertheless an efficient and rigorous ruler and a firm negotiator. She urged Antony to give her control over the lands of Lebanon, Syria, Jordan, and southern Turkey. Antony, out of love for Cleopatra, agreed to her demands.

In 35 B.C.E., Antony decided to throw his lot in with Cleopatra and abandoned Octavia. Octavius convinced the Roman citizenry that Antony was an enemy of Rome and intended to establish a capital in Alexandria. In 32, Octavius declared war against Antony and Cleopatra. Soon, with five hundred warships, seventy-five thousand legionnaires, twenty-five thousand light armed infantry, and twelve thousand cavalry, Agrippa, Octavius's leading skilled war admiral, destroyed much of Cleopatra VII's and Antony's warfleet. Octavius was able to secure new territory as he conquered Asia Minor and defeated his opponents at the Battle of Actium on September 2, 31. In the spring of 30, Octavius approached Egypt. On August 1, 30, the entire Egyptian fleet surrendered to Octavius. Antony stabbed himself and died in Cleopatra VII's arms. She, in turn, attempted to stab herself with a hidden dagger but was overpowered and taken prisoner. Later, when she asked the man guarding her to take a letter to Octavius, she killed herself, evidenced only by two scratch marks on her body. The cause was not known, although some speculated that it was the bite of a smuggled poisonous asp that killed her.

SIGNIFICANCE

Cleopatra VII was the strongest of the Ptolemaic rulers, and her influence was recorded in inscriptions on coins used in Hellenic Egypt. Fifteen coin issues bore Cleopatra VII's head. Her reign marked the culmination of the Ptolemaic era in Egypt and symbolized the confluence of both religious authority and political power. From the wall relief at Dendera, evidence indicates that she made religious offerings to the Egyptian deities of the temple, Hathor, often associated with Isis, and her son, Harsomtus. Though she was of the Hellenistic monarchical tradition, she still saw fit to identify with the religio-political traditions of classical ancient Egypt.

—*Julian Kunnie*

FURTHER READING

Chauveau, Michael. *Cleopatra: Beyond the Myth.* Ithaca, N.Y.: Cornell University Press, 1998. A concise academic text that provides a factual account and balanced analysis of Cleopatra VII's reign.

Flamarion, Edith. *Cleopatra: From History to Legend.*

100 - 1 B.C.E.

London: Thames and Hudson, 1993. Though this book focuses heavily on the legend of Cleopatra, with extensive reference to historical paintings and film depictions, it does offer some valuable historical material on Cleopatra VII.

Grant, Michael. *From Alexander to Cleopatra: The Hellenistic World*. New York: Charles Scribner's Sons, 1982. An informative work that illuminates the cultural and historical complexity of the Hellenistic world that spawned the Ptolemy era and Cleopatra VII's intriguing reign.

Hamer, Mary. *Signs of Cleopatra: History, Politics, Representation*. New York: Routledge, 1993. An important work discussing issues of gender dynamics and political depiction of Cleopatra VII, both in Egyptian history and European culture.

Hughes-Hallett, Lucy. *Cleopatra: Histories, Dreams, and Distortions*. New York: Harper and Row, 1990.

This is an insightful work clarifying issues of fiction from fact with regard to Cleopatra VII.

Weigall, Arthur. *The Life and Times of Cleopatra, Queen of Egypt: A Study in the Origin of the Roman Empire*. New York: Greenwood Press, 1968. This work attempts to provide a sensible portrait of Cleopatra VII and furnishes a historical backdrop of the Egypto-Roman monarchy of the first century B.C.E.

SEE ALSO: 323 B.C.E., Founding of the Ptolemaic Dynasty and Seleucid Kingdom; 58-51 B.C.E., Caesar Conquers Gaul; September 2, 31 B.C.E., Battle of Actium.

RELATED ARTICLES in *Great Lives from History: The Ancient World*: Marcus Vipsanius Agrippa; Marc Antony; Arsinoe II Philadelphus; Augustus; Berenice II; Julius Caesar; Cleopatra VII; Pompey the Great; Ptolemy Soter.

---

46 B.C.E.
ESTABLISHMENT OF THE JULIAN CALENDAR

The Julian calendar added ten days and a leap year to the previous calendrical system, bringing the calender into step with the solar year, and established January 1 as the beginning of the year.

LOCALE: Rome (now in Italy)
CATEGORIES: Cultural and intellectual history; science and technology

KEY FIGURES
Julius Caesar (100-44 B.C.E.), Roman general and statesman
Sosigenes (c. 90-first century B.C.E.), Alexandrian astronomer

SUMMARY OF EVENT
In the period preceding Julius Caesar's rise to power the Romans had used a calendar based on the Greek system, with each year ordinarily consisting of twelve lunar months. Four of these, March, May, July, and October, had thirty-one days each; February had twenty-eight, and the remaining seven had twenty-nine days each. Hence, a combination of the twelve months accounted for 355 days, or 10.25 less than the number of days in the solar year. The Romans were well aware of this discrepancy and had charged the *pontifices* with the responsibility of taking care of it by inserting intercalary months from

time to time in order to keep the calendar in tune with the seasons. For special reasons of their own, however, the *pontifices* often failed to insert intercalary months when they were needed, with the result that months that were supposed to be winter months eventually fell in some other season. In the year 46 B.C.E., because of the earlier failure of Julius Caesar himself to declare intercalary months in his capacity as *pontifex maximus*, the calendar was found to be sixty-seven days behind the true date as indicated by the position of the sun.

Caesar, with the help and advice of the Alexandrian astronomer Sosigenes, set out to rectify this situation. In addition to proclaiming a regular intercalary month for 46 B.C.E., he inserted two additional months between the last of November and the first of December, thereby adding sixty-seven more days to that year. Consequently, January 1 of the following year, 45 B.C.E., corresponded to the solar January 1, or *kalends* of January as the Romans named the day.

To remove the need for inserting intercalary months in the future, Caesar lengthened some of the months by one or two days. January, August, and December were given two additional days each, being changed from twenty-nine to their present thirty-one. April, June, September, and November each acquired one additional day, being changed from twenty-nine to the present thirty. These two sets of changes accounted for the addition of ten days. February retained its former quota of twenty-eight days, but the one-fourth day left over was accommodated by the inclusion of an extra day in February every fourth year in anticipation of our present leap-year arrangement.

This new Julian calendar was so nearly accurate in its measurement of the solar year that only one minor revision was required in the interval between antiquity and modern times to bring it up to date. The year is actually a little less than three hundred and sixty-five and one fourth days in length. To rectify this minor error, Pope Gregory XIII in 1582 introduced a plan of ignoring leap-year once every four hundred years.

Caesar retained, for the time being, the system that had prevailed in earlier periods whereby days of the month were designated as falling on or a certain number of days before the *kalends*, *ides*, or *nones* of a given month. The *kalends* are in all cases the first of the month, but in the case of March, May, July, and October, the *nones* fall on the seventh and the *ides* on the fifteenth, while in the other months the *nones* fall on the fifth and the *ides* on the thirteenth. January 12 is ordinarily designated as the day before the *ides* of January, but January 11, because of the inclusive system of counting used by the Romans, is designated as the third day before the *ides* of January. The names of the months as used by the Romans are actually adjectives which modify the forms of the words *kalendae*, *nonae*, and *idus* used in the formulae. In most cases, the Latin names of the months can readily be recognized from their similarity to the English names that are derived from them. It should be noted, however, that July was originally called *quinctilis* and August *sextilis*, the fifth and sixth months in a system in which the year began with March rather than with January. At a later date the names July and August were established in honor of Julius Caesar and Augustus Caesar (63 B.C.E.-14 C.E.), respectively.

In converting Roman dates listed as preceding the *nones* or *ides* of a given month, one uses the same rules for both the pre-Julian and Julian calendars. Because a date preceding the *kalends*, however, falls in the preceding month, it is necessary to take into account the number of days in that month in making the conversion. This procedure in turn means that in such cases a careful distinction must be made between the pre-Julian and Julian calendars, since the number of days for several months differs in the two cases.

SIGNIFICANCE

A calendar is an indispensable device to measure time so that people may regulate their activities. Societies have

sought from earliest times to erect a system of time based on the alternation of day and night, the rising and setting of the sun, phases of the moon, and even on the change in position of stellar constellations. Greek astronomers after the fifth century B.C.E. tried constantly to calculate the solar year more accurately. Caesar's fame in respect to the calendar rests not only on the fact that he availed himself of the latest Hellenistic knowledge to adjust the year but also on the fact that he had his system adopted as the official calendar of Rome.

Because much Roman work on the calendar has been lost, Ovid's *Fasti* (c. 8 C.E.; English translation, 1859) and certain inscriptions are invaluable. Intricacies, uncertainties, and contradictions abound in the study. It is clear enough that Rome started out with a lunar reckoning and changed to a luni-solar calendar which kept the lunar months as basic units for the year but adjusted the year to sun time by inserting intercalary months. This pre-Julian calendar was adopted by the Decemviri probably in 451 B.C.E. in connection with the Twelve Tables. In a cycle of four years, each with 355 days, or 1,420 days in all, 22 or 23 days were added to the second and fourth year. This arrangement closely approximated the solar year. The pontiffs, charged with the task of intercalation, often manipulated these additions to benefit or injure politicians and contractors.

If most calendars have religious implications so that it takes a caesar or a pope, or a French or Russian revolution, to change them, the Roman calendar was by its very nature religious. If without the approval of the gods no law could be passed, it was to be expected that all activities of the state must be carried out when the gods approve. Consequently, it was natural that the colleges of priests as official bureaus charged with divining the will of the gods should control the calendar. It has to be accepted that everything that the Roman calendar tried to regulate, whether actions at law, meetings of the assembly, market days, or festal days, was associated with religion.

All days of the calendar were religiously designated to mark their distinct character. Certain days were clearly listed as *dies nefasti* when actions at law or civil and legislative functions could not be conducted without risking divine displeasure. Some days were *nefasti* in the morning, apparently when the sacrifice was being immolated, and in the evening when the final offering of the victim was made. The period in between was *fastus*. Of the 355 days of the Republican year, the character of only 48 is uncertain. *Dies fasti*, when action at law was permitted, seem to have occurred regularly on the same dates each month. Only forty-two are listed for the year, obviously less than the demand for justice would require. Clearly other days were used for legal affairs. Since only that legal action in which the praetor played a part was forbidden on *dies nefasti*, action probably went on almost any other day in individual courts to which he referred cases. The largest group of days designated in the calendar allowed the *comitia*, the assembly of the people, to meet, although these days might be changed to a nonbusiness status if priests or magistrates announced special times to expiate prodigies or to engage in thanksgiving or supplication. The rules by which the character of comitial days could be altered were naturally used to the advantage of politicians.

Probably the *dies feriati* show best the basic religious nature of the Roman calendar. In the late Republic, these days having lost much of the original meaning, purpose, and activity became simply optional holidays of rest when courts were shut down and certain agricultural work was restricted. The fact that *dies feriati* could show a cheerful or a serious mood points to a religious origin; apparently they were days believed to be defiled by work. Since the basic pattern of the Roman calendar was no doubt dictated by rites connected with seasonal activities dealing with crops and flocks, plowing and sowing, ferial days were of agricultural origin. Because weather is important in this context, *dies feriati* were movable. As the state grew more urban and citizenship became wider, the *feriae* took on a vague religious character for the whole state and were given fixed dates. In time they came to be connected with legendary or historical events so that in 45 B.C.E. the senate honored Julius Caesar by establishing *feriae* on the anniversary of his victories. Caesar changed little. The division of the months into *ides*, *nones*, and *kalends* is of lunar origin. Moreover the civic-religious designation of each day was retained even though much of the meaning had been lost. The old designations were most likely kept to make it easier to remember the calendar.

—*Chauncey E. Finch*

FURTHER READING

Duncan, David E. *Calendar: Humanity's Epic Struggle to Determine a True and Accurate Year*. New York: Bard, 1998. This popular overview history discusses calendars and time-keeping throughout world history.

Richards, E. G. *Mapping Time: The Calendar and Its History*. New York: Oxford University Press, 2000. A very broad-based history of time-keeping, with a chapter on the Julian calendar.

Steel, Duncan. *Marking Time: The Epic Quest to Invent the Perfect Calendar*. New York: John Wiley and Sons, 2000. One chapter is devoted to Julius Caesar's reformation of the Roman calendar.

SEE ALSO: 2953-2838 B.C.E. traditionally, Reign of China's Legendary First Ruler, Fu Xi; c. 275 B.C.E., Greeks Advance Hellenistic Astronomy; 200-900 C.E., Maya Civilization Flourishes.

RELATED ARTICLE in *Great Lives from History: The Ancient World*: Julius Caesar.

43-42 B.C.E.
SECOND TRIUMVIRATE ENACTS PROSCRIPTIONS

The proscriptions of the Second Triumvirate removed many political opponents in Rome, raised funds to help pay the triumviral armies, and set a standard for ruthless bloodshed that proved to be a negative model for Western civilization.

LOCALE: Rome (now in Italy)
CATEGORY: Government and politics

KEY FIGURES
Marc Antony (c. 82-30 B.C.E.), colleague and later rival of Octavian
Cicero (106-43 B.C.E.), statesman, orator, and philosopher who was a victim of the proscriptions

Marcus Aemilius Lepidus (c. 89-12 B.C.E.), member of the Second Triumvirate who was ultimately deposed
Octavian (63 B.C.E.-14 C.E.), heir of Julius Caesar who became Augustus, first Roman emperor, r. 27 B.C.E.-14 C.E.

SUMMARY OF EVENT
The Roman Republic was increasingly troubled after 135 B.C.E. The inadequacy of its city-state constitution to meet the needs of a growing empire, the stranglehold of great families on its offices, the rise of the equites and the consequent class struggle, and the twisting of its constitution initiated already by the Gracchi between 133 and

120 B.C.E. and by Gaius Marius and Lucius Cornelius Sulla between 105 and 80 B.C.E., all contributed to the Republic's travail. Especially significant were the great rivals born in the decade between 110 and 100 B.C.E., men such as Pompey the Great (106-48 B.C.E.), Marcus Licinius Crassus (c. 115-53 B.C.E.), Julius Caesar (100-44 B.C.E.), Catiline (c. 108-62 B.C.E.), and Sertorius (c. 123-72 B.C.E.), who were ready to fulfill their ambitions between 70 and 60 B.C.E. Most of these men proved to be too big for the constitution to contain. The rise of private armies, extraordinary commands, absentee governorships, extended tenures of office, bribery, demagoguery, political manipulation, and outright violence became more and more commonplace. Marius and Sulla even dared to liquidate each other's adherents by outright purges, a precedent set for the leaders who were to emerge as the Second Triumvirate. By decimating the old patrician stock, enabling Octavian to become Augustus, the first emperor of Rome, and silencing Republican sentiments, the proscriptions of the Second Triumvirate brought an end to the civil wars.

The formation of the Second Triumvirate by Augustus, Marc Antony, and Marcus Aemilius Lepidus in 43 B.C.E. was a pragmatic arrangement of three leaders who were united by their personal connections to Julius Caesar and because of their common enemies: a faction under the leadership of Marcus Junius Brutus (c. 85-42 B.C.E.) and Cassius (d. 42 B.C.E.) and another under the leadership of Sextus Pompey (d. 35 B.C.E.), the son of Pompey the Great. Unlike the First Triumvirate, this three-man dictatorship was given legal sanction. The three leaders met on a small island in a river near Bologna and formulated a joint policy. Although in effect they established a three-man dictatorship, of necessity they avoided the term because Antony, when consul, had abolished the office of dictator for all time. They formed themselves into an executive committee that was to hold absolute power for five years in order to rebuild the Roman state. The triumvirs planned to unite their armies for a war against the republican forces in the East. The West, already under their control, was divided among themselves: Lepidus kept his provinces of Hither Spain and Narbonese Gaul and picked up Farther Spain as well; Antony took the newly conquered parts of Gaul together with the Cisalpine province; and Augustus (as junior member) was assigned North Africa, Sardinia, Corsica, and Sicily, territories largely held by Pompeian adherents. Italy itself was to be under these three men's combined rule.

At the same meeting, the triumvirs determined to en-

Augustus. (Hulton|Archive)

sure the success of their rule by declaring a proscription against their Republican enemies. In this purge, hundreds of senators and about two thousand wealthy equites were marked for destruction. The historian Livy (59 B.C.E.-17 C.E.) records that 130 senators were proscribed, Appian (c. 95-c. 165 C.E.) indicates that 300 were proscribed, and Plutarch (c. 46-after 120 C.E.) records that 200 to 300 were proscribed. The names of almost 100 of the proscribed have been recorded. Not all of these individuals were killed; a few obtained pardon and many successfully escaped from Italy. In most cases, the victims suffered only the confiscation of their properties.

In the official proclamation of the proscription, the triumvirs emphasized the injustices suffered at the hands of the enemies of the state and pointed out the necessity of removing a threat to peace at home while they were away fighting against the Republican armies. To justify their position and gain for it some semblance of respectability, they pointed out that when Julius Caesar had adopted a policy of clemency toward his enemies, he had paid for that policy by forfeiting his life.

SIGNIFICANCE

While personal vengeance and political pragmatism played a part in the proscriptions, economic necessity also played a role. Augustus, Antony, and Lepidus had bought the support of their troops with lavish promises, and it was imperative that they pay them with more than words. Altogether, the triumvirs commanded forty-three legions, and they needed their support in the impending campaign against Brutus and Cassius. However, arguments have been made that a much smaller number was actually proscribed and that, rather than the economic demands for paying the soldiers, the proscriptions were based in a political motivation to avenge Caesar and terrorize their opponents.

In drawing up the lists, each of the three triumvirs had to give up some of his friends or relatives to satisfy the vengeance of one or the other of his colleagues and to make a public demonstration of their collective "toughness." So it was that the most famous of the victims, Cicero, was found on the list of the condemned. Augustus might have spared the famous orator, but Antony insisted on his death. Although many of the proscribed acted quickly and escaped, Cicero dallied, uncertain of the best course to take, and died as a result. Livy, as quoted by Seneca, has given a full account of Cicero's death.

The bloodshed of the proscriptions, highlighted by the execution of Cicero, tainted the historical reputations of the triumvirs, and especially those of Antony and Lepidus. During the religious wars of the sixteenth century, the French painter Antoine Caron (1521-1599) produced a series of massacre paintings showing the triumvirs watching or joining in the slaughter of unarmed citizens. The proscriptions of the triumvirs thus established a pattern of rule through force and political terrorism that periodically resurfaced throughout the age of the Empire.

—*Mary Evelyn Jegen, updated by Richard D. Weigel*

FURTHER READING

Gowing, Alain. *The Triumviral Narratives of Appian and Cassius Dio*. Ann Arbor: University of Michigan Press, 1992. The author compares the accounts that Appian and Cassius Dio present of the principal personages of the triumviral period.

Huzar, Eleanor G. *Mark Antony: A Biography*. 1978. Reprint. New York: Routledge, 1986. Huzar surveys the slanted sources on Antony and sees him in a moderate light, while admitting that the proscriptions revealed him at his worst.

Mitchell, Thomas. *Cicero: The Senior Statesman*. New Haven, Conn.: Yale University Press, 1991. A biography of the orator and defender of the Republic from his consulship in 63 B.C.E. until his honorable death in the proscriptions.

Syme, Ronald. *The Roman Revolution*. 1939. Reprint. Oxford: Oxford University Press, 2002. The classic study of the transition from Republic to Empire that credits the proscriptions with a chilling, yet major, role in this process.

Weigel, Richard. *Lepidus: The Tarnished Triumvir*. London: Routledge, 1992. A biography of the "third triumvir" that attempts to reassess the biased sources and create a relatively objective account of his career.

SEE ALSO: 133 B.C.E., Tiberius Sempronius Gracchus Is Tribune; 107-101 B.C.E., Marius Creates a Private Army; Late 63-January 62 B.C.E., Catiline Conspiracy; September 2, 31 B.C.E., Battle of Actium; 27-23 B.C.E., Completion of the Augustan Settlement.

RELATED ARTICLES in *Great Lives from History: The Ancient World*: Marc Antony; Augustus; Marcus Junius Brutus; Julius Caesar; Cassius; Cicero; Marcus Licinius Crassus.

September 2, 31 B.C.E.
BATTLE OF ACTIUM

The Battle of Actium established the Roman Empire by ending the lengthy Roman civil wars with the victory of Augustus over Marc Antony and Cleopatra.

LOCALE: Ambracian Gulf, on the west coast of
   northern Greece
CATEGORY: Wars, uprisings, and civil unrest

KEY FIGURES
Marc Antony (c. 82-30 B.C.E.), Roman general, member
   of the Second Triumvirate, later rival of Augustus
Augustus (63 B.C.E.-14 C.E.), greatnephew and heir of
   Julius Caesar, first Roman emperor, r. 27 B.C.E.-14
   C.E., rival and enemy of Marc Antony
Cleopatra VII (69-30 B.C.E.), queen of Egypt, r. 51-30
   B.C.E., enemy of Augustus
Marcus Vipsanius Agrippa (c. 63 B.C.E.-12 C.E.),
   general and admiral serving Augustus

SUMMARY OF EVENT
In the decade following the assassination of Julius Caesar in 44 B.C.E., a political struggle developed between Marc Antony and Augustus. Alternately rivals for power and reluctant allies, they became bitter enemies after Antony in 34 B.C.E. openly attached himself to Cleopatra VII, thus repudiating his legal wife, who was Augustus's sister. In Italy, Augustus's supporters excoriated Antony for his liaison with Cleopatra and published a purported will of Antony deposited with the Vestal Virgins by which Antony donated eastern territories to Cleopatra and her children. In 32 B.C.E., the two consuls and three hundred senators went east to join Antony, thus terminating negotiations between him and Augustus.

Antony had recruited a heterogeneous army, variously estimated from forty thousand to a hundred thousand men, and Augustus raised an Italian force almost as large. Battle strategy eventually depended on navies, with Augustus's admiral Marcus Vipsanius Agrippa the most experienced commander at sea. Antony's fleet, perhaps at first slightly greater in size, was composed of larger, slower ships, some of his "sea castles" having eight or ten banks of oars.

In the mid-winter of 31 B.C.E., Agrippa sailed from Italy across the Ionian Sea and, after establishing Epirus as his base, began seizing important strong points along the Greek coast. At about the same time, Antony had moved his forces forward to block Agrippa's eastward advance. Antony's fleet was stationed in the Gulf of Ambracia

(now Arta) with the army occupying a fortified camp on the nearby sandy promontory of Actium, one of the two peninsulas that pointed toward each other across the mouth of the gulf. Augustus, arriving with the remainder of his forces, seized Corinth and other strategic inland positions, then occupied the northern peninsula of the gulf. Through skillful use of his cavalry, he severed Antony's communications with the interior, and when the fleet under Agrippa sealed the Gulf of Ambracia, Antony's forces were effectively blockaded. Soon, they began to suffer from hunger and disease. Significant desertions and lowered morale now impelled Antony to act.

In a council held in Antony's camp on September 1, 31 B.C.E., his officers were divided over strategy. A Roman faction advocated retreat by land; Cleopatra with some supporters favored a naval attack or an escape to Egypt. Although Antony's enigmatic aims and actions are variously reported by later historians, it seems less likely that Antony wanted a showdown by naval action than that he hoped to break out of the blockade in order to fight later in a more favorable situation. Any ships he may have burned were probably unusable. All records agree that he left some of his troops ashore to retreat by an inland route and that he kept aboard his ships the masts and sails, which were ordinarily jettisoned before action, in order to allow his fleet either to escape if the battle went against it or else pursue its defeated enemy.

The following day's battle was a chaotic imbroglio, shrouded from modern view in conflicting accounts. Antony's ships advanced through the narrow exit from the gulf, aligned so as to take advantage of an expected shift in the wind at midday. The Caesarian fleet blocked their passage. One squadron of sixty ships under Cleopatra was placed in the rear, carrying the treasure chest that undoubtedly belonged to her more than to Antony. After several hours of tense inactivity, one wing of Antony's fleet was drawn into conflict, forcing Antony to commit the remainder of his forces. His soldiers aboard the large ships hurled missiles and shot arrows into Augustus's smaller vessels, which attempted to ram or surround and capture their clumsy opponents.

Suddenly, at the height of the conflict, when a breeze rose from the northwest, Cleopatra's reserve squadron hoisted purple sails and moved through the battle line, in evident flight southward. Although Antony's flagship was entrapped, he transferred to a smaller ship and with a small portion of his fleet followed Cleopatra. The histo-

The Battle of Actium. (F. R. Niglutsch)

rian Plutarch vividly portrays the gloom of defeat on the escaping ships.

Abandoned by their leader, the remnants of Antony's fleet backed into the gulf. More than five thousand men had been killed or drowned. Augustus and Agrippa made little attempt to pursue Antony; instead, they kept their ships at sea to bottle up the enemy and thus prevented further escape. Within about a week, the ships and soldiers left behind by Antony surrendered. Augustus claimed to have captured three hundred vessels.

SIGNIFICANCE

The Battle of Actium remains one that is difficult to reconstruct and even more difficult to understand. The conflicting accounts of the battle can be interpreted either as evidence of Antony's determination to fight a serious, climactic naval battle with Augustus or as an attempt to break Augustus's blockade in order to return to Egypt. Once there, Antony and Cleopatra could have reinforced their army, resupplied their navy, and either seized the initiative or waited for Augustus to attack them at their strongest point.

Scholars who favor the decisive battle theory generally suggest that Antony attempted to turn one flank of Augustus's fleet, but that Agrippa, a solider with a first-class military mind, skillfully countered the thrust with his smaller, more maneuverable ships. As the battle unfolded, Antony's fleet began to retire in some disorder, while a gap opened in Augustus's line. Seeing the battle was going against Antony, Cleopatra fled through this gap with her ships and Antony followed.

Those who support the breakout hypothesis read the same evidence, generally the accounts of the ancient historians Plutarch and Dio Cassius, in their favor. According to this view, Antony realized that his outnumbered and blockaded fleet had no real chance of defeating Augustus and Agrippa. Therefore, he feigned an attack at one point of the line in order to open the gap through which his key units—including the ships carrying his war chest—could escape.

Whatever theory is accepted, the Battle of Actium was a decisive engagement, with profound and lasting impact on Roman and world history. Antony and Cleopatra returned to Egypt, where some final desperate expedients were contemplated but not effectively carried out. The next year, Augustus came to Egypt, where he met little resistance and precipitated the romanticized suicides of both Antony and Cleopatra. The civil wars and the Republic were at an end, for Augustus was now the undisputed ruler of the Mediterranean world.

—*Roger B. McShane, updated by Michael Witkoski*

FURTHER READING

Green, Peter. *Alexander to Actium: The Historical Evolution of the Hellenistic Age*. Berkeley: University of California Press, 1990. The political, social, and cultural undercurrents that pitted the Latin west against the Greek east during the final phases of the Roman Civil War are admirably expounded, clearly revealing the divergence of the Roman and Alexandrian worldviews.

Gurval, Robert Alan. *Actium and Augustus: The Politics and Emotions of Civil War*. Ann Arbor: University of Michigan Press, 1995. An examination of the Battle of Actium and how it is portrayed in literature.

Murray, William M., and Photios M. Petsas. *Octavian's Campsite Memorial for the Actian War*. Philadelphia: American Philosophical Society, 1989. Although this volume has archaeology as its main focus, it does provide an interesting and insightful review of the battle itself and its consequences.

Richardson, G. W. "Actium." *The Journal of Roman Studies* 27 (1937): 153-164. Accepts the traditional historical version of the battle that holds that Antony was attempting an escape, rather than a pitched battle, at Actium.

Rodgers, William. *Greek and Roman Naval Warfare: A Study of Strategy, Tactics, and Ship Design from Salamis to Actium*. Annapolis, Md.: U.S. Naval Institute, 1964. The volume as a whole places the battle within the general context of ancient naval warfare, while the specific sections on Actium are detailed and informative.

Tarn, W. W. "The Battle of Actium." *The Journal of Roman Studies* 21 (1931): 173-199. Takes the view that Antony planned to fight a decisive battle at Actium but was betrayed by disloyal or disheartened elements within his own forces. Tarn explains Cleopatra's "flight" as a valiant but failed attempt to bolster Antony's battle line.

SEE ALSO: 51-30 B.C.E., Cleopatra VII, Last of Ptolemies, Reigns; 43-42 B.C.E., Second Triumvirate Enacts Proscriptions; 27-23 B.C.E., Completion of the Augustan Settlement.

RELATED ARTICLES in *Great Lives from History: The Ancient World*: Marcus Vipsanius Agrippa; Marc Antony; Augustus; Cleopatra VII.

100 - 1 B.C.E.

27-23 B.C.E.

COMPLETION OF THE AUGUSTAN SETTLEMENT

The completion of the Augustan settlement marks a transition from the traditional res publica *to a new form of government, the principate.*

LOCALE: Rome (now in Italy)
CATEGORY: Government and politics

KEY FIGURE

Augustus (63 B.C.E.-14 C.E.), greatnephew of Julius Caesar and his son by testamentary adoption in 44 B.C.E., legally becoming Gaius Julius Caesar Octavianus; called Octavian until 27 B.C.E. and Augustus *princeps* thereafter

SUMMARY OF EVENT

For years, Julius Caesar outmaneuvered and outfought his enemies in war and politics but was never able to achieve permanent supremacy. Each victory on the bat-

tlefield and each new political office and honor produced more enemies. On March 15, 44 B.C.E., Julius Caesar was struck down in the name of liberty by a conspiracy led by men whom he had pardoned, trusted, and promoted. Caesar's plans are unknown. In 44 B.C.E., he was consul for the fifth time, *dictator perpetuo* (for life), and *pontifex maximus* (head of the state religion). Caesar had also received a number of honors deriving from Rome's kings in the sixth century B.C.E. Whether he wanted to be king is uncertain and irrelevant: Although he had publicly rejected a crown, his whole position was regal and incompatible with Roman political opinion. To the conspirators, led by Gaius Cassius Longinus and Marcus Junius Brutus, it was patriotism, not murder, to kill the tyrant.

Julius Caesar's assassins restored neither *libertas* nor the *res publica*. For months, senators who dreaded the re-

FIRST TEN EMPERORS OF IMPERIAL ROME, 27 B.C.E.-81 C.E.	
Ruler	*Reign*
Augustus	27 B.C.E.-14 C.E.
Tiberius	14-37
Caligula	37-41
Claudius	41-54
Nero	54-68
Galba	68-69
Otho	69
Vitellius	69
Vespasian	69-79
Titus	79-81

newal of civil war sought to work out a compromise. Marc Antony abolished the offensive dictatorship, but Cicero assailed him as a tyrannical threat to freedom and drove Rome to war. In November, 43 B.C.E., Caesarians came together in the Second Triumvirate: Antony, Marcus Aemilius Lepidus, and young Gaius Octavius, who had just been made consul and insisted on being called Caesar. Everyone misjudged Octavian. Cicero dismissed him as "the boy," and Antony once remarked that he owed everything to his name (Caesar). The triumvirs eliminated their domestic enemies, most conspicuously Cicero, through massive proscriptions. In 42 B.C.E., they deified Julius Caesar (permitting Octavian to style himself *divi filius*, son of the god), and then destroyed the conspirators' army at Philippi.

The triumvirate gradually failed, in good part because of the ruthless Octavian. He removed Lepidus from power in 36 B.C.E. but allowed him to live because Lepidus was *pontifex maximus*. Octavian turned public opinion against Antony, claiming that in 32 B.C.E. "all Italy" and the western provinces took an oath of loyalty to him as leader (*dux*, not a magistracy). As consul in 31 B.C.E., he destroyed Antony's forces at the Battle of Actium and drove Antony and his consort, Cleopatra VII, queen of Egypt, to suicide the next year. The young Caesar had won supremacy. He had more power than the elder Caesar had ever had but had yet to win acceptance.

Octavian wisely did not revive the dictatorship and kept clear of kingship. Yet it was not enough to avoid Caesar's errors. He had to devise a new position in the state and a new image for himself. The triumvir who had risen to power as *divi filius* moved away from his bloody Caesarian past. For a time after 31 B.C.E., he relied on

consecutive consulships. Octavian returned to Rome in 29 B.C.E., celebrated a huge triumph, proclaimed the return of peace, and spent the following year in Rome to symbolize the end of the civil wars.

Years later, he wrote that in 28-27 B.C.E., he restored the *res publica* from his control to the judgment of the senate and Roman people. Outwardly he did. On January 13, 27 B.C.E., Octavian went before the senate and renounced all extraordinary powers given him during the period of the triumvirate. The senate promptly asked him to stay on as consul and undertake the governorship of Spain, Gaul, and Syria for ten years, together with his dominion over Egypt as a kind of private possession. Octavian allowed himself to be persuaded to accede to the senate's wishes. He was a model of Roman duty: He did not grasp unprecedented powers or titles, but rather, having saved the state from its enemies, he offered to resign and then accepted a specific assignment that the senate asked him to undertake. It was a carefully scripted maneuver that he had worked out with a group of advisers. The lands given him contained about two-thirds of Rome's army and came to be designated the imperial (or armed) provinces. He governed them through legates. (A *legatus* was someone holding *imperium*, the right to command troops, delegated to him by a superior.) The senate governed all other provinces.

Three days later, the senate conferred on him a number of singular honors. The most important of them was a new name, "Augustus," chosen after rejection of an alternative, Romulus, the founder of the city. Romulus cannot have been seriously considered: A king who had supposedly been murdered by the senators and then declared a god was uncomfortably like Caesar, whose statue had stood in the Temple of Quirinus (the deified Romulus). The month Sextilis was changed to August because Augustus's greatest achievements had occurred in that month.

From then on, Augustus was widely known as *princeps*, a word long used in Roman politics but raised to a new level of meaning. Leading senators were loosely designated *principes*, the "first men" in the state; and the most distinguished member of that body was formally designated *princeps senatus*, an honor that allowed him to speak first in debate. Augustus, however, was the *princeps*, "First Man," in a way that no one had ever been. Although scholars have debated this point, the title *princeps* may have been emphasized to recall the *princeps* of Cicero's essay *De republica* (51 B.C.E.; *On the State*, 1817). The Ciceronian *princeps* was a distinguished and patriotic senator who guided the state by wisdom, not love of power, and on death won deification at the acclamation of his grateful citizens. This "settlement of 27" is generally taken as the opening of the imperial period in Roman history.

Following a long absence from Rome, suppression of a conspiracy, and recovery from a serious illness, Augustus adjusted his position on July 1, 23 B.C.E., when he resigned the consulship. This act was good propaganda: He had been consul consecutively since 31 B.C.E., which both made him appear monarchical and monopolized the office. In practical politics, however, it left Augustus without the power to control the government. The senate gave him twofold compensation: proconsular *imperium* and *tribunicia potestas*. Proconsular power enabled him to intervene and correct abuses in all provinces, for it was specified as *maius*, "greater" than of any provincial governor. Tribunician power (granted for ten years and periodically renewed) conferred the all-important right to initiate or veto measures (which he had done as consul), and made him a protector and champion of the ordinary people. Largely because of its *popularis* traditions, the tribunician power was renewed annually. Augustus emphasized this purely civilian power and downplayed his *imperium*.

Subsequent modifications in his position are minor, but two are noteworthy. After the death of Lepidus, Augustus was elected *pontifex maximus* in 12 B.C.E. In 2 B.C.E., he was hailed as *pater patriae*, "father of his country." The fundamental imperial powers thereafter were those he held, because Augustus was the first emperor: *imperium proconsulare maius*, *tribunicia potestas*, and *pontifex maximus*. (*Pater patriae* was standard but not essential.) From the late first century C.E., emperors also held the powers of the old censors, which Augustus had avoided.

SIGNIFICANCE

Scholars debate whether Augustus actually hoped to "restore the Republic." In reality there is no question. To Romans, the *res publica* was not the "Republic" in the modern sense but "the traditional state"—lawful government with the familiar magistracies and senatorial preeminence. *Res publica* was incompatible with kingship, dictatorship, or any obvious domination by a single individual. The conservative Italian upper classes and the senatorial aristocracy were emotionally attached to the ancient institutions. Julius Caesar had scorned

them as outmoded and had moved to establish some type of personal rule. His failure to appreciate the widespread devotion to the old ways and how grievously his lifelong dictatorship and quasi-royal trappings had offended the political classes put him on the wrong end of numerous daggers on the Ides of March. Augustus's genius was his ability to retain the control of the state he had won in civil war by devising a new position based on tradition. Every element of his ultimate status had "republican" antecedents, but cumulatively they were new. His position was no charade. It was the principate, and he was *princeps*. His wiser successors modeled themselves on him.

—*M. Joseph Costelloe, updated by Thomas H. Watkins*

FURTHER READING

Baker, G. P. *Augustus: The Golden Age of Rome*. New York: Cooper Square Press, 2000. An examination of the life and times of Augustus Caesar.

Lacey, W. K. *Augustus and the Principate: The Evolution of the System*. Leeds, Great Britain: Francis Cairns, 1996. An examination of Augustus and his role in developing the principate.

Millar, F., and E. Segal. *Caesar Augustus: Seven Aspects*. New York: Oxford University Press, 1984. A collection of scholarly essays by experts on Augustus.

Raaflaub, K. A., and M. Toher. *Between Republic and Empire: Interpretations of Augustus and His Principate*. Berkeley: University of California Press, 1990. Essays by experts interpret the political strength and legacy of Augustus.

Southern, Pat. *Augustus*. New York: Routledge, 1998. A biography of Augustus that covers his rise to power. Bibliography and index.

Zanker, Paul. *The Power of Images in the Age of Augustus*. Translated by Alan Shapiro. Ann Arbor: University of Michigan Press, 1988. Explores the intriguing thesis that conservatism in Roman art during the Augustan period matched that in politics.

100 - 1 B.C.E.

19 B.C.E.
ROMAN POET VERGIL DIES

Vergil requested that his poem the Aeneid *be destroyed on his death as he had not finished its revision; the intervention of the emperor Augustus preserved the Roman national epic.*

LOCALE: Brundisium (present-day Brindisi, Calabria, Italy)
CATEGORIES: Literature; cultural and intellectual history

KEY FIGURES
Vergil (Publius Vergilius Maro; 70-19 B.C.E.), Roman poet and author of the *Eclogues*, *Georgics*, and *Aeneid*
Augustus (63 B.C.E.-14 C.E.), first Roman emperor, r. 27 B.C.E.-14 C.E.
Lucius Varius (fl. first century B.C.E.), compiler, with Plotius Tucca, of the final edition of the *Aeneid* at Augustus's request
Plotius Tucca (fl. first century B.C.E.), compiler, with Lucius Varius, of the final edition of the *Aeneid* at Augustus's request

SUMMARY OF EVENT
The death of any great artist is a tragic event, but that of Vergil acquired dramatic tension as well. The poet's final wish was that his executor should ensure destruction of his masterwork the *Aeneid* (c. 29-19 B.C.E.; English translation, 1553) should Vergil be unable to give the poem its final revision. The emperor Augustus himself had to intervene to save the manuscript, and he thereby allowed Rome's great national epic to be born. This simple episode encapsulates so many of the elements that make for a compelling narrative: the death of a great man; the uncertainty of creation; the emergence of a great poem; the connection of art and the political forces of the day.

Nothing about the pattern of Vergil's life would have foreshadowed the extraordinary circumstances that surrounded his death. The specifics of his birth on the Ides of October (October 15), 70 B.C.E., were not especially distinguished: in a rural area called Andes near Mantua to an artisan potter and a mother whose name was Magia Pollia. As happens often in biography, even these humble origins became stylized, highlighted, and magnified through the prism of Vergil's death.

While she was pregnant with Vergil, Magia Pollia supposedly dreamed that she had given birth to a laurel branch, the laurel being the tree of Apollo, guardian of the Muses. As soon as the branch struck the ground it sprang up into a tree filled with different fruits and flowers. This folktale, which became current after Vergil's death, plays on the name of the poet himself, *virga* meaning "wand." It further recalls the golden bough that allows Aeneas, while still living, to enter the realm of the dead in the *Aeneid*, book 6.

It is hardly remarkable, therefore, that bibliomancy attached itself almost immediately after Vergil's death to all his poems. Both his father and his mother appear as *magi* or "sorcerers" in many of these folktales, most of which emanate from Calabria and spread quickly after the poet's death throughout the Italian peninsula. It soon became a custom among Calabrian women who had just borne children to plant a poplar sprout as a "Vergil tree" to ensure the health and fame of a newborn child. This tradition began very soon after Vergil's death and continued through the high Middle Ages, testimony to the influence Vergil had on the popular imagination.

Observers quickly noted every variety of portent connected with Vergil's life. On the day Vergil assumed the *toga virilis* (the "toga of manhood" that marked the transition from adolescence to adulthood) at the age of fifteen, the poet Titus Lucretius Carus died. Lucretius, the late Republican poet of the *De rerum natura* (c. 60 B.C.E.; *On the Nature of Things*, 1682), is identifiable with demystifying the life-death cycle. While Vergil's *Georgics* (c. 37-29 B.C.E.; English translation, 1589), his early poem on the cycle of the farmer's year, notes the symmetry of nature in the way its Greek model, Hesiod's *Erga kai Emerai* (c. 700 B.C.E.; *Works and Days*, 1618) of Hesiod (fl. c. 700 B.C.E.), does, Vergil's Homeric-inspired *Aeneid* consistently emphasizes the mystical nature of passing from this life to another.

The series of heroes who appear in the *ekphrasis* (procession) of great Romans Aeneas sees in the Underworld in the *Aeneid*, book 6, marks an important emphasis on the mystical destiny of the Roman people. This destiny is inevitably related to Cumae, the modern Cuma, a volcanically active town on the Bay of Naples and home to the Greek-founded temple of Apollo. It is here that Aeneas enters the Underworld and here that Rome's destined greatness first receives utterance. The effect is to consistently tie the prophesied greatness of Augustus's imperial city to the mythic identity of those dead centuries before.

Vergil's *Eclogues* (43-37 B.C.E., also known as the *Bucolics*; English translation, 1575), a series of ten pastoral poems inspired in their general themes by the Greek poet Theocritus (310-250 B.C.E.) that preceded the *Aeneid*, contains the so-called Messianic *Eclogue* 4, which prophesies the birth of a child who will free the land of its burdens. Christians as soon as the first century fastened on this golden child as the mystical poet's recognition of Jesus Christ's divinity nearly a half century before the fact. This served their purposes because it tied the prophet of Rome's destiny to their own fated dominance as the City of God. In actuality, the golden child of *Eclogue* 4 is the man who would become Vergil's patron, and assume extraordinary importance in his career, Augustus.

What is important to note in all of this is that the dramatic nature of Vergil's death became a filter through which the poet's work and biography achieved prophetic and mystical dimensions. Aelius Donatus (fl. 350 C.E.), the author of the first life of Vergil, collects several folk legends in which the poet becomes Augustus's personal *magus*. Vergil first shocks, then pleases the emperor

when he calls him the son of a baker, by which he meant that Augustus, who was the man leavened by the world, ordered that the poet be given bread when he was hungry. By implication, this completely apocryphal tale ascribes Christian generosity to a pre-Christian. It fastens on the fact that Augustus actually did save Vergil's homestead farm from the forced land seizures of the Roman civil wars, a fact obliquely celebrated in *Eclogue* 1.

Vergil labored painstakingly over all his poems. Having worked on the *Aeneid* for nearly eleven years, he decided, at the age of fifty-one, to make the arduous sea journey to Greece and Asia Minor to complete his final revision of the poem. Supposedly, in Athens he met Augustus, who was returning to Rome from Asia Minor, and it was the emperor himself who convinced him not to remain in Greece and Asia Minor for the three years he had planned.

En route home, Vergil caught sunstroke in the town of Megara, near Athens. He postponed his return to Italy for a time hoping that his fever would abate, but to no avail. He decided to return nevertheless, and though he reached Brundisium (modern Brindisi), he died there a few days later, on September 21, 19 B.C.E., in the consulship of Gnaeus Sentius and Quintus Lucretius. By tradition, Vergil's bones are interred on the Pozzuoli road outside Naples. The site remains Vergil's burial place by popular assent, and a famed epitaph marks the spot:

> Mantua bore me, the Calabrians snatched me,
> Now the city of Parthenope's burial holds me.
> I have sung of pastures, fields, leaders.

The epitaph is quite elegant. It touches on every facet of Vergil's life: the city of his birth; the region of his death; identification of Naples, the place of his burial, as the same as that of the siren Parthenope, who threw herself into the sea for love of Odysseus. This oblique reference to the Homeric tradition that Vergil expands in his *Aeneid* simultaneously links the two poets and identifies Vergil's poetry with the sirens' enchanting music. The final phrase sums up the three major poems of Vergil's career in three words: pastures for the *Eclogues*; fields for the *Georgics*; leaders for the *Aeneid*.

Vergil had requested Lucius Varius to destroy the entire manuscript of the *Aeneid* should he be unable to finish its revision. This request came either before leaving for his trip to the East or, more dramatically, on his deathbed at Brundisium. Donatus records that Varius refused to do this and claims that Vergil himself called for his scroll-cases while dying. By tradition, Augustus inter-

Vergil. (Library of Congress)

vened to save the poem and entrusted Varius and Plotius Tucca with the final revision. If one follows Donatus, Vergil acquiesced in this with the stipulation that nothing of the *Aeneid* appear that he himself had not revised. This is the argument scholars have used for the appearance of half-lines in the poem: that they were originally intended for completion but left unfilled by the master's direction.

The grammarian Nisus claimed that he had heard testimony that Varius made major revisions, reversing the order of *Aeneid* books 2 and 3 and subtracting the lines that appear in major Latin editions before the famous invocation *Arma virumque cano* (Arms and man I sing). Most modern scholars do not believe that Varius made any major changes and hold that the lines appended to the invocation are a scribal insertion.

SIGNIFICANCE

Vergil's works parallel the pastorals of Theocritus and Hesiod as well as the epics of Homer. If Vergil had done nothing except contribute to making Latin a recognized literary language, he would have accomplished a great deal. As it happens, the fortunate preservation of the *Aeneid* created a national epic that almost immediately after Vergil's death entered the core curriculum of the Roman schools. It remained so into the high Middle Ages, and what is more acquired the attention of the peasantry of Europe. For them, the *Aeneid* was a poem with magical qualities that could be used for prophecy.

Dante (1265-1321 C.E.) was clearly aware of the poem's immense influence. In *Inferno*, canto 20, Dante's Virgilio warns the Pilgrim to distrust any text that presents an alternate explanation for the founding of Mantua, the birthplace of Vergil. Ironically, the alternate version appears in Vergil's own *Aeneid*. One implication is that Dante's poem has replaced Vergil's, though even if this were so it would not have happened until the publication of *La divina commedia* (c. 1320; *The Divine Comedy*, 1802, 3 vols.).

—Robert J. Forman

FURTHER READING

Comparetti, Domenico. *Vergil in the Middle Ages*. Translated by E. F. M. Benecke. 1872. Reprint. Princeton, N.J.: Princeton University Press, 1997. Has remained the standard volume on Vergilian traditions, legends, and literary heirs.

Johnson, W. R. *Darkness Visible: A Study of Vergil's "Aeneid."* Berkeley: University of California Press, 1976. A revisionist approach to Vergil's poetry, particularly the *Aeneid*, that deconstructs the text to find implicit criticism of Augustus and the *pax Romana* (Roman peace) he had brought by force of arms to the Empire.

Martindale, Charles. *Cambridge Companion to Virgil*. New York: Cambridge University Press, 1997. A multi-authored guide suitable for students and general readers. Emphasis on responses to Vergil over the centuries, particularly by other creative artists.

Otis, Brooks. *Virgil: A Study in Civilized Poetry*. 1964. Reprint. Norman: University of Oklahoma Press, 1995. A classic study that emphasizes the refinement that its author sees as characteristic of both Vergil's poetry and the vision that Augustus had for Rome itself. Excellent biographical and critical examinations of all Vergil's poems.

Vergil. *Aeneid*. Translated by David West. Reprint. New York: Penguin, 2003.

_____. *The Eclogues of Virgil*. Translated by David Ferry. New York: Farrar, Straus, and Giroux, 2000.

_____. *Georgics*. Translated by L. P. Wilkinson. New York: Penguin Classics, 1983. Vergil's works in translation.

SEE ALSO: c. 438 B.C.E., Greek Lyric Poet Pindar Dies; 159 B.C.E., Roman Playwright Terence Dies; 54 B.C.E., Roman Poet Catullus Dies; November 27, 8 B.C.E., Roman Lyric Poet Horace Dies; 8 C.E., Ovid's *Metamorphoses* Is Published; 100-127 C.E., Roman Juvenal Composes *Satires*.

RELATED ARTICLES in *Great Lives from History: The Ancient World:* Augustus; Catullus; Homer; Juvenal; Lucretius; Ovid; Pindar; Sappho; Terence; Vergil.

15 B.C.E.-15 C.E.
RHINE-DANUBE FRONTIER IS ESTABLISHED

The Rhine-Danube frontier was established, fixing boundaries between the Roman Empire and European tribes to the north.

LOCALE: The Rhine and Danube Rivers and the Balkan peninsula south of the Danube valley

CATEGORIES: Expansion and land acquisition; government and politics

KEY FIGURES

Augustus (63 B.C.E.-14 C.E.), first Roman emperor, r. 27 B.C.E.-14 C.E.

Julius Caesar (100-44 B.C.E.), proconsul in Gaul, 58-50 B.C.E., and dictator of Rome, 49-44 B.C.E.

Nero Claudius Drusus (38-9 B.C.E.), brother of Tiberius and equally prominent

Tiberius (42 B.C.E.-37 C.E.), prominent general under his stepfather Augustus, whom he succeeded as emperor in 14 C.E.

Arminius (c. 17 B.C.E.-19 C.E.), chieftain of the Germanic Cherusci

Publius Quinctilius Varus (d. 9 C.E.), legate on the lower Rhine, where he directed campaigns to annex the land between the Rhine and the Elbe

Germanicus (Germanicus Julius Caesar; 15 B.C.E.-19 C.E.), Roman general and the son of Antonia Minor, father of the emperor Caligula, and brother of the emperor Claudius

SUMMARY OF EVENT

The Rhine-Danube frontier was mostly established between 15 B.C.E. and 15 C.E. through the determination of Augustus (earlier known as Octavian) to limit the boundaries of the immense empire of which he was the first emperor (*princeps*).

Julius Caesar had conquered Gaul between 58 and 50 B.C.E., thereby extending Roman rule to the Rhine. In the course of his campaigns against the Celts and the Germans who had come into eastern Gaul, Caesar came to realize the value of the Rhine as a frontier. To coerce the Germans into similar respect for this natural boundary, Caesar built a temporary wooden bridge, crossed the river in 55 B.C.E., conducted extensive raids in German lands for two weeks, and then returned to Roman territory. His intimidating campaign had the effect of keeping the Germans away from Gaul for thirty years, though there was no true frontier.

Gaul (with the Rhine valley) was one of the "impe-

rial" provinces assigned to Augustus from the start of the Roman Empire in 27 B.C.E. His enormous powers allowed him to create Rome's first unified frontier policy. Equally advantageous, all newly created provinces were automatically designated "imperial." Governors of imperial provinces were styled "propraetorian legates of the emperor" (*legati propraetore Augusti*); the emperor was commander in chief, possessed proconsular *imperium*, and delegated *imperium* to his appointees.

At the opening of Augustus's reign, Rome had extensive possessions in the west and the east but lacked control of the Alps and the Balkan peninsula. Northern Italy, Illyricum, and Macedonia could not be defended against serious attack by barbarian tribes. Augustus determined to expand Roman holdings up to the Danube and perhaps beyond. There were three theaters of campaigns. In the first theater, Augustus sent legions under the command of his capable stepsons Tiberius and Nero Claudius Drusus through the Alps to the upper Danube region in 16 B.C.E., while he himself took charge in Gaul. Within two years, Tiberius and Drusus were largely done. A legion soon occupied Vindonissa (now Windisch, on the Aare near Brugg). Modern Switzerland, southern Bavaria, and western Austria became the province of Raetia. Rome annexed Noricum (now in central Austria) and administered it through prefects (*praefecti*) headquartered at the natives' mountaintop commercial center, the Magdalensberg. Later, in 40-49 C.E., Claudius converted Noricum into a procuratorial province, so called because the governor was an equestrian *procurator* (not a senator), and moved the capital to Virunum (now Waisenberg, near Klagenfurt).

Campaigns in the second theater, south of the middle Danube, proved difficult. Augustus's son-in-law Marcus Vipsanius Agrippa was to have directed operations but died in 12 B.C.E. Tiberius took over and had apparently completed the war by 9 B.C.E. Other generals extended Roman control over the lower Danube (modern Bulgaria) to create the province of Moesia and to reduce Thrace to a client state. The Pannonians, however, rose in an extensive revolt in 6 C.E., and Tiberius, assisted by several senior commanders, took three years to crush the uprising. Illyricum was divided into two imperial provinces: Pannonia, centering on the Drava and Sava River valleys to their confluence with the Danube, and Dalmatia, in the Balkan peninsula north of Macedonia. These conquests brought Roman rule to the western coast of the Black Sea. Fortifications were established along the Danube and probably in the tributaries to its south. The location of many legionary fortresses in the early Roman Empire remains uncertain, although bases at Emona (Ljubljana) and Poetovio (Ptuj) are probable. Dalmatia had two legions: one at Burnum on the Krka and the other at Tilurium (Gardun) on the Cetina.

Meanwhile, Drusus had marched northward from Raetia along the Rhine to establish the third theater of the campaign. Because the German tribes had renewed attacks on Gaul, it was decided to invade Germany again and push back the German frontier to the Elbe (less probably as far as the Vistula). The plan was to shorten Rome's northern frontier by some three hundred miles and also to put Gaul beyond the reach of German attacks. Drusus entered the German heartland in 12 B.C.E., planting Roman eagles on the Elbe after fortifying the lower Rhine. He was accidentally killed in 9 B.C.E., and his brother Tiberius replaced him.

Rome overran but never really organized the lands east of the Rhine. The Germans revolted, and under Arminius, a young chieftain who had served with the Romans as an auxiliary commander and won Roman citizenship, they annihilated some twenty thousand Romans belonging to three legions under the command of Publius Quinctilius Varus in the famous Battle of Teutoburg Forest in 9 C.E. The site of the battle was located in the Lippe Valley. The elderly Augustus was severely shaken when news of the disaster reached him, and though Drusus's son Germanicus undertook some punitive action and restored Roman prestige in 14-17 C.E., Rome made no further effort to encompass or restrain the Germanic tribes. They remained outside the mainstream of Roman civilization.

SIGNIFICANCE

In the early Roman Empire, the Rhine commands were among the most important in the empire, and senators of consular rank held them. Two military districts, called Upper and Lower Germany (*Germania Superior* and *Inferior*), stretched along the Rhine; they became provinces only in 90 C.E. with capitals at Moguntiacum (modern Mainz) for Superior and Colonia Agrippinensis (modern Cologne or Köln) for Inferior. Each legate commanded four legions plus auxiliary troops. By the early second century, the garrison was reduced to just four.

Arminius consults a prophetess. (F. R. Niglutsch)

Other legionary fortresses along the Rhine are also the origins of modern cities: Argentorate (Strasbourg), Bonna (Bonn), Novaesium (Neuss), and Castra Vetera (Xanten). Another base was converted into a civilian colony in 49 C.E., as Colonia Claudia Ara Agrippinsium. In the 70's and early 80's, Rome occupied the Black Forest area between the Upper Rhine and Upper Danube, a noticeable shortening of the frontier. By the early second century, these garrisons had been reduced to two legions each, plus auxiliaries, as the Danube became the military center of the empire.

The Danube area had been pacified after the fall of Maroboduus as king of the Marcomanni in 19 C.E., but slowly it came to have the empire's largest concentration of forces. The bases in the Balkans were closed and their legions transferred to the Danube from Dalmatia, from the Rhine army, and even from Britain. Augusta Regina (Regensburg), Vindobona (Vienna), Aquincum (Budapest), and Singidunum (Belgrade) are legionary fortresses that have become modern cities. Trajan conquered Dacia (roughly Romania) in 101-106; his famous column in Rome commemorates the war. Ironically, it was the Marcomanni who (with the Quadi) in the reign of Marcus Aurelius (r. 161-180 C.E.) first seriously challenged the frontier after two centuries of the Pax Romana. Rome's ultimate establishment of the Rhine-Danube line as its northern frontier, the subsequent Dacian conquest notwithstanding, was not a matter of choice but of necessity. Rome's inability to conquer further was dictated by spreading internal weaknesses and . revolts, the generally troublesome Parthian frontier, and the strength of Rome's German adversaries. The establishment of the northern frontier entailed much more than the mere definition of a border; it represented both the height and the eclipse of Roman imperialism in Europe and therefore the spread of *Romanitas* as well.

—*Edward P. Keleher, updated by Thomas H. Watkins*

FURTHER READING

Alföldy, Geza. *Noricum.* Translated by Anthony Birley. London: Routledge & Kegan Paul, 1974. Part of Routledge's *History of the Provinces of the Roman Empire* series, this work is detailed and archaeological, and its scholarship is superb.

Drinkwater, J. *Roman Gaul.* London: Croom Helm, 1983. Provides an overview of activities on the Rhine frontier.

King, Anthony. *Roman Gaul and Germany.* Berkeley: University of California Press, 1990. King also treats the Rhine frontier. When compared to the work of Drinkwater, cited above, King's volume is more accessible for beginners.

Luttwak, E. *The Grand Strategy of the Roman Empire.* Baltimore: The Johns Hopkins University Press, 1976. An analyst for the Department of Defense rather than an ancient historian, Luttwak has stimulated considerable debate; many doubt Rome had a "grand strategy."

Mocsy, A. *Pannonia and Upper Moesia.* London: Routledge & Kegan Paul, 1974. Like the work by Alföldy, cited above, this well-written volume is part of Routledge's *History of the Provinces of the Roman Empire.*

Syme, Ronald. "The Northern Frontier Under Augustus." In *Cambridge Ancient History*, Vol. 10, edited by S. A. Cook et al. New York: Cambridge University Press, 1934. Syme's study remains irreplaceable; archaeological work has provided some new information.

Wilkes, J. *Dalmatia.* London: Routledge & Kegan Paul, 1969. Yet another superb entry in Routledge's *History of the Provinces of the Roman Empire* series.

Woolf, Greg. *Becoming Roman: The Origins of Provincial Civilization in Gaul.* New York: Cambridge University Press, 1998. An examination of the relationship between the Roman Empire and Gaul. Bibliography and index.

SEE ALSO: 58-51 B.C.E., Caesar Conquers Gaul; 27-23 B.C.E., Completion of the Augustan Settlement; 9 C.E., Battle of Teutoburg Forest.

RELATED ARTICLES in *Great Lives from History: The Ancient World*: Arminius; Augustus; Julius Caesar; Tiberius.

100 - 1 B.C.E.

November 27, 8 B.C.E.
ROMAN LYRIC POET HORACE DIES

By the time of his death, Horace had earned the status of one of the greatest and most distinctive lyric poets in a great age of Roman poetry.

LOCALE: Rome (now in Italy)
CATEGORIES: Literature; cultural and intellectual history

KEY FIGURES

Horace (Quintus Horatius Flaccus; 65-8 B.C.E.), Roman lyric poet
Augustus (63 B.C.E.-14 C.E.), first Roman emperor, r. 27 B.C.E.-14 C.E., celebrated by Horace in several odes
Gaius Maecenas (c. 70 B.C.E.-8 B.C.E.), wealthy patron of Horace

SUMMARY OF EVENT

The death of Quintus Horatius Flaccus, known to posterity as Horace, on November 27, 8 B.C.E., marked the end not only of a great poet's life but of a major phase of poetry. Of the great Latin poets of the Roman Golden Age of literature, Catullus (c. 84-c. 54 B.C.E.) and Vergil (70-19 B.C.E.) had already died, and Ovid (43 B.C.E.-17 C.E.), a younger man who outlived Horace, proved more often to be a brilliant entertainer than a poet of high seriousness. The accomplishments of these major poets of the first century B.C.E. set standards for European poets over the centuries that followed.

Horace was born on December 8, 65 B.C.E., in Venusia, in the Apennine Hills of southern Italy, about 80 miles (130 kilometers) east of modern Naples, but his father, a freedman, moved the family to Rome so that young Quintus might receive a good education. To complete this education, Horace was sent to Athens in 45 B.C.E. The next year he met Marcus Junius Brutus (c. 85-42 B.C.E.), who had fled to Greece after participating in the assassination of Julius Caesar (100-44 B.C.E.). Much later, in his *Odes*, book 2, poem 7, Horace tells of joining Brutus's army in its unsuccessful struggle against what they saw as another potential tyranny then being led by Mark Antony (c. 82-32 B.C.E.) and Octavian, who would become the emperor Augustus. In this ode Horace confesses that he ran away from the Battle of Philippi (42 B.C.E.), after which Brutus committed suicide.

Back in Rome, finding that his father's property had been confiscated, he found employment as a clerk and began writing poetry. This activity brought him into contact with Vergil and through him, around 38, with Vergil's wealthy patron Gaius Maecenas. At first Horace wrote *sermones*, a term that might be translated as "learned discussions," although later he would call them *Satires* (English translation, 1567). The first few of these poems establish themes that would prove important in his career and poetry to come: reasonableness, moderation, and tolerance. He published these poems in 35 B.C.E., dedicating them to Maecenas, who, two years later, made him a present of a small estate in the Sabine Hills northeast of Rome, which became his favorite dwelling place, much celebrated in his poetry. He completed another collection of satires, including his famous account of the city mouse who encourages a country mouse into town to enjoy the comfort and splendor of urban life, but as a result of the hubbub of the city, the country mouse discovers that he prefers the simplicity and quiet of his modest hole in the woods.

Around 30 B.C.E., Horace completed his *Epodes* (English translation, 1638), a collection of various experiments in verse that began to point the way to the poems of his maturity. Around this time, Horace also began to write the *Carmina*, or *Odes* (23 and 13 B.C.E.; English translation, 1621), that are his greatest poetic achievement. Like all Roman poetic forms, the ode was a Greek invention. The greatest Greek composer of odes, Pindar (c. 518-c. 438 B.C.E.), wrote elaborate, formal lyrics featuring songs of praise for triumphant athletes in the Olympic Games and other athletic competitions. In common with other Latin poets, Horace found his inspiration in the poetry of Greek poets, particularly Alcaeus and Sappho (c. 630-c. 580 B.C.E.), who wrote about a century before Pindar and are associated with the island of Lesbos. The result was a new and distinctive type of ode.

Horace used several different stanzas, often of four lines, in the *Odes*, and the poems are relatively short, few extending beyond fifty lines. His favorite subjects are love and friendship, but his love poems are radically different from the emotionally charged ones of Catullus, his great Roman predecessor in the lyric. Whereas Catullus's love lyrics express a range of emotions generated by a tempestuous relationship with a mistress whom he calls Lesbia, Horace's address several different women, none of whom can be confidently identified as a current or even former mistress. These poems tend to center on the experience of love as recollected in tranquillity and usually refer to the love affairs of friends in a detached, humorous, and delicately ironical manner.

An example is the famous "Ode," book 1, poem 5, which is addressed to one Pyrrha, whom a young man (Horace calls him a *puer*, or boy) is wooing in a rose-strewn grotto. Pyrrha is lovely, blonde, and as treacherous as a stormy sea. The emphasis on her lover's youth underscores his unawareness of the nature of the experience that awaits him. The speaker, who has been through it all, is addressing Pyrrha herself, gently chiding her rather than warning the young man directly. The lover will obviously have to learn for himself.

"Ode," book 2, poem 4 counsels, rather ambivalently, Xanthias, a friend in love. Why not, he asks, love Phyllis if that is what you wish? At the same time he slyly refers to heroes of old who were "tamed" or "undone" by women. The speaker praises Phyllis's physical attributes while assuring Xanthias that he himself has no designs on the young lady, for his days of striving to charm young women are over. The attitude toward the young friend is avuncular and encouraging, but at the same time seasoned by a recognition of the feminine guile that he knows that the latter is liable to encounter.

It would be a mistake to assume that the attitude of cool detachment in Horace's poetry on the subject of love reflects a lack of feeling. His forte is the delicate and subtle control of emotion. Feeling is more easily discernible in the poems celebrating his Sabine farm and the panoply of pleasures associated with it: tasteful and simple furnishings, good food and wine, good friends, the cultivation of his Muse. He urges moderation, modesty, the avoidance of the ambition that adds apprehensions and complications to one's life. He sums up this way of life in a poem of only eight lines, "Ode," book 1, poem 38, wherein he castigates the "Persian pomp" that he recognizes as a temptation to his countrymen. Emotion also permeates "Ode," book 2, poem 14, a lament on old age and death "whom no one conquers."

By the time of the odes Horace had forsworn his antipathy to the man who became the first Roman emperor. Now he celebrates Augustus in several odes as the embodiment of Roman glory. In "Ode," book 3, poem 2, the poet also extols the military virtues that he himself lacked, alleging the "sweetness"

of dying for one's country. Death, he points out, will overtake the coward who flees from battle. There is no reason to doubt the sincerity of Horace's admiration for the soldierly qualities so foreign to his own nature.

SIGNIFICANCE

Horace was not held in particularly high esteem in the Middle Ages, because his work could not be conveniently moralized, as Ovid's was, or given the Christian coloring that medieval classicists found that they could impose on Vergil. Beginning in the Italian Renaissance, enthusiasm for his poetry mounted and spread to Spain, France, and England. In the seventeenth century, admiration for Horace pervades the work of Ben Jonson (1572-1637), Robert Herrick 1591-1674), and Andrew Marvell (1621-1678). In that century in particular, imitations and translations of Horace's odes abounded.

Horace's lyrics are notoriously difficult to translate. Not only is the effect of Latin quantitative verse impossible to replicate in a language like English; Horace brilliantly employs the flexibility of Latin word order to create effects that can seldom be duplicated in translation. The challenge of rendering Horace's poetry effectively in English and other modern languages, however, contin-

100 - 1 B.C.E.

The poet Horace. (Hulton|Archive)

ues to attract poets. In 2002, a set of translations of the odes into English involved the participation of a number of distinguished living poets.

—*Robert P. Ellis*

FURTHER READING

Frischer, Bernard D., and Iain Gordon Brown, eds. *Allan Ramsay and the Search for Horace's Villa*. Burlington, Vt.: Ashgate, 2001. An expensively priced but handsomely illustrated collection of essays on the most important place in Horace's life: his cherished Sabine farm.

Lyne, R. O. A. M. *Horace: Behind the Public Poetry*. New Haven, Conn.: Yale University Press, 1995. Concentrating on the political poems rather than the love poems, this book studies Horace's relationship to the changing Roman sociopolitical scene.

McClatchy, J. D., ed. *Horace, the Odes: New Translations by Contemporary Poets*. Princeton, N.J.: Princeton University Press, 2002. By representing English

versions by a number of skillful poets and translators of today, this work illustrates as well as can be expected the richness of Horace's odes for readers unfamiliar with classical Latin.

Wilkinson, L. P. *Horace and His Lyric Poetry*. New York: Cambridge University Press, 1968. This useful introduction to Horace has chapters on his life, his "character and views," and the problems of translating his odes.

SEE ALSO: c. 438 B.C.E., Greek Lyric Poet Pindar Dies; 159 B.C.E., Roman Playwright Terence Dies; 54 B.C.E., Roman Poet Catullus Dies; 19 B.C.E., Roman Poet Vergil Dies; 8 C.E., Ovid's *Metamorphoses* Is Published; 100-127 C.E., Roman Juvenal Composes *Satires*.

RELATED ARTICLES in *Great Lives from History: The Ancient World*: Augustus; Callimachus; Catullus; Clodia; Juvenal; Ovid; Pindar; Sappho; Terence; Vergil.

---

c. 6 B.C.E.
BIRTH OF JESUS CHRIST

The birth of Jesus Christ heralded the foundation of one of the world's major religions, Christianity.

LOCALE: Bethlehem, Judaea
CATEGORY: Religion

KEY FIGURES
Jesus Christ (c. 6 B.C.E.-30 C.E.), religious leader whose life and teachings inspired the founding of Christianity
Mary (b. 22 B.C.E.), mother of Jesus

SUMMARY OF EVENT
The birth of Jesus has been seen as significant from the early days of the Christian community, when the story was included in traditional oral accounts recorded by the Christian apostles Luke and Matthew. From the beginning of Christianity, the birth of Jesus Christ was perceived as the entrance into the human situation of someone who, while truly human, was uniquely other and more than human. To express this perception, the tradition as handed down was colored by mythopoeic elements that suggested deeper meanings.

Jesus was born in Bethlehem, in the southern part of Palestine near Jerusalem. His parents, Mary and Joseph,

came from Nazareth in Galilee, a northern province of Palestine. The history of Jesus cannot be found in Jewish or Roman documents and annals; nevertheless, non-Christian written sources help to corroborate the at times slightly conflicting Gospel accounts that the birth occurred before the death of Herod the Great in 4 B.C.E. Because there is also strong evidence that Jesus died in full manhood during the reign of Augustus's immediate successor Tiberius, who died in 38 C.E., his birth must have occurred early in Augustus's reign. The weight of scholarly opinion favors a year between 8 and 4 B.C.E. as the time of Jesus' birth.

Christian influence on the development of the calendar has made the birth of Jesus the dividing line in occidental history, producing the temporal designations B.C., "before Christ," and A.D., from the Latin *anno Domini*, "in the year of the Lord." The "Christian" calendar was later adopted throughout the Western world. The designations B.C. and A.D., however, have been replaced by the non-religion-specific terms B.C.E., "before the Common Era," and C.E., "Common Era," but the dividing line is still the date near the traditional birth of Jesus.

Little is known about Mary and Joseph. Luke gives a picture of his mother, Mary, a young woman engaged to a local carpenter, Joseph. Luke gives an account of the miraculous conception announced by an angel, Mary's puzzlement at the news, and her act of trusting faith and willing cooperation with God's act. Matthew records Jesus' parentage from the standpoint of Joseph. The simplicity of the two accounts reveals the conviction of the early Christians who held a solid tradition of a single historical person who was really born; that is, that Jesus was not a mythical god or hero.

The circumstances surrounding the birth of Jesus in Bethlehem as recorded by Matthew and Luke also bear witness to the early Christian community's understanding of the meaning of the event. Jesus was a man whose destiny was bound up with that of every human without respect to social condition. In Luke's account, there is the manifestation of the child to the poor shepherds, while in Matthew, there is the account of the visit of the wise men from the East, in which scholars see a midrashic element, that is, a story used to carry a religious or moral truth. Other details, such as the story that there was no room at the inn and that Mary for this reason cradled the child in a manger, carry a hint of mystery that has fascinated the imagination of many people.

SIGNIFICANCE

Jesus of Nazareth, Christ (from the Greek *Christos*) or Messiah (from the Hebrew)—both of which mean the "anointed one"—is arguably the most significant person in the history of Western civilization. At the very least, he was a riveting and persuasive preacher and teacher and a gifted healer. To the Christians who follow his teachings two thousand years later, he was the son of God whose death for the sins of humans provided hope for life after death in Heaven for all. The circumstances of Jesus' birth, life and teachings, and particularly death, and how they defined Christianity, transformed the course of all occidental history.

—*Mary Evelyn Jegen*

FURTHER READING

Martin, Raymond. *The Elusive Messiah: A Philosophical Overview of the Quest for the Historical Jesus.* Boulder, Colo.: Westview Press, 2000. A good overview of the approaches and agendas of the main schools of historical research into the life of Jesus.

Meier, John P. *The Roots of the Problem and the Person.* Vol. 1 in *A Marginal Jew: Rethinking the Historical Jesus.* New York: Doubleday, 1991. The first volume of a projected four-volume study (the others published as of 2003 are *Companions and Competitors,* 2001, and *Mentor, Message, and Miracles,* 1994); discusses what is known of Jesus' life and his historical context.

Vermes, Geza. *The Changing Faces of Jesus.* Reprint. New York: Penguin, 2001. A balanced presentation of the arguments for a historical Jesus and the ways in which a human life was transformed into myth.

SEE ALSO: c. 950 B.C.E., Composition of the Book of Genesis; 250-130 B.C.E., Commissioning of the Septuagint; c. 30 C.E., Condemnation and Crucifixion of Jesus Christ; c. 30 C.E., Preaching of the Pentecostal Gospel; c. 50-c. 150 C.E., Compilation of the New Testament; 200 C.E., Christian Apologists Develop Concept of Theology; October 28, 312 C.E., Conversion of Constantine to Christianity; 313-395 C.E., Inception of Church-State Problem; 325 C.E., Adoption of the Nicene Creed; 380-392 C.E., Theodosius's Edicts Promote Christian Orthodoxy; c. 382-c. 405 C.E., Saint Jerome Creates the Vulgate; 428-431 C.E., Nestorian Controversy; October 8-25, 451 C.E., Council of Chalcedon.

RELATED ARTICLES in *Great Lives from History: The Ancient World*: David; Deborah; Ezekiel; Ezra; Herod the Great; Jesus; Saint John the Baptist; Mary; Moses; Saint Paul; Saint Peter; Pontius Pilate; Samuel; Solomon; Saint Thomas.

100 - 1 B.C.E.

Early 1st century C.E.
PYU KINGDOM DEVELOPS URBAN CULTURE

The Pyu people established the earliest known urban, advanced Iron Age civilization in Burma, profoundly influencing the first urbanized culture established by Burmese people of later ages.

LOCALE: Central Burma (now Myanmar)
CATEGORY: Prehistory and ancient cultures

SUMMARY OF EVENT

Archaeologists studying the prehistory of an area often focus on determining the point at which the first urban culture appeared. Many archaeologists define "civilization" in terms of characteristics that include urbanization; the changes in social, economic, and political organization that cause and accompany it; and important technological advances. In Burma (now Myanmar), archaeologists for decades focused almost exclusively on the cities of the Pagan Kingdom with their thousands of visible temples and monuments. Through the first half of the twentieth century it was generally accepted that the Pagan Kingdom, with its advanced agricultural technology, well-developed art, and prosperity, had emerged suddenly in Burma's central plains. The two factors most often touted as catalysts for this amazing occurrence were Theravāda Buddhism and the external influence of immigrants.

However, by the mid-twentieth century, there were some in the archaeological and historical communities who questioned these interpretations. Numerous buried sites had been occupied by the predecessors of the Pagan Kingdom. The scant evidence about them indicated the presence of both an advanced economy and Buddhism long before Pagan. Furthermore, both Burmese and Chinese ancient historical chronicles described several prosperous pre-Pagan walled cities in central Burma built of glazed bricks.

Excavations beginning in the late 1950's and early 1960's uncovered a number of cities that were built by the Pyu, a people who called themselves the Tircul and were called by the Chinese Piao (P'iao). Their sites, which include Sri Ksetra (modern-day Hmawza), Beikthano, Hanlingyi, Binnaka, and Mongamo, are located in central Burma's dry zone and thrived from at least the early first century C.E. until the mid-ninth century C.E. Archaeologists now believe that some date even earlier, from 200 B.C.E. The Pyu, like earlier prehistoric groups, migrated from Tibet or China, traveling down the western side of the Irrawaddy River into Burma. Chinese manuscripts from the fourth century C.E. list the Piao among the tribes that had inhabited China's southwestern frontier and describe their political and social organization as quite complex. All of these sites were cities with thick outer walls (some rectangular, some circular), with a walled inner citadel. The entranceways curve inward, and the principal construction materials for walls and structures are the unique Pyu bricks. They are all large compared to earlier sites, ranging from 500 to 3,500 square acres (200 to 1,400 hectares).

Among the significant finds at Pyu sites are extensive assortments of iron implements, weapons, fasteners, and other construction materials. Although there is evidence of crude ironworking in earlier Stone and Bronze Age cultures in central Burma, the Pyu utilized advanced ironworking technology. In addition, these dry-zone cities, which are located near tributaries of the Irrawaddy River, had complex irrigation systems. One water-distribution system at Hanlingyi involved nearly 200 square miles (300 square kilometers) of land.

The Pyu also worked in metals other than iron, but bronze, silver, and gold were mostly used to make artistic, ritualistic, and ornamental objects and coins. These objects are described as beautiful, ornate, and expertly crafted. Archaeologists assert that Pyu silver coins of various denominations and inscribed with several motifs may be the oldest in Southeast Asia. Their use indicates a sophisticated economy requiring a diversified medium of exchange, and their presence in countries throughout the region shows extensive economic interactions.

The strong Indian and Buddhist influences on Pyu culture are found in the use of cremation urns, the presence of Buddhist temples and monasteries, and inscriptions in both Sino-Tibetan Pyu and various Indian scripts. For decades, archaeologists hypothesized that the Pyu kingdom's impressive accomplishments were made possible because of immigrant groups who brought advanced technology, socioeconomic organization, and Buddhism. However, more recent research has generated a fairly strong consensus among scientists that, because there is no evidence of a foreign sector in Pyu cities or of Buddhism before 400 C.E., the Pyu urban culture probably developed gradually and locally. The Pyu kingdom was destroyed around 835 by invaders from Yunnan, who took thousands of prisoners back as slaves, whereupon the Burmese migrated to central Burma and established the Pagan Kingdom.

SIGNIFICANCE

The Pyu appear to have made several significant advances relative to earlier groups in central Burma. They were the region's first urban civilization; they advanced Iron Age, agricultural, and architectural technology; they created a complex economic system; and they developed several art forms. These innovations were passed on to the Pagans, who perpetuated urban civilization and built thousands of temples and massive monuments. The Pyu who survived their kingdom's downfall and remained in Burma were absorbed into Pagan culture and actively contributed to its development for hundreds of years.

The Pyu may have had more of an impact on post-Pagan cultures than on Pagan. Within their walls, Pyu cities, unlike those of Pagan, housed large, dense populations from all walks of life, not just the political and religious elite. Furthermore, Pyu citizens engaged in diverse and specialized occupations and utilized a complex monetary system. In Pagan, however, no coins were produced because the simpler economic system consisted of crops being given to the urban elite and then redistributed to the peasantry. Without a doubt, the Pyu kingdom was a major force in the progress toward the first true Burmese state.

—*Jack Carter*

FURTHER READING

Aung-Thwin, Michael. "Burma Before Pagan: The Status of Archaeology Today." *Asian Perspectives* 25, no. 2 (1982): 1-21. A detailed account of the excavations of major Pyu sites, with maps and illustrations.

Miksic, John N. "Early Burmese Urbanization: Research and Conservation." *Asian Perspectives* 40, no. 1 (2002): 88-107. Focuses on the complexity of Pyu social and economic organization.

Stargardt, Janice. *The Ancient Pyu of Burma: Early Pyu Cities in a Man-Made Landscape.* Cambridge, England: Institute on Southeast Asian Studies, 1990. Examines the history of the Pyu Kingdom and its origins. Includes maps and illustrations.

Wicks, Robert S. *Money, Markets, and Trade in Early Southeast Asia: The Development of Indigenous Monetary Systems to A.D. 1400.* Ithaca, N.Y.: Cornell University Southeast Asia Program, 1992. Details the development of very early coinage by the Pyus and its distribution throughout Southeast Asia.

SEE ALSO: 6th or 5th century B.C.E., Birth of Buddhism; 1st century C.E., Tai Peoples Migrate into Southeast Asia; 1st century-c. 627 C.E., Kingdom of Funan Flourishes.

1st century C.E.
KINGDOM OF AKSUM EMERGES

Aksum was the center of an expansive ancient kingdom that developed a civilization of considerable sophistication, one that had a lasting influence on subsequent Ethiopian polities.

LOCALE: Aksum (now in northern Ethiopia and the plateau and coastal area of present-day Eritrea)
CATEGORY: Government and politics

KEY FIGURES

Zoskales (fl. c. mid-first century-second century C.E.), king of Aksum, r. late second century C.E.
Ezana (c. 303-c. 350 C.E.), king of Aksum, r. c. 320-c. 350 C.E.

SUMMARY OF EVENT

The kingdom of Aksum grew in one of the earliest centers of plow-based agriculture. Northern Ethiopia was largely populated by peoples speaking Cushitic and Semitic languages belonging to the Afro-Asiatic family. Intimate contacts between northern Ethiopia and South Arabian communities, beginning as early as the end of the second millennium B.C.E., led to common cultural spheres on both sides of the Red Sea. This cultural fusion was in evidence in the political, religious, architectural, and linguistic features of the kingdom of Yeha (Da'amat), the first known state in Ethiopia, which arose around the mid-fifth century B.C.E.

The highlands of northern Ethiopia broke once again into petty kingdoms after the collapse of the kingdom of Yeha at the end of the first century B.C.E. One of these principalities, Aksum, emerged as the most dominant regional power in the first century C.E. The name Aksum, which initially referred to the city, came to signify also the kingdom over which it ruled. Although certain linguistic and religious features of Yeha continued to be observed throughout northern Ethiopia, many features of Aksumite civilization began to differ considerably as it encompassed increasingly diverse Cushitic and Nilo-

1 - 100 C.E.

MAJOR AKSUMITE KINGS, LATE 2D CENTURY-C. 350 C.E.

Ruler	Life	Reign
Zoskales	fl. c. mid-first century-second century	late second century C.E.
Gadar Gadarat	c. mid-second to early third century	
Sembruthes	fl. third century	
Adbaha	fl. third century	
Aphilas	fl. third century	
Endybias	fl. third century	
Wazeba	fl. third century	
Ousanas	fl. fourth century	
Ella Amida	fl. fourth century	
Ezana	c. 303-c. 350	c. 320-c. 350

Saharan cultural and ethnic groups farther south and west toward the Nile Valley.

Aksum was strategically positioned to control both the plateau and coastal regions of northeast Africa, including the shores of the Red Sea, one of the most important arteries of commerce in the ancient world. Aksum was also conveniently located within reach of the rich resource areas of the interior of northern Ethiopia.

Aksum's entry into a wider network of commerce was further stimulated by the growth of Greco-Roman interests in the Red Sea and the eastern trade. Aksum embarked on intense military and diplomatic campaigns that expanded the kingdom in the direction of the major trade routes issuing from the capital and its principal port, Adulis, to the Nile and Egypt, south toward the gold-producing areas, and southeast to the Somali Coast, where they obtained incense (a major Aksumite export commodity). By the end of the second century C.E., Aksum had begun extending its military activity into South Arabia, thereby effectively policing the Red Sea and becoming a major partner in the profitable trade in valuable goods along the routes that crisscrossed Arabia to the markets of the Roman Empire.

Aksum's hegemony on both sides of the Red Sea coast considerably enhanced its position in the growing international market. In addition to trading with Arabia and the Greco-Roman areas, the Aksumites traded with Persia, India, Sri Lanka, and China. Aksum's exports included items such as gold, emeralds, ivory, turtle shell, incense, civet, rhinoceros horn, and a variety of exotic animal skins. It imported textiles, iron, wines, olive oil, glass, and other luxury items.

Evidence of Aksum's advanced commercial economy is seen in the extensive use of locally minted currency. Most of the Aksumite kings who reigned between the second and the sixth centuries C.E. issued currencies in gold, silver, iron, and bronze. Aksumite coins depicted the effigies of the kings and bore legends in both Greek and Ge'ez. These coins were used in both external trade and internal markets. Archaeological excavations of the elaborate tombs, temples, platforms, mansions, and other material relics in the city of Aksum and in dozens of other urban centers along the trade routes, such as Adulis, Coloe, Malazo, Kaskase, Matara, Qohayto, and Tekondo, attest to a highly sophisticated and affluent urban society.

The most important testimony to Aksum's greatness is the towering obelisks that were carved from single pieces of stone. Some of these monoliths, which are thought to be among the largest single stones ever used in ancient times, weigh more than 500 tons. The tallest of them (which now is broken) was 36 yards (33 meters) high. These soaring monuments, representing an enormous display of power, resources, and skill, were probably erected to commemorate Aksum's dead rulers. They are carved to resemble conventional multistoried buildings, complete with elaborately decorated doors and windows. Only two of the obelisks remain standing, one in Aksum itself, the other in Rome, where it was transported by order of Benito Mussolini during the Italian invasion of Ethiopia in the 1930's.

Contemporary written records confirm Aksum's dominant position in the international arena. Mani, a third century C.E. Persian author, mentions Aksum as one of the four great kingdoms in the world together with Rome, Persia, and China. Increased commercial and diplomatic contacts with the Mediterranean world resulted in the spread of the Hellenic influence in Ethiopia. The

Periplus Maris Erythraei (also known as *Periplus*, first century C.E.; *Periplus of the Erythraean Sea*, 1912), a shipping guide written by a Greek merchant, mentions that the Aksumite king Zoskales was well versed in the Greek language and literature. Many inscriptions and coins dating from the second to the fourth century C.E. attest to a fairly widespread use of the Greek language in the Aksumite kingdom. Some of the Greek alphabets were absorbed into the Ethiopic (Ge'ez) script. Greek gods such as Hercules, Hermes, Zeus, Ares, and Poseidon were commonly worshiped side by side with the local and South Arabian gods.

Close interaction with the eastern Mediterranean world culminated in the introduction of Christianity into the Aksumite kingdom and its adoption as the official religion of the state by King Ezana in the middle of the fourth century C.E. With state sponsorship, Christianity began to spread deep into the interior of the kingdom, effectively replacing the worship of local, South Arabian, and Greek gods. The introduction of Christianity further stimulated the growth of the locally developed Ge'ez script (inspired by the Sabean writing system) and the evolution of a unique Ethiopian literary tradition.

The reign of Ezana marked the zenith of Aksumite power. Four of his inscriptions written in Greek and Ge'ez clearly indicate intensive military activities involving imperial expansion and consolidation. In addition to his usual titles, Ezana refers to himself as king of Himyar, Raydan, and Saba (indicating Aksum's continuing political supremacy in Arabia). It was also during this period that Aksum gave the coup de grace to the tottering kingdom of Meroë and placed much of the Sudanese region under its control. The use of the title of *nugusa nagast* (king of kings) by Aksumite rulers indicates the development of a governmental system that relied on retaining traditional rulers over the conquered territories and exacting tribute as a sign of dependence.

SIGNIFICANCE

Aksum, the precursor of the modern Ethiopian state, developed a successful urban civilization based on efficient exploitation of local resources, significant development of an internal market, and vigorous participation in the international trade. Although Aksum's political prominence had dissipated by the end of the first millennium C.E., its legacy continued to influence successive Ethiopian polities. As the center of political gravity shifted farther south in the course of the second millennium C.E., Aksum's political, literary, religious, and architectural

traditions moved along with it, providing a common reference to the diverse communities that constituted the Ethiopian state.

—*Shumet Sishagne*

FURTHER READING

Butzer, K. W. "Rise and Fall of Axum, Ethiopia: A Geo-archaeological Interpretation." *American Antiquity* 46 (1981). A concise and interesting perspective, especially on the demise of Aksumite power.

Chittick, N. "Excavations at Aksum: A Preliminary Report." *Azania* 9 (1974). A brief description of the archaeological works in Aksum undertaken by the author for the British Institute in Eastern Africa from 1972 to 1974.

Ehret, Christopher. "On the Antiquity of Agriculture in Ethiopia." *Journal of African History* 20 (1979). A history of the early beginning of agriculture in the Ethiopian highlands.

Kobishchanov, Yuri. *Axum*. University Park: Pennsylvania State University Press, 1979. One of the best standard works on the history of Aksum.

Monro-Hay, S. *Aksum: An African Civilization of Late Antiquity*. Edinburgh, Scotland: Edinburgh University Press, 1991. One of the latest and most comprehensive works on the history of the Aksumite civilization.

Periplus Maris Erythraei. Princeton, N.J.: Princeton University Press, 1989. This ancient handbook, written by a Greek merchant, describes the countries on both sides of the Red Sea. Translated with a commentary and introduction by Lionel Casson.

Sergew Hable Sellassie. *Ancient and Medieval Ethiopian History to 1270*. Addis Ababa, Ethiopia: Addis Ababa University, 1972. Covers the most important highlights of Ethiopian history from the earliest times to the medieval period, with detailed reproductions of the ancient Sabaean, Greek, and Ge'ez inscriptions and Aksumite coins.

SEE ALSO: 450-100 B.C.E., City-State of Yeha Flourishes in the Northern Ethiopian Highlands; c. 100 B.C.E.-c. 300 C.E., East African Trading Port of Rhapta Flourishes; 3d-5th century C.E., Giant Stelae Are Raised at Aksum; 4th century C.E., Ezana Expands Aksum, Later Converts to Christianity; c. 450-500 C.E., Era of the Nine Saints.
RELATED ARTICLE in *Great Lives from History: The Ancient World*: Ezana.

1 - 100 C.E.

1st century C.E.
TAI PEOPLES MIGRATE INTO SOUTHEAST ASIA

Tai tribes, linked by language and culture, migrated to Southeast Asia from what is now southwestern China in the first century C.E. to escape domination by the Chinese empire.

LOCALE: Southeast Asia and southern China
CATEGORIES: Expansion and land acquisition;
    prehistory and ancient cultures

SUMMARY OF EVENT

Today, various Tai peoples, also referred to as Dai, Siamese, Thai, and Lao, are settled over large areas of southwest China and Southeast Asia. They are linked by similarities of language as well as diet, architecture, and agricultural practices. The Yunnanese of southern China share many ethnic and cultural traits with the Tais to the south of China, while the other groups of people speaking dialects of Tai can be found within a few hundred miles of Guangzhou (Canton), in southern China.

Excavations suggest that Tai people lived in southwestern China as early as 1450 B.C.E., before ethnically Chinese people arrived in the area. However, the original location of the Tais remains uncertain. Theories place them in them in the Yangtze River Valley before the arrival of the Chinese, or in northern Laos or Vietnam, between the Song Hong and Song Da (Red and Black Rivers). The uncertainty comes in part from the wide dispersal of people speaking Tai languages and the Tais' long-standing tradition of absorbing elements from other cultures. Although a precise understanding of the movements of Tai peoples into Southeast Asia remains unknown and perhaps unknowable as a result of conflicting evidence from linguistic, archaeological, and historical sources, the fact remains that Tai people are today distributed over large areas in Southeast Asia and southern China.

Most probably, the Tai migration into Southeast Asia began as related groups of people, speaking a tonal language related to, yet distinct from, that of most Chinese, moved into Southeast Asia from southwestern China in several waves, beginning around 2,500 B.C.E. and continuing until as recently as the sixteenth century C.E. Southeast Asia had been inhabited by Malay peoples since before the Neolithic revolution. Malays had already been pushed south or absorbed by earlier invaders, mostly Mon and Khmer (Cambodian), from the north. The Khmer politically and ethnically dominated the region but were unable to halt the stream of Tais into the region.

An early appearance of the Tai in the historical record comes from the first century C.E. In 78 C.E., a Tai prince known as Lei Lao, whose predecessor had earlier submitted to the Chinese Han emperors, rebelled against Chinese rule. The subsequent military losses of the Tai to the Chinese led to a large migration of Tais from the Yangtze River Valley onto the Shan Plateau of what is now Myanmar (Burma). This account represents only a small portion of a long-term movement of Tai peoples to the south but was one of the first large-scale migrations. A more profound movement of Tais came a few centuries later, as population pressures from the Chinese pushed the Tais southward.

SIGNIFICANCE

From roughly the sixth century through the sixteenth century, a slow and steady movement occurred of Tais into Southeast Asia, out of the reaches of the Chinese emperors. They quickly dominated or drove out local peoples and began a process of adaption and assimilation into local environments. Many of the earlier inhabitants of the area, especially the Khmers, had been heavily influenced by Indian culture, which would later have a great impact on the Tai as they began to dominate the area. Tais became predominantly Theravāda Buddhists and adopted an Indian-based writing system and much of the Hindu conception of the world. However, Tais who remained geographically closer to China, such as those in the highlands of Vietnam and in southern China, remained more Chinese in their culture. By the early eleventh century, the Tais had established kingdoms in the northern reaches of the Chao Phraya River Valley. They then built a line of cities farther down the valley, culminating in the founding of Bangkok (Krung Thep) in the late eighteenth century near the mouth of the Chao Phraya River. The Tai continued to conquer and absorb Malay peoples farther south while confining the Khmers to a rump state of their former empire.

The movement of Tai peoples into Southeast Asia had profound impacts on the region and on the Tais themselves. Intermarriage between invading Tais and indigenous Malays and other earlier inhabitants seems to have occurred on a limited basis, with the Tai culturally and politically dominating large areas of the region. The movement of the Tai down the Chao Phraya Valley ended the domination of the Khmers over much of the region and reduced the once powerful Khmer Empire to the status of a vassal state of Siam until the French Empire absorbed Cambodia in the late nineteenth century. The strength of various Tai states in the Chao Phraya Valley prevented the Burmese from expanding to the east and created uncertainty over the docility of Tais of the Shan Plateau. The absorption by Tais of indigenous cultures, along with borrowing from Indian culture, most heavily through Buddhism, created the modern Thai cultural identity. The Thai dominated Siam (called Thailand since 1936) and Laos, while other Tai peoples ethnically dominated parts of southern China, Myanmar, and Vietnam.

—*Barry M. Stentiford*

FURTHER READING

Bellwood, P. *Prehistory of the Indo-Malaysian Archipelago*. New York: Academic Press, 1985. Although focused more on the area south of the main thrust of the Tai into Southeast Asia, it is useful for showing the impact of the arrival of the Tai on other peoples in the region.

Heidhues, Mary Somers. *Southeast Asia: A Concise History*. New York: Thames and Hudson, 2000. This is a good introduction to the history of the region from prehistory to the present. Bibliography and index.

Higham, C. *The Archaeology of Mainland Southeast Asia*. New York: Cambridge University Press, 1989. Higham presents archaeological evidence that occasionally disputes more traditional historical records of the area. Bibliography and index.

Jumsai, Manich. *Popular History of Thailand*. 5th ed. Bangkok: Chalermnit, 2000. Written by a Thai scholar for the Western reader.

Wood, W. A. R. *A History of Siam*. Bangkok: Wachrin, 1994. Useful for its inclusion of several differing theories of the geographic origins of the Tai people. Wood focuses mostly on turns of government and wars. Tables and indexes.

SEE ALSO: 6th or 5th century B.C.E., Birth of Buddhism; Early 1st century C.E., Pyu Kingdom Develops Urban Culture; 1st century-c. 627 C.E., Kingdom of Funan Flourishes.

1st-2d century C.E.
FOURTH BUDDHIST COUNCIL CONVENES

According to Mahāyāna Buddhist tradition, a fourth major gathering of Buddhist monks was held in Kashmir under the guidance of King Kanishka, and in the years following, Mahāyāna Buddhism spread throughout North and East Asia.

LOCALE: Kashmir, in northwestern India
CATEGORY: Religion

KEY FIGURES

Kanishka (first or second century-c. 154 C.E.), Indian emperor, r. c. 127-c. 152 C.E., who organized the Fourth Council

Vasumitra (fl. first-second century C.E.), Buddhist scholar, teacher, and leader of the Fourth Council according to one account

Aśvaghosa (c. 80-c. 150 C.E.), Buddhist scholar, dramatist, poet, and leader of the Fourth Council according to another account

SUMMARY OF EVENT

Soon after the death of the Buddha (Siddhārtha Gautama; c. 566-c. 486 B.C.E.), his followers began to take different approaches to his teachings. Buddhist tradition holds that about a year after the Buddha's passing, five hundred monks gathered for the First Council in order to establish Buddhist orthodoxy. Continuing variations in the practice and understanding of Buddhism led to the Second Buddhist Council at the city of Vesālī about 383 B.C.E. Although this council was directly concerned with a perceived loosening of monastic discipline, religious historians generally believe that at this council in Vesālī, early Buddhism split into two definable factions. One faction, known as the Mahāsāṅghika school, favored a liberal interpretation of Buddhist teachings and practice. The other, known in Sanskrit as the Sthavirada and in Pāli as Theravāda, favored a strict interpretation.

The gradual split into two major groups of believers continued over the centuries. According to many historical accounts, the Third Buddhist Council was held at Pataliputra in 250 B.C.E. to establish Buddhist orthodoxy. According to Theravāda (Hīnayāna) Buddhist sources, this council was held under the sponsorship of the great king Aśoka. One of the issues debated at the council concerned the reality of past and future states of consciousness. Those who were known as the Sarvāstivādins held that all such states were real. Another group, known as the Vibhajjavādins, maintained that these states of consciousness were unreal. This debate reflected the difference between those who advocated a liberal interpretation of Buddist doctrine (the Sarvāstivādins) and those who advocated a strict and narrow interpretation of the doctrine (the Vibhajjavādins). The Vibhajjavādins, identified as early Theravādins, were reported to have dominated the council. When missionaries went to other lands after the Second Buddhist Council was supposed to have been held, they carried the Theravāda version of Buddhism with them.

By the second century C.E., Buddhism had split into two schools, one of which came to flourish in Sri Lanka and Southeast Asia as a result of the missionary activities in the years following the time of the Third Buddhist Council and one of which came to predominate in North and East Asia. The Theravādins, following a strict interpretation of the religion, emphasized the Buddha as a historical individual and his enlightenment as an event in history. They viewed achieving personal enlightenment and nirvana, freedom from the chain of rebirth, as the goals of each Buddhist. Mahāyāna Buddhists, interpreting the teachings of the Buddha more broadly, saw the Buddha himself as the earthly representation of an abstract principle of enlightenment. In accordance with their views on the existence of a broad mental reality, the Mahāyāna believers maintained that beings who achieved enlightenment could continue to participate in the events of the world, instead of passing on to nirvana. Mahāyāna followers therefore rejected individual enlightenment as a goal, seeing this as selfish, and stressed the goal of the bodhisattva, the enlightened being who forgoes nirvana in order to care for others and lead others to eventual enlightenment. The final split between Theravāda and Mahāyāna Buddhism and the rise of Mahāyāna Buddhism as the religion of East Asia are usually traced to the last of the great legendary councils. This was said to have taken place in the region of Kashmir, in modern northwestern India under the direction of King Kanishka.

Kanishka was a member of the Kushan tribe of the Tatar ethnic group of Central Asia. In the first and second centuries C.E., the Kushāns ruled over what is now Afghanistan, much of the northern Indian subcontinent (now the northern parts of India and Pakistan), and large parts of Central Asia. Under Kanishka, whose rule dated from c. 127 to c. 152 C.E., the Kushān Empire reached its greatest power and territorial extension. During his rule, Kanishka converted to Buddhism, echoing the earlier conversion of Aśoka. The records report that Kanishka built many *viharas*, or Buddhist temples, in northwestern

India. The archaeological remains of temples attributed to him have been found, particularly in the area of Harvana Lake. As a powerful ruler in a central location, Kanishka maintained contacts with other major empires. He was in communication with the Roman Empire. The Gandhara school of art, showing Greco-Roman influences on the representation of images of the Buddha, flourished during his reign. Kanishka's links to the Chinese empire may have encouraged the movement of Buddhism into China and into areas of the Chinese cultural sphere.

Kanishka is reported to have followed the example of Aśoka in the promotion of Buddhism, as well as in the conversion to the faith. The Kushān king is supposed to have organized the Fourth Buddhist Council. It was also supposed to have begun efforts to promote the faith, just as the earlier council had. However, while an early form of Theravāda Buddhism had emerged victorious from the Third Buddhist Council, Mahāyāna Buddhism had the upper hand at the fourth. Perhaps for this reason, Theravāda Buddhists generally do not recognize the council in Kashmir. There are also questions about whether Kanishka really was the organizer and supporter of this event.

The seventh century Chinese writer Xundang (Hsüntang) is one of the most complete sources of information about the Fourth Buddhist Council and Kanishka's supposed role in it. Xundang reported that Kanishka was concerned about the conflicting sects within Buddhism. To reconcile the differences, according to this source, the king called a council modeled on the earlier ones, especially on the council at Pataliputra that had been convened by Aśoka. Monks of different schools gathered, and 499 of them were selected to represent the faith.

Xundang wrote that Kanishka built a special temple for the gathering, and Vasumitra, of the Sarvāstivādin school, became president. Under Vasumitra's leadership, the council members wrote commentaries on the *Tipiṭaka* (compiled c. 250 B.C.E.; English translation in *Buddhist Scriptures*, 1913), the three sacred books that make up the core of the Buddhist sacred writings. Kanishka had artisans engrave these commentaries on red copper sheets and built a stupa, a dome-shaped Buddhist monument, over them.

Because Xundang was writing so long after the events, his account is open to question. It may be that Kanishka was connected to the council in an effort to draw parallels between the life of the Kushān ruler and that of Aśoka. According to another version of the story of the council, it was summoned not by Kanishka but by the poet and dramatist Aśvaghosa. In this version, the council met for twelve years under Aśvaghosa's leadership. At the end of this time, the council is said to have completed the *Mahāvibhāsa* (compiled c. 100 C.E.; great commentary), a compilation of Sarvāstivādin doctrines. In other accounts of the Fourth Buddhist Council, Aśvaghosa was a councilor of Kanishka, and the association with the king led the dramatist to serve as vice president under Vasumitra. The surviving texts of the *Mahāvibhāsa* do not mention Kanishka, a fact that would be puzzling if it had been composed at a council sponsored by Kanishka.

Missionary activities were supposed to have followed the council. These took Buddhism farther from India, particularly to the north and northeast. Over the centuries, the efforts to spread Buddhism begun at the council brought the religion to China, Mongolia, Manchuria, Korea, Vietnam, and Tibet. In all of these countries, the predominant form of the religion was Mahāyāna Buddhism, as the Sarvāstivādin school that reportedly predominated at the Fourth Buddhist Council came to be called.

SIGNIFICANCE

Although there are questions about Kanishka's personal involvement in the Fourth Buddhist Council, it is evident that this was a critical period in the history of Buddhism. In earlier Buddhism, the Theravāda school tended to be stronger, and the time of the Fourth Buddhist Council marks the rise of the Mahāyāna approach. Moreover, the missionary activities that began at this time eventually brought Mahāyāna Buddhism to a huge section of Asia. It is reasonable then to identify the Third Buddhist Council as the symbolic beginning of the spread of Theravāda Buddhism in the south and the Fourth Buddhist Council as the symbolic beginning of the spread of Mahāyāna Buddhism in the north. From the time of the Fourth Buddhist Council onward, the Buddhist world would be definitively divided into two in both geography and doctrine.

—*Carl L. Bankston III*

FURTHER READING

Mitchell, Donald W. *Buddhism: Introducing the Buddhist Experience.* New York: Oxford University Press, 2002. A good general introduction to Buddhism that has chapters on its origins in India and on Mahāyāna and Theravāda Buddhism. Particularly recommended for those seeking to understand the distinctions between those two major approaches to Buddhism.

Rosenfeld, John M. *The Dynastic Arts of the Kushāns.* Berkeley: University of California Press, 1967. An art history book that contains an excellent discussion of Kanishka's life, of his representation in the arts, and of the question of his association with the Fourth Council.

Takeuchi, Yoshinori, Jan van Bragt, James W. Heisig, and James S. O'Leary, eds. *Buddhist Spirituality: Indian, Southeast Asian, Tibetan, and Early Chinese.* New York: Crossroad, 1993. A collection of studies on early Indian Buddhist spirituality, on Theravāda Buddhist practices, and on the rise of Mahāyāna in early Chinsese Buddhism.

Thakur, Manoj K. *India in the Age of Kanishka.* Rev. ed. Delhi: Worldview Publications, 1999. A general work on the historical era of the great Kushān ruler.

SEE ALSO: 6th or 5th century B.C.E., Birth of Buddhism; c. 273/265-c. 238 B.C.E., Aśoka Reigns over India; c. 250 B.C.E., Third Buddhist Council Convenes; c. 250 B.C.E., *Tipiṭaka* Is Compiled; c. 247-207 B.C.E., Buddhism Established in Sri Lanka; c. 1st century B.C.E., Indian Buddhist Nuns Compile the *Therigatha*; 1st century B.C.E.-1st century C.E., Compilation of the *Lotus Sutra*; c. 60-68 C.E., Buddhism Enters China.

RELATED ARTICLES in *Great Lives from History: The Ancient World*: Aśoka; Aśvaghosa; Buddha; Kanishka; Dēvānaṃpiya Tissa; Vattagamani.

1 - 100 C.E.

1st-3d centuries C.E.
CAṄKAM LITERATURE COMPOSED IN SOUTH INDIA

The early Caṅkam literature is poignant, often beautiful, and, most important, a relatively pure representation of Tamil culture before it was influenced significantly by northern Aryan culture.

LOCALE: Tamilnadu, South India
CATEGORY: Literature

SUMMARY OF EVENT

Caṅkam, or Śangam, refers to the earliest stratum of Tamil literature. According to legend, it was the product of an academy of poets who met under the patronage of Pāndyan kings; however, in truth, there were several patrons, including Chēra and Chola royalty. The poems were classified into two groups according to sentiment. The first were composed of *akam*, or interior, poems, usually about love or life as seen from within the family. The second type, *puram*, or exterior, poems, referred to life outside the family. *Puram* poetry dealt with such subjects as good or evil actions, war, and community or kingdom. Such public poetry celebrated the ferocity or the glory of a king, lamented the death of heroes, and mourned the poverty of poets, war, and tragic events. The two types of poems were directed to the two realms of the sacred in Tamil society, namely married life and kingship. To develop or enhance the sacred power (*aṇaṅku*) of the king, praise was given to the beat of loud drums. Love and marriage were sacred, and particular importance was placed on a woman's chastity. *Akam* poems encouraged proper behavior to protect the sacred *aṇaṅku* inherent in women.

Generally, *akam* poetry is synonymous with love poetry. The category is subdivided into two aspects: the *kalavu* and *karpu*. *Kalavu* refers to the period in which people prepare for marriage and addresses such themes as the union of hearts, trysts, meetings arranged by friends of either party, and elopement. The second aspect, *karpu*, refers to life after marriage and ideal domestic relations. Typical themes are cordial love relations, quarrels (particularly if the husband strays), reconciliation, separation, return of the husband, and the advent of the monsoon season, the best season for love. The two main aspects are subdivided further into the seven *tiṇai*, or behavioral patterns, which include unrequited love, mismatched love, and well-matched love.

The earliest Caṅkam literature consists of a group of eight anthologies of poetry referred to as the *Eṭṭuttokai*

(the eight anthologies). The dating of the material is debated among specialists, but most agree that the *Eṭṭuttokai* were composed primarily between the first and third centuries C.E. The works contain collections of poems on various topics that also are important resources for the study of Tamil history and customs, trade and commerce, economic and domestic life, various legends, and matters of love. The 740 poets who contributed to the eight collections include people of different backgrounds, with various trades, and from a number of communities. Many poets, themselves from a high class, composed in a form of oral poetry popular among the lower classes, and therefore the poems provide a comprehensive view of the language and customs of Tamil society. The earliest work was compiled at a time before any significant Aryan influence infiltrated the region; therefore, the poems are devoid of any particularly Brahmanical proclivities.

The *Eṭṭuttokai* poets came from diverse backgrounds. Some were members of royal families, and even a few women were included as contributors. The poet Naṇmullaiayār from Allur was famous for her lively descriptions of domestic life and delicate feelings. The woman poet Kākkai Pāḍiniyar wrote a poem about a crow extending invitations to guests by its cawing. It is recorded that the Chēra king Āḍu Kōṭpāṭṭu-ch-Chēralāḍaṇ rewarded her well for the popular composition. The very famous poet Kapilar was known for his loyal support of his friend, a chieftain whose cause he supported in opposition to three kings. His brilliant and imaginative poems concern both *akam* and *puram* subjects. Kōvūr Kiḷār championed humanitarian concerns in his poetry. For example, he pleaded with a king not to have elephants trample the young son of an enemy king. Another poet of note is Māmūlaṇār, whose twenty-nine poems have many historical references.

The eight anthologies reflect a broad and accurate picture of early Tamil social life and customs in a way that Sanskrit literature does not. The eight anthologies are *Narriṇai*, *Kurondokai*, *Aiṅkuṟunuṟu*, *Padiṟṟuppatta*, *Paripāḍal*, *Kalittokai*, *Akanāṉūṟu*, and *Puranāṉṉūṟu*.

The *Narriṇai* should consist of four hundred short poems, but one is missing. All verses are composed of nine to twelve lines and deal with love. The collection represents the work of 175 poets with an additional invocation by Pāradam Pāḍiya Perundēvaṇār. The collection was put together by the Pāndyan king Paṇṇāḍu Tanda Māran

Vaḷudi. The *Naṟṟiṇai* may date to the late second to early third century C.E.

The *Kurundokai* consists of 401 poems of four to eight lines each. The subject of the poems is *akam*. The collection represents the work of 205 different poets; ten verses are anonymous. Poet Pāradam Pāḍiya Perundēvaṇār contributed the invocatory stanza to Murukan. The anthology was compiled by Pūrikkō and may date to the early third century C.E.

The *Aiṅkuṟunuṟu* is possibly the earliest of the eight anthologies and may be dated to c. 100 C.E. The collection consists of five hundred short poems on love, between three and six lines each. There is also an invocation to the god Śiva by Pāradam Pāḍiya Perundēvaṇār. The work was divided into five sections by five famous poets: "Ōramobōkiyār," "Ammūvaṇ," "Kapilar," "Ōdalāndaiyār," and "Pēyaṇ." The first hundred poems dealt with the *marudam* aspect of love, or the love quarrel; the second hundred with the *neydal*, or pining for one's love; the third with *kuriñchi*, or the union of lovers; the fourth with *pālai*, or separation; and the last with *mullai*, or patient waiting. The poems were collected by Kūḍalūr Kiḷār at the insistence of the Chēra king Māndaraṇ Chēral Irumoṟai.

The *Padiṟṟuppatta* is divided into ten sections of ten poems each. The individual poems praise ten Chēra kings. As the works exists today, the first and last sections are missing. The *Padiṟṟuppatta* is an extremely valuable storehouse of historical facts about the ancient Chēra kings and the customs and manners of the people over whom they ruled. The eight surviving sections have been attributed to different poets. It is noted that the poets were rewarded well by the patron kings.

The twenty-four poems of the *Paripāḍal* were written by thirteen poets. Some of the work has been lost; originally it was said to have seventy poems. The subject of the remaining poems is mainly love. A colophon under each poem gives the author's name along with the name of the musician who set it to music and the melody in which the poem was set. One of the poets who contributed to the anthology was the well-known Nallanduvaṇar.

The *Kalittokai* took its name from the *kali* meter, in which all the poems were composed. The poems deal with incidents of love in the form of dialogues. The work has 150 poems including the stanza invoking Śiva by Perundēvaṇar, and the collection was compiled by Nallanduvaṇar. Five different authors, including the famous Kapilar, contributed to the collection as it stands today, although some specialists believe there were more contributors. The dating of the text is highly debated; some

of the poems may date to the second century B.C.E., and others may be as late as the sixth century C.E.

Akanānūṟu, also called *Neḍuntokai*, consists of four hundred poems on love with an introductory poem of invocation. The length of the poems varies from thirteen to thirty-three lines. The compilers, Uruttiracaṇmaṇ with the help of the Pāndyan king Ukkirapperuvaḷudi, assembled the work of 143 poets. There is an invocation to Śiva by Perundēvaṇār. The work was classified into three parts: *Kaḷirriyānai Nirai* (the array of male elephants), *Maṇimiḍai Pavaḷam* (string of corals interspersed with gems), and *Nittkilak Kōvai* (necklace of pearls). The anthology probably dates from the early third century C.E.

The *Puranāṇṇūru* has four hundred poems, all of which are concerned with the *puram* (war) theme. The anthology's 165 poets included kings and women. In ancient Tamil society, poets seemed to give advice to rulers on the subject of war. For example, they often intervened between angry kings and advised them. Poets were regarded as wise as well as practical and influential. Mainly the poems in the anthology are about the kings, feudatory chieftains, ministers, and warriors of the three Tamil countries. Some 139 patrons were mentioned in the poems. The *Puranāṇṇūru* is of particular historical value in that it records sentiments and facts about ancient Tamil life.

SIGNIFICANCE

The early Caṅkam poems were written during a period in which Brahmanism was not prevalent in the Tamil region. Thus, the rich language reveals more than profound sentiment; it also conveys extremely important facts about a culture that was submerged and altered in later centuries by the migrations of northern Aryans, who brought their own culture.

—*Katherine Anne Harper*

FURTHER READING

Hart, George L., III. *The Poems of Ancient Tamil: Their Milieu and Their Sanskrit Counterparts.* Berkeley: University of California Press, 1975. An excellent study of the early Caṅkam poetry with historical and literary analysis. Bibliography.

Hart, George, and Hank Heifetz, trans. and eds. *The Four Hundred Songs of War and Wisdom: An Anthology of Poems from Classical Tamil, the Puranuru.* New York: Columbia University, 1999. A translation of the *Puranāṇṇūru.* Provides information on Tamil poetry.

Marialesvam, Abraham. *The Song of Songs and Ancient Tamil Love Poems.* Rome: Editrice Pontificio Istituto Biblico, 1988. An interesting comparative study that

1 - 100 C.E.

looks at the love poems of the Bible and those of the ancient Tamils. Bibliography.

Nilakanta Sastri, A. K. *A History of South India from Prehistoric Times to the Fall of the Vijayanagar.* 4th ed. Madras: Oxford University Press, 1976. The author provides a thorough essay on the historical and social background of the Caṅkam age and also includes some discussion of the literature. Bibliography.

Zvelebil, Kamil. *Lexicon of Tamil Literature.* New York: E. J. Brill, 1995. A general work explaining Tamil terms.

SEE ALSO: c. 200 B.C.E.-200 C.E., *Bhagavad Gita* Is Created; Early 1st century B.C.E.-225 C.E., Sātavāhana Dynasty Rises to Power in South India; c. 1st century B.C.E., Indian Buddhist Nuns Compile the *Therigatha*.

1st-5th centuries C.E.
ALANI GAIN POWER

The Alani, adept at assimilation and integration, never developed a kingdom but became federated with other groups and spearheaded the movement of peoples westward into the Roman Empire.

LOCALE: Caspian Sea to Lusitania (present-day Portugal)

CATEGORY: Expansion and land acquisition

SUMMARY OF EVENT

The Alani were a loose alliance of various nomadic Indo-Iranian tribes originally from north of the Caspian Sea. They did not live in contiguous areas but were spread out in the region. They developed an identity from a mixture of different peoples joined together by virtue of their similar lifestyles, weapons, and appearance. An opportunistic rabble, they collected peoples they overcame and formed a single fearsome unit when threatened or attacking other peoples.

They were related to the Sarmatians and were described by the Roman historian Ammianus Marcellinus (330-395 C.E.) as nomads, formerly called the Massagetae, who moved about in wagons that were their permanent homes, driving their cattle before them and augmenting their diet with wild fruit. They also hunted extensively, aided by their expert hunting dogs, *Canis alani*, and used the skins of their prey as clothing and the bones and teeth as tools and ornaments.

When they camped, they put their wagons in a circle and worshiped a sword driven into the ground, which served as the image of the god of war. They divined the future by throwing down straight twigs while reciting secret incantations and examining the twigs' relative positions—something like the Chinese divination practices described in the *Yijing* (eighth to third century B.C.E.; English translation, 1876; also known as *Book of Changes*,

1986). They did not have slaves and chose as their leaders warriors of the greatest experience and success. They were expert horsemen and wore light armor, which allowed them quick movement. Described as equal to the Huns in fierceness and fighting ability but somewhat more civilized, they were tall and almost always had yellow or blond hair.

They gained influence and power in the first century C.E. by attacking the Parthians. The Jewish historian Flavius Josephus (c. 37-c. 100 C.E.) reports that they conducted border raids on Roman territory but without much success. The Alani did not make much of a distinction between enemies but always could ally themselves as friends with former enemies if their situation changed.

They are mentioned by Roman writers as early as Seneca the Younger (c. 4 B.C.E.-65 C.E.), but the Romans did not seem to have serious military contact with them until the Roman general Arrian (c. 85-c. 155 C.E.) fought them after they had invaded Cappadocia in 135 C.E. He noted that the Alani would move back in the face of an attack to draw in the enemy's infantry; then Alani horsemen would swiftly attack the flank, a tactic known as a "feigned retreat." They gained a reputation as great fighters and horsemen from these encounters, and Arrian was so impressed that he wrote about them, although unfortunately his work survives only in fragments.

At the end of the third century, when the Huns started to move against their neighbors, the Alani were defeated but made a treaty with the Huns (some of the Alani even joined the Huns). Divided and dispersed, some groups settled with the Goths in Pannonia (now western Hungary and eastern Austria), and later others joined with the Vandals and crossed into Noricum (now central Austria and southern Bavaria). Another group sought refuge in the Caucasus region and remained there.

In the late fourth century, the Alani were an important part of the army of the Roman emperor Gratian (359-383 C.E.). He showed them such favor that the other troops rebelled and elevated Magnus Maximus (r. 383-388 C.E.) as emperor. Alani were also a component of the army of Valentinian II (371-392 C.E.), further indicating their ability to collaborate when it suited them.

In 406, one of the western groups invaded Gaul with the Vandals and Suevi, crossing the Rhine and defeating the Franks. Others joined with the Romans, but the main group stayed with the Vandals and Suevi, plundering their way through Gaul; in 408, they pushed into Spain and settled in Lusitania (now Portugal). In 418, these Alani were defeated by the Visigoths, and the survivors joined again with the Vandals, where they became such an integral part of that tribe that their kings were titled *rex Vandalorum et Alanorum* (king of the Vandals and the Alanis). This group eventually moved into northern Africa, where they remained until conquered by the armies of the Byzantine emperor Justinian I (483-565) in the sixth century.

During the fifth century, the Alani who had remained in Gaul had been assimilated by the Visigoths and the local populations. Evidence of their presence survives in some modern French place-names, such as Alaincourt. The Alani who had gone west and joined with the Goths and Vandals adopted the customs and ways of their allies and lost much of their own culture, which underwent considerable change in the new environments of Gaul, Spain, and Africa. In the east, Alani troops were an important military force in the armies of the eastern empire, where they were used to fight against their former allies the Huns.

SIGNIFICANCE

Because the Alani were able to integrate themselves into the armies of stronger forces, they not only increased the power of those forces but also influenced the outcomes of many battles raging across Europe from the first to the fifth century C.E., which eventually contributed to the fall of the Roman Empire in 476 C.E. After the fifth century they are mentioned briefly by some Byzantine authors, such as Procopius (fl. early sixth century) and Menander Protector (fl. sixth century), and are considered to be the ancestors of the Ossetians who live east of the Black Sea.

—*Brian Hancock*

FURTHER READING

Alemany, Agustí. *Sources on the Alans: A Critical Compilation.* Boston: E. J. Brill, 2000. A valuable collection of primary documents and extant records on the Alani from their first appearance through the fifteenth century C.E.

Ammianus Marcellinus. *The Later Roman Empire, A.D. 354-378.* Translated by Walter Hamilton. New York: Penguin Books, 1986. The basic primary source for the history of the Alani in the west.

Bachrach, Bernard S. *A History of the Alans in the West.* Minneapolis: University of Minnesota Press, 1973. The best secondary source for the study of the Alani, with an extensive bibliography.

Matthews, John. *The Roman Empire of Ammianus.* Baltimore, Md.: The Johns Hopkins University Press, 1989. A wonderful study on the historian Ammianus and his great work on the later empire.

Procopius of Caesarea. *History of the Wars.* Translated by H. B. Dewing. 7 vols. Cambridge, Mass.: Harvard University Press, 1924. The primary source for research on the reign of Justinian and his wars against the barbarians.

Sulimirski, T. *The Sarmatians.* New York: Praeger, 1970. A good secondary source on the Sarmatians, who were closely related to the Alani.

SEE ALSO: 445-453 C.E., Invasions of Attila the Hun; September 4, 476 C.E., Fall of Rome.

RELATED ARTICLES in *Great Lives from History: The Ancient World:* Flavius Josephus; Seneca the Younger.

1 - 100 C.E.

1st century-c. 627 C.E.
KINGDOM OF FUNAN FLOURISHES

In the first century C.E. in the Mekong Delta region and the southern coast of Cambodia and Vietnam, the Funan civilization emerged, apparently a predecessor of the eleventh century Angkor, or Khmer, civilization.

LOCALE: Funan (now in Cambodia, Vietnam, Malay Peninsula)
CATEGORY: Prehistory and ancient cultures

KEY FIGURES
Kaundinya (fl. first century C.E.), legendary founder of Funan
Fan Shih-man (fl. third century C.E.), military leader of Funan

SUMMARY OF EVENT

Neolithic peoples of modern Cambodia appear to have come from India, southern China, and elsewhere in Southeast Asia. The first known civilization of this region arose in the first century C.E., formed by a people who probably were from the Khmer branch of the Mon-Khmer people, who had migrated into Southeast Asia from southwest China or from the Khasi Hills in northwest India as early as 2000 B.C.E. What is known of them is from second century Chinese chroniclers, who referred to them as the Funan (the Chinese rendering of B'iu-nam) as well as modern excavations at sites such as Oc Eo.

According to legend, the founder of the state of Funan was Kaundinya, who sailed up the Mekong River in the first century C.E., guided by a dream about his destiny. When he arrived at a place near modern-day Phnom Penh, Cambodia, the queen of the country, Liu-yeh, tried but failed to seize his ship. He then married her and founded a dynasty that ruled for nearly two centuries. The place where he arrived is known as the sacred mountain, and Liu-yeh is often called the Naga princess, or princess of the snake goddess Naga. Kaundinya's origins are unknown, although he might have come from India, as he is attributed with having brought Indianization to the region.

The original settlements were between Chaudoc and Phnom Penh. The first capital city was Vyadhapura, which is near Banam and the Ba Phnom hill in the current Cambodian province of Prey Veng. Later, the capital moved to Angkor Borei, a walled city on the margin of the Mekong Delta. Oc Eo, Funan's port city, was 55 miles (90 kilometers) south of Angkor Borei. At Oc Eo, ar-

chaeologists have found a large urban settlement, with a network of canals extending more than 120 miles (200 kilometers) that irrigated rice fields. Some canals drained swamps and some were connected to the sea, the latter permitting calm navigation that bypassed the Gulf of Siam en route to the Malay Peninsula. Oc Eo was a cosmopolitan trade center; commercial relations existed as far away as Persia, though most trade was with India. Oc Eo's Malay culture coexisted with other cultures, mostly influenced by India. As traders, the Funanese kept records and developed a unique written language based on Mon-Khmer. Funan was known for piracy as well as trading, and traders plundered wherever they could.

Excavations at Angkor Borei and Oc Eo reveal that Funan had several walled cities containing palaces and dwelling houses. The king's palace had a tiered roof, still common in Cambodia and Thailand. Houses of commoners were built on piles that afforded protection from annual monsoon floods; the roofs consisted of bamboo leaves. Settlements were fortified with wooden palisades.

The Funanese were dark-skinned, frizzy-haired people. Women put their heads through a hole in a fold of cloth, and their hair was knotted. Men wore the sampot, a piece of cloth tied around the waist. Contemporary Cambodians still practice many Funanese customs in matters of dress. The national sports were cockfighting and pigfighting. Families bathed together in large tanks. Trial was by ordeal.

Funan adapted artistic and cultural traditions from India that persist to the present, including the legends of the Naga princess and the sacred mountain. The multiheaded snake goddess, the Naga, is memorialized in statuary now found throughout much of Southeast Asia. Although Buddhism was practiced and is now the state religion of Cambodia, Hinduism was also common in Funan; the official religion by the sixth century C.E. was Saivite, which involved worship of the stars in the sky. Excavations at Angkor Borei and Oc Eo reveal that many Buddhas were carved in a distinctive Funanese style. Sky gods were carved in brass with two heads and four arms or even four heads and eight arms, replicas of which are available for sale in Cambodia today. Other jewelry was manufactured, including gold replicas of Roman coins used as pendants. The Funanese also manufactured an orange pottery.

Funan went on to become the first great power in mainland Southeast Asia. The vast irrigation works enabled agricultural plenty in rice, and the kingdom expanded as the well-fed population increased. As a trading port, Oc Eo was a cosmopolitan center, host to many cultures, languages, and peoples and a recipient of precious minerals and stones that were made into jewelry. However, Oc Eo declined as ships bypassed the inland port to sail beyond the Mekong Delta. One of Kaundinya's grandsons decided to turn over the conduct of state affairs to Fan Shih-man, who in turn built a fleet, attacked ten kingdoms, and established vassal states along the Mekong from Tonle Sap, the lake that receives the floodwaters of the Mekong River, to the Mekong Delta. During its apogee, Funan occupied the territory from what is now southern Cambodia and Vietnam through most of the Malay Peninsula, and the vassal states paid tribute.

SIGNIFICANCE

One of Funan's vassal states, Chenla, occupied what is now northern Cambodia and southern Laos. In the middle of the sixth century C.E., Chenla rebelled against its status as vassal to Funan, conquered the capital of Funan, and assumed dominance in the region. Funan then moved the capital south.

The two kingdoms of Chenla and Funan coexisted until 627 C.E., when Chenla annexed Funan. Chenla then continued conquests westward toward Thailand into the region that was to become the center of the Angkor Kingdom. However, Chenla was wracked by civil war and there was a split in 706 between Upper (Land) Chenla and Lower (Water) Chenla.

At the end of the eighth century C.E., Javanese pirates attacked the coastline of Chenla and occupied some of the Mekong Delta islands, marking the decline of Chenla. In 802, a military commander from Java consolidated control over Chenla territories on behalf of the kingdom of Angkor, which he proclaimed as an independent state. Angkor, thus, absorbed Chenla. In 877, the ruler of Angkor chose as his queen a member of the royal line of both the Funan and Chenla kingdoms. Accordingly, Angkor, the precursor to the present state of Cambodia, may be said to have grown out of both Chenla and Funan.

—*Michael Haas*

FURTHER READING

Briggs, Lawrence Palmer. *The Ancient Khmer Empire.* Philadelphia: American Philosophical Society, 1951. Reprint. Bangkok: White Lotus Press, 1999. A fascinating account of the early years of the Cambodian state.

Chandler, David P. *A History of Cambodia.* 3d ed. Boulder, Colo.: Westview Press, 2000. A history of Cambodia, including a chapter on the beginnings (from c. 2000 B.C.E.) and a bibliographic essay. Illustrations, maps.

Dega, Michael F. *Prehistoric Circular Earthworks of Cambodia.* Oxford, England: Archaeopress, 2002. Aimed at archaeologists and anthropologists, this work examines the function and timing of Cambodian earthworks and sites, casting light on the very early peoples of Cambodia and Vietnam. Includes 51 tables; 29 figures, plans, photographs, and drawings; 10 maps; and 10 appendices.

Hall, D. G. E. *A History of South-East Asia.* 3d ed. London: Macmillan, 1968. A detailed history of how modern Southeast Asia emerged from the earliest origins, with sections on Cambodia and its precursors. Illustrations, maps, and a detailed bibliography.

Higham, Charles. *The Civilization of Angkor.* London: Weidenfeld and Nicolson, 2001. The preeminent archaeologist concentrating in Southeast Asia reports on the latest archaeological evidence of Angkor and its predecessors, including Funan, where reports are often ambiguous or contradictory. Illustrations, photographs, and a glossary.

SEE ALSO: Early 1st century C.E., Pyu Kingdom Develops Urban Culture; 1st century C.E., Tai Peoples Migrate into Southeast Asia; 40-43 C.E., Trung Sisters Lead Vietnamese Rebellion Against Chinese.

1 - 100 C.E.

c. 1 C.E.
DEVELOPMENT BEGINS AT TEOTIHUACÁN

The construction of monumental religious and civic architecture, coupled with population growth at Teotihuacán, witnessed the Americas' first great experiment in urbanization and state formation.

LOCALE: Teotihuacán, Mexico, and the Central Mexican plateau

CATEGORIES: Prehistory and ancient cultures; architecture

SUMMARY OF EVENT

Ancient Teotihuacán, situated in an offshoot of the Valley of Mexico, the Teotihuacán Valley, encompasses an area of about 190 square miles (about 500 square kilometers). Perhaps one-half of the valley is arable. Water from a dozen springs, the small watercourse of the San Juan River, and rainfall provided the necessary moisture for this agricultural society. As the urban center enlarged and nutritional demands increased, the river was harnessed for canal irrigation.

The site had many advantages. It was close to sources of obsidian (a razor-sharp volcanic glass) and to trade routes, it was surrounded by good agricultural land, and the location also held religious significance. A natural cave, 330 feet (100 meters) long and later modified, provided a focus for religious ritual and the mythological past. Any understanding of the social, political, and architectural achievement at Teotihuacán requires an appreciation of the religious power exercised by the site. In ancient Mesoamerican tradition, caves provided the entry to the underworld, a region rich in spirit life and fertility. According to the local mythology, both the Sun and the Moon were born at Teotihuacán. Water was artificially channeled into the sacred cave. The sacred nature of Teotihuacán manifested in water ceremonialism that united all these mythological associations.

The Pyramid of the Sun, positioned 20 feet (6 meters) over the cave, was constructed on the east side of the main concourse, the Street of the Dead, between 1 C.E. and 150 C.E. The great pyramid is about 700 feet (215 meters) on each side, rising to slightly more than 200 feet (60 meters). It is a rubble-filled structure containing more than 1.3 million cubic yards (1 million cubic meters) of material. The smaller Pyramid of the Moon is situated at the northern end of the Street of the Dead. This dominant thoroughfare traverses the city on a north-south axis, 15.5 degrees east of north. The Street of the Dead extends about 3 miles (5 kilometers), although only

about one-half of its length has been excavated. Another major avenue bisects the Street of the Dead, dividing the city into quarters. In addition to the great pyramids, seventy-five temples, palace compounds, and administrative complexes line the Street of the Dead. Ultimately, by 500 C.E. the urban grid encompassed 8 square miles (20 square kilometers).

The Teotihuacán Mapping Project, headed by René Millon of the University of Rochester, one of the significant archaeological projects of the twentieth century, was undertaken during the 1960's and 1970's. Millon and his team discovered that the majority of the urban area comprised residential apartment compounds. Of the two thousand recognized compounds, about one hundred have been excavated. These structures would have housed twenty to one hundred individuals. The compounds, about 165 to 200 feet (50 to 60 meters) on each side, appear to have contained kin-based groups or groups who cooperated in similar productive pursuits. The majority of these compound structures were single-storied. Construction consisted of a rubble or brick wall faced with stones set in clay and coated with a lime plaster mixture. The residential compounds were constructed during the mid-third century C.E., which seems to provide a terminal date for major building projects.

The city appears to have contained distinctive ethnic barrios or neighborhoods. These kin-based groups carried out different forms of craft production within the many workshops found throughout the city. Workshops turned out manufactured goods for internal use and trade: obsidian tools, ceramic vessels and figurines, baskets, articles made of feathers or precious stones, and other goods. At the end of the first century C.E., perhaps one-quarter of the population was involved in craft production of some form. Presumably artists were in demand, given the sophisticated murals in palaces and temples and the stone sculpture that adorned temple complexes.

During the first century C.E., massive movements of population from the eastern and southern Valley of Mexico swelled the population of urban Teotihuacán. The city achieved maximum size about 500 C.E., with a population estimated between 125,000 to 200,000 individuals. The reason for this population concentration remains unknown.

The rise in occupational specialization channeled individuals away from the agrarian economy, thereby necessitating increased food production on the part of those who remained. Staple foods included the Mesoamerican triad of maize, beans, and squash, as well as amaranth and cactuses such as nopal. Hunting remained important in the Teotihuacán Valley: The only domesticated fauna were the turkey and the dog, both of which were consumed.

Archaeological work revealed evidence of trade between Teotihuacán and other regions of Mesoamerica. Small figurines exhibiting a particular facial and body style were mass-produced by the thousands and were part of the ceramic trade.

Art motifs and decorations from Teotihuacán are decidedly religious. Religious symbols are found throughout the city and adorn civic structures as well as temples, which again suggests the powerful religious forces extant in Teotihuacán society. Religious motifs and symbols from Teotihuacán have been identified at the sites of

Tikal (in modern Guatemala) and Copán (in modern Honduras).

The sophisticated grid pattern of the city reflects the high levels of precision and mathematical skill possessed by the ancient Teotihuacanos. Numerous astronomers have suggested that a strong relationship exists between astronomy and the monumental religious and administrative architecture positioned along the Street of the Dead.

The coercive mechanisms required to bring together enormous amounts of human energy, a prerequisite for the construction of the great edifices, remain a mystery. Collective labor harnessed through a powerful religious system would appear to be a key in understanding the political apparatus that controlled Teotihuacán during the centuries of its growth. It may be erroneous, however, to assume that the power base was theocratic in the conventional meaning of the term.

Elaborate carvings at Teotihuacán. (Corbis)

1 - 100 C.E.

Various groups exhibited differential access to nutritional resources that impact both health and life expectancy. Life expectancy for the poorer groups seldom exceeded age thirty. Great gaps separated social elites from the lower strata of society. Differential access to power, prestige, and wealth is evidenced in skeletal materials, in the practice of human sacrifice, and in residential compounds. Subordination is evidenced in art. The deliberate and planned bringing together of wide categories of people into an urban area was a first in the Americas.

After 1 C.E., Teotihuacán's commercial power extended beyond the heartland of the Central Plateau. The city exercised significant influence in trade as far south as modern Guatemala, as well as the Gulf Coast and lowland regions. The expansion may have involved military activity to some degree, or it may have been entirely peaceful, tied to trade and religious symbolism. Certainly Teotihuacán lacked defensive fortifications, arguing against a militaristic society, although some building complexes within the city were walled. One of these was the 38-acre (15.5-hectare) Citadel, or Ciudadela, a massive religious center containing the renowned Temple of the Feathered Serpent. Overall, the area directly controlled by the Teotihuacán polity was about 10,000 square miles (about 25,000 square kilometers). The total population in this region has been estimated at between 300,000 and 500,000 people.

During the seventh century C.E., the commercial and political influence that the city had exercised for centuries gradually declined. The reasons for the burning and destruction of the city at the beginning of the eighth century remain imperfectly understood.

SIGNIFICANCE

The visible archaeological complexes at Teotihuacán evidence a multitalented, future-oriented, self-confident people who created the first large-scale, socially stratified urban community in the Americas. Here, deliberate, long-range urban planning, hydraulic agriculture, complex mathematical skills, and architectural principles coalesced to evolve a series of innovative firsts for the New World. The precise shape of its interconnected political and religious structure remains a mystery. The scale and

success of Teotihuacán become even more apparent when it is realized that the Teotihuacanos lacked draft animals, the wheel, and metal tools, which would have facilitated both urban construction and the productive economy. Teotihuacán is without precedent in New World archaeology.

—Rene M. Descartes

FURTHER READING

Berrin, Kathleen, and Ester Pasztory, eds. *Teotihuacán: Art from the City of the Gods*. New York: Thames and Hudson, 1994. A lavishly illustrated collection of articles by principal investigators. Bibliography.

Linné, Sigvald. *Archaeological Researches at Teotihuacán, Mexico*. Tuscaloosa: University of Alabama Press, 2003. Data and analysis from the first excavations at Teotihuacán in 1932. Particularly valuable for the ethnographic research concurrently carried out among the local population, providing remnants of cultural continuity with the city's inhabitants.

Millon, René. "Teotihuacán: City, State, Civilization." In *Handbook of Middle American Indians*. Supp. 1, *Archaeology*, edited by Victoria Bricker and Jeremy Sabloff. Austin: University of Texas Press, 1981. A concise summation of what was known at the time of writing about the ancient city-state. Bibliography, index.

_____. *The Teotihuacán Map, Parts 1 and 2*. Austin: University of Texas Press, 1973. One of the great modern achievements of archaeological survey and excavation. Bibliography, indexes, maps.

Pasztory, Esther. *Teotihuacán: An Experiment in Living*. Norman: University of Oklahoma Press, 1997. A comprehensive and compelling examination of the various art forms from Teotihuacán. Bibliography, index.

SEE ALSO: c. 500 B.C.E.-c. 700 C.E., Zapotecs Build Monte Albán; c. 300 B.C.E., Izapan Civilization Dominates Mesoamerica; c. 100 B.C.E.-c. 200 C.E., Zapotec State Dominates Oaxaca; 90 C.E., Founding of the Classic Period Maya Royal Dynasty at Tikal.

8 C.E.
OVID'S *METAMORPHOSES* IS PUBLISHED

Ovid's epic of change, the Metamorphoses, *provided what became the best-known poetic accounts of Rome's gods, heroes, and history to the death of Julius Caesar.*

LOCALE: Rome (now in Italy)
CATEGORY: Literature

KEY FIGURE
Ovid (Publius Ovidius Naso; 43 B.C.E.-17 C.E.), Roman poet

SUMMARY OF EVENT
The *Metamorphoses* (English translation, 1567) by Ovid is a Latin epic poem of fifteen books, written in 11,983 lines of dactylic hexameter, the metrical form of Homer's *Iliad* (c. 750 B.C.E.; English translation, 1611) and Vergil's *Aeneid* (c. 29-19 B.C.E.; English translation, 1553). The poem is not so much a story as a collection of stories, including some fifty longer stories and two hundred shorter ones. Because many are myths that explain how things came to be as they are, they are sometimes called etiological (concerned with cause), and the same term is applied to the whole poem by extension. Because almost all the stories involve some sort of transformation (metamorphosis), the tales are collectively called the *Metamorphoses*. Ovid follows the philosophical drift of Lucretius in his *De rerum natura* (c. 60 B.C.E.; *On the Nature of Things*, 1682); however, Ovid is openly philosophical only in the last book, when the philosopher Pythagoras discourses on his doctrine of metempsychosis, and even that speech has elements of parody.

Born at Sulmo (now Sulmona, Italy), in the Appenine Hills east of Rome, into a family of equestrian rank, Ovid was educated in Rome. His rhetorical training was meant to prepare him for a career in law and politics. However, he showed an early preference for poetry. He belonged to a circle of poets patronized by Gaius Maecenas, and he counted among his friends the poet Horace (65-8 B.C.E.). After great success as a writer of amorous poems, often from the woman's point of view, Ovid began work on the *Metamorphoses* c. 2 C.E. He read various episodes in public over the next few years. He concluded the poem with praise of Julius Caesar and of his adopted son and heir, Augustus. Ironically, however, Augustus banished him from Rome in the very year when the *Metamorphoses* was officially made public. Ovid never gave the cause for his relegation to Tomis, on the Black Sea (now Constanţa, Romania), where he spent the rest of his life.

He only mentioned "a poem and a mistake," presumably his *Ars amatoria* (c. 1 B.C.E.; *The Art of Love*, 1612) and some complicity, perhaps accidental, in the notorious infidelities of Augustus's granddaughter Julia, who was exiled in the same year.

The poem is organized as a gigantic rhetorical demonstration with an introduction, three supporting arguments, and a conclusion. Ovid begins by saying, "My mind is bent to tell of bodies changed into new forms." He continues with an invocation of the gods and an account of the creation (1.2-451). He ends by predicting that his poem will defy change and will survive as long as Rome. He states finally, "Through all the ages shall I live in fame" (15.879). Ovid's first demonstration of change is an encyclopedic account of the gods (1.452-6.420), his second an equally thorough account of the ancient heroes (6.421-11.193), and his third a retelling of human history from the fall of Troy through the rise of Rome (11.194-15.870). Like Vergil, whose epic tale of Aeneas he summarizes in book 14, Ovid regards Rome as the new Troy. Unlike Vergil, he does not write anything like state propaganda. He is prepared to suggest that the Romans of his time have the same shortcomings as some of the mythological figures he describes, and that he is as deserving of apotheosis as Augustus is said to be.

Although the large narrative design is clear when the poem is viewed as a whole, it is difficult to detect in the midst of any given myth or in the transitions from one myth to another. Indeed, Ovid's invocation of the gods pretty well leaves the design in their hands, recognizing that a poem the size of his can be full of changes. Critics have accepted the *Metamorphoses* as an epic that breaks all the norms. It has no single hero, like Achilles in the *Iliad* or Odysseus in Homer's *Odyssey* (c. 800 B.C.E.; English translation, 1616), and no great action to unify the whole work, only a playful reworking of epic devices such as the extended simile and a theme worthy of epic treatment. Recent critics especially enjoy Ovid's elusiveness. He does not appeal to readers' emotions, as Vergil did, as much as to their sense of humor.

Ovid's humor includes some wicked revisions when he offers new variations on familiar myths. He states, for example, that Orpheus changed his sexual orientation after the death of Eurydice and became the "author" or inventor of pederasty (10.83). He does this largely to surprise the reader, who expects the story to end with the "ardor" of the women he shuns after Eurydice (10.81)

Ovid's epic touches on the story of Eurydice and Orpheus. (F. R. Niglutsch)

and the traditional account of dismemberment at their hands. However, he also prepares for the story of Ganymede, which follows shortly afterward.

In earlier centuries, Ovid has offended critics who want literature to provide moral lessons and not to corrupt young minds. He seems to relish the infidelities of the gods and to regard rape as the normal way for gods to interact with humans. Agriculture begins when Jupiter lusts after Io, but in order to avoid the jealousy of Juno, his wife, he turns Io into a cow. Human history begins when he disguises himself as a bull, abducts Europa, and with her sires the first Greeks. It continues when he reappears, disguised this time as a swan, to abduct Leda. It gets into full swing when Leda's daughter Helen is abducted by the prince of Troy, and her Greek husband rouses an army to reclaim her. To be sure, there are good and faithful couples such as Philemon and Baucis, but this seems to be world history as written by a love poet. Attempts to "moralize" the *Metamorphoses*, explaining the rapes and infidelities as allegories, have never succeeded for long. Ovid too obviously takes delight in the incongruous couplings.

Ovid drew from a wide variety of ancient sources, Greek and Latin, and reshaped them with considerable artistry. The mini-epic of Phaeton, who loses control of Phoebus's solar chariot (1.747-2.400), combines the tragic adult of Euripides' Greek drama with the comic child of Latin poems to create what has become the standard account of overly ambitious adolescence. It also supports the etiological purpose of the epic, helping to explain why Africa has deserts and black people.

SIGNIFICANCE

Even before the *Metamorphoses*, Ovid was the most popular poet writing in Latin. Lines from his sometimes bawdy love poems have been found on the walls of excavations at Pompeii. Although his poetry was officially banned when he was banished from Rome, the *Metamorphoses* enjoyed a large and appreciative audience of readers and listeners. The poem's last word, *vivam*, or "I shall live," was truly prophetic. Although many other pagan poets were forgotten during the Christian Middle Ages, Ovid never ceased to have his admirers, including popes such as Innocent III, theologians such as Peter Abelard, and reformers such as Martin Luther.

With the Renaissance and the revival of interest in antiquity, the *Metamorphoses* became a major focus of study and a guide to ancient myths, good Latin style, and Roman culture in general. Translated into the vernacular languages of northern Europe, the poem reached even further. Arthur Golding's English translation was one of the playwright William Shakespeare's favorite books, from which he drew such famous tales as those of Venus and Adonis, Pyramus and Thisbe, and Jason and Medea.

Ovid's influence declined as English studies replaced the classics but was still clearly evident in George Bernard Shaw's *Pygmalion* (1913) and Richard Powers's *Galatea 2.2* (1995). Ironically, Ovid's new twists on old myths such as that of Narcissus have become the standard versions.

—Thomas Willard

FURTHER READING

Grant, Michael. *Myths of the Greeks and Romans*. Rev. ed. New York: Meridian, 1995. A standard account of classical mythology with many quotations from English poetry and nearly one hundred black-and-white illustrations. Has an excellent chapter on Ovid.

Mack, Sara. *Ovid*. New Haven, Conn.: Yale University Press, 1977. Fine general introduction to the poet and his poems. Includes full chapters on his contemporary reputation, his later influence, and his epic poem. Emphasizes the humor in Ovid's storytelling.

Otis, Brooks. *Ovid as an Epic Poet*. 2d ed. New York: Cambridge University Press, 1970. Offers a chapter

on the plan behind Ovid's Epic, plus an appendix that traces the sources of major stories. The second edition points to elements of parody to show that the *Metamorphoses* is "anti-Augustan," correcting the first edition's emphasis on Augustan elements in the epic.

Ovid. *The Metamorphoses of Ovid: A New Verse Translation*. Translated by Allen Mandelbaum. New York: Harcourt, 1993. A very readable blank-verse translation. Includes a list of major stories at the start of each book.

_____. *The Metamorphoses of Ovid: Translated with an Introduction and Commentary*. Translated by Michael Simpson. Amherst: University of Massachusetts Press, 2001. Includes an extensive commentary on each book; intended for the nonspecialist.

Tissol, Garth. *The Face of Nature: Wit, Narrative, and Cosmic Origins in Ovid's "Metamorphoses."* Princeton, N.J.: Princeton University Press, 1997. A challenging but accessible study, reflecting recent interest in the ways that Ovid's poem invites yet frustrates the search for order. Like Mack, Tissol emphasizes the humor in Ovid's narrative.

SEE ALSO: c. 750 B.C.E., Homer Composes the *Iliad*; 58-51 B.C.E., Caesar Conquers Gaul; 54 B.C.E., Roman Poet Catullus Dies; 19 B.C.E., Roman Poet Vergil Dies; c. 50 C.E., Creation of the Roman Imperial Bureaucracy.

RELATED ARTICLES in *Great Lives from History: The Ancient World*: Augustus; Julius Caesar; Catullus; Homer; Lucretius; Ovid; Vergil.

1 - 100 C.E.

9 C.E.
BATTLE OF TEUTOBURG FOREST

The Roman Empire's defeat in the Teutoburg forest caused it to shift to a defensive stance after three Roman legions were ambushed on the German frontier.

LOCALE: Northwest Germany
CATEGORIES: Wars, uprisings, and civil unrest; government and politics

KEY FIGURES

Augustus (63 B.C.E.-14 C.E.), Roman emperor, r. 27 B.C.E.-14 C.E.

Publius Quinctilius Varus (d. 9 C.E.), consul in 13 B.C.E., Roman general assigned to the province between the Rhine and Elbe Rivers in 7 C.E.

Arminius (c. 17 B.C.E.-19 C.E.), chieftain of the Cherusci, a small Germanic tribe

Tiberius (42 B.C.E.-37 C.E.), Roman emperor, r. 14-37 C.E., successor to Augustus who led his troops to the Rhineland to help recover Varus's losses

SUMMARY OF EVENT

After the Battle of Actium in 31 B.C.E. and the subsequent Roman conquest of Egypt, which secured his hold on the Roman world, Octavian (hailed by the senate in 27 B.C.E. as Augustus) reduced the Roman army to almost half its former strength, leaving only twenty-eight legions in service. This was the period of the famous Pax Romana, which some historians see as a period of national fatigue and inertia, the inevitable result of more than a century of incessant civil war, rather than as a time of good will.

Because it was difficult to maintain equilibrium on the northern frontier, Augustus's policy called for an expansion into Germanic territory. By 6 C.E., the region north of the Main River between the Rhine and the Elbe was a Roman province administered by Publius Quinctilius Varus, a general chosen by Augustus and married to the emperor's grandniece. Varus appears to have been more an administrator than a soldier, a view hinted at by the Latin historian Velleius Paterculus and one that may have been shared by Arminius, who saw an opportunity to overthrow Roman imperial rule before it was firmly established in German territory. Certainly, Varus did not understand the German temperament or sufficiently appreciate its warlike nature. In 9 C.E., three legions under Varus were defeated in the Teutoburg forest by Arminius, a chieftain of the Cherusci, a small Germanic tribe, in a battle that marked a watershed in the history of the Roman Empire. From that time onward, the open secret of Roman policy in the territory beyond the Rhine was to di-vide, not conquer. Rome had changed from an offensive to a defensive position vis-à-vis the Germanic peoples.

The frontier problem was related to one of the major defects in the Roman imperial system, namely the nature of the imperial succession. Because the principle of succession by heredity was not firmly established during the early years of the Roman Empire, the ambiguity of the succession process played into the hands of strong leaders in the army, men who had little reason to be loyal to a Roman tradition that, in many cases, they did not even know. Although it was many years before a barbarian general ascended the imperial throne, the victory of Arminius signaled the growing political function of the Roman barbarized army.

Arminius was a Roman-trained soldier and, at the time of his victory over Varus, the leader of only a faction of the Cherusci. Varus's appointment as governor was an unfortunate choice. He tactlessly treated the high-spirited Germans as inferior and tried to Romanize them against their will. This policy roused resentment in the Cherusci and led to Varus's disastrous defeat. Enticed by

Varus's Roman legions meet with defeat in the Teutoburg Forest. (F. R. Niglutsch)

the report of an uprising, Varus led the seventeenth, eighteenth, and nineteenth legions out of summer quarters into the Teutoburg forest, probably located in the Lippe Valley. There, the army was ambushed and massacred, and Varus himself committed suicide. The episode can hardly be classified as a battle, for the Germans had the odds in their favor as they fell on the Roman columns encumbered by their baggage train in wooded country. The Roman cavalry attempted to escape but did not succeed.

Velleius Paterculus, in a translation by F. W. Shipley, describes the result. Hemmed in by forests and marshes and ambuscades, the column was exterminated almost to a man by the very enemy whom it had always slaughtered like cattle, whose life or death had depended solely on the wrath or the pity of the Romans. The general had more courage to die than to fight, for following the example of his father and grandfather, Varus ran himself through with his sword.

After the rout of Varus, the Germans swept on to capture Roman forts east of the Rhine. Lucius Asprenas, Varus's legate, led two legions to Mainz, but the enemy did not attempt to cross there. Having just succeeded in quelling a major revolt in Pannonia after three years of difficult fighting, the Roman general (and future emperor) Tiberius was forced to postpone a triumphal celebration in Rome to hurry to the Rhine, where the garrison was raised to eight legions. To bring the forces to this level, two Roman legions were withdrawn from the province of Raetia (modern Austria) and four were taken from Spain and Illyricum (the eastern Adriatic coast).

SIGNIFICANCE

Although the Rhine defenses were thus strengthened, the three lost legions were not replaced in the Roman army, so that its total strength was reduced to twenty-five legions. Any thought of further expansion beyond the Elbe was abandoned. Even before the disaster in the Teutoburg forest, slaves were being pressed into military service, a practice that revealed a serious shortage of Roman manpower.

Augustus, who was seventy-two years old at the time, was shocked by Varus's defeat. According to the Roman biographer and historian Suetonius, for several months Augustus cut neither his beard nor his hair, the traditional Roman sign of mourning, and sometimes would bash his head against a door, crying: "Quinctilius Varus, give me back my legions."

The major impact of the defeat, however, was to shift Roman policy to a defensive posture on the German frontier, which became fixed under Augustus's successor, Tiberius. In this sense, the defeat in Teutoburg forest was

a pivotal point in European history, allowing the Germanic tribes to remain outside Roman influence.

—Mary Evelyn Jegen, updated by Michael Witkoski

FURTHER READING

Drummond, Stephen K., and Lynn Nelson. *The Western Frontiers of Imperial Rome*. Armonk, N.Y.: M. E. Sharpe, 1994. An expansive description of the ebb and flow of Rome's borders which illustrates the long-range impact of the event in the Teutoburg forest.

Grant, Michael. *The Twelve Caesars*. New York: Charles Scribner's Sons, 1975. Written by an outstanding historian of Rome, this work contains a section on Augustus that provides a concise summary of the event and its impact.

May, Elmer C., Gerald Stadler, and John F. Votaw. *Ancient and Medieval Warfare*. Wayne, N.J.: Avery Publishing Group, 1984. Prepared for the Department of History of the United States Military Academy at West Point, this volume helps the student understand the nature of warfare on the Roman frontier.

Newark, Tim. *The Barbarians*. Poole, Dorset, England: Blandford Press, 1985. An illustrated study that discusses Germanic tactics and weapons during their contests with the imperial legions.

Scarre, Christopher. *Chronicle of the Roman Emperors*. New York: Thames & Hudson, 1995. This account of imperial Roman history provides a brief but excellent survey of the disastrous battle and its impact on Roman frontier policy.

Schlüter, W. "The Battle of the Teutoburg Forest: Archaeological Research at Kalkriese near Osnabrück." In *Roman Germany: Studies in Cultural Interaction*, edited by J. D. Creighton and R. J. A. Wilson. Providence, R.I.: Journal of Roman Archaeology, 1999. An examination of the site at which the battle is believed to have taken place.

Suetonius, Gaius. *The Twelve Caesars*. Translated by Robert Graves. Revised, with an introduction by Michael Grant. New York: Penguin, 2003. The section on "Augustus" in this illustrated version of Graves's translation memorably describes the emperor's reaction to the destruction of the frontier legions.

SEE ALSO: 58-51 B.C.E., Caesar Conquers Gaul; September 2, 31 B.C.E., Battle of Actium; 15 B.C.E.-15 C.E., Rhine-Danube Frontier Is Established; 1st-5th centuries C.E., Alani Gain Power.

RELATED ARTICLES in *Great Lives from History: The Ancient World*: Arminiums; Augustus; Julius Caesar; Tiberius.

1 - 100 C.E.

9-23 C.E.
WANG MANG'S RISE TO POWER

Wang Mang, who rose to power through his aunt, the dowager empress Wang, declared himself emperor of the Xin Dynasty, dividing the Han dynasty in two.

LOCALE: China
CATEGORY: Government and politics

KEY FIGURES
Wang Mang (45 B.C.E.-23 C.E.), usurper and ruler of the Xin Dynasty, r. 9-23 C.E., nephew of Wang Cheng-chun
Wang Cheng-chun (Wang Ch'eng-ch'un; 71 B.C.E.-13 C.E.), Xin Dynasty empress and dowager, r. 51 B.C.E.-13 C.E., Wang Mang's aunt

SUMMARY OF EVENT
Wang Mang's rise to power was due to marriage politics. Up to the mid-first century B.C.E., the Wang clan had produced only minor officials who served in the local government of the Western Han Dynasty (206 B.C.E.-23 C.E.). The clan began its rise to national prominence after Wang Cheng-chun became a concubine of a future emperor, Yuandi (Yuan-ti, r. 49-33 B.C.E.); her longevity, extraordinary for that time, contributed to their success. She was elevated to empress in 51 B.C.E. after the birth of a son, who became emperor as Chengdi (Ch'eng-ti, r. 33-7 B.C.E.). Because Chengdi was only eighteen years old when he came to the throne, his mother, now Dowager Empress Wang, asserted power over him. She entrusted the reins of government to three of her brothers, and after their passing, to her nephew Wang Mang in 16 B.C.E.

The rise of the Wang clan to dominate the government and of Wang Mang, who eventually usurped the throne and established a new dynasty, was largely because of the application of the Chinese concept of filial piety in government. A filial Chinese owes lifelong obedience to his parents. However, because an emperor usually ascends the throne after the death of his father, he can demonstrate his devotion and obedience only to his mother. If he ignores filial piety, he presents a bad example for his people and, therefore, cannot expect them to honor and obey him. Thus, ambitious dowager empresses (mothers or grandmothers of emperors) throughout the Han Dynasty were able to dominate their sons and grandsons and grant great power to male members of their families. The rise of the Wang family was a prime example of this.

Wang Mang's father had died when he was young, but he had been educated by his uncle. The longevity of his aunt, the dowager empress Wang, and a succession of young emperors on the throne, some chosen because their youth would ensure long regencies under the Wang family, culminated in power passing to Wang Mang. When his handpicked child-emperor and son-in-law Pingdi (P'ing-ti, who had been chosen to succeed the childless Chengdi) died in 6 C.E., Wang picked a two-year-old boy from the Liu clan to succeed, but instead of naming him emperor, he gave him the title of "young prince" and gave himself the title of "acting emperor." Protests by members of the Liu clan were crushed. Wang then launched a campaign to orchestrate his ascension to the throne, citing favorable omens and portents to indicate that heaven had ended its mandate to the Liu clan and given it to the worthy Wang Mang. In 9 C.E., Wang Mang declared the Han Dynasty ended and ascended the throne as emperor of the Xin (Hsin), meaning "new," dynasty.

Wang Mang ruled as the only emperor of the Xin Dynasty between 9 and 23 C.E. He attempted many changes during this period; most failed. Natural disasters, most notably the Yellow River's two changes of course during six years of his reign, caused great distress and loss of life, culminating in popular rebellion, his death, and, after a period of civil wars, the restoration of the Han Dynasty. As a result, historians did not recognize the Xin as a legal dynasty, and Wang Mang was labeled a villainous usurper.

Wang Mang began his reign with many reforms, which he claimed were a return to the institutions of the golden age of the early Zhou Dynasty (Chou; 1066-256 B.C.E.) and the true teachings of Confucius. In particular, he likened himself to the revered duke of Zhou (Chou), despite the fact that whereas the duke had acted as regent for his nephew and retired when the younger man reached maturity, Wang had deposed the young prince in whose name he had ruled and placed himself on the throne. Wang Mang degraded members of the imperial Liu clan to commoner status and elevated his family members and supporters to noble ranks. He confiscated private land holdings; nationalized forests and mines and the salt, liquor, and iron industries; and enacted laws to redistribute land to all adult males. He treated merchants harshly, debased the currency, issued new coins, and increased taxes. He also forbade the buying and selling of privately owned slaves.

Although some of his reforms were of marginal importance or merely ineffective, the overall results of Wang Mang's changes were disastrous. For example, the number of privately owned slaves was small during the Han Dynasty, and the law that forbade the buying and selling of slaves did not affect many people. The laws that confiscated private estates and distributed the land to small farmers were not enforceable and alienated the landowners whom Wang Mang tried to bring under his control. His debasement of the currency, which forced the rich to turn in their gold to the treasury in exchange for copper coins, enriched the treasury but alienated the upper classes, and his several changes of the coinage system confused the population and eroded confidence in the government. In foreign policy, however, he was fairly successful; he mobilized a large army on the frontier but was able to avoid war with the Xiongnu (Hsiung-nu).

In the end, it was nature that defeated Wang Mang. Drought and unusually bad weather resulted in poor harvests in northern China and caused serious suffering, even in the capital city Changan (now Xi'an). A series of breaks in the dikes of the Yellow River culminated in disastrous floods, followed by the mighty river changing its course, no longer entering the sea from the northern but rather the southern tip of the Shandong (Shantung) Peninsula, and trapping countless people between its two branches. No human effort could have prevented the disaster that followed: Many people were drowned or died of other causes, and many became refugees. Desperate people became bandits and rebels.

In 18 C.E., a peasant rebellion called the Red Eyebrows began. Its members painted their eyebrows red to distinguish themselves from government troops. Red was also the color of the Han Dynasty, but it is not clear whether loyalty to the Han motivated these rebels to paint their eyebrows red. Confucianism was the official state doctrine of the Han and also of Wang's regime. One Confucian tenet proclaimed: "Heaven sees as the people see; Heaven hears as the people hear." To the people of the time, what could have been a clearer declaration of Heaven's disapproval than the widespread natural disasters? Therefore, popular uprisings against the Xin emperor seemed justified.

Wang Mang's army was unable to suppress the Red Eyebrows, who moved westward from present-day Shandong Province to modern Henan (Honan) Province. At a prosperous city called Nanyang, they joined up with Liu Xiu (Liu Hsiu), the eighth-generation descendant of Liu Bang (Liu P'ang), founder of the Han Dynasty, and anti-Wang Mang gentry forces. Wang was killed in 23 C.E., ending the Xin Dynasty. Civil wars continued for

two more years before a member of the Liu clan reinstated the Han Dynasty.

SIGNIFICANCE

Because of Wang Mang's usurpation, the Han Dynasty was divided into two parts: The Western, or Former, Han, with its capital at Changan, ruled between 206 B.C.E. and 9 C.E. (sometimes this is given as 206 B.C.E.-23 C.E., incorporating the Xin Dynasty), followed by the Eastern, or Later, Han, with its capital at Luoyang (Lo-yang), which lasted from 25 to 220 C.E.

Information about Wang Mang derives from the official history of the Han Dynasty written by a famous father-son-daughter team of historians: The father was named Ban Gu (Pan Ku), the son Ban Biao (Pan Piao), and the daughter Ban Zhao (Pan Chao). They wrote a multivolume work titled the *Han Shu* (also known as *Qian Han Shu*, completed first century C.E.; *The History of the Former Han Dynasty*, 1938-1955). The section dealing with Wang Mang vilified him as a manipulative, opportunistic, and unprincipled man. Most subsequent historians have followed this assessment of Wang Mang. The short-lived Xin Dynasty was not recognized as a legitimate dynasty by traditional Chinese historians.

—*Jiu-Hwa Lo Upshur*

FURTHER READING

Ch'u, T'ung-tsu. *Han Social Structure*. Seattle: University of Washington Press, 1967. Scholarly and readable work, with documents. Bibliography and index.

Hinsch, Bret. *Women in Early Imperial China*. New York: Rowman and Littlefield, 2002. This is the first book to focus solely on Chinese women of the ancient world, mainly during the Han Dynasty. Glossary, bibliography, and index.

Jagchid, Sechin, and Van Jay Symons. *Peace, War, and Trade Along the Great Wall: Nomadic-Chinese Interactions Through Two Millennia*. Bloomington: Indiana University Press, 1989. An overview of Chinese-nomadic relations, with large sections devoted to the Han Dynasty. Glossary, bibliography, and index.

Loewe, Michael. *Crisis and Conflict in Han China, 104 B.C. to A.D. 9*. London: George Allen and Unwin, 1974. An account of court intrigues and policy conflicts in the Han court up to the rise of Wang Mang. Includes reasons for his rise. Glossary of Chinese and Japanese names and terms. Index.

Pizzoli-t'Serstevens, Michele. *The Han Dynasty*. New York: Rizzoli, 1982. Lavishly illustrated, with good maps and well-presented text. Bibliography and index.

Twitchett, Denis, and John K. Fairbank, eds. *The Ch'in*

1 - 100 C.E.

and Han Empires, 221 B.C.-A.D. 220. Vol. 1 in *The Cambridge History of China*. New York: Cambridge University Press, 1986. The definitive history of the Qin and Han Dynasties. Glossary, index, and bibliography.

Wang, Zhongshu. *Han Civilization*. New Haven, Conn.: Yale University Press, 1982. Richly illustrated account with archaeological information. Bibliography and index.

SEE ALSO: 209-174 B.C.E., Maodun Creates a Large Confederation in Central Asia; 206 B.C.E., Liu Bang Captures Qin Capital, Founds Han Dynasty; 140-87 B.C.E., Wudi Rules Han Dynasty China; 25 C.E., Guang Wudi Restores the Han Dynasty; 220 C.E., Three Kingdoms Period Begins in China.

RELATED ARTICLES in *Great Lives from History: The Ancient World*: Ban Gu; Ban Zhao.

25 C.E.
GUANG WUDI RESTORES THE HAN DYNASTY

Guang Wudi restored the Han Dynasty afer the interregnum of Wang Mang and his Xin Dynasty, establishing what became known as the Eastern, or Later, Han Dynasty.

LOCALE: China
CATEGORY: Government and politics

KEY FIGURES
Guang Wudi (Kuang Wu-ti; c. 5 B.C.E.-57 C.E.), Eastern Han emperor, r. 25-57 C.E.
Wang Mang (45 B.C.E.-23 C.E.), previous emperor of the Xin Dynasty, r. 9-23 C.E.
Guo Shentong (Kuo Shen-t'ung; fl. first century C.E.), Guang Wudi's first wife, a northerner
Yin Lihua (fl. first century C.E.), Guang Wudi's second wife, a southerner, mother of Mingdi
Mingdi (Ming-ti, born Liu Yang; 29-c. 75 C.E.), Yin Lihua and Guang Wudi's eldest son, Han Dynasty emperor, r. c. 58-c. 75 C.E.

SUMMARY OF EVENT
In 25 C.E., Liu Xiu, who received the posthumous title Guang Wudi (shining martial emperor), ascended the throne as the first ruler of the restored Han Dynasty, known as the Eastern, or Later, Han (25-220 C.E.), after the brief interregnum of Wang Mang and his Xin Dynasty (Hsin; 9-23 C.E.). Chinese civilization extended back to the third millennium B.C.E. but was first unified by Shi Huangdi (Shih Huang-ti; 259-210 B.C.E.), who established the Qin Dynasty in 221 B.C.E. It quickly disintegrated after Qin's death, to be followed by the Han Dynasty under Liu Bang (Liu P'ang; posthumous title Gaodi, r. 206-195 B.C.E.). The era of the Western, or Former, Han, was a glorious period in China's history, with the Han Empire encompassing much of modern China

and extending far into Central Asia. However, internal dynastic quarrels and a series of weak and irresponsible rulers enabled Wang Mang to proclaim himself emperor of the Xin Dynasty.

Wang Mang lacked imperial legitimacy in the opinion of the extensive Liu clan, or the Han family, and although well intentioned, his proposed reforms alienated the wealthy landowners. His difficulties were compounded by natural disasters, notably extensive flooding of the Yellow River, which resulted in the peasant rebellion known as the Red Eyebrows because of the red color they painted on their faces. During the uprising, Wang Mang was murdered in 23 C.E.

Wang's death, and the termination of his Xin Dynasty, led to an internecine civil war that lasted two years. The Red Eyebrows had gained the support of many members of the Liu-Han family in the uprising, but when the former imperial family could not agree on a single Han candidate to replace Wang Mang, in 25 C.E., Liu Xiu, a provincial landowner, declared himself emperor; he is known to history as Guang Wudi. There were numerous other claimants for the throne, and it took Guang Wudi eleven years to overcome all opposition and consolidate his rule.

The extended violence combined with floods and other natural disasters had severely affected China's economy, and Guang Wudi's reconstruction of the irrigation system led to the revival of agriculture. A land survey was initiated, at times in opposition to the largest landholders. To aid the peasants and the general populace, Guang Wudi reduced taxes to less than a tenth of harvests or profits. Agricultural surpluses were set aside to be available for relief in hard times, and the government monopoly was reasserted on liquor, iron, and salt products. Changan (now Xi'an), the old Han capital, was destroyed in the wars, and Guang Wudi moved his capital to Luoyang (Lo-yang), two hundred miles to the east, thus the designation of the Later Han Dynasty as the Eastern Han. With a population of 500,000, Luoyang was the world's most populous city at the time.

Under earlier Western Han rulers, the ideas of Confucius became paramount to Chinese culture. Guang Wudi strongly identified with Confucianism, and his reign was among the most committed Confucian regimes in China's long history. The government organized annual ceremonies honoring the memory of Confucius, and Guang Wudi visited Confucius's birthplace at Qufu. The works of Confucius and the other classic texts were diligently expounded by court-supported scholars, and schools were established with the classic texts from pre-Qin times as the focus of study. Those students who were successful in passing the Imperial Academy examinations were assigned to positions in the lower levels of the government.

Much of the governmental structure had been devastated during the violent upheavals, and Guang Wudi was able to eliminate much of the previously bloated bureaucracy. He was thus better able to center power in his own hands. However, circumstances did not allow him to become an absolute despot. Local and regional government depended on elite families and clans, but under Guang Wudi, some of the formerly powerful families were reduced in influence, and the emperor rewarded members of the lesser gentry, or lesser landlords, with governmental offices and social recognition.

With the resulting order and increasing prosperity in China, Guang Wudi pursued an activist foreign policy, launching military campaigns against China's neighbors and perceived foes. Vietnam and Korea had experienced Chinese invasions in the past, and as a result of Guang Wudi's campaigns, his forces reportedly obtained the release of Chinese slaves held in those two regions, an intimation that the Han incursion had met with considerable opposition, as it did under the Trung sisters in Vietnam. Another threat came from the northwest of China proper, or what later became much of the modern-day province of Xinjiang. The Xiongnu (Hsiung-nu), nomads of Turkic origin, had been a threat to civilized China for centuries, one of the reasons for the construction of what later became known as the Great Wall of China. In reality, the Great Wall was a series of walls built over a long period of time as a barrier to invading nomads, beginning as far back as the third century B.C.E., construction on which continued periodically through into the sixteenth century C.E. The wall known as the Great Wall today was built during the Ming Dynasty, in the sixteenth century. During Guang Wudi's reign, China was able to keep the

EMPERORS OF THE EASTERN HAN DYNASTY, 25-220 C.E.	
Ruler	*Reign*
Guang Wudi	25-57
Mingdi	c. 58-c. 75
Zhangdi	76-88
Hedi	89-105
Shangdi	106
Audi	107-125
Shudi	126-144
Chongdi	145
Zhidi	146
Huandi	147-167
Lingdi	168-189
Xiandi	190-220

Xiongnu at bay, thus ensuring trade from the famous Silk Road as well as securing other trade routes to the states of Southeast Asia and India and to the Middle East and the Mediterranean.

Internally, peace and order were often maintained throughout China's long history by royal alliances to powerful families or clans through concubinage and marriage. All Chinese emperors, including Guang Wudi, had concubines. During the Western Han era, there were about three thousand concubines in the royal harem. Among the concubines there were numerous ranks, which Guang Wudi reduced to three: honorable lady, beautiful lady, and chosen lady. A southerner, Guang Wudi, for political reasons, married Guo Shentong, a northerner, who bore him five sons. He later married a southerner, Yin Lihua, possibly because he no longer needed as much northern support. The recurrent danger was that the families of wives and favorite concubines would use their female relatives to gain political influence and economic rewards, often in bitter rivalry with the numerous court eunuchs, and generally to the detriment of the authority of the emperor. However, during his lifetime, Guang Wudi successfully retained control, limiting the ambitions and the threats of both consort families and the eunuch class, a practice that was continued by his eldest son and his heir, Liu Yang, known as the emperor Mingdi (brilliant emperor).

SIGNIFICANCE

During the Han restoration undertaken by Guang Wudi, order and considerable prosperity returned to China after the decline that had occurred under the last Western Han emperors and Wang Mang of the Xin Dynasty. During

1 - 100 C.E.

Guang Wudi's reign, China further extended its influence into southern parts of China and beyond, and there was a significant population movement of many Chinese to the south. A combination of military force and a diplomatic policy of divide and conquer reduced the threat of the Xiongnu in the northwest.

However, it took a strong individual such as Guang Wudi to maintain peace and prosperity. Under his successors, particularly after the reign of his son, Mingdi, the long decline of the Eastern Han began. A series of young emperors became subject to the ambitions of dowager empresses and consort families, who gained an overweening influence on the affairs of state. Eunuch power increased, and violence at court was not uncommon. Wealth became overly concentrated in the hands of the agricultural elite at the expense of the peasants. The continuing military costs of defending the frontiers weakened the government's financial position, and natural disasters again led to peasant uprisings. By 189 C.E., the Han Dynasty had largely collapsed, although its final end did not occur until 220.

—Eugene Larson

FURTHER READING

Harrison, James P. *The Communists and Chinese Peasant Rebellions*. New York: Atheneum, 1969. A discussion of how Chinese communists have interpreted peasant rebellions, including that of the Red Eyebrows during Guang Wudi's reign.

Paludan, Ann. *Chronicle of the Chinese Emperors*. New York: Thames and Hudson, 1998. A well-written and useful summary of China's history through biographies of its many emperors.

Pirazzoli-t'Serstevens, Michele. *The Han Dynasty*. Translated by Janet Seligman. New York: Rizzoli, 1982. A general study of Han China.

Twitchett, Denis, and John K. Fairbank, eds. *The Ch'in and Han Empires, 221 B.C.-A.D. 220*. Vol. 1 in *The Cambridge History of China*. New York: Cambridge University Press, 1978. The classic account of Chinese history in fifteen volumes, with the first volume including discussions of the Eastern Han.

Wang Zhongshu. *Han Civilization*. Translated by K. C. Chang. New Haven, Conn.: Yale University Press, 1982. A series of lectures on various aspects of the Han Dynasty.

SEE ALSO: 221 B.C.E., Qin Dynasty Founded in China; c. 221-211 B.C.E., Building the Great Wall of China; 209-174 B.C.E., Maodun Creates a Large Confederation in Central Asia; 206 B.C.E., Liu Bang Captures Qin Capital, Founds Han Dynasty; 140-87 B.C.E., Wudi Rules Han Dynasty China; 9-23 C.E., Wang Mang's Rise to Power; 40-43 C.E., Trung Sisters Lead Vietnamese Rebellion Against Chinese; 220 C.E., Three Kingdoms Period Begins in China.

RELATED ARTICLES in *Great Lives from History: The Ancient World*: Confucius; Shi Huangdi; Wudi.

---

c. 30 C.E.
CONDEMNATION AND CRUCIFIXION OF JESUS CHRIST

The Roman government crucified Jesus Christ as a threat to its hegemony over Israel. That act founded Christianity, whose adherents claim that it gained eternal salvation for them.

LOCALE: Jerusalem (now in Israel)
CATEGORY: Religion

KEY FIGURES

Jesus Christ (c. 6 B.C.E.-30 C.E.), religious leader and founder of Christianity

Pontius Pilate (d. after 36 C.E.), Roman prefect of Judah, 26-36 C.E., who ordered Jesus' crucifixion

Caiaphas (fl. first century B.C.E.), high priest in Jerusalem, c. 18-c. 36 C.E., who questioned Jesus during his trial

SUMMARY OF EVENT

The condemnation and crucifixion of Jesus Christ occurred about 30 C.E. Precision in dating is impossible because of the nature of the sources about Jesus. First, there are no reliable, extra-Christian sources on the subject. Second, while the New Testament Gospels are the basis for all Christian writing on the subject, they disagree in some details crucial to this date. They do agree that Jesus was crucified by order of Pontius Pilate, who was the governor over Jerusalem and its environs from 26 to 36 C.E., but they disagree about the date of the birth of Jesus.

In the Bible, the apostle Luke (2:1-2) places the birth of Jesus during the reign of Emperor Augustus (r. 27 B.C.E.-14 C.E.) and while Quirinius was governor of Syria (6-7 C.E.). Luke (3:23) also says that Jesus was thirty years old when he began his ministry. That date would

The crucifixion of Jesus Christ. (Library of Congress)

put the beginning of Jesus' ministry in 36 or 37 C.E., during or after the last year of Pilate's governorship, so Luke's chronology seems not to fit. Many scholars adopt a date suggested by the Gospel of Matthew, another apostle, that Jesus was born during the reign of Herod the Great (37-34 B.C.E.). Matthew's birth narrative relates the death of Herod fairly soon after the birth of Jesus. That date would fit with the ideas of Jesus' beginning his ministry at age thirty (c. 26 C.E.) and flourishing for at least three years before his crucifixion, the minimum if Jesus observed three Passovers in Jerusalem during his ministry as the Gospel of John the Apostle (2:23, 6:4, and 12:1) maintains. Thus, 30 C.E. is a plausible date for Jesus' death within the more secure parameters of 26-36 C.E.

The four Gospels record a series of trials for Jesus. They agree that Jesus was questioned at night by Jewish authorities, particularly the high priest Caiaphas. Jewish scholars sometimes object that such a trial would have been illegal under Jewish law, so perhaps the event was simply a fact-finding hearing. The Gospels say that the supreme tribunal among Jews for local affairs heard Jesus the next day. The Gospels also record a final trial under Pilate, at the end of which Jesus was condemned to be crucified, though Luke (23:6-12) has Jesus shuffled from Pilate to Herod Antipas, ruler of Jesus' home area of Galilee, and back to Herod, with neither man wishing to try Jesus. Luke implied thereby that neither Jewish nor Roman civil authorities saw grounds for condemning Jesus. Matthew (27:19) makes that same point by having Pilate's wife communicate with her husband that she had had a dream about him convincing even her that Jesus was innocent.

Instead of blaming the Romans for the death of Jesus, the Gospels blame the Jewish authorities. To be sure, the Jewish establishment had arrested and tried him, but for blasphemy, particularly for threatening (as they construed his preaching) to destroy the Temple of Jerusalem. All four gospels record an incident in which Jesus drove officials from the temple. They also record strong language on Jesus' part against some of the religious leaders. This representation suggests that at least some Jews viewed Jesus with suspicion and even hostility. It is also unclear whether the Romans would have cared if Jesus blasphemed the Jewish god, although the Romans were inclined to at least respect local deities and often incorporated them into their own pantheon. Jewish blasphemy per se might not have bothered the Romans, but causing religious unrest might well have been regarded by them as sedition.

The Gospels admitted that sedition was the real charge against Jesus, even as they attempted to show that it was groundless. John (19:19) notes that Pilate placed a sign on Jesus' cross that read: "Jesus of Nazareth, the King of the Jews." When the priests wanted him to alter the sign, he refused. John the Apostle portrayed that incident as another case of failure on the part of the Jewish leaders to see what was so obvious that even a pagan governor could see it. It also shows how firmly embedded in the tradition was the charge that Jesus gave signs of being a local rival to the power of Rome.

Jewish tradition knew of such a rival, a royal figure with the title *messiah* (anointed one). King David of the tiny Israelite state was said to have put together a small empire in the Levant between Mesopotamia and Egypt. David's successors ruled in Jerusalem from his death c. 962 B.C.E. until the Babylonians, under King Nebuchadnezzar, ended David's dynasty in 587 or 586 B.C.E. Even after that catastrophe, however, some members of the Jewish community continued to hope for a new Davidic king. The postexilic prophet Haggai (2:23) even thought a repatriated Davidite named Zerubbabel would renew the dynasty. The Jewish hope for a new David lasted into the time of Jesus and beyond. Some thought that descendant would expel the Romans and rule Israel from Jerusalem (Acts 1:6). The accounts of Palm Sunday depict Jesus entering Jerusalem on a donkey, in fulfillment of a prediction about a peaceful entry of the Messiah that appeared in Zechariah 9:9-10.

Other first century Jews, called Zealots, were less choosy about the lineage of the one who led them and would have followed any revolutionary leader against Rome. Noted for carrying concealed swords, they sometimes took deadly action when the opportunity presented itself. At least one of Jesus' disciples, Simon the Zealot (Luke 6:15), may well have belonged to this group. In addition to Zealots, a number of Jews probably hoped quietly for the overthrow of the Romans by whatever means, human or divine.

At least as the Gospels present Jesus, he had no political ambitions. Rather, he seems to have been an itinerant, apocalyptic prophet. How, then, could he have been understood as a messianic opponent of Rome? Those who preached apocalypse looked forward to a new day, a new kingdom, when the old order of things would be overturned and new order substituted for it. Although they usually depended on God to make the changes, their rhetoric could inflame action and would probably make authorities nervous. Pilate was notoriously cruel, and Jesus was by no means the only messianic pretender executed

by the Romans in the first century C.E. For instance, the famous Jewish revolutionary Bar Kokhba was killed by the Romans in 135 C.E.

Crucifixion was a particularly brutal form of capital punishment, in which prisoners were tied or nailed to a cross and left to die of exposure and thirst. People from India to Britain had practiced it for centuries before its adoption by the Romans. The Romans often used an X-shaped cross but sometimes used the T-shaped cross (with a transverse bar near the top) that Christians typically have depicted. A cross might have a seat on it, but it was less for the comfort of the prisoner than for the benefit of the soldiers, who did not want to do the job again if the prisoner's hands and feet tore through the nails. Often the bodies were left on crosses to decompose.

Jesus' crucifixion bore similarities to many others. He was stripped naked, scourged, forced to carry the transverse beam of his own cross, mocked, and draped with a placard stating the reason for his execution. His execution was public, on a hill outside Jerusalem, along with other criminals. Unlike most, he seems to have died quickly and was buried before sunset.

SIGNIFICANCE

Jesus' disciples proclaimed that he had risen from the dead, or that God had raised him as a sign of vindication of Jesus' mission and message. The result was that the crucifixion came to be understood by Christians as the means God used to offer salvation to any who would accept it, Jew or Gentile. The assimilationist character of the Christian movement would lead, over the next three centuries, to its appropriation of political power in the eastern Roman Empire and eventually to its role as a dominant force shaping Western civilization.

—Paul L. Redditt

FURTHER READING

Brandon, S. G. F. *Jesus and the Zealots*. New York: Charles Scribner's Sons, 1967. A treatment of Jesus as a zealot, opposed to the Roman government.

Brown, R. E. *The Death of Jesus the Messiah*. 2 vols. New York: Anchor-Doubleday, 1994. A thorough study of the biblical accounts of the arrest, trial, and crucifixion of Jesus.

Crossan, John Dominic. *The Historical Jesus*. San Francisco: HarperSanFrancisco, 1991. A treatment of Jesus as a wisdom teacher, not an apocalypticist.

Ehrman, Bart D. *Jesus: Apocalyptic Prophet of the New Millennium*. San Francisco: HarperSanFrancisco, 1999. A treatment of Jesus as an apocalyptic prophet.

Horsley, Richard A. *Jesus and the Spiral of Violence.* Minneapolis, Minn.: Fortress, 1993. Treatment of Jesus as an advocate of nonviolent social revolution against Rome.

Wrede, William. *The Messianic Secret.* Translated by J. C. G. Greig. 1901. Reprint. Cambridge, England: James Clark, 1971. This volume argues that the church claimed Jesus as the Messiah after his lifetime and invented the view that Jesus had secretly revealed his Messiahship before his death.

SEE ALSO: c. 135 B.C.E., Rise of the Pharisees; c. 6 B.C.E., Birth of Jesus Christ; c. 30 C.E., Preaching of the Pentecostal Gospel; c. 50-c. 150 C.E., Compilation of the New Testament; January-March, 55 or 56 C.E., Paul Writes His Letter to the Romans; 250 C.E., Outbreak of the Decian Persecution; 313-395 C.E., Inception of Church-State Problem; 325 C.E., Adoption of the Nicene Creed; 380-392 C.E., Theodosius's Edicts Promote Christian Orthodoxy; 428-431 C.E., Nestorian Controversy; October 8-25, 451 C.E., Council of Chalcedon.

RELATED ARTICLES in *Great Lives from History: The Ancient World:* David; Jesus; John the Apostle; Saint John the Baptist; Mary; Moses; Saint Paul; Saint Peter; Pontius Pilate.

c. 30 C.E.

PREACHING OF THE PENTECOSTAL GOSPEL

Saint Peter's sermon at the Jewish festival of Pentecost, fifty days after Passover, marked the initiation of the Christian faith persisting beyond the teachings and charisma of Jesus himself.

LOCALE: Jerusalem (now in Israel)
CATEGORY: Religion

KEY FIGURES

Saint Peter (d. 64 C.E.), Galilean disciple of Jesus
John the Apostle (c. 10-c. 100 C.E.), Galilean disciple of Jesus
Saint Paul (c. 10-c. 64 C.E.), apostle to the Gentiles

SUMMARY OF EVENT

Pentecost is a Jewish festival that takes place fifty days after the second day of the Passover. To Christians, Easter is the festival of the Resurrection of Jesus Christ that turned the disappointment of the Apostles into faith, while Pentecost recalls the moment in the early Church when the Holy Spirit was poured out on the Apostles so that the proclamation of Jesus as Lord and Messiah could begin.

According to Acts 2:17-21, Peter's sermon at Pentecost included the citation of Joel 2:28-32, a reference that showed clearly that the outpouring of the Holy Spirit was regarded as marking the arrival of the "last things." The Church consisted of the "end-time" people of God, the final true inheritors of all that God had promised to his people. This inheritance was given to those who faithfully believed that the life, death, and Resurrection of Jesus took place according to God's plan as announced by his prophets in the Old Testament. Admittedly Jesus' death at the hands of the very people who were listening to Peter's sermon was a shocking evil, but God had set it right by raising Jesus from the dead. The Resurrection showed that God had appointed Jesus as Lord and Messiah, the same one who was now ruling as the Lord at the right hand of God. In the name of Jesus, people were called to repentance and salvation.

Such was the substance of the Pentecostal Gospel, according to the words of Peter as recorded in Acts 2:14-40. Throughout Acts, especially in 2:9-11, Luke makes it clear that this message of good tidings was intended for all people when he recounts, according to a zodiacal list, the different peoples of the world who were present to hear the first inspired utterances of the Apostles.

The history of the primitive Church is dark. Uncertainties are caused by the character of the sources: the epistles of Saint Paul and the book of Acts. Paul's letters are the oldest books of the New Testament, the earliest dating from about 51 C.E., but his interests are not historical. Written to meet specific situations in various early Christian congregations, his letters present few details about the early history of these assemblies. Acts is a source of value, though it is also fragmentary. The apostle Luke is chiefly concerned with tracing the geographic expansion of the Church from Jerusalem throughout Palestine and with following the career of Paul as he proselytized in the eastern Mediterranean area. Luke is interested in presenting the primitive Church as a model for later church living, and he supplies surprisingly little information about Paul's teaching. Instead, he portrays a common life, a common doctrine, and a common worship unencumbered with details, so that the readers of his own day could imitate the early ideal period. The spirit of the Apostolic age is the standard that Luke would like to see adopted in the life of the Church in the last quarter of the first century C.E.

Considering the paucity and limitations of early source material, it is not surprising that little is known of the original foundation even of so important a church as that of Antioch in Syria. It can be determined from Acts 11:19-20, 28 and the probable date of Paul's conversion that Christians were in the city within three years after the first Christian Pentecost. This city was the place where regular and organized evangelization of non-Jews first took place, and it came to be the center of missionary activity throughout the Greco-Roman world. Paul was its outstanding missionary, although the see was later regarded as Petrine. Apparently the Alexandrian church was also founded before 50 C.E., though again details are missing. Some scholars profess to see evidence for the existence of Christians at Alexandria in the description of the Jewish community contained in the letter to the Alexandrians written by the emperor Claudius in 41 C.E. The capital city of Rome certainly had a Christian community by 49 C.E., even though the names of its founders have been lost.

Other data of historical interest are also lacking. The organizational structure of the earliest Christian assemblies is unknown; however, Galatians 2:1-10 describes the structure of the Church at Jerusalem. Three men were at its head: Peter, James, and John the Apostle, who were called "the pillars." Apparently the Church was thought of as God's eschatalogical temple, but little can be ascertained about the liturgical practices there or in any of the earliest churches. Some information about early worship can be learned from Paul in the tradition about the Lord's Supper as given in 1 Corinthians 11:17-33, fragments of creeds in 1 Corinthians 15:3-5 and Romans 3:24-26a, and traces of early Christian hymns in Philippians 2:6-11 and 1 Timothy 3:16. Fragments of early liturgical forms appear embedded in later documents, but valuable though such data may be, little of import can be learned. The early Church seems to have been more concerned with the spiritual impact of the Pentecostal Gospel than with the transmission of details of early institutional organization.

SIGNIFICANCE

Basically there are two approaches to reconstructing the content of the early missionary proclamation of Christianity. One view looks for fragments of earlier materials in Paul and Acts and argues their diversity. The other approach seeks to emphasize the common pattern of proclamation in what are held to be primitive New Testament materials. In the latter approach, the study of the New Testament must always remain conscious of the distinction between *kerygma* and teaching. *Kerygma*, a transliterated loan word from Greek properly meaning proclamation or public notice, has become among biblical scholars a technical term to describe a uniform missionary proclamation that can be found in the epistles of Paul, Acts, the Gospels, and elsewhere in the New Testament. As such it should be distinguished from *didache*, or the instructional function.

Certain motifs can be recovered in Paul, and Paul himself points to an earlier Christian tradition. Putting to-

Saint Paul, an early Church leader, preaches to an assembly in Athens. (F. R. Niglutsch)

gether this tradition, the *kerygma* emerges as proclaiming that the coming of Christ has fulfilled Old Testament prophecy and inaugurated the new age, that this Christ was born of the seed of David, died according to the Old Testament to deliver people from this evil age, was buried, then raised up on the third day according to the Scriptures, and was exalted to the right hand of God. Now as Lord of all humankind, God's Son, he rules and will return as judge and savior. An almost similar pattern of proclamation can be found in the great speeches or sermons in Acts, especially at 2:14-36; 2:38-39; 3:12-26; and 4:8-10. The pre-Pauline tradition and Acts agree in asserting that the decisive thing has already happened, that Jesus' return is in fact an impending advent that will corroborate the preaching of the Apostles. Acts adds the note that people are called to repent in the fact of this proclamation.

Λ study of surviving literature of a slightly later age supports this reconstruction of the primitive proclamation or *kerygma*. Naturally, when the immediate advent did not take place, a readjustment was needed. Some provided the necessary restructuring by placing a greater emphasis on the idea of the future return rather than its imminence, and consequently described it in strongly apocalyptic language as in 2 Thessalonians, Mark 13, and Revelation. Another kind of adjustment in the proclamation tended to put greater emphasis on the historical facts of the ministry of Jesus. Paul himself fits into this category of response as he rewords the primitive *kerygma*. Hebrews and 1 Peter represent similar, if schematically different, solutions.

The greatest rewriting is in the synoptic Gospels, especially in Mark. Mark is merely an expanded form of the historical section of the *kerygma*, as a comparison of its outline to Acts 10 and 13 reveals. Its stress is on fulfillment in the historical events of Jesus' life; such an emphasis naturally supports their essential historicity. Both Paul and the Fourth Gospel develop this insight still further in their emphasis on the Spirit of God as creating an abiding unity between the Messiah and the Messianic community. In both writers, the crude elements of primitive eschatology are absorbed into a doctrine of present fellowship with the Christ. The Fourth Gospel stresses a steady progression in the manifestation of the Logos or Divine Light in the darkness. Eternal fulfillment begins already on Earth through a mystical union with Christ. One looks forward not to a future great event, as the Second Coming, but rather to a resurrection and judgment that are already under way. Here the present is already part of the future and the future part of the present.

FIRST FIVE ROMAN CATHOLIC POPES (BISHOPS OF ROME), C. 33-105 C.E.	
Popes	*Dates*
Peter	c. 33-c. 67
Linus	67-76
Anacletus	76-88
Clement I	88-97
Evaristus	97-105

The approach that emphasizes disconnected and fragmentary materials can discover no recognizable unified message in the early Church. Some scholars regard the account in Acts as based on ancient reports but consider that the account reflects a stage into which legend, myth, or reflection have already entered. Moreover, Luke has shaped his material somewhat freely to serve his literary end. Indeed, there may never have been twelve apostles; Luke, in an anachronistic way, has merely joined a later idea of the apostolate to the "twelve," a group of men whose historical position is at best unclear. Some genuinely early features in the primitive Church can be recognized, such as disputes over the role of the Mosaic Law, but the general picture of Acts cannot be regarded, as it stands, as a primary source for early Church history. The major source will thus have to be the pre-Pauline material such as credal formulations, hymns, and other such literary forms found in the apostles' epistles and in other later letters.

The early Christian Church developed a self-understanding image of itself. Names such as "the holy," "the elect," and "the assembly" all emphasize the awareness of the primitive Church of its role as the community in which the hope for the gathering of Israel has been fulfilled. The subsequent organization, worship, and sacramental theology of the Church all witness its self-understanding.

The early Church's message has to do with the central affirmation of faith, with the public declaration of the one who is the community's Lord. At times the point of the confession can be gleaned from the title used for Jesus. As the "Christ," he is the expected anointed king of the Jews. In early Christian creeds, this title is often used in connection with statements saying that he died and rose again, credal assertions reflected in Romans 5:8 and 8:4, and 1 Corinthians 15:3ff. In these assertions, the death of Jesus is the central focus rather than the Resurrection. The use of other titles suggests different meanings and emphases. "Son of God" is at times a designa-

1 - 100 C.E.

765

tion used to demarcate that stage in the career of Jesus when he enters after, or through, the Resurrection. The Resurrection is seen as the exaltation of that position as stated in Romans 1:3-4 and 2 Timothy 2:8. This exaltation, in turn, is expanded into a full preexistence, humiliation, and exaltation structure in the hymn in Philippians 2:6-11. "Son of God" thus designates a position that Jesus fulfills by virtue of exaltation. The title "Lord" is similar. In 1 Corinthians 16:22, where the term occurs in Aramaic, the title refers to the coming apocalyptic judge. Elsewhere, it seems to stress the completed character of salvation and the present ruling force of Jesus. He is the one elevated to rule as stated in 1 Timothy 3:16 and 1 Peter 3:18ff. That is the sense of the miniature creed, "Jesus is Lord," found in 1 Corinthians 12:3 and elsewhere.

There is, in fact, variety in such creeds and hymns embedded in the New Testament. Out of them and other materials it is not possible to reconstruct a single pattern of proclamation or confession as it was announced by the primitive Church. Such unity as there is arises from the unity of the one to whom the creeds and hymns refer, a person known under many titles. The picture presented is of a Christianity more varied, and perhaps richer, than that given in the more conservatively reconstructed Pentecostal Gospel.

—*Edgar M. Krenz*

FURTHER READING
Bonz, Marianne Palmer. *The Past as Legacy: Luke-Acts and Ancient Epic*. Minneapolis, Minn.: Fortress Press, 2000. Illuminates the influence of literary and traditional material on Luke's Gospel.
Dunn, James D. G. *The Theology of Paul the Apostle*. Grand Rapids, Mich.: William B. Eerdmans, 1997. An extensive and detailed explication of Pauline theology.
Neill, Stephen Charles. *Jesus Through Many Eyes: An Introduction to the Theology of the New Testament*. Cambridge, England: Clarke and Co., 2002. Analyzes the differing theologies that may be discerned in the New Testament.

SEE ALSO: c. 6 B.C.E., Birth of Jesus Christ; c. 30 C.E., Condemnation and Crucifixion of Jesus Christ; c. 90 C.E., Synod of Jamnia; 200 C.E., Christian Apologists Develop Concept of Theology; 313-395 C.E., Inception of Church-State Problem; 325 C.E., Adoption of the Nicene Creed; 428-431 C.E., Nestorian Controversy; October 8-25, 451 C.E., Council of Chalcedon.
RELATED ARTICLES in *Great Lives from History: The Ancient World*: Jesus; Saint Paul; Saint Peter.

40-43 C.E.
TRUNG SISTERS LEAD VIETNAMESE REBELLION AGAINST CHINESE

Trung Trac and Trung Nhi led a rebellion against Chinese domination of Vietnam. Although the victory over China was short-lived, the sisters have remained two of Vietnam's greatest national heroes.

LOCALE: Chiao Chih (now the northern half of Vietnam)
CATEGORY: Wars, uprisings, and civil unrest

KEY FIGURES
Trung Trac (d. 43 C.E.), leader of a rebellion against Chinese domination of Vietnam
Trung Nhi (d. 43 C.E.), younger sister of Trung Trac and coleader of the Vietnamese rebellion

SUMMARY OF EVENT
The rebellion led by Trung Trac and Trung Nhi was the result of a sequence of actions by China. When Vietnam fell under the control of China in 111 B.C.E., China re-

tained the native Vietnamese aristocracy to facilitate administration of its possession. This decision, however, created an enduring hostility between the Vietnamese and Chinese upper classes.

The conflict between aristocratic classes increased when Wang Mang usurped the throne of China and declared himself emperor in 9 C.E. At that time, many of his opponents took refuge in the Circuit of Chiao Chih (Vietnamese Giao Chi), one of several names that designated Vietnam during its early history. Other early names included Au Lac, Nan Yueh, Chiao Chou, and Annam. Chiao Chih consisted of the northern part of present-day Vietnam (roughly the portion formerly known as North Vietnam) and a portion of what today is southern China. Many of the refugees were scholars who sought employment in local administration. Accommodating the additional positions required increased revenue, which led to increased taxes on salt and iron and land seizures from wealthy Vietnamese, thus setting in motion the economic reasons for the Trung sisters' rebellion.

At the same time, efforts to force Chinese customs on Vietnamese engendered additional resentment. Men were forced to grow hair, and women were required to wear pants rather than skirts. Confucian moral principles, marriages arranged by parents, and an increasingly patriarchal family system altered social life, and Vietnamese were coerced into accepting Chinese gods in place of their traditional ancestral spirits.

Wang Mang was overthrown in 23 C.E., but the change in leadership did not improve the situation for the Vietnamese. Teng Jang, the governor of Chiao Chih, after supporting restoration of the Han Dynasty, led many Chinese leaders to the emperor's court to be honored and to enjoy the royal atmosphere. Left behind to administer local government were less qualified men, such as Su Ting (To Dinh), prefect of Giao Chi. (The Circuit of Chiao Chih consisted of several prefectures, including one with the same name as the circuit.) The traditional view of Su Ting is that he was both greedy and incompetent.

Thi Sach, a prominent aristocrat at Chu Dien and husband of Trung Trac, who was from a noble family in Me Linh (near where the Hong River flows out of the mountains, with Chu Dien a short distance downriver), resisted Su Ting. Trung Trac apparently encouraged his resistance. This resulted, according to most accounts, in the prefect's execution of Thi Sach in 40 C.E. Historian Keith Weller Taylor, however, argues that there is no historical basis for this conclusion and that later chroniclers added the execution to satisfy members of patriarchal societies that would have resisted acknowledging a woman's leadership of a rebellion with her husband still living.

Historians agree that Trung Trac, aided by her younger sister, Trung Nhi, led the rebellion in 40 C.E. that quickly captured sixty-five Chinese citadels. Trung Trac is described in Vietnamese accounts as a fearless and highly effective leader. One story, probably legend rather than fact, has her killing a tiger and using its skin for a parchment on which to write her call to arms. She also is described as rejecting the traditional mourning attire of a widow in order to reflect a larger commitment to her people. The sisters led an army (described variously as thirty thousand to eighty thousand strong) that quickly overcame the opposition. Su Ting reportedly cut off his hair and beard to hide his identity and fled into China.

Many prominent Vietnamese joined the rebellion. Temples dedicated to Trung Trac cite some fifty leaders who participated, among them many women. Phung Thi Chinh is reported to have led a battle at Tay Vu in Lang

Bac Province while pregnant, giving birth during battle and immediately resuming her martial efforts. Le Chan is credited with commanding naval forces and leading a battle on the Bach Dang River. A princess named Thanh Thien is said to have triumphed over a Chinese army of twenty thousand, and one of Trung Trac's male supporters, seventy-year-old Nguyen Tam Trinh, led his martial arts students into battle. Modern historians, of course, cannot be certain that such accounts are entirely accurate. Regardless of specifics, Trung Trac clearly enjoyed considerable support or she could not have registered the major, if temporary, military success against the Chinese that history acknowledges she achieved.

Trung Trac established a royal court at Me Linh and was recognized as queen, with Trung Nhi constantly by her side. She abolished the hated taxes that had been levied by the Chinese and sought to restore traditional Vietnamese customs. An oath attributed to Trung Trac that still survives in Vietnam indicates the major goals of her rebellion: to gain revenge for wrongs committed against her country and her husband and to restore traditional Vietnamese aristocratic rule in the region.

The Chinese prepared to retaliate in 41 C.E., as the emperor appointed Ma Yüan (Ma Vien), an experienced general, to lead the counterattack. He led an army of eight thousand regular troops and some twelve thousand militiamen from eastern Chiao Chih, hoping to transport his men by boat. Finding insufficient vessels available, he marched his troops across often rough terrain, constructing roads as he went. In the spring of 42, Ma Yüan decided to pause to wait out the rainy season. At that point, Trung Trac, fearing that she would lose many of her forces if she waited longer, attacked. The results were devastating, as thousands of her Vietnamese followers were captured and beheaded, and thousands more surrendered.

Trung Trac retreated to Mount Tan Vien at Me Linh with Ma Yüan in pursuit. What happened next is in some dispute. The traditional account has Trung Trac and Trung Nhi committing suicide by throwing themselves into the Hat Giang River on February 6, 43 C.E., rather than surrendering. That account also has many of their followers, including Phung Thi Chinh and Princess Thanh Thien, following their example by also choosing death rather than being taken by the Chinese. Historian Taylor, who consistently attempts to de-romanticize the story of Trung Trac, asserts that the two sisters were captured by their adversary and beheaded, with their heads sent to the Han court. As with so much of the story, certainty remains elusive.

SIGNIFICANCE

The rebellion failed in the short term as China reasserted its rule over Vietnam. However, Trung Trac and Trung Nhi became national heroes. As the centuries progressed, they increasingly were seen as the embodiment of the country's determination to resist outside domination. They also were enshrined among the nation's national spirits, and thus their assistance was sought in times of need, such as during floods or drought.

Many temples have been constructed over the years to honor the Trung sisters, two of the most famous being the Hai Ba in Hanoi and the Hat Mon in Son Tay Province. Near Me Linh, the sisters' home, in Ha Loi village, an annual festival is held on the sixth day of the first lunar month (February 6). The Trung sisters continue to be commemorated in almost every way possible, including poems, plays, postage stamps, statues, and public ceremonies.

—*Edward J. Rielly*

FURTHER READING

Bergman, Arlene Eisen. *Women of Viet Nam*. 2d ed. San Francisco: Peoples Press, 1975. This book places the Trung sisters within the context of historical achievements of Vietnamese women and attitudes toward women throughout Vietnamese history.

Chapuis, Oscar. *A History of Vietnam: From Hong Bang to Tu Duc*. Westport, Conn.: Greenwood Press, 1995. Chapuis discusses the Trung sisters' rebellion within a scholarly examination of Vietnam from prehistoric times through the nineteenth century.

Hammer, Ellen. *Vietnam: Yesterday and Today*. New York: Holt, Rinehart and Winston, 1966. Hammer's focus is on Vietnamese culture, and her brief account of the Trung sisters is within that context.

Taylor, Keith Weller. *The Birth of Vietnam*. Berkeley: University of California Press, 1983. Taylor explores Vietnamese history through the tenth century and includes an appendix on representations of the Trung sisters in later literature.

SEE ALSO: 1st century C.E., Tai Peoples Migrate into Southeast Asia; 9-23 C.E., Wang Nang's Rise to Power; 25 C.E., Guang Wudi Restores the Han Dynasty.

43-130 C.E.
ROMAN CONQUEST OF BRITAIN

The Romans created a new province by subjugating Britain's Celtic tribes and left their cultural imprint on the island.

LOCALE: Britain south of Hadrian's Wall
CATEGORIES: Wars, uprisings, and civil unrest; expansion and land acquisition

KEY FIGURES

Julius Caesar (100-44 B.C.E.), Roman dictator, r. 49-44 B.C.E.

Claudius I (10 B.C.E.-54 C.E.), Roman emperor, r. 41-54 C.E.

Gnaeus Julius Agricola (40-93 C.E.), Roman governor (imperial legate) of Britain, 78-84 C.E.

Hadrian (76-138 C.E.), Roman emperor, r. 117-138 C.E.

SUMMARY OF EVENT

At the beginning of the Christian era, Britannia—the Roman name for England, Wales, and southern Scotland—had an Iron Age culture. Before the sixth century B.C.E., Celtic language and culture had crossed the English Channel from the Continent and, by the time of Julius Caesar, predominated throughout the island. Little is known of the Celts' history because they were preliterate, and Greek and Roman writers only wrote about them to the extent that they interacted with classical culture. Archaeology allows an estimate of their development. Tribal kingdoms dominated by warrior aristocracies fought incessantly. Possessing rich farmland, engaging in frequent trade with their Celtic kin of Gaul and the Rhineland, and sharing their La Tène culture, the tribes of the southeast were developing rapidly. Their villages approximated true towns and their kings struck coins, proof of emerging royal power. The tribes of the north and west were isolated and poorer, still relying on hill forts for defense.

Caesar's campaign against the Nervii in northern Gaul led him in 55 B.C.E. to make an expedition across the channel against their British allies. With a small force, he landed on the Kentish coast, but storm damage to his fleet and British resistance forced his withdrawal that fall. He was more successful the following year, as he defeated Cassivellaunus of the Catuvellauni near present-day St. Albans, took hostages, required payment of tribute, claimed to have conquered Britain, and left, never to return. Civil wars from 49 to 30 B.C.E. and then the organization of Gaul (which included modern France and parts of Germany and Italy) and the establishment of the Rhine frontier kept Rome out of Britain for almost a century. Diplomacy sought to maintain a rough equality among the tribes by supporting kings or factions and to prevent British assistance to revolts inside Roman Gaul. Finds of Roman coins and wine amphoras indicate a sporadic luxury trade. Anti-Roman Catuvellaunian expansion in Essex and across the south necessitated a change in Roman policies.

Claudius I decided to conquer Britain. He dispatched Aulus Plautius at the head of an army of four legions (fifty-five hundred men each) plus an equal number of auxiliary troops in 43 C.E. The force landed in Kent, crossed the Thames, and captured Camulodunum (Colchester), which had recently become the Catuvellaunian capital. Leaving Legio XX Valeria at Camulodunum, three army corps fanned out to overrun the lowlands. Legio II Augusta pacified the southern region under the command of Vespasian. Legio XIV Gemina—joined by Legio XX Valeria in 49 C.E.—thrust into the Midlands, and Legio IX Hispana marched through East Anglia.

By 47 C.E., the new province embraced lands south and east of the Humber and Severn Rivers. A military road, the Fosse Way, ran from Exeter (a base of Legio II) northeast to Lincoln (a base of Legio IX) and marked the limit of Roman control. The decommissioned fortress at Camulodunum became a *colonia* and the provincial capital; Verulamium (near St. Albans) and Londinium (London) were flourishing symbols of Roman rule. Two tribal kings surrendered in time to preserve independence as client rulers: Cogidubnus in Surrey-Hampshire and Prasutagus (d. 60 C.E.) in Norfolk.

Subsequent Roman advances were much more difficult because of highland terrain and stiffening resistance. The Silures in eastern Wales, the Ordovices in northern Wales, and the Brigantes in Yorkshire proved to be intractable. The harsh annexation of Prasutagus's kingdom after his death sparked a revolt led by his widow Boudicca in c. 60 C.E. Her army sacked Camulodunum, Londinium, and Verulamium, but the disciplined army of the governor Suetonius Paulinus destroyed it.

Under the Flavian Dynasty (69-96 C.E.), Rome expanded the province and improved the quality of its rule. The laudatory biography of Gnaeus Julius Agricola by his son-in-law Tacitus (c. 56-c. 120 C.E.) has made that governor's activities famous. His predecessors Cerealis and Frontinus (35-c. 103 C.E.) subjugated the Brigantes

SITES IN ROMAN BRITAIN, 43-130 C.E.

Roman Place Names	Modern Cities
Camulodunum	Colchester
Deva	Dover
Eburacum	York
Isca Silurum	Caerleon, Wales
Lindum	Lincoln
Londinium	London
Verulamium	St. Albans

North Sea

Hadrian's Wall

Eburacum

IRELAND

Irish Sea

Lindum

Isca Silurum

Camulodunum

Verulamium

Londinium

Deva

English Channel

1 - 100 C.E.

and the tribes of Wales, freeing Agricola to push against Caledonia (Scotland) and begin construction of a fortress for Legio XX at Inchtuthil on the Tay. It was abandoned unfinished as troubles on the Danube compelled the withdrawal from the Highlands and the reduction of the British garrison to three legions. Legion IX occupied Eburacum (York), while Legions II and XX moved to Isca (Caerleon) and Deva (Chester); all three proved to be permanent.

The cities destroyed by Boudicca were rebuilt, and Londinium, the hub of the road network and the possessor of an excellent harbor, soon became the capital. Archaeology has uncovered the governor's palace, the forum, some streets, and wharves. Two former legionary fortresses became *coloniae*: Lindum colonia (Lincoln) and Glevum *castra* (Gloucester fort). To promote Ro-

Caesar's forces land in Britain. (F. R. Niglutsch)

manization and easier provincial administration, the governors fostered Roman-style towns as *civitas*-capitals (canton-capitals), which controlled the surrounding countryside. Early examples are Canterbury and Chelmsford; more appeared under the Flavians—Chichester, Silchester, Winchester, Dorchester, Exeter, Cirencester, Caistor-by-Norwich, Leicester, and Wroxeter. Many of these places have continued to flourish as cities to modern times, so knowledge of them has increased through urban archaeology. Wroxeter and Silchester are uninhabited, and studies of them have provided the most complete information of Romano-British towns.

Literary sources necessary for narrative history practically cease at the recall of Agricola in 84 C.E. Legio IX was transferred out of Britain about 110 (the old view that it was destroyed in a rebellion around the year 117 is wrong). Hadrian came to Britain in 121, bringing a new governor (Platorius Nepos), a new legion (VI Victrix, which occupied York), and new ideas. The last *civitas*-capitals appeared in these years. Hadrian initiated the building of the famous wall, the best-known example among a number of linear barriers around the Roman

Empire and stretching some 274 Roman miles (84 miles or 135 kilometers) from coast to coast from the mouth of the River Tyne to Solway Firth. Auxiliary troops (infantry and part-mounted cohorts) garrisoned forts at 5- or 6-mile (8- or 10-kilometer) intervals. Between each pair of forts were "milecastles" housing small contingents sent out from the forts, and watchtowers rose at 0.3-mile (0.5-kilometer) intervals, thus within sight of one another. Command headquarters and the largest single unit (a "milliary" cavalry wing, or *ala*) were at Stanwix near Carlisle. There were also several cavalry forts to the north of the wall, from which mounted patrols increased Roman surveillance.

Hadrian's Wall, which marked the northern boundary of Britannia and the Roman Empire, stood guard against the tribes of the far north and prevented them from joining restless peoples within the province. The wall also allowed the Romans to collect customs. Although the wall made raids difficult, it was not intended to withstand large attacks. Invaders who overran it would have to contend with the legions moving up from York and Chester and reinforced auxiliary units closing in from behind.

SIGNIFICANCE

The reign of Hadrian marks the end of the Roman conquest of Britain. In later years there were only occasional campaigns beyond the wall. The efforts of Antoninus Pius (86-161 C.E.) to hold a line between Edinburgh and Glasgow were soon abandoned. Septimius Severus (145-211 C.E.) fought up into the Highlands and died at York; his son Caracalla (188-217 C.E.) pulled back to the wall.

The parts of Britain that had adopted Roman customs and traditions, including agricultural practices, retained this way of life after the Romans departed. The Britons continued to inhabit many of the cities and use the roads that the Romans built. However, this mode of existence began a transformation during the late fourth century, when the Angles, Jutes, and Saxons started to invade Britain.

—*Kevin Herbert and Thomas H. Watkins*

FURTHER READING

Hill, Stephen, and Stanley Ireland. *Roman Britain*. London: Bristol Classical Press, 1996. Covers the Roman conquest of Britain from beginning to end. Bibliography.

Jiménez, Ramón L. *Caesar Against the Celts*. New York: Sarpedon, 1996. An examination of Julius Caesar's campaign against the Celts. Maps, bibliography, and index.

Manley, John. *A.D. 43: The Roman Invasion of Britain, a Reassessment*. Stroud, Gloucestershire, England: Tempus, 2002. Archaeologist Manley examines the Roman invasion of Britain, casting doubt on some of the accepted beliefs in the light of archaeological discoveries.

Peddie, John *Conquest: The Roman Invasion of Britain*. New York: St. Martin's Press, 1997. Peddie describes the invasion of Britain in 43 C.E. by Roman forces. Bibliography and indexes.

Salway, Peter. *A History of Roman Britain*. New York: Oxford University Press, 1993. Classical historian Salway examines the Romans' view of Britain before the conquest, their conquest of Britain, and events during Britain's existence as a Roman province. Bibliography and index.

Salway, Peter, ed. *The Roman Era: The British Isles, 55 B.C.-A.D. 410*. New York: Oxford University Press, 2002. Covers the Roman invasion of Britain and subsequent events. Bibliography and index.

Shotter, D. C. A. *The Roman Frontier in Britain: Hadrian's Wall, the Antonine Wall, and Roman Policy in the North*. Preston, England: Carnegie, 1996. Shotter looks at how the Romans controlled Britain after the conquest, in particular, how they managed the northern border. Bibliography and index.

Todd, Malcolm. *Roman Britain*. 3d ed. Blackwell Classic Histories of England series. Malden, Mass.: Blackwell Publishers, 1999. A history of Roman Britain from the conquest to the end. Bibliography and index.

Webster, Graham. *The Roman Invasion of Britain*. 1993. Reprint. New York: Routledge, 1999. A military history of the invasion of Britain by the Romans. Bibliography and index.

SEE ALSO: 14th-9th centuries B.C.E., Urnfield Culture Flourishes in Northwestern Europe; c. 1100-c. 500 B.C.E., Hallstatt Culture Dominates Northern Europe; c. 100 B.C.E.-c. 100 C.E., Celtic Hill Forts Are Replaced by *Oppida*; c. 60 B.C.E., Druidism Flourishes in Gaul and Britain; 58-51 B.C.E., Caesar Conquers Gaul; 60 C.E., Boudicca Leads Revolt Against Roman Rule; 449 C.E., Saxon Settlement of Britain Begins.

RELATED ARTICLES in *Great Lives from History: The Ancient World:* Gnaeus Julius Agricola; Boudicca; Julius Caesar; Claudius I; Hadrian; Tacitus; Vercingetorix.

1 - 100 C.E.

c. 50 C.E.
CREATION OF THE ROMAN IMPERIAL BUREAUCRACY

The creation of the imperial bureaucracy established civil service reform within the political machinery of the Roman Empire.

LOCALE: Rome and the Roman Empire
CATEGORY: Government and politics

KEY FIGURES
Augustus (63 B.C.E.-14 C.E.), Roman emperor,
    r. 27 B.C.E.-14 C.E.
Tiberius (42 B.C.E.-37 C.E.), Roman emperor, r. 14-
    37 C.E.
Caligula (12-41 C.E.), Roman emperor, r. 37-41 C.E.
Claudius I (10 B.C.E.-54 C.E.), Roman emperor, r. 41-
    54 C.E.

SUMMARY OF EVENT
The imperial bureaucracy was the creation of the early Roman emperors, especially of the first, Augustus, and the fourth, Claudius I. Augustus's reorganization of Roman government provided the framework for the development of such a bureaucracy; Claudius's deliberate elaboration of the bureaucracy that had developed during preceding reigns brought this branch of government service to the peak of its power.

The imperial bureaucracy was comparable to, and at first existed alongside, an older and less elaborate bureaucracy of the Republican period. The Republican magistrates had drawn their supporting staffs from two sources. One was the pool of permanent employees attached to the central government treasury. The other was each magistrate's personal staff. The Roman magistrate was invariably a man of property, and it was customary for such a person to use his personal staff, composed in large part of his own slaves and freedmen, to conduct public as well as private business.

Under the political settlement effected by Augustus, the government of Italy and of about half the provinces continued to be conducted according to Republican custom, by annually elected magistrates whose supporting staff was drawn from personal employees and from employees of the treasury, which remained under the control of the senate. In the remaining provinces, government was the personal responsibility of the emperor, who governed through representatives whom he appointed. The emperor's representatives, once again men of property and political standing, may have been assisted by their personal staffs but they were not provided with personnel from the central treasury. Instead, the supporting staff for administration of the emperor's provinces was drawn from the emperor's own household and was composed, for the most part, of the emperor's slaves and freedmen.

Information about the development of the imperial bureaucracy under Augustus and under his successors Tiberius and Caligula is limited. One may assume that as an emperor gathered ever greater powers into his own hands, the bureaus that assisted him grew in number, complexity, and power. With Tiberius's retirement from Rome in his later years and with Caligula's erratic preoccupations, much of the business of the Roman Empire must have been left to the chiefs of bureaus. It is a tribute to the capabilities of the bureaucracy and of the bureau-

Tiberius. (Library of Congress)

crats that civilian government did not collapse, even under the burden of unrest and resentment that led to Caligula's assassination.

The importance of a capable imperial bureaucracy did not escape the notice of Claudius, and it is during his rule that scholars have found much evidence of the consolidation and expansion of this organization. Claudius's personal agents collected certain taxes even in provinces governed, in theory, by elected magistrates. These financial agents were granted political powers, particularly the right to preside over certain kinds of litigation, that had formerly been reserved for elected officials. The emperor's staff in Rome was organized into distinct bureaus whose chiefs, the emperor's freedmen, were granted extraordinary dignity and authority. Five chief bureaus are known: *a rationibus* dealing with finance, *ab epistulis* with state correspondence, *a libellis* with petitions, *a cognitionibus* with justice, and *a studiis* with culture.

In his elaboration of the imperial bureaucracy, Claudius was no doubt motivated by the desire to achieve efficient central administration, and there is evidence that the Roman Empire in general, and particularly the outlying regions, benefited from his reforms. Yet the population of Rome, jealous of its ancient privileges, resented the assumption of power by foreign-born former slaves. Claudius may have actually granted his ministers enough power to govern even him. Narcissus, chief of the bureau *ab epistulis*, is said to have disposed of Claudius's wife Messalina (22-48 C.E.) more or less without his consent. Pallas, chief of *a rationibus*, was believed to have cooperated with Claudius's next wife, Agrippina the Younger (15-59 C.E.), in bringing about the emperor's death by poisoning, and in establishing as next emperor not Claudius's son and heir-elect, Britannicus (c. 41-55 C.E.), but Agrippina's son, the infamous Nero (37-68 C.E.), who reigned from 41 to 68 C.E. As Nero devoted himself increasingly to his own amusement, the imperial bureaucracy continued to wield nearly unsupervised power, and there is little doubt that the abuses of the emperor's freedmen contributed to the alienation that led to open revolt and warfare in 68-69 C.E.

SIGNIFICANCE

Succeeding emperors attempted to restrain their agents without enacting any major reform of the bureaucracy, which continued to function in the form given it by Claudius until the reign of Hadrian. By that time, the principle of one-man rule was well accepted, and the service of the emperor was recognized as the service of the state. Hadrian reorganized the imperial bureaucracy accordingly, relying less on the services of his personal dependents and opening the more important positions to freeborn Roman citizens. The rift between bureaucracy and citizenry was repaired without diminishing the usefulness of the bureaucracy itself, the importance of which only increased as the Empire grew.

—Zola M. Packman, updated by Jeffrey L. Buller

FURTHER READING

Braund, David C., ed. *The Administration of the Roman Empire, 241 B.C.-A.D. 193*. Exeter, England: University of Exeter Press, 1993. A concise series of essays exploring the development of the Roman imperial bureaucracy.

Dise, Robert L. *Cultural Change and Imperial Administration*. New York: Peter Lang, 1991. Using the middle Danube provinces as an example, explores the operation of the Roman bureaucracy in outlying regions of the empire. Covers the period from the beginning of the empire to the third century C.E. and provides excellent insight into the day-to-day administration of the Roman government.

Lendon, J. E. *Empire of Honour: The Art of Government in the Roman World*. New York: Oxford University Press, 2002. Analyzes the operation of Roman government in the first four centuries C.E.

Lintott, Andrew. *Imperium Romanum: Politics and Administration*. New York: Routledge, 1993. This study of how the Romans acquired, kept, and administered their empire shows the Roman imperial bureaucracy in operation.

Lydus, Ioannes. *On Powers: Or, The Magistracies of the Roman State*. Translated by Anastasius C. Bandy. Philadelphia: American Philosophical Society, 1983. Contains both the Greek text and a good translation (in parallel columns) of an informative sixth century work on the operation of the Roman imperial bureaucracy. Also includes an introduction, critical text, and commentary.

SEE ALSO: 340-338 B.C.E., Origin of *Municipia*; 287 B.C.E., *Lex Hortensia* Reforms the Roman Constitution; 180 B.C.E., Establishment of the *Cursus honorum*; 133 B.C.E., Tiberius Sempronius Gracchus Is Tribune; 54 B.C.E., Roman Poet Catullus Dies; 43-42 B.C.E., Second Triumvirate Enacts Proscriptions; 27-23 B.C.E., Completion of the Augustan Settlement.

RELATED ARTICLES in *Great Lives from History: The Ancient World*: Agrippina the Younger; Augustus; Caligula; Catullus; Claudius I; Gracchi; Hadrian; Messalina, Valeria; Nero.

1 - 100 C.E.

c. 50-c. 150 C.E.
COMPILATION OF THE NEW TESTAMENT

The earliest Christian literature was collected as communities and their leaders decided which works should be considered authoritative, laying the foundation for the New Testament of the Christian Bible.

LOCALE: Cities of eastern Mediterranean basin, Rome (now in Italy), and southern Gaul (present-day France)

CATEGORY: Religion

KEY FIGURES

Saint Paul (c. 10-c. 64 C.E.), apostle, Christian missionary, and epistle writer

Marcion (c. 120-c. 160 C.E.), Gnostic religious leader

Saint Irenaeus (between 120 and 140-c. 202 C.E.), bishop of Lyons in southern Gaul

SUMMARY OF EVENT

The New Testament of the Christian Bible is a collection of early Christian writings that eventually supplemented the Hebrew sacred writings in constituting Christian Scripture, or the canon of what came to be accepted as divinely inspired texts. Churches that follow the decisions of the Council of Chalcedon (451 C.E.)—which include the Roman Catholic, Eastern Orthodox, and all Protestant denominations—accept twenty-seven books, while non-Chalcedonian churches, such as the Syrian Jacobite church, accept fewer.

The generally recognized canon consists of four accounts of the life and teachings of Jesus Christ, known as the Gospels ("good news"; *evangelion* in Greek); an extension of one of the Gospel accounts that describes the creation of the early Christian communities and some of the travels of Saint Paul (Acts of the Apostles); fourteen letters (epistles) originally ascribed to Paul and addressed to individuals or communities; seven other letters, two ascribed to the apostle Peter, three to John, and one each to Jesus' brother James and James's brother Jude; and an apocalyptic vision of Heaven and the end of time ascribed to Saint John the Apostle (Apocalypse or Revelation). Most scholars agree that the earliest of these writings are the Pauline epistles (c. 55-c. 68 C.E.). These were originally composed in Greek, and there is general (but by no means universal) acceptance of Paul's authorship of all except that to the Hebrews, which is now recognized as the work of someone other than Paul. The actual authorship and dating of the other, non-Pauline epistles is hotly debated, but the early Christians accepted them as authentic and quoted from them as authoritative. The latest New Testament book is probably 2 Peter, dating from perhaps as late as 125 C.E.

When Paul wrote of the Gospel of Christ he referred to the message, or "good news," because no Gospel account now recognized was written during his lifetime. The Gospels ascribed to Matthew, Mark, Luke, and John were probably composed in Greek between the late 60's C.E. and the end of the first century. Modern scholars have posited the existence of a very early written source (German *Quelle*) nicknamed "Q," which would have consisted of a list of Jesus' major teachings or sayings, perhaps known to Paul and the communities he established. The Gospel according to Mark, whose author may have been associated closely with Saint Peter or communities and traditions he established in Rome, is likely to be the earliest narrative Gospel, incorporating his own source materials. The Gospels named for Luke and Matthew apparently have their bases in Q and Mark, as well as other sources unique to each. The author of Luke appears to have strong connections with the Pauline mission, as the details on Paul's career in the Gospel's continuation, the Acts of the Apostles, makes evident, and as does mention of a Luke in three of Paul's epistles. The apostle Matthew's Gospel seems to have originated in a community of Christians with both Jewish and gentile roots, perhaps in Antioch or Palestine. Together, these three Gospels are often called the synoptics (look-alikes), since they share many common stories and essential teachings. John's Gospel, attributed by tradition to the "beloved Apostle," is structured quite differently from the other accounts and is far more concerned with complex theological teaching that clearly identifies Jesus as divine. The earliest surviving written connection of the specific authors to these works dates to about 140 C.E., but clearly the early Christian communities and writers had accepted these attributions as authentic long before this.

In the earliest Church, "Scripture" referred to the Hebrew Bible. Only slowly did specifically Christian writings come to be treated as Scripture, to be given the same respect as the Hebrew texts that guided the community from which Jesus and his apostles emerged. In large part this was due to the successes of the early faith communities, whose founders and earliest leaders died off, leaving a need for guaranteed sources of the teachings of Jesus and Paul. As long as authentic teaching remained a matter of oral preaching, the door remained open to false doctrine, against which the New Testament authors from Paul on warn their readers. Members of both the Greek-speaking gentile and the Jewish communities among whom the Christian message was spread were literate and respectful of written authority, and the direct quotation of authoritative sources such as Paul and the Gospels served the needs of Christian leaders and followers alike. However, the question remained: Which writings were truly authentic? As Christian writings increased in number, the distinction had to be made. As major differences in teachings developed by the early second century, both proto-orthodox Christians, or those whose interpretations of the Christian message eventually came to dominate, and those who would be labeled heterodox (otherwise believing), marshaled their arguments around what they considered authentic texts.

The earliest canon (list) of accepted works is probably that of Marcion, developed in Rome between 137 and 144 C.E., whose Gnostic, heterodox ideas spurred other Christian leaders to begin to create their own. Marcion

---

THE BOOKS OF THE NEW TESTAMENT

Gospel According to Matthew
Gospel According to Mark
Gospel According to Luke
Gospel According to John
Acts of Apostles
Letter of Paul to Romans
First Letter of Paul to Corinthians
Second Letter of Paul to Corinthians
Letter of Paul to Galatians
Letter of Paul to Ephesians
Letter of Paul to Philippians
Letter of Paul to Colossians
First Letter of Paul to Thessalonians
Second Letter of Paul to Thessalonians
First Letter of Paul to Timothy
Second Letter of Paul to Timothy
Letter of Paul to Titus
Letter of Paul to Philemon
Letter to Hebrews
Letter of James
First Letter of Peter
Second Letter of Peter
First Letter of John
Second Letter of John
Third Letter of John
Letter of Jude
Revelation to John

---

rejected any authority of the Hebrew Scriptures, insisting that Christian writings replace these as sources of God's message to humankind. He tried to reconcile the differences between the Gospels of Matthew and Luke and to remove any pro-Jewish elements in them, creating his own blended version of a single Gospel (ignoring Mark and John). He listed only ten Pauline epistles as authentic. Non-Marcionite Christians (and even many of Marcion's followers) rejected this approach, reasserting the importance of the Hebrew writings, of all four Gospels and Acts, and of fourteen Pauline epistles. The core of the canon is recognizable as early as the mid-second century, as Christian authors treated certain writings as authoritative and inspired sources of Christian faith and doctrine, other works as useful but not authoritative, and still others as clearly flawed or even heretical. The earliest proto-orthodox canon appears in the work of Saint Irenaeus, bishop of Lyons, France, and enemy of Gnosticism, which dates from after 180 C.E. As time went on, however, Eastern theologians and other writers, such as the fourth century Christian historian Eusebius of Caesarea (c. 260-339 C.E.), either rejected or debated the use of certain non-Pauline epistles (especially 2 and 3 John and 2 Peter) and Revelation, leaving the final definition of the canon to the Council of Chalcedon. In the Western Church, arguments over which works should be in the canon ended by the later fourth century with the creation of Saint Jerome's Vulgate (Latin) version of the Bible, which became the medieval Western Church's standard edition.

SIGNIFICANCE

The significance of the compilation of the New Testament lies in its establishment of an agreed-on set of writings whose authority would become, by the early fifth century, unquestioned among the major Christian churches. Unlike the Christian Old Testament, which differs in content among the Orthodox, Catholic, and Protestant traditions, the New Testament would prove a unifying factor in the Church's history. By rejecting Gnostic and other apparently heretical works as invalid, the proto-orthodox Church differentiated itself from the other Christian streams of the day and aided its own self-identification, a process nurtured by its evolving clerical structure and system of local and ecumenical councils. Nonetheless, canonization did not eliminate the influence of early noncanonical works, as both the Roman and Orthodox churches relied on such sources' stories, such as those about Mary's youth and Jesus' descent into Hell, in their elaboration of the Christian tradition.

—*Joseph P. Byrne*

FURTHER READING

Brown, Edward Raymond. *An Introduction to the New Testament*. New York: Doubleday, 1997. Catholic Father Brown discusses historical background of each book in clearly organized detail: date, sources, authorship, community of work's origin. Bibliographies and index.

Ehrman, Bart D. *The New Testament: A Historical Introduction to the Early Christian Writings*. New York: Oxford University Press, 1997. Full textbook treatment of the creation and reception of the recognized and rejected texts. Illustrations, bibliographies, and index.

Farmer, William R., and Denis M. Farkasfalvy. *The Formation of the New Testament Canon: An Ecumenical Approach*. Mahwah, N.J.: Paulist Press, 1983. Two self-standing, extended essays that outline the basic issues and controversies surrounding the canon's development. Notes.

Mack, Burton L. *The Lost Gospel: The Book of Q and Christian Origins*. San Francisco: HarperCollins, 1994. Introductory study and reconstruction of the conjectured controversial and lost sourcebook of the authentic sayings of Jesus and the beliefs of the communities that produced it. Short bibliography and index.

Maier, Paul. *Eusebius: The Church History*. Grand Rapids, Mich.: Kregel, 1999. New translation with book-by-book commentary of this key early history of the Church. Illustrations, bibliography, and index.

Metzger, Bruce. *The Canon of the New Testament: Its Origin, Development, and Significance*. 1987. Reprint. New York: Oxford University Press, 1997. Classic treatment of the canon's development and importance in the early Church, and beyond. Bibliography and index.

Richardson, Cyril C. *Early Christian Fathers*. 1953. Reprint. New York: Touchstone Books, 1995. Standard collection of major works of such writers as Clement, Justin, and Irenaeus. Indexed.

SEE ALSO: c. 6 B.C.E., Birth of Jesus Christ; c. 30 C.E., Condemnation and Crucifixion of Jesus Christ; c. 30 C.E., Preaching of the Pentecostal Gospel; January-March, 55 or 56 C.E., Paul Writes His Letter to the Romans; 200 C.E., Christian Apologists Develop Concept of Theology; 325 C.E., Adoption of the Nicene Creed; 413-427 C.E., Saint Augustine Writes *The City of God*; c. 382-c. 405 C.E., Saint Jerome Creates the Vulgate; 428-431 C.E., Nestorian Controversy; October 8-25, 451 C.E., Council of Chalcedon.

RELATED ARTICLES in *Great Lives from History: The Ancient World*: Saint Augustine; Saint Irenaeus; Saint Jerome; Jesus; Saint Paul; Saint Peter.

January-March, 55 or 56 C.E.
PAUL WRITES HIS LETTER TO THE ROMANS

Paul's epistle laid out his theories of postmortem judgment and marked one of Christianity's earliest attempts to distance itself from and reject Judaism.

LOCALE: Corinth (now in Greece)
CATEGORY: Religion

KEY FIGURES

Saint Paul (c. 10-c. 64 C.E.), Christian missionary
Priscilla (fl. second century C.E.) and
Aquila of Pontus (fl. second century C.E.), early Jewish converts of Paul who were living at Rome

SUMMARY OF EVENT

Saint Paul was a Jew and a Pharisee who was converted to Christianity, presumably in 33 C.E. Little is known about his life from that time until he began his first missionary journey in 47 C.E. For at least seventeen years after that, he was busy founding and visiting churches, especially in Asia Minor and continental Greece. He also wrote a number of letters which were both exhortations reflecting practical conditions in churches and expressions of his theology. His earliest letter was addressed to the church in Thessalonica about 50 C.E. During a three-month visit to the Corinthian church in the winter of 55 or 56 C.E., he wrote his most famous letter, to the Romans. Since the fourth century, this epistle has stood at the head of the Pauline corpus in the New Testament, even though it may well have been written last.

When Paul wrote to the church at Rome, which he honors as the result of others' labors, it was already widely renowned. He salutes the faith of the Romans "proclaimed all over the world," and he names some thirty people known to him as active in Christian circles, among them Priscilla and Aquila of Pontus. Some scholars, however, believe that Romans 16, which enumerates these people, really belongs to another letter, probably the one intended for the Ephesians.

Romans can scarcely be considered a summary of the whole of Paul's theology because it contains only incidental teaching on Christology and eschatology, two central concerns of the day, and nothing on the Lord's Supper or church polity. Nevertheless, Romans ranks alongside Galatians as one of Paul's most important treatises.

Judging from the contents of the letter, the writing of it was the result of controversy. After an appropriate introduction, Paul proceeds to assert that all will be rewarded or punished. The Gentiles, who have no specific moral or theological law, will be judged by the natural law written in their hearts. The Jews, who honor a specific law and yet transgress it, will also be judged. Because all have sinned, Greeks and Jews alike, it is clear that justification cannot come through the law. It brings only recognition of sin, for where there is no law there is no transgression. Justification comes rather by God's grace through redemption in Christ Jesus, whom God has sent forth as a propitiation through faith in his blood.

That man is justified by faith without the works of the law is seen, Paul contends, in the justification of Abraham, who was counted righteous by his faith and not by his legal observances. Justification, as a free gift, is mediated through the atoning death of Christ, the second Adam, who recapitulates and undoes the pernicious work of the first Adam. People, in a mystical way, are buried with Christ by baptism into death; their old selves are crucified with him so that the body of sin may be destroyed. He that is dead is free from sin. Then, just as Christ was raised up from the dead by the glory of the Father, even so people are made alive to walk in newness of life. Sin no longer has control over people because they are not under the law but under a reign of grace.

One major concern of Paul in his letter is the rejection of the Israelites and their destiny. The Jews have obviously rejected what is now offered to the Gentiles. Understandably, God will reject whom he will and show

The Romans protect Saint Paul from the mob. (F. R. Niglutsch)

mercy to whom he will; all things work together for good to those who love God and who are called. Those whom he did fore-know he predestined to be conformed to the image of his Son; those whom he predestined he also called and justified and glorified. Even though the Jews have refused to confess to the saving faith that Jesus is Lord and that God has raised him from the dead, God has not abandoned them entirely. Even now a remnant exists elected by virtue of grace and not of works. Moreover, the Jews' defection might be only temporary, so that in the meantime the Gospel can be preached to the Gentiles who should, in turn, be humble in face of their election.

At this point a section follows that deals with the practical obligations of the Christian life. Even though talents and gifts are different in different people, there must be a universal fraternal charity and tolerance. All must be subject to higher civil authorities as no authority exists except from God. Respect and forbearance must be extended to all including those who do not share the same convictions as to food and feast days. Charity, peace, self-denial, patience, and mercy must prevail.

The epistle ends with the controversial ending sending the apostle's greetings to friends supposedly in Rome.

SIGNIFICANCE

Paul's letter to the Romans, as embodying a significant draft of his theology, has always been a favorite of exegetes including Origen (c. 185-c. 254 C.E.), Saint John Chrysostom (c. 347-407 C.E.), Pelagius (c. 354-after 418 C.E.), Peter Abelard (1079-1144), and Thomas Aquinas (1224/1225-1274). Saint Augustine of Hippo was especially influenced by it in his anti-Pelagian stand, so that it has become central in any discussion of justification by faith, original sin, and to a lesser degree, of predestination. Martin Luther (1483-1546) was greatly affected by the epistle and wrote a commentary on it in 1515, which has been published only in the twentieth century. German religious reformer Phillip Melanchthon (1497-1560), too, wrote on it, as did John Calvin (1509-1564). The conversion that resulted in the establishment of Methodism by John Wesley (1703-1791) was largely effected from its study.

Romans is regarded by many scholars as the one document Paul did not write under the press of solving a problem and therefore sheds little light on the internal conditions of the Roman church with which, after all, Paul had no direct relationship. The epistle is written to secure the sympathy and hospitality of the church of Rome so it might serve Paul as a basis of operation for his subsequent work. At the same time, he hopes to make some contribution to the spiritual growth of the Roman Christians and to reap "some harvest" among them. That Romans is written for such uncomplicated and obvious reasons is not inconsistent or incongruous with the fact that the epistle stands, at the same time, as a comprehensive, planned, and carefully written statement of the fundamentals of Christianity. It is intended as an apology for Paul's understanding of the principles and methods of the Christian mission so that the Roman church can judge for itself whether he is the dangerous innovator that some Jewish Christians claimed he was, or a missionary whose gospel can command their support.

This view of Paul's purpose and the occasion of the letter naturally affects the understanding and use made of this epistle in reconstructing Paul's thought. Paul writes here for the last time as a free man and active missionary. He has completed his most successful period of missionary work and is at the height of his powers. Romans is thus the fruit of his thought and preaching, as well as his experience with controversy, suffering, trials, and spiritual buffeting. One can discern throughout the epistle traces of themes in earlier letters all brought together in a more reflective way into a finished product. Thus the concept of the "body and its members," such views as the relationship of faith and the spirit to the law and works, the promise to Abraham, and especially the matter of justification by faith are all ideas which can scarcely be understood without fuller reference to such earlier epistles as 1 Thessalonians, 1 Corinthians, and especially Galatians.

The sections in Romans that seem to stand as units, such as chapters 9-11 on the rejection of Israel and the early discourse on the universality of sin and retribution, may well represent old sermons or treatises that Paul used frequently in different contexts, which means that they may not reflect conditions in the Roman church at the time.

In Romans, then, the apologetic strain is prominent. Paul is doing more than writing something of passing historical relevance; he is, in fact, structuring a philosophy. He is arguing that a living and providential God "whose activity creates real crises in the lives of individuals and in the affairs of mankind" has broken into the course of history with the advent of Christ. It is most important, therefore, to deal with the relationship of Christianity to its parent Judaism and to expound on such meaningful matters as the merit of a legalistic religion compared to one of the free spirit, and to elucidate the doctrine of justification.

—*Edgar M. Krenz*

FURTHER READING

Bryan, Christopher. *A Preface to Romans: Notes on the Epistle in Its Literary and Cultural Setting.* New York: Oxford University Press, 2000. Attempts to show which literary type or genre would have been seen by Paul's contemporaries as being exemplified in the letter and to determine what can be surmised of Paul's attitude and approach to the Jewish Bible. The study involves discussion of and comparison with other literature from Paul's time, place, and milieu, including other writings attributed to Paul.

Dunn, James D. G. *The Theology of Paul the Apostle.* Grand Rapids, Mich.: William B. Eerdmans, 1997. An extensive and detailed explication of Pauline theology.

McRay, John. *Paul: His Life and Teaching.* Grand Rapids, Mich.: Baker Book House, 2003. An introduction to Paul's life and thought aimed at an undergraduate college audience. Includes a detailed examination of Paul's ideas, such as atonement, justification, and the Law, and what grounds these ideas in Jewish thought of the time.

Park, Eung Chun. *Either Jew or Gentile: Paul's Unfolding Theology of Inclusivity.* Louisville, Ky.: Westminster John Knox Press, 2003. Explores the evolution of Paul's understanding of the relationship between Judaism and Christianity and Jews and Christians.

Westerholm, Stephen. *Preface to the Study of Paul.* Grand Rapids, Mich.: William B. Eerdmans, 1997. Attempts to clarify Paul's assumptions about metaphysical reality, a vision derived from Jewish faith and shared with other early Christians. Paul's fundamental convic-

tions included the belief in the goodness of God and of what God has created, the belief that evil has its roots in the inappropriate responses of moral beings to what is good, and the assurance that goodness must triumph in the end. The argument of Romans takes shape within the framework of this vision.

SEE ALSO: c. 6 B.C.E., Birth of Jesus Christ; c. 30 C.E., Condemnation and Crucifixion of Jesus Christ; c. 30 C.E., Preaching of the Pentecostal Gospel; c. 50-c. 150 C.E., Compilation of the New Testament; 200 C.E., Christian Apologists Develop Concept of Theology; 325 C.E., Adoption of the Nicene Creed; 413-427 C.E., Saint Augustine Writes *The City of God*; c. 382-c. 405 C.E., Saint Jerome Creates the Vulgate; 428-431 C.E., Nestorian Controversy; October 8-25, 451 C.E., Council of Chalcedon.

RELATED ARTICLES in *Great Lives from History: The Ancient World*: Saint Augustine; Jesus; Saint Paul; Saint Peter.

---

60 C.E.
BOUDICCA LEADS REVOLT AGAINST ROMAN RULE

Boudicca's revolt, instigated by imperial disregard of her late husband's will, the rape of her daughters, and her own flogging, united southern Celtic tribes in a nearly successful attempt to resist imperial Rome rule.

LOCALE: Southeastern Britain, especially the realm of the Iceni (present-day Norfolk), Camulodunum (Colchester), Londinium (London), and Verulamium (St. Albans)

CATEGORY: Wars, uprisings, and civil unrest

KEY FIGURES

Boudicca (d. c. 60 C.E.), queen of the Iceni

Caratacus (early first century-after 51 C.E.), king of the Catuvellauni

Claudius I (10 B.C.E.-54 C.E.), Roman emperor, r. 41-54 C.E.

Catus Decianus (fl. first century C.E.), Roman procurator (tax collector) of Britain

Nero (37-68 C.E.), Roman emperor, r. 54-68 C.E.

Prasutagus (d. 60 C.E.), king of the Iceni, succeeded by Boudicca

Publius Ostorius Scapula (d. 52 C.E.), Roman governor of Britain, 50-52 C.E.

Gaius Suetonius Paulinus (fl. first century C.E.), Roman governor of Britain, 58-61 C.E.

SUMMARY OF EVENT

Queen Boudicca of the Iceni, one of the larger tribes in Britain, led a revolt against Roman rule in 60 C.E. There is greater agreement regarding the meaning of this warrior queen's name than regarding its spelling; it contains the Celtic root word for "victory." Many linguists translate Boudicca as meaning "Victory" or "the Victorious." There is little consensus regarding its proper spelling. Variations include Boudicca, Boudica, Bodicca, Boadicea, Boudicea (the spelling preferred by Tacitus, the Roman historian who provides the most information on her), Bonducca, and Bunduica. The "Boadicea" spelling was preferred by Victorian historians, but most twenty-first century scholars have adopted the more linguistically correct spelling "Boudicca."

The roots of Boudicca's rebellion were complex. Prior to the invasion of Britain in 54 B.C.E. by Julius Caesar and later in 43 C.E. by General Aulus Platius, many tribes lived in southern England. These tribes were polytheistic (believing in many deities) but were united by the priesthood of the Druids. Druidic priests could travel unharmed from one tribe to another, protected by their religious status. In this respect, they were more powerful than any tribal queen or king. They formed the one social element potentially capable of uniting the disparate tribes.

In 43 C.E., Emperor Claudius I sent Platius with four legions to conquer Britain. Many tribes, including the Iceni, welcomed the Romans or surrendered without a fight. Other tribes were defeated. Still others, including the Catuvellauni, resisted Roman rule. Resistance coalesced around Caratacus, son of the Catuvellauni king, Cunobelinus. When it became impossible to continue fighting in southeast Britain, Caratacus and his followers fled to the west, into the area now known as Wales.

Rome rewarded those who had helped them during the invasion. Emperor Claudius I loaned various chiefs the sum of forty million sesterces. King Prasutagus of the Iceni was given a client kingdom to rule with some degree of independence, an arrangement common on the borders of the Roman Empire, where pro-Roman sympathies were harnessed to create buffer zones to protect Roman territory from outside attack. For the Roman Empire, a client relationship was a tool of short-term political expedience, the achievement of rapid conquest in an area and the consolidation of Roman power therein. When the individual died with whom a client relationship had been established, the client relationship ended. From the point of view of Rome, the fortune and estates of a client king or queen reverted in full to Rome; the clients, however, often had a different understanding of their relationship to the imperial government. The situation in some ways paralleled the differing interpretations of land sales and treaties between Native Americans and Europeans in the sixteenth through nineteenth centuries.

Publius Ostorius Scapula was governor of Britain from 50 C.E. until his death in 52 C.E. Scapula unsuccessfully tried to eradicate the forces of Caratacus in Wales.

Scapula dared not count on the tribes remaining loyal to Rome while he waged battle in Wales, so preparatory to that campaign, he collected all weapons from the tribes. This search and seizure angered some of the tribes, including the Iceni. Camulodunum, the former capital city of the Trinovantes, became the capital of the new province. A large temple was built there to honor the spirit of Claudius I. The Romans also created a *colonia* at Camulodunum on lands appropriated from the tribes. Rome similarly appropriated lands from the Catuvellauni to build the city of Verulamium (St. Albans).

After the assassination of Claudius I in 54 C.E., his stepson Nero became emperor. The government under Nero seriously considered giving up Britain altogether. A decision was reached by 57 C.E. to retain Britain and to conquer and hold the whole southern area of the island. The man chosen to subdue the western areas was Gaius Suetonius Paulinus. He realized that discontent and hostility toward Rome were centered in the sacred groves of the Druids in the west, where those Britons had gathered who followed the lead of Caratacus in refusing to submit to Rome.

Prasutagus died early in 60 C.E. at a time when Suetonius, the Roman governor of Britain, was subduing Wales. His will made his two daughters co-heirs of his kingdom along with the Roman Empire. However, the chief tax collector or procurator of Britain, Catus Decianus, acted swiftly to ensure that Prasutagus's entire estate reverted

Boudicca addresses her people, seeking their help in the revolt. (Hulton Archive)

to Rome, cutting out Prasutagus's family. Decianus also declared that loans previously made by Emperor Claudius I had to be repaid immediately, with interest. Accompanied by his staff, Decianus enforced his orders. In the process, members of his staff stripped and lashed Queen Boudicca and raped her two virgin daughters, whose names were never listed in the historical record. Impelled by these outrages, Boudicca and the Iceni took up arms. They were joined by the Trinovantes and by others.

Boudicca's army of 120,000 people attacked and destroyed the *colonia* of Camulodunum, a settlement of retired Roman army veterans, along with its entire population, estimated at some 2,000 people. The Iceni and their allies then sacked and burned Londinium (London), the largest city in the province, killing its population estimated at some twenty thousand. According to Greek historian Dio Cassius (c. 150-c. 235 C.E.), the women's breasts were cut off and stuffed into their mouths, and then they were impaled on long, sharp skewers run through their bodies lengthwise. The rebels likewise killed the entire population of Verulamium, the third-largest city in the province, and burned the town to the ground. They also decimated a large part of the IX Legion. The revolt finally was defeated by the XIV and XX Legions under the command of Suetonius.

Suetonius had been in the process of eliminating the druidic stronghold on the island of Anglesey off the north coast of Wales when Boudicca rebelled. Some historians have suspected collusion between the Celts of the east and west of the island to stretch Roman forces as thin as possible by drawing the army to one of the westernmost points of Britain and then rising up in the east. Certainly Suetonius's response to Boudicca's rebellion was delayed by the necessity of marching his army most of the way across Britain to an undetermined location along Watling Street in the Midlands, possibly near modern-day Mancetter.

Tacitus describes the location of the final confrontation between the forces of Boudicca and Suetonius. Boudicca's army, estimated at this point to have numbered anywhere from 100,000 to 230,000, advanced into a front of diminishing width. Her army faced eleven thousand to thirteen thousand Roman soldiers, consisting of the XIV Legion, detachments of the II and XX at the center, and cavalry and auxiliaries on the wings. Behind the Romans lay a thick forest on rising ground that gave protection to Suetonius's rear. Ahead the ground was open, affording no cover to the advancing Britons.

Suetonius defeated Boudicca's forces and gained a massive victory. Tacitus indicates that eighty thousand Britons were killed in the battle, while Roman losses were four hundred dead and slightly more than that number wounded. Boudicca survived the battle but poisoned herself rather than face capture. Afterward, some seven thousand reinforcements were sent from Germany, and Suetonius led a systematic campaign of retaliation, from which it took ten years for the province to recover.

SIGNIFICANCE

Boudicca's revolt profoundly affected Britons and Roman imperial policy toward Britain. There was a genuine attempt by Rome to recognize the tribes as civilized peoples rather than as non-Romans. Temples were raised to Celtic gods in association with their Roman equivalents. All hopes of Roman defeat or withdrawal vanished. Not until the gradual breakup of the Roman Empire some five hundred years later did the Britons reassert themselves. The degree of assimilation between the Britons and the Romans has long been debated; it is probably significant that Britannia, unlike Gaul, reverted to speaking a Celtic language (Old Welsh) rather than a Latin-derived language. Nonetheless, the legendary history of medieval Wales presented the Welsh as the legitimate heirs of Rome.

Beginning in the eighteenth century, Boudicca became a potent icon of "Britishness," ironically, as Britain itself became increasingly imperialistic. Boudicca has also become a modern icon of the independence and power of women among the pre-Christian Celts. A statue by Thomas Thornycroft of Boudicca in her chariot, with appropriately tempestuous horses, was presented to the City of London and erected near Big Ben and the Houses of Parliament in 1902. Popular legend holds that Boudicca herself is buried beneath Track 10 at the King's Cross railway station.

—*Marjorie Donovan*

FURTHER READING

Dio Cassius. *History of Rome*. Translated by Ernest Carey. Cambridge, Mass.: Harvard University Press, 1925. At the end of the second century, the Greek historian used corroborated and uncorroborated sources to write one of two classical histories of the revolt.

Salway, Peter. *A History of Roman Britain*. 1993. Reprint. New York: Oxford University Press, 2001. A good comprehensive history of Roman involvement in Britain. Part 2 covers the events leading up to Boudicca's revolt and its aftermath.

Tacitus. *The "Annals" and the "Histories."* Translated by Alfred John Church and William Jackson Broadribb. New York: Modern Library, 2003. Tacitus, a Roman senator and consul, wrote his *Annals* just fifty

1 - 100 C.E.

years after the revolt. The noted Roman historian had access to imperial archives.

Webster, Graham. *Boudica: The British Revolt Against Rome in A.D. 60.* 2d ed. New York: Routledge, 2000. Archaeological knowledge and aerial reconnaissance join with classical sources in this indispensable narrative of the political, social, economic, and demographic factors surrounding the revolt.

_____. *The Roman Invasion of Britain.* Rev. ed. New York: Routledge, 1999. A sharply focused study of the period up to the departure of Plautius. Includes both an assessment of the Roman sources and a translation of Dio Cassius's history. Illustrations, bibliography, glossary of technical terms, glossary of Roman terms, and a table of correspondences between Roman and modern place-names.

SEE ALSO: c. 3100-c. 1550 B.C.E., Building of Stonehenge; c. 2300-c. 1800 B.C.E., Beaker People Live in Western Europe; 14th-9th centuries B.C.E., Urnfield Culture Flourishes in Northwestern Europe; c. 1100-c. 500 B.C.E., Hallstatt Culture Dominates Northern Europe; c. 100 B.C.E.-c. 100 C.E., Celtic Hill Forts Are Replaced by *Oppida*; c. 60 B.C.E., Druidism Flourishes in Gaul and Britain; 58-51 B.C.E., Caesar Conquers Gaul; 43-130 C.E., Roman Conquest of Britain; c. 50 C.E., Creation of the Roman Imperial Bureaucracy; 449 C.E., Saxon Settlement of Britain Begins.

RELATED ARTICLES in *Great Lives from History: The Ancient World*: Boudicca; Julius Caesar; Claudius I; Dio Cassius; Hadrian; Tacitus.

c. 60-68 C.E.
BUDDHISM ENTERS CHINA

Popular Buddhist legend holds that after seeing an image of the Buddha in a dream, Emperor Ming of the Han Dynasty sent envoys to India in search of Buddhist texts. Their return marked the introduction of Buddhism to China.

LOCALE: Luoyang (in Henan Province, China)
CATEGORY: Religion

KEY FIGURE

Mingdi (Ming-ti; 29-c. 75 C.E.), Chinese emperor, Han Dynasty, r. c. 58-c. 75 C.E. and introduced Buddhism to China

SUMMARY OF EVENT

According to popular legend, sometime during the seventh decade of the first century (between 60 and 68 C.E.), Emperor Ming of the Eastern, or Later, Han Dynasty (25-220 C.E.) dreamed of a tall, golden man emitting a brilliant light and hovering in the air in front of his palace. On questioning his ministers about the meaning of the dream, the emperor learned that he had seen the Buddha. Wishing to learn more about this figure, Mingdi had envoys sent to the west. They traveled as far as Yuezhi in northern India, where they met with two Buddhist monks. Together with these monks, the envoys loaded a host of images and texts onto a white horse and returned to the Han capital at Luoyang, where they took up residence at the newly built White Horse Monastery (Baima si), the

first Buddhist monastery in China. One of the texts said to have been brought back to Luoyang was the *Sutra in Forty-two Sections* (*Si shi er zhang jing*), popularly held to be the first Buddhist text translated into Chinese (although there is disagreement about whether the text was translated or composed in China). The official introduction of Buddhism to China is traditionally traced to these events.

The legend of Mingdi's dream is but one of many stories regarding the introduction of Buddhism to China found in historical texts; other accounts place the introduction as early as the third century B.C.E. Although this story has been taken as an accurate description of the introduction of Buddhism to China from at least as early as the fourth century C.E., modern scholarship suggests that it is little more than a legend. The first appearance of the story is found in the *Hou Han ji* (fourth century C.E.; record of the Later Han), written by Yuan Hong (328-397 C.E.) some three hundred years after the original event. The noted French sinologist Henri Maspero has concluded that the story of Emperor Ming's dream has no basis in historical fact and that it is a creation of the third century. In his detailed study of the early history of Buddhism in China, Erik J. Zürcher suggests that, although the actual date and details of the introduction are unknown, it must have occurred sometime between the first half of the first century B.C.E. and the middle of the first century C.E. Finally, scholar of Chinese Buddhism Kenneth Ch'en argues persuasively that Buddhism was already present in China at the time of Emperor Ming. Although the precise details of the events may never be clear, scholars agree that the introduction of the Buddhist religion, with its accompanying literature, arts, and technologies, was under way by the mid-first century C.E.

The undoubtedly long and complicated process of Buddhism's introduction to China was facilitated through Sino-Indian trade networks. It is likely that Buddhism traveled with the foreign merchants and refugees along the Silk Road, entering China in the northwest and eventually reaching the capital at Luoyang. In addition to Luoyang, there is evidence of early Buddhist communities at Pengcheng in the lower Yangtze region of east China and Tonkin in present-day coastal Vietnam. The latter location demonstrates that at an early date, Buddhism was entering China from sea via Indian traders as well as overland along the Silk Road.

At first, the religion seems to have been restricted to immigrant populations and the Chinese-born children of non-Chinese families, only later spreading to the Han Chinese. Although there is some evidence that indigenous Chinese may have converted to the Buddhist order as early as the Eastern Han Dynasty, traditional histories relate that there were no Chinese monks in China until the fourth century C.E.

The three hundred or so years after the introduction of Buddhism to China was a time of translation and assimilation. Many of the most important translators of Buddhist texts in China were of Central Asian origin rather than from the Indian subcontinent, pointing to the pivotal role played by Central Asia in the early development of Chinese Buddhism.

SIGNIFICANCE

The significance of the introduction of Buddhism to China can hardly be overstated. During the first century C. E., China had a well-established Confucian tradition as well as small but growing communities practicing Daoism. As Buddhism began to take hold and enter into dialogue with native philosophical and metaphysical systems, each tradition inspired innovations in the others. Sometimes coexisting peacefully, at others vociferously opposed to one another, all three traditions were undoubtedly shaped through their interactions. At the same time, Buddhism, like Confucianism and Daoism, was a great political and cultural force in China. Although critics would never forget Buddhism's foreign origin, they could never deny the impact the religion had on the history of China.

The introduction of Buddhism into China was also a seminal event in the history of the Asian continent as a whole. Once in China, the Buddhist religion would undergo a long and complicated development and transformation. Religious traditions inherited from India and Central Asia were assimilated into native Chinese cultural systems, resulting in what has been called the Sinification of Buddhism. Many of the uniquely Chinese schools of Buddhism that developed during the sixth and seventh centuries in China, including Tiantai and Chan (Tendai and Zen in Japanese), would later be introduced to Korea and Japan. Tibetan Buddhism was also influenced by Chinese Buddhism as well as Indian Buddhist traditions.

—*Ben Brose*

FURTHER READING

Ch'en, Kenneth. *Buddhism in China: A Historical Survey.* Princeton, N.J.: Princeton University Press, 1964. A good introduction to the history of Chinese Buddhism from its introduction through the modern period.

Hsüan-hua. *The Sutra in Forty-two Sections Spoken by Buddha.* Burlingame, Calif.: Buddhist Text Translation Society, 1994. A translation into English of one of the earliest texts available to Chinese Buddhists.

Ikeda, Daisaku. *The Flower of Chinese Buddhism.* Translated by Burton Watson. New York: Weatherhill, 1986. A selective history of Chinese Buddhism from its Indic origins through the Tang Dynasty, with special attention given to the Tiantai school.

Tsukamoto Zenryū. *A History of Early Chinese Buddhism: From Its Introduction to the Death of Hui-yüan.* Vol. 1. Translated by Leon Hurvitz. New York: Kodansha International, 1979. A detailed treatment of the early years of Chinese Buddhist communities.

Zürcher, Erik J. *The Buddhist Conquest of China: The Spread and Adaptation of Buddhism in Early Medieval China.* Leiden, Netherlands: E. J. Brill, 1972. The most authoritative and reliable work on early Chinese Buddhism available in English.

SEE ALSO: 6th or 5th century B.C.E., Birth of Buddhism; c. 247-207 B.C.E., Buddhism Established in Sri Lanka; 1st-2d century C.E., Fourth Buddhist Council Convenes; 25 C.E., Guang Wudi Restores the Han Dynasty; 399 C.E., Chinese Monk Faxian Travels to India; c. 470 C.E., Bodhidharma Brings Chan Buddhism to China.

RELATED ARTICLES in *Great Lives from History: The Ancient World*: Bodhidharma; Buddha; Faxian.

1 - 100 C.E.

64-67 C.E.
NERO PERSECUTES THE CHRISTIANS

Nero persecuted the Christians, marking the beginning of the Roman Empire's prolonged harassment of a religious group for political purposes.

LOCALE: Rome (now in Italy)
CATEGORIES: Government and politics; religion

KEY FIGURES
Nero (37-68 C.E.), Roman emperor, r. 54-68 C.E.
Saint Paul (c. 10-c. 64 C.E.), Christian apostle
Saint Peter (d. 64 C.E.), Christian apostle

SUMMARY OF EVENT
Nero, fifth emperor of Rome and the last of the Julio-Claudian line, ruled the Roman Empire from 54 to 68 C.E. and is generally considered one of the cruelest men in history. Born on December 15, 37 C.E., in Antium, Italy, to consul Gnaeus Domitius Ahenobarbus and Agrippina the Younger, daughter of Germanicus Caesar and great-granddaughter of Emperor Augustus, Nero was originally named Lucius Domitius Ahenobarbus. After the death of his father in approximately 40, Nero's scheming mother married her uncle, Emperor Claudius I, in 49, and persuaded him to adopt her son, whose name was then changed to Nero Claudius Caesar Drusus Germanicus. Nero then married Claudius's daughter Octavia, an act that marked him as Rome's next emperor, thus bypassing Claudius's biological son Britannicus. Agrippina then poisoned Claudius in 54, and the Praetorian Guard and the senate united in declaring Nero emperor at the age of seventeen. Nero had blotchy skin, a fat belly, spindly legs, and a thick neck, a feature that is recorded in his coinage.

Guided by the praetorian prefect Burrus and the Stoic philosopher-tutor Seneca, Nero began the first five years of his reign as a man of moderation, known for his clemency. He also made several popular changes within Roman government, including his proposal to abolish some forms of taxation. Although many of Nero's subjects initially received him with great enthusiasm, Burrus and Seneca were unable to hold the boy emperor's cruelty in check for long. Nero soon began to rule unrestrained, violently plotting against people he perceived as threats to his power. Britannicus, his stepbrother and rightful heir to the throne, was poisoned in 55 C.E., and Agrippina, whose plotting gained Nero the throne in the first place, was murdered in 59 after criticizing Nero's mistress, Poppaea Sabina. He later divorced and murdered his wife, Octavia, and married Poppaea. Nero later kicked Poppaea to death while she was pregnant. His third marriage was to Statilia Messalina, whose husband he had ordered to be executed.

A great fire swept through Rome in the hot July of 64 C.E. Flames raged for about ten days, burning nearly two-thirds of the city. Three of the fourteen Augustan municipal districts were completely gutted, and seven others were badly damaged. Rumors quickly circulated that Nero himself had started the fire to make room for his new palace, but most historians believe there is no factual evidence to support this theory. Some historians have suggested that Nero was away at Antium, and legend says that Nero viewed the blaze from the Tower of Maecenas, amusing himself by playing his lyre and reciting his own epic poem "The Sack of Troy" on his private stage while thousands died and Rome was reduced to ashes. This story led to the popular expression "fiddling while Rome burns," a label often bestowed on public officials who fail in their civil duty during an emergency.

According to some accounts, Nero sought to avert rumors accusing him of irresponsibility by accusing Rome's Christian inhabitants of starting the fire, thereafter making Christians the victims of vicious and cruel tortures. Up to this time, Rome had been tolerant of non-national monotheistic religions such as Judaism and Christianity but was always watchful. Jews generally were treated relatively well by Pompey the Great, Caesar, and Augustus, in part as a result of support by Herod the Great and Herod Agrippa, and were envied by other religious groups. The Christian apostle and preacher Paul enjoyed Roman protection and "appealed to Caesar" when persecuted by followers of his own Jewish heritage.

The year 64 C.E., however, marked a dramatic change in Rome's attitude toward Christians for the next 250 years. Christians were charged with incendiarism and were torn by lions and dogs, crucified, and burned alive as torches to light nocturnal games during which Nero paraded around the Palatine Gardens and Vatican Circus dressed as a charioteer. Tacitus recorded that public reaction to Nero's atrocities was generally pity of the Christians as victims of Nero's brutality, with few observers believing they were perpetrators of actual crimes. Suetonius, the other classical authority, mentions that Christians began to be driven out of Rome but does not associate them with the accusation of starting the great fire.

THE JULIO-CLAUDIAN DYNASTY, 27 B.C.E.-68 C.E.

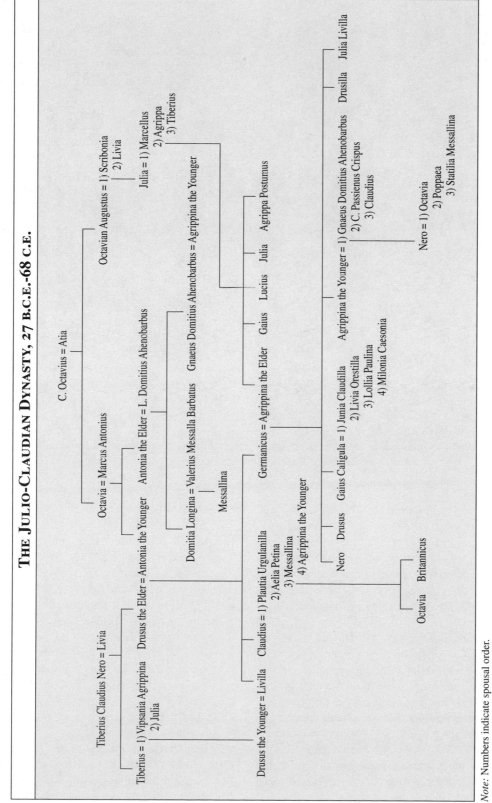

Note: Numbers indicate spousal order.

Nero and other Romans watch as the Christians are burned. (F. R. Niglutsch)

Christian executions increased in 65, when an assassination plot by a group of aristocrats, senators, and equestrians was uncovered and Nero revived the wide-ranging law of treason, under which many were executed on spurious charges or forced to commit suicide. Questions as to the legal basis behind the attacks on the Christians and the specific charges filed against them will undoubtedly never be answered.

The number and names of the early Christian martyrs under Nero and those persecuted by Roman authorities after his death were not reliably documented. Tradition beginning with Clement of Rome in approximately 95 C.E. lists Saints Peter and Paul as martyrs under Nero in Rome, whereas later tradition holds that their deaths occurred several years later and may not have even happened in Rome. Biblical references in the New Testament book of 1 Peter indicate that Nero's Christian persecutions reached far beyond the city of Rome into Asia Minor, Pontus, Galicia, and Bithynia.

SIGNIFICANCE

The trials conducted under Nero established that crimes such as secret assembly were punishable by death, with numerous Christians regularly convicted of such acts. Rome set a precedent for all its governors in that no formal law was necessary for prosecution, and proof of a definite crime was not required. Persecution of people called by the name "Christian" was begun during Nero's reign, possibly to divert attention away from the arson, and was continued with Christians being generally condemned as a sect dangerous to public safety and as permanent enemies of civilization. Orosius later popularized the idea of ten persecutions against the Christian church, which were often lackadaisically carried out by half-hearted Roman officials.

Arguably the worst period of Christian persecution occurred in 303 under Diocletian and continued under Galerius and Maximinus until 313, when the Edict of Milan gave official recognition to the Christian religion.

The total number of Christians tortured and executed between 64 and 313 C.E. remains controversial but is commonly estimated to be between 10,000 and 100,000.

—*Daniel G. Graetzer*

FURTHER READING

Bowersock, G. W. *Martyrdom and Rome*. New York: Cambridge University Press, 1995. This work, created from the Wiles lectures given at the Queen's University of Belfast, deals with the early Church and the persecution it faced. Bibliography and index.

Freud, W. H. C. *Martyrdom and Persecution in the Early Church*. 1967. Reprint. Grand Rapids, Mich.: Baker Book House, 1981. This well-written text documents numerous theories as to the underlying causes and legal basis for the sudden onset of Christian persecution in 64 C.E.

Massie, Allan. *The Caesars*. New York: Franklin Watts, 1984. This text details the relationships between Rome's first twelve emperors and the Roman Empire, including Nero's manipulative control over those by whom he felt threatened.

Novak, Ralph Martin. *Christianity and the Roman Empire: Background Texts*. Harrisburg, Pa.: Trinity Press International, 2001. Novak weaves his narrative of the

history of the Christian church from 27 B.C.E. to 419 C.E. around selections of primary sources. Bibliography and indexes.

Ramsay, William. *The Church in the Roman Empire*. 5th ed. Grand Rapids, Mich.: Baker Book House, 1954. This often-cited text, originally published in 1893, attempts to assess the meaning of the Neronian persecution and often cites writings by Tacitus and Suetonius, considered the only two reliable witnesses.

Workman, H. B. *Persecution of the Early Church*. 1923. Reprint. New York: Oxford University Press, 1980. A history of the Christian persecution under Nero.

SEE ALSO: c. 6 B.C.E., Birth of Jesus Christ; c. 30 C.E., Condemnation and Crucifixion of Jesus Christ; January-March, 55 or 56 C.E., Paul Writes His Letter to the Romans; c. 110 C.E., Trajan Adopts Anti-Christian Religious Policy; 200 C.E., Christian Apologists Develop Concept of Theology; 250 C.E., Outbreak of the Decian Persecution; 284 C.E., Inauguration of the Dominate in Rome.

RELATED ARTICLES in *Great Lives from History: The Ancient World*: Agrippina the Younger; Nero; Saint Paul; Saint Peter.

68-69 C.E.
YEAR OF THE FOUR EMPERORS

The Roman Empire experienced a period of civil wars and rule by three short-lived emperors that culminated in the establishment of the Flavian Dynasty.

LOCALE: Roman Empire and Gaul (now France)
CATEGORIES: Government and politics; wars, uprisings, and civil unrest

KEY FIGURES

Nero (37-68 C.E.), Roman emperor, r. 54-68 C.E.
Servius Sulpicius Galba (3 B.C.E.-69 C.E.), Roman emperor, r. June, 68-January, 69 C.E.
Marcus Salvius Otho (32-69 C.E.), Roman emperor, r. January-April, 69 C.E.
Aulus Vitellius (15-69 C.E.), Roman emperor, January-December, r. 69 C.E.
Fabius Valens (d. 69 C.E.), Roman general under Vitellius
Vespasian (9-79 C.E.), Roman emperor, r. 69-79 C.E.

SUMMARY OF EVENT

By 68 C.E., the Roman emperor Nero's oppressive policies and personal extravagance had caused many prominent Romans to turn against him. In March, Gaius Julius Vindex, the governor of Central Gaul, rose in rebellion against Nero. Servius Sulpicius Galba, the governor of Nearer Spain, supported Vindex's revolt; in April, Galba's troops hailed their leader as general of the senate and people of Rome. In May, Vindex's rebellion was crushed, but in June, Nero committed suicide and the Roman senate subsequently recognized Galba as emperor. After his accession, he executed some of Nero's supporters and massacred thousands of troops that Nero had assembled in Rome. Moreover, he introduced certain austere measures to stabilize imperial finances, including a refusal to pay the Praetorian Guard a special bonus promised in Galba's name by their commander in return for their desertion from Nero to Galba. As a result of these policies, Galba alienated the Praetorian Guard and most of the people of the city of Rome.

In early January of 69 C.E., the Roman legions stationed along the Rhine frontier rose in rebellion against Galba and acclaimed as emperor Aulus Vitellius, the governor of Lower Germany. Meanwhile Otho, a former governor of Lusitania (Portugal) and an early supporter of Galba, was disappointed at not being chosen to be his heir and turned against him. On January 15, the Praetorian Guard took an oath of allegiance to Otho. They then moved against Galba and killed him. The senate as well as the legions of the east recognized Marcus Salvius Otho as emperor.

In February, troops loyal to Vitellius invaded Italy. One army, led by Fabius Valens, entered from the northwest and crossed the Cottian Alps. A second army, commanded by Aulus Caecina Alienus, crossed the Pennine Alps farther to the northeast. Otho sought to delay the enemy forces by defending positions along the Po River until the arrival of reinforcements from the Danubian provinces. He also sent a small force into southeastern Gaul to delay Valens's advance. This force withdrew after an inconclusive engagement, and Vitellius's forces quickly

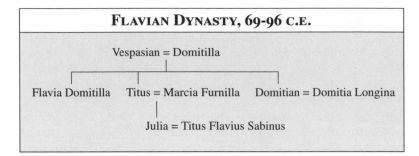

FLAVIAN DYNASTY, 69-96 C.E.

Vespasian = Domitilla

Flavia Domitilla   Titus = Marcia Furnilla   Domitian = Domitia Longina

Julia = Titus Flavius Sabinus

occupied the plain between the Alps and the Po. Meanwhile, Otho left Rome on March 14 and set out to join his forces in the north.

After an unsuccessful assault on Placentia (Piacenza), Caecina's army advanced toward Cremona, a city that was already in Vitellian hands. Caecina's army was then defeated outside Cremona but joined forces with Valens's army on April 8. Although Otho's forces were outnumbered, his generals persuaded him to permit them to attack immediately rather than wait for the arrival of reinforcements. On April 14, the Vitellian forces defeated those of Otho in the first Battle of Cremona. His army immediately took an oath of allegiance to Vitellius. On April 16, Otho committed suicide at his headquarters at Brixellum (Brescello). By April 19, both the senate and troops in Rome had acclaimed Vitellius as emperor.

Vitellius traveled to Rome at a leisurely pace, while his troops pillaged and looted all along the route of his journey. He sent the legions that had supported Otho back to their original provinces and disbanded the nine cohorts of Otho's Praetorian Guard, replacing them with a new Praetorian Guard of sixteen cohorts recruited from his own troops. He finally arrived in Rome in early July. In describing Vitellius's brief reign, ancient writers such as Tacitus and Suetonius have emphasized his gluttony and extreme cruelty toward suspected enemies. However, P. A. L. Greenhalgh argued that his alleged cruelty has been exaggerated. Moreover, he asserted that Vitellius demonstrated great respect for the senate and tried to appeal to all classes of Roman society.

Since 67 C.E., Vespasian, the governor of Judaea, had been conducting a campaign to suppress a major Jewish rebellion. In July of 69, the legions of Egypt, Judaea, and Syria acclaimed him as emperor. He also won the support of governors of other eastern provinces and various eastern native rulers, as well as the legions of the Danubian provinces. In late July, he and his generals drew up plans for the campaign against Vitellius in a war council at Berytus (Beirut). His son Titus continued operations against

Vespasian. (Library of Congress)

the Jewish rebels, while Vespasian secured Egypt to cut off Egyptian grain shipments to Rome and starve it into submission. Gaius Licinius Mucianus, the governor of Syria, led the main army against Vitellius's forces in Italy.

However, the Italian campaign was actually begun by Marcus Antonius Primus, a legionary commander in Pannonia (western Hungary). He was eager to win glory for himself and instead of waiting for Mucianus's army, he led an advance force into northwestern Italy in late August. Primus quickly gained control of Aquileia and Patavium (Padua), and in late September, he established a major base at Verona. On September 17, Caecina and his Vitellian army set out from Rome; they advanced toward Cremona and established a camp between Hostilia (Ostiglia) and Verona. On October 18, on learning of the defection of the Roman Adriatic fleet to Vespasian, Caecina and his officers also swore allegiance to him. However, Caecina's troops immediately arrested him, chose new commanders, and advanced toward Cremona to join forces with another army loyal to Vitellius.

Primus, whose army had received considerable reinforcements, decided to attack before the Vitellian armies could link up. On October 24-25, his army defeated the Vitellians in the second Battle of Cremona. After the battle, they captured the fortified camp of the Vitellians. The city of Cremona then surrendered and was sacked by Primus's troops. Vitellius's other major general, Valens, abandoned his army on learning of the defeat at Cremona. After an unsuccessful attempt to rally forces in Gaul to continue the war, he was arrested by Vespasian's troops and executed in December.

After the victory at Cremona, Primus's forces advanced down the Via Flaminia toward Rome. On December 15, a Vitellian army surrendered to him at Narnia (Narni). Meanwhile Titus Flavius Sabinus, the city prefect of Rome and brother of Vespasian, tried to persuade Vitellius to abdicate. Vitellius did so on December 18, but the people refused to accept his abdication and his troops briefly besieged Sabinus and his followers on Rome's Capitoline Hill. The next day, Vitellius's troops captured the Capitoline and Sabinus was subsequently killed by a mob of Vitellius's supporters. During the siege, a fire that broke out on the Capitoline destroyed the Temple of Jupiter Best and Greatest, a major symbol of Roman power. On December 20, Primus's forces entered Rome from the north and captured it after fierce fighting; that same day, Vitellius was arrested and killed. On December 21, the senate formally recognized Vespasian as emperor. Mucianus arrived in Rome soon after and held supreme authority in the capital until Vespasian's arrival.

Meanwhile, the Batavians, a Germanic tribe, rebelled against Roman rule and were soon joined by some Gallic tribes. By September of 70, this rebellion as well as the Jewish revolt had been crushed, although Jewish rebels at Masada held out until 73 C.E. In late September, Vespasian entered Rome and subsequently announced the restoration of peace throughout the empire.

SIGNIFICANCE

In describing the events of 68-69 C.E., Tacitus stated, "A well-hidden secret . . . had been revealed: It was possible, it seemed, for an emperor to be chosen outside Rome." For the first time since the accession of the first Roman emperor, Augustus, governors in various provinces were proclaimed emperors by their legions. This resulted in a series of bloody civil wars as well as political anarchy in the empire. Vespasian's accession marked the beginning of the Flavian Dynasty (69-96 C.E.) and a period of relative stability in the Roman Empire, which continued until the late second century.

—Thomas I. Crimando

FURTHER READING

Greenhalgh, P. A. L. *The Year of the Four Emperors*. New York: Barnes & Noble, 1975. A narrative of the events of 68-69 C.E. based on ancient sources. Maps and index.

Levick, Barbara. *Vespasian*. New York: Routledge, 1999. An account of the life and achievements of the first Flavian emperor. Maps, bibliography, and index.

Suetonius Tranquillus, Gaius. *The Twelve Caesars*. Translated by Robert Graves. Harmondsworth, Middlesex, England: Penguin, 1987. A classic work that includes biographies of Nero and the four emperors of 68-69 C.E. Maps and index.

Tacitus, Cornelius. *The Histories*. Translated by Kenneth Wellesley. Harmondsworth, Middlesex, England: Penguin, 1982. A detailed, sometimes partisan account of the events of 68-69 C.E. Maps, bibliography, and index.

Wellesley, Kenneth. *The Long Year, A.D. 69*. Boulder, Colo.: Westview Press, 1975. A narrative of the events of 68-69 C.E. based upon literary sources, documents, and ancient inscriptions. Maps and index.

SEE ALSO: c. 50 C.E., Creation of the Roman Imperial Bureaucracy; 60 C.E., Boudicca Leads Revolt Against Roman Rule; 64-67 C.E., Nero Persecutes the Christians; September 8, 70 C.E., Roman Destruction of the Temple of Jerusalem.

RELATED ARTICLES in *Great Lives from History: The Ancient World*: Nero; Vespasian.

September 8, 70 C.E.

ROMAN DESTRUCTION OF THE TEMPLE OF JERUSALEM

The destruction of the Jewish temple in Jerusalem was the final blow in the famous war that resulted from a combination of Roman political ineptness in Judaea and the upsurge of a radical Jewish nationalism.

LOCALE: Jerusalem (now in Israel)
CATEGORIES: Wars, uprisings, and civil unrest; religion

KEY FIGURES

Gessius Florus (fl. first century C.E.), procurator of Judaea, 64-66 C.E.

Herod Agrippa II (27?-c. 93 C.E.), king of Judaea under the Romans, r. 44-70 C.E.

Flavius Josephus (c. 37-c. 100 C.E.), Pharisee of the peace party, commander of Jewish forces in Galilee, and historian of the Jewish war

Vespasian (9-79 C.E.), general and Roman emperor, r. 69-79 C.E.

John of Gischala (fl. first century C.E.), leader of the Zealot group in Jerusalem

Titus (39-81 C.E.), son of Vespasian, general in the siege and capture of Jerusalem, Roman emperor, r. 79-81 C.E.

Simon ben Giora (d. 71 C.E.), Zealot leader in Jerusalem and a rival of John of Gischala

SUMMARY OF EVENT

After Judaea was made a Roman province in 6 C.E., a band of revolutionaries, better known later as Zealots, arose to challenge Roman domination. Roman misunderstanding and misgovernment added fuel to the inflammatory situation, especially between 26 and 66 C.E. Pontius Pilate, procurator of Judaea from 26 to 36, managed to outrage Jewish religious sensibilities on only a few occasions, but a series of poor governors and bad decisions led to the outbreak of actual civil war under emperor Nero.

The procuratorship of Antonius Felix, 52-60, was a turning point. A left-wing section of the Zealots, the *sicarii*, or dagger men, began a series of political assassinations. Albinus, who was procurator between 62 and 64, managed to restore some order after a previous two-year anarchy in which the old high priest Annas, or Ananus, had played a part. However, the *sicarii* ran rampant and the anti-Roman party grew while the procurator did little but fatten his pocket. The last Roman ruler, Gessius Florus, was an utterly base man who managed in May, 66, to steal seventeen talents from the treasury of

the Temple of Jeruslem. Taunting of him as a rapacious ruler by the Jews led to bloodshed; the Jews retaliated by seizing the temple, bottling up Florus in the fortress Antonia, and subsequently driving him into exile to Caesarea.

When Herod Agrippa II urged submission to Florus, the Zealots answered by seizing Masada, a strong fortress on the west shore of the Dead Sea. Cessation of the traditional sacrifices for the Roman emperor at the suggestion of Eleazar ben Ananus signified open revolt and was, as historian Flavius Josephus remarked, "the true beginning of our war with Rome."

When the Palace of Herod, which had given sanctuary to the peace party, fell in September, the Roman garrison was slaughtered and a general Jewish oppression of Gentiles arose throughout Palestine. An abortive attempt by Cestius Gallus, the legate of Syria, to put down the revolt made war inevitable. Men were drafted into the defense, and Josephus was given command of the Jewish forces in Galilee. Nero appointed Vespasian as commander of the Roman forces. As John of Gischala, a leading Zealot leader, suspected he might, Josephus defected to the Romans when Galilee was conquered in 67 C.E. by Vespasian.

The years 68-69 C.E. were ones of inactivity on the Roman side. After Vespasian subdued most of Judaea, he settled into a waiting game because of uncertainty following the suicide of Nero on June 9, 68. He could afford to wait because intra-Jewish struggles were ruining the defense of Jerusalem as rival Zealot leaders instituted a

VESPASIAN AND HIS SUCCESSORS, 69-192 C.E.	
Ruler	*Reign*
Vespasian	69-79
Titus	79-81
Domitian	81-96
Nerva	96-98
Trajan	98-117
Hadrian	117-138
Antoninus Pius	138-161
Lucius Verus	161-169
Marcus Aurelius	161-180
Commodus	180-192

reign of terror. After troops in the east acclaimed Vespasian emperor on July 1, 69, the capture of Jerusalem was turned over to his son Titus in the summer of 70 when Vespasian left for Rome. Internal Zealot strife between John of Gischala and Simon ben Giora helped to prepare the enervated Jerusalem for a fall; John even called on Idumaeans for help, and on one occasion in the civil strife, the valuable grain stores had been fired. Eventually a third faction entered the fray.

Two days before the Passover in April, 70, Titus came before the city to begin his attack on the third or outermost wall to the north. It was breached on May 25. A tightened blockade around the entire city soon brought famine; finally, after earlier attempts had failed, the great fortress Antonia fell on July 24. Twelve days later, the last morning and evening sacrifices were made, and all available men were marshaled to the defense of the temple and the upper city.

By August, four ramparts had been built against the great sanctuary of the temple, but its walls withstood the ram. The cloisters were then fired and burnt out on August 12; the gates succumbed on August 15. Later a soldier in the heat of the battle, but against the express orders of Titus, flung a torch into the temple so that a fatal fire ravaged the edifice for two days from August 29 to 30. The temple and its religion of sacrifice were ended forever. Slaughter followed, and when the last section of the city fell on September 8, the city itself was all but completely destroyed.

SIGNIFICANCE

Titus celebrated a triumph in Rome marked by the arch at one end of the Roman Forum emblazoned with a sculpture of the captured seven-branched candlestick. The Roman army wiped out remaining pockets of resistance during 71-73 C.E., the heroic defense of Masada fortress being the chief glory of the resistance. The Jewish rebellion was over. A brief, unsuccessful rally in 132-135 at last marked the end of Jewish nationalistic hopes in the ancient world.

—Edgar M. Krenz

FURTHER READING

Aberbach, Moses, and David Aberbach. *The Roman-Jewish Wars and Hebrew Cultural Nationalism.* New York: St. Martin's Press, 2000. This work on Jewish nationalism covers the Roman-Jewish war. Bibliography and index.

Bohrmann, Monette. *Flavius Josephus, the Zealots, and Yavne: Towards a Rereading of the War of the Jews.* New York: Peter Lang, 1994. An examination of Josephus's history of the war between the Romans and the Jews. Bibliography.

Hadas-Lebel, Mireille. *Flavius Josephus: Eyewitness to Rome's First Century Conquest of Judea.* New York: Macmillan, 1993. A look at the Jewish historian and an analysis of his work.

Josephus, Flavius. *The Jewish War.* 3 vols. 1927-1928. Reprint. Cambridge, Mass.: Harvard University Press, 1997. In Greek with an English translation by H. St. J. Thackeray. A classic work on the Roman-Jewish war by a participant.

Parente, Fausto, and Joseph Sievers, eds. *Josephus and the History of the Greco-Roman Period: Essays in Memory of Morton Smith.* A collection of essays on Flavius Josephus presented at the Josephus Colloquium, held in Italy in 1992. Bibliography and indexes.

Price, Jonathan J. *Jerusalem Under Siege: The Collapse of the Jewish State, 66-70 C.E.* New York: Brill, 1992. An analysis of the Roman-Jewish war, including the destruction of the temple.

SEE ALSO: c. 1280 B.C.E., Israelite Exodus from Egypt; c. 1000 B.C.E., Establishment of the United Kingdom of Israel; c. 966 B.C.E., Building of the Temple of Jerusalem; c. 922 B.C.E., Establishment of the Kingdom of Israel; 587-423 B.C.E., Birth of Judaism; c. 538-c. 450 B.C.E., Jews Return from the Babylonian Captivity; 167-142 B.C.E., Revolt of the Maccabees.

RELATED ARTICLES in *Great Lives from History: The Ancient World*: Flavius Josephus; Vespasian.

August 24, 79 C.E.
DESTRUCTION OF POMPEII

The destruction of Pompeii through the eruption of Mount Vesuvius annihilated thousands of Pompeians but preserved the remains of this former great Roman city for discovery in later archaeological excavations.

LOCALE: Pompeii (now in Campania, Italy)
CATEGORY: Cultural and intellectual history

KEY FIGURES
Pliny the Elder (23-79 C.E.), uncle of Pliny the Younger and commander of a Roman fleet who lost his life during the eruption
Pliny the Younger (c. 61-c. 113 C.E.), witness to the eruption of Mount Vesuvius and the ensuing destruction of Pompeii

SUMMARY OF EVENT
The destruction of Pompeii and two other cities as a result of the eruption of Mount Vesuvius in 79 C.E. has provided a rich archaeological treasure for excavators of the past two centuries. Pompeii was originally part of a large coastal area founded by the Greeks (c. 650 B.C.E.) called Neapolis (Naples) or "the New City," and it became a prosperous harbor town along the Sarnus (Sarno) River. The Samnites controlled the city after 420 B.C.E. until it fell to Rome in 290 B.C.E. Pompeii became a more independent colony after 91 B.C.E. and a thriving center of oil and wine production, as well as a strong exporter of fish sauce, fruit, and volcanic stone or tufa. However, the city's significance should not be overestimated, for it had a population of only twenty thousand and an importance that was solely regional. Its pleasant climate and proximity to the sea, however, made it a fashionable resort for wealthy Romans, some of whom, including the orator Cicero, maintained homes there.

During the reign of Emperor Nero on February 5, 62 C.E., a severe earthquake rocked and badly damaged towns circling Mount Vesuvius, especially Pompeii and its forum area and temples. The great reservoir near Porta Vesuvius gave way, unleashing floodwaters throughout the city, and huge chasms opened in the fields, with reports of people and flocks of sheep being swallowed.

Along with the neighboring cities of Herculaneum and Stabiae, the city came to an abrupt end on August 24 in the year 79, when the volcano Vesuvius erupted in full fury. Located some 12 miles (19 kilometers) north of Pompeii across the southern end of the Bay of Naples, the volcano, aided by strong winds, rained down tons of fiery ashes and pumice on the three helpless cities. First, a mass of lava pebbles (*lapilli*) and boulders shot thousands of feet into the sky and crashed to the surface, adding about 8 to 9 feet (about 2.5 meters) of debris on the ground. Then, a cloud of pumice covered the terrain of the city up to 6 to 8 feet (nearly 2 to 2.5 meters) in height. A new wave of earthquakes, caused by the collapse of the sides of the volcanic cone, contributed to an explosion of gaseous pumice, dust, ash, and cinders. This material eventually turned downward, adding another 7 feet (a little over 2 meters) to the ash-covered city—not to mention the addition of various lethal gases as well.

Pliny the Younger, an eyewitness, describes the event graphically. About 7:00 A.M., Pliny relates, a dark cloud shaped like a pine tree appeared over the summit of Mount Vesuvius. The volcano emitted "flashes of fire as vivid as lightning" and produced "darkness more profound than night." A thick vapor enveloped the entire area. Although all three cities were destroyed, Herculaneum appears to have received the full force of the eruption, being engulfed in a flood of volcanic waste that solidified into a level mass between 50 and 70 feet (15 and 21 meters) thick. Fortunately, the Roman fleet from Misenum commanded by Pliny the Elder, uncle of Pliny the Younger, was able to evacuate some of the inhabitants of the city. Nevertheless, the loss of life was great; by the 1990's, archaeologists had removed some two thousand bodies. Tragically, attempts to escape by sea were thwarted because of fiery stones, winds, and waves that made embarkation impossible; the burning, flowing mud and ashes also prevented ships from making any landings. Unfortunately, Pliny the Elder was overcome by the deadly fumes and died at a point near Herculaneum (west of the volcano). Indeed, the main cause of death was not incineration but asphyxiation caused by carbon monoxide or sulfur dioxide.

The submerged cities were not rebuilt. A small village did for a time occupy the site of Pompeii, but it was deserted after another eruption of Mount Vesuvius in 472 C.E. Subsequent eruptions of the volcano so changed the coastline so that by the time exploration of the region was undertaken in the mid-eighteenth century, the exact site of Pompeii and the other two cities was uncertain.

Excavation actually began in 1748, when a peasant digging a well made some interesting finds that he reported to the authorities. King Charles IV of Naples became interested in the work, and in 1755, the amphitheater and other public buildings were uncovered. During the following fifty years, little systematic excavation took place, although miscellaneous rare objects were found from time to time. Under Joachim Murat, appointed king of Naples by Napoleon, archaeologists excavated some houses and streets, but only later in the mid-nineteenth century under Giuseppe Fiorelli, professor of archaeology at the University of Naples, were extensive excavations undertaken. He wanted to maintain the historical authenticity of the site by preserving objects found on location. His great contribution to Western civilization was his invention of a way to recapture the forms, or appearances, of people and animals caught in the horror of the destruction of Pompeii. Ashes preserved the exteriors of dead bodies after decomposition, so to reveal the shape of the body, he inserted inserting a tube into hollow areas where bones no longer existed and injected a special liquid plaster that, when hardened, would assume the shape of the original body. Details of Pompeian clothes, hair texture, feet imprints, and facial expressions are amazingly preserved.

The city was shaped like an irregular oval, the length being on an east-west axis. The 1.5-mile (2.4-kilometer) wall that surrounded the town had eight gates at which sentry boxes were located. Magnificently preserved streets and homes have been unearthed, the latter containing numerous utensils, jewelry, doctors' and tradesmen's tools, lamps, and mirrors in addition to beautifully painted walls displaying frescoes that reflect various themes of Roman life. Some of the larger Pompeian homes or villas date from the second century, while the style of wall paintings in others indicate that they were built during the Augustan period. The most pretentious villas were located 2 miles (about 3 kilometers) outside Pompeii at Boscoreale. In one villa there, besides artifacts of the traditional type, numerous wine storage jars were found that could accommodate an annual production of 20,000 gallons (76,000 liters). The income from the sale of so much wine is clearly reflected in the luxurious appointments of the estate.

SIGNIFICANCE

Excavations at Pompeii, besides broadening knowledge about the daily life and routine of all ranks of Roman people, has had other unexpected repercussions. In the eighteenth century, they reinforced the neoclassical tra-

Archaeologists created plaster casts of two victims of the eruption of Mount Vesuvius. (Library of Congress)

ditions popular during the Enlightenment. In France, the discoveries influenced the so-called Imperial style of Louis XV, while in England they gave birth to the so-called Adam period of architecture and decorative art during the second half of the eighteenth century.

—Edward P. Keleher,
updated by Connie Pedoto

FURTHER READING

Ciarallo, Annamaria. *Gardens of Pompeii.* Los Angeles: J. Paul Getty Museum, 2001. A study of the gardens and of the plants depicted in Pompeii artwork. Bibliography.

Ciarallo, Annamaria, and Ernesto De Carolis, eds. *Pompeii: Life in a Roman Town.* Milano: Electa, 1999. A catalog published in conjunction with the exhibitions at the Museo Archaeologico Nazioale di Napoli and at the Los Angeles County Museum of Art in 1999 and 2000. Bibliography and index.

D'Ambrosio, Antonio. *Women and Beauty in Pompeii.* Los Angeles: J. Paul Getty Museum, 2001. An illustrated analysis of the woman of Pompeii, including their jewelry and their social lives. Glossary, bibliography, and index.

De Carolis, Ernesto. *Gods and Heroes in Pompeii.* Los Angeles: J. Paul Getty Museum, 2001. Focuses on the depiction of gods and heroes in the art of Pompeii, including its murals. Bibliography.

De Franciscis, Alfonso. *Pompeii: Monuments Past and Present.* Roma: Vision, 1995. A pictorial work examining the structures found at Pompeii. Contains transparent leaves showing artists' reconstructions of original buildings. Color illustrations.

Descourdres, Jean-Paul, et al. *Pompeii Revisited: The Life and Death of a Roman Town.* Sydney: Meditarch, 1994. This publication accompanied an exhibition on Pompeii at the Australian Museum in 1994. Sixteen pages of color plates.

Wallace-Hadrill, Andrew. *Houses and Society in Pompeii and Herculaneum.* Princeton, N.J.: Princeton University Press, 1994. An analysis of the architecture, material culture, and social life of Pompeii and Herculaneum. Bibliography and index.

Zanker, Paul. *Pompeii: Public and Private Life.* Revealing Antiquity 11. Cambridge, Mass.: Harvard University Press, 1998. A study of the political structure and social life of Pompeii. Bibliography and index.

SEE ALSO: September 2, 31 B.C.E., Battle of Actium; 68-69 C.E., Year of the Four Emperors.

RELATED ARTICLE in *Great Lives from History: The Ancient World*: Pliny the Elder.

---

90 C.E.

FOUNDING OF THE CLASSIC PERIOD MAYA ROYAL DYNASTY AT TIKAL

The establishment of a new and vigorous Maya dynastic tradition c. 90 C.E. heralded the beginning of eight centuries of divine rulership that culminated with the collapse of the ancient metropolis and kingdom of Yax Mutal, or Tikal, in 562.

LOCALE: Tikal (now in Guatemala)
CATEGORIES: Government and politics; wars, uprisings, and civil unrest

KEY FIGURES

Yax Ehb "Xook" (First Step Shark; c. 50-150 C.E.), founding *ahau* or "divine lord" of Tikal Dynasty, r. c. 90-150 C.E.

Ix Une Balam (Baby Jaguar; d. 317 C.E.), first female *ahau* or "divine lady" of Tikal, r. ?-317 C.E.

Chak Tok Ich'aak I (Great Jaguar Paw; d. 378 C.E.), *ahau* of Tikal, r. 360-378 C.E.

Nuun Yax Ayiin I (Curl Snout; d. 404? C.E.), Mexicanized *ahau* of Tikal, r. 378-404? C.E.

Siyaj Chan K'awiil II (Stormy Sky; d. 456 C.E.), Mexicanized *ahau* of Tikal, r. 411-456 C.E.

SUMMARY OF EVENT

The royal house of ancient Yax Mutal (first Mutal, top-knot), or Tikal, was founded under the leadership of the legendary Yax Ehb "Xook" c. 90 C.E. The royal lineage founded by Yax Ehb "Xook" would ultimately encompass the royal histories of some thirty-three *ahaus* (divine lords and ladies) of the house of Yax Mutal. Although little is known of the longevity and exploits of the founder of the Tikal dynastic tradition, it is known that he was the founder of a royal line that would persist in various forms for nearly eight centuries, despite foreign invasion, intermarriage, the Maya hiatus, and, ultimately, the collapse and rebirth of the ancient metropolis of Tikal.

The reign of Yax Ehb "Xook" signaled the origin and proliferation of the classic Maya dynastic tradition as it is understood today. Much of the traditional pomp and circumstance and iconographic, architectural, and symbolic conventions inherent in the warrior aristocracies and divine kingship of the later Classic era (c. 250-900 C.E.) may be traced to its earliest manifestation at the site of Yax Mutal during the first century C.E. reign of Yax Ehb "Xook." Advances in archaeology and epigraphy, or Maya glyph interpretation and translation, have enabled the detailed assessment and identification of the movers and shakers of the ancient Maya world. However, it should be noted that although precise dates are available from the interpretation of Maya glyphs derived from monuments, carved mahogany panels, and ceramic vessels, what remains as yet undetermined is the overall antiquity of the dynasty based on a specific founding date for the Tikal dynasty. Therefore, Simon Martin and Nikolai Grube, in their book *Chronicle of the Maya Kings and Queens* (2000), caution that Maya dynastic succession is necessarily limited to interpretations derived from Tikal's numbered count of kings and queens, titles of succession, and projected years in power.

Although only fragmentary glyphic histories and monuments make reference to Yax Ehb "Xook," his successors make repeated references to this founder of the dynasty that would give birth to many heirs. Among his successors may be counted two little-known kings by the names of Foliated Jaguar, or Scroll Ahau Jaguar, and Animal Headdress, whose respective periods of rule have yet to be precisely identified. The subsequent ruler, Siyaj Chan K'awiil I, or Sky-Born K'awiil Great Claw, has been identified with the period of c. 307 C.E. Siyaj Chan K'awiil I was the son of Animal Headdress and Lady Skull. As the eleventh heir of the dynasty founded by Yax Ehb "Xook," Siyaj Chan K'awiil I is thought to represent the last of a line of male heirs who ruled before the seating of Ix Une Balam, or Baby Jaguar, who died in 317 C.E. At that juncture, Ix Une Balam is believed responsible for the celebration of the K'atun ending, or twenty-

MAJOR FIGURES IN THE MAYA ROYAL DYNASTY AT TIKAL, C. 90-869 C.E.		
Mayan Name	*Common Name*	*Reign*
Yax Ehb "Xook"	Yax Moch Xok	c. 90-150
Siyaj Chan K'awiil I	Sky-Born K'awiil Great Claw	c. 300
Ix Une Balam	Baby Jaguar	d. 317
K'inich Muwaan Jol	Bird Skull	c. 330-359
Chak Tok Ich'aak I	Jaguar Paw	360-378
Nuun Yax Ayiin I	Curl Snout	378-404?
Siyaj Chan K'awiil II	Stormy Sky	411-456
K'an Chitam	Kan Boar	458-c. 486
Chak Tok Ich'aak II	Jaguar Paw Skull	c. 488-508
	Lady of Tikal	511-527
Kalomte "Balam"	Curl Head	511?-527
Wak Chan K'awiil	Double Bird	537-562
	Animal Skull	?-628?
Nuun Ujol Chaak	Shield Skull	c. 657-679
Jasaw Chan K'awiil	Ruler A	682-733
"Yik'in" Chan K'awaaiil	Ruler B	734-c. 761
Nuun Yax Ayiin II	Ruler C	768
Nuun Ujol K'inich		c. 800
	Dark Sun	810
"Jewel" K'awiil		849
Jasaw Chan K'awiil	Stela 11 Ruler	869

Source: Chronicles of the Maya Kings and Queens: Deciphering the Dynasties of the Ancient Maya (2000), by Simon Martin and Nikolai Grube.

year calendrical cycle, held sacred to Maya dynasts of the time. Her placement in that context indicates that she was in fact the queen, the twelfth successor of the founding ruler of Tikal. By 330 C.E., K'inich Muwaan Jol, or Bird Skull, was seated as the thirteenth ruler of ancient Tikal. K'inich Muwaan Jol, who died on or near May 23, 359 C.E., is cited on various monuments as having fathered his successor, the legendary fourteenth ruler of Tikal, Chak Tok Ich'aak I, or Great Burning Claw—also known as Great Jaguar Paw—who acceded to the throne on or near August 7, 360 C.E.

Perhaps the most celebrated of the early dynasts of the Petén was in fact Chak Tok Ich'aak I. His death on January 15, 378—or 8.17.1.4.12 11 Eb 15 Mak of the Maya Long Count calendar—represents a critical departure from the nearly three-hundred-year-old royal lineage cultivated by the ancestors of Chak Tok Ich'aak I and the descendants of Yax Ehb "Xook," the founder of Tikal's royal house in 90 C.E. According to Linda Schele, it was at this time that the Maya of Yax Mutal acquired the art of conquest and the use of the atlatl spear, the dart thrower identified with the ancient metropolis and state of Teotihuacán and more generally with highland Mexican civilization. Concomitantly, there was a proliferation of painted and sculpted media and writings at Tikal and nearby Uaxactún (Guatemala) that serve to document the arrival of Teotihuacán warriors or other Mexican emissaries from the central highlands.

Significantly, the death of Chak Tok Ich'aak I corresponds with the arrival at Tikal of the foreigner identified as Siyaj K'ak, or Fire Born, on January 31, 378 C.E., and the death of the royal house identified specifically with the lineage of Chak Tok Ich'aak I. According to Martin and Grube, the death of Chak Tok Ich'aak I in turn corresponds to the wholesale replacement of his lineage with that of a new male line apparently drawn directly from the ruling house of Teotihuacán itself. This displacement was in turn accompanied by the violent destruction and internment, or relocation, of virtually all monuments and artifacts pertaining to the reign of Chak Tok Ich'aak I and his predecessors. The subsequent installation of the divine lord Nuun Yax Ayiin I, or Curl Snout, on September 12, 378 C.E., ultimately set the stage for the Mexicanization of the Tikal royal house. Nowhere is this made more apparent than with the installation of the son and successor of Yax Nuun Ayiin I, the divine lord Siyaj Chan K'awiil II, or Stormy Sky, on November 26, 411 C.E.

Monuments depicting the lengthy rule of Siyaj Chan K'awiil II (411-456 C.E.) invariably depict his father Nuun Yax Ayiin I as a Teotihuacán emissary or warrior in full highland Mexican battle regalia—replete with atlatl spear throwers, rectangular shields bearing the image of the goggle-eyed war deity Tlaloc, spherical or balloon headdresses containing the Mexican crossed-trapeze year symbol, and related icons, insignia, and armaments pertaining to the war cult commanders of highland central Mexico. Stela 31, which constitutes one of the finest sculpted monuments recovered from the site of Tikal, bears a highly ornate Classic Maya portrait of Siyaj Chan K'awiil II on its frontal face flanked by two Mexicanized depictions of his father, the divine lord Nuun Yax Ayiin I, on its sides. Dated to 445 C.E., stela 31 sought to document the dynastic relationship of Stormy Sky to Yax Ehb "Xook"—the founding divine lord of the Tikal royal lineage of c. 90 C.E. Despite his derivative Mexican origins, Siyaj Chan K'awiil II is identified in other contexts as the sixteenth divine lord, or *ahau*, of Yax Mutal. Ultimately, Martin and Grube believe that stela 31 served to affirm the rebirth of "orthodox kingship" at Tikal via the proclamation that Siyaj Chan K'awiil II was a direct heir of the founding dynast Yax Ehb "Xook," despite the introduc-

tion of a foreign blood line implanted at Tikal via emissaries and warriors with ties to the distant ancient metropolis of Teotihuacán (Mexico).

Despite the fact that the metropolis of Teotihuacán lay some 630 miles (1,010 kilometers) west of Tikal, scholars have long debated the sources and affinities of Mexicanized influence on Tikal and the Petén Guatemalan lowlands. Despite glyph translations of key monuments pertaining to Uaxactún and Tikal and related lowland Maya sites; discoveries in Tikal's Teotihuacán *barrio*, or enclave, identified with the Mundo Perdido, or Lost World Complex; and newly recovered monuments depicting the "arrival" of emissaries from the Mexican highlands, some scholars continue to debate the significance of an overwhelming body of evidence that serves to document the presence of foreign intruders and the likely usurpers of the Tikal royal house. Despite some controversy over the nature and extent of Mexican or Teotihuacán influence in the architecture, iconography, ceramics, monuments, and burials recovered at Tikal, it should be noted that virtually all subsequent *ahau*, or divine lords, of Tikal would from that point onward brandish Mexicanized symbols of power and authority borne of Teotihuacán until the collapse of Yax Mutal some five centuries later.

SIGNIFICANCE

When the ill-fated final ruler of ancient Yax Mutal, Jasaw Chan K'awiil II, commissioned the installation of the final *tetun*—"stone tree" or portrait stela—for the "forest of kings" that dominated Tikal's Great Plaza of 869 C.E., one of the oldest dynastic traditions in the Americas came to an inglorious end. By that time the city's fortunes waned with the near total collapse of its political economy, the precipitous decline of its urban population, and the onslaught of a multitude of new and bellicose claimants to the throne harbored within the royal houses of those competing city-states that then occupied the former hinterlands of the late great metropolis of Yax Mutal. Despite this anticlimactic end for the ancient city and dynasty of Yax Mutal, the legendary Yax Ehb "Xook" founded what has come to be acknowledged as perhaps one of the best documented, and most emulated, early indigenous models of dynastic succession and lineage reckoning in ancient Mesoamerica.

—*Ruben G. Mendoza*

FURTHER READING

Coe, Michael D. *Breaking the Maya Code*. New York: Thames and Hudson, 1999. A chronicle of the process of discovery that led to the interpretation and subsequent translation of the ancient Maya glyph system.

_____. *The Maya*. 6th ed. London: Thames and Hudson, 1999. A classic overview of the rise and fall of Maya civilization revised to account for modern findings regarding Maya kingship and glyphic interpretations.

Coe, William R. *Tikal: A Handbook of the Ancient Maya Ruins*. Philadelphia: The University Museum, University of Pennsylvania, 1969. A review of Maya archaeology and the ruins of Tikal as seen by the lead archaeologist of the Tikal Acropolis Project.

Harrison, Peter D, Colin Renfrew, and Jeremy A. Sabloff. *The Lords of Tikal: Rulers of an Ancient Maya City*. London: Thames and Hudson, 2000. This text provides an insight-filled chronicle and useful time line documenting the evolution of the royal house of Tikal.

Martin, Simon, and Nikolai Grube. *Chronicle of the Maya Kings and Queens: Deciphering the Dynasties of the Ancient Maya*. London: Thames and Hudson, 2000. Perhaps the most authoritative, exhaustive, and up-to-date account currently available for the interpretation of the dynastic histories of the ancient city of Tikal.

Miller, Mary Ellen. *Maya Art and Architecture*. New York: Thames and Hudson, 1999. A concise overview of the origins and affinities of ancient Maya art based on both art history and archaeology.

Schele, Linda. "The Owl, Shield, and Flint Blade: In A.D. 378, the Maya Learned the Art of Conquest." *Natural History* 11, no. 4 (1991): 6. An early, albeit somewhat dated, interpretation of that Teotihuacán-inspired imagery found at Tikal and Uaxactún, Guatemala.

Schele, Linda, and David Freidel. *A Forest of Kings: The Untold Story of the Ancient Maya*. New York: Quill, William Morrow, 1990. A landmark work regarding Maya kingship based on scholarship in Maya glyph decipherment.

SEE ALSO: c. 1530 B.C.E., Mixtec Civilization Develops in Western Oaxaca; c. 1500-c. 300 B.C.E., Olmec Civilization Rises in Southern Mexico; c. 500 B.C.E.-c. 700 C.E., Zapotecs Build Monte Albán; c. 100 B.C.E.-c. 200 C.E., Zapotec State Dominates Oaxaca; c. 1 C.E., Development Begins at Teotihuacán; c. 100-200 C.E., Construction of the Pyramids of the Sun and Moon at Teotihuacán; 200-900 C.E., Maya Civilization Flourishes.

c. 90 C.E.
SYNOD OF JAMNIA

The Synod of Jamnia finalized the contents of the Jewish scripture into the three major divisions of the Old Testament: the Law, or Torah; the Prophets, or Nevi'im; and the Writings, or Kethuvim.

LOCALE: Jamnia, Palestine
CATEGORY: Religion

KEY FIGURES

Josiah (c. 648-609 B.C.E.), king of Judah, r. c. 640/649-609 B.C.E.

Ezra (fl. late sixth-early fifth century B.C.E.), leading Jewish scribe and priest

Johanan ben Zakkai (c. 1-80 C.E.), Rabbinic leader and founder of the synod

SUMMARY OF EVENT

The Synod of Jamnia finally closed the canon of Jewish Scripture, a corpus that profoundly influenced the character and content of all Western religion. The development of the Hebrew canon, like that of the Christian, was

a gradual and complicated process. Originally the message of God was preserved orally, the prophecies of Amos being the first utterance written down as a book, in the eighth century B.C.E. The notion of inspired writing appears to have grown out of prophecy. Much of the canonization process came about without datable formal pronouncements; specific synods or councils participating in canonization development merely ratified what common consent had already recognized as authoritative. The history of the canonization of the Jewish Scripture, however, can be simplified if the three major divisions of the Old Testament—the Law, or *Torah*; the Prophets, or *Nevi'im*; and the Writings, or *Kethuvim*—are isolated and studied in turn.

The core of the Pentateuch is Deuteronomy, a book discovered under strange circumstances in the Temple of Jerusalem as late as 621 B.C.E. in the reign of Josiah. It was immediately regarded as Yahweh's word and given government enforcement. By the mid-sixth century, the early history of the Jews, the story of the patriarchs, Exodus, and Kings became so popular that the Deuteronomic code was inserted into it to form a corpus. When Ezra reputedly read the book "of the law" before the people in 444 B.C.E., he gave the Pentateuch an unusual endorsement as the work of Moses and the surest bulwark of a Jewish theocratic community struggling for security and identity in the aftermath of the exile. By 250 B.C.E., when the Pentateuch was translated into Greek, it was commonly accepted as the bible of the Jews. Its canonization must have taken place about 150 years earlier, about 400 B.C.E., judging from the fact that the Samaritans knew it as Scripture before their secession from Judaism about that time. The first five books of the law (Genesis, Exodus, Leviticus, Numbers, and Deuteronomy) were apparently removed from the historical narrative of Joshua, Judges, Samuel, and Kings with which they had been associated one by one over the years, and given a unique authority never to be shared equally by later canonized books. The Torah was widely circulated as authoritative and was read extensively in synagogues.

Other books gradually began to receive recognition. The eight historical and prophetic books came to be grouped together as "the Prophets" (the former prophets: Joshua, Judges, Samuel, and Kings; and the latter prophets: Isaiah, Jeremiah, Ezekiel, and the Twelve Minor Prophets). By 200 B.C.E., their religious and patriotic popularity together with their supposed prophetic visions of a restored Jerusalem after the degradation of the exile made them desirable in synagogue worship; the four historical books, or former prophets, and the four books of latter prophets were in some sort of final edition by the same date, judging on one hand from the inclusion of definite third century materials and on the other from the absence in the corpus of Daniel, which was written in 164 B.C.E. Clearly the canonization of the law and the prophets can at best be only approximately dated because no definite event can be associated with their official recognition.

The third section to be given official status is called simply "the Writings," eleven works with little in common. Some are poetical, like Job; some are prophetic, like Daniel; and some are historical, like Chronicles. Others conveniently grouped together as "the Five Scrolls" became associated with one another merely as synagogue readings. One by one, books in this third section came to enter the canonical orbit soon after 200 B.C.E. Proverbs and Job were quickly accepted; Daniel was recognized shortly after its publication. By the beginning of the Christian era, most of the books in this third grouping were accepted as Jewish Scripture, but some were controversial, including Song of Songs with

THE JEWISH BIBLE	
TORAH	**WRITINGS (KETUVIM)**
Genesis	Psalms
Exodus	Proverbs
Leviticus	Job
Numbers	The Song of Songs
Deuteronomy	Ruth
	Lamentations
PROPHETS (NEVI'IM)	Ecclesiastes
Joshua	Esther
Judges	Daniel
Samuel	Ezra-Nehemiah
Kings	Chronicles
Isaiah	
Jeremiah	
Ezekiel	
Twelve Minor Prophets	

its love poetry, Ecclesiastes because of its skepticism and pessimism, and Esther with its secular note. By the time of Philo of Alexandria (c. 20 B.C.E.-c. 45 C.E.), the canon seems to have been well recognized; he is careful to quote no book outside the official corpus although he does not quote from all.

Between 90 and 100 C.E., the city of Jamnia or Jabneh became the scene of the last act in the process of canonization. Jamnia was a city in Palestine a few miles south of Jaffa; it had once been the property of Herod the Great (d. 4 B.C.E.), and it was later passed to Livia Drusilla, the wife of Augustus (63 B.C.E.-14 C.E.). After the time of Alexander Jannaeus (d. c. 78 B.C.E.) it became a center of Jewish culture, and it was here that Rabbi Johanan ben Zakkai, a member of the defunct Sanhedrin of Jerusalem, received permission from the emperor Vespasian (9-79 C.E.) to establish a sort of academy or sanhedrin. About 90 C.E., a synod of rabbis met in this new center of authority and learning to discuss and fix the canon. The need was urgent because of the confusion then arising through Christians quoting from books that they regarded as canonical but were not recognized as such by Palestinian Hebrews. By closing the canon of the writings, the Hebrew Bible was officially closed at twenty-four books. Flavius Josephus (c. 37-c. 100 C.E.) about the same time listed twenty-two authorized books, preferring to follow the arrangement of the Greek version.

Agreement prevailed, although there were some local variations in the list of canonical books especially among Greek-speaking Jews of Alexandria. In addition, esoteric sects often tended to give their secret writings a semi-canonical status. The Torah, however, remained the word of God par excellence to all.

SIGNIFICANCE

In all ancient religions, gods communicate with human beings spontaneously or in response to questions. This communication comes through visions or dreams, or directly through prophecy. Because the Jews enjoyed an unparalleled opportunity to hear the word of God through prophets rather than by other means, it becomes understandable why they arrived at the conclusion that God wanted his message written down in books. The unusual notion of an inspired scripture is a major contribution to religion by Judaism, one adopted later by Zoroastrianism, Hinduism, Buddhism, Christianity, and Islam. The preservation of prophetic materials seems, in retrospect, haphazard. Some were gathered together accidentally; the words of the ninth century B.C.E. prophets, Elijah, Elisha, and Micaiah ben Imlah, for instance, were incorporated in Kings. Beginning with Amos, the sayings of individual prophets were preserved in separate books. Canonization of the materials was another process, generally protracted. Thus Amos's writings were not officially recognized until five and a half centuries had elapsed; in Amos's day itself the concept of inspired scripture did not exist. The very diversity of the books in the canon is surprising when one compares the Jewish scriptures with those of Christianity or Islam. Much material was selected on the basis of patriotism, for Judaism, despite its great monotheistic thrust entailing a degree of universalism, never lost its nationalistic quality. Material of a secular nature included in the canon came to be endowed through allegory with profound religious significance originally alien to it.

Jesus himself did not regard the Scriptures as complete or a final revelation. Sometimes they contained temporary dispensations, such as divorce in the law of Moses, which were considered in opposition to the fundamental law of God. Although Paul deprecated the law and preferred to base his religion on a mystical conception of salvation through the death and resurrection of Jesus, the Old Testament Septuagint remained authoritative in the early Church because Christians needed the fulfillment of prophecies and promises in the Old Testament to guarantee the divinity of Jesus. Matthew and John especially emphasize the fulfillment of prophesy in the person of Jesus. Thus the Old Testament conversely and indirectly contributed much to Christianity. The Christians appropriated the Old Testament when the Church became in its mind the New Israel, the New Jerusalem. The institutions of Judaism outlined in the canon became forerunners, symbols, and shadows of what was to come. New Testament writers regarded the canon of the Old Testament in different ways. Paul saw the law as largely negative; while John was often anti-Jewish, the Book of Revelation was quite friendly. All, however, agreed that the old canon was divinely inspired. New Testament writers quoted widely from their predecessors, the early Church Fathers, especially those writing during the formation of the Christian scriptures, borrowing freely from the Old Testament.

It is not surprising then that the Jews at Jamnia felt the need to determine the exact content of the Hebrew canon in the face of haphazard Christian usage. Those who would impugn the historicity of Christianity by disconnecting it from the Old Testament, as Marcion (c. 120-c. 160 C.E.) and the Gnostics tried to do, were generally considered heretics. Tatian (fl. second century C.E.) recognized several important contributions of the Old Testament to Christianity: it helped to form the doctrines and institutions of the Church, it nourished piety through liturgical and private readings, it provided norms of conduct, and it opened promises of a glorious future. To the present, the Old Testament remains a pattern of faith and edification for the Jew, an ultimate source of doctrine for the Christian, and an assurance of Providence for both.

In short, the Jewish concept of a canon, of books as a norm for religion, is in itself an interesting and unique phenomenon, one far from the ancient classical mind. More significant, probably, is the closing of the canon. It implies that, since the days of Ezra, God no longer spoke to his people through prophets. Judaism became the religion of a book or *biblos*. Additional revelation had to come through exegesis, commentaries, or the employment of tradition. Acceptance of tradition in turn led inevitably to a splintering of Jewish sects. Christians, refusing to accept the thesis that God no longer walked and talked to men, felt the necessity of recognizing a "new" testament with additional insights into the psychology of the Godhead and his economy. However, adoption of the Hebrew canon with slight variations gave the new Christian community retroactive respectability in history.

—*Joseph R. Rosenbloom*

FURTHER READING

Cross, Frank Moore. *From Epic to Canon: History and Literature in Ancient Israel.* Baltimore, Md.: The Johns Hopkins University Press, 1999. Chapters 10 and 11 deal with the establishment and stabilization of the Hebrew canon. Illustrations and indexes.

1 - 100 C.E.

Davies, Philip R. *Scribes and Schools: The Canonization of the Hebrew Scriptures*. Louisville, Ky.: Westminster John Knox Press, 1998. Discusses the idea of canons generally and the control and operation of the technology of writing in the ancient world, reviews various approaches taken by scholars regarding these issues in Judaism, summarizes Israelite and Judaean history from the monarchic to the Roman periods, and considers the transition of canonical collections of literature into the Holy Books.

Grabbe, Lester L. *Judaic Religion in the Second Temple Period: Belief and Practice from Exile to Yavneh*. New York: Routledge, 2000. A holistic examination of the development of Judaism. Chapter 9 deals with the construction of the canon.

Leiman, Sid Z. *The Canonization of Hebrew Scripture: The Talmudic and Midrashic Evidence*. 2d ed. New Haven, Conn.: Connecticut Academy of the Arts, 1991. Discusses the process by which the Hebrew canon evolved and was closed.

Steinmann, Andrew. *The Oracles of God: The Old Testament Canon*. St. Louis, Mo.: Concordia Publishing House, 1999. Argues that the canon was essentially established during the Persian period. Reviews all evidence and the process of closing the canon.

Vanderkam, James C. *An Introduction to Early Judaism*. Grand Rapids, Mich.: William B. Eerdmans, 2000. A lucid yet scholarly introduction to the formation of Judaism. Discusses history, worship, and literature, explaining the process by which the Jewish canon was established.

SEE ALSO: c. 1000 B.C.E., Establishment of the United Kingdom of Israel; c. 966 B.C.E., Building of the Temple of Jerusalem; c. 950 B.C.E., Composition of the Book of Genesis; c. 922 B.C.E., Establishment of the Kingdom of Israel; 587-423 B.C.E., Birth of Judaism; c. 538-c. 450 B.C.E., Jews Return from the Babylonian Captivity; 250-130 B.C.E., Commissioning of the Septuagint; c. 200 B.C.E.-c. 100 C.E., Composition of the Intertestamental Jewish Apocrypha; c. 50-c. 150 C.E., Compilation of the New Testament; September 8, 70 C.E., Roman Destruction of the Temple of Jerusalem.

RELATED ARTICLES in *Great Lives from History: The Ancient World*: Ezra; Herod the Great; Johanan ben Zakkai; Flavius Josephus.

c. 99-105 C.E.

BAN ZHAO WRITES BEHAVIOR GUIDE FOR YOUNG WOMEN

Ban Zhao wrote a guide to proper behavior for women, in which, although upholding Confucian and classical ideals, she made a radical appeal for educating girls.

LOCALE: China
CATEGORY: Cultural and intellectual history

KEY FIGURE

Ban Zhao (Pan Chao; c. 45-c. 120 C.E.), Chinese poet, historian, educator, and moralist, often considered China's foremost woman scholar

SUMMARY OF EVENT

Ban Zhao, the first known Chinese woman historian, was born into a scholarly Chinese family, in Fufeng (Fu-feng) in modern-day Shannxi (Shensi) Province. The family had often served the Imperial Court. Ban Zhao lived during the Eastern, or Later, Han Dynasty (25-220 C.E.), a time of peace and great cultural and literary development. Rulers emphasized government by moral and cultural ideals rather than politics.

Her father, Ban Biao (Pan Piao), was a famous scholar and a popular magistrate. He had begun writing the authoritative history of the Western Han Dynasty (206 B.C.E.-23 C.E.) but died in 54 C.E., without finishing the history. At age fourteen, Ban Zhao married Cao Shou (Ts'ao Shou) from the same town, and they had several children. Her husband died early in the marriage, and Ban Zhao became a young widow, never remarrying.

She had two older twin brothers, Ban Gu (Pan Ku, 32-92 C.E.) and Ban Chao (Pan Ch'ao, 32-102 C.E.). By 76 C.E., Ban Chao had become a soldier, and Ban Gu, a poet and historian, served the Imperial Court. She and her mother also went to the capital. Ban Gu worked on the history begun by his father and titled it *Han Shu* (also known as *Qian Han Shu*, completed first century C.E.; *The History of the Former Han Dynasty*, 1938-1955). However, when in 92 C.E. the dowager empress Dou's family was accused of treason, the family's friends, including Ban Gu, were executed. Ban Gu's brother had become a great general serving on China's northwest frontier, so he was spared. Eventually, in 95 C.E., Ban Zhao's son was assigned to a distant post, and she joined him in this perceived exile.

In approximately 97 C.E., Emperor Ho (89-105 C.E.) ordered Ban Zhao to return to the capital to complete the history begun by her father and brother. She was permitted access to the Imperial Library, became de facto imperial historian, and eventually finished *The History of the Former Han Dynasty*. In addition to working on the history, Ban Zhao was appointed tutor and teacher of the dowager empress and other women of the court. One of her students was a young girl named Deng (Teng, 80-120 C.E.), who had come to the court in 96 C.E. During this time, Ban Zhao wrote *Nu jie* (c. 99-105 C.E.; *The Chinese Book of Etiquette and Conduct for Women and Girls*, 1900; also known as *Lessons for Women*) to instruct young women. In 102 C.E., the emperor ousted his empress and made Deng the new empress. When the emperor died in 106 C.E., his 100-day-old son assumed the throne, and Dowager Empress Deng served as regent. The new emperor soon died and was succeeded by another child. Again, Dowager Empress Deng was the acting sovereign. By all accounts, the Dowager Empress continued to seek advice from Ban Zhao, who was very influential in the court. Ban Zhao died in her seventies, and the exact year of her death is unknown. However, it was before 120 C.E., the year the empress died, because the empress went into mourning when Ban Zhao died.

In the introduction to *Lessons for Women*, Ban Zhao explains the purpose of her treatise as training and advice for young women at the age of marriage. "More than forty years have passed since at the age of fourteen I took up the dustpan and the broom in the Ts'ao family. . . . Day and night I was distressed in heart. . . . I taught and trained (my children) without system." She wrote this treatise to serve as a survival manual, something she never had.

In chapter 1, "Humility," Ban Zhao analyzes the traditional symbolism in birth rituals for girls and explains the value of humility in the context of cheerful labor and deferring to the wishes of others. She suggests that adherence to these ideals of conduct will bring honor to a woman's family.

In Chapter 2, "Husband and Wife," she makes her radical plea for the equal education of girls up to age fifteen.

> If a husband be unworthy then he possesses nothing by which to control his wife. If a wife be unworthy, then she possesses nothing with which to serve her husband. . . . If a wife does not serve her husband, then the proper relationship (between men and women) and the natural order of things are neglected and destroyed.

Yet only to teach men and not to teach women—is that not ignoring the essential relation between them? According to the "Rites" it is the rule to begin to teach children to read at the age of eight year, and by the age of fifteen years they ought then to be ready for cultural training. Only why should it not be [that girls' education as well as boys' be] according to this principle?

In chapter 3, "Respect and Caution," Ban Zhao states that

> As Yin and Yang are not of the same nature, so man and woman have different characteristics. The distinctive quality of the Yang is rigidity; the function of the Yin yielding. Man is honored for strength; a woman is beautiful on account of her gentleness.

Respect for others and caution in behavior and language are urged.

Chapter 4 explains the four "Womanly Qualifications": womanly virtue, words, bearing, and work. Womanly virtue means chastity, circumspect behavior, and modesty. Womanly words involves speaking with care at appropriate times and avoiding vulgar or excessive conversation. Womanly bearing consists of cleanliness in personal hygiene and dress. Finally, womanly work means devotion to sewing and weaving, clean preparation of meals for guests, and the avoidance of "gossip and silly laughter."

Chapter 5, "Wholehearted Devotion," quotes from the Confucian "Rites": "A husband may marry again, but there is no Canon that authorizes a woman to be married the second time." Ban Zhao followed this principle in her own life by never remarrying. She quotes from an ancient book: "To obtain the love of one man is the crown of a woman's life; to lose the love of one man is to miss the aim in woman's life." The best ways to keep the love of a husband are "wholehearted devotion and correct manners."

Chapter 6, "Implicit Obedience," describes how a daughter-in-law should "not lose the hearts" of her husband's parents. The advice is to always obey and not disagree with the parents-in-law, even when they are wrong.

Similarly, Chapter 7, "Harmony with Younger Brothers- and Sisters-in-law" advises the daughter-in-law to be modest and agreeable with her husband's younger siblings, in order to "win for herself the love of her parents-in-law."

SIGNIFICANCE

Ban Zhao's *Lessons for Women* served as a much-needed guide to conduct for the young women of her times and also influenced later generations. Her most quoted and most well-known work, it is the only such treatise on the

1 - 100 C.E.

education of women to come from that early period in history. Full of quotations from the classics and Confucius, it provided a theoretical system of feminine ethics and practical rules for the application of these principles in daily life. Although accepting the superiority of men, Ban Zhao made a logical, powerful appeal for equal education for girls. To do otherwise was to ignore the "essential relationship" between men and women. In this respect, she was radical and centuries ahead of her time.

—*Alice Myers*

FURTHER READING

Ayscough, Florence Wheeler. *Chinese Women, Yesterday and Today.* 1937. Reprint. New York: Da Capo Press, 1975. Includes illustrations and a translation of *Nu Jie*.

Knapp, Bettina L. *Images of Chinese Women: A Westerner's View.* Troy, N.Y.: Whitston, 1992. Includes a chapter on Ban Zhao.

Raphals, Lisa Ann. *Sharing the Light: Representations of Women and Virtue in Early China.* Albany: State University of New York Press, 1998. Includes illustrations, bibliographical references, and index. There is a section on Ban Zhao and the *Nu Jie*.

Sharma, Arvind, ed. *Women in World Religions.* Albany: State University of New York Press, 1987. Includes Theresa Kelleher's essay "Confucianism," which discusses Ban Zhao, and a bibliography.

Swann, Nancy Lee. *Pan Chao: Foremost Woman Scholar of China, First Century A.D.; Background, Ancestry, Life, and Writings of the Most Celebrated Chinese Woman of Letters.* 1932. Reprint. New York: Russell & Russell, 1968. A complete biography, written by the foremost authority on Ban Zhao. Illustrated, with bibliographies and very detailed notes with references to scholarly research.

Wills, John E. *Mountain of Fame: Portraits in Chinese History.* Princeton, N.J.: Princeton University Press, 1994. Illustrated, maps, bibliographies. Includes a chapter on Ban Zhao.

SEE ALSO: 1st century B.C.E., Sima Qian Writes Chinese History; 25 C.E., Guang Wudi Restores the Han Dynasty; c. 220 C.E., Cai Yan Composes Poetry About Her Capture by Nomads.

RELATED ARTICLES in *Great Lives from History: The Ancient World*: Ban Gu; Ban Zhao.

---

c. 100-c. 127 C.E.
KUSHĀN DYNASTY EXPANDS INTO INDIA

The Kushāns expanded trade with China and the Roman Empire and created a brilliant culture, in which the Buddhist religion and art flourished.

LOCALE: Kushān Dynasty (present-day Uzbekistan, Tajikistan, Afghanistan, Pakistan, and northern India)

CATEGORIES: Expansion and land acquisition; cultural and intellectual history; trade and commerce; religion

KEY FIGURES

Kujūla Kadphises (d. c. 80 C.E.), founder of the Kushān Dynasty, who united the five tribes of Yuezhi and expanded the Kushān realm, r. c. 30-c. 80 C.E.

Vima Takhto (d. c. 100 C.E.), son of Kujūla, whose conquests reached the plains of India, r. 80-c. 100 C.E.

Vima Kadphises I (d. c. 127 C.E.), Kushān king who instituted a new gold currency and extended Kushān rule in the subcontinent of India, r. 100-c. 127 C.E.

Kanishka (first or second century-c. 152 C.E.), Kushān king who devised a modified Greek alphabet to write the Bactrian language and favored Buddhism, r. c. 127-c. 152 C.E.

Huvishka I (d. c. 192 C.E.), Kushān king, r. c. 152-c. 192 C.E.

Vasudeva I (d. c. 225 C.E.), last of the great Kushāns, under whose reign Indianization developed and the Kushān Dynasty began a decline, r. c. 192-c. 225 C.E.

SUMMARY OF EVENT

The Kushāns were one of five tribes in a confederation, called Yuezhi in Chinese sources, who moved from Gansu Province in China to western Central Asia about 120 B.C.E. Some scholars suggest that their language was Tokharian, an Indo-European tongue, written fragments of which were found much later (seventh-eighth century C.E.) in several oases in Xinjiang Province of China. They were pushed south from the region of present-day Kazakhstan by the nomads called Xiongnu (Hsiung-nu) in Chinese sources. It is not known how or when the tribes settled and mixed with the local population, which had absorbed Hellenic culture from Seleucid, then Greco-Bactrian rulers. In their new homeland, in present-day Uzbekistan, they in turn pushed other tribes, the Śakas (Scythians), south toward India and to southeastern Iran, where the displaced tribes gave their name to the present Iranian province of Sistān (older Sakastan). The Yuezhi gradually accepted Bactrian, the language of the settled people over whom they exercised suzerainty, but almost nothing is known of this part of the world at this time. More than a century after their settlement, it seems that a Yuezhi chief, Sanab or Heraus, as the name or title appears on coins, formed a small state north of the Oxus River (Amu Dar'ya). He may have been the first chief of the tribe called Kushān in the Yuezhi confederation, flourishing at the beginning of the common era. His realm seems to have been in present-day Tajikistan, and his successor may have been Kujūla Kadphises.

In the first century of the common era, the leader of the Kushāns, Kujūla Kadphises, united the tribes, together with settled folk, to found a state that extended over most of what is present-day Afghanistan. He died at the age of eighty after a long reign of almost fifty years. His son Vima Takhto suceeded him, but his coins, both silver and copper, bore only a title in Greek, *soter megas* (great savior), rather than his name. His name and relationship to other rulers were not discovered until 1993, when an inscription was found at a site called Rabatak in Afghanistan. This inscription provided a list of Kushān kings from Kujūla to Kanishka, but without any dates. It also told how Kanishka introduced a new alphabet for writing the Bactrian language. Although the inscription provides a relative chronology of the Kushān rulers, it does not give absolute dates, so the dates of reigns are uncertain.

Vima Kadphises I followed his father and conquered part of northwest India. He was partial to the Indian deity Śiva, as is evident from his coins, although Iranian and Hellenistic deities are also found on the coins. Vima changed the monetary system by striking gold coins instead of silver, but copper coinage continued to circulate locally. The gold coins were struck in similar weight to the Roman aureus, for trade with the Roman Empire expanded greatly under Vima. He extended the Kushān domains to Mathurā in India, although in the west some territory may have been lost to the Parthians.

Kanishka mounted the throne at the death of his father Vima, and according to archaeology, he established royal sanctuaries and placed statues of his ancestors in them. One was at a site called Surkh Kotal in Afghanistan,

RULERS OF THE KUSHĀN DYNASTY, C. 30-C. 225 C.E.	
Ruler	*Reign*
Kujūla Kadphises	c. 30-c. 80
Vima Takhto	c. 80-c. 100
Vima Kadphises I	c. 100-c. 127
Kanishka	c. 127-c. 152
Huvishka I	c. 152-c. 192
Vasudeva I	c. 192-c. 225

where the first large Kushān royal inscription was excavated. Under Kanishka, the empire reached its peak, and its extent was from Samarqand in Central Asia, to Sistan in Iran, and to Pataliputra (modern Patna) on the Ganges River.

In the realm of religion, Kanishka departed from his father's partiality for Indian deities, especially Śiva, and in a spirit of tolerance included many Iranian and Greek deities on his coinage. Whether this was out of consideration for the various religions in his empire or because he believed in a syncretism of the gods is uncertain. The pantheon of deities on the coins suggests a remarkable diversity of religious cults in the empire.

Kanishka continued Vima's use of gold for coinage, together with copper but not silver. Most important was the change in language on the coins from Greek to Bactrian, probably the language of the settled people rather than the original tongue of the Yuezhi. This is the only Iranian language written in modified Greek characters, and it is possible that this introduction of a new form of writing was in imitation of Darius the Achaemenid, who initiated the writing of Old Persian in cuneiform characters.

Kanishka is mentioned in Buddhist texts as a great patron of Buddhism, and missionaries reached China during his reign. Trade with China flourished under Kanishka, and it is possible that Kushān rule in his reign extended to the oases of Kashgar and Khotan in western China. This was the period of flourishing of the Silk Road across Eurasia, and the Kushān Empire rivaled the Roman Empire, Han Dynasty China, and the Parthian state in power and in culture. The excavations at archaeological sites in Central Asia, Afghanistan, and India have revealed the high level of development of arts and crafts under the Kushāns.

Kanishka introduced a new era of time reckoning, evident from inscriptions, that lasted a century. However, it

1 - 100 C.E.

is not known when the era was founded, which makes the dates of Kanishka's rule uncertain, and dates suggested for the beginning of his reign range from 78 to 270 C.E. Under Kanishka, the power of the ruler was consolidated and became absolute. He appointed satraps (governors) over various parts of the multiethnic empire and military commanders over army units stationed in the provinces. Under his rule, new cities were founded and older cities enlarged, and irrigation and cultivation of land were greatly increased. It was a time of great prosperity, accompanied by an increase in population.

Most important, however, was the great expansion of trade and commerce, fostered by the discovery of the monsoon winds in the Indian Ocean in the first century C.E., which made sailing between India and Egypt directly across the Indian Ocean both shorter and easier. Excavations at the site of Begram in Afghanistan have uncovered carved ivories from India, glass from Alexandria, Chinese mirrors and lacquer boxes, statuettes in bronze and vessels in porphry, plaques in alabaster from the Roman Empire, and objects from nomadic tribes of Central Asia, all evidence of the far-flung trade connections of the empire.

The title "king-of-kings" is found on the coins of the Great Kushāns, probably borrowed from the Greco-Bactrian kings rather than from the Parthians. From the dynastic sanctuaries at Surkh Kotal and Mat, near Mathurā in India, one can infer that a cult of royal ancestors existed in all parts of the empire, similar to that involving Roman emperors.

After Kanishka's reign, the empire remained stable for a time, although some outlying possessions may have been lost. It is uncertain who the father of Huvishka I was, for a short period passed between the death of Kanishka and the accession of Huvishka. He continued the policies of his predecessors and supported Buddhism, although his coins show an even greater mixture of gods, including Serapis from the pantheon in Alexandria, Egypt. Under the Kushāns, Indian merchants and craftspeople moved to Central Asia, and Indian languages and religions spread with them.

The last ruler of the Great Kushāns was Vasudeva I, who ruled the large empire before it began to disintegrate. About 230 C.E., the Sāsānian ruler Ardashīr I conquered Bactria, the homeland of the Kushāns, and reduced the Kushān king, perhaps a Vasudeva II, to his vassal. Shortly afterward, a Sāsānian prince took control of the region, and Kushān rule came to an end. In India, however, Kushān rule continued, and there are inscriptions of several kings, Kanishka II and III and a Vasishka,

but their territory was much reduced as local potentates asserted their independence. It is unknown when Kushān rule came to an end in the subcontinent, but no more than a century after Vasudeva I. The prestige of the Great Kushāns remained, however, such that as late as the twelfth century, rulers of Kashmir claimed descent from the Kushān kings.

Until the discovery of inscriptions of the Kushāns, they were known primarily as the promoters of the art style called Gandharan art, which features a plethora of Buddhist statues and scenes from Buddhist history and legend. Although mainly statues and architectural features have survived, the art also included objects of gold and precious stones such as necklaces, bracelets, and horse trappings. Gandhara was a region on the northwest subcontinent with its main city Taxila, where the early Kushān art style was featured in stone (later artists worked in stucco). This style had its origins in realistic Hellenistic art, mixed with a few Central Asian and Iranian features, and it can best be described as a synthesis of various art styles. In India under the Kushāns, however, another art style evolved with a center at the city of Mathurā. This art was primarily Indian in inspiration, although it too was influenced by Greco-Roman art, especially in its portrayal of humans.

SIGNIFICANCE
The area of Central Asia, Afghanistan, and northwest India had been dominated by the Hellenistic culture of the Greco-Bactrians, but the Kushāns, with their main ruler Kanishka, created a new syncretic civilization combining Iranian, Indian, nomadic, and Hellenistic cultures, which set a model for the next half millennium. The classical portrayal of Buddha with a sculptured body and head was formed under the Kushāns, and the objects of the primarily Buddhist art called Gandharan became the basis for later Buddhist art throughout Asia. The Kushāns helped develop the Silk Road, which became the leading route for trade between China and Western countries for centuries. In many respects, the Kushān Empire was an eastern counterpart of the Roman Empire.

The later Gupta Dynasty of India (c. 321-c. 550 C.E.) owed much to the culture and organization of the Kushān Empire, and even though the Kushāns are not even mentioned in Greek and Latin writings, they left a legacy in present-day Afghanistan and Pakistan. In Kabul, an international center of Kushān studies, established in 1975, attested to the important place of the Kushāns as forefathers of the people of Afghanistan.

—Richard N. Frye

FURTHER READING

Frye, Richard. *The Heritage of Central Asia*. Princeton, N.J.: Marcus Wiener, 1998. A survey of the entire region, placing the Kushāns in relation to other states and cultures of the area.

Harmatta, Janos, ed. *History of the Civilizations of Central Asia*. Vol. 2. Paris: UNESCO, 1994. Detailed chapters on religion, economy, art, and languages of the Kushān Empire.

Lohuizen-de Leeuw, J. E. van. *The "Scythian" Period: An Approach to the History, Art, Epigraphy, and Paleography of North India from the First Century B.C. to the Third Century A.D.* Leiden: E. J. Brill, 1949. This work concentrates on the Indian heritage of the Kushāns and examines history and inscriptions.

Rosenfeld, John. *The Dynastic Arts of the Kushāns*. Berkeley: University of California Press, 1967. The classic study of Kushān art with many illustrations as well as the legacy of the Kushāns in the art of India.

SEE ALSO: c. 420 B.C.E.-c. 100 C.E., Yuezhi Culture Links Persia and China; 209-174 B.C.E., Maodun Creates a Large Confederation in Central Asia; 2d century B.C.E., Silk Road Opens; c. 155 B.C.E., Greco-Bactrian Kingdom Reaches Zenith Under Menander; 1st-2d century C.E., Fourth Buddhist Council Convenes; c. 127-c. 152 C.E., Kanishka's Reign Brings Flowering of the Arts; 224 C.E., Ardashīr I Establishes the Sāsānian Empire.
RELATED ARTICLE in *Great Lives from History: The Ancient World*: Kanishka.

100-127 C.E.
ROMAN JUVENAL COMPOSES *SATIRES*

Juvenal, the major writer of Roman satire, a unique literary achievement of the Romans, influenced numerous writers of satire from late antiquity to the modern era.

LOCALE: Rome (now in Italy)
CATEGORY: Literature

KEY FIGURES
Juvenal (60-130 C.E.), Roman satirist
Horace (65-8 B.C.E.), Roman poet
Gaius Lucilius (c. 180-c. 102 B.C.E.), Roman satirist

SUMMARY OF EVENT

Juvenal is a Roman poet who composed sixteen verse satires, the *Saturae* (*Satires*, 1693), in hexameters ranging from 60 to 660 lines. Arranged in five books, the *Satires* cover an extremely wide range of topics dealing with Roman society in the early second century C.E., including friendship, city and country, the law, food, and women. Accordingly, Juvenal calls his writing *farrago* (stuffing), a mishmash of grain fed to cattle. The *Satires* are notable especially for the poet's disgust with contemporary society and its standards. In contrast to his predecessor Horace, who produced comparatively restrained satire, Juvenal stretches the invective of Gaius Lucilius, the traditional founder of Roman verse satire, to the limit by adopting a stance of moral outrage, especially in *Satires* 1-6, to describe what he perceives as the depravity of contemporary Rome.

Very few biographical details are known about Juvenal. Any conjectures about his life and circumstances have their foundations not in irrefutable historical evidence but rather in imaginative inferences drawn from certain passages of the *Satires*. The date of Juvenal's birth is usually given as 60 C.E., but probably rests somewhere between 55 and 67 C.E. For the date of his death, evidence from the *Satires* themselves points to sometime after 127 C.E., although the date is usually given as 130. Arguments for the date of composition of the *Satires* range from 100 or as late as 117 to sometime after 127.

At the beginning of the *Satires*, Juvenal remarks, "It is difficult not to write satire." He leads his readers through an intricate yet constantly entertaining nexus of images, themes, and characters. What emerges is a picture of a society in which the established traditions and codes buttressing the Roman elite have disintegrated. As a mirror of Roman society, Juvenalian satire is powerful and direct in its portrayal. Corruption and absurdity abound at all levels from slave to emperor. The aristocratic classes are portrayed as paradigms of moral and political corruption. The wealthy are criticized for their arrogance and selfishness. Not even the emperor Domitian, depicted as a sexual hypocrite and tyrant, is immune from this criticism.

The tone of book 1, which consists of *Satires* 1-5, is one of savage indignation. Important themes include the corruption of the upper classes (*Satires* 1, 2, and 4) and the debasement of the patron-client relationship of friendship (*Satires* 1, 3, 4, and 5). *Satires* 1 serves to define Juvenal's satirical stance—his relative position in the social and literary spheres. Various manifestations of contemporary Roman vice, corruption, perversity, and absurdity pass into the sphere of his literary vision, and these are enumerated one by one. Especially important from a programmatic perspective is Juvenal's attack on the literary intelligentsia of his day. Stock themes such as those dealing with mythological subjects are disparaged as socially irrelevant as well as burdensome to those forced to sit at formal recitations of such literary treatments.

Satires 2 exposes the corruption of traditional Roman values and attacks homosexuality as a depraved social institution. This picture of social decline continues in *Satires* 3, an elaborate sketch of urban "disease" voiced by a character called Umbricius, who is quitting Rome for the simple ways of country life. Umbricius's monologue features criticisms of life in Rome, for example, the ever-present threat of fire and ruin and the prevalence of violent crime, and of its people, including criminals and the *nouveaux riches*. A prominent feature is the sustained expression of xenophobia, especially toward Greeks and Greek culture. *Satire* 4 is probably the most farcical satire in the collection, involving as it does an imperial council convened to deliberate on the grave matter of how to prepare a giant turbot presented to Domitian. *Satires* 5 describes the humiliation of clients at a dinner put on by their rich patron. Although the primary targets in these poems are the wealthy and powerful, those who are at their beck and call are equally open to condemnation because of their slavish obedience to corrupt political and social codes.

Book 1, which focuses upon the world of men, is complemented by book 2, which contains a single long poem on women, but the indignant tone continues. *Satires* 6, in superficial form an admonition against marriage, disturbs with its relentless portrayal of women as depraved freaks of nature. Practically no stone is left unturned in the misogynist's single-minded search for hideous and disagreeable feminine traits and practices.

The themes of book 3 are the same as two of those introduced in book 1: the decline of the patron-client relationship (*Satires* 7 and 9) and the corruption of the upper classes (*Satires* 8). There is a marked shift from the strident indignation of the first two books, however, especially in *Satires* 9, in which Juvenal adopts a tone of detached irony and pessimism in contrast to the anger and bitterness of his interlocutor Naevolous, who complains about the meanness of his rich patron, who rewards him stingily for his homosexual services.

There is a further shift in tone at the beginning of book 4, in which Juvenal directly opts for a more remote stance as a reaction to human absurdity. In the rest of *Satires* 10, he then proceeds to satirize the folly of human ambition and prayer, successively exposing the dangers of wealth, power, eloquence, military success, long life, and beauty. The promise of a more detached attitude is fulfilled in the succeeding satires with themes reminiscent of the more restrained satire of Horace. In *Satires* 11, Juvenal contrasts the simple dinner put on by a friend with the extravagant banquets of the wealthy, while *Satires* 12 contrasts the false friendship offered by legacy hunters with true friendship.

The authorial tone of book 5, with its themes of money, greed, and crime, becomes yet more remote, as suggested in the opening programmatic poem, *Satire* 13, which features Juvenal's criticism of anger in a mock consolation to a friend defrauded of money. *Satire* 14 treats parent's influence and the danger of teaching their children the vice of greed through their example. The antepenultimate poem, *Satire* 15, moves from a story of cannibalism in Egypt to a discourse on human nature, while the final incomplete poem, *Satire* 16, ironically explains the advantages of military life.

The compositional style of Juvenal is economical and paragraphic. Although rhetorical questions are posed in the rhetorical style, these questions in many cases lead not to logically drawn-out expositions but rather to other spheres of digressive discourse. This stylistic feature has led modern critics to examine the *Satires* for evidence of identifiable, if not predictable, structure. Lack of "logical" structure, however, is itself a poetic technique—a technique that adds spontaneity and liveliness.

Recent critical work has usually maintained either that Juvenal constructs a series of personal identities or masks (*personae*) to express his bitter denunciations of Roman society or that there is a sincerity and general consistency of authorial attitude, character, and convictions as revealed in his criticisms. The two approaches are not necessarily mutually exclusive, and the disaffection expressed for various aspects of contemporary life in the *Satires* seems to have been common among the *literati* in Rome.

SIGNIFICANCE

Juvenal is generally considered to be the primary exponent of Roman satire, a genre that appears to be a particularly Roman accomplishment. He developed a model for the satire of indignation, which included the adoption from other genres, especially epics, of an elevated style. However, Juvenal does not seem to have been extremely popular in his day, or for 250 years after his death. In the late fourth century C.E., editions and commentaries of his work began to appear, and he was cited in the Latin writings of the church fathers. Juvenal was widely read and imitated in the Middle Ages and the Renaissance. Since the sixteenth century, his popularity has been evident in the appearance of numerous editions, translations, adaptations, imitations, and citations of his work.

—*William J. Dominik*

FURTHER READING

Anderson, W. S. *Essays on Roman Satire*. Princeton, N.J.: Princeton University Press, 1982. Essays on various aspects of the satires of Juvenal and his predecessors, including influential discussions on the application of the *persona* theory to Juvenalian satire.

Braund, Susanna H. *Beyond Anger: A Study of Juvenal's Third Book of Satires*. New York: Cambridge University Press, 1988. Braund argues that Juvenal employs an ironic persona in *Satires* 7, 8, and 9 that makes his satire more nuanced and ambiguous than in the earlier books. Bibliography and indexes.

Courtney, Edward. *A Commentary on the Satires of Juvenal*. London: The Athlone Press, 1980. Contains an introduction and commentary on the *Satires* of Juvenal.

Freudenburg, Kirk. *Satires of Rome: Threatening Poses from Lucilius to Juvenal*. New York: Cambridge University Press, 2001. Freudenburg describes satire's frequent shifts in focus and tone in Juvenal and his literary predecessors. Bibliography and indexes.

Highet, Gilbert. *Juvenal the Satirist: A Study*. Oxford, England: Oxford University Press, 1954. Highet examines the life, work, and influence of Juvenal and undertakes a detailed literary analysis of each of his sixteen satires. Bibliography and indexes.

Wehrle, William T. *The Satiric Voice: Program, Form, and Meaning in Persius and Juvenal*. New York: Olms-Weidmann, 1992. A discussion of program, form, and meaning in Juvenal and his predecessor Persius. Bibliography.

Winkler, Martin M. *The Persona in Three Satires of Juvenal*. New York: Olms-Weidmann, 1983. Winkler discusses the concept of the persona in *Satires* 2, 6, and 9 of Juvenal. Bibliography.

SEE ALSO: November 27, 8 B.C.E., Roman Lyric Poet Horace Dies.

RELATED ARTICLES in *Great Lives from History: The Ancient World*: Horace; Juvenal.

c. 100-200 C.E.
CONSTRUCTION OF THE PYRAMIDS OF THE SUN AND MOON AT TEOTIHUACÁN

The construction of the Pyramids of the Sun and Moon at Teotihuacán laid the foundations for the birth and expansion of Mesoamerica's premier urban center and monumental civic-ceremonial complex.

LOCALE: Teotihuacán (now in Mexico)
CATEGORY: Architecture

SUMMARY OF EVENT

Situated in the northeast portion of the Basin of Mexico, the ancient metropolis of Teotihuacán was touted by the later Aztecs as the Place Where Men Became Gods. During the period of its earliest urban development—from 150 B.C.E. to 100 C.E.—Teotihuacán grew exponentially and came to encompass a population of some 90,000 people living within an urban landscape extending over an area of 7.5 square miles (20 square kilometers). In fact, so awesome were the monuments of the central axis of the Street of the Dead, with its Pyramids of the Sun, Moon, and Feathered Serpent, that both contemporary peoples and their descendants adopted key elements of the Teotihuacán architectural tradition for centuries to come across the length and breadth of ancient Mesoamerica.

The earliest evidence for those Mesoamerican architectural developments that culminate with the construction of the Pyramids of the Sun and Moon centers on the building of a massive causeway identified with the Street of the Dead. The construction of the core area of the 1.25-mile-long (2.5-kilometer-long) Street of the Dead was completed c. 50 C.E. The layout and building of the causeway represent the earliest civic-ceremonial planning identified with Teotihuacán. The Street of the Dead soon became the focal point for all future civic-ceremonial planning and served to structure and balance the course and character of those architectural and social developments—including the construction of some five thousand known structures—that served to define the metropolis of Teotihuacán.

The Pyramid of the Sun, also known as the Sun Pyramid, was completed c. 125 C.E. The monument was built during the course of two primary construction episodes that culminated with the erection of an earlier version of the Sun Pyramid. Built of rubble-core masonry with an adobe-block and lime-plaster veneer, the nucleus of the Sun Pyramid was stabilized through the use of massive timbers and task walls, or cell construction, used to control against the lateral flow of masonry and rubble-fill materials. The otherwise fluid nature of rubble-fill construction was checked through the inclusion of task walls, timbers, and related reinforcements that also pro-

vided safeguards against the nearly constant seismic activity in the region. The final stage of construction expanded the earlier monument from one measuring 600 square feet (56 square meters), with a height of 150 feet (46 meters), to one measuring 700 square feet (65 square meters) at its base and rising to a staggering height of 212 feet (65 meters). Incredibly, much of that construction identified with the Sun Pyramid occurred during the course of a single century, and the monument itself contains 35 million cubic feet (1 million cubic meters) of fill. That the peoples of Teotihuacán constructed their many temples—and mobilized work parties to move stones weighing between 22 and 200 tons—without the aid of draft animals or wheeled vehicles most likely earned them the admiration and wonder of many of the successor states of the Valley of Mexico and beyond.

Excavations by Rubén Cabrera Castro of Mexico's Instituto Nacional de Antropología e Historia—in collaboration with Saburo Sugiyama and George Cowgill of Arizona State University—indicate that the Pyramids of the Sun and Moon were raised to house the funerary remains of the elite overlords of the ancient metropolis. Given that initial construction of the Pyramid of the Moon antedates that of the Sun, the architect (or architects) of the original master plan are most likely buried within the Pyramid of the Moon. Moreover, the hundreds of sacrificial captives bound and buried within the nucleus of the Feathered Serpent Pyramid clearly attest that the construction of these monuments was fraught with political and military overtones during the period extending from 100 to 200 C.E.

Within and about the base of the Sun Pyramid are strewn remnants of monumental stonework that once adorned the facade of that great structure. Included within the iconographic conventions of surviving sculpture and masonry from the forecourt and facade of the Sun Pyramid are images of human skulls surrounded by circular sun shields or spoked wheels, immense representations of feathered serpents or rattlesnake motifs, and a host of architectural elements and remnants of painted plaster

The Pyramid of the Sun in Teotihuacán. (Hulton|Archive)

that similarly once adorned the massive Sun Pyramid. In its heyday, the Sun Pyramid boasted an ornate masonry and painted stucco facade of alternating sun shields, human skulls, rattlesnakes, and painted frescoed murals depicting priests, warriors, sacred animals or mascots such as the jaguar or *ocelotl*, representations of a tripartite creature thought to symbolize the planet Venus, and a host of human and nonhuman forms and other cosmological themes. Atop its 212-foot (65-meter) summit, a massive, colorful and ornate temple sanctuary or civic-ceremonial enclosure is thought to have risen an additional 40 feet (12 meters) above the summit of the platform in the period before the site's burning and destruction in 650 C.E. If images from ceramics, sculpture, and frescoes are any indication, then an ornate series of fired clay and stucco frieze elements and wall panels depicting undulating serpents, water lilies, and related imagery—like those recovered from excavations at the nearby Feathered Serpent Pyramid—probably graced the facade of the temple or *sancta sanctorum* located atop the summit of the Sun Pyramid.

One other particularly unusual dimension of the Sun Pyramid's architectural history centers on the fact that the whole of the monument was constructed immediately atop a natural cavern that extends some 330 feet (100 meters) in overall length beneath the pyramid's base. The natural cavern was modified at successive intervals, and slabs were used to diminish the height or narrow the passage into the cave. Additional modifications resulted in the opening of six cavernous enclosures, two of which were located at the midpoint of the cavern. An additional four were carved from the walls of the largest chamber, located at the eastern end of the cavern complex. The cavern located beneath the Sun Pyramid was so important that the axis of the Sun Pyramid was aligned with that of the cavern from the onset of construction. The significance of caverns in Mesoamerican cultural history and belief—with their underworld associations and ancestral and supernatural linkages to the cosmic order—suggests that the cave beneath the Pyramid of the Sun was intended to complement that course of civic planning that linked the metropolis of Teotihuacán to the cosmological order of the ancient world.

Given the extent of that iconography devoted to Teotihuacán representations of the Sun, Moon, Venus, and the stars, it should come as no surprise that scholars have identified key architectural alignments and placements correlated with astronomical phenomena deemed significant to the zenith passage of the Sun's transit. The implications and potentials for rediscovering and interpreting the significance of cosmological and astronomical relationships among the Pyramids of the Sun and Moon and the Street of the Dead have yet to be fully realized.

The end of this period of monumental construction was marked by the building and completion of the Feathered Serpent Pyramid c. 200 C.E. In fact, the construction of the Feathered Serpent monument marked the erection of the last major monument to be built in the ancient metropolis. Although archaeologist Saburo Sugiyama believes that the construction of the Feathered Serpent Pyramid may represent the first use of the hallmark *talud-tablero* architectural form, described as a recessed tablet situated atop a sloping basal platform; archaeologist Angel García Cook argues for a much earlier appearance of that style at the site of Tlalancaleca in the region of Puebla in 200 B.C.E. This early date for the appearance of the *talud-tablero* architectural style disagrees with other comparable dates and findings reported in the literature. Nevertheless, the use of a construction-cell system—or task walls—erected within the nucleus of the monuments in question followed preexisting modes of construction specific to earthquake-resistant architectural features known from throughout those regions within which Teotihuacán and its allies served as key cultural and political protagonists.

SIGNIFICANCE

The Street of the Dead was ultimately expanded some seventy-five to one hundred years after completion of the Sun Pyramid in 125 C.E. Much of the construction that occurred in the earliest years of the metropolis centered on the Street of the Dead and the civic-ceremonial heart of the city most closely associated with the monuments of the Sun and Moon. Not until the period extending from 150 to 225 C.E. were residential compounds built beyond the civic-ceremonial core of Teotihuacán. During the course of the next several centuries, Teotihuacán's political, commercial, and military might and prestige grew by leaps and bounds, and its wide-ranging influence was felt in many of the major Mesoamerican cities. The *talud-tablero* architectural tradition that is argued to have originated in 200 C.E. was soon thereafter adopted in major urban centers and outposts of Teotihuacán found throughout Mesoamerica. In 650 C.E., the palatial estates bordering the Street of the Dead and the towering monuments of the Sun and Moon were reduced to ruin in a conflagration that ultimately claimed the lives of a number of the most prominent, powerful, and elite overlords of the ancient metropolis of Teotihuacán.

—Ruben G. Mendoza

1 - 100 C.E.

FURTHER READING

Berrin, Kathleen, and Esther Pasztory, eds. *Teotihuacan: Art from the City of the Gods*. New York: Thames and Hudson, 1993. A collection of articles regarding the architectural murals and art history of the ancient metropolis of Teotihuacán.

Margain, Carlos R. "Pre-Columbian Architecture of Central Mexico." In *Archaeology of Northern Mesoamerica, Part One*, edited by Gordon F. Ekholm and Ignacio Bernal. Vol. 10 in *Handbook of Middle American Indians*. Austin: University of Texas Press, 1971. A detailed assessment and summary of the architecture of Teotihuacán and highland Central Mexico.

Millon, René. "Teotihuacan Studies: From 1950 to 1990 and Beyond." In *Art, Ideology, and the City of Teotihuacan*, edited by Janet Catherine Berlo. Washington, D.C.: Dumbarton Oaks Research Library and Collection, 1992. Provides a detailed survey of the many scholarly contributions that serve to frame the archaeological study of Teotihuacán and its art historical and architectural treasures.

Price, T. Douglas, and Gary M. Feinman. "Teotihuacan: One of the World's Largest Cities in A.D. 500." In *Images of the Past*. 3d ed. Mountain View, Calif.: Mayfield, 2001. An introductory level overview of recent perspectives on the urbanization and growth of ancient Teotihuacán.

Sprajc, Ivan. "Astronomical Alignments at Teotihuacan, Mexico." *Latin American Antiquity* 11, no. 4 (2000): 403-415. Provides a detailed analysis of the author's contentions that the Pyramid of the Sun and the *Ciudadela* complex were located so as to provide a basis for alignments with deliberate and astronomically functional orientations.

Sugiyama, Saburo. "Burials Dedicated to the Old Temple of Quetzalcoatl at Teotihuacán, Mexico." *American Antiquity* 54, no. 1 (1989): 85-106. An initial reporting of what ultimately proved to represent a mass burial of sacrificial victims under the Feathered Serpent Pyramid of Teotihuacán, Mexico.

SEE ALSO: c. 1 C.E., Development Begins at Teotihuacán; 90 C.E., Founding of the Classic Period Maya Royal Dynasty at Tikal; c. 100-c. 700 C.E., Moche Build the Huaca del Sol and Huaca de la Luna; 200-900 C.E., Maya Civilization Flourishes.

---

c. 100-c. 700 C.E.
MOCHE BUILD THE HUACA DEL SOL AND HUACA DE LA LUNA

The Moche built the temples of the Huaca del Sol and Huaca de la Luna, the largest adobe structures in the Americas.

LOCALE: Peru

CATEGORIES: Prehistory and ancient cultures; architecture

SUMMARY OF EVENT

During the Early Intermediate, or Upper Formative, period from 300 B.C.E. to 100 C.E., the Paracas, early Tiwanaku, and Moche cultures arose. In the following Florescent, or Classic, period from 100 to 700 C.E., the Nasca, Moche, and middle Tiwanaku cultures built various monuments on the Isles of the Sun and the Moon, at Sipan, and at Tiwanaku.

The Moche, as with most cultures of this region, moved from the western coastal lowlands eastward up the valleys and into the high mountains and altiplano. Originally their subsistence was based on offshore fisheries, but as they moved inland and upcountry, they developed large-scale agriculture. Once established in the mountains, they created distinctive raised-bed agriculture systems that included irrigation, made extensive use of domesticated animals, and engaged in agreements with surrounding groups that allowed them to make use of environments outside their home zones. They produced a distinctive red-on-cream pottery in figurative shapes and displaying various scenes. By linking all productive areas to form a chain of economic "islands," the Moche were able to make, or trade for, goods from all areas.

The Moche built the Huaca del Sol (temple of the Sun) and Huaca de la Luna (temple of the Moon) on the left bank of the Moche River on the plain below the Cerro Blanco. It is not known for certain what the structures represented or how they were used. Possibly, the Huacas were used for various spiritual or political functions. The Huaca de la Luna sits at the foot of the Cerro Blanco; across the valley is the Huaca del Sol. Scholars believe that the Huaca de la Luna was placed closer to the center of population because the Moche used a lunar calendar and believed the Moon to be more concerned with people and their doings; the Huaca del Sol's placement across the valley may be because the Moche viewed the Sun as remote and concerned with heavenly things. The city and towns spread down the valley, between the monument at its lower end and toward the sea from which the Moche ancestors came. The temple complex grew for hundreds of years. The Huacas were decorated with many abstract geometric designs and painted with bright colors.

The Huaca del Sol consists of several terraced structures built on a slight incline. Long causeways and passages connect buildings, platforms, and patios of various sizes. Erosion and the diversion of the Moche River by treasure hunters in colonial times reduced the Huaca in size. The complex is believed to have originally been larger, measuring about 380 by 175 yards (345 by 160 meters) and reaching as high as 33 yards (30 meters) above the surrounding farmland. The Moche used more than 140 million molded adobe bricks, often arranged in columnar segments, to create this complex, the largest adobe structure in the Americas.

The Huaca de la Luna has three major platforms connected to four secondary plazas located at different levels. The largest platform is on the southwestern corner, and two smaller ones are located on the southeastern and northeastern corners. The plazas they connect to are of varying heights and sizes, the largest measuring 198 by 110 yards (180 by 100 meters) on the northern side of the major platform (probably leading to a main entrance). A rock outcrop incorporated into the third plaza probably had a ceremonial function. All platforms and plazas were surrounded by very high, thick adobe walls. The perimeter wall on the southern side of the complex was notable for forming a long corridor, 198 by 20 yards (180 by 18 meters), facing east toward Cerro Blanco. The whole complex sits as much as 35 yards (32 meters) above the plain between the two Huacas. As this huge adobe monument was built, added onto, and rebuilt, the bones of previous generations were buried within and incorporated into the structure.

In the Huaca de la Luna are small enclosed patios characterized by gabled high windows without lintels and doors that have high thresholds. Roofs were also gabled and painted white. Human faces, bird heads, and fish are represented in relief on the outer walls. Some rooms higher up had projections similar to a balcony that overlooked the plain below. Decorated walls were sealed and painted over so that some have been preserved. Geometric designs alternated with animal and human motifs in the reliefs found on four specific walls. Yellow, red, black, and white paints were used to accentuate the carv-

ings. Some humanlike faces are similar to the faces of gods such as the Winged Decapitator and the Demon with Prominent Eyebrows. These gods are also seen among the Vicus in Piura and the Sipan in Lambayeque. Rooms and residences were well finished with flagstone floors.

SIGNIFICANCE

The complex was built in many phases over several centuries. Uses of and relationships between sections of the monument remain unclear. Some tombs found within the fill appear to be those of officials, attesting to the sacred nature of the site. The construction of some rooms suggests they may have been used in rituals related to human sacrifice.

The Huaca de la Luna shows little evidence for any kind of domestic activity, unlike the Huaca del Sol. The Temple of the Moon was the center for rites and ceremonies guaranteed to renew political power for the Moche and natural control over the irrigation and canals that channeled the waters from Heaven to Earth and kept the civilization strong. Life and death were one, so the dead were venerated and the gods given their due. However, even though the site has been researched by dozens of prominent authorities, specific cultural practices remain to this day unclear.

—*Michael W. Simpson*

FURTHER READING

Bawden, Garth. *The Moche*. Cambridge, England: Blackwell, 1996. An examination of the culture that built the Huaca del Sol and Huaca de la Luna.

Donnan, Christopher B. *Moche Occupation of the Santa Valley, Peru*. Berkeley: University of California Press, 1973. A study of the Moche culture.

Moseley, M. *The Maritime Foundations of Andean Civilization*. Menlo Park, Calif.: Cummings, 1975. Considers the ways in which the ocean-based economy influenced the development of the highly evolved civilizations that built the temples.

Richardson, James B. *People of the Andes*. Washington, D.C.: Smithsonian Books, 1994. Describes many historical and cultural details about the peoples of the Andes, including the Moche.

SEE ALSO: c. 900-c. 200 B.C.E., Chavín de Huántar Is Peru's Urban Center; 700 B.C.E.-100 C.E., Paracas Culture Develops a Sophisticated Textile Tradition; 200 B.C.E.-200 C.E., Nasca Lines Drawn in Desert Near Coast of Peru; 200-800 C.E., Lima Culture Flourishes on the Central Andean Coast.

1 - 100 C.E.

c. 105 C.E.
CAI LUN INVENTS PAPER

Cai Lun, an imperial court official and scientist during the Eastern Han Dynasty, invented paper, a material that would prove useful in communications and in many other ways.

LOCALE: China
CATEGORY: Science and technology

KEY FIGURE
Cai Lun (Ts'ai Lun; 50-121 C.E.), Chinese court
    official and eunuch during the Eastern Han Dynasty

SUMMARY OF EVENT
Cai Lun was born in Guiyang (Kuei-Yang), present-day Chenzhou City in Hunan Province. There is little information about his early life. Historical records show that in 75 C.E., he entered the service of the imperial palace and became a liaison official with the privy council and chamberlain to the royal family. Later, he became the chief eunuch under Emperor He (Liu Zhao; r. 88-105/106 C.E.) of the Eastern Han Dynasty (25-220 C.E.). Cai Lun held the high position of minister in charge of imperial edicts and documents and was adviser to the emperor on state affairs. The emperor also appointed him chief of the Imperial Supply Department and put him in charge of making swords and furniture for the royal household. Cai Lun was also assigned curatorial responsibility for the Imperial Library.

In the thirteenth year of his reign, the emperor inspected the library and directed Cai Lun to organize piles of heavy wooden board books that were rarely used. At this time, Cai Lun began research to find a lighter material for books because the large, heavy volumes were cumbersome and difficult to move and store. His research and experimentation resulted in the invention of paper, the most significant achievement in the evolution of writing materials.

Around 4000 B.C.E., the ancient Egyptians had invented papyrus, the first paperlike substance. Papyrus was a laminated substance made of thin reeds pasted together. Later, ancient western Semitic peoples and the ancient Greeks wrote on parchment made from animal skins. In China, during the Shang Dynasty (1600-1066 B.C.E.), written records consisted of inscriptions on animal bones and tortoise shells. The inscribed bones recorded important information about agricultural methods, natural phenomena, imperial life, and other events. Oracle bones were used in divination ceremonies. During the Zhou Dynasty (1066-256 B.C.E.), Chinese characters were written or cast on bronze objects such as incense burners, bells, and cooking pots. However, this process was complicated, and the bronze was expensive, so it was impractical for general use. Later, around 600 B.C.E., people carved words on wooden and bamboo strips, which were then strung together with strings to form books. These books were bulky and heavy. In 250 B.C.E., the camelhair brush was invented in China, and the art of calligraphy and the use of woven cloth to make books and scrolls advanced quickly. Silk cloth became the main writing surface, but it was expensive.

Cai Lun realized the need for a completely new writing surface that would be cheaper and more convenient than silk and more practical than wood or bamboo. It is believed that he must have observed the silk-bleaching process and realized that any material that could be beaten into fiber could be used to make a writing surface. He developed a new process, which is still used to make paper. For raw materials, he used old fish nets, mulberry bark, hemp, and rags. He cut the ingredients into small pieces and then mashed them into a paste or pulp. Then these fibers were intermixed with water. This thin layer of pulp was dried on a piece of fine cloth, which served as a sievelike screen through which the water could drain. When dried completely, these thin layers of intertwined or matted fiber became paper. This writing material was thin, light, durable, and inexpensive to produce. It was a much better-quality writing surface than bamboo, wood, or silk. About 105 C.E., Cai Lun officially presented his discovery to the emperor, who praised him for this accomplishment. Cai Lun's paper and his paper-making process immediately became popular in China.

In 106 C.E., after Emperor He died, he was succeeded by the infant emperor Shang (Liu Long), who died in his second year. Then Emperor An (Liu Shu) came to power in 107, with the dowager empress Deng (Teng) ruling for him. Cai Lun was named a lord or marquis in 114. After the empress died in 121, her enemies convinced Emperor An that the empress's relatives and supporters were plotting against him. After being accused in this plot and receiving an imperial summons to court, Cai Lun committed suicide by drinking poison in 121. (The exact year of his death, however, is not mentioned in the historical records.) After his death, people named his invention the "paper of Cai Lun," the "paper of Cai," or the "paper of Marquis Cai," in honor of his great achievement.

SIGNIFICANCE

Cai Lun's method of paper making was widely used in China and eventually became known outside China. In 751 C.E., Chinese paper makers were captured by Arabs after a battle, and the art of paper making was introduced in the Middle East. In the twelfth century, the Europeans learned the techniques from the Arabs. Paper making eventually spread to the rest of the world, and paper became the principal writing material in the West. Thus, Cai Lun's invention eventually had a worldwide impact on communications and the preservation of human knowledge.

The technique for making paper today is still the method developed by Cai Lun. Today, paper is used not only as a medium in communications and writing but also as a component in home construction materials, health and beauty products, agricultural products, packaging, and many other products.

—*Alice Myers*

FURTHER READING

Hunter, Dard. *Paper Making: The History and Technique of an Ancient Craft*. New York: Dover Publications, 1974. Includes a chapter titled, "Ts'ai Lun and the Invention of Paper: The Influence of Calligraphy Upon Paper and the Influence of Paper Upon Printing." Illustrated. Also includes a "Chronology of Paper and Allied Subjects."

Laufer, Berthold. *Paper and Printing in Ancient China*. New York: B. Franklin, 1973. Includes information on the history of paper making in China.

Narita, Kiyofusa. *A Life of Ts'ai Lung and Japanese Paper-Making*. Tokyo: The Paper Museum, 1980. Discusses the introduction of paper making in Japan by way of Korea in 610 C.E. Illustrated.

Tanenbaum, Mary, ed. *Chinese Book Arts and California*. San Francisco: Book Club of California, 1989. Although this limited edition is not easy to come by, it offers a rare illustrated overview of the Chinese book arts–not only in California but also in China. Includes an essay, "Papermaking in China," by Söören Edgren.

Veilleux, Louis. *The Paper Industry in China from 1949 to the Cultural Revolution*. Toronto: University of Toronto-York University, Joint Centre on Modern East Asia, 1978. A rare history of Chinese papermaking, with maps.

Zhong, Shizu. *Ancient China's Scientists*. Hong Kong: Commercial Press, 1984. Includes a chapter about Cai Lun. English-Chinese glossary of Chinese terms. Illustrated.

SEE ALSO: c. 3100 B.C.E., Sumerians Invent Writing; c. 2682 B.C.E., Legendary Founding of China by Huangdi; c. 1600 B.C.E., Shang Dynasty Develops Writing and Bronzework; 25 C.E., Guang Wudi Restores the Han Dynasty.

---

c. 110 C.E.
TRAJAN ADOPTS ANTI-CHRISTIAN RELIGIOUS POLICY

Trajan's religious policy established an imperial precedent for the suppression and persecution of Christians.

LOCALE: Bithynia-Pontus (now in Turkey), Roman Empire
CATEGORIES: Government and politics; religion

KEY FIGURES

Trajan (c. 53-117 C.E.), Roman emperor, r. c. 98-117 C.E.
Pliny the Younger (c. 61-c. 113 C.E.), Roman governor of Bithynia-Pontus, c. 112

SUMMARY OF EVENT

The Roman province of Bithynia-Pontus lay along the south coast of the Black Sea. King Nicomedes IV bequeathed Bithynia to Rome in 74 B.C.E. Rome governed through a dozen Hellenized cities, each of which controlled the surrounding countryside. Pompey the Great annexed Pontus at the conclusion of the war against king Mithradates VI Eupator in 63 B.C.E. This region was less urbanized, containing three Greek cities along the coast (Sinope, Amisus, and Amastris) and a few half-Hellenized places in the interior, notably Amaseia. To facilitate provincial governance, he founded a number of cities, naming some after himself (Pompeiopolis and Magnopolis). Augustus re-created the kingdom for the client ruler Polemo, but it fell under Roman rule again in 64 C.E. and was joined to Bithynia. The senate assumed supervision of this peaceful province and annually dispatched senators of praetorian rank (termed proconsuls) to govern it. Each year, the governor made a circuit of his province, holding court in the major towns, inquiring into a wide range of matters, and rendering punishments. In these *cognitiones*, the proconsuls had enormous power over ordinary provincials; they had to proceed more carefully when dealing with Roman citizens and sometimes chose to transmit their cases to Rome.

Bitter rivalries within and between cities, combined with lax senatorial supervision and corrupt governors, put urban finances in critical condition, and in about 108 C.E., Trajan intervened. Using his greater proconsular *imperium*, he removed Bithynia-Pontus from the senate, placed it under temporary imperial control, and dispatched the former consul and treasury expert Pliny the Younger as special legate. Trajan provided a broad set of instructions (*mandata*). The Tenth Book of Pliny's *Epistulae* (97-109, books 1-9; c. 113, book 10; *The Letters*, 1748) contains correspondence with the emperor; letters 15-121 are a mixture of his inquiries and Trajan's answers (*responsa*), which thus constitute imperial policy. (It is incorrect to label Pliny a *curator* or *corrector*; these officials supervised one or several cities, whereas he was in charge of the entire province.)

Pliny encountered Christians, a novel annoyance interrupting his more important concerns, while on circuit in Pontus. The location is unknown; Amastris is likely (cf. letter 98), though Amisus (numbers 92 and 110) or Sinope (number 90) are possible. Lacking personal familiarity with Christianity and possessing no guidance in his *mandata*, he relied on his *imperium* and *coercitio* (power of a legitimate authority to compel obedience and punish refusal) and then checked with the emperor whether he was correct: letters 96-97. These letters are the earliest Roman account of "the Christian problem"; a few years later, the historian Tacitus described the Neronian persecution of 64 C.E. in his *Ab excessu divi Augusti* (c. 116 C.E., also known as *Annales*; *Annals*, 1598). The Christian community was small and generally kept a low profile, though the New Testament is clear that it had been spreading through Asia Minor for years. Acts 2:9-10, Acts 18:2, and 1 Peter 1:1 mention Christians from Bithynia, Cappadocia, Galatia, Pamphylia, Phrygia, and Pontus; Paul and Barnabas had journeyed through Pisidia, Galatia, and Asia; and there are letters to Colossae, Ephesus, Galatia, and Laodicea. The notorious heretic Marcion was from Sinope, according to Eusebius

Trajan (seated) meets with a group of soldiers. (Library of Congress)

of Caesarea in his *Historia ecclesiastica* (c. 300, 324 C.E.; *Ancient Ecclesiastical Histories*, 1576-1577; better known as Eusebius's *Church History*).

Pliny the Younger's report raised three questions. First, should a distinction be made in age or sex, or "should the weakest offenders be treated exactly like the stronger?" Second, should pardon be given to those who recant, or must they be punished nevertheless for having been Christians? Third, does punishment attach to the mere name of Christian apart from the secret crimes allegedly committed by the new sect, or are Christians to be punished only for the actual crimes they may commit? In other words, was simply being a Christian a (capital) crime, or did one have to have done something more?

Pliny continued by reviewing the actions he had already taken against the Christians. Whenever accusations were made against them, he brought them to trial. Some denied that they had ever been Christians, and then offered proof by worshiping with incense and wine before a statue of the emperor; after they had reviled Christ, they were released. A second group admitting having been Christian but asserted that they had ceased to be such; these also were released after making offerings to the emperor and reviling Christ. The third group, those who confessed to being Christians, were told of the consequences of their acts and allowed three opportunities to recant. Employment of *coercitio* emerges when Pliny said that those who refused were executed: "whatever the nature of their admission, I am convinced that their stubbornness and unshakable obstinacy ought not to go unpunished." Roman citizens constituted an exception: They were remanded to Rome for sentencing.

Pliny also reported that his investigation of the Christians indicated they were a relatively harmless cult whose only guilt consisted in the habit of meeting "on a certain fixed day before it was light, when they sang in alternate verses a hymn to Christ, as to a god, and bound themselves by a solemn oath not to do any wicked deeds." The torture of two female slaves styled deaconesses revealed to the governor that the new religion was merely "a perverse and extravagant superstition." The letter concludes with the observation that because of these stringent measures against the Christians, "the almost deserted temples begin to be resorted to, long disused ceremonies or religion are restored, fodder for victims finds a market, whereas buyers until now were very few." As far as Pliny could see, Christians did not constitute a threat to public order. Yet as an unsanctioned group, a *religio illicita*, they deserved punishment. Rome tolerated far stranger beliefs and practices than Christianity. It did,

TRAJAN AND HIS SUCCESSORS, 98-194 C.E.	
Ruler	*Reign*
Trajan	98-117
Hadrian	117-138
Antoninus Pius	138-161
Lucius Verus	161-169
Marcus Aurelius	161-180
Commodus	180-192
Pertinax	193
Didius Julianus	193
Pescennius Niger	193-194
Septimius Severus	193-211

however, have a long-standing suspicion that unauthorized groups might be subversive of morality. Refusal to obey, *contumacia*, implied conspiratorial subversion. Trajan refused to permit a fire department because this seemingly commendable cause might serve to cover covert political action (letter 33). Rome's hostility toward the Bacchanalian cult in the 180's B.C.E., though tinged with hysteria because it was in Italy, is similar to its attitude toward the Christians.

Trajan's reply, embodying his statement of religious policy, was as follows:

> You have adopted the proper course, my dear Secundus, in your examination of the cases of those who were accused to you as Christians, for indeed nothing can be laid down as a general rule involving something like a set form of procedure. They are not to be sought out; but if they are accused and convicted, they must be punished—yet on this condition, that whoever denies himself to be a Christian and makes the fact plain by his action, that is by worshiping our gods, shall obtain pardon for his repentance, however suspicious his past conduct may be. Papers, however, which are presented unsigned ought not to be admitted in any charge, for they are a very bad example and unworthy of our time.

SIGNIFICANCE

This *responsum* constituted imperial precedent; although it was directed to Pliny in Bithynia-Pontus, it could be extended throughout the Roman Empire. Soon imperial *responsa* became law. Christians were not to be actively sought out. The government had more important concerns; Trajan essentially instructed Pliny not to bother unless provoked. The movement remained illegal. If

Christians caused trouble and accusers brought charges in open court (not anonymously), the authorities should suppress them. The open profession of Christianity continued to be a capital offense, apparently because it implied disloyalty in its refusal to worship the Roman gods. Punishment of Christians was local, sporadic, and, on occasion, nasty for years; the persecution of Gallic Christians at Lyon in 177 illustrates what could happen, even under the "good" Marcus Aurelius. The first empire-wide persecutions began in the crisis of the 250's.

—*Carl A. Volz, updated by Thomas H. Watkins*

FURTHER READING

Dowden, Ken. *Religion and the Romans*. 1992. Reprint. London: Bristol Classical Press, 1995. An examination of religion during the Roman Empire, including the empire's dealings with Christians. Bibliography and index.

Hopkins, Keith. *A World Full of Gods: Pagans, Jews, and Christians in the Roman Empire*. London: Weidenfeld and Nicolson, 1999. An examination of the religions of the Roman Empire. Bibliography and indexes.

Lane Fox, Robin. *Pagans and Christians*. 1987. Reprint. San Francisco: HarperSanFrancisco, 1995. Lively account of the vitality of paganism and the challenge of the new religion.

Lee, A. D. *Pagans and Christians in Late Antiquity: A Sourcebook*. New York: Routledge, 2000. Lee examines Christianity and other religions during the Roman Empire.

Pliny the Younger. *Correspondence with Trajan from Bythinia*. Translated by Wynne Williams. Warminster, England: Aris & Phillips, 1990. A translation, with commentary and introduction, of the letters of Pliny the Younger and Trajan.

Schowalter, Daniel N. *The Emperor and the Gods: Images from the Time of Trajan*. Minneapolis: Fortress Press, 1993. An analysis of Trajan and his attitude toward religion, including Christianity.

SEE ALSO: c. 6 B.C.E., Birth of Jesus Christ; c. 30 C.E., Condemnation and Crucifixion of Jesus Christ; 64-67 C.E., Nero Persecutes the Christians; 200 C.E., Christian Apologists Develop Concept of Theology; October 28, 312 C.E., Conversion of Constantine to Christianity; 313-395 C.E., Inception of Church-State Problem.

RELATED ARTICLE in *Great Lives from History: The Ancient World*: Trajan.

c. 127-c. 152 C.E.
KANISHKA'S REIGN BRINGS FLOWERING OF THE ARTS

Emperor Kanishka, the third in a line of Kushān rulers, was a prominent patron of art and scholarship.

LOCALE: Northwest and north-central India
CATEGORY: Cultural and intellectual history

KEY FIGURE

Kanishka (first or second century-c. 152 C.E.), emperor of the Kushān Dynasty, r. c. 127-c. 152 C.E.

SUMMARY OF EVENT

The Kushān Empire lasted from the late first to the third century C.E. and reached its greatest extent during the reign of Kanishka. The Kushāns were eastern Iranian people of Central Asian origin who established a large territory that extended from Varanasi on the river Ganges, through modern-day Pakistan, Afghanistan, Baluchistan, and Bactria, up to the Oxus River. They adopted Buddhism as their official religion and became active patrons of art and learning. During the early years of the reign of Kanishka, the first representations of the Buddha image in anthropomorphic form appeared. In addition, the emperor sponsored a great Buddhist event, the Fourth Buddhist Council, at which attending scholars wrote commentaries on the canon, and Kanishka became one of the vigorous supporters of the Mahāyāna doctrine.

Because of the strategic location of their empire, the Kushāns were at the crossroads of all main trade routes and had access to ports on the Arabian Sea, a vital trade link between the Roman Empire and China. Therefore, it is not surprising to recognize different religious and cultural influences in their visual art. They issued golden coins depicting Iranian and Hindu deities, Greco-Roman gods and goddesses, and images of Buddha, all accompanied with relevant inscriptions in variants of Aramaic, occasionally Greek, and predominantly Sanskrit.

Kanishka, a devoted Buddhist, was especially interested in establishing monasteries and stupas, many of which were destroyed later. Originally, the stupa was a small mound of earth sheltering a part of the relics of the Buddha. The emperor commissioned a stupa that originally rose more than 295 feet (90 meters), or according to some records, even 690 feet (210 meters), built of wood with a copper mast and thirteen copper umbrellas. Only its foundations, some 286 feet across (87 meters), can be seen today in Shahji-ki-Dheri near Peshawar. Unfortunately, none of the Kushān architecture survived intact.

The greatest achievements of Kanishka's patronage are in the area of sculpture. There are two basic styles of anthropomorphic images of Buddha produced in two distinctive art centers, Gandhara and Mathura. Artists of the Gandhara school (in present-day Pakistan) were influenced by Greco-Roman models or, more precisely, Roman sculptural and relief works created during the reign of Emperor Trajan (r. 98-117 C.E.). Accordingly, Buddha is represented as tall and slender with broad shoulders and a narrow waist, dressed in a monastic robe draped in heavy folds reminiscent of a Roman toga. He is depicted as youthful, with an expression based on classical features typical for the Apollo type of Hellenistic style, with a classical nose and curly hair. Several typical physical attributes of the Buddha image are noticeable: the *urna* (tuft of hair between the eyes), the *ushnisha* (wisdom protuberance on the crown of the head), the lotus outline on the soles of the feet, the elongated earlobes caused by the weight of earrings he wore as a prince, and the *mudra* (a symbolic hand gesture). In addition, the figure has a halo, an accepted conventional sign of divinity and kingship in India and Central Asia. Favorite media used by Gandhara masters were gray-blue and gray-black schist and stucco.

In addition to freestanding sculptures, a new conception and organization of the biography of the Buddha appeared. The earlier symbolical presentations of major events from his life such as his enlightenment, the first sermon, and his death were replaced with entire narrative cycles based on Western models, typically adorned with classical motifs of garlands, colonnades, Corinthian capitals, and figures of cupids.

On the other hand, the purely Indian version of the anthropomorphic image of Buddha appeared in the holy city of Mathura in the southern winter capital of the Kushān Empire, 100 miles (150 kilometers) south of New Delhi. Sculptors preferred red sandstone and the stela form over schist and freestanding statues. These sculptors produced a seated figure in the traditional pose of a yogi, with a halo carved into the rock behind the head. In these artworks, the Buddha is dressed in a traditional monk robe, with one shoulder bare, revealing his robust body beneath. He has a smiling face with gentle expression and bears recognizable physical attributes.

This style emerged around 80 C.E., and it derived from earlier visual representations of popular male fertility spirits.

The reliquary from Bimaran in Afganistan and now at the British Museum, London, is an excellent example of Gandhara-style metalwork. It is cylindrical in shape, made of gold with inset of garnets, and originally was used as a relics container. It is 2.75 inches (7 centimeters) high and executed in repoussé technique. It has two standing images of Buddha flanked by divine worshipers and separated by two devotees. The actual date of this work is still controversial, ranging between c. 50 C.E. and the early third century C.E., but it is most likely to have been produced c. 60 C.E.

There are a number of statues representing Kushān emperors in their native, non-Indian costumes. A typical example is the *Portrait Statue of Emperor Kanishka*, from the early second century C.E., made of red sandstone, 64 inches (163 centimeters) high, at the Archaeological Museum, Mathura. What makes this work exceptional is that although headless, it represents a portrait, quite rare in Indian art. Kanishka is depicted in the Scythian type of dress, consisting of padded boots and a heavy woolen cloak, posing fully armed with his right hand resting on a mace and the left clamping the hilt of the sword. There is an inscription identifying this statue as the emperor himself. The overall style of the work differs from the two distinctive styles originated in the Gandhara and Mathura schools. An impression of authority and power is conveyed by the hieratic rigidity of the forms. The figure is based on geometric, almost abstract shapes with rather angular and straight lines that are strikingly detached from any realism. This portrait is very similar to another portrait of Kanishka depicted on the golden coin, minted between in the second century C.E., on permanent display in the British Museum, London. On the obverse, the emperor is depicted standing in an act of sacrifice before a small altar, holding out a small elephant goad. He wears a long coat, loose trousers, a cape, and a shawl billowing out on either side. He has a sword and a spear upright in his left hand. Kanishka's bearded head is presented in a profile with a pointed hat (crown?). The inscription in Bactrian reads "Kaniska Kushāna king-of-kings." On the reverse of the coin, a local Irano-Bactrian hybrid divinity is executed.

Another work is the *Bodhisattva of Friar Bala* from Mathura, red sandstone, 8.5 feet (2.5 meters) in height, at the Archaeological Museum, Sarnath. The inscription on the image is that of bodhisattva, a future Buddha—essentially a Buddha image—dedicated by the monk

Bala. The actual date-range of this monumental sculpture is between 81 and 123 C.E. The figure of Buddha is represented frontally, dressed in a monastic garment with the right shoulder bare. His right arm is missing, and his left arm is resting on the hip. The body is a robust type with wide shoulders, prominent breasts, and a deep navel. The Buddha stands with his feet well apart and with the figure of a lion symbolizing his royal origin and indicating his status as a "lion among men." In addition, a tall shaft standing behind the figure originally supported a stone parasol that has survived and can be seen in the museum. It is decorated with signs of the zodiac and the symbols of the celestial mansions. More than any other example, the basic style of this image derived from the earlier visual representation of male fertility deities.

Because there is no consensus among scholars regarding the absolute date and provenance of the first human image of Buddha, it seems plausible that both styles, European and native, appeared at the same time but under different influences. The Gandhara masters created images modeled on typical Greco-Roman examples, while the sculptors of Mathura created an indigenous style based on local traditions.

SIGNIFICANCE

The reign of Kanishka marked the height of Kushān dominance in the cultural history of Central Asia. The emperor was a protector of art and learning, and under his patronage, the most important iconographic theme in sculpture was the creation of anthropomorphic image of Buddha.

—*Rozmeri Basic*

FURTHER READING

Czuma, Stanislaw. *Kushan Sculpture: Images from Early India*. Cleveland: The Cleveland Museum of Art, 1985. An excellent survey of Kushān sculpture. Numerous images and details of selected works. In addition, useful chronological charts with relevant examples are included.

Dehejla, Vidya. *Indian Art*. London: Phaidon Press, 1998. A comprehensive survey of all periods and styles in Indian art, including numerous color images. Bibliography and index.

Goetz, Hermann. *The Art of India*. New York: Crown, 1964. Very good discussion of selected works of Indian art. Bibliography, index, and line drawings.

Harle, J. C. *The Art and Architecture of the Indian Subcontinent*. New Haven, Conn.: Yale University Press, 1994. A comprehensive survey of the art and architecture of India. Bibliography and index.

Karetzky, Eichenbaum Patricia. "Hellenistic Influences on Scenes of the Life of the Buddha in Gandhara." *Oriental Art* 35 (1989): 163-168. A brief discussion of the Western concept of narrative in the Gandhara school of sculpture.

Krishan, Y. "The Emergence of the Buddha Image, Gandhara Versus Mathura." *Oriental Art* 34 (1988): 255-275. An excellent analysis of differences in the Gandhara and Mathura styles of depicting the human form of Buddha. Recommended selected bibliography.

Mookerjee, Ajit. *The Arts of India*. Oxford, England: Oxford and IBH Publishing, 1966. Focuses on developments in Indian art from prehistory to modern times.

SEE ALSO: 1st-2d century C.E., Fourth Buddhist Council Convenes; c. 100-c. 127 C.E., Kushān Dynasty Expands into India; Late 4th-5th century C.E., Asanga Helps Spread Mahāyāna Buddhism.
RELATED ARTICLES in *Great Lives from History: The Ancient World*: Buddha; Kanishka.

130-135 C.E.
DEDICATION OF AELIA CAPITOLINA

Hadrian's plan to build a Roman city on the site of Jerusalem caused the Jews to rise in a rebellion that was put down by the Romans.

LOCALE: Jerusalem (now in Israel)
CATEGORIES: Government and politics; wars, uprisings, and civil unrest

KEY FIGURES

Hadrian (76-138 C.E.), Roman emperor, r. 117-138 C.E.
Akiba ben Joseph (c. 40-c. 135 C.E.), rabbinical leader who proclaimed Bar Kokhba the promised Messiah
Bar Kokhba (d. 135 C.E.), leader of a Jewish rebellion
Tineius Rufus (fl. second century C.E.), governor of Palestine, 135 C.E.
Sextus Julius Severus (fl. second century C.E.), Roman general who successfully countered Jewish guerrilla tactics in 135 C.E.

SUMMARY OF EVENT

The history of the Palestinian Jews in the Roman Empire is a tragic story. Pompey the Great captured Jerusalem in 63 B.C.E., sacked the temple, and led away the Jewish leaders in chains to grace his triumph in Rome. The puppet Herodian Dynasty from 37 B.C.E. to 44 C.E. did Rome's will. Judaea, disrupted by partisan disagreements of the Sadducees, Pharisees, and Zealots, was controlled by the Roman provincial administration. Despite some autonomy under the Sanhedrin, the supreme Jewish council and court in Jerusalem, open rebellion broke out in 66 C.E. It was put down by Titus, son of the emperor Vespasian, in 70 C.E. with the sacking of Jerusalem and the destruction of the temple.

The Jewish population in the area of Jerusalem was decimated and scattered. Vespasian ordered all Jews in the empire to pay a special tax of two drachmae, *fiscus Judaicus*, for the rebuilding of the temple of Jupiter Capitolina in Rome, a tax that had formerly gone toward the maintenance of the temple in Jerusalem. The Jewish communities outside Palestine did not, however, submit quietly to Roman authority, especially when they were forced to pay what they regarded as an idolatrous tax. In 115-117 C.E., rebellions erupted in Cyrene, Cyprus, Egypt, and Mesopotamia, a result of the contemporary Jewish Messianism. In Cyrene, the Jewish leader, "King" Lukuas, proclaimed the renewal of the Jewish state. The emperor Trajan was forced to use his most experienced generals, Quintus Marcius Turbo and Lusius Quietus;

loss of life in the rebellions of 115-117 was even greater than that of 66-70, and Lusius Quietus ruled over Palestine with an iron hand.

Hadrian at first seemed a deliverer, for in the early years of his reign, his governor Tineius Rufus pursued a moderate policy toward the Jews, but after 125 C.E., matters deteriorated. When Hadrian forbade any form of mutilation of the human body, a reflection of his Hellenic notion that the body was a divine creation, the Jews were understandably disturbed because circumcision could be interpreted as mutilation of the natural body. Overt opposition to Rome, however, was retarded by Rufus, who kept Jewish leadership scattered in various centers around Jerusalem such as Jabna and Ludd. Rufus also encouraged partisan division among the Jews, and he was apparently well acquainted with the then moderate rabbinical leader Akiba ben Joseph.

The cosmopolitan emperor Hadrian arrived in Palestine in 130 C.E. amid wild rumors and expectations that he would restore Jerusalem and its temple. It was soon clear, however, that he was proposing a new city, dedicated by his familial name, Aelia, to the Jupiter Capitolina. Within two years, a resurgent nationalistic movement arose under Simeon ben Kosiba (later Bar Kokhba).

The story of this last Jewish rebellion against Roman rule in Palestine has been pieced together from scant mention in the works of historian Dio Cassius and from references in the Talmud and the Midrash, Jewish holy books. Bar Kokhba apparently led a successful offensive in the early stages of the rebellion, as evidenced in Rufus's inability to control the situation and his call for help from the Syrian legate, Publius Marcellus. The Jewish resistance seized nearly all the undefended towns and villages, as well as some fifty fortified positions. The learned and highly respected Rabbi Akiba ben Joseph, infected with the Messianism of the age, proclaimed Simeon ben Kosiba to be Bar Kokhba, the Star, the Promised One, and the latter apparently assumed the role willingly. He issued coins commemorating the liberation of Jerusalem, and dispatches disclose that he considered himself absolute ruler of the recovered land, the prince of Israel. He had a well-organized military administration that he controlled with strict discipline. Rebuilding of the temple was to have been among his programs, and the high priest Eleazar was appointed to resume the sacrificial system.

The resources for resistance were, however, too meager. Roman forces of nearly four legions, consisting of 20,000-25,000 troops, were commanded by Hadrian's greatest general, Sextus Julius Severus, who had been recalled from Britain to quell the uprising. During 134-135 C.E., he systematically reduced the rebel strongholds, including Jerusalem. Bar Kokhba was captured at Bethar and executed. The Jews who survived the fighting and famine were either sold into slavery or forced to migrate. The Roman victory was complete. Dio Cassius relates that in the three-and-one-half-year war about a thousand villages and nearly 600,000 people were destroyed.

SIGNIFICANCE

Hadrian apparently never understood the importance of Jerusalem to the Jews. Because of his passion for building and his program for revitalizing the empire, he saw in Aelia Capitolina only another city to be reestablished. The Jews, however, having become ossified in the exclusiveness of their religion, would accept only full autonomy, an autonomy inappropriate to Hadrian's synthetic system. Hadrian was too Greek in his social ideas and in his religion to sympathize with the Jewish aspirations.

Aelia Capitolina was built and a temple therein was dedicated to Jupiter. The city did not prosper, however, because the major cities of Antioch and Alexandria were more cosmopolitan and pivotal to Roman affairs in the southeastern Mediterranean. Eusebius of Caesarea states that the entire Jewish race was forbidden even to set foot in the neighborhood of Jerusalem. Gentile Christians, not so restricted, in time caused Jerusalem to take on a larger significance as one of the major early sees in the Church.

—*Richard J. Wurtz*

FURTHER READING

Aberbach, Moses, and David Aberbach. *The Roman-Jewish Wars and Hebrew Cultural Nationalism.* New York: St. Martin's Press, 2000. An examination of the Bar Kokhba rebellion and the Roman and Jewish interactions of the time. Bibliography and index.

Marks, Richard Gordon. *The Image of Bar Kokhba in Traditional Jewish Literature: False Messiah and National Hero.* University Park: Pennsylvania State University Press, 1994. An analysis of the major figure in the Bar Kokhba rebellion, particularly his heroic status. Bibliography and index.

Nadich, Judah. *Rabbi Akiba and His Contemporaries.* Northvale, N.J.: Jason Aronson, 1998. A discussion of Akiba ben Joseph and his life. Bibliography and index.

Reznick, Leibel. *The Mystery of Bar Kokhba: An Historical and Theological Investigation of the Last King of the Jews.* Northvale, N.J.: Jason Aronson, 1996. Reznick examines Bar Kokhba and the rebellion from the historic and religious perspectives. Bibliography and index.

Yadin, Yigael, et al., eds. *The Documents from the Bar Kokhba Period in the Cave of Letters.* 2 vols. Jerusalem: Israel Exploration Society, 2002. These volumes are the second and third in the series on the discoveries made by Yadin's expedition. The first volume was published in 1963 under a slightly different title.

_____. *The Finds from the Bar Kokhba Period in the Cave of Letters.* Jerusalem: Israel Exploration Society, 1963. The first volume of three on the documents and artifacts discovered in the Cave of Letters in Nahal Hever.

SEE ALSO: c. 966 B.C.E., Building of the Temple of Jerusalem; 587-423 B.C.E., Birth of Judaism; 167-142 B.C.E., Revolt of the Maccabees; September 8, 70 C.E., Roman Destruction of the Temple of Jerusalem.

RELATED ARTICLES in *Great Lives from History: The Ancient World*: Akiba ben Joseph; Hadrian.

142 C.E.
ZHANG DAOLING FOUNDS THE CELESTIAL MASTERS MOVEMENT

Zhang Daoling received a mandate from Lord Lao and founded the Celestial Masters movement, the first organized sect of Daoism.

LOCALE: Sichuan Province, China
CATEGORIES: Religion; philosophy

KEY FIGURES

Zhang Daoling (Chang Tao-ling; fl. second century C.E.), philosopher and fortune-teller who was a spiritual link between Daoist believers and heaven

Laozi (Lao-tzu; 604-sixth century B.C.E.), legendary sage whose thoughts and teachings are venerated in Daoism

Cao Cao (T'sao T'sao; 155-220 C.E.), military and political leader who supported Daoism

SUMMARY OF EVENT

Zhang Daoling was a fortune-teller in southwestern China's Sichuan Province. In 142 C.E., Zhang had a vision, in which Laojun (Laozi), the deified founder of the Daoist religion, revealed that Zhang was to serve as the spiritual link between earth and heaven. As patriarch on earth of the faithful, he was to be given the title of Celestial Master and granted the authority to establish and rule a community of believers that would be saved at the end of the world because of its faith. Awakening from his vision, Zhang carried out the instructions of Laojun, and in doing so, he fundamentally changed the direction of the religion of Daoism and therefore the course of Chinese history.

Daoism is one of the three great religions of China, the other two being Confucianism and Buddhism. The religion venerates the thoughts and teachings of Laozi, a legendary sage who may not have really existed. Daoists believe that Laozi was a god who descended to earth to be born as a human and spent his time in the world delivering his mission of living with *dao*, or the Way. After several decades on earth, Laozi was said to have "ridden off to the West," this being a metaphor for transcending the physical world and returning to the spiritual realm. After he did so, followers gave him the deified name of Laojun.

In its initial phases, the religion took as its focus two main books: the *Dao De Jing* (possibly sixth century B.C.E., probably compiled late third century B.C.E.; *The Speculations on Metaphysics, Polity, and Morality of "the Old Philosopher, Lau-Tsze,"* 1868; better known as the *Dao De Jing*), a complex work that uses anecdotes

about Laozi to describe the *dao*, and the *Zhuangzi* (traditionally c. 300 B.C.E., probably compiled c. 285-160 B.C.E.; *The Divine Classic of Nan-hua*, 1881; also known as *The Complete Works of Chuang Tzu*, 1968; commonly known as *Zhuangzi*, 1991), a collection of stories about the philosopher Zhuangzi, which often evoke metaphysical descriptions of the world. Believers used meditation techniques and special diets to achieve longevity and ultimately live in peaceful harmony with the world around them.

Daoists believe in the purity of things unconstrained by human manipulation. A recurring theme in Daoism is that of the "uncarved" block, signifying the purity of things before they are manipulated. Whereas Confucianists believed that rules were necessary for order and harmony, Daoists advocated as few rules as possible to achieve precisely the same end. A common Daoist saying is that "the Dao does nothing, yet leaves nothing undone." Adherents believed that to attempt any action without the Way was futile, but acting in accordance with the Way allowed graceful and simple solutions to problems.

Zhang Daoling's mandate came during the end of the Han Dynasty (206 B.C.E.-220 C.E.), which many in China viewed as a millenarian event. By establishing a separate "heavenly" kingdom, it would be certain that those living with the Way would be spared in the next world. Over the next fifty years, the community established by Zhang Daoling evolved into a fully fledged state, with tax levies and an independent monetary system. Initially the religious founders accepted offerings of five pecks of rice in exchange for their instruction, leading to the name that the movement first took: Wudoumi Dao, or Five Pecks of Rice Dao. However, as the sect prospered and evolved its own bureaucracy and legal system, it took the name of Zhengyi, or True Path, before finally settling on Tianshi, Celestial Masters. At the height of the community, perhaps as many as 500,000 people lived in Sichuan as adherents to the Tianshi.

The final collapse of the Han Dynasty in 220 C.E. signaled the evolution of China into the Three Kingdoms, a period that heralded an age of chivalry and romance. The famous novel written about this period, *San guo zhi yan yi* (fourteenth century C.E.; *San Kuo: Or, Romance of the Three Kingdoms*, 1925, known as *Romance of the Three Kingdoms*) by Luo Guanzhong (Lo Kuan-chung), covers some of the more impressive events, but the history has remained much more complicated and interesting than the fiction. The collapse of the Han had two separate but equally important ramifications to the development of Daoism.

The first movement came from the intellectual class, who with the collapse of the Han had become disillusioned with Confucianism. The escape that was permitted them in Daoism was to concern themselves with alchemy, the search for immortality, and the ability to perfect their bodies through diets and exercise. The ability to co-opt the intellectual class was an important precursor to the religion's gaining greater appeal.

The second development was that Zhang Daoling's creation of a Daoist state in Sichuan became politically important to the new would-be dynasts. The warlords of the Three Kingdoms were each attempting to prove that they had inherited the mandate of heaven, which had been lost by the Han, and were therefore the rightful rulers of China. Zhang Daoling's Daoist state, which had by this time come into the control of his grandson, Zhang Lu, allied itself to the warlord of the Wei state, Cao Cao. Grasping this opportunity to receive a heavenly mandate, Cao Cao took control of the state, moving some of the population to his capital but leaving others in place. Daoism received imperial investiture and many of the Celestial Masters were enfeoffed.

With resources and time, the religious elite were able to establish and collate a canon for the religion that would allow its faithful to be able to discuss doctrine with Buddhism, a creed that entered China with a full and rich body of religious literature. The ability to set down and design its canon was a significant outcome for the Tianshi. In China, where the written text is all but revered, a canon was important to the intellectual classes.

One key difference between the Daoist canon and the Buddhist canon was the number and type of texts. In the Buddhist canon, numerous sutras, or parables about the Buddha, could be added as later patriarchs of the faith composed new prayers; however, the Daoist canon had only two main texts: the *Dao De Jing* and the *Zhuangzi*.

In addition to allowing stronger interaction with the Buddhist community, the written Daoist canon paved the way for the future growth of the religion. The Tianshi movement eventually gave way to the Shangqing (Highest Clarity) school, and finally the Lingbao (Numinous Treasure or Sacred Jewel) school. Today, Daoism draws from all three traditions, but has again melded with numerous animist traditions from both Buddhism and other Chinese folk traditions. Although Daoism survives in a distinct organized form in Taiwan, in mainland China, the religion's mixing with Buddhism—which produced

the Chan, or Zen, school of Buddhism—has obscured the distinct thought process and value system that coalesced under Zhang Daoling's Celestial Masters.

SIGNIFICANCE

The revelation of Zhang Daoling inspired him to lay the foundation for one of the most deep-rooted and spiritual of Chinese religions. The revelation of Laozi to Zhang Daoling occupies in the history of Daoism a similar position to that of the visions of Paul on the road to Tarsus in Christianity or that of the revelation granted to the Prophet Muḥammad in Islam. Each event was characterized by a sudden awakening of the individual with regard to his religion; and the subsequent actions of each individual forever changed the direction of his faith.

In the case of Daoism, the establishment of an organized religious state served two main purposes. First, it permitted a loose affiliation of practitioners to become a nationally recognized religion with great political control. The need for national communication led to the creation of a codified Daoist canon, which enabled the religion to begin comparing its beliefs to that of Buddhism. Second, Daoism came to be placed in a position nearly equal to Confucianism, which ensured the religion's long-term success. Although Buddhism would briefly become the dominant faith in China, it was continually criticized as an "alien" religion, whereas Confucianism and Daoism could point to their Chinese heritage as irrefutable proof of their pedigree.

—*Jason D. Sanchez*

FURTHER READING

Bokenkamp, Stephen R. *Early Daoist Scriptures*. Berkeley: University of California Press, 1997. An introduction to and translation of many of the most famous texts from the three traditions included in the Daoist canon.

Graham, A. C. *Disputers of the Tao*. Chicago: Open Court Publishing, 1989. Graham's book is subtitled "philosophical argument in ancient China" and includes many sections on the debates between Confucianists and Daoists as well as an excellent bibliography.

Henricks, Robert G. *Lao Tzu's "Tao Te Ching."* New York: Columbia University Press, 2000. A translation of a version of the *Dao De Jing* discovered in a tomb in Guodian in 1993. The bamboo-slip copy of the Guodian *Dao De Jing* is the earliest version known, interred in the third century B.C.E.

Lynn, Richard John. *A New Translation of the "Tao-te Ching" of Laozi as Interpreted by Wang Bi*. New York: Columbia University Press, 1999. Lynn translates and offers a new interpretation of the Wang Bi version of the *Dao De Jing*, which is today the most predominantly studied version of the text.

Robinet, Isabelle. *Taoism: Growth of a Religion*. Translated by Phyllis Brooks. Stanford, Calif.: Stanford University Press, 1997. A masterful survey of the history of Daoism, from c. 300 B.C.E. to c. 1400 C.E.

Schipper, Kristofer. *The Taoist Body*. Translated by Karen C. Duval. Berkeley: University of California Press, 1993. An insight into the thought systems and popular values of the Daoist religion in everyday life in China.

SEE ALSO: 3d century B.C.E. (traditionally 6th century B.C.E.), Laozi Composes the *Dao De Jing*; 285-160 B.C.E. (traditionally, c. 300 B.C.E.), Composition of the *Zhuangzi*; 139-122 B.C.E., Composition of the *Huainanzi*; 25 C.E., Guang Wudi Restores the Han Dynasty; c. 3d century C.E., Wang Bi and Guo Xiang Revive Daoism; 220 C.E., Three Kingdoms Period Begins in China.

RELATED ARTICLES in *Great Lives from History: The Ancient World*: Cao Cao; Laozi; Wang Bi; Zhuangzi.

---

c. 150 C.E.

AŚVAGHOSA COMPOSES COMPLETE BIOGRAPHY OF THE BUDDHA

Aśvaghosa composed Buddhacarita, *the complete biography of the Buddha, and achieved a reputation as one of the great poets of world literature and as one of the founders of Sanskrit drama.*

LOCALE: Peshawar (in modern Pakistan)
CATEGORY: Religion

KEY FIGURES
Aśvaghosa (c. 80-c. 150 C.E.), Buddhist scholar, poet, dramatist, and biographer of the Buddha
Buddha (Siddhārtha Gautama; c. 566-c. 486 B.C.E.), founder of Buddhism
Kanishka (first or second century-c. 152 C.E.), emperor of Kushān Dynasty, patron of Buddhism, r. c. 127-c. 152 C.E.

SUMMARY OF EVENT
The dates of the birth and death of the poet Aśvaghosa are uncertain, but historians generally suggest that he was born c. 80 C.E. in the Indian city of Ajodhya. He was a Brahman, a member of the hereditary priest caste of the Vedantic religious tradition that eventually became known as Hinduism. Members of the Brahman caste were usually hostile to Buddhism, which challenged the caste system and the religious orthodoxy of India. Educated in the Vedas, the holy books of India, Aśvaghosa was a strong opponent of Buddhism. Legend holds that Aśvaghosa defended the Vedantic faith in a debate on Buddhism with the sage Parsva, religious adviser of the ruler Kanishka. After losing the debate, Aśvaghosa converted and became an eloquent spokesperson for his new religion.

Aśvaghosa's probable lifetime was a period of political and religious change in the Indian subcontinent. A people known as the Kushān ruled over what is now Afghanistan, much of the northern Indian subcontinent (now the northern parts of India and Pakistan), and large parts of central Asia. The Kushān Empire reached its greatest power and territorial extension under Kanishka, whose rule dated from c. 127 to c. 152, or a good portion of Aśvaghosa's career. In addition to greatly extending his inherited kingdom through conquest, Kanishka was known as a great patron of Buddhism. Kanishka reportedly called the Fourth Buddhist Council, a critical event in the emergence of Mahāyāna Buddhism, in Kashmir. The emperor's contacts with the Chinese empire may have encouraged the movement of Buddhism into China. He also maintained communication with the Roman Empire, and the Gandhara school of art, which produced images of the Buddha that exhibited Greco-Roman influences, flourished during his reign.

There are reports that Aśvaghosa was a councillor at the court of Kanishka at Peshawar. Some historians place Aśvaghosa a generation earlier and argue that attempts to connect the great poet and the great leader are simply reflections of popular desires to put these two prominent figures together. It is also possible that claims of Aśvaghosa's connections to the Kushān ruler were caused by a confusion of Aśvaghosa with the Buddhist sage Sangharaksa, who was a teacher of Kanishka and who wrote a life of the Buddha with the same title as the biography written by Aśvaghosa.

Aśvaghosa is supposed to have helped organize the Fourth Buddhist Council and to have spoken in defense of Mahāyāna Buddhist doctrine at this council. If so, this would suggest that the poet must have known Kanishka. However, at least one account of the council holds that it was Aśvaghosa, not Kanishka, who called a great council to discuss religious doctrine. In this version of events, the council met for twelve years under Aśvaghosa's direction to produce the *Mahāvibhāsa* (compiled c. 100 C.E.; great commentary), an encyclopedia of religious tenets. Because even the dates of Aśvaghosa's life are uncertain and most of the claims about the events in that life were set down long after it ended, it may not be possible to resolve all of the questions about the poet's connections to the Kushān king and the Fourth Buddhist Council.

Aśvaghosa's best known work was his *Buddhacarita* (first or second century C.E.; *Buddhacharitam*, 1911; commonly known as *Buddhacarita*). Consisting of twenty-eight cantos, this epic poem told the story of the Buddha's life, from his birth until his passing into nirvana. It was the first complete biography of the Buddha and has therefore formed the basis for most of the tales of the Buddha's life that appeared later.

The work was divided into four parts of seven cantos each. The first told of Gautama Śākyamuni's birth as a young prince, of his youth, and of his renunciation of a life of privilege. The second told of his journeys, hardships, and his struggles with the representation of death, ending in the awakening that made him the Buddha (the Enlightened One, or the Awakened One). The third recounted his mission to humankind after his enlightenment and how his message spread in the four directions. The fourth section told of the Buddha's final journey, his passing over into nirvana, and of the establishment of the faith that followed. Scholars of religious literature observe that each part of the *Buddhacarita* corresponds to one of the main places of Buddhist pilgrimage in India: Kapilavastu, the Buddha's place of origin; Bodh Gayā, where the Buddha received enlightenment; Varanasi, where he preached his first sermon; and Kuśinagara, where he died.

A shorter epic poem, the *Saundarānanda* (first or second century C.E.; *The Saundarananda of Asvaghosa*, 1928), tells the story of the Buddha's half-brother and disciple Nanda. In this poem, Nanda is a handsome and worldly man, greatly attracted to sensual pleasures, who decides to become a monk and follow the Buddha. Gradually, life in the company of monks enables Nanda to renounce the appeals of the senses and to follow the true path.

Aśvaghosa's style in both of these epics was the elaborate form known as the *kavya*, and his work offers the earliest known examples of this style. The *kavya* is an ornate literary language that relies heavily on metaphor and simile and makes use of complicated meters. Aśvaghosa

helped popularize this type of writing, which influenced Indian literature down to the present.

In addition to the epic poems, a number of fragments of plays and two complete plays written by Aśvaghosa have survived. Manuscripts of the two complete plays were discovered at Turfan in Central Asia early in the twentieth century. Aśvaghosa's plays strictly followed the rules laid down earlier by the *Nātya-śāstra* (between 200 and 300 C.E.; *The Nātyashāstra*, 1950), a text attributed to a sage named Bharata Muni. According to this classical work on drama, plays should be composed by specially educated members of the priest caste with a complete knowledge of dance, music, and ritual. Works should treat sacred matters and be performed for knowledgeable audiences. In composing his works on Buddhist themes, Aśvaghosa created an important place for Buddhism in the Indian tradition of Sanskrit drama and linked Buddhism to Vedantic ideas about drama.

In the traditions of China and other parts of Eastern Asia, Aśvaghosa came to be regarded as a boddhisattva, or enlightened being, and he was the subject of a number of legends. Many of these dwelt on his supposed relationship with Kanishka. According to one story in a Chinese text, in his early career, Aśvaghosa lived at the court of the king of Pataliputra in eastern India. After the king was defeated by the Kushāns under Kanishka, the Indian king had to sue for peace and was required to pay 900,000 pieces of gold. Instead, he gave up the equivalent by handing over the begging bowl of the Buddha, a special rooster, and Aśvaghosa. Another legend holds that on death, Kanishka was condemned to hell for the violence of his conquests but was saved from this fate because he had heard Aśvaghosa preach. The words of the religious poet managed to deliver the powerful king to the apparently lesser punishment of being reborn in the ocean as a fish with a thousand heads that were continually cut off.

SIGNIFICANCE

Aśvaghosa's historical importance was both artistic and religious. His poetry and drama influenced Sanskrit literary style and helped to make the *kavya* a widely used form. The *Buddhacarita* and *The Saundarananda of Asvaghosa* both inspired works of Buddhist sculpture, an art that was making great advances in Aśvaghosa's era by drawing on models from Greek civilization. Aśvaghosa's plays became an important part of Sanskrit dramatic tradition.

The *Buddhacarita* was not only the first complete biography of the Buddha but also one of the most influential in passing down the story of the Buddha's life and work. Whether Aśvaghosa actually knew Kanishka or took part in the Fourth Buddhist Council, the poet achieved reverence throughout Eastern Asia as a great religious figure.

●   *—Carl L. Bankston III*

FURTHER READING

Rosenfeld, John M. *The Dynastic Arts of the Kushans.* Berkeley: University of California Press, 1967. Although chiefly concerned with Kushān art, the book also contains a good deal of information on Aśvaghosa's legendary association with the Kushān ruler Kanishka. Readers will want to look in particular at chapter 2.

Stryk, Lucien. *World of the Buddha: An Introduction to Buddhist Literature* New York: Grove Press, 1987. Gives selections of classical Buddhist literature, in-

cluding part of the *Buddhacarita*, with introduction and commentary on each selection.

Thakur, Manoj K. *India in the Age of Kanishka.* Rev. ed. Delhi: Worldview, 1999. A general work on the historical era during which Aśvaghosa lived.

Winternitz, Maurice. *History of Indian Literature: Buddhist and Jain Literature.* New Delhi: Motilal Banarsidass, 1999. Part of a massive history of Indian literature that will enable readers to place Aśvaghosa's work in its historical context.

SEE ALSO: 6th or 5th century B.C.E., Birth of Buddhism; c. 100-c. 127 C.E., Kushān Dynasty Expands into India; 1st-2d century C.E., Fourth Buddhist Council Convenes; c. 127-c. 152 C.E., Kanishka's Reign Brings Flowering of the Arts.

RELATED ARTICLES in *Great Lives from History: The Ancient World*: Aśvaghosa; Buddha; Kanishka.

---

c. 157-201 C.E.

GALEN SYNTHESIZES ANCIENT MEDICAL KNOWLEDGE

Galen synthesized ancient medical knowledge, combining preexisting medical knowledge with his own ideas in writings that dominated European medical thinking for some fifteen hundred years after his death.

LOCALE: Rome (now in Italy)

CATEGORIES: Health and medicine; cultural and intellectual history; science and technology

KEY FIGURES

Galen (129-c. 199 C.E.), Roman physician and medical author

Hippocrates (c. 460-c. 370 B.C.E.), Greek physician, considered the Greek father of medicine

SUMMARY OF EVENT

Galen, a Greek subject of the Roman Empire, was born in 129 C.E. in Pergamon, a city in Asia Minor considered to be second only to Alexandria as a great center of learning in the Roman Empire. After studying philosophy in Pergamon and serving as a surgeon to gladiators, he moved to Alexandria to study anatomy. In 169, Galen took a position as the personal physician of the Roman emperor Marcus Aurelius, and his eminence as a medical teacher was widely recognized. At Rome, he had access to the imperial library's vast collection of medical writings from the farthest reaches of the empire. Combining his

own observations and research with this great store of medical knowledge, Galen's writings, more than any other source, influenced Western medical thinking for approximately fifteen hundred years after his death.

Galen wrote down for posterity the accomplishments of the great early figures of medicine. Hippocrates, the father of medicine, is largely known to the modern world through the writings of Galen. The Hippocratics, followers of Hippocrates, built on the scientific foundation laid by Hippocrates. Their collections of observations and research were kept alive by Galen for subsequent generations. If not for Galen, most of the Hippocratic literature would have perished, and the modern world would know nothing about the work of the great Alexandrian anatomists of the fourth and third centuries B.C.E. such as Herophilus and Erasistratus who pioneered work on the nervous and circulatory systems. Galen's seventeen-volume medical treatise *De usu partium corporis humani* (written between 165 and 175 C.E.; *On the Usefulness of the Parts of the Body,* 1968) summarized the medical knowledge of his day and preserved the medical knowledge of his predecessors.

Galen, in his book *De naturalibus facultatibus* (c. late second century C.E.; *On the Natural Faculties,* 1916) expanded on Hippocrates' theory of the four humors, or bodily wet substances: black bile, yellow bile, blood, and phlegm. According to Galen, in addition to the physiological abnormalities caused by imbalances of these humors, psychological differences would also result. Furthermore, overabundances of different humors were linked with distinct temperaments (personality predispositions). Thus, excess black bile could result in sadness (melancholic temperament); too much yellow bile in excitability and being easily angered (choleric temperament); excess phlegm in sluggishness and introversion (phlegmatic temperament); and too much blood in cheerfulness and extroversion (sanguine temperament). The influence of this theory is still seen in the contemporary use of words such as sanguine and phlegmatic and in expressions such as, "Are you in a good humor today?" Even the red-striped barber's pole was originally the sign of an individual who would drain blood to improve the health of others.

Although he was not a Christian, Galen was strongly opposed to atheistic, materialistic explanations of nature and the human body. He believed that nature reflects a divine design and so does the body. God breathes life into nature, and according to Galen, the divine life-giving principle in humans is called *pneuma* (from the Greek "breeze"). Three adaptations of *pneuma* give the following attributes of living creatures: the natural spirit produces growth; the vital spirit causes locomotion; and the animal (from the Latin term *anima*, meaning soul) spirit is what makes intellectual functioning possible. Galen's studies of anatomy and physiology were often conducted to determine the flow of these spirits throughout the human body. *Pneuma* theory dominated Western medical thinking until well into the eighteenth century.

Galen not only wrote on the impact of physiological factors on mental activities but also concluded that thinking could affect physiology. This is illustrated in an incident in which Galen was treating a female patient. Galen noticed that when the name of Pylades, a male dancer, was mentioned, the patient's heart rate became irregular. When the names of other male dancers were mentioned, there were no effects on her pulse. Galen concluded from this that the patient was "in love" with the dancer and that thinking can lead to physiological consequences. Thus, the first clear description of a psychosomatic (mind-body) relationship can be said to originate with Galen.

Dealing with psychological problems was also a concern of Galen. He wrote of the importance of counsel and education in treating psychological problems. Therapy, according to Galen, should involve a mature, unbiased older person, confronting clients whose passions, such

Galen. (Library of Congress)

as anger and jealousy, were thought to be primarily responsible for their psychological problems. Such advice by Galen illustrates an ancient idea of psychotherapy. Other advice by Galen on psychological matters is contained in his books *De propriorum animi cujusque affectuum dignotione et curatione* and *De cujuslibet animi peccatorum dignotione atque medela* (c. late second century C.E.; translated together as *On the Passions and Errors of the Soul*, 1963).

SIGNIFICANCE

Galen's ideas dominated Western medical thinking from his era until the Renaissance. His strongly theistic attitudes were embraced by the Christian thinkers who began to prevail over the affairs of the later Roman Empire. Early Christian writers from the second to the fourth centuries C.E., such as Tertullian, Lactantius, Nemesius, and Gregory of Nyssa, integrated Galen's ideas into many of their works. Unfortunately, Galen's numerous medical treatises (more than four hundred) were often summarized and distorted by other, inferior, writers, and the Galenism that dominated Western medical thinking from the Dark Ages through medieval times was often far removed from Galen's original writings. Nevertheless, Galen's influence was so profound that even many Renaissance texts began with an acknowledgment to the great contributions of Galen, particularly his emphasis on observation and experimentation.

The profound impact of Galen on subsequent Western thinking is demonstrated most clearly in examining the influence of his theories of *pneuma* and humors. The three adaptations of *pneuma* can be seen to be influential in the writings of the great theologian Saint Thomas Aquinas (1224/1225-1274) in his description of the faculties (or powers) of the soul. The philosophy of René Descartes (1596-1650) is often considered to mark the beginning of the modern period of philosophy. He has also been called the father of physiology for his descriptions of the workings of the human body. These descriptions contained something new, the demonstration of the circulation of the blood by William Harvey (1578-1657), and something old, the animal spirits from Galen's writings.

The old theory of humors, expanded on by Galen, resurfaced in the twentieth century in the work of two noted psychologists. Ivan Petrovich Pavlov (1849-1936), whose work on classical conditioning is one of the greatest contributions to the history of psychology, accepted Galen's classification of temperaments and even extended the theory to dogs, the primary subjects of his research. The distinguished British psychologist Hans Eysenck presented a personality theory in 1964 that incorporated some of Galen's ideas. Indeed, modern research on introversion and extroversion can be seen to have its philosophical antecedents in Galen's theory of humors.

The work of Galen united philosophy with science and rationalism (major source of knowledge is reason) with empiricism (major source of knowledge is experience). His writings are a connection to ancient thinkers and yet his influence on twentieth century theories can be seen. Galen was a practical man dedicated toward discovering the facts of medicine, and his influence is likely to continue to be found in future medical practices.

—*Paul J. Chara, Jr.*

FURTHER READING

Eysenck, Hans J. "Principles and Methods of Personality Description, Classification, and Diagnosis." *British Journal of Psychology* 55 (1964): 284-294. A description of twentieth century personality theory in consideration of Galen's theory of humors.

Galen. *On the Natural Faculties*. Translated by Arthur John Brock. New York: Putnam, 1916. Considered Galen's most important psychological work.

_____. *On the Passions and Errors of the Soul*. Translated by Paul W. Harkins. Columbus: Ohio State University Press, 1963. This work shows Galen's interest in psychology.

_____. *On the Usefulness of the Parts of the Body*. Translated by M. T. May. Ithaca, N.Y.: Cornell University Press, 1968. A seventeen-volume work containing Galen's most extensive description of the ancient anatomical literature.

García-Ballester, Luis. *Galen and Galenism: Theory and Medical Practice from Antiquity to the European Renaissance*. Burlington, Vt.: Ashgate, 2002. An examination of ancient medicine, focusing on Galen and his influence. Bibliography and index.

Nutton, Vivian, ed. *The Unknown Galen*. London: Institute of Classical Studies, University of London, 2002. A collection of papers presented at a joint symposium on Galen held in 1999.

Robinson, Daniel N. *An Intellectual History of Psychology*. 3d ed. Madison: University of Wisconsin Press, 1995. A brief description of Galen is presented, emphasizing his scientific thinking.

Viney, Wayne. *A History of Psychology: Ideas and Context*. Boston: Allyn & Bacon, 1993. Contains a summarization of Galen's life with unique (such as his influence on Pavlov) emphasis on his contributions to psychology.

SEE ALSO: 6th-4th century B.C.E. (traditionally, 1st millennium B.C.E.), Suśruta, Indian Physician, Writes Medical Compendium; c. 500 B.C.E., Acupuncture Develops in China; c. 500-400 B.C.E., Greek Physicians Begin Scientific Practice of Medicine.

RELATED ARTICLES in *Great Lives from History: The Ancient World*: Erasistratus; Galen; Herophilus; Hippocrates.

101 - 200 C.E.

c. 165 C.E.
GAIUS CREATES EDITION OF THE *INSTITUTES* OF ROMAN LAW

Gaius's edition of the Institutes *of Roman law codified classical Roman law in textbook form and survived as the only authentic work of classical legal scholarship still extant and unaltered by the ministers of Justinian.*

LOCALE: Rome (now in Italy)
CATEGORIES: Laws, acts, and legal history; cultural and intellectual history

KEY FIGURE
Gaius (fl. second century C.E.), Roman jurist and author

SUMMARY OF EVENT
When Justinian published *Corpus Juris Civilis* (body of civil law), his monumental codification of Roman law, in the sixth century C.E., he proscribed the use of any other legal texts. As a result, the older collections lay unused and forgotten, falling prey during the course of centuries to the ravages of time. Because Justinian also ordered that all excerpts included in his *Codex Iustinianus* (529, 534 C.E.; English translation, 1915; better known as *Justinian's Codification*) should be altered if necessary to make them consistent with contemporary legal practice, it seemed impossible for modern scholars to ascertain the ancient texts. It was therefore of some importance to legal historians when B. C. Niebuhr, a German scholar of the early nineteenth century, discovered a fifth century C.E. copy of Gaius's *Institutiones* (second century C.E.; *Institutes of Gaius*, 1946-1953, also known as *Institutes*), which up to that time was known only from fragments in Justinian's *Digesta* (533 C.E., also known as *Pandectae*; *The Digest of Justinian*, 1920) and barbaric codes of the sixth century C.E.

Gaius, the author of this textbook of Roman law, is a shadowy figure. Although his *Institutes* was prescribed as a basic text in the law schools of the Western Roman Empire and citations from eighteen of his works appear in Justinian's code, he does not seem to have been cited by other jurists. From the text, it would appear that the *Institutes* was compiled shortly after 162 C.E. Other than this dating, and the conjecture that he may have studied and taught in Rome, little else is known about Gaius. Even his complete name remains unknown.

Because it was meant to be used as a textbook, the *Institutes* is devoid of penetrating analyses of law or profound solutions to complex legal problems. Nevertheless, it is important to legal historians and students for several reasons. It remains the only authentic work of

classical legal scholarship still extant and unaltered by the ministers of Justinian. Beyond that, however, it provides insights into classical Roman law that would not otherwise be available. It is from the *Institutes* of Gaius, for example, that scholars have obtained knowledge of the *legis actiones* (actions of law) of ancient Roman law. Apparently in early Roman law, a plaintiff could initiate an action or claim of law only by using one of the five distinct ritual modes, or *actiones*, recognized as legal. As might be expected, these ritual formulas did not cover all possible situations. Even when the situation was covered by an appropriate action, the plaintiff had to take care to state his claim in words acceptable to the formula pertinent to his situation.

Gaius gives a clear example of this anomaly in the *Institutes* 4:11, when he states that "the actions of the practice of older times were called *legis actiones* either because they were the creation of statutes . . . or because they were framed in the very words of statutes and were consequently treated as no less immutable than statutes." He cites the case of a man who, when suing for the cutting down of his vines, would lose his claim if he referred to trees, since "the law of the Twelve Tables, on which his action for the cutting down of his vines lay, spoke of cutting down trees in general."

These actions were probably a form of verbal combat, the vestigial remains of a time when Roman society had emerged from a primitive state and was making its first attempts to regulate self-help. Although the *legis actiones* had become obsolete by Gaius's time, his discussion of this ancient form of legislation has provided valuable knowledge of ancient Roman law and has contributed to an understanding of the concepts that shaped development of the Roman legal system and determined its form.

SIGNIFICANCE
Even a cursory reading of Gaius's *Institutes* indicates that it is the model followed by Justinian in his own *Institutiones* (533 C.E.; *Justinian's Institutes*, 1915), published as an introduction to his *Corpus Juris Civilis*. Following Gaius, Justinian divided Roman law into three main categories: the law of persons, the law of things, and the law of obligations. Although there is some overlap among these categories, the first section contains those laws referring to people, the second refers to the rights and duties of persons, and the third contains laws

relating to remedies, or the way in which rights and duties are to be enforced or protected. This last section involves legal concepts that fall under the modern category of procedural law. As a result of Justinian's borrowings from Gaius, nearly all modern legal systems are generally divided into these three categories. Although Gaius was not clear about these divisions, he nevertheless bequeathed a method of studying and teaching law that has endured, clarifying and making legal concepts more concise and manageable.

Gaius's *Institutes* offers modern readers more than an opportunity to read an authentic document of ancient classical law; it also allows them to understand more about Roman law in general and about contemporary approaches to modern law and legal philosophy.

—*J. A. Wahl, updated by Jeffrey L. Buller*

FURTHER READING

Borkowski, J. A. *Textbook on Roman Law.* London: Blackstone Press, 1994. A general work on Roman law that provides information about Gaius.

Gaius. *The Institutes of Gaius and Justinian.* 1882. Reprint. Translated by T. Lambert Mears. Holmes Beach, Fla.: Gaunt, 1994. A reprint of an early translation of the *Institutes.* Includes introduction and index.

Lambiris, Michael A. *The Historical Context of Roman Law.* Sydney: LBC Information Services, 1997. A general history of Roman law that covers Gaius and Justinian. Bibliography and index.

Leage, R. W. *Roman Private Law.* 2d ed. 1932. Reprint. Holmes Beach, Fla.: Gaunt, 1994. Using the *Institutes* of Gaius and the legal code of Justinian as a basis, this work provides an extensive introduction and discussion of Roman private law and its impact on modern legal systems.

Robinson, O. F. *The Sources of Roman Law: Problems and Methods for Ancient Historians.* New York: Routledge, 1997. An analysis of Roman law, with an eye to its development and how historians view sources. Bibliography and indexes.

Sohm, Rudolf. *The "Institutes": A Textbook of the History and System of Roman Private Law.* 1901. Reprint. Holmes Beach, Fla.: Gaunt, 2001. In this classic work, Sohm examines early Roman private law. Includes introduction, bibliography, and index.

SEE ALSO: 451-449 B.C.E., Twelve Tables of Roman Law Are Formulated; 445 B.C.E., Establishment of the Canuleian Law; 90 B.C.E., Julian Law Expands Roman Citizenship.

184-204 C.E.
YELLOW TURBANS REBELLION

This short-lived, Daoist peasant rebellion signaled the demise of the Eastern Han Dynasty.

LOCALE: Henan and Shandong provinces in eastern China

CATEGORY: Wars, uprisings, and civil unrest

KEY FIGURES

Lingdi (Ling-ti; 156-189 C.E.), Eastern Han emperor, r. 168-189 C.E.

Zhang Jue (Chang Chüeh; d. c. 184 C.E.), Daoist faith healer and leader of Yellow Turbans with his two brothers, Zhang Liang and Zhang Bao

Cao Cao (Ts'ao Ts'ao; 155-220 C.E.), Han general

SUMMARY OF EVENT

After the death of the Han emperor Wu (Wu-ti; 156-87 B.C.E.), for about eighty years, a succession of weak emperors nominally ruled while the families of consorts controlled the empire. Toward the end of the Western Han Dynasty (206 B.C.E.-23 C.E.), a relative of the empress dowager, Wang Mang, usurped the throne and created the Xin Dynasty (Hsin; 9-23 C.E.). He adopted Confucianism to promote a social hierarchy of relationships that would regain dynastic glory and eventually lead to a reunification of the empire. Wang Mang attempted substantial reforms such as the nationalization of land, manumission of slaves, stabilizing market prices on commodities, placing taxes on mining and on slaveholders, and offering loans for a limited time at low percentage rates. Unfortunately for Wang, a major flood devastated the agricultural economy near the Yellow River, and in 17 C.E., rebellions had broken out in the countryside. Eight years later, forces led by Liu Xiu (Liu Hsiu), a member of the Han, defeated Wang's army. Liu Xiu (Guang Wudi) reestablished the Han Dynasty and made Luoyang (Loyang), in present-day Henan Province, its capital.

The Eastern, or Later, Han Dynasty (25-220 C.E.), lasted 195 years under twelve emperors. During the first half of the Eastern Han Dynasty, the empire flourished, largely because of five changes. First, paper began to

101 - 200 C.E.

be used in 105 C.E. for tax-keeping purposes. Second, alliances were made with Central Asian tribes to defend the northern borders against barbarian invaders. Third, military campaigns secured the Silk Road so that commercial trade in luxury goods with other parts of Asia and the Roman-controlled Mediterranean could be carried on safely. Fourth, the sociopolitical policy remained Confucianism, which emphasized a strict division between superiors and inferiors. Fifth, men training to be civil servants were required to study and pass an examination. They were placed in academies to learn not only Chinese law, history, and culture but also Confucian ideals. However, beginning in the first century C.E., the dynasty's stability began to weaken.

Over time, political turmoil ensued among the ruling classes and landlords. Three powerful families of the imperial court eventually controlled the central government. Eunuchs began trading favors with emperors for court positions. Corruption was rampant, and when Emperor Huan died in 168 C.E., a twelve-year-old boy, Lingdi inherited the position. Lingdi proved to be a weak ruler who placed far too much trust in the eunuchs in the palace. Clashes continued to worsen among the ruling classes as eunuchs and bureaucrats vied for control of the government. Economic problems arose. Because of extended military campaigns, taxation increased for the lower classes. In addition, a series of natural disasters—floods, droughts, and famines—affected the agricultural regions, causing unrest among the peasantry. Often the peasantry interpreted such pestilence as a sign that the ruling dynasty had lost its mandate from heaven (divine approval of leadership), a main tenet of the Confucian system. Daoism, a counterpart to Confucianism, had also been gaining momentum during this time period.

Zhang Jue, a Daoist faith healer, became the leader of the Yellow Turbans (Huang-jin) along with his two brothers, Zhang Liang (Chang Liang) and Zhang Bao (Chang Pao). Jue proclaimed that the Great Peace (*taiping*) would occur, and China would become a utopian society based on universal equality. Using medical charms, chants, and religious rites, his Daoist message gained widespread appeal and spread throughout central China. The color of the headdress, yellow, was the color of the soil that blew into the Yangtze region from deserts to the north and northwest and represented a return to the earth and a symbolic rejection of Confucian notions of hierarchy. Each brother assumed the title of general to signify the relationship between heaven, man, and earth. Jue was the general of heaven; Liang became the general of earth; and Bao was the general of man.

The armed insurrection began in 184 C.E., a *jizai* year; the rebels believed that a new cycle of renewal began every sixty years and that this year was significant. They seized provincial offices, drove out or killed government officials, and appointed their followers to these positions. However, retribution was swift. Eastern Han armies rallied and suppressed the resistance. Lu Zhi (Lu Chih) attacked Jue at Guangzong; Jue died of natural causes during the siege of the city. His brother, Liang, assumed command but was killed shortly before the fall of Guangzong. The last of the brothers, Bao, was killed by Huangfu Song (Huang-fu Sung) a few months later.

SIGNIFICANCE

The Yellow Turbans rebellion, although short-lived, had devastating effects on the Eastern Han Dynasty. Followers of the sect continued to be a military threat until 205 C.E. Lingdi died in 189, and because there was no direct heir in line for the throne, the empress dowager chose a successor, but the eunuchs did not support her choice. An army, commanded by General He, the brother of the empress, assembled outside the capital. The general decided to take matters into his own hands and walked into the palace alone to confront the eunuchs. The eunuchs lay in wait for the general and murdered him as he entered the courtyard. The general's troops, on hearing of his death, stormed the palace and killed every eunuch in the building. This event caused civil war to break out between local landholders and the eunuchs for the next thirty years. The dynasty continued to disintegrate as military generals (*condottieri*) who once fought against the peasants shifted their allegiances away from the Han.

In 190, Dong Zhuo (Tung Cho) pillaged and destroyed Luoyang by setting fire to the palace, temples, ministries, libraries, and archives. Dong Zhuo also killed reigning emperor Shao and replaced him with a nine-year-old boy named Liu Xie (Xiandi as emperor). Dong Zhou's puppet regime and ruthless tactics would last only two years; his officers eventually assassinated him.

In the meantime, another brilliant Han general, Cao Cao, unifed the area north of the Yangtze River. After Cao Cao's death, his son Cao Pei (Ts'ao P'ei) deposed the last Eastern Han emperor, Xiandi (Hsien-ti) and founded the Wei Dynasty, ruling from 220-265. Two other dynasties came to power as well: Shu Han in the west and Wu in the south. This period is referred to by historians as the Three Kingdoms Period (220 to 280 C.E.). Three centuries would pass before a reunification in China occurred under the Sui Dynasty (581-618).

—*Gayla Koerting*

FURTHER READING

Barnhill, David L., and Rogert S. Gottlieb, eds. *Deep Ecology and World Religions: New Essays on Sacred Grounds*. Albany: State University of New York Press, 2001. Three essays, "Chinese Religion," "Daoism," and "Deep Ecology," by Barnhill provide a good explanation of Daoism and its tenets. The work examines the relationship between spirituality, ethics, and the natural world.

Debaine-Francfort, Corinne. *The Search for Ancient China*. New York: Harry N. Abrams, 1999. This work is a general encyclopedia of archaeological discoveries in China. Includes sections on the Han Dynasty and 150 color illustrations.

Gernet, Jacques. *Ancient China from the Beginnings to the Empire*. Berkeley: University of California Press, 1968. The author provides a general introduction to fifteen hundred years of Chinese civilization, from its beginnings to the establishment of an empire in 221 B.C.E. Includes chronological table and maps.

Loewe, Michael. *Records of the Han Administration*. 2 vols. New York: Cambridge University Press, 1967. Primary source materials for researchers. Volume 1 is directed to students of Chinese history and focuses on the development of written communication and the growth of government institutions. Volume 2 is intended for scholars of the Han period. It includes notes on texts and inscriptions.

Murphey, Rhoads. *East Asia: A New History*. 2d ed. New York: Longman, 2001. This work is a comprehensive history of China, Japan, Korea, and Vietnam. Chapter 4 is entitled, "Qin and Han: The Making of an Empire." Includes color illustrations and an excellent bibliography of sources.

Pirazzoli-t'Serstevens, Michele. *The Han Dynasty*. Translated by Janet Seligman. New York: Rizzoli, 1982. Provides an excellent political, economic, cultural, and military overview of the Han Dynasty period. Includes numerous illustrations and color photographs. The author asserts that the Han period reflected an age of consolidation, change, and experimentation in China.

Ssu-ma Ch'ien. *Early Years of the Han Dynasty*. Vol. 1 in *Records of the Grand Historian of China: Translated from the Shih chi of Ssu-ma Ch'ien*. New York: Columbia University Press, 1961. Primary source material for researchers. Sima Qian was the court historian of Wudi. The work includes 130 chapters and is divided into the following sections: Basic Annals, Chronological Tables, Treatises, Hereditary Houses, and Biographies.

Yü, Ying-Shih. *Trade and Expansion in Han China: A Study in the Structure of Sino-Barbarian Economic Relations*. Berkeley: University of California Press, 1967. Focuses on the Han Dynasty's ability to conduct foreign relations in developing and expanding trade networks. Economic and military issues are also addressed in this work.

SEE ALSO: 206 B.C.E., Liu Bang Captures Qin Capital, Founds Han Dynasty; 140-87 B.C.E., Wudi Rules Han Dynasty China; 9-23 C.E., Wang Mang's Rise to Power; 25 C.E., Guang Wudi Restores the Han Dynasty; 40-43 C.E., Trung Sisters Lead Vietnamese Rebellion Against Chinese; 142 C.E., Zhang Daoling Founds the Celestial Masters Movement; c. 220 C.E., Cai Yan Composes Poetry About Her Capture by Nomads; 220 C.E., Three Kingdoms Period Begins in China.

RELATED ARTICLES in *Great Lives from History: The Ancient World*: Cao Cao; Wudi.

101 - 200 C.E.

200 C.E.
CHRISTIAN APOLOGISTS DEVELOP CONCEPT OF THEOLOGY

Christian apologists developed a concept of theology, providing the young Christian Church with a solid core of durable beliefs about humans and their relationship to God.

LOCALE: Rome (now in Italy) and the eastern Mediterranean region
CATEGORY: Religion

KEY FIGURES

Saint Paul (c. 10-c. 64 C.E.), Christian convert who helped create the early church through his teaching efforts and powerful personality

Marcion (c. 120-c. 160 C.E.), Greek Christian who came to Rome and helped establish the New Testament canon

Montanus (fl. late second century C.E.), charismatic teacher whose appeal to many female followers resulted in women being banned from the ministry

Tertullian (c. 155-160-after 217 C.E.), eloquent Carthaginian polemicist and believer in the importance of faith as a force in the lives of the elect

Origen (c. 185-c. 254 C.E.), founder of the science of biblical theology

SUMMARY OF EVENT

Christian theology begins with Saint Paul's trip around 49 C.E. from Antioch to Jerusalem to meet with the surviving followers of Jesus, the founder of Christianity. According to the Acts of the Apostles, this conference, or the Council of Jerusalem, came about because of the insistence of James, Jesus' brother, and others of the Jerusalem church that circumcision was demanded by the law. Disputing this, Paul went from Antioch with Barnabas to settle the issue and left with a compromise dispensing with circumcision, while agreeing to Jewish laws governing sex and diet. However, in chapter 2 of his epistle to the Galatians, Paul mentions no compromise on the law, stating only that his congregation would go to the heathens (Gentiles) while the Jerusalem church went to the circumcised, or the Jews.

For Paul, the Apostolic conference raked over no mere legal dispute among sects but forced a momentous showdown over the importance of Jesus' life. He insists in Galatians 2, verse 16 that "man is not justified by the works of the law, but by the faith of Jesus Christ," adding later (chapter 3, verse 13) that "Christ hath redeemed us from the curse of the law." In Paul's theology, Jesus of Nazareth was descended from David and born of a woman, but through his resurrection he proved himself the Son of God. He was crucified for humankind's sins and was raised to the throne at God's right hand. He was Jesus Christ, or the Messiah, whose death redeemed all humanity. This world would fade away and Christ would return from heaven as the Son of Man. Much of this new salvationist theology is outlined in Paul's epistle to the Romans.

The success of Paul's revolutionary vision was guaranteed by the political unrest in Jerusalem and the city's subsequent destruction by Titus in 70 C.E. after four years of civil war. In 135, Hadrian put down another revolt and built a new Roman colony on the site of the old city. These events destroyed the Jewish-Christian congregation, leaving Rome to become the center for the propagation of Paul's teachings. Certain fringe sects soon condemned Paul as a heretic, and although these charges introduced the notion of heresy into the new church, just what constituted heresy was not clear.

Saint Paul. (Library of Congress)

The emerging church was threatened by external foes. Greek philosophy, for instance, would have rationalized the Gospels, Hellenizing them. Another Greek element that persists to this day among many Christians is a sharp conflict between matter and spirit, with a concomitant conviction that salvation demands the spirit's escape from the bondage of the human flesh.

Further competition came from Gnosticism, a combination of beliefs from many Mediterranean and Eastern sources. The Greek word *gnosis*, or "knowledge," denotes a direct apprehension of spiritual truth, and the Gnostics received their name from their belief in a secret knowledge that can be passed on to initiates. They also stressed the dualism of flesh and spirit, teaching that the emancipation of the spirit could be accomplished only by initiation into the Gnostic mysteries.

One powerful thinker influenced by Gnosticism was Marcion. Marcion was wealthy, and he gave generously to the church in Rome when he gravitated there from the Black Sea region around 140 C.E. Marcion's preaching attracted enough followers that he could begin his own church. Although he believed in the dualism of the Gnostics, he supplanted Gnostic insistence on initiation with a radical faith in the Gospel. Marcion preached a God of love who revealed himself in Christ, who, in Marcion's Gnostic-influenced theology, only seemed to have a physical body (an argument called docetism).

Marcion's emphasis on salvation through faith made him a natural follower of Paul, and he collected Paul's letters and edited the Gospel of Luke to his own taste. This work made Marcion one of the earliest collectors of Christian documents. Although Marcion was also an effective organizer who brought his followers together into churches, his insistence on absolute celibacy and the separation of husbands and wives spelled eventual doom for his teachings.

Another group that flourished in the late second century C.E. were the Montanists, named after their leader, Montanus. They were also known as Phrygians after the region of Asia Minor from which they came. They were chiliasts, or believers in the imminent second coming of Christ. Montanus spoke in tongues, declaring that the Paraclete, the Holy Spirit, spoke through him. Montanus had two women disciples who also claimed to speak for the Holy Spirit, but ironically it was opposition to Montanus's women followers that helped bar women from the ministry.

Montanism had a wide following in Asia Minor and North Africa as late as the fifth century C.E., including among its converts the wealthy Carthaginian-born Tertullian. Well educated in philosophy and history, Tertullian practiced law in Rome until he converted to Christianity in middle age and returned to Carthage to spend his remaining years writing on questions of theology. Tertullian wrote beautiful prose, which he used to condemn heretics and to attack Marcion and his teaching that love is sufficient to guide rational human beings through life. Tertullian's innate pessimism reflected his conviction of human corruptibility and his contempt for Greek philosophy and rational inquiry in general. Like Paul, Tertullian valued most highly the faith of the elect and proclaimed the absolute necessity of the individual spirit in direct, unmediated communion with God.

Among the early shapers of Christian theology, none was more intellectually gifted and creative than the Alexandrian scholar Origen. He identified three levels of meaning in the scriptures: a surface meaning accessible to any common reader; a didactic sense offering moral edification; and a hidden, allegorical meaning available only to the spiritually pure. Origen was a prodigious scholar whose thinking was shaped by Greek as well as Hebrew thought, and his fluent writings did much to give the young Christian Church a coherent vision of God and humanity by the time he died around 254 C.E.

SIGNIFICANCE

The need to harmonize the clamor of competing voices within the church led to the shaping of an apostolic succession that created an episcopate, to the stabilization of a New Testament canon, and to the formulation of the Apostles' Creed.

The first of these demands was met partly by Ireneaus, a native of Smyrna and an outstanding theologian who became bishop of Lyons. He stressed the reliability of the apostles' accounts and the validity of the line of bishops descended from them. Ireneaus exerted a vital influence in establishing a secure episcopacy. The episcopal system was strengthened by the insistence of Cyprian, bishop of Carthage, that the impossibility of salvation through direct communion with God necessitated the mediation of bishops.

The need for a New Testament canon was partly met by Marcion's work with Paul's letters and the Gospel of Luke, and it was furthered by Irenaeus's firm insistence on a total of four Gospels. By 200 C.E., the final canon of twenty-seven works was fairly well settled as a companion to the Jewish scriptures.

Although the declaration known as the Apostles' Creed was not fixed in its present form before the sixth century C.E., an early version, the Roman Symbol, was known in part by Tertullian and Irenaeus. The Roman Symbol may have evolved from the primitive baptismal statement, altered in response to Marcion's idiosyncratic view on God's role in the creation of the universe.

—*Frank Day*

FURTHER READING

Barnhart, Joe E., and Linda T. Kraeger *In Search of First Century Christianity*. Burlington, Vt.: Ashgate, 2000. A look at early Christianity and Saint Paul.

Harnack, Adolf von. *Marcion: The Gospel of the Alien God*. Durham, N.C.: Labyrinth Press, 1990. An examination of this early Christian thinker.

Hoffman, Daniel L. *The Status of Women and Gnosticism in Irenaeus and Tertullian*. Studies in Women and Religion 36. Lewiston, N. Y.: Edwin Mellen Press, 1995. An examination of Tertullian and Irenaeus and their effect on women in Christianity.

Johnson, Paul. *A History of Christianity*. 1976. Reprint. New York: Simon and Schuster, 1995. Part 1, "The Rise and Rescue of the Jesus Sect (50 B.C.E.-250 C.E.),"

is an excellent source, especially good on the genius of Paul.

Osborn, Eric Francis. *Tertullian, First Theologian of the West*. New York: Cambridge University Press, 1997. A look at Tertullian and his role in forming the doctrine of the early Christian church.

Rankin, David. *Tertullian and the Church*. New York: Cambridge University Press, 1995. A look at the early doctrines of the Christian church and Tertullian's role.

SEE ALSO: c. 6 B.C.E., Birth of Jesus Christ; c. 30 C.E., Condemnation and Crucifixion of Jesus Christ; c. 50-c. 150 C.E., Compilation of the New Testament; January-March, 55 or 56 C.E., Paul Writes His Letter to the Romans; 130-135 C.E., Dedication of Aelia Capitolina; 313-395 C.E., Inception of Church-State Problem; 325 C.E., Adoption of the Nicene Creed; 380-392 C.E., Theodosius's Edicts Promote Christian Orthodoxy; 428-431 C.E., Nestorian Controversy; October 8-25, 451 C.E., Council of Chalcedon.

RELATED ARTICLES in *Great Lives from History: The Ancient World*: Jesus; Origen; Saint Paul; Tertullian.

200-800 C.E.
LIMA CULTURE FLOURISHES ON THE CENTRAL ANDEAN COAST

When Aymara invaders settled in the river valleys of central Peru, they laid the foundation, through their Lima culture, for the demographic and economic transformation of the central coast and developed the Pachacámac shrine.

LOCALE: Along the coast of central Peru, near modern-day Lima

CATEGORIES: Prehistory and ancient cultures; religion

SUMMARY OF EVENT

In the second century C.E., the Lima culture emerged in the Lurín, Rimac, and Chillón River Valleys of the central Peruvian coast. The area had previously come under the influence of the Chavín culture as it spread its religious and artistic influences over much of northern and central Peru. With the collapse of the Chavín, however, Aymara immigrants moved to the central coast, perhaps as invaders. These newcomers established the Lima culture, which bore linguistic, technological, and ceramic similarities to the Aymara altiplano (high plateau). The Lima rulers, probably a warrior elite, dominated the region's indigenous population. They built *huacas*, or shrines, with accompanying towns at Copacabana in the Chillón valley,

Caxamarquilla and Maranga (probably the political center) along the Rimac, and Ychma (later to be known as Pachacámac, the ceremonial center dedicated to the worship of Pacha Kamaq) near the Lurín River.

Lima culture is marked by the adobe pyramids (the Temple of Cerro Culebras and the Trujillo Huaca) with surrounding auxiliary buildings; roads to facilitate trade and pilgrimages; thick, somewhat crude Playa Grande and Maranga ceramics, with red, black, and white decorations that sometimes depicted interlocking animals or persons; finer ceramics with a highly polished orange tint; textiles, often painted rather than made with dyed yarn; and very primitive metallurgy. The culture's burials demonstrated its belief in an afterlife. During the early Lima period, the deceased were laid out on stretchers for burial, and wives and servants of the elite were often killed and buried with them. As the culture reached maturity (c. 500 C.E.), that practice was replaced by the burial of figurines representing those who in earlier centuries had been sacrificed to serve the lords in the afterlife.

Although heavily influenced by religion, Lima culture appears to have been more secular than the culture that had flourished during the Chavín period. Along the arid coast, the need for extensive irrigation systems to grow crops of maize, beans, and peanuts required further political organization. Canals and dams diverted the rivers and spread life-giving water over the parched coastal lands. Food surpluses permitted part of the population to specialize in nonagricultural tasks. Some limeño towns lacked important shrines or temple complexes, although the region had major *huacas*, particularly that at Ychma where the god Pacha Kamaq gained widespread fame as an oracle (the site may have initially been a shrine to Kon, an earlier creator deity).

The Lima culture lasted until c. 800 C.E., when it suddenly disappeared as a result of its conquest by the Wari. During the Wari or Middle Horizon period, the central coast underwent a dramatic transformation. Towns grew (Cajamarquilla preserves the most evidence of Wari occupation), and interregional trade flourished, with large warehouse complexes built to store food and other goods. The limeña region became a commercial entrepot between the population centers of the Pacific coast and the Andean highlands. With the Wari as the elite, social stratification grew. Burials practices changed; the deceased was interred in a seated position, with the knees drawn up against the chest and the body wrapped in textiles much superior in quality to those produced by the limeños. The Wari promoted the worship of Viracocha, their creator deity, but this seemed also to increase the influence of the Pacha Kamaq cult. Coastal peoples perhaps conflated the two deities. By this time, the ceremonial center of Ychma had become known as Pachacámac, in recognition of the creator/earthquake deity and oracle worshiped there. The Wari period ended c. 1100, perhaps when economic malaise in the Andes undermined the commerce on which the central coast depended. Wari Cajamarquilla declined, replaced by Pachacámac as the region's major center. In fact, Pachacámac flourished despite Wari despotism and political centralism.

SIGNIFICANCE

Pachacámac continued to prosper, even when the Incas conquered the central coast in the fifteenth century. Pacha Kamaq's great shrine became a political tool. To augment his power and legitimacy, Topa Inca Yupanqui aligned himself with the Pachacámac *huaca*. In part, he did this to gain allies in his military campaign against the Chimu peoples to the north. According to some accounts, Topa's mother, while pregnant with him, had a vision that Pacha Kamaq was the creator deity. Consequently, when Topa Inca gained power, he lavished gifts and prestige on Pachacámac. Topa Inca built a great pyramid to the Sun at Pachacámac, near the ancient shrine of Pachacámac. He also established affiliated *huacas* for the worship of Pacha Kamaq elsewhere in the Andes, as the god allegedly directed him. Some of these lay in unconquered areas and consequently gave Topa Inca a means to begin the political penetration of those regions in a religious guise. Of course, these branch *huacas* also provided the priests of Pachacámac with a means of extending their influence and garnering more sacrificial offerings. Topa Inca's actions probably also reveal the Incas' inability to impose their owns gods completely on the coastal peoples and to suppress the Pacha Kamaq cult.

After the death of Topa Inca (c. 1493) and the succession to power of Huayna Capac, the great *huaca* at Pachacámac remained tremendously influential. Andeans from distant regions knew of the creator deity, and many traveled to Pachacámac as pilgrims, bringing sacrificial offerings with them. Pacha Kamaq was revered as a powerful oracle, consulted by rulers and commoners alike. When Huayna Capac fell ill in the mid-1520's, he sought advice from Pachacámac shortly before dying. During the civil war that followed Huayna Capac's unexpected death (c. 1525), the oracle incorrectly predicted the triumph of Huascar, whose mother belonged to the *panaca* (royal clan) founded by Topa Inca.

Thus, when the Spaniards invaded, took Huascar's rival Atahualpa prisoner at Cajamarca in 1532, and demanded gold and silver, Atahualpa sent them to Pachacámac to plunder its riches. Miguel de Estete accompanied Hernando Pizarro to Pachacámac and described the oracle. Pilgrims, he noted, came from great distances bearing rich gifts to seek the oracle's advice. On arrival they made their petitions to the priests, who insisted the pilgrims fast and abstain from sexual relations for weeks before their questions were presented to the god. Only Pacha Kamaq's priests dared enter the sanctuary itself. The Spaniards wanted gold, not oracular divinations, and forced their way into the sanctuary. Opening a jewel-encrusted door into a dark, foul-smelling room, they found the wooden idol, which to them was the devil. Offerings of gold, silver, and cloth lay about the sanctuary. The carved wood idol had two faces representing Pacha Kamaq's dual nature: sometimes blessing his worshipers with bountiful harvests and good health but also causing earthquakes, floods, and tidal waves. Pizarro ordered the sanctuary destroyed, and two years later, the Spaniards founded their capital, the city of the kings (Lima), a few miles to the north of the ancient *huaca*.

By the eighteenth century, the *huaca* of Pacha Kamaq was in ruins, through abandonment and depredations

101 - 200 C.E.

caused by grave robbers seeking treasures. Max Uhle initiated the first serious archaeological excavations there in the late 1800's. Peru declared it a national monument in 1929.

—*Kendall W. Brown*

FURTHER READING

Cobo, Bernabé. *Inca Religion and Customs*. Translated and edited by Roland Hamilton. Austin: University of Texas Press, 1990. A seventeenth century Spanish priest describes Pachacámac's oracular function and displays Catholic prejudices regarding Andean *huacas*.

Keatinge, Richard W. *Peruvian Prehistory: An Overview of Pre-Inca and Inca Society*. New York: Cambridge University Press, 1988. A general survey of cultural development in the Andes before the Spaniards' arrival.

Lumbreras, Luis G. *The Peoples and Cultures of Ancient Peru*. Translated by Betty J. Meggers. Washington, D.C.: Smithsonian Institution Press, 1974. A summary of pre-Hispanic Peru, with some attention given to developments along the central coast.

MacCormack, Sabine. *Religion in the Andes: Vision and Imagination in Early Colonial Peru*. Princeton, N.J.: Princeton University Press, 1991. Describes the cult of Pacha Kamaq and Spanish interpretations of it.

Patterson, Thomas C. "Pachacámac: An Andean Oracle Under Inca Rule." In *Recent Studies in Andean Prehistory and Protohistory*, edited by D. Peter Kvietok and Daniel H. Sandweiss. Ithaca, N.Y.: Cornell University Latin American Studies Program, 1983. Insightful analysis of how the Inca rulers and the priests of Pachacámac used each other for political and religious ends.

Rostworowski de Diez Canseco, María. *History of the Inca Realm*. Translated by Harry B. Iceland. New York: Cambridge University Press, 1999. Shows how the central coastal populations and the great shrine of Pachacámac fit into the Inca realm.

Uhle, Max. *Pachacámac: A Reprint of the 1903 Edition*. Philadelphia: University Museum of Archaeology and Anthropology, University of Pennsylvania, 1991. Sometimes called the father of Peruvian archaeology, Uhle undertook the first excavations at Pachacámac.

SEE ALSO: c. 13,000 B.C.E., Humans Enter the South American Continent; c. 8000 B.C.E., Permanent Settlement of the Andean Altiplano Begins; c. 5800-c. 3700 B.C.E., Chinchorro Inhabit the Peruvian and Chilean Coasts; c. 2500 B.C.E., Construction of Monumental Architecture at Caral in Peru; 700 B.C.E.-100 C.E., Paracas Culture Develops a Sophisticated Textile Tradition; 200 B.C.E.-200 C.E., Nasca Lines Drawn in Desert Near Coast of Peru; c. 100-c. 700 C.E., Moche Build the Huaca del Sol and Huaca de la Luna.

200-900 C.E.
MAYA CIVILIZATION FLOURISHES

The ancient Maya made profound achievements in art, mathematics, astronomy, and architecture.

LOCALE: Mesoamerica
CATEGORY: Prehistory and ancient cultures

SUMMARY OF EVENT
Maya history is divided into three periods: Preclassic (2000 B.C.E.-200 C.E.), Classic (200-900 C.E.), and Postclassic (900 C.E. to the Spanish conquest). The Maya lived in an area that included the present-day Mexican states of Chiapas, Tabasco, Campeche, Yucatán, and Quintana Roo, in addition to the countries of Belize, Guatemala, Honduras, and El Salvador. Scholars who study the Maya have divided the entire region into three subregions: the southern subregion of Guatemala highlands and the Pacific coast; the central subregion of northern Guatemala, its adjacent lowlands, and the Petén region; and the northern subregion of the Yucatán Peninsula. The highland areas of southern Guatemala and Chiapas flourished during the late Preclassic period; lowland areas in the Petén region reached their height during the Classic period; and the area in the Yucatán Peninsula prospered in the late Classic and Postclassic periods.

The end of the Preclassic period and the beginning of the Classic period, when the Maya flourished, had formerly been defined by the appearance of vaulted stone architecture, monumental inscriptions, and polychrome pottery. However, subsequent finds have revealed that each of these traits appeared at different times during the Terminal Preclassic. Consequently the "official" end of the Preclassic period and beginning of the Classic period has been changed from 300 C.E. to 250 or 200. During the late Preclassic period, writing, mathematics, architec-

Mayan ruins at Chichén Itzá. (PhotoDisc)

ture, astronomy, and calendars were used, but these were all more fully developed in the Classic period.

A few city-states, such as El Mirador and Kaminaljuyu, developed in the Preclassic period, but it was the Classic period that witnessed the rise of the larger, more advanced city-states for which the Maya are known. One of the earliest and largest of the Classic-period centers was Tikal, located in the Petén region of Guatemala. It covered a 6-square-mile (16-square-kilometer) area, contained more than three thousand constructions, and had an estimated forty thousand inhabitants. One pyramid, 224 feet high (68 meters), is the tallest pre-Columbian edifice in America. Copán, which was in Honduras, 250 miles (402 kilometers) southeast of Tikal, may have been a scientific center specializing in astronomy. Although the Maya did not have telescopes, jade tubes were used, which helped to concentrate their vision on selected celestial bodies. Their knowledge of astronomy was such that they not only had an accurate calendar of 365 days but also were able to predict solar and lunar eclipses, as well as the movement of Venus.

Palenque, in Chiapas, Mexico, had an aqueduct to direct water from a nearby stream to the center of the city and contained a building called the Palace, which was 228 feet (69 meters) long and 180 feet (55 meters) deep, with a four-story tower with an internal stairway. Perhaps its most famous feature is the tomb of the ruler Pacal, who died in 683 C.E. after ruling for sixty-eight years. The lid of the sarcophagus was a five-ton, twelve-foot slab of limestone carved with a bas-relief image of the ruler as he entered the jaws of death in the underworld. Palenque also is special because two women ruled before Pacal assumed the throne.

Bonampak, also located in Chiapas, is best known for its Temple of Frescoes. The frescoes depict many activities and scenes of daily life not represented elsewhere. Some of these representations have helped scholars to realize that the Maya were not the peaceful people they once were believed to be.

Other important centers in the Yucatán Peninsula, such as Chichén Itzá, began in the Classic period but continued to flourish in the Postclassic period under the influence of the Toltecs, who invaded Maya territory in the tenth century C.E. Some of the aforementioned centers had previously experienced a foreign influence early in the Classic period. In the fifth century, Teotihuacán, which was located in the central basin of Mexico, began to spread its influence throughout southern Mesoamerica, including the Maya cities of Kaminaljuyu, Copán, and Tikal. This influence ended in the eighth century, and there has been speculation that this was a factor in the demise of the Classic period at the end of the ninth century.

The Classic period was characterized by the construction of impressive structures, often one on top of the other. Either existing structures were demolished and the material was used in the new construction, or a new and larger structure enveloped the older one. Buildings were typically covered with stucco. If it was an important structure, the date would be recorded, and the event would be celebrated with a religious ceremony that included bloodletting. Some of the main features of Maya architecture were large, flat-topped stone pyramids with steps that led to a temple decorated with tiled pediments known as "roof combs"; buildings covered with bas-reliefs; jutting corbeled arches or vaults; ball courts; large public squares or plazas; and stelae, altars, and monoliths inscribed with names, dates, and important events. A major feature of the large ceremonial centers was the formal plaza lined by public buildings. Much of this was made possible by the Maya practice of cementing the cut stones together. They had perfected the use of mortar, plaster, and stucco.

Society was highly stratified. At the top was an elite who ruled and enjoyed special privileges. It was the function of the common people to provide not only necessities but also luxuries for the elite. There were probably a number of strata between the royal family and the common farmers, based on birth or occupation, which may have been hereditary. Each city-state had its own ruling dynasty, which is believed to have been by patrilineal primogeniture accessible to others only through marriage. The inequality of treatment did not end with death; while the nobility were buried in tombs, the peasants were buried under the floor in their homes.

Religion was of central importance to Maya culture. Myriad gods controlled everything and therefore had to be consulted and appeased constantly. Maya religious concerns encouraged the development of astronomy and mathematics. Each day and number had its patron deity. When a child was born, a priest would predict its future with the aid of astrological charts and books. Depending on the exact day and time of its birth, a child would owe a special devotion to the ascendant deity throughout his or her lifetime. Religious ceremonies were of the utmost importance. An important aspect of some religious ceremonies was the practice of shedding human blood.

Bloodletting took the form of human sacrifices—either of enemies or possibly of devout martyrs—and nonfatal self-immolation. The latter seems to have been a common practice, which entailed the piercing of the tongue, lips, earlobes, or penis. The blood was sometimes dripped onto paper strips that then were burned. In addition to giving nurture and praise to the gods, the Maya believed contact could be made with gods or deceased ancestors by the letting of blood.

The Classic period was marked by competition and conflict. There was an extensive system of short- and long-distance trade, not only among the Maya but with other indigenous peoples as well. Economic success brought growth and prosperity to the many city-states, but it also brought increased competition for territory and power. Warfare was a frequent outcome. Some of the conquered rivals provided sacrificial victims to satisfy the gods; others were beheaded, with the heads possibly used as trophies. During this period, Tikal was defeated by Caracol, which later was defeated by Dos Pilas. Thus fortunes changed for communities and individuals alike.

SIGNIFICANCE

The end of the classic Maya civilization was both swift and mysterious. Numerous theories attempt to explain the rather sudden and widespread demise of the prosperous lowland Maya communities. Undoubtedly, there were both internal and external causes. The former may have included environmental degradation, overpopulation relative to the food supply, disease and malnutrition, a revolution of peasants against the elite, and decay of the artistic, political, and intellectual superstructure of society. Invasion and economic collapse due to changes in other parts of Mesoamerica are possible external causes. While the southern past of the Maya civilization was undergoing collapse and depopulation, the centers in northern Yucatán continued to prosper and some southward migration occurred to fill the vacuum. The succeeding Postclassic period, which witnessed the dominance of the Yucatán area, continued until the Spanish conquest in the mid-sixteenth century.

—Philip E. Lampe

FURTHER READING

Arden, Traci, ed. *Ancient Maya Women*. Gender and Archaeology series 2. Walnut Creek, Calif.: AltaMira Press, 2002. A collection of essays examining Mayan women in many aspects, including their portrayal in hieroglyphic texts and their roles as royals and women of power.

Coe, Michael D. *The Maya*. 6th ed. London: Thames and

Hudson, 1999. The Maya civilization, from beginning to end, revised to incorporate modern discoveries regarding the Maya kings.

Harrison, Peter D. *The Lords of Tikal: Rulers of an Ancient Maya City*. New York: Thames and Hudson, 1999. Harrison focuses on the Maya kings at Tikal, using information from modern archaeological discoveries and interpretations of glyphs. Bibliography and index.

Hughes, Nigel. *Maya Monuments*. Woodbridge: Antique Collectors' Club, 2000. Hughes looks at the monuments created by the Maya. Illustrations and index.

Inomata, Takeshi, and Stephen D. Houston, eds. 2 vols. *Royal Courts of the Ancient Maya*. Boulder, Colo.: Westview Press, 2001. Essays on the Maya royalty, providing a comparison and synthesis of the various

theories. Volume 2 is data and case studies. Bibliography and index.

Miller, Mary Ellen. *Maya Art and Architecture*. New York: Thames and Hudson, 1999. An examination of the architecture and art of the Maya. Illustrations, bibliography and index.

SEE ALSO: c. 1530 B.C.E., Mixtec Civilization Develops in Western Oaxaca; c. 1500-c. 300 B.C.E., Olmec Civilization Rises in Southern Mexico; c. 500 B.C.E.-c. 700 C.E., Zapotecs Build Monte Albán; c. 100 B.C.E.-c. 200 C.E., Zapotec State Dominates Oaxaca; c. 1 C.E., Development Begins at Teotihuacán; 90 C.E., Founding of the Classic Period Maya Royal Dynasty at Tikal; c. 100-200 C.E., Construction of the Pyramids of the Sun and Moon at Teotihuacán.

200-1250 C.E.
ANASAZI CIVILIZATION FLOURISHES IN AMERICAN SOUTHWEST

This Basket Maker civilization of the American Southwest emerged, advanced architecture and agriculture, and then vanished.

LOCALE: Four Corners area of New Mexico, Arizona, Utah, and Colorado
CATEGORY: Prehistory and ancient cultures

SUMMARY OF EVENT

The Anasazi, believed to be descendants of ancient Desert Archaic people, are one of the best-known prehistoric cultures of the American Southwest. Different groups of Anasazi spoke at least six languages, which were not mutually understood. The term "Anasazi" derives from an English-language corruption of a Navajo term, Anaasa'zi, which describes the many stone ruins of the Four Corners region and may mean "ancient ones," "enemies of the ancient ones," or "ancient enemy."

The earliest Anasazi are known as the Basket Makers because of their extraordinary skill in basketry. Initially, these early people occupied a few cave sites and rock shelters along the San Juan River and open sites in the Rio Grande Valley. Inhabitants of these early villages planted maize and squash, a skill learned from their ancestors, and hunted and foraged.

The villages, perhaps occupied seasonally, consisted of a few pit houses: low, circular houses dug into the ground, approximately 7 feet (2 meters) across. Stone slabs were used for some houses. Upper walls and roofs

of many dwellings were made of wood and adobe or wattle and daub. The houses had fire pits and were entered by ladders placed in the smokehole of the roof. Tunnel-like side entries faced the east. Larger pit houses were for ceremonial use. Smaller slab-lined structures were used for storing food. Baskets (some woven tightly enough for cooking), sandals, and other articles were of high caliber, highly stylized with geometric motifs. These designs gave rise to later Anasazi pottery painting traditions. Anasazi rock art of the period shows humans with broad shoulders, trapezoid-shaped bodies, and very large hands and feet. Elaborate headdresses, hair ornaments, necklaces, earrings, and sashes adorn the figures. Found near the villages, the art appears to have been part of community life.

As the Basket Maker Anasazi population grew and their territory expanded, their villages became larger. Almost all had ritual rooms, which the later Hopi called kivas. Pit houses became deeper, more complex, and spacious. Earth-covered wooden roofs were supported by four posts with crossbeams. Some houses were dome-shaped. Storage bins, benches, a central fire pit, and a draft deflector between the fire and the ventilator shaft were found in many dwellings. Roof or side entrances were retained.

Within the village were many outdoor work and cooking areas. Slab-lined storage buildings and ramadas (roofed, open-walled structures shading work and living areas) were built on the surface. Some kivas were modified houses, but many were larger, some 35 feet across (11 meters). Excavated holes called *sipapu* were dug near the center of the floor in many homes and in most kivas. Turquoise or other offerings were placed in the *sipapu*, the opening to the underworld from which people emerged.

Farming became increasingly important to the Anasazi. To ensure successful crops, check dams and devices were used in fields near villages. By 600 C.E., beans, introduced from Mexico, were cultivated. By 700 C.E., cotton, the bow and arrow, and stone tools were used generally. Maize was ground on large stone mortars using two-handed grinding stones.

Basketry, sandal making, and weaving also became increasingly elaborate. Feathers and rabbit fur were woven into robes. Pottery making developed as both an occupation and a basis for trade. Pots were used for rituals, storing food and water, and cooking and serving food.

The great houses in Chaco Canyon, in New Mexico, were built by the Anasazi between 1000 and 1250 C.E. (Digital Stock)

The quantity and variety of rock art increased. Rock art was near or in villages, on mesa boulders, near hunting trails, or in other open locations. Subjects included birds, animals, hunting scenes, and figures playing the flute. Human handprints covered some cliff walls in mass profusion. Home, village, and the kiva were the focus of community life, which endeavored to encourage and ensure agricultural prosperity.

The Pueblo period of the Anasazi began about 700 C.E. Villages varied in size from small complexes to those with more than a hundred dwellings. Architecture gradually developed into rectangular surface buildings of dry masonry or stone and adobe that followed a linear arrangement with multiroom units. Buildings usually faced a plaza located to the south or southeast. One or more kivas were built in the plaza. Kiva architecture included an encircling bench attached to the wall, roof support poles, a central fire pit, a ventilator shaft, and a *sipapu*. The kiva was entered by ladder through a roof opening that also allowed smoke to escape. Jars, bowls, and ladles were frequent forms for pottery. Turkeys and dogs were domesticated. Infants were bound to cradle boards so that the child could be near the mother. By 900 C.E., trade activities and movement of the people had engendered a certain amount of cultural uniformity, although some local differences occurred in agriculture, architecture, and pottery.

The Anasazi realized their cultural apogee between 1000 and 1300. The building of Chaco Canyon, the cliff houses of Mesa Verde, and the ruins of Kayenta date from this time. Many communities of this period and virtually all of the Chaco-style "great houses" were planned or renovated into single, self-enclosed structures. New rooms were attached to older ones. Linear units grew into L-shapes when a room was added at the end of a row to enclose space. L-shapes became U's and U's turned into rectangles. If a village grew or became old enough, the public space of the plaza was enclosed. "Great kivas" were usually built in the Chaco plazas in addition to smaller ones. Rooms were organized into units of two or three, with a doorway facing the plaza. Ladders led to upper-level units.

The Chaco Canyon district included nine great houses and eighteen great kivas within an eight-mile area. Families occupied suites of rooms in the great houses. Other rooms were for storage, turkey pens, trash, or sometimes burial chambers. Anasazi ate stews of meat, corn mush, squash, and wild vegetables and cornmeal cakes.

Beginning about 1050, the Chaco Anasazi built a complex of twelve elaborate towns that became their religious, political, and commercial center. Grandest of all the great houses was Pueblo Bonito, a five-story D-shaped structure with eight hundred rooms and thirty-seven kivas, covering three acres (a little over a hectare). It took 150 years before the planned village of Pueblo Bonito realized the conceptions of the original designers.

Skilled as astronomers, the Anasazi built celestial observatories on clifftops. Of these, Fajada Butte is the most famous. Three stone slabs lean against a vertical cliff face on which two spiral petroglyphs are carved. Each day before noon, sun daggers fall through the slabs onto the spirals in different places and, depending on the time of year, mark the solstices and equinoxes.

The Chaco Anasazi built an elaborate road system of about 1,500 miles (2,400 kilometers). The 30-foot-wide (9-meter-wide) roads were paved and curbed. Straight paths cut through or were built over gullies, hills, or cliffs. Roadside shrines were constructed in widened parts of the road. These roads may have served some ceremonial purpose.

SIGNIFICANCE

By 1150, the Chacoan culture began to decline. The people of Pueblo Bonito walled up the doors and windows facing the outside of the great houses. Stones closed the entrance to the pueblos, leaving access by ladder only. Slowly the people left the basin, never to return.

About 1100, the Mesa Verde Anasazi began to abandon many small settlements in the mesa. Large pueblos developed, which initially followed the traditional Mesa Verde pattern with the kiva in front of the main dwelling. Soon, the kivas were enclosed within the circle of houses and walls. Stone towers were built, perhaps as watchtowers. Walls were made of large rectangular sandstone blocks with little mortar. Mud plaster was applied inside and out. One hundred years later, the Mesa Verde Anasazi moved into the caves below the mesa, although they continued to farm the mesa. Some of the cliff dwellings became quite large. Cliff Palace numbered two hundred rooms with twenty-three kivas. The Mesa Verde Anasazi prospered for some time in their cliff dwellings, but decline fell on these Anasazi, too. A savage, twenty-three-year drought occurred in the

Southwest. The Mesa Verdeans left as the crisis intensified.

By 1300, few Anasazi remained in their once-large domain. As their legacy they left descendants who became the Hopi, Zuñi, and other Pueblo peoples, as well as some of their religious and social traditions. Today the adobe pueblos of the Southwest serve as reminders of the great stone houses of their Anasazi forebears.

—Mary Pat Balkus

FURTHER READING

Brody, J. J. *The Anasazi*. New York: Rizzoli International Press, 1990. Presents a definitive view of the Anasazi, from prehistoric tribes to modern Pueblo people. Color photographs and illustrations.

Bullock, Peter Yoshio, ed. *Deciphering Anasazi Violence: With Regional Comparisons to Mesoamerican and Woodland Cultures*. Santa Fe, N.Mex.: HRM Books, 1998. A collection of essays examining the signs of violence at Anasazi sites and the possible meanings. The cannibalism theory, along with others, is discussed.

Gabriel, Kathryn. *Roads to Center Place*. Boulder, Colo.: Johnson Books, 1991. Provides insight into the development of the Chaco roads. Photographs and illustrations.

Reed, Paul F., ed. *Foundations of Anasazi Culture: The Basketmaker-Pueblo Transition*. Salt Lake City: University of Utah Press, 2000. An analysis of the early Anasazi, in particular the Basket Maker culture.

Roberts, David. *In Search of the Old Ones: Exploring the Anasazi World of the Southwest*. New York: Simon and Schuster, 1996. A history of the Pueblo Indians, in particular the Anasazi. Bibliography and index.

Sebastian, Lynne. *The Chaco Anasazi: Sociopolitical Evolution in the Prehistoric Southwest*. New York: Cambridge University Press, 1992. A look at the government and social conditions of the Anasazi in Chaco Canyon.

Turner, Christy G., II, and Jacqueline A. Turner. *Man Corn: Cannibalism and Violence in the Prehistoric American Southwest*. Salt Lake City: University of Utah Press, 1999. Anthropologist Turner asserts that the signs of violence at Anasazi and other sites in the American Southwest are evidence of human sacrifice and cannibalism.

SEE ALSO: c. 9000-c. 8000 B.C.E., Cochise Culture Thrives in American Southwest; c. 2100-c. 600 B.C.E., Mogollon Culture Rises in American Southwest; c. 300 B.C.E., Hohokam Culture Arises in American Southwest.

c. 3d century C.E.
WANG BI AND GUO XIANG REVIVE DAOISM

Wang Bi and Guo Xiang provided insightful commentaries on the two foundational works of Daoism, the Dao De Jing *and the* Zhuangzi. *Their works were instrumental in the revival of Daoism in the third century C.E. and charted a new course for the development of Chinese philosophy.*

LOCALE: China
CATEGORIES: Cultural and intellectual history; philosophy

KEY FIGURES
Wang Bi (Wang Pi; 226-249 C.E.), philosopher and leader of the revival of Daoism
Guo Xiang (Kuo Hsiang; d. 312 C.E.), philosopher and leader of the revival of Daoism

SUMMARY OF EVENT

The third century C.E. in Chinese history was a period of great political uncertainty and military strife, characterized with rebellion, usurpation, civil war, invasion, and desperate economic conditions. However, it was also an era of great intellectual vitality and achievement, which was particularly marked by the revival of Daoist thought.

This revival of Daoism was a reaction to the scholastic tendencies of Confucian learning in the earlier period, the Han Dynasty (206 B.C.E.-220 C.E.), and to the decline of the credibility of Confucianism in the late Han and the immediate post-Han period. Confucianism was adopted by the Han rulers as an official ideology, and the study of Confucian classics constituted the primary academic endeavor during the Han. Han Confucian learning emphasized the correspondence between the human and the heavenly realms, which tended to render Confucianism superstitious and mystical. It attached more importance to grammatical or lexical explanations than to the meaning of a text as a whole—this often led to inordinately long and cumbersome discussions on the multiple meanings of a particular word or phrase. This kind of Confucian learning proved unable to provide a moral basis for human conduct. It only served to stifle intellectual creativeness and was used by unscrupulous politicians and partisans to justify their various "unethical" activities. To the young generation of scholars in the post-Han era, the Han-style Confucianism seemed both superficial and hypocritical. Seeking an ideological or philosophical alternative, these scholars turned to Daoism and put new insight into it. The result was the revival and development of Daoist philosophy.

The Daoist revival was led and represented especially by Wang Bi and Guo Xiang, commentators on the two earliest Daoist classics, the *Dao De Jing* (possibly sixth century B.C.E., probably compiled late third century B.C.E.; *The Speculations on Metaphysics, Polity, and Morality of "the Old Philosopher, Lau-Tsze,"* 1868; better known as the *Dao De Jing*) and the *Zhuangzi* (traditionally c. 300 B.C.E., probably compiled c. 285-160 B.C.E.; *The Divine Classic of Nan-hua*, 1881; also known as *The Complete Works of Chuang Tzu*, 1968; commonly known as *Zhuangzi*, 1991), respectively. In their commentaries on the two classics, Wang and Guo expressed their own ideas about Daoism. Their discourse on Daoism has been more commonly known as "profound learning" (*xuanxue*, also translated as "mysterious learning" or "the learning of dark)—profound" because the discourse addressed fundamental concepts and meanings not easily intelligible to the common people.

Wang Bi's Daoist discourse focused on the concept of nonbeing or nothingness (*wu*). Wang took this concept from Laozi, but gave it a different understanding. In Wang's commentary on the *Dao De Jing*, "nonbeing" was used to describe the nature of Dao. Without physical form or image, nonbeing constitutes the "ultimate source" or "fundamental substance" (*ben*) of the myriad things (*wanwu*) in the universe. All things or beings (*you*) with names and forms are only "branch tips" (*mo*) and originate from nonbeing and depend on it for their utility. Instead of being independent of the myriad things, nonbeing covers and permeates them and actually exists in them; it can only be understood through these things. Because nonbeing is so important, it should be venerated or enhanced (*chong*).

Some scholars identify Wang Bi's "nonbeing" with the concept of "abstract," as opposed to "concrete"; and thus they believe that Wang's "nonbeing" does not mean nothingness (or emptiness) in the real sense of that word but actually means something, something that is abstract (for example, principle) as the opposite of what is concrete (the myriad things). They also insist that Wang Bi's understanding of nonbeing is ontological, for it is concerned with the question of being, its nature and source. It thus differs from previous philosophical analyses including Laozi's, which are cosmological, for they concentrate on the question of how the universe comes into being and of its makeup.

Although viewing nonbeing as the source of all things,

Wang did not identify it with a god or a divine creator. Nonbeing does not produce these things nor does it interfere with them. Instead of being designed or created artificially, the myriad things came into existence (from nonbeing) naturally and spontaneously; and they function by following the course of nature. This is what Wang meant by the terms "naturalness" (*ziran*) and "nonaction" or "nonassertive or deliberate action" (*wu wei*). These terms are identical in meaning and were all used by Wang to reveal the attribute of *dao*. For all things in the universe including humans, to act naturally (or by way of nonaction) results in success, safety, contentment, and happiness, while to act with design and effort leads to failure, danger, dissatisfaction, and misery.

Applying his ideas about nonbeing to politics, Wang Bi advocated governing by means of nonaction. According to him, an ideal ruler remains tranquil and refrains from actively making plans; he gains without seeking and achieves without action; he repudiates intelligence by displaying pristine simplicity and gets rid of cleverness and craft by minimizing his own personal desires. Such a ruler can be regarded as possessing the highest virtue. Following his model, people also will be simple and without excessive desires and therefore will not commit any treacherous activities. The result will be the achievement of order and peace.

Wang opposed the use of Legalist ruling techniques such as laws and systems and rewards and punishments as artificial and intrusive. He also rejected Confucian "benevolence and righteousness" and "rituals" (or propriety) as hypocritical and causes of disorder. For this reason, Wang was accused by one of his contemporaries of abandoning the way of Confucius. According to other scholars, however, Wang only attempted to reconcile Confucianism and Daoism and reinterpret Confucianism in a Daoist manner: Confucian ethics or morals should be treated as "branch tips" and be based on its "root" or source, namely, the Daoist nonbeing.

Another leading figure of the revival of Daoism was Guo Xiang, whose major intellectual effort was compiling and commenting on the *Zhuangzi*. Through his interpretation of this classic, Guo put forward his own philosophical ideas, which are essentially Daoist.

The core of Guo Xiang's philosophy was the stress on "self-production" and "self-satisfaction" of the myriad things (beings). Guo insisted that everything in the universe spontaneously produces itself and is by no means produced by others. In other words, the source or root of everything lies in the thing itself, and there is no external reason for its existence. Guo denied the existence of any

divine creator and even did not accept that things were produced by *dao*. He also rejected Wang Bi's nonbeing as the source of all things. According to him, *dao* and nonbeing all represent nothingness or emptiness, and nothingness cannot exist before something is created and cannot produce things. Guo Xiang further argued that everything is spontaneously what it is and has its own nature and capacity. Following its own nature and allowing full play to its natural capacity, everything enjoys satisfaction and happiness in its own way. All things can be equally happy if they are allowed to act in accordance with their own natural capability. On the other hand, troubles will ensue if they act beyond their natural ability.

Guo Xiang's concern with individual and concrete things (beings), their nature and happiness, resonates with the individualistic spirit expressed by Zhuangzi. However, there are some differences between Guo Xiang and Zhuangzi in their understanding of what is natural. For instance, Zhuangzi held that a horse's nature is to gallop and graze at ease on its own, and it is against the horse's nature for human beings to harness and ride it. However, to Guo Xiang, being harnessed and ridden by human beings is utterly in accordance with the horse's nature, for the horse by nature exists for people to ride. Thus Guo Xiang's "nature" actually contains something artificial. Zhuangzi regarded the pursuit of external things (for example, wealth and fame) as unnatural and an obstacle to achieving personal happiness, whereas Guo Xiang saw no contradiction between the two—external things and personal happiness. He believed that a person can be an accomplished ruler and a Daoist sage simultaneously.

Guo Xiang embraced the concept of nonaction as a major governing principle. By nonaction, Guo meant that the ruler should act or govern according to his natural ability. If he is endowed with great ability, he should do more; if not, then he should do less. Refraining from using his natural ability is unnatural. This perception of nonaction allows room for rulers' initiatives and thus departs from Zhuangzi's view, which discourages rulers from taking any initiatives.

Guo Xiang did not oppose institutions (government, laws, and morals). He believed that institutions are, like all other things, part of natural existence and that they spontaneously produce themselves. He also insisted that institutions are not immutable but transform with the passage of time and the change of social circumstances. New times require new institutions, and it is inappropriate to turn to ancient times for models of governing. In all these respects, Guo's views differ from those of Zhuangzi and seem more realistic Daoist theories.

201 - 300 C.E.

SIGNIFICANCE

More speculative and metaphysical than all previous philosophical discussions, the Daoist thought elaborated by Wang Bi and Guo Xiang represented a new stage in the development of Daoist philosophy and influenced not only Daoist thinking but also Confucian learning in later generations. It particularly contributed to the rise of the New-Confucianism.

Wang and Guo demonstrated a tendency to reconcile different alternatives: Daoism and Confucianism, being a sage and being a king, and political career and quiet personal life. This orientation had significant impact on Chinese scholars, scholar-officials in particular and on Chinese culture in general in that one major feature of Chinese culture is the emphasis on harmony.

— *Yunqiu Zhang*

FURTHER READING

Chan, Alan K. L. *Two Visions of the Way*. Albany: State University of New York Press, 1991. Contains chapters about Wang Bi's commentary on the *Dao De Jing*.

Fung, Yu-lan. *Chuang-Tzu: A New Selected Translation with an Exposition of the Philosophy of Kuo Hsiang*. Beijing: Foreign Languages Press, 1989. An English translation of the first seven chapters of the *Zhuangzi* with commentaries by Fung Yu-lan and Guo Xiang.

Guo Xiang. *Nanhuo zhenjing zhu*. Reprint. Beijing: Zhonghua Shuju, 1987. Chinese version of the *Zhuangzi* with commentaries by Guo Xiang.

Lin, Paul J. *A Translation of LaoTzu's "Tao Te Ching" and Wang Pi's Commentary*. Ann Arbor: Center for Chinese Studies, University of Michigan, 1977. An English version of the *Dao De Jing* and Wang Bi's commentary.

Lynn, Richard John. *A New Translation of the "Tao-te ching" of Laozi as Interpreted by Wang Bi*. New York: Columbia University Press, 1999. Contains Wang Bi's essay, *Laozi zhilue* (outline introduction to the *Dao De Jing*), which highlights the main theme of the *Dao De Jing*.

Wagner, Rudolf G. *Language, Ontology, and Political Philosophy in China: Wang Bi's Scholarly Exploration of the Dark (xuanxue)*. Albany: State University of New York Press, 2003. Focuses on Wang Bi's views on nonbeing and government.

SEE ALSO: 479 B.C.E., Confucius's Death Leads to the Creation of *The Analects*; 3d century B.C.E. (traditionally 6th century B.C.E.), Laozi Composes the *Dao De Jing*; 285-160 B.C.E. (traditionally, c. 300 B.C.E.), Composition of the *Zhuangzi*; 206 B.C.E., Liu Bang Captures Qin Capital, Founds Han Dynasty; 139-122 B.C.E., Composition of the *Huainanzi*.

RELATED ARTICLES in *Great Lives from History: The Ancient World:* Confucius; Laozi; Wang Bi; Zhuangzi.

---

c. 3d-4th century C.E.
HUNS BEGIN MIGRATION WEST FROM CENTRAL ASIA

The westward migration of the Huns eventually became a major factor contributing to the fall of the Roman Empire.

LOCALE: Central Asia to the Danube River region of Romania

CATEGORY: Expansion and land acquisition

KEY FIGURES

Theodosius the Great (346/347-395 C.E.), emperor of the Eastern Roman, r. 379-395 C.E.

Arcadius (c. 377-408 C.E.), emperor of the Eastern Roman Empire, r. 395-408 C.E., son of Theodosius the Great

Honorius (384-423 C.E.), emperor of the Western Roman Empire, r. 395-423 C.E., son of Theodosius the Great

Theodosius II (401-450 C.E.), emperor of the Eastern Roman Empire, r. 408-450 C.E., son of Arcadius

Attila (c. 406-453 C.E.), king of the Huns, r. 435-453 C.E.

Marcian (c. 392-457 C.E.), emperor of the Eastern Roman Empire, r. 450-457 C.E.

SUMMARY OF EVENT

The Huns were one of several nomadic tribes that by the fourth century C.E. had come to populate the plains of southwestern Russia and southeastern Europe. They most likely originated in the steppe region of central Asia in what is now Mongolia and northwestern China. Chinese records of the second century B.C.E. refer to the Xiongnu (Hsiung-nu), or Huns, who had posed a serious threat to the security of China. In response, the Chinese, through war and the building of the Great Wall, repelled

The Huns are depicted plundering a Roman villa in Gaul. (F. R. Niglutsch)

the Xiongnu, forcing them west beyond the Asian steppe. An illiterate people, the Huns left no written legacy. Consequently, the scant record of these nomadic people's westward migration before the late fourth century C.E. is attributed to Roman historian Ammianus Marcellinus (c. 330-c. 395 C.E.). Although Ammianus's record is sketchy, modern archaeological evidence suggests that the Hunic migration west began sometime between the third and fourth centuries C.E. By about 374 C.E., the Huns had advanced as far as the Don River in southern Russia. There, they formed an alliance with the Alani, another nomadic people. The newly formed alliance pushed west, by 376 C.E. reaching the banks of the Danube River, the northeastern frontier of the Roman Empire. For the hundred years to follow, the Huns would influence the political dynamics of the region, eventually becoming a significant factor in the fall of Rome.

The Huns were a predatory people who often allied with other tribes as a way to secure loot and dominate enemy lands. Not only were the spoils of war an incentive for conquest, but the Huns' vast herds of sheep, cattle,

and horses kept them in constant search for new pasture lands to sustain their livestock. At times, Hunnish alliances were nothing more than short-term arrangements forged as a matter of convenience; it was not uncommon for Huns to fight their former allies for control of territory. Eventually, the Huns would even serve under Roman command in wars against the Visigoths and Franks.

The westward migration of the Huns pushed aside Ostrogoths, Visigoths, and less well-known tribes that occupied the plains of southeastern Europe. Because these tribes were displaced from their homelands, they had no choice but to penetrate beyond the Roman frontier. Thus, Rome entered an era of invasions by nomadic tribes (barbarians) that drained the resources of its empire. By 378 C.E., the Huns had advanced beyond the Danube. The Romans, already at war with the Visigoths, feared the formation of a barbaric alliance against their northern frontier. To quell the possibility of such an alliance, Emperor Valens set out to crush the Visigoths on the open plains south of the Danube before they could unite with the Huns. In the end, this decision proved a

201 - 300 C.E.

costly mistake. The Visigoths had the advantage on the open plains. Their superb horsemanship and their weapons, which were designed for horse-mounted combat, won the day. The army of the Eastern Roman Empire was defeated. The Battle of Adrianople (378 C.E.; now Edirne, Turkey), as it became known, left Valens's forces so devastated that Rome would no longer be able to field its own army. Likewise, the defeat at Adrianople opened the door for the Huns to penetrate the northern and western reaches of the Roman frontier.

In 382 C.E., the Roman emperor Theodosius the Great made peace with the Visigoths and immediately enlisted their support against the Huns. By this time, it had become clear that the Roman Empire had to rely on barbarians to field an army to defend its borders against other barbarians, especially the Huns. The cost of this arrangement would put a severe strain on Theodosius the Great's treasury. From 382 to the mid-fifth century, the Roman world would see mixed alliances among Huns, Goths, and Romans despite their costly, destabilizing, and tenuous arrangements.

Theodosius the Great died in 395 C.E. leaving the Roman Empire divided between his two sons Arcadius and Honorius. Honorius became emperor of the western empire and Arcadius emperor of the eastern empire. Arcadius and his successor, Theodosius II, continued to pay tribute to the Huns. In the meantime, the Huns became united under Attila, controlling vast stretches of the Hungarian plains, east to the region north of the Black Sea.

When Theodosius II died in 450 C.E., his successor, Marcian, refused to continue paying tribute to the Huns. Instead, Marcian used his empire's resources to fortify the east and enlarge his army. Attila, recognizing the potential costs and returns of invading Marcian's territory, reasoned against invasion. By then the riches of the Eastern Roman Empire had become so depleted that the booty of war would not likely be worth the effort. The lands of the Western Roman Empire looked more fruitful. Turning west, Attila met tough resistance from an alliance of Romans and Gauls, strong enough that it repelled the Huns back into Hungary.

Within a year, a determined Attila set his sights on Rome itself. In the west, Rome's strength had begun to deteriorate from constant invasions by Germanic tribes. Attila saw in this deterioration an opportunity to take the Eternal City for himself. Beginning in 452 C.E., the Huns claimed easy victories in northern Italy. These successes would be short-lived because the Hunnish army fell victim to the plague just as it was about to lay siege to Rome. In the meantime, Marcian's army, fresh from victory

over the Persians, marched west to rescue the Romans. Marcian's advancing army and the plague were enough to convince Attila to retreat back across the Danube. Attila died in 453 C.E. before he could resurrect another invasion. Although Rome had been spared the wrath of the Huns, the empire had reached a state of internal decay that within a quarter of a century would see its final collapse at the sword of Germanic tribes.

After Attila's death, internal dissension broke out among Attila's heirs for control over their father's empire. These fights left the Huns disunited, creating an opportunity for the Germanic tribes, particularly the Gepids and Ostrogoths, to revolt against Hunnic domination. In 454 C.E., the Germanic tribes defeated the Huns at the Battle of the Nedal River somewhere in Hungary. Defeated, the Huns retired east of the Carpathian Mountains in modern-day Ukraine, leaving the victorious Gepids to occupy the lands east of the Danube and the Ostrogoths the lands west of the river.

SIGNIFICANCE

As the Huns migrated west, they set in motion the westward migration of other steppe tribes who were pushed closer and closer to the borders of the Roman Empire. As these tribes penetrated beyond these borders, they forced Rome to respond militarily, straining the resources of the empire, both politically and economically. As Rome weakened internally in response to the barbaric invasions, the empire faltered, collapsing in 476 C.E.

The Huns left another legacy that would be adopted by the later Byzantium Empire: the mounted archer. This mounted warrior would prove himself paramount in defending the new empire against Vandals, Persians, and Goths and sustain the integrity of Byzantium for the next five centuries.

—*Michael J. Garcia*

FURTHER READING

Hildinger, Erik. *Warriors of the Steppe: A Military History of Central Asia, 500 B.C. to A.D. 1700.* Cambridge, Mass.: DaCapo Press, 1979. Examines the military history of several nomadic tribes of the Eurasian steppe.

Lyttle, Richard B. *Land Beyond the River: Europe in the Age of Migration.* New York: Atheneun, 1986. Covers the various barbaric tribes that affected Europe from the third to the sixteenth centuries.

McGovern, William Montgomery. *The Early Empires of Central Asia.* Chapel Hill: University of North Carolina Press, 1939. Examines the Asian origins of the

Huns and their eventual impact on China, their westward migration into Europe, and their eventual influence on the Roman Empire. Bibliography and Index.

Maenchen-Helfen, Otto J. *The World of the Huns.* Berkeley: University of California Press, 1973. A thoroughly referenced history of the Huns with particular reference given to Roman historical sources. Bibliography and Index.

SEE ALSO: c. 2000 B.C.E., Mongols Inhabit Steppes North of China; c. 420 B.C.E.-c. 100 C.E., Yuezhi Culture Links Persia and China; 209-174 B.C.E., Maodun Creates a Large Confederation in Central Asia; 15 B.C.E.-15 C.E., Rhine-Danube Frontier Is Established; 1st-5th centuries C.E., Alani Gain Power; 9 C.E., Battle of Teutoburg Forest; August 9, 378 C.E., Battle of Adrianople; August 24-26, 410 C.E., Gothic Armies Sack Rome; 439 C.E., Vandals Seize Carthage; 445-453 C.E., Invasions of Attila the Hun; September 4, 476 C.E., Fall of Rome.

RELATED ARTICLES in *Great Lives from History: The Ancient World:* Attila; Theodosius the Great.

3d-5th century C.E.
GIANT STELAE ARE RAISED AT AKSUM

Large monuments constructed of single stones were placed on the northern edge of the city of Aksum.

LOCALE: Northern Ethiopia
CATEGORY: Architecture

KEY FIGURE
Ezana (c. 303-c. 350 C.E.), Aksumite king who converted to Christianity, r. c. 320-c. 350 C.E.

SUMMARY OF EVENT
The history of the almost impenetrable, mountainous region that consists of modern-day Ethiopia and Eritrea spans three thousand years. The biblical queen of Sheba is believed to have come from this region, which embraced Judaism around 900 B.C.E. The most important of the ancient Ethiopic states was Aksum. The Aksumite people were a mixture of Cushitic-speaking peoples from the Ethiopian highlands and Semitic-speaking southern Arabians who settled the territories around the Red Sea about 500 B.C.E. Roman and Greek sources indicate that Aksum, a city near the center of the current Ethiopian-Eritrean border from which an empire bearing its name arose, was thriving by the first century C.E. Over mountains to the north, the empire's port, Adulis, noted as the most important harbor on the Red Sea, enjoyed a strategic position on trade routes between Yemen and the Indian Ocean to the east and Nubia, Egypt, and the Mediterranean to the north. In the second century C.E., Aksum acquired Sabaean and Himyarite tributary states in Yemen across the Red Sea and conquered the coast of what is now Sudan.

The Aksumite Empire was wealthy, cosmopolitan, and culturally important. In its marketplaces, Ethiopians, Egyptians, Indians, Arabs, Greeks, Romans, and Africans speaking Sudanic and Cushitic tongues traded ideas and exotic products, such as gold dust, ivory, leather, hides, and aromatics. Jews, Christians, and even Buddhists interacted with followers of Africa's religious traditions. Coins bearing the inscriptions of some twenty kings have been found throughout the region. Both Semitic, the Aksumite language and its written script, Ge'ez, are part of the longest continuous literate traditions in Africa. They were the forerunners of Amharic, Ethiopia's modern language.

The Aksumites' polytheistic beliefs were closely related to pre-Islamic Arabian religion. However, in 330 C.E., under the influence of Syrian bishop Frumentius, newly converted Aksumite king Ezana declared his realm a Christian state. Therefore, Ethiopia is often cited as history's first Christian country. However, its Christianity differed from that followed in other areas. Because of their Semitic origins, Aksumite and other Ethiopian Christians have viewed themselves as heirs to God's Old Testament covenant with the Hebrews. Since the fifth century C.E., Ge'ez, rather than Greek, has been the liturgical script of the Ethiopian church. Influenced by Egypt's Coptic Church, the Aksumites were Monophysites who believed that Christ had a single rather than a dual nature. Until the twentieth century, the Abuna or patriarch of the Ethiopian church, was chosen by the Coptic patriarch in Alexandria. Because the Aksumites had sheltered Muḥammad's first followers, the Arabs never attempted to overthrow Aksum as they spread across North Africa. Even after its prosperity and power had waned, Aksum enjoyed good relations with its Muslim neighbors. Hence, Ethiopia's form of Christianity has survived to the present day.

201 - 300 C.E.

847

The focus of worship as well as power, Aksum became a holy city in which emperors were crowned. Beneath a lofty peak of the Adwa Mountains, the city lies in a *kloof*, or valley, over a vast plain at 7,545 feet (2, 300 meters) above sea level. Until the sixteenth century, Aksum was both the civil and religious center of Ethiopia, despite its destruction by ninth century Jewish queen Judith, who slaughtered all the royal princes. In 1538, it was captured by Muslim general Mohammed Gragn (also known as Ahmed Ibrahim al-Ghazi), prince of Leïla, and the Ethiopian monarchy moved to a new capital at Gonder, deep in the Abyssinian Highlands.

According to local traditions, the queen of Sheba's palace and bath are in Aksum. Its valley's entrance is dominated by a large thickly wooden enclosure, nearly a mile in circumference, in the center of which rises the city's cathedral, a monastery and its bishop's residence. Running up the valley is the long line of monuments and beyond is the ancient reservoir that supplied the city with water until recent times. On a nearby hill are the sixth century ruins of King Kaleb's Palace.

However, from an architectural perspective, Aksum's most impressive and best-preserved structures are the roughly 120 granite monoliths that dominate the northern edge of the city. Rising like stone skyscrapers above the city, these stelae are single stone blocks. No one knows exactly when or how they were quarried and erected. Their construction employed considerable manpower and artistic ability with advanced knowledge of architectural, engineering, and mathematical skills. Traditionally, Ethiopians believed that the mystical powers of the Ark of the Covenant, the box that holds the original Ten Commandments, raised the stones after they were carved. Many thought that the stelae were erected some time between 1000 and 700 B.C.E., before Ethiopia's Jewish era. This may be true of some in a small field near Sheba's palace, but not of the larger monuments of the northern field.

Modern scholars have estimated their construction to be more recent. All agree that these monuments graced Aksum at the height of its power under Ezana in the fourth century C.E. Although they memorialize the city's

A camel walks past some of the stelae at Aksum. (AP/Wide World Photos)

rulers, the intended purpose of certain features of these structures remains a mystery. Nonfunctional doors and windows are carved on their surfaces. Each is crowned with a semicircular finial, on which a disk representing the Sabaean sun god and a crescent moon are often carved. These symbols and numerous Himyaritic (Arabic) inscriptions on the stelae and throughout the city reveal a mingling of Arabian and African influences. About fifty stone pedestals on the stelae are believed to have held metal statues of Aksum's pre-Christian kings. Metal plates bearing the faces of kings were riveted to the stelae. Altars for animal sacrifices were fitted to their bases.

Now lying broken on the ground in three pieces and totaling 234 feet (71 meters), the tallest stela originally weighed some 500 tons, the largest single piece of stone ever quarried. It may have broken during its erection in the second quarter of the fourth century C.E. Some scholars suggest that the disastrous collapse, which might have been interpreted as a failure of old religious practices, may have contributed to Aksum's conversion to Christianity. The second largest stela is about 80 feet (24 meters) tall and was taken by the Italians during Benito Mussolini's invasion of Ethiopia in 1937. An international campaign was begun in the late twentieth century for its return to Ethiopia from Rome, where it graces a square. Many other stelae are no longer standing. However, of those standing, the tallest is 69 feet (12 meters) and weighs 300 tons.

SIGNIFICANCE

Isolated and protected by its mountains for centuries, Ethiopia's mixture of Middle Eastern and African cultures is exemplified by the mysterious stelae of Aksum. Archaeologists believe the city sits on extensive ruins, which cannot be excavated because of the expense of such a project and the need to relocate the current population. To Ethiopia's millions, Aksum, now the capital of Ethiopia's Tigré Province, is the seat of their country's glorious past and a sacred, inviolable refuge with a tranquillity unknown elsewhere.

—Randall Fegley

FURTHER READING

Bent, J. Theodore. *The Sacred City of the Ethiopians*. London: Longmans, 1896. A detailed account of Aksum by a European traveler.

Bruce, James. *Travels to Discover the Source of the Nile*. 1788. Reprint. New York: Horizon Press, 1964. One of the first accounts of European exploration, this Scottish traveler's work contains important descriptions of Aksum.

Munro-Hay, Stuart. *Aksum: An African Civilisation of Late Antiquity*. Edinburgh, Scotland: Edinburgh University Press, 1991. An excellent study of Aksum's history.

Pankhurst, Richard. *The Ethiopians: A History*. Oxford, England: Blackwell, 2001. This excellent history of Ethiopia surveys Aksum's place in the ancient past.

Phillipson, David W. *Ancient Ethiopia*. London: British Museum Press, 1998. This survey of ancient Ethiopia is centered on Aksum.

_____. *Archaeology at Aksum, Ethiopia, 1993-1997*. 2 vols. London: Society of Antiquaries, 2001. The best, most thorough study of archaeological finds in Aksum.

Salt, Henry. *Travels in Abyssinia*. London: Frank Cass, 2001. Salt's nineteenth century account provides a valuable description of Aksum.

SEE ALSO: 450-100 B.C.E., City-State of Yeha Flourishes in the Northern Ethiopian Highlands; 1st century C.E., Kingdom of Aksum Emerges; 4th century C.E., Ezana Expands Aksum, Later Converts to Christianity; c. 450-500 C.E., Era of the Nine Saints.

RELATED ARTICLE in *Great Lives from History: The Ancient World*: Ezana.

c. 220 C.E.
CAI YAN COMPOSES POETRY ABOUT HER CAPTURE BY NOMADS

Cai Yan, a Chinese woman, wrote poems about her capture by the nomadic Xiongnu, her subsequent ransom, and the heartache she felt at leaving two sons behind.

LOCALE: China and the northwest frontier territory
CATEGORY: Literature

KEY FIGURES
Cai Yan (Ts'ai Yen; c. 176-early third century C.E.), Chinese poet
Cao Cao (Ts'ao Ts'ao; 155-220 C.E.), Chinese general

SUMMARY OF EVENT
The story of the life of the Chinese poet Cai Yan (or Cai Wenji, lady of refinement) is the locus of an important moment in both history and literature. Cai Yan's experience has served until this day as an avatar of narratives about the tensions between cultures and peoples. The daughter of Cai Yong (Ts'ai Yong), an influential Han Dynasty (206 B.C.E.-220 C.E.) Chinese administrator and poet, Cai Yan was born in Yu of Chenliu. She was well educated and possessed a keen ear for both music and poetry, which she studied formally. She is believed to have used these talents in later life, to record her troubles in poetry and music. Cai Yong found a husband for Cai Yan, but he died after only a few years of marriage. This event was the first of many steps by which the young aristocratic lady became ever more vulnerable to the vicissitudes of the world around her. Indeed, she seemed surrounded by threats; the prestige of her family within the Han ruling class was threatened by civil uprisings that would eventually supplant the Han Dynasty, Chinese tradition left little opportunity for a widow to remarry, and her father had no male heirs. When her father, a political prisoner in the wake of the uprising led by Dong Zhou (Tung Chou), died in 192, Cai Yan knew that she had become the last generation of her family. However, her challenges in finding a place in the world were only just beginning.

In operations against the Han emperor, the Chinese general Dong Zhou had employed a mercenary army of southern Xiongnu (Hsiung-nu) nomads. Many of these soldiers were given general orders to spread terror in the Chinese areas in which they were operating; their raiding parties typically slaughtered men and took women as captives. The Chinese were terrified of these aggressive invaders who seemed totally foreign to them. Unfortunately for Cai Yan, she was one of the women whom the Xiongnu soldiers captured, probably not long after the death of her father. Her captors forced her and many others to march long distances under conditions of constant pain and fear away from China into the northwest territories. The captives were beaten and threatened with death, and none could know who would survive the journey or the day. Once in Xiongnu territory, however, Cai Yan was treated reasonably well. She was given as a bride to Prince Zuoxian of the southern Xiongnu. Although the cultural divide between the Chinese and Xiongnu never allowed Cai Yan to feel a part of the foreign people, Zuoxian was fond of her, and together they had two sons.

Cai Yan raised the boys well; they were the only source of joy for her as she lived in a foreign and inhospitable place far from her home and familiar traditions. She was a Chinese woman, but she was not in China; she was a mother in a Xiongnu household, but she was not a Xiongnu woman. For twelve years, she hoped every day for an opportunity to return home, or at least for news from her people. At last, in 206 C.E., a messenger arrived from the famous general Cao Cao, who would later be the founder of the Wei Dynasty (posthumously styled Wudi, Wei emperor, by his son). Cao Cao had been a close friend of Cai Yan's father and, out of loyalty, had offered one thousand gold pieces to the Xiongnu in exchange for the return of the late official's daughter. The offer was accepted, and the messenger prepared horses with which to transport Cai Yan back to her native land.

It was now that Cai Yan faced yet another trial: the separation from her beloved sons. If she returned to China, she would be compelled to leave them behind. The boys clung to her and begged her to stay. She embraced them and hesitated repeatedly in her anguish in choosing between her two families. In the east, her Chinese ancestors called her home, and in the west, her children begged her not to leave. As she rode away to China, she knew that all her days would be filled with regret and longing for her children. She knew also that she would never see them again. Back in China, her home village had fallen into ruin, and she was left without hope once again. Cao Cao, however, was concerned with her fate and had her married to Dong Si (Tung Ssu), who served in Cao Cao's court. Even so, the reception of Cai Yan in palace society was a cold one. She had been married three times, once to a foreigner; the traditional association of her father's family with the Han did not work to her advantage under the new imperial power structure; and Dong Si himself was sometimes at odds with Cao Cao. In fact, Cao Cao at one time threatened to execute Dong Si, who was saved only through the intervention of Cai Yan, who asked Cao Cao if he planned to supply her with yet a fourth husband.

SIGNIFICANCE

Cai Yan came to symbolize the challenges posed by different cultures coming into contact. She was a woman who could not find a single place on earth in which she wholly belonged, and she ended her life an outsider in her own country. However, Cai Yan was also a poet, and all the suffering and complexity of her story become the foundation of some of the world's most poignant literature. Three lengthy poems are ascribed to her, two of which are called *Ben fen shi* (song of grief and resentment), and the last, *Hu jia shi ba pai* (third century C.E.?; "Eighteen Songs of a Nomad Flute," published in English in *Women Writers of Traditional China*, 1999), is a cycle of eighteen songs written for the "nomad," or "traverse," flute, which was the traditional instrument of the Xiongnu. The attribution of the eighteen songs has been called into question in the last century, but whether or not the voice is actually hers, the poem eloquently expresses her story and the complexity of the suffering she endured. Indeed, the story of Cai Yan would inspire many subsequent writers, who created poetry, drama, and art.

—*Wells S. Hansen*

FURTHER READING

Chang, Kang-i Sun, and Haun Saussy, eds. *Women Writers of Traditional China*. Stanford, Calif.: Stanford University Press, 1999. A fine anthology of verse in translations, this volume also provides an excellent and readable introduction to the history of women's writing in China. Bibliography and index.

Frankel, Hans H. "Cai Yan and the Poems Attributed to Her." *Chinese Literature: Essays, Articles, Reviews* 5 (1983): 133-56. A seminal paper on the current thought about the authenticity of the Cai Yan poems.

Levy, Dore J. "Transforming Archetypes in Chinese Poetry and Painting." *Asia Major* 6, no. 2 (1993): 147-68. A brief look at some of the artistic impact of Cai Yan's work.

Rouzer, Paul F. *Articulated Ladies: Gender and the Male Community in Early Chinese Texts.* Cambridge, Mass.: Harvard-Yenching Institute, 2002. Provides literary context for Cai Yan's poems. Bibliography and index.

SEE ALSO: 209-174 B.C.E., Maodun Creates a Large Confederation in Central Asia; 206 B.C.E., Liu Bang Captures Qin Capital, Founds Han Dynasty; 140-87 B.C.E., Wudi Rules Han Dynasty China; 25 C.E., Guang Wudi Restores the Han Dynasty; c. 99-105 C.E., Ban Zhao Writes Behavior Guide for Young Women; 184-204 C.E., Yellow Turbans Rebellion; 220 C.E., Three Kingdoms Period Begins in China; c. 405 C.E., Statesman Tao Qian Becomes Farmer and Daoist Poet.

RELATED ARTICLES in *Great Lives from History: The Ancient World*: Cao Cao; Wudi.

201 - 300 C.E.

220 C.E.
THREE KINGDOMS PERIOD BEGINS IN CHINA

After the death of General Cao Cao and the fall of the Han Dynasty, China experienced three-and-a-half centuries of disunion and civil war.

LOCALE: Most of central and northern modern-day China

CATEGORIES: Government and politics; wars, uprisings, and civil unrest

KEY FIGURES

Cao Cao (Ts'ao Ts'ao; 155-220 C.E.), military and political leader who attempted to unify China at the end of the Han Dynasty

Xiandi (Hsien-ti, also Liu Xie, or Liu Hsieh; 173-220 C.E.), emperor of the Han Dynasty, r. 190-220 C.E.

SUMMARY OF EVENT

The fall of the Han Dynasty in 220 C.E. was the result of a number of domestic and international problems that the dynasty was unable to solve. In the international arena, its traditional adversaries, the northern nomadic tribes threatened China's national security. By the last decade of the Han Dynasty, a nomadic confederacy known as the Xiongnu had been established and was threatening the security of the northern section of the empire. The Han Dynasty tried to counter the strength of this formidable military alliance by instituting a massive arms buildup, the most important aspect of which was the enlargement of its cavalry forces. The cost of rearmament was expensive, and most of the tax burden fell upon the lower classes of Chinese society. This added fuel to an already combustible situation, and the empire was ravaged by a series of uprisings.

Domestically, the empire had been ravaged by epidemic disease, especially smallpox, measles, and bubonic plague. People traveling along the Silk Road, which connected East Asia to the Roman Empire, introduced these pathogens into China. These diseases were so virulent that China's population dropped by 25 percent. This demographic catastrophe also caused the contraction of China's commercial economy just at the time when the agricultural sector was being ravaged by internal strife. During the last century of the Han Dynasty, the empire also suffered from a number of peasant uprisings. These revolts were the result of the growing gap between the rich, landholding aristocracy and the increasingly

disadvantaged peasants who provided most of the empire's agricultural labor. Over time, a small but powerful group of aristocratic families had accumulated large tracts of productive farmland, which led to the development of an agricultural monopoly. The wealth generated by these large landholdings allowed these families to become extremely powerful, while the peasants sank deeper into poverty.

Emperor Wang Mang, known to Chinese historians as the "socialist emperor," attempted to reverse this situation in the second decade of the common era, but the cancer on the body politic had metastasized, and Wang Mang was overthrown by a revolt in 23 C.E. The most significant uprising, the Yellow Turbans Rebellion, occurred 184-204 C.E. in the northern provinces of the Han Empire and was a reaction to both widespread poverty and excessive taxation. A coalition of powerful aristocrats put down the rebellion; this ensured there would be little chance for meaningful reform.

These problems undermined the security of the Han Dynasty; eventually the military intervened, and the emperor was reduced to a figurehead under the control of his generals. Finally in 220 C.E., the Chinese military abolished the Han Dynasty, and China broke into three separate regional kingdoms, the Wei, Shu Han, and Wu.

Cao Cao, who was born in the middle of the second century C.E., was the son of a powerful court official. He used his connections and China's internal chaos to establish himself as an important figure in Chinese politics. Through a series of strategic alliances and bold political maneuvering, Cao Cao would eventually become the most powerful figure in northern China. He began his march to greatness in the last decade of the second century, when his small but effective fighting force defeated a coalition of aristocratic warlords at the Battle of the Yellow River. By 195 C.E., Cao Cao had established a secure, strategically located base of operations and attempted to reunite all of China under his control. His first step was to usurp the power of the new emperor, Xiandi. Because Xiandi was young and inexperienced, Cao Cao was able to use military power to intimidate him into following his political dictates, which in reality made Xiandi Cao's political puppet.

Cao Cao then relocated thousands of peasants who had lost their homes because of the civil wars onto fertile land around the Yellow River that had been abandoned because of the recent fighting that had occurred there.

The land was placed under the direct control of Cao Cao's government, which prevented the wealthy aristocrats from regaining control. The peasants responded to their new economic security by creating bountiful harvests that were used to feed Cao Cao's ever-expanding army. In times of trouble when rival armies attempted to bring these fertile lands under their control, the peasants could always be counted on to fight with great courage and determination because they knew they were spilling their blood for land from which they themselves would benefit. One of the many reasons Cao Cao was so successful was that none of his rivals could replicate the loyalty and productivity of his peasants.

Cao Cao also undertook major military reforms that increased the effectiveness of his army. He created a military system in which, for the first time, Chinese and foreign troops fought side by side. Most important, he realized that military tactics were changing and that if he did not adapt to this new reality, the likelihood of his success would be greatly diminished.

The most significant change occurred in the use of the cavalry. A well-disciplined cavalry unit could easily demoralize and defeat China's traditional infantry units. Cao Cao made great efforts to recruit the best nomadic warriors from the regions north of China. These tribes

had developed a mobile warrior culture that made them the most devastating force in East Asia. For centuries, these nomadic groups had lived on horseback, dominating the great steppe lands of central and northern Asia. Cao Cao's light horse calvary consisted of the best archers on the continent, who could fire volleys of arrows with unprecedented accuracy from atop a swiftly moving horse. The volley of arrows was meant to shock the enemy with a demonstration of superior power.

Warfare in East Asia was forever changed as a result of Cao Cao's tactics. The use of these nomadic warriors also initiated the diffusion of Chinese culture into the northern and central regions of Asia. This in turn allowed Chinese ideas, philosophy, and literature to be transported by horse across much of the eastern and central portion of the Eurasian landmass. Cao Cao also set the stage for increased diplomatic activity with Korea, Vietnam, and Japan.

Cao Cao's fortunes began to decline with his defeat at the Battle of Red Cliffs (208 C.E.). This was his attempt to gain control of the central portion of the Yangtze River, which was of great strategic and tactical significance. Strategically, the Yangtze provided an avenue of transportation stretching from the East China Sea completely across the south central portion of the Han Empire. It was this territory that the successors to the Han wanted because it gave them access to the rich agricultural land of southern China. Control of that territory would enhance the economic and military power of anyone wishing to become the next emperor. Tactically, the control of the Yangtze would enable any general to move his troops at will throughout this very important part of China.

Most historians agree that Cao Cao's defeat at Red Cliffs was mostly caused by bad timing. His troops were always loyal and ready to go anywhere and fight for their general. At the time of the battle, his troops had been campaigning steadily for five years against brutal competition in the area around the Great Wall. His overwhelming success in those campaigns made him momentarily overconfident, and a series of poor tactical maneuvers turned what should have been a fairly easy victory into a tactical defeat. Cao Cao realized his mistake, and instead of compounding his error by engaging the enemy the next day, he instead decided on a tactical retreat. He believed that if he rested his troops, he could return and defeat the enemy forces. In retrospect, Cao Cao had squandered his best chance of gaining control of the Yangtze River. Cao Cao's withdrawal gave the defenders time to reinforce their defensive structures; this,

THREE KINGDOMS PERIOD, 220-280 C.E.

WEI KINGDOM

Ruler	Reign
Wendi (Cao Pei)	220-226
Mingdi	227-239
Cao Fang (Feidi), king of Qi	240-253
Shaodi, duke of Gao Gui	254-259
Yuandi	260-265

SHU HAN DYNASTY

Ruler	Reign
Zhaoliedi (Liu Bei)	221-223
Hou Zhu (last ruler)	223-263

WU KINGDOM

Ruler	Reign
Dadi (Sun Quan)	222-252
Feidi, king of Kuaiji	252-258
Jingdi	258-264
Modi (Sun Hao)	264-280

201 - 300 C.E.

853

together with the natural barriers of the river itself proved too much for Cao Cao's forces to overcome.

SIGNIFICANCE

Cao Cao's defeat at the Battle of Red Cliffs would ultimately prevent anyone from uniting China for the next three and a half centuries and initiated the historical era of the Three Kingdoms (Wei, Shu Han, and Wu). At the time of Cao's death, China had slipped into a time of political and economic chaos that in many ways mirrored the Warring States Period after the fall of the Zhou Dynasty 1066-256 B.C.E. This resemblance is most striking in the elegance of its prose, especially in the area of military tactics and philosophy.

—*Richard D. Fitzgerald*

FURTHER READING

Gernet, Jacques. *A History of Chinese Civilization.* New York: Cambridge University Press. 1990. The best single-volume account of Chinese cultural history. Maps, index, bibliography.

Graff, David A. *Medieval Chinese Warfare 300-900.*

New York: Routledge Press, 2002. An excellent overview of medieval Chinese military history. Maps, index, bibliography.

Graff, David A., and Robin Higham. *A Military History of China.* Boulder, Colo.: Westview Press, 2002. Possibly the best survey of Chinese military history to date. Maps, index, and bibliography.

Hucker, Charles O. *China's Imperial Past: An Introduction to Chinese History and Culture.* Stanford, Calif.: Stanford University Press, 1975. An excellent historical overview of Chinese cultural history. Index, pictures, and bibliography.

SEE ALSO: 209-174 B.C.E., Maodun Creates a Large Confederation in Central Asia; 9-23 C.E., Wang Mang's Rise to Power; 25 C.E., Guang Wudi Restores the Han Dynasty; 184-204 C.E., Yellow Turbans Rebellion; 265 C.E., Sima Yan Establishes the Western Jin Dynasty; 316 C.E., Western Jin Dynasty Falls; 420 C.E., Southern Dynasties Period Begins in China.

RELATED ARTICLE in *Great Lives from History: The Ancient World*: Cao Cao.

---

c. 220 C.E.
ULPIAN ISSUES DICTUM IN ROME

Ulpian's dictum constituted an early statement on theories of government, clothing an absolutist reality with a veneer of constitutionalism.

LOCALE: Rome (now in Italy)
CATEGORIES: Laws, acts, and legal history; government and politics

KEY FIGURE
Ulpian (172?-223 C.E.), classical jurist

SUMMARY OF EVENT

One of the most famous phrases in the *Digesta* (533 C.E., also known as *Pandectae*; *The Digest of Justinian*, 1920) of Justinian's *Corpus Juris Civilis*, or body of civil law, is Ulpian's statement concerning the origin of the emperor's authority: "What pleases the prince has the force of law since by the *lex regia* which was passed concerning his authority, the people transfer to him and upon him the whole of its own authority and power."

Early Roman law asserted that law was an enactment of the whole people in assembly. In time, however, de-

crees of the senate were accepted as replacements for laws because of the impracticality of calling together and consulting the entire populace. By the first century C.E., however, the power of the *princeps* had so overshadowed the authority not only of the people but also of the senate that it could no longer be ignored. While it was an established fact of political life that imperial decrees were also laws, Ulpian attempted to protect the ancient popular rights by assuming that this authority rested on a grant of power by the people through a so-called *lex regia*. There is no evidence of such a law except possibly an extant "*lex de imperio Vespasiani*" (69-70 C.E.), whereby Emperor Vespasian was granted sovereignty and in which the rights held by his predecessors are mentioned. It is doubtful that any such formal grant was made later than that. In this fiction of the *lex regia*, Ulpian clothed an absolutist reality with a veneer of constitutionalism.

Thus, two apparently contradictory concepts are contained in this one statement: unlimited imperial authority and the ultimate sovereign rights and power of the people. This opinion of Ulpian caused the Roman people no difficulty because the power of the emperor was a fact, while the sovereignty of the people was a theory accepted by all, even the emperors.

SIGNIFICANCE

In the course of the Middle Ages, however, two divergent traditions developed from Ulpian's statement: the absolutist and the constitutional concepts of monarchy. Ulpian's dictum did not create these terms of reference, but supporters on either side of the issue made use of his authority after the rediscovery of Roman law in the eleventh century.

In the twelfth century, a doctrine of sovereignty arose that ascribed to the ruler an absolute plenitude of power; all inferior authority came by way of delegation. The adherents of this doctrine pointed to the first part of Ulpian's statement that the prince's will has the force of law. Not only was he unfettered by any statute but he could also apply or break them as he believed the circumstances warranted.

One such proponent was Henry de Bracton, a jurist of King Henry II of England and a writer on English law, who concluded from the "quod principi" dictum that the king as supreme lawgiver could not be legally bound by any earthly authority or the law even though he was morally bound to obey the law. Legally, the ruler was an absolute ruler; morally, he was a constitutional monarch.

Opposition to this exalted view of the monarchical office took the form of an emphasis on popular sovereignty. The proponents of this view also relied upon Ulpian's dictum, laying their stress on the second part. According to them, the king's power rested on a grant of authority by the people. Should the people be convinced that he was not acting in their interests, they could legally depose him and choose a new ruler.

Because both camps appealed with equal vehemence to Ulpian in support of their arguments, the discussion quickly began to revolve around the question of the nature of the cession of authority to the king by the people. The proponents of the absolutist view, while conceding that a grant of authority had been made, insisted that it was irrevocable and complete. The people not only were powerless to rescind the grant they had made but also no longer possessed any legislative power. Among the advocates of this view was Accursius, who wrote what became the standard gloss, or commentary, on Justinian's *Codex Iustinianus* (529, 534 C.E.; English translation, 1915; better known as *Justinian's Codification*), and Hostiensis, one of the foremost canonists of the thirteenth century.

Hostiensis, who studied at Bologna and lectured in Paris, was particularly influential. He served King Henry III of England and Pope Innocent IV and became cardinal bishop of Ostia. His two commentaries on the Decretals, written between 1250 and 1271, assured his fame. Bartolus of Sassoferrato and Baldus de Ubaldis, two of the greatest Roman lawyers of the fourteenth century, also supported the absolutist powers of the prince.

The Enlightenment did much to settle the question by advocating the doctrine that the will of the people was the ultimate authority in government. Modern democratic countries have determined that, in the final analysis, Ulpian was correct when he proposed that the ruler's authority was founded ultimately on the will of the people.

—*J. A. Wahl, updated by Jeffrey L. Buller*

FURTHER READING

Honore, Tony. *Ulpian: Pioneer of Human Rights*. 2d ed. New York: Oxford University Press, 2002. The most complete scholarly resource available on the contributions of Ulpian to the Roman legal system. Going far beyond the importance of Ulpian's dictum, this work summarizes all that is known about the early third century C.E. jurist.

McIlwain, Charles Howard. *Constitutionalism: Ancient and Modern*. Rev. ed. Reprint. Ithaca, N.Y.: Great Seal Books, 1961. Traces the impact of Ulpian's dictum on the development of constitutionalism in the West.

Scott, S. P. *The Civil Law*. 1932. Reprint. Cincinnati: Central Trust Company, 1973. Provides a translation of *Domitii Ulpiani Fragmenta* (1874; *Rules of Ulpian*, 1880) along with other legal codes, including the Twelve Tables and works by Gaius and Justinian.

Ullmann, Walter. *Principles of Government and Politics in the Middle Ages*. 2d ed. New York: Barnes & Noble, 1966. An excellent presentation of medieval political theory, including the influence that various doctrines of the Roman Empire had upon it.

SEE ALSO: 54 B.C.E., Roman Poet Catullus Dies; c. 165 C.E., Gaius Creates Edition of the *Institutes* of Roman Law.

201 - 300 C.E.

224 C.E.
ARDASHĪR I ESTABLISHES THE SĀSĀNIAN EMPIRE

Ardashīr I took over the Parthian monarchy and established the powerful empire of the Sāsānians, which experienced a cultural revival.

LOCALE: Sāsānian Empire (now in Iran)
CATEGORIES: Wars, uprisings, and civil unrest; government and politics

KEY FIGURE
Ardashīr I (d. c. 241 C.E.), ruler of Persia,
r. 224-c. 241 C.E.

SUMMARY OF EVENT
During the third century B.C.E., Persia and Mesopotamia were conquered by the Parthians, cattle- and horse-breeding nomads whose original home lay between the Caspian and Aral Seas. Their royal house, the Arsacids, ruled for nearly five centuries (c. 247 B.C.E.-224 C.E.), but by the end of the second century C.E., protracted dynastic conflicts and rivalry with Rome left the regime fragmented and exhausted. In these circumstances, Ardashīr I, a local leader from Persis (modern Fārs Province, Iran), was able to challenge Parthian hegemony and establish in its place the formidable empire of the Sāsānians (224-651 C.E.).

The final century of Parthian rule involved periods of disastrous warfare with the Romans. Trajan captured Ctesiphon, the Parthian capital, in 115 C.E., and there were further Roman occupations in 165 and 198. In 216, there was yet another Roman incursion into Mesopotamia during the reign of Caracalla, by which time warfare and plague had ravaged the Parthian kingdom, and the last Parthian monarch, Artabanus V (r. 213-224) was losing control. The time was ripe for Ardashīr to challenge his overlord.

Ardashīr was a member of an influential family in Persis, where his grandfather, Sāsān (after which the Sāsānian Dynasty was named), was custodian of the temple of the goddess Anahita at Istakhr. Ardashīr's father, Bābak, established himself as an independent ruler in Persis. According to one account, Ardashīr seized the fortress of Dārābgerd (near modern Dārāb, Iran), overcoming several local rulers (Parthian vassals), and incited his father to rebel. However, it is more likely that Bābak himself initiated the revolt, making his elder son, Shāpūr, co-ruler. Numismatic evidence confirms that Bābak and Shāpūr were co-rulers for a time, but when Shāpūr died or was killed, Ardashīr took his place. Coins survive showing Ardashīr on the obverse, either full face or in profile, with Bābak on the reverse. On both sides, there occurs the Middle Persian *MLK*, meaning "king."

The date of Bābak's death is not recorded, but Ardashīr I may have been the sole ruler for a decade before his final victory over Artabanus V in 224 C.E. He certainly acted as an independent ruler, extending his control over Khūzestān and Kermān (both in Iran), minting coins in his name, and undertaking the founding of new cities, an activity for which he would become famous. Probably, it was at this time that he selected what is now Fīrūzābād, India, southwest of Istakhr, as the site for the circular city of Gur, where his well-preserved palace still stands and where he constructed a cliff-top fortress above the gorge leading into Fīrūzābād.

What triggered the final confrontation between Ardashīr and Artabanus is unknown. Probably the time came when Artabanus felt the need to confront this overpowerful subject, or Ardashīr felt himself strong enough to confront his nominal overlord. The precise location of the Battle of the Plain of Hormizdagān is unknown, but it was somewhere in Media, perhaps between Hamadān and Eṣfahān. It was fought on April 28, 224, a date confirmed by an inscription of Ardashīr's son, Shāpūr I (r. 240-272), at Bishapur. No contemporary description survives, but if the scene portrayed on a Sāsānian rock carving at Bishapur is reliable, Ardashīr slew Artabanus in hand-to-hand fighting, and the heir-apparent, Shāpūr I, killed the Parthian vizier, Darbendam.

On the battlefield, Ardashīr assumed the lofty title of *shahanshah*, or "king of kings," justified by the presence

MAJOR RULERS OF THE EARLY SĀSĀNIAN EMPIRE, 224-379 C.E.

Ruler	Reign
Ardashīr I	224-c. 241
Shāpūr I	240-272
Hormizd I	272-273
Bahrām I	273-276
Bahrām II	276-293
Bahrām III	293
Narses	293-302
Hormizd II	302-309
Shāpūr II	309-379

of subordinate allies, the subkings of Adiabene (ancient Assyria) and Kirkuk (ancient Arrapha) and perhaps others. As the founder of a new dynasty, Ardashīr marched into lower Mesopotamia and in 226 held his coronation at Ctesiphon, which became the Sāsānian capital. He then advanced into upper Mesopotamia but failed to take the great fortress of Hatra (now Al Ḥḍr, Iraq), an undertaking that had twice frustrated the Romans, and in Armenia, he met with fierce resistance from an Arsacid collateral. Moreover, from 226 to 227, a son of Artabanus, Artavasdes, continued to resist.

For Ardashīr, political legitimation was a priority, and he initiated vigorous propaganda, including a claim of descent from the ancient Achaemenids, who ruled from c. 705 to 330 B.C.E. He commissioned a series of rock sculptures in the tradition of the Bisitun inscription of Darius the Great (r. 522-486 B.C.E.), but these cannot be precisely dated. The combat scene at Bishapur has already been mentioned. At Naqsh-i Rustam, where several of the Achaemenids were commemorated, and close to the Achaemenid ceremonial capital of Persepolis, Ardashīr commissioned the carving of an investiture scene in which he receives a ring, symbol of sovereignty, from Ahura Mazda (supreme deity of the ancient Iranians and the "good" god of Zoroastrianism). Both figures are on horseback. Beneath the feet of Ardashīr I's horse lies the prostrate figure of the dead Artabanus V, while at the feet of Ahura Mazda's mount is stretched Ahriman, embodiment of evil in Zoroastrian dualism. The names of both Ardashīr and Ahura Mazda are inscribed on their horses' breasts, and the inscription is trilingual: in Middle Persian, Parthian, and Greek. It is likely that this relief was commissioned soon after the victory of the Plain of Hormizdagān.

Close to Naqsh-i Rustam is the grotto known as Naqsh-i Rajab, which holds a second investiture scene: In this instance, Ardashīr is on foot, receiving the ring of sovereignty from Ahura Mazda, observed by Shāpūr, his son; a wife of Ardashīr and Shāpūrur; and two of Ardashīr's grandsons. A similar investiture scene at Fīrūzābād shows Ardashīr receiving the ring of sovereignty from Ahura Mazda, with a fire altar between them; there are other surviving examples.

These reliefs proclaim Ardashīr as reigning under the protection of Ahura Mazda, and convey the idea that he was endowed with that special quality of *hvarna*, a term denoting the imperial glory of Iran. The full extent of Ardashīr's conquests cannot be precisely delineated. Before 224 C.E., the eastern Iranian lands had drifted out of Parthian control, and Ardashīr had to reconquer much of

what is now central and western Afghanistan from the Kushāns. These conquests were confirmed by the use of the title *Kushanshah*, or "king of the Kushāns," by the heir apparent, Shāpūr, and successive Sāsānian crown princes.

Control of upper Mesopotamia was crucial. In 230 C.E., Ardashīr sent troops to besiege Nisibin (now Nusaybin, Turkey), and western sources mention raids into Syria and Cappadocia. The Roman emperor, Severus Alexander (r. 222-235), assembled an army in Antioch, but war was avoided. In a year or so, however, the strategic fortress of Hatra, between the upper Tigris and the Euphrates, went over to the Romans. Ardashīr embarked on his last and most successful campaign, taking advantage of Severus Alexander's assassination in 235. Hatra fell after a protracted siege, Dura-Europos (in Mesopotamia, now Salahiyeh, Syria) was raided, and in 240, Ardashīr's army captured both Carrhae (now Haran, Turkey) and Nisibin.

Sources for Ardashīr's reign occur in Latin, Greek, Armenian, Syriac, Arabic, and Middle and New Persian, but are of a fragmentary character. The *Taʿrikh al-rusul wa-al-muluk* (c. late ninth, early tenth century C.E.; *The History of al-Tabari*, 1985) of Tabari (d. 923) contains a detailed narrative of Ardashīr's career, and the *Shahnama* (compiled late tenth and early eleventh centuries C.E.; *The Epic of Kings*, 1926) of Firdausi (d. 1030), Iran's national poet, includes both historical and legendary material about him. Ardashīr's prestige in later times is exemplified by his spurious "Testament of Ardashīr" (third century C.E.) and the *Letter of Tansar* (third century C.E.; English translation, 1968).

SIGNIFICANCE

Ardashīr ended the disintegrating Parthian regime and laid the foundations for the mighty Sāsānian Empire of the future. At his death, he bequeathed to his experienced successor, Shāpūr I, an imperial regime of great ethnic, linguistic, and cultural diversity, which Shāpūr would further expand and consolidate. Not surprisingly, future generations would revere Ardashīr as a model ruler of beneficence and wisdom, a reputation that the seventh century Islamic conquest of Iran would do nothing to diminish.

—Gavin R. G. Hambly

FURTHER READING

Frye, Richard N. "The Political History of Iran Under the Sāsānians." In Vol. 3 of *The Cambridge History of Iran*. New York: Cambridge University Press, 1982. A detailed narrative history of the Sāsānians.

Herrmann, Georgina. *The Iranian Revival*. Oxford, England: Elsevier-Phaidon, 1977. Well-illustrated. Contains much information on art and archaeology.

Levy, Reuben, trans. *The Epic of the Kings*. 2d ed. Costa Mesa, Calif.: Mazda, 1996. A partial translation of the *Shahnama*, including sections on the early Sāsānians.

Shepherd, D. "Sāsānian Art: Rock Reliefs and Sculpture." In Vol. 3 of *The Cambridge History of Iran*. New York: Cambridge University Press, 1982. A detailed account of Ardashīr's reliefs.

Wiesehöfer, Josef. *Ancient Iran*. New York: I. B. Tauris, 1996. An excellent account of the Sāsānian period.

SEE ALSO: c. 705-330 B.C.E., Founding and Flourishing of the Achaemenian Dynasty; 245-140 B.C.E., Rise of Parthia; c. 230-1300 C.E., Manichaeanism Begins in Mesopotamia; 309-379 C.E., Shāpūr II Reigns over Sāsānian Empire.

RELATED ARTICLE in *Great Lives from History: The Ancient World*: Shāpūr II.

c. 230-1300 C.E.

MANICHAEANISM BEGINS IN MESOPOTAMIA

In the third century C.E., the self-proclaimed apostle Mani founded a dualistic religion that rivaled Christianity and spread from the Middle East to Africa, Europe, and China.

LOCALE: Mesopotamia
CATEGORIES: Religion; cultural and intellectual history

KEY FIGURE
Mani (216-c. 277 C.E.), founder of Manichaeanism

SUMMARY OF EVENT

Mani was born of Persian parents in southern Mesopotamia. His father, Patek (Patekios), was a member of a religious community preaching baptism and penance. Through his mother, Mani was related to the Parthian royal family, who were overthrown by the Sāsānians in 224 C.E. He was raised in southern Mesopotamia in a Judaeo-Christian Baptist community, speaking Aramaic.

At the age of twelve, Mani underwent some type of religious experience accompanied by a vision of an angel, later referred to as his "twin." Twelve years later, he experienced another vision, his "annunciation," and he went forth to preach a new religion under the spiritual guidance of his twin. Mani viewed himself as the final successor in a long line of prophets including Buddha and Zoroaster; he especially acknowledged his debt to Jesus Christ, referring to himself as an "apostle of Jesus." However, he viewed earlier revelations of the true religion as limited because they were local in scope, taught usually to only one people in one language. Mani also believed that all earlier religions had lost sight of the truth, and he regarded himself as the carrier of the universal message. As such, he wrote down his teachings, encouraged their translation into other languages, and vigorously engaged in missionary activity.

After receiving instruction, Mani preached throughout the Mesopotamian area of the recently established Sāsānian Empire. He sent early converts to Alexandria and Afghanistan to engage in missionary activities. In 240 or 241 C.E., he sailed to India, where he obtained many new converts, including a Buddhist king. After the death of King Ardashīr I and the coronation of his successor Shāpūr I (r. 240-272), Mani traveled to the Sāsānian capital and was favorably received by the king. Although the king did not convert, he permitted Mani to preach his religion throughout the realm. This event is remembered as the Manichaean Day of Pentecost. Mani's privileges were renewed under the reign of Shāpūr's successor, Hormizd I (r. 272-273). However, after the latter's reign, Bahrām I (r. 273-276) ascended the throne. Representatives of the Zoroastrian church persuaded Bahrām to withdraw Mani's privileges, and the Sāsānians began to persecute the Manichaeans. Mani was imprisoned, and after twenty-six days of trials, known as the Passion, he delivered a final message to his disciples and died in chains c. 277.

The persecution drove his adherents far and wide, and the religion soon spread eastward in Asia and westward toward North Africa and Europe. For a decade, Saint Augustine was a Manichaean "hearer," or one who followed the teachings of Mani, before he converted to Christianity.

Mani's teachings fall under the broad realm of Gnostic because they offered salvation through special knowledge (*gnosis*) of spiritual truth. As with all forms of Gnosticism, Mani taught that human life consists of suffering and evil; illumination can be attained only by means of *gnosis*.

Mani taught a dualistic religion consisting of the two eternal roots, or principles of light (good) and dark (evil). These two principles brought the world into being and would remain primary forces until the end. Mani devised a universal chronology consisting of three time periods with respect to the two principles: In the first time period, the kingdoms of light and dark existed apart; in the second, the darkness invaded the light and created a mixture; and in the third, future period, the two kingdoms would once again be separate.

According to Mani's teachings, a cosmic conflict existed between the Prince of Light and the Demon of Darkness. Light had created only the spiritual; all matter was attributed to darkness. The two realms had become fused in an event known as "the seduction of the demons." The forces of the dark stole some of the divine substance of light and used it to fashion the earth and all the organic and inorganic objects contained in it. Thus human beings are a mixture of the two opposing forces: spiritual substances trapped within an evil material shell. The goal of human beings is therefore to do good and to eliminate the material in their lives by means of fasting, abstinence, and relinquishing material possessions. At death, the soul of the righteous person returns to the light. The soul of a person who persists in things of the flesh is condemned to rebirth in a succession of bodies.

Mani's community existed of a tripartite group of the faithful. The first, the elect, lived ascetic lives based on the belief that excessive speech, food, worldly acts, and desires were essentially evil. The second, the hearers, had to abjure magic and idolatry, follow Mani's teachings, and support the elect with work and alms. The third, the adherents, were those who were interested in Mani's teachings but undertook no obligations. Although the members of the elect were grouped at the apex of the Manichaean hierarchy, Manichaeanism never developed an organized priesthood.

SIGNIFICANCE

In the nineteenth century, scholars studied Manichaeanism from material gleaned primarily from Greek and Latin sources and secondarily from Syriac and Arabic ones. All these sources were generally hostile to Manichaeanism. However, in the twentieth century, scholars unearthed a veritable plethora of Manichaean treatises in myriad languages including Bactrian, Chinese, Coptic, Old Turkic, Parthian, Middle Persian, New Persian, Sogdian, and Tokharian. The extant Manichaean corpus is extensive, consisting of hymn books, catechism, theological tractates, homilies, epistles, liturgies, prayers, po-

etry, and historical fragments. The Manichaean written record is still being discovered and translated; it provides an ample testament to the popularity and the extent of Mani's religion.

Manichaeanism spread rapidly. In the West, Manichaeanism was a religious force by the end of the third century C.E.; it is mentioned in an edict of the emperor Diocletian in 297. Around the year 300, the Neoplatonist Alexander of Lycopolis in Upper Egypt wrote a treatise against the teachings of the Manichaeans, and in the fourth and fifth centuries, Christian theologians, both in the East and West, vigorously attacked Mani's doctrines. By the fourth century, the Manichaeans had founded churches in Spain and southern Gaul, but because of attacks by both the Christian Church and a Christianized Roman Empire, Manichaeanism disappeared from Western Europe by the fifth century. Although it was ousted from the Eastern Roman Empire through the combined pressure of church and state by the sixth century, it continued to thrive in Asia, notably in China, for another thousand years.

Mani's teachings spread through Persia throughout his own lifetime. Despite frequent persecutions, Manichaeanism survived in the Middle East until the persecutions of the Muslim ʿAbbāsids in the tenth century. As a result of these persecutions, the Manichaeans moved northward out of Persia and toward Samarqand in modern Uzbekistan.

Manichaeanism spread yet farther east in the seventh century C.E. along the caravan routes following China's conquest of east Turkestan. By 694, a Manichaean missionary had reached the Chinese court; in 732, an edict ensured its followers the freedom to worship in China. Although Manichaeanism was prohibited in China in 843 and afterward persecuted, it endured there at least until the fourteenth century. The Italian traveler Marco Polo found Manichaean communities there at the end of the thirteenth century.

In the eighth century C.E., when the Uighur Turks conquered east Turkestan, one of the leaders leaders converted to Manichaeanism, which remained the state religion of the Uighur kingdom until its overthrow in 840. Manichaeanism probably survived in east Turkestan until the Mongol invasion of the thirteenth century.

Various dualistic sects surfaced throughout the Middle Ages in a variety of guises; however, it is difficult to ascertain exactly the nature of their relationship to Manichaeanism. The Paulicians appeared in Armenia (seventh century), the Bogomils in Bulgaria (tenth/eleventh century), and the Albigensians (Cathars) in

201 - 300 C.E.

France (twelfth century). Although contemporaries noted their similarities to Manichaeanism, no direct historical links have been established with the religion of Mani.

—*Andrew G. Traver*

FURTHER READING

BeDuhn, Jason. *The Manichaean Body: In Discipline and Ritual*. Baltimore: The Johns Hopkins University Press, 2000. A scholarly treatment of Manichaean religion.

Mirecki, Paul, and Jason BeDuhn, eds. *Emerging from Darkness: Studies in the Recovery of Manichaean Sources*. Leiden, Netherlands: Brill, 1997. An important collection of essays on Manichaean sources and the state of Manichaean studies at the end of the twentieth century.

_____. *The Light and the Darkness: Studies in Manichaeism and Its World*. Leiden, the Netherlands: Brill, 2001. A scholarly collection of essays dealing with the reconstruction of Manichaean literary sources.

Oort, Johannes van, Otto Wermelinger, and Gregor Wurst, eds. *Augustine and Manichaeism in the Latin West: Proceedings of the Fribourg-Utrecht International Symposium of the IAMS*. Leiden, Netherlands: Brill, 2001. A scholarly series of essays concerning Manichaean penetration of North Africa during the period of Saint Augustine.

Widengren, Geo. *Mani and Manichaeism*. Translated by Charles Kessler. New York: Holt, Rinehart, and Winston, 1965. An excellent survey of Mani's life and teachings.

SEE ALSO: c. 600 B.C.E., Appearance of Zoroastrian Ditheism; 224 C.E., Ardashīr I Establishes the Sāsānian Empire; 309-379 C.E., Shāpūr II Reigns over Sāsānian Empire; 413-427 C.E., Saint Augustine Writes *The City of God*.

RELATED ARTICLES in *Great Lives from History: The Ancient World*: Saint Augustine; Zoroaster.

---

c. mid-3d century C.E.
HIMIKO RULES THE YAMATAI

Himiko, the legendary sovereign/shaman of Yamatai, was duly recognized by the Chinese emperor as ruler of Wa, or Japan.

LOCALE: Yamatai (now in Japan)
CATEGORIES: Prehistory and ancient cultures; government and politics

KEY FIGURE

Himiko (third century-after 238 C.E.), legendary first emperor of Wa (Japan), r. third century C.E.

SUMMARY OF EVENT

Much of Japanese history before the sixth century C.E. is shrouded in uncertainty, including the question of the precise origins of the Japanese people. Because writing came late to Japan, no indigenous historical accounts of this period exist, but there are references in Chinese chronicles to Wa (the archaic name given to Japan), beginning in 57 C.E. One of the most significant descriptions of early Japan occurs in the *Wei Zhi* (written between 280 and 297 C.E.; "The History of the Wei Kingdom," 1951). According to these annals, the kingdom of Wa, consisting of more than thirty domains, previously

had a male sovereign in the second century, but for some seventy years afterward, there was chaos and conflict. The people agreed on a woman as ruler, Himiko (also Pimiko or Pimeho) of the domain of Yamatai, described in the chronicle as "the Queen's country," an area within Japan identified as being either in the Yamato region located in modern-day Nara Prefecture on the main island of Honshū or somewhere in the northern portion of Kyūshū Island. Himiko was adept at sorcery (*kido*: the way of occult magic), with which she mesmerized the people. She remained unmarried and reigned with a thousand female servants in attendance but only one man, who served her meals and functioned as her liaison with the outside world. While she remained cloistered in her palace conducting rites, her younger brother aided her in the day-to-day matters of governing. The chronicle describes her palace as consisting of fortified buildings with watchtowers and stockades presided over by guards.

In 238 C.E., Himiko sent a delegation to the Wei emperor in China, who formally accepted her tribute of slaves and textiles. In the following year, he issued an edict in which he bestowed on Himiko the title "Queen of Wa, Friend of the Wei Kingdom," sent her presents, including bronze mirrors, and admonished her to rule her people peaceably. She sent other emissaries to China subsequently to request aid in her battle with Kuna, a rival domain.

When Himiko died, a funerary tumulus or tomb mound was erected, said to be more than 164 yards (150 meters) across. One hundred male and female attendants accompanied her to the grave. After her death, a king was enthroned, but once more civil strife and violence ensued. In his stead, Iyo, a young girl said to be a relative of Himiko, was named as ruler and peace was reestablished.

SIGNIFICANCE

The story of Himiko raises a number of issues, the first having to do with the nature of early Japan. Speculating about the origins of Japan, scholars have sought to link Himiko and early Japanese society with various other shamanistic cultures on the continent of Asia. Also the question remains whether the narrative of Himiko should be considered legend, history, or a combination of the two. The two earliest Japanese histories, the *Kojiki* (712 C.E.; *Records of Ancient Matters*, 1883) and the *Nihon shoki* (compiled 720 C.E.; *Nihongi: Chronicles of Japan from the Earliest Times to A.D. 697*, 1896), generally ignore the Chinese accounts of the Yamatai state. The latter, however, quotes passages from the *Wei Zhi* but attributes them to another ruler, Empress Jingū, who putatively ruled in the third century C.E. and is referred to as the Queen of Wa. This identification of Himiko with Empress Jingū was later debunked by historians but suggests how powerful the mystique of an inviolable and powerful queen was in establishing the authenticity of the early Japanese nation. The linking between political and sacerdotal power in the early Japanese state develops eventually into the institution of the imperial line, in which the emperor of Japan until 1945 functioned both as an earthly ruler and as the divine shaman-priest of the nation.

Feminists have viewed the description of Himiko as attesting to the importance of women in early Japan, which some scholars have suggested was matrilineal and matriarchal. A number of parallels have been drawn with Amaterasu, the sun goddess who is the central figure of the Shinto pantheon. Like Himiko, Amaterasu is described as being supreme, performing various esoteric magical rituals and also possessing a younger brother, the deity Susanoo, who is subservient to her.

Finally, there remains the question of identifying the country of Yamatai. Scholars have debated whether

Yamatai, based on the description in the *Wei Zhi*, was located in the northern part of Kyūshū or if it was located in the area known as Yamato (thought to be cognate with Yamatai) on the main island of Honshū. Although the description corresponds more closely with the Kyūshū venue, the funerary tumulus mentioned in connection with Himiko's burial provides some evidence for the Yamato site because that kind of burial mound had generally been unearthed on the main island.

During the last decades of the twentieth century, archaeological evidence was uncovered in Kyūshū, specifically in Yoshinogari (present-day Saga Prefecture) that includes a double moat, watchtowers, and storehouses as well as clothing and jewelry from a burial mound said to be nearly two thousand years old, prompting some scholars to argue that this might have been the center of the Yamatai domain. To complicate matters, in the early twenty-first century, researchers have claimed to found the remains of Yamatai in a burial mound in Nara Prefecture, Katsuyama Mound in Makimuku, ascertained as the oldest in the country, and another in the Nara region, the Hokenoyama burial mound in Sakurai, which dates to the middle of the third century. Whether any of these can be categorically demonstrated to be the site of Himiko's palaces in Yamatai remains to be seen.

—*Meera S. Viswanathan*

FURTHER READING

Aoki, Michiko. "Empress Jingū: The Shamaness Ruler." In *Heroic with Grace: Legendary Women of Japan*, edited by Chieko Irie Mulhern. Armonk, N.Y.: M. E. Sharpe, 1991. Focuses on the legend of the Empress Jingū and possible connections with Pimiko (Himiko) and Amaterasu.

Edwards, Walter. "In Pursuit of Himiko: Postwar Archaeology and the Location of Yamatai." *Monumenta Nipponica* 51, no. 1 (1996): 53-79. Scholarly analysis of archaeological remains that have been linked to Himiko and Yamatai.

Tsunoda, Ryusaku, et al., eds. *Sources of Japanese Tradition*. New York: Columbia University Press, 1958. Translation of portions of the *Wei Zhi* and other Chinese chronicles dealing with early Japan and the story of Himiko.

Young, John. *The Location of Yamatai: A Case Study in Japanese Historiography, 720-1945*. Baltimore: The Johns Hopkins University Press, 1958. Historical examination of various theories about Yamatai and the identity of Himiko.

201 - 300 C.E.

SEE ALSO: c. 10,000-c. 300 B.C.E., Jōmon Culture Thrives in Japan; c. 7500 B.C.E., Birth of Shintō; c. 300 B.C.E., Yayoi Period Begins; 3d century B.C.E. (traditionally 660 B.C.E.), Jimmu Tennō Becomes the First Emperor of Japan; c. 300-710 C.E., Kofun Period Unifies Japan; 390-430 C.E. or later, traditionally r. 270-310, Ōjin Tennō, First Historical Emperor of Japan, Reigns.

RELATED ARTICLES in *Great Lives from History: The Ancient World*: Jimmu Tennō; Jingū; Ojin Tennō.

250 C.E.
OUTBREAK OF THE DECIAN PERSECUTION

The Roman emperor Decius organized the first systematic attack on Christianity that encompassed the entire empire.

LOCALE: Roman Empire, especially Rome, Carthage, and Alexandria

CATEGORIES: Religion; government and politics

KEY FIGURES

Decius (c. 201-251 C.E.), Roman emperor, instituted persecution of Christians, r. 249-251 C.E.

Saint Fabian (d. 250 C.E.), bishop of Rome, 236-250 C.E.

Saint Cyprian of Carthage (c. 200-258 C.E.), bishop of Carthage, 248-258 C.E.

Saint Cornelius (d. 253 C.E.), bishop of Rome, 251-253 C.E.

Novatian (c. 200-c. 258 C.E.), Roman presbyter who became a schismatic bishop (251-c. 28 C.E.) on the election of Saint Cornelius

Valerian (d. 260 C.E.), chief lieutenant of Decius, emperor, r. 253-260 C.E.

SUMMARY OF EVENT

The persecution of the church under Decius was the first systematic attack on Christianity throughout the Roman Empire. The earlier attacks, beginning with that of the emperor Nero, had been sporadic, local efforts, often prompted by mob pressure. Except for a brief outburst under Maximinus in 235 C.E., the church had enjoyed peace since the reign of Septimius Severus, a period of about forty years. In fact, the first half of the third century was so favorable to the expansion of Christianity that a tradition grew up claiming that the emperor during that time was Christian.

While the church was prospering, the empire was collapsing. Philip the Arabian celebrated the one thousandth anniversary of the founding of Rome in 248 with great magnificence, but the pageantry did not match the reality of the situation. The Goths on the Danube and the Parthians in the east were threatening a complete breakthrough, and the economy of the empire was in chaos. Decius, proclaimed emperor by his Illyrian troops in 249, interpreted the dire times to be the result of neglect and profanation of the traditional gods of Rome.

There were two phases to the persecution of Christians under Decius. The actual decrees are not extant, but their contents can be reconstructed from various sources. The first action was arrest of the higher clergy, and the first martyr was Saint Fabian, bishop of Rome, in January, 250 C.E. Many, such as Saint Cyprian, bishop of Carthage, chose to flee and to direct the affairs of their churches from hiding. Decius's second order was a universal command that all inhabitants of the empire participate in sacrifice to the gods by pouring a libation, burning incense, or tasting sacrificial meat. Commissions were set up throughout the state to supervise the sacrifices and to grant certificates of participation to those who complied. More than forty of these *libelli*, mostly from Egypt, have survived. In form, they are petitions to the authorities asking that by signing their name they witness the individual's declaration of loyalty to the gods and that they attest the sacrifice duly performed in their presence.

Thousands refused to comply with Decius's order and were martyred. In some localities, large numbers of the Christians "lapsed" by participating in the sacrifices or by securing a certificate of sacrifice through bribery or subterfuge. Others fled or went into hiding. Only a small percentage of the Christian population stood firm in confessing its faith or dying for it; however, this might reflect more a laxity in enforcing Decius's order on the part of officials than a lack of steadfastness on the part of Christians.

Confusion reigned in the churches, but the government did not follow up its initial advantage, and the following year, 251 C.E., Decius was killed on the frontier. A plague spread over the empire, and Christians distinguished themselves in ministering to the needs of the populace while the "lapsed" flocked back to the church lest they die outside it without grace. Confessors, by virtue of their merits, claimed the right to reconcile their weaker brethren and freely restored them to communion. This practice, strangely suggestive of later indulgences, threatened the disciplinary authority of the bishops because it was carried out by unauthorized personnel and without established liturgical forms. Veneration of martyrs during the persecution became so popular that the practice entrenched itself permanently.

SIGNIFICANCE

Decius's persecution, the first great confrontation with Christianity and the model for the still more drastic attack by Diocletian, did much to encourage the development of the penitential system of the church. Cyprian's correspondence reveals conditions in North Africa and Rome. On his return from hiding, Cyprian found himself challenged by "laxists" who wanted to readmit apostates to communion and by "rigorists" who would deny reconciliation to them. Cyprian was able to reestablish his authority and gain support for a middle course. Apostasy was now added officially to the list of forgivable sins. All deserters were placed under discipline, the duration of which varied according to the gravity of their sin as judged by the bishop and presbyters. At Rome, the issue of granting forgiveness for apostasy caused a more serious schism. When the moderate Saint Cornelius was elected to succeed Fabian, Novatian, who as a leading local presbyter had dominated the Roman see after Fabian's death, placed himself at the head of the rigorist party and had himself ordained as a rival bishop in Rome. The Novatianists, holding that only God could forgive the sin of apostasy, demanded that the lapsed remain permanently excluded from the church. Their puritan stand won a considerable following, and the Novatianist church remained for several centuries as a rival to the more lenient catholic body.

The Roman emperor Valerian in 257 C.E. resumed the persecution. His first edict sent all bishops into exile and forbade assemblies of the Christians. In 258, more stringent measures ordered the execution of all bishops and other clergy. Christians of high rank were to be degraded and their property seized. Christians in the imperial service were sent in chains to work the imperial estates. Among the victims was Cyprian, long chided for his flight under Decius. His martyrdom is still commemorated in the canon of the Roman Mass.

Valerian's son, Gallienus, in 260 C.E. issued a rescript that, in effect, is the first official declaration of toleration for Christianity. The policy of suppression had failed, but it was not until Constantine that Caesar came to terms with the Galilean.

—Everett Ferguson

FURTHER READING

Bowersock, G. W. *Martyrdom and Rome.* New York: Cambridge University Press, 1995. A collection from the Wiles lectures at the Queen's University of Belfast on martyrdom, Rome, and the early Christian church.

Ferguson, Everett, ed. *Church and State in the Early Church.* New York: Garland, 1993. A collection of articles on the early church, originally published 1935-1987. Bibliography.

Frend, W. H. C. *Martyrdom and Persecution in the Early Church.* 1965. Reprint. Grand Rapids, Mich.: Baker Book House, 1981. Frend's massive work amounts to a full-scale history of the early church organized around the theme of martyrdom and persecution.

Lesbaupin, Ivo. *Blessed Are the Persecuted: Christian Life in the Roman Empire, A.D. 64-313.* Maryknoll, N.Y.: Orbis Books, 1987. A look at the early persecution of Christians, including the Decian persecution.

Workman, H. B. *Persecution in the Early Church.* 1906.

Saint Cornelius. (Hulton|Archive)

Reprint. New York: Oxford University Press, 1980. An old but still widely read history centering around the disunion caused by Christianity within the state.

SEE ALSO: c. 6 B.C.E., Birth of Jesus Christ; c. 30 C.E., Condemnation and Crucifixion of Jesus Christ; 64-67 C.E., Nero Persecutes the Christians; c. 110 C.E., Trajan Adopts Anti-Christian Religious Policy; October 28, 312 C.E., Conversion of Constantine to Christianity; 313-395 C.E., Inception of Church-State Problem; 380-392 C.E., Theodosius's Edicts Promote Christian Orthodoxy.

c. 250 C.E.
SAINT DENIS CONVERTS PARIS TO CHRISTIANITY

In Christian tradition, Saint Denis was named bishop of Paris c. 250 C.E. and martyred at some point thereafter; Paris, then the rest of Gaul, were converted to Christianity.

LOCALE: Paris, Gaul (later in France)
CATEGORIES: Religion; government and politics

KEY FIGURES
Saint Denis (d. c. 250 C.E.), bishop of Paris, third century C.E.
Saint Fabian (d. 250 C.E.), bishop of Rome, 236-250 C.E.

SUMMARY OF EVENT
The earliest reference to Saint Dionysius, who is known in France as Saint Denis or Saint Denys, is found in the "Vita Genovefae" (sixth century C.E.; life of Saint Geneviève) written by an anonymous author. It mentions a place several miles north of Paris called Catulacum, "where Saint Dionysius was martyred and buried." However, the story of Saint Denis and the conversion of Gaul to Christianity is described most fulsomely by bishop Gregory of Tours (539-594 C.E.), who composed *Historia Francorum* (late sixth century C.E.; *History of the Franks*, 1916), ten books dealing with Roman, Christian, and barbarian Gaul.

Gregory reports that "in the consulship of Decius and Gratus" (250 C.E.), seven bishops were sent to various cities in Gaul: Trophimus to Arles, Paul to Narbonne, Saturninus to Toulouse, Dionysius (Denis) to Paris, Stremonius to Clermont, and Martial to Limoges. Gregory, therefore, believed that Denis's mission to Paris (which in the third century was a city of but middling importance) was part of a more broadly conceived plan to convert Gaul to Christianity. Even though Gregory does not specifically say so, it has been assumed that the seven were sent by the bishop of Rome, in this case Pope Fabian. Subsequently, Gregory briefly notes, "The blessed Dionysius, bishop of Paris, having suffered diverse pun-ishments for the sake of the name of Christ, ended his present life by means of the threatening sword." Later elaborations of the story included the co-martyrdom of two of Denis's colleagues, the priest Rusticus and the deacon Eleutherius, and the report that the body of Saint Denis got up, took its head in its hands, and accompanied by a choir of angels singing "Alleluia," carried it a couple of miles from Montmartre to Catulacum. The date of Denis's martyrdom is unknown, but some scholars argue that it must have occurred long enough after 250 (perhaps c. 275) to allow him to accomplish his work of evangelization. Denis's tomb at Catulacum became the site of a small shrine.

Many aspects of the cult of Saint Denis derived from Paris's pagan past. For example, the name of the site of Denis's martyrdom, Montmartre, was thought in the Middle Ages to be derived from the Latin *mons martyris* (hill of the martyr), but probably actually came from Mons Martis (the hill of Mars). Also, the traditional date of Denis's martyrdom, October 8, is coincidentally the same as the date of the vintage festival of the Roman wine god Dionysus (Bacchus), which was celebrated on October 8-9.

Denis was not the only early Gallic Christian to suffer martyrdom. In 177 C.E., Bishop Irenaeus and forty-eight Christians of Lyon were either decapitated or thrown to the beasts in the arena. In the next century, Denis's companion Saturninus of Toulouse also was executed. According to Gregory, "He was tied to the feet of a mad bull, and being sent headlong from the capitol he ended his life."

However, in other regards, the Christianization of Gaul proceeded peacefully. Gregory notes that Denis's five other companions "lived in the greatest sanctity, winning people to the church and spreading the faith of Christ among all, and died in peace, confessing the faith." Their disciples established churches in other Gallic cities. In these early years of Gallic Christianity, there were no large churches; Christians met in private homes or in small shrines, like that of Saint Denis, outside the city walls located on the sites of cemeteries and earlier martyrdoms. Gaul was largely spared during the great persecution of Diocletian (c. 245-316 C.E.). In 314, when sixteen Gallic bishops attended the first imperial-sponsored church council, which was held at Arles under Constantine the Great (r. 306-337), Gaul was well on its way to becoming Christianized. Fourth century bishops such as Hilary of Poitiers and Martin of Tours played leading roles in establishing the authority of the Church both inside and outside Gaul.

SIGNIFICANCE

It was not until the sixth century C.E., when Paris became one of the capitals of the Merovingian kingdom of the Franks, that Denis's cult began to expand. By the end of the sixth century, the church of Saint Denis in Paris had become a burial place for French kings, and as of the tenth century, he was the patron saint of France. The relics of Saint Denis and his companions survived the French Revolution and are still preserved in his church. In general, the evangelization of Paris by Saint Denis is but one of the many manifestations of the spread of Christianity throughout the Mediterranean world.

—*Ralph W. Mathisen*

According to legend, the martyred Saint Denis picked up his severed head and, accompanied by singing angels, carried it in his hands from Montmartre to Catulacum. (F. R. Niglutsch)

FURTHER READING

Duchesne, Louis. *Early History of the Christian Church*. 4th ed. New York, 1920. A thorough discussion of the conversion of the Roman Empire to Christianity, with full attention given to the conversion of Roman Gaul.

Herrin, Judith. *The Formation of Christendom*. Princeton, N.J.: Princeton University Press, 1987. A masterful discussion of the development of the Christian Mediterranean world, from its origins to the ninth century.

MacMullen, Ramsay. *Christianizing the Roman Empire, A.D. 100-400*. New Haven, Conn.: Yale University Press, 1984. A survey of the means by which the Roman Empire became Christianized.

Sharp, Mary. *A Traveler's Guide to Saints in Europe*. London: Hugh Evelyn, 1964. A collection of saints' lives that includes Dionysius (Denis).

Van Dam, Raymond. *Saints and Their Miracles in Late Antique Gaul*. Princeton, N.J.: Princeton University Press, 1993. The role of saints in the religious and secular life of early medieval France.

SEE ALSO: c. 6 B.C.E., Birth of Jesus Christ; c. 30 C.E., Condemnation and Crucifixion of Jesus Christ; October 28, 312 C.E., Conversion of Constantine to Christianity; 4th century C.E., Ezana Expands Aksum, Later Converts to Christianity; c. 450 C.E., Conversion of Ireland to Christianity.

RELATED ARTICLES in *Great Lives from History: The Ancient World:* Saint Denis; Ezana; Saint Irenaeus; Jesus.

201 - 300 C.E.

265 C.E.
SIMA YAN ESTABLISHES THE WESTERN JIN DYNASTY

Sima Yan attempted to use the establishment of the Western Jin Dynasty to unify China.

LOCALE: The western and northwestern portion of modern-day China

CATEGORIES: Government and politics; wars, uprisings, and civil unrest

KEY FIGURES

Sima Yi (Ssu-ma I; 179-251 C.E.), military general who began the Sima family's rise to power

Sima Yan (Ssu-ma Yen; 236-290 C.E.), military general, Sima Yi's grandson, founded the Western Jin Dynasty in 265, first emperor, r. 265-290 C.E.

SUMMARY OF EVENT

The period after the fall of the Han Dynasty in 220 C.E. was one of great political and social chaos. The old empire was fractured by a series of internal uprisings and invasions by nomadic tribes from central and northern Asia. With the defeat of the forces of Cao Cao (Ts'ao Ts'ao; 155-220 C.E.) at the Battle of Red Cliffs (208 C.E.), China's chance for reunification ended. The old empire broke apart, and this political breakdown ushered in the Three Kingdoms Period (220-280 C.E.), in which China divided into the Wei, Wu, and Shu Han Dynasties. This period witnessed a renewed interest in the martial arts, especially in the areas of military philosophy and strategy. This was an era of great turmoil but also one of significant intellectual accomplishment. Scholars created a vast number of written works that reflected the uncertainty and violence of the period. These treatises focused on the development of new tactical and strategic doctrines that reflected the emphasis placed on the use of cavalry formations by general Cao Cao during the decline and fall of the Han Dynasty.

The Three Kingdoms Period also witnessed a rise in the practice of Buddhism. Merchants and missionaries who traveled along the Silk Road initially brought this South Asian belief system to China. As social conditions declined, many of China's intellectual elite looked for alternatives to their traditional Confucian model. Buddhism provided an optimistic alternative centered on the belief that a life based on strong ethical principles would be rewarded.

This is the world in which the Sima family rose to prominence. Sima Yan's grandfather, Sima Yi, began the family's quest for power as a military bureaucrat for the state of Wei. He became prominent at the royal court as the result of a number of important military victories against the northern nomadic tribes and other rivals of the state of Wei who coveted the rich agricultural land under its control. Sima Yi acquired his political and military skill serving as an adviser to general Cao Cao. When Cao Cao died, his son Cao Pei (Ts'ao P'ei; 187-226 C.E.) openly broke with the Han Dynasty and created the state of Wei. Sima Yi would prove to be Cao Pei's most reliable and successful general, scoring victory after victory on behalf of his emperor for the next two decades.

Sima Yi's sons inherited their father's position after his death, and they proved to be just as successful in their military accomplishments. Most important, they led a successful campaign against the Shu Han Dynasty and were rewarded with aristocratic status. The family grew in prominence and created a power base that would eventually allow the Sima family to challenge the emperor for control of the state.

Sima Yan (Jin Wudi) rose to power in 265 C.E. when he forced the emperor of Wei to abdicate. He then declared that he had received the mandate of heaven (a divine authority to rule) and became the first emperor of the Western Jin Dynasty (265-316 C.E.). Sima Yan's rise to power, like that of his grandfather, was based on his great military skill. In the preceding decade, Sima Yan had led a large expeditionary force exceeding 200,000 men in a successful campaign against the Wu Dynasty. His great victory was based on the successful implementation of a number of military technologies that enhanced the impact of light horse cavalry that had been introduced into Chinese warfare a generation earlier.

Advances in metallurgy allowed for the creation of lighter and stronger weapons and armor. When the Chinese cavalry went into battle, both the warrior and his horse were protected with armor that made it almost impossible to stop their assault. Sima Yan's cavalry also took advantage of a new, important piece of equipment, the stirrup. This allowed the mounted warrior, moving at speeds up to 25 miles (40 kilometers) per hour, to attack any formation—or any opponent—at a full gallop. Until the invention of the stirrup, the cavalry had been used as moving artillery, essentially archers on horseback. The stirrup allowed cavalry to be used to break infantry formations without the fear of the rider being knocked off his horse by the force generated by the impact of a

EMPERORS OF THE WESTERN JIN DYNASTY, 265-316 C.E.

Ruler	Reign
Sima Yan (Jin Wudi)	265-290
Huidi	290-306
Huaidi	307-312
Mindi	313-316

handheld weapon hitting its target. Sima also supported the growth of a professional military class. These hereditary warriors became a social institution set apart from the rest of society. They were permanent members of the military establishment subjected to regular training; individual positions within the military were passed on to the eldest son on the death of his father.

The world inherited by the Western Jin Dynasty was one ravaged by civil war. Years of fighting had destroyed the basic infrastructure, and Sima Yan was continually facing challenges to his power. Sima reacted to this by adapting the Legalist model for his government. This theory was based on the belief that people were basically bad and if left on their own would always choose selfish interests over the well-being of the community. Practitioners of Legalism established a strict legal code and enforced it by executing harsh punishments on anyone who broke the law. Sima also instituted the practice of creating a number of feudal estates and distributing them to his relatives as insurance against anyone's challenging his power.

SIGNIFICANCE

The success of the Western Jin Dynasty was short-lived. The incessant warfare prevented the dynasty from instituting measures that would provide enough security to reestablish a strong, well-functioning economy. The dynasty was also cursed with a series of weak, inefficient emperors who would be manipulated by military strongmen for personal gain. In time, the dynasty would splinter and another attempt at the reunification of China would be thwarted.

—*Richard D. Fitzgerald*

FURTHER READING

Gernet, Jacques. *A History of Chinese Civilization*. New York: Cambridge University Press, 1990. The best single-volume account of Chinese cultural history. Maps, index, and bibliography.

Graff, David A. *Medieval Chinese Warfare, 300-900*. New York: Routledge, 2002. An excellent overview of medieval military history. Maps, index, and bibliography.

Graff, David A., and Robin Higham. *A Military History of China*. Boulder, Colo.: Westview Press, 2002. The best survey of Chinese military history on the market. Maps, index, and bibliography.

SEE ALSO: 25 C.E., Guang Wudi Restores the Han Dynasty; 184-204 C.E., Yellow Turbans Rebellion; 220 C.E., Three Kingdoms Period Begins in China; 316 C.E., Western Jin Dynasty Falls; 386 C.E., Toba Establishes the Northern Wei Dynasty in China; 420 C.E., Southern Dynasties Period Begins in China.

RELATED ARTICLE in *Great Lives from History: The Ancient World*: Cao Cao.

201 - 300 C.E.

284 C.E.
INAUGURATION OF THE DOMINATE IN ROME

The inauguration of the dominate placed the rule of the Roman Empire on a formally and explicitly authoritarian basis to provide stability in a troubled political climate.

LOCALE: Roman Empire
CATEGORY: Government and politics

KEY FIGURES
Diocletian (c. 245-316 C.E.), Roman emperor, r. 284/
    285-305 C.E.
Maximian (c. 250-308/310 C.E.), son-in-law of and co-
    emperor with Diocletian, r. 293-305 C.E.

SUMMARY OF EVENT
The Roman Empire has been traditionally divided into two great periods: the principate as founded by Augustus and the dominate as reconstituted by Diocletian. The difference in tone between the two periods is well indicated by their separate names: Principate, derived from *princeps*, or first man, indicates that the emperor was, at least in theory, a constitutional magistrate. Dominate, on the other hand, taken from *dominus*, meaning lord or master, acknowledges the fact that the emperor was an absolute ruler.

From the assassination of Severus Alexander in 235 C.E. to the accession of the Dalmatian peasant and successful general Diocletian in 284, the Roman Empire had been in a state of almost continuous anarchy. Thanks to assassinations and wars, only one of the more than twenty emperors who ruled during this period had died a natural death. Ruinous taxes, a plague that lasted from 253 to 268, wars with the Persians, and barbarian threats further afflicted the empire.

In the face of these difficulties, Diocletian effected a series of controversial reforms. Changes to make the army more mobile, arrangement for planned retirement of emperors after twenty years and for peaceful successions by trained caesars, and division of the state into four major districts with courts and capitals in Nicomedia, Milan, Trier, and Sirmium were ways in which Diocletian further divided the empire for administrative purposes into twelve dioceses. Each diocese was under a vicar subject to the praetorian prefect of his respective augustus or caesar, and Diocletian enlarged the number of provinces to one hundred. In the new provincial arrangement, military authority was separated from the civil, the former under *duces*, or "dukes," the latter under *comites*, or "counts." The old haphazard land tax was replaced with a new system based on a division of land into *juga* of uniform value in each diocese and a similar division of men and animals into units known as *capita*. At stipulated periods, praetorian prefects had to estimate the budget in terms of goods and make an assessment, or *indictio*, according to *juga* and *capita*.

These reforms, however wise or necessary, were not made without cost. Already during the Severi, the emperorship and the state had been brutalized by falling under military domination. The state had to resort to liturgies to bolster the flagging collection of taxes. Rich men and members of *collegia* were forced to provide free services and supplies to balance the budget. During the Severi, moreover, Roman jurisprudence divorced both criminal and civil jurisdiction from vestiges of Republican institutions such as the senate of Rome, which under Diocletian became a provincial city. Ulpian's dictum well presaged the absolutism of Diocletian in asserting that the "will of the prince has the force of law." It was becoming more and more obvious that citizens were existing for the benefit of the state rather than the other way around.

Diocletian's reign can readily be seen as representative of this trend toward totalitarian control. The cost of supporting four elaborate courts and the enlarged army added to the burden of the already impoverished economy. Inadequate issuance of new gold and silver coins

ROMAN EMPERORS FROM CARUS TO CONSTANTINE THE GREAT, 282-337 C.E.	
Ruler	*Reign*
Carus	282-283
Numerian (East)	283-284
Carinus (West)	283-285
Diocletian (East)	284-305
Maximian (West)	293-305
Constantius (West)	305-306
Galerius (East)	305-315
Severus (West)	306-307
Maxentius (West)	306-312
Constantine the Great (East)	306-337
Licinius (East)	308-324
Constantine the Great (all)	324-337

and overdevaluation of others encouraged rapid inflation. Consequently in 301 C.E., Diocletian attempted to control the economy by issuing his famous Edict of Prices, fixing the maximum that could be paid for all kinds of goods and services. Despite severe penalties, the law proved to be unworkable and eventually had to be permitted to lapse. To prevent people from avoiding the more thorough collection of taxes, farmers became bound to their land and workmen to their trades. Moreover, sons had to take up the same labors as their fathers, thereby creating a kind of serfdom in the country and a caste system in the cities.

SIGNIFICANCE

Historians have often tended to overemphasize the rigidity of Diocletian's regime. Whether because of a misleading comparison with twentieth century socialism or a dislike of Diocletian's persecution of the Christians, historians have underestimated the significance of Diocletian's constitutional reforms. These reforms proceeded from a genuine vision of how the Roman Empire could be reconstituted and once again be made a formidable and cohesive force.

Particularly important was the mechanism Diocletian devised for the imperial succession. Typically, the reigning emperor had been suspicious of any particularly strong man among those who served him; this suspicion led either to the elimination of the rivals or their preemptive overthrow of the emperor. By granting ambitious, energetic men a junior share in government and promising them eventual leadership, Diocletian defused the air of suspicion and intrigue that had plagued Roman statesmanship for several decades. Although his system ultimately collapsed, it still provided the Roman Empire with twenty years of good government, and the imperial succession would never again be so unstable as it had been in the third century.

Also notable (and rare in Roman imperial history) was Diocletian's willingness to abdicate the throne after serving his twenty years. This action, which hearkened back to the old Roman virtues of rectitude and patriotic self-sacrifice and was only reluctantly emulated by Maximian, indicates that Diocletian adhered to his own standards of conduct and was not merely an opportunistic dictator. Diocletian's authoritarianism, unlike so many others, possessed a rationale and a logic.

Indicative of the new atmosphere, Diocletian introduced an elaborate ceremonial protocol into his court borrowed from Persian and earlier Hellenistic rulers. On formal occasions, he wore a robe of purple silk and shoes adorned with jewels and was seated on a throne. He insisted upon being styled *dominus*, or lord, and those admitted to his presence had to perform the *proskynesis*, or prostration, to kiss the hem of his robe. Many historians profess to see in the declining art of the period the trend toward domination by the emperor.

Finally, although not as an innovator, Diocletian took control over the consciences of his subjects. Diocletian believed in using the prestige of the classical gods to buttress his own power; thus he allowed himself to be described as "Jove" and Maximian as "Hercules." A conservative polytheist convinced that the prosperity of the state depended on the favor of the gods, Diocletian issued decrees against Manichaeans in 297 C.E. and instituted the great persecution against the Christians in 303-304. This dragnet, which required all to display a certificate of sacrifice to the gods, came to a permanent end only with the Edict of Milan in 313 and the so-called Peace of the Church.

—*M. Joseph Costelloe,*
updated by Nicholas Birns

FURTHER READING

Barnes, Timothy. *The New Empire of Diocletian and Constantine*. Cambridge, Mass.: Harvard University Press, 1982. A compendium of laws and records make this source useful for research on Diocletian.

Cameron, Averil. *The Later Roman Empire A.D. 284-430*. London: Fontana, 1993. Cameron provides a crisply written and cogent analysis of the period.

Corcoran, Simon. *The Empire of the Tetrarchs: Imperial Pronouncements and Government, A.D. 284-324*. Oxford, England: Clarendon Press, 1996. Explores the legal and political basis of the Dominate.

Jones, A. H. M. *The Later Roman Empire, 284-602*. Baltimore: The Johns Hopkins University Press, 1986. Describes Diocletian's impact on the entire period of late antiquity.

Southern, Pat. *The Roman Empire from Severus to Constantine*. New York: Routledge, 2001. A look at the Roman Empire from the viewpoint of its rulers. Covers Diocletian.

Victor, Sextus Aurelius. *Liber de Caesaribus of Sextus Aurelius Victor*. Translated with an introduction and commentary by H. W. Bird. Liverpool, England: Liverpool University Press, 1994. Bird has provided a fine translation of the main primary source for Diocletian, accompanied by an excellent, modern-day commentary.

Williams, Stephen. *Diocletian and the Roman Recovery*.

201 - 300 C.E.

London: B. T. Batsford, 1985. This source is particularly recommended as the most thorough analysis available of Diocletian and his time.

SEE ALSO: 133 B.C.E., Tiberius Sempronius Gracchus Is Tribune; 43-42 B.C.E., Second Triumvirate Enacts Proscriptions; 27-23 B.C.E., Completion of the Augustan Settlement; c. 220 C.E., Ulpian Issues Dictum in Rome; c. 230-1300 C.E., Manichaeanism Begins in Mesopotamia.

RELATED ARTICLES in *Great Lives from History: The Ancient World*: Augustus; Diocletian; Gracchi.

c. 286 C.E.
SAINT ANTHONY OF EGYPT BEGINS ASCETIC LIFE

Saint Anthony's religious hermitage inspired others to live a solitary life of religious devotion and began the anchoritic form of Christian monasticism.

LOCALE: Mount Pispir, Egypt
CATEGORY: Religion

KEY FIGURE
Saint Anthony of Egypt (c. 251-probably 356 C.E.), teacher of the Gospels and known as the father of Christian monasticism

SUMMARY OF EVENT
Around 286 C.E., a Christian ascetic named Anthony (or Antony) went to live on Mount Pispir, a mountain near the Nile River. His settlement on Mount Pispir began an entire movement, the anchoritic form of Christian monasticism. Within his lifetime, Anthony drew great numbers of followers, as monks flocked to the desert to live the life of Christian hermits. By the time of his death, Anthony was styled the father of monks by his biographer Saint Athanasius of Alexandria.

Anthony was born to Christian parents in Coma, in Middle Egypt. His parents both died when he was around twenty years of age, and he received a substantial inheritance. Soon after he came into this inheritance, Anthony heard Matthew 19:21 read in church, in which Christ had told a rich young man to seek perfection by selling his possessions and giving the money to the poor. Anthony took those words to heart. He sold his possessions, and after providing for his younger sister by placing her in a convent, he gave his money away to the poor. Anthony began his life of asceticism by moving to the fringe of his old community. From local hermits, Anthony gained a wisdom and experience that would, around the year 286 C.E., lead Anthony to Mount Pispir and his vision of Christian anchoritic monasticism.

Anthony's monasticism had much in common with other early existing forms, including the practice of celibacy and a personal striving for spiritual perfection. Anthony's monastic vision differed from that of his fellow Egyptian and contemporary Pachomius, recognized as the founder of cenobitic, or communal, monasticism. What made Anthony's approach unique was his goal of withdrawal and isolation from the world. Anthony chose to live separated from what he saw as the constraints of family and society to be able to concentrate more clearly on his goal of spiritual perfection.

On Mount Pispir, Anthony settled into a deserted fort, where he lived the life of a hermit. While he practiced a monastic discipline in isolation from others, that isolation was not total. Over the years, many, including bishops, philosophers, and emperors came or wrote to Anthony for advice and counsel. People came out to be taught and to be healed and to be prayed over. Others came to imitate his anchoritic lifestyle. By his teaching and example, the desert was said to have become "a city of monks."

Like other Christian monks, Anthony saw himself as a successor of the martyrs and of their struggle for faithfulness in the midst of adversity. In common with other Christian monks, Anthony also saw his anchoritic discipline as a war against the devil and his demons. According to his biographer, Saint Athanasius, Anthony fought battles of the spirit against demons who tried to tempt him away from his life of spiritual perfection. These demons appeared in many forms, as women, fellow monks, and wild animals. According to Athanasius in his *Vita S. Antonii* (c. 357 C.E.; *The Life of Saint Anthony the Great*, 1850), Anthony defeated these demons while he fought himself and the passions of the flesh. Anthony is reported to have used various means of fighting these demons, such as invocation of the name of Christ, recitation of verses of Scripture, praying, and making the sign of the cross. Athanasius also offered accounts of Anthony's healing miracles and his visions of the future. These miracles and visions were presented by Athanasius as further evidence of Christ's power, which he saw active in Anthony's life. Athanasius recorded elements of Anthony's teaching. Anthony is recorded refuting the heretical Arians on three occasions, and at least one of Anthony's sermons (delivered in Coptic) is presented.

Athanasius's biography is not the only source for Anthony's life. There are seven extant letters, most likely originally written in Coptic, bearing Anthony's name. These letters indicate the variety of his correspondents as well as the practical and theological issues that occupied his attention (from monastic advice, to Trinitarian reflections, and to renunciations of Arius). Tradition claims that Anthony was illiterate. Athanasius, and later Saint Jerome, stated that Anthony wrote his letters by means of an interpreter or translator. These letters are a significant source for understanding the father of anchoritic monasticism.

Another source for Anthony is the collection of *Apophthegmata Patrum* (fourth century C.E.; *The Wisdom of the Desert: Sayings from the Desert Fathers of the Fourth Century,* 1961). Anthony is the second most frequently cited father in this collection. Many of these "sayings" of Anthony are recognized as genuine, while some are not. References to Anthony also appear in other early monastic literature and church histories.

Although Anthony is remembered for his seclusion on Mount Pispir, he made several journeys back into the world—for example, visiting Alexandria both during the Maximian persecutions at some point between 311-313 C.E. and again possibly as early as 337 or as late as shortly before his death around 356, to battle the Arians.

SIGNIFICANCE

By the time he died, Anthony's settlement on Mount Pispir had spawned the anchoritic form of monasticism. Within his lifetime, Anthony developed an international fame that built an entire movement. Anthony's temptations served as an inspiration to artists from the fourth to the twenty-first centuries, and his biography became the model for Christian hagiography.

—*J. Francis Watson*

FURTHER READING

Athanasius. *The Life of Antony and the Letter to Marcellinus.* Translated by Robert C. Gregg. New York: Paulist Press, 1980. A modern translation of Anthony's life by Athanasius, with an introduction by the translator.

Brown, Peter. *Society and the Holy in Late Antiquity.* Berkeley: University of California Press, 1982. This volume, especially the chapter "The Rise and Function of the Holy Man in Late Antiquity," presents the context for Anthony and the rise of Christian monasticism.

The Desert Fathers. Translated by Helen Waddell. New York: Vintage Books, 1998. A translation of a collection of sayings of the desert fathers and a good introduction into Egyptian monasticism in general.

Quasten, Johannes. *Patrology.* Vol. 3 in *The Golden Age of Greek Patristic Literature.* Westminster, Md.: Christian Classics, 1983. A major study of the Patristic period, including a treatment of Anthony and works associated with his name.

Saint Anthony of Egypt. (Library of Congress)

201 - 300 C.E.

Queffélec, Henri. *Saint Anthony of the Desert*. New York: E. P. Dutton, 1954. A readable biography of Anthony.

Rubenson, Samuel. *The Letters of Saint Antony: Monasticism and the Making of a Saint*. Minneapolis: Fortress Press, 1995. A thorough study of Anthony and his letters.

SEE ALSO: c. 6 B.C.E., Birth of Jesus Christ; c. 30 C.E., Condemnation and Crucifixion of Jesus Christ; c. 382-c. 405 C.E., Saint Jerome Creates the Vulgate; 413-427 C.E., Saint Augustine Writes *The City of God*.

RELATED ARTICLES in *Great Lives from History: The Ancient World*: Saint Athanasius of Alexandria; Saint Augustine; Saint Jerome; Jesus.

290-300 C.E.
WEST AFRICAN GOLD FIRST REACHES NORTH AFRICA

In the third century C.E., gold began to be transported from the West African mines near Buré and Bambuk through Ghana into North Africa.

LOCALE: Bambuk (Bambouk), Buré (Bouré), Inter-Senegal-Niger River region, modern-day Guinea, Senegal, southern Mauritania, and Mali

CATEGORY: Trade and commerce

SUMMARY OF EVENT

By the third century C.E., gold was being transported into North Africa via Ghana from fields in Buré and Bambuk. The gold fields were located near the upper Senegal River in the forest regions of modern-day Guinea. Ghana came into being at the beginning of the common era, when a confederation of Soninke clans came together under a politico-religious leader. The consolidation of populations in the inter-river region may have been a response to climate change and resulting socioeconomic pressures that caused Takrur, Berbers, Soninke, and others to contest control over land and resources. The empire that emerged from the confederation derived power and wealth from gold. The gold trade was primarily controlled by the ancient kingdom of Ghana, which had begun to emerge as a powerful centralized state through a concentration of wealth as early as the fourth century C.E.

The early occupation of land between the Senegal and Niger Rivers may have had little to do with the presence of gold; however, the emergence of a strong centralized state in this region is not incidental to the presence of gold. Gold served as the primary basis of the wealth that financed the strong, centralized state of Ghana. Archaeological evidence demonstrates that Kumbi Saleh, which become the capital of Ghana in the eighth century C.E., had been occupied by at least the fifth century. The available evidence suggests that a population was present in the area before it became a centralized state.

Ancient Ghana lies about 400 miles (650 kilometers) northwest of modern Ghana and is not related to modern Ghana geographically, politically, or ethnically. The old Ghana Empire was located just north of the gold fields in Bambuk and Buré. Ancient Ghana's borders extended across the southern borderlands between modern-day Mauritania and Mali and into the northern parts of modern-day Senegal. Ancient Ghana stretched across the territory between the two major rivers of western Africa, the Niger and Senegal, and was just south of major Sahelian market towns and key transshipment points on the trans-Saharan caravan route such as Awdaghust. The kingdom was just west of important pre-Islamic, pre-Arab Middle Niger towns such as Gao, Timbuktu, and Jenne (Djenné), which also served as the southernmost points on various caravan routes. Ancient Ghana was thus ideally located for transportation of goods between forest, Sahara, Niger River, and Senegal River populations, and it was located in the midst of densely populated urbanizing regions that produced large food surpluses.

In the western Sudan, gold dust was used as a valuable item of trade, similar to a currency. Internal African trade among inhabitants of the forest, savanna, Sahel, and inter-river communities preceded the trans-Saharan gold trade and made ancient Ghana attractive to the Roman gold markets and in medieval times attracted Arab and Islamic traders. Gold was mined in woodland savannas of the upper Niger and Senegal Rivers and then traded north to the Sahel in the first three centuries C.E. Available evidence demonstrates that the arrival of West African gold in North Africa coincides with the use of the camel to cross the Sahara into the Sahel from the third century C.E. The camel facilitated long-distance trade of heavy commodities such as salt, gold, and cloth across the desert. With the increased use of the camel after the fourth century in the Sahara and Sahel, the amount of goods—particularly gold—that was transported on caravans across the desert increased significantly.

The gold region of the Ghana Empire, also known as Wangara, was the foundation and starting point of the later trans-Saharan trade routes. The gold produced there was the main commodity sought by trans-Saharan traders. The king of Ghana maintained tight control over the gold production. To keep gold prices high, common folk could possess gold dust, but only the king could possess gold nuggets, which allowed him to accumulate great wealth. By the Islamic age, when large caravans traversed the Sahara, the king had begun levying tariffs on traders who used trade routes that passed through the Ghana Empire, particularly those caravans passing to Sijilmasa and the salt regions of Taghaza.

SIGNIFICANCE

Ancient Ghana's early wealth came from the state's ability to control the distribution of gold as it was passed from mining areas in the Bambuk and Buré regions to Jenne and further north. Ancient Ghana is an example of a state in ancient times collecting taxes to ensure its own political and economic strength.

By the third century C.E., trans-Saharan gold trade was creating strong commercial links between the forests of western Sudanic Africa and the Sahara-Sahel. These early commercial links were the foundation of a large and prosperous medieval trans-Saharan trade system. Gold from western Africa helped fuel commerce in the Mediterranean world. Coins began to appear in the eastern Mediterranean and the Horn of Africa as currency for commerce early in the first millennium C.E. By the third century, gold was in great demand at the Roman mint in Carthage. Beginning in the late third century, trans-Saharan trade from West Africa supplied the Roman Mediterranean world with a proportion of its gold resources from the bullion and gold dust of Guinea, just south of ancient Ghana.

By the eighth century C.E., the trans-Saharan trade routes were highly lucrative, and this trade intensified the Ghana Empire's success. Merchants from the north brought foodstuffs and salt to the kingdom to exchange for locally produced goods such as cotton, leather, metal, and, most important, gold. The increased demand for gold from the northern Islamic states after the eighth century brought great attention to medieval Ghana, which came to be referred to by the Islamic states as "the Land of Gold."

—*Catherine Cymone Fourshey*

FURTHER READING

Andah, B. Wai. "West Africa Before the Seventh Century." In *Ancient Civilizations*, edited by G. Mokhtar. Berkeley: University of California Press, 1981. Includes a section on ancient trade in western Africa. Excellent resource on the history of ancient Africa. Many bibliographic references.

Phillipson, David. *African Archaeology.* 2d ed. New York: Cambridge University Press, 2000. Includes brief discussion of early gold trade, including a map of ancient Ghana. The primary focus of the sections on the gold trade is post-Islamic rather than the ancient trade.

Posnansky, Merrick. "Aspects of Early West African Trade." *World Archaeology* 5, no. 2 (1973): 149-162. Includes maps and a discussion of key issues to consider in West African trade history.

Schneider, Klaus. "Das Gold der Lobi: Aspekte historischer und ethnologischer Interpretation." *Afrika-Studien* 36 (1990): 277-290. Schneider examines the place of Lobi gold within the larger historical picture of trading systems in the Sahel. The Lobi gold mine is less known than Bambuk, Buré, or the Akan gold-fields in terms of West African economic history. In German.

SEE ALSO: 3d century B.C.E., Commercial City of Jenne Is Founded on Niger River; c. 100 B.C.E.-c. 300 C.E., East African Trading Port of Rhapta Flourishes; 4000.

201 - 300 C.E.

c. 300 C.E.
LICCHAVI DYNASTY BEGINS IN THE KATHMANDU VALLEY, NEPAL

The advent of the Licchavi rule brought Nepal into the historical world. The Licchavis introduced many important innovations, including writing, the Sanskrit language, an organized government with a code of laws, and the formal worship of Hindu deities.

LOCALE: Kathmandu Valley, Nepal
CATEGORIES: Government and politics; cultural and intellectual history; religion

KEY FIGURES

Mānadeva I (fl. mid-fifth to early sixth century C.E.), Licchavi king, r. 465-505 C.E.

Aṁśuvarman (fl. late sixth-early seventh century C.E.), Licchavi king, r. c. 605-621 C.E.

Narendradeva (fl. seventh century C.E.), Licchavi king, r. 643?-679? C.E.

SUMMARY OF EVENT

It is not known precisely when the Licchavis penetrated into Nepal. Inscriptions and records are fragmented, and much of the data conflicts. There is, however, a consensus among specialists that their rule must have taken hold of the Kathmandu Valley no later than the beginning of the fourth century C.E. A precise chronology of kings and the period of their rule is problematic because the remaining inscriptions and chronicles are fragmentary and do not provide a coherent account. Before the Licchavis, the region was inhabited by a group of people called the Kirātas, a remarkable people known for their skill in archery and warfare, who had held sway in the region for centuries. One record asserts that a Licchavi king who came from the south overthrew a Kirāta king named Galija. Religion in Nepal before the Licchavis largely consisted of a mixture of Buddhism and popular atavistic deities.

The Licchavis came from the south, probably from the Vaisali region in India's Gangetic Plain. They introduced Indo-Aryan religion, and although Hindu, they were tolerant of other forms of worship. One theory asserts that the Licchavis entered Nepal after their homeland fell to the control of the Kushān Empire of north India in the first century C.E. In that case, they may have been living on Nepali soil for some time before taking full control over the region. Although historical records provide the names of the first four rulers, Haridattavarman, Vasurāja, Vṛsadeva, and Śaṅkaradeva, the dates of their rule are not certain. The political authority of the

early dynasty, however, can be surmised from the marriage of a Licchavi princess to King Chandragupta I of north India at the end of the third century C.E. The marriage alliance, referred to frequently in Gupta inscriptions, served to enhance greatly the prestige of the Imperial Gupta Dynasty.

Only with King Mānadeva I does a clear picture of Licchavi rule begin to emerge. He has a heroic place in Nepal's history. Regarded as the preeminent Licchavi king, he continues to live in the folk memory as sovereign of a golden age. He was the first Nepali king to mint his own coins and to have royal edicts inscribed on stone. His inscription on the Changunārāyana pillar at Changu (464 C.E.) is the earliest dated Licchavi historical account available. His various stone edicts reveal that he loved his subjects and looked after the poor. He was devoted to his mother, Rājyavatī, and persuaded her not to immolate herself on her husband's funeral pyre because he needed her wise counsel in administering the country. By quelling rebellious feudatories, he brought the country under his full control. Mānadeva was a devotee of the Hindu god Viṣṇu, and he set up two famous stone images of the deity that are splendid examples of Licchavi art. The historical data indicates that he also consecrated images dedicated to Śiva and established a Buddhist monastery and two stupas (Buddhist funerary monuments). He also built the Mānagṛha, the famous palace and administrative center used by Licchavi kings until the mid-seventh century.

Aṁśuvarman, one of the greatest rulers, technically was not of the Licchavi line. It is said that he belonged to the Vaiśya Ṭhakurī clan and started out as an influential officer of King Śivadeva's court. In time, he rose to be a co-ruler. Finally, after the death of Śivadeva, he became the sole monarch of the country. His inscriptions cover a sixteen-year period; he also produced coins bearing his name and the royal title "most venerable king of kings," a designation later assumed by each Licchavi ruler.

A great builder, Aṁśuvarman was known for his many architectural and sculptural achievements. He constructed a beautiful palace called Kailāskūṭa Bhavana that served as his residence and administrative center of the government. He supported major irrigation projects in the kingdom. Many fountains and water conduits were built during his reign; some are still in existence today. The famous seventh century Chinese traveler Xuanzang (Hsüan-tsang) mentioned Aṁśuvarman in his account of his travels. Although Aṁśuvarman had died a few years previously, his reputation was great and he was respected as a man of great bravery, learning, and piety. Aṁśuvarman worked tirelessly to subdue rival feudatories and to ensure a harmonious and prosperous kingdom. Aṁśuvarman was a religious man, constantly engaged in the study of books. Although a follower of Śiva, he set up generous trusts to meet the expenses of many various Hindu temples and Buddhist monasteries. A compassionate king, he wrote, "I am always thinking of how I can make my people happy."

Aṁśuvarman was followed by Udayadeva (r. 621 C.E.), a Licchavi and the legitimate heir. Udayadeva's reign was very brief. He was overthrown by a rival clan, the Ābhīra Guptas, who, although seizing the full and real

---

KINGS OF THE LICCHAVI DYNASTY, C. 300-879 C.E.

Ruler	Reign
Haridattavarman	
Vasurāja	
Vṛsadeva	c. 400
Śaṅkaradeva	c. 425
Dharmadeva	c. 450
Mānadeva I	465-505
Mahīdeva	505-506
Vasantadeva	506-532
Manudeva	
Vāmanadeva	538
Rāmadeva	545
Ganadeva	560-565
Gaṅgādeva	567
Bhaumagupta	567-590
Mānadeva II	c. 575
Śivadeva I	590-604
Aṁśuvarman*	605-621
Udayadeva	621
Dhruvadeva and Jiṣṇugupta*	624-625
Bhīmārjunadeva and Jiṣṇugupta*	c. 631-633
Viṣṇugupta*	633
Bhīmārjunadeva and Viṣṇugupta*	640-641
Viṣṇugupta*	641-643
Narendradeva	643?-679?
Śivadeva II	694-705
Jayadeva II	713-733
Mānadeva III	756
Balirāja	826
Baladeva	847
Mānadeva IV	877

Note: Asterisk indicates rulers not of the Licchavi line.

---

power, established puppet Licchavi rulers on the throne. Although the records of the period seem to suggest joint rule between Guptas and Licchavis, the fragmentary data does not provide a definite picture as to why the Guptas did not seize exclusive control for themselves.

In 643 C.E., Narendradeva, Udayadeva's son, finally crushed the Guptas and their ambitions to rule. When his father was overthrown, Narendradeva had avoided Gupta machinations and escaped to Tibet. Later, with Tibetan help, he returned to recover his rightful place on the throne. About this time, a new route was forged through the Himalayas between China and India going through Lhasa, the Tibetan capital, and the Kathmandu Valley to north India. Once it was established, Chinese pilgrims were able to visit sacred Buddhists sites more easily by following the Himalayan route and avoiding the treacherous Central Asian routes through the Taklamakan Desert. Opening the mountain route greatly stimulated the growth of commercial and cultural interaction in Nepal. The Licchavi Kingdom flourished because of the frequent, rich trade. During his stay in Tibet, Narendradeva learned of the wealth and splendor of China. Once he regained control of his kingdom, he sent a mission to China with gifts and established cordial relations with the Chinese court. Both Nepali and Chinese records refer to their mutual warm relations.

There is documentation of a very peculiar event relating to Narendradeva's rule. A Chinese mission had been attacked in north India while attempting to visit the court of King Harṣvardhana. The king had died and his throne was seized by a usurper named Arjuna. The Chinese ambassador Wang Xuance (Wang Hsüan T'se) and his entourage had been attacked, and many on the mission had been killed. Wang managed to flee to Kathmandu where he found refuge at the Licchavi court. Subsequently, Narendradeva and the king of Tibet, Song-tsen Gampo, sent troops to avenge the wrongful treatment of the Chinese mission. The guilty party was captured with his family and brought to China for retribution. The event sealed the friendship between China and Nepal, and the Chinese government was grateful to Nepal for vindicating China's honor. Having regained Licchavi suzerainty, Narendradeva's kingdom was wealthy, flourishing, and powerful.

By the ninth century C.E., the Licchavi state had begun to disintegrate. The few and fragmentary records that remain from the period indicate that central authority was severely compromised. Feudal lords and the monasteries may have appropriated political power. Some scholars believe that Nepal must have fallen under foreign domination of some sort. Whatever the facts, it is clear that Nepal suffered a decline in power and entered into a dark period in its history for the next two and a half centuries.

SIGNIFICANCE

It is difficult to define the geographical and political boundaries of Nepal during the Licchavi period. During the reign of Mānadeva, the kingdom may have included parts of eastern Assam and West Bengal. There is no doubt that, with the Licchavis, the region entered not only the historical era but also the mainstream of classical South Asian culture with a sophisticated urban society and refined material culture. The region had been largely Buddhist until the Licchavi's introduction of formal Hinduism with its concomitant caste system, temple architecture, and religious texts and rituals.

Brahman priests working for the Licchavis accelerated the process of Sanskritization. In fact, Sanskrit became the courtly and literary language of Nepal and was used exclusively for inscriptions and royal edicts of the time. The Licchavi period is known for its brightly painted multistoried wooden architecture and sculptural achievements. The stone works of the Licchavi period are remarkable for their sophisticated form, elegant proportions, and harmony. Sculptures from the seventh century in particular are the masterpieces that established high artistic standards that influenced artists for centuries to come. It was in the field of governance that the Licchavis made the greatest impact in Nepal because they set a precedent for what thereafter became the standard pattern in which Hindu kings claiming high-caste Indian origin ruled over a population that was neither Indo-Aryan nor Hindu. Nepal today continues to have an ethnically diverse population that is half Hindu and half Buddhist.

—*Katherine Anne Harper*

FURTHER READING

Jha, Hit Narayan. *The Licchavis (of Vaisali)*. Varanasi, India: The Chowkhamba Sanskrit Series Office, 1970. This excellent study considers the two phases of Licchavi history, as rulers of an important kingdom in Vaisali, north India, and later as the first dynasty of the Kathmandu Valley. Reviews Licchavi social, religious, and economic life as well as administrative systems.

Regmi, D. R. *Ancient Nepal*. Calcutta: Firma K. L. Mukhopadhyay, 1960. Overview of early Nepali culture and life as well as the history of the Licchavi Dynasty. Bibliography.

Slusser, Mary Shepherd. *Nepal Mandala: A Cultural Study of the Kathmandu Valley*. Princeton, N.J.: Princeton University Press, 1982. Excellent two-volume treatise that reviews archaeological, inscriptional, and textual evidence to construct a definitive history of Nepal. Bibliography.

SEE ALSO: c. 321 B.C.E., Mauryan Empire Rises in India; c. 200 B.C.E., Birth of Hinduism; c. 100-c. 127 C.E., Kushān Dynasty Expands into India; c. 127-c. 152 C.E., Kanishka's Reign Brings Flowering of the Arts; 220 C.E., Three Kingdoms Period Begins in China.

300-400 C.E.
BANTU PEOPLE INVENT COPPER METALLURGY

The independent invention of copper metallurgy took place among the Bantu people of the Copper Belt of Zambia, in the far southern Congo.

LOCALE: Copper Belt along upper Lualaba River (now in Zambia, far southern Congo)
CATEGORIES: Science and technology; trade and commerce

SUMMARY OF EVENT

The independent invention of copper metallurgy took place among Bantu people in the Lualaba-Upemba region around the fourth century C.E. and had a far-reaching long-term impact on their economic and political institution building. The development of copper mining and smithing appeared in central Africa (present-day Zambia and southern Congo) in the pre-Kisalian (Kamilambian) era. The Kisalian era is defined by the spread of this pottery tradition, created by the ancestral Luba (of Bantu origins), between 600 and 1000 C.E. The early Luba spread toward the southeast beginning as early as 300 C.E., migrating toward the Upemba Depression, south of the Lualaba River. In the process of settling frontier lands, the early Luba incorporated other groups of people into their communities, most prominently Sabi speakers, also of Bantu origins. One consequence of these population movements was the essentially interethnic mixing of communities of people of Bantu heritage with diverse cultural systems and different Bantu languages. The cross-cultural integration that was prominent in the territory around the Lualaba River and the Upemba Depression during this period resulted in new economic, social, and political traditions.

In addition to the cultural and intellectual crosspollination during this period, access to essential resources of copper, salt, and iron—all found in abundance near the Upemba Depression—facilitated the emergence of copper working. Copper in particular is found 325 to 480 miles (200 to 300 kilometers) to the south of the Upemba Depression in what is today referred to as the Copper Belt of Zambia. Copper was being mined and smelted on a limited scale by the fourth century C.E., and after 300 C.E. emerged as a major trade commodity traversing the Lualaba region. By the end of the first millennium, copper became a key symbol of wealth and was typically fashioned into modestly sized *croisettes* that could be used as a currency throughout the region. The small copper crosses are prominent in the Classical Kisalian archaeological record, and their common placement in burial mounds in the hands of the deceased suggests that the crosses were used as a currency for trade. Certainly in later periods it is known that small copper and iron ingots and crosses were used for commercial exchange.

While mining, transport, and smelting copper ore were time-consuming processes, the region's bayous and tributaries provided additional economic activities focused on the waterways. People of the Kisalian era built levees along rivers and tributaries and utilized riverbanks for village cites. The marshlands were used to produce floating farm plots. These communities relied on the importance of copper production and trade as only one segment of the economy. They also controlled their environment to maximize desirable riverbank and stream niches for agriculture and fishing. Riverine villages were somewhat isolated on the wetlands, although there was outward trade in products such as reeds for baskets, mats, and thatching; meat and fish; medicinal products; and other resources desired by nearby communities.

SIGNIFICANCE

Copper production contributed to the accumulation of wealth and creation of stately regalia, as well as providing the first metal currency of central Africa. The early era of copper production was the foundation for the larger-scale economic and political growth that materialized over the next five centuries. The era of copper smelting was the beginning of a new phase in central African history, as skillful metalworking produced both the

means and the incentive for a state apparatus to safeguard accumulated wealth.

In the territories south of the Congo River Basin along the Lualaba River, multifaceted political organization developed between the seventh and ninth centuries C.E. The production of wealth through metalworking allowed for greater social and economic variation and integration, as well as a degree of social stratification. In this period, perhaps for the first time in this region, individual leaders were able to utilize their political power, social status, and economic networks to integrate communities over a broader territorial expanse, beyond the localized kingroup, and as a result political hierarchies emerged. Secondary artisan classes specializing in various crafts and trades emerged to support the production of metal. For example, leatherworking, which produced among other things the bellows essential to the smelting of metals, came into being primarily because of its usefulness in metalworking. Additionally, professional craftpeople who produced mats, baskets, pottery, ivory products, tools, small jewelry such as bangles, and fishhooks increasingly contributed to economic diversification and social stratification. The new artisan professions contributed to the production of material goods representative of wealth and to prosperity and affluence among those who created the items of display.

The most powerful political leaders controlled the economies of the Copper Belt. It seems that the advent of copper increasingly provided the basis for the political hierarchy in the Lualaba-Upemba region. By the Classic Kisalian era, in the twelfth century, central control of the copper, iron, and salt trades were established, and through the collection of tribute the Luba chiefs were able to extract a great deal of wealth. Power was delegated among a hierarchy of subordinate and dependent local chiefs who each acknowledged the king's power through paying tribute in exchange for access to resources in the territory.

Excavation by Pierre de Maret around Lake Kisale in the vicinity of the southeastern edges of the forest reveals that by the eleventh and twelfth centuries there had been a great accumulation of wealth in metal, including the flange-welded bells and ceremonial axes that, in later eras, were central to the pageantry and display of wealth associated with political power. The assumption is that the importance of metal items increased over time and spread into new regions as the smelters of the Copper Belt traded their product more widely. In fact, by the fourteenth century the kingdoms of Malawi, north of the Zambezi Valley between the Shire River and the Indian

Ocean, began to link themselves to the Luba, as recorded in Lunda and Phiri oral traditions. Copper as a currency moved from the Lualaba-Upemba areas of production into Indian Ocean and internal African trade networks throughout the late first millennium into the later half of the second millennium C.E. Thus, the advent of copper smelting in the Upemba region had major long-term and far-reaching political and economic consequences. Copper served as the foundation of economic affluence and political esteem in the second millennium kingdoms and empires of the region.

—*Catherine Cymone Fourshey*

FURTHER READING

Connah, Graham. *African Civilizations: Precolonial Cities and States in Tropical Africa, an Archaeological Perspective*. New York: Cambridge University Press, 1994. A historical account of ancient African towns which draws from archaeological data.

Ehret, Christopher. *The Civilizations of Africa*. Charlottesville: University of Virginia Press, 2002. A text-book survey of Africa before, during, and after the agricultural revolution.

Herbert, Eugenia. *Iron, Gender, and Power: Rituals of Transformation in African Societies*. Bloomington: Indiana University Press, 1993. An analysis of the industry, ceremony, and ideology surrounding Iron Age metalworking in Africa.

_____. *Red Gold of Africa: Copper in Precolonial History and Culture*. Madison: University of Wisconsin Press, 1984. An examination of the mining, trade, and social customs associated with copper production in Africa.

Phillipson, David W. *African Archaeology*. New York: Cambridge University Press, 2000. A survey of African history through archaeological data.

SEE ALSO: c. 1000-c. 700 B.C.E., Mashariki Bantu Establish Chifumbaze Ironworking Culture; c. 400 B.C.E.-c. 300 C.E., Bantu Peoples Spread Farming Across Southern Africa; c. 5th century C.E., Lydenburg Bantus Sculpt Life-Size Terra-cotta Heads.

c. 300-600 C.E.
THREE KINGDOMS PERIOD FORMS KOREAN CULTURE

During the Three Kingdoms Period in Korean history, Buddhism and Confucianism were introduced, and with some influence from China, Koreans developed the foundation for their contemporary culture.

LOCALE: Korean peninsula
CATEGORY: Prehistory and ancient cultures

SUMMARY OF EVENT
The Three Kingdoms Period in Korean history is named for three great kingdoms that emerged in the first century B.C.E., rose to prominence by the third century C.E., and reached their peak in the sixth century, before all of them were unified under one kingdom in the seventh century. Despite the name of this period, there was a fourth region on the Korean peninsula that did not belong to any of the kingdoms at first. This area comprised the Kaya (Gaya) states. It was located in the south central part of the peninsula and wedged between two kingdoms. The kingdoms that define the period are known as the Koguryŏ (Goguryeo), the Paekche (Baekje), and the Silla (Shilla).

The Koguryŏ Kingdom was the largest of the three kingdoms. It extended from the central part of what is now the Republic of Korea (south of the Han River) northward to the Sungari River, today part of China. Its origins are shrouded in old stories of Korea's early history and Chinese colonization of the region by the Han Dynasty in the first century B.C.E. The first royal family was likely named Hae-si, and it had close ties to the Han Chinese. As the royal family's power expanded, so did the Koguryŏ kingdom, finally pushing out the last Chinese colony in 313 C.E. Because of its proximity to and early control by China, the Koguryŏ culture borrowed liberally from Chinese civilization until the collapse of the Han in the third century C.E. China broke up into many kingdoms itself, which allowed the Koguryŏ to form their own civilization without interference. The Koguryŏ were in constant conflict with several groups of people in the region, such as the Puyŏ people and several nomadic groups. This conflict eventually led to moving the Koguryŏ capital southward to P'yŏngyang, and this put pressure on another kingdom on the peninsula: the Paekche Kingdom.

The Paekche Kingdom was situated on the southwest corner of the Korean peninsula. A confederacy of clans called the Chin occupied the southern part of the peninsula until the first century B.C.E., when conflict from the north spilled into the southern region. Puyŏ refugees from the north migrated to the southwest and established the Paekche Dynasty in 18 B.C.E. under the rule of King Onjo. Because of continuing conflict with the Koguryŏ, the Paekche moved their capital several times. They also formed alliances with the Chinese in the lower Yangtze Valley and with the Japanese, mainly the Asuka culture in the southwest. As a result, the Paekche acted as a conduit for the transfer of Chinese culture to Japan. This relationship was formalized in 367 C.E. when diplomats, cultural envoys, and craftspeople were exchanged. Interestingly, the third kingdom did not participate in these exchanges at first.

The Silla Dynasty formed the third kingdom. Their strength began in the walled town of Saro (now called Kyŏngju) during the collapse of the Chin confederacy. The first Silla king was Pak Hyŏkkŏse (r. 57 B.C.E.-4 C.E.). The early years of this dynastic rule were confined mainly to the walled city of Kyŏngju, but by the middle of the third century C.E. their power expanded to the largest part of what is today the southeastern corner of South Korea. In part because of a degree of isolation from Paekche in the early centuries of development, the Silla had little Chinese influence on their culture. This limited isolation was caused by the Kaya states wedged between Silla and Paekche as well as the southern extension of the T'aebaek Mountains. This isolation eventually changed. In 247, the Silla formalized state relations with the Koguryŏ, although this did not prevent the Koguryŏ from making periodic incursions into Silla territory. Moreover, the Paekche also started to put pressure on the Silla's northwest boundary. The combination of these problems with periodic raids by Japanese bands led the Silla to develop a militaristic culture called the *hwarang*, an institution of elite soldiers with a strong sense of chivalry and unquestioned commitment to the king. They were so successful in responding to attacks from all directions that by the middle of the sixth century C.E. they had expanded the Silla Kingdom by absorbing the Kaya states, the northern part of Paekche, and the eastern part of Koguryŏ. In the process, the Silla were exposed to Chinese culture. This had an important impact on their own culture as well as the future of Korea as a whole.

All three of the kingdoms and the loose collection of city-states in Kaya were definable and separate entities from at least the first century C.E. to the middle of the sixth century C.E. The rise of Silla, especially through the *hwarang*, changed the political and cultural conditions of the Korean peninsula for many centuries to come. The Silla had absorbed the Kaya states by 532 C.E., slowly absorbed Paekche between the mid-sixth century and 660 C.E., and finally absorbed the largest part of Koguryŏ by 668 C.E. This date, 668 C.E. heralds a new period in Korean history called the United Silla, contemporaneous with the Tang Dynasty (618-907) of China, with which it had close ties. The United Silla period lasted until 935 and was the golden age of Korean culture and history. It was also the first time that most of the Korean peninsula was under a single, centralized government.

SIGNIFICANCE

The significance of the Three Kingdoms Period in Korean history cannot be underestimated. The foundation of modern Korean culture was formed in the Three Kingdoms. Key elements of Chinese civilization were absorbed during this period. Most important among these were the writing system, ceramics, astronomy, Buddhism, and Confucianism. Later, Korean-style, developments of these elements during the United Silla period and the Koryŏ Dynasty (918-1392) were based largely on Chinese prototypes. For example, Koreans created their own writing system, called *hangul*, in the medieval period but they retained Chinese characters for proper names and calligraphic art. Once Koreans learned the craft of making ceramics, they went on to create their own, highly evolved styles and colors in the later periods. Most famous is Korean celadon. Confucianism slowly seeped into Korean social behavior at this time, but eventually Koreans created their own version, Neo-Confucianism. Buddhism was adopted by the Koguryŏ in 372 C.E., by the Paekche in 384 C.E., and by the Silla in 528 C.E., where, by the time of unification, it became the state religion. Most important, however, is that Korean interpretations of Buddhist texts contributed to the development of Zen Buddhism (called Sŏn in Korean), and the desire to spread Buddhist ideas to as many people as possible led to the development of early woodblock printing, as well as the first metal, movable type nearly two hundred years before Johannes Gutenberg in Europe. The oldest known woodblock print, called the Darani sutra, was found inside the Seokga Pagoda of Bulguksa Temple in Kyŏngju in 1966. It is believed to have been made at the end of the seventh century.

Another reason for the significance of this period is the establishment of a unique sense of Korean history separate from the cultural groups that surrounded the peninsula. The origin stories of the Korean people focus on a heroic progenitor named Tangun Wanggom, who is believed to have lived in the time just before the Three Kingdoms emerged. Many Koreans believe the first king of Koguryŏ was a son of Tangun. Although this belief is most likely based in mythology and legends of the time, its importance in forming a strong sense of Korean identity throughout the ages cannot be dismissed.

—*Carolyn V. Prorok*

FURTHER READING

Adams, Edward B. *Korea's Golden Age: Cultural Spirit of Silla in Kyongju*. Seoul, Korea: Seoul International Publishing House, 1991. Adams shows us the extraordinary cultural development of the Silla in their capital city of Kyŏngju through detailed descriptions and hundreds of photographs. Index.

Covell, J. Carter. *Korea's Cultural Roots*. Elizabeth, N.J.: Hollym International, 1981. Covell presents the ancient roots of Korea's culture through its art work and religious materials. Index.

Il-Yon. *Samguk Yusa: Legends and History of the Three Kingdoms of Ancient Korea*. Translated by Ha Tae-Hung and Grafton K. Mintz. Seoul, Korea: Yonsei University Press, 1986. Il-Yon was a thirteenth cen-

tury Buddhist monk who collected stories and documents from the Three Kingdoms Period. These are collected in this volume. Bibliography and index.

Kim, Duk-Whang. *A History of Religions in Korea*. Seoul, Korea: Daeji Moonhwa-sa, 1990. Kim describes the history and beliefs of the many religious traditions in Korea from ancient times to the current era.

Koo, John H., and Andrew C. Nahm, eds. *An Introduction to Korean Culture*. Elizabeth, N.J.: Hollym International, 2000. Chapter 3 in the history section covers the Three Kingdoms Period, but other relevant material is also to be found in topical sections on Confucianism, Buddhism, literature, and elsewhere. A substantial survey, with index.

SEE ALSO: 6th or 5th century B.C.E., Birth of Buddhism; 479 B.C.E., Confucius's Death Leads to the Creation of *The Analects*; Early 1st century C.E., Pyu Kingdom Develops Urban Culture; c. 470 C.E., Bodhidharma Brings Chan Buddhism to China.

c. 300-710 C.E.
KOFUN PERIOD UNIFIES JAPAN

The Kofun period, named after the keyhole-shaped tomb mounds constructed for the local elite, marked Japan's increased contacts with the continent and its development into a unified state.

LOCALE: Japan
CATEGORY: Prehistory and ancient cultures

SUMMARY OF EVENT

A distinctive funeral custom of burying their elite in large mounded tombs, or *kofun*, appeared in the protohistoric period of Japan, which is known as the Kofun period. The period is traditionally dated from 300 to 710 C.E.; however, research suggests that it may have begun as early as the latter half of the third century and ended in the late seventh century. Some scholars would date the period's end even earlier, in 552, when Buddhism was officially introduced to Japan.

The distribution of *kofun* extends throughout the nation, centering on the Kinai region. Although various shapes of mounded tombs have been discovered, the keyhole-shaped burial mounds, often surrounded by moats, are notable for their enormous scale. Burial mounds had been constructed in Japan since the Paleolithic period.

Square mounds appeared in western Japan early in the Yayoi period (300 B.C.E.-300 C.E.) and spread widely in the main parts of Japan during the middle Yayoi period. Moats have been discovered surrounding square burial mounds at some Yayoi sites. The distinction between the tombs of the Kofun period and earlier tombs lies primarily in the shape of the mound itself. Although a variety of mound shapes were used during the period, keyhole-shaped, mounded tombs are the dominant and defining type of the Kofun period. The significant sociopolitical and cultural meanings behind the construction of these mounds indicate a change in society as well as a change in tomb shape.

Furthermore, the mounded tombs of the Kofun period are an independent and permanent type of burial mound, occupying the space above ground level and recognizable without excavation. In the *kofun* burial, the remains were placed in the top of the mound, unlike the Yayoi custom of burying the dead under it. The *kofun* was also the place where the rites of royal succession were held, in addition to funerary and mortuary rituals. Local rulers were religiously authorized to protect their people's lives by their magical power. The *kofun* therefore symbolizes the highest sociopolitical power and religious or magical power of the times. Thus, its size and shape had to be impressive, and each tomb must have been made for a single ruler.

There are three phases of the Kofun period: Early (the late third to the fourth century), Middle (the end of the fourth to the fifth century), and Late (the sixth to the seventh century). Between the phases, distinct shifts are found in the structure, dimension, number, and location of mounded tombs, burial goods, and *haniwa* (clay cylinders), which were placed over the surface of the mound to divide the sacred space for the dead from the outer world. The changes in these elements reflect Japan's gradual evolution toward a unified state and its close contacts with China and Korea.

The tomb mounds of the Early Kofun period developed from the burial customs of the Late Yayoi, when the deceased were buried on hills, using geographical advantage. The representative keyhole-shaped Kofun period mound was composed of a circular mound joined with a triangular one, creating a keyhole shape when viewed from above. The burial chamber, located near the top of the mound, was closed with ceiling rocks and covered by earth. One of the early tombs, Hashihaka *kofun* in modern-day Nara Prefecture, is dated around the late third or the beginning of the fourth century. It is the oldest massive *kofun* tomb yet discovered, measuring 912 feet (278 meters) in length, and it is often considered to be the origin of that type. It is also the first known tomb of a local great king, suggesting the birth of the Yamato kingdom in the Nara region. The typical burial objects found in tombs of this period, symbolizing the social status of the deceased, include bronze mirrors, ornaments made of jade, jasper, and glass, iron weapons such as swords and knives, and ceramic vessels. Such burial goods do not appear to have been provided in the case of the Hashihaka *kofun*; however, the excavation of specific types of cylindrical and pot-shaped *haniwa*, which were originally developed for ritual use in Okayama Prefecture during the Late Yayoi period, indicates an early date and use of ritual at the tomb.

In the Middle Kofun period, keyhole-shaped mounds spread widely in other parts of Japan. *Kofun* construction reached its peak in number and dimension during this period. By the fifth century, *kofun* construction moved from hillsides to flat land, where the mounds were artificially made out of earth. The moats surrounding the mounds clearly distinguish the burial mounds from other areas. In the Kinki region, *kofun* began to concentrate in the plains of the Ōsaka area. The Daisen *kofun*, also

This haniwa, *a terra-cotta warrior, is typical of the figurines found during the later Kofun period.* (Corbis)

known as the Mausoleum of Emperor Nintoku, is located at Sakai, Ōsaka. Although there is no archaeological basis for the identity of the deceased, the tomb is the largest keyhole-shaped mound, measuring 1,600 feet (486 meters) in length and covering 80 acres (32 hectares). It is surrounded by three moats and accompanied by fifteen smaller tombs in which close relatives and attendants of the deceased were supposedly buried. It is estimated that about twenty thousand *haniwa* were placed on the surface of the mound, and illustrations of the stone chamber, drawn at the time of the mound's collapse in 1872, record some significant burial objects including bronze armor, iron swords, and glass vessels. This huge fifth century tomb manifests the power of the imperial line.

From the latter half of the fifth century, monumental tomb mounds diminished in scale and, at the same time, mounds in clusters appeared. It became popular to abandon pit-shaft-styled stone chambers in favor of tombs

201 - 300 C.E.

881

with a Korean-style corridor leading to the chamber. This suggests that the tombs were being used for multiple burials, such as family burials. Also, a strong military cast to the period becomes clear. The number of horse trappings and military hardware increased in burial goods, and in addition to simple cylindrical *haniwa*, figure *haniwa* in the shapes of warriors and military shields became common. In the Imashirozuka *kofun* in Ōsaka, 113 enormous *haniwa* were placed in a regular, fencelike arrangement, with palace buildings, warriors and shrine maidens, and horses and chickens representing a scene of the central court of the early sixth century. In addition to the military equipment and horse-riding goods, the Sue ware pottery is another indicator of the influx of foreign, especially Korean, culture into Japan during this time. The pottery is often found as offering vessels in the tombs. Unlike Haji ware, which was in continual casual use from the Yayoi period, Sue ware is much more refined. The pottery found in the tombs is identical to Korean vessels, and the technology must have been brought to Japan by Korean immigrants.

Around the end of the sixth century, the keyhole-shaped mounds began to disappear nationwide, suggesting the rapid centralization of Japan. The tombs of the final stage of the Kofun period are replaced by square or round mounds and are often characterized by wall paintings in the chamber. Two especially popular mounds, Takamatsuzuka *kofun* (late seventh century) and Fujinoki *kofun* (late sixth century), both in Nara Prefecture, show strong foreign influences. The designs of cosmology and figures on the wall paintings at Takamatsuzuka suggest a direct link with Chinese and Korean tomb paintings. Elaborate gold openwork crowns and the gilt bronze rear saddle bow at Fujinoki display continental motifs including those of India and Central Asia. The Kofun period ended as the result of the intense influence of continental culture, especially Buddhism and the practice of cremation.

SIGNIFICANCE

The Kofun period is Japan's protohistoric period, bridging the gap between the end of the prehistoric and the opening of the new, historic Japan. The four hundred years during which these tombs were constructed manifest a revolution in sociopolitical structure, during which the nature of Japanese leaders changed from charismatic to political, aiming for the centralization of Japanese government.

—*Yoshiko Kainuma*

FURTHER READING

Aston, W. G. *Nihongi: Chronicles of Japan from the Earliest Times to A.D. 697.* Revised by Terence Barrow. Rutland, Vt.: Tuttle, 1972. A translation of *Nihon Shoki*, an important early chronicle, from the original Chinese and Japanese writing.

Barnes, Gina L. *Protohistoric Yamato: Archaeology of the First Japanese State.* Ann Arbor: University of Michigan Press, 1988. A study of early state emergence in Nara after a long-term social change. Bibliography.

Brown, Delmer M., ed. *Ancient Japan.* Volume 1 in *The Cambridge History of Japan.* New York: Cambridge University Press, 1988. Discusses Japan's radical sociopolitical change between 300 B.C.E. to 784 C.E. Index and glossary.

Kondō, Yoshirō, ed. *Zenpō kō enfun Shūsei.* 6 vols. Tokyo: Yamakawa Shuppansha, 1992-2000. A collection of more than forty-six hundred keyhole-shaped mound tombs. Although written in Japanese, the illustrations are good for technical studies. Bibliography and index.

Pearson, Richard. *Ancient Japan.* New York: George Braziller, 1992. The lavishly illustrated catalog to accompany an exhibit at the Smithsonian Institution. The commentary is intended for nonspecialist readers, and the Kofun period is one of the eras covered.

Piggott, Joan R. *The Emergence of Japanese Kingship.* Stanford, Calif.: Stanford University Press, 1997. Analyzes the political changes of the Kofun period.

SEE ALSO: c. 10,000-c. 300 B.C.E., Jōmon Culture Thrives in Japan; c. 7500 B.C.E., Birth of Shintō; c. 300 B.C.E., Yayoi Period Begins.

4th century C.E.
EZANA EXPANDS AKSUM, LATER CONVERTS TO CHRISTIANITY

Under Ezana's leadership, Aksum became a major power in the ancient world, developing international commercial routes and firmly establishing Christianity in the Ethiopian area.

LOCALE: Aksum (now northern Ethiopia, Eritrea, probably parts of southern Arabia and Sudan)
CATEGORIES: Cultural and intellectual history; religion; trade and commerce

KEY FIGURES
Ezana (c. 303-c. 350 C.E.), king of Aksum, r. c. 320-c. 350 C.E.
Saint Frumentius (fl. fourth century C.E.), first bishop of the Abyssinian church, probably converted Ezana to Christianity

SUMMARY OF EVENT
When Ezana (also known as Ēzānā, Ezanas, Aezana) ruled Aksum, the state was considered to be one of the most powerful empires of the ancient world. The kingdom was named after the city of Aksum, its ceremonial and secular capital. Because Aksumite kings' titles listed many of the regions they ruled, it is known that Ezana controlled or had political bases in an enormous territory that included most of present-day Ethiopia and Eritrea. His titles and the circulation of his coins indicate an Aksumite foothold across the Red Sea in South Arabia. His titular claim to be "king of Kasa" (Kush) suggests suzerainty over the Upper Nile River Valley.

Historical information on Ezana's reign, although incomplete, has been gleaned from studies of coins, references from ancient classical and Christian literature, modern archaeology, and inscriptions. Ezana most likely assumed power sometime in the 320's C.E. A letter addressed to him by Roman emperor Constantius II shows that he was still on the throne c. 350. According to inscriptions, he was the son of Ella Amida (Ella Allada), who was probably his royal predecessor. Based on early Christian writing, it is believed that Ezana succeeded to the kingship as a child and was guided in his minority by his mother, the queen regent. Although it has been suggested that Ezana shared his throne with his brother, contemporary inscriptions on coinage indicate a single ruler. No portraits or personal descriptions of Ezana have been uncovered.

Fourth century C.E. Aksum was a prosperous and sophisticated civilization, noted for its stone buildings and monuments. It had its own language and system of writing. Official inscriptions appeared in two languages and three scripts: Ge'ez (old Ethiopic), written both in its own cursive and South Arabian script, and Greek, the common language of the Hellenized world. The kingdom issued its own coinage. At this time, Aksum occupied an important position in international commerce that incorporated overland trails and Red Sea routes to link the Horn of Africa to the Mediterranean world, the Nile Valley, sub-Saharan Africa, and kingdoms across the Red Sea. Through its major port city of Adulis, the Aksumite kingdom diverted commerce from Meroë and supplanted its western neighbor as the main exporter of African goods such as ivory, animal skins, ebony, gold, tortoise shell, incense, and spices. Imports included pottery, glassware, textiles, silver and gold vessels, iron, and brass.

Achievements of the period—especially military capability, the issuance of coinage, and monumental construction—indicate a consolidation of power rather than a loose political configuration. Ezana's additional title "king of kings" suggests a quasi-federal system of government with the Aksumite monarch ruling over a number of vassal states. Aksum's kings oversaw military operations aimed at pacification, subjugation, and payment of tribute. Descriptions of these royal campaigns were inscribed on stone slabs, which were displayed on the sides of public commemorative thrones or mounted beside major roadways.

Such inscriptions indicate that in the early years of his reign, Ezana undertook a series of military campaigns to reestablish control that perhaps had been challenged during his minority. According to these texts, he suppressed separatist groups one by one. He defeated and relocated the nomadic Beja people. He led a punitive expedition against the Afan who had raided and destroyed an Aksumite trading caravan. The inscriptions generally followed a formula listing the king's credentials, justifications for war, Aksum's diplomatic endeavors to avoid hostilities, details of the war itself, results of the conflict, a credit to the deities, and finally, a warning about vandalism. Although they sometimes mention groups and locations that can no longer be identified, these descriptions of campaigns and spoils provide important glimpses into fourth century C.E. Aksumite culture.

After consolidating his power in the Ethiopian highlands and subjugating neighboring desert cultures, Ezana launched a large-scale expedition against the territories of the Meroitic Empire (Kush) c. 350 C.E. In the second and third centuries, Aksum's westward expansion led to conflicts between these two African rivals. The discovery of fragments from two earlier Aksumite victory inscriptions at the city of Meroë and references to Ezana as "king of Kasu" (Kush) suggest that Aksum had already established suzerainty over its western neighbor sufficient to justify a campaign to maintain authority. The Upper Nile Valley's fertile lands, wealth, and trade routes into the African interior made it a valuable asset. According to Ezana's lengthy victory inscription, the Noba had insulted his ambassadors and refused to submit to Aksumite authority. Although this campaign has been cited as the coup de grâce to the Meroitic Empire, it is noteworthy that the inscription made no actual mention of the kingdom or its rulers. The enemy was described as the Noba. This indicates that Meroë already had been overtaken by this nomadic group and was in decline.

A recent theory suggests that the Ethiopian highlands, rather than the Nile Valley, was the theater of operations against the Noba; it is generally held, however, that Ezana's armies defeated the Noba in former Meroitic territory along the Nile. Although people and place-names are not clearly identifiable, it is believed that after a battle at the confluence of the Nile and Atbara Rivers, Aksumite troops went upstream, where they destroyed the trading cities of Alva and Daro. As some of the remaining Kushites had attempted to block Aksum's advancing forces, Ezana's troops moved downstream to remnant Meroitic territories in central Nubia. The resulting devastation was vividly described: Leaders were killed, and temples and buildings were destroyed.

Of more lasting importance than his territorial expansion was Ezana's conversion to Christianity, c. 333 C.E. Saint Frumentius, a Syrian Christian who rose to a position of influence in the Aksumite court, was involved with the conversion of the local populace and laid the foundation of the region's Christian community. It is likely that Frumentius converted Ezana, but it remains unclear how quickly this was publicly proclaimed. Roman historian Tyrranius Rufinus recounted that Frumentius visited the Alexandrian patriarch Athanasius in the 330's and was appointed Aksum's first bishop. Saint Athanasius of Alexandria later described the Roman emperor Constantius II's unsuccessful attempt c. 356 to enlist Ezana's support against Frumentius in an ecclesiastical dispute. It seems the emperor's request was ignored, as Frumentius is still revered as the founder of the Ethiopian church.

Ezana's conversion to Christianity was indicated by changes in his inscriptions and coinage. Halfway through his reign, the crescent-and-disc symbol of earlier Aksumite religion was replaced by the Christian cross. Whereas early inscriptions were dedicated to traditional gods, with Ezana identified as the son of Mahrem (counterpart to the Greek Ares, god of war), the inscription celebrating victory over the Noba denoted a shift in religious ideas. This monotheistic invocation to the "lord of all," and the "lord of the heavens" suggests that Ezana was by then indebted to a single god and appeared as that god's deputy on earth. As the role of deputy to a single, all-powerful god added significance to the monarch's status, the introduction of monotheism possibly strengthened Ezana's political position. Although many have stressed that this inscription is monotheistic but not unambiguously Christian, it is important to note that the Greek and South Arabian scripts describing Ezana's victory make specific references to Christ.

SIGNIFICANCE

Although Aksum was one of the most powerful empires of its time, its greatness and cultural richness have not been fully considered in accounts of Africa or the ancient world. Aksum was certainly connected to the decline of the Meroitic Empire. The Aksumite kingdom took control of the Red Sea trade and supplanted its western neighbor as the main supplier of African goods. Ezana's campaign has been cited as the official end of the Meroitic Empire as an independent political entity, but Aksum's role in regional commerce had already pushed the Upper Nile Valley into economic decline.

Regardless of Ezana's personal commitment to his new religion, his conversion to Christianity had significant political and cultural implications. It forged links with Christianized Rome, Egypt, and the Byzantine world that were key components of Aksum's commercial prosperity. It also weakened Aksumite links with South Arabia. From the time of Ezana and Frumentius, Christian ideas were tightly woven into the fabric of this area's culture. The city of Aksum came to be venerated as the religious center of Ethiopia, the oldest Christian state in Africa.

—*Cassandra Lee Tellier*

FURTHER READING

Burnstein, Stanley, ed. *Ancient African Civilizations: Kush and Axum*. Princeton, N.J.: Marcus Wiener, 1998. A compilation of primary sources including geographic and ethnographic texts, secular and church histories, inscriptions, and commercial documents. Notes, bibliography, and index.

Marcus, Harold G. *A History of Ethiopia*. Berkeley: University of California Press, 1994. Surveys the history of Ethiopia from prehistory to the present. Maps, bibliography, and index.

Munro-Hay, S. C. *Aksum: An African Civilization of Late Antiquity*. Edinburgh, Scotland: Edinburgh University Press, 1991. A good overall history of Aksum. Bibliography and index.

Munro-Hay, S. C., and B. Juel-Jensen. *Aksumite Coinage*. London: Spink, 1995. Shows how the study of coins reveals historical information.

Phillipson, David W. *Ancient Ethiopia: Aksum—Its Antecedents and Successors*. London: British Museum Press, 1998. Applies recent research to develop understanding of ancient Ethiopia. Notes, bibliography, and index.

SEE ALSO: 450-100 B.C.E., City-State of Yeha Flourishes in the Northern Ethiopian Highlands; 1st century C.E., Kingdom of Aksum Emerges; 3d-5th century C.E., Giant Stelae Are Raised at Aksum; c. 450-500 C.E., Era of the Nine Saints.
RELATED ARTICLE in *Great Lives from History: The Ancient World*: Ezana.

4th-11th centuries C.E.
ANCIENT GHANA EMERGES

Ghana, identified in Arabic historic accounts dating from the ninth to seventeenth centuries C.E. and in archaeological remains, became the first state established in West Africa.

LOCALE: Present-day western Mali and southwestern Mauritania, West Africa
CATEGORY: Government and politics

SUMMARY OF EVENT

The ancient state of Ghana arose in the land-locked Sahel region of western Mali and southwestern Mauritania, West Africa (not in Ghana, the contemporary nation situated on the shores of the Atlantic Ocean farther south, which nonetheless took its name from the ancient empire). Ancient Ghana is important because it was the first West African state-level society, emerging possibly as early as the fourth century C.E. Contrary to earlier suppositions that white Islamic nomads founded the state, it is now generally accepted that Ghana was an indigenous cultural development based on West African antecedents. This fits with the established convention that the rulers of Ghana were a Soninke people. Contemporary speakers of Soninke languages are found in Mali, Mauritania, the Ivory Coast, Guinea-Bissau, Senegal, and Gambia.

Some scholars have suggested that Ghana's location was a crucial factor in the development of its sophisticated state-level organization. The Sahel's name comes from Arabic *sāhil*, "shore." This is the transitional zone of dry scrubland located between the Sahara Desert and the southern tropical forests, and environmental deter-

minism may help to explain the formation and development of the Ghana state in this region. Nehemia Levtzion analyzed the underlying metaphor of the desert as a sand sea and the camel that traverses it as a ship, leading to the towns of the region being seen as comparable to ports. The state arose as the leaders in the towns along trade routes attempted to extend their authority, and thus trade nurtured increasing political organization, and power followed the changing trade routes across the Sahara and throughout the continent.

In addition to extensive trade across the territory, it has also been suggested that microtrade across different ecozones in the Sahel also played a significant role in the development of the region's political cohesion. There is archaeological evidence for local exchange networks operating prior to the far-reaching trans-Saharan ones.

Ancient Ghana was extensively documented in the writings of Arab historians and geographers but has received little archaeological field investigation. The Arabic accounts, dating between c. 800 and 1650 C.E., are of variable quality, since many of them are compilations of rumors and travelers' tales by men who did not actually explore West Africa themselves. For example, Ibn al-Faqīh produced an encyclopedia in approximately 900 C.E. that contained many unacknowledged and unverified stories from earlier writers. His failure to evaluate carefully these implausible tales accounts for his acceptance of the claim that "in the country of Ghāna gold grows in the sand as carrots do, and is plucked at sunrise."

However, a few of these stories probably have some basis in fact. For example, it seems likely that Ghana did control access to gold, since other Arab scholars also mention its presence there, although in more credible contexts. For example, the earliest reference to Ghana presents it as "the land of gold," from the works of al-Fazārī, an Arab geographer whose writings date to the early ninth century, although the original materials are now lost and his words only survive because al-Masʿūdī quoted him many years later. An additional difficulty with the Arabic sources is that documentary references to Ghana may postdate the actual events by many years, which means that the accounts may be blurred by temporal as well as geographical distance.

Because of these problems with the Arabic sources, they cannot be accepted as valid but must be evaluated in combination with other historic documents and with evidence from the physical remains of the ancient settlements. The lack of extensive archaeological research in West Africa makes this difficult, especially because only some of the results from these investigations have been published. For example, the spectacular desert ruins of Koumbi Saleh in southern Mauritania consist of a 109-acre (44-hectare) tell incorporating more than sixty mounds. It was discovered in 1914 and tentatively identified as the remains of the Muslim portion of the early capital of Ghana. Despite many years of archaeological fieldwork, the results have not been made readily available (a few brief reports were published in Senegal). This situation improved in 1997 with the publication of Sophie Berthier's work. However, her analysis concentrates on a single building and its architectural development, rather than on the site as a whole. Radiocarbon dates suggest that Koumbi Saleh flourished between the sixth and eighteenth centuries C.E.

If the identification of Koumbi Saleh with the Ghanaian capital is correct, then some material from the historic annals may prove useful in comprehending the archaeological remains. Nehemia Levtzion and J. F. P. Hopkins, in their 1981 collection *Corpus of Early Arabic Sources for West African History*, offer a description by al-Bakrī, an eleventh century Arab writer:

> The city of Ghāna consists of two towns situated on a plain. One of these towns, which is inhabited by Muslims, is large and possesses twelve mosques. . . . The king's town is 6 miles [10 kilometers] distant. . . . Between these two towns there are continuous habitations. The houses of the inhabitants are of stone and . . . wood. The king has a palace and a number of domed dwellings all surrounded with an enclosure like a city wall.

Al-Bakrī also provided much information concerning local geography and customs. He recounted that the king wore golden jewelry and elaborate clothing and that he was not Muslim but followed a religion characterized by idol worship and the presence of sorcerers. According to his account, the economy of the state included a vast trade in salt, copper, and gold, all of it taxed by the king. Al-Bakrī documented the political power of the empire, controlled by the king's vast army of 200,000 men.

Al-Bakrī also wrote about the burial practices in Ghana, specifically those relating to the kings. This information correlates well with the remains of burial mounds found in Mali, some of which have been excavated. Continuing his description, Al-Bakrī stated that

> when their king dies they construct . . . an enormous dome of . . . wood. Then they bring him on a bed. . . . At his side they place his ornaments, his weapons, and the vessels from which he used to eat and drink. . . . They place there too the men who used to serve his meals. They close the door . . . and cover it with mats and furnishings. Then the people . . . heap earth upon it until it becomes like a big hillock.

Unfortunately, there is inadequate information about how the kings and commoners of Ghana lived and died, and similarly, a lack of data and scholarly consensus concerning the underlying factors for the success and later decline of the Ghana state. Ibn Khaldūn (1332-1406 C.E.), the renowned Arab historian, provides some relevant information, although it is difficult to date the events he reported. He suggests that a group of radical Muslims called the Almoravid emerged as an active military force in the mid-eleventh century and that they played a major role in the collapse of Ghana. He notes that

> the authority of the people of Ghāna waned and their prestige declined as that of the veiled people . . . grew. These extended their domination . . . and pillaged, imposed tribute . . . and converted many of them to Islam. Then the authority of the rulers of Ghāna dwindled away and . . . a neighbouring people . . . subjugated and absorbed them.

SIGNIFICANCE

Ghana was regionally important not only at the time during which it was active but also for many centuries after it collapsed. Many of the political and cultural institutions established by Ghana were adopted and further developed by later West African states, such as Mali and Songhai. Ghana continues to be important as a symbol of indigenous cultural achievement, which is why the name of this ancient kingdom was adopted by the current nation of Ghana.

—*Susan J. Wurtzburg*

FURTHER READING

Berthier, Sophie. *Recherches archéologiques sur la capitale de l'empire de Ghana: Étude d'un secteur d'habitat à Koumbi Saleh, Mauritanie. Campagnes II-III-IV-V (1975-1976)-(1980-1981).* Cambridge Monographs in African Archaeology 41. Oxford, England: Archaeopress, 1997. Although written in French, this is a rich source of maps, drawings, and photographs.

Connah, Graham. *African Civilizations: Precolonial Cities and States in Tropical Africa—An Archaeological Perspective.* New York: Cambridge University Press, 1987. Covers state formation in general. Bibliography and index.

Davidson, Basil. *West Africa Before the Colonial Era: A History to 1850.* New York: Addison Wesley Long-man, 1998. A chapter covers Ghana. Bibliography and index.

Fisher, Humphrey J. "Early Arabic Sources and the Almoravid Conquest of Ghana." *Journal of African History* 23 (1982): 549-560. Extensive review of *Corpus of Early Arabic Sources for West African History* (see below).

Levtzion, Nehemia. *Ancient Ghana and Mali.* Studies in African History 7. London: Methuen, 1973. History of Ghana based primarily on the Arabic sources. Bibliography and index.

Levtzion, Nehemia, and J. F. P. Hopkins, eds. *Corpus of Early Arabic Sources for West African History.* New York: Cambridge University Press, 1981. Hopkins's translations of the original Arabic historic accounts with annotations by both editors.

Shinnie, Margaret. *Ancient African Kingdoms.* London: Edward Arnold, 1965. Early account of Ghana.

SEE ALSO: 1st century C.E., Kingdom of Aksum Emerges; 290-300 C.E., West African Gold First Reaches North Africa.

309-379 C.E.
SHĀPŪR II REIGNS OVER SĀSĀNIAN EMPIRE

Shāpūr II, a warrior king of Persia, expanded the confines and influence of Persia from Syria to Afghanistan and ushered in a lengthy period of cultural and religious growth.

LOCALE: Persia (modern-day Iraq, Iran, and Armenia)
CATEGORIES: Religion; wars, uprisings, and civil unrest; expansion and land acquisition

KEY FIGURES

Shāpūr II (309-379 C.E.), king of Persia, r. 309-379 C.E.
Constantine the Great (c. 272-285 to 337 C.E.), sole emperor of the Roman Empire, r. 324-337 C.E.
Constantius II (317-361 C.E.), sole Roman emperor, r. 353-361 C.E.
Julian the Apostate (331-363 C.E.), Roman emperor, r. 361-363 C.E.

SUMMARY OF EVENT

Shāpūr II was born in 309 C.E., the third son of King Hormizd II and a Jewish mother. According to legend, his father died before he was born and he was pronounced king while still in the womb. Persian matters of state reverted to a regency in the form of the Council of Nobles headed by Shahroy, an elder councilor, until 325 C.E. Shāpūr assumed his throne at the age of sixteen, becoming the tenth monarch of the vigorous Sāsānian Empire; he would later be counted among its most successful.

From the onset, Shāpūr II proved adept at military affairs and led successful forays against Arab marauders advancing from the south. He subsequently seized the initiative by collecting forces and a fleet near the Gulf of Hormuz and driving deeply into the Arabian peninsula. The Persians proved completely victorious, and the king paraded his captives in an impressive triumph held at Ctesiphon. However, relations with the neighboring Roman Empire remained tense and deteriorated over religious issues. Constantine the Great reached an accord with Christians at the Council of Nicaea in 325 C.E. and granted that creed both official recognition and tolerance. Christianity had long flourished in Persia, but Shāpūr, mindful of a potential fifth column in his kingdom, began systematically converting its adherents to Zoroastrianism. Tensions increased further in 337 C.E., when Shāpūr's half brother, Hormazd, fled to Constantinople seeking Roman protection. Sensing the inevitabil-

MAJOR RULERS OF THE LATER SĀSĀNIAN EMPIRE, 309-651 C.E.	
Ruler	**Reign**
Shāpūr II	309-379
Kavadh I	488-531
Khosrow I	531-579
Khosrow II	590-628
Yazdgard III	633-651

ity of conflict, the king suddenly renounced the forty-one-year-old peace treaty between Persia and Rome and invaded Mesopotamia that same year. He intended to recapture all the land lost to Rome during the previous century.

In 338 C.E., Shāpūr commenced his long conflict with Rome by attacking numerous fortifications across the Tigris River. The Persians stormed several smaller positions but failed to take the commercial metropolis of Nisibis (now Nusaybin, Turkey) after three costly sieges. Shāpūr was nonetheless aided by the fact that Constantine the Great had died the previous year and his successor, Constantius II, was preoccupied with civil wars and Germanic invaders. The king accordingly wheeled his forces north into Armenia in 341 C.E., conquered the province, and appointed his ally, Arsaces, as king. The Romans could not mount an effective response until 348 C.E., when Constantius II arrived and personally directed an invasion of Persia. This offensive came to grief that year amid the hills of Singara when Shāpūr, feigning defeat, attacked the unsuspecting Roman camp at night and drove off the confused enemy. This victory temporarily secured his left flank, and the king hurried off to the northeast to confront an invading horde of Scythians. The Persians were hard-pressed to cope with their hit-and-run guerrilla tactics, and seven years lapsed before the nomads were subdued and incorporated into the expanding Sāsānian Empire.

In 359 C.E., Shāpūr returned to the west, eager to retry conclusions with Rome. Between 359 and 360 C.E., he successfully besieged and took the fortified cities of Amida (now Diyarbakir, Turkey), Singara, and Edessa (now Urfa, Turkey). Constantius II, aged and infirm, dispatched envoys seeking peace, but Shāpūr's intention was no less than to reconstitute the ancient Persian empire. It fell on Constantius II's successor, the energetic emperor Julian the Apostate, to renew the struggle on Rome's behalf. Through the winter of 362 C.E., he

amassed a huge army of ninety-five thousand men, including a fleet of warships and supply ships, and began systematically advancing down the Euphrates River. The Romans expertly brushed aside Persian resistance and defeated Shāpūr's army beneath the walls of Ctesiphon in June, 363. The king then hastily withdrew, but Julian decided he lacked the manpower for a formal siege and likewise retreated before the onset of winter. Shāpūr then suddenly turned on his antagonists and doggedly harassed his fleeing columns. When Julian was killed in a minor skirmish on June 26, 363 C.E., command passed to his senior general Jovian, who sought peace talks. Shāpūr imposed a humiliating treaty on Jovian, which secured five additional provinces east of the Tigris River and a thirty-year truce. The episode was thoroughly humiliating to Rome's military prestige and confirmed Shāpūr's reputation as a skilled commander and negotiator.

For the remainder of his long reign, Shāpūr was occupied with securing his northern flank in Armenia. Arsaces, whom he had placed on the throne, changed sides and joined the Romans until a successful Persian invasion deposed him in 370 C.E. However, Shāpūr's policy of forced conversions incited resistance and allowed Roman influence to reassert itself. A five-year impasse ensued before the disputed province was divided between Rome and Persia.

Domestically, Shāpūr's reign coincided with a great cultural and religious flowering throughout the kingdom. Persian art, coinage, and sculpture had become particularly ornate and imparted influence throughout the Middle East as far as India. Zoroastrianism also flourished as a state religion and was accompanied by the persecution of Christians as official policy. However, Shāpūr proved more hospitable to the Jewish community residing in Babylon, from which his mother probably originated. He also rebuilt the ancient city of Susa, founded a new commercial center at Nishapur (now Neyshābūr, Iran), and left the Sāsānian Empire on a much sounder footing than when he had assumed the throne. The empire endured for another three centuries.

SIGNIFICANCE

Shāpūr II ruled the Sāsānian Empire for seventy years and outlasted the eight Roman emperors with whom he dealt. By the time he died in 379 C.E., the Sāsānian Empire was at its height and stretched more than two thousand miles (thirty-two hundred kilometers) from Syria to India. Persia also reaped the profits of controlling the fabled Silk Road between China and the West.

The Sāsānian Empire was the last great Persian monarchy before the advent of Islam. It arose following the overthrow of the Parthian Empire, to which Persia was a vassal state, by Ardashīr I in 226 C.E. His son Shāpūr I initiated a long and costly war against the Roman Empire that culminated in the capture of Emperor Valerian in 260 C.E. and recognition of Sāsānian conquests. The process was further abetted by his grandson, Shāpūr II, who also reduced Roman influence in Armenia and the Middle East. His relentless wars with Rome, and the numerous battles this incurred, drained the Roman Empire of valuable men and resources. His reign can be considered a significant factor in the Roman Empire's weakening and eventual overthrow.

The Eastern Roman Empire's successor, Byzantium, fought the Sāsānians to a standstill for three centuries. The triumph of Emperor Heraclius over Khosrow II (r. 590-628 C.E.) ultimately and fatally weakened the Persian Empire after 628 C.E. Within two decades, the onslaught of Islam from the south proved irresistible, and in 651, the last Sāsānian king, Yazdgard III (r. 633-651 C.E.), died a fugitive in Ctesiphon. Nonetheless, the Sāsānian Dynasty made Persia a leading power in the Middle East and exerted great influence from Syria to Afghanistan and from the Persian Gulf to the Black Sea.

—*John C. Fredriksen*

FURTHER READING

The Cambridge History of Iran. 7 vols. New York: Cambridge University Press, 1968-1991. Volume 3, edited by Ehsan Yarshater, is an extremely erudite account of Shāpūr II's time with great emphasis on primary evidence. Numerous maps, bibliography, and index.

Dodgeon, Michael H., Samuel N. C. Lieu, and Geoffrey Greatrex, eds. *The Roman Eastern Frontier and the Persian Wars.* 2 vols. London: Routledge, 1991-2000. Indispensable collection of period documents and early narrative historical accounts covering Shāpūr II's entire reign.

Neusner, Jacob. *Judaism, Christianity, and Zoroastrianism in Talmudic Babylonia.* Lanham, Md.: University Press of America, 1986. An important narrative of the interaction between three prevalent creeds in ancient times and their political ramifications.

Nicolle, David. *Sassanian Armies: The Iran Empire Early Third to Mid-Seventh Centuries A.D.* Stockport, England: Montvert, 1996. A useful overview of military considerations, replete with excellent color illustrations.

Stark, Freya. *Rome on the Euphrates: The Story of a Frontier.* New York: Harcourt, Brace, and World, 1967. Somewhat dated but still a useful introduction to problems faced by Rome while containing Persia by force.

Tafazzoli, Ahmad. *Sāsānian Society.* New York: Bibliotheca Persica Press, 2000. A brief but very scholarly account of societal classes, including the warrior-aristocrats that formed the bulk of Shāpūr II's army.

Wilcox, Peter. *Parthians and Sassanid Persians.* London: Osprey, 1986. A useful introductory survey of military considerations accompanied by color uniform plates.

SEE ALSO: c. 600 B.C.E., Appearance of Zoroastrian Ditheism; 245-140 B.C.E., Rise of Parthia; 95-69 B.C.E., Armenian Empire Reaches Its Peak Under Tigranes the Great; 224 C.E., Ardashīr I Establishes the Sāsānian Empire; October 28, 312 C.E., Conversion of Constantine to Christianity.

RELATED ARTICLES in *Great Lives from History: The Ancient World*: Constantine the Great; Shāpūr II; Zoroaster.

October 28, 312 C.E.
CONVERSION OF CONSTANTINE TO CHRISTIANITY

The conversion of Constantine marked the emergence of Christianity as the dominant religion of the slowly disintegrating Roman Empire, a development that led to the creation of a common European culture.

LOCALE: Milvian Bridge, a few miles north of Rome (now in Italy)

CATEGORIES: Religion; government and politics

KEY FIGURES

Constantine the Great (c. 272-285 to 337 C.E.), sole emperor of the Roman Empire, r. 324-337 C.E.

Maxentius (d. 312 C.E.), self-proclaimed Roman emperor, r. 306-312 C.E.

Licinius (mid-third century-325 C.E.), Roman emperor, r. 308-324 C.E.

SUMMARY OF EVENT

By the end of the third century C.E., the Roman Empire was politically and religiously divided and in decline. Diocletian, one of the claimants to the title of Roman emperor, in an attempt to create religious and cultural unity, issued a series of decrees beginning in 303 C.E. against Christianity. The decrees included instructions to burn churches, destroy copies of the Scripture, and eventually to murder Christians themselves. After the abdication of Diocletian in 305, at least eight rivals emerged to claim the imperial title. By 312, only four remained: Maxentius and Maximinus Daia were aligned against Constantine and Licinius and continued the policy of encouraging religious unity by persecuting Christians. After Constantine defeated Maxentius at the Battle of Milvian Bridge (312) and Licinius conquered Maximinus Daia, the two

Constantine (seated). (Library of Congress)

victors divided the Roman Empire between them. The division lasted for ten years until Constantine defeated Licinius in 324 and became sole ruler.

At noon on the day before the battle against Maxentius at Milvian Bridge, Constantine, according to Eusebius of Caesarea's *Vita Constantini* (339 C.E.; *Life of Constantine*, 1845), saw a sign appearing in the sky as a fiery cross with the legend: "Conquer by this." The same night, the Christian God allegedly appeared to him in a dream and instructed him to place the Christian emblem on the imperial standards if he wished to be victorious. Eusebius claims that he heard the story from the lips of Constantine, but he wrote after the emperor's death and he does not tell the same tale in his *Historia ecclesiastica* (c. 300, 324 C.E.; *Ecclesiastical History*, 1576-1577, better known as Eusebius's *Church History*). At the head of his legions, Constantine placed the *labarum* displaying the first two letters of the word "Christ" in Greek, combined to form a cross. Subsequent victory against Maxentius convinced Constantine that the Christian God was more powerful than the classical deities worshiped by his rivals. Clearly Constantine was taking a risk because only about one-tenth of the Roman Empire was Christian at the time.

Whether the emperor's conversion was contrived or genuine is still a matter of debate, but there can be no doubt that his rule was beneficial for Christianity. In 313 C.E., Licinius agreed on the terms of the Edict of Milan, which granted toleration to Christianity, reimbursed Christians for losses suffered in recent persecutions, and exempted the clergy from certain compulsory civil obligations. Although the edict continued to provide support for the continuance of traditional forms of Roman religion and simply affirmed toleration of Christianity, subsequent legislation certainly provided Christianity with a favored status. In 315, Constantine enacted legislation that prohibited retribution against Jewish converts to Christianity, and in 318, the emperor ordained, in a precedent-making decree, that a civil suit might, with the consent of both litigants, be removed to the jurisdiction of a bishop, whose verdict would be final. By 321, the Church could inherit property, and bishops could manumit slaves. Sunday was declared a holiday for imperial employees. By convening councils at Arles and Nicaea, Constantine set up ecclesiastical machinery for the adjudication of problems caused by dissenting groups such as Donatists and Arians. At the first ecumenical council, the emperor himself put his prestige behind the *homoousian* formula (the idea that Jesus Christ, the Son, had the same essence or substance as the Father, or God), which has re-

ROMAN EMPERORS FROM CONSTANTINE THE GREAT TO THEODOSIUS THE GREAT, 306-395 C.E.	
Ruler	*Reign*
Constantine the Great (East)	306-337
Licinius (East)	308-324
Constantine the Great (all)	324-337
Constantine II (West)	337-340
Constans I (West)	337-350
Constantius II (East)	337-361
Magnentius (West, usurper)	350-353
Julian (all)	361-363
Jovian (all)	363-364
Valentinian I (West)	364-375
Valens (East)	364-378
Procopius (East)	365-366
Gratian (West)	375-383
Valentinian II (West)	375-392
Theodosius I (all)	379-395

mained Christian dogma ever since. Associating his Christian piety with the welfare of the state, Constantine built basilicas, composed prayers, and paid for translations of the Christian Scriptures. Finally, he was baptized on his deathbed by Eusebius, bishop of Nicomedia.

SIGNIFICANCE

Christianity's sudden change in fortune from a persecuted, outlawed sect to a tolerated and favored religion posed special problems. Christianity's strong commitment to pacifism and its status as a religion of the lower classes were both significantly modified. The attitude of the Church toward the Roman Empire also underwent a drastic change. The seventeenth chapter of Revelation, probably written at the end of the first century C.E., is generally supposed to refer to Rome when it speaks of the woman "drunk with the blood of saints," but Eusebius of Caesarea now saw the emperor as the vice-regent of God. Nevertheless, the dilemma had to be faced concerning where jurisdictional lines should be drawn between church and the state. Because Christians enjoyed political preferment in the imperial government after the conversion of Constantine, the Church in the fourth century was inundated with large numbers of half-convinced pagans. This mixed blessing led to early reform movements in the Church and the institution of monasticism.

The favored position of Christianity in the Roman Empire also led to a different interpretation of history.

Whereas Christians during the persecutions had looked for the immediate return of Christ and the establishment of the new Jerusalem to replace the vicious rule of Rome, it now appeared that the golden age had dawned. Eusebius saw in Constantine the fulfillment of God's promises to his chosen people through Abraham. Such a sanguine view of the state remained typically eastern; in the West, the view that became dominant was dualist in nature, seeing a constant tension between church and state.

Clearly the conversion of Constantine was a turning point in imperial and Christian history, which ultimately affected the entire Western world. Historians have variously interpreted the sincerity of Constantine's change of heart. One view holds that his conversion was motivated by political expediency so that he might use the Church for purposes of state. The opposite position maintains that Constantine's acts can be explained only in the light of a genuine change of heart and full conversion. A mediating position attempts to postulate a gradual change in the emperor from that of a deistic humanitarian trying to integrate Christianity with the current paganism, to one of nominal conversion by the time of his death. It should be noted that Constantine was known to place for placing great significance on dreams and visions, and one legend reports an earlier experience in which Constantine adopted Apollo as his god because of a promise that he would prosper in Apollo's name. It is noteworthy that Apollo was linked to the Sun god, a form of monotheistic faith that Constantine seems to have adopted, perhaps preparing the ground for his conversion to Christianity, also a monotheistic religion.

— *Carl A. Volz, updated by Charles L. Kammer III*

FURTHER READING

Elliott, T. G. *The Christianity of Constantine the Great.* Scranton, Pa.: University of Scranton Press, 1996. An examination of Constantine's conversion and his attitude toward Christianity.

Eusebius. *Life of Constantine.* Oxford, England: Clarendon Press and Oxford University Press, 1999. A translation of Eusebius of Caesarea's account of Constantine's life. Introduction, translation, and commentary by Averil Cameron and Stuart G. Hall.

Grant, Michael. *Constantine the Great: The Man and His Times.* New York: Maxwell Macmillan International, 1994. Focuses especially on the complex religious policies and personal development of Constantine.

Kousoulas, D. George. *The Life and Times of Constantine the Great: The First Christian Emperor.* Danbury, Conn.: Rutledge Books, 1997. A biography of Constantine the Great that focuses on his role as a converted Christian.

Lieu, Samuel N. C., and Dominic Montserrat, eds. *Constantine: History, Historiography, and Legend.* New York: Routledge, 1998. An examination of Constantine's life that attempts to differentiate between legend and history.

Pohlsander, Hans A. *The Emperor Constantine.* New York: Routledge, 1996. A biography of Constantine that examines his role as Roman emperor.

Reuver, Marc. *Requiem for Constantine: A Vision of the Future of Church and State in the West.* Kampen, the Netherlands: Kok, 1996. Reuver examines Constantine the Great's role in the establishment of relations between church and state.

SEE ALSO: 64-67 C.E., Nero Persecutes the Christians; c. 110 C.E., Trajan Adopts Anti-Christian Religious Policy; 250 C.E., Outbreak of the Decian Persecution; 313-395 C.E., Inception of Church-State Problem; 325 C.E., Adoption of the Nicene Creed; 380-392 C.E., Theodosius's Edicts Promote Christian Orthodoxy.

RELATED ARTICLES in *Great Lives from History: The Ancient World*: Constantine the Great; Diocletian; Eusebius of Caesarea.

313-395 C.E.
INCEPTION OF CHURCH-STATE PROBLEM

The church-state problem developed from conflicting interpretations of the relationship between the organized church and civil government concerning the extent of their powers within each other's sphere of activity.

LOCALE: Roman Empire
CATEGORIES: Government and politics; religion

KEY FIGURES

Constantine the Great (c. 272-285 to 337 C.E.), sole emperor of the Roman Empire, r. 324-337 C.E.

Constantius II (317-361 C.E.), son of Constantine and emperor of the Eastern Roman Empire, r. 337-353 C.E., sole Roman emperor, r. 353-361 C.E.

Constans I (c. 323-350 C.E.), son of Constantine and emperor of the Western Roman Empire, r. 337-350 C.E.

Saint Athanasius of Alexandria (c. 293-373 C.E.), bishop of Alexandria, 328-373 C.E.

Saint Ambrose (c. 339-397 C.E.), bishop of Milan, 374-397 C.E.

Gratian (359-383 C.E.), emperor of the Western Roman Empire, r. 375-383 C.E.

Theodosius the Great (346/347-395 C.E.), emperor of the Eastern Roman Empire, r. 379-395 C.E., sole Roman emperor, 393-395 C.E.

Saint Augustine (354-430 C.E.), bishop of Hippo, 396-430 C.E.

SUMMARY OF EVENT

The phrase "church and state" represents a framework for understanding how religion and politics are related when both institutions are allowed to make formal jurisdictional claims within the same society. Historians have recognized that church and state have managed to coexist in three basic ways: totally detached, distinguished but not necessarily separated from each other, and joined together as one. Since the time of the Roman Empire, Christian theology has swung back and forth between viewing the Church as supreme, with the state merely a vassal of the Church, to viewing the state as supreme, with the Church purely a spiritual power. Most societies exist with a mutually dependent church and state, as in the United States, in which church-state issues have centered on the U.S. Constitution and its First Amendment freedom of religion clause, interpreted by a large body of constitutional law.

The inception of church-state problems occurred with the organization of the early Christian Church within the Roman Empire and its recognition of the existence and legality of the state by praying for the good of the state and its magistrates. The empire, however, did not begin to acknowledge the legality or authority of the Church until the Edict of Milan in 313 C.E., which gave official recognition to the Christian religion. Before the edict, there was essentially no common ground of acknowledgment on which conflicts of jurisdiction could be settled or even discussed. Thus, the persecuted Church enjoyed considerable early freedom in its doctrinal formulations and other functions mainly because Rome denied its legal existence. The coming age of toleration made it evident that both church and state would soon find it necessary to define the limits of their respective boundaries. During the fourth century C.E., some church fathers adopted the stance that the two institutions should remain fundamentally separate, particularly in matters of faith. Others developed the opinion that the Church should be subject to the state, assuming that the major state religion was Christianity.

One controversial issue that emerged as organized Christianity developed within the Roman Empire involved the emperor's title and influence as *pontifex maximus*. Beginning in 12 B.C.E., Roman emperors claimed this position with authority over all religious activities within the Roman Empire. When Christianity was recognized as the official state religion under Theodosius the Great, controversy developed as to whether Christianity should and could be governed by the same public laws as the earlier pagan cults. Before Christianity, Roman emperors and other secular rulers held religious and civil authority either in a priestly role as intermediaries between people and gods, or as actual gods themselves.

The inception of church-state problems was furthered by the teaching of the church and state as dual authorities, known as the two swords doctrine, and the activities of Constantine the Great, the first public leader to convert to Christianity. Tradition relates that Constantine became converted when he saw a vision of a cross in the sky on which were written the words "By this sign, thou shalt conquer." The dualistic view advanced by Constantine actually began much earlier with the Jewish nation, which was forced to submit to conquerors from Egypt, Assyria, Babylon, Medeo-Persia, and Greece but man-

Saint Athanasius of Alexandria, who favored a separation of church and state. (Library of Congress)

aged to retain an independent religious identity and thus a separation between spiritual and worldly matters.

Growing out of Judaism, Christianity preserved this distinction in the words of Jesus Christ recorded in the book of Saint Matthew, "Render to Caesar the things that are Caesar's, and to God the things that are God's." Constantine assisted the new state religion not only by convening councils and actively supporting its propaganda but also by threatening heretics and implementing social restrictions against them. Constantine did not aspire to act as head of the Church, and he disclaimed any rights to define dogma or judge bishops in matters of the Christian faith. Under Constantine's leadership, church and state first recognized each other as legal and independent institutions, clearly setting the stage for later jurisdictional conflicts. After Constantine's death, the Roman Empire was divided among his three sons, Constantine II,

Constantius II, and Constans I, which served to create three weak governments out of one relatively strong one.

Strife between church and state became inevitable when Constantius II sought to assume numerous controversial ecclesiastical prerogatives that his father, Constantine, had not attempted to claim. One notable example is that Constantius II sought to impose an Arian creed on all bishops, quickly bringing the protest of several Western clerics. The basis for Constantius's attempts at controlling Christianity was derived from the same constitutional rules that previously had placed paganism under imperial control. The Arian incident resulted in conclusions from Saint Athanasius of Alexandria, Hilary, and Saint Ambrose that only a true and complete separation of church and state would avert further conflict. Problems initiated by church-state issues became more volatile with a trend toward Church leaders resisting the emperor's authority in the spiritual domain, while allowing him more extensive jurisdiction in civil matters. The duties of defending and propagating the Christian faith and of taking disciplinary action against paganism were included under imperial authority and later began to be expected by the Church.

After Gratian became the first Roman emperor to refuse the title of *pontifex maximus*, future Christian emperors claimed their right to authority over the Church by saying that their office was conferred directly by God for the welfare of the Church. With decrees by Gratian and Theodosius making the empire legally Christian, the relationship between church and state became more confrontational, with intense disagreements between Bishop Ambrose and Emperor Theodosius. The theology of fourth century fathers, such as Athanasius, Hilary, and Ambrose, rejected the attempt to unite Church and Roman Empire within one institution but sought independent juristic existence, as long as the empire continued to guarantee the Church's integrity.

SIGNIFICANCE

The principle of separation between church and state became well established in the Western Roman Empire by the end of the fourth century C.E., but the Christian Church in the Eastern Roman Empire still looked to the emperor for guidance and approval in Church matters. The Western tradition of separation between the two powers was bequeathed to the medieval Church largely through Saint Augustine's *De civitate Dei* (413-427 C.E.; *The City of God*, 1610). Augustine considered all earthly governments, regardless of their form, as representative of the fallen and imperfect "city of man." Under his theology, the state was necessary to provide the "sword" to discipline fallen humankind through law and education. Augustine's church represented the perfect and eternal "city of God" set up to preserve the divine values of peace, hope, and charity. Church and state were separate in that they occupied different realms and held different values but remained very much related. Gelasius, pope in the late fifth century, laid down many of Augustine's principles for separate spiritual and temporal jurisdiction.

With the fall of the Roman Empire in 476 C.E., the Church gained enormous political and administrative power as it had become the main source of educated leaders. Charlemagne, Frankish emperor from 800 to 814 who greatly influenced Western civilization during the early Middle Ages, sought to subordinate ecclesiastical power and advance an independent secular state by personally appointing bishops and requiring political allegiance from them. Pope Gregory VII attempted to reverse Charlemagne's trend and excommunicated Emperor Henry IV for his resistance. The Protestant Reformation, begun by Martin Luther in 1520, replaced the medieval doctrine of two swords with the doctrine of the sovereign state, under which the Church was clearly subordinated to secular authority in worldly matters.

—*Daniel G. Graetzer*

Further Reading

Barnes, Timothy David. *Athanasius and Constantius: Theology and Politics in the Constantinian Empire.* Cambridge, Mass.: Harvard University Press, 1993. An examination of church and state in the time of Constantine the Great and Saint Athanasius. Bibliography and indexes.

Ferguson, Everett, ed. *Church and State in the Early Church.* Studies in Early Christianity 7. New York: Garland, 1993. A collection of articles, published 1935-1987, on church and state in the Roman Empire.

Free, Katherine B., ed. *The Formulation of Christianity by Conflict Through the Ages.* Lewiston, N.Y.: Edwin Mellen Press, 1995. A collection of papers delivered at a conference held at Loyola Marymount University, Los Angeles, in 1993 on early Christianity and its relations with the state.

Keresztes, Paul. *Imperial Rome and the Christians.* 2 vols. Lanham, Md.: University Press of America, 1989. An examination of the relationship between the Roman Empire and the Christian Church, from Herod the Great to Constantine the Great. Bibliography and indexes.

O'Grady, Desmond. *Beyond the Empire: Rome and the Church from Constantine to Charlemagne.* New York: Crossroad, 2001. An examination of how the Church shaped the role that Rome played in Western civilization.

Picket, H. W., ed. *Aspects of the Fourth Century A.D.: Proceedings of the Symposium Power and Possession.* Leiden, the Netherlands: AGAPE, 1997. A collection of essays from the symposium held by the debating society AGAPE in 1993. Centers on the Church in the fourth century C.E. and its relations to the state and society.

Rahner, Hugo. *Church and State in Early Christianity.* San Francisco: Ignatius Press, 1992. An analysis of how church and state interacted in the early history of the Church.

See also: c. 30 C.E., Condemnation and Crucifixion of Jesus Christ; January-March, 55 or 56 C.E., Paul Writes His Letter to the Romans; 64-67 C.E., Nero Persecutes the Christians; c. 110 C.E., Trajan Adopts Anti-Christian Religious Policy; 250 C.E., Outbreak of the Decian Persecution; October 28, 312 C.E., Conversion of Constantine to Christianity; 361-363 C.E., Failure of Julian's Pagan Revival; 380-392 C.E., Theodosius's Edicts Promote Christian Orthodoxy; 413-427 C.E., Saint Augustine Writes *The City of God.*

Related articles in *Great Lives from History: The Ancient World*: Saint Ambrose; Saint Athanasius of Alexandria; Saint Augustine; Constantine the Great; Theodosius the Great.

316 C.E.
WESTERN JIN DYNASTY FALLS

After the fall of the Western Jin Dynasty in 316 C.E., China experienced more than two hundred years of turmoil, political division, and a series of weak, short-lived dynasties.

LOCALE: China
CATEGORIES: Wars, uprisings, and civil unrest; government and politics

KEY FIGURES

Sima Yan (Ssu-ma Yen; d. 290 C.E.), founded the Jin Dynasty in 265 C.E., which fell into civil war after his death

Liu Yuan (Liu Yüan; d. 310 C.E.), self-proclaimed emperor of the Han Dynasty whose invasion of Western Jin began more than two hundred years of turmoil in China, including short-lived dynasties

SUMMARY OF EVENT

Toward the end of the Han Dynasty (206 B.C.E.-220 C.E.), it was almost overthrown by the rebellion of the Yellow Turbans (184-204). After the defeat of the Yellow Turbans, the generals assigned to put down the rebellion were unwilling to give up their power. They became stronger than the emperor and fought among themselves. In the north, the general Cao Cao (Ts'ao Ts'ao) became a dictator; and in 220 C.E., the last Han emperor gave up power to Cao Cao's son, Cao Pei (Ts'ao P'ei), who became the first ruler of the Wei Dynasty (220-265) at the old capital of Luoyang (Lo-yang). Two other military leaders proclaimed themselves emperors, one in the west (the Shu Han Dynasty; 221-263) in present-day Sichuan (Szechwan) Province, and one in the south (the kingdom of Wu; 222-280), in the Yangtze River Valley.

The period of rivalry among these kingdoms is known as the Three Kingdoms Period (220-280 C.E.; also sometimes given as 220-265). None of these kingdoms achieved any great political power or centralized bureaucratic government such as had existed in the Qin (Ch'in) and Han Dynasties. This period of battles, alliances, betrayals, and bloody civil warfare has been romanticized as an age of chivalry in Chinese history and fiction. Events from the period are immortalized in a popular novel by Luo Guanzhong (Lo Kuan-chung) called *San guo zhi yan yi* (fourteenth century C.E.; *San Kuo: Or, Romance of the Three Kingdoms*, 1925, known as *Romance of the Three Kingdoms*).

In 263 C.E., the Wei Dynasty, having the largest population and army, conquered Shu Han. Two years later, Sima Yan, the son of the victorious general, defeated the Wei emperor and founded the Jin Dynasty (later called the Western Jin) in 265. After a naval campaign, the Jin crossed the Yangtze River and defeated the southern Wu Dynasty in 280. The Western Jin Dynasty (Chin; 265-316 C.E.) thus temporarily reunited China, and the central goverment sought to rein in the power of the great landowners and restore feudalism to China.

The Western Jin Dynasty was a brief period of calm, order, and prosperity. It seemed the magnificence of the former Han Dynasty might be revived. However, the Western Jin Dynasty was in a weakened condition. The years of warfare had greatly decreased the population. The rulers could not establish a strong, central imperial government that could maintain power for the emperor and prevent feuding and struggles for power from members of the imperial family.

A system of filling government posts on the basis of character and merit according to the Confucian system (the Nine Rank System) declined to one of filling places according to the rank of one's family. Government therefore became corrupt, and the population suffered from increased taxes and other obligations. Giving out vast holdings of land to the princes only encouraged the princes to form alliances and fight one another for the throne. After Sima Yan's death in 290 C.E., the empire fell into civil war, the Rebellion of the Eight Princes (291-306).

During the second and third centuries C.E., hundreds of thousands of the Xiongnu (Hsiung-nu), ancestors of the Turks and possibly related to the Huns, and other non-Chinese nomadic peoples had been settling inside China south of the Great Wall, as it was easier to absorb them than defend against them. They were often recruited as soldiers but, in general, were poorly treated by the aristocracy.

With the Western Jin Dynasty descending into internal warfare, the danger of having the Xiongnu tribes within China became apparent. The non-Chinese tribal chiefs saw the opportunity for rebellion, and in 304 C.E., the sinified (Chinese-assimilated) king Liu Yuan (Liu Yüan) declared himself emperor of Han and started the conquest and destruction of the north. The year 304 marks the beginning of a long period of chaos and disorder in northern China. The Xiongnu overran the northern capital Luoyang in 311 and Changan (now Xi'an) in 316. The destruction of these capitals ended Chinese rule in the north for centuries. According to the Chinese annals, only one hundred families were left in Changan.

China became divided along north-south lines. The north was ruled by a series of short-lived, non-Chinese dynasties known as the Sixteen Kingdoms of the Five Barbarians (304-439). The south was ruled by a series of native Chinese dynasties, also short-lived. In the south, this led to the Eastern Jin Dynasty (317-420) and the period of the Southern Dynasties (420-588). These native Chinese dynasties, along with the earlier Wu Dynasty (222-280), which all had their capital at Jiankang, are sometimes referred to as the Six Dynasties.

During the period of the Sixteen Kingdoms of the Five Barbarians, the Northern China Plain became a battle ground as a multitude of various barbarian warlords invaded and succeeded each other in establishing a variety of overlapping and short-lived non-Chinese dynasties. The exact ethnicity of all these invading tribes is not clear, but they included Turkish, Tibetan, and Mongol tribes. The people in the countryside defended themselves with forts and their own small armies or sought the protection of great local families. The land saw famine, banditry, and collapse of the economy. Millions of northern Chinese, including the wealthy and high ranking, fled south of the Yangtze River. The survival of Chinese civilization in the north seemed in doubt as rulers lost the sense of public service and indulged in extravagant living.

In the north, the first invasion was by the Xiongnu, who founded the Earlier Zhao Dynasty (Chao; 304-320). The second wave of invaders were the Di (Ti) and Qiang

(Ch'iang), proto-Tibetan tribes from the west. The Di founded the Earlier Qin (Ch'in) Dynasty in 351 and conquered much of the north. However, when they invaded the south in 383, they were defeated, and more than half the army was slaughtered. The collapse of the Earlier Qin led to the rise of numerous states that fought among themselves for mastery over northern China. The third and longest-lasting invasion was the Turkish or Mongol Toba (T'o-pa) tribe, who destroyed all their rivals and tried to establish control over the peasants; once more the north was unified under the Northern Wei Dynasty (386-534).

All these invading tribes faced the same problem, whether to maintain their own tribal customs or adopt Chinese culture (become sinified) in order to rule. Most tribes had been somewhat sinified before their rise to power, so the states they set up were part barbarian, part Chinese. The nomadic rulers set up military aristocracies that formed the core of the military. Because they did not have the experience or institutions to rule large agricultural territories whose population greatly outnumbered their own, they adopted traditional Chinese methods of government. Thus, much of the governing was done by the literate, established Chinese families.

In the south, at Jiankang (Chien-k'ang), now modern Nanjing (Nanking), local leaders set up a surviving Jin prince on the throne at the head of a court of the emigre aristocrats from the north. This first Eastern Jin Dynasty (317-420) was toppled in 420 by Liu Yu (Liu Yü), one of the generals who founded the Liu-Song Dynasty (Liu-Sung; 420-479), the first of the Southern Dynasties. Founded by generals who were unable to create long-lasting imperial institutions and consolidate power, these dynasties were short-lived.

SIGNIFICANCE

The Western Jin Dynasty was a brief period of stability and prosperity. Internal squabbling led to the breakup of the Western Jin. After the fall of the Jin, China was plunged into more than two hundred years of turmoil, political division, and weak governments. Waves of nonnative tribes invaded the north, and China was divided along north-south lines. The two regions, greatly different in geography and climate, developed cultural differences and attitudes toward each other, which often survive today. The north was ruled by a series of barbarian, non-Chinese dynasties, while the south was ruled by a series of native Chinese dynasties, also short-lived. The south became the most important location for the preserving of Chinese culture for more than 250 years.

EMPERORS OF THE EASTERN JIN DYNASTY, 317-420 C.E.

Ruler	Reign
Yuandi	317-322
Mingdi	323-325
Chengdi	325-342
Kangdi	343-344
Mudi	345-361
Aidi	362-365
Hai Xi Gong (Di Yi)	366-370
Jian Wendi	371-372
Xiao Wudi	373-396
Andi	397-418
Gongdi	419-420

301 - 400 C.E.

Life for the people was hard during this time. Transportation, communication, and commerce fell apart. Instead of a monetary system, the economy turned to a barter system, which usually means a fall in the standard of living. Social stratification increased, with the populace at the bottom increasingly falling into bondage or servitude. Belief in the Confucian view of order declined, and people of all stations of life took solace in new religions such as Buddhism (introduced by the nomadic invaders) and new Daoist cults, which promised salvation and transcendence from worldly turmoil.

Traditional Chinese civilization survived in the Southern Dynasties, and China was reunified again in 581 with its culture largely intact, though now with the influences of the nomads and Buddhism.

—*Thomas McGeary*

FURTHER READING

Ebrey, Patricia B. *The Cambridge Illustrated History of China.* New York: Cambridge University Press, 1996. Presents a brief account of the period but contains good maps, illustrations, coverage of the arts and culture of the period, and further readings.

Gernet, Jacques. *A History of Chinese Civilization.* Translated by J. R. Foster. New York: Cambridge University Press, 1989. Extended account of the history of the period, along with a full treatment of its culture and civilization.

Hook, Brian, ed. *The Cambridge Encyclopedia of China.* 2d ed. New York: Cambridge University Press, 1991. Chronological entries with numerous maps, charts, illustrations, and tables.

Huang, Ray. *China: A Macro History.* Armonk, N.Y.: East Gate, 1988. Good overview of the history of the period with attempts to explain the events.

Hucker, Charles O. *China's Imperial Past: An Introduction to Chinese History and Culture.* Stanford, Calif.: Stanford University Press, 1975. General history of the period interspersed with accounts of society, philosophy, literature, religions, and arts.

Roberts, J. A. G. *A Concise History of China.* Cambridge, Mass.: Harvard University Press, 1999. As its title suggests, contains a concise summary of the period.

_____. *A History of China: Prehistory to c. 1800.* New York: St. Martin's Period, 1996. A good general history.

Schirokaur, Conrad. *A Brief History of Chinese Civilization.* New York: Harcourt Brace Jovanovich, 1991. Textbook that gives a good historical survey, as well as treatment of arts, society, science, religion, and technology.

SEE ALSO: 209-174 B.C.E., Maodun Creates a Large Confederation in Central Asia; 25 C.E., Guang Wudi Restores the Han Dynasty; c. 60-68 C.E., Buddhism Enters China; 142 C.E., Zhang Daoling Founds the Celestial Masters Movement; 184-204 C.E., Yellow Turbans Rebellion; c. 220 C.E., Cai Yan Composes Poetry About Her Capture by Nomads; c. 3d century C.E., Wang Bi and Guo Xiang Revive Daoism; 220 C.E., Three Kingdoms Period Begins in China; 265 C.E., Sima Yan Establishes the Western Jin Dynasty; 397-402 C.E., Ge Chaofu Founds the Lingbao Tradition of Daoism; 386 C.E., Toba Establishes the Northern Wei Dynasty in China; 420 C.E., Southern Dynasties Period Begins in China.

RELATED ARTICLES in *Great Lives from History: The Ancient World*: Cao Cao; Wang Bi; Wudi.

325 C.E.
ADOPTION OF THE NICENE CREED

The Nicene Creed attempted to standardize Christian doctrine and restore Christian unity; it became the only creed accepted by all major bodies of the Christian church: Catholic, Orthodox, and Protestant.

LOCALE: Nicaea, Asia Minor (now Turkey)
CATEGORY: Religion

KEY FIGURES

Arius (c. 250-336 C.E.), presbyter of Alexandria, 313-325 C.E.

Saint Alexander (c. 250-328 C.E.), bishop of Alexandria, 313-328 C.E.

Eusebius of Caesarea (c. 260-339 C.E.), Eastern bishop and supporter of Arius

Eusebius of Nicomedia (d. c. 342 C.E.), bishop and supporter of Arius; bishop of Constantinople, 339-c. 342 C.E.

Constantine the Great (c. 272-285 to 337 C.E.), sole Roman emperor, r. 324-337 C.E.

Hosius of Córdoba (c. 256-357/358 C.E.), bishop of Córdoba, c. 295 C.E., and ecclesiastical adviser to Constantine, 312-326 C.E.

Saint Athanasius of Alexandria (c. 293-373 C.E.), deacon of Alexandria, 319-328 C.E., bishop, 328-373 C.E.

SUMMARY OF EVENT

At the beginning of the fourth century C.E., faith in the divinity of Jesus Christ was firmly established in Christian worship, but it was not precisely defined theologically, especially in relation to the divinity of God the Father. Arius, a presbyter in the Baucalis district of Alexandria, hoped to clarify these matters and, in line with a strong trend in Hellenistic philosophy, was anxious to assert the unity and immutability of God. For Arius, God must of necessity be one, alone, and eternal. The world, the realm of change so completely foreign to the nature of God, must be created by an intermediary being, the Son, or Word. Arius was willing to countenance the worship traditionally given the Son because as Son he was a perfect creature standing in such a special relation to God that he might well be called "only begotten God." Yet he remained a creature whose "substance," or nature, was separate and related to the eternal Father. Unlike God the Father, the Son had a beginning, and in the words of a popular Arian slogan concerning the Son, "There was when he was not."

Alexander, the bishop of Alexandria, totally rejected Arius's denial of the full divinity of Christ. When Arius made an appeal for popular support by composing theological songs based on his teachings, such as *Thalia* or *Spiritual Banquet*, Saint Alexander denounced him, took steps to depose him, and forced him into exile in Syria where he had powerful friends in Bishops Eusebius of Caesarea, Theodotus of Laodicea, and Eusebius of Nicomedia.

The dispute, which by now had assumed serious proportions, came to the attention of Emperor Constantine. While Constantine the Great seems to have had little understanding of the complex issues that were being debated, he was anxious to secure theological agreement within the Church as a bulwark of political stability. Because both sides in the dispute could find both Scriptural support and support from earlier theological writers for their positions, there was no immediate way to resolve the dispute. When imperial letters and the efforts of his ecclesiastical adviser Bishop Hosius of Córdoba failed to end the contention, Constantine decided, with little or no precedent, to call together a council of all Christian bishops. In taking such action, he established the precedent of calling Church councils to resolve theological disputes as a means of preserving ecclesiastical unity. To facilitate matters, he extended to the bishops the courtesy of the imperial coach service.

On May 20, 325 C.E., the council opened in Nicaea near Constantinople with about three hundred bishops in attendance. Except for seven bishops from the Western Roman Empire and a few from beyond the Eastern Roman Empire frontier, all were from the East. For the most part, they were not learned theologians. The absent Arius had his mouthpieces in Eusebius of Caesarea and Eusebius of Nicomedia; Alexander had at his elbow his deacon and successor Saint Athanasius of Alexandria, who was later to play the leading part in the post-Nicene disputes with the Arians.

The council, which opened with great splendor with Constantine's greetings and admonitions, was presided over by Hosius of Córdoba. The actual course by which the council drafted a creed is obscure. It appears that a radical Arian creed was almost unanimously rejected early in the course of debate, but the formulation of the orthodox belief proved to be more difficult.

As a number of anti-Arian phrases attest, the creed represents a complete condemnation of the teachings of

Bishop Arius, founder of Arianism. (Hulton|Archive)

Arius. The term "begotten, that is, from the substance of the Father," directly rejected the Arian position that the Son was created out of nothing. The Nicene Creed further asserts that the Son was "Very God of very God," denying the Arian stand that God the Father was unique and that the Son was God in some secondary sense, not "true God." The phrase "begotten not made" again states the belief that the Son was one in nature with the Father and related to him in a way that the Creation was not. In response to the Arian objection that the begetting of the Son required a Father who was prior, the Nicene defenders referred to Origen's teaching of the eternal generation of the Son by the Father. The wording "of one substance with the Father" asserted the full deity of the Son in a way which admitted no Arianizing interpretation. However, the word *homoousios*, "of the same substance," presented certain difficulties. It was not a biblical term and moreover had been condemned in another context by an earlier synod. To some, it suggested a materialistic concept of God and courted the danger of the Sabellian heresy, which completely identified the persons of the Father and the Son. Later, in the 350's, the word *homoousios* became the keynote in a three-way struggle between the radical Arians, who said that the Son was not

of the same substance as the Father; the conservatives, who believed that the Son was of "like" substance with the Father; and the defenders of the Nicene formula. Finally, the creed explicitly condemned a number of Arian teachings. When the supporters of Arius at the council were given the choice of signing the creed or going into exile, all but two signed. Arius himself was banished and his writings burned by imperial order. The Church also anathematized all those who claimed there was a time when the Son did not exist.

SIGNIFICANCE

Before Nicaea, Christian symbols had been primarily local and liturgical creeds, used for the instruction of catechumens. The Nicene formula was a theological creed intended for universal subscription, not as a replacement for the older creeds but as a theological test for Church leaders.

The council, however, did not finally end the dispute. Arius's followers were able to exert pressure on the emperor and the Church, and Arius was readmitted in 327 C.E. At the Council of Tyre in 335, Athanasius was banned from the Church. The dispute continued until a further council was called at Constantinople in 381, the Second Ecumenical Council. It was there that the more fully developed Nicene Creed was formally adopted. It included the provisions of the Creed adopted by the Council of Nicaea and enlarged the section on the Holy Spirit.

The creed formulated by the two councils of Nicaea and Constantinople is the Nicene, or Niceno-Constantinopolitan, Creed found in the liturgy of most Christian churches, including Roman Catholic, Greek Orthodox, and Protestant faiths.

—David Charles Smith,
updated by Charles L. Kammer III

FURTHER READING

Barnes, Timothy D. *Athanasius and Constantius: Theology and Politics in the Constantinian Empire.* Cambridge, Mass.: Harvard University Press, 1993. An examination of the relationship between Constantine the Great and Saint Athanasius of Alexandria. Bibliography and indexes.

_____. *Constantine and Eusebius.* Cambridge, Mass.: Harvard University Press, 1981. Contains a discussion of the Council of Nicaea as part of Constantine's attempt to create a unified Roman Empire.

Burrus, Virginia. *Begotten, Not Made: Conceiving Manhood in Late Antiquity.* Stanford, Calif.: Stanford University Press, 2000. An examination of the Nicene

Creed, Arianism, and the roles of Saint Athanasius of
Alexandria and Saint Ambrose.

Grant, Michael. *Constantine the Great: The Man and His
Times*. New York: Maxwell Macmillan International,
1994. Discusses the Council of Nicaea in terms of
Constantine's concern for a unified faith.

Hebblethwaite, Brian. *The Essence of Christianity: A
Fresh Look at the Nicene Creed*. London: SPCK,
1996. Contains a discussion of the contemporary significance of the Nicene Creed.

SEE ALSO: c. 6 B.C.E., Birth of Jesus Christ; c. 30 C.E.,
Condemnation and Crucifixion of Jesus Christ; Oc-
tober 28, 312 C.E., Conversion of Constantine to
Christianity; 313-395 C.E., Inception of Church-State
Problem.

RELATED ARTICLES in *Great Lives from History: The
Ancient World*: Saint Ambrose; Saint Athanasius
of Alexandria; Constantine the Great; Eusebius of
Caesarea; Jesus.

November 24, 326-May 11, 330 C.E.
CONSTANTINOPLE IS FOUNDED

*Constantine the Great founded Constantinople, the
capital city of the Eastern Roman Empire, which became
instrumental in the survival of the Byzantine Empire and
the extinction of the Western Roman Empire.*

LOCALE: Constantinople (now Istanbul, Turkey)
CATEGORIES: Cultural and intellectual history;
government and politics

KEY FIGURE

Constantine the Great (c. 272-285 to 337 C.E.), sole
emperor of Rome, r. 324-337 C.E., and founder of
Constantinople

SUMMARY OF EVENT

During the third century C.E., the Roman Empire faced a
crisis. Beginning in the year 235, armies around the empire acclaimed their generals as emperors, leading to
constant civil wars as each new emperor attempted to
gain control of Rome, the capital, for only the emperor
who controlled Rome was the legitimate emperor. Furthermore, with the armies engaged in civil wars, the borders were left unguarded, and the empire was attacked on
all sides, by Franks and Alamanni on the Rhine, Goths on
the Danube, and Persians in the east. During the 250's,
with the empire at its lowest ebb, the emperor Valerian
turned the western part over to his son and took the east
for himself. This marked the beginning of a trend toward
multiple emperors and an administrative splitting of the
empire, although officially there was only one empire
and only one capital city, Rome.

Beginning in the year 284 C.E., the emperor Diocletian was able to reestablish control of the entire empire,
defeat all the invaders, and put an end to the interminable
warfare. At the same time, he instituted a number of re-

forms that were so overwhelming that his reign has been
called the beginning of the Late Roman Empire. Diocletian formalized the practices of having two emperors (au-
gustuses), each with a junior emperor (caesar), in charge
of the eastern and western parts of the empire. As senior
emperor, Diocletian took control of the more populous
and prosperous eastern part of the empire and established
his court at Nicomedia in Asia Minor. Rome, however,
remained the official capital of the entire empire.

After Diocletian retired in 305 C.E., civil war broke
out again. The victor this time was Constantine, the son
of one of Diocletian's junior emperors. In 324, Constantine defeated Licinius, his last rival, and he continued,
and even expanded on, Diocletian's reforms. Like Diocletian, Constantine the Great recognized that the eastern
section of the empire—the Balkans, Asia Minor, Syria-
Palestine, and Egypt—was strategically, politically, and
economically more important than the west. In recognition of this reality—not because of dislike of the Romans of Rome, as some later commentators thought—
Constantine decided to establish not merely another
court-city but an actual second capital city of the empire,
located in the east. This step was a sharp blow to the status and prestige of Rome. By this time, however, Rome
was living on its past glories, a backwater area in which
nothing of significance happened any longer.

The selection of a site was accompanied by a good bit
of soul-searching. After deciding against places such as
Serdica (modern Sofia) near the Danube, Thessalonica in
northern Greece, and Chalcedon in northern Asia Minor,
Constantine initially decided to found his city on the site
of ancient Troy. This was the home of Aeneas, the legendary ancestor of the ancient Romans, and would have
been a worthy site for a second Rome. Constantine even

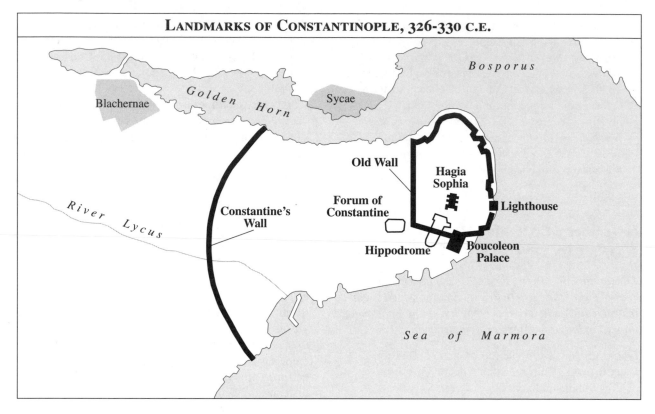

LANDMARKS OF CONSTANTINOPLE, 326-330 C.E.

went so far as to lay out the city and build the city gates. It was later said, however, that God came to him in a vision and told him to abandon this pagan site and select another. Another legend said that eagles carried the measuring tapes from the proposed site at Chalcedon north to the old Greek city of Byzantium.

Byzantium was strategically located on the north side of the Bosporus, the strait that linked the Aegean and Black Seas and separated Europe from Asia. It was surrounded on three sides by water: the Golden Horn on the north, the Bosporus on the east, and the Sea of Marmora on the south. This was where the land route from Europe to Asia crossed the sea route from the Aegean to the Black Sea. Whoever controlled the site controlled both commercial and military traffic going east and west and north and south. As long as the crossing could be held, Rome's eastern, and richest, domains were protected from invasion from the north.

The new capital was officially "founded" on November 24, 326, at an astrologically auspicious time with the sun in Sagittarius and Cancer ruling the hour. At this time, only the western wall was laid out. Constantine himself, spear in hand, marked out the remaining extent of the city. According to a later legend, his courtiers thought he

was incorporating too much ground and asked, "How much further, my Lord?" Constantine replied, "Until he who walks before me stops walking." Work then proceeded apace—some said too quickly, for Constantine subsequently was accused of wasting public funds and shoddy construction. The latter charge, at least, has some substance, for some of the buildings had to be propped up, and others soon had to be reconstructed.

The new city was encompassed by a wall that extended north to south and quadrupled the previous size of the city. In many regards, it was an imitation of Rome. Like Rome, it was built, allegedly, on seven hills, and it had fourteen districts and a forum. In the forum stood a porphyry column of Constantine, nearly 100 feet (30 meters) tall, which had on top a gold encrusted statue of Constantine with a nail from the true cross embedded in its diadem and a piece of the cross in the orb that he held. To emphasize the city's role as the new Rome, Constantine placed beneath the column the *palladium*, an ancient wooden statue of Athena said to have been brought from Troy to Rome by Aeneas himself, the legendary ancestor of the Romans.

Toward the eastern end of the peninsula, the imperial palace and the 440-yard-long (400-meter-long) hippodrome (racing course for chariots) adjoined each other, just as the imperial palace and Circus Maximus adjoined in Rome. The city was decorated with monuments removed from other famous sites. In the hippodrome stood the famous serpent column, which had been dedicated at Delphi after the Greek victory over the Persians at Plataea in 479 B.C.E. Also there was the *milarion*, the milestone from which the distances of all roads in the east were measured. Many statues of pagan gods, including the Pythian Apollo, the Samian Hera, and the Olympian Zeus, were removed from their temples and brought to the city, where they could be appreciated for their material beauty rather than their divine power. Indeed, Saint Jerome noted in his chronicle under the year 330, "Constantinople is dedicated, while almost all other cities are stripped."

Unlike old Rome, however, Constantinople was a Christian city from the very beginning. Constantine built three churches in honor of Dynamis (power), Irene (peace), and Sophia (wisdom), the last of these with 427 pagan statues aligned in front. At a later time, the last two were combined into a much larger church of Saint Sophia (Hagia Sophia). The only pagan temples in the city were those of Castor and Pollux in the hippodrome and of Tyche, the patron goddess of the city—and even she had a cross incised in her forehead.

Although it was yet incomplete, the new city was officially dedicated on May 11, 330, and endowed with the name "Constantinople," that is, "the city of Constantine." The celebrations lasted forty days, and the pagan writer Zosimus later reported that they included further astrological ceremonies and that the Neoplatonist philosopher Sopatros took part. On the Christian side, processions left the forum singing *Kyrie eleison*. There were chariot races in the Hippodrome, the Baths of Zeuxippus were officially opened, and commemorative coins were issued—one for the old capital of Rome, showing the wolf and twins, the other for Constantinople, with a depiction of the goddess Victoria.

As for the name of his foundation, Constantine himself stated that he "bestowed upon it an eternal name by the commandment of God." What this name was is uncertain. It was not "Constantinople," although it may have been "New Rome" or "Second Rome," names by which the city was also known. Yet the "eternal name" may have been *Flora, Anthusa* in Greek, which means "flourishing," and which also had been the sacred, occult name of Rome itself.

For Constantinople to be a true city, moreover, a population was necessary. Settlement by influential individuals was encouraged by promises of land grants and tax remissions. A later legend recounted, "Wishing to populate his city, and in particular to draw Romans to Byzantium, the great Constantine secretly took their signet rings from senators, one from each, and sent them [to fight] against the king of the Persians, who was called Sarbarus." Meanwhile, he moved the families of these men to Constantinople and built houses for them, and on their return from the east, they decided to remain there as well. In spite of such efforts, it was not until about ten years later that the city received its own senate. Even this senate had the image but not the substance of the Roman one. The new senators gained social rank and prestige but no political power.

Another thing Constantinople had in common with Rome was an increasingly large population of urban poor who were fed and entertained at imperial expense. The foodstuffs came largely from Egypt, and the entertainment was provided primarily by the chariot races in the hippodrome. The four teams (blues, greens, reds, and whites) each gained large cheering sections. The "blues" and "greens," as the fans of these teams were known, were the most numerous and most vociferous and given to expressing opinions on matters not merely athletic but political as well.

SIGNIFICANCE

In later years, Constantinople justified Constantine's choice of a site. The population expanded rapidly, approaching one million. In the early fifth century C.E., there were 20 public bakeries, 120 private bakeries, 9 public baths, 153 private baths, and 4,388 houses (not including apartment buildings). Constantine's walls were demolished in the year 413, and the famous "land walls" were built, doubling the size of the city. During the barbarian invasions of the late fourth and the fifth centuries, Constantinople protected the rich provinces of the east, with the end result that the western part of the empire fell, but the eastern section—later known as the Byzantine Empire—survived. Another reason for the fall of the Western Roman Empire was that the establishment of a second capital effectively split the empire in two, and left each to fend for itself. Thus, it was no surprise that the more populous, more "civilized," and more financially sound portion survived.

During the same period, Constantinople also appropriated status from old Rome in another way, for the bishops of Constantinople laid claim to first rank among Christian bishops. The result was a festering quarrel with Rome that ultimately led, in 1054, to the Great

903

Schism, and the development of separate Greek Orthodox churches in the eastern empire and Roman Catholic
in the western empire.

In 1204, Constantinople was captured for the first
time in its history, by treacherous western crusaders with
no stomach for fighting the Muslims. When it was re-
taken by the Byzantines in 1261, it was but a shadow of
its former self. The shrunken Byzantine Empire, now under constant attack by the Turks, held out until 1453,
when the city finally fell. The last emperor, appropriately
named Constantine XI, died defending the walls and was
recognized in death only by his red shoes.

Despite its conquest, the city's importance did not
end. Under the name Istanbul, Constantinople became
the capital of the Ottoman Empire and as such continued to be one of the most important cities in the world. It
has been said that the building of Constantinople alone
would place Constantine among the great figures of history. Given the significance of the city through subsequent ages, few would deny this claim.

—*Ralph W. Mathisen*

FURTHER READING

Eusebius. *Life of Constantine*. Oxford, England: Clarendon Press and Oxford University Press, 1999. A translation of Eusebius of Caesarea's account of Constantine's life by Averil Cameron and Stuart G. Hall.
Includes an introduction and commentary.

Grant, Michael. *Constantine the Great: The Man and
His Times*. New York: Maxwell Macmillan International, 1994. A biography of Constantine that touches
on many accomplishments and his religious conversion.
Kousoulas, D. George. *The Life and Times of Constantine the Great: The First Christian Emperor*. Danbury,
Conn.: Rutledge Books, 1997. The story of Constantine's life and his activities as a Christian emperor.
Lieu, Samuel N. C., and Dominic Montserrat, eds. *Constantine: History, Historiography, and Legend*. New
York: Routledge, 1998. An attempt to examine the life
of Constantine with an eye to separating legend and
history.
Mango, Cyril A. *Studies on Constantinople*. Brookfield,
Vt.: Variorum, 1993. A collection of studies on Con-
stantinople. Bibliography and index.
Pohlsander, Hans A. *The Emperor Constantine*. New
York: Routledge, 1996. A biography of Constantine
that examines his role in history as emperor of the
Eastern Roman Empire.

SEE ALSO: October 28, 312 C.E., Conversion of Constan-
tine to Christianity; August 24-26, 410 C.E., Gothic
Armies Sack Rome; 445-453 C.E., Invasions of Attila
the Hun; September 4, 476 C.E., Fall of Rome.
RELATED ARTICLES in *Great Lives from History: The
Ancient World*: Constantine the Great; Diocletian.

361-363 C.E.
FAILURE OF JULIAN'S PAGAN REVIVAL

*The failure of Julian's pagan revival represented an
attempt to replace Christianity with a government-
sponsored pagan renaissance.*

LOCALE: Eastern Roman Empire
CATEGORIES: Government and politics; religion

KEY FIGURE
Julian the Apostate (331-363 C.E.), Roman emperor,
r. 361-363 C.E.

SUMMARY OF EVENT
Julian, known as Julian the Apostate for his renunciation
of Christianity, was a descendent of Constantine the
Great, the emperor who first adopted the Christian faith
as the state religion. Educated in the classical traditions
of rhetoric and philosophy, Julian found Christianity intellectually and morally lacking; once he became em-

peror of the Roman Empire in 361 C.E., he pursued two
goals: the rejection of Christianity in favor of classical
paganism and the renewal of the empire through a vigorous campaign against the Persians in the east. He failed at
both endeavors.

His attempts, however, began well. In 355 C.E., Constantius II, Julian's cousin and the ruling emperor, summoned Julian from his studies in Milan to serve as caesar,
or junior emperor. At the same time, Julian was married
to Constantius's daughter Helena and sent to Gaul. There,
Julian defeated an invading force of the Alemanni, then
conducted two years of vigorous and successful campaigning against the Germans. In 360, the troops of
Julian declared him emperor against Constantius. The
two rivals were marching toward one another when
Constantius died suddenly, naming Julian as his successor.

Julian the Apostate, as his soldiers declare him emperor. (F. R. Niglutsch)

Julian, once dutiful in his outward obedience to Christianity, now revealed his allegiance to paganism. He had studied the Neoplatonic philosophy of the noted scholars Iamblichus (c. 250-c. 330 C.E.) and Maximus (d. 370 C.E.) and had developed an advanced, mystical paganism. A monotheist, he regarded paganism as a unified system of worship that needed its moral dimension expanded and strengthened to combat the Christian faith. Julian believed in one, abstract deity of whom the individual gods and goddesses represented various aspects or qualities. The combined influence of Iamblichus's Neoplatonism and Maximus's eastern mystery religions are clearly seen in Julian's own thoughts and writings.

When he became emperor, Julian was able openly to champion paganism against Christianity, which he sincerely regarded as a corrupting influence in society. While carefully avoiding the persecution of Christians, he used legal and political measures to destroy the Church. He removed the privileges extended to the Christian institution by Constantine the Great, granting toleration for all in the late Roman Empire—Jews, Christians, and heretics alike. The clergy were no longer exempt from such civil duties as the office of *curiale*, or member of a municipal council, a position that was often incompatible with their pastoral responsibilities. Pagan temples were reopened, temple lands were restored, and public cults of the gods were reestablished.

The step that caused the greatest reaction was Julian's edict forbidding Christians to teach literature in the schools. By this measure, the emperor planned, astutely enough, to cut off Christians from a chief source of influence and ultimately to destroy their social position. The rationale behind his edict assumed that those who did not subscribe to the pagan system of values as expressed in classical letters had no right to teach literature because they could not do so with integrity. Julian maintained that Christians who insisted on their own form of worship in their own churches should likewise maintain their own schools. He knew that upper-class Christians would not sacrifice their children's chances for an education that would prepare them for high positions in society by exposing them to makeshift training. It is impossible to know how Julian's strategy would have worked because he died within two years and his plans never materialized. Attempts of two Christian professors to translate the Scriptures into classical verse forms and Platonic dialogues proved a waste of time in the face of standard pagan educational fare.

Julian brought other pressure to bear against the Christians. Pagans were preferred in the emperor's service, and cities that cooperated with the restoration of pagan worship were favored. Although Julian never implemented a vicious imperial policy of open persecution, there were petty attacks in some provinces. A punitive action was taken on at least one loyally Christian city, and private acts of vindictiveness were perpetrated by both Christians and pagans.

At the same time, paganism was actively promoted in many ways. Pagan rites were made part of civic celebrations and military ceremonies. Official sacrifices celebrated for the army included lavish and attractive feasts of sacrificial meat. Julian also attempted to provide the pagan revival with a trained elite corps of pagan clergy. He appointed a priest for each city and a high priest of each province; he wrote personally to several of his high ecclesiastics, outlining for them the courses they were to follow. Several of these extant letters show the high ideal and the elevated ethical code that Julian proposed for his revival. His instructions were remarkably parallel to the teachings of Christian morality in that he encouraged his pagan bishops to lead holy and austere lives, to avoid the theater and races, and to organize works of social welfare for the poor and unfortunate. The social welfare program was supplemented by state grants. On one occasion, Julian instructed his pagan high priest of Galatia to spend at least a fifth of a government subsidy on the poor who served the priests and to distribute the rest to strangers and beggars. "For it is a disgrace," wrote Julian, "that no Jew is a beggar, and the impious Galileans feed our people in addition to their own, whereas ours manifestly lack assistance from us." The emperor insisted that pagans must be taught to subscribe to such services and benefits to humanity.

Julian was deeply interested in classical learning and literature. His own writings include orations, letters, satires, and pagan hymns. Only fragments of his most famous piece, the satire *Against the Galileans* (English translation, 1913), have survived, and the work is known primarily from the refutation written by Cyril, bishop of Alexandria.

SIGNIFICANCE

It is possible that Julian's campaign against Persia was motivated partly by his desire to find a location outside the Christian Roman orbit where his pagan renaissance might have a better chance of success. At any rate, when Julian met his death on his Persian campaign in 363 C.E.,

his pagan revival ended with him. It is possible that Julian may have been mortally wounded by one of his own soldiers, for many of them deeply resented his paganism. Although sincere, Julian apparently did not understand the hold of Christianity on the popular mind and imagination. His own religion was largely negative, a revulsion against what he saw as a barbarism and the loss of classical values; his pagan revival was chiefly an attempt to retain the Hellenistic cultural heritage. His efforts were further hampered by the fact that his personal religion was esoteric and appeared bizarre to his contemporaries. If Julian's attempt proved anything, it showed that the day of paganism as a formative cultural influence was past, although pockets of paganism remained in both the East and West for centuries.

—*Mary Evelyn Jegen, updated by Michael Witkoski*

FURTHER READING

Athanassiadi-Fowden, Polymnia. *Julian: An Intellectual Biography*. 1981. Reprint. New York: Routledge, 1992. An examination of Julian's thought as it was influenced by the Greek experience and how he wished to extend that heritage throughout the empire.

Head, Constance. *The Emperor Julian*. Boston: Twayne, 1976. A good, basic introduction to the man and his times.

Ricciotti, Guiseppe. *Julian the Apostate*. Translated by M. Joseph Costelloe. Milwaukee: Bruce Publishing, 1959. Using contemporary sources, this study provides a good examination of how Julian was perceived during his own times and the impact, or lack of impact, of his pagan revival.

Smith, Roland. *Julian's Gods: Religion and Philosophy in the Thought and Action of Julian the Apostate*. New York: Routledge, 1995. An ambitious review of Julian's career in terms of his religious and philosophical influences.

Vidal, Gore. *Julian*. New York: Ballantine, 1986. First published in 1964, this novel remains the finest recreation of Julian and his times. Deeply and at times passionately informed on the religious and philosophical debates of the age.

SEE ALSO: October 28, 312 C.E., Conversion of Constantine to Christianity; 313-395 C.E., Inception of Church-State Problem; 380-392 C.E., Theodosius's Edicts Promote Christian Orthodoxy.

RELATED ARTICLES in *Great Lives from History: The Ancient World*: Saint Augustine; Constantine the Great.

Late 4th-5th century C.E.
ASANGA HELPS SPREAD MAHĀYĀNA BUDDHISM

Asanga revived Mahāyāna Buddhism, which was in decline, and founded the Yogācāra school of Mahāyāna Buddhism.

LOCALE: India
CATEGORIES: Religion; philosophy

KEY FIGURES
Asanga (c. 365-c. 440 C.E.), Buddhist philosopher of religion
Vasubandhu (fl. fourth-fifth century C.E.), Buddhist philosopher, brother of Asanga

SUMMARY OF EVENT
According to Tārānātha, Asanga's mother was of the Brahman caste of the Kauśika clan, Prasannaśīla. She conceived Asanga with a man who belonged to the warrior (Kṣatriya) caste, whereas her two other sons were fathered by a Brahman. According to Paramārtha's *Basohanzu hoshiden* (sixth century C.E.; *The Biography of Vasubandhu*, 1995), three sons were born to a Brahman woman of the Kauśika clan in Puruṣapura (modern Peshawar, Pakistan). All three were given the name Vasubandhu. The eldest became known as Asanga, the middle son retained the name Vasubandhu, and the third son became known as Viriñcivatsa. In Paramārtha's account, there is no indication that Asanga was the stepbrother of the other two. All three sons are said to have entered the Sarvāstivādin sect of Hīnayāna Buddhism. Not much else is known about the youngest son, Viriñcivatsa.

Asanga reportedly studied under Piṇḍola. According to Tārānātha, Asanga, dissatisfied with his understanding of the Prajñāpāramitā sutras, retreated to a cave in the mountain Kukkuṭapāda until the bodhisattva Maitreya took him up to the Tuṣita Heaven and expounded the Mahāyāna sutras and doctrine to him. (A bodhisattva is a being who strives for enlightenment for himself but who also remains in this world to help others advance toward enlightenment.) According to Paramārtha, Asanga reached the Tuṣita Heaven through his own powers and received instruction from Maitreya. Scholars have debated whether Maitreya was the bodhisattva or a historical person who happened to be named after the bodhisattva.

Returning from Tuṣita Heaven, Asanga set about spreading the Mahāyāna doctrine. The sources agree in stating that at this time, the Mahāyāna was in decline. In this respect, Asanga was reported to have set up various monasteries (*vihāras*) throughout India to disseminate the teachings of the Mahāyāna. It is reported that the number of practitioners of Mahāyāna increased through the influence of Asanga. One of the monasteries set up by Asanga was the Dharmāṅkura-vihāra, in which he composed his works.

In spreading the Mahāyāna doctrine, Asanga enlisted the help of his brother, Vasubandhu, who had been a vehement expounder of the Sarvāstivādin sect and who had denounced the teachings of the Mahāyāna. Entreating Vasubandhu to come to him because of illness, Asanga in the end converted Vasubandhu to the Mahāyāna. After Asanga's death in Rajagṛha, Vasubandhu became a major proponent of the Mahāyāna and in particular the Yogācāra school.

Although exact dates vary, most scholars place Asanga's lifetime spanning the fourth and fifth centuries C.E. The attribution of writings to Asanga has been much debated. Most scholars would agree that at least the following were composed by Asanga: the *Abhidharmasamuccaya* (fourth-fifth centuries C.E.; *Compendium of the Higher Teaching*, 2001); the *Xianyang shengjiao lun* (fourth-fifth centuries C.E.; a Chinese translation of the *Āryadeśanāvikhyāpana*), an abridgment of the *Yogācārabhūmi* (fourth century C.E.); and *Mahāyānasaṃgraha* (fourth century C.E.; *The Summary of the Great Vehicle*, 1992). Traditionally the *Yogācārabhūmi*, the foundation text of Yogācāra, is the most well-known work attributed to Asanga; however, it is also assigned to the historical Maitreya or is taken as a compilation of several sources.

Asanga's most significant achievement is the founding of the Yogācāra school. The Yogācāra and the Mādhyamika, founded by Nāgārjuna (second-third century C.E.), are the major schools of Mahāyāna thought.

The Yogācāra philosophy posited three aspects of consciousness: *vijñāna*, *manas*, and *citta*. Earlier Buddhist thinkers treated these terms as synonyms. Asanga, however, looked on *vijñāna* as the consciousness related to the sense organs (for example, visual and auditory consciousness). *Manas* was the seat of discursive reasoning, connected with the illusion of self. *Citta* was the *ālayavijñāna*, the store-consciousness, which contained traces from one's past lives and potentialities for future actions. It is through the "revolution" or "uprooting" of the *ālayavijñāna* that one attains enlightenment. The seeds of defilement of the *ālayavijñāna* must be purified.

The uprooting of the *ālayavijñāna* ultimately amounts to the realization of the emptiness (*śūnyatā*) of all phenomena. Earlier, Nāgārjuna, the founder of the Mādhyamika school, had offered a devastating critique in which he argued that all phenomena were "empty" of any permanent substance or essence. In doing this, many thought that he was advocating some form of nihilism because he was arguing that there was no permanent substance. However, Nāgārjuna was very careful to point out that he was following the middle way (*mādhyama*) between essentialism and nihilism. The phenomena exist as transforming and changing forms without substance or essence.

Asanga's approach was somewhat different. He advanced the doctrine of three natures (*trisvabhāva*). According to this doctrine, phenomena have an "imaginary" nature (*parikalpita-svabhāva*); a dependent nature (*paratantra-svabhāva*); and a "perfected" nature (*parinispanna-svabhāva*). It is people's past experiences in the *ālayavijñāna* that impose the imaginary nature on phenomena. The imposition of constructions on the phenomena gives them the appearance of independent substances. Thus the belief that people perceive independently existing things is reducible, according to Asanga, to constructions of the mind. (This school of thought is also known as the mind-only—*cittamātra*—school.) However, phenomena are empty; they exist only in their relative, dependent nature. Moreover, when the phenomena are seen without the superimposition of the imagination, when they are viewed in their undifferentiated relativity, then the phenomena are seen in their perfected nature. It is through the uprooting of the *ālayavijñāna* that a person attains this vision.

This vision of the perfected nature of phenomena forms an important part of the understanding of reality that the bodhisattva has. Asanga contributed to the Mahāyāna understanding of the bodhisattva by positing ten stages in the development of the bodhisattva toward this understanding of reality. These stages are not found in earlier Buddhism.

Another important aspect of the Yogācāra view of Buddhas is the doctrine of the three bodies of Buddhas. The first body is the *Dharmakāya*, the truth or essence body of Buddhas. Also there is the *Sambhogakāya*, the enjoyment body, through which the Buddhas enjoy the doctrine and assemblies of the Buddhas. Finally, there is the *Nirmanakāya*, the appearance body of Buddhas, which is the physical form in which Buddhas appear among people. These latter two bodies are dependent on the essence body.

SIGNIFICANCE

Vasubandhu, Asanga's brother, continued to propagate the Yogācāra philosophy after Asanga's death. After Vasubandhu's death, various branches of the Yogācāra school were formed. One branch was formulated by Sthiramati (510-570 C.E.). Paramārtha (499-569) introduced Sthiramati's system into China in the fifth century. This branch formed the basis of the Shelun sect. The name is an abbreviated form of the Chinese name for Asanga's *The Summary of the Great Vehicle*. Dignāga (400-480) and Dharmapāla (530-561) set up another branch, and Xuanzang (more well known as the Chinese pilgrim who visited India, brought it to China. This school was called Faxiang (Fa-hsiang; Dharma characteristic). In the eighth century, it arrived in Japan, where it was called the Hossō school.

—Albert T. Watanabe

FURTHER READING

Asanga. *La Somme du Grande Véhicule d'Asanga (Mahāyānasaṃgraha)*. Louvain-la-Neuve, France: Univeristé de Louvain, Institut Orientaliste, 1973. Translation into French with notes of this major work of Asanga. Tibetan and Chinese texts are included. Bibliography.

Griffiths, P. J., N. Hakayama, J. P. Keenan, and P. L. Swanson. *The Realm of Awakening: Chapter Ten of Asanga's "Mahāyānasaṃgraha."* Oxford, England: Oxford University Press, 1989. Text, translation, and commentary on this text, which explains the Yogācāra doctrine of the three bodies of the Buddhas. Bibliography and indexes.

Paramartha. "'The Life of Vasu-bandhu' by Paramartha (A.D. 499-569)." Translated by Junichiro Takakusu. *T'oung Pao* 2, no. 5 (1904): 269-296. A translation of the biography of Asanga's brother; it also gives the most authoritative information on the life of Asanga.

Willis, J. D. *On Knowing Reality: The "Tattvartha" Chapter of the Asanga's Bodhisattvabhūmi*. New York: Columbia University Press, 1979. A translation with commentary of the text, which explains in what way a bodhisattva apprehends reality. The introduction gives a good general overview of Yogācāra philosophy. Willis argues strongly for the view that Asanga's philosophy should not be regarded as idealistic. Glossary and bibliography.

SEE ALSO: 6th or 5th century B.C.E., Birth of Buddhism; c. 250 B.C.E., Third Buddhist Council Convenes; c. 250 B.C.E., *Tipiṭaka* Is Compiled; 1st century B.C.E.-1st century C.E., Compilation of the *Lotus Sutra*; 1st-

2d century C.E., Fourth Buddhist Council Convenes; c. 60-68 C.E., Buddhism Enters China.

RELATED ARTICLES in *Great Lives from History: The Ancient World*: Asanga; Buddha; Vasubandhu.

August 9, 378 C.E.

BATTLE OF ADRIANOPLE

The Battle of Adrianople marked the first time that tribal invaders from outside Rome's borders managed to inflict a full-fledged defeat on the Roman army and gained permission to enter the Roman Empire as refugees.

LOCALE: Adrianople (now Edirne, Turkey)
CATEGORY: Wars, uprisings, and civil unrest

KEY FIGURES

Valens (c. 328-378 C.E.), Roman emperor in the east, r. 364-378 C.E.

Sebastian (d. 378 C.E.), commander of the Roman infantry

Fritigern (fl. fourth century C.E.), leader of the Visigoths

Gratian (359-383 C.E.), Roman emperor in the west, r. 367-383 C.E.

SUMMARY OF EVENT

The group that historians eventually termed the Visigoths (they called themselves the Tervingi) first came into contact with the Roman Empire because the Huns, a group of powerful Asian nomads, were pushing them westward. The Goths were less an ethnically homogeneous nation than an armed group consisting of various peoples, largely Germanic in origin but containing peoples from other backgrounds as well. At first, the Goths had contracted to serve in the imperial armies but later had accumulated many grievances against the Romans and had begun to rebel.

For almost two years, rebellious Visigoths had spread death and destruction throughout the Roman provinces that made up the area of modern Bulgaria. The emperor Valens was in residence at Antioch pursuing his campaign against the Persians, and it was there in 376 C.E. that he learned of the disastrous breakdown of his agreement with the Visigoths. Without undue haste, he arranged a truce with Persia so that he might deal with the Germanic threat; it was not until April, 378, that he departed for Constantinople. Dissatisfied with the efforts of his commander Trajan against the Visigoths, he replaced

him with a capable officer recently arrived from the Western Roman Empire, Sebastian, who had a distinguished military record. To him, Valens entrusted a selected infantry force that Sebastian quickly whipped into shape and then led off toward the troubled provinces. Sebastian experienced no difficulty in clearing the countryside of the roving bands of marauders, but he was not prepared for a major engagement. With additional troops, Valens himself left his headquarters near Constantinople at the end of June and advanced toward Adrianople to join his general in preparation for a decisive blow.

Fritigern, the Visigothic leader, became alarmed. He realized that his scattered countrymen, impeded by the presence of their wives, children, and possessions, were highly vulnerable. They were more like a group of refugees on the move than an army. Fritigern therefore ordered his people to concentrate near Cabyle, and at the same time, he sent out agents to enlist auxiliaries for the impending clash with the Romans. Bands of Huns and Alanis from beyond the Danube River joined him, and a wandering contingent of Ostrogothic cavalry under the ethnic Alanis Alatheus and Saphrax promised to do the same. Fritigern had already recruited runaway slaves and a variety of discontented Roman subjects, and although these additions to his fighting force swelled his numerical strength, the diversity of their interests and their undisciplined nature placed heavy demands on his leadership. Food supplies were uncertain because the Germans were living off the countryside, and time worked against them.

Unfortunately for the Romans, Emperor Valens threw away his advantages. Reinforcements from the west led by his nephew, the co-emperor Gratian, were marching eastward; a small advance unit reached Adrianople about August 7, while Valens and his officers were discussing strategy. Some urged caution and delay until the western army arrived. Sebastian and others, however, favored an immediate attack, and their advice confirmed Valens's own inclination. He had been incorrectly informed that the Visigoths numbered only ten thousand men. No figures are available about the numerical strength of either side, but the Roman army probably totaled at least twenty thousand. At the same time, unknown to Valens, the Goths actually outnumbered the Romans.

Possibly Valens was also motivated in his decision by jealousy. Gratian had shortly before achieved a notable victory over the Germans in the Western Roman Empire, a feat that Valens seems to have desired to emulate. Gratian was vastly preferred by the majority of the Roman people because he was an orthodox, Catholic Christian whereas Valens was an Arian heretic. Ironically, the Goths were also Arian Christians, having been converted a generation before by the Gothic missionary Ulfilas, so Valens was in religious communion with the barbarians who opposed him in battle. His religious differences with Gratian made Valens less inclined to cooperate. To wait for the Gallic reinforcements would mean sharing the glory of victory rather than enjoying it alone. Whatever the reason, Valens decided on an immediate offensive.

While these councils were being held, Fritigern sent an Arian Christian priest as an envoy to negotiate with Valens. The envoy promised peace in return for a guarantee of land in Thrace for the Visigoths to settle on as their own, together with an adequate food supply. In effect, this had been Valens's original agreement with the Goths two years earlier, so that Fritigern asked little more than what had been previously conceded. Yet Valens rejected any talk of a truce or treaty. Perhaps he was convinced that the rebellious depredations of the Germans could not be left unpunished. Perhaps, too, he doubted Fritigern's sincerity, for the Visigothic leader was awaiting the arrival of the Gothic cavalry of Alatheus and may have been stalling for time.

Early on the morning of August 9, 378 C.E., the Romans broke camp and advanced 8 miles (13 kilometers) out from Adrianople to within sight of the Visigoths. Fritigern had drawn up his forces in a defensive position with his wagon train forming a circle enclosing his noncombatants and supplies. Tired from their morning's march, the Roman soldiers also suffered from the summer heat as well as from the smoke and heat of the fires that the Visigoths set in the surrounding fields to confuse and discomfit them. A second offer of negotiations from Fritigern induced Valens to dispatch one of his officers toward the Visigothic camp for a consultation. Before the officer could reach the camp, some of the Roman troops impetuously opened the attack.

The details of the battle cannot be reconstructed accurately. The Gothic army, largely cavalry, overwhelmed the Roman infantry, who evidently broke under the shock and the superior numbers of the Visigoths. By nightfall, scarcely one-third of the Romans survived. Among the slain were Valens and Sebastian. The emperor's body was never recovered. Two stories circulated about his death: one that he had been killed by an arrow while fleeing in a band of common soldiers, the other that he had been carried wounded into a farmhouse that the Visigoths destroyed by fire, not knowing the identity of the Romans within who refused to surrender.

Fritigern's victory at Adrianople did not solve his problem. Even with numerical superiority, the Visigoths could not follow up their success properly because they lacked the equipment and knowledge needed to conduct siege operations. As a result, they could not strike at the towns in which Roman wealth and power were concentrated. Two days after the battle, they tried to take Adrianople itself but had to abandon this effort. They soon made their way southward and reached the outskirts of Constantinople before retiring.

Essentially, the Visigoths desired land on which to settle and make new homes for themselves, but they could attain their objective only by coming to terms with the Roman authorities. Shrewdly understanding this aim, Theodosius the Great, the new emperor of the Eastern Roman Empire, combined diplomacy with military pressure and subdued the barbarians with a treaty in 382 C.E. They received what they desired and also the right to rule themselves. They agreed to pay an annual tribute in return for peace and guaranteed they would serve in the Roman army whenever called on.

SIGNIFICANCE

Valens's Arianism made him hated by Catholic historians; thus the calamitous nature of his loss at Adrianople has perhaps been exaggerated in the historical record. However, it cannot be denied that there were two significant results of the Battle of Adrianople. First, the Visigoths became the first Germanic tribe to win territory within the Roman Empire and a degree of autonomy that placed them generally beyond the government's control. This situation portended the future dismemberment of the Roman Empire. Second, the destruction of a Roman army on its own soil demonstrated the deterioration of the once-powerful legions, thereby encouraging the Visigoths and later other Germanic tribes to risk further campaigns against Rome. The period of the peaceful penetration of the Roman Empire by the Germans thus came to an end, and the age of invasions by conquest and force began on the battlefield of Adrianople.

—Raymond H. Schmandt, updated by Nicholas Birns

FURTHER READING

Ammianus Marcellinus. *The Later Roman Empire*. Selected and translated by Walter Hamilton. New York: Penguin, 1986. The major primary source of knowledge about the Battle of Adrianople. Of necessity, it emphasizes the Roman perspective and is not sympathetic to Valens.

Gibbon, Edward. *The Decline and Fall of the Roman Empire*. 3 vols. Reprint. New York: Modern Library, 1995. This work by the great eighteenth century British historian places Adrianople within a general account of the Roman Empire's collapse.

Grant, Michael. *The Fall of the Roman Empire*. London: Weidenfeld & Nicolson, 1990. Grant reevaluates whether Adrianople constituted a crucial loss for the Roman Empire.

Heather, P. J. *The Goths*. Cambridge, Mass.: Blackwell, 1996. An overall history of the Goths, which includes the Roman period.

_____. *Goths and Romans, 332-489*. New York: Oxford University Press, 1991. Provides a close examination of Gothic history during the migration period.

Nicasie, Martinus Johnannes. *Twilight of Empire: The Roman Army from the Reign of Diocletian Until the Battle of Adrianople*. Amsterdam: J. C. Gieben, 1998. An examination of the Battle of Adrianople and the history that led up to it.

Williams, Stephen, and Gerard Friell. *Theodosius: The Empire at Bay*. 1994. Reprint. New Haven, Conn.: Yale University Press, 1995. A provocative and detailed account of the Battle of Adrianople and its aftermath.

SEE ALSO: c. 3d-4th century C.E., Huns Begin Migration West from Central Asia; 380-392 C.E., Theodosius's Edicts Promote Christian Orthodoxy; August 24-26, 410 C.E., Gothic Armies Sack Rome; 439 C.E., Vandals Seize Carthage; 445-453 C.E., Invasions of Attila the Hun; September 4, 476 C.E., Fall of Rome.

RELATED ARTICLES in *Great Lives from History: The Ancient World*: Attila; Ulfilas.

380-392 C.E.

THEODOSIUS'S EDICTS PROMOTE CHRISTIAN ORTHODOXY

Theodosius's edicts promoted Christian orthodoxy by establishing Nicene Christianity as the state religion of the Roman Empire.

LOCALE: Roman Empire
CATEGORIES: Government and politics; religion

KEY FIGURES

Theodosius the Great (346/347-395 C.E.), Roman emperor in the east, r. 379-395 C.E., sole ruler, 393-395 C.E.

Gratian (359-383 C.E.), Roman emperor in the west, r. 375-383 C.E.

Saint Ambrose (339-397 C.E.), bishop of Milan, 374-397 C.E.

Damasus I (c. 304-384 C.E.), bishop of Rome, 366-384 C.E.

SUMMARY OF EVENT

In the late fourth century C.E., government policies made one form of Christianity a mainstay of a troubled Roman Empire. The reign of Theodosius the Great brought to a close the turbulent controversy over the nature of the Trinity (the Father, the Son, and the Holy Ghost). Basically the question revolved around the issue of relation-

ships within the trio. Arius had said that the Son and the Holy Ghost, because not fully spirit and eternal, were inferior to the Father, whereas the bishops assembled in the First Ecumenical Council at Nicaea in 325 had affirmed the equality of the Son and the Father. In succeeding years, many of these bishops also agreed that the Holy Ghost shared essential deity with the Father and the Son. Argument raged throughout the empire for years, aggravated by religious splits among the successors of Constantine the Great.

After the death of Jovian in 364 C.E., the Roman Empire became divided politically between Valentinian (364-375) in the Western Roman Empire and his brother Valens (364-378) in the Eastern Roman Empire. The western emperor was little inclined toward interfering in Church affairs, but in the east, Valens adopted a modified form of Arianism and harassed Christians who adhered to the Nicene formula. Gratian, succeeding his father Valentinian, refused to become *pontifex maximus*, an imperial title since 12 B.C.E., and in 382 C.E. ordered that the statue of Victory be removed from the Senate House in Rome, the citadel of conservatism and paganism. In general, he supported the Nicene faith and began to place both heretics and pagans under civil penalties. In 382 and

384, delegations of senators pleaded for the traditional freedom to allow all people to seek "the Divine Mystery" (in the words of Symmachus) in their own way. Damasus I and Saint Ambrose opposed the petitions, and the government remained firm.

When Valens was killed by the invading Goths at Adrianople in 378 C.E., Gratian appointed Theodosius (later the Great) to succeed him. Theodosius, of Iberian family origin and whose father (*comes*, or Count, Theodosius) had been a distinguished general, was a devout adherent of the Nicene views espoused by most western bishops. At the same time, a Nicene group was emerging in the east, and Theodosius evidently felt the time was ripe for his own vigorous participation in the controversy among the Christians. He issued his edict of Febru-

ary 27, 380 C.E., from Thessalonica (Salonika), one month after baptism at the hands of the Nicene bishop of the city and recovery from illness. It has come to be known as *Cunctos Populos* from its opening words. The text of the edict is translated as follows:

> It is our pleasure that all the nations which are governed by our clemency and moderation should steadfastly adhere to the religion which was taught by Saint Peter to the Romans; which faithful tradition has preserved; and which is now professed by the pontiff Damasus I and by Peter, Bishop of Alexandria, a man of apostolic holiness.

In accordance with the teaching of the Gospel and of the early apostles, Theodosius enjoined belief in the sole deity of the Father, the Son, and the Holy Ghost, "under an equal majesty and a pious Trinity." Only followers of this doctrine could assume the title of "Catholic Christians"; all others were judged extravagant madmen and were branded with the "infamous title of heretics." Under the Theodosian Code 16.1.2, their conventicles would no longer be called churches, and they could expect to suffer the penalties that the emperor, under divine guidance, would deem justifiable. By imperial edict, orthodox ("correct") Christianity was established, and deviationists were threatened with penalties. In 381, the government convened the second ecumenical council at Constantinople. It reissued the Nicene Creed, and the emperor gave the force of civil law to the council's canons.

Arianism faded away inside the empire, but missionaries spread it among the Germans. After 400 C.E., Visigoths settled in southern Gaul and Spain, Ostrogoths in Italy, and Vandals in North Africa. Religious hostility exacerbated the tensions between the heretical invaders and the mostly Nicene natives.

Although Theodosius took a rigid attitude toward Christian heretics, he allowed considerable latitude to non-Christians during the first twelve years of his reign. In 391 C.E., however, two edicts were issued against the pagans, and the following year, a more comprehensive law was promulgated. In this decree, which came to be known as *Nullus Omnino*, he ordered that no one was to kill innocent victims in the worship of idols, nor was anyone henceforth permitted to venerate *lares*, *genii*, or *penates*. The reading of entrails was likewise forbidden, and he en-

Saint Ambrose bars Theodosius the Great from entering the Church. (F. R. Niglutsch)

ROMAN EMPERORS FROM THEODOSIUS THE GREAT TO LEO I, 379-474 C.E.

Ruler	Reign
Theodosius the Great (East)	379-395
Maximus (West, usurper)	383-388
Eugenius (West, usurper)	392-394
Honorius (West)	393-423
Arcadius (East)	395-408
Theodosius II (East)	408-450
Constantius III (East)	421
Valentian III (West)	425-455
Marcian (East)	450-457
Petronius Maximus (West)	455
Avitus (West)	455-456
Majoran (West)	457-461
Leo I (East)	457-474

couraged informers to reveal infractions of the law. Idol worship was ridiculed as a violation of true religion. Houses in which pagan rites were conducted were to be confiscated, and a fine of twenty-five pounds in gold was to be imposed on all who sacrificed to idols or circumvented the law. The edict concluded with threats against officials who might be lax in enforcing this law (Theodosian Code 16.10.12).

Theodosius's solicitude for Christianity was not confined to the promulgation of these two edicts. By *Nullus Haereticis* in 381 C.E., he ordered that there be "no place left to the heretics for celebrating the mysteries of their faith," and he went on to assign the name Catholic only to those who believed in the Trinity. Heretics were forbidden to conduct assemblies within the limits of towns. During the next two years, the emperor set aside wills of apostate Christians, and he denied them the rights of inheritance. Likewise, his attitude toward pagans resulted in the laws of 391, which prohibited sacrifices and the visiting of shrines. Possibly as a result of these laws, the great temple to Serapis in Alexandria was destroyed about 391.

The pretender Magnus Maximus eliminated Gratian in 383 C.E., but Theodosius took revenge. While in Italy from 388 to 391, he had several disputes with Saint Ambrose, the west's most prominent bishop. In 390, Saint Ambrose refused to allow the emperor to receive communion until he accepted responsibility and did penance for the massacre of civilians at Thessalonica by imperial troops. Theodosius also ended the pagan Olympic

Games (considered immoral because participants competed naked); those held in 392 were the last to be staged until the modern Olympic Games were revived in 1896. Valentinian II, brother of Gratian, was murdered or committed suicide in 392, but Theodosius eliminated the pretender Eugenius and the Frankish general Arbogast. Theodosius was the last emperor to rule the entire Roman Empire.

SIGNIFICANCE

Theodosius's policies went beyond those of Constantine, who had been content to legalize Christianity and endow the Church with wealth, buildings, and legal privileges. Damasus I and Saint Ambrose convinced Gratian and Theodosius that diversity in belief was wrong now that the truth was known. Theodosius ended Rome's traditional religious toleration when he decreed the Nicene-Catholic form of Christianity to be the official religion of the state and made liable to the harsh penalties of the law all who did not accept it. This established two enduring principles: religious persecution and the state church. Temples of the old gods were reconsecrated to the Christian God or fell into disrepair; Christian mobs destroyed others in riots their bishops encouraged and the government permitted. Imperial religious processions, occasions of display to the people, were henceforth only to Christian basilicas. For centuries, Europe regarded diversity as synonymous with disunity. Accepting the proposition that political and social unity required religious uniformity, governments enforced such uniformity through a state church. The policy began to break down with the Edict of Nantes in France in 1598, but the constitutional separation of church and state established in the United States two centuries later constituted the clearest rejection of the Theodosian policy.

—*Carl A. Volz, updated by Thomas H. Watkins*

FURTHER READING

Barnes, T. D. "Religion and Society in the Age of Theodosius." In *Grace, Politics and Desire: Essays on Augustine*, edited by H. A. Maynell. Calgary: University of Calgary Press, 1990. Judicious, traditional scholarship.

Brown, P. *Power and Persuasion in Late Antiquity: Toward a Christian Empire*. Madison: University of Wisconsin Press, 1992. Bishops, some with access to the emperors, became the elite of society as Christianity superseded paganism.

Cochrane, C. N. *Christianity and Classical Culture*. Rev. ed. 1944. Reprint. New York: Oxford University Press, 1957. An older study that contains a masterful summary of the topic. Chapters 5-9 argue that Theodosius completed the revolution begun by Constantine.

McLynn, N. B. *Ambrose of Milan: Church and Court in a Christian Capital*. Berkeley: University of California Press, 1994. Chapters 3 and 7 analyze the Altar of Victory controversy, the relationship between Saint Ambrose (as Nathan) and Theodosius (as David), and reinterpret the events of 390-391.

SEE ALSO: c. 110 C.E., Trajan Adopts Anti-Christian Religious Policy; 250 C.E., Outbreak of the Decian Persecution; 313-395 C.E., Inception of Church-State Problem; 325 C.E., Adoption of the Nicene Creed; 428-431 C.E., Nestorian Controversy; October 8-25, 451 C.E., Council of Chalcedon.

RELATED ARTICLES in *Great Lives from History: The Ancient World*: Saint Ambrose; Theodosius the Great.

c. 380-c. 415 C.E.
GUPTA DYNASTY REACHES ITS PEAK UNDER CHANDRAGUPTA II

The Gupta era was India's golden age, a time when arts and literature flourished under the rule of enlightened kings. Chandragupta II reigned at the very apex of the dynasty's glory.

LOCALE: North India

CATEGORIES: Cultural and intellectual history; government and politics

KEY FIGURES

Chandragupta I (fl. fourth century C.E.), Gupta ruler, r. c. 321-330 C.E.

Samudragupta (d. 380 C.E.), Chandragupta I's son, Gupta ruler, r. c. 330-c. 380 C.E.

Chandragupta II (fl. fourth-fifth century C.E.), Samudragupta's son, Gupta ruler, r. c. 380-c. 415 C.E.

SUMMARY OF EVENT

Although the names of the Gupta rulers are celebrated throughout the annals of Indian history, regrettably little is known about the individual kings. Most of the available information has been recovered from fewer than thirty fragmentary inscriptions. Archaeological materials and literature, both sacred and secular, provide, however, tantalizing glimpses of a highly refined and sophisticated world.

There is no doubt that Chandragupta II ruled the Gupta Empire (c. 321-c. 550 C.E.) at the height of its glory. It was, however, Chandraupta I, his grandfather and a ruler of a small principality located in either modern-day Bengal or Bihar, who envisioned an empire that reclaimed Indian soil from the foreign Kushān Dynasty that had ruled for more than three hundred years. The Guptas were also fervent Hindus who sought to reestablish their Brahmanical religion as the primary spiritual authority in the land. Toward these goals, the first

king began his program of westward expansion of the ancestral kingdom through war and the politics of marriage. He is represented on one side of his minted coins and his queen Kumāradevī on the other. A princess of the esteemed Licchavi line, her marriage alliance with the ruler brought prestige and undoubtedly great tracts of land. It is assumed that the Gupta era, which began on February 26, 321 C.E., was founded by Chandragupta I to commemorate his coronation, and probably at that time, he took the regal title Mahārājādhirāja (great king of kings). He chose Pataliputra as his capital, a city associated with the earlier imperial Mauryan Dynasty.

On his accession, Samudragupta, son of Chandragupta I and Kumāradevī, inherited his father's dreams and his titles but added the epithets Digvijaya and Dharnībhanda, meaning "conquest in all directions to bind the country as a single unit." His imperial ambitions were made clear by the titles. Inaugurating a series of military campaigns throughout his long reign, Samudragupta expanded his control over a large part of north India, but it was his son Chandragupta II who finally realized the imperial mandate to exterminate foreign rule in the west and extend the empire from sea to sea. Uniting all of ancient Bhārata (India) from the Himalayan Mountains in the north to the Vindhya Mountains to the south and from the Arabian Sea in the west to the Bay of Bengal in the east, he had driven out the last of the foreign rulers. Reconquest of western India, land crossed by the major trade routes, meant increased revenues, particularly through possession of important ports and harbors connecting India with the outside world. Also the long-held city of Ujjayini in western Malwa was so strategic to trade that Chandragupta later designated it as his second capital after he captured the region.

More important than recovering the trade revenue from foreigners was the establishment of dominion over

EMPERORS OF THE GUPTA DYNASTY, C. 321-550 C.E.

Emperor	Reign
Chandragupta	c. 321-330 C.E.
Samudragupta	c. 330-c. 380
Chandragupta II	c. 380-c. 415
Kumāragupta I	c. 415-455
Skandagupta	455-467
Kumāragupta II	467-477
Budhagupta	477-496
Chandragupta III?	496-500
Vainyagupta	500-515
Narasimhagupta	510-530
Kumāragupta III	530-540
Vishnugupta	540-550

the ancient land by a righteous Hindu king. Hindu treatises on governance such as the *Arthaśāstra* (dates vary, c. fourth century B.C.E.-third century C.E.; *Treatise on the Good*, 1961) by Kauṭilya and the *Manusmṛti* (probably compiled 200 B.C.E.-200 C.E.; *The Laws of Manu*, 1886) set down the ideal standards for sovereigns and stated unequivocally that a righteous king's foremost duty was to preserve the purity and the integrity of Hindu society and culture throughout the land. In other words, the kings were responding to a divine mandate to ensure the purity of Bhārata. Like his grandfather, Chandragupta II formed marriage alliances with some powerful ruling families as a way to extend his influence across the land. His marriage to Kuveranāgā of the Nāga family was a political maneuver. They had a daughter named Prabhāvatīgupta, who, when she came of age, was married to the Vākāṭaka king Rudrasena II, who ruled a kingdom in the western Deccan. Both the Nāgas and Vākāṭakas were rulers of important feudatory states, whose support augmented Gupta prestige and at least indirect control across the subcontinent.

A Chinese pilgrim named Faxian (Fa-hsien) traveled through India between 400 and 411 C.E. Although he never mentioned Chandragupta's name, he described his rule and realm in his journal. He related that the people whom the monarch governed were happy and, among other things, were not subject to taxes or corporal punishments. The pilgrim's chronicle provided glimpses of an empire in which peace and prosperity prevailed.

Having expelled the foreign interlopers, Chandragupta set about creating a model Hindu state, one in which the caste system was affirmed. Despite the Guptas' strong

personal Hindu affiliation, the rulers were tolerant of all religions. The archaeological remains of the Gupta Empire indicate that the country was secure, peaceful, and exceedingly prosperous.

Part of Chandragupta's drive against foreign adversaries included the creation of stone temples and icons. Chandragupta's patronage is largely responsible for the inauguration and development of Hindu art and architecture. Although Buddhists and Jains had been creating stone monuments for centuries, only a few small stone icons of Hindu deities had been created before the time of Chandragupta II. During his reign, a new tradition of creating impressive and enduring Hindu monuments was formulated. The first artistic campaign occurred at Udayagiri near modern-day Bhopal. The twenty-some cave temples there have the distinction of being the only works that can be personally associated with a Gupta monarch. An inscription dated to 401-402 C.E. attests to the king's presence at the site.

For the first time, an elaborate exegesis in stone gave visual form to the major Hindu deities, including representations of the goddess Durga with ten arms, the Saptamātṛkās, Śiva in his *linga* form, Viṣṇu, Varāha, Brahma, Skanda, Gaṇeśa, and a host of supportive figures. From that point on, religious monuments were erected throughout the Gupta kingdom. The temples were decorated with icons imbued with a numinous beauty, achieving such a degree of aesthetic perfection that they serve as the classical standard by which all Indian art is evaluated.

The astonishing beauty of Gupta painting is demonstrated by the paintings in the Ajanta Caves in the Deccan; they are among the greatest surviving paintings of any ancient civilization. Most of the caves were excavated and decorated with great murals during the reign of King Hariṣena Vākāṭaka, whose family line was allied with the Guptas through marriage. Although the caves are Buddhist, the painting style nevertheless is highly evolved and sophisticated. In the paintings, thousands of figures, in courtly dress and ornaments, are rendered with supreme mastery and lyrical grace. These vivid paintings reveal courtly Indian life in the fifth century C.E. in minute detail. Although the Ajanta caves technically are not located within the borders of the Gupta Empire, it can be assumed that the elegant paintings represented there were like those used to ornament Gupta temples and palaces.

During the reigns of the early Gupta kings, the great two Indian epics, *Rāmāyaṇa* (c. 550 B.C.E.; English translation, 1870-1889) and *Mahābhārata* (c. 400 B.C.E.-400 C.E.; *The Mahabharata of Krishna-Dwaipayana Vyasa*,

1887-1896) with its famous sermon, *Bhagavadgītā* (c. 200 B.C.E.-200 C.E.; *The Bhagavad Gita*, 1785; literally the divine song or song of the lord), are believed to have seen their final development. This same period fostered the compilation of several major Hindu texts known as Purāṇas. In the field of literature, Gupta poetry, prose, and drama are regarded as works of a great intellectual renaissance.

The language of the court was classical Sanskrit and the works were written mainly for recitation or performance at court, or for an elite circle of literati, well versed in the canon of the courtly, flowery conventions. Generally, the subjects of the poets included love, nature, moralizing, and storytelling. Religious subjects relating the legends of the divine were common as well.

Kālidāsa was the best-known and greatest Sanskrit poet/dramatist of his day; his reputation is celebrated even today. He probably flourished during the reigns of the emperors Chandragupta II and his son Kumāragupta. Works that have survived the centuries are: *Abhijñāna-śākuntala* (c. 45 B.C.E. or c. 395 C.E.; *Śākuntala: Or, The Lost Ring*, 1789), *Kumārasambhava* (c. 60 B.C.E. or c. 380 C.E.; *The Birth of the War-God*, 1879), *Raghuvaṃśa* (c. 50 B.C.E. or c. 390 C.E.; *The Dynasty of Raghu*, 1872-1895), *Meghadūta* (c. 65 B.C.E. or c. 375 C.E.; *The Cloud Messenger*, 1813), and *Ṛtusaṃhāra* (c. 75 B.C.E. or c. 365 C.E.; English translation, 1867). Kālidāsa's masterpieces brought the classical courtly Sanskrit tradition to a state of perfection. Daṇḍin, Subandhu, and Bāṇabhaṭṭa were other great writers of the age; many of their works have survived the centuries.

Indian intellectual progress soared during the Gupta era, especially in the fields of science, medicine, mathematics, and astronomy. In the fifth century C.E., it was recognized that Earth revolved around the Sun and rotated on its axis, facts not acknowledged in the West for centuries. Although generally the Arabs are credited with the invention of the decimal system and other mathematical notions, Arabs called mathematics an Indian lore (*hindisat*). Much of the mathematical investigations date to the Gupta era.

The peaceful empire secured by Chandragupta II was severely disturbed during the reign of his son Kumāragupta I when the empire suffered a severe blow. Late in his reign, a new group of foreign invaders swept across the land. A central Asian people known as the Huns conducted brutal raids, decimating many of the great institutions of the previous centuries. Their incursions were the death blow to India's greatest empire, which completely vanished by 550 C.E.

SIGNIFICANCE

The names of the great rulers of the Gupta Dynasty dominate the history of India. It is an age as memorable as the time when Aryan Brahmanical religion evolved into Hinduism and the three great cults of Viṣṇu, Śiva, and the goddess Durga took final shape. During the 250 years that the Guptas held sway over north India, Hinduism became the state religion, Sanskrit became the dominant and official language, and all of the arts achieved classical perfection. Chandragupta II, in particular, established a righteous Hindu rule and an affluent, prosperous, and efficiently administered kingdom that became the model for later rulers throughout India.

—*Katherine Anne Harper*

FURTHER READING

Dikshitar, V. R. R. *The Gupta Polity*. Delhi: Motilal Banarsidass, 1993. Excellent study of Gupta military and civil organization as well as religious policies. Bibliography.

Khosla, Sarla. *Gupta Civilization*. Delhi: Motilal Banarsidass, 1989. Focuses on the emergence of the Gupta Dynasty and its importance as a model for later Hindu civilization. Bibliography.

Smith, Bardwell L. *Essays on Gupta Culture*. Delhi: Motilal Banarsidass, 1983. Collection of informed essays by specialists on various aspects of Gupta history, art, literature, and culture. Bibliography.

Sudhi, Padma. *Gupta Art: A Study from Aesthetic and Canonical Norms*. New Delhi: Galaxy Publications, 1993. A consideration of major Sanskrit textual references to Indian aesthetics as applied to various fields and particularly as they relate to Gupta art and architecture. Bibliography.

SEE ALSO: 6th-4th century B.C.E. (traditionally, 1st millennium B.C.E.), Suśruta, Indian Physician, Writes Medical Compendium; c. 550 B.C.E., Vālmīki Composes the *Rāmāyaṇa*; c. 4th century B.C.E.-3d century C.E., Kauṭilya Compiles a Treatise on Practical Statecraft; c. 400 B.C.E.-400 C.E., Composition of the *Mahābhārata*; c. 321 B.C.E., Mauryan Empire Rises in India; c. 200 B.C.E.-200 C.E., *Bhagavad Gita* Is Created; c. 300 C.E., Licchavi Dynasty Begins in the Kathmandu Valley, Nepal; 399 C.E., Chinese Monk Faxian Travels to India; c. 400 C.E., Kālidāsa Composes Sanskrit Poetry and Plays; 460-477 C.E., Buddhist Temples Built at Ajanta Caves in India.

RELATED ARTICLES in *Great Lives from History: The Ancient World*: Chandragupta Maurya; Faxian; Kālidāsa.

c. 382-c. 405 C.E.
SAINT JEROME CREATES THE VULGATE

Jerome, an influential Christian scholar whose life blended several ideals of late antique Christendom, created a Latin translation of the Old Testament and Gospels, which along with translations of the remaining New Testament books by other scholars, became known as the Vulgate and remained the standard translation of the Bible until the sixteenth century.

LOCALE: Bethlehem (now in Israeli-occupied West Bank)
CATEGORY: Religion

KEY FIGURES
Saint Jerome (between 331 and 347-probably 420 C.E.), Christian scholar, notable translator, and a father of the Christian church
Damasus I (c. 304-384 C.E.), bishop of Rome, 366-384 C.E., encouraged Jerome's Latin translation of Greek scriptures
Paula (d. 404 C.E.), a woman of the aristocracy who · became Jerome's colleague in Bethlehem
Eustochium (d. 419 C.E.), established monastic houses for men and women in Bethlehem with her mother Paula
Saint Augustine (354-430 C.E.), bishop of Hippo, 396-430 C.E., who questioned Jerome's translations

SUMMARY OF EVENT
By Saint Jerome's death, the Roman world in its former glory had come unraveled, and so had Jerome. His life's pursuit of holiness and spiritual perfection was instead filled with rancor and conflict, but on the anvil of his sharp letters and other writings was forged the teaching authority that earned him a place among the fathers of the Christian Church.

Born in north Italian obscurity, Jerome (originally Eusebius Hieronymus) set out on a lifelong journey across the Roman Empire. Rome was the first stop, where he received his primary training. This initial foray into classical learning later blossomed into fluency in Hebrew and Greek, enabling his master achievement, the translation of the Bible into Latin.

A trip to Gaul introduced him to monasticism. He joined a group of men in the common life, separated from the world through fasting, prayer, and study. He would wrestle with the memory of Roman dancing girls and worldly pleasures, both of which entranced his imagination as he pursued holiness. This form of self-renunciation, known as asceticism, had gained impetus across the ancient church through the early example of Antony of Egypt, who was popularized by Saint Athanasius of Alexandria.

The young scholar-monk crossed the Roman Empire to Asia Minor in 370 C.E., pagan and Christian books in tow. From Antioch, he retreated to the desert for two years, all the while honing his linguistic skills and wrestling with temptation. Eastern desert hermits lived in solitude, repudiating worldly company. Such a life was too much of a stretch for the more social Jerome, and he did not stay long. The monks he did meet found his western theological views troublesome. Significant during his sojourn there was his dream that, at the Last Judgment, Christ accused him of having given in to another temptation, worldly learning. "You are a Ciceronian," said the Christ of his nightmare, "not a Christian." This curse on his learning never troubled him enough to discard it.

Jerome returned the thirty miles to Antioch and was ordained to the priesthood there by his friend, Bishop Paulinus. There, he was introduced to the writings of Origen (c. 185-c. 254), the Alexandrian theologian whose ideas would have a profound effect on him. Origen's methods of biblical interpretation and his particular sort of asceticism were to prove troublesome for Jerome in time. He moved to Constantinople in 380 C.E., in time for the Second Ecumenical Council the following year. He studied there with another great church father, Gregory of Nazianzus, and began translating Greek texts for a western audience. Such translation occupied much of his career and formed a cross-cultural bridge within the Roman Empire.

Pope Damasus I in Rome called him to be his personal secretary in 382 C.E. Recognizing his abilities, Damasus embarked the scholar on the biblical translation project that would be his greatest contribution. He was commissioned to produce a Latin translation of the Greek scriptures. He began in Rome with the Gospels. This project would span his stay in Rome and much of his later career in Bethlehem. It would also win him disapproval from readers who questioned everything from his word choices to his authority for altering the Bible.

Pope Damasus also opened the door for him to noblewomen in Rome whose asceticism and learning made Jerome their apt companion. These aristocratic women included Paula and daughters Blesilla and Eustochium, Marcella, Asella, and Lea. Anxiety over sex did not keep him from retaining the company of this circle of Roman women. These widows, unmarried daughters, and others devoted to the consecrated life came to know a side of the fiery Jerome rarely exposed to his intellectual opponents, who felt the satirical lash of his tongue in the letters they received from him on theological controversy, asceticism, and churchly politics. A lion to his enemies, he was a lamb among these women who shared his interest in biblical study.

Jerome was prepared to grant women a privileged place in conversation because he was steeped in Origen's thought. Origen taught that human bodies were but temporary homes for eternal spirits. Male and female minds were not essentially different. Borrowing this idea, Jerome thought that men and women could commune together intellectually without succumbing to temptation because the intellect kept the lower appetites subdued.

However, if he affected a cool demeanor in his relationships with women, he wrote to other ascetics of the constant battle they should wage with fleshly desire. The Roman monk Jovinian declared that all forms of life, married or celibate, were equally virtuous. One estate was no higher than another. Jovinian's egalitarianism

earned a stern rebuttal from Jerome, who denigrated marriage in his reply. To marry once, he wrote, was a compromise with the physical state. To marry a second time was little better than prostitution.

When Origen's views fell out of favor in the late fourth century C.E., Jerome abandoned them in writing, but no change resulted in his ascetic practices. Now, however, the virgin physical body would rise not to a world of ethereal spirits in eternity, as Origen had suggested, but rather to a Paradise resembling a great monastery, a desert in bloom with virginal, embodied holiness.

Jerome merited Roman disfavor, this time from among the aristocracy, who were realizing that his asceticism disrupted families and made folly of the social stability they underwrote. Damasus died in 384, leaving Jerome without a sponsor, so Jerome set sail to the Holy Land the following year. Paula and her daughter Eustochium met him there, and together they established monastic houses for men and women in Bethlehem. He spent the remainder of his life there, mostly involved in translating the scriptures into Latin, writing commentaries on biblical books, and sending and receiving letters far and wide. Commentaries on the text served to bolster his transla-

Saint Jerome, in his study. (Hulton|Archive)

tion and distinguish himself as not simply a grammarian, but a scholar worthy of wealthy patronage. Thus, in no way did the move afford isolation and that was not his desire. Rather, westerners flocked to his monastery, and the ink flowed long from his pen. The crowds, some days, became too much for the productive scholar.

In Bethlehem, he continued to translate scripture and Greek theologians, especially Origen, into Latin, but by 393 C.E., Origen was under fire. Theologians began to criticize his views. Bishops denounced the new heretic's memory. Jerome did not stand against the prevailing tide but instead laid aside his admiration for the bygone teacher. If Jerome valued one thing above Origen's writings, it was orthodoxy. He would not suffer himself to be remembered as the advocate of a heretic.

That Jerome could choose different words for familiar passages in his Latin Bible raised the eyebrows, and ire, of some opponents. Among them was the rising star of North Africa, Bishop Augustine of Hippo (later Saint Augustine), who questioned points of his translation. The two scholars maintained a peppery correspondence for more than a decade. The approbation Jerome later extended the bishop was rare. Augustine and Jerome joined ranks on a new Western controversy, the idea of the monk Pelagius that human beings were capable of meriting divine grace. Augustine countered Pelagius's stress on human freedom to choose good over evil with the doctrine that, in the absence of human ability to choose God, God chooses some humans for eternal life apart from their own merits. Jerome's opposition to Pelagius was not quite as adamant as Augustine's. Jerome believed that the human will was capable of joining with the divine in working out salvation. Nevertheless, Pelagius's teaching was an extreme.

If Jerome was sustained by the friendship of Paula and Eustochium, their deaths in 404 and 419, respectively, enervated him. In between, the end of the Roman Empire in 410 cut empire flesh from empire spirit. Similarly spent and left alone, Jerome died, probably in 420.

SIGNIFICANCE

Saint Jerome's legacy would extend far into the Middle Ages, as the Vulgate (Latin Bible) remained the standard Latin biblical text. The Protestant Reformation of the sixteenth century brought new biblical translations. The Vulgate continued to be used in the Roman Catholic Church until superseded by newer translations in the twentieth century.

Jerome's career marks the symbiosis of two ideals celebrated among Christians of late antiquity. The ideal of asceticism, or self-renunciation, was a key determinant in his career. However, he is not distinguished by this common mode of life in his age. It is when his particularly stringent asceticism is combined with the intellectual ideal taken over by Christians from Greek culture that Jerome's achievement stands forth. His powerful mind was not devoted to theology in any systematic sense but instead to linguistics, biblical translation, and commentary. He finds a place among the four Latin doctors of the Church, with Saint Augustine, Saint Ambrose, and Gregory the Great. Among them, he represents the importance of biblical scholarship to the overall theological enterprise.

Much has been made of Jerome's stridency, sexual anxiety, and intellectual abilities. Balanced scholarship avoids reductionism in estimating the impact of this complex figure. His letters provide excellent examples of the art of polemic in late antiquity. His varied relationships with men and women are a study in social location in his time, and his scholarship provided a benchmark for centuries of biblical interpreters.

—*William P. McDonald*

FURTHER READING

Brown, Peter. *The Body and Society: Men, Women, and Sexual Renunciation in Early Christianity.* New York: Columbia University Press, 1988. This collection of essays by the author links Jerome with his ascetic milieu. Virginity and other forms of renunciation are viewed both socially and intellectually.

Gonzalez, Justo L. *The Early Church to the Dawn of the Reformation.* Vol. 1 in *The Story of Christianity.* San Francisco: Harper and Row, 1984. Gonzalez provides the general reader with a broad introduction to the early church and its key figures. Illustrations and maps included.

Kelly, J. N. D. *Jerome: His Life, Writings, and Controversies.* New York: Harper and Row, 1975. Kelly provides a detailed account of Jerome as a great mind of the patristic era.

Rebenich, Stefan. *Jerome.* London: Routledge, 2002. This study provides selections from Jerome's writings and an analysis of his biblical interpretation and interactions with those he mentored.

SEE ALSO: c. 50-c. 150 C.E., Compilation of the New Testament; c. 286 C.E., Saint Anthony of Egypt Begins Ascetic Life; 413-427 C.E., Saint Augustine Writes *The City of God*.
RELATED ARTICLES in *Great Lives from History: The Ancient World*: Saint Augustine; Saint Jerome.

386 C.E.
TOBA ESTABLISHES THE NORTHERN WEI DYNASTY IN CHINA

During the Period of Disunity, a nomadic tribe established a dynasty in Northern China that lasted until 534 C.E. and acted as the precursor to the reunification of China under the Sui.

LOCALE: Northern China
CATEGORIES: Expansion and land acquisition; government and politics

KEY FIGURES
Wendi (Wen-ti; fl. fifth century C.E.), emperor, r. 471-499 C.E.
Li Anshi (Li An-shih, fl. fifth century C.E.), founder of land equalization system

SUMMARY OF EVENT

Following the demise of the Han Dynasty (206 B.C.E.-220 C.E.), China was plunged into three and a half centuries of division, commonly referred to as the Period of Disunity. In the first stage, the Three Kingdoms Period (220-280 C.E.), three kingdoms established hegemony in the southwest, southeast, and northern regions of China. This was followed by a tentative reunification under the Western Jin (Chin) from 280-316. (The Jin Dynasty was founded in 265 and became known as the Western Jin in 280, after conquering the Wu Dynasty.)

With the fall of the Jin, China again became divided between north and south (with the Huai River serving as the traditional line of demarcation). Starting in about 304, a succession of non-Chinese nomads established the so-called Sixteen Kingdoms of the Five Barbarians in the north (304-439), while the south was ruled by a bewildering array of Chinese factions, each of whom installed their own dynasties. Amidst the social, political, and economic chaos of the period, one nomadic tribe, the Toba (T'o-pa), succeeded in establishing the longest dynasty of the period, effectively ruling northern China from 386-534 as the Northern Wei.

The ethnic origins of the Toba (a variant of their own name for themselves, Tabgatch) is still a matter of some controversy. One of three members of the Xianbei tribal confederation, consisting of nomadic herdsmen from southern Manchuria who had settled in southeastern Mongolia in the third century C.E., the Toba moved into northern modern-day Shanxi Province by 315. The Toba confederacy appears to have been composed of tribal units of Mongol and Turkish origins. Briefly establishing a small state in north-central China, known as the Dai, in

338, the Toba had capitulated to Tibetan rule (Earlier Qin, or Ch'in, Dynasty, 350?-394) in 376. Although subdued, the Toba were never effectively destroyed, and when the Qin, seeking to invade southern China, met with defeat in 383 at the Battle of the Fei River, the Toba quickly reasserted themselves. By 386, enjoying a strategic position along one of the principal invasion routes into north China, they had succeeded in gaining control over much of the region.

Abandoning their traditional nomadic lifestyle, the Toba established their capital at Datong (Ta-t'ung) in northern Shanxi. Faced with the need to feed a settled community, the Toba spent the next decade securing control of the fertile plains of eastern China. By 430 C.E., they had conquered all of northern China, moving as far south as the former Han capital of Luoyang, abandoned in 311. Mass migrations to the south following the chaos of the Han's fall had severely depleted the population base in the north, leaving vast amounts of arable land abandoned. To reclaim the arid land, the Toba pursued a policy of mass deportation of conquered peoples into the region around Datong. An estimated 460,000 people were uprooted and moved during the reign of Dao Wudi, the first Toba emperor (r. 386-409).

Unlike their nomadic predecessors, the Toba began a deliberate process of sinicization from the outset. Datong was built in traditional Chinese style; the walled, rectangular city was oriented to the four compass points and included such features as an Ancestral Hall and Great Earth Mound. Lacking the administrative skills necessary to effectively govern an agricultural state, the Toba quickly turned to the Chinese landowning gentry. Cui Hao (Ts'ui Hao; 381-450) introduced Chinese administrative and penal codes into the new dynasty, and the Toba appointed resident Chinese gentry to governmental positions as representatives of the capital in their local district. This close collaboration would continue throughout the period and would prove to be both beneficial and detrimental to the Toba. In addition, the nomadic conquerors abandoned their traditional religion of shamanism and animism in favor of Buddhism and the indigenous tradition of Daoism, both of which would enjoy state support at various times.

In an effort to raise agricultural production, increase the tax base, provide tillable land for those deported and prevent farmer migration, the Toba introduced their most significant, and longest lasting, institution in 486 C.E.

The land equalization system (*juntian*), created by Li Anshi, would remain in effect until 750. Under this plan, every adult (male and female) was entitled to a standard allotment of agricultural land, the typical family receiving approximately 14 acres (6 hectares). Eighty percent of the land was to be reserved for grain cultivation and ideally would gradually revert back to the state as the farmer grew older or became disabled, until at the individual's death, all the land would be back in state control and subsequently redistributed to the young. The state collected an annual tax in grain from this "personal share land," usually no more than one-thirtieth of the yield. The remaining 20 percent, the so-called "mulberry land" was to be held by the family in perpetuity, as long as it was maintained. This land was to be dedicated to permanent crops, most often mulberry trees, whose leaves would feed silkworms. A second tax in kind from the silkworm production was also collected. However, any crops grown under the trees were not taxable, thus effectively stimulating the creation and cultivation of very diversified crops.

In addition to the taxes in kind, every farmer owed the state twenty days of labor, or the payment of an extra tax. Most scholars doubt that the Toba were ever completely successful in carrying out this policy, necessitating as it did both zero population growth and strict continuous census taking, but it did serve as an effective check on the growth of the Chinese gentry and was practiced in various forms for nearly three centuries.

As the administrative apparatus grew, a steadily rising number of Chinese reclaimed prominence and power, while the Toba, at least those at the capital, increasingly viewed themselves as Chinese. The apex came during the reign of Emperor Wen (r. 471-499 C.E.). For both practical and political reasons, in 493, Wendi ordered the capital moved six hundred miles south of Datong, to the abandoned Han capital of Luoyang. From a practical standpoint, Datong was situated at the end of a very long supply line, perfectly appropriate for a seminomadic, steppe empire, but wholly inadequate for a new urbanized society. Luoyang, located on the Yellow River, provided easy access to waterborne transportation and was strategically positioned in the center of the most productive agricultural zone. In addition, from a political perspective, the growing Chinese contingent convinced the emperor that tradition and prestige dictated such a move. Wendi, who went by the extended name Xiao Wendi (Filial Cultured Emperor, reflective of the Chinese emphasis on filial piety), concurred, and ordered the immediate reconstruction of Luoyang on a grand scale; when finished, the new capital stretched 6 miles (nearly 10 kilometers)

THE NORTHERN DYNASTIES AND THEIR RULERS, 386-581 C.E.

NORTHERN WEI DYNASTY

Ruler	Reign
Dao Wudi	386-409
Ming Yuandi	409-423
Tai Wudi	424-41
Toba Yu, king of Nan'an	452
Wen Chengdi	452-265
Xian Wendi	466-470
Xiao Wendi	471-499
Xuan Wudi	500-515
Xiao Mingdi	516-528
Xiao Zhuangdi	528-529
Yuan Ye, king of Changguang	530
Jie Mindi	531
Yuan Lang, king of Anding	531
Xiao Wudi	532-534

EASTERN WEI DYNASTY

Ruler	Reign
Xiao Jingdi	534-550

WESTERN WEI DYNASTY

Ruler	Reign
Wendi	535-552
Feidi (overthrown emperor)	552-554
Gongdi	554-556

NORTHERN QI DYNASTY

Ruler	Reign
Wen Xuandi	550-560
Feidi (overthrown emperor)	560
Xiao Zhaodi	560-561
Wuchengdi	561-565
Houzhu (the later ruler)	565-577
Youzhu (the infant ruler)	577

NORTHERN ZHOU DYNASTY

Ruler	Reign
Xiao Mindi	557
Mingdi	557-561
Wudi	561-579
Xuandi	579
Jingdi	579-581

east to west, and 4.5 miles (more than 7 kilometers) north to south, containing a reported 1,367 monasteries. Wendi proclaimed that henceforth Chinese was to be the official language, all were to adopt Chinese dress, Chinese family names were to replace old tribal affiliations, and intermarriage was strongly encouraged. Wendi himself took the lead, changing the imperial family name to Yuan.

These events served as the death knell for the Toba nobility. Six hundred miles from their original tribes, unable to transfer their herds over such a distance, forbidden to return north, and ultimately left with nothing to do, they quickly became impoverished and resentful. While the court and its largely Chinese bureaucracy flourished, the Toba who remained on the steppe for defense grew to despise those in the capital, disgusted with their sinicized and sedentary life of luxury. The combination of disgruntled nobility and apprehensive military commanders, who viewed the rise of the Chinese bureaucracy as a threat to their own traditional power, would lead to the eventual downfall of the Northern Wei.

In 523, with the support of Toba nobility, the Rebellion of Six Garrisons, involving more than one million Toba, erupted onto the North China Plain. A ten-year civil war followed, in the course of which the Empress Regent Hu had Emperor Xiao Mingdi assassinated and replaced with a child. In response, the rebellious armies captured Luoyang, and drowned Hu and the child in the Yellow River; two thousand of her courtiers also perished. Finally, in 534, the two most powerful military leaders divided the kingdom between themselves, with the resultant Eastern Wei (534-550) reverting back to a nomadic, militaristic lifestyle, and the Western Wei (535-557) continuing as a sinicized state.

SIGNIFICANCE

The Northern Wei emerged in the midst of political and social chaos to establish the longest single dynasty during the Period of Disunity. Politically, it provided an era of stability and prosperity for north China. Its economic policy and creation of the land equalization system not only benefited the peasant population but also laid the foundation for similar policies over the next three hundred years. The Toba's self-conscious, and highly successful, sinicization would be repeated numerous times over the course of ensuing Chinese history, with the last, and perhaps most notable example being the Manchu/Qing Dynasty (1644-1911).

Culturally, the Northern Wei also created some of the most remarkable Buddhist cave temples and sculptures

in the world. Begun in 460 C.E. at Yungang, about 10 miles (16 kilometers) west of Datong, the first caves were dug by Buddhist monks under the leadership of Tanyao, appointed as head Buddhist monk by the emperor. Carved out of sandstone cliffs, there are fifty-three caves containing more than 51,000 (out of an estimated 100,000) statues and bas-reliefs of the Buddha and other figures, the largest a seated Buddha measuring 56 feet (17 meters) high and 52 feet (16 meters) wide. Once the capital was moved to Luoyang, work stopped at Yungang, and a new cave complex begun at Longmen near the capital. Here, more than 1,300 caves contain 100,000 scultures, several Buddhist pagodas and numerous inscriptions distributed through 2,100 grottoes and niches. The work in both of these complexes represents some of the earliest examples of stone carving in China and are considered the high point of Buddhist artistic expression.

—Jeffrey W. Dippmann

FURTHER READING

Eberhard, Wolfram. *A History of China*. Berkeley: University of California Press, 1977. A concise history with a well-balanced section on the Northern Wei.

Jenner, W. J. F. *Memories of Loyang: Yang Hsüan-chih and the Lost Capital (493-534)*. Oxford, England: Oxford University Press, 1981. A highly readable and interesting account of the new capital at Luoyang.

Mather, Richard B. "K'ou Ch'ien-chih and the Taoist Theocracy at the Northern Wei Court, 425-451." In *Facets of Taoism*, edited by Holmes Welch and Anna Seidel. New Haven, Conn.: Yale University Press, 1979. An excellent study of the impact Daoism had on the early history of the dynasty.

Rodzinski, Witold. *A History of China*. New York: Pergamon Press, 1979. Another good account of the basic history of this period.

SEE ALSO: 206 B.C.E., Liu Bang Captures Qin Capital, Founds Han Dynasty; 140-87 B.C.E., Wudi Rules Han Dynasty China; 9-23 C.E., Wang Mang's Rise to Power; 25 C.E., Guang Wudi Restores the Han Dynasty; 220 C.E., Three Kingdoms Period Begins in China; 265 C.E., Sima Yan Establishes the Western Jin Dynasty; 316 C.E., Western Jin Dynasty Falls; 420 C.E., Southern Dynasties Period Begins in China.
RELATED ARTICLE in *Great Lives from History: The Ancient World*: Wudi.

390-430 C.E. or later, traditionally r. 270-310
ŌJIN TENNŌ, FIRST HISTORICAL EMPEROR OF JAPAN, REIGNS

Ōjin was the first Japanese emperor who clearly was not legendary but an actual historical figure, and his reign saw a consolidation of power and economic and cultural development

LOCALE: Japan
CATEGORY: Government and politics

KEY FIGURES

Ōjin Tennō (fl. late fourth-early fifth century C.E.; traditionally 201-310 C.E.), emperor of Japan, r. 390-430 C.E., traditionally r. 270-310 C.E.

Nintoku (375?-427 C.E.; traditionally 290-399 C.E.), Ōjin's favorite son and successor, traditionally r. 313-399 C.E.

Kaminaga Hime (fl. late fourth-early fifth century C.E.), a woman with whom Ōjin falls in love but who marries Nintoku

Yehime (fl. late fourth-early fifth century C.E.), a favorite concubine romanced by Ōjin

Wani (fl. late fourth-early fifth century C.E.), a Korean scribe who introduced writing to Japan

SUMMARY OF EVENT

Ōjin Tennō, that is, Emperor Ōjin (also known as Homuda or Homutawake no Mikoto before his death), is the first such ruler who is actually a historical person. Although the oldest surviving written accounts of his reign, the *Kojiki* (712 C.E.; *Records of Ancient Matters*, 1883) and the *Nihon shoki* (compiled 720 C.E.; *Nihongi: Chronicles of Japan from the Earliest Times to A.D. 697*, 1896) still include some events that are either purely mythical, or a mix of legend and history, scholars agree that Ōjin lived and ruled Japan, albeit much later than these eighth century sources calculated. His reign thus marks the shift of protohistorical to historical Japan.

Contemporary scholars have an inkling that Ōjin was a relative outsider who took over rule in the Yamato region of Japan and established his own reign there in one of the cradles of Japanese civilization. The ancient Yamato region encompasses the fertile Nara plain and is in the part of Japan's central island of Honshū where the modern cities of Nara, Ōsaka, and Kobe are located, as well as the ancient shrine of Ise, dedicated to the emperor's mythical ancestor, the sun goddess Amaterasu.

Some historians who subscribe to the hotly disputed "horse rider theory" even believe that Ōjin was part of this hypothetical Asian people theorized to have conquered Japan because of their superior weapons technology around the fourth century C.E. However, most historians believe that the indigenous Yayoi culture of Yamato and Kyūshū evolved to a higher state without outside invaders and that Ōjin was a member of this civilization.

According to tradition, Ōjin assumed the imperial throne as the fifteenth of Japan's emperors in the year 270 C.E. About his real parents, nothing is known. However, myth has it that he was born to the legendary Empress Jingū (also known as Jingō) in 271, a few months after his father, the legendary fourteenth emperor Chūai, had either died in battle in Kyūshū or succumbed to a sudden illness. For the next sixty-nine years, until her death, his mother, Jingū, ruled as a regent, refusing to let her son be enthroned.

As emperor, Ōjin's children became imperial princes and princesses, and many noble families of the seventh and eighth century later claimed one of them as their genuine first ancestor. Thus, the sources spend considerable attention to his ample offspring. Altogether, Ōjin had either twenty or twenty-six children. They were born to him by his wife, Empress Nakatsuhime, and his imperial concubines, two of whom were the younger sisters of the empress.

In the first years of his reign, Ōjin consolidated his power and dedicated himself to domestic politics. He used the workforce of tributary people to build roads and ponds, improving the Yamato region. He also organized the *be*, or guilds, of the fishermen and gamekeepers, securing a food supply for his domain. As such, Ōjin stands out compared with most other emperors, who performed fewer practical tasks and concerned themselves mostly with religious ceremonies.

Ōjin also became involved in foreign affairs in Korea. The Japanese were pursuing interests of their own and intervened in the affairs of the three Korean kingdoms of the period. Japanese and Korean sources vary considerably about the nature of these struggles and their exact date. Japanese tradition, for example, has it that Sinsă, the king of Paekje, disrespected Ōjin and was killed by his own people to atone for this transgression in 272 C.E. A Korean source states that Sinsă died in his traveling palace while hunting, in the year 392. Although the Korean date is believed to be correct, the nature of the king's death is still subject to historical debate.

Ōjin continued his program of domestic improvements, often with foreign labor sent as tribute; shipbuild-

IMPORTANT CHILDREN OF EMPEROR ŌJIN

With his wife, Empress Nakatsuhime:
  Imperial Princess Arata
  Imperial Prince Ohosazaki, later Emperor Nintoku
  Imperial Prince Netori

With his concubine Takaki Iribime
(younger sister of the empress):
  Imperial Prince Nukada no Ohonakahiko
  Imperial Prince Ohoyamamori
  Imperial Prince Iza no Mawaka
  Imperial Princess Ohohara
  Imperial Princess Komida

With his concubine Otohime
(younger sister of the empress):
  Imperial Princess Ahe
  Imperial Princess Ahaji no Mihara
  Imperial Princess Ki no Uno

With his concubine Miyanushiyaka Hime:
  Imperial Prince Uji no Wakairatsuko, designated
    successor of Ōjin
  Imperial Princess Yata
  Imperial Princess Medori

With his concubine Oname Hime:
  Imperial Prince Uji no Wakairatsume

With his concubine Oto Hime:
  Imperial Prince Wakanoke Futamata

With his concubine Mago Hime:
  Imperial Prince Hayabusa Wake

With his concubine Naga Hime:
  Imperial Prince Ohohaye
  Imperial Prince Wohaye

ing; and consolidation of his rule. There were also intrigues among the nobles, such as when Takechi no Sukune was accused by his own brother of planning to usurp the throne. Sent to subdue the southwestern Japanese island of Kyūshū, Takechi returned to the palace to defend himself. A judgment by ordeal involving boiling water was won by Takechi, but the emperor prevented him from killing his brother, indicating Ōjin's emphasis on domestic peace.

The emperor's private life fascinated his contemporaries. After falling in love with the beautiful Kaminaga Hime in 282 C.E., Ōjin nevertheless yielded the young woman to his favorite son Ohosazaki no Mikoto (later the emperor Nintoku). He presented her to his son at a special banquet, and father and son expressed their desire in poems recorded for eternity. When Kaminaga responded to Ohosazaki without resistance, his status at court rose accordingly. Later, Ōjin allowed his beloved concubine Yehime, whom he had romanced with songs reminiscent of the songs of Salomon in the Bible, to visit her parents. Thus he showed humanity to his subjects.

Ōjin's efforts at improving Yamato civilization also gained from his desire to have skilled professionals sent to Japan from Korea as tribute. The Korean seamstress Maketsu founded an important trade school, and the learned scribe Wani introduced writing to Japan. Historically, the Japanese acquired writing through the Korean scribe Wani from the Chinese around 404 C.E., even though the Japanese traditional account uses the older, incorrect date of 284. By using Chinese characters to correspond phonetically to spoken Japanese, Japan finally became literate, a key event of Ōjin's reign.

Throughout his remaining years, Ōjin continued to intervene in Korea, occasionally sending Japanese troops to install his Korean protégés as kings there. He also demanded skilled immigrants to improve Japan's manufacture and infrastructure.

At the end, Ōjin gave clear preferences to Ohosazaki. Even as he appointed another son as heir apparent, he gave Ohosazaki a powerful position of his own, from which he would eventually become the emperor Nintoku. When Ōjin died, in 310 according to legend, he left behind an empire of considerable power.

SIGNIFICANCE

There may be a certain irony in the fact that later generations would make Ōjin the god of war, called Yahata or Hachiman—for his most enduring accomplishments lie in improving the domestic situation of his empire and in introducing writing to Japan. His interventions in Korean politics brought Ōjin many skillful immigrants from this area. Traditionally, his reign also provided Japan's noble houses with many illustrious ancestors to claim for themselves, solidifying their position in Japan's rank-conscious feudal society.

Indicative of the power, resources, and skills of the emperors of Yamato of Ōjin's time are the many impressive burial mounds of the period. One of the earliest and largest mausoleums, in Habikino in Ōsaka prefecture, is traditionally believed to be Ōjin's tomb. Like many of the others, it is shaped like a keyhole lying on the earth. It possesses three tiers, two moats, and two dikes. It is 1,362 feet (415 meters) long and rises over the plain landscape. Ōjin and his contemporaries' graves gave the period of his reign its name, Kofun, which is Japanese for keyhole.

With Ōjin, Japanese imperial history leaves the realm of legend and enters that of history. Although there are still shrines in Japan venerating this emperor as the god of war, it is clear that he was a real person. His emphasis on domestic development and the improvement of the skills of his people advanced his nation, even though his office would become much more ceremonial in the decades and centuries to come, until the Meiji Restoration of 1868. Ōjin's kindness to his concubine Yehime is remembered as an important personal trait of this emperor.

—*R. C. Lutz*

FURTHER READING

Aston, W. G., trans. *Nihongi: Chronicles of Japan*. London: George Allen and Unwind, 1956. Reprint of the original 1896 text. Still the only translation of this Japanese text, compiled in 710 and also called *Nihon Shoki*, which contains one of the two original accounts of Ōjin's reign.

Brown, Delmer M., ed. *Ancient Japan*. Vol. 1 in *The Cambridge History of Japan*. New York: Cambridge University Press, 1993. A collection of contemporary

essays covering the latest scholarship on the rise of early imperial Japan, with an interesting reflection on ancient Japanese historical consciousness; discusses the historical facts of Ōjin's reign.

Philippi, Donald L., trans. *Kojiki*. Princeton, N.J.: Princeton University Press, 1968. English translation of the first surviving Japanese account of Ōjin's reign, compiled in 712. The reader has to get used to Philippi's unique style of transcribing ancient Japanese names into Roman letters, which alters the spelling of most, but this is the only English text of the Japanese original.

Reischauer, Robert Karl. *Early Japanese History: Part A*. Princeton University Press, 1937. Reprint. Gloucester, Mass.: Peter Smith, 1967. A pre-World War II compilation of Japanese sources telling of mostly legendary events, including those that occurred during Ōjin's reign.

Sansom, George B. *A History of Japan to 1334*. Stanford, Calif.: Stanford University Press, 1958. Still valuable study of the earliest, legendary period of Japanese history.

SEE ALSO: 3d century B.C.E. (traditionally 660 B.C.E.), Jimmu Tennō Becomes the First Emperor of Japan; c. 300 B.C.E., Yayoi Period Begins; c. mid-3d century C.E., Himiko Rules the Yamatai; c. 300-600 C.E., Three Kingdoms Period Forms Korean Culture; c. 300-710 C.E., Kofun Period Unifies Japan.

RELATED ARTICLES in *Great Lives from History: The Ancient World*: Jimmu Tennō; Jingū; Ojin Tennō.

301 - 400 C.E.

397-402 C.E.
GE CHAOFU FOUNDS THE LINGBAO TRADITION OF DAOISM

Ge Chaofu attributes a series of scriptural texts to ancient revelations representing the first significant melding of Daoist and Buddhist thought, resulting in a new, liturgical tradition within Daoism.

LOCALE: Southeast China
CATEGORY: Religion

KEY FIGURES

Ge Xuan (Ko Hsüan; c. 164-244 C.E.), magical practitioner
Ge Hong (Ko Hung; 283-343 C.E.), aristocrat and author of religious texts
Ge Chaofu (Ko Ch'ao-fu; fl. 400 C.E.), purported author, compiler and disseminator of Lingbao scriptures

SUMMARY OF EVENT

According to several sources, between 397 and 402 C.E., an otherwise little-known member of China's southern gentry, Ge Chaofu, transmitted a set of scriptures to two Daoist priests, Xu Lingqi and Ren Yanqing. Known as the Lingbao (Numinous Treasure or Sacred Jewel) scriptures, their appearance elicited such enthusiasm that they were widely disseminated within a decade and prompted the creation of dozens of similar texts. The texts' unique merger of Daoist and Buddhist thought, along with a well-developed liturgical system, gave rise to a new movement within Daoism, the high religion of China. Although scholars differ on whether this movement ever solidified into a distinct school, it is clear that the Lingbao tradition dramatically changed the nature of

925

Daoist practice and expanded its fundamental world view. Drawing on Mahāyāna Buddhism, the Lingbao scriptures shifted Daoist practice from the individual pursuit of transcendence or immorality to universal salvation and the emancipation of one's own ancestors from the travails of reincarnation.

Ge Chaofu was part of the Ge family, aristocrats from southeastern China, whose most famous member, Ge Hong, had amassed an extensive library of alchemical and magical texts devoted to the pursuit of longevity and immortality. Ge Hong's major work, *Baopuzi* (c. 320 C.E.; *Alchemy, Medicine, Religion in the China of A.D. 320*, 1966; commonly known as the *Baopuzi*), synthesized these traditions and presents numerous practices, talismans (abstract depictions of the universe used by adepts to gain power over its elements), and formulas for achieving immortality. Such practices have a long history in Chinese religion, dating as far back as the third century B.C.E. and associated with a group of magical practitioners known as *fangshi*. *Fangshi* actively served the Han emperor Wu (r. 140-87 B.C.E.), and were responsible for discovering the secrets of immortality, controlling demons through the use of talismans, and performing prognostication via cosmic charts.

Ge Chaofu, grandnephew of Ge Hong, inherited his ancestor's celebrated library and religious techniques. He also carefully studied Buddhist texts, particularly those of the so-called Great Vehicle, or Mahāyāna tradition, Han cosmological texts on the Five Phases, and the scriptures of another early Daoist school, the Shangqing (Highest Clarity). Then, between 397 and 402, Ge Chaofu claimed to have discovered the Lingbao corpus, purportedly revealed to his distant ancestor, Ge Xuan.

According to the *Baopuzi*, Ge Xuan received three alchemical texts from Zuo Ci (Tso Tz'u; c. 200 C.E.), who himself had been given the scriptures by a god. He then transmitted them to his disciple, Zheng Yin (Cheng Yin), who subsequently passed them on to his student, Ge Hong, Xuan's nephew. While Ge Hong identifies the specific texts transmitted, along with several "Lingbao" manuscripts, none of them correspond to the scriptures Ge Chaofu claimed he inherited in his great-uncle's collection, nor do they appear to exist in the extant scriptural corpus. However, the most important of Ge Chaofu's alleged scriptures are based on another text, the *Wufujing* (n.d.; five talismans scripture). Most scholars believe that this is a relatively ancient text that was expanded and added to over the centuries.

The basic premise of the text, fragments of which can be found in the Daoist canon, is built upon the Han cosmological scheme of the five phases. As developed in the first two centuries of the common era, the theory of the five phases (wood, fire, earth, metal, water) sought to understand the cosmic correspondences between these fundamental building blocks of the universe, and a bewildering array of natural elements. For example, each phase came to be associated with a specific color, direction, season, bodily organ, sacred mountain, musical note, etc. According to the *Wufujing*, by controlling these elements through the ritualized use of a corresponding talisman, it was believed that one could heal, dispel demons, achieve longevity, or protect the adept from serpents, dragons, and other natural dangers. Composed in three chapters, the text centers around the five Lingbao talismans, and offers a variety of meditation and ritualistic practices based on the five phases, along with additional talismans, dietary measures, invocations, and prescriptions for health and immortality. This basic framework permeates and informs the remaining Lingbao texts.

Contemporary scholarship has convincingly demonstrated that Ge Chaofu himself authored the earliest text that he claimed was revealed to Ge Xuan. This text, the *Perfect Script in Five Tablets* (fifth century C.E.), establishes the basic structure and philosophy of subsequent Lingbao writings. Heavily influenced by Mahāyāna Buddhism, whose principal philosophical texts and sutras were just becoming widely disseminated in China, the Lingbao scriptures represent the first significant fusion of Daoist and Buddhist elements. Neither of the previous Daoist movements, the Celestial Masters (founded in 142 C.E.) and Shangqing (founded c. 370), had addressed or incorporated the teachings of the foreign religion. The Lingbao tradition—apparently working from the premise that Buddhism was nothing more than an Indianized form of Daoism, created after Laozi traveled to the west and converted the barbarians (that is, the Buddha)—freely adapted and borrowed numerous ideas based on a rather superficial understanding of Buddhism.

Thus the Lingbao scriptures introduce the notion of punishments in hell, reincarnation, and the practicing of five or ten precepts, copied almost verbatim from the original formulation in Buddhism. Time is divided into four kalpas, or ages, directly patterned on the Indian notion of successive ages, each more corrupt and degenerative than its predecessor. At the conclusion of each, the world collapses, and the scriptures vanish. Like the Buddhist sutras, many of the Lingbao scriptures opened with a god proclaiming the text in the presence of a multitude of other heavenly beings and worthies. Lingbao also adopted the traditional Buddhist worldview in which rebirth occurred in one of five realms: earth prisons, hungry ghost, animal, human, and celestial. Because the Chinese were initially repulsed by the idea of reincarnation, emphasizing as they did the ancestral obligations incumbent on every individual, the Lingbao emphasized that proper ritual will benefit the adept and his or her ancestors. For example, the proper recitation of the *Wondrous Scripture of the Upper Chapters on Limitless Salvation* (fifth century C.E.; English translation, 1997), assures the release of the souls of myriad ancestors, who will ascend to the Vermillion Palace and have their souls refined for rebirth. Thus, the adept is able to fulfill his or her familial responsibilities while simultaneously gaining better rebirth for the self.

The most significant adaption came with the related idea of universal salvation. Most Daoist practice up to this time centered on the individual's pursuit of immortality, or transcendence. Emulating the Buddhist notion of the bodhisattva, who forgoes his or her own salvation until all beings are enlightened, Lingbao liturgical ritual increasingly incorporated the idea that individual practice should be directed toward universal salvation. Vows to devote one's coming lives to the salvation of the world become commonplace, and every monk entering Lingbao orders took an oath to relieve suffering for hundreds of thousands of kalpas. The majority of Lingbao ritual, which centered on purification ceremonies, also revolved around the concept of universal repentance, cleansing, and establishment of harmony and well-being.

SIGNIFICANCE

Through the efforts of later Daoists such as Lu Xiujing, cataloguer, compiler and ritual specialist, the Lingbao corpus became a major portion of the developing Daoist canon. Its worldview and emphasis on universal salvation; its incorporation, rather than rejection of Buddhism; and the liturgical tradition it established are all prominent features of Daoism down to the present day. The use of talismans and charms, rituals involving the Big Dipper and other stars, the presentation of petitions to the celestial bureaucracy on behalf of the community, all owe their existence in part to the Lingbao movement. Its texts are cherished and used by practitioners of many other forms of Daoism. The present-day liturgy is a direct result of the Lingbao revelations. By combining the Celestial Master emphasis on petitioning the Heavenly Bureaucracy, the Shangqing belief in body gods, and Buddhist notions of reincarnation and universal salvation, and by adding the power of talismanic control over the

universe, the Lingbao tradition effectively established the parameters of Daoist ritual. Although variations naturally crept in over the centuries, based on new revelations, Daoism today is essentially of Lingbao origin.

—*Jeffrey W. Dippmann*

FURTHER READING

Bokenkamp, Stephen R. *Early Daoist Scriptures*. With a contribution by Peter Nickerson. Berkeley: University of California Press, 1997. A selection of scriptures from the three major schools of early Daoism (Celestial Masters, Highest Clarity, and Numinous Treasure). Along with an excellent historical and philosophical introduction, Bokenkamp translates perhaps the most important Lingbao text, the *Wondrous Scripture of the Upper Chapters on Limitless Salvation*.

_____. "Sources of the Ling-pao Scriptures." In *Tantric and Taoist Studies*, edited by Michel Strickmann. Brussels, Belgium: Institut Belge des Hautes Etude Chinoises, 1983. A very important study on the Buddhist and Highest Clarity influences on the formation of the Lingbao scriptures.

Robinet, Isabelle. *Taoism: Growth of a Religion*. Translated by Phyllis Brooks. Stanford, Calif.: Stanford University Press, 1997. Contains an excellent chapter on the growth and history of the Lingbao school by one of the world's foremost scholars on Daoism. Doctrines, practices, and the school's place within the broader context of Daoism are clearly and succinctly discussed.

Yamada, Toshiaki. "The Lingbao School." In *Daoism Handbook*, edited by Livia Kohn. Boston: Brill, 2000. A seminal summary by one of the leading experts on the Lingbao school. In addition to this particular article, the *Daoism Handbook* is the single most comprehensive volume on the Daoist tradition. Supplemental information can be found on ritual, the use of talismans, and everything else Daoist.

SEE ALSO: 6th or 5th century B.C.E., Birth of Buddhism; 3d century B.C.E. (traditionally 6th century B.C.E.), Laozi Composes the *Dao De Jing*; 285-160 B.C.E. (traditionally, c. 300 B.C.E.), Composition of the *Zhuangzi*; 139-122 B.C.E., Composition of the *Huainanzi*; c. 60-68 C.E., Buddhism Enters China; 142 C.E., Zhang Daoling Founds the Celestial Masters Movement; c. 3d century C.E., Wang Bi and Guo Xiang Revive Daoism; c. 470 C.E., Bodhidharma Brings Chan Buddhism to China.

RELATED ARTICLES in *Great Lives from History: The Ancient World*: Laozi; Wang Bi; Zhuangzi.

399 C.E.
CHINESE MONK FAXIAN TRAVELS TO INDIA

Faxian, the first Chinese monk to travel from China to India and back, brought a wealth of Buddhist texts back to his homeland and left a narrative account of his journey.

LOCALE: Changan, China (now Xi'an, China), India
CATEGORIES: Religion; cultural and intellectual history

KEY FIGURES

Faxian (Fa-hsien; c. 337-c. 422 C.E.), Chinese Buddhist monk
Buddhabhadra (d. 429 C.E.), Indian Buddhist monk, helped Faxian translate Buddhist texts

SUMMARY OF EVENT

In 399 C.E., the Buddhist monk Faxian and four companions left the Chinese capital of Changan by foot on their way to India. The purpose of their journey was to obtain copies of the monastic rules of discipline (*vinaya*) and return with them to China. By the end of the fourth century, a handful of Chinese monks had made the journey to Central Asia to study with flourishing Buddhist communities there, but no one had ever successfully traveled to India, the heartland of Buddhism, and returned to tell about it.

Most of what is known about Faxian and his travels comes from his autobiographical account, *Fo guo ji*, also known as *Faxian Zhuan* (fourth century C.E.; *Fo Koue Ki*, 1836; also known as *The Travels of Fa-hsien*) written after his return to China. Although the precise dates of his birth and death are unknown, most scholars agree that Faxian must have been close to sixty when he left on his historic journey. His biography in the *Gao seng zhuan* (seventh century C.E.; biographies of eminent monks) relates that his surname was Gong (Kung) and that his family was from present-day Shanxi Province. He received full ordination into the Buddhist order when he was twenty. Nothing is known about the intervening forty-odd years, but at the close of the fourth century, he left the Chinese capital, heading west along the northern Silk Road. The dangers of the first leg of his tour were vividly described by Faxian, who said the route was plagued by evil spirits and burning winds, marked only by the bones of the dead. His small party of travelers, eleven at this point, passed the Buddhist cave temples at Dunhuang (Tun-huang) and continued on to the Central Asian king-

doms of Shanshan and Agni. Faxian's group remained in the kingdom of Khotan for three months in order to attend an important festival and image procession. Continuing west, they passed through Chakarka and made the dangerous crossing of the Pamir Mountains, at the far west of the Tarim Basin. After Faxian's party crossed the harrowing Hanging Passage, a series of scaffolds and suspension bridges along the upper reaches of the Indus River, they had finally reached India proper, the ultimate goal of their travels and the farthest place any Chinese pilgrim had ever ventured. Three years had passed since they had first left Changan.

Faxian then traveled south through Gandhara to Peshawar, where three members of the party turned back toward China. The group was further reduced by the death of another companion during the difficult crossing of the Little Snow Mountains. In the early phases of his travel in India, Faxian traveled to many of the sites associated with the life of the historical Buddha, and the corresponding passages of his autobiographical *The Travels of Fa-hsien* are filled with tales regarding the events of the Buddha's life rather than detailed descriptions of the sites themselves. The group traveled to Mathura and Sankisa, where the monastic communities were thriving. In Savatthi, he visited the site of Jetavana Monastery, a longtime residence of the Buddha. Moving east, Faxian went to Kapilavastu and Kuśinagara, the locations of the Buddha's birth and death, respectively. Next he visited Eagle Peak in Rajagaha, the site of many of the Buddha's sermons, Bodh Gayā, where the Buddha was enlightened, and Deer Park, where he first began to teach.

It was during this time in northern India that Faxian and his party arrived at Mahāyāna Monastery in Pataliputra, where they would remain for more than two years. Six years earlier, Faxian had lamented the incomplete condition of the Buddhist monastic code in China and decided to undertake the journey to India. It was here that Faxian was finally able to obtain copies of several versions of the Buddhist monastic code. In addition to learning Sanskrit, Faxian was occupied with the copying of texts. At least four of these are mentioned in his narrative: the monastic code of the Sarvāstivāda in six or seven thousand verses, the *Samyutābhidharma-hrydaya Śāstra* in six thousand verses, the *Mahāparinirvāna Sūtra* in five thousand verses, and the *Mahāsāmghika Abhidharma*.

Faxian left Pataliputra alone. The last remaining

member of his original party had decided to remain in India. He traveled to Tāmraliptī, where he would remain for another two years, making copies of scriptures and images. From there, Faxian set sail for Sri Lanka, where he obtained additional texts, unknown in China: the *Dīrghāgama*, the *Samyuktāgama*, and the *Zazang jing*. Like Central Asia and North India, the island of Sri Lanka had a flourishing Buddhist community. For two years, Faxian visited famous sites said to be associated with the historical Buddha, observed various festivals, and attended lectures. Once his work there was complete, he began what was an arduous return journey by sea to China. Encountering terrible storms, his ship was forced to land at the island of present-day South Sumatra. After another five months, the ship set sail once again. More bad weather drew the journey out to three months before they finally landed on the Shandong Peninsula in 412 C.E. Some fifteen years and thirty kingdoms later, Faxian had returned home.

The remainder of Faxian's life was spent translating many of the texts he brought back with him from India and Sri Lanka. In this, he was aided by the Indian Buddhist missionary Buddhabhadra. More of these texts were translated after his death by other Indian monks. It is known that Faxian died at Xin Monastery in Jing Zhou (Hubei Province), but the precise date of his death has not been recorded (the scholar Jan Yün-hua gives 418; some Chinese sources place it between 418 and 423).

SIGNIFICANCE

By the time Faxian left for India at the close of the fourth century C.E., more than three hundred years had passed since the introduction of Buddhism to China in the first century. The centuries that followed saw Buddhism transformed from an exotic faith practiced by foreigners to an intellectual pursuit of the upper classes, and finally to a living practice carried out by a large population of native Chinese monks, nuns, and lay people. When Faxian left on his journey, he was motivated by a desire to learn from great Indian masters and to retrieve the rules for monastic discipline (*vinaya*) that he felt were an essential element to the proper practice of Chinese Buddhism. He was not unique in this concern. When Kumārajīva, the famous Central Asian translator of Sanskrit texts, arrived in Changan in 402, one of his first tasks was to translate the ten verses of the *vinaya* of the Sarvāstivāda school, in sixty-one volumes. Thus the establishment and observance of the *vinaya* was a primary concern for the Chinese Buddhist community. The success of Faxian's journey, along with the activity of translators such as

Kumārajīva, can be viewed as the culmination of a unique phase in the history of Chinese Buddhism, when the faith became irrevocably grounded in Chinese soil.

Faxian's account of his travels is a great mine of information for anyone interested in the history of Buddhism in general or the history of South Asia in particular. Not only do his interests and motivations provide insight into what was important to Chinese Buddhists of his time, but also Faxian's descriptions of the kingdoms, monks, ministers, kings, and the customs he observes also afford a rare glimpse into these ancient cultures. At the time of his journey, Buddhism was flourishing throughout Central Asia, India, and Sri Lanka. Faxian recounted visiting monasteries whose populations ranged into the thousands and whose needs were looked after by the king and the local populace. Nowhere is he detained by war or unrest, but rather everywhere Faxian visited on his long journey, he was welcomed as an honored guest and provided with provisions for the remainder of his travels. In contrast, many of the Chinese monks who later were inspired to make similar journeys, such as Xuanzang (602-664) and Yijing (635-713), found that the state of Buddhism in India never again attained the prosperity described by Faxian.

—Ben Brose

FURTHER READING

Faxian. *The Pilgrimage of Fa Hian.* Translated by J. W. Laidley. 1848. Reprint. Delhi: Cosmo, 2000. The first English translation of Faxian's *Fo guo ji*, which was translated from the 1836 French translation, *Foé Koué Ki: Ou, Relation des royaumes boudhiques: Voyages dams la tartarie, dans l' Afghanistan et dans l'Inde.*

_____. *A Record of Buddhistic Kingdoms.* 1886. Reprint. Translated by James Legge. New York: Dover, 1991. This translation of Faxian's *Fo guo ji* is both reliable and easily available.

_____. *A Record of the Buddhist Countries.* Translated by Li Yongxi. Peking: Chinese Buddhist Association, 1957. A twentieth century translation of Faxian's *Fo guo ji.*

Ikeda, Daisaku. *The Flower of Chinese Buddhism.* Translated by Burton Watson. New York: Weatherhill, 1986. A selective history of Chinese Buddhism from its Indic origins through the Tang Dynasty, with special attention given to the Tiantai school. Contains a map showing the locations visited by Faxian during his journey.

Tsukamoto, Zenryū. *A History of Early Chinese Bud-*

dhism: *From Its Introduction to the Death of Hui-yüan.* Translated from the Japanese by Leon Hurvitz. New York: Kodansha International, 1979. A useful summary of the major events of the early phases of Chinese Buddhism in general and the life of Faxian in particular.

SEE ALSO: 6th or 5th century B.C.E., Birth of Buddhism; 2d century B.C.E., Silk Road Opens; c. 60-68 C.E., Buddhism Enters China; c. 470 C.E., Bodhidharma Brings Chan Buddhism to China.

RELATED ARTICLES in *Great Lives from History: The Ancient World*: Buddha; Faxian.

c. 400 C.E.
KĀLIDĀSA COMPOSES SANSKRIT POETRY AND PLAYS

Considered by Indian scholars to be the greatest of Sanskrit poets, Kālidāsa is best known today for his dramas, which capture the essence of aristocratic society in the golden age of the Gupta Dynasty in India.

LOCALE: India
CATEGORY: Literature

KEY FIGURE
Kālidāsa (c. 340-c. 400 C.E.), Indian poet and dramatist

SUMMARY OF EVENT
The death of Kālidāsa marks a literary end to the golden age of the Gupta Dynasty (c. 321-c. 550 C.E.), which occurred during the reign of Chandragupta II (c. 380-c. 415), according to Sanskrit scholar K. Krishnamoorthy. His epic, lyric, and dramatic poetry captures the aristocratic culture of that era, a high point in artistic and literary development in India, that resulted from nearly a century of relative peace, stability, and prosperity. Because the Gupta kings taxed imports and exports rather than their people and maintained roads connecting India with Byzantium and Persia to the west and China to the east, trade thrived, producing a leisure class that supported scientific, mathematical, and artistic development. This period of intellectual achievement continued until the invasion of the Huns in the latter part of the fifth century C.E. The foremost literary figure of this Gupta renaissance was Kālidāsa.

Although Kālidāsa's works reflect his time and class, they are not parochial. They embody the ideals of his age but not necessarily the people. Rather, his characters are almost exclusively chosen from the classical Sanskrit epics *Rāmāyaṇa* (c. 550 B.C.E.; English translation, 1870-1889) and *Mahābhārata* (c. 400 B.C.E.-400 C.E.; *The Mahabharata of Krishna-Dwaipayana Vyasa*, 1887-1896), and express the religious and cultural themes of those works: love, honor, duty, and right action—universal human concepts that speak to all nations and times.

Because almost nothing is known of Kālidāsa outside of his works and his works contain no contemporary references, there is no sure way of determining the order of their composition. Nevertheless, it is almost universally conceded that the lyric poem *Ṛtusaṁhāra* (c. 75 B.C.E. or c. 365 C.E.; English translation, 1867) is his earliest surviving work because of relative infelicities of style noticeable only by comparison with his presumably more mature works. *Ṛtusaṁhāra* is a lyric description of the six seasons identified by the Indian calendar: summer, rains, autumn, prewinter, winter, and spring. The description in the poem is simultaneously internal and external, interweaving physical description of each season with its corresponding emotional effect.

Kālidāsa's other known lyric poem, *Meghadūta* (c. 65 B.C.E. or c. 375 C.E.; *The Cloud Messenger*, 1813), is generally considered his masterpiece. Though lyric in nature, it has a narrative frame involving an exiled *yaksa* (demigod) who, unable to return to his grieving wife, begs a cloud to carry his message of comfort to her. The first half is a stirring description of his Himalayan home, artfully disguised as the *yaksa's* directions to the cloud messenger. The second half is the *yaksa's* moving message to his wife.

Kālidāsa also attempted two epic poems in the style of the *Rāmāyaṇa*: *Kumārasambhava* (4th century C.E.; *The Birth of the War-God*, 1853) and *Raghuvaṁśa* (c. 50 B.C.E. or c. 390 C.E.; *The Dynasty of Raghu*, 1872-1895). *The Birth of the War-God* details an intricate conflict between destiny and religious devotion. The world is urgently in need of deliverance from the terrible demon Taraka, who can be defeated only by a hero born of the god Śiva and his wife. The first impediment, his wife's death, is overcome by her reincarnation as Pārvati. However, on her death Śiva had sworn celibacy. Śiva thwarts the attempts of the love god Kama to overcome his vows of celibacy and destroys Kama. Yet Pārvati's own spiritual self-control captivates Śiva, and he re-marries her and begets the needed hero.

930

The Dynasty of Raghu, the second epic, involves political rather than mythological matter, though it continues the theme of self-control explored in *The Birth of the War-God* (generally considered the earlier of Kālidāsa's two epics). This time, the virtue of self-control is emphasized by its absence in the corrupt King Agnivarna, whose degeneracy brings an end to the Raghu line (hence the title). What makes Agnivarna's corruption all the more reprehensible is the fact, reflected throughout the poem, that the king is the unworthy descendent of the great Rama, hero of the Sanskrit epic that bears his name.

Three dramas by Kālidāsa survive: *Abhijñānaśākuntala* (c. 45 B.C.E. or c. 395 C.E.; *Śākuntala: Or, The Lost Ring*, 1789), *Mālavikāgnimitra* (c. 70 B.C.E. or c. 370 C.E.; English translation, 1875), and *Vikramorvaśīya* (c. 56 B.C.E. or c. 384 C.E.; *Vikrama and Urvaśī*, 1851). All exhibit similar plots, starting with the love at first sight of a king for a simple maiden. *Śākuntala*, Kālidāsa's best drama and probably his best-known work, takes its plot from an incident in the Sanskrit classical epic *The Mahabharata of Krishna-Dwaipayana Vyasa*. King Dusyanta falls in love with Śākuntala, daughter of a remote Himalayan hermit, and secretly marries her. An evil curse causes Dusyanta to forget Śākuntala until he sees the ring he has given her. A poignant scene of renunciation under the curse is followed by an equally moving scene of reconciliation when the king's memory returns and the lovers are reunited.

The love at first sight in *Mālavikāgnimitra* occurs not in a hermitage as in *Śākuntala* but in a harem. The king falls in love with Mālavikā after seeing her picture and arranges to meet her. His jealous queen imprisons Mālavikā, but when the girl causes the queen's aśoka tree to blossom, she is forgiven and reunited with the king and elevated to the status of one of his wives.

The least successful of the three love plots, that of *Vikrama and Urvaśī*, goes through the same sequence of meeting, separation, and reunion—in fact, repeatedly—but the separations do not seem to arise from circumstance as in the other two but rather from whim. The story, adapted from the *The Mahabharata of Krishna-Dwaipayana Vyasa*, involves Purūravas yearning for Urvaśī, who four times eludes him before the final obligatory reunion.

SIGNIFICANCE

Kālidāsa's genius was felt in his own era. No fewer than forty-five commentaries of his lyric masterpiece *The Cloud Messenger* survive from his century. His works became instant classics, standard reading in schools throughout medieval India. In the West, Kālidāsa's dramas were among the first non-Western works translated in the romantic rediscovery of the East. The German poet Johann Wolfgang von Goethe (1749-1832) made the enthusiastic and seemingly extravagant claim that Kālidāsa's masterpiece *Śākuntala* contains everything that charms the soul, and the first English translator of that classic, William Jones (1746-1794), called Kālidāsa the Shakespeare of India. Jones's comparison is probably not fair to either poet, as Elizabethan and Sanskrit dramas differ widely in form and convention. However, as the twentieth century Indian poet Rabindranath Tagore asserted, Kālidāsa could match Shakespeare in emotional depth.

One of the reasons for Kālidāsa's success at exploring human emotion is that such exploration is one of the central aims of the form in which his most famous works were written. Two of Kālidāsa's surviving dramas are in the *nāṭaka* form, a high dramatic genre depicting great events from Indian legend or history. What makes them effective emotional windows is that the form dictates that each scene be governed by a predominant *rasa*, or emotional mood. Hence the very success of the work depends on the extent to which it renders that emotion poetically.

In *Śākuntala*, for example, Kālidāsa explores the *rasa* of human love in such a way that it builds on Kālidāsa's complex exploration in *The Birth of the War-God* of one of the central paradoxes of Hindu culture. In that epic, as in the drama *Śākuntala*, erotic desire leading to procreation is conflated with sensual renunciation leading to enlightenment. When the German romantics encountered Indian, especially Gupta, culture, this coincidence of opposites was puzzling. How could a highly-developed Hindu theology of renunciation and an equally highly developed erotic art both arise from the same source? An answer can be found in the work of Kālidāsa, which orchestrated the erotic and the spiritual into a pastiche of emotions that are proper to both.

A second aspect of the Gupta Dynasty that makes Kālidāsa virtually its spokesperson is its extraordinary religious tolerance. Chandragupta II, the emperor under whom Kālidāsa most likely wrote, worshiped Krishna, though his ministers were devotees, variously, of Buddha and Śiva, with no perceived conflict. Kālidāsa seems to honor all the Hindu gods equally, with perhaps a personal preference for Śiva. Yet even though the source material of his poetry dates from before Buddhist times, his *Mālavikāgnimitra* includes a sympathetic portrait of a Buddhist nun. Finally, Kālidāsa's works offer insight into the Gupta era by reflecting the great variety of its dialects, departing from the classical language of the traditional epics to produce dialogue that, if not exactly colloquial, at least reflected the variety of class and character that was Gupta India.

—John R. Holmes

FURTHER READING

Krishnamoorthy, K. *Kālidāsa.* Boston: Twayne, 1972. Though dated, this volume in a standard series is still quoted and is the best starting point for studying Kālidāsa.

Mandal, Paresh Chandra. *Kālidāsa as a Dramatist: A Study.* Dhaka, India: University of Dhaka, 1986. Establishes the probable chronology of Kālidāsa's dramas.

Shastri, Satya Vrat. *Kālidāsa in Modern Sanskrit Litera-*

ture. Columbia, Mo.: South Asian Books, 1992. Explores the influence of Kālidāsa on later writers.

Stoller-Miller, Barbara. *The Plays of Kālidāsa: Theatre of Memory.* Ottowa, Ont.: Laurier Books, 1999. A very readable modern translation, with a useful introduction and notes geared to the nonspecialist.

SEE ALSO: c. 550 B.C.E., Vālmīki Composes the *Rāmāyaṇa*; c. 400 B.C.E.-400 C.E., Composition of the *Mahābhārata*; c. 150 C.E., Aśvaghosa Composes Complete Biography of the Buddha; c. 380-c. 415 C.E., Gupta Dynasty Reaches Its Peak Under Chandragupta II.

RELATED ARTICLE in *Great Lives from History: The Ancient World*: Kālidāsa.

c. 5th century C.E.
LYDENBURG BANTUS SCULPT LIFE-SIZE TERRA-COTTA HEADS

The discovery of the "Lydenburg heads" testifies to the cultural life and society of the peoples inhabiting southern Africa by the sixth century C.E.

LOCALE: Transvaal and Natal regions in northeastern South Africa

CATEGORIES: Prehistory and ancient cultures; cultural and intellectual history

SUMMARY OF EVENT

Seven life-size terra-cotta sculpted heads were discovered in the eastern Transvaal region of South Africa in the 1950's by K. L. von Bezing. Metal ornaments, beads, and pottery shards were located with these heads. Von Bezing reported his find to Ray Inskeep, an archaeologist from the University of Cape Town, South Africa, which led to an excavation and study of the site. Radiocarbon dating has placed these intricate sculptures in the period between the fifth and sixth centuries C.E., which was the height of the Late Iron Age on the continent of Africa. Archaeologists named the sculptures the Lydenburg heads after the place where Von Bezing discovered them. Historians believe that the site where the heads were located was the territory settled by early Bantu-speaking immigrants in southern Africa.

In the last thousand years B.C.E., Bantu speakers migrated in multiple phases to southern Africa from the eastern Congolese rainforests and became the leading force of change on the southern African economic scene. The range of communities that existed in southern Africa resulted from the semidesert, shrubland ecology of the

region. The hunting-and-gathering practices of the ancestral Khoikhoi, who most likely populated these regions before the arrival of the Bantu, required dispersed, sparsely populated groups of people as one means of managing the semidesert environment. Communities of southern Africa, in the early first millennium C.E. and earlier, were typically based on economies and lifestyles of hunting and gathering, but the Bantu immigrants established themselves in farming, iron smelting, and basketry. The Bantu agriculturalists facilitated the transfer away from an economic concentration on gathering and hunting to a complex mixed economy of cattle raising and grain cultivating. The innovations brought in with the southeastern Sala-Shona Kusi Bantu included cultivation techniques developed by ancestral Bantu-speaking peoples of the west-central African forests as well as methods of grain and cattle raising that were viable in the semi-arid vegetation zones of southern Africa.

The hollow sculpted heads themselves were elaborately designed and showed evidence of having been painted. Several of the sculptures are large enough to have been worn by an adult person, but the majority are significantly smaller. The smaller heads have notches in the necks, suggesting that were attached to some type of fixture for display or use in festivities or rituals. Carved and sculpted clay was added to create detailed facial designs. Examples of the meticulous facial expressions include a temple to define the hair line, wide mouths, oval eyes, and raised bars across the forehead, suggestive of facial creases. The two largest heads have animal figures on the top, likely signifying wealth or religious or political authority. Typically, the balance of the head and neck are covered with designs, including geometric shapes, that are common in material culture found in other Bantu-influenced Iron Age archaeological sites. The makers of these remarkable sculptures were most likely the southeastern Sala-Shona Bantu ancestors, who themselves emerged from Kusi Bantu communities in the Transvaal region.

SIGNIFICANCE

The discovery of the Lydenburg heads gives evidence of the earliest known settled agricultural civilization in southern Africa and has revealed much about the Africans south of the equator from ancient times. Because there is no written evidence of the Bantu from the early first millennium, the importance of the heads is situated not only in their intrinsic value as art objects but also in the evidence they provide of the Bantu presence, cultural developments, and adaptations in southern Africa. These sculpted heads were created in the initiation period of farming in southern Africa, which hints that the early Kusi Bantu civilizations were more sophisticated and culturally complex than assumed by early scholars. The terra-cotta style suggests the work of a sedentary agricultural people inhabiting southern Africa by the fifth century C.E. Because of the similarity to other Bantu inspired potteries, the Lydenburg heads suggest that they were created by agriculturalists speaking Bantu languages.

Attribution of cultural meaning and social significance of the Lydenburg pieces has been based on comparative evidence collected and analyzed by archaeologists and historians. Authorities in the field of southern African history and archaeology have inferred that the heads were used for ceremonial rites in initiation rituals, which were common in Iron Age Bantu cultures. The heads would have been used as ceremonial objects or possibly to signify a particular cult or religious affiliation. This interpretation is supported by the numerous beaded decorations found on the masks. The beads would have caught the sunlight and shimmered, creating luminous ritual regalia. The masks may also have displayed the wealth and social prominence of their owners.

The fact that the Lydenburg heads and other artifacts were found together in an underground cavity suggests that they were hidden or protected when not being used, further testament to their likely ritual importance.

—Sheena L. Binkley

FURTHER READING

Connah, Graham. *African Civilizations: Precolonial Cities and States in Tropical Africa: An Archaeological Perspective.* New York: Cambridge University Press, 1987. Provides a detailed account of archaeological finds in the African continent and how archaeologists interpret the continent's historical cultures. Contains information on the early Bantu peoples as determined from their archaeological remains.

Ehret, Christopher. *The Civilizations of Africa: A History to 1800.* Charlottesville: University Press of Virginia, 2002. A textbook examination that covers early African civilizations and the cultures they introduced. Includes bibliography and study questions.

Evers, T. M. "Excavations at the Lydenburg Heads Site, Eastern Transvaal, South Africa." *South African Archaeological Bulletin* 37 (1982): 16-30. Addresses the archaeological importance of the terra-cotta sculptures found in the Transvaal.

Maggs, T., and P. Davison. "The Lydenburg Heads and the Earliest African Sculpture South of the Equator." *African Arts* 14, no. 2 (1981): 28-33. Discusses the discovery and importance of the Lydenburg heads, including their significance as evidence of an artistic society.

Mokhtar, G. *General History of Africa II: Ancient Civilizations of Africa.* Berkeley: University of California Press, 1981. This work contains an analysis of ancient Africa well before colonial forces arrived in Africa. Provides a detailed report of ancient activities throughout the continent.

SEE ALSO: c. 1000-c. 700 B.C.E., Mashariki Bantu Establish Chifumbaze Ironworking Culture; c. 400 B.C.E.-c. 300 C.E., Bantu Peoples Spread Farming Across Southern Africa; 300-400 C.E., Bantu People Invent Copper Metallurgy.

401 - 476 C.E.

5th or 6th century C.E.
FIRST MAJOR TEXT ON HINDUISM'S GREAT GODDESS IS COMPILED

A remarkable work, the Devī Māhātmyam *was the major and foundational text relating to the great goddess of Hinduism. It was the first text to explore the wonder of the goddess in her myriad forms.*

LOCALE: North India
CATEGORY: Religion

SUMMARY OF EVENT

The *Devī Māhātmyam* (also known as the *Śrī Durgā Saptaśatī*, or "the seven hundred verses to Durga," and translated into English in 1963 as *Devī Māhātmyam: The Glorification of the Great Goddess*), is the earliest extant text specifying the complex nature of the great goddess of Hinduism and recounting the three most important myths associated with the goddess, or Devī. The proposed dates for the compilation of the work, based on linguistic studies, spans two centuries between 400 and 600 C.E. The language of the work is classical Sanskrit, arranged in verse. Perhaps as a way of sanctioning some of the revolutionary notions put forth, the *Devī Māhātmyam* was appended to an orthodox Hindu text, the *Mārkaṇḍeya Purāṇa* (c. 300-600 C.E.; English translation, 1904). Although the name of the author is not known, he was probably a learned Brahman priest, versed in Tantric teachings, and was undoubtedly connected to the court of the powerful imperial Guptas of north India. The text may have had a long oral tradition before it was rendered in written form. Originally and to this day, the text is chanted on sacred occasions, particularly during the Durgā Puja, the major festival in the northeastern part of India.

Devī Māhātmyam is divided into thirteen chapters and consists of seven hundred mantras or verses. It describes the three primary aspects of the divine goddess and the astounding events associated with each manifestation. Although the text provides many names, manifestations, and embodiments for the goddess, it is made clear that there is only *one* great divine mother goddess; she is a tremendous force that explodes into a thousand forms. The three aspects of the goddess depicted are Mahāmāyā, also called Svāhā (chapter 1); Caṇḍikā or Chaṇḍikā, also called Durgā (chapters 2-4); and Ambikā, also called Kālī (chapters 5-13).

The story of *Devī Māhātmyam* is told to a disenfranchised king and a disillusioned merchant by a great sage named Medhas. He implored the disheartened king and merchant to meditate on the great goddess because only she could bestow all blessings as well as spiritual liberation. So that his listeners might understand her true and complex nature, he expounded on her three greatest accomplishments, explaining that she is the very embodiment of the universe and that she manifests in order to accomplish deeds no other can attempt.

To illustrate the point, Medhas related the following tale. While the god Viṣṇu (the preserver) slumbered on a serpent raft in the primordial ocean at the beginning of time, Lord Brahma (the creator) emerged from a lotus sprouting from Viṣṇu's navel. Soon thereafter, two horrible demons, Madhu and Kaiṭabha, were born from the wax of Viṣṇu's ear. They were determined to kill Brahma. Unable to take action, Brahma evoked the goddess Mahāmāyā. It was she, the embodiment of universal power (*śakti*), who was able to awaken (enliven) Viṣṇu so that he could destroy the terrible demons that threatened the destruction of the universe.

The second myth is of the famous battle between the goddess Caṇḍikā and the horrifying demon king Mahiṣa. Having conquered the army of the gods, Mahiṣa seated himself on the divine throne and claimed sovereignty over all while the gods were forced to wander the earth as mortals. The gods met, and from their collective fury, each issued forth a fiery force (*śakti*) that collectively combined to form the goddess Caṇḍikā. After she was outfitted with their weapons, she was ready to undertake what they were unable to accomplish. Immediately, she began battling the demonic forces. She exterminated, without effort, millions on millions of demons. Once Mahiṣa's forces were destroyed, Caṇḍikā came after the evil demon king. Each time she administered a fatal blow, the fiend immediately arose in another shape. Finally, as she decapitated the head of the demon who had taken the form of a powerful buffalo, Mahiṣa began to leap from the buffalo carcass in a human form. Before he could emerge fully, however, she annihilated him.

The third event concerns the two most formidable demons of all, Śumbha and Niśumbha, who had taken over the world of the gods. The gods invoked the mighty goddess Ambikā. Answering their pleas for help, she commenced a battle that raged, creating a horrible field of slaughter. Ambikā, by calling forth her own darkest essence, enticed the terrible black goddess Kālī to emerge from her body in order to take on the slaughter of the demon generals Caṇḍa and Muṇḍa. Also, among the terrible fiendish forces was one in particular, Raktabīja

(Bloodseed) whose drops of blood multiplied into many hundred more demons. Kālī lapped up Raktabīja's blood before it hit the earth and demolished him easily. Also joining battle with the goddess were the eight goddesses called Śaktis, the life force of eight gods; their fierce natures easily helped crush the demonic forces.

The text ends with the goddess granting boons to the king and merchant. The king desired his kingdom restored to him; the merchant sought supreme enlightenment.

SIGNIFICANCE

The work is not only innovative but also groundbreaking. Until *Devī Māhātmyam*, goddesses in India were largely overshadowed by the mighty presence of the gods. Although goddesses occasionally were mentioned in the Hindu religious writings known as the Vedas and Upaniṣads and many were the focus of local cults across India, their relative status was minor. The text was the first to address matters of gender. Its proclamation is loud and clear, and it presents the revolutionary view of the ultimate reality as being feminine. The great goddess is the source of all creation. For the first time, the most ancient fertility goddesses, revised and newly exalted, were given full recognition in the patriarchal Brahmanical religion. The text presents a structure in which the many names and forms of the goddesses are united in a comprehensive and complex organization. Most important,

Devī Māhātmyam provides an underlying philosophical foundation for the worship of the goddess. The concept of *śakti*, female energy that gives birth to and enlivens the entire universe including the male gods, is the vital core of the sophisticated Tantric philosophical teaching.

—*Katherine Anne Harper*

FURTHER READING

Coburn, Thomas B. *"Devī Māhātmyam": The Crystallization of the Goddess Tradition*. Delhi: Motilal Banarsidass, 1984. Exploration of the Hindu concept of the feminine as being the ultimate view of reality. Provides a careful scriptural analysis of the text. Bibliography.

_____. *Encountering the Goddess: A Translation of the "Devī Māhātmyam" and a Study of Its Interpretation*. Albany, N.Y.: State University of New York Press, 1991. An excellent translation from the Sanskrit of the *Devī Māhātmyam* with important insights into the text. Bibliography.

Jagadisvarnanada, Swami, trans. *Devī Māhātmyam*. Madras: Sri Ramkrishna Math, 1972. An important early translation into English with the accompanying Sanskrit text.

SEE ALSO: 1500-1100 B.C.E., Compilation of the Vedas; c. 1000-c. 200 B.C.E., Compilation of the Upaniṣads; c. 200 B.C.E., Birth of Hinduism; c. 200 B.C.E.-200 C.E., *Bhagavad Gita* Is Created.

---

c. 405 C.E.

STATESMAN TAO QIAN BECOMES FARMER AND DAOIST POET

The most famous pre-Tang Chinese poet, Tao Qian, gave up official government work in favor of an impoverished life as a farmer and poet during the Eastern Jin Dynasty.

LOCALE: China
CATEGORIES: Cultural and intellectual history; literature; philosophy

KEY FIGURE
Tao Qian (T'ao Ch'ien; 365-427 C.E.), Chinese poet and essayist of the Eastern Jin Dynasty

SUMMARY OF EVENT

In 365 C.E., Tao Qian (Tao Yuanming; T'ao Yüan-ming) was born in Xinyang (Hsin-yang) in what is now Henan Province. Although some of his ancestors held high gov-

ernment posts, his family had become impoverished minor aristocrats by the time he was born. Nevertheless, from childhood, Tao Qian was well read and classically educated, with an interest in poetry.

Following the Confucian tradition of service and duty to the sovereign, family, and country, in 393 C.E., Tao Qian started a career in government. He also needed to provide financial support for his family and an elderly parent. He soon resigned, and his first wife died. He remarried and by 402 had four sons with his second wife. For a decade, he worked in various local government positions such as district magistrate and secretary to generals. In the winter of 401, his mother died, and Tao resigned from an official government post. He went into mourning and seclusion for two years and later attained another position. However, he was discouraged and disappointed in each of these government positions and each time resigned and returned home after working a short period of time. He also refused numerous governmental offers. This period in medieval China was a time of social upheaval and political corruption, including civil war, peasant revolts, assassinations, and palace revolutions.

Finally, in 405 C.E. Tao was appointed prefect but resigned after eighty days; this was his last official post. Although his family was destitute, he felt a sense of relief on leaving office and returning home to stay. He expressed this in his essay, "Homeward Ho" (as translated by Tan Shilin):

> Homeward ho! Let me cut off all social ties! Since worldly wisdom disagrees with me, why seek the society of men? . . . To free myself from cares, on books and the zither I rely. . . . I glory in the timely blessing Nature bestows upon all creation, yet bemoan the numbered days of this my transient life.

This was the major turning point in his life. Because of the troubled times, Tao was unable to realize the Confucian ideal of a scholar pursuing high rank in public life. Unwilling to continue compromising his principles, Tao chose a life of poverty and hardship as a reclusive farmer. He did not value fame or fortune, and his choice represented a complete break with conventional practice.

Thus, in the remaining twenty-two years of his life, Tao turned to Daoism to help him attain inner peace and spiritual freedom. Many of his poems reflect a Daoist philosophy and naturalist perception of life. The ancient Daoists believed that rural work was humankind's natural occupation. His "pastoral poetry" praised the solitary life and the joys of nature and simple living. His writings reflect a harmony of Confucian and Daoist sentiments, but they also relate inner conflict and struggle. Tao's writing style was plain and unadorned but at the same time emotional and often deeply philosophical. In poems such as "The Hibiscus" and "The Body, Shadow, and Soul," he reflected seriously on his life.

There were crises and difficulties such as a fire in which Tao lost everything, crop failures, and near-starvation. For example, in the poem, "Awareness," he describes his growing hunger and weakness after a blighted crop. In another poem, "Fire in the Sixth Lunar Month of the Year Wu-Shen," he describes a tragic fire:

> My straw-hut was nestled in a narrow lane,
> I lived in its sweet seclusion.

> The wind blew strong at midsummer,
> House and garden disappeared in flames.
> Not a single room was spared;
> The boat lay moored by the shady gate.

Two of his most well-known prose works are "Peach Blossom Spring" and the biographical sketch of "The Man of Five Willows." "Peach Blossom Spring," a prose narrative followed by a poem, is set during the reign of Xiao Wudi (r. 372-396 C.E.) of the Eastern Jin. The story is about a lost fisherman, who follows a stream along a peach orchard and accidentally discovers a hidden land. In this land lives a society of happy people, whose ancestors escaped from tyranny to this beautiful, hidden utopia. Here, people live and work together harmoniously, and there is no war, hatred, oppression, or even taxes. When the fisherman leaves and finds his way home, he tells others about his experience in this paradise. Although many go searching for this place, no one can ever find this utopia again.

In the autobiographical story of "The Man of Five-Willows," Tao portrays his main characters as a man who has leisure or idleness in his heart (as translated by Roland C. Fang).

> Tranquil and spare of speech, he covets neither fame nor profit. . . . Four bare walls enclose his rooms; the wind and sun find free access through the roof and the chinks. His clothes are ragged, his dishes usually empty. But he takes it perfectly at ease. Sometimes he writes to amuse himself, to express what is in his mind. He cares little for worldly gain or loss. It is thus he passes his allotted span on earth.

Finally, "A Lamentation Upon My Own Death," written in the year of his death, shows the rich imagery, wisdom, honesty, and sincerity typical of his works (as translated by Fang).

> When spring and autumn came round
> I labored in the fields.
> I plowed and sowed, and watched
> the growth of the grain.
> Happy was I in reading the books,
> and in playing on the seven-strings.
> I basked myself in the winter sun,
> and cleaned my feet in summer streams.
> Though my toils so taxed my strength,
> my light heart often gave me leisure.
> I would gladly resign myself to Heaven's will
> and live my mortal days in contentment.

SIGNIFICANCE

Tao Qian remains one of the greatest and most respected Chinese writers. His poetry influenced the famous Tang Dynasty poets Li Bai (Li Po), Du Fu (Tu Fu), and Wang Wei. Song Dynasty poets Su Dongpo (Su T'ung-po) and Lu You (Lu Yu) also admired Tao Qian's writings. More than 120 of Tao Qian's works have survived. He was a pastoral poet and one of the first nature poets, writing about country life, drinking, and nature, but he was also a philosophical poet, reflecting on his life and spiritual values. His self-doubt, questioning, and anxiety expressed a modern consciousness, and he is considered the first great modern poet of China. His "Peach Blossom Spring" is the Chinese Shangri-la, and has become the classic poetic expression of the search for utopia.

According to translator David Hinton, Tao was the "first writer to make a poetry of his natural voice and immediate experience, thereby creating the personal lyricism which all major Chinese poets inherited and made their own." Subsequent generations of poets have found inspiration in his writings, and Tao's appeal and popularity have continued through the centuries.

—*Alice Myers*

FURTHER READING

Kwong, Charles Yim-tze. *Tao Qian and the Chinese Poetic Tradition: The Quest for Cultural Identity.* Ann Arbor: University of Michigan, 1994. Interprets the poetry and poet within historical and cultural contexts. Includes detailed notes, bibliography, and a glossary.

Tao Qian. *The Complete Works of Tao Yuanming.* Translated and annotated by Tan Shilin. Hong Kong: Joint Publishing, 1992. Includes Tao Qian's poems in Chinese, as well as helpful biographical information and extensive annotations.

_____. *Gleanings from Tao Yuan-ming.* Translated by Roland C. Fang. Hong Kong: The Commercial Press, 1980. This book includes a biographical sketch of the poet by Prince Xiao Dong (Hsiao Tung; 527 C.E.) and the poems in their full Chinese versions.

_____. *The Poetry of T'ao Ch'ien.* Translated by James Hightower. Oxford, England: Clarendon Press, 1970. This is a translation of all of the poet's surviving poetry, with extensive commentary, annotations, and background information useful for the Western reader.

_____. *The Selected Poems of T'ao Ch'ien.* Translated by David Hinton. Port Townsend, Wash.: Copper Canyon Press, 1993. A translation of selected poems of Tao Qian. Includes biography and notes.s

_____. *T'ao Yüan-ming, A.D. 365-427: His Works and Their Meaning.* 2 vols. Translated by A. R. Davis. New York: Cambridge University Press, 1983. The two volumes include poems in Chinese, as well as the English translation, with extensive commentary and notes.

SEE ALSO: c. 3d century C.E., Wang Bi and Guo Xiang Revive Daoism; 265 C.E., Sima Yan Establishes the Western Jin Dynasty; 316 C.E., Western Jin Dynasty Falls; 397-402 C.E., Ge Chaofu Founds the Lingbao Tradition of Daoism; 420 C.E., Southern Dynasties Period Begins in China.

RELATED ARTICLES in *Great Lives from History: The Ancient World*: Laozi; Tao Qian; Wang Bi; Zhuangzi.

401 - 476 C.E.

August 24-26, 410 C.E.
GOTHIC ARMIES SACK ROME

Gothic armies sacked Rome and revealed the crisis afflicting the Roman Empire in the west, shattering the myth of Rome's invincibility and security.

LOCALE: Rome (now in Italy)
CATEGORY: Wars, uprisings, and civil unrest

KEY FIGURES
Alaric I (c. 370-410 C.E.), leader of the Visigoths, r. 395-410 C.E.
Honorius (384-423 C.E.), Roman emperor in the west, r. 395-423 C.E.
Flavius Stilicho (c. 365-408 C.E.), Vandal general in control of Rome as regent for Honorius, 395-408 C.E.

SUMMARY OF EVENT
When Emperor Theodosius the Great died in 395 C.E., the breakup of the Roman Empire into eastern and western halves was inevitable. From that time onward, the civil rulers in the west were under the power of barbarian leaders. The sack of Rome by the Visigoths under Alaric I in 410 should be seen as one episode in the final stages of the disintegration of the united empire.

Theodosius's successors were his sons: eighteen-year-old Arcadius, who was designated augustus in the east; and Honorius, a mentally impaired child of eleven who was designated augustus in the west. Actual rule in the west was in the hands of the army under the leadership of a Vandal, Flavius Stilicho, chosen by Theodosius as regent for Honorius.

Alaric, a member of the Balth Dynasty of Gothic kings and a leader of the Visigothic allies of the Romans, took advantage of the death of Theodosius to make a bid for power in the Balkans and southern Greece. Stilicho tried to stop Alaric in the north but was deflected by an order from Arcadius to lead his army back to Constantinople. Later, Stilicho managed to come to terms with Alaric in Greece. Alaric and his Goths settled in Epirus, and Alaric had the satisfaction of receiving the title *magister militum*, or master of the soldiers, from the eastern court. This title was tantamount to official recognition as a military dictator.

The Visigoths have often been pictured in popular lore and culture as an aggressive, war-hungry group of barbarian invaders. Modern historians, however, have stressed the one-sidedness of this view. Far more than invaders, the Goths were refugees fleeing the turmoil in their homelands, which were being invaded by waves of nomads from the east. The Goths were not an ethnically homogeneous group; they were a collection of warriors and their dependents, who were largely Germanic but included Alani and Sarmatian elements as well. By the time Alaric became Visigothic leader, the Goths had lived within Roman borders for a generation. They were no longer fully "barbarians"; they were far more interested in gaining a piece of Roman prosperity than in destroying the empire by warfare and looting. The Visigoths were Christians, although they adhered to the Arian heresy. Despite their acculturation into Roman ways, however, the Goths still constituted a large group on the move, hungry and skilled at fighting. Their management presented a formidable challenge to Stilicho and the other Roman authorities.

In 401 C.E., Alaric first invaded Italy but was forced to withdraw by Stilicho. Stilicho checked a similar attempt in 403. For a time, Alaric joined forces with Stilicho to help him in taking Illyricum, which Stilicho was attempting to restore to Honorius. News of an uprising in Gaul, however, caused Alaric to sense an opportunity for advancing his own cause. He hurried north, demanded employment for his troops, and succeeded in obtaining four thousand pounds of gold from the senate. Alaric's adviser in this negotiation was Stilicho, who soon after, in 408, was killed by enemies in court who thought he was plotting to make his own grandchild emperor. Stilicho's murder was an imprudent action accompanied by an antibarbarian purge in which soldiers, along with their wives and children, were brutally murdered. The result was that barbarian troops defected to Alaric.

With Stilicho out of the way, Italy was defenseless, and Alaric had his opportunity to strike at the heart of the Western Roman Empire. He demanded lands and supplies for his men. Honorius refused and barricaded himself at Ravenna, northeast of Rome. In 408 C.E., Alaric and his Goths marched on Rome but were bought off. They marched on Rome again in 409, and Alaric set up a rival emperor, Priscus Attalus. Having secured supporting troops from the Eastern Roman Empire, however, Honorius refused to capitulate. Indeed, Honorius sought to counter Alaric by setting up Sarus, a Gothic bandit, as a rival candidate for chieftain of the Goths, and internal dissension between Alaric and his puppet Attalus led to the latter's deposition.

Finally, on August 24, 410 C.E., Alaric and some forty

thousand Goths seized Rome and plundered it for three days. The actual physical destruction was relatively slight, but the impression on contemporaries was shattering. The event marked the first time in more than eight hundred years that Rome had been taken by an enemy. It appeared that an era or even a civilization had come to an end. When the news reached Bethlehem in Palestine, the scriptural scholar Saint Jerome wrote that all humanity was included in the ruins of Rome. Saint Augustine was moved by the event to write his great masterpiece of political and historical theory, *De civitate Dei* (413-427 C.E.; *The City of God*, 1610), in which he answered those who charged that Christianity was the cause of Rome's decline.

SIGNIFICANCE

After his attack on Rome, in which he took Honorius's sister Galla Placidia as one of his prizes, Alaric attempted to invade Africa, the granary of Italy. This invasion failed when his ships were wrecked in a storm. Alaric died soon after and was buried in the Busento River, near modern Cosenza, by followers who were killed thereafter to prevent anyone from knowing the exact location of the body and desecrating the remains.

If Alaric had any consistent policy, it seems to have been the acquisition of lands in the Roman Empire, preferably in Italy, where his people might settle. In this attempt, he failed. According to Jordanes, historian of the Goths, another aim of Alaric was the union of the Goths and the Romans as a single people. In this, Alaric had unrealistic expectations in terms of his own time, although later generations saw the assimilation of the two peoples in Spain and southern Gaul. Alaric's successor, his brother-in-law Ataulf (r. 410-415 C.E.), married Honorius's sister, Galla Placidia, and thus cemented the terms of peaceful coexistence between Goths and Romans. Ataulf led the Goths into Gaul and from there into Spain, where he died in 415. The next Visigoth leader, Wallia, negotiated with the Romans and was given lands in southern Aquitania, in Gaul, in 418. Spasmodic struggles between Goths and Romans continued for another sixty years, but after 477, with the total collapse of Ro-

Alaric I receives presents from the Athenians. (F. R. Niglutsch)

man authority in the West, the Goths' sovereignty in southern Gaul and Spain—the so-called kingdom of Toulouse—was assured.

　　—Mary Evelyn Jegen, updated by Nicholas Birns

FURTHER READING

Grant, Michael. *The Fall of the Roman Empire.* London: Weidenfeld, 1990. Good discussion of Honorius's relationships with Flavius Stilicho and Alaric.

Heather, P. J. *The Goths.* Cambridge, Mass.: Blackwell Publishers, 1996. An overall history of the Goths, which includes the Roman period.

＿＿＿. *Goths and Romans, 332-489.* New York: Oxford University Press, 1991. In contrast to Wolfram below, Heather seeks to diminish the emphasis on Alaric's belonging to the Balth Dynasty of Gothic rulers.

Herrin, Judith. *The Formation of Christendom.* 1987. Reprint. Princeton, N.J.: Princeton University Press, 1989. Emphasizes Alaric as a historical participant in fifth century Roman politics.

O'Flynn, John M. *Generalissimos of the Western Roman Empire.* Edmonton: University of Alberta Press, 1983. The definitive source on Stilicho.

Orosius, Paulus. *The Seven Books of History Against the Pagans.* Translated by Roy J. Deferrari. Washington, D.C.: Catholic University of America Press, 1964. This fifth century historian established the theme of Alaric's sack as the calamitous end of Roman greatness.

Wolfram, Herwig. *History of the Goths.* Berkeley: University of California Press, 1988. A detailed and well-researched account of the Gothic migrations.

SEE ALSO: c. 3d-4th century C.E., Huns Begin Migration West from Central Asia; August 9, 378 C.E., Battle of Adrianople; 439 C.E., Vandals Seize Carthage; 445-453 C.E., Invasions of Attila the Hun; September 4, 476 C.E., Fall of Rome.

RELATED ARTICLES in *Great Lives from History: The Ancient World*: Attila; Saint Augustine; Saint Jerome.

413-427 C.E.
SAINT AUGUSTINE WRITES *THE CITY OF GOD*

Saint Augustine wrote The City of God, *a key work that embodied the transformation from the humanistic, world-centered viewpoint of classical thought to the God-centered concept of eternity that characterized the Christian Middle Ages.*

LOCALE: Hippo Regius, North Africa
CATEGORIES: Cultural and intellectual history; religion

KEY FIGURES

Alaric I (c. 370-410 C.E.), leader of the Visigoths, r. 395-410 C.E.

Honorius (384-423 C.E.), Roman emperor in the west, r. 395-423 C.E.

Saint Augustine (354-430 C.E.), bishop of Hippo, 396-430 C.E.

Marcellinus (fl. mid-fourth to mid-fifth century C.E.), Roman imperial tribune and friend of Augustine who suggested writing *The City of God*

SUMMARY OF EVENT

Under their chieftain Alaric I, the Visigoths captured the city of Rome in August, 410 C.E. For almost eight hundred years, Rome had escaped the ravages of invaders, but at last the Germans succeeded where even Hannibal's military genius had failed. The event was not totally unexpected. For two years, the Visigoths had been tramping practically at will through central Italy. In Ravenna, then the capital of the Western Roman Empire, the timorous emperor Honorius cowered in fright, having himself ordered the murder of Flavius Stilicho, the general who might have delivered Italy from the barbarian menace. When Innocent I, the bishop of Rome, came to beg military assistance for his flock, Ravenna had nothing to offer.

The physical damage was relatively light, but the psychological shock was great. If the Eternal City was no longer safe, doom seemed to threaten civilization itself. Saint Jerome, far off in his murky cave in Bethlehem, reacted typically: He poured out his heart in lamentation to one of his correspondents, prophesying the imminent end of the world. For Rome was the ideological heart of all that was mighty and worthwhile in secular life and culture.

How could the disaster be explained? One interpretation that quickly made itself heard traced Rome's misfortune to the displeasure of the ancient deities who had stood guard over the city during its long history before being displaced by the Christian God. Scarcely a generation had passed since Emperor Theodosius the Great had proscribed the ancient cults and declared Christianity to be the Roman Empire's official faith. Mars, Jupiter, and the old pantheon had been discarded; and now they were having their revenge. It was not the first time that Christianity had been blamed for calamities of one sort or another. The writings of Tertullian, Cyprian of Carthage, and Arnobius of Sicca testify to similar accusations during the preceding centuries, and the Church Fathers had striven to counter the charges.

One of the last significant groups of Romans still privately holding fast to the old paganism was an educated cultured elite, men of good lives and sound learning who grasped the true grandeur of the empire and its civilization and who formed an influential body of conservative public opinion that continually looked back nostalgically to the past. These men felt the fall of Rome acutely, and the last gasp of dying paganism was their protest against the new religion that they held responsible for the decay that was everywhere evident. Christianity to these conservative minds seemed completely incompatible with the best interests of the state and its culture. The events of 410, to them, unmistakably confirmed their diagnosis.

This sentiment was voiced forcefully among the refugees from Rome who had fled to the security of North Africa when the Visigoths approached. Volusianus, the imperial proconsul in the province, shared their views. When his friend Marcellinus tried to convert him to Christianity, Volusianus let it be known that his reluctance stemmed not from doctrine but from cultural and historical reasons. Marcellinus, another imperial official but a fervent Christian, had been sent to North Africa by Emperor Honorius for the purpose of mediating between orthodox Christians and Donatist heretics. He had become a close friend of the bishop of Hippo Regius, Saint Augustine, and he turned to him for help in answering Volusianus's objections.

As a result, Augustine was alerted to the larger issue of the relations between Christianity and Rome within the newest context of the barbarian menace. With Marcellinus urging him on, he decided to defend his faith in the volume entitled *De civitate Dei* (413-427 C.E.; *The City of God*, 1610), which he began in 413 and finished in twenty-two books thirteen years later. When Marcellinus approached him, Augustine already enjoyed a reputation as one of the most penetrating of Christian thinkers. More than half his numerous books, many sermons, and hundreds of letters had already been written. Most of this material sprang from an immediate challenge. Always an unsystematic, intuitive thinker, Augustine wrote best when responding to an immediate problem. Proof of his greatness is the fact that his responses generally had much more than a circumstantial value or application;

Saint Augustine. (Library of Congress)

ephemeral circumstances elicited from him immortal replies. This was certainly true of *The City of God*.

Augustine started with the intention of answering the current charge against Christianity, but he soon gave up such a limited plan and turned that project over to the Spanish priest Paulus Orosius who stopped by for a visit and an exchange of ideas in 414. Augustine delegated to him the purely historical task. As Orosius related in his *Historiarum adversus paganos libri VII* (after 417 C.E.;

Seven Books of History Against the Pagans, 1936), Augustine had directed him to "discover from all the available data of histories and annals whatever instances past ages have afforded of the burdens of war, the ravages of disease, the horrors of famine, of terrible earthquakes, extraordinary floods, dreadful eruptions of fire, thunderbolts and hailstorms, and also instances of the cruel miseries caused by parricides and disgusting crimes." This sort of information would demonstrate how miserable the world had actually been under the tutelage of the old gods. With Orosius composing this sort of book, Augustine felt justified in devoting his energies to a more philosophical approach to the subject.

For himself, Augustine decided to take up the vaster burden of interpreting the whole of human history in the light of the principles of Christian theology. He would write not history, but a philosophy or a theology of history. He desired to show that everything had its place in the divine plan. Himself one of the greatest of Romans, he labored to reconcile Roman culture with Christianity, not to drive them apart. His vehicle was an analogy that he apparently found in the writings of another African, the Donatist intellectual Tyconius: the scheme of the organization of all people and human events into two vast groups, the City of God and the Worldly City, the society of those who lived in conformity with divine law and the society of those who did not.

It is difficult to re-create the precise stages of composition and evolution of Augustine's thought during the thirteen years that he wrote *The City of God*. As a bishop in an unsettled time for the Christian church, he had many preoccupations and duties that kept him from devoting full attention to this particular work. The completed treatise, which consists of twenty-two books, has two major compositional parts. The first, consisting of books 1-10, primarily defends Christianity and counters pagan accusations, especially relating to the recent attack on Rome. The second part, books 11-22, presents Augustine's new view of history in Christian terms. He sees history as a progressive course leading from Creation to the ultimate end in the city of God.

SIGNIFICANCE

Using all the secular learning at his disposal, Augustine wrote a theological tract of universal value, creating an ideology that became a satisfactory substitute for the classical polis. Still regarded as one of the greatest books of Western civilization, it has taken a remarkable share in the shaping of Christendom.

—*Raymond H. Schmandt, updated by Karen K. Gould*

FURTHER READING

Bonner, Gerald. *Saint Augustine of Hippo: Life and Controversies*. 3d ed. Norwich, England: Canterbury, 2002. An examination of the life of Saint Augustine, with special attention paid to controversies surrounding the bishop.

Brown, Peter. *Augustine of Hippo: A Biography*. Rev. ed. Berkeley: University of California Press, 2000. A new edition of the most complete biography of Augustine by a scholar with a thorough knowledge of Christianity in late antique culture. *The City of God* is discussed in several chapters within the context of Augustine's life.

Fitzgerald, Allan D., ed. *Augustine Through the Ages: An Encyclopedia*. Grand Rapids, Mich.: W. B. Eerdmans, 1999. An encyclopedic treatment of Saint Augustine that covers his life and his influence. Bibliography and index.

Kaye, Sharon M., and Paul Thomson. *On Augustine*. Belmont, Calif.: Wadsworth/Thomson Learning, 2001. A basic biography of Saint Augustine, which covers his writing of *The City of God*. Bibliography.

Stump, Eleonore, and Norman Kretzmann, eds. *The Cambridge Companion to Augustine*. New York: Cambridge University Press, 2001. An encyclopedic treatment of Saint Augustine's life, his writings, and his influence.

Van Oort, Johannes. *Jerusalem and Babylon: A Study into Augustine's "City of God" and the Sources of His Doctrine of the Two Cities*. Leiden, the Netherlands: E. J. Brill, 1991. A complete study of *The City of God* from multiple standpoints: compositional structure, the meaning of the two cities, its character as an apologetic and theological work, and the sources of Augustine's ideas.

Vessey, Mary, Karla Pollman, and Allan D. Fitzgerald, eds. *History, Apocalypse, and the Secular Imagination: New Essays on Augustine's "City of God."* Bowling Green, Ohio: Philosophy Documentation Center, 1999. A collection of essays presented at a colloquium on *The City of God* and Saint Augustine at the University of British Columbia in 1997.

SEE ALSO: 313-395 C.E., Inception of Church-State Problem; c. 382-c. 405 C.E., Saint Jerome Creates the Vulgate; August 24-26, 410 C.E., Gothic Armies Sack Rome.

RELATED ARTICLES in *Great Lives from History: The Ancient World*: Saint Augustine; Saint Jerome.

415 C.E.

MATHEMATICIAN AND PHILOSOPHER HYPATIA IS KILLED IN ALEXANDRIA

A fanatical Christian mob attacked and killed the first known woman mathematician, head of the Neoplatonist school of philosophy at the Alexandrian museum.

LOCALE: Alexandria, Egypt
CATEGORIES: Cultural and intellectual history; science and technology; mathematics

KEY FIGURES

Hypatia (c. 370-415 C.E.), teacher and head of the Neoplatonist school at Alexandria
Theon (c. 335-c. 405 C.E.), teacher at the Alexandrian museum and father of Hypatia
Synesius of Cyrene (c. 370-413 C.E.), student of Hypatia, Neoplatonist, and bishop of Ptolemais (Libya), from c. 410 C.E.
Saint Cyril of Alexandria (c. 375-444 C.E.), theologian and patriarch of Alexandria, 412-444 C.E.

SUMMARY OF EVENT

Ancient Greek philosophy moved toward a greater emphasis on science and mathematics after the death of Alexander the Great in 323 B.C.E. His empire was divided among his generals, and Ptolemy Soter established a dynasty of Greek-speaking kings in Egypt with his capital at the still unfinished city of Alexandria, where the western branch of the Nile River empties into the Mediterranean Sea. He also founded the Museum of Alexandria, which was similar to a modern research university and lasted for seven hundred years. Scholars from all around the Greek-speaking world were invited to join the museum on the condition that they would deposit their scrolls and manuscripts in its library, which at its highest point included some 600,000 volumes. Among its greatest mathematicians and scientists were Euclid, Aristarchus of Samus, Apollonius of Perga, Diophantus, Hipparchus, and the astronomer Ptolemy.

Hypatia was one of the last significant mathematicians associated with the Alexandrian museum and the earliest known woman mathematician and astronomer. By her time, Alexandria was the third largest city in the Roman Empire, having been conquered by Julius Caesar some four centuries earlier. The museum had diminished in importance, many of its books having been burned by Roman soldiers, and there were separate schools for Jews, pagans, and Christians. Although Hypatia's origi-

nal writings have not survived, she is known from letters that she received from her student Synesius of Cyrene and from references in the *Historia ekklesiastike* (fifth century C.E.; *Ecclesiastical History*, 1844) of Socrates Scholasticus. She was born about 370 C.E., but estimates range from as early as 355, based on the fact that Synesius studied under her, to 390 to 395, when she was an established scholar.

Hypatia's father, Theon of Alexandria, was a member of the museum and a prominent teacher of mathematics and astronomy. His writings describe a solar and a lunar eclipse he predicted at Alexandria in 364 C.E. He is best known for his student commentaries on Euclid's works on geometry and optics and on Ptolemy's works on astronomy, but he also wrote poetry and interpretations of omens. Theon raised Hypatia to be strong in both mind and body. He taught her mathematics and astronomy as well as the arts, literature, speech, philosophy, and such disciplines as swimming, horseback riding, and mountain climbing. She eventually surpassed her father's mathematical skills.

Although Hypatia was considered to be both bright and beautiful, she was also known for prudence and self-control and avoided the marital expectations of her time in favor of scholarship. She was soon recognized as a gifted scholar, and by 390 C.E., she was well established as a teacher. By 400, she became the salaried head of the Neoplatonist school, where the emphasis on Platonic philosophical ideas supported her interest and gifts in mathematics. She is thought to have assisted her father in writing an expanded version of Euclid's *Stoicheia* (compiled c. 300 B.C.E.; *Elements*, 1570), which was the only known Greek text of this important synthesis of Greek geometry until the discovery of an earlier one in the Vatican in the late nineteenth century. She also assisted him in his commentary on Ptolemy's influential astronomical treatise, *Mathēmatikē syntaxis* (c. 150 C.E.; *Almagest*, 1948).

Hypatia's students were aristocratic young men from Egypt, Cyrene (Libya), Syria, and as far away as Constantinople (now Istanbul, Turkey). Although she was pagan, her students were both pagans and Christians, and many of them became important civil and ecclesiastical leaders. Some continued to look to her for guidance for many years after studying with her. A long correspondence with Synesius of Cyrene lasted even beyond his conse-cration in 410 as bishop of Ptolemais by Theophilus, the patriarch of Alexandria. His letters show that she had ex-tensive knowledge of Greek philosophy and literature as well as mathematics and science. He often asked for her advice on his own writings and even sought her politica influence on occasion. The Byzantine church his-torian Socrates Scholasticus wrote that her knowledge exceeded all other contemporary philosophers, and there is general agreement that she surpassed her father in mathematics and astronomy.

In addition to collaborations with her father Theon, Hypatia is known to have written several works on math-ematics and astronomy that have not survived. Her most important work was in the new field of algebra, expanding and commenting on the third century work of Diophantus of Alexandria on indeterminate equations (with multiple solutions) and on quadratic equations. She also wrote a treatise on planetary motion entitled *Astronomical Canon* and *Treatise on the Conics of Apollonius*, which devel-oped Apollonius's third century geometry of the curves formed by the intersections of a plane with a cone. Her interest in scientific instruments is clear from some of Synesius's letters. In one, he inquires about the construc-tion of a hydroscope for measuring the density of liquids. In another, he asks about the construction of an astrolabe for measuring the positions of stars and planets. She is also credited with an apparatus for distilling sea water.

By the time of Hypatia, Christianity had become the official religion of the Roman Empire. As Christianity became established in Alexandria at the end of the fourth century C.E., rioting often erupted between those of op-posing religions. In the year 412, Cyril (later Saint Cyril) became patriarch of Alexandria and began a campaign opposing schismatic Christian groups and driving many Jews from the city. This led to hostility between Cyril and Orestes, the Roman prefect of Egypt and a good friend of Hypatia. Five hundred monks from the Nitrian desert as-sembled to defend Cyril of Alexandria, and one of them threw a stone that wounded Orestes. The monk was ar-rested and tortured and then died, but Cyril hailed him as a martyr.

Because of her friendship with Orestes, Hypatia came to be viewed by some Christians as not only a pagan phi-losopher but also as an obstacle to friendship between the patriarch and the prefect. During Lent in March of 415 C.E., a fanatical mob of antipagan Christians led by a church reader named Peter dragged Hypatia from her chariot into the Caesarium, then serving as a church. There, according to Socrates Scholasticus, they stripped her and scraped her skin with sharp shells until she died. They then dismembered her body and burned it to ashes at a place called Cinaron. Many of her students then left to study in Athens, which gained a reputation in mathe-matics by 420. The Alexandrian Neoplatonic school con-tinued until the Arab invasion of 642, when the remain-ing books in the library were used to fuel the city's baths for six months; probably among them were the works of Hypatia.

SIGNIFICANCE

Hypatia was the only female scientist of the ancient world whose life is well documented, and perhaps the most famous of all women scientists until Marie Curie. As one of the last pagan scientists in the Western world, her death also came in the last years of the Roman Em-pire. Her life and death mark the beginning of the end of ancient Greek science and more particularly the end of the Alexandrian tradition that had flourished in its mu-seum and libraries for some seven hundred years. Be-cause of her qualities of beauty and intellect, she has been romanticized in historical and fictional accounts.

Hypatia's early work with her father Theon in correct-ing and commenting on Ptolemy's *Almagest* helped to preserve it as the standard reference on astronomy for a thousand years. Their version of Euclid's *Elements* be-came the basis for all later editions of Euclid. Even though Hypatia's own works did not survive, they have still had an important influence. Her careful commentary on the algebraic work of Diophantus most likely led to the survival of most of his original thirteen books of the *Arithmetica* (c. 250 C.E.; "Arithmetica" in *Diophantus of Alexandria: A Study in the History of Greek Algebra*, 1885). Six of the surviving works are in Greek and four are translations in Arabic, all of which contain notes and interpolations that probably come from Hypatia's com-mentary.

—*Joseph L. Spradley*

FURTHER READING

Alic, Margaret. *Hypatia's Heritage*. Boston: Beacon Press, 1986. Includes a chapter on Alexandrian sci-ence highlighting the life and work of Hypatia.

Duckett, Eleanor Shipley. *Medieval Portraits from East and West*. Ann Arbor: The University of Michigan Press, 1972. A chapter on Synesius of Cyrene and Hypatia contains several excerpts from the letters of Synesius to Hypatia.

Dzielska, Maria. *Hypatia of Alexandria*. Translated by F. Lyra. Cambridge, Mass.: Harvard University Press,

1995. The most complete and authoritative biography of Hypatia.

Osen, Lynn M. *Women in Mathematics*. Cambridge, Mass.: The MIT Press, 1974. A chapter on Hypatia emphasizes her mathematical work.

Porter, Neil A. *Physicists in Conflict*. Philadelphia: Institute of Physics Publishing, 1998. A chapter on medieval conflicts has a short section on Hypatia's conflict with Saint Cyril.

SEE ALSO: 332 B.C.E., Founding of Alexandria; c. 300 B.C.E., Euclid Compiles a Treatise on Geometry; c. 275 B.C.E., Greeks Advance Hellenistic Astronomy; 380-392 C.E., Theodosius's Edicts Promote Christian Orthodoxy.

RELATED ARTICLES in *Great Lives from History: The Ancient World*: Euclid; Hypatia; Ptolemy (astronomer).

420 C.E.
SOUTHERN DYNASTIES PERIOD BEGINS IN CHINA

Liu Yu usurped the throne and established the Liu-Song Dynasty, the first of a series of dynasties known as the Southern Dynasties. Though politically unstable, these dynasties maintained traditional Chinese culture.

LOCALE: Present-day southern China
CATEGORY: Wars, uprisings and civil unrest

KEY FIGURES
Liu Yu (Liu Yü; 355-423 C.E.), founder of the Liu-Song (Liu-Sung) Dynasty, r. 420-423 C.E.
Xiao Daocheng (Hsiao Tao-ch'eng; 423-483 C.E.), founder of the Southern Qi (Ch'i) Dynasty, r. 479-483 C.E.
Xiao Yan (Hsiao Yen; 464-550 C.E.), founder of the Liang Dynasty, r. 502-550 C.E.
Chen Baxian (Ch'en Pa-hsien; 500-560 C.E.), founder of the Chen (Ch'en) Dynasty, r. 557-560 C.E.

SUMMARY OF EVENT
After the breakup of the Western Jin Dynasty (Chin; 265-316 C.E.), which was a brief period of stability and prosperity, China was plunged into more than one hundred years of turmoil, political division, and weak governments. Waves of nonnative tribes invaded the north, and China was divided between north and south. The north was ruled by a series of barbarian, non-Chinese dynasties.

During the chaos and invasions that occurred in the north, millions of Chinese, including the wealthy and high-ranking, fled south of the Yangtze River. At Jiankang (Chien-k'ang), now Nanjing (Nanking), local leaders set up a surviving Jin prince on the throne at the head of a court of the exiled aristocrats and great landlords from the north. This was the Eastern Jin Dynasty (Chin; 317-420).

An insurrection led by Sun En that threatened the capital was crushed in 402 C.E.; but the instability brought power to the generals in charge of repressing it. One general, Huan Xuan (Huan Hsüan), seized power in 420 C.E. However, in the same year, Liu Yu, a general from a humble family who had won great popularity for his victories in the north, seized power, proclaimed himself Emperor Wu (Wudi; Wu-ti), and founded the Liu-Song Dynasty (Liu-Sung; 420-479), the first of the Southern Dynasties.

These Southern Dynasties were founded by generals or warlords who could maintain rule only for a generation or two. Lacking political skill, the rulers were unable to create long-lasting imperial institutions and consolidate power; these short-lived dynasties were constantly subject to feuds and civil unrest and were soon overrun.

Because of the general instability and weakness of the central governments, the countryside was ruled by aristocratic, landowning families. Using the Nine Rank System for selecting high government officials, these families managed to limit possession of powerful bureaucratic positions to their own family members and maintain their exemption from taxes. At court, they were often forceful enough to frustrate the emperor's wishes in appointments or promotions.

By the time Liu Yu came to power, the northern immigrants had been merged into the southern population. After fending off several attacks, the Song enjoyed a period of peace and developed relations with Central Asia and Japan. However, attacks from the north weakened the dynasty, which was split by conflicts. General Xiao Daocheng, who suppressed one of the rebellious princes, finally seized power and established the Southern Qi Dynasty (Ch'i; 479-502). This dynasty was especially unstable, broken by conflict within the imperial family and between the aristocrats and military men.

SOUTHERN DYNASTIES AND THEIR RULERS, 420-581 C.E.

LIU-SONG DYNASTY

Ruler	Reign
Liu Yu (Wudi)	420-423
Shaodi	423-424
Wendi	424-454
Xiao Wudi	454-465
Qian Feidi (first overthrown emperor)	465
Mingdi	465-473
Hou Feidi (second overthrown emperor)	473-477
Shundi	477-479

SOUTHERN QI DYNASTY

Ruler	Reign
Xiao Daocheng (Gaodi)	479-483
Wudi	483-494
Xiao Zhaoye, king of Yulin	493-494
Xiao Zhaowen, king of Hailing	494
Mingdi	494-499
Xiao Baojuan, marquis of Donghun	499-501
Hedi	501-502

LIANG DYANSTY

Ruler	Reign
Xiao Yan (Wudi)	502-550
Jian Wendi	550-552
Yuandi	552-555
Jingdi	555-557

CHEN DYNASTY

Ruler	Reign
Chen Baxian (Wudi)	557-560
Wendi	560-567
Feidi (overthrown emperor)	567-569
Xuandi	569-583
Houzhu (the last ruler)	583-589

Nonetheless, during this short-lived dynasty, trade was greatly expanded on the Yangtze River and into southern China, and the power of the aristocracy was limited and the central government was strengthened by the promotion of commoners to positions of authority. However, the suppression and massacres of the nobles bred discontent, and Xiao Yan, a cousin of the emperor who ruled in one of the distant courts, marched on the capital and forced himself on the throne, even though he was not the legitimate successor. He secured his rule by murdering all the surviving Qi Liu family.

Xiao Yan, known as Emperor Wu, or Liang Wudi (Wu-ti), established the Liang Dynasty (502-557 C.E.). His rule was longer and more stable than that of any other southern ruler, lasting from 502 to 550. The chaos of the north, along with his lack of interest in military conquest, gave the south a brief rest from constant warfare. He converted to Buddhism and is known as its great protector. Three times he expressed a desire to retire to a monastery. However, he also established institutes for the study of Confucian ethics for those entering government. He was a scholar, poet, and patron of literature, and under him, Chinese civilization flourished. Expansion of the economy continued, especially because of the increased commerce with Southeast Asia, the South Seas, and the Indian Ocean.

Meddling by the Liang in affairs of the north led to invasion by a non-Chinese northern general, Hou Jing (503-552), who besieged the capital in 548 and, after five months, overran and devastated it in 549. During the siege, many of the aristocratic families starved to death in their mansions. Emperor Wu died shortly afterward, and his heirs fought Hou Jing for the throne. During his uprising, the Western Wei attacked the Liang, seized Sichuan (Szechwan), and advanced as far as the middle Yangtze, where they installed a puppet ruler. From this time in the south, there was a Northern (or Later) Liang regime (555-587), subservient to the north. During the warfare between Hou Jing and the Wudi heirs, Liang general Chen Baxian seized power, assumed the throne, and founded the Chen Dynasty (Ch'en; 557-589), the last of the Southern Dynasties.

Most of the aristocracy of the south had been eliminated by the time of the Chen Dynasty, and power moved back to the local landlords, weakening the central government, which was corrupt and inefficient. Weak and disorganized, the south was threatened by attacks from the west and north. A victory in retaking Shouyang (modern Shouxian) gained nothing. The dynasty was easily overrun in 589 by a swift invasion by the Sui Dynasty (581-618) from the north, which finally reunited China.

SIGNIFICANCE

The Southern Dynasties marked a period of transformation of Chinese society and an increase in the economic and political power of the south. Although politically unstable, the Southern Dynasties continued the brilliance of Chinese culture in art, literature, philosophy, and religion. The aristocratic families saw themselves as the embodiment of Chinese civilization and tried to foster its great cultural achievements. The life of the upper classes became more cultivated and refined. During the Southern Dynasties, the native people in the south were brought into the mainstream of Chinese civilization, and Buddhism was integrated into Chinese culture. The south became the economic center of China. The immigrants from the north developed the technological and economic potential of southern China and provided manpower for the thinly populated area. The population is estimated to have increased fivefold from 280 to 464 C.E. The southern capital, Jiankang, became one of the world's greatest cities and a center of waterborne trade.

The wealth of the great ruling families was based on their large estates and improvements in agriculture. Agriculture was extended by bringing marshlands into cultivation, and feudal economic patterns became established in the countryside. Large portions of the previously landowning peasant population were transformed into tenant farmers on large estates; they lost their freedom and could be sold or transferred at will by their landlords.

Trade routes were expanded southward, and along these routes, Buddhism entered China. In the south, Buddhism remained apart from the centers of political power and developed monastic and philosophic traditions that provided an alternative to traditional, mainstream Confucianism.

—Thomas McGeary

FURTHER READING

Chinese Academy of Social Science. "Feudal Society." In Vol. 1 of *Information China: The Comprehensive and Authoritative Reference Source of New China*. Oxford, England: Pergamon Press, 1989. A positive and nationalistic account of the period's accomplishments.

Ebrey, Patricia B. *The Cambridge Illustrated History of China*. New York: Cambridge University Press, 1996. Brief account of the period, but good maps, illustrations, coverage of the arts and culture of the period, and further readings.

Gernet, Jacques. *A History of Chinese Civilization*. Translated by J. R. Foster. New York: Cambridge University Press, 1989. Extended account of the history of the period, along with full treatment of culture and civilization.

Hook, Brian, ed. *The Cambridge Encyclopedia of China*. 2d ed. New York: Cambridge University Press, 1991. Brief chronological entries with numerous maps, charts, illustrations, and tables.

Huang, Ray. *China: A Macro History*. Armonk, N.Y.: East Gate, 1988. Good overview of history of the period with attempts at historical explanation of events.

Paludan, Ann. *Chronicle of the Chinese Emperors: The Reign-by-Reign Record of the Rulers of Imperial China*. London: Thames and Hudson, 1998. Thumbnail sketches of all the emperors.

Roberts, J. A. G. *Prehistory to c. 1800*. Vol. 1 in *A History of China*. New York: St. Martin's, 1996. A good general history.

Schirokaur, Conrad. *A Brief History of Chinese Civilization*. New York: Harcourt Brace Jovanovich, 1991. Textbook that gives good historical survey, as well as treatment of arts, society, science, religion, and technology.

SEE ALSO: 25 C.E., Guang Wudi Restores the Han Dynasty; 220 C.E., Three Kingdoms Period Begins in China; 265 C.E., Sima Yan Establishes the Western Jin Dynasty; 316 C.E., Western Jin Dynasty Falls; 386 C.E., Toba Establishes the Northern Wei Dynasty in China.

401 - 476 C.E.

428-431 C.E.
NESTORIAN CONTROVERSY

The Nestorian controversy heralded the beginning of a long series of political and theological controversies concerning the divine and human natures of Christ.

LOCALE: Antioch, Syria, and Alexandria (now in Egypt)
CATEGORIES: Government and politics; religion

KEY FIGURES
Saint Cyril of Alexandria (c. 375-444 C.E.), bishop of Alexandria, 412-444 C.E.
Nestorius (c. 381-c. 451 C.E.), bishop of Constantinople, 428-431 C.E.
Theodosius II (401-450 C.E.), Roman emperor in the east, r. 408-450 C.E.
Celestine I (d. 432 C.E.), Roman Catholic pope, 422-432 C.E.

SUMMARY OF EVENT
In the early fifth century C.E., there were two rival theological schools of thought concerning Jesus Christ. The theologians in Alexandria in Egypt, led by Saint Cyril of Alexandria, held that Jesus was the eternal Word of God, living under the conditions of humanity. The other school, based in Antioch, in Syria, believed that Jesus was the result of a union between the divine Son of God and the human Jesus. In Alexandria, more emphasis was placed on the divinity of Christ, whereas Antioch feared that too much emphasis on divinity would obscure Jesus' humanity.

In 428 C.E., Nestorius, a Syrian, became bishop of Constantinople, the eastern capital of the Roman Empire, a position that ranked second only to Rome itself in ecclesiastical prestige. Following the school of Antioch, he preached that Jesus had two distinct natures, human and divine. He also preferred the term "christotokos" (mother of Christ), for Jesus' mother, rather than the more popular "theotokos" (mother of God), because, he said, "theotokos" implies that Mary gave birth to God. To Cyril, denial of the concept of "theotokos" meant that Mary was not the mother of God and hence that God had not become human in Jesus. Nestorius seemed to be teaching that there were two persons in Christ, the human Jesus and the divine Son of God.

Nestorius was quickly challenged by Cyril, who considered it his duty to strike down heresy wherever it might appear. Nestorius retaliated by encouraging renegade Egyptians living in Constantinople to file charges of misconduct against Cyril. Cyril complained to Emperor

Theodosius II, who had appointed Nestorius. During the Easter season in 430 C.E., Cyril convoked a synod of all the bishops under his jurisdiction, and after a formal investigation, they condemned Nestorius as a heretic.

Early in his term of office, Nestorius had written to the pope about various matters and had incidentally mentioned something of his novel opinions. Concerned about these opinions, Pope Celestine I kept Constantinople under observation. The pope took no action until Cyril sent him a dossier of the documents that had been used at his synod, along with information of that body's verdict. Celestine then brought together the Italian bishops during August of 430, studied the matter, and concurred in the Egyptian decision. In a letter to Nestorius, Celestine informed the bishop of Constantinople of his verdict and gave Nestorius ten days after receiving the letter to repudiate the erroneous doctrine or suffer excommunication. To see to it that Nestorius obeyed, Celestine commissioned Cyril to enforce his decision. Meanwhile, however, Theodosius II intervened; on November 19, he summoned a general council to meet in Ephesus early

Saint Cyril of Alexandria. (Library of Congress)

in 431 to investigate the controversy. The pope tacitly agreed to suspend his sentence in the interval.

On June 7, 431, the date set by Theodosius for the opening of the council, Nestorius and Cyril were in Ephesus. Each had a coterie of supporters, but the pope's legates were absent, as were the delegates in the jurisdiction of John, bishop of Antioch. Although this last group did not support Nestorius, they also did not care for Cyril's theology. During his anti-Nestorian campaign, Cyril had drawn up a list of theses, known as the Twelve Anathemas, in an effort to pinpoint the errors of Nestorius. The language of these propositions, however, was equivocal and suspicious to the Antiochene theologians.

After waiting two weeks for the tardy bishops, and against the protests of the emperor's civil supervisor, Cyril opened the council on June 22. Summoned officially to account for his ideas and defend himself, Nestorius refused to attend, so his views were studied in his written documents. The assembled theologians found him guilty of advocating heretical ideas, excommunicated him, and declared him deposed.

During the course of the remaining sessions of the council, all the latecomers finally arrived, and immediately the Antiochenes quarreled with Cyril and those who accepted his leadership. They declared him excommunicated and proclaimed themselves a rival council. In the end, the emperor ordered the arrest of both Cyril and John of Antioch; irritated and somewhat puzzled, he wanted time to conduct a personal investigation. Cyril lavishly distributed money and gifts to the important people at Theodosius's court, but whether this activity influenced the emperor cannot be determined. With the advice of the pope's legate and of others whom he consulted, Theodosius ratified the condemnation of Nestorius and exonerated the other two bishops. Not until 433 C.E. did Antioch and Alexandria reach an agreement that removed all suspicion from Cyril.

SIGNIFICANCE

As a result of these controversies, a reaction set in against Nestorianism called monophysitism, a Greek term meaning "a single nature." Whereas Nestorians believed that Jesus had two separate natures, Monophysites stressed his predominately divine nature. In 451 C.E., the Council of Chalcedon finally declared Jesus to be both fully human and fully divine and that he was one person who was divine.

Nestorian supporters thought that their views were vindicated by this council. Nevertheless, Nestorius was exiled by the emperor's order, at first back to his home near Antioch and then to a distant oasis in Upper Egypt. Some twenty years later, he died in obscurity. His ideas, however, did not die. They fell on fertile ground outside the Roman Empire in Armenia and Persia; from there, Nestorianism penetrated eastward as far as China. Europeans visiting Beijing (Peking) in the time of Marco Polo found Nestorian Christians there. Of even greater significance for Christianity was the legacy of ill will created by the Nestorian affair. The virulent theological hostilities that it engendered released a current of controversy that swept over the Roman world during the following century.

—*Raymond H. Schmandt,*
updated by Winifred O. Whelan

FURTHER READING

Constas, Nicholas. "Weaving the Body of God: Proclus of Constantinople, the Theotokos, and the Loom of the Flesh." *Journal of Early Christian Studies* 3 (Summer, 1995): 169-194. Constas describes the conflict between Nestorius, who did not believe in honoring Mary as Mother of God, and Proclus, his successor, who defended the Theotokos title.

Kee, Howard Clark, et al. *Christianity: A Social and Cultural History.* New York: Macmillan, 1991. This book includes a short section telling the story of the Nestorian controversy. It describes the role of the emperor's sister Pucheria in the event, and the blustery personality of Nestorius.

LaPorte, Jean. "Christology in Early Christianity." In *Christology: The Center and the Periphery*, edited by Frank K. Flinn. New York: Paragon House, 1988. LaPorte describes the bitter conflict between Cyril and Nestorius. The Council of Chalcedon in 451 actually agreed with Nestorius that there are two natures in Christ, but said that the two natures are united in a "hypostasis" or person.

L'Huillier, Peter. *The Church of the Ancient Councils: the Disciplinary Work of the First Four Ecumenical Councils.* Crestwood, N.Y.: St. Vladimir's Seminary Press, 1995. An examination of the work of the first four ecumenical councils, including the discussion about the Nestorian controversy. Bibliography and index.

Morris, Thomas V. *The Logic of God Incarnate.* Ithaca, N.Y.: Cornell University Press, 1986. This work constitutes a useful reference for a more complete discussion of the arguments on both sides of the God-human debate.

Sellers, R. V. *The Council of Chalcedon.* London: Society for Promoting Christian Knowledge, 1961. A more lengthy and thorough explanation of the Nestorian controversy, which was a catalyst for a series of political and theological debates. These debates resulted in the official clarification of the Church's doctrine of the single person of Christ.

SEE ALSO: 200 C.E., Christian Apologists Develop Concept of Theology; 325 C.E., Adoption of the Nicene Creed; October 8-25, 451 C.E., Council of Chalcedon.
RELATED ARTICLE in *Great Lives from History: The Ancient World*: Jesus.

439 C.E.
VANDALS SEIZE CARTHAGE

Vandal forces seized Carthage, seriously expediting the erosion of Roman authority in the Western Roman Empire.

LOCALE: Carthage, on the northwest coast of Africa
CATEGORIES: Expansion and land acquisition; wars, uprisings, and civil unrest

KEY FIGURES
Wallia (d. 418 C.E.), Visigoth leader, r. 415-418 C.E., who was authorized by Rome to attack the Vandals in Spain
Genseric (c. 390-477 C.E.), king of the Vandals, r. 428-477 C.E., leader of the attack on Carthage in 439 C.E., sacked Rome in 455 C.E.
Bonifacius (d. 432 C.E.), Roman general and governor in Africa, 425-431 C.E., alleged to have sought the Vandals as allies in rebellion against Rome, 429 C.E.
Valentinian III (419-455 C.E.), Western Roman emperor, r. 425-440 C.E.
Galla Placidia (c. 390-450 C.E.), Roman princess, regent for her son, Emperor Valentinian III, 425-c. 440 C.E.
Flavius Aetius (c. 300-c. 454 C.E.), master-general and chief minister to Valentinian III

SUMMARY OF EVENT
The Vandals appear to have entered the stage of European history suddenly and with little prior attestation, aside from various legends that point to a sometime residence in the area that later became modern Poland. In the mid-fourth century C.E., the Vandals split into two groups, the Asding and the Siling. It is the Asding Vandals who participated in the events of the fifth century C.E. Driven west by the swiftly moving Huns, the Vandals crossed the Rhine River near Mainz in 406. For several years, the Vandals ravaged Gaul and at one point seemed poised to cross the English Channel and invade Britain. Instead, they crossed the Pyrenees and settled in Spain in 409. In 411, the Vandals became *foederati*, or official allies of the Romans. The Vandals remained in

Spain for twenty years, but the Roman-Vandal peace was an uneasy one. It was broken in 416, when Rome authorized the Visigoths, under Wallia, to attack the Vandals in the name of the emperor. The Vandals suffered severely under this treatment but recovered their strength within a decade.

Under the leadership of their king, Genseric, the Vandals crossed to North Africa in 429 C.E., lured by the prospect of controlling the rich grain lands there. Conditions in Africa made an invasion an attractive prospect for the enterprising Vandals, because the local ruler, Bonifacius, had rebelled against Galla Placidia, regent for the child emperor Valentinian III. It cannot be proved that Bonifacius actually invited the Vandals as allies; nevertheless, an estimated eighty thousand Vandals arrived, of whom twenty thousand were fighting men. The Vandals found further advantages in the restlessness of the native Berbers and in the turmoil fomented by the religious discord of the Donatists, a group of schismatic Christians.

Although Genseric did not capture any of the chief cities of North Africa then, he did ravage the country and defeat Bonifacius's troops in battle in 431 C.E. Genseric also laid siege to Hippo for fourteen months, during which time the city's great bishop and writer, Saint Augustine, died. Finally in 435, terms of peace were concluded by which the Vandals were permitted to settle in Numidia.

In 439 C.E., Genseric threw off the Roman yoke and seized Carthage, the leading city and key to the control of North Africa and the Mediterranean. Next, a fleet was organized to operate off the Sicilian coast. In 442, despite the vigorous efforts of Flavius Aetius, the generalissimo and chief minister to Valentinian III, Rome was forced to acknowledge the independence of the Vandal kingdom.

For the next century, under Genseric and four of his successors, the Vandals ruled independently in North Africa, holding Sicily, Corsica, and Sardinia as well, thus controlling the Mediterranean. In 455, when Valentinian III was assassinated, Genseric descended on Rome. The Vandals spared the buildings and monuments but otherwise plundered the city's art treasures.

Shortly after becoming emperor of the Eastern Roman Empire in 457 C.E., Leo I sent a fleet to try to reconquer Carthage; his troops suffered a humiliating defeat, and Genseric was left in total control of the province of Africa. The Vandals continued to administer the rich, grain-producing North African territory in much the same manner as had the Romans, even using the same administrative personnel. The significant differences were to be seen in the confiscation of large landed estates (which became properties of the Vandals), in the independent stance toward the Roman emperor in Constantinople, and in the religion of the people. The Vandals were Arian Christians, and Genseric and several of his successors waged bitter persecution against the non-Arian Christians; they were largely successful in destroying orthodox Christianity and replacing it with Arianism. This attitude was different from the policies of other barbarian kingdoms, such as the Visigoths and Ostrogoths, who, although adherents of Arianism themselves, were tolerant of the religions of their Catholic subjects. The Vandals' hollow victory over Catholicism proved to be the seed of their own undoing.

Carthage is destroyed by the Vandals. (F. R. Niglutsch)

SIGNIFICANCE

Vandal control of Africa came to an end when the emperor Justinian decided to reincorporate the western portion of the old Roman Empire and to enforce orthodoxy throughout his dominions. Belisarius, Justinian's general, defeated the Vandals at Ad Decimam and soon after captured Gelimer, the Vandal king, thus bringing Vandal rule in Africa to a close. The Vandals who survived became slaves of the Romans and disappeared as a people from history.

Although the Vandals held North Africa for more than a century, their influence was more negative than positive. They made little or no lasting cultural contribution to North Africa and left almost no records. The coming of the Vandals marked the denouement of Roman culture in North Africa, which had been among its most advanced areas. The career and writings of Saint Augustine of Hippo serve as a reminder of the achievements and potential of North African civilization, had the Roman-

Christian synthesis there persisted. There were exceptions, such as the work of the poet Luxorius and the allegorist Fulgentius, that showed the spirit of Roman culture could still flourish in Vandal-occupied Africa, but a full-scale cultural revival was impossible. Justinian's recovery of North Africa in 534 C.E. proved ephemeral, for the area was taken over by the Muslims in the seventh century, permanently destroying the economic, cultural and political unity of the Mediterranean under the Romans.

—*Mary Evelyn Jegen, updated by Nicholas Birns*

FURTHER READING

Cameron, Averil. *The Later Roman Empire: A.D. 284-430.* Cambridge, Mass.: Harvard University Press, 1993. Cameron focuses his story on the latter part of the Roman Empire, including the barbarian invasions.

Clover, Frank. *The Late Roman West and the Vandals.* Aldershot, England: Variorum, 1993. A collection of essays, ranging from general to more specialized topics, written by the late twentieth century's leading historian of the Vandals.

Grant, Michael. *The Fall of the Roman Empire.* London: Weidenfeld, 1990. Grant analyzes the Vandal invasion in light of the dissolution of Roman rule in the West.

_____. *From Rome to Byzantium: The Fifth Century A.D.* New York: Routledge, 1998. An examination of the history of the Roman Empire after the fall until it became the Byzantium Empire. Covers Vandals and other barbarians. Bibliography and index.

Isidore of Seville. *History of the Goths, Vandals, and Suevi.* Translated by Guido Donini and Gordon B. Ford. Leiden, the Netherlands: E. J. Brill, 1970. A leading primary source on the Vandals.

O'Flynn, John M. *Generalissimos of the Western Roman Empire.* Edmonton: University of Alberta Press, 1983. Good coverage of the relationship between Genseric and Flavius Aetius.

SEE ALSO: c. 3d-4th century C.E., Huns Begin Migration West from Central Asia; August 24-26, 410 C.E., Gothic Armies Sack Rome; 445-453 C.E., Invasions of Attila the Hun; September 4, 476 C.E., Fall of Rome.

RELATED ARTICLE in *Great Lives from History: The Ancient World*: Genseric.

445-453 C.E.
INVASIONS OF ATTILA THE HUN

Invasions of Attila the Hun highlighted Roman weakness, pushed some German tribes into new regions, and dislocated much of the population of Italy.

LOCALE: Eastern and Western Roman Empires
CATEGORIES: Expansion and land acquisition; wars, uprisings, and civil unrest

KEY FIGURES

Attila (c. 406-453 C.E.), king of the Huns, r. 435-453 C.E.

Honoria (fl. fifth century C.E.), Roman princess, sister of Valentinian III

Valentinian III (419-455 C.E.), Western Roman emperor, r. 425-440 C.E., Honoria's brother

Flavius Aetius (c. 300-c. 454 C.E.), master-general of the joint Roman-Visigothic army at Châlons and chief minister to Valentinian III

Theodoric I (d. 451 C.E.), king of the Visigoths, r. 419-451 C.E.

Saint Leo I (c. 400-461 C.E.), Roman Catholic pope, 440-461 C.E.

SUMMARY OF EVENT

Although the connection is disputed by some, the Huns are generally identified with the Xiongnu (Hsiung-Nu), a nomadic tribe from the Gobi Desert who first attracted the attention of the civilized world when they attacked Han Dynasty China in the second and first centuries B.C.E. According to historian Edward Gibbon, the Xiongnu were ultimately defeated by the Han emperor, precipitating the permanent division of the tribe. One group remained in the Gobi Desert where they were soon conquered by another Mongol tribe called the Sienpi. Another group settled in southwestern China on land allotted to them by the emperor. A third group, however, headed west and split into a northern and a southern branch as they left central Asia. The southern branch eventually settled around the Caspian Sea while the northern branch, the Huns who so disrupted the late Roman Empire, headed for Europe.

The Huns advanced very rapidly across the Ukraine, central Europe, and as far south as the junction of the Rhine and Danube Rivers. They organized the territory they conquered into a loose confederation of subservient tribes. The Alani, Scythians, Ostrogoths, and many other lesser tribes were subjected to Hunnish rule in this manner. Other tribes, such as the Visigoths, fled their homelands to avoid a similar fate and thereby contributed to increasing German pressure on Roman territory. The Visigoths fled en masse to the banks of the Danube and begged the Roman emperor Valens to allow them to enter the relative safety of the empire. He agreed and thereby introduced a dangerous and unstable element into the Western Roman Empire that many Roman leaders would later regret.

When Attila assumed leadership of the Hunnish empire, it was at its greatest extent, with all German tribes, except the Frisians and Salian Franks, bound to the Huns

Attila and the Huns attack. (Library of Congress)

in one way or another and the Eastern Roman Empire reduced to paying annual bribes to keep them at bay (a policy introduced by the emperor Theodosius the Great). Attila originally assumed kingship of the Huns jointly with his brother, Bleda, in 435 C.E. The two men ruled together until 444, when Attila murdered his brother and seized exclusive control of the tribe and its extensive possessions.

Attila became involved shortly thereafter in the internal politics of the family of the Western Roman emperor, Valentinian III. The emperor's sister, Honoria, had disgraced herself by having an affair with one of her servants and had been excluded from her inheritance and former position within the royal family. She appealed to Attila for aid and seems to have promised him her hand in marriage and a tremendous amount of money if he would help her regain her lost prominence and prestige. This offer seems to have flattered Attila, and he began to demand that Valentinian hand Honoria over to him so that

he could formalize her marriage offer. He also began to claim that half of the Western Roman Empire was his by right of the fact that he was Honoria's fiancé. Valentinian rejected these demands, and the uneasy truce that had existed between the Huns and the Western Roman Empire steadily deteriorated.

This deterioration culminated in Attila's invasion of Gaul in 451 C.E. The king of the Franks had just died, and a dispute over his throne had erupted among several of his sons. Attila hoped to take advantage of this confusion to add this valuable piece of the Western Roman Empire to his possessions. At the same time, he once again repeated his demand that Valentinian surrender Honoria to him and give him half of the Western Roman Empire. The ensuing campaign has been described as one of the decisive events in European history. Attila was more than simply a danger to Roman political control of the west. He also represented a serious threat to Latin civilization and to the Christian religion. Even though most of the Germanic tribes who had settled in Gaul were independent in a political sense, most of them had adopted Christianity and were at least to a degree appreciative of the merits of Roman civilization. Attila possessed no such appreciation and had no use at all for Christianity, preferring his own customs and beliefs.

In the end, all the Germanic tribes in the region—the Salian Franks, Burgundians, and Visigoths—joined together with Roman forces to stop Attila. This combined force was commanded by the Roman master-general Flavius Aetius and the king of the Visigoths, Theodoric I. In 451 C.E., this army met Attila's force near Châlons in a bloody battle that cost, according to contemporary sources, between 162,000 and 320,000 lives. Theodoric himself was mortally wounded during the battle, but the joint German-Roman army did manage to halt Attila's advance in Gaul and force him to retreat back beyond the Rhine River. It did not, however, have the strength left to follow Attila and finish him off.

Attila's defeat at Châlons did nothing to weaken his powerful ambitions. The very next year, 452 C.E., he invaded Italy and laid siege to the large and prosperous city of Aquileia, on the northern Adriatic coast. After a three-month siege, the city fell to the Huns and was so thoroughly destroyed by them that it never rose again. Attila then headed south toward Rome, destroying any other city in his path that did not immediately surrender to him. His original intention was to capture and sack Rome but he began to waver in this goal after some of his advisers warned him that every other invader who had sacked Rome (most notably, Alaric I, former king of the Visigoths) had died shortly thereafter. At this point, an embassy, led by Pope Leo I (later Saint Leo), met Attila north of Rome and offered him a substantial bribe if he would spare the city. This bribe, combined with the fact that a famine was ravaging Italy and making it difficult for the Huns to support themselves, convinced Attila to alter his plans, and he withdrew from the peninsula shortly thereafter.

SIGNIFICANCE

One long-term consequence of Attila's invasion of Italy was that a large number of refugees settled on the low islands on the northern Adriatic coast. They became the nucleus of what would become the future republic of Venice.

After his withdrawal from Italy, Attila made another attempt to invade Gaul, only to be stopped by the forces of the new Visigothic king, Thorismund. He then began to threaten to invade the Eastern Roman Empire. Before he could carry this threat out, however, he died suddenly of a hemorrhage after excessive drinking during one of his frequent wedding celebrations. Attila's empire quickly disintegrated after his death in 453 C.E., with many of the survivors drifting back into Central Asia, and the Huns ceased to be a force in world history. The Roman Empire and the Visigoths and the other Germanic tribes of Europe were saved from further invasions and free to maintain their civilizations and culture.

—Christopher E. Guthrie

FURTHER READING

Gibbon, Edward. *The Decline and Fall of the Roman Empire*. Reprint. New York: Modern Library, 1995. A classic account of the collapse of the Roman Empire that contains several interesting and valuable sections on the impact of Attila and the Huns on this event.

Goffart, Walter. *Rome's Fall and After*. London: The Hambledon Press, 1989. An excellent collection of essays that place the invasions of the Huns within the larger context of Rome's problems during the third and fourth centuries C.E.

Howarth, Patrick. *Attila, King of the Huns: Man and Myth*. New York: Carroll and Graf, 2001. A biographical treatment of Attila that covers the history of the Huns. Bibliography and index.

Thompson, E. A. *The Huns*. London: Blackwell, 1996. A reissue of the author's 1948 classic, *A History of Attila and the Huns*, this revised edition is one of the best sources in English on the history of both the Huns as a people and Attila as a leader.

SEE ALSO: 209-174 B.C.E., Maodun Creates a Large Confederation in Central Asia; 1st-5th centuries C.E., Alani Gain Power; c. 3d-4th century C.E., Huns Begin Migration West from Central Asia; August 24-26, 410 C.E., Gothic Armies Sack Rome; 439 C.E., Vandals Seize Carthage; July, 451 C.E., Battle of Châlons.

RELATED ARTICLE in *Great Lives from History: The Ancient World*: Attila.

---

449 C.E.
SAXON SETTLEMENT OF BRITAIN BEGINS

The Saxon settlement of Britain began, bringing an end to Roman occupation and establishing the origins of English language and culture.

LOCALE: Britain
CATEGORIES: Expansion and land acquisition; wars, uprisings, and civil unrest

KEY FIGURES

Vortigern (fl. fifth century C.E.), British warlord indirectly responsible for the establishment of the first Saxon settlement in Britain in 450 C.E.

Hengist (c. 420-c. 488 C.E.), Jutish leader responsible for establishing the first Saxon settlement in Britain in 450 in the vicinity of modern Kent, r. c. 456-c. 488 C.E.

Ambrosius Aurelianus (fl. fifth century C.E.), surviving member of the Roman ruling class, organized the Britons against the Saxon invaders

Artorius (fl. fifth century C.E.), Roman British leader and successor of Ambrosius Aurelianus, said to be the prototype of the medieval King Arthur

SUMMARY OF EVENT

Three separate tribes make up what is now referred to as the Anglo-Saxons. Beginning in about 250 C.E., three disparate but racially and culturally similar groups—the Angles, the Saxons, and the Jutes—invaded and settled in different parts of Britain. The Angles (whose name serves as the origin for the word "English") settled in the north of Britain. A similar tribe known as the Saxons settled in the southern part of the island, and the Jutes, whom some scholars believe originated in Jutland (Denmark), settled in the middle. Although these were the major invading groups, there were also a small percentage of Frisians from the northern part of what is now the Netherlands, Swabians from the innermost parts of Germany, and very likely some smaller tribes that had originally inhabited Sweden. The causes for this geographical migration were overcrowding, poor farmland, and the constant battles with nature in their homelands in Northern Europe. At this point in history, the land held by these groups was literally shrinking as sections of the northern German coasts sank into the sea.

The first Anglo-Saxon raids began around 259 C.E. with small raiding parties that also invaded the opposite coasts of Gaul. These raiders surprised the native Britons and carried off plunder and captives. Although its hold was weakening, the Roman Empire, which dominated Britain at this time, was still strong enough to fight back. The real invasions, however, started about 449 and lasted for more than one hundred years. First called Saxons, the German invaders were later referred to as Angles. By 601, the pope referred to the leader of southern Britain, Aethelbert of Kent, as *rex Anglorum* (king of the Angles).

Arriving without warning in their long boats, the Saxons first landed on the southern and eastern coasts of Britain and then moved to the island's interior. Some of the boats that the Saxons used to invade Britain have been preserved in peat bogs. The Nydam boat, named for its place of discovery, was 77 feet (23 meters) long and up to 11 feet (3.4 meters) wide. It used oars for propulsion and resembled a long rowboat. These invaders carried thrusting spears, bows, swords, and Roman-made armor. Their shields were round and made of wooden planks with a large metal spike in the center.

In the year 400 C.E., Britain was still a Roman province, with Roman-style towns, villas, roads, and armies. Unlike the Romans, who had earlier invaded Britain with strong and highly trained armies, the Saxons carried out their invasion of Britain more slowly with wave after wave of invaders. Also, unlike the Romans, who desired to overthrow the native Celtic Britons and absorb them into the vast Roman Empire, the Saxons wanted to stay, cultivate the earth, and prosper in a new land. When the

Hengist (right) with Horsa, meets with British warlord Vortigern. (Hulton Archive)

Saxon warrior-adventurers first arrived, they were repelled by the Roman army. By the early fifth century, however, Roman Britain had reached the point of collapse. By 410, the British people found themselves without Roman protection on an isolated and vulnerable island at the edge of the empire. Emperor Honorius, who was under attack from the Goths, was unable to send Roman military forces. Slowly, the Saxons made their way up the British rivers, plundering and taking captives all the way, but always returning to their native country.

The first permanent Saxon settlement was not established until about 450, when the British warlord, Vortigern, presented a tract of land to a group of Saxons in return for protection from other native warlords. Although the Jutish leader, known as Hengist, provided protection for awhile, he soon turned against Vortigern and quickly conquered Kent for himself. Soon after, the next wave of Saxon invaders were made up of farmers and their families intent on seizing rich farmland, instead of warrior-adventurers and plunderers. By the second half of the fifth century, the Saxons had gained settlements along the rivers and coasts without much opposition from the native British people. They wanted peace and were intent on gaining land and farming it well. They were prepared to fight only if necessary. Although the native Britons traditionally farmed on the lighter soil found on hill slopes, the newcomers preferred the clay soil, similar to that found in their native land. In many parts of England, the two peoples were able to coexist peacefully for a time.

At the end of the fifth century, however, the Britons rallied around a leader, a survivor of the Roman ruling class named Ambrosius Aurelianus. Some scholars believe Aurelianus held the Anglo-Saxons at bay for forty years. His successor, Artorius (thought to be the model for the mythical King Arthur), is said to have replaced Aurelianus as leader of the Britons. Riding into battle in Roman-style chain-mail armor, Artorius defeated the Saxons at Mount Badon. To the Anglo-Saxons, who fought only on foot, the Britons, who sometimes fought in Roman-style cavalry units, must have seemed quite formidable. It is said that Artorius halted the Saxon invasion for fifty years. However, the British people, who were broken up into at least five separate kingdoms, could not unite under a single leader. By the middle of the sixth century, the temporary British revival had ended.

The fair-haired Anglo-Saxons eventually claimed victory and rapidly moved inland, erecting their timber huts many times among Roman ruins. They lived side by side and intermarried with the darker-haired Celtic-speaking British peasantry. Although the Celtic language was eventually replaced by the language of the Angles, Saxons, and Jutes, it continued to survive in various forms in Ireland, Wales, and Scotland. By the seventh century C.E., there were seven Saxon kingdoms in Britain: Kent, Essex, Sussex, Wessex, Mercia, East Anglia, and Northumberland.

Early Anglo-Saxon society was built on families and clans, or tribes, and centered on the warrior and a method of reciprocity that was to lead to the medieval feudal system known as the *comitatus*. The lord (earl) expected the service and loyalty of his thanes (similar to the later feudal knights), who expected the reciprocal protection from the lord. The West Germanic language of the invaders has been always referred to as English, whether spoken by Angles, Saxons, or Jutes, but it was not until about 890 that the name "Engla lande" (the land of the Angles) became popular.

The Saxon culture maintained a strong oral tradition rich in poetic form. Saint Bede the Venerable, who completed his famous *Historia ecclesiastica gentis Anglorum* (731 C.E.; *The Ecclesiastical History of the English Nation*, 1723) in Latin, is chiefly responsible for preserving in written form the legends of England reaching as far back as the Roman occupation. In addition, the *Anglo-Saxon Chronicle* (assembled 871-899 C.E.), written in Old English, has provided scholars with many incidents of Anglo-Saxon life and history. Although the famous epic *Beowulf* (c. 700-750 C.E.; first printing 1815) is set in Scandinavia, it is written in English and gives modern readers a glimpse of Anglo-Saxon life.

SIGNIFICANCE

The decline and fall of the Roman Empire ensured the success of the Anglo-Saxon invasion of Britain. The geographical movement of the Anglo-Saxons from what later became Germany, Denmark, and the Netherlands to the British Isles was only part of the general upheaval that affected Europe for generations. With the introduction of Christianity in 597 C.E., the Anglo-Saxons began using the Latin alphabet. By the end of the seventh century, the Saxons had been converted to Christianity by Saint Augustine of Canterbury and other missionaries from the European continent.

—*M. Casey Diana*

FURTHER READING

Bazelmans, Jos. *By Weapons Made Worthy: Lords, Retainers, and Their Relationship in "Beowulf."* Amsterdam: Amsterdam University Press, 1999. An examination of *Beowulf* and what it reveals about relationships between lords and retainers in the Anglo-Saxon world.

Bredehoft, Thomas A. *Textual Histories: Readings in the "Anglo-Saxon Chronicle."* Buffalo, N.Y.: University of Toronto Press, 2001. An analysis of the *Anglo-Saxon Chronicle* that examines it as literature and as a historical document.

Ellis, Peter Berresford. *Celt and Saxon: The Struggle for Britain, A.D. 410-937.* London: Constable, 1993. An examination of the relationship between the invading Saxons and the Celts in Britain. Bibliography, index, and map.

Higham, N. J. *Rome, Britain, and the Anglo-Saxons.* London: Seaby, 1992. An analysis of the end of the Roman period in Britain and how the Saxons came to settle there.

Hines, John, ed. *The Anglo-Saxons from the Migration Period to the Eighth Century: An Ethnographic Perspective.* Rochester, N.Y.: Boydell Press, 1997. A collection of papers presented at a conference of the Center for Interdisciplinary Research on Social Stress, in 1994. Focuses on the Anglo-Saxons from their migration to England to their settlement there.

Karkov, Catherine E., ed. *The Archaeology of Anglo-Saxon England: Basic Readings*. New York: Garland, 1999. A collection of essays on the archaeological findings regarding the Anglo-Saxon period.

SEE ALSO: 43-130 C.E., Roman Conquest of Britain; 60 C.E., Boudicca Leads Revolt Against Roman Rule.
RELATED ARTICLE in *Great Lives from History: The Ancient World*: Hengist.

c. 450 C.E.
CONVERSION OF IRELAND TO CHRISTIANITY

The conversion of Ireland precipitated a form of monasticism that ensured the preservation of the records and literature of Western civilization after the Fall of Rome.

LOCALE: Ireland and the Celtic parts of the British Isles

CATEGORIES: Religion; cultural and intellectual history

KEY FIGURES

Pelagius (c. 355-c. 435 C.E.), British monk whose heretical beliefs (Pelagianism) upheld the essential goodness of human nature

Celestine I (d. 432 C.E.), Roman Catholic pope, 422-432 C.E., and first Roman bishop interested in the Irish

Saint Patrick (c. 418/422-493 C.E.), semilegendary missionary bishop traditionally associated with the conversion of Ireland

SUMMARY OF EVENT

The Irish of history have their roots in the Celtic La Tène civilization, which was probably established in Ireland by the end of the third century B.C.E. The Celtic cultural base remained predominant through the first millennium C.E., virtually the only modification being the introduction of Christianity.

Christianity certainly existed in Ireland before the fifth century C.E., although it was probably limited to the southern part of the island, where it had presumably been carried by inhabitants of Britain and Gaul who had fled to Hibernia from the Vandals and Huns. Saint Augustine of Hippo (a city in Roman Africa) believed that his rival, the arch-heretic Pelagius was from Hibernia, and Gallic bishops such as Victricius of Rouen, Lupus of Troyes, and Germanus of Auxerre journeyed to the British Isles in the late fourth and early fifth centuries to counter Pelagianism, which taught that salvation could be achieved by the exercise of human powers. Pope Celestine I commissioned Palladius, a Roman deacon, to convert Ireland in 431 C.E. Little is known about this missionary bishop other than that he was either the original Saint Patrick or, more likely, a predecessor. On the death of Palladius, Patrick was ordained a bishop and set out for Ireland.

Research on Patrick trying to establish a chronology for his life and work has yielded few positive results. His own writings, his *Confessio* (fifth century C.E.; *The Confession* in *Saint Patrick, the Writings*, 1887), a reply to his detractors, *Epistola ad milites Corotici* (fifth century C.E.; *Letters to the Soldiers of Croticus*, 1953), and several letters, date from the fifth century, but the earliest extant biographies come from the seventh century. Patrick was born in Roman Britain where, at the age of sixteen, he was captured and sold into slavery in Ireland. During his captivity, he turned to religion. After six years of labor as a shepherd, he returned to Britain determined eventually to convert the Irish to Christianity. Although the record of his actual missionary activity among the Irish is not clear, Patrick is credited with securing toleration for Christians, developing a native clergy, fostering the growth of monasticism, and establishing dioceses. Patrick's doctrine is considered orthodox and has been interpreted as anti-Pelagian. There is no account of his immediate successors nor any knowledge of ecclesiastical establishments attributable to him.

SIGNIFICANCE

The ecclesiastical polity introduced by Palladus and Patrick was probably episcopal, but their establishment of monasticism was to influence Irish Christianity profoundly. By the sixth century C.E., the Irish church became a monastic church under the control of powerful abbots within a system closely akin in tone to the Eastern anchoritic traditions that had filtered into Ireland by way of Wales; Aquitaine, a region in present-day southwestern France; and Galicia in Spain. The monasteries were organizational centers for the *paruchiae*, or parishes, areas often corresponding to the boundaries of the tribe from which the founder had sprung, or that tribe that pa-

401 - 476 C.E.

tronized the establishment. Powerful personages of the tribes became abbots.

The monasteries were centers of learning, and the Irish monks transmuted the law and poetry of their pagan predecessors into a rich literary style with Christian implications. These transmuted works included the *brehon*, whose ancient Irish customary Brehon laws were used to arbitrate claims, and the *filidh*, which was made up of bardic poets, physicians, and druids. Latin learning in Ireland in the fifth and sixth centuries laid solid foundations in grammar and rhetoric, as well as knowledge of the scriptures, church fathers, and lives of saints.

As noteworthy as their zest for learning was the Irish monks' penchant for poverty, asceticism, contemplation, and solitude. This form of monasticism, reminiscent of earlier *brehon* and *filidh* spartan characteristics, reflects the Celtic spirit of individualism. During the sixth century C.E., this ascetic spirit of the Irish was manifest in the activities of Finnian at Clonard, Cieran at Clonmacnoise, and Comgall at Bangor. Of particular note were Briget of Kildare, a miracle-working transmutation of the Celtic goddess Ceridwen, who founded four monasteries, and Brendan at Clonfert, the subject of the Irish

Saint Patrick. (Library of Congress)

epic *Navigatio Brendani* (n.d.; *An Old Italian Version of the Navigation Sancti Brendani*, 1931), who is rumored to have traveled to North America. For the sake of solitude more than for proselytizing, Irish outposts were founded on pagan frontiers. Therefore, in the British Isles, monasteries were founded by Columba in 563 on Iona, an island off the coast of western Scotland, and by Aidan in 634 at Lindisfarne, an island off the northeast coast of England. These centers were responsible for the spread of the Christian faith into Scotland and Northumbria. On the Continent, the works of Columba at Luxeuil and Bobbio, Gall in Switzerland, and Kilian at Wurzburg were similar in method and intent. Each of these foreign missions provided a great stimulus for the maintenance of Latin learning and Christian ascetic piety in Western Europe in the early Middle Ages.

In the realm of spiritual discipline, Irish innovations made a lasting impression. The Irish monks first replaced public penance with private penance, consisting of prayers and works of mortification directed by the confessor for the penitent.

By the mid-seventh century, certain practices of Irish and the whole of Celtic Christendom were considered irregular in the eyes of the Roman Church, which was then episcopally governed and Benedictine in its monasticism. Differences between Irish and Roman practices included peculiarities of liturgy and rituals in the Mass, single immersion in baptism, extensive rites for ordinations, procedures in episcopal consecration, and especially differences in the celebration of Easter, the Irish tonsure, and the use of leavened bread in the communion. England was the scene of the clash between the Roman and the Celtic (Irish) traditions in the fifty years following Augustine of Canterbury's mission and the death of Columba at Iona (597). The Synod of Whitby in 664, witnessed the debate between the Roman Wilfrid and the Celtic Colman, but the resolution resulted in King Oswald of Northumbria's preference for Roman practices. By the beginning of the eighth century, the Irish had conformed to Roman practices as they understood them, and Armagh, a district of Northern Ireland said to be the site of Patrick's first mission settlement, emerged as the chief episcopal center. The harsh rules of innovators such as Columba made the more moderate papal-sponsored Benedictine form of monasticism seem attractive by comparison. Complete alignment with continental practices was impeded, however, by Viking invasions beginning in 795 C.E.

What was for most of Europe the Dark Ages was for Ireland the golden age. During this era, religious art, such as the Ardagh Chalice and the *Book of Kells* (1914) and other illuminated manuscripts, flourished. As the invading Germanic tribes burned the books of the Roman cities, the Irish monk scribes, perched on remote islands, copied all the Western literature they could obtain, thereby preserving Western civilization.

—Richard J. Wurtz, updated by M. Casey Diana

FURTHER READING

Cahill, Thomas. *How the Irish Saved Civilization: The Untold Story of Ireland's Heroic Role from the Fall of Rome to the Rise of Medieval Europe.* New York: Doubleday, 1995. Scholarly yet approachable work that argues that although Ireland knew neither Renaissance nor Enlightenment, its monks refounded Western civilization by preserving Western literature. Contains a pronunciation guide to Irish words, illustrations, a bibliography for each chapter, and a chronology from approximately 3000 B.C.E. to 1923.

Da Paor, Liam, trans. *Saint Patrick's World: The Christian Culture of Ireland's Apostolic Age.* Dublin: Four Courts Press, 1993. A collection of early sources on Ireland's early Christian church, with translations and commentaries by De Paor. Bibliography and index.

Dumville, David N., et. al. *Saint Patrick, A.D. 493-1993.* Rochester, N.Y.: Boydell, 1993. A general biography of Saint Patrick that also covers early church history in Ireland. Bibliography and index.

O'Laughlin, Thomas. *Saint Patrick: The Man and His Works.* London: Triangle, 1999. A biography of Saint Patrick that also examines his writings. Bibliography and index.

Thompson, E. A. *Who Was Saint Patrick?* 1986. Reprint. Rochester, N.Y.: Boydell, 1999. Uses both primary and secondary sources to account for Saint Patrick's life, including his own written works. Reconstructs the conversion of Ireland.

SEE ALSO: c. 6 B.C.E., Birth of Jesus Christ; c. 30 C.E., Condemnation and Crucifixion of Jesus Christ; c. 250 C.E., Saint Denis Converts Paris to Christianity; October 28, 312 C.E., Conversion of Constantine to Christianity; 4th century C.E., Ezana Expands Aksum, Later Converts to Christianity; c. 450-500 C.E., Era of the Nine Saints.

RELATED ARTICLE in *Great Lives from History: The Ancient World*: Saint Augustine.

c. 450-500 C.E.
ERA OF THE NINE SAINTS

Syrian monks, later known as the Nine Saints, preached Monophysite Christianity in the kingdom of Aksum and began the conversion of the rural population.

LOCALE: Aksum (now in Ethiopia)
CATEGORY: Religion

KEY FIGURES

Aragawi, Syrian monk and translator, traditional leader of the Nine Saints, started elimination of pagan cultic practice
Pantalewon,
Guba,
Yemata,
Alef,
Sahma,
Afse,
Garima, and
Liqanos (all fl. fifth century C.E.), Syrian monks, translators

SUMMARY OF EVENT

Between 450 and 500 C.E., nine Syrian monks, later designated the Nine Saints, arrived in the kingdom of Aksum in present-day Ethiopia, bringing with them their Syrian Monophysite form of Christianity. The precise date of their arrival in Aksum and the dates of their deaths are not known. The Nine Saints revolutionized Ethiopian Christianity in a number of ways. Besides promulgating Monophysite theology, the Nine Saints helped shape the Ethiopian liturgy. They translated the Bible and other Christian books into Ethiopian (Ge'ez). They founded monasteries, establishing a Syrian type of monasticism that replaced an older Alexandrian form. The Nine Saints also helped put monasticism in the central place it continues to hold in Ethiopian society. Furthermore, the Nine Saints helped to Christianize Ethiopia more deeply, working as missionaries to spread Christianity into previously pagan portions of the Aksum kingdom.

When the Nine Saints arrived in Aksum in the later half of the fifth century C.E., they found a kingdom that was already Christianized. Indeed, Christianity had been introduced into Ethiopia fairly early. A passage in the New Testament (Acts 8:26-39) presents the story of Saint Philip's baptism of an Ethiopian eunuch. Nonetheless, Church historians, starting with Rufinus, have traditionally traced the introduction of Christianity into Ethiopia in the first half of the fourth century C.E., through the work of two shipwrecked brothers from Roman Syria, Frumentius and Aedesius. Arriving as prisoners, they soon won the respect and trust of the royal family in Aksum. The brothers were eventually released from captivity. Aedesius returned to Tyre, where he was ordained a priest, and Frumentius, after converting the royal house of Aksum to Christianity, traveled to Alexandria in Egypt, where he was ordained by Saint Athanasius as the first bishop of the Ethiopian Church. Archaeological and numismatic evidence supports the contention that Christianity arrived in Ethiopia during the fourth century.

With the arrival of the Nine Saints later in the next century, Ethiopian Christianity traveled in a different direction. The nine Syrian monks who came to the Aksum kingdom were Monophysites. This meant that they rejected the Christological decree of the Fourth Ecumenical Council that had been held in Chalcedon in 451 C.E. The Monophysites rejected the Christological decision of Chalcedon that asserted that Christ is one person who exists "unconfusedly, unalterably, undividedly, inseparably" in two natures. The Chalcedonians tried to maintain both the full humanity as well as the full divinity of Jesus. The Monophysites also tried to maintain the full humanity and divinity of Jesus but saw themselves as being faithful to the teaching of Patriarch Cyril of Alexandria (whose basic teachings had been upheld as orthodox at the third ecumenical council in Ephesus in 431). Strictly speaking, the Monophysites held to the belief that Christ existed in "one incarnate nature." To the Chalcedonians, Christ was one person "in" two natures, while to the Monophysites, Christ was one person "out of, or from" two natures.

In the aftermath of the Council of Chalcedon in 451, Monophysite Christians found refuge in areas such as Ethiopia, which were removed from the centers of ecclesiastical and political intrigue in the Byzantine world. Although Ethiopian tradition has called them the Nine Roman Saints, scholarly consensus holds that they came from Syria, which was a territory of the Eastern Roman, or Byzantine, Empire. The Monophysite movement was strong in Syria, and individuals such as the Nine Saints were able to find a welcome in the Aksum kingdom. Therefore, in the later half of the fifth century C.E., nine Syrian monks arrived in the Aksum kingdom: Aragawi

(Za-Mikael), Pantalewon, Guba, Yemata (Mata), Alef, Sahma, Afse (Os), Garima (Isaak), and Liqanos.

The Nine Saints appear to have been led by Aragawi, and they are believed to have arrived in Ethiopia by way of Egypt. Like the Syrian Church, the Egyptian Coptic Church was also Monophysite in its theology. Since the time of Saint Frumentius (and up into the twentieth century), the bishop of the Ethiopian Church had been a Copt appointed by the patriarch of Alexandria, and thus there had always been a measure of Coptic influence on the Ethiopian Church. Although in their organization of Ethiopian monastic life, Aragawi and the other members of the Nine Saints developed a monastic rule based on the Egyptian *Rule of Saint Pachomius*, they modeled Ethiopian monastic life on the basis of the Syrian form.

A number of monasteries were established by the Nine Saints. At times, the work of establishing monasteries was closely connected with missionary work among Ethiopian pagan enclaves. This was the case at Debre Damo, where Aragawi is said to have eradicated pagan cultic practice and then to have founded the renowned monastery. Pantalewon and Afse are also said to have eliminated pagan practices and to have turned pagan temples into churches. This missionary work was carried out with royal support from Aksum.

These Syrian monks also helped shape Ethiopian culture in succeeding centuries by translating the Bible into Ge'ez, the native language of Ethiopia. Scholars generally hold that the Nine Saints brought a Syrian or Greek biblical text with them when they traveled to the Aksum kingdom and that they used this as the basis for their translation of the Bible into Ge'ez. Ethiopian tradition asserts that the task of translating the Bible began during the time of Frumentius and that the Nine Saints completed this translation task later in the fifth century C.E. Ethiopian tradition also holds that each of the nine monks translated a portion of the biblical text, thus explaining the differences in style and translation that exist in the Ethiopian renderings of the biblical books. It seems that this translation of the Bible introduced a number of new words into the Ethiopian language.

The Nine Saints also translated a number of other Christian books into Ge'ez, such as writings of the Church Fathers. Among the more significant of these translations were the works of Cyril of Alexandria, as well as Saint Athanasius of Alexandria's *Vita S. Antonii* (c. 357 C.E.; *The Life of Anthony*, 1697). They greatly influenced the worship life of the Ethiopian Church as well. Their disciple Yared is credited with developing Ethiopian Church music. Finally, the personal piety of the Nine Saints deeply affected the people of the Aksum kingdom, and the Syrian monks were believed to have worked miracles. For example, Pantalewon was said to have both healed the sick and raised the dead.

SIGNIFICANCE

The deep impression the Nine Saints left on the Ethiopian Church has remained to the present day. Christianity first spread in the kingdom of Aksum in the fourth century C.E. through the conversion of the royal household. In the fifth century, a more thorough Christianization of the kingdom was accomplished by the nine Monophysite Syrian monks. Their translations of the Scriptures and other Christian texts helped transform Ethiopia's cultural and intellectual heritage, and their Monophysite theology and monastic ideals revolutionized church life among the Aksumite population.

—*J. Francis Watson*

FURTHER READING

Frend, W. H. C. *The Rise of the Monophysite Movement: Chapters in the History of the Church in the Fifth and Sixth Centuries.* New York: Cambridge University Press, 1972. A thorough presentation of the Monophysite churches and their theology, including a discussion of the Nine Saints' work in Ethiopia.

Haymanot, Ayala Takla. *The Ethiopian Church and Its Christological Doctrine.* Rev. ed. Addis Ababa: Graphic Printers, 1981. A detailed study of the development of Ethiopian Monophysitism, including an overview of the work of the Nine Saints.

Isaac, Ephraim. *The Ethiopian Church.* Boston: Henry N. Sawyer, 1968. A general study of the Ethiopian Church intended for the general reading public.

McCullough, W. Stewart. *A Short History of Syriac Christianity to the Rise of Islam.* Chico, Calif.: Scholars Press, 1982. A detailed study of the Syrian Church, offering insight into the ecclesiastical background of the Nine Saints.

Metzger, Bruce M. *The Early Versions of the New Testament: Their Origin, Transmission, and Limitations.* Oxford, England: Clarendon Press, 1977. Presents a comprehensive analysis of the development of Ethiopian versions of the Bible and treats the arrival of Christianity into that country together with the work of the Nine Saints.

O'Leary, De Lacy. *The Ethiopian Church: Historical Notes on the Church of Abyssinia.* London: SPCK, 1936. A basic history of the Ethiopian Church.

Roberson, Ronald G. *The Eastern Christian Churches.* Rome: Edizioni Orientalia Christiana, 1993. A presentation of the theological and historical development of the Oriental Orthodox Churches, including the Ethiopian Church.

Selassie, Sergew Hable, ed. *The Church of Ethiopia: A Panorama of History and Spiritual Life.* Addis Ababa: Haile Sellassie I University Press, 1971. An Ethiopian study of church life and history.

Wallis Budge, E. A., ed. *The Book of the Saints of the Ethiopian Church.* Cambridge: Cambridge University Press, 1928. Reprint. New York: Georg Olms Verlag, 1976. Volumes 1-4 describe the traditional Ethiopian hagiographic traditions associated with the Nine Saints.

SEE ALSO: 3d-5th century C.E., Giant Stelae Are Raised at Aksum; 4th century C.E., Ezana Expands Aksum, Later Converts to Christianity; October 8-25, 451 C.E., Council of Chalcedon.

RELATED ARTICLE in *Great Lives from History: The Ancient World*: Saint Athanasius of Alexandria.

401 - 476 C.E.

July, 451 C.E.
BATTLE OF CHÂLONS

The Battle of Châlons, also known as the Battle of the Catalaunian Plain, stopped the advance of the Huns into Europe and was the last effective act of the Roman Empire in the west.

LOCALE: The Mauriac Plain, northwest of Troyes (now in France)
CATEGORY: Wars, uprisings, and civil unrest

KEY FIGURES

Attila (c. 406-453 C.E.), king of the Huns, r. 435-453 C.E.
Theodosius II (401-450 C.E.), Eastern Roman emperor, r. 408-450 C.E.
Honoria (fl. fifth century C.E.), Roman princess, sister of Valentinian III
Valentinian III (419-455 C.E.), Western Roman emperor, 425-440 C.E., Honoria's brother
Flavius Aetius (c. 300-c. 454 C.E.), Roman master-general of the Roman-Visigothic army at Châlons and chief minister to Valentinian III
Sangibanus (fl. fifth century C.E.), king of the Alans, r. c. mid-fifth century C.E.
Theodoric I (d. 451 C.E.), king of the Visigoths, r. 419-451 C.E.
Thorismund (d. 453 C.E.), king of the Visigoths, 451-453, son of Theodoric I

SUMMARY OF EVENT

The Huns appear to have been related to the Xiongnu (Hsiung-Nu), a Turkish-Mongolian people who appear in Chinese records of the early centuries C.E. They eventually made their way across Central Asia and acquired a fearsome reputation as savage warriors who lived out their lives on horseback. They defeated and absorbed one barbarian group after another, and in the process, they created a nomad horde. Pressure from the Huns forced other barbarian groups into the Roman Empire and has even been blamed for the so-called barbarian invasions.

In the 370's C.E., the Huns halted their advance north of the Danube River. For a time, their relations with the Romans were like those of other barbarians, and they often served as auxiliaries in the Roman army. In the fifth century, however, they once again grew restive. In the early 420's, the Hun king Rua had to be bought off by the Romans with a subsidy of 350 pounds (160 kilograms) of gold per year. This created an unfortunate precedent, for the barbarian taste for gold obtained in this manner could never be satiated.

In the late 430's C.E., the brothers Attila and Bleda, sons of Rua, succeeded to the throne. Sometime around 445, Attila murdered his brother and became sole king. He imposed increasingly severe terms on the Eastern Roman emperor Theodosius II, raising the yearly subsidy first to 700 pounds (320 kilograms) of gold, and then to 2,100 pounds (950 kilograms). In 447, the Romans even agreed to evacuate a strip south of the Danube five-days' march wide.

Subsequently, Attila's interests seem to have turned toward the west and to the Princess Honoria, elder sister of Emperor Valentinian III. Around 449 C.E., she had been apprehended in an illicit love affair and exiled to Constantinople. She then sent her ring to Attila and appealed to him for help. At this, Theodosius II, who already had enough problems with the Huns, immediately dispatched her back to Italy—with the recommendation that Valentinian turn her over to Attila.

Valentinian refused, and what happened next is described by the historian Priscus, who had visited Attila's camp in 448 C.E. According to Priscus, Attila

> sent men to the ruler of the western Romans to argue that Honoria, whom he had pledged to himself in marriage, should in no way be harmed. . . . He sent also to the eastern Romans concerning the appointed tribute, but his ambassadors returned from both missions with nothing accomplished. . . . Attila was of two minds and at a loss which he should attack first, but finally it seemed better to him to enter on the greater war and to march against the west, since his fight there would be not only against the Italians but also against the Goths and Franks. . . . He sent certain men of his court to Italy that the Romans might surrender Honoria. . . . He also said that Valentinian should withdraw from half of the empire. . . . When the western Romans held their former opinion, he devoted himself eagerly to preparation for war.

Meanwhile, in the western part of the empire, things were not going well. Britain, Africa, and much of Gaul (modern-day France) had been lost to the barbarians. By mid-century, only a shadow of the Western Roman Empire was held together by the patrician and master of soldiers (field marshal) Flavius Aetius, a hostage of Attila in his youth, who for twenty-five years had skillfully played one barbarian group against another.

When Attila led the Huns and their subject peoples across the Rhine into Gaul in 451 C.E., the situation looked bleak for the Romans. The Roman army consisted of little more than barbarian mercenaries in the personal service of Aetius. The other powers in western Europe, the Visigoths in Aquitania and the Franks in the Rhineland, could be expected only to use to their own advantage a further weakening of the Romans. As things turned out, however, the western barbarians decided they had more to fear from the Huns than the Romans, and Aetius became the leader of an unlikely coalition of what remained of the Roman army, Visigoths, and Franks.

Scholars have pieced together the progress of the invasion from several sources. The Gallic chronicler Prosper, writing only a few years later, noted, "Once the Rhine had been crossed, many Gallic cities experienced Attila's most savage attacks." The Spaniard Hydatius, writing in the 460's C.E., reported, "Having broken the peace, the nation of the Huns ravaged the provinces of Gaul; many cities were destroyed"; he names Metz in particular. In the next century, Gregory of Tours related that after destroying Metz, the Huns "ravaged a great number of other cities" before finally attacking Orléans. Other reports from about the same time tell of an attack on Rheims and an approach toward Paris. It would seem, therefore, that the Huns crossed the Roohine near Strasbourg, traveled west by way of Metz and Rheims, but then turned south before reaching Paris and so came to Orléans.

At that time, Orléans was under the protection of a group of barbarian Alani in Roman service. The mid-sixth century C.E. historian Jordanes, a Goth himself, reports, "Sangibanus, the king of the Alani, terrified by fear of the future, promised to surrender himself to Attila and to betray into his power the Gallic city of Orléans, where he then was stationed." In the meantime, however, Anianus, bishop of Orléans, had gone south to seek the aid of Aetius, and the imperial coalition arrived in the nick of time, apparently after a breach had already been made in the walls.

Unable to take the now strongly defended city and not having expected to be resisted in force, Attila began a strategic retreat northward. In July, it seems, between Troyes and Châlons-sur-Marne (ancient Catalauni), Attila was brought to battle. The actual location of the battle, which traditionally has been referred to as the Battle of Châlons, is in some doubt. Jordanes says, "They came together in the Catalaunian Plain, which also is called Mauriac. It is one hundred leagues in length and seventy in breadth." This is a large

area, about 150 by 105 miles (240 by 170 kilometers), which demonstrates even Jordanes's uncertainty about the location of the battle. Among other sources, the Spaniard Hydatius says the battle took place "in the Catalaunian fields," but the Gallic sources all agree that it occurred "at Troyes in the place called Mauriac." Modern scholars have favored the French view that the battle took place on the Mauriac Plain (modern Mery-sur-Seine), about 20 miles (32 kilometers) northwest of Troyes, 35 miles (58 kilometers) south of Châlons, and next to the Catalaunian fields.

The only detailed account of the ensuing "battle of the nations" comes, again, from Jordanes. He reports that on the night before the general engagement, the Franks, perhaps under king Merovech, and Gepids fell on each other, and that fifteen thousand were slain. On the next day, the Roman battle line consisted of the Visigoths under their king, Theodoric I, on the right wing and the Romans under Aetius on the left, with the unreliable Alani under Sangibanus in the center. The location of the Franks is unspecified, suggesting that they may have received the worst of the fighting the night before. Perhaps they were stationed behind the Alani. On the other side, the Huns took the center, with the wings occupied by the Ostrogoths, under Valamer, on the left, and the remaining Gepids, under Ardaric, on the right. The rest of the

Thorismund, king of the Visigoths. (Hulton|Archive)

"crowd of kings," says Jordanes, "attended to Attila's whims like lackeys."

The battle proper began rather late, at the "ninth hour" (that is, at about 5:00 P.M.), with a skirmish for the possession of a strategic ridge of high ground. The Romans, led by the Visigothic prince Thorismund, reached the summit first, and were able to repel the Huns as they came up the slope. Stung by this initial reverse, Attila gave his soldiers a brief pep talk, concluding, "I shall hurl the first spear against the enemy, and if any man thinks to take his leisure while Attila fights, he is a dead man."

Next, there ensued "a battle ghastly, confused, ferocious, and unrelenting, the like of which history has never recounted." The streams, it was said, ran red with blood. Initially, the motley Roman forces retained their line. The Visigoths were able to drive back the Ostrogoths, although in the course of this fighting the aged Visigothic king Theodoric was thrown from his horse and trampled to death by his own men. The Visigoths then separated from the Alani on their left and fell on the left flank of the Huns themselves. In the ensuing melee, Attila was nearly slain, and the Huns then retreated to their camp, which had been fortified by their encircled wagons. As darkness fell, the Visigoths made an attack on the Hun camp but were repulsed. On the Roman right, meanwhile, Aetius and his forces seem to have broken through the weakened Gepids; Aetius himself became separated from his men and only after wandering through enemy lines did he return safely to camp.

The next day, neither side felt strong enough to resume the battle—it was later said that 165,000 men had been slain. While the members of the Roman coalition debated what to do next, Attila himself, it was said, stood atop a funeral pyre threatening to immolate himself rather than be taken captive. According to Jordanes, Aetius, fearful that if the Huns were destroyed totally, the Visigoths would be left with a free hand in Gaul, advised Thorismund, the new Visigothic king, to return home to consolidate his own place on the throne. Gregory of Tours reports that Aetius also persuaded the Franks to leave—so that he could claim all the booty. Perhaps a more realistic reconstruction is that both the Visigoths and Franks, weakened themselves, departed because they believed that their job was complete. Attila had been weakened to the point where he no longer posed a threat, and to continue to fight would only be to serve Roman interests.

Neither Attila nor Aetius was in any condition to carry on the fight. Attila withdrew back across the Rhine to fight another day. Indeed, in the next year, he returned and passed through the inexplicably undefended Alps into Italy. Aquileia was destroyed, and Milan was captured. Then, according to a pious legend, the Huns were induced to withdraw by an embassy of Pope Leo I, who was assisted in his efforts by apparitions of Saints Peter and Paul. Disease, starvation, and the rumored arrival of reinforcements from the east also would have influenced the decision. In 453 C.E., Attila died on his wedding night, and in 454, the subject peoples of the Huns revolted, inflicting a disastrous defeat on their erstwhile masters at the Battle of the Nedao River. The Huns never again posed a serious threat to the Roman Empire.

SIGNIFICANCE

The Battle of Châlons subsequently assumed a prodigious place in the popular imagination. A fifteenth century writer, for example, listed Rheims, Cambrai, Trier, Tetz, Arras, Tongres, Tournai, Therouanne, Cologne, Amiens, Beauvais, and Paris, not to mention Worms, Strasbourg, and Langres, as having been destroyed by Attila. Attila himself subsequently obtained a reputation as a barbarian par excellence. Christian moralists referred to him as the "scourge of God" for his perceived role in punishing sinful Christians. In modern times, it has been suggested that a victory by the Huns would have caused irreparable damage to the future of Western civilization. The battle has been portrayed as a victory of civilization over barbarism, and a major turning point in history.

—*Ralph W. Mathisen*

FURTHER READING

Gordon, C. D. *The Age of Attila: Fifth Century Byzantium and the Barbarians*. Ann Arbor: University of Michigan Press, 1966. This classic work on Attila provides the commentary of Priscus.

Gregory of Tours. *The History of the Franks*. Translated by L. Thorpe. London: Penguin, 1974. A modern translation of the history of the battle as written by Gregory of Tours.

Howarth, Patrick. *Attila, King of the Huns: Man and Myth*. New York: Carroll and Graf, 2001. A biographical treatment of Attila. Bibliography and index.

Jordanes. *The Origin and Deeds of the Goths*. Translated by C. C. Mierow. Princeton, N.J.: Princeton University Press, 1915. A translation of Jordanes's account of the battle.

Thompson, E. A. *The Huns*. London: Blackwell, 1996. A reissue of the author's 1948 classic, *A History of Attila and the Huns*, this revised edition is one of the best sources in English on the history of both the Huns as a people and Attila as a leader.

SEE ALSO: 209-174 B.C.E., Maodun Creates a Large Confederation in Central Asia; 1st-5th centuries C.E., Alani Gain Power; c. 3d-4th century C.E., Huns Begin Migration West from Central Asia; August 24-26, 410 C.E., Gothic Armies Sack Rome; 439 C.E., Vandals Seize Carthage; 445-453 C.E., Invasions of Attila the Hun.
RELATED ARTICLE in *Great Lives from History: The Ancient World*: Attila.

October 8-25, 451 C.E.

COUNCIL OF CHALCEDON

The Council of Chalcedon settled the controversy in the early Christian Church concerning the person of Jesus Christ, declaring that Christ is one person with both a human nature and a divine nature.

LOCALE: Chalcedon, Bithynia, Asia Minor (now Kadiköy, Turkey)
CATEGORY: Religion

KEY FIGURES

Eutyches of Constantinople (c. 378-453/454 C.E.), a leader of the church in Constantinople
Saint Flavian (d. 449 C.E.), bishop of Constantinople, 446-449 C.E.
Saint Leo I (c. 400-461 C.E.), bishop of Rome, 440-461 C.E.

SUMMARY OF EVENT

The Council of Chalcedon, the Fourth Ecumenical Council of the early Christian Church, was the culmination of the debate concerning whether, during the Incarnation of Jesus Christ, he was human, divine, a mixture of each, or fully each at the same time. This debate was a result of the First Ecumenical Council in Nicaea in 325 C.E. At Nicaea, not far from Chalcedon, the council decided that Christ was both complete God and complete man but did not clarify how that could be possible. The Nicene Creed condemned Arianism, the teaching of Arius in Alexan-

Bishops resolve questions regarding the nature of Jesus Christ at the Council of Chalcedon. (Library of Congress)

THE TOME OF LEO

"The Tome of Leo" is one of the most elegantly worded documents in the early Christian Church. In it, Pope Leo I declared that Eutyches of Constantinople should have studied the Old Testament prophesies that Christ would be the seed of David, as well as the New Testament Gospel of Matthew, which begins with "The book of the generation of Jesus Christ, the son of David, the son of Abraham" (Matthew 1:1). Leo then emphasized that had Christ not had a human nature, he could not have died to pay the penalty of sin for the entire human race. Christ also had to be God in order to live a sinless life and then by his death reestablish unity between God and the human race. In the elegant words of Leo, "The same one is true God and true man. There is nothing weird about this oneness, since both the lowliness of the man and the grandeur of the divinity are in mutual relation. As God is not changed by showing mercy, neither is the humanity devoured by the dignity received."

dria that Christ was created by God the Father out of nothing and was therefore neither God nor man. The Nicene Creed was reaffirmed by the Second Ecumenical Council in Constantinople in 381 C.E.

The issue was then confused by Apollinarius (c. 310-390 C.E.), the bishop of Laodicea in Syria, who said that Christ was human in body and soul but that his mind (human spirit) was replaced by a divine *Logos* (word). This position was condemned at Constantinople in 381. Then came Nestorianism, which overly emphasized the humanity of Christ and was condemned at the Third Ecumenical Council at Ephesus in 431.

The next to enter the debate, and whose views precipitated the calling of the Council of Chalcedon, was Eutyches of Constantinople. Eutyches was a pious presbyter and the leader of a monastery of three hundred monks near Constantinople. He strongly opposed Nestorianism, which had been condemned in 431 C.E. Although reluctant to leave his monastery, Eutyches was drawn into the controversy by the Alexandrians, led by Cyril of Alexandria, who had led the opposition to Nestorianism. Eutyches held partially to the already condemned views of Apollianarius. He believed that Christ was human in body, soul, and mind but that his humanity was still subordinate to his deity. In reality, Eutyches believed that Christ had only one nature, which was divine; in other words, the body of Christ was the body of God. Eutyches was strongly opposed and eventually deposed

and excommunicated by Saint Flavian, the patriarch of Constantinople in a local council in 448. For this council, Eutyches had left his monastery for the first time in many years.

In 449 C.E., a new council was held in Ephesus, the infamous Robber Synod, or Council of Robbers. This meeting, in which many delegates carried weapons under their cloaks, reinstated Eutyches and thereby "robbed" Christ of his humanity. Patriarch Flavian denied the authority of this council and was deposed as patriarch. Soldiers were called in to enforce the council's decision. Flavian was severely beaten and died soon thereafter. This meeting is not recognized as a legitimate church council.

At this point in the controversy, Leo I, bishop of Rome (the first of that office to be called pope), entered the debate. He was brought in by a letter written by Flavian shortly before his death. Leo seemed surprised by the seriousness of the controversy, assuming that the issue had been long settled, and by the accusations against Eutyches. Because Eutyches was a priest and a respected monastic leader, Leo had regarded him as a man of honor. However, when informed that Eutyches believed that Christ had only a divine nature, he described Eutyches, in his response to Flavian, as "very rash and extremely ignorant."

Leo's response was his famous "Tome," (449; "The Tome of Leo," 1899), a letter in which he referred back to the Nicene Creed as the definition of orthodoxy. He defined heretics such as Eutyches as those who use their own ideas rather than established truth. "The Tome of Leo" established the basis for the decision at Chalcedon by explaining in many ways, from the Virgin Birth to the Resurrection, how Christ had to have a complete human nature as well as a divine nature. Flavian died soon after receiving the "The Tome of Leo," and it eventually was taken to the Council of Chalcedon by three of Leo's leading aides. Their task was to secure the correct decision at the council. Leo at first had opposed a council, fearing a repeat of Ephesus in 449 C.E. and hoping that his letter would settle the issue.

The council was originally scheduled to meet at Nicaea in September, 451 C.E. It was rescheduled for Chalcedon in October to be closer to Constantinople. Both Roman emperors, Valentinian III in the west and Marcion in the east, issued the call for the council. Their interest was primarily religious, and therefore political, unity.

"The Tome of Leo" was specifically mentioned in the final decrees of the council. Eutychianism was condemned, and Eutyches himself was eventually deposed and exiled shortly before he died. The final decrees began by stating that Christ had come to bring peace and, therefore, that all Christians should agree on doctrine and that an official council had the authority to define that doctrine. The Creed of Chalcedon did end the major debate on the person of Christ, although Eutychianism was not entirely stamped out, by declaring,

> Our Lord Jesus Christ: the same perfect in divinity and perfect in humanity, the same truly God and truly man, of a rational soul and body; consubstantial with the Father as regards His divinity, and consubstantial with us as regards His humanity.

SIGNIFICANCE

Both the church in the Western Roman Empire, which became the Roman Catholic Church, and the church in the Eastern Roman Empire, which became the Eastern Orthodox Church, accepted the decision at the Council of Chalcedon. That decision survived centuries of controversy, including the Reformation of the sixteenth century. It has remained the orthodox Christian position on the person of Jesus Christ.

However, two variations of Eutychianism also remained as minority positions. In Egypt and Palestine, Monophysitism, meaning one nature, became a powerful force. Byzantine emperor Justinian (r. 527-565) tried to win them back to the Creed of Chalcedon and was assisted by a scholarly monk, Leontius of Byzantium. The Monophysites refused to be reconciled. Their ideas remain active in the Coptic, Ethiopian, and Armenian churches.

The second variation was Monotheletism, meaning one will, which tried to reconcile Monophysitism to the Creed of Chalcedon by stating that Christ completed his work of redemption through one divine-human will. It began in Armenia and Syria in 633 C.E. Many bishops believed that this position was in agreement with the Creed of Chalcedon. Monotheletism even gained the support of Pope Honorius, Patriarch Sergius, and the Byzantine emperor Heraclius. However, the Sixth Ecumenical Council at Constantinople in 680 debated and rejected Monotheletism and anathematized many of its adherents, including Pope Honorius.

—*Glenn L. Swygart*

FURTHER READING

"Council of Chalcedon." *The Ecumenical Review.* 22, no. 4 (October, 1970). Gives a detailed doctrinal evaluation of the issues involved in the Council of Chalcedon and of the final decision.

Gray, Patrick. *The Defense of Chalcedon in the East.* Leiden, the Netherlands: E. H. Brill, 1979. Focuses primarily on the aftermath of the Council of Chalcedon in the Eastern Orthodox Church.

Percival, Henry R. *The Seven Ecumenical Councils.* New York: Edwin C. Gorham, 1901. A historical and theological analysis of the Council of Chalcedon within the context of the seven major church councils between 325 and 787 C.E.

Sellers, R. V. *The Council of Chalcedon.* London: Society for Promoting Christian Knowledge, 1953. A thorough historical and doctrinal study of the council and the full debate concerning the person of Christ.

Stevenson, J. *Creeds, Councils, and Controversies: Documents Illustrating the History of the Church A.D. 337-461.* London: Society for Promoting Christian Knowledge, 1966. Includes many documents relating to the Council of Chalcedon, including the *Tome* of Leo that formed the basis of the final decision of the council.

Wand, J. W. C. *The Four Councils.* London: The Faith Press, 1951. Published on the fifteenth century anniversary of the Council of Chalcedon to commemorate the end of the four councils that are recognized by the Church of England.

SEE ALSO: 200 C.E., Christian Apologists Develop Concept of Theology; 325 C.E., Adoption of the Nicene Creed; 428-431 C.E., Nestorian Controversy.

RELATED ARTICLE in *Great Lives from History: The Ancient World*: Jesus.

460-477 C.E.

BUDDHIST TEMPLES BUILT AT AJANTA CAVES IN INDIA

The architecture, sculpture, and painting of the Ajanta caves mark a high point in the art of ancient India and in the development of Buddhist art.

LOCALE: Ajanta, India
CATEGORIES: Architecture; cultural and intellectual history; religion

KEY FIGURE
Hariṣeṇa (d. 477 C.E.), Vākāṭaka king of central India, r. c. 460-477 C.E.

SUMMARY OF EVENT
When the Vākāṭaka king Hariṣeṇa began his rule over much of central India around 460 C.E., his reign brought a cultural flowering, and the Buddhist site at Ajanta became the focus of intense artistic activity. More than five hundred years earlier in the second century B.C.E., several cave prayer halls (*chaityas*) and monastic residences (*vihāras*) had been excavated into the rock cliff at Ajanta, located in the Deccan plateau along a horseshoe-shaped gorge created by the Waghora River. In the second phase of activity, more than twenty new caves were added. The reasons for an artistic revival at Ajanta include the natural magnificence of the site, its location near trade routes, and changes in the Buddhist religion that promoted donations and expansion of Buddhist iconography.

Surviving inscriptions identify the major donors of these rock-cut prayer halls and monasteries. Varāhadeva, minister of King Hariṣeṇa, was the patron of Cave 16. A feudatory prince of Hariṣeṇa named Upendragupta donated a group of caves now numbered 17, 18, 19, and 20. A highly placed Buddhist monk, Buddhabhadra, with the support of a feudatory dynasty, the Aśmakas, sponsored the magnificent *chaitya*, Cave 26. Although no inscription identifies Hariṣeṇa as a donor, Walter Spink, the leading authority on Ajanta, associates Cave 1 with the patronage of this king. These inscriptions, combined with the scale and high artistic quality of the work, demonstrate that royal patronage was a key inspiration in the second phase at Ajanta.

In their plan and elevation, the caves resemble architecture. The *chaityas* are long, rectangular halls that terminate in a rounded apse, where the stupa (mound with relics) is located. The *vihāras* are more square, with a large central hall, small monastic cells to either side of the hall, and a recessed area for a Buddha shrine. Many of the caves have portico entrances. Columns subdivide

spaces in the large halls. All of these architectural features, including roof beams that resemble wooden structures, are carved out of the rock itself. The stonecutters worked from top to bottom and from front to back.

Sculpture and painting cover many of the surfaces within these cave halls. Some of this artistic embellishment is decorative. However, much of the art is devoted to Buddhist imagery. Statues of the Buddha are placed within shrines of the *vihāras* and in front of the stupas in the *chaityas*. Relief scupture depicts various Buddhist scenes. One famous example from Cave 26 is the *Parinirvana* (the Buddha's death and attainment of nirvana), which features a 23-foot-long (7-meter-long) reclining figure of Buddha, with a row of smaller mourning monks underneath.

Paintings cover the walls of many caves. These paintings were executed with water-based earth pigments and lapis lazuli for the blues on dry plaster. Most of the paintings are narrative scenes whose subjects often were drawn from the *jātakas*, parable stories about the Buddha's previous lives. The rich details of people from all walks of life engaged in many activities provide a glimpse of Indian life and culture at this period.

Although there is some disagreement about the amount of time it took to complete this impressive group of rock-cut caves, most scholars now accept Spink's chronology, in which the work was accomplished in a short burst of creative activity from the accession of Hariṣeṇa around 460 C.E. until shortly after the king's death in 477. By 500, Ajanta was abandoned. After it was discovered in 1819 by British soldiers on a hunting expedition, Ajanta has become the subject of scholarly study as well as a tourist attraction. The United Nations Educational, Scientific, and Cultural Organization (UNESCO) has designated Ajanta as a World Heritage Site.

SIGNIFICANCE
Because of the collapse of the Vākāṭaka Empire around 480 C.E. and the abrupt abandonment of Ajanta, these caves had modest immediate influence on Indian religion and culture. The craftspeople that worked at Ajanta migrated to other centers. Some stylistic influences from Ajanta appear at rock-cut cave complexes such as those at Aurangabad, Elephanta, and Ellora in neighboring regions.

From a historical perspective, Ajanta has major significance. After the Ajanta caves were abandoned, their remote location preserved them until their discovery in the nineteenth century. In stone and paint, the Ajanta caves bear witness to the importance and high cultural achievement of the Vākāṭaka Empire in central western India. The art not only provides a sense of daily life and the richness of the Vākāṭaka courts that has otherwise perished but also represents a pinnacle of aesthetic quality in ancient Indian art. Ajanta documents an important phase in Buddhism, particularly of Mahāyāna Buddhism, by showing how monks lived, the growing importance of donations to secure individual karma, and the evolution of statues of the Buddha along with the multiplication of narratives to explicate the faith and enhance personal devotion.

—*Karen K. Gould*

FURTHER READING

Behl, Benoy K. *The Ajanta Caves: Artistic Wonder of Ancient Buddhist India*. New York: Harry N. Abrams, 1998. Introduction to Ajanta accompanied by color photographs of the major painted caves. Bibliography and index.

Pant, Pushpesh. *Ajanta and Ellora: Cave Temples of Ancient India*. New Delhi: Lustre Press, 1998. Introduction to Ajanta with color photographs.

Parimoo, Ratan, et al., ed. *The Art of Ajanta: New Perspectives*. 2 vols. New Delhi: Books and Books, 1991. A collection of essays by leading scholars on all aspects of Ajanta's art.

Schlingloff, Dieter. *Narrative Wall Paintings*. Vol. 1 in *Guide to the Ajanta Paintings*. New Delhi: Munshiram Manoharlal Publishers, 1999. Diagrams and plans identifying the narrative subjects of the Ajanta paintings.

Spink, Walter. "The Achievement of Ajanta." In *The Age of the Vākāṭakas*, edited by Ajay Mitra Shastri. New Delhi: Harman Publishing House, 1991. Argues for the significance of Ajanta in its historical context.

_____. "The Archaeology of Ajanta." *Ars Orientalis* 21 (1991): 67-94. Explains the chronological sequence of work at Ajanta.

SEE ALSO: 6th or 5th century B.C.E., Birth of Buddhism; c. 5th-4th century B.C.E., Creation of the *Jātakas*; 2d century B.C.E., Silk Road Opens; c. 380-c. 415 C.E., Gupta Dynasty Reaches Its Peak Under Chandragupta II.

RELATED ARTICLE in *Great Lives from History: The Ancient World*: Buddha.

c. 470 C.E.
BODHIDHARMA BRINGS CHAN BUDDHISM TO CHINA

Bodhidharma brought the Chan form of Buddhism to China, where it eventually became the dominant religion.

LOCALE: China
CATEGORIES: Religion; cultural and intellectual history

KEY FIGURE
Bodhidharma (fifth-sixth century C.E.), considered traditional founder of the Chan school

SUMMARY OF EVENT
Bodhidharma is said to be the founder of the Chan school of Buddhism, which was a blend of the dominant Mahāyāna school with the Daoist tradition of China. Bodhidharma's Chan school helped to bring Buddhism to its pinnacle in China, as the dominant state religion, and continues to influence the beliefs of the Buddhist religion to this day.

The Buddhist religion began in India, with the enlightenment of Prince Siddhārtha Gautama, the histori-

cal Buddha, in the fifth century B.C.E. The followers of the Buddha quickly spread the religion throughout India and gained significant strength with the ascension of the Mauryan emperor Aśoka (r. c. 273/265-c. 238 B.C.E.), a patron of Buddhism.

Contact between India and China was helped during the historical Buddha's life through the end of the third century C.E. by a combination of the Pax Romana in the West and the Pax Sinica in the East. The Roman Empire in the Mediterranean and the Han Dynasty in China had developed road and caravan systems that traveled between the two large empires; these trade and travel routes have become known as the Silk Road. Traffic on the silk routes was brisk and prolific and carried much more than silks to Rome or wine to Changan (modern-day Xi'an). Missionaries, pilgrims, merchants, itinerant artisans, and others traveled the silk routes in search of fortune or to spread the word of their faith. Travelers went two ways: The Indian Buddhists went into China, and Chinese interested in Buddhism, such as Faxian (Fa-hsien) and

Xuanzang (Hsüan-tsang), went to India in search of better scriptures and to further their religious understanding.

Among the first references to Buddhism in China is the dream of Mingdi (Ming-ti; 29-c. 75 C.E.), the Eastern Han Dynasty emperor. The emperor claimed that he had a vision in which he saw "a golden god who could fly" in his palace. Despite this early vision, Mingdi was a strict Confucian, and Buddhism's early impact on China was quite limited, owing to the religion's conflicts with Confucianism.

Confucianism's main argument with Buddhism was its view that worldly involvements, including service to the state, marriage, and procreation, were of little significance and were not the path to enlightenment. Because Confucian dogma held that to be virtuous, one had to serve the emperor, be faithful to one's parents, and procreate, Buddhism was in diametric opposition to the beliefs of the Chinese creed.

It was not until the establishment of the Mahāyāna (Greater Vehicle) school of Buddhism, which emphasized the ability of an individual to become enlightened and be reborn into a paradise filled with beings similarly freed from the world that Buddhism was able to begin to succeed in China. The Mahāyāna school became established in China in about 148 C.E., when Parthian Buddhist scholar An Shigao arrived in the capital of Luoyang (Lo-yang) with a Buddhist canon that could be translated into Chinese.

The Buddhist canon, known as the *Tipiṭaka* (collected c. 250 B.C.E.; English translation in *Buddhist Scriptures*, 1913), literally, the "three baskets" of wisdom, had an immediate impact on the Daoists. Although an ethnic Chinese religion, Daoism had heretofore not had an organized literature of its own. As the Celestial Masters (Tianshi) movement of Daoism began, a vital task for the early Daoists was to codify their own religious views to better articulate to the Buddhist community the precepts of Daoism. Because in Chinese the Buddhist canon was translated as the *sanzang* (three baskets), the Daoists called their canon the Daozang.

As the two traditions began to compare their methods and beliefs, the Buddhist canon began to undergo changes; texts were sinicized and made more palatable to the Daoist intellectuals. This was the situation that existed c. 401 C.E. when the next great translator of Buddhist texts, Kumārajīva, arrived on the silk routes. Kumārajīva's translation of the *Lotus Sutra* (1st century B.C.E.-1st century C.E.) marked an important milestone on the path of the creation of Chan. The *Lotus Sutra* is one of the most important texts of the Mahāyāna school, and the symbolism of the *Lotus Sutra* was a perfect meld of both Daoist and Buddhist tradition and was greatly studied by both faiths.

The *Lotus Sutra* is a complex parable about the Buddha delivering a sermon on Vulture peak, surrounded by his disciples, while twirling a lotus blossom between his fingers. Other followers of the Buddha questioned his teaching, but it was Mahākāshyapa who recognized that the real teaching of this particular episode was the silent twirling of the flower in the Buddha's hand. During the sutra, Mahākāshyapa stayed silent and smiled, and the Buddha recognized that he alone had learned the lesson. The story in the *Lotus Sutra* would prove to be pivotal in the formation of Chan Buddhism.

When Bodhidharma arrived in China around 470 C.E., it was an auspicious time to complete the marriage of Daoism and Buddhism to form a completely new school of thought. Bodhidharma's lineage was impeccable: He was recognized as the twenty-eighth patriarch of the Mahāyāna school of Buddhism. The patriarchy counted Mahākāshyapa, the "constant companion" of the Buddha on earth, as its first patriarch.

The traditional story of Bodhidharma's enlightenment places him at a monastery in China. Reportedly, Bodhidharma entered the Shaolin monastery, sat, and did nothing but meditate before a wall, not moving for nine years. After the end of the nine years, he was enlightened. Sculptures of Bodhidharma often show him with legs withered by the years that he spent in sitting in meditation.

The method of Bodhidharma's enlightenment marked a major change from the traditional Buddhist path to nirvana, a state of escape from the world. Previously, Buddhism had emphasized the Eightfold Path, which stated that enlightenment came from a process in which one followed the eight correct views: right beliefs, right resolve, right speech, right actions, right livelihood, right effort, right mind, and right meditation. In addition, Buddhist adepts were to follow the Five Precepts of not killing, not stealing, not lying, not consuming alcohol, and chastity. This meant that those who followed certain occupations, such as fisherman and stock herders, could never become enlightened because of their professions, which obligated them to kill living things. Emperors, who were obligated to procreate to produce a successor, also were unlikely to achieve nirvana.

The Chan enlightenment of Bodhidharma was a sudden, abrupt change from this tradition. It implied that sudden enlightenment could happen to anyone, regardless of whether they followed the Five Precepts and Eightfold Path. Removing these obstacles for the elite class greatly improved the potential for Bodhidharma to find followers for his faith in China. Another factor that appealed to the intellectual elite was that the Chan school emphasized study with a master—if at all possible, with the patriarch himself. In playing on Mahākāshyapa's pivotal role in the *Lotus Sutra*, the Chan school emphasized that the patriarch had esoteric knowledge, passed down through the line of patriarchs from the Buddha himself, which could guide the novitiate into enlightenment. These esoteric teachings were not written down but were transmitted orally or in secret from master to disciple.

The concept of studying with a master was an extremely old Chinese value, beginning with the Confucian bureaucracy. The Chan school was able to tap into this concept by emphasizing the private learning that a student did with his master and the fact that the master taught the student things that could not be learned merely by reading the literature. This opened the way for the bureaucrats, long the intellectual elite of China, to be able to study with a Chan master in a manner that would give great kudos to the student. Teachers often taught their students through *gong-an* (known as *kōan* in Japanese), cryptic questions that encouraged students to break the bounds of logic and dogma to obtain the "flash" of wisdom that led to enlightenment.

The rise of the Chan school is strongly associated with the Tang Dynasty (T'ang; 618-907 C.E.), which is regarded as the greatest epoch in Chinese history economically, militarily, and culturally. The literature created

A Japanese politician celebrates an election victory with a Daruma doll. The legless doll represents Bodhidharma, who supposedly meditated for so long that he lost his legs. The doll's ability to take a hit without falling down makes it a symbol of perseverance and ultimate victory. (AP/Wide World Photo)

during the dynasty and the government reforms that were instituted became the benchmarks for all successive Chinese governments. During the Tang Dynasty, Buddhism became the dominant religion in China, helped by the patronage of the religion under the emperor Taizong (T'aitsung; r. 627-650 C.E.). Taizong's investiture of monasteries and monks and the recognition he gave to the religion allowed Buddhism to usurp both Confucianism and Daoism as the dominant religion in practice. During the Tang Dynasty, Buddhism achieved its aim of obtaining imperial investiture on a scale it had never previously attained, whether in India or Central Asia, and Chan Buddhism became the preferred school of Buddhism in China.

SIGNIFICANCE

Although credited as the founder of the Chan school, Bodhidharma did not really create the school as such. Bodhidharma's two great contributions to the Chan school were the concept of sudden enlightenment through everyday tasks and the establishment of his successor and a patriarchy of his own. The melding of Buddhist and Daoist philosophy, combined with the concept of learning from a master, made the religion extremely attractive to the Chinese.

Although later dynasties directly proscribed Buddhism, the Chan school survived and thrived, in particular when monks brought the religion to Japan, where it became known as Zen and today is still the dominant religion in that country. In the West, Zen teachings became popular during the 1960's, when *kōan* were translated and popularized. Buddhism remains the dominant religion throughout East Asia, and after the Open Door policy was instituted in China in 1900, it staged a remarkable comeback in that country.

—*Jason D. Sanchez*

FURTHER READING

Faure, Bernard. *Chan Insights and Oversights*. Princeton, N.J.: Princeton University Press, 1996. One of the best overall approaches to the formation of the Chan school.

Lopez, Donald S., Jr., ed. *Religions of China in Practice*. Princeton, N.J.: Princeton University Press, 1996. An excellent survey on the many religions of China, with a special emphasis on Buddhism.

Verellen, Franciscus. *Buddhism in Chinese Society*. New York: Columbia University Press, 1995. A fascinating study of the wealth created by the amassing of largess from donors in Buddhist monasteries.

Yampolsky, Philip. *The Platform Sutra of the Sixth Patriarch*. New York: Columbia University Press, 1978. The sixth patriarch, Huineng, is revered as one of the most important Chan teachers. Includes critical background detail on the formation of the Chan school.

Zürcher, Erik. *The Buddhist Conquest of China*. 2 vols. 1959. Reprint. Leiden, the Netherlands: E. J. Brill, 1972. Zürcher's work is quite possibly the single most definitive study of the history of Chinese Buddhism.

SEE ALSO: 6th or 5th century B.C.E., Birth of Buddhism; 479 B.C.E., Confucius's Death Leads to the Creation of *The Analects*; 285-160 B.C.E. (traditionally, c. 300 B.C.E.), Composition of the *Zhuangzi*; c. 273/265-c. 238 B.C.E., Aśoka Reigns over India; c. 250 B.C.E., *Tipiṭaka* Is Compiled; 2d century B.C.E., Silk Road Opens; 1st century B.C.E.-1st century C.E., Compilation of the *Lotus Sutra*; c. 60-68 C.E., Buddhism Enters China; 399 C.E., Chinese Monk Faxian Travels to India; 460-477 C.E., Buddhist Temples Built at Ajanta Caves in India.

RELATED ARTICLES in *Great Lives from History: The Ancient World*: Aśoka; Bodhidharma; Buddha; Confucius; Faxian; Laozi; Zhuangzi.

September 4, 476 C.E.
FALL OF ROME

The Fall of Rome occurred as the result of internal strife and external attacks and resulted in a transfer of imperial power to Constantinople.

LOCALE: Ravenna (now in Italy)
CATEGORY: Wars, uprisings, and civil unrest

KEY FIGURES

Julius Nepos (d. 480 C.E.), Roman emperor in the west, r. 474-480 C.E.
Zeno (d. 491 C.E.), Roman emperor in the east, r. 474-491 C.E.
Odoacer (c. 435-493 C.E.), Scirian warlord, first barbarian ruler of Italy, r. 476-493 C.E.
Romulus Augustulus (fl. fifth century C.E.), son of Orestes, usurper of the position of Roman emperor in the west, r. 475-476 C.E.

SUMMARY OF EVENT

The decline and eventual fall of the powerful Roman Empire can be traced back to severe problems beginning with the reign of Marcus Aurelius, a brutal persecutor of the Christians. His violent reign (r. 161-180 C.E.) experienced increased interior rebellions in addition to attacks on the empire's borders. The subsequent reign of his brutal and incompetent son Commodus from 180 to 192 (when he was strangled) is regarded by many historians as the beginning of Rome's long decline.

The third century C.E. saw increased tension between the opulent city-dwellers and the barely civilized peasants. Caracalla reigned from 211 to 217 and granted Roman citizenship to all freemen living in the Roman Empire, with the intent of imposing additional taxes on them. Severus Alexander ruled with "wisdom and justice" from 222 to 235, with his death beginning a period of great confusion throughout all Italy. Of his twelve successors who ruled in the next thirty-three years, all but one died a violent death, usually at the hands of the soldiers who had established them. The internal strife that began under Aurelius continued, and the increased taxation necessary to finance the military resulted in economy-crippling inflation. The defenses of the empire on the Rhine and Danube collapsed under the attack of Germanic and other tribes, and the eastern provinces were invaded by the Persians.

A very temporary restoration of peace and prosperity was achieved by the Illyrian emperors Claudius II Goth-icus (r. 268-270), who drove back the Goths, and by Aurelian (r. 270-275), who was victorious over the Goths, Germans, and Zenobia, queen of Palmyra, who had occupied Egypt and Asia Minor. This brief restoration lasted until the accession of Diocletian, who ruled from 284 to 305. Diocletian introduced many social, economic, and political reforms, including removal of many political and economic privileges that Rome and Italy had enjoyed at the expense of the provinces. He sought to regulate rampant inflation by controlling prices on many necessary goods and on the maximum wages of workers.

Diocletian controlled Thrace, Egypt, and Asia. He assigned control of Italy and Africa to Maximian, control of Gaul, Spain, and Britain to Constantius, and control of Danubian provinces to Galerius. This system created a strong administration but greatly increased the size of the already monstrous governmental bureaucracy, thus creating a tremendous financial burden on the empire's resources.

The abdication in 305 of Diocletian and Maximian, who both had taken the title of augustus, resulted in the outbreak of several civil wars that did not end until the accession of Constantine the Great in 312. Constantine the Great, who had previously become caesar of the army in Britain, overcame all rivals and reunited the Western Roman Empire under his rule. The defeat of Eastern emperor Licinius in 324 made Constantine the sole ruler of the Roman world.

Christianity had recovered from Diocletian's attempts to destroy it by persecution, and the politically minded Constantine adopted Christianity, claiming a personal conversion and proclaiming it the official religion of the Roman Empire. The other event of far-reaching significance during Constantine's reign was his establishment of a new governmental seat in Byzantium, which eventually was named in his honor as Constantinople (later called Istanbul). Constantine reigned from 306 to 337 C.E. and is often regarded as the second founder of the empire. He successfully fought off numerous opponents; reorganized local government into prefectures, dioceses, and provinces; legalized Christianity after his self-proclaimed conversion; and enlisted the church in service to the state. The death of Constantine in 337 began more civil wars between the rival caesars, which continued until Constantine's only surviving son, Constantius II, was successful in briefly uniting the empire. Constantius II was followed by Julian, who ruled from 361 to 363 and was known as the Apostate because of his renunciation of Christianity. The reforms begun under Constantine, however, proved to be far from successful enough to halt the fall of the empire.

On the death of Theodosius the Great in 395 C.E., the empire was permanently divided into the Latin Western and the Greek Eastern Byzantine empires. The Eastern Roman Empire, with its capital at Constantinople, lived on until 1435, when it was conquered by the Turks. The Western Roman Empire was overrun and gradually dismembered by Germanic tribes with various Roman leaders initially conciliating a victorious invader with mili-

tary commands and administrative offices. The conquest of Africa by the Vandals under Genseric and the seizure of Gaul and Italy by the Huns soon followed. Led by their famous leader Attila, the Huns ruled central and northern Europe and confronted the emperors of east and west alike as an independent power. The city of Rome was plundered by the Visigoths in 410 and by the Vandals in 455, after which Julius Nepos and Leo I briefly held the Western and Eastern thrones, respectively. The death of Leo I passed the Eastern throne to his seven-year-old grandson, Leo II, whose father, Zeno, became the Eastern emperor when Leo II died in 474. Nepos's insecure

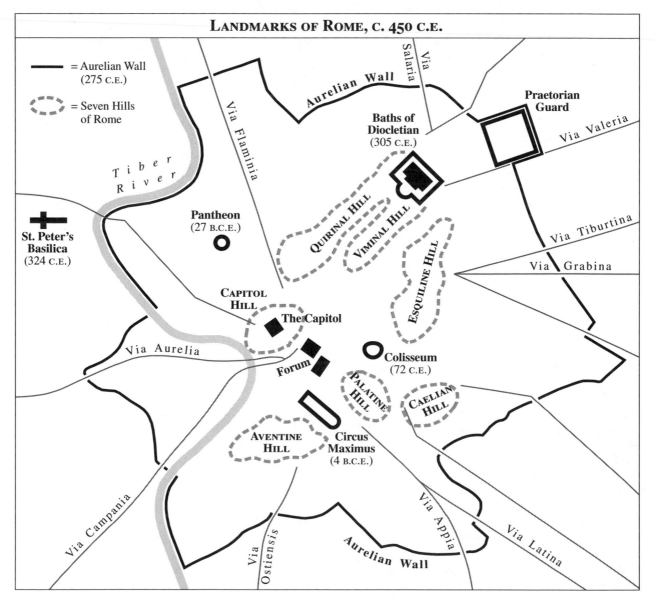

LANDMARKS OF ROME, C. 450 C.E.

= Aurelian Wall (275 C.E.)

= Seven Hills of Rome

The last Roman emperor, Romulus Augustulus, surrenders his crown. (F. R. Niglutsch)

rule in Rome was highlighted by his appointment of Orestes, a former lieutenant of Attila the Hun.

It quickly became evident that Orestes desired the imperial throne for his son Romulus, and when Nepos fled Rome, Orestes crowned his young son in late 475 C.E. The crowning of Romulus was without any legal authority, but historians from the sixth century on have accepted that the boy was the last emperor of the Western Roman Empire. Orestes was soon at odds with his Germanic army and was slain in 476. A leader of this rebellious army was the mercenary Herulian leader Odoacer (sometimes called Odovacer), who is credited with overthrowing the child Romulus Augustulus on September 4, 476, thus finalizing the fall of ancient Rome.

SIGNIFICANCE

Historians have been analyzing the world-changing decline and fall of ancient Rome ever since the founding of the science of history in the eighteenth and nineteenth centuries. Their work probably will never result in a single definitive answer to the complex question of what caused the decline of the mighty Roman Empire. Any answer to this question must take into account the fact that the Eastern Roman Empire in Constantinople did not decline simultaneously with the Western Roman Empire but endured almost another thousand years.

Some scholars have stressed that the well-documented sharp decline in population in the Western regions severely limited agricultural and industrial growth as well as defense against invasion. Economic explanations were initially accepted as adequate, but nearly all have since been refuted or seriously weakened. Some scholars have looked for evidence that the soil of the western provinces

was of poorer quality than that of the eastern provinces, and others have tried to show that patterns of rising and ebbing rainfall made the region fluctuate in prosperity. Furthermore, most barbarians invaded Europe from the west along the flatter regions as compared with the mountain ranges of southeastern Europe.

Geographically speaking, it is obvious why invaders appeared in Germany along the Danube River and in Italy itself, while Byzantium lay protected by the Balkan Mountain ranges. One scholar points to data that suggest that a contributing factor to Rome's fall was widespread lead poisoning among the Roman upper class. The richer citizens consumed a Greek diet, with their food cooked in lead containers or lead-glazed pottery and drinking water that flowed through lead pipes. As they ingested diluted lead, they may have sterilized themselves and thus prevented the survival of the more talented men and women.

Regardless of how historical theories are evaluated, what is well documented in history are the numerous ideas of Rome that survived its decline and fall. Many scholars contend that the mighty Roman Empire did not fall but was merely transformed as a result of the merging of the papacy, Holy Roman Empire, Papal States, Italy, and various German elements into the nation-states of medieval Europe.

—Daniel G. Graetzer

FURTHER READING

Gibbon, Edward. *The Decline and Fall of the Roman Empire*. 2d ed. 2 vols. Chicago: Encyclopaedia Brittanica, 1990. Acclaimed as a masterpiece by other historians and literary critics, Gibbon's work was first published in seven volumes.

Grant, Michael. *The Collapse and Recovery of the Roman Empire*. New York: Routledge, 1999. An analysis of the Roman Empire that examines the period of military anarchy between 235 and 284 C.E., the empire's recovery, and the growth of the Byzantine Empire.

_____. *The Fall of the Roman Empire*. Rev. ed. London: Weidenfeld and Nicolson, 1990. Grant's earlier work on the Fall of Rome.

Kagan, Donald, ed. *The End of the Roman Empire: Decline or Transformation?* 3d ed. Lexington, Mass.: Heath, 1992. A revision of *Decline and Fall of the Roman Empire* (1962). Discusses whether the Fall of Rome marked the end of the Roman Empire or a transformation into a new country.

Liebeschuetz, J. H. W. G. *Decline and Fall of the Roman City*. New York: Oxford University Press, 2001. An examination of the history of the Roman Empire during its decline. Bibliography and index.

Moorhead, John. *The Roman Empire Divided, 400-700*. New York: Longman, 2001. This history of the Roman Empire focuses on the division into eastern and western empires and the role of the Germanic invasions. Bibliography and index.

Williams, Stephen, and Gerard Friell. *The Rome That Did Not Fall: The Survival of the East in the Fifth Century*. New York: Routledge, 1999. An examination of the division of the Roman Empire into eastern and western empires. Argues that the western empire fell, while the eastern empire continued. Bibliography and index.

SEE ALSO: August 24-26, 410 C.E., Gothic Armies Sack Rome; 439 C.E., Vandals Seize Carthage; 445-453 C.E., Invasions of Attila the Hun; July, 451 C.E., Battle of Châlons.

RELATED ARTICLES in *Great Lives from History: The Ancient World*: Attila; Constantine the Great; Diocletian; Marcus Aurelius.

TIME LINE

The time line below includes the events and developments covered in the essays in this publication as well as more than 275 other important events and developments. The abbreviation B.P. is used for "before the present." Events are organized by type of development.

LIST OF TIME LINE CATEGORIES

AGRICULTURE, MIGRATION, AND THE CREATION OF COMMUNITIES

c. 4 million B.P.	*Australopithecus*, a genus of semi-upright apes, is spreading throughout southern Africa.
c. 1 million B.P.	*Homo erectus*, the first *hominid* with a notably large brain, begins to migrate into Asia.
c. 100,000 B.P.	Anatomically modern humans (*Homo sapiens*) are migrating throughout Africa and into Asia.
c. 40,000 B.P.	A branch of anatomically modern humans, often labeled Cro-Magnon, are living in western Europe. Neanderthals are becoming relatively rare.
c. 35,000 B.P.	People have already moved into Australia, probably from Southeast Asia.
c. 18,000-11,000 B.C.E.	Early ancestors of American Indians are thought to be entering Alaska by way of an Ice Age land bridge in the Bering Sea.
c. 16,000-c. 3000 B.C.E.	BaTwa people, a hunter-gather group, form one of the earliest African communities in the forests of Central Africa.
c. 13,000 B.C.E.	People first arrive on the South American continent.
c. 13,000-c. 7000 B.C.E.	The Paleo-Indians display highly varied technology and lifestyles in North America.
c. 10,000 B.C.E.	People begin to domesticate wolves in Mesopotamia.
c. 9500-c. 5000 B.C.E.	The settlement at Abu Hureyra in northern Syria demonstrates a shift from hunting and gathering to a lifestyle based on farming and animal husbandry.
c. 9000-c. 8000 B.C.E.	The Cochise in the American Southwest begin cultivating corn and creating pottery.
c. 8000 B.C.E.	People establish permanent settlements on the high grasslands of the Andes in South America.
c. 8000-c. 1000 B.C.E.	As the climate warms, North American Archaic Indians evolve into organized groups that cultivate plants, create artwork, and form trade networks.
c. 7700-c. 1000 B.C.E.	The northern Pacific coast provides a fertile ground for the mixing of peoples from a number of different areas, including Siberia, China, and Oceania
c. 7500 B.C.E.	People in southeastern Asia begin to cultivate rice and millet.
c. 7200 B.C.E.	Kennewick Man lives in North America; his relation to present-day Native Americans remains unknown.

c. 7000-c. 4900 B.C.E.	The level of development in the Neolithic city of Çatalhüyük in Anatolia indicates that the birth of civilization was not limited to the Fertile Crescent.
c. 7000 B.C.E.	People in central Persia begin to domesticate goats, making herding possible.
c. 7000 B.C.E.	People in the Middle East region are developing Neolithic cultures, which include agriculture, pottery, and small sedentary villages.
c. 7000-c. 6000 B.C.E.	Khoisan peoples spread from the Kalahari desert throughout Southern Africa, becoming the dominant group.
c. 6500-c. 5000 B.C.E.	Nilo-Saharan peoples spread cultivation and herding across the Sahara and the Sudan Belt into the Eastern Sahara and across the upper Nile plains.
c. 6000 B.C.E.	People of Peru begin to cultivate potatoes and beans.
c. 6000 B.C.E.	People in Thailand begin to domesticate pigs.
c. 6000-c. 1500 B.C.E.	The Yangshao and Longshan are the earliest known farming cultures in China.
c. 6000-c. 1000 B.C.E.	Omotic peoples in the Horn of Africa create an elaborate agricultural system that uses irrigation, plowing, fertilizing, and stone-terraced mountainsides.
c. 5500 B.C.E.	The fair-skinned Ainu settle in Japan.
c. 5500-c. 4500 B.C.E.	The Niger-Congo spread the practice of agriculture into the tropical rainforest along the western and southern Sahara.
c. 5000 B.C.E.	Hunter-gatherers from Siberia cross the Bering Strait land bridge into Alaska, eventually establishing the Aleutian coastal culture.
c. 5000-c. 3000 B.C.E.	The Kelteminar establish the first extended settled civilization in the western part of Central Asia.
c. 4500 B.C.E.	People in the region of Turkey domesticate cattle, probably from wild oxen.
c. 4000 B.C.E.	The Sahara of Africa is turning into a desert.
c. 3800 B.C.E.	Wild horses are domesticated in west-central Asia.
c. 3800 B.C.E.	The city of Uruk develops civil institutions and becomes a model for other large cities in Sumer.
c. 3000 B.C.E.	The Canaanites in the Levant engage in large-scale trade with Egypt and Mesopotamia.
c. 3,000 B.C.E.	Peoples in Mesopotamia and Egypt invent irrigation, which allows for the growth of vibrant villages when rainfall is uncertain.
c. 3,000 B.C.E.	Africans begin to plant crops and domesticate animals.
c. 3,000 B.C.E.	Most large mammals of America become extinct, forcing aboriginal peoples to diversify their food sources.
c. 3000 B.C.E.	Polynesians are migrating to the Samoan Islands, probably coming from Fiji.
c. 2700-c. 1400 B.C.E.	The Gash civilization, located at a delta and near several important cultures in Africa, becomes a center for trade.
c. 2500 B.C.E.	The camel is domesticated in Arabia.
c. 2500-c. 1500 B.C.E.	Skilled navigators from Southeast Asia settle the islands of the South Pacific.
c. 2300-c. 2000 B.C.E.	Berber peoples undertake first great expansion across North Africa.
c. 2100-c. 600 B.C.E.	The Mogollon culture, identified by its pit houses and brown and dark red pottery, arises in the American Southwest.
c. 2000 B.C.E.	Cities and sea trade appear in northern Africa.
c. 2000 B.C.E.	Mon-Khmer migrate into Southeast Asia.
c. 1900-c. 1400 B.C.E.	Villages form in Oaxaca, allowing for the development of agriculture and political organization.
1750-800 B.C.E.	The Andronovo culture, a pastoral people, represent the movement of Indo-Europeans eastward across Siberia to Xinjiang and Mongolia.
c. 1500 B.C.E.-c. 500 C.E.	Lapita culture colonizes the South Pacific.
c. 1200 B.C.E.	Hebrew people are invading Palestine.

c. 1200 B.C.E.	The Egyptians dig the first canal from the Nile River to the Red Sea.
c. 1200-c. 1000 B.C.E.	Berbers expand across North Africa; some become Egyptianized.
c. 1100 B.C.E.	Arameans settle in Syria-Palestine and Mesopotamia in the wake of a political vacuum in the area.
c. 1000 B.C.E.	The Maori people are beginning to migrate to New Zealand.
c. 1000 B.C.E.-c. 300 C.E.	Urban commerce develops in the Sudan Belt.
c. 1000 B.C.E.-c. 900 C.E.	The Woodland Indians in Northern America establish a long-lasting hunting and gathering lifestyle.
c. 734-c. 580 B.C.E.	Greeks and Phoenicians begin to establish settlements and trading posts throughout the Mediterranean region.
c. 733 B.C.E.	The Greeks found Syracuse.
c. 700 B.C.E.	Clans and tribes from the Asian mainland migrate to Japan and force the Ainu to move north.
c. 700-c. 500 B.C.E.	Dorset culture extends into Labrador, Newfoundland, and Greenland.
c. 600 B.C.E.	The agriculturist Bantu-speaking peoples of western Africa are beginning to migrate southward.
c. 500 B.C.E.-c. 200 C.E.	Libyan Garamantes flourish as farmers and traders.
c. 500 B.C.E.-c. 300 C.E.	Socially stratified kingdoms arise around the Middle Niger River.
450-100 B.C.E.	City-state of Yeha flourishes in the northern Ethiopian highlands.
c. 420 B.C.E.-c. 100 C.E.	Yuezhi culture links Persia and China.
c. 400 B.C.E.-c. 300 C.E.	Bantu peoples spread farming across southern Africa.
312 B.C.E.	Roman censor Appius Claudius Caecus begins construction of the Appian Way, a paved road uniting Rome and Capua.
3d century B.C.E.	Commercial city of Jenne is founded on the Niger River.
c. 300 B.C.E.	Izapan civilization dominates Mesoamerica.
c. 300 B.C.E.	Hohokam culture arises in American Southwest.
c. 300 B.C.E.-c. 100 C.E.	Khoikhoi and Kwadi adopt pastoral lifestyle in Africa.
2d century B.C.E.	The Silk Road from China to Europe is opened during the reign of Wudi of China's Han Dynasty.
c. 100 B.C.E.-c. 300 C.E.	East African trading port of Rhapta flourishes.
c. 3d-4th century C.E.	The Huns move westward into Europe and attack Germanic peoples.
290-300 C.E.	West African gold first reaches North Africa.
370's C.E.	Large numbers of Visigoths move into the Balkans.
c. 400 C.E.	Small numbers of Bantu-speaking peoples are moving into the region of present-day Malawi.
c. 400 C.E.	As Roman power decreases, Germanic tribes—Angles, Saxons, Frisians, and others—invade Britain, forcing indigenous Celtic peoples to move into western and northern regions.

ARTS AND ARCHITECTURE

c. 30,000 B.P.	Old Stone Age artists make the earliest known wall paintings in a cave near Avignon, France.
c. 28,000 B.P.	Old Stone Age craftsmen in Europe make the first known sculptures from bone, stone, and antlers.
c. 25,000 B.C.E.	San peoples create earliest rock paintings known in Africa.
c. 15,500 B.C.E.	Early Australians create petroglyphs known as the Bradshaw paintings.
c. 15,000 B.C.E.	Artists of the Paleolithic Age paint animal representations on the cave walls at Lascaux, France.
c. 10,000-c. 300 B.C.E.	Jōmon culture of Japan produces distinctive pottery with cord markings.

c. 10,000 B.C.E.-c. 1 C.E.	Saharans create petroglyphs and pictographs that reflect their changing climate and culture.
c. 9000-c. 7000 B.C.E.	Nilo-Saharans produce Wavy Line pottery, the first pottery made in Africa.
c. 6000 B.C.E.	Peoples of Asia Minor (Turkey) make fertility goddesses of baked clay.
c. 5500-c. 4500 B.C.E.	The Halafian culture in Mesopotamia produces highly sophisticated ceramics fired at high temperatures to create a porcelain-like finish.
c. 4000 B.C.E.	Mesopotamians fire building bricks in kilns.
c. 4000 B.C.E.-c. 100 C.E.	The Ban Chiang in Thailand create elaborate bronze and iron jewelry as well as elegant pottery.
c. 3300 B.C.E.	Peoples of Sumer (southern Iraq) invent the pottery wheel. The Chinese perhaps make the invention at about the same time.
c. 3100-c. 1550 B.C.E.	Stonehenge is constructed in southwestern England.
c. 3050 B.C.E.	The Egyptians of the Predynastic Period begin to use bronze tools for carving stone.
c. 3050 B.C.E.	The Egyptians begin to paint human representations in their wall paintings in tombs.
c. 3000 B.C.E.	Aboriginal peoples in Australia paint mythical cultural heroes called Wandjina on cave walls.
c. 3000-c. 500 B.C.E.	The Elamites in Mesopotamia create the sanctuary of Dur Untash, a complex containing a ziggurat and a number of temples dedicated to the gods.
c. 2686 B.C.E.	The Egyptians construct the tomb of king Khasekhemui, the earliest stone building that can be accurately dated.
c. 2650 B.C.E.	The Egyptians invent the chair, the earliest known piece of furniture.
c. 2575-c. 2566 B.C.E.	Egyptian king Khufu of the Old Kingdom constructs the Great Pyramid at El Giza, the largest pyramid ever built.
c. 2550 B.C.E.	Egyptian pharaoh Khafre builds the temple of the Great Sphinx.
c. 2500 B.C.E.	Egyptian artists construct the Great Sphinx of Giza, which will be repaired many times.
c. 2500 B.C.E.	Pyramids, residences, altars, tombs, and an amphitheater, part of a large ceremonial complex, are constructed at Caral, Peru.
c. 2300 B.C.E.	The Egyptians make a stature of King Pepi I using the lost-wax method, the earliest known example of the method.
c. 2300 B.C.E.	Mesopotamians begin to make maps of cities and regions.
c. 2100 B.C.E.	At Ur, the Sumerians build a large ziggurat, a temple erected on a pyramidal brick platform.
c. 2000 B.C.E.	Minoan artists on the island of Crete are decorating walls on buildings with lively representations of animals and humans.
c. 1800-c. 1500 B.C.E.	El Paraíso, a large residential site with multiple complexes, is constructed in Peru.
c. 1800-c. 700 B.C.E.	Poverty Point culture builds earthworks in Northern America.
c. 1600 B.C.E.	Chinese artists of the Shang dynasty produce bronze containers and make three types of pottery.
c. 1550 B.C.E.	The Mycenaeans begin to bury their dead with metal artifacts in shaft graves on the Greek mainland. About the same time, Mycenaean artists carve the Lion Gate of Mycenae.
c. 1504 B.C.E.	Thutmose III becomes Egyptian pharaoh and initiates an art style of great decoration, monumentality, and fluidity of movement.
c. 1500-c. 300 B.C.E.	The Olmecs of Mexico and Central America build mammoth stone carvings in the shape of human heads.

c. 1370 B.C.E.	Egyptian pharaoh Akhenton builds a monumental temple to the sun-disk god Aton at Tell el-ʿAmârna.
c. 1352 B.C.E.	Egyptian pharaoh Tutankhamen dies and is buried with superb works of art, which are discovered by Howard Carter in 1922.
c. 1250-c. 700 B.C.E.	The Eurasian Karasuk, a group of aggressive horsemen, produces skillfully wrought bronze bracelets, rings, knives, daggers, and horse bridles.
c. 1213 B.C.E.	Death of Egyptian king Ramses II, builder of Abu Simbel and the Temple of Al Karnak.
c. 1000-c. 500 B.C.E.	Nok artists in Africa develop terra-cotta sculpture.
c. 1000 B.C.E.-c. 100 C.E.	The Adena, a prehistoric North American society, creates large earthen mounds, including one shaped like a sepent.
700 B.C.E.-100 C.E.	Paracas culture develops a sophisticated textile tradition and complex mortuary rites.
c. 700 B.C.E.-c. 500 C.E.	The earliest architects in North America build elaborate burial mounds in the Ohio Valley.
c. 550 B.C.E.	Greek sculptors and painters of the classical period are displaying more realism and life than found in the archaic period. Notable artists include Kritios, Nesiotes, and Polygnotus.
c. 550 B.C.E.	The Etruscans of northern Italy are burying their dead in elaborate sarcophagi decorated with relief sculpture.
c. 500 B.C.E.-c. 700 C.E.	Zapotecs build Monte Albán, the first and largest urban center in the Oaxaca Valley of Mexico.
447 B.C.E.	Pericles begins construction of the Parthenon in Athens.
430 B.C.E.	The death of Greek sculptor Myron, whose works include the *Discus Thrower* and *Athena and Marsyas*.
c. 400 B.C.E.-c. 300 C.E.	Dong Son in Vietnam create bronze drums, apparently used in rituals.
c. 323 B.C.E.	Following the death of Alexander the Great, Hellenistic artists excel in portraying deeply emotional scenes.
300 B.C.E.	King Ptolemy Soter establishes a museum in Alexandria, Egypt.
c. 221 B.C.E.	Shi Huangdi, Qin Dynasty emperor, begins construction of the Great Wall.
c. 212-202? B.C.E.	The Qin tomb is constructed; at his death, Shi Huangdi is buried with 6,000 life-size terra-cotta figures.
200 B.C.E.-200 C.E.	Nasca lines drawn in desert near coast of Peru.
c. 200 B.C.E.-c. 500 C.E.	Hopewell people construct earthworks.
170's B.C.E.	Eumenes II, king of Pergamum in western Asia Minor, initiates a grand building program featuring an altar to Zeus with a sculpture of the god as its centerpiece.
c. 150 B.C.E.	Indian artists begin to paint frescos depicting Buddhist themes near the village of Ajanta.
27 B.C.E.	Roman engineer and general Marcus Vipsanius Agrippa builds the Pantheon, a large domed building.
19 B.C.E.	The gigantic Roman aqueduct across the Gard River (called the Pont du Gard) is completed near Nimes, France.
79 C.E.	An eruption of Italy's Mount Vesuvius buries Pompeii and Herculaneum, a tragedy that will preserve much of the art and architecture of the period.
80 C.E.	The monumental Colosseum at Rome is dedicated by the emperor Titus.
98-117 C.E.	Roman emperor Trajan builds an aqueduct, a theater, and an immense forum in Rome.
c. 100 C.E.	Pyramids of the Sun and Moon are built at Teotihuacán (near Mexico City).

c. 100-c. 700 C.E.	Moche build the Huaca del Sol and Huaca de la Luna in Peru.
c. 118-128 C.E.	Roman emperor Hadrian rebuilds the Pantheon in Rome.
122 C.E.	Romans build the 72-mile Hadrian's Wall in Britain to defend against tribes of present-day Scotland.
c. 127-c. 152 C.E.	Kanishka's reign brings flowering of the arts.
180 C.E.	Roman artists complete a monumental bronze equestrian statute of Marcus Aurelius.
c. 200 C.E.	The decentralized Mayan Civilization of Central America and southern Mexico begins its classic age, with monumental pyramid structures decorated in carved stones.
200-800 C.E.	Lima culture in Peru develops the a ceremonial center known as the Pachacamac shrine.
200-900 C.E.	The ancient Maya in Mesoamerica made profound achievements in art, mathematics, astronomy, and architecture.
200-1250 C.E.	The Anasazi in the American Southwest are known for their basketry, sandal making, and weaving.
3d-5th century C.E.	Giant stelae are raised at Aksum in Africa.
c. 321 C.E.	The beginning of India's Gupta period marks a flourishing of the arts under imperial patronage.
333 C.E.	Romans begin to construct St. Peter's Church, which will often serve as a model for later churches.
386 C.E.	Saint Ambrose, bishop of Milan, introduces hymn singing to the West.
c. 400 C.E. or later	Humanlike megaliths are constructed on Easter Island in the South Pacific.
c. 5th century C.E.	Lydenburg Bantus sculpt life-size terra-cotta heads.
460-477 C.E.	Buddhist temples are built at Ajanta Caves in India.

GOVERNMENT, POLITICS, AND WARS

c. 4000 B.C.E.	The world's first organized state emerges in Sumer, Mesopotamia.
c. 3500 B.C.E.	Dravidian peoples of the Indus Valley begin to construct cities of Harappā and Mohenjo Daro.
c. 3050 B.C.E.	The legendary king Menes unites Upper and Lower Egypt into a single kingdom.
c. 3000 B.C.E.	The southern cities of Sumer form a federation under holy city of Nippur, but it is soon disbanded.
c. 2687 B.C.E.	Zoser founds the Third Dynasty of Egypt, which marks the beginning of the Old Kingdom (c. 2687-c. 2125)
2500-1900 B.C.E.	Wawat chiefdom in lower Nubia provides soldiers for the Old Kingdom.
c. 2340 B.C.E.	Sumerian Uruk-Agina becomes the first ruler to initiate social reforms in an attempt to alleviate the oppression of people in Lagash by the priestly class.
c. 2334 B.C.E.	Sargon unifies Mesopotamia and thus establishes the world's first large empire in Akkad.
c. 2333 B.C.E.	Semilegendary Tangun Wanggom founds Korea by establishing a kingdom now known as Old Chosōn.
c. 2200-1500 B.C.E.	Kerma kingdom develops and dominates Lower Nubia.
c. 2160 B.C.E.	The collapse of the central government of Egypt marks the beginning of the First Intermediate Period (c. 2160-c. 2055).
c. 2112 B.C.E.	Ur-Nammu, king of the Mesopotamian city of Ur, establishes a code of law.
c. 2100 B.C.E.	Legendary Chinese hero Yu is said to begin the Xia Dynasty (c. 2100-1600), but the historical evidence for the dynasty is unreliable.

c. 2055 B.C.E.	Egyptian king Montuhotep II reunites the country and centralizes control over the nobles, which marks the beginning of the Middle Kingdom (c. 2055-c. 1650).
c. 2000 B.C.E.	Minoans of Crete begin to use wooden ships and become the world's first sea power.
c. 2000 B.C.E.	Mongols, a nomadic group that engages in raiding, grows powerful in the steppes north of China.
c. 1900 B.C.E.	The Nubian kingdom of Kerma is established south of Egypt.
c. 1900-1527? B.C.E.	Kerma kingdom rules Nubia, acts as a trading center.
c. 1770 B.C.E.	King Hammurabi of Babylon establishes one of the most detailed written legal codes of the ancient world.
c. 1700 B.C.E.	Chinese people of the Huangdi Valley found the Shang Dynasty (c. 1600-1066), which is the first recorded dynasty of China.
c. 1650 B.C.E.	The Hyksos ("foreign princes") take over Egypt, beginning a rule that will last more than a century and a half.
1650-1620 B.C.E.	Hattusilis I establishes the Old Hittite kingdom.
c. 1600-c. 1300 B.C.E.	Hurrians establish the Mitanni kingdom in upper Mesopotamia.
c. 1570 B.C.E.	The rulers of Thebes reunite Egypt by driving out the Hyksos, which marks the beginning of the New Kindom (c. 1570-c. 1069).
c. 1530 B.C.E.	Mixtec replace the Zapotec as the dominant power in Western Oaxaca.
c. 1514 B.C.E.	Egyptian pharaoh Amenhotep I ascends to the throne and begins to colonize Nubia in the south and the upper Euphrates in the northeast.
c. 1450 B.C.E.	International Age of Major Kingdoms begins in the Near East.
c. 1370 B.C.E.	The palace on the island of Crete is destroyed.
c. 1275 B.C.E.	Egyptian king Ramses II defeats the Hittites in the Battle of Kadesh in Syria.
c. 1250 B.C.E.	Fall of Troy marks end of Trojan War.
c. 1200 B.C.E.	The Sea Peoples invade the Mediterranean region, which contributes to the decline of Egypt.
1069 B.C.E.	Third Intermediate Period begins in Egypt.
c. 1066 B.C.E.	The Zhou people in alliance with other ethnic groups in China begin the Western Zhou Dynasty (c. 1066-771).
c. 1000 B.C.E.	The Israelites of Palestine establish a united kingdom under the legendary king Saul.
c. 1000-900 B.C.E.	Ionian confederacy forms.
c. 900-c. 200 B.C.E.	Chavín de Huántar, known for its temple complex, becomes an important urban and religious center in Peru.
c. 883 B.C.E.	Ashurnasirpal II establishes second Assyrian Empire.
8th century B.C.E.	Kushite king Piye establishes rule over Egypt, which is maintained for nearly a century.
8th century B.C.E.	Scythians drive the Cimmerians from Central Asia.
8th-6th century B.C.E.	The Phrygians found a kingdom in western Anatolia.
c. 800 B.C.E.	Phoenicians from Tyre found Carthage.
c. 783-c. 591 B.C.E.	Napata kingdom flourishes in Kush.
770 B.C.E.	After Western Zhou king You is killed, the capital is moved to Louyi, and the Eastern Zhou period (770-256) begins.
753 B.C.E.	Romulus, according to legend, founds the Roman monarchy.
745 B.C.E.	Tiglath-pileser III rules Assyria.
c. 736-716 B.C.E.	Spartans conquer Messenia.

c. 721 B.C.E.	The Assyrians conquer Israel (the Northern Kingdom) and take many Israelites into captivity.
c. 712-698 B.C.E.	Shabaka reunites the Nile Valley.
c. 705-330 B.C.E.	Founding and flourishing of the Achaemenian Dynasty.
701 B.C.E.	Sennacherib invades Syro-Palestine.
664 B.C.E.	Saite Dynasty begins in Egypt.
c. 650 B.C.E.	Cypselus rebels against the oligarchy and becomes a popular "tyrant" in Corinth, Greece.
c. 645-546 B.C.E.	Lydia rises to power under the Mermnad family.
625-509 B.C.E.	Rise of Etruscan civilization in Rome.
621 or 620 B.C.E.	Draco creates a strict legal code for the Athenians.
c. 607-562 B.C.E.	Nebuchadnezzar creates the first Neo-Babylonian state.
c. 6th century B.C.E.-c. 350 C.E.	Meroitic Empire rules from southern Egypt to the Blue Nile.
c. 594-580 B.C.E.	Athenians appoint Solon to reform their laws in an attempt to end social unrest.
587 B.C.E.	The Babylonians under Nebuchadnezzar capture Jerusalem and take many of the Jews into captivity.
547 B.C.E.	Cyrus the Great founds the Persian Empire.
539 B.C.E.	Cyrus of Persia captures Babylon and allows the Jews to return to Palestine.
520-518 B.C.E.	Darius the Great conquers the Indus Valley.
c. 509 B.C.E.	The Romans oust the monarchy and establish a Republic.
508-507 B.C.E.	Cleisthenes reforms the Athenian constitution, making it more democratic.
c. 500 B.C.E.	The Latins defeat the Etruscans and gain control of northern Italy.
499-494 B.C.E.	The Ionian Greek-speaking city-states of Asia Minor rebel against Persian rule, and Athens sends troops to aid the rebels.
494/493 B.C.E.	A new Roman law requires that a plebeian must be one of two consuls elected each year.
490 B.C.E.	The Persian invaders, led by Darius the Great, are defeated by the Greeks at the Battle of Marathon.
483 B.C.E.	Naval law of Themistocles is instituted.
480-479 B.C.E.	King Xerxes I sends a Persian force to invade Greece but meets with defeat in Plataea in 479.
478-448 B.C.E.	Athenian Empire is created.
475-221 B.C.E.	China enters chaotic Warring States Period.
459 B.C.E.	Corinth, an ally of Sparta, declares war on Athens, beginning the Great Peloponnesian War (459-445)
451-449 B.C.E.	The Roman Republic promulgates the Twelve Tables, Rome's first written legal code.
445 B.C.E.	Establishment of the Canuleian law.
431 B.C.E.	Athenian imperialism leads to the Peloponnesian War (431-404), with Sparta victorious over Athens.
429 B.C.E.	Pericles dies during an epidemic in Athens.
June, 415-Sept., 413 B.C.E.	Athens invades Sicily.
403 B.C.E.	The Athenians overthrow the Thirty Tyrants and restore democracy.
401-400 B.C.E.	March of the Ten Thousand.
386 B.C.E.	King's Peace ends Corinthian War.
359 B.C.E.	Philip II becomes king of Macedonia and reorganizes the government.
340-338 B.C.E.	Romans incorporate towns, creating *municipia*.
338 B.C.E.	King Philip II establishes Macedonian hegemony over Greece at the Battle of Chaeronea.

336 B.C.E.	Philip II is murdered and Alexander III replaces him as king of Macedonia.
334 B.C.E.	Alexander begins his conquests by leading an army of Greeks and Macedonians against the Persian Empire.
333 B.C.E.	Battle of Issus.
332 B.C.E.	City of Alexandria is founded.
October 1, 331 B.C.E.	Battle of Gaugamela.
327-325 B.C.E.	Alexander the Great invades the Indian subcontinent.
323 B.C.E.	Alexander the Great dies in Babylon without a successor.
c. 323-275 B.C.E.	Alexander's generals divide up the kingdom and make themselves the kings, founding the Ptolemaic Dynasty and Seleucid Kingdom.
c. 321 B.C.E.	Indian ruler and warrior Chandragupta Maurya establishes the Mauryan Dynasty (c. 321-c. 185), which will eventually control most of India.
3d century B.C.E.	Jimmu Tennō becomes the first emperor of Japan.
c. 300 B.C.E.,	Yayoi period begins in Japan.
c. 300-c. 100 B.C.E.	Berber kingdoms of Numidia and Mauretania flourish.
287 B.C.E.	*Lex Hortensia* reforms the Roman constitution.
264 B.C.E.	The Carthaginians clash with the Roman forces in Sicily, beginning the First Punic War (264-225).
c. 273/265-c. 238 B.C.E.	Mauryan Empire flourishes culturally and artistically under King Aśoka.
c. 245 B.C.E.	Diodotus I founds the Greco-Bactrian kingdom.
245-140 B.C.E.	Rise of Parthia.
221 B.C.E.	Shi Huangdi centralizes the government and establishes the Qin Dynasty (221-206) in China.
221-206 B.C.E.	Legalist movement dominates Chinese thought.
218-201 B.C.E.	Second Punic War.
209-174 B.C.E.	Maodun creates a large confederation in Central Asia.
206 B.C.E.	Chinese warrior Liu Pang establishes the Han Dynasty (206 B.C.E.-220 C.E.), which soon becomes a powerful empire.
202 B.C.E.	Battle of Zama.
180 B.C.E.	Establishment of the *Cursus honorum*.
167-142 B.C.E.	Revolt of the Maccabees.
c. 155 B.C.E.	Greco-Bactrian kingdom reaches its zenith under Menander.
146 B.C.E.	Sack of Corinth marks the end of Greek political autonomy.
146 B.C.E.	The Third Punic War (149-146) ends when Rome destroys Carthage.
140-87 B.C.E.	Wudi rules Han Dynasty China.
c. 135 B.C.E.	The Pharisees advocate a flexible Judaism that incorporates aspects of Hellenistic civilization.
133 B.C.E.	Political control of Pergamum is tranferred from the Seleucid Empire to Rome.
133 B.C.E.	Roman tribune Tiberius Sempronius Gracchus gets legislation redistributing public lands but then dies in riots.
122 B.C.E.	Roman tribune Gaius Sempronius Gracchus dies in a civil war provoked by his progressive reforms.
107-101 B.C.E.	Marius creates a private army.
Early 1st century B.C.E.-225 C.E.	Sātavāhana Dynasty rises to power in South India.
c. 100 B.C.E.-c. 100 C.E.	Celtic hill forts are replaced by *oppida*, unfortified religious and commercial centers.
c. 100 B.C.E.-c. 200 C.E.	Zapotec state dominates Oaxaca and the surrounding areas in Mesoamerica.
c. 100 B.C.E.-c. 100 C.E.	Tiwanaku becomes the second great empire in the Andes Mountains of South America, with the world's highest capital city.

95-69 B.C.E.	Armenian Empire reaches its peak under Tigranes the Great.
90 B.C.E.	Julian law expands Roman citizenship.
89 B.C.E.	Mithradates VI, the greatest king of Pontus, conquers Asia Minor (Turkey) and threatens Roman power in Greece.
81 B.C.E.	Roman general Lucius Cornelius Sulla begins a dictatorship notable for its cruelty and extra-legal procedures.
71 B.C.E.	Roman slave rebel Spartacus is defeated and killed by troops led by Crassus.
64 B.C.E.	Roman commander Pompey the Great takes over the last part of the Seleucid Empire in Syria and Palestine.
63 B.C.E.	Pompey defeats Pontus king Mithradates VI in the third Mithradatic War (74-63), giving the Romans control over Asia Minor (Turkey).
Late 63-January 62 B.C.E.	Senator Catiline conspires to overthrow the Roman Republic.
60 B.C.E.	Julius Caesar, Pompey, and Crassus form the First Triumvirate.
58-51 B.C.E.	Roman commander Caesar conquers Gaul and invades Britain for a second time, gaining limited control over the southeast portion of the island.
51-30 B.C.E.	Cleopatra VII, last of Ptolemies, reigns.
44 B.C.E.	After Julius Caesar is appointed Roman dictator for life, he is assassinated.
43-42 B.C.E.	The Second Triumvirate—Octavian, Marc Anthony, and Lepidus—enacts proscriptions.
31 B.C.E.	Octavian defeats Marc Anthony and Cleopatra in the Battle of Actium, giving Rome control over the Ptolemaic empire.
27-23 B.C.E.	Completion of the Augustan settlement marks a transition to a new form of government, the principate.
15 B.C.E.-15 C.E.	Rhine-Danube frontier fixes the boundaries between the Roman Empire and European tribes to the north.
Early 1st century C.E.	Pyu kingdom develops urban culture.
1st century C.E.	The kingdom of Aksum is established in Ethiopia.
1st century C.E.	Tai peoples migrate into Southeast Asia.
1st-5th century C.E.	Alani, a European nomadic group, gain power.
1st century-c. 627 C.E.	Kingdom of Funan flourishes in Southeast Asia.
c. 1 C.E.	Development begins at Teotihuacán in Mesoamerica.
9 C.E.	Battle of Teutoburg Forest.
9-23 C.E.	Wang Mang usurps throne and creates the Xia Dynasty in China.
14 C.E.	Roman emperor Augustus dies and is succeeded by Tiberius, which begins the Julio-Claudian dynasty (14-68).
25 C.E.	Guang Wudi restores the Han Dynasty in China.
41 C.E.	Roman emperor Caligula is murdered and succeeded by Claudius.
43 C.E.	Roman troops gain control over most of the tribes of southern Britain, but some chieftains continue to fight the invaders.
c. 50 C.E.	Creation of the Roman imperial bureaucracy.
64-67 C.E.	Nero persecutes the Christians.
68-69 C.E.	Year of the four emperors.
69 C.E.	Following a civil war among four Roman generals, Vespasian emerges as emperor, which begins the Flavian Dynasty (69-96).
August 24, 79 C.E.	Destruction of Pompeii after a volcanic eruption.
90 C.E.	Founding of the Classic Period Maya Royal Dynasty at Tikal.
96 C.E.	After the murder of Roman emperor Domitian, Nerva becomes the first of the Five Good Emperors.
c. 100-c. 127 C.E.	Kushān Dynasty expands into India.

122 C.E.	Roman emperor Hadrian orders the building of a stone wall in Britain to defend against northern tribesmen. The 172-mile wall will be completed in five years.
132 C.E.	Jewish leader Bar Kokhba begins a rebellion against the Romans that will last three years.
180 C.E.	The death of Roman emperor Marcus Aurelius, last of the Five Good Emperors, is followed by a period of instability and civil war.
184-204 C.E.	Yellow Turbans Rebellion signaled the end of the Eastern Han Dynasty.
220 C.E.	China's Han Dynasty falls apart, and the country is divided into three kingdoms: the Wei Dynasty (220-265), the Shu Han Dynasty (221-263), and the Wu Dynasty (222-280).
c. 220 C.E.	Ulpian issues dictum, an early statement on theories of government, in Rome.
224 C.E.	Ardashīr I establishes the Sāsānian Empire.
c. mid-3d century C.E.	Himiko rules the Yamatai in Japan.
265 C.E.	Sima Yan establishes the Western Jin Dynasty.
284 C.E.	The dominate is inaugurated in Rome.
264 C.E.	Chinese general Sima Yan overthrows the Wei Dynasty and founds the Western Jin Dynasty (265-316).
293 C.E.	Diocletian divides Rome into four administrative districts, called the Tetrachy.
c. 300 C.E.	The Licchavi Dynasty establishes its authority in the Kathmandu Valley of Nepal.
c. 300-600 C.E.	Three Kingdoms period forms Korean culture.
c. 300-710 C.E.	Kofun Period unifies Japan.
4th-11th century C.E.	Ancient Ghana emerges.
309-379 C.E.	Shāpūr II reigns over Sāsānian Empire.
313 C.E.	Roman emperor Constantine I legislates the Edict of Milan, which officially recognizes and gives special support to the Christian Church.
316 C.E.	Western Jin Dynasty falls, initiating period of chaos in China.
c. 321 C.E.	Chandragupta I founds the Gupta dynasty (c. 321-c. 550), initiating one of India's classical periods.
324-330 C.E.	Roman Emperor Constantine the Great establishes Constantinople as his capital.
August 9, 378 C.E.	At the Battle of Adrianople, tribal invaders from outside Rome's borders first manage to completely defeat the Roman army.
c. 380 C.E.	Chandragupta II becomes emperor of India, and his 35-year reign will see imperial expansion and a flowering of art, architecture, and sculpture.
386 C.E.	Toba establishes the Northern Wei Dynasty in China.
390-430 C.E. or later	Ōjin Tennō, first historical emperor of Japan, reigns.
395 C.E.	Following the death of Roman emperor Theodosius the Great, the empire is divided into western and eastern spheres.
410 C.E.	The Visigoth king Alaric captures the city of Rome.
c. 410 C.E.	Romans abandon Britain after almost four centuries of occupation.
418 C.E.	Western emperor Honorius is forced to allow the Visigoths to settle in southwestern Gaul (now France).
420 C.E.	Southern Dynasties Period begins in China.
430 C.E.	Vandals led by king Genseric invade North Africa.
438 C.E.	Eastern Roman Emperor Theodosius II issues the Theodosian Code, which reduces and systematizes Roman law.
439 C.E.	Vandals seize Carthage.
445-453 C.E.	Attila the Hun invades Rome.

July, 451 C.E.	Battle of Châlons stops the advance of the Huns into Europe.
455 C.E.	The Vandals, who already control North Africa, plunder Rome.
474 C.E.	Theodoric the Great is elected king of the Ostrogoths.
476 C.E.	The Goth leader Odoacer deposes the last Roman emperor, Romulus Augustus, and Rome falls.

LITERATURE, HISTORIOGRAPHY, AND PHILOSOPHY

c. 2500 B.C.E.	Babylonians in the city of Nippur make the first known library with a collection of clay tablets.
c. 2400 B.C.E.	*The Instruction of Ptahhotep*, composed of maxims of practical morality, is one of the first known works of Egyptian wisdom literature.
c. 2300 B.C.E.	Enheduanna, an Akkadian poet, becomes first named author.
c. 2000 B.C.E.	Sumerians begin to write early versions of the Gilgamesh epic, the oldest known story.
1400-1300 B.C.E.	Aqhat epic is composed in Ugarit.
c. 1000 B.C.E.	With the fall of the Mycenaean civilization, the Greeks enter their so-called "dark age," and for the next three hundred years they apparently lose their knowledge of writing.
776 B.C.E.	Olympic Games are first recorded.
c. 750 B.C.E.	The *Iliad* and later the *Odyssey* (725), attributed to Homer, are recorded after the Greeks rediscover how to write, now using a modified Phoenician alphabet.
c. 700 B.C.E.	Hesiod's epic poems, *Theogony* and *Works and Days*, appear.
c. 580 B.C.E.	Greek poet Sappho dies.
c. 585 B.C.E.	Thales predicts a solar eclipse, which is often considered the beginning of the Milesian school of philosophy.
c. 550 B.C.E.	The Sanskrit epic poem, the *Rāmāyaṇa*, is composed in India.
c. 530 B.C.E.	Founding of the Pythagorean brotherhood.
c. 525 B.C.E.	Sibylline books are compiled.
520-518 B.C.E.	Scylax of Caryanda voyages the Indian Ocean, writes an account of his travels.
5th century B.C.E.	Composition of the *Spring and Autumn Annals*, attributed to Confucius
c. 5th-3d century B.C.E.	Composition of *The Art of War*, attributed to Sunzi.
5th-1st century B.C.E.	Composition of *The Great Learning*, attributed to Confucius.
c. 500 B.C.E.	Pāṇini composes Sanskrit work of grammar.
c. 500-470 B.C.E.	Hecataeus of Miletus writes the first geography book.
500-400 B.C.E.	Creation of the *Wujing*, the Five Classics.
c. 479 B.C.E.	The disciples of Confucius begin collecting his teachings into *The Analects*.
c. 456/455 B.C.E.	Death of Greek playwright, Aeschylus, known as "the father of Greek tragedy."
c. 450 B.C.E.	Greek rational philosopher Leucippus asserts that every event has a natural cause, ruling out supernatural intervention.
c. 450-c. 425 B.C.E.	History develops as a scholarly discipline.
c. 440 B.C.E.	Greek philosopher Democritus theorizes that matter is composed of invisible particles called atoms.
c. 440 B.C.E.	Sophists train the Greeks in rhetoric and politics.
c. 438 B.C.E.	Death of Pindar, often considered the greatest lyric poet of ancient Greece.
c. 430 B.C.E.	The Sophist Protagoras is thought to have asserted that the brain is the center of intellectual activity.
c. 424 B.C.E.	The Greek historian Herodotus completes his monumental history of the Persian wars, which earns him the title, "father of history."
411 B.C.E.	Greek playwright Aristophanes presents his antiwar comedy, *Lysistratē*, in which women withhold sex to end war.

c. 410 B.C.E.	Athenian general and historian Thucydides writes *History of the Peloponnesian War*, famous for its precision and attempt at objectivity.
c. 406 B.C.E.	Death of Greek tragic playwright Sophocles, author of *Oedipus Rex* and more than one hundred plays.
c. 406 B.C.E.	Death of Greek tragic playwright Euripedes, author of *Medea* and about eighty other dramas.
c. 4th century B.C.E.-3d century C.E.	Kauṭilya compiles a treatise on practical statecraft.
Early 4th century B.C.E.	Founding of Mohism.
c. 400 B.C.E.-400 C.E.	Composition of the *Mahābhārata*.
399 B.C.E.	Socrates is found guilty of impiety and put to death by drinking hemlock.
Between 394 and 371 B.C.E.	Xenophon writes the *Anabasis*; he is later banished from Rome.
c. 388 B.C.E.	Greek philosopher Plato founds the Academy at Athens, where he teaches and writes his dialogues for the remainder of his life.
c. 385 B.C.E.	Greek playwright Aristophanes dies.
c. 380 B.C.E.	Plato develops his theory of Ideas.
c. 350 B.C.E.	Diogenes popularizes cynicism.
335 B.C.E.	Aristotle founds the Lyceum in Athens, where he and his disciples produce many classical works of philosophy.
c. 335-323 B.C.E.	Aristotle writes the *Politics*.
c. 322 B.C.E.	The dramatist Menander presents the first of his hundred comedies in Athens.
c. 310 B.C.E.	Greek philosopher Euhemerus writes his *Sacred Scripture*, suggesting that the gods were once human heroes.
307 B.C.E.	Philosopher Epicurus, remembered for his theories about pain and happiness, establishes his school at "the Garden" in Athens.
c. 300 B.C.E.	Greek philosophers Zeno, Citium, and Chrysippus develop an approach to life called Stoicism, emphasizing the duty to live rationally according to principles of natural law.
c. 289 B.C.E.	Death of Chinese Confucian scholar Mencius, proponent of a positive view of human nature.
c. 285-c. 255 B.C.E	Xunzi develops teachings that lead to Legalism.
285-160 B.C.E.	Composition of the *Zhuangzi*, an important Daoist work.
c. 270's B.C.E.	Greek innovative poet Theocritus is writing pastoral poetry, which will later have many imitators.
272 B.C.E.	Greek skeptical philosopher Pyrrhon of Elis dies, and soon thereafter his admirer, Sextus Empiricus, summarizes his ideas in *Outlines of Pyrrhonism*.
c. 260 B.C.E.	Mauryan emperor of India Aśoka becomes a Buddhist and orders construction of the great *stupa* (domed structure for relics) at Sanchi.
c. 235 B.C.E.	Death of Chinese Confucian scholar Xunzi, proponent of a negative view of human nature.
c. 240 B.C.E.	Death of Callimachus, a Greek poet, grammarian, and critic.
159 B.C.E.	Roman playwright Terence dies.
139-122 B.C.E.	Composition of the *Huainanzi*, a Chinese philosophical treatise.
c. 118 B.C.E.	Death of Greek politician and historian Polybius, author of a highly prized history about the rise of Roman power.
c. 104 B.C.E.	The death of Dong Zhongshu, a Chinese Confucian scholar who synthesized the views of Mencius and Xuanzi.
1st century B.C.E.	Sima Qian writes the first significant dynastic history of China, the *Records of the Grand Historian of China*.
1st-3d century C.E.	Caṅkam literature composed in South India.

c. 60 B.C.E.	Roman philosopher Lucretius writes *On the Nature of Things*, a poem that popularizes the "atomic theory" of Epicurus.
54 B.C.E.	Roman poet Catullus dies.
51 B.C.E.	Cicero, the famous Roman writer and orator, writes *De republica*. In 43, he is murdered by Marc Anthony's soldiers.
c. 26 B.C.E.	Livy begins to write his monumental history of Rome.
19 B.C.E.	Roman poet Vergil dies before completing the *Aeneid*.
8 B.C.E.	Roman lyric poet Horace dies.
8 C.E.	Roman poet Ovid composes his mythological collection, *Metamorphoses*, and is banished from Rome.
75-79 C.E.	Flavius Josephus, Jewish historian and general, writes *History of the Jewish War*.
c. 99-105 C.E.	Ban Zhao writes behavior guide for young Chinese women.
2d century C.E.	Nāgārjuna founds the Mādhyamika ("of the middle"), a philosophical school of Mahāyāna Buddhism.
100-127 C.E.	Roman Juvenal composes *Satires*.
c. 105-115 C.E.	Greek Plutarch completes his *Parallel Lives*, biographies of prominent Greeks and Romans.
c. 120 C.E.	Roman historian Suetonius composes *History of the Twelve Caesars*.
c. 138 C.E.	Death of Epictetus, whose maxims were collected in the *Encheiridion*.
c. 150 C.E.	Aśvaghosa composes the first complete biography of the Buddha.
c. 165 C.E.	Gaius creates edition of the *Institutes* of Roman law.
c. 171-180 C.E.	Roman emperor Marcus Aurelius, an adherent of Stoic Philosophy, writes his *Meditations*.
c. 180 C.E.	The death of Greek writer Lucian, author of dialogues, poetry, and fantastic tales.
c. 220 C.E.	Chinese noblewoman Cai Yan composes poetry about her capture by nomads and separation from her sons.
c. 229 C.E.	Roman politician and historian Dio Cassius retires from public life and is too ill to continue working on his *Roman History*.
c. 250 C.E.	Roman mystic Plotinus formulates a quasi-religious philosophy inspired by Plato, which is later called Neoplatonism.
c. 300 C.E.	The Indian sage Vatsyayana writes the *Kama Sutra*, a handbook on sexual love.
c. 305 C.E.	Death of Greek philosopher Porphyry, editor of Plotinus's works into the *Enneads* and author of an introduction to Aristotle's logic.
c. 400 C.E.	Kālidāsa composes Sanskrit poetry and plays.
c. 405 C.E.	Statesman Tao Qian becomes farmer and Daoist poet.
413-427 C.E.	Bishop Augustine of Hippo, North Africa, finishes *The City of God*, which denies that Christianity was the cause of Rome's fall.

MEDICINE AND HEALTH

27th century B.C.E.	Egyptian physician, Imhotep, often called the world's first scientist, writes the first known medical text.
c. 2700 B.C.E.	Legendary Chinese emperor Shen Nong, considered the founder of Chinese medicine, describes the medicinal powers of numerous plants.
c. 2600 B.C.E.	Egyptian dentist Neferites makes artificial teeth out of ivory.
c. 1770 B.C.E.	The laws of Hammurabi establish the first known code of medical ethics and outline a fee schedule for surgery.
c. 1000 B.C.E.	The developing Mosaic Code of the Hebrews include sanitary measures and dietary restrictions.

6th-4th century B.C.E	Suśruta, Indian physician, writes a medical compendium.
600 B.C.E.	Historical records indicate that Hindu communities in India operate hospitals for the sick.
c. 500 B.C.E.	Chinese physicians begin the practice of acupuncture.
500 B.C.E.	Some Greek city-states take care of sick people in hospitals called Aesculapia (named after Aesclepius, the god of medicine).
c. 500 B.C.E.	The Greek physician and scientist Alcmaeon of Croton makes the first known dissections of dead human bodies.
c. 500-400 B.C.E.	Greek physicians begin scientific practice of medicine.
c. 370 B.C.E.	Death of Greek physician Hippocrates, author of many books with detailed case histories and proposed physical explanations for diseases. The Hippocratic Oath, which appears later, represents his principles.
c. 325 B.C.E.	Greek physician Praxagoras of Cos discovers the value of measuring the pulse when diagnosing diseases.
c. 300 B.C.E.	*The Yellow Emperor's Classic of Internal Medicine*, a compilation attributed to Chinese emperor Huangdi, contains references to the function of the heart and the circulation of the blood.
2d century C.E.	The Taoist religious leader, Zhang Daoling, composes a guide of charms and incantations that presumably cure diseases.
c. 157-201 C.E.	Greek physician and anatomist Galen proves that the arteries carry blood but incorrectly explains how the blood passes through the heart.
369 C.E.	Saint Basil erects a hospital at Caesarea.

RELIGION

50,000 B.C.E.	There is some evidence that the human subspecies called Neanderthals are burying their dead, which perhaps suggests some notion about an afterlife.
20,000 B.C.E.	Surviving artifacts and paintings in numerous locations suggest that humans have developed a large diversity of beliefs about humanlike, animal-like, and nature deities.
c. 7500 B.C.E.	Shintō religion arises in Japan.
c. 6200-c. 3800 B.C.E.	The Ubaid culture builds mud-brick rectangular temples, the first sacred public architecture to appear in Mesopotamia.
c. 6000-c. 5000 B.C.E.	The Niger-Congo religion, which recognizes a creator god, ancestral spirits, and territorial spirits, takes hold across West Africa.
c. 5800-c. 3700 B.C.E.	The Chinchorro, fisher folk living along the Peruvian and Chilean coasts, mummify their dead, probably for spiritual or religious reasons.
c. 5000 B.C.E.-c. 1 C.E.	The Red Paint culture in North America buries their dead with gifts and then covers both with red ocher pigment.
c. 3500 B.C.E.	People of Mesopotamia (modern Iraq) are making small humanlike statutes of deities in stone and pottery.
c. 3300-c. 1500 B.C.E.	The Valdivia culture in the tropical forest of northwestern South America creates ceremonial centers, evidence of religious and ritual activity.
c. 3200 B.C.E.	The predynastic Egyptians have a rich variety of tribal and local deities, with the dominance of a god following the political dominance of a city or region.
c. 2687 B.C.E.	By the Third Dynasty (c. 2687-c. 2613) of Egypt's Old Kingdom, the government is emphasizing the king's divinity and placing mummified bodies of dead kings in graves containing useful objects and religious art. Major deities and religious practices are crystalizing in forms that will continue for about three thousand years.

c. 2000 B.C.E.	The legendary Abraham, later recognized as the first Hebrew patriarch, leaves southern Mesopotamia and moves to Syria and Canaan.
c. 1500 B.C.E.	Aryan invaders in western India are formulating religious and social duties that will later crystallize in Hinduism.
c. 1500 B.C.E.	Egyptians are using written funeral texts, called the Book of the Dead.
c. 1500-1000 B.C.E.	Hindu priests of India create religious hymns later called the *Rigveda*.
14th-9th century B.C.E.	Urnfield culture, known for its cremations and field cemetaries, flourishes in northwestern Europe.
c. 1374 B.C.E.	Egyptian pharaoh Amenhotep IV changes his name to Akhenaton and begins a near-monotheistic religion that venerates the Sun god Aton.
c. 1280 B.C.E.	Moses, a legendary religious and political leader, probably leads the Hebrews (Israelites) out of Egypt, although some modern historians argue that the Hebrews never lived in Egypt.
c. 1000 B.C.E.	Hebrew priests and prophets are making a gradual transition to consistent monotheism. About the same time, the "J" document, one of the major sources of the Hebrew Bible, is recorded.
c. 1000-c. 200 B.C.E.	Hindu mystics of India write early versions of the Upaniṣads.
c. 966 B.C.E.	King Solomon constructs a Hebrew temple in Jerusalem.
c. 950 B.C.E.	Composition of the Book of Genesis.
775 B.C.E.	Delphi Oracle provides guidance for city-states.
Before 600 B.C.E.	Celebration of the Eleusinian mysteries.
6th century B.C.E.	The semi-historical Laozi introduces the doctrines of Daoism. Perhaps three centuries later, the *Dao De Jing* appears and is attributed to him.
6th or 5th century B.C.E.	Birth of Buddhism.
c. 600 B.C.E.	The Persian prophet Zoroaster develops a ditheistic religion, later called Zoroastrianism.
587-423 B.C.E.	Birth of Judaism.
c. 539 B.C.E.	Indian mystic Vardhamāna, founder of Jainism, renounces his family and spends the next twelve years developing the doctrine of *ahiṁsā* (or nonviolence).
c. 538 B.C.E.	Persian King Cyrus the Great allows the Jewish people to return to their homeland in Palestine.
c. 525 B.C.E.	The Sibylline Books, a collection of oracles, make their appearance in Rome.
c. 524 B.C.E.	The traditional date when Siddhārtha Gautama (the Buddha) is believed to have obtained enlightenment near Benares, India.
c. 5th-4th century B.C.E.	Creation of the *Jātakas*.
c. 500 B.C.E.	The cult of Mithra, called Mithraism, grows out of the Zoroastrian system and becomes a major religion of Persia.
c. 480 B.C.E.	Following the Buddha's death, the First Buddhist Council meets at Rājagṛha, India, and adopts rules of monastic discipline.
c. 467 B.C.E.	Gośāla Maskarīputra, founder of Ājīvika sect, dies.
c. 450 B.C.E.	The first five books (the Torah) of the Hebrew Bible (Christian Old Testament) have probably been written in their modern form.
c. 391 B.C.E.	Chinese philosopher Mozi, the founder of Mohism, dies, and his followers begin to collect his teachings in the *Mozi*.
c. 383 B.C.E.	The elders at the Second Buddhist Council at Vesālī, India, affirm principles of Theravāda orthodoxy.
c. 300's B.C.E.	Buddhist monks of India, including Maitreya and Asanga, develop the Yogācāra ("consciousness only") school of Buddhism.

c. 300's B.C.E.	Chinese scholar Huiyuan begins a devotional society for meditation in the name of Amitbha Buddhia (the Buddha of Infinite Light).
c. 300's B.C.E.	Indian scholar Patanjali develops the system of *raja* (royal) yoga, which will be recorded in the *Yoga Sutras* a few hundred years later.
c. 300's B.C.E.	Chinese philosopher Zhuangzi further develops the tenants of classical Daoism. A collection of parables and allegories, called the *Zhuangzi* (285-160), is attributed to him.
300 B.C.E.-600 C.E.	Construction of the Māhabodhi Temple, commemorating the place where the Buddha attained enlightenment.
c. 260 B.C.E.	Indian king Aśoka is converted to Buddhism and begins a policy based on toleration and benevolence.
c. 250 B.C.E.	Third Buddhist Council convenes.
c. 250 B.C.E.	Buddhist monks begin to write down the *Tipiṭaka* (three baskets), which contains the teachings and meditations attributed to the Buddha and his followers.
250-130 B.C.E.	Jewish scholars create the Septuagint, a translation of the Hebrew scriptures into Greek.
c. 250 B.C.E.-70 C.E.	Dead Sea Scrolls are composed.
c. 247-207 B.C.E.	Buddhism is established in Sri Lanka.
c. 200 B.C.E.	Birth of Hinduism.
c. 200 B.C.E.	Devout Hindus of India compose early versions of the poem *The Bhagavad Gita* (Song of the Lord).
c. 200 B.C.E.-c. 100 C.E.	Composition of the Intertestamental Jewish Apocrypha.
168-167 B.C.E.	Judas Maccabaeus ("the Hammer") rededicates the Temple of Jerusalem to the Jewish religion (now celebrated in Hanukkah).
c. 1st century B.C.E.	Indian Buddhist nuns compile the *Therigatha*, a collection of poems.
1st century B.C.E.-1st century C.E.	Compilation of the *Lotus Sutra*, one of the most important of Mahāyāna Buddhist texts.
c. 100's B.C.E.	Mahāyāna ("greater vehicle") Buddhism emerges with beliefs about bodhisattvas ("enlightened beings").
c. 70 B.C.E.	The Persian cult Mithraism is introduced to the Romans and spreads rapidly among the people.
c. 60 B.C.E.	Druidism flourishes in Gaul and Britain.
23 B.C.E.	The practice of deifying living emperors begins with the veneration of Caesar Augustus.
c. 6 B.C.E.	Jesus is born to Joseph and Mary, probably in Bethlehem of Judaea.
1st century-2d century C.E.	Fourth Buddhist Council convenes.
c. 27 C.E.	The Jewish ascetic John the Baptist is put to death by Herod Antipas, tetrarch of Galilee.
c. 30 C.E.	Jesus of Nazareth is condemned and crucified in Jerusalem.
c. 30 C.E.	Preaching of the Pentecostal Gospel.
c. 33 C.E.	Following a mystical religious experience, Saul of Tarsus converts to Christianity and changes his name to Paul.
c. 46 C.E.	Paul begins his travels in Asia Minor seeking converts to Christianity.
c. 50 C.E.	The leaders of the Christian church hold their first doctrinal council at Jerusalem, deciding that gentile converts are not obligated to be circumcised or to follow all of the Torah.
c. 55 or 56 C.E.	Paul develops Christian doctrine in his letter to the church at Rome.
c. 60-68 C.E.	According to tradition, Emperor Mingdi introduces Buddhism to China.

64 C.E.	Emperor Nero begins a persecution of Christians following the burning of Rome.
c. 65 C.E.	The Christian Gospel of Mark is completed, which influences the later accounts of Matthew, Luke, and John.
70 C.E.	Roman commander Titus destroys the Jewish temple at Jerusalem.
c. 73 C.E.	The Romans destroy the Jewish stronghold at Masada and community at Qumran, both located near the Dead Sea. The people of Qumran hide their religious texts in caves.
c. 90 C.E.	A synod of rabbis establishes the canon of Jewish scriptures at Jamnia, Palestine.
2d century C.E.	Many apocryphal Christian writings, attributed to the Apostles, are being written, especially in Egypt and Syria.
c. 110 C.E.	Trajan adopts anti-Christian religious policy.
c. 120 C.E.	Christian churches are using early versions of the Apostles' Creed in religious ceremonies.
130-135 C.E.	Hadrian's plan to build a Roman city at Jerusalem brings about the Second Jewish Revolt, which results in the Jews being banished from Jerusalem.
142 C.E.	The Daoist religious leader Zhang Daoling founds the Celestial Masters movement.
c. 150 C.E.	All of the New Testament books have probably been written. Most churches recognize the Gospels and Paul's letters as scripture, but the canonical status of other books is unclear.
c. 150 C.E.	Marcion, a Christian Gnostic, formulates the first known New Testament canon, which included ten of Paul's letters and an edited version of Luke.
180 C.E.	Irenaeus, Christian theologian and bishop of Lyons, writes *Against Heresies*, which defends the doctrine of apostolic succession.
c. 3d century C.E.	Wang Bi and Guo Xiang revive Daoism.
c. 230-1300 C.E.	Manichaeanism, a dualistic religion that rivaled Christianity, begins in Mesopotamia.
250 C.E.	Outbreak of the Decian persecution of Christians.
c. 250 C.E.	Saint Denis converts city of Paris to Christianity.
c. 250 C.E.	Badarayana writes a mystical summary of the Upaniṣads in the *Vedānta Sutras*.
c. 250 C.E.	The Christian Montanist sect teaches that Priscilla and Maximilla, two female prophets, receive revelations by the Holy Spirit.
c. 286 C.E.	Saint Anthony of Egypt begins ascetic life.
c. 300, 324 C.E.	Eusebius, bishop of Caesarea, writes his *Church History*, the first major historical account of the Christian Church.
October 28, 312 C.E.	Conversion of Constantine to Christianity.
313-395 C.E.	Inception of the church-state problem in the Roman Empire.
321 C.E.	Arius, a priest of Libya, teaches that Jesus is not fully divine, a doctrine that bishop Athanasius of Alexander and other Christian theologians condemn as heretical.
c. 323 C.E.	Christian ascetic Pachomius organizes the first monastic community in Upper Egypt.
c. 325 C.E.	With the conversion of king Tiridates III, Armenia becomes the first country to make Christianity its official religion.
325 C.E.	Roman emperor Constantine I sponsors the Council of Nicaea in Asia Minor, which condemns Arianism and adopts the Nicene Creed.
c. 333 C.E.	The kingdom of Aksum (now Ethiopia) is converted to Christianity.

c. 350 C.E.	Gnostic writings, condemned by orthodox Christians, are hid in Nag Hammadi, Egypt.
350 C.E.	The Christian Church establishes Christmas as a major religious festival.
360 C.E.	Christian ascetic Basil the Great writes rules of monastic life that require monks to do charitable works.
361 C.E.	The new Roman emperor, known as Julian the Apostate, initiates a vigorous policy of reviving the old pagan cults.
Late 4th-5th century C.E.	Asanga helps spread Mahāyāna Buddhism.
c. 370 C.E.	Chinese Buddhist missionaries introduce Buddhism into Korea.
380-392 C.E.	Emperor Theodosius makes Christianity the official religion of the Roman Empire.
382 C.E.	A Synod of Rome approves the current New Testament canon of 27 books, and the North African Church will follow suit at the Synod of Hippo ten years later.
c. 382-c. 405 C.E.	Saint Jerome translates the Bible into the Latin language (the Vulgate).
397-402 C.E.	Ge Chaofu founds the Lingbao tradition of Daoism.
399 C.E.	Chinese Buddhist monk Faxian travels to India.
5th or 6th century C.E.	First major text on Hinduism's great goddess is compiled.
428 C.E.	Nestorius, an unorthodox Christian theologian, becomes bishop of Constantinople, and the Nestorian Controversy begins.
c. 450 C.E.	Saint Patrick begins to spread Christianity throughout Ireland.
October 8-25, 451 C.E.	Council of Chalcedon.
459 C.E.	Christian ascetic Simeon Stylites dies after living thirty years atop a pillar of stones.
461 C.E.	Leo I (later called "the Great") becomes Pope of the Roman Catholic Church and consolidates the primacy of the papacy over the other bishops.
c. 470 C.E.	Bodhidharma brings Chan Buddhism to China.

SCIENCE AND TECHNOLOGY

c. 2.5 million B.P.	Small groups of the hominid species *Homo habilis* make simple stone tools in East Africa.
c. 500,000 B.P.	The hominid *Homo erectus* discovers the use of fire in China and perhaps Europe.
c. 25,000 B.P.	People in western Europe and perhaps northern Africa invent the bow and arrow.
c. 9,000 B.C.E.	Aboriginal peoples in the Central Plains of North America are hunting large game with chipped flint points known as Clovis points and Folsom points (named after places of discovery in New Mexico).
c. 8000-c. 4000 B.C.E.	Plano cultures in Northern America develop method of chipping stone to produce projectile points that differ from the fluted points of earlier periods.
c. 6800-c. 4900 B.C.E.	The Kitoi, hunter-fishers in central Siberia, produce stone-polished ceramics and slate fishhooks, adzes, and knives as well as perforators, drills, and harpoon heads.
c. 4,000 B.C.E.	Egyptians begin to smelt copper ores.
c. 4000-c. 1000 B.C.E.	The Old Copper complex, Archaic Indian cultures in the western Great Lakes, mine copper to produce tools and ornaments.
c. 3400 B.C.E.	Peoples of the Middle East region invent bronze, an alloy of copper and tin.
c. 3300 B.C.E.	Southern Mesopotamians invent the wheel and use it for transporting objects in carts.
c. 3100 B.C.E.	The Sumerians of Mesopotamia begin to use simple picture writings that eventually develop into cuneiform.

c. 3000 B.C.E.	Mediterranean peoples begin to use metal nuggets of copper for ornamentation and soon thereafter for tools and weapons.
c. 3000 B.C.E.	The Egyptians develop a system of picture writing that develops into hieroglyphs. Soon thereafter they use a local reed to form papyrus as a writing material.
c. 3000 B.C.E.	The Egyptians devise the cubit, the distance from the elbow to the extended finger tips, as a standard unit of linear measurement.
c. 3000 B.C.E.	Dravidian peoples of the Indus valley in India weave cotton fabrics.
c. 3000 B.C.E.	People in both China and the Eastern Mediterranean invent an abacus, using rods and beads.
2953-2838 B.C.E.	China's mythical first ruler, Fu Xi, reportedly develops the calendar, musical instruments, animal husbandry, and the eight trigrams of the *Yijing* divination text.
c. 2900 B.C.E.	The Sumerians, in the Early Dynastic Period c. 2900-c. 2340), develop symbols for syllables, making writing more efficient.
c. 2700 B.C.E.	The Mesopotamians develop a lunar calendar, using 354 days for a year. Egyptians begin to quarry limestone and use it for constructing pyramids.
c. 2600 B.C.E.	Eastern Mediterranean peoples begin to utilize iron, without at first recognizing its advantages.
c. 2600 B.C.E.	Death of China's legendary emperor Huangdi (the Yellow Emperor), said to have invented the compass. His wife, Leizu, is said to have introduced silkworm production.
c. 2550 B.C.E.	The Greeks of Troy begin to make and use lead.
c. 2500 B.C.E.	Peoples of the Mediterranean region are making bronze tools and weapons.
c. 2400 B.C.E.	The Sumerians develop a calendar consisting of 12 months of 30 days each.
c. 2300 B.C.E.	The Babylonians invent the first maps, portraying canals, rivers, and mountains on clay tablets.
c. 2300-c. 1800 B.C.E.	The Beaker people introduce metallurgy to Western Europe.
c. 2100 B.C.E.	The Sumerians add an intercalated month to their lunar calendar to harmonize it with the solar year.
c. 2000 B.C.E.	The Bronze Age begins in Europe.
c. 1800 B.C.E.	The Chinese begin to make bronze weapons and chariots.
c. 1800 B.C.E.	Babylonian astronomers begin to record their celestial observations.
c. 1800 B.C.E.	Mesopotamians improve their writing system with the rebus principle, using simple pictures for ideas.
c. 1700 B.C.E.	Egyptian mathematicians develop a table of values for fractions and a system of geometry.
c. 1600 B.C.E.	The Phoenicians invent a phonetic alphabet using only symbols for sounds.
c. 1450 B.C.E.	The Hittites of Asia Minor (modern Turkey) are perhaps the first to smelt iron, a process that will spread to Europe within a few hundred years.
c. 1300 B.C.E.	Some peoples of northeastern Africa are beginning to produce smelt iron.
c. 1250 B.C.E.	The European alphabet, which can be used by a number of languages, is developed.
c. 1200 B.C.E.	Peoples of the Middle East and southern Europe are beginning to make useful iron tools and weapons.
c. 1100-c. 500 B.C.E.	Hallstatt culture ushers in the Iron Age in northern Europe.
c. 1000 B.C.E.	The earliest known sites for making iron in sub-Saharan Africa appear in the Lake Chad and Rwanda regions.
c. 1000 B.C.E.	The Chinese learn to burn coal for fuel and to store ice for refrigeration.

c. 1000 B.C.E.	The Greek alphabet, from which the English alphabet is derived, is developed.
c. 1000-c. 700 B.C.E.	Mashariki Bantu establish Chifumbaze ironworking culture.
c. 1000-c. 690 B.C.E.	The Cimmerians in Russia are the first to use the horse in warfare.
c. 800-c. 600 B.C.E.	Iron production gradually extends from North Africa and into East and West Africa, eventually covering the entire continent.
763 B.C.E.	The Babylonians are the first to record a solar eclipse.
c. 750-c. 500 B.C.E.	Marib dam is built in Yemen.
c. 700-330 B.C.E.	Phalanx is developed as a military unit.
c. 640 B.C.E.	The first stamped coins made of gold and silver are made in Lydia, and their use quickly spreads around the Mediterranean.
6th century B.C.E.	Greek philosopher Anaximander teaches the plurality of worlds and recognizes the complex sources of matter.
585 B.C.E.	Thales of Miletus, a Greek philosopher, predicts a solar eclipse. About the same time he theorizes that water is the fundamental element for all substances.
c. 550 B.C.E.	Construction of trireme changes naval warfare.
c. 550 B.C.E.	Greek philosopher and astronomer Anaximander proposes a theory of biological evolution.
c. 530 B.C.E.	Greek mathematician and philosopher Pythagoras invents the Pythagorean theorem. He also argues that the earth is a sphere and that the Sun, stars, and planets revolve around it.
5th century B.C.E.	Greek philosopher Anaxagoras writes *On Nature*, arguing that mind exists and that matter is composed of an infinite number of atomic elements.
c. 430 B.C.E.	Death of Greek philosopher Empedocles, who held that all matter is made from four elements: water, fire, air, and earth.
c. 400 B.C.E.	Greek philosopher Philolaus is the first known person to argue that Earth orbits around the Sun.
325-323 B.C.E.	Aristotle isolates science as a discipline.
c. 320 B.C.E.	Theophrastus initiates the study of botany.
312 B.C.E.	First Roman aqueduct is built.
300 B.C.E.	Babylonian mathematicians develop a symbol for zero.
c. 300 B.C.E.	Greek mathematician Euclid of Egypt writes *Elements*, which includes a summary of plane and solid geometry.
early 3d century B.C.E.	Greek astronomer Aristarchus of Samos writes *On the Size and Distance of the Sun and the Moon*, arguing that the earth revolves around the Sun.
c. 275 B.C.E.	Greeks advance Hellenistic astronomy.
c. 250 B.C.E.	Greek scientist Archimedes discovers the law of specific gravity, later known as Archimedes' principle.
From 240 B.C.E.	Romans learn to use the arch in building.
240 B.C.E.	Chinese astronomers make the first known observation of Haley's comet.
240 B.C.E.	Eratosthenes of Cyrene, librarian of Alexandria, Egypt, correctly calculates the circumference of the earth at about 25,000 miles.
221 B.C.E.-220 C.E.	Advances are made in Chinese agricultural technology.
200 B.C.E.	The Greeks invent the astrolabe to determine the positions of the stars.
165 B.C.E.	The Chinese make the first known observations of sunspots.
150 B.C.E.	Greek astronomer Hipparchus of Nicaea calculates that the moon is about 240,000 miles from the earth.
100 B.C.E.	The Romans begin to use water power to mill flour.
c. 100 B.C.E.	Greek philosopher Poseidonius shows correlation between tides and the lunar cycle.

46 B.C.E.	Establishment of the Julian calendar.
7 B.C.E.	Greek philosopher Strabo summarizes geographical knowledge in his *Geography*.
c. 62 C.E.	Hero of Alexander invents a simple steam engine, which is never found to have a practical use.
77 C.E.	Roman natural philosopher Pliny the Elder publishes *Natural History*, which will serves as a standard scientific handbook until the Renaissance.
c. 105 C.E.	Chinese inventor Cai Lun makes paper out of wood, rags, or other materials containing cellulose.
c. 150 C.E.	Alexander scientist Ptolemy argues that all heavenly bodies revolve around a fixed Earth in the *Almagest*.
c. 250 C.E.	The Maya in Mexico and Central America are beginning scientific and technological advances that will continue for about six hundred years.
c. 350 C.E.	The Chinese invent an early form of printing.
c. 400 C.E.	The Chinese invent the wheelbarrow.

WOMEN'S ISSUES

c. 2687 B.C.E.	Upper-class women of Egypt have the title "priestess of Hathor" in the Old Kingdom (c. 2687-c. 2125).
c. 2600 B.C.E.	Some Egyptian medical texts explain means of contraception, although induced abortions are illegal.
c. 2300 B.C.E.	Sumerian priestess Enheduanna, the first known female poet, composes a hymn to the goddess Inanna.
c. 2000 B.C.E.	The nine Greek muses become identified with specific arts and sciences.
c. 2000 B.C.E.	Egyptian wives can inherit property from their husbands in the Middle Kingdom (c. 2055-c. 1650).
c. 1290 B.C.E.	Queen Nefertari, chief wife of Ramses II, is presented with a large tomb in the Valley of the Queens, west of Thebes.
c. 1200 B.C.E.	Fu Hao, consort of Chinese emperor Wu Ding, leads military expeditions.
c. 1200-1125 B.C.E.	Deborah leads the Israelites to defeat the Canaanite king Jabin.
c. 10th century B.C.E.	Queen of Sheba legends arise.
c. 800 B.C.E.	Queens Jezebel and Athaliah establish worship of the mother goddess Asherah in Israel and Judah, but they are eventually defeated by followers of the male god Yahweh.
c. 800 B.C.E.	Hebrews compose the "second" creation story that presents Eve as weak and sinful.
c. 712 B.C.E.	Japan's *Kojiki*, a historical record, presents the Shinto deity Amaterasu as ruler of the heavens.
c. 700 B.C.E.	Egyptian men who divorce their wives are required to give them money, except when the wife is unfaithful.
c. 700 B.C.E.	The "standard" version of the Gilgamesh epic converts the Mesopotamian goddess into a weak and fickle "goddess of love."
c. 600 B.C.E.	Sappho of Lesbos, a female Greek poet, writes lyric poems about erotic love between women.
c. 509 B.C.E.	Lucretia, a chaste Roman woman, is said to have committed suicide after being raped by the son of king Tarquin.
c. 440 B.C.E.	The legendary Esther, Hebrew wife of the Persian king, is said to have saved her people from the evil plans of Haman.
c. 400 B.C.E.	The Greek physician Hippocrates proposes theories about women's physiology and diseases that influence medicine until the eighteenth century.

c. 380 B.C.E.	Axiothea and Lastheneia are students of the Greek philosopher Plato, at a time in which women are usually not allowed to study philosophy.
c. 350 B.C.E.	Greek sculptor Praxitiles creates a nude statue of Aphrodite, considered the first nude female statute in Greece.
330 B.C.E.	Athenian female physician Agnodike successfully challenges a law that had forbidden women to practice medicine.
270 B.C.E.	After the death of Arsinoe II Philadelphus, the strong Egyptian queen of the Potlemaic dynasty, a shrine is built in her honor and many cities are named for her.
204 B.C.E.	Romans celebrate arrival of the black stone of the mother goddess Cybele.
c. 195 B.C.E.	Chinese Empress Lu Zhi, following the death of Liu Bang (the emperor Gaozu), ruthlessly eliminates her rivals and rules effectively.
195 B.C.E.	Rome's short-lived Oppian Law forbids women from wearing jewelry and openly displaying wealth.
165 B.C.E.	Rome's Voconian Law prohibits fathers and husbands from making women their heirs.
c. 100 B.C.E.	Roman midwife Metrodora writes a book about the practice of midwifery.
30 B.C.E.	Queen Cleopatra VII of Egypt dies, probably by suicide.
18 B.C.E.	A Roman law (*lex Julia*) penalizes women who do not marry and have children.
2 B.C.E.	Julia, daughter of Roman emperor Augustus, is exiled as punishment for adultery.
1st century C.E.	Ban Zhao, the first know woman historian, writes the *Han Shu*, a respected history of the Han dynasty of China.
40-43 C.E.	Trung sisters lead Vietnamese rebellion against Chinese.
60 C.E.	Warrior queen Boudicca, wife of a Celtic king, leads a revolt against Roman rule.
88 C.E.	Dou Xian, dowager empress of the Eastern Han Dynasty, begins her nine-year reign.
c. 180 C.E.	Priscilla and Maximilla help found Montanism, a non-orthodox version of Christianity.
235 C.E.	Julia Mamaea, regent for the young emperor Alexander Severus, is defeated militarily in Persia, for which she is executed by the soldiers.
c. 320 C.E.	Zhong Lingyi becomes the first Chinese Buddhist nun.
324 C.E.	Helena, mother of Constantine, makes a pilgrimage to Palestine, where she establishes several Christian churches.
415 C.E.	Mathematician and philosopher Hypatia is killed in Alexandria.
c. 450 C.E.	Greek-speaking Christian churches are ordaining women, whose public roles are increasingly being restricted.

—Thomas Tandy Lewis

GLOSSARY

Although most of the unfamiliar and foreign words are explained within the text of this encyclopedia, this glossary serves to highlight some of the more important terms.

Advaita (Hinduism): literally, "without a second"; nondualism; the view that the only reality is *brahman*, the primary origin and essence of all things, and that the multiplicity of the universe as it is perceived is the result of illusion and ignorance

ahaus (Maya): divine lords and ladies of the Classic period Maya Royal Dynasty

ahiṁsā (Hinduism/Jainism): principle of nonviolence, with the corollary practice of compassion for all living beings

Ahura Mazda (Persia): supreme god of Zoroastrianism; subordinate to him are all Ahuras (responsible for the creation of all that is good in this world) and the Daivas (demons)

akam (Tamil): genre in Caṅkam literature consisting of poems that describe inner and personal human experiences such as love and its emotional phases

Amaterasu (Japan, Shintō): Sun goddess who, upset by her brother's actions, retreated into a cave and had to be coaxed out by the other gods

Amen (Egypt): also Amen-Ra, Sun god worshiped by Egyptians

anātman (Hinduism): the idea that there is no real self (personality or soul) that exists, that there is only the ultimate reality or "true suchness" of being

anekāntvādis (Jainism): limitations of human perception, illustrated by the blind men whose perceptions of the elephant are all different

Apedemak (Africa): Nubian war god most often represented with the head of a lion and a human body, although sometimes with the body of a serpent

apirigraham (Jainism): the principle that greed and the desire for material possessions entangles and limits humans; the absence of such a desire frees humans not only in this world but also from the endless cycle of birth, suffering, and death

Apollo (Greece): god known for healing, purification, prophecy, care for the young, poetry, and music; portrayed as a young, handsome athletic man; many cults arose around him

archon (Greece, Athens): civilian head of state in sixth century B.C.E. Athens

Aristotle's Lyceum: Athenian school founded by the philosopher Aristotle

Artemis (Greece): goddess of the hunt and women's rites of passage (as from virginity into womanhood); many cults arose around her

asceticism: a simple way of life, usually involving self-denial, that is often followed by religious figures who renounce materialism and sensualism to pursue a higher level of spirituality

Asclepius (Greece): god of healing, often depicted as a mature, bearded man holding a staff with a snake coiled around it

Ashur (Assyria): god who ruled and controlled the land of Assyria and had supreme power over other deities, including Ishtar (goddess of love and war), Ninurta (warfare and hunting), Shamash (Sun), Adad (storm), and Sin (Moon)

Athena (Greece): goddess of war and crafts, known for patronage of crafts including carpentry and metalworking as well as for helping heros

atlatl: spear thrower; implement that can enable a hunter to throw a projectile with up to 150 times the force of a hand-thrown spear

ātman (Hinduism): the transpersonal aspect of the self, a person's spiritual component

Attic orators: ten Athenian orators given status of classics by the second century C.E.: Lysias, Isaeus, Hyperides, Isocrates, Dinarchus, Aeschines, Antiphon, Lycurgus, Andocides, and Demosthenes

Aton (Egypt): "solar disk"; Sun god, object of worship by Egyptian pharaoh Akhenaton

augusta (Rome): title used to describe the wife of the Roman emperor

augustus (Rome): title given to Roman emperors; used to denote the higher position in the tetrarchy established by Diocletian

avatar (Hinduism): incarnation of a deity, often Viṣṇu

avidyā (Hinduism): ignorance

Āyurveda (India): the science of longevity, a kind of alternative medicine

bas-relief: sculptural relief; the raised part of the sculpture is shallow, without undercutting

bhakti (Tamil): genre in Caṅkam literature consisting of devotional poems

biface: a stone tool having two faces

bishop of Rome: head of the Catholic Church; also pope

bodhi (Buddhism): wisdom

Bodhi tree (Buddhism): tree under which the historical Buddha reached enlightenment

bodhisattva (Mahāyāna Buddhism): "enlightened being"; individual who has achieved enlightenment but delays passing over into nirvana in order to help with the salvation of others

boustrophedon: a writing technique in which alternate lines are written in different directions

Brahmā (Hinduism): "the creator"; deity in Hinduism regarded as the supreme being, the source of all reality

brahman (Hinduism): the primary origin and essence of all things

Brahman: priestly caste, the most favored of the four main hereditary groupings of people within India's traditional caste system

Bronze Age: period between 4000 and 3000 B.C.E. and the start of the Iron Age in which human cultures used bronze for tools and other objects

Buddha (Buddhism): "enlightened one"; name for Indian prince Siddhārtha Gautama after he gained enlightenment

Caesar (Rome): title given to Roman emperors, used during the tetrarchy established by Diocletian to denote a position lower than that of Augustus

camelid (Andes): *Camelidae*, family of animals including alpacas, llamas, vicunas, and guanaco, often used as pack animals

castes: hereditary groupings of people by social status and rank

celadon: greenish ceramic glaze, originated in China; also a name for pottery bearing this glaze

censor (Rome): Republic official responsible for citizen and senate rolls

Chan Buddhism: also Zen Buddhism; form of Buddhism in which meditation is used to reach spiritual enlightenment

church: building in which worship (usually Christian) takes place

city-state (Greece): an independent state consisting of a city and its environs

coloniae (Rome): colonies of the Roman Empire

concubine: mistress, woman included in household who performs many functions of a wife but has lower status than a spouse

consul (Rome): the Republic's highest office; position was reduced in power after Rome became an empire

cremation: the burning of a body after death

cultigen: cultivated or domesticated version of an unknown wild plant

cuneiform: rigid and angular wedge-shaped characters or the script that was produced using them

Dao (Daoism): literally "road" or "way"; the source and principle of everything in the universe, which cannot be defined in a positive manner as it is not anything concrete, tangible, or fixed, although it is at work in everything

deme (Greece): local territorial district, unit of government in Attica

democracy: a government ruled by the people, usually through majority rule

dendrochronology: a method of dating artifacts by studying tree ring growth in wood samples

despotism: rule by a despot, or autocrat; a ruler with absolute power

dharma (Buddhism): also dhamma; divine law; the teachings of the Buddha, the truth, ultimate reality, the moral law or the right way

dharma (Hinduism): law of the universe, to be followed by those wishing to fulfill their duties

-di (China): suffix meaning emperor

Dionysus (Greece, Rome): Roman name Bacchus; god of wine and intoxication, also ritual madness, ecstasy, the mask (theater), realm of the dead; object of many cults

dithyramb (Greece, Athens): song sung by a chorus to honor Dionysus; performed in contests at festivals such as the City Dionysia

dolmen: monument consisting of two or more upright stones holding up a horizontal slab; thought to be tombs or burial sites

earthenware: pottery; low-fired wares, relatively soft and porous, suitable for funerary vessels and tomb sculptures

Eightfold Path (Buddhism): the path to nirvana, consisting of right views, right resolve, right speech, right action, right work, right effort, right mindfulness, and right concentration

enlightenment (Buddhism): also nirvana, *satori*, a state of freedom from desire and suffering

epinician ode (Greece, Athens): *epinikia*; victory odes, choral songs usually performed after an athlete's victory, either at the festival or upon his return home

equites (Rome): equestrian class, positioned between the senate and citizens in the Republic, they filled bureaucratic posts in the empire

Eros (Greece): god of love; depicted as a young, beautiful man; numerous cults arose around him

eunuch: castrated man, often employed around women in a palace

fauna: animals characteristic of a period or region

fluting: the removal of large flakes with stone implements

foederati (Rome): allies of Rome whose relationship was established through treaty

Four Noble Truths (Buddhism): first truth is that life is suffering, which continues through an endless chain of rebirths; second, that suffering is caused by desire; third, that desire can be ended; fourth, that right living according to Buddhist precepts (the Eightfold Path) is the way to end desire and enter nirvana

frieze: a highly ornamented or sculpted band, usually on a structure or furnishings

fu (China): form of poetry that mixes prose with verse

gens (Rome): clan, a group of families that share a name and a male ancestor

geoglyphs (Andes, Nasca culture): large-scale line drawings of birds, monkeys, spiders, and plants, scratched into the surface of the earth and visible only from the sky

haniwa (Japan): unglazed terra-cotta cylinders and figurines placed on burial mounds during the Kofun period; their significance is unknown

harmost (Greece, Sparta): title of Spartan garrison commanders or military governors when abroad

helots (Greece, Sparta): *heilōtai*, state-owned serfs; believed to have a status between free men and slaves

henotheism: the worship of a single god while acknowledging the existence of other gods

heresy: religious teaching or belief deemed contrary to accepted dogma of the faith

hieroglyphs (Egypt): "sacred inscriptions"; Egyptian hieroglyphs contained three types of signs: pictograms, phonograms, and determinatives, clarifying symbols that indicated the category of ideas pictured; also used to describe scripts that use mostly pictorial characters

Hīnayāna Buddhism: "the lesser vehicle", also known as Theravāda; a form of Buddhism in which each individual must achieve enlightenment and salvation by his or her own efforts

hoplites: heavily armored infantrymen

Ionic column (Greece): column produced by ancient Greek architectural order in Ionia; designed as a fluted column with scroll-like ornamentation at its top

iconography: traditional symbols or pictures associated with a religious or legendary subject; also pictorial material illustrating a subject

ideograms: pictures or symbols used in a writing script to represent a concept or object but not the word used for that concept or object

imperator (Rome): originally an honor given to a victorious general during the Roman Republic; title presented to the head of the Roman Empire

inhumation: burial of the deceased in the ground

Iron Age: historical period beginning around 1000 B.C.E. in western Asia and Egypt in which people smelted iron and used it in industry; followed Bronze Age

Isis (Egypt): goddess who was the exemplary wife and mother, the healer, the bestower of fertility and prosperity, the patroness of the dead, and the great magician; a large cult developed around her and spread to Greece and Rome

jātakas (Buddhism): birth stories of the past lives of the Buddha

juzi (China): a leader of a Mohist group

kāma (Hinduism): desire

kami (Japanese): god, as well as gods in the traditional sense, includes local spirits, half-human, half-devine heros and heroines, forces in natural phenomena such as thunder

karma (Hinduism, Buddhism): the concept that all actions produce consequences and that the way a person leads his or her life determines the individual's chance for deliverance through reincarnation

Kṣatriya (India): caste of nobles and warriors (administrators), the second-ranked caste in the four main hereditary groupings of people within India's traditional caste system

knapping: shaping of fluted points

kofun (Japan): keyhole-shaped tomb mounds constructed for the local elite

lithic technology: stone tool technology

logogram: letters, sign, or symbols representing an entire word

Mahāyāna Buddhism: "the great vehicle"; a form of Buddhism in which individuals can reach enlightenment through the assistance of bodhisattvas, individuals who have achieved enlightenment but delay passing over into nirvana in order to help with the salvation of others

mandate of heaven (China): authorization by heaven to rule, could be taken away if the emperor did not act properly

mastaba (Egypt): tomb structure that predated the pyramids, consisted of oblong structure with sloping sides and a flat roof

māyā (Hinduism): illusion

megafauna: fauna (animals) large enough to be visible to the naked eye

megaliths: large stones used in massive prehistoric structures

menhir: a single standing stone monolith

microlith: tiny blade tool, sometimes triangular, often set into a bone or wooden haft

Middle Way (Buddhism): spiritual journey, neither ascetic nor self-indulgent, to achieving nirvana, a state of liberation, peace, and joy

mokṣa (Jainism): enlightenment, liberation from the cycle of rebirth, suffering, and death

monarchy: absolute rule by a single individual

monasticism: a way of life that involves seclusion or asceticism in a monastery

monoliths: single great stones often in the shape of columns or obelisks

monotheism: worship of a single god, admitting of no other gods

municipia (Rome): towns incorporated into the city of Rome, with their inhabitants becoming citizens of Rome

necropolis: literally "city of the dead"; expansive and elaborate ancient cemetery

Neolithic Age: late Stone Age, historical period of time in which people used polished stone implements

New Comedy (Greece, Athens; Rome): comic plays or poems using situation comedy; many examine relationships, love, and family life

nirvana (Buddhism): a state in which a person is freed from all desires and attachments, a state of release from existence

nomes: (Egypt) administrative or geographical unit of area

Old Comedy (Greece, Athens): carnivalesque form of poetry/drama that made fun of topical people, institutions, and issues; its origins were in rituals of fertility and verbal abuse and its defining features were

grotesque costumes, obscene language, and fantastic plots

oligarchy: rule by a small group, often for selfish or corrupt purposes

Panchamas (India): Untouchables, who were without inherited status or caste

papyrus: writing material made from the pith of the papyrus plant, a tall sedge

pater patriae (Rome): "father of the country"; prestigious title given to some emperors

patriarch (Christianity): bishops in the church who headed the most important sees or areas and therefore had special rights and powers

patricians (Rome): *Patricii*; noble class of Rome, highest strata in the Republic

Pax Romana (Rome): period of peace within the Roman Empire beginning after Augustus claimed victory at the Battle of Actium (31 C.E.)

phalanx (Greece): body of heavily armed infantry in close formations

pharaoh (Egypt): ruler of ancient Egypt

phonograms: characters used to represent phonetic elements, syllables, or words

pictograms: drawings or pictures used to represent words or parts of words

Plato's Academy: school of philosophy established by Plato and located in Athens

plebeians (Rome): plebs; general population of Rome, apart from the elites

polis, poleis (plural): city

polytheism: worship of more than one god

pontifex maximus (Rome): chief priest, head of Rome's state religion and all its establishments

pope: head of the Catholic Church; also bishop of Rome

porcelain: high-fired wares (pottery), which are relatively hard, durable, and impervious to water, suitable for everyday use

praetor (Rome): title used first for a consul, then a magistrate dealing with justice in Rome

Praetorian Guard (Rome): elite guard force of the Roman Empire created by Augustus

prefect of the Praetorian Guard (Rome): commander of the Praetorian Guard; the post gradually grew in power during the Roman Empire

princeps (Rome): "first man in the state"; unofficial honorary title given during the Republic

proconsul (Rome): governor of a province serving in place of a consul during the Roman Republic; governor of a senatorial province during the Roman Empire

projectile points (Americas): arrowheads; stone points fastened to the end of projectiles (weapons)

puram (Tamil): genre in Caṅkam literature consisting of poems that extol the virtues of heroism

quaestor (Rome): lowest-ranked magistrate, often associated with finances

quern: a handmill used to grind grain

radiocarbon dating: a method of dating artifacts that measures the amount of the radioactive isotope of carbon (C-14) in organic material

reincarnation (Hinduism, Buddhism, Jainism): rebirth of a person into another life (body) after death; part of the cycle of death and rebirth

relic: object (sometimes a bone) venerated or held in high regard because of its association with a religious figure

saint (Christian): a holy person, living or dead

samsāra (Hinduism, Buddhism): the world in which the cycle of birth and rebirth continually repeats itself; reincarnation

Saṅgha (Buddhism): community of monks, nuns, and lay people

satrap (Persia): provincial governor in ancient Persia

satya (Jainism): a renunciation of secular life

schism: a break between subgroups within a religious body

shaman: high priest or priestess, uses magic or rituals to heal people, predict the future, and control events (rain)

Shamash (Aramea, Babylonia, Sumer): also Samash; Sun god

shrine: place hallowed by its religious associations, often where a deity or religious figure is worshiped

Śiva (Hinduism): "the destroyer"; deity associated with cosmic change

socii (Rome): allies of Rome

sophists (Greece): itinerant teachers giving lectures throughout Greece

stela: stelae (plural); stone slab or pillar, usually with commemorative inscription

Stone Age: historical period preceding the Bronze Age; distinguished by peoples' use of tools and weapons made of stone

stratum: stratum (plural); a chronologically distinct layer, typically in an archaeological dig

stratēgos (Greece): military commander or general; in fifth century C.E. Athens, they also had political importance

stupa (Buddhism): structure, usually in the shape of a dome, often containing a relic

Śūdras (India): caste of peasants, the fourth-ranked caste in the four main hereditary groupings of people within India's traditional caste system

śūnyatā (Buddhism): emptiness, which is without origin or decay and beyond all description and is pure consciousness and the essence of phenomena

sutra (Buddhism, Hinduism): Sanskrit, also *sutta*; a precept or aphorism; in Buddhism, a discourse of the Buddha

swidden: agricultural field created by cutting and burning the vegetation covering the area

tell: archaeological site

temple: building in which religious exercises take place, usually not Christian

tennō (Japan): emperor or empress

terra-cotta: glazed or unglazed fired clay

tetrarchy (Rome): system of collegiate government created by Diocletian in which two Augusti shared power with two junior Caesars

Three Jewels (Buddhism): the first was the Buddha; the second, the dharma; the third, the Saṅgha (community of monks)

Three Jewels (Jainism): *ratna traya*; three religious practices of right perception (*samyagdarśana*), right knowledge (*samyagjñāna*), and right conduct (*samyagcāritra*)

threnoi (Greece): songs of lament for deceased men

torii (Japan): sacred gateway to a shrine

totem: plant or animal that represents a clan or family

trireme: galley (ship) with three banks of oars

tumulus: burial mound

tyrannicides (Greece): killers of tyrants; often used to refer to those who killed Julius Caesar and Hipparchus of Athens

tyranny (Greece): monarchy set up by those who seized power (usually fringe member of the ruling aristocracy) in the city-states of seventh-sixth century B.C.E.

Vaiśya (India): caste of farmers and merchant, the third-ranked caste in the four main hereditary groupings of people within India's traditional caste system

vegeculture: the cultivation of multiple species within a single field

vinaya (Buddhism): rules for monastic discipline

Viṣṇu (Hinduism): also Vishnu; "the preserver"; deity who personifies eternal, unchanging qualities

viziers (Egypt): king's highest officials, acted as judges and collected taxes

wang (China): king

wu wei (Daoism): the principle of noncontention; to be waterlike, to follow the flow of nature and not to oppose it, to be flexible and yet to accomplish one's goals

yin and yang (Chinese): two forces, one passive and negative (yin), and the other active and positive (yang), that are to be balanced in life

yoga (Hinduism): mental and spiritual exercises designed to enable a person to reach spiritual enlightenment

Yogācara (Buddhism): a form of Buddhism that involves metaphysical idealism and meditation and stresses that only thought exists and that the external world is an illusion; the only reality is *śūnyatā*, or emptiness

Zeus (Greece): primary god of the Greek pantheon; father of the gods who rules from Mount Olympus

ziggurat: Mesopotamian temple tower, built in pyramid form with a shrine at the top

BIBLIOGRAPHY

This bibliography of secondary sources is directed toward the general reader, high school student, and undergraduate student. It contains books that are general histories or that focus on some aspect of history and cover more than one geographic or cultural area; books on women of the ancient world, and books that focus on specific geographic and cultural areas: the Americas; Asia Minor; China, Japan, and Korea; Egypt and North Africa; Britain, Ireland, and Prehistoric Europe; Greece; India; Mesopotamia, Persia, and the Ancient Middle East; Oceania; and the Roman Empire. No primary sources have been included, and all entries are in English. The time period represented in the bibliography is from prehistory to the Fall of Rome in 476 C.E.

GENERAL TOPICS

Dalby, Andrew. *Food in the Ancient World, A-Z.* New York: Routledge, 2003. Dalby examines food and related concepts in ancient Greece and Rome. Entries range from several lines to several pages and cover specific food items, ancient culinary writers, and archaeological approaches to the question of what the Greeks and Romans ate.

Gebauer, Anne Birgitte, and T. Douglas Price, eds. *Transitions to Agriculture in Prehistory: Monographs in World Archaeology.* No. 4. Madison, Wis.: Prehistory Press, 1992. Work consists of eleven scholarly papers on the prehistoric transitions to agriculture presented at the 1991 meeting of the Society of American Anthropology. Papers discuss the major theories about the adoption of food production by human groups. Regions addressed in the papers are the Mediterranean Levant, Japan, Mexico, American Southwest, Eastern Sahara, Western and Northern Europe. Includes site maps and graphs.

Maisels, Charles Keith. *Early Civilizations of the Old World: The Formative Histories of Egypt, the Levant, Mesopotamia, India, and China.* New York: Routledge, 1999. Traces the structural development of early civilizations through economic, ecological, geological, cultural, and social interactions. Maisels surmises that complex societies can exist without class structure and the state. He also employs Hughsey Childe's urban revolution theory in his analyses. Includes glossary of terms.

Raaflaub, Kurt, and Nathan Rosenstein. *War and Society in the Ancient and Medieval Worlds: Asia, the Mediterranean, Europe, and Mesoamerica.* Washington, D.C.: Center for Hellenic Studies; Cambridge, Mass.: Harvard University Press, 1999. A collection of thirteen papers presented at Harvard's Center for Hellenic Studies in June, 1996, that presents a comparative social history of war and military organization from the third millennium B.C.E. to the tenth century C.E. Includes maps.

Saggs, H. W. F. *Civilization Before Greece and Rome.* New Haven, Conn.: Yale University Press, 1989. Explores the following ancient civilizations and peoples: Egypt, Mesopotamia, Crete, Indus Valley, Hittites, Hurrians, Canaanites, Phoenicians, Aramaeans, and Arabs. Topics include city-states and kingdoms, pyramids and ziggurats, education, city life, trade, law, national alliances, natural resources, mathematics and astronomy, medicine, and ancient religion. Includes list of illustrations, chronological chart, index of biblical references, and a select bibliography

Starr, Chester. *A History of the Ancient World.* 4th ed. New York: Oxford University Press, 1991. Starr's history begins with early man and finishes with the decline of the Roman Empire. Areas covered include Greece, Rome, Mesopotamia, India, and China. Illustrated.

Yoffee, Norman, and George L. Cowgill. *The Collapse of Ancient States and Civilizations.* Tucson: University of Arizona Press, 1988. Work is based on seminar sessions at the School of American Research in Santa Fe, New Mexico, in 1982. Explores socio-political, economic, military, and cultural reasons why certain civilizations collapsed over a period of centuries. Civilizations discussed are Mesopotamia, Maya, Teotihuacán, Roman Empire, and the Han Dynasty in China. Role of barbarian invaders is also addressed in the book.

AMERICAS

Blanton, Richard E., ed. *Ancient Mesoamerica: A Comparison of Change in Three Regions.* 2d ed. Cambridge, England: Cambridge University Press, 1993. Addresses human behavior and cultural evolution in pre-Hispanic societies of ancient Mesoamerica over a period of ten thousand years. This work updates developments and findings in the field since the first edition was published in 1981. Includes detailed maps of settlements and bibliography.

Cordell, Linda S., and George J. Gumerman, eds. *Dynamics of Southwest Prehistory.* Washington, D.C.: Smithsonian Institution Press, 1989. Compilation of papers presented at a seminar for the School of American Research in Santa Fe, New Mexico, six years earlier. Groups addressed in the papers are the Hohokam, Mogollon, Anasazi, and Sinagua.

Ericson, Jonathon E., and Timothy G. Baugh, eds. *The American Southwest and Mesoamerica: Systems of Prehistoric Exchange.* New York: Plenum Press, 1993. Addresses North American socio-political trade or exchange economies from the Archaic through the Late Prehistoric periods. Commodities such as marine shells, turquoise, and pottery are topics of discussion.

Folan, William J., ed. *Contributions to the Archaeology and Ethnohistory of Greater Mesoamerica.* Carbondale: Southern Illinois University Press, 1985. A collection of papers presented at a conference in honor of Carroll L. Riley, a preeminent researcher in the field. These papers apply prehistoric, ethnohistoric, and ethnographic data in order to analyze ancient peoples in Mesoamerica and the American Southwest, particularly with settlement patterns.

Hassig, Ross. *War and Society in Ancient MesoAmerica.* Berkeley: University of California Press, 1992. Discusses how warfare shaped the socio-cultural history of Mesoamerican peoples from 2500 to 400 B.C.E. Major articles and books from 1961 to 1990 are cited in the reference section. Sixteen pages of black-and-white photographic plates.

ASIA MINOR

Canby, Jeanny Vorys, Edith Paroda, Brunilde Sismondo Ridgway, et al., eds. *Ancient Anatolia: Aspects of Change and Cultural Development, Essays in Honor of Machteld J. Mellink.* Madison: University of Wisconsin Press, 1986. Collection of papers in honor of Mellink, a renowned archaeologist from Bryn Mawr College. Work updates archaeological research conducted in Asia Minor at various sites on food production and iconographical and ethnic questions. Includes photographs of artifacts and a bibliography of major articles and books written on the subject from 1943 to 1984.

Kondoleon, Christine, ed. *Antioch: The Lost Ancient City.* Princeton, N.J.: Princeton University Press, 2000. Ten essays by scholars regarding the ancient city of Antioch in Turkey near the Mediterranean Sea. Published in conjunction with an exhibition of items in the Worcester Art Museum in Massachusetts. Color photographic plates of maps, artwork, and artifacts are used throughout the work.

Ma, John. *Antiochus III and the Cities of Western Asia Minor.* New York: Oxford University Press, 1999. Addresses the relationship between the Hellenistic empire and the structures of control for the polis in Asia Minor. Focuses on epigraphical material and historiographical approaches in the analysis. Includes two regional maps and an extensive bibliography.

Mitchell, Stephen. *Anatolia: Land, Men, and Gods in Asia Minor.* 2 vols. Oxford, England: Clarendon Press, 1993. Comprehensive study of the history of Asia Minor from Alexander the Great to the Byzantine Empire. Part 1 examines Celtic tribes that settled into this area during the Hellenistic period. Part 2 addresses how Roman imperial rule changed this region. Includes a list of figures and a list of maps in each volume.

BRITAIN, IRELAND, AND PREHISTORIC EUROPE

Cunliffe, Barry. *The Oxford Illustrated Prehistory of Europe.* Oxford, England: Oxford University Press, 1994. Consists of thirteen scholarly essays on the social, political, and economic development of Europe from 700,000 B.C.E.-700 C.E. Authors emphasize that local networks of interaction and exchange allowed European communities to expand. Includes maps, color plates, and illustrations of artifacts.

Freeman, Philip. *Ireland and the Classical World.* Austin: University of Texas Press, 2001. Interdisciplinary study of the relationship between Ireland and Mediterranean civilizations using archaeological finds as well as literary evidence in Greek and Latin texts. Includes three appendices: Greek Alphabet, Classical References to Scotland, and Names of Ireland.

Green, Miranda J., ed. *The Celtic World.* New York: Routledge, 1995. A collection of papers by scholars addressing social, political, economic, religious, and military topics of Celtic history from ancient times to 1000 C.E. Maps, photographs, and illustrations are included.

Salway, Peter. *The Oxford Illustrated History of Roman Britain.* Oxford, England: Oxford University Press, 1993. Provides an overview of the relationship between Roman-occupied Britain from the first to the fifth century C.E. Explains how Roman occupation shaped the island's history in political and economic thought. Includes thirty-four color plates and ten maps.

Snyder, Christopher A. *An Age of Tyrants: Britain and the Britons,* A.D. *400-600.* University Park: Pennsylvania State University Press, 1998. Synder explores the history of sub-Roman Britain from archeological and literary perspectives. He contends that Britain developed unique social, political, and religious institutions, resulting in a hybrid of Celtic, Roman, and Christian elements. Includes maps, black-and-white photographs, and an extensive bibliography.

Thomas, Charles. *Christianity in Roman Britain to* A.D. *500.* Berkeley: University of California Press, 1981. Asserts that Christianity maintained a consistency in Britain for three hundred years, c. 300-500 C.E. The Christian element even survived the Saxon conquests in the early fifth century, and the faith continued to spread into Scotland and Ireland. Includes illustrations, maps, and an extensive bibliography.

CHINA, JAPAN, AND KOREA

Cook, Constance A., and John S. Major. *Defining Chu: Image and Reality in Ancient China.* Honolulu: University of Hawaii Press, 1999. Addresses the sociopolitical, religious, and military aspects of the Chu culture in southern China from the eighth through the third centuries B.C.E. A major part of the work explains why this culture did not survive. Includes color photographs of artifacts.

Farris, William Wayne. *Sacred Texts and Buried Treasures: Issues in the Historical Archaeology of Ancient Japan.* Honolulu: University of Hawaii Press, 1998. Using recent archaeological discoveries, Farris renews debate in the lost location of Yamatai, ancient Japan's relations with Korea, its creation of Chinese-style capitals, and government organization. Includes Japanese character list and an extensive bibliography.

Gernet, Jacques. *Ancient China: From the Beginnings to the Empire.* Berkeley: University of California Press, 1968. Covers ancient China from prehistory to the beginnings of the unified empire in 221 B.C.E. Chapters examine the prehistory and origins of Chinese civilization, the archaic period, the Shang and Western Zhou, the Warring States Period, and the empire. Includes short bibliography of sources.

Kim, Yung-Chung, ed. *Women of Korea: A History from Ancient Times to 1945.* 2d ed. Seoul, Korea: Ewah Womans University Press, 1979. Analyzes the status, role, and activities of Korean women from a historical perspective. Parts 1 and 2 of the work focus on the ancient period.

Maspero, Henri. *China in Antiquity.* Rev. ed. Boston: University of Massachusetts Press, 1978. Work is a history of China before the ninth century C.E. divided into five sections. Book 1 addresses the Yin Dynasty and Zhou Empire; book 2 addresses social and religious life; book 3 address the hegemonies under Qi, Jin, and Wu; Book 4 addresses the warring kingdoms; and book 5 addresses ancient literature and philosophy. Includes extensive end notes and a bibliography of writings by Henri Maspero.

EGYPT AND NORTH AFRICA

Burnstein, Stanley Mayer. *Ancient African Civilizations: Kush and Axum.* Princeton, N.J.: Markus Wiener, 1998. Kush and Aksum were highly developed ancient civilizations south of Egypt in the Nile Valley from 300 B.C.E. to 300 C.E. Discusses the gold mines of Nubia, the Hellenistic city of Meroë, and the capital of the Ethiopian empire of Kush. Includes a select bibliography of sources.

_____. *Graeco-Africana: Studies in the History of Greek Relations with Egypt and Nubia.* New Rochelle, N.Y.: A. D. Caratzas, 1995. Discusses the relations between the Greeks and the ancient northeast civilizations of Africa, Egypt, and Nubia. Includes chapters on the birth of Greek Egyptology, the organization of the Nubian slave trade, Aksum, and the fall of Meroë.

Hodel-Hoenes, Sigrid. *Life and Death in Ancient Egypt: Scenes from Private Tombs in New Kingdoms Thebes.* Ithaca, N.Y.: Cornell University Press, 2000. Intended to provide information about Theban private tombs during the New Kingdom period to the general reader. Tombs addressed in chapters are Nakht, Ramose, Userhat, Menna, Sennefer, Rekhmire, Neferhotep, Kheruef, Samut, Deir el-Medineh, Sennedjem, and Inher-kha. Includes a select bibliography, chronological table, maps, color plates, and illustrations.

O'Connor, David B. *Ancient Nubia: Egypt's Rival in Africa.* Philadelphia: University of Pennsylvania, 1993. Work is based on an exhibit of Nubian artifacts at the University Museum of Archaeology and Anthropology at the University of Pennsylvania. Provides general overview of Nubian history in ancient times. Book contains illustrative drawings of Nubian buildings, cemeteries, and maps. Thirty-five color plates of Nubian objects are also featured in the book.

Redford, Donald B. *Egypt, Canaan, and Israel in Ancient Times.* Princeton, N.J.: Princeton University Press, 1993. Presents an overview of the relationships between Egypt and Western Asia from the Paleolithic period to the destruction of Jerusalem in 586 B.C.E. Includes maps of regions and tables chronicling various dynasties.

Robins, Gay. *Women in Ancient Egypt.* Cambridge, Mass.: Harvard University Press, 1993. Depicts the role of women in Egyptian society. Its ten chapters examine royal women; queens and the assumption of kingship; marriage; fertility, pregnancy, and childbirth; the family; women outside the home; the economic and legal position of women; women and temple ritual; religion and death; and women in literature and art. Includes illustrations.

Shaw, Ian, ed. *The Oxford History of Ancient Egypt.* Oxford, England: Oxford University Press, 2000. Overview of the emergence and development of the ancient Egyptian civilization from its prehistoric origins to its domination by the Roman Empire. Chapters are divided chronologically. Includes color photographs of artifacts, a glossary of terms, maps, and tables.

Wilkinson, Richard H. *The Complete Temples of Ancient Egypt.* New York: Thames & Hudson, 2000. Excellent reference book describing the construction, function, and symbolism of Egyptian temples. Includes reconstructive diagrams of temples, color maps, and 535 illustrations of ruins, 173 of which are in color. Book also contains a chronology of the temple builders with span dates.

GREECE

Adkins, Lesley, and Roy A. Adkins. *Handbook to Life in Ancient Greece.* New York: Facts on File, 1997. Presents information relating to Greek history from the Minoan period to the Roman conquest. Chapters are organized thematically: "Civilizations, City-states, and Empires," "Rulers and Leaders," "Military Affairs," "Geography of the Greek World," "Economy, Trade, and Transport," "Towns and Countryside," "Written Evidence," "Religion and Mythology," "Art, Science, and Philosophy," and "Everyday Life." Includes extensive bibliography and index.

Bremen, Riet van. *The Limits of Participation: Women and Civic Life in the Greek East in the Hellenistic and Roman Periods.* Amsterdam: J. C. Gieben, 1996. Chronicles why women became dominant in civic life and office in the Greek cities of Asia Minor during the late Hellenistic period. Part 1 of the work addresses the political, economic, and social changes that allowed women to enter public service. Part 2 looks at the financial and legal benefits for women benefactors.

Flensted-Jensen, Pernille, Thomas Heine Nielsen, and Lene Rubinstein, eds. *Polis and Politics: Studies in Ancient Greek History.* Copenhagen: University of Copenhagen Press, 2000. Papers presented in honor of Mogens Herman Hansen on his sixtieth birthday. Work is divided into two parts, part 1 addresses physical and community aspects of the polis, and part 2 delves into the ideological and practical politics of the polis.

Georges, Pericles. *Barbarian Asia and the Greek Experience: From the Archaic Period to the Age of Xenophon.* Baltimore, Md.: The Johns Hopkins University Press, 1994. Interprets Greek ideas and attitudes toward ancient peoples in Asia. Chapters titles are "Mythology and Representation: The Greek Appropriation of the Word," "Asia and the Image of Tyranny," "Tabula Rosa: The Invention of the Persia," "Aeschylus: The Human Fabric of Persae," "Herodotus' Typology of Hellenism," "Herodotus's Typology of Barbarism," and "Xenophon: The Satrap of Scillus." Extensive bibliography.

Martin, Thomas R. *Ancient Greece from Prehistoric to Hellenistic Times.* New Haven, Conn.: Yale University Press, 1996. Provides an overview of the history of ancient Greece from the prehistory of Europe to the end of the second century B.C.E. Chapters cover ancient Greek history; Mycenaeans; the dark age; the archaic age; oligarchy, tyranny, and democracy; the Persian Wars and the Athenian Empire; culture and society in ancient Athens; the Peloponnesian War; Alexander the Great; and the Hellenistic age. Includes a "Suggested Reading" section for each chapter.

Price, Simon. *Religions of the Ancient Greeks.* Cambridge, England: Cambridge University Press, 1999. Book delves into the religious and spiritual life of the Greeks from the eighth century B.C.E. to the fifth century C.E. Chapters cover gods, myths, and festivals; religious places; authority and control; youths and adults; elective cults; Greek thinkers; and reactions to Greek religions. Includes an excellent bibliography.

Rihll, T. E. *Greek Science.* Published for Classical Association. Oxford, England: Oxford University Press, 1999. For a general audience. Explains scientific developments in physics, mathematics, astronomy, geography, biology, and medicine. Includes six illustrations: Greek alphabetic numerals, Pythagoras's theorem, celestial north pole in 400 B.C.E., Aristarchus's proposition on the distance to the Sun from Earth, the Mediterranean Sea, and ancient whaling gear.

INDIA AND SOUTH ASIA

Chakrabarti, Dilip K. *The Archaeology of Ancient Indian Cities*. Delhi, India: Oxford University Press, 1995. Work delves into an evaluation of archeological data on the early urban history of India—protohistoric to 300 C.E. Chapters are divided by region and cities. Includes twenty-eight pages of maps (site and excavation plans).

Raychaudhuri, Hemchandra. *Political History of Ancient India: From the Accession of Parikshit to the Extinction of the Gupta Dynasty*. 3d ed. New York: Oxford University Press, 1996. Work addresses ancient India from the ninth century B.C.E. when Parikshit established a thriving kingdom to the end of the Gupta Dynasty. Book focuses on kingdoms and empires that proved to have lasting political effects in India's national development. Includes three foldout maps and a genealogical/synchronistic table.

Singh, Upinder. *Ancient Delhi*. New York: Oxford University Press, 1999. Explains history of ancient Delhi, India, and the surrounding areas of the Faridabad district of Haryana and the Ghaziabad district of Uttar Pradesh. Singh utilizes archaeological evidence and literary texts in his analysis. Includes maps, list of illustrations, and twelve color plates.

MESOPOTAMIA, PERSIA, AND THE ANCIENT MIDDLE EAST

Brosius, Maria. *Women in Ancient Persia, 559-331 B.C.* New York: Oxford University Press, 1996. Explains Greek attitudes toward royal women in the Achaemenid court from 559-331 B.C.E. Includes list of royal marriage alliances in appendix and an extensive bibliography. Work is based on Brosius's dissertation research.

Charvat, Petr. *Mesopotamia Before History*. Rev. ed. New York: Routledge, 2002. Interprets archaeological pilot sites found on the Mesopotamian alluvial plain during the Paleolithic, Mesolithic, Neolithic, and Chalcolithic eras. Work also addresses the rise of the Uruk civilization. Includes maps and illustrations of artifacts.

Dolukhanov, Pavel. *Environment and Ethnicity in the Ancient Middle East*. Worldwide Archaeology Series, Vol. 7. Great Britain: Athenaeum Press, 1994. Explores how societies developed in the Middle East during the Neolithic Revolution. Argues that unique landscape patterns, along with the predominant theory of ecological factors, helped settlement in the "cradle of civilization." Includes graphs, tables, and site maps.

Fraser, P. M. *Cities of Alexander the Great*. Oxford, England: Clarendon Press, 1996. Addresses cities founded by Alexander the Great, king of Macedonia, from 359-323 B.C.E. Maps of Iran, Central Asia, and Afghanistan are included. There is also an index of Greek and Latin authors mentioned in the book.

Maisels, Charles Keith. *The Emergence of Civilization: From Hunting to Gathering to Agriculture, Cities, and the State in the Near East*. New York: Routledge, 1990. Argues that scholarly assumptions about state formation in the Near East, based on nineteenth century scholarship, are incorrect. He analyzes this topic from a new anthropological perspective. Includes maps, charts, and tables. Colored map is featured on both end papers of the book. Extensive bibliography.

Shanks, Hershel, ed. *Ancient Israel: A Short History from Abraham to the Roman Destruction of the Temple*. Washington, D.C.: Biblical Archaeology Society, 1988. Compilation of eight scholarly articles regarding the history of ancient Israel from 70 C.E. to when the Romans burned Jerusalem. Chapters are divided chronologically: "The Patriarchal Age," "Israel in Egypt," "The Settlement in Canaan," "The United Monarchy," "The Divided Monarchy," "Exile and Return," "The Age of Hellenism," and "Roman Domination." Intended for the general reader. Includes list of illustrations, color plates, maps, and charts.

Silver, Morris. *Prophets and Markets: The Political Economy of Ancient Israel*. Boston: Kluwer-Nijhoff, 1983. Silver, a market-oriented economist, delves into the political economy of ancient Israel. He challenges the assumption that classical prophets were poor eccentrics; rather, he says, they were well-educated members of the established government who initiated social reforms and programs. Includes an extensive bibliography.

Soden, Wolfram von. *The Ancient Orient: An Introduction to the Study of the Ancient Near East*. Grand Rapids, Mich.: William B. Eerdmans, 1994. Soden, a renowned Assryriologist, presents a comprehensive overview of the ancient Mesopotamian civilization. Chapters include "The Term 'Ancient Orient' and its Demarcation," "The Scene," "Peoples and Cultures in the Ancient Orient," "Writing and Systems of Writing," "The History of Ancient Western Asia: The Historical Sources," "State and Society," "Nutrition and Agriculture," "Artisanry," "Trade and Commerce," "Law," "Sumerian and Babylonian Science," "Religion and Music," " Literature," "Building, Art, and Music," and "Concluding Observations and Remarks." Includes a select bibliography.

OCEANIA

Kirch, Patrick Vinton. *On the Road of the Winds: An Archaeological History of the Pacific Islands Before European Contact.* Berkeley: University of California Press, 2000. Using linguistic, ethnographic, and biological evidence from archeological excavations, the author traces the history of the Pacific Islands from their settlement to European conquest. Extensive bibliography. Includes list of maps, tables, and figures.

Lourandos, Harry. *Continent of Hunter-Gatherers: New Perspectives in Australian Prehistory.* Cambridge, England: Cambridge University Press, 1997. Author surmises that Australian Aboriginal prehistory is more complex than once thought by scholars. Lourandos challenges the idea that hunter-gatherer societies were egalitarian, and he believes that changes in the natural, economic, demographic, and natural environment were significant factors shaping the societies. Includes site maps and illustrations.

Mulvaney, John, and Johan Kamminga. *Prehistory of Australia.* Washington, D.C.: Smithsonian Institution Press, 1999. Comprehensive volume that explores 40,000 years of Australian Aboriginal cultures, languages, and practices. Authors use a chronological and regional approach to the subjects of colonization, extinction of marsupials, prehistoric rock art, tool-making, and ceremonies. Includes maps, illustrations, black-and-white photographs, and an extensive reference section.

Terrell, John. *Prehistory in the Pacific Islands: A Study of Variation in Language, Customs, and Human Biology.* Cambridge, England: Cambridge University Press, 1986. Author uses a thematic approach for each chapter: "Portraits of the Past," "Peopling the Islands," "Language Origins," "By Accident or Design?" "Life and Death," "Isolation," "Change and Adaptation," "Living Together," "Structure and Function," and "Science and Prehistory." Includes black-and-white photographs, illustrations, and settlement distribution plot maps. Excellent reference section.

White, J. Peter, and James F. O'Connell. *A Prehistory of Australia, New Guinea, and Sahul.* Sydney: Academic Press, 1982. Authors use a regional approach to discuss issues of society, settlement patterns, white contact, stone tools, and death. Includes large-scale maps and illustrations. Extensive reference section.

ROMAN EMPIRE

Allason-Jones, Lindsay. *Women in Roman Britain.* London: British Museum Publications, 1989. Examines social, political, economic, and military roles for women in Roman Britain. Chapters cover birth, marriage, and death; home life; women and the army; women in the countryside and in towns; fashion; religion; and entertainment and recreation. Includes sixty-eight black-and-white illustrations and a list of women mentioned in the text with brief descriptions of occupations.

Ando, Clifford. *Imperial Ideology and Provincial Loyalty in the Roman Empire.* Berkeley: University of California Press, 2000. Explores why the Roman Empire lasted for so many centuries. Ando argues that ideological, political, and administrative justification for Roman rule was just as important as Roman military might. Ideas by modern theorists such as Max Weber, Jürgen Habermas, and Pierre Bourdieu are used to support the argument.

Ball, Warwick. *Rome in the East: The Transformation of an Empire.* New York: Routledge, 2000. Overview of the economic, political, social history of the Roman Empire in the East from the conquest by Pompey the Great in 63 B.C.E. until its demise under Heraclius in 636 C.E. Focuses on Near Eastern kingdoms, cities, and towns. Includes photographs, illustrations, maps, bibliography, and index.

Casson, Lionel. *Everyday Life in Ancient Rome.* Rev. ed. Baltimore, Md.: The Johns Hopkins University Press, 1998. Addresses daily life at every social level—aristocrat, solider, engineer, and slave—in Roman society. Casson added two chapters for this edition.

Grandazzi, Alexandre. *The Foundation of Rome: Myth and Legend.* Ithaca, N.Y.: Cornell University Press, 1997. Author depicts historiographical and ideological accounts of Rome's origins. He focuses on nineteenth century philology and recent archaeological discoveries in the analysis of the birth of Rome. Includes chronologies and maps.

Habinek, Thomas, and Alessandro Schiesaro, eds. *The Roman Cultural Revolution.* New York: Cambridge University Press, 1997. A series of articles by scholars. States that the transformation for the Roman revolution was dependent on cultural changes as evidenced by literary and artistic works. Part 1 explains changes in the cultural systems of gender, sexuality, status, and space in the city of Rome. Part 2 analyzes specific texts and artifacts.

Huskinson, Janet, ed. *Experiencing Rome: Culture, Identity, and Power in the Roman Empire*. New York: Routledge, 2000. Twelve essays that explore these three topics during the first three hundred years of the Roman Empire. Preface includes sections on key dates, four maps, and a list of emperors with reign-span dates.

Jones, Michael E. *The End of Roman Britain*. Ithaca, N.Y.: Cornell University Press, 1996. Contends that the end of Roman Britain was caused by internal problems in the Romanization process that were linked to external economic, societal, and environmental factors. Extensive bibliography.

Kallet-Marx, Robert Morstein. *Hegemony to Empire: The Development of Roman Imperium from 148 to 62 B.C.* Berkeley: University of California Press, 1995. Author contends that the Roman evolution of power was a complex, adaptive, and integrative process in the Balkans, Greece, and Asia Minor. Excellent bibliography.

Kamoo, Ray. *Ancient and Modern Chaldean History: A Comprehensive Bibliography of Sources*. The ATLA Bibliography Series, No. 43. Lanham, Md.: Scarecrow Press, 1999. Bibliography of sources for Chaldean history—Aramaic speaking people in Mesopotamia. Part 1 addresses books and periodical literature on ancient Chaldean history; part 2 addresses books and periodical literature on modern Chaldean history; part 3 addresses dissertations, theses, and papers on the subject.

Lancon, Bertrand. *Rome in Late Antiquity: Everyday Life and Urban Change, A.D. 312-609*. New York: Routledge, 2001. Addresses the history of daily life in Rome from the third to the seventh centuries C.E. Book is divided into four major topics: the majesty of the Quirinal, plebs and patricians religion and religiousity, and worldly concerns. Includes illustrations and maps.

Laurence, Ray, and Joanne Berry, eds. *Cultural Identity in the Roman Empire*. New York: Routledge, 1998. A compilation of scholarly articles regarding cultural identity and acculturation in the Roman Empire presented at the Theoretical Roman Archaeology Conference of 1995. Includes illustrations and maps.

Leibeschuetz, J. H. W. G. *The Decline and Fall of the Roman City*. Oxford, England: Oxford University Press, 2001. Discusses de-urbanization in Roman cities from 400-650 C.E., administration, Christianization of education, and economic and social life. Includes list of illustrations and a list of maps and plans.

Potter, D. S., and D. J. Mattingly. *Life, Death, and Entertainment in the Roman Empire*. Ann Arbor: University of Michigan Press, 1999. A series of ten essays exploring Roman societal issues such as family structure, gender identity, food supply, religion, and entertainment. Includes an extensive bibliography.

Webster, Leslie, and Michelle Brown, eds. *The Transformation of the Roman World A.D. 400-900*. Berkeley: University of California Press, 1997. Features essays contributed by a team of distinguished scholars: Evangelos Chrysos, Javeir Arce, Walter Pohl, Max Martin, Stephane Lebecq, Averil Cameron, Ian Wood, Alan Dierkens, and Patrick Perin. The essays look at the significant aspects of the transition from late Antiquity to the Middle Ages. Includes general bibliography for each essay, illustrations, and color plates.

Wells, Peter S. *The Barbarians Speak: How the Conquered Peoples Shaped the Roman Empire*. Princeton, N.J.: Princeton University Press, 1999. Author examines indigenous peoples of Europe before, during, and after Roman conquest. Using archaeological evidence, he contends that native peoples played a greater role in the formation of societies. Includes list of figures and tables. Extensive bibliography.

WOMEN OF THE ANCIENT WORLD

Cameron, Averil, and Amelie Kuhrt, eds. *Images of Women in Antiquity*. Detroit, Mich.: Wayne State University Press, 1993. Work is a compilation of scholarly articles written on the diverse roles of women in ancient societies. Chapters are divided thematically: "Perceiving Women," "Women and Power," "Women at Home," "The Biology of Women," "Discovering Women," "The Economic Role of Women," and "Women in Religion and Cult."

Ehrenberg, Margaret. *Women in Prehistory*. Norman: University of Oklahoma Press, 1989. Using archeological, anthropological, and classical sources from the Paleolithic era to the Iron Age, Ehrenberg contends that women were significant contributors to the discovery and development of agriculture. Chapter titles include "The Search for Prehistoric Woman," "The Earliest Communities," "The First Farmers," "The Bronze Age," and "The Celtic Iron Age." Regions discussed are Minoan Crete, Scandinavia, and Britain. Includes maps, illustrations, and glossary of terms.

Fantham, Elaine, Helene Peet Foley, and Natalie Boymel Kampen, et al. *Women in the Classical World: Image and Text*. Oxford, England: University of Oxford

Press, 1994. Provides overview of ancient women in a cultural and historical context for general readers. Part 1 addresses women in the Greek world, focusing on Sparta, Athens, Amazons, and cosmopolitan regions. Part 2 addresses women in the Roman world, focusing on Republican Rome, Etruscan society, the age of Augustus and the Julio-Claudians, Pompeii, and the High and Later Empire. Includes maps, photographs, chronological table, and an extensive index.

Vivante, Bella, ed. *Women's Roles in Ancient Civilizations: A Reference Guide.* Westport, Conn.: Greenwood Press, 1999. Great overview of subject for readers. Consists of twelve essays written by scholars on topics of women in ancient China, Indian, Japan, Mesopotamia, the Levant, Egypt, West Africa, Greece, Rome, Mesoamerica, Andes, and North America. Includes bibliographical references.

—Gayla Koerting

WEB SITES

This list of Web sites dealing with the ancient world lists the name of the person or organization responsible for the site followed by the site's official title and its address (URL). The URLs for these sites were active as of February, 2004.

GENERAL

Ancient and Lost Civilizations
Ellie Crystal
http://www.crystallinks.com
> A massive and very elaborate site that provides many links to ancient Web sites.

Ancient Civilizations Themes Page
http://www.cln.org/themes/ancient.html
> Useful for students and teachers alike. There are links to informational resources as well as lesson plans.

Ancient History
British Broadcasting Corporation
http://www.bbc.co.uk/history/ancient/
> Through the British Broadcasting Corporation (BBC), this Web site allows a student to learn more about the Anglo Saxons, Egyptians, Greeks, Romans, and Vikings. There is also a wealth of material that can be located by clicking on timelines, historic figures, history trails, talk history, and multimedia zone. Some of the multimedia highlights include finding out the color of Anglo-Saxon coins, discovering treasures from Mesopotamia, and planning a Viking raid.

Ancient History, Archaeology, and Biblical Studies
Bruce J. Butterfield
http://mcadams.posc.mu.edu/txt/
> Useful for providing online texts by ancient writers and archaeologists. Some of the texts included are Tacitus's *History of Rome*, Herodotus's *History of Persian Wars*, and some of Plutarch's biographies.

Ancient History Museums and Links
http://www.museumstuff.com/museums/types/
   history_ancient/
> Serves as a gateway to museums of ancient history and other related resources.

Ancient Near East.net
http://www.ancientneareast.net/
> This constantly updated site is valuable for scholars and students alike.

The Ancient World
http://www.fsmitha.com/h1/
> Designed to connect the student to many sites devoted to ancient civilizations. Includes links to maps, books, and images.

Ancient World History
Discovery Communications
http://www.dsc.discovery.com
> The "History" section of "Explore by Subject" features a very useful introduction to the ancient world for students.

Ancient World Web
Julia Hayden
http://www.julen.net/aw
> Created in 1994, this site is divided into such categories as Buildings, Monuments and Cities; Daily Life; Language and Literature; Law and Philosophy; Mythology and Religion; and Science.

AncientWorlds
http://www.ancientsites.com/
> A subscription-based site that has been created for those who love ancient hitory.

Awesome Library: Ancient Civilizations
R. Jerry Adams
 http://www.awesomelibrary.org/Classroom/
    Social_Studies/Ancient_Civilizations/
    Ancient_Civilizations.html
> Under the main topic of Ancient Civilizations, a student can click on fifteen subtopics of particular ancient civilizations. This site was created by Adams and sponsored by Continuing Teacher Education and Keystone Family Protection.

The British Museum: World Cultures
British Museum
http://www.thebritishmuseum.ac.uk/world/world.html
> The world-respected British Museum has a wealth of information available for any serious student of ancient cultures. The museum states that it exists "to illuminate the histories of cultures, for the benefit of present and future generations." The researcher can

access any of the following regions: Africa, Americas, Asia, Britain, Egypt, Europe, Greece, Japan, Near East, and the Pacific.

Classic Links

Classics Department at the University of Texas, Austin

http://www.utexas.edu/depts/classics/links.html

Contains e-mail discussion lists recommended by the University of Texas and classical resources. The classical resources include directories of electronic resources and classical organizations; course materials in language and literature, art and archaeology, and classical civilizations; and electronic journals/bibliographies.

Classics Subject Guide

Lyle Ford and Joan Martin

http://www.ualberta.ca/~slis/guides/classics/
      home.htm

Created by Ford and Martin as part of their Master of Library and Information Studies program at the University of Alberta. This guide must be thought of as merely a starting point for classics sites on the Internet. The categories included in the guide are: Art in the Ancient World, Archaeology, History, Listservers and E-Journals, University Classics Departments, Classics Societies, Other Classics Resources, Photograph Gallery, and Search Tools.

Diotima

http://www.stoa.org/diotima/

A extremely useful site for the study of women in the ancient world.

Encyclopedia Mythica

M. F. Lindermans

http://www.pantheon.org/information/about.html

This popular encyclopedia was created by the scholar Lindermans and contains definitions of more than six thousand gods, goddesses, supernatural beings, legendary creatures, and monsters from around the world. Specific areas include mythology, folklore, bestiary, heroes, image gallery, genealogy tables, and featured items.

Exploring Ancient World Cultures

Anthony F. Beavers and University of Evansville

http://eawc.evansville.edu/

Created by Beavers and funded by the University of Evansville, this is an ever-expanding site that features essays and primary texts and is adding extended histories of the Near East, India, Egypt, China, Greece,

Rome, Early Islam, and Medieval Europe. Over the years, the site has won numerous awards for the quality of its scholarship.

Internet Ancient History Sourcebook

Fordham University

http://www.fordham.edu/halsall/ancient/asbook.html

This Web site contains more than a hundred links to sources that concern themselves with ancient civilizations and is divided into sections such as Studying Ancient History, Human Origins, and the Ancient Near East. Within a section such as the Ancient Near East, one can investigate ancient Egypt and look at detailed maps, discover what Egyptians thought of death and resurrection, and look into everyday life.

The Internet Classics Archive

http://classics.mit.edu

Created in 1994, this archive provides access to more than four hundred works of classical literature in English translation.

Mr. Donn's Ancient History

Don Donn

http://members.aol.com/donnandlee/

Includes a wealth of information on ancient history as well as lesson plans and activities.

Odyssey Online

http://carlos.emory.edu/ODYSSEY/
      MidElem_Home.html

Created to help students explore the Near East, Egypt, Greece, Rome, and Africa. Includes objects from the Michael C. Carlos Museum at Emory University (Atlanta, Georgia), the Memorial Art Gallery of the University of Rochester (Rochester, New York), and the Dallas Museum of Art (Dallas, Texas). There is also a useful "Teacher Resource Site."

The Perseus Digital Library

Perseus Project

http://www.perseus.tufts.edu/

The Perseus Project receives funds from the National Endowment for the Humanities, the National Science Foundation, the Digital Libraries Initiative Phase 2, Tufts University, and private contributions. It is a nonprofit enterprise and is run by the Department of the Classics at Tufts University. This is an extraordinary source for Greek and Latin texts, English translations, archaeological sites, maps, art, reference grammars, and more.

Shalom

http://www.geocities.com/Athens/Olympus/5993/

Provides the student with many ancient Near East resources and links found on the World Wide Web. Links to archaeology, mythology, biblical criticism, history, a book store, and a photo gallery are provided. Specific civilizations covered are Sumer, Assyria, Babylon, and Persia.

Texts for Ancient History Courses

University of Calgary

http://www.acs.ucalgary.ca/~vandersp/Courses/texts/
texts.html

Works by such noted ancient authors as Thucydides, Aeschylus, Plutarch, Tacitus, and Eusebius have been made available for students through the University of Calgary.

Virtual Ancient Civilizations

Urbana Middle School

http://www.cmi.k12.il.us/Urbana/projects/AncientCiv/

Considered one of the best learning resources on the Internet, this site is listed in the BBC Education Web Guide. A student can access the following topics: early man; Mesopotamia; Egypt; China; Greece; Rome; Maya and Inca; Ancient Africa; and Middle Ages.

Women in the Ancient World

James C. Thompson

http://www.womenintheancientworld.com/

Scholar Thompson created a site that details "the status, role and daily life of women in the ancient civilizations of Egypt, Rome, Athens, Israel, and Babylonia."

AFRICA

African Timelines

Cora Agatucci

http://www.cocc.edu/cagatucci/classes/hum211/
timelines/

Created by Professor Agatucci at Central Oregon Community College, this site offers timelines that look at ancient Africa and African empires.

National Museum of African Art

National Museum of African Art

http://www.nmafa.si.edu/

As part of the Smithsonian Institution, this museum is dedicated to bringing a greater understanding of Africa's vast array of visual arts and diverse cultures.

The Nubia Salvage Project

Oriental Institute Museum

http://www.-oi.uchicago.edu/OI/PROJ/NUB/
Nubia.html

Created by the Oriental Institute Museum of the University of Chicago, this is an important resource for the study of ancient Nubians.

THE AMERICAS

American Indian History and Related Issues

Troy Johnson of the California State University at
Long Beach

http://www.csulb.edu/projects/ais/

This site does a marvelous job of gathering together a wealth of research on native tribes.

Ancient Mesoamerican Civilizations

Kevin L. Callahan

http://www.angelfire.com/ca/humanorigins/index.html

This site introduces a student to the diverse cultures that existed in ancient Mesoamerica.

The Maya Astronomy Page

Michael Berger

http://www.michielb.nl/maya/

An extraordinary site created for all those who are interested in Mayan astronomy.

ASIA

Ancient Japan

Richard Hooker

http://www.wsu.edu:8080/~dee/ANCJAPAN/
ANJAPAN1.HTML

This educational site delves into the world of ancient Japan from various angles.

Asian Historical Architecture

http://www.orientalarchitecture.com/

This site includes a comprehensive photographic survey of the architecture that is unique to Asia. It is possible to view more than six thousand photographs that can be found at more than 450 web sites.

Center for Chinese Studies Library, Berkeley

http://www.lib.berkeley.edu/CCSL/

This site lists hundreds of links that specialize in Chinese history; includes the center's own catalog and bibliography.

Chinese Dynasties

Ming L. Pei

http://www.chinapage.com/dyna1.html

China expert Pei has created an invaluable site on the Chinese dynasties.

Chinese Philosophy Page

Stephen A. Brown

http://main.chinesephilosophy.net/index.html

This site serves as a useful introduction into everything related to Chinese philosophy.

Manas

Vinay Lal of the University of California at Los Angeles

http://www.sscnet.ucla.edu/southasia/History/Ancient/ancient.html

A marvelous site for students of Indian history.

EGYPT

Ancient Egypt

The British Museum

http://www.ancientegypt.co.uk

Although designed for children, this site provides valuable information and many photographs.

Tour Egypt

Egyptian Ministry of Tourism

http://touregypt.net

A valuable site created by the Ministry of Tourism in Egypt.

EUROPE

Ancient Europe

E. L. Knox

http://history.boisestate.edu/westciv/ancient/

This site offers a fascinating glimpse into the world of ancient Europe.

Encyclopedia of the Celts

Knud Mariboe

http://celt.net/Celtic/celtopedia/indices/encycintro.html

This online encyclopedia serves as an invaluable resource for everything Celtic.

GREECE

Ancient Greece

http://www.ancientgreece.com/

A student can search on many aspects of ancient Greece, including geography, mythology, wars, people, Olympics, and history.

Ancient Greek (Hellenic) Sites on the World Wide Web

John Fisher

http://www.webcom.com/shownet/medea/grklink.html

This gateway site serves as a valuable starting point for a study of ancient Greece.

MESOPOTAMIA AND THE MIDDLE EAST

Hittite Home Page

Billie Jean Collins

http://www.asor.org/HITTITE/HittiteHP.html

A survey of the world of the Hittites.

The Temple Mount in Jerusalem

Tuvia Sagiv

http://www.templemount.org/index.html

Provides a valuable look at this sacred location.

RELIGION AND PHILOSOPHY

Academic Info: Religion Gateway

Michael Madin

http://www.academicinfo.net/religindex.html

A useful gateway to information on the world's religions.

Bible History Online

http://www.bible-history.com/

An indepth database that provides access to such topics as ancient documents, ancient Israel, languages, maps and geography, rabbinical works, and study tools.

Buddhanet.net

Buddha Dharma Educational Association

www.buddhanet.net/

A nonsectarian Australia-based Buddhist site providing basic information on Buddhism, electronic books, a worldwide Buddhist directory, a Buddhism-in-schools program for teachers, links to Buddhist online magazines, and extensive links to other Buddhist sources.

Buddhist Studies WWW Virtual Library
T. Matthew Ciolek, Joe Bransford Wilson, and Jerome Ducor
http://www.ciolek.com/WWWVL-Buddhism.html
> This site provides links to information on Buddhism.

Hindu Resources Online
http://www.hindu.org/
> This site offers links to Hindu or Hindu-related Web sites.

The Internet Encyclopedia of Philosophy
James Fieser, Ph.D., general editor
http://www.utm.edu/reserach/iep/
> Articles for this encyclopedia are either original entries written by philosophers, adaptations from public domain sources, or adaptations of entries written for the classroom by the editors of the encyclopedia. The encyclopedia is updated on a regular basis.

Judaism 101
Tracey Rich
http://www.jewfaq.org/
> Created and maintained by law librarian Tracey Rich, this site is an online encyclopedia of Judaism. Includes information on Jewish beliefs, people, places, scripture, practices, and customs.

Stanford Encyclopedia of Philosophy
Edward N. Zalta, principal editor
http://plato.stanford.edu/
> This invaluable reference source is run by the Metaphysics Research Lab at the Center for the Study of Language and Information (CSLI) at Stanford University.

ROME

Ancient Rome
History Link 101
http://www.historylink101.com/ancient_rome.htm
> Provides links to Web sites on Roman daily life, art, and biography as well as links to photographs, maps, and research.

Link to Ancient Rome
http://www.ghgcorp.com/shetler/rome/
> Allows students of ancient Rome to get connected to links that contain a wealth of information on various aspects of Rome, including history, religion, warfare, literature, art, and architecture.

—Jeffry Jensen

The Ancient World

Prehistory - 476 C.E.

CHRONOLOGICAL LIST OF ENTRIES

25,000-10,001 B.C.E.

c. 25,000 B.C.E., San Peoples Create Earliest African Art
c. 18,000-c. 11,000 B.C.E., Bering Strait Migrations
c. 16,000-c. 3000 B.C.E., BaTwa Peoples Thrive in Central Africa
c. 15,500 B.C.E., Early Australians Create the Bradshaw Rock Paintings

c. 15,000 B.C.E., Early Europeans Create Lascaux Cave Paintings
c. 13,000 B.C.E., Humans Enter the South American Continent
c. 13,000-c. 7000 B.C.E., Paleo-Indian Culture Flourishes in North America

10,000-5001 B.C.E.

c. 10,000-c. 300 B.C.E., Jōmon Culture Thrives in Japan
c. 10,000 B.C.E.-c. 1 C.E., Saharan Peoples Create Rock Art
c. 9500-c. 9000 B.C.E., Clovis Culture Rises in New Mexico
c. 9500-c. 5000 B.C.E., Settlement Established at Abu Hureyra in Syria
c. 9000-c. 8000 B.C.E., Cochise Culture Thrives in American Southwest
c. 9000-c. 7000 B.C.E., Nilo-Saharan Peoples Produce Food and Pottery
c. 8800-c. 8500 B.C.E., Folsom People Flourish in New Mexico
c. 8000 B.C.E., Permanent Settlement of the Andean Altiplano Begins
c. 8000-c. 4000 B.C.E., Plano Culture Flourishes in Great Plains Area
c. 8000-c. 1000 B.C.E., Archaic Indians Adapt to Warmer Climates
c. 7700-c. 1000 B.C.E., Native Cultures Flourish on the North Pacific Coast
c. 7500 B.C.E., Birth of Shintō
c. 7500 B.C.E., East Asian Grain Cultivation Begins

c. 7200 B.C.E., Kennewick Man Lives in North America
c. 7000-c. 6000 B.C.E., Khoisan Peoples Disperse Throughout Southern Africa
c. 7000-c. 4900 B.C.E., Çatalhüyük Flourishes as Center of Anatolian Culture
c. 6800-c. 4900 B.C.E., Kitoi People Live Near Lake Baikal in Siberia
c. 6500-c. 5000 B.C.E., Nilo-Saharan Farmers Spread Cultivation and Herding
c. 6200-c. 3800 B.C.E., Ubaid Culture Thrives in Mesopotamia
c. 6000-c. 5000 B.C.E., Niger-Congo Religion Takes Hold Across West Africa
c. 6000-c. 1500 B.C.E., Yangshao and Longshan Cultures Flourish in China
c. 6000-c. 1000 B.C.E., Omotics Advance Farming Practices in Horn of Africa
c. 5800-c. 3700 B.C.E., Chinchorro Inhabit the Peruvian and Chilean Coasts
c. 5500-c. 4500 B.C.E., Halafian Culture Flourishes in Northern Mesopotamia
c. 5500-c. 4500 B.C.E., Niger-Congo Peoples Spread Agriculture in Africa

5000-3001 B.C.E.

c. 5000 B.C.E., Aleutian Coastal Hunters Flourish
c. 5000-c. 3000 B.C.E., Kelteminar Culture Flourishes in Central Asia
c. 5000 B.C.E.-c. 1 C.E., Red Paint Culture Flourishes in Eastern North America

c. 4000 B.C.E., Horse Is Domesticated
c. 4000 B.C.E., Sumerian Civilization Begins in Mesopotamia
c. 4000-c. 1000 B.C.E., Old Copper Complex Flourishes in North America

III

c. 4000 B.C.E.-c. 100 C.E., Ban Chiang Culture Flourishes in Thailand

c. 3800 B.C.E., Cities and Civic Institutions Are Invented in Mesopotamia

c. 3500 B.C.E., Indus Valley Civilization Begins in South Asia

c. 3300-c. 1500 B.C.E., Valdivia Culture Forms Villages in Coastal Ecuador

c. 3100 B.C.E., Sumerians Invent Writing

c. 3100-c. 1550 B.C.E., Building of Stonehenge

c. 3050 B.C.E., Unification of Lower and Upper Egypt

3000-2001 B.C.E.

c. 3000 B.C.E., Australian Aborigines Create Wandjina Cave Paintings

c. 3000 B.C.E., Canaanites Inhabit the Levant

c. 3000-c. 500 B.C.E., Elamite Empire Rises in Near East

2953-2838 B.C.E. traditionally, Reign of China's Legendary First Ruler, Fu Xi

c. 2900-c. 2340 B.C.E., Early Dynastic Period Flourishes in Southern Mesopotamia

c. 2700-c. 1400 B.C.E., Gash Civilization Thrives in Africa

c. 2687 B.C.E., Old Kingdom Period Begins in Egypt

c. 2682 B.C.E., Legendary Founding of China by Huangdi

c. 2600 B.C.E., Leizu Discovers Silk Making

c. 2575-c. 2566 B.C.E., Building of the Great Pyramid

c. 2500 B.C.E., Construction of Monumental Architecture at Caral in Peru

2500-1900 B.C.E., Wawat Chiefdom Flourishes in Lower Nubia

c. 2500-c. 1500 B.C.E., Southeast Asians Migrate into the South Pacific

c. 2340 B.C.E., Sumerian Uruk-Agina Makes Social and Political Reforms

c. 2334-c. 2279 B.C.E., Sargon of Akkad Establishes the Akkadian Dynasty

c. 2333 B.C.E., Old Chosŏn State Founded in Korea

c. 2300 B.C.E., Enheduanna Becomes First Named Author

c. 2300-c. 2000 B.C.E., First Great Expansion of Berber Peoples Across North Africa

c. 2300-c. 1800 B.C.E., Beaker People Live in Western Europe

c. 2200-1500 B.C.E., Kerma Kingdom Develops and Dominates Lower Nubia

c. 2160 B.C.E., First Intermediate Period Begins in Egypt

c. 2112 B.C.E., Ur-Nammu Establishes a Code of Law

c. 2100 B.C.E., Xia Dynasty Marks Start of Historical China

c. 2100-c. 600 B.C.E., Mogollon Culture Rises in American Southwest

c. 2055 B.C.E., Middle Kingdom Period Begins in Egypt

2000-1501 B.C.E.

c. 2000 B.C.E., Composition of the Gilgamesh Epic

c. 2000 B.C.E., Mon-Khmer Migrate into Southeast Asia

c. 2000 B.C.E., Mongols Inhabit Steppes North of China

c. 1900-1527? B.C.E., Kerma Kingdom Rules Nubia

c. 1900-c. 1400 B.C.E., Early Villages Form in Oaxaca

c. 1800-c. 1500 B.C.E., Construction of El Paraíso in Peru

c. 1800-c. 700 B.C.E., Poverty Point Culture Builds Earthworks

c. 1770 B.C.E., Promulgation of Hammurabi's Code

1750-800 B.C.E., Andronovo Culture Rises in Central Asia

c. 1650 B.C.E., Hyksos Create Second Intermediate Period

1650-1620 B.C.E., Hattusilis I Establishes the Old Hittite Kingdom

1500-1001 B.C.E.

1000-801 B.C.E.

800-701 B.C.E.

8th century B.C.E., Kushite King Piye Conquers Upper Egypt

8th century B.C.E., Scythians Drive the Cimmerians from Central Asia

8th-6th century B.C.E., Phrygian Kingdom Rises

c. 800 B.C.E., Phoenicians from Tyre Found Carthage

c. 800-c. 600 B.C.E., Ironworking Spreads into Sub-Saharan Africa

c. 783-c. 591 B.C.E., Napata Kingdom Flourishes in Kush

776 B.C.E., Olympic Games Are First Recorded

775 B.C.E., Delphic Oracle Provides Guidance for City-States

770 B.C.E., Eastern Zhou Dynasty Begins in China

c. 750 B.C.E., Homer Composes the *Iliad*

c. 750-c. 500 B.C.E., Marib Dam Is Built in Yemen

745 B.C.E., Tiglath-pileser III Rules Assyria

c. 736-716 B.C.E., Spartan Conquest of Messenia

c. 734-c. 580 B.C.E., Greeks Colonize the Mediterranean and Black Sea Regions

c. 733 B.C.E., Founding of Syracuse

c. 712-698 B.C.E., Shabaka Reunites the Nile Valley

c. 705-330 B.C.E., Founding and Flourishing of the Achaemenian Dynasty

701 B.C.E., Sennacherib Invades Syro-Palestine

700-601 B.C.E.

c. 700 B.C.E., Hesiod Composes *Theogony* and *Works and Days*

c. 700-c. 500 B.C.E., Dorset Culture Extends into Labrador, Newfoundland, and Greenland

c. 700-330 B.C.E., Phalanx Is Developed as a Military Unit

700 B.C.E.-100 C.E., Paracas Culture Develops a Sophisticated Textile Tradition

c. 700 B.C.E.-c. 500 C.E., Mound Builders Rise in Ohio Valley

664 B.C.E., Saite Dynasty Begins in Egypt

c. 645-546 B.C.E., Lydia Rises to Power Under the Mermnad Family

c. 640 B.C.E., Greek City-States Use Coins as Means of Exchange

625-509 B.C.E., Rise of Etruscan Civilization in Rome

621 or 620 B.C.E., Draco's Code Is Instituted

c. 607-562 B.C.E., Nebuchadnezzar Creates the First Neo-Babylonian State

Before 600 B.C.E., Celebration of the Eleusinian Mysteries

600-501 B.C.E.

6th or 5th century B.C.E., Birth of Buddhism

c. 6th century B.C.E.-c. 350 C.E., Meroitic Empire Rules from Southern Egypt to the Blue Nile

6th-4th century B.C.E. (traditionally, 1st millennium B.C.E.), Suśruta, Indian Physician, Writes Medical Compendium

c. 600 B.C.E., Appearance of Zoroastrian Ditheism

600-500 B.C.E., Greek Philosophers Formulate Theories of the Cosmos

c. 594-580 B.C.E., Legislation of Solon

587-423 B.C.E., Birth of Judaism

c. 580 B.C.E., Greek Poet Sappho Dies

c. 550 B.C.E., Construction of Trireme Changes Naval Warfare

c. 550 B.C.E., Vālmīki Composes the *Rāmāyaṇa*

547 B.C.E., Cyrus the Great Founds the Persian Empire

October, 539 B.C.E., Fall of Babylon

c. 538-c. 450 B.C.E., Jews Return from the Babylonian Captivity

c. 530 B.C.E., Founding of the Pythagorean Brotherhood

527 B.C.E., Death of Vardhamāna, Founder of Jainism

c. 525 B.C.E., Sibylline Books Are Compiled

520-518 B.C.E., Darius the Great Conquers the Indus Valley

520-518 B.C.E., Scylax of Caryanda Voyages the Indian Ocean

509 B.C.E., Rape of Lucretia

c. 509 B.C.E., Roman Republic Replaces Monarchy

508-507 B.C.E., Reforms of Cleisthenes

500-401 B.C.E.

5th century B.C.E., Composition of the *Spring and Autumn Annals*

c. 5th-4th century B.C.E., Creation of the *Jātakas*

c. 5th-3d century B.C.E., Composition of *The Art of War*

5th-1st century B.C.E., Composition of *The Great Learning*

c. 500 B.C.E., Acupuncture Develops in China

c. 500 B.C.E., Pāṇini Composes Sanskrit Work of Grammar

c. 500-470 B.C.E., Hecataeus of Miletus Writes the First Geography Book

500-400 B.C.E., Creation of the *Wujing*

c. 500-400 B.C.E., Greek Physicians Begin Scientific Practice of Medicine

c. 500 B.C.E.-c. 200 C.E., Libyan Garamantes Flourish as Farmers and Traders

c. 500 B.C.E.-c. 300 C.E., Socially Stratified Kingdoms Arise Around the Middle Niger River

c. 500 B.C.E.-c. 600 C.E., Mithraism Emerges as Significant Religion

c. 500 B.C.E.-c. 700 C.E., Zapotecs Build Monte Albán

499-494 B.C.E., Ionian Revolt

494/493 B.C.E., Institution of the Plebeian Tribunate

September 17, 490 B.C.E., Battle of Marathon

483 B.C.E., Naval Law of Themistocles Is Instituted

480-479 B.C.E., Persian Invasion of Greece

479 B.C.E., Confucius's Death Leads to the Creation of *The Analects*

478-448 B.C.E., Athenian Empire Is Created

475-221 B.C.E., China Enters Chaotic Warring States Period

c. 467 B.C.E., Gośāla Maskarīputra, Founder of Ājīvika Sect, Dies

c. 456/455 B.C.E., Greek Tragedian Aeschylus Dies

451-449 B.C.E., Twelve Tables of Roman Law Are Formulated

c. 450-c. 425 B.C.E., History Develops as a Scholarly Discipline

450-100 B.C.E., City-State of Yeha Flourishes in the Ethiopian Highlands

447-438 B.C.E., Building of the Parthenon

445 B.C.E., Establishment of the Canuleian Law

c. 440 B.C.E., Sophists Train the Greeks in Rhetoric and Politics

c. 438 B.C.E., Greek Lyric Poet Pindar Dies

May, 431-September, 404 B.C.E., Peloponnesian War

c. 420 B.C.E.-c. 100 C.E., Yuezhi Culture Links Persia and China

June, 415-September, 413 B.C.E., Athenian Invasion of Sicily

406 B.C.E., Greek Dramatist Euripides Dies

September, 404-May, 403 B.C.E., Thirty Tyrants Rule Athens for Eight Months

401-400 B.C.E., March of the Ten Thousand

400-301 B.C.E.

c. 4th century B.C.E.-3d century C.E., Kauṭilya Compiles a Treatise on Practical Statecraft

Early 4th century B.C.E., Founding of Mohism

c. 400 B.C.E.-c. 300 C.E., Bantu Peoples Spread Farming Across Southern Africa

c. 400 B.C.E.-c. 300 C.E., Dong Son Culture Appears in Vietnam

c. 400 B.C.E.-400 C.E., Composition of the *Mahābhārata*

399 B.C.E., Death of Socrates

Between 394 and 371 B.C.E., Xenophon Writes the *Anabasis*
386 B.C.E., King's Peace Ends Corinthian War
c. 385 B.C.E., Greek Playwright Aristophanes Dies
c. 380 B.C.E., Plato Develops His Theory of Ideas
359-336 B.C.E., Philip II Expands and Empowers Macedonia
c. 350 B.C.E., Diogenes Popularizes Cynicism
340-338 B.C.E., Origin of *Municipia*
August 2, 338 B.C.E., Battle of Chaeronea
336 B.C.E., Alexander the Great Begins Expansion of Macedonia
c. 335-323 B.C.E., Aristotle Writes the *Politics*
333 B.C.E., Battle of Issus
332 B.C.E., Founding of Alexandria

October 1, 331 B.C.E., Battle of Gaugamela
327-325 B.C.E., Alexander the Great Invades the Indian Subcontinent
325-323 B.C.E., Aristotle Isolates Science as a Discipline
323 B.C.E., Founding of the Ptolemaic Dynasty and Seleucid Kingdom
c. 323-275 B.C.E., Diadochi Divide Alexander the Great's Empire
c. 321 B.C.E., Mauryan Empire Rises in India
c. 320 B.C.E., Theophrastus Initiates the Study of Botany
312 B.C.E., First Roman Aqueduct Is Built
312-264 B.C.E., Building of the Appian Way

300-201 B.C.E.

3d century B.C.E., Commercial City of Jenne Is Founded on Niger River
3d century B.C.E. (traditionally 660 B.C.E.), Jimmu Tennō Becomes the First Emperor of Japan
3d century B.C.E. (traditionally 6th century B.C.E.), Laozi Composes the *Dao De Jing*
c. 300 B.C.E., Euclid Compiles a Treatise on Geometry
c. 300 B.C.E., Izapan Civilization Dominates Mesoamerica
c. 300 B.C.E., Hohokam Culture Arises in American Southwest
c. 300 B.C.E., Stoics Conceptualize Natural Law
c. 300 B.C.E., Yayoi Period Begins
c. 300-c. 100 B.C.E., Berber Kingdoms of Numidia and Mauretania Flourish
c. 300 B.C.E.-c. 100 C.E., Khoikhoi and Kwadi Adopt Pastoral Lifestyle
300 B.C.E.-600 C.E., Construction of the Māhabodhi Temple
287 B.C.E., *Lex Hortensia* Reforms the Roman Constitution
c. 285-c. 255 B.C.E., Xunzi Develops Teachings That Lead to Legalism
285-160 B.C.E. (traditionally, c. 300 B.C.E.), Composition of the *Zhuangzi*

c. 275 B.C.E., Greeks Advance Hellenistic Astronomy
c. 273/265-c. 238 B.C.E., Aśoka Reigns over India
264-225 B.C.E., First Punic War
c. 250 B.C.E., Discoveries of Archimedes
c. 250 B.C.E., Third Buddhist Council Convenes
c. 250 B.C.E., *Tipiṭaka* Is Compiled
250-130 B.C.E., Commissioning of the Septuagint
c. 250 B.C.E.-70 C.E., Dead Sea Scrolls Are Composed
c. 247-207 B.C.E., Buddhism Established in Sri Lanka
c. 245 B.C.E., Diodotus I Founds the Greco-Bactrian Kingdom
245-140 B.C.E., Rise of Parthia
From 240 B.C.E., Exploitation of the Arch
221 B.C.E., Qin Dynasty Founded in China
c. 221-211 B.C.E., Building the Great Wall of China
221-206 B.C.E., Legalist Movement in China
221 B.C.E.-220 C.E., Advances Are Made in Chinese Agricultural Technology
218-201 B.C.E., Second Punic War
c. 212-202? B.C.E., Construction of the Qin Tomb
209-174 B.C.E., Maodun Creates a Large Confederation in Central Asia
206 B.C.E., Liu Bang Captures Qin Capital, Founds Han Dynasty
202 B.C.E., Battle of Zama

c. 29 C.E., Condemnation and Crucifixion of Jesus Christ

c. 30 C.E., Preaching of the Pentecostal Gospel

40-43 C.E., Trung Sisters Lead Vietnamese Rebellion Against Chinese

43-130 C.E., Roman Conquest of Britain

c. 50 C.E., Creation of the Roman Imperial Bureaucracy

c. 50-c. 150 C.E., Compilation of the New Testament

January-March, 55 or 56 C.E., Paul Writes His Letter to the Romans

60 C.E., Boudicca Leads Revolt Against Roman Rule

c. 60-68 C.E., Buddhism Enters China

64-67 C.E., Nero Persecutes the Christians

68-69 C.E., Year of the Four Emperors

September 8, 70 C.E., Roman Destruction of the Temple of Jerusalem

August 24, 79 C.E., Destruction of Pompeii

90 C.E., Founding of the Classic Period Maya Royal Dynasty at Tikal

c. 90 C.E., Synod of Jamnia

c. 99-105 C.E., Ban Zhao Writes Behavior Guide for Young Women

c. 100-c. 127 C.E., Kushān Dynasty Expands into India

100-127 C.E., Roman Juvenal Composes *Satires*

c. 100-200 C.E., Construction of the Pyramids of the Sun and Moon at Teotihuacán

c. 100-c. 700 C.E., Moche Build the Huaca del Sol and Huaca de la Luna

101-200 B.C.E.

c. 105 C.E., Cai Lun Invents Paper

c. 110 C.E., Trajan Adopts Anti-Christian Religious Policy

c. 127-c. 152 C.E., Kanishka's Reign Brings Flowering of the Arts

130-135 C.E., Dedication of Aelia Capitolina

142 C.E., Zhang Daoling Founds the Celestial Masters Movement

c. 150 C.E., Aśvaghosa Composes Complete Biography of the Buddha

c. 157-201 C.E., Galen Synthesizes Ancient Medical Knowledge

c. 165 C.E., Gaius Creates Edition of the *Institutes* of Roman Law

184-204 C.E., Yellow Turbans Rebellion

200 C.E., Christian Apologists Develop Concept of Theology

200-800 C.E., Lima Culture Flourishes on the Central Andean Coast

200-900 C.E., Maya Civilization Flourishes

200-1250 C.E., Anasazi Civilization Flourishes in American Southwest

201-300 C.E.

c. 3d century C.E., Wang Bi and Guo Xiang Revive Daoism

c. 3d-4th century C.E., Huns Begin Migration West from Central Asia

3d-5th century C.E., Giant Stelae Are Raised at Aksum

c. 220 C.E., Cai Yan Composes Poetry About Her Capture by Nomads

220 C.E., Three Kingdoms Period Begins in China

c. 220 C.E., Ulpian Issues Dictum in Rome

224 C.E., Ardashīr I Establishes the Sāsānian Empire

c. 230-1300 C.E., Manichaeanism Begins in Mesopotamia

c. mid-3d century C.E., Himiko Rules the Yamatai

250 C.E., Outbreak of the Decian Persecution

c. 250 C.E., Saint Denis Converts Paris to Christianity

265 C.E., Sima Yan Establishes the Western Jin Dynasty

284 C.E., Inauguration of the Dominate in Rome

c. 286 C.E., Saint Anthony of Egypt Begins Ascetic Life

290-300 C.E., West African Gold First Reaches North Africa

c. 300 C.E., Licchavi Dynasty Begins in the Kathmandu Valley, Nepal

300-400 C.E., Bantu People Invent Copper Metallurgy

c. 300-600 C.E., Three Kingdoms Period Forms Korean Culture

c. 300-710 C.E., Kofun Period Unifies Japan

CATEGORY INDEX OF ENTRIES

LIST OF CATEGORIES

AGRICULTURE

c. 9500-c. 5000 B.C.E.: Settlement Established at Abu Hureyra in Syria, 24

c. 9000-c. 7000 B.C.E.: Nilo-Saharan Peoples Produce Food and Pottery, 28

c. 8000 B.C.E.: Permanent Settlement of the Andean Altiplano Begins, 32

c. 7500 B.C.E.: East Asian Grain Cultivation Begins, 42

c. 6500-c. 5000 B.C.E.: Nilo-Saharan Farmers Spread Cultivation and Herding, 51

c. 6000-c. 5000 B.C.E.: Niger-Congo Religion Takes Hold Across West Africa, 56

c. 6000-c. 1500 B.C.E.: Yangshao and Longshan Cultures Flourish in China, 58

c. 6000-c. 1000 B.C.E.: Omotics Advance Farming Practices in Horn of Africa, 60

c. 5500-c. 4500 B.C.E.: Halafian Culture Flourishes in Northern Mesopotamia, 65

c. 5500-c. 4500 B.C.E.: Niger-Congo Peoples Spread Agriculture in Africa, 67

2953-2838 B.C.E.: Reign of China's Legendary First Ruler, Fu Xi, 102

c. 2600 B.C.E.: Leizu Discovers Silk Making, 114

c. 1900-c. 1400 B.C.E.: Early Villages Form in Oaxaca, 161

c. 750-c. 500 B.C.E.: Marib Dam Is Built in Yemen, 299

c. 500 B.C.E.-c. 200 C.E.: Libyan Garamantes Flourish as Farmers and Traders, 416

c. 400 B.C.E.-c. 300 C.E.: Bantu Peoples Spread Farming Across Southern Africa, 485

c. 300 B.C.E.-c. 100 C.E.: Khoikhoi and Kwadi Adopt Pastoral Lifestyle, 566

221 B.C.E.-220 C.E.: Advances Are Made in Chinese Agricultural Technology, 612

ARCHITECTURE

c. 3300-c. 1500 B.C.E.: Valdivia Culture Forms Villages in Coastal Ecuador, 87

c. 2575-c. 2566 B.C.E.: Building of the Great Pyramid, 116

c. 2500 B.C.E.: Construction of Monumental Architecture at Caral in Peru, 119

c. 1800-c. 1500 B.C.E.: Construction of El Paraíso in Peru, 163

c. 966 B.C.E.: Building of the Temple of Jerusalem, 263

c. 900-c. 200 B.C.E.: Chavín de Huántar Is Peru's Urban Center, 270

c. 700 B.C.E.-c. 500 C.E.: Mound Builders Rise in Ohio Valley, 326

c. 500 B.C.E.-c. 700 C.E.: Zapotecs Build Monte Albán, 422

447-438 B.C.E.: Building of the Parthenon, 457

300 B.C.E.-600 C.E.: Construction of the Māhabodhi Temple, 568

From 240 B.C.E.: Exploitation of the Arch, 603

c. 221-211 B.C.E.: Building the Great Wall of China, 607

c. 212-202? B.C.E.: Construction of the Qin Tomb, 618

c. 100 B.C.E.-c. 100 C.E.: Celtic Hill Forts Are Replaced by *Oppida*, 682

c. 1 C.E.: Development Begins at Teotihuacán, 748

EXPANSION AND LAND ACQUISITION

GOVERNMENT AND POLITICS

RELIGION

SCIENCE AND TECHNOLOGY

GEOGRAPHICAL INDEX OF ENTRIES

LIST OF GEOGRAPHICAL CATEGORIES

AFRICA. *See also* **ALEXANDRIA, EGYPT, MEDITERRANEAN**

c. 25,000 B.C.E.: San Peoples Create Earliest African Art, 1

c. 16,000-c. 3000 B.C.E.: BaTwa Peoples Thrive in Central Africa, 6

c. 10,000 B.C.E.-c. 1 C.E.: Saharan Peoples Create Rock Art, 20

c. 9000-c. 7000 B.C.E.: Nilo-Saharan Peoples Produce Food and Pottery, 28

c. 7000-c. 6000 B.C.E.: Khoisan Peoples Disperse Throughout Southern Africa, 46

c. 6500-c. 5000 B.C.E.: Nilo-Saharan Farmers Spread Cultivation and Herding, 51

c. 6000-c. 5000 B.C.E.: Niger-Congo Religion Takes Hold Across West Africa, 56

c. 6000-c. 1000 B.C.E.: Omotics Advance Farming Practices in Horn of Africa, 60

c. 5500-c. 4500 B.C.E.: Niger-Congo Peoples Spread Agriculture in Africa, 67

c. 2700-c. 1400 B.C.E.: Gash Civilization Thrives in Africa, 107

2500-1900 B.C.E.: Wawat Chiefdom Flourishes in Lower Nubia, 121

c. 2300-c. 2000 B.C.E.: First Great Expansion of Berber Peoples Across North Africa, 134

c. 2200-1500 B.C.E.: Kerma Kingdom Develops and Dominates Lower Nubia, 138

c. 1900-1527? B.C.E.: Kerma Kingdom Rules Nubia, 159

c. 1650 B.C.E.: Hyksos Create Second Intermediate Period, 173

c. 1200-c. 1000 B.C.E.: Berbers Expand Across North Africa, 227

1069 B.C.E.: Third Intermediate Period Begins in Egypt, 234

c. 1000 B.C.E.: Sub-Saharan Ironworking Begins, 245

c. 1000-c. 700 B.C.E.: Mashariki Bantu Establish Chifumbaze Ironworking Culture, 249

c. 1000-c. 500 B.C.E.: Nok Artists Develop Terra-cotta Sculpture, 253

c. 1000 B.C.E.-c. 300 C.E.: Urban Commerce Develops in the Sudan Belt, 260

8th century B.C.E.: Kushite King Piye Conquers Upper Egypt, 275

c. 800 B.C.E.: Phoenicians from Tyre Found Carthage, 281

c. 800-c. 600 B.C.E.: Ironworking Spreads into Sub-Saharan Africa, 284

c. 783-c. 591 B.C.E.: Napata Kingdom Flourishes in Kush, 286

c. 712-698 B.C.E.: Shabaka Reunites the Nile Valley, 309

c. 6th century B.C.E.-c. 350 C.E.: Meroitic Empire Rules from Southern Egypt to the Blue Nile, 348

c. 500 B.C.E.-c. 200 C.E.: Libyan Garamantes Flourish as Farmers and Traders, 416

ISRAEL

JAPAN

KOREA

MEDITERRANEAN. *See also* **AFRICA, ALEXANDRIA, ASIA MINOR, EGYPT, GREECE, ISRAEL, ROMAN EMPIRE**

PERSONAGES INDEX

SUBJECT INDEX